1,000,000 Books

are available to read at

Forgotten Books

www.ForgottenBooks.com

Read online
Download PDF
Purchase in print

ISBN 978-0-266-02034-9
PIBN 10960404

This book is a reproduction of an important historical work. Forgotten Books uses state-of-the-art technology to digitally reconstruct the work, preserving the original format whilst repairing imperfections present in the aged copy. In rare cases, an imperfection in the original, such as a blemish or missing page, may be replicated in our edition. We do, however, repair the vast majority of imperfections successfully; any imperfections that remain are intentionally left to preserve the state of such historical works.

Forgotten Books is a registered trademark of FB &c Ltd.
Copyright © 2018 FB &c Ltd.
FB &c Ltd, Dalton House, 60 Windsor Avenue, London, SW19 2RR.
Company number 08720141. Registered in England and Wales.

For support please visit www.forgottenbooks.com

1 MONTH OF FREE READING

at
www.ForgottenBooks.com

By purchasing this book you are eligible for one month membership to ForgottenBooks.com, giving you unlimited access to our entire collection of over 1,000,000 titles via our web site and mobile apps.

To claim your free month visit: www.forgottenbooks.com/free960404

* Offer is valid for 45 days from date of purchase. Terms and conditions apply.

English
Français
Deutsche
Italiano
Español
Português

www.forgottenbooks.com

Mythology Photography **Fiction** Fishing Christianity **Art** Cooking Essays Buddhism Freemasonry Medicine **Biology** Music **Ancient Egypt** Evolution Carpentry Physics Dance Geology **Mathematics** Fitness Shakespeare **Folklore** Yoga Marketing **Confidence** Immortality Biographies Poetry **Psychology** Witchcraft Electronics Chemistry History **Law** Accounting **Philosophy** Anthropology Alchemy Drama Quantum Mechanics Atheism Sexual Health **Ancient History Entrepreneurship** Languages Sport Paleontology Needlework Islam **Metaphysics** Investment Archaeology Parenting Statistics Criminology **Motivational**

ON THE

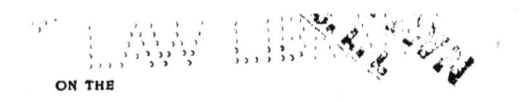

LAW OF RAILROADS

CONTAINING A CONSIDERATION OF THE ORGANIZATION, STATUS AND
POWERS OF RAILROAD CORPORATIONS, AND OF THE RIGHTS
AND LIABILITIES INCIDENT TO THE

LOCATION, CONSTRUCTION AND OPERATION
OF RAILROADS

AND ALSO THE

DUTIES, RIGHTS AND LIABILITIES OF RAILROAD COMPANIES

AS CARRIERS

UNDER THE RULES OF THE COMMON LAW AND THE
INTERSTATE COMMERCE ACT

BY

BYRON K. ELLIOTT

AND

WILLIAM F. ELLIOTT

Authors of Roads and Streets, Appellate Procedure and
General Practice

In Four Volumes

VOLUME II

INDIANAPOLIS AND KANSAS CITY
THE BOWEN-MERRILL COMPANY
1897

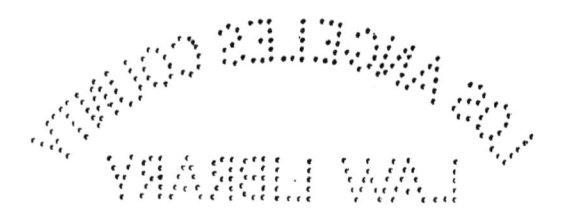

Copyright 1897
BY
THE BOWEN-MERRILL CO.

TABLE OF CONTENTS.

VOLUME II.

THE CORPORATION.

CHAPTER XV.

CONSOLIDATION.

	PAGE.
§ 322. Consolidation must be authorized by legislature	443
323. Statutory mode must be pursued—Collateral attack	445
324. Intention to consolidate—Difference between succession and consolidation	448
325. Right of majority to effect consolidation—When minority may prevent—Release of dissenting subscribers	449
326. Statutory provisions for consolidation	451
327. Rights of old stockholders and their relation to the new company	452
328. Remedies of old stockholders	454
329. Consolidated company succeeds to rights and liabilities of the old companies	455
330. Special privileges and immunities—When they pass to the new company	457
331. When special privileges do not pass	458
332. Duties and obligations of new company	459
333. Liability of new company on old contracts	460
334. Liability of new company for torts—Extent of liability—Generally	461
335. Constituent companies are usually dissolved—When not	462
336. Effect of consolidation upon liens	464
337. *De facto* consolidation—Estoppel—Liability of constituent companies where consolidation is set aside	466
338. Effect of consolidation upon pending suits	467
339. Consolidation with foreign corporations	469

CHAPTER XVI.

CONTRACTS.

	PAGE.
§ 340. Contracts—Power to make—Generally	474
341. Contracts—Scope of corporate power	475
342. General power to contract—Illustrative instances	476
343. Power to contract—Control of by courts	478
344. Effect of changes in charter	479
345. Contracts—Formal requisites of	480
346. Formal defects	481
347. Contracts—Who may make—Generally	481
348. Contracts by interested persons	482
349. Mode prescribed must be pursued	483
350. Contracts—Parties bound to take notice of charter provisions	484
351. Contracts—Unauthorized—Notice	485
352. Estoppel—Generally	487
353. Ratification of unauthorized acts—Rights of the public and of creditors	488
354. Contracts in conjunction with other parties	489
355. Pledge of corporate securities	489
356. Contracts between connecting lines—Division of fares	490
357. Contracts permitting use of part of road	491
358. Contracts regarding terminal facilities	491
359. Traffic contracts—Surrender to competing line	492
360. Contracts with municipal corporations for terminal facilities	493
361. Use of tracks constructed under grant from municipal corporation	493
362. Contracts for location of stations	494
363. Location of tracks, switches and the like	495
364. Contracts that may be made by railroad companies—Particular instances	496
365. Pooling contracts—Generally	497
366. Pooling contracts—The authorities	499
367. Pooling contracts—Presumption	500
368. Contracts—*Ultra vires*	501
369. Contracts—*Ultra vires*—General doctrine	503
370. Contracts—What are *ultra vires*—Generally	504
371. Contracts—*Ultra vires*—Estoppel	505
372. Contracts—*Ultra vires*—Executed and executory contracts	507
373. Contracts—*Ultra vires*—Cases discriminated	509
374. Contracts—*Ultra vires*—Illustrative instances	511
375. Contracts—*Ultra vires*—Rule where statute prescribes consequences	514
376. Contracts—*Ultra vires*—Injunction	514
377. Contracts—*Ultra vires*—Denial of relief—Laches	516
378. Contracts—*Ultra vires*—Who may contest	516
379. Contracts—*Ultra vires*—Creditors	518

TABLE OF CONTENTS—VOL. II. v

PAGE.
§ 380. Contracts—*Ultra vires*—Non-assenting stockholders............... 519
381. Prohibited contracts—Effect of prescribing penalties............. 520
382. Illegal contracts—Generally 522
383. Illegal contracts and *ultra vires* contracts discriminated.......... 522
384. Classes of illegal contracts 524
385. Contracts void because against public policy..................... 524
386. Contracts against public policy—Location of stations and tracks.. 526
387. Contracts void as against public policy—General conclusions..... 529
388. Contracts void as against public policy—Illustrative cases........ 531

CHAPTER XVII.

REAL ESTATE.

389. What railroad property is real estate........................... 535
390. Statutory authority requisite 536
391. Power to acquire real estate—Implied power—Generally......... 537
392. Implied power to acquire—General rule........................ 538
393. Implied power—Illustrative instances 538
394. Power to acquire real estate—Instances of denial of power....... 540
395. Title to real estate is in the company........................... 541
396. Title once vested not divested because property subsequently becomes unnecessary.. 541
397. Effect of conveyance to corporation of land it has no power to hold 542
398. Right of foreign corporation to hold real estate 543
399. The power to acquire by grant broader than the power to acquire by condemnation 544
400. Acquisition of the fee by private grant 544
401. Acquisition of title by adverse possession....................... 546
402. Possession of land—To what right referred 548
403. Rights of company where land is owned in fee................... 549
404. Effect of conveyance of property the company is not authorized to acquire.. 549
405. Questioning the right to hold real estate........................ 550
406. Enjoining purchase of real estate where no power to receive and hold 550
407. Executory contract of purchase not enforceable where there is no power to hold the land....................................... 551
408. Estoppel of parties to deeds to deny corporate existence.......... 551
409. Deed to company not in existence 551
410. Formal execution of conveyances and agreements relating to real estate 553
411. Contracts under corporate seal—Effect as evidence.............. 554
412. Acceptance of deed.. 555
413. Distinction between a donation of lands and a sale 556
414. Deeds of company—By whom executed........................ 556

		PAGE.
§ 415.	Construction of deeds to railroad companies—Generally	557
416.	Deeds to railroad companies—Construction of conditions	558
417.	Grants—Beneficial—Presumption of acceptance	559
418.	Incidents pass with principal thing granted	560
419.	Effect of designating in the deed the purpose for which the land is granted	560
420.	Covenants that run with the land	561
421.	Merger of preliminary agreement in deed	562
422.	Bonds for conveyance—Specific performance	562
423.	Presumption that there is power to hold the land	563
424.	Power to convey real estate	563
425.	Dedication of land for use as a highway	564
426.	Disposition of property corporation has no power to receive and hold—Escheat	565

CHAPTER XVIII.

LEASES.

427.	Power to lease—Generally	567
428.	What the legislature may prescribe	568
429.	Power to lease not an implied one—Legislative authority requisite	568
430.	The power to lease—General rule	569
431.	The foundation of the rule	570
432.	Power to accept a lease	570
433.	Statutes asserted to confer power to lease are not aided by construction	571
434.	Statutes strictly construed—Illustrative instances	572
435.	Statutes—Construction of	573
436.	What is included in the authority to execute a lease	574
437.	Scope of authority to lease	575
438.	Statutes conferring power to lease must be strictly followed	575
439.	Consent of stockholders—Statutory requirement must be obeyed	576
440.	Concurrence of stockholders necessary	576
441.	What number of stockholders must assent to the lease	580
442.	Consent of stockholders—Waiver of objections	581
443.	Lease where parties are corporations of different states	581
444.	Authority to execute lease has no extra-territorial effect	582
445.	Rights of foreign lessors	582
446.	Leases to connecting lines	583
447.	Lease to competing lines—Effect of statutes prohibiting	584
448.	Effect of executing unauthorized lease	585
449.	Lease—Construction	586
450.	Lease—Dependent and independent contracts	587
451.	Contract to permit use of track not necessarily a lease	589
452.	Traffic contract not valid if it is in effect a lease	590
453.	Contract granting right to use—Effect and construction of	591
454.	Part performance—Effect of	592

TABLE OF CONTENTS—VOL. II.

PAGE.

§ 455. Duration of lease.. 593
456. Effect of lease on taxation...................................... 593
457. Public duties of lessee under an unauthorized lease—Mandamus. 595
458. Authorized lease—Duty of lessee to operate the road—Mandamus 595
459. Lessee not liable for wrongs committed prior to the execution of the lease.. 596
460. Effect of a lease upon rights of creditors....................... 597
461. Authorized lease—Rights and duties to which lessee company succeeds... 598
462. Contract obligation of lessor—Lessee not liable thereon.......... 599
463. Recovery of rent under unauthorized lease....................... 600
464. Improvements of road by lessee operating under an unauthorized lease.. 600
465. Receiver's power to lease... 601
466. Unauthorized lease—Liability of lessor—Generally.............. 601
467. Authorized lease—Liability of lessor for injuries caused by negligence of lessee—Cases holding lessor liable................... 603
468. Authorized lease—Liability of lessor for negligence of lessee in operating the road—Authorities................................. 604
469. Authorized lease—Liability of lessor for negligence of lessee in operating the road—Views of the authors...................... 605
470. Control reserved by lessor.. 607
471. Liability of lessee under authorized lease—Illustrative cases...... 608
472. Unauthorized lease—Liability of lessor to employes of lessee—Generally.. 609
473. Unauthorized lease—Liability of lessor—General rule............ 611
474. Liability of lessee for injuries resulting from negligence in operating the road... 612
475. Contracts of the lessee.. 613
476. Joint liability... 613
477. Liability of company where it permits another company to use track in common with itself..................................... 614
478. Fraudulent leases... 615
479. Unauthorized lease—Injunction................................... 616

CHAPTER XIX.

RAILROAD SECURITIES.

480. Power of railroad companies to issue notes and bonds............ 618
481. Power to guarantee bonds... 620
482. Income bonds... 621
483. Convertible bonds... 623
484. Negotiability of bonds—*Bona fide* purchasers..................... 625
485. Form and manner of issuing bonds—Effect of irregularities....... 630
486. Interest coupons.. 632
487. Payment of bonds and interest.................................... 635
488. No power to mortgage without legislative authority.............. 637

	PAGE.
§ 489. Legislative authority to mortgage	638
490. Distinction between authority to mortgage franchises and authority to mortgage property	639
491. Who may execute the mortgage	640
492. Ratification by stockholders of unauthorized or improperly executed mortgage	642
493. When *ultra vires* mortgage may be made effective	643
494. Recording mortgages	644
495. Generally as to what property is covered by the mortgage	645
496. What is covered by a mortgage of the undertaking	649
497. Mortgage of after-acquired property	650
498. Fixtures	654
499. Reserved power to create prior lien or dispose of unnecessary property	655
500. Priority of mortgages	655
501. Trust deeds	658
502. Equitable and defective mortgages	659
503. Statutory mortgages	660
504. Debentures	661

CHAPTER XX.

FORECLOSURE.

505. Foreclosure—Default	662
506. Option to declare whole debt due—Election	664
507. Foreclosure for default in payment of interest	666
508. Parties to foreclosure suit—Plaintiffs	668
509. Bondholders as plaintiffs	669
510. Pledgees, assignees and others as plaintiffs	674
511. Defendants in foreclosure suits—Generally	676
512. When other lien-holders should be made defendants	678
513. Defenses to foreclosure suit	681
514. Effect of provisions giving trustees the right to take possession and sell	682
515. The decree	686
516. Consent decree	687
517. Deficiency decree	688
518. Final and appealable decrees	689

CHAPTER XXI.

SALE AND REORGANIZATION.

519. Railroad company can not sell franchise and necessary property without statutory authority	692
520. Execution sales	695
521. Foreclosure sales—Authority—Purchasers	697

		PAGE.
§ 522.	Sale on default in payment of interest—Sale of road as an entirety	698
523.	Sale of consolidated road—Sale by receiver pending foreclosure..	700
524.	Discretion of trustees and officers as to time and manner of sale..	700
525.	Effect of sale—Purchaser's title	701
526.	When purchaser takes title free from liabilities and liens	703
527.	Disposition of proceeds of sale	706
528.	Preferred claims—Six months' rule	707
529.	Setting sale aside	710
530.	Redemption	715
531.	Reorganization by purchasers at sale—Power of legislature to provide for	717
532.	Statutory reorganization—Liability of new corporation	719
533.	Reorganization by agreement—Rights of minority	722
534.	Rights and obligations of the parties—Laches and estoppel	724
535.	Fraud in the sale or reorganization	725
536.	Reorganization by the courts	728

CHAPTER XXII.

RECEIVERS.

537.	Receivers generally	731
538.	Jurisdiction of courts of equity—Statutory provisions	732
539.	Jurisdiction is sparingly exercised—Purpose of appointment	735
540.	General rules as to when receivers of railroads will be appointed.	736
541.	Receivers will not be appointed merely because parties consent..	739
542.	Extent to which jurisdiction has been exercised	740
543.	Insolvency as ground for appointment of receiver	741
544.	When insolvency is sufficient without default	742
545.	Default in payment of indebtedness as ground for appointment...	743
546.	Appointment in foreclosure proceedings	745
547.	Other grounds for appointment	748
548.	Appointment upon application of unsecured creditor	750
549.	Appointment upon application of secured creditor	753
550.	Appointment upon application of stockholders	757
551.	Appointment upon application of corporation	758
552.	What court may appoint	760
553.	Court first obtaining jurisdiction retains it—Conflict of jurisdiction	762
554.	Extra-territorial jurisdiction	767
555.	Ancillary appointment—Comity	769
556.	Procedure—*Ex parte* application	773
557.	Parties to proceedings for appointment of receiver	775
558.	Appointment upon motion or petition and notice—Affidavits	776
559.	Who may appoint—Appointment in vacation	778
560.	Suit must generally be pending	779
561.	Who may be appointed receiver	780
562.	Order appointing receiver	783
563.	Effect of appointment	784

		PAGE.
§ 564.	Collateral attack on appointment	786
565.	Title and possession of receiver	787
566.	Authority, rights and duties of receiver—Control by court	788
567.	Contracts of receiver	790
568.	Suits by receivers—Authority to sue	792
569.	When receiver may maintain suit—Defenses to receiver's suit	795
570.	Right of receiver to sue in other jurisdictions—Comity	796
571.	Suits against receivers—Leave to sue must be obtained	799
572.	Effect of failure to obtain leave to sue	802
573.	Effect of recent act of congress	804
574.	Rule where suit has been commenced before appointment of receiver	807
575.	Protection of receiver by the court	808
576.	Liability of receivers—Generally	811
577.	Liability for torts	812
578.	Receiver is bound to perform public duties—Mandamus	815
579.	Liability on contracts	816
580.	Liability on claims arising from operation of the road	817
581.	Liability of corporation	819
582.	Receivers of leased lines	821
583.	Receivers' accounts	822
584.	Compensation of receiver	824
585.	Attorney's fees	826
586.	Removal and discharge	828
587.	Effect of removal or discharge	831

CHAPTER XXIII.

RECEIVER'S CERTIFICATES.

588.	Definition and nature of receiver's certificates	832
589.	Power of courts to authorize	833
590.	Purposes for which receiver's certificates may be issued—Extent of power	834
591.	Order giving authority to issue	838
592.	Lien created by receiver's certificates	840
593.	Statutory provisions as to lien	841
594.	Negotiability of receiver's certificates	842
595.	Rights of holders of receiver's certificates	843
596.	Who may question validity of receiver's certificates	844
597.	Payment and redemption of certificates	846

CHAPTER XXIV.

INSOLVENCY AND DISSOLUTION.

598.	Scope of the chapter	848
599.	Railroad company is subject to state insolvency law	848

PAGE.
§ 600. Trust fund doctrine... 849
601. When a corporation is deemed insolvent—Effect of insolvency... 851
602. Assignments by corporations..................................... 853
603. Preferences by corporations...................................... 854
604. Preference of stockholders and officers......................... 854
605. Statutory preference of employes................................ 857
606. What constitutes a dissolution 858
607. Judicial determination of dissolution............................ 860
608. Voluntary dissolution—Surrender of charter..................... 861
609. Proceedings to dissolve 863
610. Dissolution in case of consolidated company..................... 865
611. Effect of dissolution 865
612. Corporation may have a qualified existence after dissolution...... 866
613. Disposition of property on dissolution........................... 868
614. Rights of creditors upon dissolution............................. 869

CHAPTER XXV.

ACTIONS BY AND AGAINST CORPORATIONS.

615. Generally—Suits by corporations................................. 871
616. When incorporation must be alleged 872
617. Actions and suits against corporations........................... 874
618. Power of corporation over litigation—Power to compromise and arbitrate 875
619. Estoppel to deny corporate existence............................. 876
620. When stockholders may sue 877
621. Service of process 878
622. Return of service.. 882
623. Venue of actions against corporations 883
624. Attachment and garnishment.................................... 886
625. Duty and liability of garnishee................................... 889
626. What may be reached in garnishment........................... 890
627. Garnishment of employes' wages................................ 893
628. Injunction—Generally.. 895
629. Injunction where the company seeks to take or condemn lands... 897
630. Injunction where railroad is laid in a street..................... 899
631. Enjoining a nuisance 902
632. Injunction at suit of the company............................... 904
633. Enjoining strikers... 908
634. Injunction at suit of stockholder 911
635. Mandatory injunction—English cases 913
636. Rule in the United States—Illustrative cases 913
637. Mandamus—Generally... 915
638. Mandamus to compel completion and operation of road.......... 916
639. Mandamus to compel restoration of highway and construction of crossings or viaducts.. 918
640. Mandamus to compel carriage of freight........................ 919

§ 641. Mandamus to compel the company to maintain stations and furnish increased facilities.................................... 920
642. When mandamus will not lie 923
643. Who may be relator... 925
644. *Quo warranto*.. 926

CHAPTER XXVI.

REMOVAL OF CAUSES.

645. When removal is authorized—Statutes now in force 928
646. What are suits of a civil nature under the removal acts........... 929
647. Parties.. 932
648. Rights of removal as affected by amount in controversy.......... 934
649. Diverse citizenship as a ground for removal 935
650. Separable controversy 937
651. Prejudice or local influence as a ground for removal 939
652. Removal where federal question is involved.................... 941
653. Time and manner of making application for removal............. 943
654. Effect of application on jurisdiction of state and federal court 945
655. Remanding and dismissing cause.............................. 947
656. Pleading and practice in federal court after removal 949

CHAPTER XXVII.

GOVERNMENTAL CONTROL.

657. Introductory 950
658. Effect of the commerce clause of the federal constitution upon the power of the states 951
659. Legislative power over private rights of railroad companies—Nature of 952
660. Constitutional protection 954
661. The limits of legislative power unduly extended 955
662. Regulations affecting acts and duties of a public nature 956
663. Corporate rights are subject to the police power 958
664. The police power is fettered by limitations 959
665. The subject must be one over which the police power extends— Cases adjudging statutes invalid.............................. 962
666. Police power—Legislative and judicial questions................ 964
667. The police power and the commerce clause of the federal constitution... 966
668. Regulations that have been held valid.......................... 967
669. The power to impose penalties in favor of private persons—Constitutional questions 972
670. Regulating speed of trains 974
671. Grade crossings 974

TABLE OF CONTENTS—VOL. II. xiii

PAGE.

§ 672. Requiring services and denying compensation.................... 975
673. Federal corporations—State can not transform into a domestic corporation.. 976

CHAPTER XXVIII.

STATE RAILROAD COMMISSIONERS.

674. Introductory.. 978
675. Nature of state railroad commissions............................. 979
676. The power to create railroad commissions........................ 980
677. Strictly judicial powers can not be conferred upon administrative or ministerial officers.. 982
678. Granting authority to make regulations not a delegation of legislative power... 983
679. Legislature can not authorize a railroad commission to make unjust discriminations... 983
680. Members of railroad commission are public officers.............. 985
681. Qualifications of commissioners................................... 986
682. Powers of railroad commissioners—Illustrative cases............. 986
683. Jurisdiction of railroad commissioners............................ 988
684. Jurisdiction of commissioners not extended by implication—General rule.. 990
685. Incidental powers of a railroad commission....................... 991
686. Right of railroad companies to a hearing......................... 991
687. Orders of commissioners not contracts............................ 992
688. Certificates of commissioners that rates are reasonable—Effect of. 992
689. Regulation of charges for transporting property and passengers.. 993
690. Domestic commerce... 994
691. Reasonableness of freight and fare tariff of rates—How far a judicial question... 996
692. Regulation of charges—Test of resonableness..................... 998
693. Tariff of rates—Test of resonableness............................ 998
694. Stations—Power to order company to provide....................1002
695. Procedure before the commissioners..............................1004
696. Effect of the decision of the commissioners that a company has not committed an act authorizing a forfeiture...................1005
697. Enforcing the orders of the commissioners—Generally............1006
698. Enforcing the orders of the commissioners—Mandamus...........1007
699. Mandamus enforcing orders of commissioners—Illustrative cases.1008
700. Suits against railroad commissioners are not ordinarily suits against the state...1010
701. Remedies for illegal acts of railroad commissioners..............1011
702. Specific statutory remedy..1011
703. Parties to suits against railroad commissioners..................1013
704. Review by *certiorari*...1014
705. Injunction against commissioners—Generally.....................1014
706. Where commissioners exceed their jurisdiction injunction will lie.1015

xiv   TABLE OF CONTENTS—VOL. II.

PAGE.
§ 707. Vacating orders of commissioners on the ground of fraud........1016
  708. Federal question—Removal of causes from state courts..........1016

CHAPTER XXIX.

PENAL OFFENSES BY AND AGAINST RAILROAD COMPANIES.

709. Penal offenses by railroad companies—Generally................1018
710. Penal statutes strictly construed—No extra-territorial effect.......1021
711. Right of action as affected by penal statutes—Effect of violation as proof of negligence...1023
712. Action for enforcement of penal statutes......................1026
713. The informer's rights—Parties.................................1027
714. The penalty—Computation.....................................1029
715. When "penalty" and when "liquidated damages"...............1031
716. Indictment of railroad companies for causing death.............1034
717. Violation of Sunday laws......................................1035
718. Indictment of railroad company for maintaining a nuisance......1036
719. Obstruction of highways.......................................1038
720. Failure to maintain accommodations at stations.................1040
721. Statutory signals—Stops at crossings..........................1041
722. Blackboards and bulletins at stations..........................1042
723. Unlawful speed..1043
724. Other penal regulations.......................................1044
725. Violation of federal regulations...............................1046
726. Penalty for confinement of live stock..........................1046
727. Offenses against railroads—Obstructing mails and interfering with interstate commerce...1047
728. Sale of tickets without authority—Scalpers....................1047
729. Climbing on car—Evading payment of fare....................1048
730. Placing obstruction on track...................................1048
731. Shooting or throwing missiles at car..........................1051
732. Breaking into depot or car—Burglary..........................1052
733. Injury to railroad property—Malicious trespass.................1052
734. Other crimes against railroad companies.......................1053

CHAPTER XXX.

TAXATION OF RAILROAD PROPERTY.

735. Taxation of railroads—Preliminary............................1055
736. Legislative power...1056
737. Appropriate method of assessing...............................1057
738. Methods of taxation...1058
739. Statutory method of assessment exclusive......................1059
740. Legislative discretion—Classification..........................1059
741. Equality and uniformity 1060
742. Duties of corporation—Rights of stockholders..................1060

PAGE.
§ 743. Failure of the corporation to make return—Effect on stockholder.1061
744. Discrimination..1062
745. Lien of assessment..1063
746. Relinquishment of the power of taxation........................1063
747. Exemption from taxation—Consolidation..........................1064
748. Right of exemption non-assignable...............................1066
749. Immunity from taxation not a franchise..........................1066
750. Exemption of property used in operating railroad 1067
751. Remedies—Injunction 1069
752. Tender of amount of taxes owing is required 1071

CHAPTER XXXI.

TAXATION AS AFFECTED BY THE FEDERAL CONSTITUTION.

753. Taxing interstate commerce railroads 1072
754. Interstate commerce—Obstruction of.............................1073
755. Railroad property used in interstate commerce is taxable by the states 1074
756. Interstate commerce—Taxation of property brought from one state into another..1076
757. Railroad in more than one state.................................1076
758. Mileage basis of valuation 1077
759. License tax 1078
760. Privilege tax on interstate railroads...........................1079
761. Privilege tax discriminated from a property tax 1079
762. Excise tax 1081
763. Tax on passengers carried 1083
764. Tax on interstate freight.......................................1083
765. Tax on gross receipts of interstate commerce corporations 1084
766. Fees for the right to be a corporation not taxes................1085
767. Municipal tax as compensation for use of streets 1085
768. Impairing obligation of a contract..............................1086
769. Impairing obligation of contracts—Tax on bonds 1088
770. Exemption of railroad property—Contract—Alteration of charter.1089
771. Due process of law in tax proceedings...........................1091
772. Equal protection of the laws 1091
773. Equal protection of the laws—Corporations are persons..........1092
774. Equal protection of the laws—What is a denial of 1093
775. Fourteenth amendment—Unequal protection generally..........1094
776. Classification not a denial of equal protection.................1095
777. Fourteenth amendment—Tax for salaries of railroad commissioners 1095
778. Corporations deriving rights from the United States 1096
779. Land grants..1096
780. Domestic commerce 1097

CHAPTER XXXII.

LOCAL ASSESSMENTS.

	PAGE.
§ 781. Assessments and taxes—Distinction	1099
782. Local assessments—Power to levy	1101
783. Statute must be complied with	1103
784. Property subject to local assessment—General rule	1105
785. Property of railroad companies	1106
786. Right of way—Whether subject to assessment	1107
787. Abutting property—Right of way is not	1110
788. Right of way—Mode of assessing	1111
789. Lien of the assessment	1112
790. Assessment of right of way—Enforcing assessment	1114
791. Procedure	1116

CHAPTER XXXIII.

LAND GRANTS.

792. The ground upon which public aid to railroads rests	1117
793. Land grants	1118
794. Construction of land grants	1118
795. Construction of land grants—Illustrative cases	1120
796. Effect of grant	1123
797. Effect of grant—Illustrative cases	1125
798. Reserved lands	1126
799. Indemnity lands	1127
800. Priority of rights	1128
801. Breach of condition—Forfeiture	1129
802. Legislative declaration of forfeiture	1130
803. Cancellation of grants and entries	1131
804. Staking and surveying line does not conclude the company	1132
805. Aid to two companies by same grant	1132
806. Grants by the government—Estoppel	1132
807. Where state renders performance of condition impossible grant is not defeated	1134
808. Partial failure to perform conditions	1134
809. Notice by possession	1135
810. Injunction on the application of company	1135
811. Effect of reservation of right to use railroad as a highway	1136

CHAPTER XXXIV.

PUBLIC AID.

812. State aid	1138
813. State aid—Lien of state	1139

TABLE OF CONTENTS—VOL. II. xvii

PAGE.
- § 814. Constitutionality of statutes authorizing municipal aid to railroads.1139
- 815. Construction of constitutional provisions 1141
- 816. Corporate power—Constitutional limitation......................1141
- 817. Constitutional prohibitions 1143
- 818. Direct limitations upon the state not limitations upon power to authorize municipalities to grant aid 1143
- 819. Constitutional restrictions operate prospectively.................1145
- 820. Limitation upon the power of municipalities to incur debts.......1146
- 821. Constitutional questions—Delegation of legislative power 1147
- 822. Submission to vote..1147
- 823. Submission to popular vote—Constitutional requirements 1148
- 824. Constitutional power—Compelling public corporations to aid railway companies...1149
- 825. Scope of the legislative power....................................1150
- 826. Scope of the legislative power—Illustrative cases................1151
- 827. Power to aid railroads—Statutory authority......................1153
- 828. Power to grant aid is continuous.................................1154
- 829. Railroad aid laws not restricted to new companies...............1156
- 830. Taxing the property of one railroad company to aid in the construction of the road of another company.....................1156
- 831. Construction of statutes conferring authority to aid railroad companies..1157
- 832. Impairment of contract rights...................................1158
- 833. Impairment of contract rights—Illustrative cases.................1159
- 834. Construction of statutes—Implied powers........................1160
- 835. Construction of statutes conferring authority to aid railroad companies—Illustrative instances...............................1161
- 836. Construction of enabling acts—Adjudged cases....................1163
- 837. Means and methods..1166
- 838. Requirements of statute—Classes of cases........................1166
- 839. Power to aid by subscription does not authorize the execution of bonds..1167
- 840. Levy of taxes—Withdrawal of power—Time.....................1168
- 841. Donations and subscriptions.....................................1169
- 842. Repeal of enabling act—Withdrawal of authority................1170
- 843. Validating proceedings—Retrospective laws......................1171
- 844. Legislative power to authorize ratification.......................1174
- 845. Curative statutes—Requisites of.................................1176
- 846. Division of municipality for purpose of voting....................1177
- 847. What corporations may be authorized to grant aid...............1178
- 848. Subscription to unorganized company............................1178
- 849. Votes—Voters—Majority of votes................................1179
- 850. Failure to conform to the requirements of the enabling act—Illustrative cases..1181
- 851. Conditions—Performance of—Excuse for non-performance—Illustrative cases...1183
- 852. Conditions—Power of municipality to prescribe..................1185

xviii   TABLE OF CONTENTS—VOL. II.

                                   PAGE.

§ 853. Change of municipality..1186
854. Limitations upon the amount...................................1187
855. Valuation of property..1188
856. Conditions must be performed..................................1189
857. Preliminary survey..1190
858. Petition—Requisites of—Petitioners—Qualifications of...........1191
859. Notice of election...1194
860. Influencing voters...1195
861. Vote does not of itself constitute a contract...................1196
862. Aid authorized by popular vote—Duty of local officer...........1197
863. Contract granting aid—Subscription—Enforcement................1198
864. Power of municipal officers where statute required submission to popular vote..1201
865. Decision of local officers as to jurisdictional facts.................1201
866. Acceptance of aid...1203
867. Ratification of subscription.....................................1204
868. Stock subscribed by municipality—Legislative control of.........1204
869. Rights and liabilities of municipal corporations as stockholders..1206
870. Defenses to municipal subscriptions............................1206
871. Estoppel of tax-payers...1207
872. Remedies of tax-payers..1208
873. Remedies of municipalities....................................1210
874. Remedies of railroal companies................................1211

CHAPTER XXXV.

MUNICIPAL AID BONDS.

875. Power to issue aid bonds......................................1215
876. Legislative authority requisite.................................1216
877. Constitutional questions—Completed road......................1217
878. Governmental subdivision may be authorized to issue bonds.....1218
879. Execution of the power to issue aid bonds—Generally...........1218
880. Execution of the power to issue aid bonds—Implied powers......1219
881. Formal execution of bonds....................................1220
882. Nature of municipal aid bonds................................1220
883. Proceedings of municipal officers must conform to the statute....1222
884. Want of power—Definition....................................1222
885. Conflict of authority..1223
886. Consolidation does not take away right to bonds................1223
887. Purchasers of aid bonds—Duty to ascertain that power to issue bonds exists..1225
888. Bonds issued in excess of the limits prescribed by the constitution..1225
889. Limitation of amount—Construction of statute..................1226
890. Bonds in excess of the limit prescribed by statute...............1227
891. Bonds running beyond time prescribed........................1228
892. Bonds payable out of a specific fund...........................1228

		PAGE.
§ 893.	Performance of conditions	1229
894.	Ratification of bonds irregularly issued	1230
895.	When bonds are void	1231
896.	*Bona fide* holders of aid bonds	1234
897.	Estoppel by recitals in bonds—General doctrine	1235
898.	Estoppel by recitals in bonds—Illustrative cases	1237
899.	Recitals in bonds not always conclusive	1240
900.	Official certificates—Conclusiveness of	1241
901.	Recitals in bonds to constitute an estoppel must be of facts	1242
902.	No estoppel where the officer ordering bonds to issue had no jurisdiction	1243
903.	Estoppel otherwise than by recital—Illustrative instances	1244
904.	Estoppel by retention of stock	1246
905.	Recitals in bonds—Effect of against bondholders	1247
906.	Refunding—Substitution	1248
907.	Discretionary powers and peremptory duty	1249
908.	Registration	1250
909.	Rights of *bona fide* holders not affected by sale of bonds at less sum than that prescribed by statute	1251
910.	Subrogation of holder of invalid bonds	1251
911.	Liability of municipality to purchaser of invalid bonds	1252
912.	Right of municipality to recover money paid because of wrongful acts of the railroad company	1252
913.	Defenses to aid bonds	1253
914.	Bondholders not bound by proceedings to which they are not parties	1255
915.	Following state decisions	1255
916.	Jurisdiction of federal courts	1255
917.	Compelling the issue of bonds	1257
918.	Remedies of bondholders	1257

THE CORPORATION.

CHAPTER XV.

CONSOLIDATION.

§ 322. Consolidation must be authorized by legislature.
323. Statutory mode must be pursued—Collateral attack.
324. Intention to consolidate—Difference between succession and consolidation.
325. Right of majority to effect consolidation — When minority may prevent—Release of dissenting subscribers.
326. Statutory provisions for consolidation.
327. Rights of old stockholders and their relation to the new company.
328. Remedies for old stockholders.
329. Consolidated company succeeds to rights and liabilities of the old companies.
330. Special privileges and immunities—When they pass to the new company.

§ 331. When special privileges do not pass.
332. Duties and obligations of new company.
333. Liability of new company on old contracts.
334. Liability of new company for torts—Extent of liability—Generally.
335. Constituent companies are usually dissolved—When not.
336. Effect of consolidation upon liens.
337. *De facto* consolidation—Estoppel—Liability of constituent companies where consolidation is set aside.
338. Effect of consolidation upon pending suits.
339. Consolidation with foreign corporations.

§ 322. Consolidation must be authorized by legislature.— In the absence of legislative authority a railroad company can not consolidate with another company so as to form a single corporation,[1] although the legislature may, by a subsequent

[1] Clearwater *v.* Meredith, 1 Wall. (U. S.) 25; Pearce *v.* Madison, etc., R. Co., 21 How. (U. S.) 441; Green- ville, etc., Co. *v.* Planters', etc., Co., 70 Miss. 669, s. c. 35 Am. St. R. 681; Aspinwall *v.* Ohio, etc., R. Co., 20

act, render valid an unauthorized consolidation.[1] Most of the states, however, now make provision for the consolidation of railroad companies owning roads which form a continuous or connecting line,[2] while some of the states permit consolidation wherever the two consolidating roads connect to form a continuous line by means of an intervening railroad, and others do not require any connection at all between existing roads as a prerequisite to a valid consolidation of their lines.[3] This general authority, however, is subject to the provisions of the constitutions[4] and laws[5] of many of the states, which forbid the

Ind. 492; Blatchford v. Ross, 5 Abb. Pr. N. S. (N. Y.) 434, 54 Barb. (N. Y.) 42; New York, etc., Canal Co. v. Fulton Bank, 7 Wend. (N. Y.) 412; Black v. Delaware, etc., Canal Co., 24 N. J. Eq. 455; Charlton v. Newcastle, etc., R. Co., 5 Jur. N. S. 1096. But if one company is given power to consolidate with any other it may choose, the company it selects is thereby authorized to unite with it in the consolidation. *In re* Prospect Park, etc., R. Co., 67 N. Y. 371.

[1] Bishop v. Brainerd, 28 Conn. 289; Mead v. New York, etc., R. Co., 45 Conn. 199; McAuley v. Columbus, etc., R. Co., 83 Ill. 348; Mitchell v. Deeds, 49 Ill. 416; Fisher v. Evansville, etc., R. Co., 7 Ind. 407, 413. But a general law authorizing railroad corporations to consolidate their roads, which is prospective in its language and terms, will not be construed to have a retrospective operation. Hatcher v. Toledo, etc., R. Co., 62 Ill. 477; 1 Rorer on Railroads, 591. Informal consolidation has been held validated by subsequent legislation. Mead v. New York, etc., R. R. Co., 45 Conn. 199; McCauley v. Columbus, etc., R. R. Co., 83 Ill. 348, 352.

[2] Stimson's Am. Stat. (1892), § 8730. Two or more railroad corporations, whose roads form a continuous line, may enter into an arrangement for operating both roads as one and thus become jointly liable for debts incurred in borrowing money to be used in furtherance of the business of such line. Chicago, P. & St. L. Ry. Co. v. Ayres, 140 Ill. 644, 30 N. E. 687.

[3] Stimson's Am. Stat. (1892), § 8730. The statutes of many of the states also authorize consolidation when the roads *cross or intersect* each other.

[4] Stimson's Am. Stat. (1886), § 467, citing constitutions of Pennsylvania, Illinois, Michigan, Nebraska, West Virginia, Missouri, Arkansas, Texas, Colorado.

[5] Stimson's Am. Stat. (1892), § 8730. A railroad need not necessarily be parallel to or connected with another road in order to be a "competing road" within the statute forbidding the consolidation of competing roads. East Line & R. R. Co. v. State, 75 Tex. 434, 12 S. W. R. 690. The Missouri statute, which prohibits any railroad company within the state from owning, operating, or managing any other parallel or competing railroad within the state, applies only where both the roads are situated within the state, and where the competition is of some practical importance, such as is liable to affect rates. Kimball v. Atchison, T. & S. F. R. Co., (C. C. U. S.) 46 Fed. R. 888.

consolidation of companies owning or operating parallel and competing lines.[1] In addition to the powers conferred by such general statutes, authority to consolidate is sometimes given in the company's charter,[2] or is contained in a special act of the legislature in states where special acts are not forbidden by the constitution.[3] A state has a right to prescribe the conditions upon which a consolidation may be had under its laws, and a statute requiring the payment of a fee upon filing an agreement of consolidation is not unconstitutional or invalid as imposing a tax on interstate commerce.[4]

§ 323. **Statutory mode must be pursued — Collateral attack.**—These enabling statutes are construed to authorize a consolidation only in cases where the companies seeking to combine come fairly within the terms of the statute. And a statute which provides for the consolidation of companies owning lines that have been so constructed as to admit

---

[1] In West Virginia and Maryland, the consolidation of such companies is forbidden without the consent of the legislature, and in Florida the consent of the railroad commission is required. Stimson's Am. Stat. (1892), § 8730. The constitution of Texas forbids consolidation with any other railroad company organized under the laws of another state. Art. 10, § 6. In New Jersey, consolidation with a corporation of another state can only be effected with the consent of the legislature. N. J. Supp. (1886), R. R's., § 91. As to what are and what are not competing lines, see Kimball v. Atchinson, etc., R. Co., 46 Fed. R. 888; People v. O'Brien, 111 N. Y. 1; County of Leavenworth v. Chicago, etc., R. Co., 25 Fed. R. 219; Currier v. Concord, etc., R. Co., 48 N. H. 321, and authorities cited in preceding note.

[2] Nugent v. Supervisors, 19 Wall. (U. S.) 241; Archer v. Terre Haute, etc., R. Co., 102 Ill. 493.

[3] R. S. Ill. 1889, Ch. 114, §§ 3941 and 196,197; Black v. Delaware, etc., Canal Co., 24 N. J. Eq. 455; Fisher v. Evansville, etc., R. Co., 7 Ind. 407. Power given by statute to one railroad to consolidate with another has been held to authorize any other to join with it. In the matter of Prospect Park, etc., R. Co., 67 N.Y. 371; Mitchell v. Deeds, 49 Ill. 416. A law prohibiting a particular railroad company from consolidating with any parallel or competing line does not violate any contract or other right vested in another railroad company, authorized generally by a former statute to consolidate with any connecting company, the company prohibited not yet being in existence at the time of passage of the prohibitory statute and there being at that time no contract authorizing such consolidation of the two roads. East Line, etc., R. R. Co. v. Rushing, 69 Tex. 306.

[4] Ashley v. Ryan, 153 U. S. 436, s. c. 14 Sup. R. 865, affirming 49 O. St. 504, 31 N. E. R. 721.

the passage of cars over such lines of road continuously without break of gauge or interruption, does not authorize the consolidation of companies whose roads can not be so combined as to form substantially a single line of road.[1] But statutes authorizing the consolidation of connecting or continuous lines do not always require that one should connect with the other at its terminus.[2] It has been held that the organization of a railroad company with the view of ultimately consolidating upon equitable terms and in accordance with the provisions of an existing statute with another already in existence, is not contrary to public policy, and a railroad corporation organized for such purpose may, with a view to accomplishing such consolidation and carrying out the object for which it was created, purchase the stock of such other road.[3] Where the statute provides for the mode of consolidation, that mode must be substantially, if not strictly, pursued,[4] although the courts will usually presume in favor of

[1] State v. Atchison, etc., R. Co., 24 Neb. 143, s. c. 38 N. W. R. 43; East Line, etc., R. Co. v. State, 74 Tex. 434, 12 S. W. R. 690; State v. Vanderbilt, 37 Ohio St. 590. In the latter case, the court says: "That the mere physical ability to pass cars from one road to the other satisfies the statute is a construction of it which is wholly inadmissible, for the provision requiring such connection would be without meaning. In imposing that restriction upon consolidation, the legislature intended, not merely that the physical fact should exist, but that such consolidation should *only* be made for the very purpose of passing freight and passengers over both lines, or some material parts thereof—not necessarily in a direct or straight line, but continuously." The court can not know judicially that roads sought to be consolidated would, if completed, form a continuous line. Georgia Pacific R. Co. v. Gaines, 88 Ala. 377.

[2] Hancock v. Louisville, etc., R. Co., 145 U. S. 409, s. c. 12 Sup. Ct. R. 969; Wallace v. Long Island R. Co., 12 Hun (N. Y.) 460. See, also, Buck v. Seymour, 46 Conn. 156; Humphreys v. St. Louis, etc., R. Co., 37 Fed. R. 730; Union Trust Co. v. Illinois Mid. Ry. Co., 117 U. S. 434, s. c. 6 Sup. Ct. R. 809; Atchison, etc., R. Co. v. Fletcher, 35 Kan. 236; Mayor, etc., v. Baltimore, etc., R. Co., 21 Md. 50.

[3] Hill v. Nisbet, 100 Ind. 341. It was held by the supreme court of Michigan that a certain statute of that state authorized a railroad company to purchase the stock of another company for the purpose of acquiring its road-bed and right of way. Dewey v. Toledo, A. A. & N. M. Ry. Co., 91 Mich. 351, s. c. 51 N. W. 1063. See, *ante*, § 95, note 3, on page 142, where the provisions of the statute are quoted.

[4] Rodgers v. Wells, 44 Mich. 411; Mansfield, etc., R. Co. v. Drinker, 30 Mich. 124; Peninsular R. Co. v. Tharp, 28 Mich. 506; Commonwealth v. At-

§ 323   CONSOLIDATION.   447

the validity of a consolidation in the absence of evidence to the contrary,[1] and will not permit it to be questioned collaterally,[2] at least by the corporation and its stockholders, where it assumes to act as a consolidated company under the law and issues bonds and mortgages as such without any objection on the part of the state or the stockholders.[3] But where the constitution of a state provided that no railroad corporation should consolidate its stock, property, franchises or earnings, in whole or in part, with any other railroad company owning a parallel or competing line, it was held that the word "consolidate" was

---

lantic, etc., R. R. Co., 53 Pa. St. 9; State v. Vanderbilt, 37 Ohio St. 590. An agreement for consolidation of two railroad companies, duly executed after the meetings of the stockholders of both companies had been held, in which the consolidation was ordered, is not rendered invalid by the fact that it bears date prior to the meetings. Wells v. Rodgers, 60 Mich. 525, 27 N. W. R. 671. Substantial compliance with an act authorizing consolidation is sufficient. County of Leavenworth v. Chicago, etc., R. Co., 25 Fed. R. 219.

[1] Sparrow v. Evansville, etc., R. Co., 7 Ind. 369; Farmers' L. & T. Co. v. Toledo, etc., R. Co., 67 Fed. R. 49, 55; Swartwout v. Michigan, etc., Railroad Co., 24 Mich. 389. See Wells v. Rodgers, 60 Mich. 525. But in Georgia Pacific R. Co. v. Gaines, 88 Ala. 377, the supreme court of Alabama held that it must affirmatively appear that several companies consolidated under the laws of that state are so joined as to form a continuous line, or the consolidated company can not claim to succeed to the rights of the constituent companies. See, also, Georgia Pac. R. Co. v. Wilks, 86 Ala. 478; Brown v. Dibble, 65 Mich. 520, 30 Am. & Eng. R. Cas. 241.

[2] Pittsburgh, etc., R. Co. v. Rothschild, 26 Am. & Eng. R. Cas. 50. See, also, Wallace v. Loomis, 97 U. S. 146; Dallas Co. v. Huidekoper, 154 U.S. 654, s. c. 14 Sup. Ct. R. 1190; Casey v. Galli, 94 U. S. 673. A *de facto* consolidated corporation can not set up the illegality of the consolidation to defeat a recovery against it upon the contracts of one of its constituent companies. Chicago, etc., R. Co. v. Putnam, 36 Kan. 121, 12 Pac. R. 593. Only the state can attack the validity of a consolidation, apparently regular, which has existed and been acted upon by the companies for five years. Atchison, etc., R. Co. v. Board Comrs. Sumner Co., 51 Kan. 617, 33 Pac. R. 312. See, also, Bell v. Pennsylvania, etc., R. R. Co. (N. J.), 10 Atl. R. 741. But see, as to right of stockholder in the original corporation to question the existence of the consolidated corporation when sued on his subscription, *post*, § 307; 1 Thomp. Corp., §§ 357, 358.

[3] Phinizy v. Augusta, etc., R. Co., 62 Fed. R. 678; Farmers' L. & T. Co. v. Toledo, etc., R. Co., 67 Fed. R. 49. See, also, Ashley v. Supervisors, 60 Fed. R. 55; Close v. Glenwood Cemetery, 107 U. S. 466, s. c. 2 Sup. Ct. R. 267; Douglas Co. v. Bolles, 94 U. S. 104; Bradford v. Frankfort, etc., R. Co., (Ind.) 40 N. E. R. 741.

used "in the sense of join or unite," and that the constitution could not be evaded by substituting a lease instead of a conveyance.[1] The case just referred to was a *quo warranto* proceeding by the attorney-general to oust the lessor company from its franchises, and the court held that they were subject to forfeiture, but refused to decree a forfeiture in the first instance and merely declared the lease void.

§ 324. **Intention to consolidate — Difference between succession and consolidation.**—Where a general power to consolidate is given without any specific provision as to the terms or mode, it is held that the companies may unite upon such terms and in such mode as they choose,[2] so long as they do not exceed the statutory authority. But a clear intention to consolidate, together with the performance of acts reasonably appropriate to that end, must be shown in order to establish a consolidation,[3] and the mere purchase by one railroad corporation of the franchise and property of another at a sale on execution does not operate to make the purchaser the successor by consolidation of the purchased road.[4] A consolidated corpo-

---

[1] State *v.* Atchison, etc., R. Co., 24 Neb. 143, s. c. 38 N. W. R. 43, 32 Am. & Eng. R. Cas. 388.

[2] Dimpfel *v.* Ohio, etc., R. Co. (U. S. C. C. S. D. Ill.), 8 Rep. 641, s. c. 9 Biss. 127.

[3] 1 Thomp. Corp., §§ 327, 328, 329; Shrewsbury, etc., R. R. Co. *v.* Stour Valley Ry. Co., 21 Eng. L. & Eq. 628. See, also, Hart *v.* Rensselaer, etc., R. R. Co., 8 N. Y. 37. The union of name, officers, business and property of corporations, does not, it has been held, change their distinctive character as separate corporations. Nashua & L. R. Corp. *v.* Boston & L. R. Corp. 136 U. S. 356, 42 Am. & Eng. R. Cas. 688. Nor is a temporary co-operation under one management a consolidation. Archer *v.* Terre Haute, etc., R. R. Co., 102 Ill. 493, s. c. 7 Am. & Eng. R. R. Cas. 249. And the identity of the stockholders, or the fact that one of the corporations, by means thereof, or by means of the ownership of the stock of the other, exercised a controlling influence over it, does not make either the agent of the other, nor merge them into one, so as to make the contract of one binding upon the other, where they are separately organized under distinct charters. Richmond, etc., Const. Co. *v.* Richmond, etc., R. Co., 68 Fed. R. 105; Central Trust Co. *v.* Bridges, 57 Fed. R. 753.

[4] Gulf, etc., R. Co. *v.* Newell, 73 Tex. 334; Gulf, etc., R. Co. *v.* Morris, 67 Tex. 692; Houston, etc., R. R. Co. *v.* Shirley, 54 Tex. 125. But consolidation by purchase may be expressly authorized. Williamson *v.* New Jersey, etc., R. R. Co., 26 N. J. Eq. 398; Eaton, etc., R. Co. *v.* Hunt, 20 Ind. 457.

ration may usually be said to be the successor of the original or constituent companies,[1] but succession is not necessarily consolidation, and a corporation may have authority to become the successor of another without having any authority to consolidate. Succession by purchase, or in any other manner than by consolidation, is usually a very different thing from the latter and gives rise to different rights and liabilities.[2]

§ 325. **Right of majority to effect consolidation—When minority may prevent—Release of dissenting subscribers.**—Where the law under which a corporation is formed provides generally for its consolidation with other companies, such consolidation may be effected at the pleasure of the majority of the corporation.[3] But where the power to consolidate was not contained in the charter or governing law, a consolidation can not be effected without the consent of all the stockholders,[4]

---

[1] United States v. Southern Pac. R. Co., 14 Sawy. (U. S.) 620.

[2] See Taylor on Priv. Corp., § 415-418; Wait Insolv. Corp., § 428. Thus, the successor by purchase may acquire the property free from debts and liabilities already created. Hoard v. Chesapeake & O. Ry., 123 U. S. 222; Pennsylvania Transp. Co.'s Appeal, 101 Pa. St. 576; Cook v. Detroit, etc., Ry. Co., 43 Mich. 349; Hammond v. Port Royal, etc., R. R. Co., 15 S. Car. 10, and 16 So. Car. 567. And while it is usually bound by restrictions on the old company, it does not always acquire the special privileges and franchises of the old company. Thus, if an individual purchaser becomes the successor, the franchise to be a corporation may not pass to him. See Chaffe v. Ludeling, 27 La. Ann. 607; Pittsburgh, Cin., etc., Ry. Co. v. Moore, 33 Ohio St. 384; Campbell v. Marietta, etc., R. R. Co., 23 O. St. 168; Daniels v. St. Louis, etc., R. Co., 62 Mo. 43; Pennsylvania R. R. Co. v. Sly, 65 Pa. St. 205; Ragan v. Aiken, 9 Lea (Tenn.) 609.

[3] Sparrow v. Evansville, etc., R. Co., 7 Ind. 369; Bish v. Johnson, 21 Ind. 299; Atchison, etc., R. Co. v. Phillips Co., 25 Kan. 261; Cork, etc., R. Co. v. Paterson, 37 Eng. L. & Eq. Rep. 398; Mansfield, etc., R. R. Co. v. Stout, 26 Ohio St. 241; Nugent v. Supervisors, 19 Wall. (U. S.) 241; Hale v. Cheshire R. R. Co., 161 Mass. 443, 37 N. E. R. 306.

[4] Thomp. Corp., § 343. See, also, Chapman v. Mad River, etc., R. R. Co., 6 Ohio St. 119; Botts v. Simpsonville, etc., Co., 88 Ky. 54, s. c. 10 S. W. R. 134; Illinois, etc., R. R. Co. v. Cook, 29 Ill. 237; Indianola R. Co. v. Fryer, 56 Tex. 609; Compare Lauman v. Lebanon Valley R. R. Co., 30 Pa. St. 42. The stockholder may be estopped by his acquiescence for a term of years to deny the validity of a consolidation effected without his express consent. Boston, etc., R. Co. v. New York, etc., R. Co., 13 R. I. 260; Bell

even though the legislature may have passed a subsequent statute authorizing the consolidation of all railroad companies.[1] In other words, there must be the unanimous consent of all the stockholders, unless the right to consolidate was given by the law or the "constating instruments" at the time the corporation was created.[2] If a consolidation be effected under legislative authority given after subscriptions are made but without the consent of subscribers who have not yet paid for stock in the original companies, the consolidated company can not enforce such subscriptions.[3] It has also been held that a municipal corporation has no power to give its consent to or acquiesce in a consolidation by which the enterprise is so far changed that the vote authorizing a subscription does not apply to the road of the new company.[4]

v. Pennsylvania, etc., R. R. Co., (N. J.), 10 Atl. R. 741. The consent of the bondholders and other creditors is not necessary to a consolidation. 2 Morawetz Priv. Corp., § 953.

[1] McCray *v.* Junction R. Co., 9 Ind. 358; Sparrow *v.* Evansville, etc., R. Co., 7 Ind. 369; Kean *v.* Johnson, 9 N. J. Eq. 401. And the fact that the legislature has reserved the right to amend or repeal the original charter does not, ordinarily, give it a right to authorize a consolidation against the will of the minority. Mayor, etc., Knoxville *v.* Knoxville, etc., R. Co., 22 Fed. R. 758; Cross *v.* Peach Bottom R. Co., 90 Pa. St. 392. But see Pennsylvania College Cases, 13 Wall. (U. S.) 190; Bishop *v.* Brainerd, 28 Conn. 289. "Whether or not the legislature can authorize the consolidation of a corporation, under the general power reserved to alter or annul the charter, is not necessary to be decided. It is certain that it can not be done when it affects the right of stockholders, by increasing their liability as such, or diminishing the value of their stock. * * The act in this case is void unless made by the unanimous consent of the stockholders." Botts *v.* Simpsonville & B. C. Turnp. Co., 88 Ky. 54; 2 L. R. A. 594, Blatchford *v.* Ross, 54 Barb. (N. Y.) 42, s. c. 37 How. Pr. (N. Y.) 110. But see Beal *v.* New York, etc., R. Co., 4 N. Y. S. Rep. 174, s. c. 41 Hun 172.

[2] Earle *v.* Seattle, etc., R. Co., 56 Fed. R. 909, 912.

[3] Booe *v.* Junction R. Co., 10 Ind. 93; Harshman *v.* Bates Co., 92 U. S. 569; McCray *v.* Junction R. R. Co., 9 Ind. 358; Clearwater *v.* Meredith, 1 Wall. (U. S.) 25; 1 Thomp. Corp., § 75. See *ante*, §§ 43, 45.

[4] State *v.* Commissioners of Nemaha Co., 10 Kan. 569. See, also, Harshman *v.* Bates Co., 92 U. S. 569; Board of Commissioners of Hamilton Co. *v.* State, 115 Ind. 64, s. c. 4 N. E. R. 589, and 17 N. E. R. 855. But compare New Buffalo *v.* Iron Co., 105 U. S. 73; Livingston County *v.* Portsmouth Bank, 128 U. S. 102, s. c. 9 Sup. Ct. R. 18; Mayor *v.* Dennison, 69 Fed. R. 58. See other authorities in note to Cantillon *v.* Dubuque, etc., R. Co., 78 Iowa 48, 5 L. R. A. 278.

§ 326. **Statutory provisions for consolidation.**—The laws of the various states for the consolidation of railroad companies generally provide that an agreement for a consolidation must be entered into by the directors of the several companies[1] and ratified by a vote of stockholders.[2] In Indiana the statute provides that any railroad corporation in that state may consolidate with a railroad corporation in an adjoining state "upon such terms as may be by them mutually agreed upon, in accordance with the laws of the adjoining state," and it is held that this does not require that the meeting of the stockholders to act upon the proposition to consolidate shall be called and conducted in accordance with the laws of such adjoining state.[3] The agreement of consolidation as entered into by the directors and ratified by the stockholders is usually required to be filed with the secretary of state,[4] and it is held in Ohio that until this is done the consolidation is not actually completed so as to effect a dissolution of the old companies,

[1] Stimson's Am. Stat. (1892), § 8731.

[2] Stimson's Am. Stat. (1892), § 8732. The agreement for a consolidation must be ratified by a state board before it is of any force in Michigan. Howell's Stat., § 3344. In New Hampshire, application must be made to the supreme court, which may, after notice and hearing, authorize the consolidation, " if the public good will be promoted by such union." Pub. Stat. 1892, Ch. 156, § 22.

[3] Bradford v. Frankfort, etc., Co., (Ind.) 40 N. E. R. 741.

[4] Stimson's Am. (1892), § 8732; Trester v. Missouri Pac. R. Co., 33 Neb. 171, 49 N. W. R. 1110. See article by Judge Thompson in 31 Cent. L. Jour. 5. Notice is also required in some states. The certificate so filed is made evidence of a lawful consolidation by a statute in some states. A copy of the articles of consolidation between two railroads, duly certified under the seal of the secretary of state, is *prima facie* evidence of the existence of the consolidated corporation. East St. Louis C. Ry. Co. v. Wabash, St. L. & P. Ry. Co., 24 Ill. App. 279. A certified copy from the secretary of state's office of an agreement for consolidation was held by the Supreme Court of the United States to be *conclusive* evidence of the consummation of the consolidation of corporations in Missouri, under a similar statute, in suits between the consolidated company and individuals or other corporations. Leavenworth County v. Chicago, R. I. & P. R. Co., 134 U. S. 688, s. c. 10 Sup. Ct. Rep. 708. The filing of the certificate of consolidation may be made a condition precedent. Commonwealth v. Atlantic, etc., R. R. Co., 53 Pa. St. 9; Peninsular R. R. Co. v. Tharp, 28 Mich. 506. But see Leavenworth County v. Chicago, etc., Ry. Co., *supra*. Other steps may also be required as condition precedent. Mansfield, etc., R. R. Co. v. Drinker, 30 Mich. 124.

but that they still remain competent to accept subscriptions to their capital stock until the agreement is actually filed.[1] The supreme court of Pennsylvania, however, holds that the consolidated corporation is so far created by the execution of an agreement of consolidation by the constituent corporations that a valid subscription to its stock may be made before the agreement is recorded.[2] And in a recent case in one of the federal courts it was held that where the agreement was recorded in the office of the secretary of state and it appeared from the minutes of three of the companies that it had been ratified and accepted by the stockholders, and the new company assumed and exercised for several years entire charge and control of all the roads without objection, this was sufficient to show an acceptance by all of them, although the minutes of the fourth company were lost and although the agreement did not have upon it the certificates of the several secretaries of the different companies, which the statute made conclusive evidence of such acceptance.[3] A statute granting railroad companies power to consolidate, but coupling the grant with a condition or proviso that the consolidated company shall not have power to create any lien which shall be valid as against a specified class of creditors is not in violation of a constitutional provision that statutes shall embrace but one subject, which must be expressed in the title.[4]

§ 327. **Rights of old stockholders and their relation to the new company.**—The stockholders of the constituent corporations can not be compelled to become stockholders of the new

---

[1] Mansfield, etc., R. Co. v. Brown, 26 Ohio St. 223. See, also, State v. Vanderbilt, 37 Ohio St. 590.

[2] McClure v. People's Freight R. Co., 90 Pa. St. 269. The provision requiring each company to file with the secretary of state a resolution accepting the provision of the act under which the two companies have consolidated, is merely directory, and a disregard of it will not invalidate the agreement of consolidation, if all other provisions of the act have been complied with.

[3] Phinizy v. Augusta, etc., R. Co., 62 Fed. R. 678. As to proof of consolidation, see Columbus, etc., R. Co. v. Skidmore, 69 Ill. 566; Commonwealth v. Carroll, 145 Mass. 403, s. c. 14 N. E. R. 618; Kinion v. Kansas City, etc., R. Co., 39 Mo. App. 382.

[4] Frazier v. East Tenn., etc., R. Co., 88 Tenn. 138, s. c. 12 S. W. R. 537, **40** Am. & Eng. R. Cas. 358.

corporation without their consent, unless otherwise provided, and do not become such, as a rule, until the surrender of their old stock in exchange for new.[1] And, although the old corporation may be dissolved by the act of consolidation the property interests of its stockholders remain unchanged until divested by their own act or in some manner provided by law.[2] Several of the states, however, provide for the purchase by the company of the shares of stockholders who decline to become members of the consolidated company.[3] And, as a general rule, unless otherwise provided by contract or the governing statute, when the consolidation is duly perfected stockholders in the old companies become stockholders in the new,[4] which may usually enforce the unpaid subscriptions to the stock of the old corporations.[5] But, if the subscription was made upon a valid condition, it passes to the new company subject to such condition.[6]

[1] 1 Beach Priv. Corp., § 351; State v. Bailey, 16 Ind. 46, s. c. 79 Am. Dec. 405; Gardner v. Hamilton, etc., Ins. Co., 33 N. Y. 421.

[2] Philadelphia, etc., R. Co. v. Catawissa R. Co., 53 Pa. St. 20. It has been held in Massachusetts that the holder of bonds convertible into the stock of a road which had consolidated with another to form a new corporation, expressly charged with the performance of its obligations and liabilities, was entitled to demand stock in the new corporation, as for the purposes of this contract the old corporation continued under the new name. Day v. Worcester, etc., R. Co., 151 Mass. 302.

[3] Stimson's Am. Stat. (1892), § 8732. But this does not prevent a resort to the courts in a proper case. Langan v. Francklyn, 20 N. Y. Supp. 404. See, also, as to right to arbitrate. Pittsburgh, etc., Ry. Co. v. Garrett, 50 Ohio St. 405, 34 N. E. R. 493.

[4] Ridgway Township v. Griswold, 1 McCrary (U. S.) 151; 1 Thomp. Corp., § 355. In Fee v. New Orleans, etc., Co., 35 La. Ann. 413, it was held that a stockholder in one of the old companies could sue the consolidated company for stock which he was entitled to in exchange. So, under the agreement in Anthony v. American Glucose Co., (N. Y.) 41 N. E. R. 23.

[5] Wells v. Rodgers, 60 Mich. 525, s. c. 27 N. W. Rep. 671; Cooper v. Shropshire, etc., R. R. Co., 13 Jur. 443, s. c. 6 Eng. Ry. & Canal Cas. 136; Hanna v. Cincinnati, etc., R. R. Co., 20 Ind. 30; Swartwout v. Michigan, etc., R. R Co., 24 Mich. 389; Pope v. Board of Com'rs, 51 Fed. R. 769; Nugent v. Supervisors, 19 Wall. (U. S.) 241; Sprague v. Illinois, etc., R. Co., 19 Ill. 174; Ottawa, etc., R. Co. v. Black, 79 Ill. 262. As to when this can not be done, see *ante*, § 325. Here, of course, we refer to a consolidation authorized by charter or statute at the time the subscription was made.

[6] 1 Thomp. Corp., § 360; Mansfield, etc., R. R. Co. v. Pettis, 26 Ohio St. 259.

§ 328. **Remedies of old stockholders.**—As elsewhere stated,[1] a dissenting stockholder can not always be compelled to become a shareholder in the new consolidated company, nor held liable upon his original subscription, and he may, in some instances, entirely defeat or prevent the consolidation. Thus, he may enjoin an *ultra vires* consolidation,[2] inimical to him; at least until his interest is purchased or secured.[3] He may, however, lose the right to enjoin a consolidation which could not be made without his consent by acquiescence or laches.[4] It is also said that where a consolidation is wrongfully effected by the shareholders, over the objection of a dissenting shareholder, who has partly paid for his stock, the consolidated company is liable to him therefor, but he can not sue the directors personally for damages.[5] We have already referred to the general rule prohibiting collateral attacks upon consolidated corporations as well as other corporations, but this rule ought not, it seems to us, to be applied so as to prevent a subscriber to stock in one of the original corporations from questioning, under certain circumstances, the corporate existence or title of the new consolidated corporation by way of defense to an action by the new company to enforce such subscription.[6]

---

[1] *Ante,* § 325.

[2] Charlton v. New Castle, etc., R. R. Co., 5 Jur. (N. S.) 1096; Watson v. Harlem, etc., Co., 52 How. Pr. (N. Y.) 348; Nathan v. Tompkins, 82 Ala. 437. See, also, Stevens v. Rutland, etc., R. R. Co., 29 Vt. 545; Mowrey v. Indianapolis, etc., R. R. Co., 4 Biss. (U. S.) 78; Botts v. Simpsonville, etc., Co., 88 Ky. 54, s. c. 10 S. W. Rep. 134; Mills v. Central R. R. Co., 41 N. J. Eq. 1; 1 Beach. Priv. Corp., § 356. But not, it is held, on the ground that one of the constituent companies was illegally organized. Bell v. Penn., etc., R. Co., (N. J.) 10 Atl. R. 741.

[3] Lauman v. Lebanon, etc., R. R. Co., 30 Pa. St. 42; State v. Bailey, 16 Ind. 46, s. c. 79 Am. Dec. 405.

[4] Deaderick v. Wilson, 8 Baxt. (Tenn.) 108; Zabriskie v. Hackensack, etc., R. R. Co., 18 N. J. Eq. 178; Bell v. Pennsylvania, etc., R. R. Co., (N. J.) 10 Atl. Rep. 741; 1 Beach Priv. Corp., § 356. See, also, Boston, etc., R. Co., v. New York, etc., R. Co., 13 R. I. 260.

[5] International, etc., R. R. Co. v. Bremond, 53 Tex. 96; Taylor Priv. Corp., § 536, note 3.

[6] See Mansfield, etc., R. R. Co. v. Stout, 26 Ohio St. 241; Mansfield, etc., R. R. Co. v. Brown, 26 Ohio St. 223; Tuttle v. Michigan Air Line R. R. Co., 35 Mich. 247. But see Ottawa, etc., R. Co. v. Black, 79 Ill. 262.

§ 329. **Consolidated company succeeds to rights and liabilities of the old companies.**—As a general rule the consolidated company is vested with all the rights, property, privileges and franchises of the several companies of which it is formed,[1] and is subject to the debts and liabilities of such companies.[2] But it is not liable for a penalty incurred by the lessee of one of the constituent companies.[3] Even in the absence of express statutory provisions on the subject the property and franchises of the old companies will usually vest in the new corporation,[4] and it

---

[1] Stimson's Am. Stat. (1892), § 8734; note to Louisville, N. A. & C. R. R. Co. v. Boney, 117 Ind. 501, s. c. 3 L. R. A. 435; Mt. Pleasant v. Beckwith, 100 U. S. 514; Crawfordsville, etc., Co. v. Fletcher, 104 Ind. 97; 1 Thomp. Corp., § 365, et seq.; 1 Beach Priv. Corp., § 342; Taylor Priv. Corp., § 424. In State v. Maine Central R. Co., 66 Me. 488, it is held that where a new corporation is formed by the consolidation of two or more previously existing corporations, and by the act is to "have the powers, privileges and immunities possessed by each of the corporations," the new corporation will have only the privileges, powers, and immunities possessed by the one of such corporations having the fewest privileges, powers and immunities, and which were common to all. But see Natchez, etc., R. R. Co. v. Lambert, 70 Miss. 779, 13 So. R. 33.

[2] Stimson's Am. Stat. (1892), § 8734; note to McMahan v. Morrison, 79 Am. Dec. 424, 426; Louisville, N. A. & C. R. R. Co. v. Boney, 117 Ind. 501, 3 L. R. A. 435, and note; Beach Priv. Corp., § 343; Taylor Priv. Corp., § 425. See Harrison v. Arkansas, etc., Co., 4 McCrary (U. S.) 264. Pullman Car Co. v. Missouri Pac. Co., 115 U. S. 587; Thompson v. Abbott, 61 Mo. 176; Berry v. Kansas City, etc., R. R. Co., 52 Kan. 759. The new company cannot aver ignorance of an unrecorded mortgage given by one of its constituent companies. Mississippi, etc., Co. v. Chicago, etc., R. Co., 58 Miss. 846. See, also, Bloxam v. Florida, etc., R. Co., (Fla.) 17 So. R. 902. The New York statute authorizing the consolidation of railroad companies, and providing that all debts and liabilities of either company, except mortgages, shall attach to the new corporation, and be enforced against it and its property to the same extent as if created by it, allows an action against the new company on bonds and coupons of one of the former companies, though secured by a mortgage on the property of the orignal debtor corporation. Polhemus v. Fitchburg R. Co., 123 N. Y. 502, 26 N. E. 31. See Town of Plainview v. Winona, etc., R. Co., 36 Minn. 505, 32 N. W. 745. Such liability attaches unless there is a special agreement to the contrary. Berry v. Kansas City, etc., R. Co., 52 Kan. 759, 774.

[3] State v. Pittsburgh, etc., R. Co., 135 Ind. 578, s. c. 35 N. E. R. 700.

[4] Meyer v. Johnston, 53 Ala. 237; Green County v. Conness, 109 U. S. 104; South Carolina R. R. Co. v. Blake, 9 Rich. L. (S. Car.) 228; Trester v. Missouri Pac. R. R. Co., 33 Neb. 171; Zimmer v. State, 30 Ark. 677; Daniels v. St. Louis, etc., R. Co., 62 Mo. 43; Mayor, etc., of Baltimore v. Baltimore, etc., R. R. Co., 6 Gill (Md.) 288,

will succeed to all the rights of each of such companies, and may compromise and settle a claim against one of them and enforce the settlement by suit.[1] Where the law under which the corporation was organized authorizes a consolidation, the consolidated company may recover on the contracts of subscription given to the original companies, since the subscriptions will be held to have been made with reference to the law as it then existed.[2] The consolidated company may accept a continuing offer to subscribe made to one of the original companies, and may, when authorized to do so, perform any conditions annexed to a subscription given to such company.[3] A valid consolidation or a right as successor may, however, be required to be shown to enable the consolidated company or

---

s. c. 48 Am. Dec. 531; State v. Seaboard, etc., R. R. Co., 52 Fed. 450; Cashman v. Brownlee, 128 Ind. 266. In this latter case it is held that where land is conveyed in fee-simple to a railroad company, and afterward the company is consolidated with another, and further consolidations take place from time to time, the new companies formed by the successive consolidations succeed to the said real estate, and may recover it from the grantor or those to whom he afterward transfers it, although he has remained in possession of the premises for more than twenty years after the conveyance was made; since the possession of a grantor can not be adverse to the title of his grantee.

[1] Paine v. Lake Erie, etc., R. Co., 31 Ind. 283. The consolidated company may collect municipal aid voted to one of the companies of which it is formed, where the consolidation was authorized at the time it was voted. Scott v. Hansheer, 94 Ind. 1; Atchison, etc., R.Co. v. Phillips Co., 25 Kan. 261; Town of East Lincoln v. Davenport, 94 U. S. 801. See, also, Pope v. Board of Comrs, 51 Fed. R. 769 (holding in accordance with the Indiana decision that the tax must be levied and collected or there is no legal right to it). The Pennsylvania statute governing the consolidation of connecting railroad companies provides that the new company shall possess all the rights theretofore vested in either of them; and all the property and rights of actions shall be deemed to be transferred to the new company. It was held that the consolidated company could recover on an indemnity bond given by a passenger agent to one of the old companies, its attorney, successors, or assigns, prior to the act of consolidation, where such agent continues in his position and discharges substantially the same duties as before. Pennsylvania & N. W. R. Co. v. Harkins, 149 Pa. St. 121, 50 Am. & Eng. R. Cas. 587. The new company may lawfully use a patent axle box which the old companies were licensed to use. Lightner v. Boston, etc., R. R. Co, 1 Lowell 338.

[2] Bish v. Johnson, 21 Ind. 299; Atchison, etc., R. Co. v. Phillips Co., 25 Kan. 261; Nugent v. Supervisors, 19 Wall. (U. S.) 25; *ante*, § 309.

[3] Mansfield, etc., R. Co. v. Brown, 26 Ohio St. 223.

its assignee to maintain an action upon the contracts of one of the roads out of which it was formed.[1] But it is sufficient, in pleading such a consolidation, to show the organization of the original companies into the consolidated company by a given name and as a corporate body by authority of law, without setting out the steps taken to effect the same.[2]

§ 330. **Special privileges and immunities—When they pass to the new company.**—Special privileges possessed by all of the consolidating companies will pass to the new company, where the statute provides that it shall have all the "franchises, privileges and immunities of the constituent companies."[3] Thus, it has been held that an exemption from taxation will pass to the new company so far as the property originally covered by the exemption is concerned.[4] But, in

[1] Brown v. Dibble, 65 Mich. 520, s. c. 30 Am. & Eng. R. Cas. 241. After a railroad company has been merged by consolidation with another railroad company, and such new corporation is carrying on a railway business, and is a *de facto* corporation, the existence and validity of the corporation can only be attacked in a direct proceeding brought for that purpose; such a matter will not be the subject of a collateral attack by way of defeating the right to recover on bonds of the merged railroad subscribed to by a county in aid of railroad construction. Chicago, K. & W. R. Co. v. Putnam, 36 Kan. 121, 12 Pac. R. 593.

[2] Collins v. Chicago, etc., R. Co., 14 Wis. 492. In pleading the consolidation of two railway corporations under the statutes of another state, it is sufficient to set out a copy of the statutes, and to allege that their provisions have been complied with, and the consolidation effected; it is not necessary to set out the steps taken under the statutes, such steps being evidence of the consolidation. Rothschild v. Rio Grande W. Ry. Co., 18 N. Y. Supp. 548, 63 Hun (N. Y.) 632.

[3] In State v. Maine, etc., R. Co., 66 Me. 488, it was held that the consolidated company took only such privileges and immunities as were common to all of the constituent companies. It could, however, doubtless be given all that any one of them possessed.

[4] International, etc., R. Co. v. Anderson Co., 59 Tex. 654; Natchez, etc., R. R. Co. v. Lambert, 70 Miss. 779, 13 So. R. 33. Where two companies, whose charters exempt their capital stock from taxation, consolidate to form a single corporation, it has been held that the shares of stock of such consolidated company are not subject to taxation. Tennessee v. Whitworth, 117 U. S. 139, affirming State v. Whitworth, (U. S. C. C. E. D. Tenn.) 22 Féd. R. 81; State v. Whitworth (U. S. C. C. E. D. Tenn.) 22 Fed. R. 75. See Philadelphia, etc., R. Co. v. Maryland, 10 How. (U. S.) 376; Tomlinson v. Branch, 15 Wall. (U. S.) 460; Central R., etc., Co. v. Georgia, 92 U. S. 665; Chesapeake, etc., R. Co. v. Virginia, 94 U. S. 718; Atlantic, etc., R. Co. v

the absence of such a provision, it seems that a special immunity of exemption from taxation enjoyed by one of the original companies will not pass to the consolidated company.[1] It has been held that a right to take land for a right of way,[2] or to borrow money or mortgage the road as security,[3] or to charge a certain rate for transportation,[4] will pass to the consolidated company. So, it has been held that the right conferred by special charter upon a street railway company to operate a street railway upon all or any of the streets of a city, survives to the company in which it is merged by consolidation.[5] And where the officers and servants of a company are exempt from jury duty, it has likewise been held that the officers and servants of the company into which it is merged by consolidation will possess the same privilege.[6]

§ 331. When special privileges do not pass.—A surrender by the companies of all special privileges is sometimes made the condition of a grant by the state of authority to consolidate, in which case the new company will have only the special privileges conferred by its charter.[7] And, when the consolidation under the law giving the power to consolidate operates in effect as a charter, and the company formed by the consolidation is a new corporation organized under that charter,[8] no special privileges or exemptions will be transmitted to the new company which the legislature could not confer at the

---

Georgia, 98 U. S. 359; State Treasurer v. Auditor-General, 46 Mich. 224. But compare State v. Maine Central R. R. Co., 66 Me. 488, s. c. affirmed in 96 U. S. 499; State v. Keokuk, etc., R. R., 99 Mo. 30, 12 S. W. R. 290; Morgan v. Louisiana, 93 U. S. 217; Railroad Co. v. Gaines, 97 U. S. 697.

[1] See *ante*, § 63, note 2; Keokuk, etc., R. Co. v. Missouri, 152 U. S. 301, s. c. 14 Sup. Ct. R. 592, in which attention is called to the apparent conflict in the decisions of the Supreme Court of the United States.

[2] South Carolina R. Co. v. Blake, 9 Rich. (S. C.) 228.

[3] Mead v. New York, etc., R. Co., 54 Conn. 199.

[4] Fisher v. New York Central, etc., R. Co., 46 N. Y. 644. But see Covington, etc., Co. v. Sanford, (Ky.) 20 S. W. R. 1031.

[5] Citizens' Street R. Co. v. City of Memphis, 53 Fed. R. 715.

[6] Zimmer v. State, 30 Ark. 677.

[7] State v. Keokuk, etc., R. Co., 99 Mo. 30.

[8] The consolidation of a railroad corporation with companies organized under the laws of other states is not an incorporation within the meaning of laws requiring the payment of an

time the consolidation was effected.[1] This is in accordance with the rule announced in a previous section.[2]

§ 332. **Duties and obligations of new company.**—Not only does the new company possess all of the rights and privileges of the original companies not expressly taken from it, but it is subject in general to all the duties imposed upon them by the law or laws of their creation, except so far as the law under which the consolidation is effected relieves it from the performance of such duties.[3] It is bound to perform the duties resting upon the original companies as common carriers, and any agreement to avoid such duties is contrary to public policy and void.[4] So, it has been held liable for a failure to restore a stream crossed by one of the constituent companies to its

organization tax. People v. New York, etc., R. Co., 129 N. Y. 474, 654. See Opinion of the justices, 65 N. H. 673, to the same effect as to the union of two domestic corporations.

[1] St. Louis, etc., R. Co. v. Berry, 113 U. S. 465, s. c. 5 Sup. Ct. R. 529; Keokuk, etc., R. Co. v. Missouri, 152 U. S. 301, s. c. 14 Sup. Ct. R. 592; State v. Keokuk, etc., R. Co., 99 Mo. 30; Keokuk, etc., R. Co. v. County Court of Scotland Co., 41 Fed. Rep. 305. In these cases it is held that the corporation formed by a consolidation effected after the state has adopted a constitution prohibiting the legislature from granting any exemption from taxation can not claim the benefit of an exemption previously granted to the companies of which it is composed. But in Citizens' Street R. Co. v. City of Memphis, 53 Fed. Rep. 715, Judge Hammond held that a consolidation did not have the effect to destroy the special privileges and immunities held by the consolidating companies where the consolidation was effected under a law passed after the adoption of a constitution providing "that the legislature shall have no power * * * to pass any law granting to any individual or individuals rights, privileges, immunities, or exemptions other than such as may be, by the same law, extended to any member of the community who may be able to bring himself within the provisions of such law. No corporation shall be created, or its powers increased or diminished by special laws, but the general assembly shall provide by general laws for the organization of all corporations hereafter created, which laws may at any time be altered or repealed."

[2] See *ante*, § 325.

[3] Chicago, etc., R. Co. v. Moffitt, 75 Ill. 524; Tomlinson v. Branch, 15 Wall. (U. S.) 460; State v. Northern Pac. R. R. Co., 36 Minn. 207; Charity Hospital v. New Orleans, etc., Co., 40 La. Ann. 382, 4 So. R. 433.

[4] Peoria, etc., R. Co. v. Coal Valley Min. Co., 68 Ill. 489; People v. Louisville, etc., R. Co., 120 Ill. 48, s. c. 10 N. E. R. 657.

former condition,[1] and for the continuance of a nuisance erected by such company.[2]

§ 333. Liability of new company on old contracts. — The contracts entered into by the constituent railroad companies may be enforced against the new company to the extent that it is capable of performing their conditions.[3] But, while the contracts of the original companies may be binding upon the corporation formed by their consolidation to the same extent and in the same manner that they were binding upon the original companies respectively, the new company, ordinarily, assumes no greater obligations than rested upon those companies at the time of the consolidation. Thus, in a suit to compel a railroad company formed by consolidation to perform a contract made by one of the original companies to use the complainant's cars on its entire line of railway, and on all roads which it might thereafter control by ownership, lease, or otherwise, the court held that the new company must use the plaintiff's cars upon all roads owned or controlled at the time of the consolidation by the company which had made the contract, but that the contract did not apply to roads acquired after the consolidation.[4]

---

[1] Chicago, etc., R. Co. v. Moffitt, 75 Ill. 524; Cott v. Lewiston R. Co., 36 N. Y. 214.

[2] Eyler v. County Comrs., 49 Md. 257; Wellcome v. Leeds, 51 Me. 313; Central R. Co. v. State, 32 N. J. L. 220.

[3] Pullman Palace Car Co. v. Missouri Pac. R. Co., 115 U. S. 587; 2 Morawetz Priv. Corp. (2d ed.), § 955; Smith v. Los Angeles, etc., R. Co., 98 Cal. 210, 33 Pac. R. 53 (liable for breach of contract); Union Pac. R. Co. v. McAlpine, 129 U. S. 305. See, also, Columbus, etc., Ry. Co. v. Skidmore, 69 Ill. 566; Thompson v. Abbott, 61 Mo. 176; Day v. Worcester, etc., R. R. Co., 151 Mass. 302; Hancock, etc., Ins. Co. v. Worcester, etc., R. R. Co., 149 Mass. 214, s. c. 21 N. E. R. 364. Under a statute authorizing the consolidation of a railroad company, which is the grantee of a right of way, with another company, a section of the statute providing that the consolidation shall not affect the rights of creditors of the companies, the new company is not protected, as an innocent purchaser, against the enforcement of covenants entered into by the grantee of the right of way, and which run with the land, even though the breach occurred after the consolidation was effected. Mobile & M. Ry. Co. v. Gilmer, 85 Ala. 422.

[4] Pullman's Palace Car Co. v. Missouri Pac. R. Co., 115 U. S. 587; 2 Morawetz Priv. Corp. (2d ed.), § 955.

§ 334. **Liability of new company for torts — Extent of liability—Generally.**—The consolidated company is liable for the torts of the original companies as well as upon their contracts.[1] Where suit is brought directly against the consolidated company upon a demand against one of its constituent corporations, the fact of the consolidation should be averred in the complaint, declaration, or bill, in order to avoid a variance in the proof.[2] The debts and liabilities may be enforced against the consolidated company into which it is merged, without any statute imposing such liability,[3] at least to the extent of the property received by it from the old corporation. For equity will consider the effects of a merged or dissolved corporation as a trust fund for the payment of creditors, into whosoever

---

[1] Indianapolis, etc., R. Co. v. Jones, 29 Ind. 465 (stock killing case); Columbus, etc., R. Co. v. Powell, 40 Ind. 37 (personal injuries); Jeffersonville, etc., R. Co. v. Hendricks, 41 Ind. 48 (personal injuries); Cleveland, etc., R. Co. v. Prewitt, 134 Ind. 557, 33 N. E. R. 367, s. c. 54 Am. & Eng. R. Cas. 198; Warren v. Mobile, etc., R. Co., 49 Ala. 582 (personal injuries); Railroad Co. v. Hutchins, 37 Ohio St. 282 (conversion); Texas, etc., R. Co. v. Murphy, 46 Tex. 356; Coggin v. Central R. Co., 62 Ga. 685; Chicago, etc., R. Co. v. Moffitt, 75 Ill. 524; New Bedford R. Co. v. Old Colony R. Co., 120 Mass. 397; State v. Baltimore, etc., R. Co., 77 Md. 489, 26 Atl. R. 865. It is the identity of the corporation, and not of the name, that determines the liability of a railroad company for a trespass. De Lissa v. Missouri P. R. Co., 36 Mo. App. 706.

[2] Indianapolis, etc., R. Co. v. Jones, 29 Ind. 465. A variance arising from such omission can not be taken advantage of for the first time in an appellate court. Indianapolis, etc., R. Co. v. Jones, 29 Ind. 465.

[3] The consolidated company, it is said, should be deemed to be merely the same as each of its constituents, their existence continued in it, under the new form and name, their liabilities still existing as before, and capable of enforcement against the new company in the same way as if no change had occurred in its organization or name. Indianapolis, etc., R. Co. v. Jones, 29 Ind. 465; Columbus, etc., R. Co. v. Powell, 40 Ind. 37; Thompson v. Abbott, 61 Mo. 176; Miller v. Lancaster, 5 Coldw. (Tenn.) 514; Louisville, etc., R. Co. v. Boney, 117 Ind. 501, s. c. 3 L. R. A. 435. There can be no loss of identity of the original companies in the consolidation to the prejudice of the rights of prior creditors, or the destruction of prior liens. Hamlin v. Jerrard, 72 Me. 62; Central R., etc., Co. v. Georgia, 92 U. S. 665. Where one railroad company terminates its existence by being consolidated with another, and no arrangements are made respecting the property and liabilities of the first company, the consolidated company will succeed to all the property and be answerable for all the liabilities of the consolidating companies. Louisville, N. A. & C. Ry. Co. v. Boney, 117 Ind. 501.

hands they may come.[1] But is held that where the act of consolidation merely merges the identity of one railroad company into that of another which has already become the owner of its property and franchises freed from liens, this rule does not apply. For the foundation of the liability of a consolidated corporation for the debts and liabilities of the constituent corporations must rest, it is said, upon an agreement either express or implied from its further act in taking possession of all means of meeting those liabilities. And no assumption of liability can be implied from a consolidation by which no assets pass to the corporation sought to be charged.[2]

§ 335. Constituent companies are usually dissolved—When not.—There is, it seems, a clear distinction between a consolidation whereby the several corporations are merged into a new one and the union or combination of two or more corporations by dissolving all but one into which the others are merged.[3] And the fact that the company absorbing the others

[1] Powell v. North Missouri R. Co., 42 Mo. 63. The creditors have not only a remedy at law against the new company, but also may enforce their claims in equity against the assets of the original company; for it is not competent for the legislature by law to compel the creditors of a company to accept the liability of a new company formed of the stockholders of their debtor company and others, in substitution for their original rights. Morawetz Priv. Corp. (2d ed.), §§ 808, 954; Harrison v. Arkansas Valley R. Co., 4 McCrary (U. S.) 264; Barksdale v. Finney, 14 Gratt. (Va.) 338; Montgomery, etc., R. R. Co. v. Branch, 59 Ala. 139. In some jurisdictions it is held that the new company, in the absence of a statute or contract to the contrary, does not assume the debts and liabilites of the old, and is liable only to the extent of the property which it has received from the debtor company. Prouty v. Lake Shore R. Co., 52 N. Y. 363; Boardman v. Lake Shore, etc., R. R. Co., 84 N. Y. 157; Shackleford v. Miss. Cent. R. R. Co., 52 Miss. 159; Shaw v. Norfolk County R. R. Co., 16 Gray (Mass.) 407.

[2] Houston, etc., R. Co. v. Shirley, 54 Tex. 125. See, also, Hatcher v. Toledo, etc., R. R. Co., 62 Ill. 477, where the debts of the old company having been wiped out by foreclosure and sale, were held not to be fastened upon the new by a subsequent statute making consolidated companies liable for the debts of the constituent companies.

[3] See United States v. Southern Pac. R. Co., 46 Fed. R. 683; Tomlinson v. Branch, 15 Wall (U. S.) 460; Central R., etc., Co. v. Georgia, 92 U. S. 665; Philadelphia, etc., R. R. Co. v. Maryland, 10 How. (U. S.) 376; Citizens' Street R. Co. v. City of Memphis, 53 Fed. R. 715.

§ 335　　　　　　　CONSOLIDATION.　　　　　　　463

is given a new name and enlarged powers will not, necessarily, affect its identity, but a mortgage upon its property, together with all future acquisitions executed before such other companies were absorbed or merged into it will, it has been held, attach to the entire line of road as it exists after the merger.[1] Ordinarily, the effect of a consolidation is to dissolve the old companies and form a new one;[2] but this result does not always follow, for it depends largely upon the terms of the consolidation and the legislative intent as manifested in the statute under which the consolidation takes place,[3] and the constituent companies usually have at least a qualified existence for the purpose of winding up their affairs and preserving the rights of their creditors.[4] The term "consolidation" is an elastic one and may include a union of two or more corporations into a new one with a different name, with or without extinguishing the constituent corporations, or the merger of two or more corporations into another existing corporation under the name of the latter.[5] There is, as we have already said, a distinction between these modes of consolidation. In the latter case, if the merger is complete, it is evident that the one

---

[1] Meyer v. Johnston, 64 Ala. 603, s. c. 8 Am. & Eng. R. Cas. 584.

[2] McMahan v. Morrison, 16 Ind.172, s. c. 79 Am. Dec. 418, and note; St. Louis, etc., R. Co. v. Berry, 41 Ark. 509; Railroad Co. v. Georgia, 98 U. S. 359, 363; Keokuk, etc., R.R.Co. v. Missouri, 152 U. S. 301, s. c. 14 Sup. Ct. R. 592; Clearwater v. Meredith, 1 Wall. (U. S.) 25; Shields v. Ohio, 95 U. S. 319, 325; Fee v. New Orleans, etc., Co., 35 La. Ann. 413; Miner v. New York, etc., R. R. Co., 123 N.Y. 242; Cheraw, etc., R. R. Co. v. Commissioners, 88 N. Car. 519; Note to Louisville, N. A., etc., R. R. Co. v. Boney, 3 L. R. A. 435; Note to State v. Chicago, etc.,R. R. Co., 2 L. R. A. 564; Ashley v. Ryan, 49 Ohio 504, 31 N. E. R. 721, 725, 726.

[3] Wabash, etc., Ry. Co. v. Ham, 114 U. S. 587, 595; Central R. R. Co. v. Georgia, 92 U. S. 665, 670. See, also, ante, § 324, note 3.

[4] Edison Electric Light Co. v. New Haven, etc., Co., 35 Fed. R. 233; Eaton, etc., R. Co. v. Hunt, 20 Ind. 457; 1 Beach Priv. Corp., § 339; Compton v. Wabash, etc., Ry. Co., 45 Ohio St. 592, s. c. 16 N. E. R. 110, 117. See ante, § 334, note.1, p. 462.

[5] In Powell v. North Mo. R. Co., 42 Mo. 63, however, it is said that a union by which several companies are merged into and constituted one body, corporate under the name of one of them, and all are continued in existence, is a consolidation proper, while it is not a mere consolidation where one is extinguished and the other continued in existence.

corporation is extinguished, unless kept alive for certain purposes, while it is equally clear that the other, in which it is merged, is not dissolved.[1] In other words, the legislative intention in such a case would seem to be to unite the two companies under the old charter of one of them, while statutes authorizing the consolidation of two or more corporations in the ordinary way are generally construed as authorizing the formation of a new and distinct corporation, thus extinguishing all the constituent companies unless a contrary intention is manifest. It all depends, however, upon the intention of the legislature, as shown in the statute authorizing the consolidation, and the agreement of consolidation in pursuance of the statute. "There is nothing in the nature of the subject-matter, nor of the process of consolidation, that requires the extinction of the old corporations to make the new. It may be done, or it may not."[2] So far at least as domestic corporations are concerned, it is for the state to say upon what terms they may consolidate and it may thus determine the effect of the consolidation. As said in a recent case, "It is perfectly competent for the legislature, in consolidation acts, to declare what shall be the status of the domestic corporations which shall avail themselves of their provisions, and also of the consolidated company. Whether the new consolidation shall create a mere business union between the constituent companies, leaving them in existence as corporations, or whether it shall operate as a surrender of the corporate franchises and an extinguishment of their corporate existence, and as creating a new corporation combining, to the extent permitted by the act, the powers of the corporations out of which it is formed, and vesting in it the property of the constituent companies, depends upon the legislative intention."[3]

§ 336. **Effect of consolidation upon liens.**—A mortgage

[1] Central R., etc., Co. v. Georgia, 92 U. S. 665; Meyer v. Johnston, 64 Ala. 603, s. c. 8 Am. & Eng. R. Cas. 584.
[2] Citizens' St. R. Co. v. City of Memphis, 53 Fed. R. 715, 718.
[3] People v. New York, etc., R. Co., 129 N. Y. 474, 482, s. c. 29 N. E. R. 959. To the same effect is Day v. Worcester, etc., R. Co., 151 Mass. 302, s. c. 23 N. E. R. 824.

placed upon the property by the original corporation remains a lien upon it in the hands of the consolidated company,[1] and where the mortgage so provides, it will cover all acquisitions of the consolidated company which become a part of the property to which it originally attached.[2] It has been held, however, that a mortgage executed by a consolidated corporation will take priority over unsecured debts of one of the consolidating companies, contracted while the company possessed the power to enter into an agreement of consolidation, and transfer all of its assets and liabilities to the new company thereby formed.[3] Where a person purchases unsecured bonds of a railroad company which is authorized by law to consolidate with other companies he will be held to have made the pur-

[1] Hazard v. Vermont, etc., R. Co., 17 Fed. R. 753; Rutten v. Union Pac. R. Co., 17 Fed. R. 480; Mississippi Valley Co. v. Chicago, etc., R. Co., 58 Miss. 846; Eaton, etc., R. Co. v. Hunt, 20 Ind. 457; Compton v. Wabash, etc., Ry. Co., 45 Ohio St. 592, 16 N. E. R. 110. But see Wabash, etc., Ry. Co. v. Ham, 114 U. S. 587, s. c. 5 Sup. Ct. R. 1081. And the consolidated company will not be permitted to aver ignorance of such mortgage, though unrecorded. Miss. V. R. Co. v. Chicago, etc., R. Co., supra; The Key City, 14 Wall. (U. S.) 653. See, also, North Carolina R. R. Co. v. Drew, 3 Woods (U. S.) 691. A railroad company with notice of plaintiff's lien on the road entered into a consolidation with another company. The property of the consolidated company was leased to a canal company. Held, that neither the consolidated company nor its lessee, the canal company, was, in respect to plaintiff's lien, a purchaser for value without notice. Vilas v. Page, 106 N. Y. 439.

[2] Central R., etc., Co. v. Georgia, 92 U. S. 665, 98 U. S. 359; Hamlin v. Jervard, 72 Me. 62; Hamlin v. European, etc., R. Co., 72 Me. 83; Compton v. Jesup, 68 Fed. R. 263.

[3] Wabash, etc., R. Co. v. Ham, 114 U. S. 587; Tysen v. Wabash, etc., R. Co., 15 Fed. R. 763; Indianapolis, etc., R. Co. v. Jones, 29 Ind. 465. In the first case just cited the old bondholders were given an opportunity to exchange their bonds for bonds secured by a mortgage of the consolidated company, but failed to do so for six years, after which the mortgage in question was executed. See Blair v. St. Louis, etc., R. Co., 24 Fed. R. 148. But where a consolidated company stipulated that certain bonds of the old company should be protected by the new company, it was held that the holders of these bonds acquired the right to require the property of the company issuing them to be applied to their payment in preference to mortgagees of the consolidated company. Compton v. Wabash, St. L. & P. R. Co., 45 Ohio St. 592. This case grew out of the same transaction as the first case above cited and the supreme court of Ohio refused to follow the Supreme Court of the United States.

chase in contemplation of a possible consolidation;[1] but liens created by the constituent companies and existing at the time of the consolidation are superior to those of the same class created by the consolidated company.[2] So, where the act of consolidation provides that the old companies shall remain in existence to preserve the rights of creditors, they are not relieved from liability on previously issued bonds by reason of the fact that their property has passed into the hands of the consolidated company.[3] It has been held, however, that where several railroad companies are consolidated the bonded indebtedness of each, although secured by mortgage on its property and franchises, may be enforced against the new corporation, under a statute providing that "all debts and liabilities incurred by either of said corporations, except mortgages, shall thenceforth attach to such new corporation."[4]

§ 337. **De facto consolidation—Estoppel—Liability of constituent companies where consolidation is set aside.**—Railroad companies which, being authorized by law to consolidate their lines, enter into a *de facto* consolidation, and transact business in the name of the consolidated company, will be estopped to deny the validity of the consolidation in a suit to enforce liabilities incurred in the transaction of such business and upon the faith of their legal existence as a consolidated company.[5]

---

[1] Tysen v. Wabash, etc., R. Co., 15 Fed. R. 763; Montgomery, etc., Railroad Co. v. Branch, 59 Ala. 139.

[2] Shackleford v. Miss. Cent. R. R. Co., 52 Miss. 159; Hazard v. Vermont, etc., R. R. Co., 17 Fed. R. 753.

[3] Gale v. Troy, etc., R. Co., 51 Hun (N. Y.) 470, s. c. 4 N. Y. Supp. 295; Indianapolis, etc., R. Co. v. Jones, 29 Ind. 465; Jones Corp. Bonds and Mort., § 362.

[4] Polhemus v. Fitchburg R. Co., 123 N. Y. 502, s. c. 26 N. E. R. 31. The court held that the words, "except mortgages," confined the mortgage lien to the property owned by the company which had executed the mortgage prior to the consolidation without affecting the other property of the consolidated company, but did not prevent the latter from becoming liable for the debt of the old company secured by such mortgage.

[5] Racine, etc., R. Co. v. Farmers', etc., Co., 49 Ill. 331, 347, s. c. 95 Am. Dec. 595; Reynolds v. Myers, 51 Vt. 444; Southern Kan., etc., R. Co. v. Towner, 41 Kan. 72, s. c. 21 Pac. R. 221; Callender v. Painesville, etc., R. Co., 11 Ohio St. 516; Tagart v. Northern Central R. Co., 29 Md. 557; Farmers' L. & T. Co. v. Toledo, etc., R. Co., 67 Fed. R. 49, 55. *Ante*, § 323.

This rule has been said to be applicable where business within the ordinary powers of the constituent companies was transacted by a company into which they had formed themselves without legislative authority.[1] This decision rests upon the theory that the companies, having power to do the acts, could not deny a liability incurred thereby upon the ground that they exceeded their charter powers in selecting the means by which the acts should be done. Possibly it may be upheld on this ground, but, in any event, it is an extreme application of the doctrine. Where an ineffectual attempt is made to effect a consolidation, and the attempted consolidation is afterward set aside by the court as being null and void, it has been held that the several companies are individually liable for liabilities contracted by the consolidated company; and execution may be had against them upon a judgment recovered against the consolidated company before it was judicially dissolved.[2]

§ 338. **Effect of consolidation upon pending suits.**—It is sometimes provided by statute that pending suits against a corporation shall not be affected by its consolidation with other companies.[3] And, even in the absence of such a provision, the action of the state in granting authority to consolidate and the action of the corporation in effecting a consolidation under that

---

[1] Bissell v. Michigan Southern, etc., R. Co., 22 N. Y. 258.

[2] Ketcham v. Madison, etc., R. Co., 20 Ind. 260. Where two competing railway lines executed an illegal consolidation, and defendant has derived all the benefits arising from the contract of consolidation, its illegality is no defense to a bill in equity for an accounting and a return of the consideration to plaintiff whose property passed to defendant under the contract. Manchester & L. R. R. v. Concord R. R., (N. H.) 20 Atl. R. 383, 47 Am. & Eng. R. Cas. 359.

[3] Baltimore, etc., R. Co. v. Musselman, 2 Grant's Cas. 348; East Tennessee, etc., R. Co. v. Evans, 6 Heisk. (Tenn.) 607; Shackleford v. Mississippi, etc., R. Co., 52 Miss. 159. Under a New York statute, which provided that actions pending against either of the consolidating companies should not abate, but might be conducted to final judgment in the name of the existing company, and the rights of creditors preserved unimpaired, and the corporations continued in existence to preserve the name, it was held that an action could be brought after the consolidation against one of the consolidating companies on its bonds previously executed. Gale v. Troy, etc., Co., 51 Hun 470.

authority can not affect the rights of the plaintiff in a suit pending against it. The corporation can not, by its own act, defeat the right of persons to maintain suits actually begun.[1] The identity of the old corporation may be considered, in some jurisdictions, at least, as continued for the purposes of the suit.[2] But it has been held that the new company should be made a party to the suit by substitution, and that all proceedings against the original company after consolidation without bringing the consolidated company into court are void.[3] Where such a substitution is made the substituted defendant may treat the pleadings filed by the original defendant as its own and avail itself of the exceptions reserved by the original defendant before the substitution.[4] There is conflict among the authorities as to whether an action at law can be instituted against

---

[1] Shackleford v. Mississippi, etc., R. Co., 52 Miss. 159. See, also, Kinion v. Kansas City, etc., R. R. Co., 39 Mo. App. 574; Evans v. Interstate, etc., R. Co., 106 Mo. 594, s. c. 17 S. W. R. 489. It is no defense that defendant has no property, but that the property it formerly possessed had vested in the new company. Gale v. Troy, etc., R. Co., 51 Hun (N. Y.) 470.

[2] Shackleford v. Mississippi, etc., R. Co., 52 Miss. 159; East Tennessee, etc., R. R. Co. v. Evans, 6 Heisk. (Tenn.) 607; Baltimore, etc., R. R. Co. v. Musselman, 2 Grant Cas. (Pa.) 348. But see Kansas, etc., R. R. Co. v. Smith, 40 Kan. 192, s. c. 19 Pac. R. 636.

[3] Selma, etc., R. Co. v. Harbin, 40 Ga. 706; Prouty v. Lake Shore, etc., R. R. Co., 52 N. Y. 363. But compare Kinion v. Kansas City, etc., R. R. Co., 39 Mo. App. 382; Indianola R. R. Co. v. Fryer, 56 Tex. 609; Indianapolis, etc., R. R. Co. v. Jones, 29 Ind. 465. A railroad company which has consolidated with other railroad companies under a new name ceases to exist as a corporation, and a suit by or against such railroad company before consolidation can not afterwards be prosecuted by or against it or in its original name. Kansas, O. & T. R. Co. v. Smith, 40 Kan. 192, 19 Pac. 636. Under the Missouri statute, which provides that the consolidated company succeeds to the liabilities of the consolidating corporations where such a consolidation takes place pending a suit against one of the consolidating companies, the complaint may be amended by substituting the consolidated company as defendant, and judgment may be entered against it without further notice to it. Kinion v. Kansas City, F. S. & M. R. Co., 39 Mo. App. 574. It has been held that judgment against the consolidated company on a claim against a constituent company, afterwards dissolved, may be enforced against the property which the latter received and held from both of the constituent companies. Ketcham v. Madison, etc., R. R. Co., 20 Ind. 260.

[4] Louisville, etc., R. Co. v. Utz, 133 Ind. 265, s. c 32 N. E. R. 881.

§ 339 · CONSOLIDATION. 469

the consolidated company after the consolidation. Some of the courts hold that it is only liable to the extent of the property received from the constituent company, against which the liability existed, and that it can only be reached by suit in equity,[1] but the better rule seems to be that an action at law can be maintained against the consolidated company for the prior torts or debts of the constituent companies, for which it is made liable under the statute or agreement of consolidation.[2] It has been held, however, that even where an action might have been maintained against either the constituent company committing a tort or against the consolidated company, at the election of the plaintiff, he can not sue both in one action.[3]

§ 339. **Consolidation with foreign corporations.**—The legislature of a state may authorize corporations of that state to consolidate with those of other states.[4] Railroads of other states are generally permitted to consolidate with roads within

[1] See *ante*, § 334, note.

[2] Langhorne v. Richmond Ry. Co., 91 Va. 369, 22 S. E. R. 159, citing 1 Thomp. Corp., §§ 372, 395; 1 Beach Priv. Corp., § 344; 2 Morawetz Priv. Corp., § 955; Taylor Priv. Corp., § 666; New Bedford R. Co. v. Old Colony R. Co., 120 Mass. 397; Columbus, etc., Railroad Co. v. Skidmore, 69 Ill. 566; Arbuckle v. Illinois, etc., Railroad Co., 81 Ill. 429; Montgomery, etc., Railroad Co. v. Boring, 51 Ga. 582; Thompson v. Abbott, 61 Mo. 176; Houston, etc., Railroad Co. v. Shirley, 54 Tex. 125; Warren v. Mobile, etc., Railroad Co., 49 Ala. 582; State v. Baltimore, etc., R. Co., 77 Md. 189, 26 Atl. 865; Berry v. Kansas City, etc., Railroad Co., 52 Kan. 774, s. c. 36 Pac. R. 724. See, also, *ante*, § 334, note. The right to bring an action at law against the consolidated company is placed upon various grounds. It avoids circuity of action, and the necessary privity is created, according to some of the decisions, by the statute and consolidation thereunder, or, according to others, the right to maintain such an action may be supported upon the theory that the old corporations are continued in existence in the new for the purpose of enforcing such liability.

[3] Langhorne v. Richmond Ry. Co., 91 Va. 369, 22 S. E. R. 159.

[4] Chicago, etc., R. Co. v. Lake Shore, etc., R. Co., 5 Fed. Rep. 19; Peik v. Chicago, etc., R. Co., 94 U. S. 164; Maine Central R. Co. v. State of Maine, 96 U. S. 499; Ohio, etc., R. Co. v. Weber, 96 Ill. 443; Boardman v. Lake Shore, etc., R. Co., 84 N. Y. 157; Richardson v. Vermont, etc., R. Co., 44 Vt. 613; Ellis v. Boston, etc., R. Co., 107 Mass. 1; Bishop v. Brainerd, 28 Conn. 289. But a state may, of course, permit a railroad of another state to acquire the property and franchises of domestic corporations and to operate their roads by other means than consolidation. Copeland v. Memphis, etc., R. Co., 3 Woods (U. S.) 651.

the state upon the same terms as domestic corporations,[1] if the laws of such states also authorize the consolidation.[2] But the new company so formed is a domestic corporation, in each state within which its property lies, so far as the ownership and use of such property is concerned,[3] and it is subject to the jurisdiction of the courts of the several states, so far as its property and the operation of its road in them respectively is concerned.[4] One state, while it may fix the status of domestic companies which consolidate under its laws, has no power to authorize the consolidation of domestic corporations with those of another state, without the consent of the latter state, in such a manner as to vest the franchises, rights and property of the foreign corporations in the consolidated company, or to authorize the conversion of the stock of all the constituent corporations into that of the consolidated company.[5] Where a corporation is formed by the consolidation of corporations of several states it

---

[1] The consolidation of a domestic corporation with a corporation organized under the laws of another state or the United States is prohibited in Texas. Constitution, Art. 10, § 6. R. S. Texas (1879), § 4247. And in New Jersey the consent of the legislature is necessary to such a consolidation. N. J. Supp. (1886), R. R. § 91.

[2] Pennsylvania and South Carolina expressly provide so. Dig. (1883), Pa. R. R., § 79. Laws 1885, S. C. Ch. 96, § 5. The laws of Indiana require the consolidation to be made in accordance with the laws of the adjoining state. R. S. 1894, § 5257.

[3] Eaton, etc., R. Co. v. Hunt, 20 Ind. 457; Delaware, etc., Tax Cases, 18 Wall (U. S.) 206; State v. Chicago, etc., R. R. Co., 25 Neb. 156, 2 L. R. A. 564, and note; Graham v. Boston, etc., R. Co., 14 Fed. R. 753; 2 Cook on Stock and Stockholders, § 909. It has been held that the corporation can not be sued in the Federal courts of one state by a citizen of that state for injuries received in another state, into which the consolidated line extends. See Nashville, etc., Railway Co. v. Edwards, 91 Ga. 24, 16 S. E. R. 347; Western, etc., R. Co. v. Roberson, 61 Fed. R. 592; Memphis, etc., R. Co. v. Alabama, 107 U. S. 581, s. c. 2 Sup. Ct. R. 432. As to whether the result of the consolidation is one or two companies, see *ante*, §§ 26, 28. See, also, Central Trust Co. v. Chattanooga, etc., R. Co., 68 Fed. R. 685, 693; Burger v. Grand Rapids, etc., R. Co., 22 Fed. R. 561, 20 Am. & Eng. R. Cas. 607.

[4] So provided by law in many of the states. Stimson's Am. Stat. (1892) § 8734. The courts of a state will still retain jurisdiction of a corporation after its consolidation with a foreign corporation unless an express surrender of jurisdictional power is shown. Eaton, etc., R. Co. v. Hunt, 20 Ind. 457.

[5] People v. New York, etc., R. Co., 129 N. Y. 474, s. c. 29 N. E. R. 959.

generally acts as a unit in the transaction of its business, and, in the absence of a statutory provision to the contrary, it has been held that it may transact its corporate business in one state for all, and the contracts it enters into, and the liabilities it incurs in one state are binding upon it in all the states, and may be enforced against it in any one of them when the action is transitory.[1] Yet, as the laws of a state have no effect outside of its limits, it is held that the consolidated corporation in one state acts under the authority of the charter of that state, and is not affected by the legislation of another state in which a part of its line lies,[2] and that it may be dissolved and its business wound up in one state by the courts of that state without affecting its franchise in another.[3] It is not safe, however, to

---

[1] Fitzgerald v. Missouri Pac. R. Co., 45 Fed. Rep. 812; Graham v. Boston, etc., R. Co., 118 U. S. 161; Horne v. Boston, etc., R. Co., 62 N. H. 454, *ante*, § 27. The provision in the constitution of Illinois requiring a majority of the directors of any company incorporated under the laws of that state to be residents thereof, does not apply to a corporation formed by the consolidation of an existing corporation of that state with similar corporations of other states. Ohio, etc., R. Co. v. People, 123 Ill. 467, s. c. 14 N. E. R. 874. A railroad corporation, chartered and operated in two states, consolidated and made subject to all the duties and liabilities, under one charter and the laws of one state, as if wholly located therein, is an entity, and it is responsible as a whole for its acts and its negligence. Providence Coal Co. v. Providence & W. R. Co., 15 R. I. 303, s. c. 4 Atl. R. 394.

[2] Pittsburgh, etc., R. Co. v. Rothschild, (Pa.), 26 Am. & Eng. R. Cas. 50, s. c. Pittsburgh, etc., Co.'s Appeal, 4 Atl. R. 385, affirming 1 Pa. County Ct. R. 620; Eaton, etc., R. Co. v. Hunt, 20 Ind. 457; Mead v. New York, etc., R. Co., 45 Conn. 199; Quincy R. Bridge Co. v. Adams Co., 88 Ill. 615; State v. Northern Central R. Co., 18 Md. 193; Gardner v. James, 5 R. I. 235; *ante*, § 27. In Ohio, etc., R. Co. v. People, 123 Ill. 467, s. c. 14 N. E. R. 874, it is said explicitly that the consolidated corporation has in each state all the rights, powers and franchises that the constituent company of that state had therein, but will not have therein the rights, powers and franchises of the constituent company of the other state, or, in other words, that the new corporation will stand in each state as the original company had stood in the same state. This, however, can not be affirmed as an invariable rule, for much depends upon the statute and consolidation agreement. The legislature of each state could give, and often does give, the new company the right to exercise in its own jurisdiction all the powers and franchises that any or all of the constituent companies may have possessed.

[3] Hart v. Boston, etc., R. Co., 40 Conn. 524. For a further and fuller treatment of the subject-matter of this section, see *ante*, §§ 26, 27, 28.

lay down any unqualified general rules upon these **subjects**. In order to determine, with any degree of certainty, the effect of a consolidation, and the rights, powers, duties and liabilities of the consolidated company, in any particular case, resort must be had to the legislation of the states in which the company is consolidated and the agreement of consolidation **in** pursuance thereof.

CHAPTER XVI.

CONTRACTS.

§ 340. Contracts—Power to make—Generally.
341. Contracts—Scope of corporate power.
342. General power to contract—Illustrative instances.
343. Power to contract—Control of by courts.
344. Effect of changes in charter.
345. Contracts—Formal requisites of.
346. Formal defects.
347. Contracts—Who may make—Generally.
348. Contracts by interested persons.
349. Mode prescribed must be pursued.
350. Contracts—Parties bound to take notice of charter provisions.
351. Contracts — Unauthorized — Notice.
352. Estoppel—Generally.
353. Ratification of unauthorized acts—Rights of the public and of creditors.
354. Contracts in conjunction with other parties.
355. Pledge of corporate securities.
356. Contracts between connecting lines—Division of fares.
357. Contracts permitting use of part of road.
358. Contracts regarding terminal facilities.
359. Traffic contracts — Surrender to competing line.

§ 360. Contracts with municipal corporations for terminal facilities.
361. Use of tracks constructed under grant from municipal corporation.
362. Contracts for location of stations.
363. Location of tracks, switches and the like.
364. Contracts that may be made by railroad companies—Particular instances.
365. Pooling contracts—Generally.
366. Pooling contracts—The authorities.
367. Pooling contracts — Presumption.
368. Contracts—*Ultra vires*.
369. Contracts—*Ultra vires*—General doctrine.
370. Contracts—What are *ultra vires*—Generally.
371. Contracts — *Ultra vires* — Estoppel.
372. Contracts— *Ultra vires*—Executed and executory contracts.
373. Contracts—*Ultra vires*—Cases discriminated.
374. Contracts—*Ultra vires*—Illustrative instances.
375. Contracts— *Ultra vires* — Rule where statute prescribes consequences.
376. Contracts— *Ultra vires* — Injunction.

§ 377. Contracts—*Ultra vires*—Denial of relief—Laches.
378. Contracts—*Ultra vires*—Who may contest.
379. Contracts—*Ultra vires*—Creditors.
380. Contracts—*Ultra vires*—Non-assenting stockholders.
381. Prohibited contracts—Effect of prescribing penalties.
382. Illegal contracts — Generally.
§ 383. Illegal contracts and *ultra vires* contracts discriminated.
384. Classes of illegal contracts.
385. Contracts void because against public policy.
386. Contracts against public policy—Location of stations and tracks.
387. Contracts void as against public policy—General conclusions.
388. Contracts void as against public policy—Illustrative cases.

§ 340. Contracts—Power to make—Generally.—A railroad company has the implied or incidental power to enter into any and all contracts necessary to enable it to carry out the purposes of its organization, except so far as it is restrained by its charter or the general law. The presumption is in favor of the power of the corporation to make any contract, which is regular on its face and is not in conflict with any prohibition of law, and is within the scope of the general powers conferred upon the corporation.[1] Within the scope of the corporate powers the right to contract is much the same as that of natural persons,[2] but as corporate powers are derivative and not inherent, the authority of a corporation to contract is limited by the charter or act of incorporation. It is, of course, competent for

---

[1] Mayor, etc., of Baltimore v. Baltimore, etc., R. R. Co., 21 Md. 50; South Wales R. R. Co. v. Redmond, 10 C. B. N. S. 675; Shipper v. Pennsylvania R. Co., 47 Pa. St. 338; Stewart v. Erie Trans. Co., 17 Minn. 372; Davis v. Old Colony R.R. Co., 131 Mass. 258; Mitchell v. Rome, etc., R. Co., 17 Ga. 574; Rider Life Raft Co. v. Roach, 97 N. Y. 378; Morris, etc., R. Co. v. Sussex R. Co., 20 N. J. Eq. (5 C. E. Green), 542. The burden of proof is upon the person asserting the illegality or *ultra vires* character of a contract made by a corporation. Morris, etc., R. Co. v. Sussex R. Co., 20 N. J. Eq. (5 C. E. Green), 542; Ohio, etc., R. Co. v. McCarthy, 96 U. S. 258; Alabama Gold Life Ins. Co. v. Central, etc., Assn., 54 Ala. 73. *Prima facie* all its contracts are valid, and it lies on those who would impeach any contract to make out that it is invalid. Scottish North Eastern R. Co. v. Stewart, 3 Macqueen 382, 415.

[2] Hand v. Clearfield, etc., Co., 143 Pa. St. 408, s. c. 22 Atl. R. 709; Tennessee, etc., Co. v. Kavanaugh, 93 Ala. 324, s. c. 9 So. R. 395; Fitzgerald, etc., Co. v. Fitzgerald, 137 U. S. 98, s. c. 11 Sup. Ct. R. 36; Hall v. Tanner, etc., Co., 91 Ala. 363, s. c. 8 So. R. 348; Gloninger v. Pittsburgh R. Co., 139 Pa. St. 13, s. c. 21 Atl. R. 211.

the legislature to limit the power to contract and to designate the mode in which corporations may contract, and where a limitation is imposed or a mode prescribed the corporation can not rightfully make a contract beyond the limits fixed by the statute, nor can it regularly contract in any other mode than that prescribed by law in cases where a specific mode is prescribed.[1]

§ 341. Contracts—Scope of corporate power.—The power of a railroad company to make contracts is limited by the act of incorporation, but is, nevertheless, very broad and comprehensive. Every charter granted a railroad corporation invests it with implied as well as with express powers. The doctrine seems to have been asserted in England, and receives some support in this country, that the legislature, when it creates a corporation, gives to that body an absolute right of contract, except so far as it may be restrained by positive law.[2] It can not, however, be true that a corporation has an absolute right to contract, for it can not make a contract entirely foreign to the object for which it was created.[3] It is generally held in the United States, and it is the only defensible doctrine, that

---

[1] Central, etc., Co. v. Pullman Car Co., 139 U. S. 24, s. c. 45 Am. & Eng. R. Cases 607; Pearce v. Madison, etc., Co., 21 How. (U. S.) 441; Zabriskie v. Cleveland, etc., Co., 23 How. (U. S.) 381, 398; Thomas v. West Jersey, etc., Co., 101 U. S. 71; Branch v. Jesup, 106 U. S. 468; Penn. R. Co. v. St. Louis, etc., Co., 118 U. S. 290; Salt Lake City v. Hollister, 118 U. S. 256; Green Bay, etc., R. Co. v. Union, etc., Co., 107 U. S. 98; Pittsburgh, etc., R. Co. v. Keokuk, etc., Co., 131 U. S. 371; Oregon, etc., Co. v. Oregonian R. Co., 130 U. S. 1; City of New London v. Brainard, 23 Conn. 522; Perrine v. Chesapeake, etc., Co., 9 How. (U. S.) 172; Commonwealth v. Erie, etc., Co., 27 Pa. St. 339.

[2] Shrewsbury, etc., R. Co. v. Northwestern R. Co., 6 H. L. Cas. 113; Riche v. Ashbury R. Car Co., L. R. 9 Ex. 224, citing case of Sutton's Hospital, 10 Coke 1; Mayor, etc., of Norwich, v. Norfolk, etc., R. Co., 4 El. & Bl. 397.

[3] This is an old and familiar doctrine, for it has long been settled that a corporation can not make a contract beyond the sphere of corporate power, as defined by the act of incorporation. Utica Ins. Co. v. Scott, 19 Johns 1; Lawler v. Walker, 18 Ohio 151; Dublin Corp. v. Attorney-General, 9 Bligh. N. S. 395; Webb v. Manchester, etc., 4 Mylne & Craig 116; Peirce v. New Orleans, etc., Co., 9 La. 397.

the power of a corporation to make contracts is limited to the making of contracts which it is expressly authorized to enter into and such as are reasonably necessary or incident to the enjoyment of the express powers granted by its charter, and its officers and agents can only bind it to this extent.[1] It is not necessary that the powers of a corporation should be enumerated, nor is it necessary that the power to contract should be expressly conferred, for the power to make such contracts as will promote the corporate welfare and enable the corporation to conduct its corporate affairs is implied.[2]

§ 342. General power to contract—Illustrative instances.—Railroad companies, unless forbidden by statute, may borrow money for corporate purposes and issue negotiable instruments.[3] It is held, however, that under a power to borrow money and issue negotiable bonds a railroad company can not issue perpetual or irredeemable bonds.[4] A railroad company

---

[1] Mobile, etc., R. Co. v. Franks, 41 Miss. 494; Winter v. Muscogee R. Co., 11 Ga. 438; Bowling Green R. Co. v. Warren County, 10 Bush (Ky.) 711; Downing v. Mt. Washington R. Co., 40 N. H. 231; Vandall v. South San Francisco Dock Co., 40 Cal. 83.

[2] Smith v. Nashua, etc., R. Co., 27 N. H. 86; Brown v. Winnisimmet Co., 11 Allen 326; Buffit v. Troy, etc., Co., 36 Barb. 420. Some of the cases affirm that the inquiry which the courts are to make is whether the power to make the contract is forbidden, not whether it is granted. Taylor v. Chichester, etc.,R..Co.,L. R. 2 Exch. 356, 384; Scottish, etc., R. Co. v. Stewart, 3 Macq. 382, 415; Eastern, etc., R. Co. v. Hawkes, 5 H. L. Cas. 331. See Cary v. Cleveland, etc., R. Co., 29 Barb. 35, 52; Bateman v. Mayor, etc., Ashton, etc., 3 Hurl. & N. 323; Kitchen v. Cape Girardeau, etc., Co., 59 Mo. 514; South Yorkshire R. Co. v. Great Northern R. Co., 9 Exch. 55, 88; South Wales R. Co. v. Redmond, 10 C. B. N. S. 675; Mississippi, etc., R. Co. v. Howard, 7 Wall. 392; Ohio, etc., R. Co. v. McCarthy, 96 U. S. 258; Norwich v. Norfolk R. Co., 4 El. & Bl. 397, 432; Madison, etc., Co. v. Watertown, etc., Co., 5 Wis. 173.

[3] White Water Valley R. Co. v. Vallette, 21 How. (U. S.) 414; Mississippi, etc., R. Co. v. Howard, 7 Wall. 392; Gloninger v. Pittsburgh, etc., R. Co., 139 Pa. St. 13 , s. c. 46 Am. & Eng. R. Cas. 276; Richards v. Merrimack, etc., R. Co., 44 N. H. 127, 135; Olcott v. Tioga R. Co., 27 N. Y. 546; Marion, etc., Co. v. Hodge, 9 Ind. 163; Frye v. Tucker, 24 Ill. 180; Goodrich v. Reynolds, 31 Ill. 490; Philadelphia, etc., Co. v. Hickman, 28 Pa. St. 318; Pierce v. Emery, 32 N. H. 484; Galveston, etc., Co. v. Cowdrey, 11 Wall. 459; Dupee v. Boston, etc., Co., 114 Mass. 37; Butler v. Rahm, 46 Md. 541.

[4] Taylor v. Philadelphia, etc., R.Co., 7 Fed. R. 386, s. c. 1 Am. & Eng. R. Cases 616, citing Thomas v. West Jer-

§ 342   CONTRACTS.   477

has power to compromise all controversies relating to corporate affairs.[1] A contract to haul a designated quantity of goods each month is one that may be lawfully made, provided no discrimination is made against other shippers.[2] There can, of course, be no doubt as to the power to employ and contract to pay a compensation to such agents and officers as may be required to conduct the corporate business, and it has been held that two companies may employ one general manager.[3] A contract between two railroad companies, wherein they agreed to establish and maintain a dispatch line for the transportation of freight, was recognized as valid, but there seems to have been no discussion of the question whether the contract was or was not against public policy.[4] An arrangement by which the receiver of existing companies was to receive all the stock and bonds of a proposed railroad, to be used in constructing the road-bed, leaving no funds for building side-tracks or purchasing equipment, was held to be invalid and the organization of the proposed company a fraud upon the statute.[5] A railroad company may contract with a municipal corporation to erect a depot at a designated place, but in the absence of clear words constituting a covenant to perpetually maintain the depot at the designated place the company is not bound to do so.[6] It seems to us doubtful whether an agreement to perpetually maintain a depot at a designated place would be valid, since the changes wrought by time and progress may make it necessary for the public interest and the promotion of the public welfare

---

sey, etc., R. Co., 101 U. S. 71. *Contra,* Phila., etc., R. R. Co.'s Appeal, (s. c. Phila., etc., R. Co. *v.* Stichter), 11 W. N. C. (Pa.) 325, 4 Am. & Eng. R. R. Cas. 118, 21 Am. L. Reg. 713.

[1] Philadelphia, etc., Co. *v.* Hickman, 28 Pa. St. 318; Macon, etc., R. Co. *v.* Vason, 57 Ga. 314. See, generally, Bath's Case, L. R. 8 Ch. Div. 334; Kipling *v.* Todd, L. R. 3 C. P. Div. 350.

[2] Harrison *v.* New Orleans, etc., Co., 28 La. Ann. 777; Chicago, etc., R. Co. *v.* Chicago, etc., R. Co., 79 Ill. 121.

[3] State *v.* Concord R. Co., 62 N. H. 375, s. c. 13 Am. & Eng. R. Cas. 94.

[4] Chicago, etc., R. Co. *v.* New York, etc., R. Co., 22 Am. & Eng. R. Cas. 265.

[5] Chicago, etc., R. Co. *v.* Miller, 91 Mich. 166, s. c. 51 N. W. R. 981.

[6] Texas, etc., R. Co. *v.* City of Marshall, 136 U. S. 393, s. c. 10 Sup. Ct. R. 846, 42 Am. & Eng. R. Cas. 637, citing Mead *v.* Ballard, 7 Wall. 290.

to locate the station elsewhere. We suppose that when parties enter into a contract they must be held to contract with reference to such matters. It is held that one railroad company may grant to another the right to use the track without pecuniary compensation and that where such a contract is made by the general superintendent with the knowledge of the board of directors, it will be enforced.[1]

§ 343. Power to contract—Control of by courts.

The business policy of a corporation is a matter for the management and control of the corporation, and the courts will not dictate the policy to be pursued in such a matter, nor exercise surveillance over the corporation in regard to mere matters of business policy or expediency.[2] Where the action is lawful and not beyond the power of the corporation, the courts will not examine "into the affairs of the corporation to determine the expediency of its action, or the motives for it."[3] Courts will not control corporate action where the matter is one of pure discretion, but may interfere where there is a palpable abuse of discretion which causes a legal injury to the person who seeks judicial assistance.[4] To justify interference upon the

---

[1] Alabama, etc., R. Co. v. South, etc., R. Co., 84 Ala. 570, s. c. 5 Am. St. R. 401, 3 So. R. 286. Some of the expressions used in the opinion delivered in the case cited indicate that the directors may make a donation of the property rights of the company, but we think that the agreement before the court disclosed a consideration, so that it can not be said that there was an entire absence of consideration. We do not believe that the officers of a railroad company have power to make a gift of any material part of the corporate property.

[2] Evans v. Union Pacific R. Co., 58 Fed. R. 497. See, generally, Willoughby v. Chicago, etc., Co., 50 N.J.Eq. 656, s. c. 25 Atl. R. 277, 39 Am. & Eng. Corp. Cas. 153; Sewell v. East Cape May Co., 50 N. J. Eq. 717, s. c. 25 Atl. R. 929.

[3] Oglesby v. Attrill, 105 U. S. 605; Bailey v. Birkenhead, etc., R. Co., 12 Beav. 433.

[4] Davis v. Mayor, etc., 1 Duer (N. Y.) 451; Methodist, etc., Church v. Mayor, etc., of Baltimore, 6 Gill 391; Baldwin v. Bangor, 36 Me. 518. See Williams v. New York, etc., R., 16 N. Y. 97; Western Union, etc., Co. v. Mayor, etc., 38 Fed. R. 552, s. c. 3 L. R. A. 449; Montgomery, etc., Co. v. City Council of Montgomery, 87 Ala. 245, s. c. 4 L.R. A. 616; Des Moines, etc., Co. v. City of Des Moines, 44 Iowa 505, s.c. 24 Am.R. 756; City of Chicago v. Evans, 24 Ill. 52; Smith v. McCarthy, 56 Pa. St. 359; City of Richmond v. Davis, 103 Ind. 449.

ground of an abuse of discretion, a very strong and clear case must be made by the complainant, for it is only where there is palpable abuse and manifest injury that courts will give relief.[1]

§ 344. **Effect of changes in charter.**—A party who contracts with a railroad company deals, as he is bound to know, with a creature of the law invested with limited powers. He can not successfully insist that it possesses unlimited power to enter into contracts, and he must take notice of the general power of the legislature over the corporation. It is in accordance with this principle that all parties contracting with a corporation must take notice of the conditions on which it holds its franchises, and of its subjection to the legislative will, and that executory contracts for the construction of the road may be annulled or rendered less profitable by the act of the legislature in amending the charter under a reserved power so as to change the route and render the performance of such contracts impossible, or more expensive.[2]

---

[1] Wilder v. Rural, etc., Co., (N. J.) 32 Atl. R. 676.

[2] Macon, etc., R. Co. v. Gibson, 85 Ga. 1. Bleckly, J., said: "Nor is the right of the state so to amend or modify the charter abridged or in any manner affected by executory contracts, entered into by the company with third persons, before the amending act was passed. The Macon Construction Company, in dealing with the railroad company, was bound to take notice of the general law of the state, under which the right and power were reserved which have been exercised. A tenant at will can not make contracts with reference to the estate, which will limit the power of the landlord to terminate the estate by means compatible with its nature. So a corporation in the possession of franchises held at the will of the state can not hinder the resumption or modification of those franchises by entering into executory contracts with third persons. Nor can that effect be wrought by like contracts between the parties immediately contracting with the corporation, and subcontractors under them. On no contract whatsoever does the amendment now in question have any direct effect. Its only effect upon contracts is incidental, and, if they can not be performed consistently with the alteration in the charter made by the amending statute, their performance, in so far as thus hindered or obstructed, will be excused; the rule of law being that performance of contracts, when rendered impossible by act of law, stands excused. (Citing Bish. Cont., § 594, and other authorities.) Under these authorities, if the Macon Construction Company, or a subcontractor under it, was under a stipulation to complete the railway by a given time, and if time was of the essence of the contract, a valid excuse for failing so to do would be furnished by this subse-

§ 345. Contracts — Formal requisites of. — The old doctrine that a corporation could only contract under its common seal does not, as every one knows, any longer prevail. Some contracts must be evidenced by the corporate seal, but the instances in which a seal is essential to the validity of a corporate contract are comparatively few, for in the vast majority of cases no seal is required. It is not required where the contract relates to ordinary corporate business. The legislature may, of course, require that all contracts shall be attested by the corporate seal, but a provision in the charter requiring the corporation to have a common seal does not require all contracts to be under seal.[1] In considering the authority of corporate representatives, we referred to the familiar rule that where the charter prescribed the mode of contracting, that mode must be pursued, and also said that the general rule is that corporations are not bound by contracts executed by persons having no authority from the

quent legislation, in that legislation has rendered, or should render, it impossible to complete the work by the stipulated time. In so far as this or any other executory contract has been rendered less valuable or profitable to the parties concerned by the legislation in question, that is a consequence which should have been foreseen as possible, and which must be accepted by the parties as an incident of the exercise by the legislature of its rightful legislative power. Surely, it can not rationally be contended that because the alteration of charters with respect to the latitude of the franchises granted may or does operate unfavorably upon executory contracts made by or under the corporations, the charters must remain unaltered in this respect, and the reserved power in the legislature be reduced to a power in name only."

[1] Sarmiento v. Davis, etc., Co., 105 Mich. —, s. c. 63 N. W. R. 205. See Cary, etc., Co. v. Cain, 70 Miss. 628, s. c. 13 So. R. 239. The seal, where one is required, may be attached by a person whom the governing board recognizes as secretary, although such a person is not secretary *de jure*. Augusta, etc., R. Co. v. Kittel, 52 Fed. R. 63, 2 C. C. A. 615. A contract not required to be under seal, which professes to be executed by the president in behalf of the corporation, is presumptively a corporate contract. National, etc., Assn. v. Prentice, etc., Co., 49 Minn. 220, s. c. 51 N. W. R. 916. See Muscatine, etc., Co. v. Muscatine Lumber Co., 85 Iowa 112, s. c. 52 N. W. R. 108. Of course a corporate contract must possess the essential elements of a contract between natural persons, such as a consideration and the like. It is barely necessary to suggest that where the statute requires a contract to be in writing, or requires it to be under seal, the statutory requirement must be obeyed. Pauling v. London, etc., R. Co., 8 Exch. 867. See Chase v. Second Av. R. Co., 97 N. Y. 384.

corporation, or by agents who transcended the authority conferred upon them. It is not necessary to add anything to what has been said upon those subjects, for they are familiar ones and our consideration of them has been as full as is consistent with the scope of our work.[1]

§ 346. Formal defects.—Merely formal defects in a corporate contract not affecting the substantial rights of the parties will be disregarded by the courts. If there is no defect affecting substantial rights the courts will ascertain and carry into effect the intention of the contracting parties.[2] But, of course, if the defects are of such a character as to render the contract nugatory, or so vague and uncertain that the intention of the parties can not be discovered, it will not be enforced.

§ 347. Contracts—Who may make—Generally.—The general power of a railroad company to enter into contracts may be exercised by the board of directors.[3] The general rule is that in the board is vested the paramount power of making corporate

---

[1] In addition to the authorities heretofore cited, see Missouri Pacific R. Co. v. Sidell, 67 Fed. R., 464; Leroy, etc., R. Co. v. Sidell, 66 Fed.R. 27; Canda, etc., Co. v. Inhabitants, etc., (N. J.) 32 Atl. R. 66; Tulleys v. Keller, 45 Neb. 220, s. c. 63 N. W. R. 388; Eaton v. Robinson, (R. I.), s. c. 31 Atl. R. 1058; Bradford v. Frankfort, etc., R. Co., 142 Ind. 383, s. c. 40 N. E. R. 741; National, etc., Bank v. Vigo County, etc., Bank, 141 Ind. 352, s. c. 40 N. E. R. 799; First National Bank v. Asheville, etc., Co., 116 N. C. 827, s. c. 21 S. E. R. 948. Effect of notice by one who takes promissory note executed by treasurer of corporation in fraud of its rights. In re Millward, etc., Co., 161 Pa. St. 157, s. c. 28 Atl. R. 1072, 1077. Authority to an agent to execute a mortgage empowers him to insert usual conditions therein. Gribble v. Columbus, etc., Co., 100 Cal. 67; Vincent v. Snoqualmie, etc., Co., 7 Wash. 566, s. c. 35 Pac. R. 396. Acts in excess of authority may be ratified where they are within scope of corporate power. People v. Eel River, etc., R. Co., 98 Cal. 665, s. c. 33 Pac. R. 728; Nebraska, etc., Co. v. Bell, 58 Fed. R. 326, 7 C. C. A. 253; Thomas v. City, etc., Bank, 40 Neb. 501, s. c. 58 N. W. R. 943, 24 L. R. A. 263.

[2] Underhill v. Santa Barbara, etc., Co., 93 Cal. 300, s. c. 28 Pac. R. 1049. See Seymour v. Spring Forest, etc., Assn., 19 N. Y. Supp. 94; Hasselman v. Japanese, etc., Co., 2 Ind. App. 180, s. c. 27 N. E. R. 718, 28 N. E. R. 207; Dexer v. Long, 2 Wash. 435, s. c. 27 Pac. R. 271.

[3] Bank of Middlebury v. Rutland, etc., R. Co., 30 Vt. 159; Wright v. Oroville, etc., Co. 40 Cal. 20.

contracts, but other officers may contract on behalf of the corporation.[1] As was said at another place, there are some contracts which the board of directors must make, but ordinary corporate contracts relating to the usual business of the corporation may be made by other officers, or by duly appointed agents acting within the scope of their employment.[2]

§ 348. **Contracts by interested persons.**—The general rule is that a corporate agent can not act for the corporation in a matter where his interests are antagonistic to those of the corporation. This rule is one of wide sweep. Thus it is held, in accordance with this rule, that corporations having common officers and trustees can not enter into valid contracts with each other.[3] Nor can an officer or agent of the company bind

---

[1] A president who has general managing authority may assent to the reformation of a contract, in case of a mistake therein, executed by him in behalf of the corporation. Nichols v. Scranton, etc., Co., 137 N. Y. 471, s. c. 33 N. E. R. 561.

[2] Where the purchasing agent of a railway has apparent authority to make contracts for supplying the company with stationery, a third person, who has dealt with him a number of years on the faith of his having such authority, can enforce a contract with said purchasing agent as against the company, and the defense that the agent had no authority is not a good one. Levey v. New York Cent. & H. R. R. Co., 4 Misc. R. 415, 24 N. Y. S. 124.

[3] Stokes v. Phelps Mission, 47 Hun 570, 14 N. Y. S. R. 901; Barr v. New York, L. E. & W. R. Co., 52 Hun 555, 24 N. Y. S. R. 188. A contract leasing cars from one railroad company to another, whose officers are substantially the same, will not be recognized on a claim for compensation against a receiver of the lessee railroad company, though a reasonable compensation for the use of the cars will be allowed. Thomas v. Peoria & R. I. R. Co., (C. C. N. D. Ill.) 36 Fed. R. 808. Four persons, common directors of two different railroads, became assignees of a construction contract made by one of the companies, by which they received its stocks and bonds, thereby making a large profit. Afterwards acting for the two companies, they executed a lease of the road and franchises of the company whose bonds and stocks they held to the other company, binding it to pay as rental certain sums to meet interest on the bonds and dividends on the stocks. The lease was held invalid as an attempt by the directors to impose obligations on the lessee company for their own private benefit and no formal rescission of the lease was necessary. Barr v. New York, L. E. & W. R. Co., 5 N. Y. S. 623, 52 Hun 555. Certain persons, being stockholders and directors of both a railroad company and an iron company, negotiated in good faith a contract between the railroad company and the iron company, which took the form of a resolution by the railroad

it by a contract in which he is personally interested.[1] It is, therefore, to be understood that when it is said that a corporation may be bound by the act of its agent performed within the scope of his authority the meaning is that he must be acting for the corporation and not in a matter in which his interests and those of the corporation are in conflict.

§ 349. **Mode prescribed must be pursued.**—The requirements of the charter must be observed, when it prescribes a mode of contracting, since it is from the charter alone that the corporation derives power to enter into contracts.[2] This elementary rule applies to provisions respecting the designation of the officers by whom the contract shall be made, as well as to other matters. The stockholders of a corporation can not, by a majority vote, bind the corporation to a contract, when the charter lodges the power of contracting with the board of

---

company to lease a railroad owned by the iron company and pay in stocks and bonds, and of a subscription by the iron company to be paid in property, viz., a lease of their railroad, the contract was unanimously ratified by a vote of all the stockholders of the railroad company. The contract was held to be, at worst, only voidable, and as no fraud or intentional overvaluation appeared, and the consideration was nearly adequate, the bonds issued were held valid. Coe v. East & W. R. Co. of Alabama, (C. C.) 52 Fed. R. 531. In Chicago, etc., Co. v. Yerkes, 141 Ill. 320, s. c. 30 N. E. R. 667, it is held that where authority to sell corporate property was conferred upon the president and secretary a sale to the secretary was ineffective.

[1] Sargent v. Kansas Midland R. Co., 48 Kan. 672. See *ante*, §§ 276, 290. The fact that the president of a railroad company, without the knowledge of the other directors, is interested in a construction contract let by the company, does not in itself make the contract void, but simply voidable. Augusta, T. & G. R. Co. v. Kittel, (C. C. A.) 52 Fed. R. 63, 2 C. C. A. 615, 2 U. S. App. 409; Langan v. Francklyn, 29 Abb. (N. Y.) N. Cas. 102. A corporation which sells certain of its bonds to its directors, for less than par, but for their actual value, is estopped from attacking the validity of the sale. Union Loan & Trust Co. v. Southern California Motor Road Co., (Cir. Ct.) 51 Fed. R. 840. See Skinner v. Smith, 134 N. Y. 240. The rule prohibiting persons in a fiduciary relation from contracting for their own advantage in the name of the beneficiaries does not apply to directors who own all the stock of the corporation, and such contracts are not void as against public policy. McCracken v. Robison, 57 Fed. R. 375, 6 C. C. A. 400.

[2] Head v. Providence Ins. Co., 2 Cranch (U. S.) 127.

directors.[1] But if a contract were adopted by a unanimous vote of the stockholders, they would, no doubt, be estopped to deny the binding force of the contract.[2] Although the acts, doings and declarations of individual members of a corporation, unsanctioned by the body, are not binding upon it, yet, in the absence of any vote, a contract may be shown by inferences drawn from corporate acts, the same as in the case of an individual.[3]

§ 350. **Contracts — Parties bound to take notice of charter provisions.**—The constitution of a corporation, and the powers which it possesses under its constitution, are presumed to be known as matters of law to its members and to all persons dealing with the corporation.[4] It is a logical conclusion from

---

[1] Gulf, etc., R. Co. v. Morris, 67 Tex. 692; McCullough v. Moss, 5 Denio (N. Y.) 567; Gashwiler v. Willis, 33 Cal. 11. But at common law a corporation may contract by a vote accepting a proposal made in a meeting. Maxwell v. Dulwich College, 1 Fonbl. Eq. 306, n. o, s. c. 7 Simons 222, n.; Essex Turnpike Corp. v. Collins, 8 Mass. 292.

[2] The act of incorporation furnishes no security to persons assenting to unauthorized acts. Kearny v. Buttles, 1 Ohio St. 362. But the creditors or a receiver acting for their interests may dispute the corporate liability on such a contract so far as it tends to impair the ability of the corporation to pay its valid obligations. Bank of Chattanooga v. Bank of Memphis, 9 Heisk. (Tenn.) 408; National Trust Co. v. Miller, 33 N. J. Eq. 155. A shareholder ratifying, participating in or acquiescing in the acts of a corporation will be bound by such acts and his trustee can not bring action adversary to said acts, in his favor. Memphis & C. R. Co. v. Grayson, 88 Ala. 572, 7 So. 122.

[3] New York, etc., R. Co. v. New York, 1 Hilton (N. Y.) 562; Proprietors of Canal Bridge v. Gordon, 1 Pick. (Mass.) 297; Gowen Marble Co. v. Tarrant, 73 Ill. 608; Goodwin v. Union Screw Co., 34 N. H. 378.

[4] Spence v. Mobile, etc., R. Co., 79 Ala. 576; Davis v. Old Colony R. Co., 131 Mass. 258; Pearce v. Madison, etc., R. Co., 21 How. (U. S.) 441; Kraniger v. People's, etc., Society, 60 Minn. 94, s. c. 61 N. W. R. 904; Western Nat. Bank v. Armstrong, 152 U. S. 346, s. c. 14 Sup. Ct. R. 572; Alexander v. Cauldwell, 83 N. Y. 480; Hoyt v. Thompson, 19 N. Y. 207; Relfe v. Rundle, 103 U. S. 222; Leonard v. American Insurance Co., 97 Ind. 299; Jemison v. Citizens' Savings Bank, 122 N. Y. 135, s. c. 3 American R. & Corp. Cases 285. In Jenkins v. Gastonia, etc., Co., 115 N. C. 535, s. c. 20 S. E. R. 724, it is held that where the statute requires the corporate contract to be in writing it can not be ratified by silence. See, also, Spence v. Wilmington, etc., Mills, 115 N. C. 210, s. c. 20 S. E. R. 372. These cases seem to us to go very far.

this general rule that parties contracting with a railroad company can not successfully aver that they were ignorant of the nature of the powers conferred upon it by the legislature, but, nevertheless, the courts do in some measure at least depart from this general doctrine, since they do protect persons who contract with the company. The doctrine, however, exerts an important influence on almost all cases. The general principle stated leads to the conclusion that the corporation is not bound by any act of the board of directors, or any other corporate agent, done in excess of the charter powers, since a person dealing with the corporation is bound to know that no agent can exceed the powers of the corporation itself.[1] And, of course, nobody can hold a principal bound by a contract made with his agent in excess of that agent's known powers, much less can the corporation be held on the contract where the contract is one which the corporation had no power to make. The same general rule holds as to an *ultra vires* act of the majority of the stockholders, for the majority can bind absent or dissenting stockholders only by acts done under sanction of the charter.[2] While a person dealing with the corporation is held to be affected with notice of the corporate powers as indicated by the law of its incorporation, he is not, as a rule, bound to take notice of extraneous circumstances upon which the right to exercise those powers may depend.[3]

§ 351. Contracts — Unauthorized — Notice.—A party who deals with a corporation is bound to take notice of the powers conferred upon it by the act of incorporation, but is not bound to take notice of the purpose of the corporation in making the contract unless that purpose is made apparent by the nature of the transaction. There is, it is obvious, a clearly marked distinction between cases where a party asserts that he was igno-

[1] Elevator Co. *v.* Memphis, etc., R. Co., 85 Tenn. 703; Davis *v.* Old Colony R. Co., 131 Mass. 258.

[2] Bird *v.* Bird's Patent, etc., Co., L. R. 9 Ch. 358.

[3] Madison, etc., R. Co. *v.* Norwich Sav. Soc., 24 Ind. 457; Thompson *v.* Lambert, 44 Iowa 239; Express Co. *v* Railroad Co., 99 U. S. 191, 199; Galveston Railroad *v.* Cowdrey, 11 Wall. (U. S.) 459; Oxford Iron Co. *v.* Spradley, 51 Ala. 171; Gano *v.* Chicago, etc., R. Co., 60 Wis. 12; Eastern Counties Ry. *v.* Hawkes, 5 H. L. C. 331.

rant of extrinsic facts or circumstances, and cases where he avers ignorance of the provisions of a charter or statute.[1] Although the purpose of the corporation be to do an illegal act, the person will be unaffected by that fact unless he had notice of it. Thus, if a contract in the form of a negotiable corporate security, issued by a corporation having authority to issue such paper, gives no suggestion that it was issued as accommodation paper, an innocent holder will not be affected by the fact that it was issued for accommodation and without consideration,[2] but it would be otherwise if the person who took the paper had actual knowledge of its character.[3] If it is within the scope of the power of the corporate agents to issue such securities, the purchaser may assume that they were properly issued.[4] A person who sells to a corporation property which it has power to purchase, will not be affected by the circumstance that it was purchased for an unauthorized purpose, if he has no knowledge of such fact.[5] The general doctrine applies to a loan of money which is afterward misapplied. If the corporation had general authority to borrow money the lender is not

[1] It was held in Kuser v. Wright, (N. J.), 31 Atl. R. 397, that a person receiving a mortgage is not bound to know that sufficient notice was given corporate directors.

[2] Madison, etc., R. Co. v. Norwich Sav. Soc., 24 Ind. 457; National Bank v. Young, 41 N. J. Eq. 531; Farmers', etc., Bank v. Empire Stone Dressing Co., 5 Bosw. (N.Y.) 275; Bird v. Daggett, 97 Mass. 494; Bank of Genesee v. Patchin Bank, 19 N. Y. 312; Ex parte Estabrook, 2 Lowell 547; Farmers', etc., Bank v. Sutton, etc., Co., 52 Fed. R. 191; Monument, etc., Bank v. Globe Works, 101 Mass. 57; Lafayette, etc., Bank v. St. Louis, etc., Co., 2 Mo. App. 299. But see McLellan v. Detroit, etc., Works, 56 Mich. 579.

[3] National Bank v. Wells, 79 N. Y. 498; West St. Louis, etc., Bank v. Shawnee, etc., Bank, 95 U. S. 557.

[4] Hackensack Water Co. v. DeKay, 36 N.J. Eq. 548; Ellsworth v. St. Louis, etc., R. Co., 98 N. Y. 553; Eastern Counties R. Co. v. Hawkes, 5 H. L. C. 331; London, etc., R. Co. v. McMichael, 5 Ex. 855. A corporation having power to execute negotiable paper may bind itself, by becoming an indorser or guarantor of bonds received by it in the course of business, with a view to increasing the value of such bonds. Railroad Co. v. Howard, 7 Wall. 392; Tod v. Kentucky Union Land Co., (C. C.) 57 Fed. R. 47.

[5] And in case the property is such as the corporation is authorized to purchase, the vendor is under no obligation to inform himself as to whether this particular purchase was a proper one for it to make. Eastern Counties R. Co. v. Hawkes, 5 H. L. C. 331.

§ 352   CONTRACTS.   487

bound to supervise its application.[1] It is held that if a corporation, with authority to borrow not more than a certain sum, borrows in excess of that sum, the lender may recover provided he made the loan in ignorance that the excess was already reached.[2] It may be well enough to suggest, in passing, that the rules respecting rights depending upon the ignorance of the party dealing with the corporation, are subject to the further rule that he must have acted in good faith and as a prudent man, and his ignorance must not be due to his own fault or negligence.[3]

§ 352. **Estoppel—Generally.**—A corporation may estop itself to deny the existence and binding force of a contract, the same as an individual, provided that the contract is not entirely beyond the scope of its corporate powers. Where a corporation voluntarily accepts the benefit arising from the performance of a contract made on its behalf by one who was not authorized to represent it, it can not afterward deny its liability on the contract.[4] A railroad company may, of course, be estopped by acts or conduct, as well as by matter of record. It may be

[1] Thompson v. Lambert, 44 Iowa 239; Tracy v. Talmage, 14 N. Y. 162.

[2] Ossipee, etc., Mfg. Co. v. Canney, 54 N.H. 295; Auerbach v. LeSueur Mill Co., 28 Minn. 291; New Providence v. Halsey, 117 U. S. 336, s. c. 6 Sup. Ct. R. 764; Cotton v. New Providence, 47 N. J. Law 401; Mutual Benefit, etc., Co. v. Elizabeth, 42 N. J. Law 235. See Coffin v. City of Indianapolis, 59 Fed. R. 221.

[3] Express Co. v. Railroad Co., 99 U. S. 191, 199.

[4] Bonner v. Spiral Hinge Mfg. Co., 81 N. Y. 468; Little Rock, etc., R. Co. v. Perry, 37 Ark. 164. See Weatherford, etc., R. Co. v. Granger, 85 Tex. 574, 86 Tex. 350, 22 S. W. Rep. 70, 22 S. W. R. 959, 23 S. W. Rep. 425. When a natural principal would be estopped under similar circumstances, to deny his liability on a contract made in his name by his agent, a corporation will be estopped in like manner, provided the contract is not in the proper sense *ultra vires*. Foulke v. San Diego, etc., R. Co., 51 Cal. 365; Hayden v. Middlesex Turnp. Co., 10 Mass. 397; Tyler v. Trustees, 14 Oreg. 485; Kellogg Bridge Co. v. Hamilton, 110 U. S. 108; Taylor Priv. Corp. 249. Where the president and general manager of a company borrowed money and executed notes in the corporate name, the corporation is not estopped from attacking the validity of the notes, even though one member of the board of trustees knew of the transaction and though the money was used for the company's benefit. Dunbar, C. J., dissenting. Elwell v. Puget Sound & C. R. Co., 7 Wash. 487, 35 P. 376.

estopped to deny that it has ratified the unauthorized act of a person who has assumed to represent it. It is not necessary to show a formal ratification of a contract by a board of directors of a corporation, but it is sufficient to render it binding upon the corporation if it accepted and acted under it and performed its terms, with full knowledge of its import.[1]

§ 353. **Ratification of unauthorized acts—Rights of the public and of creditors.**—So far as concerns the corporation and its stockholders, there can be no doubt that the unauthorized acts of the company's officers and agents may be ratified by the stockholders, so as to render them valid and binding upon the corporation and its stockholders. This is elementary doctrine.[2] But, as we have elsewhere said, we do not believe that an act entirely outside of and beyond the scope of the powers conferred upon the corporation can be ratified so as to give vitality to the contract, for what could not be done directly by entering into contract can not be accomplished by ratification.[3] We make a distinction between acts performed by agents outside of the scope of their authority, and acts en-

---

[1] Taylor v. Albemarle Steam Nav. Co., 105 N. C. 434; Gulf C. & S. F. Ry. Co. v. Pittman, 4 Tex. Civ. App. 167, 23 S. W. 318. The acceptance of a bonus by a railroad company ratifies the representations made by a director, while soliciting the bonus from the citizens of a town.

[2] Hitchings v. St. Louis, etc., Trans. Co., 68 Hun (N. Y.) 33; Branch v. Jesup, 106 U. S. 468; Taylor v. Chichester, etc., R. Co., L. R. 2 Ex. 356, 380; Taylor v. S. & N. Alabama R. Co., 13 Fed. R. 152; Kelley v. Newburyport, etc., R. Co., 141 Mass. 496; Augusta, etc., R. Co. v. Kittel, 52 Fed. R. 63. If stockholders of a corporation stand by and sanction, or seem by their silence to sanction unauthorized acts of the officers of the company, they must abide by such acts. Burgess v. St. Louis County R. Co.,

99 Mo. 496. But in Weatherford, etc., R. Co. v. Granger, 86 Tex. 350, it was held, reversing s. c. 23 S. W. R. 425, that a corporation accepting a bonus on its organization is not liable on the contract of the promoter for services in procuring the bonus, in the absence of a statutory provision or an express agreement to that effect.

[3] *Post*, § 371; Kelner v. Baxter, L. R. 2 C. P. 174; Scott v. Lord Ebury, 36 L. J. C. P. 161; Melhado v. Porto Alegre, etc., R. Co., L. R. 9 C. P. 503; Spiller v. Paris Rink Co., L. R. 7 Ch. D. 368; *In re* Empress Eng. Co., L. R. 16 Ch. D. 125; *In re* North'd Ave. Hotel Co., L. R. 33 Ch. D. 16. See Gooday v. Colchester & S. W. R. Co., 15 Eng. L. & Eq. 596; Preston v. Liverpool M., etc., R. Co., 7 Eng. L. & Eq. 124; Webb v. Direct L. & P. R. Co., 9 Hare 129.

tirely beyond the scope of the powers conferred upon the corporation by the legislature. The question of the right to ratify and of the effect of a ratification is radically different in cases where the interests of creditors are involved, and in cases where the state assails the contract from what it is where the corporation or its stockholders seek to avoid the contract. The state, and in some instances the creditors of the company, may object to the enforcement of such a contract, although the corporation and its stockholders may have assumed to ratify it.[1]

§ 354. **Contracts in conjunction with other parties.**—The power to unite with other corporations or with natural persons in making contracts required by legitimate corporate business is one of the implied powers of a railroad company. The general power to contract authorizes the execution of all such contracts as are necessary to enable the corporation to successfully and properly conduct its corporate business. Thus a railroad company may unite with natural persons in a contract for the maintenance of crossings.[2]

§ 355. **Pledge of corporate securities.**—A party who, in good faith, receives from the board of directors of a corporation bonds in pledge, will be protected provided the directors had authority to issue such bonds.[3] The general doctrine is that the power to sell carries with it the power to pledge.[4] But an officer or agent who has no power to sell or negotiate the bonds can not, of course, pledge them, and the decisions in analogous cases clearly establish the doctrine that neither the

---

[1] Oil Creek, etc., R. Co. v. Pennsylvania Trans. Co., 83 Pa. St. 160; Kelly v. People's Transportation Co., 3 Ore. 189; Shewalter v. Pirner, 55 Mo. 218. As to the rights of creditors, see Bank of Chattanooga v. Bank of Memphis, 9 Heisk. (Tenn.) 408; National Trust Co. v. Miller, 33 N. J. Eq. 155; Abbott v. Baltimore, etc., Co., 1 Md. Ch. 542; Talmage v. Pell, 7 N. Y. 328.

[2] Chattanooga, etc., R. Co. v. Davis, 89 Ga. 708, s. c. 15 S. E. R. 626.

[3] Farmers' Loan, etc., Co. v. Toledo, etc., R. Co., 54 Fed. R. 759; Duncomb v. New York, etc., Railroad Co., 84 N. Y. 190; Beecher v. Marquette, etc., Mill Co., 45 Mich. 103, s. c. 7 N. W. R. 695.

[4] Platt v. Union Pac. Railroad Co., 99 U. S. 48; Leo v. Union Pac. Railway Co., 17 Fed. R. 273; Farmers' Loan, etc., Co. v. Toledo, etc., R. Co., 54 Fed. R. 759.

president nor any other executive or ministerial officer has authority, merely by virtue of his office, to pledge the bonds of the company.[1] The board of directors, if it has the power to issue and sell bonds, may authorize the president or other representative of the company to pledge them. If the course of business has been such as to warrant the inference that the president or other representative has authority to pledge the bonds, and such an act is not *ultra vires* in the proper sense, then a pledge by the president would be upheld for the protection of a *bona fide* pledgee.

§ 356. Contracts between connecting lines—Division of fares.—In the absence of a statute interdicting it, one railroad company may rightfully enter into a contract with another for the purpose of making a through line, and agree upon a division of the fares according to local rates.[2] Where the object of such a contract is to secure through connections and not to stifle competition, there is, it is obvious, no violation of the principles of public policy. If, however, under the guise of securing a through connection, one railroad company should contract with another for the purpose of shutting off all competition and enabling one of the companies to charge unreasonable fares, the contract would be illegal. Where there is a statute forbidding combinations and the division of fares an essentially different question is presented, and that question is not here considered.

---

[1] Potts v. Wallace, 146 U. S. 689, s. c. 13 Sup. Ct. R. 196, 40 Am. & Eng. Corp. Cas. 286; Burke v. Smith, 16 Wall. 390; Bank of U. S. v. Dunn, 6 Pet. 51; Famous etc., Co. v. Eagle Iron Works, 51 Mo. App. 66; Blanding v. Davenport, etc., R. Co., 88 Iowa 225, s. c. 55 N. W. R. 81; Chemical, etc., Bank v. Wagner, 93 Ky. 525, s. c. 20 S.W. R. 535; Davis v. Rockingham, etc., Co., 89 Va. 290, s. c. 15 S. E. R. 547.

[2] Hartford, etc., R. Co. v. New York, etc., R. Co., 3 Robt. (N. Y.) 411; Stewart v. Erie, etc., Co., 17 Minn. 372; Sussex, etc., Co. v. Morris, etc., Co., 19 N. J. Eq. 13; Columbus, etc., R. Co. v. Indianapolis, etc., R. Co., 5 McLean 450; Androscoggin, etc., Co. v. Androscoggin R. Co., 52 Me. 417; Great Northern R. Co. v. Manchester R. Co., 10 Eng. Law & Eq. 11. See Bartlette v. Norwich, etc., R. Co., 33 Conn. 560; Munhall v. Pa. R. Co., 92 Pa. St. 150; Perkins v. Portland, etc., R. Co., 47 Me. 573; Pennsylvania, etc., Co. v. Delaware, etc., Co., 1 Keyes (N. Y.) 72.

§ 357. **Contracts permitting use of part of road.**—A distinction is made between the lease of the entire road and a contract granting permission to one railroad company to use part of the road of another.[1] Where the company granting the permission does not disable itself from performing its duty to the public, there is no reason for holding invalid a contract which simply grants the use of part of the road. It would be otherwise if one of the companies by such a contract should disable itself from performing the duties enjoined upon it by law. If the governing statute authorizes the execution of a lease, then, of course, there can be no question as to the power of one company to lease all of its road to another.

§ 358. **Contracts regarding terminal facilities.**—A contract by one railroad company to permit the use of its terminal facilities by another company is valid, provided the company owning the terminal facilities does not by the terms or the effect of the contract disable itself from performing its corporate functions.[2] But under guise of such a contract, a railroad company can not so divest itself of its property and franchises as to incapacitate itself from discharging the duties resting upon it. The paramount rule that railroad corporations can not abdicate their functions, nor surrender their powers without the consent of the legislature is not impinged by a reasonable contract granting to another company use of its tracks and stations.

---

[1] Chicago, etc., R. Co. v. Ayres, 140 Ill. 644, s. c. 30 N. E. R. 687; Union Pacific R. Co. v. Chicago, etc., R. Co., 51 Fed. R. 309; Chicago, etc., R. Co. v. Denver, etc., R. Co., 143 U. S. 596, s. c. 12 Sup. Ct. R. 479.

[2] Union Pac. R. Co. v. Chicago, etc., R. Co., 51 Fed. R. 309, s. c. 2 C. C. A. 174, 51 Am. & Eng. R. Cas. 162; Chicago, etc., R. Co. v. Union Pacific R. Co., 47 Fed. R. 15. In the case first cited the court referred to Oregon, etc., Co. v. Oregonian R. Co., 130 U. S. 1, s. c. 9 Sup. Ct. R. 409; Central Transp., etc., Co. v. Pullman, etc., Co., 139 U. S. 24, s. c. 11 Sup. Ct. R. 478, and other cases of like character, and discriminated them from the case where there was a grant of a right to use terminal facilities. The court cited, in support of its conclusion, the following cases: Joy v. City of St. Louis, 138 U. S. 1, 43, s. c. 11 Sup. Ct. R. 243; Brown v. Bellows, 4 Pick. 179; Gregory v. Mighell, 18 Vesey 328; City of Providence v. St. John's Lodge, 2 R. I. 46; Dike v. Greene, 4 R. I. 285; Brown v. Winnisimmet Co., 11 Allen

§ 359. **Traffic contract—Surrender to competing line.**—A traffic contract which destroys the independence of a railroad company and disables it from performing its duties can not be enforced, except where such a contract is authorized by statute.[1] The policy of the law is to prevent the creation of monopolies and to foster fair competition, and hence one railroad company has no implied power to absorb another, but such power may be granted by the legislature. The rule that a railroad company can not "absolve itself from the performance of its functions without the consent of the legislature,"[2] is a general one applicable to all classes of contracts made by railroad corporations. An arrangement by which one company grants to another a right to use its track, the purpose of the two companies being to secure an interchange of traffic is not a mere naked license but is an enforceable contract.[3] Trackage contracts, unless forbidden by statute, may be made between railroad companies.[4] Railroad companies have general power to

326; Midland R. Co. v. Great Western R. Co., 8 Ch. App. 841, 851; Simpson v. Westminster Hotel Co., 8 H. L. Cas. 712; Hendee v. Pinkerton, 96 Mass. 381, 386. See, generally, Harper v. Cincinnati, etc., Co., (Ky.) 22 S. W. R. 849.

[1] Earle v. Seattle, etc., R. Co., 56 Fed. R. 909.

[2] Fisher v. West Virginia, etc., Co., 39 W. Va. 366, s. c. 23 L. R. A. 758, 19 S. E. R. 578; Ricketts v. Chesapeake, etc., R. Co., 33 W.Va. 433, s. c.7 L.R.A. 354; New York, etc., R. Co. v. Winans, 17 How. (U. S.) 30; Washington, etc., R. Co. v. Brown, 17 Wall. 445; Pennsylvania, etc., Co. v. St. Louis, etc., Co., 118 U. S. 290; Grand Tower, etc., Co. v. Ullman, 89 Ill. 244. See George v. Central, etc., R. Co., 101 Ala. 607, s. c. 14 So. R. 752. Biles v. Tacoma, etc., Co., 5 Wash. 509, s. c. 32 Pac. R. 211; In Galveston, etc., Co. v. Davis, 4 Texas Cir. App. 468, s. c. 23 S. W. R. 301, and in Galveston, etc., Co. v. Arispe, 5 Texas Civ. App. 611, s. c. 23 S. W. R. 928, 24 S. W. R. 33, it was held that an arrangement by which several companies lease their roads to one company for ninety-nine years, is an agreement of partnership and not a lease. We very much doubt the soundness of those decisions, for, as we believe, the contract, whether technically a lease or not, was ineffective.

[3] Louisville, etc., R. Co. v. Kentucky, etc., R. Co., 95 Ky. 55, s. c. 26 S. W. R. 532.

[4] Boston, etc., R. Corp. v. Nashua, etc., R. Corp., 157 Mass. 258, citing Nashua, etc., R. Co. v. Boston, etc., R., 136 U. S. 356, s. c. 10 Sup. Ct. R. 1004. Contract granting right to use railroad and appurtenances is governed by ordinary rules of construction. Chicago, etc., Co. v. Denver, etc., R. Co., 143 U. S. 596, s. c. 12 Sup. Ct. R. 479, 50 Am. & Eng. R. Cas. 60. See St. Paul, etc., R. Co. v. St. Paul, etc., Co., 44 Minn. 325, s. c. 46 N. W. R. 566.

make contracts to build, repair and restore public or private crossings.[1]

§ 360. Contracts with municipal corporations for terminal facilities.—A contract may be made between a railroad company and a municipal corporation, by which the company is granted terminal facilities.[2] The grant is taken with the burdens imposed upon it by the town or city,[3] and all companies claiming through the company to which the grant is made take subject to the burdens so imposed.[4] It is true of all grants of rights to use public parks, streets or roads, that the grantee takes with the burdens imposed by the municipal authorities, and all parties whose claims are founded upon the grant are bound by its terms and conditions.

§ 361. Use of tracks constructed under grant from municipal corporation.—It is common for municipal corporations to grant the right to use its streets to one railroad company upon a condition that other companies may be permitted to use the track.[5] The power to make such a contract is unquestionable, and the disputes that the courts have been called upon to adjudicate generally are as to the construction to be given such

---

[1] Post v. West Shore, etc., R. Co., 123 N. Y. 580, s. c. 26 N. E. R. 7. See Atchison, etc., R. Co. v. Lenz, 35 Ill. App. 330; Elgin v. Baltimore, etc., R. Co., 74 Md. 61, s. c. 21 Atl. R. 688.

[2] Louisville, etc., Co. v. Mississippi, etc., Co., 92 Tenn. 681, s. c. 59 Am. & Eng. R. Cas. 99; Chicago, etc., Co. v. St. Paul, etc., R.Co., 54 Minn. 411; Baltimore, etc., R. Co. v. Pittsburgh, etc., R. Co., 55 Fed. R. 701; St. Paul, etc., v. Minnesota, etc., R. Co., 47 Minn. 154, s. c. 50 Am. & Eng.R. Cas. 55, 49 N. W. R. 646.

[3] Hayes v. Michigan Cent. R. Co., 111 U. S. 228, s. c. 15 Am. & Eng. R. Cas. 394.

[4] Joy v. City of St. Louis, 138 U. S. 1, s. c. 45 Am. & Eng. R. Cas. 655, citing Tulk v. Moxhay, 2 Phil. Ch. 774; Luker v. Dennis, 7 Ch. Div. 227; Bronson v. Coffin, 108 Mass. 175; Parker v. Nightingale, 6 Allen 341; Van Doren v. Robinson, 16 N. J. Eq. 256; Kirkpatrick v. Peshine, 24 N. J. Eq. 206; Western v. Macdermott, L. R. 2 Ch. 72; Trustees of Watertown v. Cowen, 4 Paige 510; Randall v. Latham, 36 Conn. 48; City of Cincinnati v. Lessee of White, 6 Pet. 431; Drew v. Van Deman, 6 Heisk. 433; Winfield v. Henning, 21 N. J. Eq. 188; Verplanck v. Wright, 23 Wend. 506; Stockett v. Howard, 34 Md. 121.

[5] We merely touch upon the general question here, as we have considered the subject more at length in discussing the subject of railroads in streets.

contracts.¹ Ordinarily, the municipal corporation may impose such conditions as in its discretion it deems expedient, and the company accepting such a grant, as well as such companies as avail themselves of the benefit of it, must accept the benefit with its conditions and burdens.² A municipal corporation may contract with a railroad company to pay part of the expense of changing a grade crossing, and in making such a contract the municipality does not loan its credit.³

§ 362. Contracts for location of stations.—Elsewhere we have directed attention to the cases which hold that a railroad company can not enter into a valid contract to locate a station at a designated place, and have said that in our opinion such a contract may be made if no public interest is prejudiced. If the contract is made solely to promote private interests at the expense of the public welfare, the contract should, as we think, be held to be illegal. But if public interests are not prejudiced, or the power of the company to do what the public welfare requires is not abridged, we believe the contract should be regarded as valid. Many cases hold that a railroad corporation may contract for the erection and maintenance of a station at a certain point,⁴ where its right to maintain stations at

---

¹ Chicago, etc., R. Co. v. Kansas City, etc., R. Co., 52 Fed. R. 178, s. c. 38 Fed. R. 58; Central, etc., Co. v. Wabash, etc., R. Co., 29 Fed. R. 546. The power of determining where tracks shall be located, unless an express provision to the contrary is made by the legislature, resides in the municipal corporation. Booth on Street Railways, §§ 855, 856; Chicago, etc., R. Co. v. People, 73 Ill. 541; West End, etc., R. Co. v. Atlanta, etc., Co., 49 Ga. 151; State v. Henderson, 38 Ohio St. 644; Citizens', etc., Co. v. Jones, 34 Fed. R. 579; Elliott on Roads and Streets, p. 573.

² Louisville, etc., Co. v. Mississippi, etc., Co. 92 Tenn. 681, s. c. 22 S. W. R. 920; Joy v. City of St. Louis, 138 U. S. 1, s. c. 45 Am. & Eng. R. Cas. 655.

³ Brooke v. City of Philadelphia, 162 Pa. St. 123, s. c. 24 L. R. A. 781, 29 Atl. R. 387.

⁴ Currier v. Concord R. Co., 48 N. H. 321; McClure v. Missouri River, etc., R. Co., 9 Kan. 373; Kansas Pac. R. Co. v. Hopkins, 18 Kan. 494; Cedar Rapids, etc., R. Co. v. Spafford, 41 Iowa 292; First Nat. Bank v. Hendrie, 49 Iowa 402; Louisville, etc., R. Co. v. Sumner, 106 Ind. 55; Martindale v. Kansas City, etc., R. Co., 60 Mo. 508; Kinealy v. St. Louis, etc., R. Co., 69 Mo. 658; Missouri Pac. R. Co. v. Tygard, 84 Mo. 263; Vicksburgh, etc., R. Co. v. Ragsdale, 46 Miss. 458; Cumberland Valley R. Co. v. Baab, 9 Watts

other points is not thereby impaired.[1] This we believe to be the sound doctrine.

§ 363. **Location of tracks, switches and the like.**—The first duty of a railroad company in the location of tracks and switches is to the public, and it can not rightfully make any contract which will prevent it from performing this duty. Where, however, no public interest is affected, a railroad company may bind itself to locate a switch at a designated place.[2] If, however, it appears that the company is governed by a consideration of self-interest, and that the interest of the public will be prejudiced by such a contract, it should be regarded as illegal. It has been held that a railroad company may make a valid agreement to stop its trains at a certain point at specified times for the receipt of freight.[3] But in our opinion such contracts can not be upheld if it is shown that they are materially injurious to the interests of the public, for the public welfare can not be sacrificed for mere private benefit. It has also been adjudged that a railroad company may agree with the lessee of refreshment rooms at a point upon its line for the stoppage of its trains at such point for a reasonable time to enable the pas-

(Pa.) 458; Texas, etc., R. Co. v. Robards, 60 Tex. 545; Jessup v. Grand Trunk R. Co., 28 Grant's Ch. (U. C.) 583; Township of Wallace v. Great Western R. Co., 3 Ont. App. R. 44; Caldwell v. East Broad Top, etc., R. Co., 169 Pa. St. 99, s. c. 32 Atl. R. 85. Contra, Pacific R.Co. v. Seely, 45 Mo. 212; Clark on Contracts, 424, and cases there cited.

[1] Williamson v. Chicago, etc., R. Co., 53 Iowa 126; St. Louis, etc., R. Co. v. Mathers, 72 Ill. 592. Where a right of way and ground for the erection of station were granted to a railroad at a nominal quit rent in consideration that "all passenger trains should stop regularly" at such station, it was held on appeal to the House of Lords that the company was bound to stop all trains passing through said station for the conveyance of passengers, excepting trains chartered by individuals for their own use, and special excursion trains. Burnett v. Great North of Scotland R. Co., L. R. 10 App. Cas. 147, 24 Am. & Eng. R. Cas. 647.

[2] Lydick v. Baltimore, etc., R. Co., 17 W. Va. 427.

[3] Lydick v. Baltimore, etc., Co., 17 W.Va. 427; Lindsay v. Great Northern R. Co., 17 Jur. 522. In these cases it was held that such an agreement could be specifically enforced, and a court of equity will restrain a breach thereof.

sengers to obtain refreshments there,[1] and that a recovery may be had for a breach of such agreement.[2]

§ 364. Contracts that may be made by railroad companies —Particular instances.—We have called attention to the general and familiar rule that all railroad companies possess implied and incidental contract powers, and we do not attempt to give many cases illustrating the general rule, but shall refer to some cases possessing peculiar features. A railroad company may contract to carry a person and his family upon its trains free during his life,[3] or for any period of time,[4] subject to any prescribed legal conditions.[5] It may make special contracts for the carriage of passengers,[6] provided that it makes

---

[1] Phillips v. Great Western R. Co., L. R. 7 Ch. 409.

[2] Flanagan v. Great Western R. Co., L. R. 7 Eq. 116; Rigby v. Great Western R. Co., 4 Eng. R. & Canal Cas. 190. But we think that such contracts are to be carefully scrutinized and not upheld where they materially infringe the rights of the public. The public interest is always, as it seems to us, the paramount consideration. Contracts to stop trains at designated places, or to do like acts, may in many instances be detrimental to the public welfare, and in such instances they should not be enforced.

[3] Grimes v. Minneapolis, etc., R. Co., 37 Minn. 66. See Pennsylvania Co. v. Erie, etc., R. Co., 108 Pa. St. 621; Rice v. Illinois Cent. R. Co., 22 Ill. App. 643. Where right of way is granted to a railroad company in consideration of a free pass for the grantor during his life, the purchaser of the road at a foreclosure sale can not be held liable for failure to grant such pass. Helton v. St. Louis, K. & N. W. R. Co., 25 Mo. App. 322.

[4] Knopf v. Richmond, etc., R. Co., 85 Va. 769.

[5] In Knopf v. Richmond, etc., R. Co., 85 Va. 769, it was decided that, under the circumstances, the company was not at fault for failing to issue a pass which had not been applied for, and that the company's agents rightfully ejected the plaintiff on his failure to produce and show a pass. In Grimes v. Minneapolis, etc., R. Co., 37 Minn. 66, it was held that the defendant, having contracted to carry the members of the family of plaintiff's father, in consideration of a conveyance of land for a right of way, and making it a rule to issue no passes, was under an obligation to inform the conductors of plaintiff's rights, and instruct them to allow them.

[6] Gulf, etc., R. Co., v. McGown, 65 Tex. 640; Bates v. Old Colony R. Co., 147 Mass. 255: Johnson v. Philadelphia, etc., R. Co., 63 Md. 106; Mosher v. St. Louis, etc., R. Co., 127 U. S. 390; Pennington v. Philadelphia, etc., R. Co., 62 Md. 95. See, also, Quimby v. Boston, etc., R. Co., 150 Mass. 365; Griswold v. New York, etc., R. Co., 53 Conn. 371; Ulrich v. New York., etc., R. Co., 108 N. Y. 80.

no unjust discrimination and violates no rules of law. This is true also respecting the carriage of goods.[1] It may, by contract, extend its duties and liabilities to the carriage of goods beyond its own line.[2] Many cases hold that where no statutory provisions control, a railway company may contract to carry for less than a reasonable compensation, though it may not charge more.[3]

§ 365. **Pooling contracts — Generally.** — There is much diversity of opinion as to the wisdom or expediency of permitting railroad companies to enter into pooling contracts,[4] and there is some diversity of opinion among authors and judges as to the validity of such contracts.[5] It seems to us

---

[1] Ball v. Wabash, etc., R. Co., 83 Mo. 574; Bartlett v. Pittsburgh, etc., R. Co., 94 Ind. 281; Chicago, etc., R. Co. v. Abels, 60 Miss. 1017; Brown v. Manchester, etc., R. Co., L. R. 9 Q. B. Div. 230, 10 Q. B. D. 250, affirmed, L. R. 8 App. Cas. 703; Black v. Wabash, etc., R. Co., 111 Ill. 351; Sprague v. Missouri Pac. R. Co., 34 Kan. 347; Louisville, etc., R. Co. v. Sherrod, 84 Ala. 178, 35 Am. & Eng. R. Cas. 611.

[2] Houston, etc., R. Co. v. Hill, 63 Tex. 381; Cummins v. Dayton, etc., R. Co., (Marion Co., Ind., Super. Ct.) 9 Am. & Eng. R. Cas. 36; Beard v. St. Louis, etc., R. Co., 79 Iowa 527; Atlanta, etc., R. Co. v. Tex. G. Co., 81 Ga. 602; Hanson v. Flint, etc., R. Co., 73 Wis. 346; St. Louis, etc., R. Co. v. Larned, 103 Ill. 293; Pereira v. Central Pac. R. Co., 66 Cal. 92; Swift v. Pacific Mail, etc., Co., 106 N. Y. 206; Dardanelle, etc., R. Co. v. Shinn, 52 Ark. 93.

[3] Toledo, etc., R. Co. v. Elliott, 76 Ill. 67; Christie v. Missouri Pac. R. Co., 94 Mo. 453. But it may not unjustly discriminate in favor of certain shippers, so as to foster a monopoly. Scofield v. Lake Shore, etc., R. Co., 43 Ohio St. 571. See Houston, etc., R. Co. v. Rust, 58 Texas, 98, 9 Am. & Eng. R. Cas. 123.

[4] Railway Review, April 26, 1884.

[5] Mr. Morawetz says: "It is impossible to support the proposition that all agreements among railroad companies which restrict competition are condemned by law. Some such agreements may be contrary to public policy and unlawful, but if an agreement of this character is a reasonable business arrangement to protect the shareholders and creditors of the companies from loss, and does not cause unreasonably high charges, or violate any duty which the companies owe the public, it should be sustained and enforced by the courts." 2 Morawetz Corp. (2d ed.), 1131. See Greenhood Public Policy, 660–666; Redfield Railways, § 146, par. 2, where it is said: "There is no principle of public policy which renders void a traffic arrangement between two lines of railway for the purpose of avoiding competition." Beach on Railways, § 528; Wood on Railroads, 590–600; Taylor Private Corp. (2d ed.), § 309; 2 Cook on Stockholders, § 897.

that some confusion has been caused by the failure to clearly discriminate a pooling contract from a contract for the maintenance of fair rates and the prevention of ruinous competition. If a contract is simply one wherein provision is made for preventing ruinous competition and is neither intended to nor does limit or suppress fair competition and is neither intended to nor does fix or maintain unreasonable rates of fare, then it can not be regarded as an illegal pooling contract, but must be regarded as a valid traffic contract. If there is no restraint placed upon any one of the contracting companies, if all are left free to perform their duties, and if there is no incentive or inducement to any one of them to neglect or refuse to perform its duty there is not, as it seems to us, any illegal element in the contract. But if the contract either in terms or in effect disables any one of the contracting companies from performing its duty or makes it to its interest not to perform its duty the contract should, as we believe, be held void as against public policy. Whether the contract does or does not disable some one of the contracting companies, or whether it makes it to its interest not to perform its duty, or limits fair competition, or tends to enable the companies, or some one of them, to obtain unreasonable fares, are questions to be determined from the facts of the particular case. Where the constitution or statute prohibits contracts between competing or rival lines then, of course, no such contract can be valid.[1] If the policy of the state as indicated by its laws is against such contracts they are not, it is obvious, of any validity.[2] We do not at this place enter upon a consideration of the effect of the federal interstate commerce law, or of the federal statute directed against trusts, or the effect of state statutes directed against trusts and combinations, but confine our discussion to

---

[1] In some of the states railroad companies are forbidden to enter into any contract for pooling their earnings. Stimson's Am. Stat., § 8839.

[2] Morrill v. Boston, etc., R. Co., 55 N. H. 531. But see Manchester, etc., R. Co. v. Concord R. Co., (N. H.) s. c. 20 Atl. R. 383, 47 Am. & Eng. R. Cas. 359, 3 Am. R. & Corp. R. 22; Currier v. Concord R. Co., 48 N. H. 321.

the subject of what are commonly called pooling contracts without regard to constitutional or statutory provisions.

§ 366. **Pooling contracts—The authorities.**—The rule which seems to be sanctioned by the weight of authority is that contracts between railroad companies providing for the regulation of charges and preventing ruinous competition are not in themselves illegal, but they are illegal if they are intended to suppress fair competition or have that effect, and so they are if they disable any of the contracting companies from performing their duty or make it to the interest of any one of them not to perform the duty enjoined upon them by law.[1] We have

[1] Shrewsbury, etc., R. Co. v. London, etc., R. Co., 17 Q. B. 652, s. c. 21 L. J. Q. B. 89; Hare v. London, etc., R. Co., 2 J. & H. 80, 30 L. J. Ch. 817; Lancaster, etc., Co. v. Northwestern, etc., Co., 2 K. & J. 293, 25 L. J. Ch. 223; Eclipse, etc., Co. v. Pontchartrain R. Co., 24 La. Ann. 1; Stewart v. Erie, etc., Co., 17 Minn. 372; Sussex, etc., R. Co. v. Morris R. Co., 19 N. J. Eq. 13; United States v. Trans-Missouri, etc., Assn., 58 Fed. R. 58; Manchester, etc., R. Co. v. Concord R. Co., — N. H. —, s. c. 20 Atl. R. 383, 47 Am. & Eng. R. Cas. 359, 3 Am. R. & Corp. Cases 22; Ex parte Koehler, 23 Fed. R. 529; Central Trust Co. v. Ohio Central R. Co., 23 Fed. R. 306; Burke v. Concord R. Co., 61 N. H. 160; Pittsburgh, etc., R. Co. v. Keokuk, etc., Co., 131 U. S. 371. In Ives v. Smith, 3 N. Y. Supp. 645, a violation of such a contract by a company was enjoined at the suit of a stockholder. A contract between railroad companies, members of a freight association, binding them to establish and maintain such rates, rules and regulations on freight traffic between competitive points, as a committee of their choosing shall recommend, providing for monthly meetings of the association, and that each company shall give five days' notice before a monthly meeting of every reduction of rates or deviation from the rules it proposes to make; that it will advise with the representatives of the other members at the meeting relative to proposed changes, and, if the proposition is voted down, that it will then give ten days' notice that it will make the changes, notwithstanding the vote, if it will not abide by the vote; that no member will bill any freight falsely, or at a wrong classification; and, providing that any member may withdraw from the association on a notice of thirty days, does not substantially disable the parties to the contract from the performance of their public duties. United States v. Trans-Missouri Freight Assn., 58 Fed. R. 58, 7 C. C. C. A. 15. In this case there is a strong dissenting opinion by Shiras, J. See Texas, etc., R. Co. v. Southern Pacific R. Co., 41 La. Ann. 970, s. c. 40 Am. & Eng. R. Cas. 475, 6 So. R. 888; Kettle River R. Co. v. Eastern R. Co., 41 Minn. 461, s. c. 40 Am. & Eng. R. Cas. 449, 43 N. W. R. 469.

stated the doctrine in somewhat narrower terms than some of the cases declare it, but we believe our statement to be a fair expression of the prevailing opinion. If the purpose of the contract between the companies is to stifle competition so as to obtain unreasonable fares, or if its effect be to disable one of the contracting companies from performing the duty enjoined upon it, the contract should be condemned as illegal.[1]

§ 367. **Pooling contracts—Presumption.**—It seems to us that when it appears that several railroad companies have entered into an agreement to establish and maintain rates the presumption should be against its validity, and that the contracting companies should be required to show that it was not intended to unjustly stifle fair competition or disable any one of the companies from performing its duty. *Prima facie* such a contract should be regarded as against public policy.[2] The

---

[1] In the case of Chicago, etc., R. Co. v. Wabash, etc., Co., 61 Fed. R. R. 993, s. c. 10 Lewis' Am. R. & Corp. R. 173, the court said: "A railroad company is a *quasi* public corporation and owes certain duties to the public, among which are the duties to afford reasonable facilities for the transportation of persons and to charge only reasonable rates for such service. Any contract by which it disables itself from these duties, or which makes it to its interest not to perform them, or removes all incentive to their performance, is contrary to public policy and void, and the obvious purpose of this contract being to suppress or limit competition between the contracting companies, in respect to the traffic covered by the contract, and to establish rates without regard to the question of their reasonableness, it is contrary to public policy and void." The court cited Cleveland, etc., Co. v. Closser, 126 Ind. 348, s. c. 26 N. E. R. 159; Gulf, etc., R. Co. v. State, 72 Tex. 404, s. c. 10 S. W. R. 81; State v. Standard Oil Co., 49 Ohio St. 137, s. c. 30 N. E. R. 279; Texas, etc., Co. v. Southern Pacific R. Co., 41 La. Ann. 970, s. c. 6 So. R. 888; Gibbs v. Consolidated Gas Co., 130 U. S. 396, s. c. 9 Sup. Ct. R. 553; Morris Run Co. v. Barclay, etc., Co., 68 Pa. St. 173; Central, etc., Co. v. Guthrie, 35 Ohio St. 666; Stanton v. Allen, 5 Denio 434; Hooker v. Vandewater, 4 Denio 349; Chicago, etc., Co. v. People's, etc., Co., 121 Ill. 530, s. c. 13 N. E. R. 169; West Va., etc., Co. v. Ohio River, etc., Co., 22 W. Va. 600; Western Union Tel. Co. v. American, etc., Co., 65 Ga. 160; Sayre v. Louisville, etc., Assn., 1 Duvall (Ky.) 143; United States v. Trans-Missouri, etc., Assn., 58 Fed. R. 58, 7 C. C. A. 15. The court denied the doctrine of Central, etc., Co., v. Ohio Central R. Co., 23 Fed. R. 306. Mr. Lewis, in his note to the case from which we have quoted, cites and comments upon many cases. 10 Lewis' Am. R. & Corp. R. 181-184.

[2] Cleveland, etc., R. Co. v. Closser, 126 Ind. 348, s. c. 26 N. E. R. 159.

presumption against such a contract may doubtless be removed, but the contract should be jealously scrutinized and not upheld if it be not made to appear that it was not entered into in order to prevent ruinous or, as some of the cases say, unhealthy competition. The burden of making this appear should be placed on the party who asserts the validity of the contract.[1]

§ 368. **Contracts—Ultra vires—Definitions.**—In discussing many of the subjects which have been considered in the preceding pages we have referred to the doctrine of *ultra vires*, and so we shall do in other parts of our work, but it seems appropriate to treat briefly of the general doctrine of *ultra vires* at this place. The term *"ultra vires"* is one very frequently employed and not always with strict accuracy. Roughly defined the term, when applied to a corporation, means beyond the powers of the corporation.[2] It may be here noted that the doctrine of *ultra vires* is applicable as a defense on the part of the corporation only to actions arising out of contract.[3] Contracts and other acts of the corporation which are outside or in excess of the corporate powers are *ultra vires*. The term is sometimes applied to acts which corporations, as well as natural persons, are forbidden by law to do,[4] and when so used it means illegal contracts, but this is not, in strictness, an accurate use of the

[1] In a subsequent part of our work, we have discussed the effect of the interstate commerce law and other statutes upon the question of the validity of pooling arrangements between railroad companies.

[2] In the case of National, etc., Bank v. Porter, 125 Mass. 333, s. c. 28 Am. R. 235, the court said: "There is nothing of mystery or sanctity in the use of the words of a dead language, *ultra vires;* and although it is a concise and convenient form by which to indicate the unauthorized action of artificial persons with limited powers, still it is as applicable to individual as to corporate action. An illegal act of an individual is as really *ultra vires* as the unauthorized act of a corporation."

[3] National Bank v. Graham, 100 U. S. 699; Hussey v. Norfolk, etc., R. Co., 98 N. C. 34; Hutchinson v. Western, etc., R. Co., 6 Heisk. (Tenn.) 634; 'Gruber v. Washington, etc., R. Co., 92 N. C. 1; Central, etc., R. Co. v. Smith, 76 Ala. 572.

[4] East Anglian R Co. v. Eastern Counties R. Co., 11 C. B. 775; South Yorkshire R. Co. v. Great Northern R. Co., 9 Ex. 55, 84. It is held that the word "unlawful," as applied to the purposes for which corporations are formed, is not used exclusively in the sense of *malum in se* or *malum prohibitum*, but is also used to des-

term. Acts may be *ultra vires* and yet not be illegal, for acts in excess of the corporate powers, although entirely honest and moral, may be *ultra vires*.[1] If the corporation is not invested with power to make the contract or perform the act which is the subject of controversy, the contract or act is *ultra vires*, although it may be free from any taint of fraud. The term *ultra vires* is often used as denoting contracts voidable because of their violation of public policy, but, as said by an eminent English judge, the term "illegality" is the better one.[2] The term *ultra vires* is sometimes used to characterize a contract made by a corporate officer, who has no authority to act for the corporation in the transaction out of which the contract arises, but this is not an accurate use of the term. A president of a railroad company, for example, may have no authority to contract for the construction of the road, because such authority is vested in the board of directors, but such a contract could not be justly said to be *ultra vires*.[3]

ignate such acts, powers, and contracts as are *ultra vires*. People, *ex rel.* Peabody *v.* Chicago Gas Trust Co., 130 Ill. 268, s. c. 8 L. R. A. 497, 22 N. E. R. 798.

[1] In Whitney Arms Co. *v.* Barlow, 63 N. Y. 62, s. c. 20 Am. R. 504, it was said: "When acts of corporations are spoken of as *ultra vires*, it is not intended that they are unlawful or even such as the corporation can not perform, but merely those which are not within the powers conferred upon the corporation by the act of its creation, and are in violation of the trust reposed in the managing board by the shareholders, that the affairs shall be managed and the funds applied solely for carrying out the objects for which the corporation was created." The court cited Earl of Shrewsbury *v.* North Staffordshire, etc., R. Co., L. R. 1 Eq. 593; Tyler *v.* Chichester, etc., Co., L. R. 2 Exch. 356; Bissell *v.* Mich., etc., R. Co., 22 N. Y. 258. In Bissell *v.* Mich., etc., R. Co., *supra*, the court said: "The words *ultra vires* and illegality represent totally different and distinct ideas. It is true that a contract may have both these defects, but it may also have one without the other." See, generally, Ashbury, etc., Co. *v.* Riche, L. R. 7 H. L. 653; Kent *v.* Quicksilver, etc., Co., 78 N. Y. 159; Taylor Private Corp., § 592.

[2] Cairns, L. C., in Ashbury, etc., R. Co. *v.* Riche, L. R. 7 H. L. 653.

[3] An agent may exceed his authority, but the contract entered into by him not be *ultra vires* as to the corporation. The distinction between cases where an agent exceeds the authority conferred upon him and cases where the act is beyond the corporate power or capacity is often of importance. It is especially so in cases where the question is whether the agent's act has been ratified; if the agent simply transcended his authority his act may be

§ 369. **Contracts — Ultra vires — General doctrine.**—Contracts which are beyond the scope of the powers granted by the act of incorporation or outside of the objects for which it was created, are, in the just sense, *ultra vires,* but they are not necessarily illegal.[1] An illegal contract, that is, a contract condemned or prohibited by law, differs from a contract made by a corporation in excess of its corporate powers, but involving no moral turpitude or wrong, and this difference leads to important practical results. If a party engages with a corporation in an illegal contract, that is, a contract involving moral turpitude, the courts will not aid him to enforce the contract nor to recover money or property yielded the corporation under it. Where, however, a corporation obtains money or property under a contract that is not illegal, the party from whom such money or property is obtained will be aided by the courts, although the contract was *ultra vires.*[2] It is held upon the

---

validated by ratification, but if the act was beyond the corporate power, ratification will not always validate it.

[1] Lord Chancellor Selborne in Great Eastern, etc., R. Co. *v.* Turner, L. R. 8 Ch. 149, said: "The company is a mere abstraction of law. All that it does, all that the law imputes to it as its act, must be that which can be legally done within the powers vested in it by law. Consequently, an act which is *ultra vires* and unauthorized is not an act of the company in such a sense as that the consent of the company to that act can be pleaded."

[2] Pullman, etc., Co. *v.* Central, etc., Co., 65 Fed. R. 158; New Castle, etc., Railroad Co. *v.* Simpson, 23 Fed. R. 214; Manchester, etc., Co. *v.* Concord, etc., Co., (N. H.), s. c. 20 Atl. R. 383; Memphis, etc., R. Co. *v.* Dow, 19 Fed. R. 388; Parrish *v.* Wheeler, 22 N. Y. 494; Bissell *v.* Michigan, etc., Co., 22 N. Y. 258; Hays *v.* Galion, etc., Co., 29 Ohio St. 330, 340; Attleborough Bank *v.* Rogers, 125 Mass. 339; Rutland, etc., R. Co. *v.* Proctor, 29 Vt. 93; Central Transportation Co. *v.* Pullman Car Co., 139 U. S. 24, s. c. 11 Sup. Ct. R. 478; Pennsylvania, etc., Co. *v.* St. Louis, etc., Co., 118 U. S. 290, s. c. 6 Sup. Ct. R. 1094; Union Trust Co. *v.* Illinois Midland, etc., Co., 117 U. S. 434; DeGroff *v.* American, etc., Co., 21 N.Y. 124; Franklin Co. *v.* Lewiston, etc., Bank, 68 Me. 43, 49; Dill *v.* Inhabitants of Wareham, 7 Metcf. (Mass.) 438; Morville *v.* American, etc., Co., 123 Mass. 129; Oil Creek, etc., Co. *v.* Penn. Transportation Co., 83 Pa. St. 160; Bradley *v.* Ballard, 55 Ill. 413; Hazlehurst *v.* Savannah, etc., R. Co., 43 Ga. 13; Argenti *v.* City of San Francisco, 16 Cal. 255; State Board, etc., *v.* Citizens, etc., Co., 47 Ind. 407; Miners', etc., Co. *v.* Zellerbach, 37 Cal. 543; Northwestern, etc., Co. *v.* Shaw, 37 Wis. 655; County of Wapello *v.* Burlington, etc., Co., 44 Iowa 585; Atlantic, etc., Co. *v.* Union Pacific R. Co., 1 Fed. R. 745; Wright *v.* Pipe Line Co., 101 Pa. St. 204; Miller *v.* American, etc., Co., 92 Tenn. 167, s. c. 21 S. W. R. 39.

same general principle that if the party contracting with a corporation retains the property obtained from the corporation, thus securing a benefit under the contract, he can not escape payment of the value of the property so obtained on the ground that the contract was *ultra vires*.[1] A contract expressly forbidden by statute or one *malum in se* is not enforceable, but is to be regarded as void, for in such cases the corporation does more than perform an act in excess of its corporate powers.[2] Some of the cases hold that contracts executed in a mode different from that prescribed by the act of incorporation are *ultra vires*,[3] but this doctrine we regard as untenable. It is, no doubt, true that the contract should be made in the mode prescribed by the charter,[4] but the fact that the contract was not made in the prescribed mode does not authorize the conclusion that the corporation had no power to enter into the contract. It is probably true that an executory contract, made in a mode different from that prescribed, will not be obligatory upon the corporation, but, nevertheless, such a contract is not void and may therefore be ratified.

§ 370. Contracts—What are ultra vires—Generally.—The familiar elementary rule is that the corporate powers are such only as are expressed in the charter, or in the act of incorporation and the articles of association, together with such implied powers as are proper and necessary to the enjoyment of those which are expressly conferred,[5] and acts of the corpora-

---

[1] Bath Gaslight Co. v. Claffy, 56 N. Y. S. R. 426; Ashenbroedel Club v. Finlay, 53 Mo. App. 256; Whitney Arms Co. v. Barlow, 63 N. Y. 70. See Belcher, etc., Co. v. St. Louis, etc., Elevator Co., 101 Mo. 192; Baker v. Northwestern, etc., Co., 36 Minn. 185; Salmon, etc., Co. v. Dunn, 2 Idaho 30.

[2] Root v. Godard, 3 McLean (U. S. Cir.) 102; Hayden v. Davis, 3 McLean (U. S. Cir.) 276; Root v. Wallace, 4 McLean (U. S. Cir.) 8; Davis v. Bank, 4 McLean (U. S. Cir.) 387; New York State, etc., Co. v. Helmer, 77 N. Y. 64; *In re* Jaycox, 12 Blatch. (U. S. Cir.) 209; Philadelphia, etc., Co. v. Towner, 13 Conn. 249; Talmage v. Pell, 7 N. Y. 328.

[3] Farmers', etc., Bank v. Harrison, 57 Mo. 503; Matthews v. Skinker, 62 Mo. 329, s. c. 21 Am. R. 425; McSpedon v. New York, 7 Bosw. (N. Y. Superior Ct.) 601.

[4] Bank of U. S. Dandridge, 12 Wheat. 64; Hannibal, etc., Co. v. Marion County, 36 Mo. 294; Head v. Providence, etc., Co., 2 Cranch 127.

[5] Thomas v. Railroad Co., 101 U. S.

tion or its agents in excess of such powers will not impose an obligation upon the corporation by express contract.[1] It is, of course, not difficult to state, as a general rule, that contracts beyond or outside of the scope of the powers bestowed on the corporation are *ultra vires*, but it is not always easy to say just what contracts are beyond the scope of the powers expressly or impliedly conferred upon the corporation. It is, to be sure, not difficult in all cases to conclude that a contract is *ultra vires* since there are many cases in which the contract is so plainly beyond the corporate power that it may, without doubt or hesitation, be adjudged to be *ultra vires*. In many instances a careful study of the charter or act of incorporation is necessary in order to determine whether the contract is one the corporation had power to make, in others a bare knowledge of the nature and character of the corporation is all that is required in order to determine whether the contract is beyond the scope of the powers conferred upon the corporation by the legislature. A study of the decided cases will give a clearer conception of the law upon the subject than the statement of general rules can do.

§ 371. Contracts — Ultra vires—Estoppel.—It is held in some of the cases that a corporation may be estopped to make the defense that the contract was *ultra vires*,[2] but this doctrine

71; Mobile, etc., R. Co. *v.* Franks, 41 Miss. 494, 511; State *v.* Atchison, etc., R. Co., 24 Neb. 143; Lower *v.* Chicago, etc., R. Co., 59 Iowa 563.

[1] Lucas *v.* White Line Transfer Co., 70 Iowa 541; Mayor, etc., of Knoxville *v.* Knoxville,etc.,R. Co.,22 Fed.R. 758. No corporation, either public or private, can exercise any power not expressly conferred or necessarily implied to enable it to carry into effect the purposes for which it was created. First M. E. Church *v.* Atlanta, 76 Ga. 181; Oregon R. & Nav. Co.*v.*Oregonian R. Co., 130 U. S. 1, s. c. 9 Sup. Ct. R. 409; Beers *v.* Dalles City, 16 Ore. 334, s. c. 18 Pac. 835; State *v.* Atchison & N. R. Co., 24 Neb. 143, s. c. 38 N. W. 43; Chewacla Lime Works *v.* Dismukes, 87 Ala. 344, 6 So. 122. An *ultra vires* contract can not, as we have seen, impose an obligation by express contract on the corporation, but property or money received by the corporation, under color of the contract, may be recovered back.

[2] State Board *v.* Citizens', etc., Co., 47 Ind. 407; Whitney Arms Co. *v.* Barlow, 63 N. Y. 62. See authorities cited in the notes to the next section which follows. See, also, *post*, § 374.

is, as we believe, radically unsound. We do not doubt that a corporation receiving and retaining a benefit under an *ultra vires* contract may be compelled to do equity, but we do not see how it is legally possible to hold that a corporation can be estopped to deny that it had no power to make the contract. If a contract is *ultra vires* in the true sense, that is, a contract entirely beyond and outside of the corporate powers, it can not be made effective by an estoppel although the party contracting with the corporation may be protected from loss or injury upon equitable principles. Where the contract is not beyond the scope of the corporate powers, but is executed in a mode different from that prescribed by law, or is executed by officers or agents without authority from the corporation, then it may be ratified or the corporation may be bound by an estoppel. Where, however, the contract is in the true sense *ultra vires* it is void and relief is granted a party against the corporation not upon the ground of estoppel or of ratification, but upon equitable principles, and in granting relief the courts in effect treat the contract as disaffirmed.[1]

[1] The doctrine, which rests on solid principle, is that declared in Central Transportation Co. *v.* Pullman, etc., Co., 139 U. S. 24, s. c. 11 Sup. Ct. R. 478, where it was said: "A contract of a corporation which is *ultra vires* in the proper sense, that is to say outside of the object of its creation as defined in the law of its organization, and, therefore, beyond the powers conferred upon it by the legislature, is not voidable only, but wholly void, and of no legal effect. The objection to the contract is not merely that the corporation ought not to have made it, but that it could not make it. The contract can not be ratified by either party, because it could not have been authorized by either. No performance on either side can give it validity, or be the foundation of any right of action upon it. When a corporation is acting within the general scope of the powers conferred upon it by the legislature, the corporation, as well as persons contracting with it, may be estopped to deny that it has complied with the legal formalities, which are prerequisite to its existence or to its action, because such prerequisites might in fact have been complied with. But when the contract is beyond the powers conferred upon it by the legislature, neither the corporation, nor the other party to the contract, can be estopped by assenting to it, or by acting upon it, to show that it was prohibited by those laws." It was also said: "A contract *ultra vires* being unlawful and void, not because it is in itself immoral, but because the corporation, by the law of its creation, is incapable of making it, the courts, while refusing to maintain any action upon the unlawful contract, have always striven to do justice between the

§ 372. **Contracts—Ultra vires—Executed and executory contracts.**—The authorities discriminate between executed and executory contracts. There is substantial agreement upon the proposition that *ultra vires* contracts which are wholly executory can not be enforced against the corporation,[1] but as intimated in the preceding paragraph there is conflict as to the effect of such a contract after it has been executed and the party contracting with the corporation has parted with money or property. The performance of an executory *ultra vires* contract may be enjoined by a dissenting stockholder or other interested parties, so far as could be done, consistently, with adherence to the law, by permitting money or property, parted with on the faith of the unlawful contract, to be recovered back or compensation to be made for it. In such a case, however, the action is not maintained upon the unlawful contract, nor according to its terms." The court cited many cases, among them City of Parkersburg v. Brown, 106 U. S. 487, s. c. 1 Sup. Ct. R. 442; Chapman v. Board, etc., 107 U. S. 348, s. c. 2 Sup. Ct. R. 62; Pittsburgh, etc., R. Co. v. Keokuk, etc., Co., 131 U. S. 371, s. c. 9 Sup. Ct. R. 770; Hitchcock v. Galveston, 96 U. S. 341; Union Trust Co. v. Illinois Midland,etc.,Co., 117 U. S. 434, s. c. 6 Sup. Ct. R. 809. This doctrine, asserted in the case from which we have quoted, is sustained by well reasoned cases. Brunswick, etc., Co. v. United Gas, etc., Co., 85 Me. 532, s. c. 35 Am. St. R. 385; Marble Co. v. Harvey, 92 Tenn. 115, s. c. 36 Am. St. R. 71; Franco, etc., Co. v. McCormick, 85 Tex. 416, s. c. 34 Am. St. R. 815; Chicago, etc., Co. v. People's, etc., Co., 121 Ill. 530, s. c. 2 Am. St. R. 124; Long v. Georgia, etc., Co., 91 Ala. 519, s. c. 24 Am. St. R. 931; Bank of Chillicothe v. Swayne, 8 Ohio 257, s. c. 32 Am. Dec. 207; Eastern Counties Railway v. Hawkes, 5 H. L. Cases 331, per Lord Cranworth; Bagshaw v. Eastern Union R. Co., 7 Hare 114, per Wigram, V. C.; Ashbury Ry., etc., Co. v. Riche, L. R., 7 H. L. Cas. 653; Morris, etc., R. Co. v. Sussex R. Co., 20 N. J. Eq. 542, 562; Central Transportation Co. v. Pullman Car Co., 139 U. S. 24, but these cases hold the several contracts to be opposed to public policy, and the opinions expressed as to the effect of contracts to which this objection can not be made, may therefore be considered as mere *dicta*. Rorer on Railroads, 941, 942.

[1] Greens Brice's Ultra Vires, 607. See State Board of Agriculture v. Citizens' Street R. Co., 47 Ind. 407; Parish v. Wheeler, 22 N. Y. 494; Hazlehurst v. Savannah R. Co., 43 Ga. 13; Nassua Bank v. Jones, 95 N. Y. 115; Wilkes v.Georgia Pacific R.Co.,79 Ala. 180; Day v.Spiral Springs Co., 57 Mich. 146; Simpson v. Building Assn., 38 Ohio St. 349. Such executory contracts as are entirely foreign to the objects and purposes for which the corporation was formed, or which are outside its express or implied powers, are void and can not be enforced against it. Rock River Bank v. Sherwood, 10 Wis. 230.

party, who would be injured if it were carried into effect.[1] Many cases hold that after a contract has been executed, in whole or in part, a new element is introduced into the transaction. It would, they assert, be clearly unjust to permit the members of a corporation to take the benefits of a performance of the contract by the other party and then refuse performance on its part.[2] The fallacy in this reasoning, as it seems to us, is in assuming that a contract may be valid although there was no power whatever to make it, and that unless the contract is upheld, the party will be remediless. The party is not without remedy because the courts decline to hold the contract valid, for it is clearly within the power of the court to do complete justice by compelling the restoration of the property or by awarding damages. We fully agree that in all cases where the corporation has received money or property or the fruits of labor, as a result of a performance of the contract by the other party, it should not be permitted to retain the benefits received, without making reparation, but we can not agree that a contract made where there is an entire absence of power can be enforced. The members of the corporation are held by many of the courts to be estopped, not only individully, but collectively, to set up the defense,[3] but as we have said in the preceding section we can not yield assent to this.

[1] A contract for the purchase of steamboats to run in connection with the line may be set aside at the suit of a stockholder. Hoagland v. Hannibal & St. Joseph R. Co., 39 Mo. 451; Colman v. Eastern Counties R. Co., 10 Beav. 1. So of a contract to improve a harbor. Munt v. Shrewsbury, etc., R. Co., 13 Beav. 1. Or to build the main line by the use of money raised for the construction of a branch line. Bagshaw v. Eastern Union Railway, 7 Hare 114. So of an *ultra vires* lease. Board, etc., Tippecanoe Co. v. Lafayette, etc., R. Co., 50 Ind. 85. See, also, Central R. Co. v. Collins, 40 Ga. 582; Cumberland Valley R. Co.'s Appeal, 62 Pa. St. 218; Stewart v. Erie, etc., Trans. Co., 17 Minn. 372, 398; Stevens v. Rutland, etc., R. Co., 29 Vt. 545; Mills v. Central R. Co., 41 N. J. Eq. 1; March v. Eastern R. Co., 40 N. H. 548, 43 N. H. 515.

[2] State Board of Agriculture v. Citizens' Street R. Co., 47 Ind. 407; Oil Creek, etc., R. Co. v. Pennsylvania Trans. Co., 83 Pa. St. 160; Peoria, etc., R. Co. v. Thompson, 103 Ill. 187; Camden, etc., R. Co. v. Mays Landing, etc., R. Co., 48 N. J. L. 530; Denver Fire Ins. Co. v. McClelland, 9 Col. 11.

[3] State Board of Agriculture v. Citizens' Street R. Co., 47 Ind. 407; Bradley v. Ballard, 55 Ill. 413; Cary v. Cleveland, etc., R. Co., 29 Barb.

§ 373. **Contracts—Ultra vires — Cases discriminated.**—We think that it will be found upon an analysis of many of the cases often cited as holding that a corporation may be estopped to aver that it had no power to enter into the contract which is beyond its corporate capacity, that they are not, in fact, cases in which the contract was in the proper sense *ultra vires*. They are cases of the defective exercise of power, not cases where (N. Y.) 35; Argenti *v.* San Francisco, 16 Cal. 255; McCluer *v.* Manchester, etc., R. Co., 13 Gray (Mass.) 124; Hale *v.* Mutual Fire Ins. Co., 32 N. H. 295; Rutland, etc., R. Co. *v.* Proctor, 29 Vt. 93; Louisville, etc., R. Co. *v.* Flanagan, 113 Ind. 488; Texas Western R. Co. *v.* Gentry, 69 Tex. 625. In one case it was held that where two street-car companies, organized under the general laws of the state, enter into a contract by which the first is to pay the second a certain rental for the use of the latter's track, the lessor can not, while exercising and enjoying the right, refuse to pay the sum agreed on the ground that the contract was *ultra vires* of its officers. Canal & C. R. Co. *v.* St. Charles St. R. Co., 44 La. Ann. 1069, 11 So. R. 702. So it has been held that a corporation which accepts and uses money loaned in good faith on a mortgage upon its property, and pays interest on such money after notice of the mortgage, can not escape liability on such mortgage by the passage of a resolution disapproving and annulling the president's authority, especially where the mortgage was executed by the president by the authority of the board of directors and no steps were taken to disaffirm the mortgage until long after its execution. Augusta, etc., R. Co. *v.* Kittel, 52 Fed. R. 63. The cases which follow also oppose the doctrine we favor. In one case it was held that after a corporation has received the fruits which grow out of the performance of an act *ultra vires*, and the mischief has all been accomplished, it comes with an ill grace then to assert its want of power to do the act or make the contract in order to escape the performance of an obligation it has assumed. Wright *v.* Hughes, 119 Ind. 324. The same general doctrine is held in other cases. Owen Sound S. S. Co. *v.* Canadian Pac. R. Co., 17 Ont. R. 691, 40 Am. & Eng. R. Cas. 593. A corporation, having enjoyed the benefits of a contract, can not plead that it was *ultra vires* in the absence of fraud. Sherman Center Town Co. *v.* Morris, 43 Kan. 282, 23 Pac. R. 569; People's Gaslight & C. Co. *v.* Chicago Gaslight & C. Co., 20 Ill. App. 473; First Nat. Bank of Monmouth *v.* Brooks, 22 Ill. App. 238; Sheridan Electric Light Co. *v.* Chatham Nat. Bank, 52 Hun 575, 24 N. Y. S. R. 622, 5 N. Y. Supp. 529; Hubbard *v.* Camperdown Mills, 26 S. Car. 581, 2 S. E. R. 576. This rule applies where a corporation attempts to deny the authority of an agent or officer. Peck *v.* Doran & W. Co., 57 Hun 343, 32 N. Y. S. R. 405, 10 N. Y. Supp. 401; Lancaster County *v.* Cheraw & C. R. Co., 28 S. Car. 134, 5 S. E. R. 338. A railroad company can not plead that its contract to build and operate a telegraph line was *ultra vires* as a defense to an action by the builder of the line for his compensation. Pittsburgh & C. R. Co. *v.* Shaw, (Pa.) 13 Cent. R. 220, 14 Atl. 323.

there is an entire want of power.[1] Some of the cases are really cases where the act was performed in violation of the corporate by-laws,[2] or by an agent in excess of his authority, and not cases where the act was wholly and entirely beyond the scope of the powers conferred upon the corporation by the legislature.[3] It may, perhaps, be true in a limited or qualified sense that where the contract is made by an agent who exceeds his authority, or is made in violation of corporate by-laws, that there is a contract *ultra vires*, but it is not true in the proper or just sense, for it is not a contract made where the corporation itself had no capacity whatever to contract, and it is only to cases where there is an entire absence of power to contract that the doctrine of *ultra vires* justly applies. Some of the decisions treat cases where the contract in question was made in some mode other than that prescribed by

[1] This is true of the case of Bensiek v. Thomas, 66 Fed. R. 104, and of the cases of Aurora, etc., Horticultural Society v. Paddock, 80 Ill. 263; Kent v. Quicksilver Mining Co., 78 N. Y. 159. The reasoning of the decision in Sheldon, etc., Co. v. Eickemeyer, etc., Co., 90 N. Y. 608, is, we venture to say, founded on the erroneous assumption that an *ultra vires* contract is "but the case of an agent making a contract in excess of his authority," for, as it seems to us, where the corporation itself acts and the contract is entirely outside of the scope of the powers conferred upon the corporation, the case is that of a corporation attempting to make a contract it had no power to make. We believe the conclusion reached in the case upon which we are commenting is right, but think the reasoning fallacious.

[2] Roy, etc., Co. v. Scott, etc., 11 Wash. 399, s. c. 39 Pac. R. 679.

[3] In the case of Missouri Pac. R. Co. v. Sidell, 67 Fed. R. 464, the court pointed out the difference between cases where there is an entire absence of power and cases where the power is abused or not properly exercised. The court cited the cases of Davis v. Old Colony Railroad Co., 131 Mass. 258; Pennsylvania, etc., Co. v. Keokuk, etc., Co., 131 U. S. 371, s. c. 9 Sup. Ct. R. 770; Louisiana v. Wood, 102 U. S. 294; City of Parkersburg v. Brown, 106 U. S. 487, 1 Sup. Ct. R. 442; Pennsylvania R. Co. v. St. Louis, etc., R. Co., 118 U. S. 290; Zabriskie v. Cleveland, etc., Railroad Co., 23 How. (U. S.) 381. The court quoted with approval from Davis v. Railroad Co., *supra*, the following: "There is a clear distinction between the exercise of a power not conferred upon, varying from the objects of its creation as declared in the law of its organization, of which all persons dealing with it are bound to take notice, and the abuse of a general power, or the failure to comply with prescribed formalities or regulations in the particular instance, when such abuse or failure is not known to the other contracting parties."

the charter as *ultra vires;* but this certainly is erroneous, for the defect in such cases is in the execution of a power granted; the power itself is not absent. Other cases cited as affirming that a corporation may be estopped to deny the validity of an *ultra vires* contract really decide nothing more than that the corporation must restore the property it received or make compensation, and in such cases there is no question of estoppel involved. Still other cases are placed under the doctrine of *ultra vires* where there was in fact nothing more than a failure to hold a directors' meeting, or give a notice, or do some such act in the mode prescribed by law,[1] but such cases are not justly cases within the doctrine of *ultra vires.*

§ 374. **Contracts—Ultra vires—Illustrative instances.**— A charter incorporating a company to build and operate a railroad, does not by implication confer power to purchase and run a line of steamboats,[2] but, of course, such a company may be invested with power to own and operate a line of steamboats in connection with its railroad. Such a charter does not by implication confer power to engage in the business of trading in

---

[1] Farmers', etc., Co. v. Toledo, etc., 67 Fed. R. 49. The case cited holds *inter alia,* that parties, by unreasonable delay, may lose the right to successfully complain of an irregular or unauthorized act, citing Allis v. Jones, 45 Fed. R. 148; Reed's Appeal, 122 Pa. St. 565, s. c. 16 Atl. R. 100; Fidelity, etc., Co. v. West Pennsylvania, etc., R. Co., 138 Pa. St. 494, s. c. 21 Atl. R. 21; Wood v. Corry Water-Works Co., 44 Fed.R. 146; Hackensack Water Co. v. DeKay, 36 N.J. Eq. 548.

[2] Central R., etc., Co. v. Smith, 76 Ala.572; Gunn v. Central R., etc., Co., 74 Ga. 509; Hoagland v. Hannibal, St. Joseph R. Co., 39 Mo. 451; Pearce v. Madison, etc., R. Co., 21 How. (U. S.) 441; Colman v. Eastern Counties R. Co., 10 Beav. 1. But authority to contract for the transportation of its passengers beyond its own line will enable it to make a valid contract guaranteeing the profits of a steamboat line connecting with it at its terminus. Green Bay, etc., R. Co. v. Union Steamboat Co., 107 U. S. 98. But see Colman v. Eastern Counties. R. Co., 10 Beav. 1. And a railroad company can purchase and operate such boats as are necessary to carry its traffic from the end of its line across an intervening navigable water to the "ostensible and substantial termini of their route." Wheeler v. San Francisco, etc., R. Co., 31 Cal. 46. Where the road has authority to contract for transportation and delivery of persons and property beyond its own termini, it may run boats from its termini to other points. Shawmut Bank v. Plattsburgh, etc., R. Co., 31 Vt. 491; South Wales R. Co. v. Redmond, 10 Com. B. N. S. 675.

coal,[1] nor to purchase and hold for speculative purposes lands not needed for the purposes of the corporation.[2] A railroad can not contract to extend its line beyond the limits defined in the charter,[3] nor construct branch roads not authorized by its charter,[4] nor make any material change in its route where the charter prescribes what the route shall be,[5] nor expend its funds in the construction of a line essentially different from that for which they were raised;[6] so it has been held that it can not use corporate funds to improve the navigation of a stream upon which it had erected wharves and warehouses.[7] A railway company has no implied power to build a canal basin,[8] nor to aid improvement, gas, water, or land companies, or the like.[9] Corporate funds can not be used for lobbying purposes,[10] nor, as a rule, used to purchase stock in another company.[11] Corporate

[1] Attorney-General v. Great Northern R. Co., 1 Dr. & S. 154.

[2] Pacific R. Co. v. Seely, 45 Mo. 212; Rensselaer, etc., R. Co. v. Davis, 43 N. Y. 137; Waldo v. Chicago, etc., R. Co., 14 Wis. 575. A contract whereby one railroad company agrees not to oppose the passage of a law giving land to another company, on condition that the land shall be subsequently divided, is not enforceable. Chippewa, etc., R. Co. v. Chicago, etc., R. Co., 44 N.W. R. 17; 75 Wis. 224. A railroad corporation has no power to take by gift, lands lying along its route. Case v. Kelly, 133 U. S. 21.

[3] Bagshaw v. Eastern Union R. Co., 7 Hare 114. See Stevens v. Rutland, etc., R. Co., 29 Vt. 545.

[4] Knight v. Carrollton R. Co., 9 La. Ann. 284; Morris, etc., R. Co. v. Central R. Co., 31 N. J. L. 205.

[5] Chartiers R. Co. v. Hodgens, 77 Pa. St. 187; see Central Plank R. Co. v. Clemens, 16 Mo. 359; Rives v. Montgomery, etc., R. Co., 30 Ala. 92; Mississippi, etc., R. Co. v. Cross, 20 Ark. 443.

[6] See Bagshaw v. Eastern Union Railway, 7 Hare 114, where, at the suit of a stockholder, the railway company was enjoined from using for the completion of its main line, funds raised under authority of an act of parliament to construct a branch line.

[7] Munt v. Shrewsbury, etc., R. Co., 13 Beav. 1.

[8] Plymouth R. Co. v. Colwell, 39 Pa. St. 337.

[9] City of Chicago v. Cameron, 120 Ill. 447.

[10] Shea v. Mabry, 1 Lea (Tenn.) 319, where the directors were held liable for using the corporate funds for this purpose.

[11] Central R. Co. v. Collins, 40 Ga. 582; Salomons v. Laing, 12 Beav. 339; Mannsell v. Midland, etc., R. Co., 1 Hem. & Miller 130. Though the purchase by a corporation of stock in another corporation is *ultra vires*, the objection can not be raised by the stockholders of the company whose stock is so purchased. Oelbermann v. New York & N. R. Co., 7 Misc. R. 352, 27 N. Y. Supp. 945. In some states railway corporations are given a limited power to purchase stock in other railway companies. Stimson's Am. Stat. (1892), § 8720, citing laws of

funds, it is held, may not be donated to an exhibition,[1] nor to a musical concert, even though it is expected that the receipts of the corporation from its business of carrying will be thereby materially increased.[2] The directors can not legally use the corporate funds to induce promoters to abandon a proposed rival

Pennsylvania, Kansas, Nebraska, Tennessee, Missouri, North Dakota, Idaho, Montana, South Carolina, Florida, Ohio, Michigan, Wyoming, New Mexico; Pub. Stat., 1891, Mass. Ch. 112, § 74; Laws 1891 (Ex. Sess.), Ill., p. 185. While other states expressly forbid such a purchase. Stimson, *supra*, citing laws of New York, Illinois, Arkansas, Texas. See, also, Oelbermann v. New York & N. Ry. Co., 77 Hun (N. Y.) 332.

[1] See Tomkinson v. South, etc., R. Co., 56 L. T. R. 812, where such a donation was enjoined at the suit of a stockholder.

[2] Davis v. Old Colony R.Co.,131 Mass. 258, where a subscription in aid of the "World's Peace Jubilee and International Musical Festival" at Boston was held not binding upon the corporation, although the concert had been held on the faith of the subscription guarantees. In this case, Gray, J., after an exhaustive review of the cases both of this country and England, says: "But when the corporation has actually received nothing in money or property, it can not be held liable upon an agreement to share in or to guarantee the profits of an enterprise which is wholly without the scope of its corporate powers, upon the mere ground that conjectural or speculative benefits were believed by its officers to be likely to result from the making of the agreement, and that the other party has incurred expenses upon the faith of it. East Anglian R. Co. v. Eastern Counties R. Co., 11 C. B. 775; MacGregor v. Dover & Deal R. Co., 18 Q. B. 618; Ashbury Ry. Carriage & Iron Co. v. Riche, L. R. 7 H. L. 653; Thomas v. Railroad Co., 101 U. S. 71; Downing v. Mount Washington Road Co., 40 N. H. 230; Franklin Co. v. Lewiston Institution for Savings, 68 Me. 43." See, however, State Board of Ag. v. Citizens' St. R. Co., 47 Ind. 407, s. c. 17 Am. Rep. 702, where the court, in construing a subscription contract, conditioned upon the location of the state fair upon its line, says: "It is not claimed in the case under consideration that there was any statute by which the Street Railway Company was prohibited from entering into the contract in question or, in other words, that in making the contract that company violated any statute by which the act was prohibited. All that is claimed is that there was a want of power on the part of the corporation to bind itself by the contract. It is fully shown on the part of the plaintiff that the State Board of Agriculture performed the contract on its part. The Street Railway Company has thus received the benefits and advantages of the contract, but seeks to avoid paying the consideration promised, because it had not the legal power to contract for the benefits which it has actually received. In our opinion the Street Railway Company is not at liberty to assume this position. It has received the profits resulting from the compliance of the plaintiff with the contract. These profits, we are at liberty to presume, have gone to swell the dividends of

company,[1] nor to buy land at an exorbitant price of one who, as part consideration, withdraws opposition to the charter,[2] or lends his influence to the scheme.[3]

§ 375. Contracts—Ultra vires—Rule where statute prescribes consequences.—It is generally held that where the legislature specifically prescribes the consequences that shall follow from an act *ultra vires*, the act is not to be regarded as void.[4] Where the statutory prohibition is clearly for the benefit of a designated class of persons and no others, only members of that class can take advantage of a violation of the statute. Where the manifest intention of the statute would be defeated by adjudging an *ultra vires* contract void it will not be so adjudged.[5]

§ 376. Contracts — Ultra vires — Injunction. — A contract which a corporation has no power to make can not be enforced by injunction.[6] The doctrine that an *ultra vires* contract can not be enforced directly or indirectly by injunction is so clearly sound that there is no room for fair debate, but as to the power

the stockholders in that corporation. It would be unjust for their company now to escape performance of the contract by which these profits have been realized."

[1] Russell *v.* Wakefield W. W. Co., L. R. 20 Eq. 474.

[2] Gage *v.* New Market R. Co., 18 Q. B. 457. Cases such as the above are usually treated as coming under the doctrine of *ultra vires*, and many of them with reason since such contracts as they involve are tainted with the vice of illegality and are also beyond the corporate power. A contract may, it is evident, have more than one defect or vice.

[3] Earl of Shrewsbury *v.* North Staffordshire R. Co., L. R. 1 Eq. 593.

[4] Pratt *v.* Short, 79 N. Y. 437, 445; Lester *v.* Howard Bank, 33 Md. 558. In Chattanooga, etc., R. Co. *v.* Evans, 66 Fed. 809, it is held that non-compliance with a statute requiring certain acts to be done by a railroad company and prescribing a penalty to be imposed upon persons for a violation of the statute does not invalidate a purchase of land by the company.

[5] Gold Mining Co. *v.* National Bank, 96 U. S. 640; Duncomb *v.* New York, etc., Co., 84 N. Y. 190; Farmington, etc., Bank *v.* Fall, 71 Me. 49; National Bank *v.* Matthews, 98 U. S. 621.

[6] Greenville, etc., Co. *v.* Planters', etc., Co., 70 Miss. 669, s. c. 13 So. R. 879, citing Pennsylvania Co. *v.* St. Louis, etc., Co., 118 U. S. 290, s. c. 6 Sup. Ct. R. 1094; Davis *v.* Old Colony Railroad, 131 Mass. 258; Pearce *v.* Madison, etc., Railroad Co., 21 How. (U. S.) 451; *In re* Cork, etc., R. Co., 4 Ch. App. 748; Ashbury, etc., Co. *v.* Riche, L. R. 7 H. L. 653, 672.

to prevent a corporation from entering into such a contract there is perhaps room for debate, since such a contract if entered into is not, as a contract, effective. In our opinion, however, both principle and authority require the conclusion that injunction will lie to restrain a corporation from making such a contract.[1] The modern cases, with good reason, are inclined to extend the remedy by injunction,[2] and it seems to us that sound reason authorizes interference to prevent a corporation from entering into a contract that it has no power to make rather than to permit the contract to be made and after it is made contest its validity. The state may, in the proper case, secure relief in equity against a corporation that attempts to exercise a power that it does not possess.[3] Stockholders may maintain injunction to prevent corporate officers from materially deviating from the objects for which the corporation was formed.[4]

---

[1] Attorney-General v. Chicago, etc., R. Co., 35 Wis. 425; Fishmongers Co. v. East India Co., 1 Dickens 163; Agar v. Regents' Canal, Cooper Ch. 77; Latimer v. Richmond R. Co., 39 So. Car. 44; Beman v. Rufford, 6 Eng. L. & Eq. 106; Colman v. Eastern, etc., R. Co., 10 Beav. 1; Coats v. Clarence R. Co., 1 Russell & M. 181; Attorney-General v. Delaware, etc., R. Co., 27 N. J. Eq. 631; Stockton v. Central R. Co., 50 N. J. Eq. 489, s. c. 17 L. R. A. 97; Board v. Lafayette, etc., R. Co., 50 Ind. 85; Thomas v. Railroad Company, 101 U. S. 71; 2 Redfield on Railways 307; 2 Story's Eq. 920, 923; Pomeroy Eq. Juris., § 1093. See, however, Graham v. Birkenhead, etc., R. Co., 6 Eng. L. & Eq. 132; Ffooks v. London, etc., Co.,19 Eng. L. & Eq. 7.

[2] Champ v. Kendrick, 130 Ind. 549; Pomeroy Equity Juris., § 1357.

[3] Stockton v. Central R. Co., 50 N. J. Eq. 489, s. c. 17 L. R. A. 97; Columbian Athletic Club v. State, 143 Ind. 98, s. c. 40 N. E. R. 914. See Attorney-General v. Great Northern R. Co., 4 De Gex & S. 75; Taylor v. Salmon, 4 Myl. & C. 134; Attorney-General v. Chicago, etc., R. Co., 35 Wis. 425; Ware v. Regent's, etc., Co., 3 De Gex. & J. 212; River Dun, etc., Co. v. North Midland R. Co., 1 Eng. Ry. & Canal Cas. 135; Attorney-General v. Johnson, Wilson's Ch. pt. 2, 87; Attorney-General v. Birmingham, etc., Co., 4 De Gex. & S. 490; Attorney-General v. Forbes, 2 Mylne & C. 123; Attorney-General v. Eastern Counties R. Co., 3 Eng. Ry. & Canal Cas. 337; Attorney-General v. Sheffield, etc., Co., 3 De Gex, M. & G. 304; Attorney-General v. Mid-Kent R. Co., 3 Ch. App. Cas. 100. See People v. North River, etc., Co., 121 N. Y. 582, s. c. 9 L. R. A. 33; People v. North River, etc., Co., 22 Abbott New Cas. 164, s. c. 2 L. R. A. 33.

[4] Kean v. Johnson, 9 N. J. Eq. 401; Livingston v. Lynch, 4 Johns. Ch. 573; Ware v. Grand Junction R. Co., 2 Russ. & M. 470. See Sparhawk v. Union, etc., R. Co., 54 Pa St. 401.

§ 377. **Contracts—Ultra vires—Denial of relief—Laches.—** It is held that if there is inexcusable delay in seeking relief the courts will refuse to interpose, although the contract may be *ultra vires*.[1] The decisions proceed upon the general doctrine that a party guilty of laches can not successfully invoke the assistance of the courts. The courts in refusing to grant relief do not affirm the validity of the contract, but leave the parties where it found them because of the laches of the complainant.[2]

§ 378. **Contracts—Ultra vires—Who may contest.—**A person not a corporate stockholder, or one not having a right to or interest in corporate property, can not dispute the right of a corporation to make contracts of a certain kind upon the ground that they are *ultra vires*. Thus, a wharfinger will not be permitted to dispute the right of a railroad company to rent its wharf in competition with his own, by showing that its charter does not authorize it to keep a wharf for rent.[3] A person who is sued for damage done to real estate held by a corporation can not successfully defend by showing that the charter of the corporation does not permit it to hold such real estate, or that it is not authorized to take and hold land for the purposes for which the real estate in question is acquired.[4] Even with regard to stockholders and officers of the corporation the rule obtains that a person whose rights are in no way infringed by the doing of an *ultra vires* act can not found an action or defense upon the doing of that act.[5] Upon this principle, it is held that the

---

[1] St. Louis, etc., Co. v. Terre Haute, etc., Co., 145 U. S. 393, s. c. 12 Sup. Ct. R. 953; St. Louis, etc., Co. v. Terre Haute, etc., Co., 33 Fed. R. 440.

[2] In the case first cited the court placed stress upon the principle that where both parties are in fault the courts will not give aid to either of them.

[3] New Orleans, etc., R. Co. v. Ellerman, 105 U. S. 166, 9 Am. & Eng. R. Cas. 144; see Oelbermann v. New York, etc., R. Co., 7 Misc. R. 352, 27 N. Y. Supp. 945; Tomlinson v. Bricklayers' Union, 87 Ind. 308; Farmers', etc., Bank v. Detroit, etc., R. Co., 17 Wis. 372; St. Louis Drug Co. v. Robinson, 81 Mo. 18; Gifford v. New Jersey R. Co., 10 N. J. Eq. 171; New Haven Wire Company Cases, 57 Conn. 352.

[4] Farmers' Loan and Trust Co. v. Green Bay, etc., R. Co., 11 Biss. (U. S.) 334.

[5] Taylor on Priv. Corp. 281.

title acquired by the vendee of land from a railroad company is good, although it was *ultra vires* the company's charter to purchase the land in the first instance.[1] And the officers of a corporation who have bought stock for the company can not plead as a defense to an action for conversion of the stock to their own use, that the original purchase made by them on behalf of the corporation was *ultra vires*.[2] The rule as asserted by many of the adjudged cases is that, after the corporation has performed its part of the contract, the other party will not be permitted to interpose the plea that it had no power to make such a contract.[3] The rule has been thus stated: "Without deciding whether or not it was within the corporate power of the railway company to become a party to such bond or contract, we are clearly of opinion that, after full performance by the company of the stipulations of such bond or contract on its part to be done and performed, and after the appellees have received in full the benefits they bargained for, they can not be permitted to escape or avoid the obligation of their contract, upon the ground that the company had possibly exceeded its corporate power, or that such contract, as to it, was possibly *ultra vires*."[4] We have elsewhere said that we believe that the contract is not enforceable and the right of the party to protection from loss or injury does not rest upon the contract, but upon general equitable principles.

[1] Walsh *v.* Barton, 24 Ohio St. 28.

[2] St. Louis Stoneware Co. *v.* Partridge, 8 Mo. App. 217.

[3] Whitney Arms Co. *v.* Barlow, 63 N. Y. 62; Parish *v.* Wheeler, 22 N. Y. 494; Hamilton, etc., Hydraulic Co. *v.* Cincinnati, etc., R. Co., 29 Ohio St. 341. In this case the defendant was permitted to fill up a water-course in consideration that it would re-open and restore the water-course when requested. The defendant was held estopped to set up that the ownership and maintenance of the water-course by the plaintiff was *ultra vires*. Three years of performance of a contract by which the railway company demised its road, privileges, and franchises for ninety-six years to the defendant does not render it so far an executed contract that a party thereto is estopped to deny its validity and to repudiate it. Oregon R. & Nav. Co. *v.* Oregonian R. Co., 130 U. S. 1, 9 Sup. Ct. R. 409; Pennsylvania R. Co. *v.* St. Louis, etc., R. Co., 118 U. S. 290, 630.

[4] Chicago, etc., R. Co. *v.* Derkes, 103 Ind. 520, 525. See, also, Louisville, etc., Co. *v.* Flanagan, 113 Ind. 488, 493; Steam Nav. Co. *v.* Weed, 17 Barb. 378.

§ 379. Contracts—Ultra vires—Creditors.—Corporate creditors occupy an essentially different position from that occupied by the corporation or its stockholders. They have no part in the management of the affairs of the corporation, and receive no direct benefit from a successful prosecution of its enterprises. Their contracts are made in reliance upon the fact that the corporate fund is a primary fund for the payment of the corporate debts. Accordingly the assent of all the shareholders can not render valid as against the creditors, a contract not within the corporate powers; and a partial performance by the other contracting party can not make the corporation liable to an action that will jeopardize their interests.[1] The position of the creditors is so essentially different from that of the corporation and its shareholders that the rules which apply to the one class can not unqualifiedly apply to the other. The rule asserted in well considered decisions is that in cases where the corporation is insolvent, the claims of parties founded upon an *ultra vires* contract will be set aside in favor of creditors claiming under valid contracts.[2] The corporate creditors, of course, have no rights to be protected in cases where the corporation is clearly solvent, for in such a case payment of the debt due under an *ultra vires* contract will not menace its ability to pay its other debts, and they can not complain of such payment. But where the payment of the claims of creditors founded upon contracts valid in all respects will be endangered by the enforcement of what are called *ultra vires* contracts the latter class of contracts will not be enforced. Where the contract is *ultra vires* in the proper sense of the term, then, as we have elsewhere shown, there can be no re-

---

[1] National Trust Co. v. Miller, 33 N. J. Eq. 155.

[2] The receiver of such a corporation may repudiate claims arising out of *ultra vires* contracts. Abbott v. Baltimore, etc., Steam Packet Co., 1 Md. Ch. 542. He may repudiate a transfer of mortgages by the corporation made to secure such claims. Talmage v. Pell, 7 N. Y. 328. The corporation is not estopped to set up the defense of *ultra vires* in favor of its creditors whose debts were created under lawful power, where it is insolvent, and the object is to prefer such creditors to others claiming under unauthorized contracts. Bank of Chattanooga v. Bank of Memphis, 9 Heisk. (Tenn.) 408.

covery upon it. The contract itself is void, but there may be in many cases a recovery upon the *quantum valebat* or *quantum meruit*. If there is a right to recover on the *quantum meruit*, for the reasonable value of the property received and appropriated by the corporation, there is reason for doubting whether creditors can defeat the claims of parties having such a right of recovery, for, in such a case, the property received and appropriated becomes part of the corporate assets and increases the security of the creditors. Where there is an executory contract merely there is no difficulty, for it is clear that such a contract can not be enforced nor damages recovered for its breach. It is held that creditors may be estopped by the fact that they have received the benefits of the unauthorized act and their dealings have been with reference thereto.[1]

§ 380. **Contracts—Ultra vires—Non-assenting stockholders.** —It is reasoned that as corporations act only by their officers and agents, and are controlled by majorities, and as the interests of the minority stockholders and the creditors are not always respected by the managers, the rule that the corporation is bound by contracts of its agents, is not of universal application. It would seem to be clear upon principle that a stockholder would not be bound by any *ultra vires* contract entered into by the directors, of which he had no knowledge, even though a benefit accrued to the corporation by reason of the performance of such a contract.[2] There is, however, difficulty in practically applying this general doctrine. If the corporation does actually receive and retain property of value it should be compelled to make just and equitable compensation, although some of the stockholders may assail the transaction. It is, however, quite clear on principle that where the contract is executory a non-assenting stockholder, who promptly assails it, is entitled to relief. But since the books of the company are at all times open for their inspection, it may be presumed that the members of the corporation are cognizant of its acts, and a ratification of such acts will be presumed from acquiescence

---

[1] Tone v. Columbus, 39 Ohio St. 281.   [2] Taylor on Priv. Corp. 278.

on their part.[1] It is so difficult to permit a contract to be set aside by a dissenting stockholder without at the same time relieving those by whom it was made, that the courts refuse to entertain his objections on the ground that a contract is *ultra vires*, unless he moves promptly to prevent its execution. He will not, as a general rule, be heard to express, after the contract is executed, a dissent which he has not made known until it was apparent that the contract would operate against his interests,[2] unless he has done equity or caused equity to be done by the corporation.

§ 381. Prohibited contracts—Effect of prescribing penalties.

—Where a contract is illegal because prohibited by legislative enactment, it is not void if the legislature has specifically provided what the consequences of a violation of the statute shall be. The general rule upon this subject seems to be that where the statute which prohibits the contract expressly prescribes the consequences of its violation the contract is not void, since the consequences expressly prescribed are exclusive.[3] But this rule can

---

[1] Thompson *v.* Lambert, 44 Iowa 239; Taylor on Priv. Corp. 279.

[2] Thompson *v.* Lambert, 44 Iowa 239; Bradley *v.* Ballard, 55 Ill. 413.

[3] Where a corporation was forbidden by law to issue notes or other evidences of debt, to be loaned or put in circulation as money, the statute declaring that all notes or other securities for the payment of money "made or given to secure the payment of any money loaned or discounted by any incorporated company, contrary to the provisions of the [statute] shall be void," it was held that the notes or securities so taken were void, but the money loaned on them could be recovered. The court said: "A prohibitory statute may itself point out the consequences of its violation, and if, on a consideration of the whole statute, it appears that the legislature intended to define such consequences, and to exclude any other penalty or forfeiture than such as is declared in the statute itself, no other will be enforced, and if an action can be maintained on the transaction of which the prohibited transaction was a part without sanctioning the illegality, such action will be entertained." Pratt *v.* Short, 79 N. Y. 437, 445; Taylor on Priv. Corp. (2d ed.), 299. In Edison General Electric Co. *v.* Canadian Pac. Nav. Co., 8 Wash. 370, 36 Pac. R. 260, the supreme court of Washington held that although a statute provides a penalty for a foreign corporation doing business without first having registered, contracts by such corporation are not thereby rendered void. The court said: "There is some diversity among the cases in the construction of laws of this kind, but the weight of authority seems to establish the doctrine that it is the duty of the

not govern where there is simply a general penalty prescribed. Where a penalty is declared the general rule is that a contract to do the forbidden act is void. As is well known the accepted doctrine is that the imposition of a penalty for doing the act operates as such an implied prohibition as to bring the case within this rule.[1] It is sometimes provided that only specified persons courts to look at the whole statute, and therefrom determine as to what was the intent of the legislature. If, by the terms thereof, the act is made unlawful, it will usually be construed to amount to a prohibition of said act, and the imposition of a penalty will also amount to a prohibition if, from the language used, such seems to have been the intent of the legislature. But in the case at bar, while the company is liable to the penalty provided in the statute, there is nothing in the act which in terms prohibits the transaction of business or declares it to be unlawful, and the particular language of the clause which imposes the penalty has no tendency to establish either of said propositions. On the contrary, its language, fairly construed, would seem to contemplate that the company might do business without such registration, but that, if it did, it should pay the penalty therein prescribed for the privilege of so doing. The cases cited by appellant, when applied to the facts of this case, have little tendency to sustain its contention. The investigation which we have been able to give to the adjudged cases tends to support the statement made by respondent, in its brief, that a provision like the one under consideration has never been held to render contracts void, though entered into without the authority of the statute. Some of the cases cited by appellant contain expressions to the effect that the imposition of a penalty for the performance of an act is equivalent to declaring it unlawful; but an examination of the facts will show that the provisions which they were construing were clothed in far different language than the one under consideration." Where a corporation loans money in excess of the prescribed limit to be loaned to an individual, the corporation can recover the money. "We do not think that public policy requires, or that congress intended that an excess of loans beyond the proportion specified should enable the borrower to avoid the payment of the money actually received by him. This would be to injure the interests of creditors, stockholders and all who have an interest in the safety and prosperity of the bank." Gold Min. Co. v. National Bank, 96 U. S. 640; Duncomb v. New York, etc., R. Co., 84 N. Y. 190. And a provision in the charter of a corporation, prohibiting any director or other officer, under penalty of fine or imprisonment, from borrowing money from the bank, does not exempt a director from liability for money loaned to him in violation of the prohibition. Farmington Sav. Bank v. Fall, 71 Me. 49. Ante, § 375.

[1] Ohio L. Ins., etc., Co. v. Merchants' Ins. Co., 11 Humph. (Tenn.) 1; Mitchell v. Smith, 1 Binney (Pa.) 110; Seidenbender v. Charles, 4 Serg. & R. (Pa.) 151; Wilson v. Spencer, 1 Randolph (Va.) 76; Sharp v. Teese, 9 N. J. Law, 352; O'Donnell v. Sweeney, 5 Ala. 467; Woods v. Armstrong, 54 Ala. 150.

shall be entitled to the protection of a special prohibition of the statute, and when this is so only such persons can take advantage of it.[1]

§ 382. Illegal contracts—Generally.—It is hardly necessary to say that a railroad company has no more right to enter into an illegal contract than a natural person or a corporation of any kind. If an act be *malum in se* or *malum prohibitum* a railroad company can not perform it.[2] Where a contract is illegal and for that reason void, no action can be maintained upon it, for the courts will decline to assist either party in enforcing it.[3] But it is unnecessary to do more than suggest these general rules and add that all of the fundamental rules regarding illegal contracts apply to contracts by railroad companies.

§ 383. Illegal contracts and ultra vires contracts discriminated.—At another place we have directed attention to the difference between contracts that are *ultra vires* and contracts that are illegal.[4] It is obvious that a contract may be beyond

---

[1] "Courts often speak of acts and contracts as void, when they mean no more than that some party concerned has a right to avoid them. Legislators sometimes use language with equal want of exact accuracy; and when they say that some act or contract shall not be of any force or effect, mean perhaps no more than this; that at the option of those for whose benefit the provision was made it shall be voidable, and have no force or effect as against his interests. * * * * * If it is apparent that an act is prohibited and declared void on grounds of general policy, we must suppose the legislative intent to be that it shall be void to all intents, while if the manifest intention is to give protection to determinate individuals who are *sui juris*, the purpose is sufficiently accomplished, if they are given the liberty of avoiding it." Beecher v. Marquette, etc., Co., 45 Mich. 103, 108, per Cooley, J.; Earle v. Earle, 91 Ind. 27; Taylor on Priv. Corp. (2d ed.), 300.

[2] Chippewa, etc., Co. v. Chicago, etc., R. Co., 75 Wis. 224; Marshall v. Baltimore, etc., R. Co., 16 How. (U. S.) 314; Pueblo, etc., R. Co. v. Rudd, 5 Colo. 270; Pueblo, etc., R. Co. v. Taylor, 6 Colo. 1; Morris, etc., R. Co. v. Sussex, etc., R. Co., 20 N. J. Eq. 542; Ashbury Ry., etc., Co. v. Riche, L. R. 7 H. L. C. 653.

[3] Ohio, etc., Co. v. Merchants', etc., Co., 11 Humph. (Tenn.) 1; Wilson v. Spencer, 1 Rand. (Va.) 76; O'Donnell v. Sweeney, 5 Ala. 467; Woods v. Armstrong, 54 Ala. 150; Webb v. Tulchire, 3 Ired. (N. C.) Law 485.

[4] *Ante*, § 373; Woodruff v. Erie R. Co., 93 N. Y. 609, 618. The modern cases deny that there is any essential difference between contracts to perform acts *malum in se* and contracts to

§ 383 CONTRACTS.

the scope of the corporate powers and yet not be illegal in the proper sense of the term. The term "illegal contract," as we employ it, means a contract forbidden by legislative enactment or condemned by some general rule of law. It is true, of course, that a contract which is against public policy is illegal, but we can see no valid reason for making an independent and distinct class of contracts against public policy, for public policy is settled and determined by general rules of law, so that such a contract is really an illegal one and is, therefore, properly a member of the general class designated by the term illegal contracts. What the term "public policy" means has not been precisely determined by the judicial decisions.[1] Illegal contracts are, in a sense, *ultra vires*, but they are something more, they are contracts of "an evil tendency." It is hardly necessary to say that a railroad corporation has no more right to enter into an illegal contract than an individual. It is to be remarked that a positive legislative enactment may confer authority to make a contract which, but for the statute, would be regarded as illegal because against public policy.[2]

---

do that which is *malum prohibitum*. Evans v. City of Trenton, 24 N. J. L. 764.

[1] In Richardson v. Mellish, 2 Bing. 229, 9 E. C. L. 557, Burroughs, J., said: "Public policy is a very unruly horse, and when once you get astride of it you never know where it will carry you. Public policy does not admit of definition and is not easily explained." See, generally, Egerton v. Earl Brownlow, 4 H. L. Cas. 1; Smith v. Arnold, 106 Mass. 269; Durgin v. Dyer, 68 Me. 143; Burkholder v. Beetem, 65 Pa. St. 496; Pierce v. Evans, 61 Pa. St. 415; Bank of United States v. Owens, 2 Pet. 527; Bishop v. Palmer, 146 Mass. 469, 474; Brown v. New York, etc., Co., 75 Hun 355, s. c. 27 N. Y. Supp. 69; Florida, etc., R. Co. v. State, 31 Fla. 482, s. c. 20 L. R. A. 419, s. c. 13 So. R. 103; Pennsylvania Co. v. Dolan, 6 Ind. App. 109, s. c. 32 N. E. R. 802; Griswold v. Illinois, etc., R. Co., (Iowa) 53 N. W. R. 295 (reversed on rehearing, in 57 N. W. R. 842); Farmers', etc., R. Co. v. White, 5 Col. App. 1, s. c. 31 Pac. R. 345; Providence, etc., Co. v. Norris, 2 Wall. 45, 56.

[2] Donaldson v. Jude, 2 Bibb (Ky.) 57; Brown v. Anderson, 1 T. B. Monr. (Ky.) 198; Vermont, etc., R. Co. v. Vermont, etc., R. Co., 34 Vt. 1. Where there is no legislation it is for the courts to decide whether a contract is or is not "at war with any established interest of society," and, therefore, illegal. Kellogg v. Larkin, 3 Pinney (Wis.) 123, s. c. 3 Chand. 133, 56 Am. Dec. 164; Boardman v. Thompson, 25 Iowa 487, 501. Legislation, however,

§ 384. **Classes of illegal contracts.**—We have said that in our judgment a contract void because against public policy is an illegal contract. Some of the cases, however, do not class such contracts as illegal, but make of them a separate and distinct class. We think that illegal contracts, as distinguished from ordinary *ultra vires* contracts, may be divided into (1) those which are immoral in themselves, and forbidden by law to persons as well as corporations; (2) those which the corporations in question are forbidden to make by statute, and (3) those which public policy forbids them to make.[1] The latter class of contracts, that is, contracts against public policy, have been discussed principally in cases where corporations charged with the performance of certain public duties have entered into contracts whereby they are disabled to perform such duties, or the rights of the public are infringed,[2] but the principle has a somewhat wider range.

§ 385. **Contracts void because against public policy.**—The settled doctrine is that railroads and other corporations which are created with special powers and privileges, and charged with certain duties to the public, are held bound by considerations of public policy to refrain from doing any acts which may disable them from performing their duties to the public.[3]

settles questions of policy. Speaking of the power of the legislature in this regard the supreme court of the United States said: "Questions of this sort determined there are conclusive here." License Tax Cases, 5 Wall. 462, 469. See, also, Hadden *v.* Collector, 5 Wall. 107; Magee *v.* O'Neill, 19 S. Car. 170.

[1] Taylor on Priv. Corp. (2d ed.), 292.

[2] New York, etc., R. Co. *v.* Winans, 17 How. (U. S.) 30, 39; Pearce *v.* Madison, etc., R. Co,. 21 How. (U. S.) 441; Thomas *v.* Railroad Co., 101 U. S. 71; Branch *v.* Jesup, 106 U. S. 468, 478; Pennsylvania R. Co. *v.* St. Louis, etc., R. Co., 118 U. S. 290; Pittsburgh, etc., R. Co. *v.* Keokuk, etc., Bridge Co., 131 U. S. 371, 384; Central Trans. Co. *v.* Pullman P. Car. Co., 139 U. S. 34; Hazlehurst *v.* Savannah, etc., R. Co., 24 Ga. 13; Elkins *v.* Camden, etc., R. Co., 36 N. J. Eq. 5; New England Express Co. *v.* Maine Central R. Co., 57 Me. 188.

[3] Daniels *v.* Hart, 118 Mass. 543; Abbott *v.* Johnstown, etc., R. Co., 80 N. Y. 27; Central Trans. Co. *v.* Pullman Car. Co., 139 U. S. 24. A corporation can not disable itself by contract from performing its public duties, or, by agreement, compel itself to make public accommodation subordinate to its private interests. Gibbs *v.* Consolidated Gas Co., 130 U. S. 396, s. c. 9 Sup. Ct. Rep. 553.

This familiar principle is applied to various classes of cases, but while there is no diversity of opinion as to the principle itself there is some conflict among the cases as to its application. It is held, in accordance with the general principle stated,[1] that a railroad can not mortgage, lease or sell its railroad, nor any property essential to the operation of its railroad,[2] in the absence of authority from the state.[3] So contracts by which it is undertaken to stifle competition between parallel roads, which would, in the natural order of things, be competing lines, are illegal and void.[4] One road will not be per-

[1] Daniels v. Hart, 118 Mass. 543; State v. Morgan, 28 La. Ann. 482; Winchester, etc., Turnp. Co. v. Vimont, 5 B. Mon. (Ky.) 1; Black v. Delaware, etc., Canal Co., 22 N. J. Eq. 130, 399. But see Memphis, etc., R. Co. v. Dow, 19 Fed. Rep. 388; Kelly v. Trustees, etc., 58 Ala. 489; Miller v. Rutland, etc., R. Co., 36 Vt. 452, 488, holding that it may mortgage its property to purchase necessary rails, without which it could perform none of its public duties.

[2] Pierce v. Emery, 32 N. H. 484; Singleton v. Southwestern R. Co., 70 Ga. 464; Board, etc., v. Lafayette, etc., R. Co., 50 Ind. 85, 110; Abbott v. Johnstown, etc., R. Co., 80 N. Y. 27; Freeman v. Minnesota, etc., R. Co., 28 Minn. 443; Middlesex R. Co. v. Boston, etc., R. Co., 115 Mass. 347; Peters v. Lincoln, etc., R. Co., 2 McCrary (U. S.) 275; Thomas v. Railroad Co., 101 U. S. 71; Pennsylvania R. Co. v. St. Louis, etc., R. Co., 118 U. S. 290; Oregon Railway, etc., Co. v. Oregonian Railway Co., 130 U. S. 1; Morawetz on Priv. Corp. 1120. See opinion of Chief Justice Ruger, in Woodruff v. Erie Railway Co., 93 N. Y. 609, 618.

[3] In Maine, it is held to be the policy of the state to permit railroads to mortgage their property at will. Kennebec, etc., R. Co. v. Portland, etc., R. Co., 59 Me. 9. Nearly all the states permit railroads to mortgage their property for any purpose for which they are allowed to borrow money. Stimson's Am. Stat. (1892), §§ 8642, 1840. Most of the states now offer every advantage to non-competing roads to unite by lease, sale or consolidation. Stimson's Am. Stat. (1892), §§ 8721, 8722, 8730. Mr. Charles Francis Adams, president of the Union Pacific Railroad, in an address at Boston, on December 15, 1888, said: "I am very sure now, as I have been for the last twenty years, and as I long ago expressed myself, that a great consolidated corporation, or even trust, can be held to a far stricter responsibility to the law than numerous smaller and conflicting corporations." Mr. Justice Brewer, in United States v. Western Union Tel. Co., 50 Fed. R. 28, 42, said: "It may be true, as contended, and, not disturbed by the common hue and cry about monopoly, I am disposed to believe that it is true—that the real interests of the public are subserved by the consolidation of the various transportation systems."

[4] Cleveland, etc., R. Co. v. Closser, 126 Ind. 348; Hooker v. Vandewater, 4 Denio (N. Y.) 349; Central Ohio Salt Co. v. Guthrie, 35 Ohio St. 666; Morrill v. Boston, etc., R. Co., 55 N.

mitted to contract for the purchase of stock of a competing road, with a view to gaining control of it, and so preventing competition between the two roads.[1]

§ 386. **Contracts against public policy—Location of stations and tracks.**—True principle requires, as it seems to us, that contracts for the location of depots and stations should be held illegal where they are made for the advancement of mere private interest, and are prejudicial to the public interest. Where, however, there is no contravention of the public interest, we can see no valid reason for condemning such a contract. We believe that whether public interests are or are not sacrificed to purely private interests is a question to be determined upon the facts of the particular case. The cases which

---

H. 531; Craft v. McConoughy, 79 Ill. 346; Morris Run Coal Co. v. Barclay Coal Co., 68 Pa. St. 173; Gibbs v. Consolidated Gas Co., 130 U. S. 396. In announcing the opinion of the court in this case Chief Justice Fuller said: "In the instance of business of such a character that it presumably can not be restrained to any extent whatever without prejudice to the public interest, courts decline to enforce or sustain contracts imposing such restraint, however partial, because in contravention of public policy." Texas, etc., R. Co. v. Southern Pacific R. Co., 41 La. Ann. 970; Gulf, etc., R. Co. v. State, 72 Tex. 404. See United States v. Trans-Missouri Freight Assn., 58 Fed. R. 58.

[1] Central R. Co. v. Collins, 40 Ga. 582; Elkins v. Camden, etc., R. Co., 36 N. J. Eq. 5; Pennsylvania R. Co. v. Commonwealth, (Pa.) 29 Am. & Eng. R. Cas. 145, 154. An insolvent construction company contracted to build a railway for a corporation, and received nearly all of the latter's stocks, bonds, and assets as security for its outlay. Without beginning the work the construction company transferred all the stock to the persons managing another railway already in operation, among whom were the president and many of its directors, the funds of the latter corporation being used in purchasing the stock of the construction company. So that the stock of both the construction company and the projected road was controlled by the same management as the road then in operation, and ran for nearly the same distance, and in the same general direction, as the projected line, which would be a competitor. The court held that the evident purpose and effect of the transaction was to violate by indirection the section of the Georgia constitution prohibiting the purchase of the stock of one corporation by another, and any contract between them tending to lessen competition in their respective businesses or to encourage monopoly, and that equity would interfere and seize the assets of the insolvent construction company, which stood in the position of derelict trustees. Langdon v. Branch, 37 Fed. R. 449.

hold that subscriptions upon condition that the road shall be built upon a designated line are valid,[1] as well as cases which uphold municipal aid to railroad companies, can not be supported if it be conceded that all contracts to locate a road on a designated line, or build stations at a particular place are void. It has been held that contracts requiring a railroad company to establish its depot at a certain point are against public policy, and not enforceable.[2] There is, however, conflict of authority upon this question.[3] Contracts made to influence the location of the route of a projected road are held to be illegal by some of the courts.[4] In our opinion, however, a con-

[1] Rhey v. Ebensburg, etc., Co., 27 Pa. St. 261; Evansville, etc., Co. v. Shearer, 10 Ind. 244; Martin v. Pensacola, etc., R. Co., 8 Fla. 370; Ashtabula, etc., R. Co. v. Smith, 15 Ohio St. 328; Taggart v. Western Md. R. Co., 24 Md. 563; Burlington, etc., R. Co. v. Boestler, 15 Iowa 555; Detroit, etc., Co. v. Starnes, 38 Mich. 698; Spartanburg, etc., R. Co. v. De Graffenreid, 12 Rich. L. (S. C.) 675; Bucksport, etc., Co. v. Brewer, 67 Me. 295; McMillan v. Maysville, etc., R. Co., 15 B. Mon. 218; O'Neal v. King, 3 Jones (N. C.) 517; North Mo. R. Co. v. Winkler, 29 Mo. 318.

[2] Pacific R. Co. v. Seely, 45 Mo. 212; Florida Cent. R. Co. v. State, 31 Fla. 482, s. c. 13 So. R. 103.

[3] Bestor v. Wathen, 60 Ill. 138; Currier v. Concord R. Co., 48 N. H. 321; Williamson v. Chicago, etc., R. Co., 53 Iowa 126, s. c. 36 Am. R. 206; Kansas Pac. R. Co. v. Hopkins, 18 Kan. 494; Vicksburgh, etc., R. Co. v. Ragsdale, 54 Miss. 200; Missouri Pac. R. Co. v. Tygard, 84 Mo. 263; Texas, etc., R. Co. v. Robards, 60 Tex. 545; Cedar Rapids, etc., R. Co. v. Spafford, 41 Iowa 292; Louisville, etc., R. Co. v. Sumner, 106 Ind. 55; Marsh v. Fairbury, etc., Co., 64 Ill. 414; International, etc., Co. v. Dawson, 62 Tex. 260; Chapman v. Mad River, etc., R. Co., 6 Ohio St. 119. A provision in such a contract that another depot should not be established within certain limits is illegal and void. St. Joseph, etc., R. Co. v. Ryan, 11 Kan. 602; Williamson v. Chicago, etc., R. Co., 53 Iowa 126; St. Louis, etc., R. Co. v. Mathers, 104 Ill. 257; St. Louis, etc., R. Co. v. Mathers, 71 Ill. 592.

[4] Woodstock Iron Co. v. Richmond, etc., Co., 129 U. S. 643, s. c. 9 Sup. Ct. R. 402. In announcing the opinion of the court in the case cited, Mr. Justice Field said: "The business of the extension company was one in which the public was interested. Railroads are for many purposes public highways. They are constructed for the convenience of the public in the transportation of persons and property. In their construction, without unnecessary length between designated points, in their having proper accommodations, and in their charges for transportation, the public is directly interested. * * * All arrangements, therefore, by which directors or stockholders or other persons may acquire gain by inducing corporations to disregard their duties to the public, are illegal and lead to unfair dealing, and, this being against public

tract to locate a railroad upon a designated line can not be adjudged void as a matter of law without regard to extrinsic facts. Such a contract may or may not be void, depending upon the facts of the particular case. If the public interests are not prejudiced, and there is no corrupt conduct, such contracts are not illegal, but if the public interests are sacrificed, the charter violated, or corrupt influences exerted, the contract should be adjudged illegal. A stipulation in a contract that no side track shall be built by the railroad company in a certain town is sufficient to render the entire contract illegal and void.[1]

policy, will not be enforced by the courts. In this case, the extension company, to which the duty of locating and constructing the railroad between its termini was intrusted, in agreeing, for a consideration offered by a third party, to disregard that duty, and locate and construct the road by a longer route than was required, not only committed a wrong upon the railroad company by imposing unnecessary burdens upon it, to meet which larger charges for transportation might be called for, but also a wrong upon the public." Fuller v. Dame, 18 Pick. (Mass.) 472; Bestor v. Wathen, 60 Ill. 138; St. Louis, etc., R. Co. v. Mathers, 71 Ill. 592; Holladay v. Patterson, 5 Or. 177.

[1] Pueblo, etc., R. Co. v. Rudd, 5 Colo. 270; Pueblo, etc., R. Co. v. Taylor, 6 Colo. 2. In this case the court said: "Railroad companies are held to be quasi public corporations and agencies, their directors, acting in the double capacity as agents for the company and trustees for the public, clothed with an important public trust. These roads subserve public purposes to such an extent that the public may impose upon itself the burden of taxation to aid in their construction (St. Joseph & Denver City R. Co. v. Ryan, 11 Kan. 602), and the lawful exercise of the rights of eminent domain in the taking of private property for the purpose of their construction is put solely upon the ground of public use. When, therefore, the public interests are brought in conflict with the private interests of the company, or of private individuals with whom such companies deal, such private interests must yield to those of the public. It logically follows that the public has a right to say that such companies shall not be permitted to make any contract which would prevent them from accommodating the public, where entitled to it in the matter of transportation and travel. In the case of the St. Joseph, etc., R. Co. v. Ryan, 11 Kan. 602, which arose upon a contract containing a stipulation that the railroad company would not have or use any other depot within three miles of the depot agreed to be established by the contract, the court says: 'Railroads are public agencies and perform a public duty. They are agencies, created by the public, with certain privileges, and subject to certain obligations. A contract that they will not discharge, or by which they can not discharge those obligations, is

§ 387. **Contracts void as against public policy—General conclusions.**—It may be laid down as a general rule that any contract by which the rights of the public are infringed is void as against public policy; but the decisions as to what are public rights and what is the public policy upon which those rights are founded, depend so much upon the peculiar circumstances of each case that it is not an easy matter to state a general rule that will justly govern any given contract.[1] A contract which on its face assumes to bind the parties to an act hostile to the public interest may, doubtless, be adjudged void as a matter of law. But it can not be justly said that every contract

a breach of that public duty, and can not be enforced. They are under obligations to employ skillful and competent engineers and other competent employes to superintend and take care of the running of their trains. A contract that they will not employ such agents and servants is certainly void. They are bound to furnish reasonable facilities for the transportation of freight and passengers, both as to number and quality of cars and coaches, and the number of trains, and a contract not to furnish such facilities will not be tolerated. * * * Upon the same principle it is the duty of a railroad company to furnish reasonable depot facilities. The number and location of the depots so as to constitute reasonable depot facilities vary with the changes and amount of population and business. A contract to leave a certain distance along the line of the road destitute of depots is a contravention of this duty.' In addition to the foregoing, the same doctrine is laid down in the following, among other cases: Marsh v. Fairbury and Northwestern R. Co., 64 Ill. 414; St. Louis, Jacksonville and Chicago R. Co. v. Mathers, 71 Ill. 592; Pacific R. Co. v. Seely, 45 Mo. 212; Fuller v. Dame, 18 Pick. (Mass.) 472;

Holladay v. Patterson, 5 Ore. 177. Upon both principle and authority, we think it beyond serious question that the condition in this contract, whereby it was sought to prevent a neighboring town through which the railroad passed from having the facilities of even a side track, and to prevent the railroad company from the exercise of discretion in providing such facilities for the public, is illegal and void, by reason of its clear contravention of the public interests, and the duty of such company in their relations to the public."

[1] In proof of this statement of the text we refer to the conflict of authority as to whether a railroad company may make a valid contract with a telegraph company to allow no other telegraph company to construct a line along its road. The following authorities hold that, under the circumstances of those cases, it may. Western Union Tel. Co. v. Atlantic, etc., Tel. Co., 7 Biss. (U. S.) 367; Western Union Tel. Co. v. Chicago, etc., R. Co., 86 Ill. 246. The case of Western Union Tel. Co. v. Burlington, etc., R. Co., 3 McCrary (U. S.) 130, holds that it may not. See Atlantic, etc., Tel. Co. v. Union Pac. R. Co., 1 McCrary (U. S.) 541.

providing for the construction of a railroad upon a given line, or for the building of a station at a particular place is opposed to the interests of the public. It may well be that such a contract will promote and not prejudice the public welfare. So, too, it may be true that such a contract in no manner violates the provisions of the corporate charter, but, on the contrary, justly aids in carrying those provisions into effect. In such cases, or in cases of a similar character, there is no valid reason for adjudging the contract void. We believe that a contract providing for the location of a station at a given place should be regarded with something akin to suspicion and that it should be carefully scrutinized, but we do not think that it should be regarded as illegal *per se* without looking to attendant circumstances or regarding extrinsic evidence.[1] As we have substantially said, such a contract may be regarded as *per se* illegal where a corrupt purpose is disclosed by its terms, or where it appears from its provisions that public interests will be unduly prejudiced, but we do not believe that such a contract is under all circumstances to be regarded as illegal. We know that the general rule is that the validity of a contract is to be determined not by considering whether it does injury in the particular case, but whether it is such as might be injurious.[2] But we do not believe that the rule applies to all contracts belonging to the class of which we are speaking, for such contracts are not always opposed to the public interests. The cases which hold that officers can not contract for their own benefit to secure a particular location are not in point, for they rest upon a different principle; nor are the cases which hold that a contract to pay a person a sum of money to secure the location at a particular place, since such cases are different from those in which there is a direct and open agreement with the railroad company.[3] Where a party under a contract to build

---

[1] *Ante*, § 362.
[2] Holladay v. Patterson, 5 Ore. 177, 180; Oscanyan v. Arms Co., 103 U. S. 261, 274; Providence Tool Co. v. Norris, 2 Wall. 48, 56; Elkhart County Lodge v. Crary, 98 Ind. 238.

[3] The case of Fuller v. Dame, 18 Pick. 472, was that of a person agreeing for a designated sum to secure the location at a particular place, and is not, when justly interpreted, against the doctrine of the text. It seems to

a railroad enters into an agreement to deviate from the line fixed, it is entirely just to adjudge such an agreement void, but such an agreement is essentially different from one openly and directly made with the railway company.[1] The doctrine we have ventured to advocate is, perhaps, opposed by the weight of authority, if regard be had only to the number of the cases, but there are well-reasoned cases which give our views full support.[2]

§ 388. **Contracts void as against public policy—Illustrative cases.**—A contract by which a railway corporation undertakes to convey to a telegraph company such exclusive rights in that portion of its right of way not occupied by its track as to prevent the erection of a competing line thereon is invalid.[3] An

us that some of the courts have given an effect to the case cited far beyond that which can be fairly assigned it. A doctrine has been deduced from it which it does not declare.

[1] The agreement held void in Woodstock, etc., Iron Co. v. Richmond, etc., Co., 129 U. S. 643, s. c. 9 Sup. Ct. R. 402, was between a construction company and a land-owner, so that the decision can not be regarded as opposing the statements of the text.

[2] Louisville R. Co. v. Sumner, 106 Ind. 55, s. c. 5 N. E. R. 404; Swartwout v. Michigan, etc., Railroad Co., 24 Mich. 389; Williamson v. Chicago, etc., R. Co., 53 Iowa 126, s. c. 4 N.W. R. 870; First National Bank v. Hendrie, 49 Iowa 402; Taylor v. Cedar Rapids, etc., R. Co., 25 Iowa 371; Harris v. Roberts, 12 Neb. 631, s. c. 41 Am. R. 779, 12 N. W. R. 89; McClure v. Mo. River R. Co., 9 Kan. 373.

[3] Pacific Postal Tel. Co. v. Western Union Tel. Co., 50 Fed. R. 493, s. c. 50 Am. & Eng. R. Cas. 665. This was a proceeding by bill in equity for an injunction to prevent the Western Union Telegraph Company from constructing and operating a telegraph line on the right of way of the Seattle, Lake Shore and Eastern Railway Company between certain stations. The plaintiff based its claims upon a contract entered into by the defendant's grantor, which provided as follows: "The railway company hereby grants right of way for said line of telegraph along the route of its road, and upon its grounds, * * * and the railway company hereby agrees that it will not grant right of way along its road for the construction of the line of any other telegraph company." Judge Hanford said: "The argument is that the contract is a conveyance, and that it vests in the complainant the exclusive right to the entire strip of land for telegraph purposes during the term specified, which right amounts to an interest in the land, and is a legal estate. * * * If the contract, in explicit terms, granted such an interest in the premises as the plaintiff claims, I should have to hold it to be *ultra vires* and void, for the reason that the laws of the territory of Washington, in force when it was made, did not authorize a railway corporation to transfer land acquired for

agreement, which, by its terms, gives the exclusive right to a railway corporation in or through a certain tract of land, in so far as it attempts to exclude other railway corporations from

railroad purposes, by lease, so as to divest itself of its duties and obligations to the public as to the use of such property * * * Telegraph lines are to serve the public, and wherever they are connected with a railroad as incidental to the railway business, the rights of the public respecting the same must be governed by the principles applicable to other branches of the service; and the public policy which underlies the numerous decisions of the courts of this country denying the right of railway corporation to divest itself of responsibility and invest another with its powers and functions, touches directly the question in this case as to the right of one corporation to transfer to another an exclusive right for telegraph purposes to the occupancy and control of property acquired as a necessary means of serving the public. A contract made by a railway company, whereby it attempts to create a monopoly in the use of its property for the transmission of news and intelligence, is just as invalid as a contract would be whereby a railway corporation should attempt to confer upon one individual or corporation an exclusive right to have any particular commodity transported as freight over its railway. Whether this contract be regarded as an intended conveyance of an interest in the property, or as a covenant affecting the title to the right of way, or as a contract creating simply a personal liability, it is not such a contract as a court of equity can uphold or decree to be specifically performed; and at least as against the defendant the Western Union Telegraph Company, it is void, except in so far as it confers upon the plaintiff the right to maintain unmolested its telegraph line and conduct its business without interruption." It has been laid down as a general rule that contracts, the object of which is to secure to the obligee a monopoly or an exclusive use for public purposes of land held by other corporations or by a private owner if subject to the right of eminent domain, are void. See American Rapid Tel. Co. v. Connecticut Telephone Co., 49 Conn. 352; Western Union Tel. Co. v. Am. Tel. Co., 19 Am. L. Reg. (N. S.) 173; Western Union Tel. Co. v. Atlantic, etc., Tel. Co., 5 Nev. 102; Western Union Tel. Co. v. Americal Tel. etc., Co., 65 Ga. 160; Skrainka v. Scharringhausen, 8 Mo. App. 522; Pensacola Tel. Co. v. Western Union Tel. Co., 96 U. S. 1; Western Union Tel. Co. v. St. Joseph, etc., R. Co., 1 McCrary (U. S.) 565; Western Union Tel. Co. v. Burlington, etc., R. Co., 3 McCrary (U. S.) 130; Western Union Tel. Co. v. American U. Tel. Co., 9 Biss. (U. S.) 72; Western Union Tel. Co. v. Baltimore, etc., Tel. Co. of Texas, 22 Fed. R. 133; Western Union Tel. Co. v. Baltimore, etc., Tel. Co., 23 Fed. R. 12. In Fort Worth St. R. Co. v. Queen City R. Co., 71 Tex. 165, 9 S. W. R. 94, the court in construing a contract by which a railroad company owning a tract of land upon which its depot is located undertakes to give to a horse railway company an exclusive right to build its road to the depot over the land, held that such a contract is not a monopoly, but an easement granted by the owner of the fee, and can be taken for public use only by due process of law, but that the acquiring a right of way over the same tract, upon land not appropriated or required for its use by the company, is against public policy and void.[1] A contract by which a corporation, chartered to perform certain duties to the public, agrees that it will not perform those duties at all, for a term of years is void.[2] A stipulation in a contract by which a railroad common carrier seeks to protect itself from liability for the negligence of itself or its servants will not be enforced by the courts.[3] And a contract by which a common carrier undertakes to carry for one person or corporation to the exclusion of all others,[4] or to carry for them on more favorable terms than are accorded others, thereby fostering a monopoly and destroying the business of those less favored[5] is contrary to public policy and void.[6]

rights of the company can not be divested by any act of the original grantors.

[1] Kettle River R. Co. v. Eastern R. Co., 41 Minn. 461.

[2] Central Trans. Co. v. Pullman's Palace Car. Co., 139 U. S. 24; Gibbs v. Consolidated Gas. Co., 130 U. S. 396, 408; Oregon Steam Nav. Co. v. Winsor, 20 Wall. (U. S.) 64. This principle applies to all cases where the corporation assumes to contract that it will not perform the duties imposed upon it, no matter what the form of the contract may be, but it finds, perhaps, its most frequent illustration and application in cases where corporations assume to transfer their property by way of lease. See Leases, Chapter XVIII.

[3] Railroad Company v. Lockwood, 17 Wall. (U. S.) 357. This topic is considered in treating of liability of employer to employe.

[4] New England Express Co. v. Maine Central R. Co., 57 Me. 188; Sandford v. Railroad Co., 24 Pa. St. 378; Dinsmore v. Louisville, etc., R. Co., 2 Flippin (U. S.) 672; Southern Express Co. v. Memphis, etc., R. Co., 2 McCrary (U. S.) 570, holding that a discrimination against an express company is unlawful.

[5] Scofield v. Railway Co., 43 Ohio St. 571; Messenger v. Pennsylvania R. Co., 37 N. J. L. 531, 36 N. J. L. 407 Stewart v. Lehigh Valley R. Co., 38 N. J. L. 505. Every common carrier must carry for all to the extent of his capacity, without undue or unreasonable discrimination either in charges or facilities. Atchison, etc., R. Co. v. Denver, etc., R. Co., 110 U. S. 667, 674.

[6] But it is held that a common carrier which charges no more than a reasonable sum for carrying may charge one person more than it does another. Munhall v. Pennsylvania R. Co., 92 Pa. St. 150; Johnson v. Pensacola, etc., R. Co., 16 Fla. 623, 667; Fitchburg R. Co. v. Gage, 12 Gray (Mass.) 393; Houston, etc., R. Co. v. Rust. 58 Tex. 98. The granting of a rebate contrary to the provisions of the interstate commerce law does not render the bill of lading void, so that no action can be maintained against the carrier for loss of the goods by negligence. Merchants' Cotton Press, etc., Co. v. Ins. Co. of North America, 151 U. S. 368, 14 Sup. Ct. R. 367.

CHAPTER XVII.

REAL ESTATE.

§ 389. What railroad property is real estate.
390. Statutory authority requisite.
391. Power to acquire real estate— Implied power—Generally.
392. Implied power to acquire— General Rule.
393. Implied power — Illustrative instances.
394. Power to acquire real estate— Instances of denial of power.
395. Title to real estate is in the company.
396. Title once vested not divested because property subsequently becomes unnecessary.
397. Effect of conveyance to corporation of land it has no power to hold.
398. Right of foreign corporation to hold real estate.
399. The power to acquire by grant broader than the power to acquire by condemnation.
400. Acquisition of the fee by private grant.
401. Acquisition of title by adverse possession.
402. Possession of land — To what right referred.
403. Rights of company where land is owned in fee.
404. Effect of conveyance of property the company is not authorized to acquire.

§ 405. Questioning the right to hold real estate.
406. Enjoining purchase of real estate where no power to receive and hold.
407. Executory contract of purchase not enforceable where there is no power to hold the land.
408. Estoppel of parties to deeds to deny corporate existence.
409. Deed to company not in existence.
410. Formal execution of conveyances and agreements relating to real estate.
411. Contracts under corporate seal — Effect as evidence.
412. Acceptance of deed.
413. Distinction between a donation of lands and a sale.
414. Deeds of company—By whom executed.
415. Construction of deeds to railroad companies—Generally.
416. Deeds to railroad companies— Construction of conditions.
417. Grants—Beneficial—Presumption of acceptance.
418. Incidents pass with principal thing granted.
419. Effect of designating in the deed the purpose for which the land is granted.
420. Covenants that run with the land.

(534)

§ 389   REAL ESTATE.   535

421. Merger of preliminary agreement in deed.
422. Bonds for conveyance—Specific performance.
423. Presumption that there is power to hold the land.
424. Power to convey real estate.
425. Dedication of land for use as a highway.
426. Disposition of property corporation has no power to receive and hold—Escheat.

§ 389. **What railroad property is real estate.**—There is no contrariety of opinion as to the nature of land and "annexed permanent immovable structures," for that kind of property is so clearly real estate that there is no room for doubt as to its character.[1] The question of difficulty most often encountered is as to the nature of what is commonly called "rolling stock," that is, locomotives, cars and the like. These things are essential to the operation of a railroad and it is difficult to conceive the existence of a railroad without incorporating in the conception locomotives and cars. Locomotives and cars are not, to borrow a term from logic, accidents, but inseparable incidents. There is reason supporting the cases which adjudge that the rolling stock is personal property, but, on the other hand, there is reason supporting the cases which adjudge it to be real estate. The weight of authority is that where the statute does not otherwise provide, rolling stock is personal property and not real estate,[2] but upon this question

[1] Palmer v. Forbes, 23 Ill. 301; Hunt v. Bullock, 23 Ill. 320. See, Front, etc., Co. v. Johnson, 2 Wash. 112, s. c. 25 Pac. R. 1084; St. Louis, etc., Co. v. Donahue, 3 Mo. App. 559, Appendix; McIlvain v. Hestonville, etc., R. Co., 5 Phila. 13. Iron rails laid on road bed are held to be real estate unless made personal property by agreement. Hunt v. Bay State, etc., Co., 97 Mass. 279.

[2] Judge Minor is very decided in his opinion that rolling stock is personal property. He says, "As the rolling stock is not *attached* to the realty it seems to be an extraordinary anomaly to treat it as constituting a part thereof, merely because the road can not be operated without it. With equal reason a cart, a plough, a mule, a wheelbarrow or a spade might be deemed part of a farm inasmuch as a farm can not be operated without such appliances." Minor's Inst. (top) 609. The conclusion of the justly respected and able author is sustained by the weight of authority, but, with sincere deference, we venture to say that the fact that the things he mentions are not *attached* to the land is not sufficient to characterize them as personal property. The character of property is by no means always determined by the answer to the question whether it is or is not attached to the land. As shown in the argument of Mr. Carpenter, elsewhere quoted from, many things are regarded as real

there is a direct conflict. Whether rolling stock is or is not real estate depends in a great measure upon the statute. But where the question is not influenced by statute the weight of authority is that it is personal property,[1] but there has been much diversity of opinion.[2] The right of way of a railroad company is real estate.[3]

§ 390. **Statutory authority requisite.**—The rule is well established that a railroad corporation can not acquire and hold lands for any purposes except such as are authorized by statute.[4] The authority must be conferred by legislation or it does not exist. It is, however, not necessary that the authority should be expressly conferred. It may be implied.

estate although not permanently annexed to the land. Farrar v. Stackpole, 6 Greenl. 154; Rogers v. Gilinger, 30 Pa. St. 185; Colegrave v. Dias Santos, 2 B. & C. 76; Siford's Case, 11 Coke 46; House v. House, 10 Paige Ch. 158; Gile v. Stevens, 13 Gray 146; Rogers v. Cox, 96 Ind. 157, and cases cited.

[1] *Ante*, § 31; Randall v. Elwell, 52 N. Y. 521, s. c. 11 Am. R. 747; Hoyle v. Plattsburg, etc., R. Co., 54 N. Y. 314, s. c. 13 Am. R. 595; Stevens v. Buffalo, etc., R. Co., 31 Barb. 590; Williamson v. New Jersey, etc., R. Co., 29 N. J. Eq. 311; Chicago, etc., Co. v. Ft. Howard, 21 Wis. 44. See, generally, Beardsley v. Ontario Bank, 31 Barb. 619; State Treas. v. Somerville, etc., R. Co., 28 N. J. L. 21; Boston, etc., R. Co. v. Gilmore, 37 N. H. 410; Coe v. Columbus, etc., R. Co., 10 Ohio St. 372, s. c. 75 Am. Dec. 518; Neilson v. Iowa, etc., R. Co., 51 Iowa 184, s. c. 33 Am. R. 124; Meyer v. Johnston, 53 Ala. 237, 353; Grand Trunk, etc., R. Co. v. Eastern Township Bank, 10 Lower Canada Jur. 11; Louisville, etc., R. Co. v. State, 25 Ind. 177.

[2] Phillips v. Winslow, 18 B. Monr. 431; Minnesota Co. v. St. Paul Co., 2 Wall. 644; Farmers', etc., Co. v. Hendrickson, 25 Barb. 484; Palmer v. Forbes, 23 Ill. 301; State v. Northern, etc., R. Co., 18 Md. 193; Railroad Co. v. James, 6 Wall. 750; Pennock v. Coe, 23 How. (U. S.) 117; Farmers', etc., Co. v. St. Joseph, etc., R. Co., 3 Dill. (U. S.) 412; Morrill v. Noyes, 56 Me. 458; Titus v. Mabee, 25 Ill. 257; Farmers', etc., Co. v. Commercial Bank, 11 Wis. 207; Scott v. Clinton, etc., R. Co., 6 Biss. 529.

[3] President, etc., v. Sipe, 11 Ind. 67; Timmons v. Switzer, 11 Ind. 363; Vaughn v. Dayton, 12 Ind. 561; New Albany, etc., R. Co. v. Huff, 19 Ind. 444.

[4] Coleman v. San Rafael Turnpike Co., 49 Cal. 517; Taber v. Cincinnati, etc., R. Co., 15 Ind. 459; New York, etc., R. Co. v. Kip, 46 N. Y. 546; Case v. Kelly, 133 U. S. 21; Overmyer v. Williams, 15 Ohio 26; Pacific R. Co. v. Seely, 45 Mo. 212; Waldo v. Chicago, etc., R. Co., 14 Wis. 575; Eldridge v. Smith, 34 Vt. 484; Eastern Counties R. Co. v. Hawkes, 5 H. L. Cas. 331.

§ 391. **Power to acquire real estate—Implied power—Generally.**—The rule as generally expressed is that a railroad company has the implied power to acquire and hold such real estate as is reasonably necessary to enable it to perform its corporate duties and exercise its corporate functions. Where there is no statute specifically defining the power of the company to hold real estate, the question is to be solved by ascertaining what is reasonably necessary to enable it to accomplish the purpose for which it was organized. The object for which the corporation was created is, of course, to be determined from the statute authorizing its existence. This object being ascertained then it follows that such incidental powers as are reasonably necessary to enable the corporation to accomplish the object for which it was created vest in it by necessary implication. Analogous cases adjudge that the power of a corporation is not confined to authority to do that which is absolutely or indispensably essential to the performance of the acts and duties specified in the statute from which it derives its powers,[1] but extends to such things as are reasonably and fairly necessary. The law, however, has always jealously regarded the power of corporations to hold real estate and the courts are reluctant to enlarge the power by implication. It has been again and again affirmed that there is serious danger to be apprehended from corporate acquisition of land, and that the power should be carefully limited.[2] It is, therefore, true that the cases relating to implied powers where ordinary business contracts or acts performed in conducting ordinary corporate affairs are involved can hardly be taken as safe guides for the government of cases where the question is as to the power of a railroad company to acquire and hold real estate.[3]

[1] Smith v. Nashua, etc., R. Co., 27 N. H. 86, 94; Brown v. Winnisimmet Co., 11 Allen 326; Buffett v. Troy, etc., R. Co., 40 N. Y. 168, s. c. 36 Barb. 420.

[2] The statutes enacted by the British parliament and by the legislatures of some of the American states, evidence the opposition to the policy of allowing corporations to become owners of real estate. Angell on Private Corp., § 177. The public grant of land by the United States and by the states to railroad companies is a departure from the ancient policy of the law.

[3] In Case v. Kelly, 133 U. S. 21, s. c.

§ 392. **Implied power to acquire — General rule.** — The general rule that a corporation has the right to take and hold real estate reasonably necessary to the purpose of its creation is asserted by many of the courts. There is no substantial diversity of opinion.[1] This is implied as an incident of the principal power granted.[2] But as corporate grants are always strictly construed, the right to acquire and hold real estate can not be extended by liberal construction.[3] If it appears from the express provisions of the statute that to deny the power to hold real estate would defeat the object for which the corporation was created, then, in the absence of countervailing provisions, the power to hold real estate will be implied. In the case of a railroad corporation the implied power is broad enough to authorize the acquisition of land for any structures that are reasonably necessary for the proper construction and operation of the road.[4]

§ 393. **Implied power—Illustrative instances.**—A railroad company may acquire land for the erection of engine houses and shops for the repair of cars and engines used on the road.[5]

10 Sup. C. R. 216, it was held that a railroad company could only receive and hold lands for the defined purposes of the road.

[1] Asheville Division, etc., v. Aston, 92 N. C. 578; Ossipee, etc., Co. v. Canney, 54 N. H. 295; Callaway, etc., Co. v. Clark, 32 Mo. 305; Page v. Heineberg, 40 Vt. 81; State v. Madison, 7 Wis. 688; Old Colony, etc., R. Co. v. Evans, 6 Gray (Mass.) 25; 2 Kent's Comm. 227; 1 Bl. Comm. 475, 478; Morawetz on Priv. Corp. Sec. 327.

[2] The question as to the right to hold real estate is, as is well known, a question between the sovereign and the corporation. The title which the corporation obtains even where it has no authority to own the land is a peculiar one. It does, it seems, acquire a title, but, of course, not a complete one. It is held that "a corporation might purchase and take title to the real estate, its title, however, like that of an alien being defeasible at the pleasure of the commonwealth." Leazure v. Hillegas, 7 Sergt. & R. 313; Goundie v. Northampton Water Co., 7 Pa. St. 233; Hickory Farm, etc., Co. v. Buffalo, etc., R. Co., 32 Fed. R. 22; Runyan v. Coster, 14 Pet. 122; Hamsher v. Hamsher, 132 Ill. 273, s. c. 23 N. E. R. 1123.

[3] Eversfield v. Mid-Sussex, etc., R. Co., 1 Giff. 153, s. c. 3 DeG. & J. 286; Dodd v. Salisbury, etc., R. Co., 1 Giff. 158, s. c. 5 Juris. (N. S.) 782; Bostock v. North Staffordshire, etc., R. Co., 5 DeG. & S. 584, s. c. 4 El. & B. 798; Browne & Theobald's Ry. Law, 96.

[4] Chicago, etc., R. Co. v. Wilson, 17 Ill. 123; Low v. Galena, etc., R. Co., 18 Ill. 324; In re New York, etc., R. Co., 46 N. Y. 546; Bangor, etc., R. Co. v. Smith, 47 Me. 34.

[5] Southern Pac. R. Co. v. Raymond, 53 Cal. 223; Hannibal, etc., R. Co. v.

§ 393   REAL ESTATE.   539

It may buy and hold property for docks and warehouses reasonably necessary for the storage of property entrusted to it for carriage.[1] It may buy land for freight and passenger depots and the necessary approaches thereto,[2] for the building of turnouts and side tracks to accommodate the business of the company.[3] It may acquire land in order to procure materials for the economical construction of the road.[4] It has been held that it may buy land in order to furnish gravel to persons who are to transport it over the company's road, thereby adding to its revenues.[5] It may acquire land for the purpose of erecting thereon a dinner house for its employes.[6] It may provide offi-

Muder, 49 Mo. 165; State v. Mansfield, 23 N. J. L. 510; Virginia, etc., R. Co. v. Elliott, 5 Nev. 358.

[1] 1 Morawetz Private Corp., § 268.

[2] Mansfield, etc,, R. Co. v. Clark, 23 Mich. 519; Protzman v. Indianapolis, etc., R. Co., 9 Ind. 467; Graham v. Connersville, etc., R. Co., 36 Ind. 463; Nashville, etc., R. Co. v. Cowardin, 11 Humph. (Tenn.) 348; Reed v. Louisville Bridge Co., 8 Bush. (Ky.) 69; South Carolina, etc., R. Co. v. Blake, 9 Rich. L. (S.C.) 228; Hamilton v. Annapolis, etc., R. Co., 1 Md. 553; Cumberland Valley R. Co. v. McLanahan, 59 Pa. St. 23; In re New York Cent., etc., R. Co., 77 N. Y. 248; Giesy v. Cincinnati, etc., R. Co., 4 Ohio St. 308; Hannibal, etc., R. Co. v. Muder, 49 Mo. 165; Weir v. St. Paul, etc., R. Co., 18 Minn. 155. A railroad company may use the land acquired by it for a right of way in any manner which contributes to the safe and efficient operation of the road, and does not interfere with the rights of adjacent property and the erection of a freight depot and other structures thereon is not a misuser. Elyton Land Co. v. South & North Ala. R. Co., 95 Ala. 631, 10 So. 270. We cite some cases where the land was acquired by condemnation, since they serve to show the general scope of the term corporate purposes.

[3] Protzman v. Indianapolis, etc., R. Co., 9 Ind. 467; Cleveland, etc., R. Co. v. Speer, 56 Pa. St. 325; Toledo, etc., R. Co. v. Daniels, 16 Ohio St. 390.

[4] Overmyer v. Williams, 15 Ohio 26. But see New York, etc., R. Co. v. Gunnison, 1 Hun (N. Y.) 496. See, in general, New York, etc., R. Co. v. Kip, 46 N. Y. 546; McClure v. Missouri River R. Co., 9 Kan. 373; Lake Shore, etc., R. Co. v. Cincinnati, etc., R. Co., 30 Ohio St. 604; Land v. Coffman, 50 Mo. 243; Blunt v. Walker, 11 Wis. 334.

[5] Old Colony, etc., R. Co. v. Evans, 6 Gray, 25. It has been suggested that a railway company may supply a chapel or theater for the benefit of its workmen. East Anglian R. Co. v. Eastern Counties R. Co., 11 C. B. 775. There is reason, in our judgment, for holding that railway companies may within reasonable limits, provide for the comfort and welfare of their employes.

[6] Gudger v. Richmond, etc., R. Co., 106 N. C. 481; Texas, etc., R. Co. v, Robards, 60 Tex. 545; United States. etc., Co. v. Wabash, etc., R. Co., 32 Fed. R. 480.

ces for the transaction of its business, although such offices are located in a foreign state, and it has been held that it may buy mines.[1]

§ 394. **Power to acquire real estate—Instances of denial of power.**—We have called attention to the fact that the power to acquire property by purchase is broader than the power to acquire it by the virtue of the right of eminent domain,[2] and it is obvious that cases bearing on the power to acquire by condemnation can not be accepted as safe guides where the question is as to the power to obtain land by purchase. But those cases do serve to mark the general nature of the power, so that it is proper to cite them in this connection, as we are here discussing the general power to acquire land. It is held that a railroad company can not acquire land by condemnation for the construction of a temporary track while the main track is building,[3] but it seems to us that the doctrine of the cases cited goes too far. We think that where a temporary track is essential to the proper construction of the main line or to its operation, it is competent for the company to acquire land for that purpose. It is not competent for a railroad company to condemn land for the erection of dwellings for the workmen employed by it.[4] It is

---

[1] Lyde v. Eastern, etc., R. Co., 36 Beav. 10, 17. See Attorney-Gen. v. Great Northern, etc., R. Co., 6 Jurist N. S. 1006. See, generally, Attorney-Gen. v. Great Eastern, etc., R.Co., L. R. 11 Ch. D. 449, 505; Holmes v. Eastern Counties, etc., R. Co., 3 K. & J. 675; Flanagan v. Great Western, etc., R. Co., 7 Eq. 116; Shrewsbury, etc., R. Co. v. Stour Valley, etc., R. Co., 2 De G. M. & G. 866; East, etc., Docks R. Co. v. Dawes, 11 Hare 363; Cother v. Midland R. Co., 2 Phill. 469; Moses v. Boston, etc., R. Co., 24 N. H. 71; Smith v. Nashua, etc., R. Co., 27 N. H. 86, 95; Western Union, etc., Co. v. Rich, 19 Kan. 517; New York, etc., R. Co. v. Kip, 46 N. Y. 546.

[2] The rights acquired by purchase are regarded as more complete than those acquired by condemnation. Thus where a railroad company acquires land upon which to build its road by purchase of the fee, it is not bound, in its dealings with such land, by restrictions upon its authority to use its "right of way." Calcasieu Lumber Co. v. Harris, 77 Tex. 18.

[3] Currier v. Marietta, etc., R. Co., 11 Ohio St. 228; Gray v. Liverpool, etc., R. Co., 9 Beav. 391.

[4] Nashville, etc., R. Co. v. Cowardin, 11 Humph. (Tenn.) 348; Eldridge v. Smith, 34 Vt. 484; State v. Mansfield, 23 N. J. L. (3 Zab.) 510.

clear that a railroad company has no implied power to acquire lands by eminent demain or otherwise for speculative purposes, or to prevent competition, or to aid in collateral enterprises remotely connected with the road.[1]

§ 395. **Title to real estate is in the company.**—Title to real estate acquired by a railroad company vests in the company and not in its stockholders. The stockholders have an interest in corporate property which interest is represented by their shares of capital stock, but they are not the owners of the real estate of the company. The corporation while composed of its shareholders is a distinct legal entity having an individuality of its own.[2] It is of itself a person although it is the creature of statute. We do not mean to say that the term "corporations" always includes natural persons, but so far as the ownership of property is concerned a corporation such as a railroad company is a person. Conveyances of corporate real estate must be executed by the company,[3] and, ordinarily, actions for injuries to its property must be prosecuted by the corporate entity. There are cases where, upon the wrongful refusal of the corporation to act, equity will interfere for the protection of the stockholders, but these cases form exceptions to the general rule.

§ 396. **Title once vested not divested because property subsequently becomes unnecessary.**—Where property at the time of its acquisition is reasonably necessary for the legitimate corporate purposes the fact that the necessity subsequently ceases does not always make the holding wrongful nor divest the title. The question of the right to hold property acquired

---

[1] Rensselaer, etc., R. Co. v. Davis, 43 N.Y. 137; Iron R. Co. v. Ironton, 19 Ohio St. 299; Vermont, etc., R. Co. v. Vermont Cent. R. Co., 34 Vt. 1; New York, etc., R. Co. v. Kip, 46 N. Y. 546; Baltimore, etc., R. Co. v. Union R. Co., 35 Md. 224.

[2] Regina v. Arnaud, 16 L. J. Q. B. 50; Rand v. Hubbell, 115 Mass. 461.

[3] Ante, § 237. There are cases of a very peculiar nature in which equity will enforce a conveyance made by individual stockholders, but they are exceedingly rare. American, etc., Co. v. Taylor, etc., Co., 46 Fed. R. 152; Society, etc., v. Abbott, 2 Beav. 559.

by a railroad company must, as a rule, be determined by the situation and condition at the time of its acquisition, and complete title once acquired is not taken away by future events. There is no wrong in holding real estate where a complete title is rightfully obtained, although changes wrought by subsequent action, taken under authority of law, may have the effect to render the property not necessary to the attainment of corporate objects or the exercise of corporate functions. But the general doctrine stated does not ordinarily apply where the property is acquired by virtue of the right of eminent domain and the fee is not taken. If, however, the law authorizes the taking of the fee and a fee is taken, it is not divested by the fact that it has ceased to be necessary to the accomplishment of corporate objects.[1] If an absolute title vests, no matter how acquired, the company, it is obvious, secures an indefeasible estate.

§ 397. **Effect of conveyance to corporation of land it has no power to hold.**—A conveyance to a corporation of land it has no power to hold is voidable at the suit of the state, but it is not void.[2] Such a conveyance is so far effective that it vests in the corporation a title which will empower it to convey the land, provided the conveyance is made prior to a judgment against it in a proceeding by the state. The authorities declare the title acquired by the corporation to be similar to that obtained by an alien in a jurisdiction where aliens are forbidden to hold land.[3]

---

[1] Page v. Heineberg, 40 Vt. 81, s. c. 94 Am. Dec. 378.

[2] In National Bank v. Matthews, 98 U.S. 621, 627, it was said: "Where a corporation is incompetent by its charter to take a title to real estate a conveyance to it is not void, but voidable, and the sovereign alone can object. It is valid until assailed by a direct proceeding instituted for that purpose." See, to the same effect, National Bank v. Whitney, 103 U. S. 99; Swope v. Leffingwell, 105 U. S. 3; Reynolds v. Crawfordsville, etc., Bank, 112 U. S. 405, s. c. 5 Sup. Ct. R. 213; Smith v. Sheeley, 12 Wall. 358, 361; Myers v. Croft, 13 Wall. 291; Fortier v. New Orleans, etc., Bank, 112 U. S. 439, s. c. 5 Sup. Ct. R. 234.

[3] Fritts v. Palmer, 132 U. S. 282, s. c. 10 Sup. Ct. R. 93, citing Cross v. De Valle, 1 Wall. 1, 13; Governeur v.

§ 398. **Right of foreign corporation to hold real estate.—** It was adjudged in an early case by the Supreme Court of the United States that a corporation of one state can not be the owner of land in another state without the assent of the state in which the land lies.[1] But while it is true that the state in which the land is situated may deny the right to a foreign corporation to hold land within the state limits, the corporation may hold such lands, if it has power from the state that created it,[2] unless the right is denied by the state in which the land is situated.[3] In one of the cases it is held that in favor of a grantee a foreign corporation will be presumed to have power to hold real estate under the laws of the state by which it was incorporated.[4] The state in which the land lies may impose such limitations and restrictions upon the right of a foreign corporation to acquire and hold land situated within its borders as it deems proper.[5] The doctrine of the cases is that an individual can not successfully assail the right of a foreign corporation to hold lands.[6]

Robertson, 11 Wheat. 332; National Bank v. Matthews, 96 U. S. 621, 628; Phillips v. Moore, 100 U. S. 208. See, also, Leazure v. Hillegas, 7 Sergt. & R. 313; Goundie v. Northampton Water Co., 7 Pa. St. 233; Hickory Farm, etc., Co. v. Buffalo, etc., R. Co., 32 Fed. R. 22; Hamsher v. Hamsher, 132 Ill. 273, s. c. 23 N. E.R. 1123.

[1] Runyan v. Coster, 14 Pet. 122; Carroll v. East St. Louis, 67 Ill. 568, s. c. 16 Am. R. 632; United States, etc., Co. v. Lee, 73 Ill. 142, s. c. 24 Am. R. 236; Pennsylvania Co., etc., v. Bauerle, 143 Ill. 459; Barnes v. Suddard, 117 Ill. 237; Cowell v. Colorado, etc., Co., 100 U. S. 55.

[2] Diamond, etc., Co. v. Powers, 51 Mich. 145; Metropolitan Bank v. Godfrey, 23 Ill. 579. See Blair v. Perpetual Ins. Co., 10 Mo. 559, s. c. 47 Am. Dec. 129; Ohio, etc., Co. v. Merchants', etc., Co., 11 Humph. 1, s. c. 53 Am. Dec. 742.

[3] New York, etc., Dock v. Hicks, 5 McLean 111; Lumbard v. Aldrich, 8 N. H. 31, s. c. 28 Am. Dec. 381; Thompson v. Waters, 25 Mich. 214, s. c. 12 Am. R. 243; Baltimore, etc., S. Co. v. McCutchen, 13 Pa. St. 13; Northern Transportation, etc., Co. v. Chicago, 7 Biss. 45; Lathrop v. Commercial Bank, 8 Dana 114, s. c. 33 Am. Dec. 481; Alward v. Holmes, 10 Abbott (N. C.) 96; Claremont, etc., v. Royce, 42 Vt. 730; Lancaster v. Amsterdam, etc., Co., 140 N. Y. 576, s. c. 24 L. R. A. 322; New Hampshire, etc., Co. v. Tilton, 19 Fed. R. 73; White v. Howard, 46 N. Y. 144.

[4] Tarpey v. Deseret, etc., Co., 5 Utah 494. See New Hampshire, etc., Co. v. Tilton, 19 Fed. R. 73; Realty Co. v. Appolonio, 5 Wash. 437.

[5] Diamond, etc., Co. v. Powers, 51 Mich. 145.

[6] Lancaster v. Amsterdam, etc., Co., 140 N. Y. 576, s. c. 24 L. R. A. 322;

§ 399. **The power to acquire property by grant broader than the power to acquire by condemnation.**—The authorities with good reason discriminate between the power to acquire property by grant and the power to obtain by the exercise of the right of domain. Statutes conferring the authority to condemn property are, as is well known, strictly construed and their operation is seldom enlarged by implication. Where property is seized by virtue of the eminent domain, it is taken against the owner's will, while in the case of a grant he voluntarily conveys to the company. Property legitimately connected with the purpose of the corporation may be rightfully acquired, although the connection be remote. It is not essential, in case of purchase, that the property be immediately connected with the corporate purpose; it is sufficient if it be reasonably necessary to the convenience of the company and those dealing with it. They may acquire land by purchase for many purposes that would not be sufficient to warrant the seizure under the right of eminent domain. Refreshment stands, dining places, book stalls, and like conveniences, may be provided by railroad companies for the use of travelers and, as we believe, employes, and as there is power to provide such things there is also power to acquire land for such purposes. But the power to acquire by purchase does not imply the power to seize under the right of eminent domain.

§ 400. **Acquisition of the fee by private grant.**—A railroad company may acquire a fee in lands by grant, unless forbidden by statute or by some rule of law.[1] Where there is authority to receive and hold real estate by private grant, and there is neither an express nor an implied limitation upon the authority, a fee may be taken. But where there is an implied restriction, as is often the case in regard to the right of way, or the like, of a railroad company, the grant does not ordinarily vest a fee in the company, but vests such an estate, usually an easement, as is requisite to effect the purpose for which the

---

Bank of Toledo v. International Bank, 21 N. Y. 542; Methodist, etc., Church v. Pickett, 19 N. Y. 482.

[1] Hill v. Western, etc., R. Co., 32 Vt. 68; State v. Brown, 27 N. J. L. 13; Holt v. Somerville, 127 Mass. 408.

property is required. Where the grant is of "surplus real estate,"[1] as it is often called, that is of real estate not forming part of the railroad or its appendages, a deed effective to vest a fee in a natural person will vest that estate in a railroad company. The acquisition of land for a corporate purpose, such as the use in constructing and operating a railroad, conveys the property for the time the company has a right to operate the road, but unless the fee is clearly granted we suppose that the title does not extend beyond that period. It is held that even though the corporation is chartered for a limited period, it may take a conveyance of lands in fee in so far that it can convey the fee to another, although for the purposes of enjoyment, its estate must necessarily be limited to the term of its corporate existence.[2] It may well be doubted whether the doctrine of the cases referred to can be sustained.[3] It may well be held that where the statute gives a right to renew or extend the term of the corporate existence the grant extends to that time, for the law in force at the time of the execution of the contract enters into it as a silent but important factor; but where

---

[1] Mulliner v. Midland, etc., R. Co., 11 Ch. Div. 611. See as to the authority to hire out property not needed by the company, Forrest v. Manchester, etc., R. Co., 30 Beav. 40; Brown v. Winnisimmet Co., 11 Allen 326.

[2] Nicoll v. New York, etc., R. Co., 12 N. Y. 121; Rives v. Dudley, 3 Jones Eq. (N. C.) 126. The charter of the Tonawanda R. Co. (Laws N. Y. 1832, c. 241) limited its existence to fifty years, and authorized the company to acquire lands by eminent domain "for the use or accommodation of such railroad or its appendages;" and "to appropriate so much of such lands as may be necessary to its own use for the purposes contemplated by this act." It also conferred the "right to construct and during its existence to maintain and continue a railroad." It was held that the use of the land taken was not limited to the fifty years of corporate existence, but was to continue as long as it should be devoted to such public purpose; and that, as this company was afterwards consolidated by legislative act with another company, the owners of the fee can not recover the land at the expiration of the fifty years. Miner v. New York Cent. & H. R. R. Co., 46 Hun 612; Davis v. Memphis, etc., R. Co., 87 Ala. 633. Since a corporation organized under the general railroad act (2 Rev. St. N. Y., 7th ed., 1569) ceases to exist within five years after its articles of association are filed, unless it begins the construction of its road, a grant to such a corporation ten years after its organization, and before it had constructed any road conveys no title. Greenwood Lake & P. J. R. Co. v. New York & G. L. R. Co., 8 N. Y. S. 26.

[3] 1 Redfield on Railways, § 265.

there is an express limit to the term of the corporate existence, we think that it can not be justly held that the grant extends beyond that period. A grant to a corporation is a grant for the purpose specified in the charter, and when the right of the corporation to use the property ceases the estate terminates. We are not speaking of "surplus real estate," nor of deeds where there is an express conveyance of an absolute fee, but of cases where from the situation and agreement of the parties it satisfactorily appears that the land was granted for use in constructing and operating the road, and not absolutely and unconditionally. Where the fee is acquired it may, of course, be transferred, and so may any other estate.[1] But it is to be understood that, as to the conveyance of property essential to enable the company to perform the duties imposed upon it by law, the right to transfer does not exist unless conferred by statute, for, as we have elsewhere shown, a railroad company can not disable itself from discharging its duty by transferring its property, except in cases where the transfer is authorized by statute.[2]

§ 401. Acquisition of title by adverse possession.—There can be no doubt that title to surplus real estate may be acquired by limitation. It may upon the same principle acquire an easement by possession.[3] We suppose that where the possession consists in the use of the lands as a right of way an easement and not the fee would be acquired.[4] The general

---

[1] New Jersey, etc., R. Co. v. Van Syckle, 37 N. J. Law, 496; Pollard v. Maddox, 28 Ala. 321; Harrison v. Lexington, etc., R. Co., 9 B. Mon. 470.

[2] The subject of acquisition of the right of way by purchase is discussed in the chapter entitled "Purchase of right of way."

[3] Sherlock v. Louisville, etc., R. Co., 115 Ind. 22. Where a railroad company, with the consent of a landowner, staked off a strip of ground as a right of way, and entered thereon and occupied so much thereof as was needed for the construction of its road, and remained in possession thereof under claim of title to the entire strip, exercising over it such acts of ownership as the nature of the property permitted for twenty years, the railroad company acquired a title to the entire strip laid off. Hargis v. Kansas City, etc., R. Co., 100 Mo. 210.

[4] Organ v. Memphis, etc., R. Co., 51 Ark. 235, s. c. 39 Am. & Eng. R. Cas. 75. In Texas, etc., R. Co. v. Wilson, 83 Texas 153, s. c. 51 Am. & Eng. R. Cas. 364, it was held that if the company was a mere trespasser it could

§ 401				REAL ESTATE.				547

rule is that where an easement is claimed by user the easement can be no broader than the use. The extent of the easement in such a case is to be determined by the actual use and possession. Upon the general principle stated it is held that adverse use of railroad tracks for more than twenty years is not shown if it appears that the particular tracks, the use of which constituted a nuisance, had been laid a much shorter time than that, although other tracks had been used a longer time.[1] The quantity of land taken under a grant is determined from the terms of the deed or from the attendant circumstances and not simply from actual user. Thus it is held in Pennsylvania that a railroad company authorized to take for its right of way a strip not exceeding sixty feet in width is, in the absence of any designation of its boundaries, presumed to have taken the full sixty feet, though the road be located in a street less than sixty feet wide, and the company in the construction of its road does not take actual possession of the land outside of the street.[2] But where the railroad claims under a grant or release of the right of way by a private land-owner in which the width is not specified the width of the strip conveyed may be shown by proof of the contemporaneous acts and declarations of the parties.[3]

not acquire title. The court cited Hays v. Texas, etc., R. Co., 62 Texas 397. As to what acts are sufficient to constitute possession, see Emery v. Raleigh, etc., R. Co., 102 N. C. 209, s. c. 37 Am. & Eng. R. Cas. 253. See, generally, American Bank Note Co. v. New York, etc., R. Co., 50 Am. & Eng. R. Cas. 292; Erie, etc., R. Co. v. Rousseau, 17 Ont. App. 483, s. c. 46 Am. & Eng. R. Cas. 539; Chicago, etc., R. Co. v. Galt, 133 Ill. 657, s. c. 44 Am. & Eng. R. Cas. 43.

[1] Thompson v. Pennsylvania R. Co., s. c. 14 Atl. R. 897, s. c. on appeal, Penn. R. Co. v. Thompson, 54 N. J. Eq. 870, 19 Atl. R. 622.

[2] Jones v. Erie, etc., R. Co., 144 Pa. St. 629. In Indiana the court will presume, from the fact that a railroad appropriated a right of way under the general railroad law, that it took the full width (100 feet) which that law authorized it to take. Campbell v. Indianapolis, etc., R. Co., 110 Ind. 490. And the same is true where the land was taken possession of under a special charter. Indianapolis, etc., R. Co. v. Rayl, 69 Ind. 424; Prather 'v. Western Union Tel. Co., 89 Ind. 501. To the same effect see Duck River Valley, etc., R. Co. v. Cochrane, 3 Lea (Tenn.) 478; Day v. Railroad Co., 41 Ohio St. 392.

[3] Indianapolis, etc., R. Co. v. Reynolds, 116 Ind. 356; Indianapolis, etc., R. Co. v. Lewis, 119 Ind. 218. If the grant of a right of way by a private

§ 402. **Possession of land—To what right referred.**—Where there is a right to take land for a designated purpose and the land is used for that purpose, the possession will be referred to that right.[1] From this doctrine, which we regard as well-founded, it follows that a railroad company, in taking possession of land, will ordinarily take an easement and not the fee, for the reason that the right to take an easement is the right to which possession must be referred. The fee is not acquired by possession unless the right to which the possession is referable authorizes the acquisition of a fee.[2] A corporation can not, by exceeding its power, enlarge its rights.

land-owner does not specify the width of the strip granted, the railroad company will only acquire a right to such land as is actually taken and used. Fort Wayne, etc., R. Co. v. Sherry, 126 Ind. 334; Vicksburg, etc., R. Co. v. Barrett, 67 Miss. 579. Where a right of way is granted,"with right to to use such additional land as may be necessary for the construction and maintenance" of the road, the company is bound only to use ordinary care in constructing its road; and the necessity for taking additional land is to be determined by ordinary care. Gulf, C. & S. F. R. Co. v. Richards, 83 Tex. 203, 18 S. W. R. 611. Staking off the full width permitted by law, with the land-owner's permission, and the subsequent occupation of so much as the needs of the road required, under claim of title to the whole, gives a railroad company a right of way of the width originally staked off. Hargis v. Kansas City, etc., R. Co., 100 Mo. 210.

[1] Proprietors,etc., v. Nashua, etc., R. Co., 104 Mass. 1.

[2] Peirce v. Boston, etc., R. Co., 141 Mass. 481, s. c. 6 N. E. R. 96. In speaking of the use and occupancy of property, the court said: "The manner in which it shall be used for the designated purposes is in the discretion of the corporation and is no concern of the land-owner. Even if the corporation exceeds its franchise in the manner of such occupancy, it does not thereby disseize the owner of the fee. If a railroad corporation fits its station-house with conveniences for furnishing lodging and food necessary for the comfort of its passengers, it does not claim the fee of the land, allowing others than passengers to use them. It is not a claim in the fee of the land that it does not distinguish between the public and its passengers in the use of the refreshment table, news stand or telegraph office kept there. The building is none the less a station-house, and the fitting it for use and providing conveniences for passengers and the public alike, is an incident of its use for the business of the corporation, and, in doing it, the corporation asserts no right except to maintain a station-house and what it deems incidental to that. It may exceed its corporate rights in the use of the station-house, but it does not thereby claim the fee in the land on which it stands."

§ 403. **Rights of company where land is owned in fee.**—
Where a railroad company becomes the owner of land in fee simple it has all the ordinary rights of a natural person, except in so far as those rights are abridged by statutory provisions. The difficulty is to determine when the title of the company is in fee, for, as we have seen, a conveyance which would convey an absolute fee to a natural person does not always convey such an estate to a railroad company since the situation of the parties and attendant circumstances may exert an important influence, as, for instance, where a deed is made of land for a right of way and the company is not authorized to take a fee, or where the term of the corporate existence is limited to a specified term of years. In all such cases the law is to be considered as an element of the contract, for the law is always a part of the contract unless excluded by valid stipulations,[1] so that a conveyance, although apt words for the creation of a fee, and such as would create a fee if the transaction were between natural persons, are used, will not invariably vest a fee in the corporation. Some of the courts make a distinction between cases where there is a grant of the fee for a right of way and cases where the right of way is acquired under the eminent domain. Thus in one case it was held that a statute prohibiting a railroad company from erecting buildings on its right of way did not apply where the right of way was acquired by grant.[2]

§ 404. **Effect of conveyance of property the company is not authorized to acquire.**—As we have seen, a railroad company does acquire a title to land conveyed to it, although the title is a peculiar one. As it acquires a title it possesses something which it may convey, so that, in cases where it does convey, the question is as to the title its grantee takes under the deed. The adjudged cases hold, and with reason, that the conveyance

---

[1] Foulks v. Falls, 91 Ind. 315, 321; Long v. Straus, 107 Ind. 94, s. c. 57 Am. R. 87.

[2] Calcasieu, etc., Co. v. Harris, 77 Texas 18, s. c. 43 Am. & Eng. R. Cases 570.

carries to the grantee a full and valid title.[1] The conveyance can not, it is obvious, have such an effect unless made before the state has assailed the right of the company to hold the land.

§ 405. **Questioning the right to hold real estate.**—The rule that the right to hold land can only be questioned by the state is a familiar one.[2] The legislature may, of course, authorize an individual having an interest or suffering an injury to assail the right of a railroad company to hold land. But where there is no legislation modifying the rule the right to hold land can be successfully challenged only by a proceeding in the name of the state in the nature of a *quo warranto*. The attack must be direct and not collateral. Upon this principle it is held that a party against whom a railroad company seeks an injunction to restrain interference with land of which it is in possession by grant can not successfully defend upon the ground that the railroad company had no power to acquire the land.[3]

§ 406. **Enjoining purchase of real estate where no power to receive and hold.**—The familiar and long-settled rule stated in the preceding section does not preclude a stockholder from enjoining the purchase of property which the company has no power to receive and hold. It is one thing to prevent the expenditure of corporate funds for an unauthorized purpose and quite another to question the right to hold property already acquired by the corporation. There is, therefore, sound reason for discriminating between the two classes of cases.

---

[1] Walsh *v.* Barton, 24 Ohio St. 28; Ragan *v.* McElroy, 98 Mo. 349.

[2] Cowell *v.* Colorado Spring Co., 100 U. S. 55; Jones *v.* Habersham, 107 U. S. 174, s. c. 2 Sup. Ct. R. 336: Fritts *v.* Palmer, 132 U. S. 282, s. c. 10 Sup. Ct. R. 93; Mackall *v.* Chesapeake, etc., Co., 94 U. S 308; Toledo, etc., R. Co. *v.* Johnson, 49 Mich. 148; Van Wyck *v.* Knevals, 106 U. S. 360. See, generally, Hackensack Water Co. *v.* De Kay, 36 N. J. Eq. 548; Osborn *v.* People, 103 Ill. 224; Truckee, etc., Co. *v.* Campbell, 44 Cal. 89; Freeland *v.* Penna., etc., Co., 94 Pa. St. 504; Keene *v.* Van Reuth, 48 Md. 184; Denver, etc., R. Co. *v.* Denver, etc., Co., 2 Colo. 673; Pixley *v.* Roanoke, etc., Co., 75 Va. 320; North *v.* State, 107 Ind. 356; Cincinnati, etc., R. Co. *v.* Danville, etc., R. Co., 75 Ill. 113.

[3] Kansas City, etc., R. Co. *v.* Kansas City, etc., Co., 118 Mo. 599, s. c. 34 S. W. R. 478.

§ 407. **Executory contract of purchase not enforceable where there is no power to hold the land.**—The general principle that an individual can not question the power of a corporation to hold real estate except in cases where the statute authorizes it[1] does not apply to a case where a corporation seeks to enforce a contract for real estate which it has no power to hold.[2] A corporation can not invoke judicial aid where the purpose of the suit or action is to secure property of which the law does not permit it to become the owner. It would be strange, indeed, if a corporation could obtain a judgment or decree investing it with land which the law commands it not to take, since such a judgment or decree would make the court the agent of a party in violating the law. "Better is the condition of the defendant" in such a case.

§ 408. **Estoppel of parties to deeds to deny corporate existence.**—The well known general rule is that a person who contracts with a corporation is estopped to deny that it is a corporation, and this rule applies to a grantor who conveys land to a corporation.[3] It may be true that where there is no statute authorizing the organization of a corporation of such a general class or nature as that named as grantee there can not be an estoppel, but if there can be a corporation of the general class or nature then the grantor will be estopped. In other words, if there can be a *de facto* corporation the doctrine of estoppel will effectively operate. An estoppel can not arise where there is a clear and explicit statute governing the subject and its provisions are such as to preclude the operation of an estoppel.[4]

§ 409. **Deed to company not in existence.**—The doctrine of many of the cases is that as a deed is a contract there must be two

---

[1] Martindale *v.* Kansas City, etc., R. Co., 60 Mo. 508.

[2] Case *v.* Kelly, 133 U. S. 21, s. c. 13 Am. & Eng. R. Cas. 70.

[3] Close *v.* Glenwood Cemetery, 107 U. S. 466; Swartwout *v.* Michigan, etc., R. Co., 24 Mich. 389. In Winget *v.* Quincy Building Assn., 128 Ill. 67, it is held that there is an estoppel, even if the statute be unconstitutional.

[4] Workingmen's Bank *v.* Converse, 29 La. Ann. 369.

parties and hence there must be a grantee.[1] This doctrine has been applied to deeds to corporations not having a legal existence.[2] There is reason for holding that where it appears that there is no statute authorizing the creation of any such corporation as the one named in the deed the grant is ineffective, but where there is a statute authorizing the organization of any such corporation it seems to us that the deed can not be regarded as void or even voidable in all cases. If there is a statute under which such a corporation may exist, the doctrine of estoppel may well be applied in many instances. A deed is valid if the corporation be one *de facto*.[3] There is some diversity of opinion as to whether a deed executed before the formation of a corporation which is subsequently organized is valid.[4] Our opinion is that such a deed may be valid where the parties all know that a corporation is to be organized, intend that the deed shall be effective when the corporation comes into existence, and the corporation is organized, as all the parties in-

---

[1] Harriman v. Southam, 16 Ind. 190; Lyles v. Lescher, et al., 108 Ind. 382; Huss v. Stephens, 51 Pa. St. 282; Stephens v. Huss, 54 Pa. St. 20; Hall v. Leonard, 1 Pick. 27. See Hogan v. Page, 2 Wall. 605; Gage v. Newmarket, etc., R. Co., 18 Q. B. 457; Hunter v. Watson, 12 Calf. 363; Morris v. Stephens, 46 Pa. St. 200; Douthitt v. Stinson, 63 Mo. 268; German, etc., Assn. v. Scholler, 10 Minn. 331; Russell v. Topping, 5 McLean (U. S.) 194; 3 Washburn Real Prop. (5th ed.), 567.

[2] In Harriman v. Southam, 16 Ind. 190, the court held that a deed to a corporation which had no existence was a nullity and did not estop the grantor, but in Snyder v. Studebaker, 19 Ind. 462, the earlier case was overruled and it was held that the grantor was estopped to deny the existence of the corporation to which the deed was made. See Russell v. Topping, 5 McLean 194; Douthitt v. Stinson, 63 Mo. 268; German, etc., Association v. Scholler, 10 Minn. 331; Jackson v. Cory, 8 Johns. 385. The court, in the case of Provost v. Morgan, etc., R. Co., 42 La Ann. 809, s. c. 8 So. R. 584, 46 Am. & Eng. R. Cas. 535, reaches a correct conclusion upon the facts, but we doubt the soundness of some of the broad statements contained in the opinion. See 2 Am. Law Reg. & Rev. 296; 2 Morawetz on Corp., Chap. IX.

[3] Myers v. Croft, 13 Wall. 291; Smith v. Sheeley, 12 Wall. 358. As we have elsewhere shown such a deed does pass title, and as no one but the state can question the right to exercise corporate powers or hold property a deed to a *de facto* corporation can not be treated as a nullity.

[4] Clifton Heights, etc., Co. v. Randell, 82 Iowa 89, s. c. 47 N. W. R. 905; Philadelphia, etc., Assn. v. Hart, 4 Wheat. 1; Rotch's Wharf. Co. v. Judd, 108 Mass. 224.

tended it should be.[1] If a deed is delivered in escrow to be held until the formation of the proposed corporation, it will be valid if the corporation is formed as contemplated and a delivery made to it after its organization.[2]

§ 410. **Formal execution of conveyances and agreements relating to real estate.**—The ancient and well known rule is that where the statute prescribes a specific mode for the execution of corporate contracts that mode must be substantially pursued,[3] but it does not follow that in all cases the failure to pursue the prescribed rule will render the contract voidable. Where no specific mode is prescribed the company may contract in the usual mode. Where the law requires a seal then

---

[1] Rathbone v. Tioga, etc., Co., 2 Watts & S. (Pa.) 74. We do not believe, however, that where there is no statute authorizing the organization of such a corporation as that contemplated a deed would be valid. Subscriptions to a contemplated corporation may be valid and upon the same principle a deed may be valid.

[2] In the case of Spring Garden Bank v. Hulings Lumber Co., 32 W.Va. 357, s. c. 3 L. R. A. 583, 9 S. E. R. 243, the court conceded the rule to be that if there is no grantee *in esse* the deed would be inoperative, citing Hulick v. Scovil, 4 Gilm.(Ill.) 159; Harriman v. Southam, 16 Ind. 190, and Russell v. Topping, 5 McLean 194, but held that a delivery in escrow made the deed operative. In the course of the opinion the court quoted from the opinion in Rotch's Wharf Co. v. Judd, 108 Mass. 224, 228, the following: "The acceptance of the deed will be presumed as soon as the plaintiffs (the corporation) were competent to take it. Concord Bank v. Bellis, 10 Cush. 276; Bank of U. S. v. Dandridge, 12 Wheat. 64, 70." The cases of Drury v. Foster, 2 Wall. 24, was also cited. In support of the rule that it is the duty of the court to uphold rather than destroy deeds the court cited Sherwood v. Whiting, 54 Conn. 330; Flagg v. Eames, 40 Vt. 16, s. c. 94 Am. Dec. 363; African, etc., Church v. Conover, 27 N. J. Eq. 157; Shed v. Shed, 3 N. H. 432.

[3] Beatty v. Marine, etc., Co., 2 Johns. 109, s. c. 3 Am. Dec. 401; Salem Bank v. Gloucester Bank, 17 Mass. 1, s. c. 9 Am. Dec. 111. The courts are generally reluctant to adjudge a contract ineffective because of a defect in the mode of executing it. Some of the courts hold that the rule that contracts must be executed in the mode prescribed applies only to executory contracts. Pixley v. Western Pacific, etc., R. Co., 33 Calf. 183; City of Cincinnati v. Cameron, 33 Ohio St. 336; Foulke v. San Diego, etc., R. Co., 51 Calf. 365. Sée Rumbough v. Southern, etc., R. Co., 106 N. C. 461, s. c. 11 S. E. R. 528; Curtis v. Piedmont, etc., Co., 109 N. C. 401, s. c. 13 S. E. R. 944. In the absence of statutory restrictions a corporation may make every kind of a deed. Angell & A. Corp., § 220."

the contract, in order to be effective, should be attested by the seal of the corporation, but even in cases where a seal is required the conveyance may be upheld, although no seal is attached. If its enforcement be required by the general principles of equity the absence of a seal will not defeat the title of the grantee. The requirement of the statute of frauds that conveyances of land shall be under seal applies to corporations, and deeds conveying real estate should be under the corporate seal, but while such an unsealed deed does not satisfy the statute there may often be such circumstances connected with the execution as will operate to estop the corporation from alleging its invalidity. A deed defectively executed is voidable, not void, for as the general power to execute deeds exists the act of the corporation in executing it is not *ultra vires*. A defectively executed deed may be made good by ratification. Where the statute requires conveyances of land to be under seal corporate deeds must be under the seal of the corporation.[1] Where there is an agreement and part performance, although the agreement may not be such as to satisfy the statute of frauds, the grantee may enforce the contract substantially under the same rules as those which govern similar contracts between individuals. An agreement to convey land, although not under the corporate seal, may be enforced where the rules which apply to contracts between natural persons entitle the party to enforce a contract of a similar nature.[2] A distinction is made between an agreement to convey or lease land and the deed or lease, and it is held that although the deed in the one case must be executed under seal an unsealed agreement is effective.[3]

§ 411. **Contracts under corporate seal—Effect as evidence.** —An agreement evidenced by the corporate seal is *prima facie* evidence that the instrument was executed by the corporation.[4]

[1] Crawford *v.* Longstreet, 43 N. J. Law 325. A valuable collection of authorities upon the subject of the effect of the statute upon the execution of leases will be found in Mr. Freeman's note to Wallace *v.* Scoggins, 17 Am. St. R. 752.

[2] Banks *v.* Poitiaux, 3 Rand. (Va.) 136, s. c. 15 Am. Dec. 706; Legrand *v.* Hampden, etc., College, 5 Munf. (Va.) 324.

[3] Conant *v.* Bellow's Falls, etc., Co., 29 Vt. 263.

[4] Crescent City, etc., R. Co. *v.* Simp-

§ 412 REAL ESTATE.

Where the seal is affixed to an instrument which is within the power of the corporation to execute, that is, where there is not an entire absence of power to execute it, the presumption is that it was duly executed by the corporation. But, of course, a seal will not give even *prima facie* validity to the instrument where it appears from an inspection of the instrument itself that the contract in question is *ultra vires* in the proper sense of the term. If the person who affixes the seal has no authority to do so the seal will not make the contract effective.[1] Where the signatures of the officers are shown to be genuine the authenticity of the seal will be presumed.[2]

§ 412. **Acceptance of deed.**—A deed may be accepted by parol.[3] A parol acceptance of a deed binds the grantee accepting it to a performance of the covenants and conditions written in the deed.[4] The statute of frauds can not be made available to defeat the performance of the agreements which the deed contains. The authorities establish the doctrine that the person for whose benefit the promise is made may enforce it.[5]

son, 77 Cal. 286, s. c. 19 Pac. R. 426; Reed v. Bradley, 17 Ill. 321; Leggett v. New Jersey, etc., Co., 1 N. J. Eq. 541, s. c. 23 Am. Dec. 728; Burrill v. Nahant Bank, 2 Metc. 163, s. c. 35 Am. Dec. 395; Morse v. Beale, 68 Iowa 463; Indianapolis, etc., R. Co. v. Morganstern, 103 Ill. 149; Union, etc., Co. v. Bank, 2 Colo. 226; Boyce v. Montauk, etc., Co., 37 W. Va. 73, s. c. 16 S. E. R. 501; Missouri, etc., Works v. Ellison, 30 Mo. App. 67; Mickey v. Stratton, 5 Sawyer (U. S. C. C.) 475.

[1] In Luse v. Isthmus, etc., R. Co., 6 Oreg. 125, s. c. 25 Am. R. 506, the president affixed the seal to a mortgage of one of the company's locomotives, and it was held that he had no authority to use the seal. The court cited Fink v. Canyon, etc., Co., 5 Oreg. 301; Hoyt v. Thompson, 5 N. Y. 320; Angell & A. Corp., §§ 223, 224. A somewhat similar ruling was made in Gibson v. Goldthwaite, 7 Ala. 281, s. c. 42 Am. Dec. 592.

[2] Josey v. Wilmington, etc., R. Co., 12 Rich. Law (So. Car.) 134; Phillips v. Coffee, 17 Ill. 154, s. c. 63 Am. Dec. 357; Solomon's Lodge v. Montmollin, 58 Ga. 547; Evans v. Lee, 11 Nev. 194; Susquehanna, etc., Co. v. Gen. Ins. Co., 3 Md. 305, s. c. 56 Am. Dec. 740. *Re* Barned's Banking Co., L. R. 3 Ch. 105.

[3] Smith's Appeal, 69 Pa. St. 474; Tripp v. Bishop, 56 Pa. St. 424; Swisshelm v. Swissvale, etc., Co., 95 Pa. St. 367.

[4] Harlan v. Logansport, etc., R. Co., 133 Ind. 323; Lake Erie, etc., R. Co. v. Priest, 131 Ind. 413.

[5] Lawrence v. Fox, 20 N. Y. 268; Moore v. Ryder, 65 N. Y. 438; Douglass v. Wells, 57 How. Pr. R. 378; Stevens v. Flannagan, 131 Ind. 122; Jones on Mortgages, §§ 763, 764.

Corp. 36

§ 413. **Distinction between a donation of lands and a sale.**—
The courts make a distinction between a donation of land to a railroad company and a sale of land to it.[1] The distinction exerts an important influence in many cases. Where property is purchased the estate of the purchasing company is, ordinarily, greater than it is in cases where the land is acquired by condemnation, so the use to which property acquired by purchase may be devoted is often less limited than it is in cases where the acquisition is by virtue of the power of eminent domain, and so, too, the power to purchase property for a corporate purpose is much less fettered than the power to acquire it by proceedings to condemn.[2]

§ 414. **Deeds of company—By whom executed.**—Where the statute expressly designates the officers or agents by whom deeds shall be executed its provisions should be followed. We do not mean to say that a deed executed by other officers or agents would be void, for deeds executed within the corporate power are not void, although executed by other officers or agents than those designated by statute. Such deeds may be ratified and so, too, they may become practically effective where there are present the requisite elements of an estoppel. A deed executed by officers other than those designated by the statute is not an *ultra vires* act. Where the power to perform the act exists, the fact that it is not performed by the proper officers is a defective or improper execution of a power, but it is nothing more. There is a clear distinction between the defective execution of a power and an act beyond the scope of the powers of the corporation. A railroad company having power to convey property may, in the absence of statutory provisions, convey it by such officers or agents as it may select.[3] There is no conflict upon the general question, and the doctrine is so well settled that we deem it unnecessary to cite many authorities.

[1]. Roberts *v.* Northern Pacific, etc., R. Co., 158 U. S. 1, s. c. 15 Sup. Ct. R. 756; Northern Pacific R. Co. *v.* Roberts, 42 Fed. R. 734.

[2] *Ante*, § 399.

[3] Morris *v.* Keil, 20 Minn. 531, Bason *v.* King's, etc., Mining Co., 90 N. C. 417.

§ 415. Construction of deeds to railroad companies—Generally.

—Deeds, conveying to a railroad company what is called "surplus real estate," that is, real estate not essential to the construction or operation of the road are to be construed by substantially the same rules as those which govern the construction of ordinary private grants, but conveyances granting to the company property essential to the construction and operation of the road are, in many respects, so peculiar that the ordinary rules for the construction of deeds do not supply the means of solving questions which arise in cases involving the construction and effect of such conveyances. Many deeds convey land for "a right of way," and the extent of the estate conveyed by such a deed is to be determined by ascertaining what constitutes a right of way. In an Iowa case the landowner conveyed, by deed of quit claim, "a right of way for all purposes connected with the construction, use or occupation of said railroad," and it was adjudged that the grantee could not take sand from the land for use in the erection of a roundhouse, and that the grantor might take sand for any purpose provided he did not interfere with the legitimate use of the land by the company.[1] The decision in the case cited may be supported upon the theory that the words "right of way" are controlling, and are not modified or limited by the words with which they are associated. It can not be supported upon the theory that the construction of a round-house is not a purpose connected with the construction, use and operation of a railroad. Providing a place for sheltering the locomotives used in operating the road is executing a purpose reasonably connected with the construction and use of the road.[2] The rulings in similar cases authorize and support this conclusion.[3] The

---

[1] Vermilya v. Chicago, etc., R. Co., 66 Iowa 606, s. c. 55 Am. R. 279, 23 Am. & Eng. R. Cas. 108.

[2] New York, etc., R. Co. v. Kip, 46 N. Y. 546, s. c. 7 Am. R. 385; Hannibal, etc., R. Co. v. Muder, 49 Mo. 165.

[3] Mallett v. Simpson, 94 N. C. 37, s. c. 55 Am. R. 594; Lyde v. Eastern, etc., R. Co., 36 Beav. 10; Grand Trunk R. Co. v. Richardson, 91 U. S. 454; Old Colony, etc., R. Co. v. Evans, 6 Gray 25, s. c. 66 Am. Dec. 394; Cumberland, etc., R. Co. v. McLanahan, 59 Pa. St. 23; Spofford v. Bucksport, etc., R. Co., 66 Me. 26; Chicago,

necessity which will authorize a railroad company to receive and hold land need not be an absolute one, nor need it appear that the land is indispensable to the construction or operation of the road, but it is sufficient if there is a reasonable necessity for taking and holding the land,[1] so that where a conveyance is made granting such property as is necessary for the construction and operation of the road, it conveys such property and estate as is reasonably necessary for the construction or operation of the road. The term "right of way," it has been held, describes the tenure and not the land granted.[2] We suppose, however, that the term "right of way" may sometimes mean the land occupied by the company,[3] but ordinarily it can not be regarded as descriptive of the real estate conveyed. The meaning of the term may be controlled by associated words and sometimes by the circumstances under which the deed is executed.[4]

§ 416. Deeds to railroad companies—Construction of—Conditions.—The acceptance of a deed containing conditions imposes upon the company accepting it the duty of performing such covenants and conditions.[5] Thus a condition in a deed granting land to a railroad company for a right of way, "providing the same does not interfere with buildings," and providing also that in the event that the right of way shall interfere with buildings the grantee shall pay damages, is binding upon the grantee.[6] In one case it was held that where the convey-

etc., R. Co. v. Wilson, 17 Ill. 123; Strohecker v. Alabama, etc., R. Co., 42 Ga. 509.

[1] State v. Hancock, 35 N. J. Law 537; State v. Commissioners, etc., 23 N. J. Law 510; Inhabitants of Worcester v. Western R. Co., 4 Metc. (Mass.) 564; Curtis v. Leavitt, 15 N. Y. 9.

[2] Atlantic, etc., R. Co. v. Lesueur, (Ariz.) 19 Pac. Rep. 157, 37 Am. & Eng. R. Cas. 368. In the case cited, in speaking of the argument of counsel, the court used this language: "It is said that the term right of way is used to describe the land granted; that is, that these are words of description rather than of tenure. We can not concur with this view, and no authority can be found which so holds."

[3] See *ante*, § 5.

[4] Reidinger v. Marquette, etc., R. Co., 62 Mich. 29, s. c. 14 Am. & Eng. Corp. Cas. 394; Hall v. City of Ionia, 38 Mich. 493.

[5] Inhabitants of Cambridge v. Charlestown, etc., R. Co., 7 Metc. (Mass.) 70.

[6] Rathbone v. Tioga, etc., Co., 2 Watts & S. (Pa.) 74.

ance contained a condition requiring the company to construct cattle guards at crossings the grantor might enforce specific performance of the contract or enforce a lien for the expense of constructing proper cattle guards.[1] A condition that the grantee shall fence is operative upon the grantee although there is nothing more than a parol acceptance of the deed.[2] The result to which the authorities lead is this, a railroad company can not be permitted to enjoy the easement and yet refuse to perform the conditions of the contract which created the easement or vested the estate conveyed in the grantee.[3] The condition must, of course, be a valid one, for an illegal condition has no effect.[4]

§ 417. **Grants—Beneficial—Presumption of acceptance.**— The general rule is that where a grant to a railroad company is beneficial no formal acceptance is required, and that in the absence of countervailing facts an acceptance of a beneficial grant will be presumed.[5] If the statute requires an acceptance to be evidenced in a prescribed mode there must, as a rule, be an acceptance in the mode prescribed; in other words, there must be a substantial compliance with the provisions of the statute. The rule is that deeds will be upheld where it can

[1] Dayton, etc., R. Co. v. Lewton, 20 Ohio St. 401. In Davies v. St. Louis, etc., R. Co., 56 Iowa 192, it was held that the grantor has a vendor's lien if the grantee fails to pay the purchase money. See, on the general subject, Kansas Pacific R. Co. v. Hopkins, 18 Kans. 494.

[2] Midland, etc., R. Co. v. Fisher, 125 Ind. 19, s. c. 43 Am. & Eng. R. Cas. 578. See, generally, Louisville, etc., R. Co. v. Power, 119 Ind. 269.

[3] Donald v. St. Louis, etc., R. Co., 52 Iowa 411; Huston v. Cincinnati, etc., R. Co., 21 Ohio St. 235; Atlantic Dock Co. v. Leavitt, 50 Barb. 135; Duffy v. New York, etc., R. Co., 2 Hilton, (N.Y.) 496; Cincinnati (Pittsburg), etc., R. Co. v. Bosworth, 46 Ohio St. 81, s. c. 38 Am. & Eng. R. Cas. 290; Midland, etc., R. Co. v. Fisher, 125 Ind. 19, s. c. 43 Am. & Eng. R. Cas. 578.

[4] St. Louis, etc., R. Co. v. Mathers, 71 Ill. 592; Hammond v. Port Royal, etc., R. Co., 15 So. Car. 10; Lynn v. Mount Savage, etc., R. Co., 34 Md. 603; Kettle River, etc., R. Co. v. Eastern, etc., R. Co., 41 Minn. 461, s. c. 40 Am. & Eng. R. Cas. 449.

[5] Bangor, etc., R. Co. v. Smith, 47 Me. 34; Charles River Bridge v. Warren Bridge, 7 Pick. 344; Rathbone v. Tioga, etc., R. Co., 2 Watts & S. (Pa.) 74.

be justly and reasonably done, and presumptions in favor of their effectiveness are generally made.

§ 418. Incidents pass with principal thing granted.—Where there is a grant of a principal thing all the necessary incidents essential to the enjoyment of the principal thing pass to the grantee.[1] Where there is a grant of land for use by a railroad company in operating its road the grant conveys the right to use the land for that purpose and the grantee can not recover damages for injuries caused by a reasonably careful operation of the road.[2] The principle asserted in the cases to which we have referred is one of practical importance and leads to material results. It prevents a grantor from successfully asserting a claim for damages for injuries from noise, smoke and the like, resulting from the proper operation of the road, and it precludes him from successfully prosecuting an action for a nuisance, although annoyance from smoke, noise and similar things necessarily incident to the operation of the road is suffered by him.[3] But the grant does not exonerate the company from liability for injury caused by its negligence, nor, it may be said in passing, do the damages assessed in condemnation proceedings cover loss caused by the negligence of the company.

§ 419. Effect of designating in the deed the purpose for which land is granted.—The designation of the purpose for which the land is granted is sometimes regarded as creating a

[1] Reidinger v. Marquette, etc., R. Co., 62 Mich. 29, s. c. 29 Am. & Eng. R. Cas. 611; Babcock v. Western, etc., Corp., 9 Metcf. (Mass.) 553, s. c. 43 Am. Dec. 411.

[2] Chicago, etc., R. Co. v. Smith, 111 Ill. 363, s. c. 29 Am. & Eng. R. Cas. 558, citing Chicago, etc., R. Co. v. Springfield, etc., R. Co., 67 Ill. 142; Keithsburg, etc., R. Co. v. Henry, 79 Ill. 290; Norris v. Vermont, etc., R. Co., 28 Vt. 99. See, also, Chicago, etc., Co. v. Loeb, 118 Ill. 203, s. c. 8 N. E. R. 460; Lafayette, etc., v. New Albany, etc., Co., 13 Ind. 90; Swinney v. Fort Wayne, etc., R. Co., 59 Ind. 205; Lafayette, etc., Co. v. Murdock, 68 Ind. 137; Indiana, etc., R. Co. v. Allen, 113 Ind. 308; White v. Chicago, etc., R. Co., 122 Ind. 317.

[3] Dunsmore v. Central R. Co., 72 Iowa 182, s. c. 33 N. W. R. 456; Randle v. Pacific, etc., R. Co., 65 Mo. 325; Cosby v. Owensboro, etc., Railway Co., 10 Bush. 288; Struthers v. Dunkirk, etc., Railway Co., 87 Pa. St. 282.

§ 420   REAL ESTATE.   561

condition subsequent and as defining and limiting the title of the grantee.[1] The effect of a deed is not, as a rule, to be determined from a single clause, but the whole instrument must be considered. It is to be read by the light of surrounding circumstances,[2] and given such effect as the parties intended it should have.[3]

§ 420. **Covenants that run with the land.**—Many covenants peculiar to conveyances to railroad companies run with the land. If the covenant is a direct and not a collateral one it runs with the land and binds remote grantees.[4] The weight of authority is that a covenant to fence runs with the land.[5] A parol agreement to maintain a fence does not run with the land.[6]

---

[1] Ottumwa, etc., R. Co. v. McWilliams, 71 Iowa 164, s.c. 29 Am. & Eng. R. Cas. 544; Robinson v. Missisquoi R. Co., 59 Vt. 426, s. c. 30 Am. & Eng. R. Cas. 299. See, generally, Gadberry v. Sheppard, 27 Miss. 203; Adams v. Logan Co., 11 Ill. 336; Harris v. Shaw, 13 Ill. 456; State v. Brown, 27 N. J. Law 13; Wiggins Ferry Co. v. Ohio, etc., R. Co., 94 Ill. 83; Morrill v. Wabash, etc., R. Co., 96 Mo. 174, s. c. 9 S. W. R. 657.

[2] It has been held that a deed for a nominal consideration, to railroad companies, which recites that the conveyance is "for the erection and maintenance thereon of the freight-houses which said companies or either of them * * * and for such other general railroad purposes as may be necessary"—conveys absolute title, and is not conditioned upon the erection of said freight-houses, so as to enable the grantor to have it canceled upon failure to erect them. Noyes v. St. Louis, A. & T. H. R. Co., 21 N. E. R. 487.

[3] Louisville, etc., R. Co. v. Koelle, 104 Ill. 455, s. c. 11 Am. & Eng. R. Cas. 301; Koelle v. Knecht, 99 Ill. 396; Hadden v. Shoutz, 15 Ill. 582; Newaygo, etc., Co. v. Chicago, etc., R. Co., 64 Mich. 114, s. c. 29 Am. & Eng. R. Cas. 505.

[4] Easter v. Little Miami, etc., R. Co., 14 Ohio St. 48; Kellogg v. Robinson, 6 Vt. 276; Hazlett v. Sinclair, 76 Ind. 488, and authorities cited; Hartung v. Witte, 59 Wis. 285; Bronson v. Coffin, 108 Mass. 175; Burbank v. Pillsbury, 48 N. H. 475; Countryman v. Deck, 13 Abb. (N. C.) 105; Cincinnati (Pittsburg), etc., Co. v. Bosworth, 46 Ohio St. 81, s. c. 38 Am. & Eng. R. Cas. 290; Blain v. Taylor, 19 Abb. Pr. 228; Midland, etc., R. Co. v. Fisher, 125 Ind. 19, s. c. 43 Am. & Eng. R. Cas. 578; Fresno, etc., Co. v. Rowell, 80 Cal. 114, s. c. 13 Am. St. R. 254; Scott v. Stetler, 128 Ind. 385.

[5] Cincinnati (Pittsburg), etc., R. Co. v. Bosworth, 46 Ohio St. 81, s. c. 38 Am. & Eng. R. Cas. 290; Midland, etc., R. Co. v. Fisher, 125 Ind. 19, s. c. 43 Am. & Eng. R. Cas. 578; Countryman v. Deck, 13 Abbott N. C. 105.

[6] Kentucky Central, etc., R. Co. v. Kenney, (Ky.), s. c. 20 Am. & Eng. R. Cas. 458; Morss v. Boston, etc., R. Co., 2 Cush. 536; Wilder v. Maine

§ 421. **Merger of preliminary agreement in deed.**—The general rule is that a preliminary agreement providing for the conveyance of land is merged in the deed.[1] This rule applies to a contract made with a railroad company for the conveyance of land.[2] The rule is a familiar one and is one of great practical importance in cases where the question relates to the grant of a right of way.

§ 422. **Bonds for conveyance — Specific performance.**— A railroad company acting within the scope of its authority may take a bond, often called "a title bond," for the conveyance of land. If the bond is sufficiently specific and certain, presents the necessary equitable elements and the conditions on the part of the company are performed, specific performance will be decreed.[3] The rule which requires contracts to be specific and certain will defeat a specific performance where the price is not agreed upon but is left to be fixed by an umpire.[4] If, however, the price has been definitely and finally fixed by the umpire, specific performance may be decreed.[5] There must be such a consideration as the court can justly regard as equitable; but where the contract recites that the agreement to

Central R. Co., 65 Me. 332; Vandegrift v. Delaware, etc., R. Co., 2 Houst. (Del.) 287; Pitkin v. Long Island, etc., R. Co., 2 Barb. Ch. 221; Day v. New York Central R. Co., 31 Barb. 548.

[1] Twyford v. Wareup, Cases temp. Finch 310; Bailey v. Snyder, 13 Sergt. & R. 160; Williams v. Morgan, 15 Q. B. 782; Frederick v. Campbell, 13 Sergt. & R. 136; Smith v. Evans, 6 Binney 102; Houghtaling v. Lewis, 10 Johns. 297; Haggerty v. Fagan, 2 Penrose & W. 533; Phillbrook v. Esmwiler, 92 Ind. 590.

[2] Waldron v. Toledo, etc., R. Co., 55 Mich. 420, s. c. 20 Am. & Eng. R. Cas. 348; Druse v. Wheeler, 22 Mich. 439.

[3] Walker v. Eastern, etc., R. Co., 6 Hare 594; Sanderson v. Cockermouth, etc., R. Co., 11 Beav. 497; Boston, etc., R. Co. v. Babcock, 3 Cush. 228; Chicago, etc., R. Co. v. Swinney, 38 Iowa 182; Byers v. Denver, etc., R. Co., 13 Colo. 552. As to what is a sufficient description of the land, see Ottumwa, etc., R. Co. v. McWilliams, 71 Iowa 164, s. c. 29 Am. & Eng. R. Cas. 544, citing Pursley v. Hayes, 22 Iowa 11; Beal v. Blair, 33 Iowa 318; Barlow v. Chicago, etc., R. Co., 29 Iowa 276; Spangler v. Danforth, 65 Ill. 152; Mead v. Parker, 115 Mass. 413; Hurley v. Brown, 98 Mass. 545.

[4] Milnes v. Gery, 14 Vesey 400. See Tillett v. Charing Cross Co., 26 Beav. 419.

[5] Brown v. Bellows, 4 Pick. 179.

§ 423 REAL ESTATE. 563

build the road forms part of the consideration, the fact that the land agreed to be conveyed is much more valuable than the price named will not defeat the suit.[1] It has been held that the fact that the road has not been completed within the time limited by the statute will not avail the obligor as a defense for the reason that only the state can make that question,[2] but the failure may, as it seems to us, be of such a character as to render it inequitable to enforce the contract, and if that be so, then, upon well-established principles, specific performance will not be decreed.[3]

§ 423. **Presumption that there is power to hold the land.**— Where a corporation is authorized to hold land for certain purposes, a conveyance of land to it will be presumed to be for some purpose within the corporate powers, unless the contrary is clearly shown.[4] The presumption can not obtain where it appears upon the face of the deed and from a reference to the statute that the company had no power to acquire and hold the property, but there are very few cases in which the presumption will not be made.

§ 424. **Power to convey real estate.**—A railroad company has power to convey lands of which it is the owner, except where some rule of law or some statute prohibits it from conveying its property. It is to be remembered, however, that the rule to which we have often referred, prohibiting a railroad company from disabling itself from performing its duties, operates as a limitation upon the power of disposition. The power of a railroad company is, therefore, not so unfettered as

---

[1] Ottumwa, etc., R. Co. v. McWilliams, 71 Iowa 164, s. c. 29 Am. & Eng. R. Cas. 544.

[2] Ross v. Chicago, etc., R. Co., 77 Ill. 127. See Atlantic, etc., R. Co. v. St. Louis, 66 Mo. 228.

[3] Coe v. New Jersey Midland R. Co., 31 N. J. Eq. 105; Webb v. Direct London, etc., R. Co., 9 Hare 129; Clarke v. Rochester, etc., R. Co., 18 Barb. 350; Gooday v. Colchester, etc., R. Co., 17 Beav. 132; Edwards v. Grand Junction, etc., R. Co., 1 Myl. & C. 650 (13 Eng. Ch. 559); Hawkes v. Eastern, etc., R. Co., 1 DeG., M. & G. 737; Wycombe, etc., R. Co. v. Donnington Hospital, L. R. 1 Ch. 268.

[4] McCarty v. St. Paul, etc., R. Co., 31 Minn. 278; Ohio, etc., R. Co. v. McCarthy, 96 U. S. 258; Yates v. Van DeBogert, 56 N. Y. 526.

that of a purely private corporation. The right to convey its surplus land, that is, land not essential to enable it to perform its corporate duties, is substantially the same as that of a strictly private business corporation. A private business corporation has general power to convey,[1] and it follows from what we have said that as to surplus property the power of railroad companies is one of a general nature.

§ 425. **Dedication of land for use as a highway.**—A railroad corporation may dedicate to public use a highway across lands owned by it and used for its railroad tracks.[2] Indeed, it is a general rule that either public or private corporations may make dedications unless they are forbidden by their charter or the governing statute.[3] Thus, where the Northern Pacific Railroad Company made an addition to a town on a section of land granted to it by congress, and sold lots with reference to a recorded plat thereof, it was held that a street which was shown on the plat as extending across the railroad track must be regarded as dedicated to the public use, that this was not *ultra vires* as an alienation of its right of way so as to interfere with the purpose of the grant made by congress, and that it had no right to block the street by the erection of a depot at that point.[4] So, where a railroad company for eighteen years permitted the public to use a crossing as a street, parted its trains to let vehicles through, allowed it to be improved as a street, and made a map showing the existence of such a street, it was held that a valid dedication was shown and that

---

[1] *In re* Patent, etc., Co., L. R. 6 Ch. 83; Aurora, etc., Co. v. Paddock, 80 Ill. 263; White Water, etc., Co. v. Vallette, 21 How. (U. S.) 414; Barry v. Merchants', etc., Co., 1 Sandf. Ch. 280; Dupee v. Boston, etc., Co., 114 Mass. 37; Buell v. Buckingham, 16 Iowa 284; Town Council of Town of Newark v. Elliott, 5 Ohio St. 113; Miners', etc., Co. v. Zellerbach, 37 Cal. 543.

[2] Central R. Co. v. Bayonne, 52 N. J. L. 503.

[3] Elliott on Roads and Streets, § 107, citing, as to private corporations, Williams v. New York, etc., Co., 39 Conn. 509; Green v. Canaan, 29 Conn. 157; Grand Surrey Canal v. Hall, 1 M. & Gr. 392. The rule stated in the text-book above referred to was approved in Lake Erie, etc., R. Co. v. Town of Boswell, 137 Ind. 336, 36 N. E. 1103.

[4] Northern Pac. R. Co. v. City of Spokane, 56 Fed. R. 915.

the company was estopped from denying the existence of the street, especially as persons had bought lots and built houses on both sides of the street upon the faith that it extended across the company's right of way.[1] In another case it was held that the dedication of a portion of its land by a railroad company to the public as a highway was not *ultra vires*, and that its uninterrupted use as a highway for four years by the public was sufficient to show a complete dedication and acceptance.[2]

§ 426. Disposition of property corporation has no power to receive and hold—Escheat.—The question as what disposition shall be made of property purchased by a company which it has no power to receive and hold is an interesting one. Whether the property shall escheat to the state upon judgment in a proceeding by the state assailing the right of the company to hold it, may, of course, be controlled by statute, but if there be no statute then the question is to be determined upon general principles. We suppose that if there is a statute providing that it shall escheat to the state, creditors dealing with the corporation, as well as stockholders, must take notice of the statute and must know, as matter of law, that they can not successfully assert a right to the property. In considering the effect of a dissolution we have discussed the cases bearing upon the question and stated the general doctrine relating to the disposition of property upon the dissolution of the corporation.[3] In Pennsylvania the question came before the court and it was held that the property did not escheat to the state but went to the stockholders.[4]

[1] Lake Erie, etc., R. Co. v. Town of Boswell, 137 Ind. 336, s. c. 36 N. E. R. 1103.

[2] People v. Eel River, etc., R. Co., 98 Cal. 665, s. c. 33 Pac. R. 728.

[3] Greenwood v. Freight Co., 105 U. S. 13; Owen v. Smith, 31 Barb. 641; Heath v. Barmore, 50 N. Y. 302; McCoy v. Farmer, 65 Mo. 244.

[4] Commonwealth v. New York, etc., R. Co., 132 Pa. St. 591, s. c. 7 L. R. A. 634; Commonwealth v. New York, etc., R. Co., 114 Pa. St. 340. See, generally, Heman v. Britton, 88 Mo. 549; St. Louis, etc., Coal Co. v. Sandival, etc., Co., 116 Ill. 170; Hightower v. Thornton, 8 Ga. 486; Asheville, etc., v. Aston, 92 N. C. 578; Burrall v. Bushwick R. Co., 75 N. Y. 211; Wheeler v. Pullman, etc., Co., 143 Ill. 197.

CHAPTER XVIII.

LEASES.

§ 427. Power to lease—Generally.
428. What the legislature may prescribe.
429. Power to lease not an implied one—Legislative authority requisite.
430. The power to lease—General rule.
431. The foundation of the rule.
432. Power to accept a lease.
433. Statutes asserted to confer power to lease are not aided by construction.
434. Statutes strictly construed—Illustrative instances.
435. Statutes—Construction of.
436. What is included in the authority to execute a lease.
437. Scope of authority to lease.
438. Statutes conferring power to lease must be strictly followed.
439. Consent of stockholders—Statutory requirement must be obeyed.
440. Concurrence of stockholders necessary.
441. What number of stockholders must assent to the lease.
442. Consent of stockholders—Waiver of objections.
443. Lease where parties are corporations of different states.
444. Authority to execute lease has no extra-territorial effect.
445. Rights of foreign lessors.
446. Leases to connecting lines.

§ 447. Lease to competing lines—Effect of statutes prohibiting.
448. Effect of executing unauthorized lease.
449. Lease—Construction.
450. Lease—Dependent and independent contracts.
451. Contract to permit use of track not necessarily a lease.
452. Traffic contract not valid if it is in effect a lease.
453. Contracts granting right to use—Effect and construction of.
454. Part performance—Effect of.
455. Duration of a lease.
456. Effect of lease on taxation.
457. Public duties of lessee under an unauthorized lease—Mandamus.
458. Authorized lease—Duty of lessee to operate the road—Mandamus.
459. Lessee not liable for wrongs committed prior to the execution of the lease.
460. Effect of a lease upon rights of creditors.
461. Authorized lease—Rights and duties to which lessee company succeeds.
462. Contract obligation of lessor—Lessee not liable thereon.
463. Recovery of rent under unauthorized lease.
464. Improvements of road by lessee operating under an unauthorized lease.

§ 465. Receiver's power to lease.
466. Unauthorized lease—Liability of lessor—Generally.
467. Authorized lease—Liability of lessor for injuries caused by negligence of lessee—Cases holding lessor liable.
468. Authorized lease—Liability of lessor for negligence of lessee in operating the road—Authorities.
469. Authorized lease—Liability of lessor for negligence of lessee in operating the road—Views of the authors.
470. Control reserved by lessor.
471. Liability of lessee under authorized lease—Illustrative cases.

§ 472. Unauthorized lease—Liability of lessor to employes of lessee—Generally.
473. Unauthorized lease—Liability of lessor—General rule.
474. Liability of lessee for injuries resulting from negligence in operating the road.
475. Contracts of the lessee.
476. Joint liability.
477. Liability of company where it permits another company to use track in common with itself.
478. Fraudulent leases.
479. Unauthorized lease — Injunction.

§ 427. Power to lease—Generally.—The legislative power respecting the creation of railroad corporations is of such a plenary nature that statutes may be enacted authorizing one company to lease its road equipments and appurtenances to another company. The whole subject is in the main a legislative one. Where there is no constitutional provision interdicting it the authority to lease may be conferred by a special act, but where the constitution of the state requires that all laws for the organization and government of corporations shall be general and not special or local, the authority to execute a lease of a railroad and its equipments must be conferred by a general law. The authority to lease the road is to be discriminated from the authority to lease property not forming part of the railroad or essential to its operation, for a railroad company authorized to own and hold property not forming part of its line of railroad or essential to the operation thereof, is, as to such property, invested with the rights of an ordinary owner of land, and as such owner may lease or sell it. Property forming part of the railroad, or essential to its operation, is not held as property is held by ordinary owners, but is held under the grant to the corporation for the purpose of enabling it to perform its corporate duties and functions, and, as the law forbids a railroad corporation from conveying or transferring such of its property as would disable it from performing such duties and functions it has no power to transfer by way of lease property essential to enable it to perform such functions or duties.

§ 428. What the legislature may prescribe.—Within the limitations imposed by the constitution the legislature may prescribe by whom and to whom leases may be executed. The legislative determination, where no constitutional provision is violated, is conclusive. The legislative judgment (when expressed in a valid enactment), as to the parties to whom leases may be made,[1] as to the terms and conditions of leases, and as to the duties and obligations of parties thereto can not be reviewed by the courts. If the power, which the legislature assumes to exercise, is vested in it by the organic law, it is master of its own discretion and is the exclusive judge of all questions of expediency or policy.

§ 429. Power to lease not an implied one—Legislative authority requisite.—As the power to lease property essential to the operation of a railroad is not an implied or incidental power, it would seem to necessarily follow that it does not exist except by virtue of an effective statute. The rule that a railroad company can not execute a lease is generally placed upon the ground of public policy, but it is frequently said that in the absence of a statute there is no power to execute a lease. One who asserts that a railroad corporation has power to lease its railroad or property essential to the operation thereof must show an effective legislative enactment granting the power to lease, otherwise his assertion will be unavailing.[2]

---

[1] Where the statute authorized a lease to another company but gave no express authority to lease to an individual, it was held that such a lease was neither *malum in se* nor *malum prohibitum*, that it was not void as contrary to public policy, and that, after the individual lessee had operated the road under the lease, he could not defend against an action to recover the stipulated rent. Woodruff v. Erie R. Co., 93 N. Y. 609. But the decision referred to is of doubtful soundness. See Abbott v. Johnstown, etc., R. Co., 80 N. Y. 27.

[2] It seems that there are really two

§ 430. **The power to lease—General rule.**—Whatever difference of opinion there may be as to the grounds upon which the rule rests, the rule itself is firmly established. That rule, as asserted in very numerous cases, is that a railroad corporation can not, without express legislative permission, lease its road, franchises and equipments to another corporation and transfer to its lessee the privilege of operating the road.[1] It

grounds upon which the prevailing doctrine may be supported namely, the rule of public policy and the rule that corporate charters are to be strictly construed and corporations possess only such powers as their charters confer. In St. Louis, etc., Co. v. Terre Haute, etc., Co., 145 U. S. 393, s. c. 12 Sup. Ct. R. 953, the court, speaking of the contract between the two corporations, said: "In short, by this contract one railroad company undertook to transfer its whole railroad and equipments and its privileges and franchises to maintain and operate the road to another company for a term of 999 years in consideration of the payment from time to time by the latter to the former of a portion of the gross receipts. This was, in substance and effect, a lease of the railroad and franchise for a term of almost a thousand years, and was a contract which neither of the companies had power to enter into unless expressly authorized by the state which created it, and which, if beyond the scope of the lawful powers of either corporation was wholly void, could not be ratified or validated by either or both, and would support no action or suit by either against the other."

[1] Thomas v. West Jersey R. Co., 101 U. S. 71; Pennsylvania R. Co. v. St. Louis, etc., R. Co., 118 U. S. 290; Oregon R., etc., Co. v. Oregonian, etc., R. Co., 130 U. S. 1; Pittsburg, etc., R. Co. v. Allegheny Co., 63 Pa. St. 126; Middlesex R. Co. v. Boston, etc., R. Co., 115 Mass. 347; Board Com'rs Tippecanoe Co. v. Lafayette, etc., R. Co., 50 Ind. 85; Memphis, etc., R. Co. v. Grayson, 88 Ala. 572; Mills v. Central R. Co., 41 N. J. Eq. 1; International, etc., R. Co. v. Underwood, 67 Tex. 589; Troy, etc., R. Co. v. Boston, etc., R. Co., 86 N. Y. 107; State v. Atchison, etc., R. Co., 24 Neb. 143; Great Northern R. Co. v. Eastern Counties R. Co., 12 Eng. L. & Eq. 224; Fisher v. West Virginia, etc., R. Co., 39 W. Va. 366, 19 S. E. Rep. 578; Earle v. Seattle, etc., R. Co., 56 Fed. R. 909; Ricketts v. Chesapeake, etc., R. Co., 33 W. Va. 433, s. c. 10 S. E. R. 801, 1 Lewis' Am. R. & Corp. R. 455; Grand Tower, etc., Co. v. Ullman, 89 Ill. 244; Abbott v. Johnstown, etc., R. Co., 80 N. Y. 27, s. c. 36 Am. R. 572; People v. Albany, etc., R. Co., 77 N. Y. 232; East Anglian, etc., R. Co. v. Eastern, etc., R. Co., 11 Com. B. 775; Pittsburg, etc., R. Co. v. Columbus, etc., R. Co., 8 Biss. (U. S.) 456; Briscoe v. Southern Kansas, etc., R. Co., 40 Fed. R. 273; Wabash, etc., R. Co. v. Payton, 106 Ill. 534; Norwich, etc., R. Co. v. Worcester, 147 Mass. 518; Hamilton v. Savannah, etc., Co., 49 Fed. R. 412; Harmon v. Columbia, etc., R. Co., 28 S. Car. 401; Memphis, etc., R. Co. v. Grayson, 88 Ala. 572; Hays v. Ottawa, etc., R. Co. 61 Ill. 422; Stewart & Foltz's Appeal, 56 Pa. St. 413; Nelson v. Vermont, etc., R. Co., 26 Vt. 717.

can not, by way of lease, transfer a corporate franchise or privilege to another company nor impose upon another its own corporate duties except in cases where the statute so provides.

§ 431. **The foundation of the rule.**—It seems to us, as we have said, that the rule forbidding a railroad company from leasing its railroad may be rested on two grounds. The rule, however, is usually put upon the ground that public policy forbids one company from transferring its railroad to another. It is unquestionably true that a railroad corporation has no power to relieve itself of the duties and obligations which it owes to the public by a voluntary surrender of its property and franchises.[1] A railroad company can not escape its charter obligations by an abandonment of its road, or the like, for that public policy forbids,[2] and there is no reason why the same general principle should not apply to transfers by way of lease.

§ 432. **Power to accept a lease.**—The principle which underlies the doctrine that a railroad company can not lease its railroad without direct legislative authority supports the rule that a railroad company can not, without legislative authority, take a grant or lease of the property and franchises of another

---

[1] Gulf, etc., R. Co. v. Morris, 67 Tex. 692; International, etc., R. Co. v. Moody, 71 Tex. 614; Harmon v. Columbia, etc., R. Co., 28 S. Car. 401; Balsley v. St. Louis, etc., R. Co., 119 Ill. 68; Palmer v. Utah, etc., R. Co., 2 Idaho 290, 16 Pac. R. 553, 36 Am. & Eng. R. Cas. 443; Ricketts v. Chesapeake, etc., R. Co., 33 W. Va. 433. The obligation of one of two contracting railroads to fulfill the duties of its charter by completing the unbuilt part of its road is inconsistent with a contract for a long time—such as twenty years—by which it contracts to deliver all its traffic over that part of its road to another company. Des Moines & Ft. D. R. Co. v. Wabash, St. L. & P. R. Co., 135 U. S. 576, 43 Am. & Eng. R. Cas. 694.

[2] The principle to which we refer is illustrated by such cases as State v. Dodge City, etc., R. Co., 53 Kan. 377, s. c. 61 Am. & Eng. R. Cas. 631; Erie, etc., Railroad Co. v. Casey, 26 Pa. St. 287; State v. Sioux City, etc., R. Co., 7 Neb. 357; People v. Louisville, etc., R. Co., 120 Ill. 48. See, generally, Railroad Commissioners v. Portland, etc., R. Co., 63 Me. 269; Gates v. Railroad, 53 Conn. 333; Pierce v. Emery, 32 N. H. 484; People v. New York, etc., R. Co., 28 Hun 543.

company.[1] The power to accept franchises granted to another company is not an implied or incidental power. Public policy forbids that one company should, without legislative sanction, assume the duties imposed by law upon another corporation.

§ 433. **Statutes asserted to confer power to lease are not aided by construction.**—The power to lease is not, as a rule, favored by the courts, at least they are not inclined to adjudge that it exists unless the statute in clear terms confers it. The power to lease does not exist unless it clearly appears that the legislature intended to confer it upon the corporation. Construction will be strict, not liberal, as against a party who asserts that the corporation has power to lease its railroad and equipments.[2] The power to transfer property essential to the operation of a railroad is one of great importance and the policy of the law has always been against such transfers, so that there is strong reason for the conclusion that the power must be clearly and expressly conferred.

---

[1] Oregon R., etc., Co. v. Oregonian R. Co., 130 U. S. 1; St. Louis, etc., R. Co. v. Terre Haute, etc., R. Co., 145 U. 393, s. c. 12 Sup. Ct. 953; Pennsylvania, etc., R. Co. v. St. Louis, etc., R. Co., 118 U. S. 290, s. c. 6 Sup. Ct. R. 1094. See, also, Central Transportation Co. v. Pullman's, etc., Co., 139 U. S. 24, s. c. 11 Sup. Ct. R. 478. We mean by the statement in the text that one corporation can not take, by lease, property of another corporation in cases where the property assumed to be leased is essential to the performance of corporate duties by the company which undertakes to execute the lease, but we do not mean that corporate property other than that of the character indicated may not be leased.

[2] Oregon R., etc., Co. v. Oregonian R. Co., 130 U. S. 1, s. c. 9 Sup. Ct. R. 409; Thomas v. West Jersey, etc., R. Co., 101 U. S. 71. In the first case cited the court commented upon the doctrine that corporate charters are to be strictly construed, referred to the cases Charles River Bridge v. Warren River Bridge, 11 Pet. 420; Dubuque, etc., Railroad Co. v. Litchfield, 23 How. 66, and Turnpike Co. v. Illinois, 96 U. S. 63, and, in the course of the opinion, said: "One of the most important powers with which a corporation can be invested is the right to sell out its whole property, together with the franchises under which it is operated, or the authority to lease its property for a long term of years. In the case of a railroad company these privileges, next to the privilege to build and operate its railroad, would be the most important which could be given it, and this idea would impress itself upon the legislature. Naturally, we should look for the authority to do these things in some *express provision* of the

§ 434. **Statutes strictly construed—Illustrative instances.**
—A power conferred upon a corporation to consolidate with other roads,[1] or to sell its road,[2] or to acquire other lines of railroad by purchase,[3] or to make contracts with another railroad company for the use of its road,[4] does not necessarily include authority to lease its road. A general statute authorizing the formation of a corporation for any lawful purpose does not authorize a railroad company to insert in its articles of association authority to make such a lease.[5]

law. We would suppose that if the legislature saw fit to confer such rights it would do so in terms which could not be misunderstood."

[1] Archer v. Terre Haute, etc., R Co., 102 Ill. 493; Mills v. Central R. Co., 41 N. J. Eq. 1; St. Louis, etc., R. Co. v. Terre Haute, etc., R. Co., 145 U. S. 393; State v. Vanderbilt, 37 Ohio St. 590; Board, etc., v. Lafayette, etc., R. Co., 50 Ind. 85.

[2] Oregon, etc., R. Co. v. Oregonian R. Co., 130 U. S. 1, s. c. 9 Sup. Ct. R. 409; Pennsylvania Co. v. St. Louis, etc., R. Co., 118 U. S. 290; Thomas v. West Jersey, etc., R. Co., 101 U. S. 71.

[3] Mills v. Central R. Co., etc., 41 N. J. Eq. 1.

[4] Rev. St. Ind., 1881, §§ 3971,3973, authorize any railroad company of Indiana "to intersect, join and unite" with any railroad of an adjoining state constructed to the state line, and "to make such contracts and agreements with any such road * * * for the transportation of freight and passengers, or for the use of road, as to the board of directors may seem proper." This statute has been held not to authorize one railroad corporation to lease the road of another. St. Louis, V. & T. H. R. Co. v. Terre Haute & I. R. Co., 145 U. S. 393. The power conferred by the New York act of 1839 upon a railroad corporation to contract with another for the use of their respective roads in such manner as the contract may prescribe has been held to involve the power to make a lease for a term of years. Beveridge v. New York Elev. R. Co., 112 N. Y. 1; Woodruff v. Erie R. Co., 93 N. Y. 609. By the laws of New York, 1839, c. 218, providing that "it shall be lawful hereafter for any railroad corporation to contract with any other railroad for the use of their respective roads, and thereafter to use the same in such manner as may be prescribed in such contract," a railroad company is authorized to lease its road and franchise to another railroad company, though the roads of the lessor and lessee are parallel and competing lines, and their merger or consolidation is prohibited by the laws. New York. 1869, c. 917, § 9; Gere v. New York Cent. & H. R. R. Co., 19 Abb. N. C. 193.

[5] Oregon, R., etc., Co. v. Oregonian R. Co., 130 U. S. 1. In announcing the opinion of the court in this case, Mr. Justice Miller said: "Another important consideration to be observed, peculiarly applicable to the acts of corporations formed by the corporators themselves, declaring what business they are about to pursue, and the powers which they purpose to exercise in carrying it on, is, that while the thing to be done may be lawful, in

§ 435. **Statutes — Construction of.** — While the construction of statutes conferring the power to execute leases is, as against the power, always strict, still the legislative intention is not to be defeated by an unreasonably strict construction. The grant of a principal power will carry with it such necessary incidental powers as are requisite to effectuate it. In accordance with this principle a grant of power wherein is manifested the intention of the legislature to enable a railroad company to secure a continuous line of transportation and to make contracts with other railroad companies or with steamboat lines to effect that object authorizes the railroad corporation to contract with a steamboat line and confers authority to execute and accept a lease.[1] The express grant of a right to lease a railroad authorizes the transfer by way of lease of all such incidents and appurtenances as are reasonably necessary to the operation of the demised road.[2] This must, on principle, be the correct rule. If the legislature authorizes the execution of a lease it is necessarily implied that the lease shall be an effective one, and in order to make it effective it is essential that all incidents neces-

a general way, there are and must be limitations upon the means by which it is to be done or the purpose carried out, which the articles can not remove or violate. A company might be authorized by its articles to establish a large manufactory in a particular locality, and might be held to be a valid incorporation with sufficient powers to prosecute the business described; but such articles, although mentioning the particular place, would not empower the company in the exercise of the power thus conferred, to carry on a business injurious to the health or comfort of those living in that vicinity. Instances might be multiplied in which powers described in general terms as belonging to the objects of the parties who thus become incorporated would be valid; but the corporation, in carrying out this general purpose, would not be authorized to exercise the powers necessary for so doing in any mode which the law of the state would not justify in any private person or any unincorporated body. The manner in which these powers shall be exercised, and their subjection to the restraint of the general laws of the state and its general principles of public policy, are not in any sense enlarged by inserting in the articles of association the authority to depart therefrom."

[1] Green Bay, etc., R. Co. v. Union, etc., Co., 107 U. S. 98, s. c. 13 Am. & Eng. R. Cas. 658; Pittsburgh, etc., R. Co. v. Keokuk, etc., R. Co., 131 U. S. 371, s. c. 39 Am. & Eng. R. Cas. 213; Branch v. Jesup, 106 U. S. 468, s. c. 9 Am. & Eng. R. Cas. 558.

[2] Simpson v. Denison, 10 Hare 51, s. c. 16 Jurist 828, 1 Redfield Ry. 616, 2 Shelford Ry. (Ben. ed.) 694.

sary to a proper operation of the road shall pass to the lessee. The legislative sanction implies the authority to properly operate the leased road, and so, too, the public welfare demands that it shall be properly operated. It must be true that necessary incidents pass to the lessee, since the lessor, by executing a lease under legislative sanction, parts with all control and the lessee must operate the road or else it must cease to do business. That it must cease to do business can not be affirmed, since the cessation of business would be the defeat of the legislative purpose in creating the corporation and authorizing it to lease its road.

§ 436. What is included in the authority to execute a lease.—In a preceding paragraph of this chapter we said that authority to execute a lease carried such incidental powers as were necessary to make the lease effective, and this principle authorizes the conclusion that authority to lease, given in general and unrestricted terms, confers authority to assign a lease or accept an assignment. The matter of form is of comparatively little importance, for the courts will look through the form to the substance. Upon this principle it is held that a railroad company which is authorized to take a lease of another line may take an assignment of such a lease from the lessees of such other line.[1]

---

[1] Stewart v. Long Island R. Co., 102 N. Y. 601. Where a railroad is sold under foreclosure, a new corporation acquiring all of the property of the old except a leased line, not included in the transfer, but of which, nevertheless, the new company actually takes possession and operates, the new company must be regarded as the assignee of the lease, and, by virtue of its possession, is liable for the rent, which in this case was the interest on first mortgage bonds, which the original lessee had agreed to pay; and the succeeding company is liable as long as it occupies the road. Frank v. New York, etc., R. Co., 122 N. Y. 197; Jacksonville, etc., R. Co. v. Louisville, etc., R. Co., 47 Ill. App. 414, 150 Ill. 480, 37 N. E. R. 924. A railroad company, having issued to plaintiff a perpetual pass over its road in consideration of a right of way given it through plaintiff's land, subsequently sold its road, the purchaser assuming none of its debts or obligations, and not using the right of way. Held, that the purchaser was not bound to honor plaintiff's pass. Dickey v. Kansas City & I. R. T. Ry. Co., 122 Mo. 223, 26 S. W. R. 685.

§ 437. **Scope of authority to lease.**—Some of the cases give a very wide and liberal construction to the express grant of authority to execute a lease. In some of the cases very broad language is used, broader than true principle warrants. While it is true that incidents pass by the grant of a principal power purely collateral powers do not. The courts hold that under a statute giving a railroad company power to lease, maintain and operate another railroad upon such terms and conditions as may be agreed upon between the companies respectively,[1] the lessee company may guarantee the payment of interest coupons of bonds issued by the lessor company, which are equal in amount and times of payment to the reserved rent.[2] The general authority to lease implies the incidental authority to agree upon the consideration, terms and conditions of the lease, and hence the contracting companies may agree that part or all of the consideration agreed upon may be yielded by guarantying payment of bonds.

§ 438. **Statutes conferring power to lease must be strictly followed.**—It is held that statutes conferring power upon a railroad company to lease its road must be strictly followed,[3] but

---

[1] This is substantially the language of the statute in New Hampshire, Vermont, New York, New Jersey, Pennsylvania, Nebraska, West Virginia, California, Oregon, Idaho, Wyoming, Utah, South Carolina, Georgia, New Mexico and Arizona. Stimson's Am. Stat. (1892), § 8722.

[2] Eastern Townships Bank v. St. Johnsbury, etc., R. Co., 40 Fed. R. 423, 40 Am. & R. Cas. 566; Day v. Ogdensburg, etc., R. Co., 107 N. Y. 129, aff'g 42 Hun 654. An agreement by the lessor company, guarantying to the lessee a sum of money equal to ten per cent. of the latter's capital stock, to be paid in equal quarterly installments, and an unsigned clause printed on the margin of such stock, in pursuance of the agreement, that lessor "has agreed to pay to [the lessee] an amount equal to ten per cent. per annum on the capital stock," do not constitute any contract to which a holder of such stock is a party or privy. Beveridge v. New York El. R. Co., 112 N. Y. 1. An agreement by a railroad company, in leasing property and franchises from another company, to pay as rent the interest on certain liabilities of the lessor during term of the lease, and to pay the principal of such liabilities at the expiration of the lease is not *ultra vires*. Gere v. New York Cent. & H. R. R. Co., 19 Abb. N. C. 193.

[3] In Humphreys v. St. Louis, etc,. R. Co., 37 Fed. R. 307, the president of the company signed a certificate that a majority of the shareholders had assented to the lease, and it was evidence of the assent of all share-

we suppose that if all the material requirements of the statute are substantially complied with the lease would not be void. The power to lease is, however, not favored, and a material departure from the provisions of the statute would make the lease ineffective. Where conditions are imposed by the statute they must be complied with or the lease may be avoided.[1]

§ 439. Consent of stockholders — Statutory requirement must be obeyed.—Many of the states make the consent of a designated number of the stockholders requisite to the effective execution of a lease.[2] Where the mode of assenting is prescribed by statute there must be a substantial compliance with its requirements. It has been decided that where the statute requires that "no lease shall be perfected until a meeting of the stockholders shall have been called by the directors," and the "holders of at least two-thirds of the stock," voting "at such meeting, shall have assented thereto," the requirement that the assent shall be given by voting at a stockholders' meeting is of the essence, and the assent of the individual stockholders given otherwise than in such meeting is of no effect.[3]

§ 440. Concurrence of stockholders necessary.—We regard the concurrence of the stockholders as essential to the validity

holders and was a compliance with the statutory requirement that the assent of a majority of the shareholders to the execution of the lease should be given in writing.

[1] Peters v. Lincoln, etc., R. Co., 14 Fed. R. 319; Peters v. Lincoln, etc,. R. Co., 12 Fed. R. 513; Kent, etc,. R. Co. v. London, etc., Co., Law R. 3 Ch. R. 656.

[2] Two-thirds are required to vote for the lease in New Hampshire, Connecticut, New York, Nebraska, West Virginia, Colorado, New Mexico and Arizona. Three-fifths in Montana and a majority in Massachusetts and Wyoming. Stimson's Am. St. (1892),

§ 8722. A certificate signed by the president, who owns nearly all the stock, to the effect that a majority of the stockholders have assented to the lease is sufficient evidence of a compliance with the statute of Missouri, which requires the majority of the stockholders to give their assent in writing. Humphreys v. St. Louis, etc., R. Co., 37 Fed. R. 307. See Peters v. Lincoln, etc., R. Co., 12 Fed. R. 513.

[3] Peters v. Lincoln, etc., R. Co., 12 Fed. R. 513. See Smith v. Hurd, 12 Metc. (Mass.) 371; Humphreys v. McKissock, 140 U. S. 304, s. c. 11 Sup. Ct. R. 779.

of the lease of a railroad and its equipment. There is, however, conflict of authority upon this question which can not be reconciled. It is held in a New York case that where a general power to lease its road is given by the law of its incorporation to a railroad company whose directors are charged with the government and direction of its affairs, a contract for such leasing is within the original power of the board of directors, and may be exercised without the concurrence of the stockholders.[1] We can not assent to the doctrine of the case referred to. The execution of a lease of the entire road is a matter in its nature fundamental and organic, and where there is a mere grant of authority to execute a lease, we think that the consent of the stockholders is necessary, but if the power is by statute lodged in the governing board then, of course, the concurrence of the stockholders is not required. The New York case to which reference has just been made,[2] does not, we venture to say with due respect for the able court by which the case was decided, correctly express the general rule of law. We do not believe that the board of directors is, in name or in power, the corporation, for as we have elsewhere shown,[3] the board is the representative of the corporation. The courts do certainly apply to corporate directors the rule *respondeat*

---

[1] Beveridge *v.* New York El. R. Co., 112 N. Y. 1. It was held in the case cited that an agreement on the part of the lessor company, made in good faith and on account of the financial embarrassment of the lessee, to reduce the amount of rental under the lease, is within the powers of the directors. We think that some of the statements in the opinion made in the case above cited, and in the cases of Leslie *v.* Lorillard, 110 N. Y. 536, and Hoyt *v.* Thomson's Ex., 19 N. Y. 216, go much too far. We do not believe that merely conferring upon the board of directors the power to manage corporate affairs constitutes the board the corporation or invests it with power to make fundamental or organic changes in the constitution of the corporation. If it can be said that the statute vests the whole and entire power of conducting the corporate business in the board of directors, including that of radically changing the corporate objects, then it may properly be held that a lease of the whole road may be made without the concurrence or assent of the stockholders, but if the power is to manage ordinary corporate affairs, we think the assent of the stockholders is necessary.

[2] Beveridge *v.* New York, etc., R.Co., 112 N. Y. 1.

[3] *Ante*, §§ 236, 237, 249, 252, 254.

superior, and this is a recognition of the fact that they are the mere agents of the corporation.[1] Their powers to a great extent are delegated and not original powers. Doubtless the directors do acquire power from the corporate charter, but not such power as is required to make an organic and fundamental change in the objects and purposes of a corporation.[2] The object of the formation of a railroad company is to itself operate the road and not to lease to another company and thereby

---

[1] The New York cases assert the doctrine stated in the text. Abbott *v.* American Hard Rubber Co., 33 Barb. 578; Cumberland, etc.,Co. *v.* Sherman, 30 Barb. 553; Metropolitan, etc., Co. *v.* Manhattan, etc., Co., 15 Am. & Eng. R. Cas. 1; Twin, etc., Co. *v.* Marbury, 91 U. S. 587; Angell & A. Corp., § 771; Stark Bank *v.* United States, etc., Co., 34 Vt. 144; State *v.* Smith, 48 Vt. 266; Branch Bank *v.* Collins, 7 Ala. 95; Simons *v.* Vulcan Oil, etc., Co., 61 Pa. St. 202, s. c. 100 Am. Dec. 628; Brokaw *v.* New Jersey, etc., Co., 32 N. J. Law 328, s. c. 90 Am. Dec. 659; Bank of Middlebury *v.* Rutland, etc., Co., 30 Vt. 159; Lindley Company Law, (5th ed.) 155; Burmester *v.* Norris, 6 Exch. 796; Colman *v.* Eastern, etc., R. Co., 10 Beav. 1; Rollins *v.* Clay, 33 Me. 132; Clay *v.* Rufford, 19 Eng. L. & E. 350.

[2] Railroad Co. *v.* Allerton, 18 Wall. (U. S.) 233; Cass *v.* Manchester, etc., R. Co., 9 Fed. R. 640; Penobscott, etc., R. Co. *v.* Dunn, 39 Me. 587; Bedford, etc., Co. *v.* Bowser, 48 Pa. St. 29; Burke *v.* Smith,16 Wall.390; Bank *v.* St.John, 25 Ala. 566; Alford *v.* Miller, 32 Conn. 543; Marlborough, etc., Co. *v.* Smith, 2 Conn. 579; White Mountain, etc., Co. *v.* Eastman, 34 N. H. 124; Gill *v.* Balis, 72 Mo. 424; State *v.* Chamber of Commerce, 20 Wis. 68; Alford *v.* Miller, 32 Conn. 543. Mr. Taylor ably discusses the general subject; says that there are four things the board of directors can not do, and affirms that it "can not, ordinarily, lease the whole plant of the corporation," and refers to Cass *v.* Manchester, etc., Co., 9 Fed. R. 640. See Taylor Priv. Corp., § 229. The case referred to directly decides that even if the corporation has authority to lease its property the board of directors can not execute a lease if the stockholders protest. In Stevens *v.* Davison, 18 Gratt. 819, s. c. 98 Am. Dec. 692, the court held that a lease does involve a franchise, and that it could not be executed by the board of directors under a statute providing that no contract shall be made "involving the franchise of said road," without the consent of the stockholders. See Kersey, etc., Co. *v.* Oil Creek, etc., R., 12 Phila. 374; Bedford, etc., R. Co. *v.* Bowser, 48 Pa. St. 29, 37; Penobscott, etc., R. Co. *v.* Dunn, 39 Me. 587, 601. Judge Rorer says that, "The leasing of a railroad with authority in the lessee to take tolls involves the franchise and requires the action and consent of the stockholders formally expressed, at a stockholders' meeting." Rorer on Railroads 603. The opinion of Mr. Wood is thus expressed: "The consent of a majority of the stockholders, fairly obtained, is always essential to the validity of a lease. The consent must be expressed at a stockholders' meeting." 3 Wood on Railroads (2d ed.) 2053, note.

cease to conduct the business for which the corporation was organized and assume the position of a landlord. The effect of a railroad lease is an organic change. The law forbids the leasing of a railroad, except where the power is given by express legislative enactment, and one of the grounds upon which this rule of law rests is that the execution of a lease, is an act fundamental and organic in its nature.[1] In granting authority to lease, the legislature grants authority to radically change the character of corporate business, rights and liabilities and it seems to us that the directors must have the concurrence of the stockholders. We do not mean to say that the stockholders can directly execute a lease, but what we mean is that the directors can not execute a lease without the concurrence of the stockholders. The directors must, as we believe, formally execute the contract, and must directly represent and act for the corporation in making it,[2] but they must also have the assent of the stockholders. Where, as we have elsewhere remarked, the board of trustees, or the board of directors is incorporated there is reason for a different rule from that which we have here stated to be the sound one. Incidental or ordinary corporate powers may, as a rule, be exercised by the board of directors without any interference on the part of the stockholders, and a contract for the right to use part of a railroad may, perhaps, be regarded as an ordinary corporate contract,[3] but a lease for a long period of years vesting entire and exclusive possession and control in another corporation is essentially

---

[1] If the power to lease were an ordinary corporate power it would not be necessary to enact a statute conferring the power, but a statute is necessary because the power is in its nature fundamental and organic. Thomas v. West Jersey, etc., R. Co., 101 U. S. 71, and cases cited.

[2] Ante, § 170.

[3] Green Bay, etc., R. Co. v. Union, etc., Co., 107 U. S. 98, s. c. 2 Sup. Ct. R. 221. See Davis v. Old Colony, etc., R. Co., 131 Mass. 258; York, etc., R. Co. v. Winans, 17 How. (U. S.) 30; Pearce v. Madison, etc., Railroad Co., 21 How. 441. See, generally, Eastern, etc., R. Co. v. Hawkes, 5 H. L. Cas. 331, 371–381; Ashbury, etc., Co. v. Riche, L. R. 7 H. L. 653; MacGregor v. Dover, etc., R. Co., 18 Q. B. 618; East Anglian, etc., R. Co. v. Eastern Counties R. Co., 11 C. B. 775.

different from trackage, traffic, or other contracts of a similar nature.

§ 441. **What number of stockholders must assent to the lease.**—Where the statute designates the number of stockholders that must assent to a lease in order to render it effective there is no difficulty, for it is clear that the assent of the prescribed number will make the lease effective, although the number may be less than the whole number of stockholders. But where no number is designated by the statute, and a general authority to lease is granted there is difficulty. Some of the courts hold that where a general authority is granted to execute a lease, the lease is not effective unless the stockholders unanimously assent to its execution.[1] Other courts hold that where there is general authority to execute the lease and no provision is made as to the number that must assent, a majority may authorize the execution of the lease.[2] It seems to us that where the lease transfers the entire road for a long term of years the consent of all the stockholders is required unless the statute otherwise provides. The general rule is that after the shareholders have entered into a contract among themselves, under legislative sanction, and have made investments and expended their money in execution of the plan agreed upon, the plan can not, even by virtue of legislative enactment, be radically changed by the act of a bare majority. A lease does work a radical change in many respects, notably in the respect that the character of the stockholders' investment is radically altered, for the lease places them substantially in the position of a landlord whose income is derived from rents, whereas the income of a stockholder is derived from the profits of the road. There is, however, reason for a different conclusion from that which we favor. A lease for a limited period is not the same thing as a sale, but in cases where the term is a long one it is not very different

---

[1] Mills v. Central R. Co., 41 N. J. Eq. 1. See Boston, etc., R. Co. v. New York, etc., R. Co., 13 R. I. 260; Zabriskie v. Hackensack, etc., R. Co., 18 N. J. Eq. 178.

[2] Inhabitants of Waldoborough v. Knox, etc., R. Co., 84 Me. 469.

in its practical consequences from a sale; for it yields possession and control to the lessee, and takes the entire operation and control from the lessor, although it does not terminate the lessor's ownership. But while the ownership remains, its rights and incidents for the term fixed by the lease are entirely different from those which attach to the ownership of a railroad where there is no lease.

§ 442. Consent of stockholders—Waiver of objections, formal execution of lease.—The provisions of a statute requiring the consent of the stockholders confer a personal privilege which they may waive by acquiescence in a lease executed without their consent.[1] The fact that the board of directors agree upon the terms of the lease before submitting it to the stockholders does not invalidate the lease where the stockholders assent to its execution.[2] Where no special mode for executing a lease is provided by statute, an authorized lease executed in the usual form, or in such a form as to express the contract of the parties will be sufficient.

§ 443. Lease where parties are corporations of different states.—As appears from what has been said in a preceding section, and as is indeed clear upon general principles, in order to make an effective lease, it is necessary that there should be power in the one company to execute a lease and in the other to accept it. If the company to which the lease is made has no power to accept a lease, the lease is ineffective. This principle governs cases where leases are executed by corporations of different states. In a very ably reasoned opinion it was affirmed by the supreme court of the United States that a lease executed by an Illinois railroad company to an Indiana company was not valid for the reason that the Indiana company was not authorized by statute to accept a lease from the Illinois corporation.[3]

[1] St. Louis, etc., R. Co. v. Terre Haute, etc., R. Co., 33 Fed. R. 440, affirmed 145 U. S. 393. The lease had been suffered to stand for seventeen years, and the court held the stockholders barred by laches.

[2] Jones v. Concord, etc., R. Co., (N. H.), s. c. 30 Atl. R. 614.

[3] St. Louis, etc., R. Co. v. Terre Haute, etc., R. Co., 145 U. S. 393, s. c. 12 Sup. Ct. R. 953, 6 Lewis' Am. R. & Corp. R. 439.

§ 444. **Authority to execute lease has no extra-territorial effect.**—State laws, as is well known, have no force or effect outside of the limits of the state. Laws conferring authority upon a corporation to do prescribed acts, operate only upon state corporations. We do not mean, of course, that a state has no control over foreign corporations doing business within its borders; our meaning is that its laws conferring authority upon a corporation do not carry that authority into other states. The principle stated requires the conclusion that a state can not, by chartering a corporation, confer upon it a legal right to act within the jurisdiction of another state,[1] and that authority granted to a corporation to lease its road can not have any effect outside of the state giving such authority.[2] The authority does not extend beyond the state limits. Upon the principle stated, it was held that the charter granted by the state of Kansas to a railroad corporation formed under its laws, conferred upon such corporation no power to lease that part of its road lying in the Indian territory; and that, in the absence of a grant of power to lease contained in the act of Congress authorizing the building of that part of the road, a lease of its whole road would be invalid as to the part lying in the territory.[3]

§ 445. **Rights of foreign lessors.**—The rights of a corporation of one state that becomes the lessee of a railroad of another state are such as are conferred by the laws of the state from which the lessor received its charter.[4] This must necessarily be true, for the lessor derives all its powers from the state in which it was incorporated, and, of course, can grant no other rights than such as were conferred upon it by the statute

---

[1] 2 Morawetz Priv. Corp. (2d ed.), § 958. The law of New Jersey prohibits the lease of a railroad within the state to a foreign corporation, and it is held that under this statute a lease to a domestic corporation whose stock is owned by a foreign corporation is invalid. Stockton v. Central R. Co., 50 N. J. Eq 52.

[2] Oregon R., etc., Co. v. Oregonian R. Co., 130 U. S. 1.

[3] Briscoe v. Southern Kansas R. Co., 40 Fed. R. 273, 40 Am. & Eng. R. Cas. 599.

[4] McCandless v. Richmond, etc., R. Co., 38 S. C. 103, s. c. 61 Am. & Eng. R. Cas. 524.

to which it owes its existence and powers. What the lessor was required to do by the state which created it must be done by its lessee.

§ 446. **Leases to connecting lines.**—In some of the states the statutes grant a right to lease to connecting lines. Where there is such a grant, then, upon the principle that statutes granting authority to execute a lease are to be strictly construed, it is implied that there is no authority to lease to other lines. It is held that under such a statute it is not essential to the validity of a lease that the leased road shall be an extension from either terminus of the main line, but it may be merely a collateral branch, forming a continuous road, by way of the junction, to either terminus of such main line, in as direct a route as the average railroad.[1] The pivotal question under

[1] Hancock v. Louisville, etc., R. Co., 145 U. S. 409, construing the Kentucky Act of January 22, 1858. The court says: "The main line of the lessee's road extends in a northeasterly direction from Louisville to Cincinnati. At Anchorage, about twelve miles east of Louisville, the Shelbyville road touches it. At the time of the lease the latter road was completed from the place of junction to Shelbyville, a distance of about eighteen miles, the general course being a trifle south of east. There was a physical connection between the two roads at Anchorage, the latter being the western terminus of the Shelbyville road. From this point the main line of the lessee road extends northeasterly, and the Shelbyville road southeasterly, making two forks of the letter 'V.' Shelbyville is nearly due east from Louisville, and the Shelbyville road, together with twelve miles of the lessee's road, makes a continuous line between Shelbyville and Louisville in a route about as straight as the average railroad. But Anchorage is not a terminus of the lessee road, and the contention is that, under the statute, the leased line must touch one of the termini of the lessee's road so as to make an extension of it. * * * We think it is enough that by the lease the connected roads form a continuous line, and it is not essential that the leased line be an extension from either terminus of the lessee's road. The evil which was intended to be guarded against by this limitation was the placing of parallel and competing roads under one management and the control by one company of the general railroad affairs of the state through the leasing of roads remote from its own and with which it has no physical or direct business connection. It was not intended to prevent a company with a long road, like the lessee company, from leasing branches by means of which it establishes continuous lines from their several termini to each of its own."

such statutes is whether the line to which the lease is executed is a connecting line.

§ 447. Lease to competing lines—Effect of statutes prohibiting.—Many of the states now provide by general laws for the transfer by lease,[1] of a railroad to another corporation which does not own a parallel or competing line.[2] The effect of these statutes is, generally speaking, to confer power to lease to any other than competing or rival lines, so that the validity of the lease depends upon whether the lines are rival or competing lines within the meaning of the statute. Such statutes are to be strictly construed; as some of the courts say, a railroad company is required to "be able to point to the exact provisions granting authority" to make any given lease.[3] It is clear from the trend of the judicial decisions that as in favor of the power to lease, there is no elasticity in such statutes. A statute authorizing a railroad to lease its track to another company, when the respective lines "are continuous or connected," authorizes a lease only when the two roads form one continu-

---

[1] Stimson's Am. Stat. (1892), § 8722.

[2] Leases of parallel or competing lines are forbidden by the constitutions of Pennsylvania, West Virginia, Missouri, Arkansas and Texas. Stimson's Am. Stat., § 467. A line of railroad may be competing within the meaning of a statute which forbids railroad companies from purchasing or leasing a competing line, though the competing points are reached by trackage arrangements with other lines. Hafer v. Cincinnati, H. & D. R. Co., (Ohio Com. Pl.) 29 Wkly. Law Bul. 68.

[3] State, ex rel., v. Atchison, etc., R. Co., 24 Neb. 143; Pennsylvania, etc., R. Co. v. St. Louis, etc., R. Co., 118 U. S. 290. A railroad corporation, whose power of eminent domain necessary to the construction of a branch road conferred by charter is extinct by reason of non-user during the term prescribed for its exercise, can not purchase or lease the branch road subsequently built, on the foundation of the right of eminent domain which is extinct. Such lease is therefore *ultra vires*. Camden & A. R. Co. v. May's Landing & E. H. C. R. Co., 48 N. J. L. 530, 7 Atl. R. 523. It was held that neither Rev. St. Ohio, § 3300, providing that any railroad may lease or purchase the road of another company, not competing, nor § 3409, providing that a company, not able to complete the construction of its line, may transfer its property to another, which transfer "shall include all work done, together with all rights, privileges, and easements," confers authority to sell and transfer a company's contracts of subscription payable on completion of the road. Toledo, C. & St. L. R. Co. v. Hinsdale, 45 Ohio 556, 15 N. E. 665.

ous line, between points not otherwise connected by either separately,[1] over which freight and passengers may be carried without transfer.[2] The principle asserted by the courts in the cases referred to, as in many others, forbids transfers to rival lines except where the statute clearly and unequivocally confers the right to make such transfers, but where there is statutory power the transfer to a rival line is valid.[3] It is held that a statute which forbids railroad companies to purchase or lease competing lines renders void a lease of a railroad by another, which reaches competing points by means of trackage arrangements with other lines.[4]

§ 448. Effect of executing unauthorized lease.—The au-

[1] State, ex rel., v. Atchison, etc., R. Co., 24 Neb. 143; Smith v. Reading City, etc., R. Co., 13 Pa. Co. Ct. R. 49. Two lines which can not be operated together without a transfer of passengers and freight do not form a "continuous line." Hampe v. Mt. Oliver I. R. Co., (Pa. Com. Pl.) 24 Pittsb. Leg. J. (N. S.) 330.

[2] State v. Vanderbilt, 37 Ohio St. 590.

[3] In the case of the Catawissa, etc., R. Co. v. Philadelphia, etc., R. Co., 14 Pa. Co. R. 280, it was held that where one railroad company acquired, by virtue of a valid lease, the right to the railroad of another company, the former, in building a line parallel with the road acquired, did not violate the constitutional provision, prohibiting one company from acquiring the rights of a parallel and competing road. In the course of the opinion, it was said: "Was it in any sense a competing road the acquisition of which is prohibited by Article XVII, of the constitution. The object of the prohibition was clearly to prevent one independent corporation from acquiring the possession of the road of another company, which is operating a competing line. It was to prevent the buying up by one railroad corporation of a competing line and the establishment thereby of a monopoly. The building of one road by another for the purpose of facilitating and enlarging its own business, can by no fair process of reasoning be contended to be within the constitutional prohibition, unless, indeed, a man be said to compete with himself, when he enlarges his own business or enters into a new one."

[4] Hafer v. Cincinnati, etc., R. Co. (Ohio Com. Pls., 1893), 29 Weekly Law Bul. 68. In the case of Louisville, etc., R. Co. v. Commonwealth, (Ky.) 31 S. W. R. 476, it was held that a statute authorizing a railroad company to purchase and own a road constructed by another company did not confer authority to purchase a competing line in violation of a constitutional provision adopted subsequent to the enactment of the statute prohibiting railroad companies from purchasing competing lines. See Missouri Pacific, etc., Co. v. Sidell, 67 Fed. R. 464.

thorities generally affirm that an unauthorized lease is void,[1] but some of the cases seem to hold that rent provided for by such a lease may be recovered where the road is operated under the lease and benefit is actually received by the company which has possession and use of the road. Our opinion, elsewhere expressed and elaborated, is that such a lease is void[2] and no recovery can be had upon it, but that in the proper case there may perhaps be a recovery upon an implied contract. Some of the courts hold that the abandonment of its road to the lessee is sufficient grounds for the institution of *quo warranto* proceedings on the part of the state.[3]

§ 449. Lease—Construction.—The doctrine of some of the courts is that the terms of a lease made under legislative authority will be strictly construed, and their meaning will not be extended by implication.[4] We can see no reason, however, for applying to railroad leases any other rules of construction than those which govern in the construction of

---

[1] We think that principle and authority require the conclusion that the unauthorized lease by which a railroad seeks to turn over its entire road to another is *ultra vires* and void, and may be set aside at the suit of a dissenting stockholder. Ante, §§ 368, 373.

[2] State, *ex rel.*, v. Atchison, etc., R. Co., 24 Neb. 143. An Illinois railroad corporation is bound to take notice that its lease to an Indiana corporation is *ultra vires* of the latter, so that, where the lease becomes an executed contract by the delivery of the leased property, the lessor is *in pari delicto* with the lessee, and can not maintain a suit to recover possession. So far as the lessor corporation can be regarded as representing its nonconsenting stockholders in their efforts to set aside the lease, it and they are barred by laches in failing to bring an action to set it aside for seventeen years, and by accepting the rentals during that time. St. Louis, V. & T. H. R. Co. v. Terre Haute & I. R. Co., 145 U. S. 393.

[3] Board Comrs. Tippecanoe Co. v. Lafayette, etc., R. Co., 50 Ind. 85. But, it is held that a contract whereby another railroad is permitted to use a track jointly with the lessor, in such a manner as not to interfere with the lessor's use thereof, is valid unless expressly forbidden. Union Pac. R. Co. v. Chicago, etc., R. Co., 51 Fed. Rep. 309. Such a contract is not within the rule forbidding a railroad company from transferring property essential to the performance of its corporate duties, since the company does not by permitting another company to make a limited and qualified use of its tracks, disable itself from performing the duties imposed upon it by law.

[4] Chicago, etc., R. Co. v. Denver, etc., R. Co., 143 U. S. 596.

similar contracts executed under statutory authority. The terms must, of course, be such as the statute authorizes, but, within the limits of the power conferred, the contracting parties may agree upon such terms and conditions as they deem proper, provided, of course, no rule of law is violated.

§ 450. **Lease—Dependent and independent contracts.**—The question whether a contract relating to a lease and in a measure connected with it is dependent or independent, is sometimes an important one, for a lease may be void and the contract relating to the same subject, executed by the same parties, may be valid.[1] If the contract is independent of the lease it may be valid, although the lease is void. Reference in the independent contract to the lease does not necessarily make the lease part of it, but, of couse, the reference may be such as to incorporate the lease in the contract, and whether it does or not is to be determined in each particular case from the language employed in the instrument.[2] Whether the contract is or is not a dependent one depends, of course, upon the language employed by the parties, and the ordinary doctrines of law, applicable to the subject of dependent and independent contract provisions govern cases in which the construction of such leases are involved and supply the rules of decision. In an Illinois case, the agreement in the form of a lease was that the

---

[1] Pittsburgh, etc., R. Co. v. Keokuk, etc., Co., 155 U. S. 156; Pittsburgh, etc., R. Co. v. Keokuk, etc., Co., 131 U. S. 371, s. c. 39 Am. & Eng. R. Cas. 213.

[2] Pittsburgh, etc., R. Co. v. Keokuk, etc., Co., 131 U. S. 371, s. c. 39 Am. & Eng. R. Cas. 213. Ordinarily the reference would make the lease part of the contract. The maxim is, "Instruments to which reference is made in another instrument have the same effect and operation as if they were inserted in the clause referring to them." In applying this ancient and well-settled rule in the case of Fitmaurice v. Bayley, 9 H. L. Cases 78, Compton, J., said: "By referring in a document signed by the party to another document, the person so signing in effect signs a document containing the terms of the one referred to." The rule applies to references made by acts of parliament. North British, etc., Co. v. Tod, 12 Cl. & Fin. 722; Ware v. Regents's Canal Co., 28 L. J. Ch. 153; Galwey v. Baker, 5 Cl. & Fin. 157; Brain v. Harris, 10 Exch. 908; Reg. v. Caledonia R. C., 16 Q. B. 19.

CORP. 38

railroad company should deliver to the other party a designated quantity of grain, which the other should accept and store, and it was held that the promises to deliver and to accept and store were dependent promises.[1] Covenants in leases executed by railroad companies are construed and enforced as are covenants in leases executed by natural persons, that is, the same general principles of law govern in such cases,[2] but the nature of the business of such companies and the limited powers with which they are invested, necessarily render their leases different in some respects from those of natural persons. A reasonable construction is to be given covenants in railroad leases and such covenants are held to require that to be done, which "is reasonable and which would be so accounted by reasonable men."[3] In a New Hampshire case, the subject of covenants in leases executed by one railroad company to another is very fully discussed, and the effect of such covenants clearly stated.[4] Where the contracting parties have, by a settled course of dealing, given a construction to the lease, that construction will be upheld by the courts, unless it is in violation of the clear words of the contract or infringes the rights of others.

[1] Dunlap v. Chicago, etc., R. Co., 151 Ill. 409, citing Hough v. Rawson, 17 Ill. 588; Porter v. Rose, 12 Johns. 209.

[2] Boston, etc., R. Co. v. Boston, etc., R. Co., 65 N. H. 393, s. c. 51 Am. & Eng. R. Cas. 106.

[3] In the case of Catawissa, etc., R. Co. v. Philadelphia, etc., R. Co., 14 Pa. Co. Ct. R. 280, the lease contained a covenant that the lessee should maintain the leased road in good condition, operate it with reasonable care, and "use all proper and reasonable means to maintain and increase the business thereof." It was held that this covenant was not broken by the construction of a parallel road. The court said, *inter alia:* "The defendants are required to use all reasonable means to maintain and increase the business of the road. This means that they will do what is usually accounted reasonable, and what ought to be so accounted by reasonable men. It is difficult, perhaps impossible, to bring within the limits of a precise definition exactly what is required by an undertaking in such general terms. It can only be determined when questions arise in regard to the particular actions and conduct of the party, and their result." We agree with the court that the solution of the question generally depends upon the facts of the particular case, but it seems to us that a covenant such as that contained in the lease before the court prohibits the lessee from building a road parallel with that leased to it.

[4] Boston, etc., R. Co. v. Boston, etc., R. Co., 65 N. H. 393, s. c. 51 Am. & Eng. R. Cas. 106.

Thus, where a railroad company which has granted to another company the right to the joint use of its track and depots, allows the grantee and assignee of the latter to enter upon and continue in such possession and use, it is practically a construction of the power of the company to assign its rights under the contract.[1]

§ 451. **Contract to permit use of track not necessarily a lease.**—A contract between two railroad companies wherein one company agrees to permit another company to use its tracks, station, buildings or the like, is not necessarily a lease within the meaning of the rule prohibiting a railroad company from transferring its property by way of lease. There is a distinction between a lease and a traffic, or trackage contract.[2] A lease transfers control from the lessor to the lessee, and the former is thereby disabled from performing the duties imposed upon it by law, whereas a contract granting the privilege of using tracks, station buildings and the like does not divest the company granting such use or control, nor disable it from discharging its corporate duties or exercising its corporate functions.[3] There is solid foundation for the distinction between

---

[1] Chicago, etc., R. Co. v. Denver, etc., R. Co., 46 Fed. R. 145.

[2] *Ante*, §§ 356, 357, 358, 359; Union Pac. R. Co. v. Chicago, etc., R. Co., 51 Fed. R. 309, s. c. 2 C. C. A. 174, 51 Am. & Eng. R. Cas. 162; Chicago, etc., Co. v. Union Pac. Co., 47 Fed. R. 15. See Langley v. Railroad Co., 10 Gray 103; Humphreys v. St. Louis, etc., R. Co., 37 Fed. R. 307. A contract wherein one company agrees to permit another company at the expense of the latter to connect with the main track of the former, the object being to facilitate an interchange of business, is more than a mere revocable license. It is an enforceable contract founded on a valuable consideration. Louisville, etc., R. Co. v. Kentucky, etc., Co., 95 Ky. 550, 26 S. W. R. 532.

[3] The reasoning upon which a denial of the right of a railroad company to transfer its property and franchises so as to disable itself to perform its public duties is based does not, it is obvious, apply to a contract whereby a railroad company lets another company into joint possession of part of its line for a term of years at an agreed rental; and such a contract is not, as between the parties, *ultra vires*, where such joint possession does not interfere with the present use of such line by the company that owns it. Chicago, etc., R. Co. v. Union Pac. R. Co., 47 Fed. R. 15, affi'd, 51 Fed. R. 309, 10 U. S. App. 98. It has been held that a contract whereby a railroad company is granted "the perpetual and free use" of the right of way of another railroad company, within a specified distance, means that the

a contract whereby one company simply permits use to be made of its railroad, and a contract whereby the one company transfers to the other its railroad through the instrumentality of a lease. The right to do such things as are reasonably necessary to the successful operation of a railroad is implied in the grant of a franchise to build and operate a railroad, and it may well be held in cases where the object to be attained advances the interests of the contracting companies and the contract which they enter into does not disable either from performing its corporate duties, that in making such a contract the companies have not exceeded the power conferred upon them. There is, it is obvious, no rule of public policy which forbids one company from granting to another a mere right to use tracks, depots or the like. If, however, under the guise of a contract permitting one company to use the property of another, there should, in fact, be a transfer from one to the other, the contract would be *ultra vires*, and against public policy.

§ 452. **Traffic contract—Not valid if it is in effect a lease.**—A traffic contract may be rightfully entered into, but, under the guise of a traffic contract, a railway company can not, except where the statute authorizes it, turn over its road to another company. In other words, a railroad company can not, under the form of a traffic contract, make a lease of its road, except where there is statutory authority to execute the lease.[1] If the professed traffic contract is, in fact, a lease, it is *ultra vires*, but where the contract is in the proper sense a traffic contract, then, as we believe, it may be effective.

grantee of such privilege is to have, not merely the uninterrupted use of such right of way but is to have it free of compensation. Alabama G. S. R. Co. *v.* South & N. A. R. Co., 84 Ala. 570, 5 Am. St. Rep. 401.

[1] In the case of Nashua, etc., R. Co. *v.* Boston, etc., 164 Mass. 222, s. c. 41 N. E. 268, the question was stated but not decided. The court, however, referred to the cases of Burke *v.* Concord, etc., R. Co., 61 N. H. 160, and Boston, etc., R. Co. *v.* Boston, etc., R. Co., 65 N. H. 393, s. c. 23 Atl. R. 529. In the first of the cases cited the court held that the joint manager of two roads both operated by one company under a contract had no right to use the joint funds in improving the road of the operating company and that the other company might recover it in a proper action In support of this ruling the court cited Slater Woollen Co. *v.* Lamb, 143

§ 453. **Contracts granting right to use—Effect and construction of.**—It is held that an agreement between two railroad companies, conferring on each the right to run its cars over the tracks of the other, each retaining absolute control over its road for all other purposes, confers no interest which can be assigned or leased.[1] It is obvious that such a contract can not be regarded as a lease since there is nothing more than an agreement permitting one company to use the tracks of another, but it is difficult to determine just what the specific nature of the contract is and what are the rights of the parties. It is a contract for joint use, and the company owning the road does not fully part with possession or control, so that the rights and obligations of the parties are not the same as those of a lessor and lessee in an authorized lease. Some of the courts hold that an agreement by one railroad company that another, "and its assigns," may use one of its tracks on certain conditions, is a mere license and not a lease.[2] We incline

Mass. 420, s. c. 9 N. E. R. 823; Nims v. Mount Hermon, etc., 160 Mass. 177, s. c. 35 N. E. R. 776; L'Herbette v. Pittsfield, etc., Bank, 162 Mass. 137, s. c. 38 N. E. R. 368; Central, etc., Co. v. Pullman's, etc., Co., 139 U. S. 24, s. c. 11 Sup. Ct. R. 478; Manchester, etc., R. Co. v. Concord, etc., R. Co., 66 N. H. 100, s. c. 20 Atl. R. 383; Central Trust Co. v. Ohio, etc., R. Co., 23 Fed. R. 306.

[1] Brooklyn Crosstown R. Co. v. Brooklyn City R. Co., 51 Hun (N. Y.) 600.

[2] Coney Island, etc., R. Co. v. Brooklyn Cable Co., 53 Hun (N. Y.) 169. In a reported case the president of the plaintiff railroad company testified that the vice-president of the defendant railroad company promised that plaintiff should have, free of charge, full terminal facilities at the junction of the two roads. A director of plaintiff testified that it was asssumed, rather than expressly agreed, that plaintiff should have such terminal facilities. Several officers of plaintiff testified that they had heard of no claim that said agreement had been made until about twenty years after the organization of plaintiff, when it was deprived of such terminal facilities. It appeared that the plaintiff company had been operated by defendant for five years, and that on being reorganized, it consented that a charge should be made for the use of the terminal facilities; that at a subsequent reorganization a higher charge was paid for eighteen months; and that two years later the charge was increased, and one payment made under protest. No action was ever taken by the directors of either company upon the subject. It was held, in an action for damages for severing the connection between the two companies, and depriving the plaintiff of such facilities, that the evidence justified a finding that the agreement was

to the opinion that where there is a valid consideration for such an agreement it is not a mere revocable license but is an enforceable contract.[1] If there is a sufficient consideration for the agreement, we can see no reason why it should not be regarded as a contract in all that the term implies. If, however, there is no consideration the agreement may well be treated as a mere license. If there is nothing more than a license then there is reason for holding that the licensee can not enjoy the privileges conferred by such agreement and at the same time confer the right to do so on other companies, since this would be to impose greater burdens on the licensor than the agreement contemplated.[2] We do not believe that there can be an assignment, even if there be a contract, where the original company also retains the right to make use of the right or privilege granted it, for the grant implies that the right to exercise the privilege is only conferred upon the company to which it is granted. The parties may, of course, provide for an assignment by the stipulations of their contract.

§ 454. Part performance—Effect of.—The partial performance of a contract of lease, executed without legislative authority, confers no rights under the lease. Thus, where a void lease is made by a railroad company for a term of ninety-six years, at a certain yearly rental, the use of the road by the lessee and payment of the rental for three years, does not make the contract so far an executed one as to estop the lessee to deny its validity.[3] This doctrine results from the principle elsewhere

temporary and permissive only. Port Jervis, etc., R. Co. v. New York, etc., R. Co., 132 N. Y. 439. Where one railroad company has permission by parol to extend its track upon the right of way of another company for the purpose of making a connection, such permission is a mere license, and, although valuable improvements have been made, may be revoked at the will of the licensing company. Richmond & D. R. Co. v. Durham & N. R. Co., 104 N. C. 658, 40 Am. & Eng. R. Cas. 488.

[1] Louisville, etc., R. Co. v. Kentucky, etc., R. Co., (Ky.), 26 S. W. R. 532.

[2] Coney Island, etc., R. Co. v. Brooklyn Cable Co., 53 Hun 169.

[3] Oregon Ry. & Nav. Co. v. Oregonian Ry. Co., 130 U. S. 1, s. c. 9 Sup. Ct. R. 409; Oregon Ry. & Nav. Co. v. Oregonian Ry. Co., 145 U. S. 52, s. c. 12 Sup. Ct. R. 814.

considered that where the contract is, in a proper sense, *ultra vires*, no right can be founded on the contract itself. If the contract be absolutely void and not merely voidable, it can not be made effective by the acts of the contracting parties.[1]

§ 455. **Duration of a lease.**—Where there is no authority to sell, there is, as it seems to us, no right to execute a lease the practical effect of which is equivalent to a sale.[2] This principle would prohibit a railroad company from leasing its road for such a length of time as would clearly deprive it of possession and use for a palpably unreasonable period. We do not believe that a transfer can be made which is in substance a sale, although in form a lease. Of course, where there is authority to sell, a sale may be made. It has been held in New York that a lease of its road by a railroad company for a longer term than the period of its corporate existence is not void, since the laws of that state provide for an extension of the charter.[3] There is, as it seems to us, reason for the conclusion that a railroad corporation can not make a lease extending beyond its corporate life. One would think that in authorizing a lease the legislature had in mind the statute fixing the duration of corporate existence, and that it did not mean that any corporate act should be effective after corporate death.

§ 456. **Effect of lease on taxation.**—Where the statute authorizes the execution of a lease and also provides that the leased road shall become the property of the lessee company, the road is assessable as the property of the lessee and not as the property of the lessor.[4] It may well be doubted whether

[1] *Ante*, §§ 372, 383, and §§ 356, 357, 358, 359.

[2] St. Louis, etc., R. Co. v. Terre Haute, etc., R. Co., 145 U. S. 393, s. c. 12 Sup. Ct. R. 953, and cases cited.

[3] Gere v. New York Cent., etc., R. Co., 19 Abb. N. C. 193. The fact that a lease by a railroad company was for 999 years, while the charter of the *lessee* would expire in about forty years, did not render it void, especially as the charter contained a provision that it might be renewed from time to time, and as the lease was expressly made binding upon the assigns and successors of the parties. Union Pac. R. Co. v. Chicago, etc., R. Co., 51 Fed. R. 309, 10 U. S. App. 98.

[4] Huck v. Chicago, etc., R.,Co., 86 Ill. 352; Hagan v. Hardie, 8 Heisk. 812. See,generally, Philadelphia, etc., R. Co. v. Appeal Tax Court, 50 Md.

this result would follow where the lessor remains the owner and only transfers the road for a limited time. If the lessor remains the owner the principle which ordinarily prevails would require that taxes be assessed against it and not against its lessee. We suppose that where there is simply an authority to lease and no provision vesting the lessee with the ownership the property must be treated for the purpose of taxation as that of the lessor. Authority to execute a lease implies that the lessor retains the ownership of the demised property, but grants to the lessee use, possession and control for a designated term. A person, natural or artificial, who executes a lease, does not sell or convey the property, but simply transfers use, possession and control for the term designated in the lease. It is competent for the legislature in conferring authority to lease to prescribe the terms and conditions upon which the authority shall be exercised, and hence it may provide that the lessee company shall be treated as the owner or that it shall pay all taxes. In every authorized lease there are two estates, that of the lessor and that of the lessee, and where both are of value both may be assessed, but each estate must be assessed against its owner unless the statute otherwise provides. It is probably true that if under the form of a lease a sale is made, the company acquiring the property is liable to taxation as owner,[1] but to have this effect the contract, although in form a lease, must be, in legal contemplation, a sale. Where the statute provides for a tax upon the earnings of the road the lessee company is, ordinarily, the party against which the assessment should be made.[2] The earnings are part of the estate of the lessee company and not of the estate of the lessor. The earn-

---

397; Appeal Tax Court v. Western, etc., R. Co., 50 Md. 274. Such a contract is practically a contract of sale, or rather, in its practical effect is equivalent to a sale in cases where the term is one of great length; while nominally a lease it is practically a sale in its effects and consequences. Where the contract is for a short term it is a lease rather than a sale, but if for a great number of years it would be substantially a sale of the property. St. Louis, etc., R. Co. v. Penn. Co., 118 U. S. 290.

[1] Commonwealth v. Nashville, etc., R. Co., 93 Ky. 430, s. c. 54 Am. & Eng. R. Cas. 254.

[2] Vermont, etc., R. Co. v. Vermont, etc., R. Co., 63 Vt. 1, s. c. 46 Am. & Eng. R. Cas. 646.

ings are derived from the possession and use of the road, and hence are the property of the lessee. The question, however, is one depending almost entirely upon the statute governing the particular case, for, as we have said, the legislature may lay the tax upon either company as it deems proper, since it has full power to prescribe the terms and conditions upon which the authority to lease shall be exercised.

§ 457. **Public duties of lessee under an unauthorized lease— Mandamus.**—It by no means follows from the rule that the lessee operating a road under an unauthorized lease is liable for torts in the management of the leased road, that it can be compelled to perform the duties imposed upon the lessor company. It is evident that it may be liable for its torts in operating the road and yet not bound to perform the obligations which the law requires the lessor to perform. If the lease is void it neither confers a right nor creates a duty. In a well reasoned opinion it was adjudged that where a lease was executed without authority the lessee could not be compelled to operate the leased road and that mandamus would not lie.[1]

§ 458. **Authorized lease—Duty of lessee to operate the road —Mandamus.**—Where the lease is authorized a very different question is presented from that which arises in cases where the lease is unauthorized. If it is the imperative duty of the lessor company to operate the road and it has no discretionary power in the matter and that duty was transferred to the lessee by the lease, it would seem clear that the lessee could be compelled by mandamus to perform the duty. This conclusion is supported by decisions in analogous cases.[2] It is settled that a railroad

---

[1] People v. Colorado, etc., R. Co., 42 Fed. R. 638. In the course of the opinion Caldwell, J., said: "As the relator and the respondents are agreed that the lease was void that ends the case as to the Union Pacific Railroad Company, for if the lease is void it imposes no obligation on the Union Pacific Railroad Company to operate the road." The decision was placed on the ground that the lease was void, for it was affirmed that mandamus lies where there is a duty to operate a railroad. The court cited State v. Sioux City, etc., R. Co., 7 Neb. 357; Commonwealth v. Fitchburgh, etc., R. Co., 12 Gray 180.

[2] State v. Sioux City, etc., R. Co., 7

company in possession of its road may be compelled by mandamus to operate its road in accordance with the positive requirements of its charter, and we can see no reason why this principle should not apply to a company in full possession of a road under an authorized lease. In authorizing the lease the legislature empowered the transfer of the duty of operating the road to the lessee, and, with the duty, authorized the transfer of important rights and privileges, so that the duty of the lessee accepting the lease with its benefits becomes imperative. The lessor having rightfully transferred possession to the lessee company can not operate the road, and hence the duty necessarily devolves on the lessee.[1]

§ 459. **Lessee not liable for wrongs committed prior to the execution of the lease.**—The lessee does not become liable for injuries inflicted by the lessor before the execution of the lease, unless it expressly assumes such liability.[2] Where there is an assumption of liability the extent and nature of the liability of the lessee company depends upon the provisions of the contract. In saying that the lessee is not liable for wrongs committed prior to the execution of the lease we do not mean to convey the impression that for a continuing wrong the lessee is not liable, for our opinion is that where the lessor company is the original wrong-doer and the lessee continues the wrong after the execu-

Neb. 357; Commonwealth v. Fitchburg, etc., R. Co., 12 Gray 180; Farmers', etc., Co. v. Henning, 17 Am. Law Reg. (N. S.) 266; State v. Nebraska Tel. Co., 17 Neb. 126; Mobile, etc., R. Co. v. Wisdom, 5 Heisk. 125; State v. Hartford, etc., R. Co., 29 Conn. 538; Union Pacific R. Co. v. Hall, 91 U. S. 343; King v. Severn, etc., R. Co., 2 Barn. & Ald. 646; People v. Albany, etc., Co., 24 N. Y. 261; People v. Rome, etc., R. Co., 103 N. Y. 95; Railroad Commissioners v. Portland, etc., R. Co., 63 Me. 269; State v. New Haven, etc., R. Co., 41 Conn. 134; New Haven, etc., R. Co. v. State 44 Conn. 376; Chicago, etc., R. Co. v. People, 56 Ill. 365; Chicago, etc., R. Co. v. Crane, 113 U. S. 424; People v. New York, etc., R. Co., 28 Hun 543; Talcott v. Township of Pine Grove, 1 Flip. 120.

[1] There may, possibly, be exceptional cases, as where the operation of a line would exhaust the corporate capital, in which a mandamus would not lie. Commonwealth v. Fitchburg, etc., R. Co., 12 Gray 180. But where there is not a clear, valid and sufficient reason shown excusing the company there can, as we believe, be no doubt of the power to coerce a performance of duty by mandamus.

[2] Pittsburgh, etc., R. Co. v. Kain, 35 Ind. 291; Little Miami, etc., R. Co. v. Hambleton, 40 Ohio St. 496.

tion of the lease it is liable.[1] But this rule can not apply where there was a single transient wrong and the injury was complete prior to the execution of the lease.

§ 460. **Effect of a lease upon rights of creditors.**—The question whether a railroad company which acquires by an authorized lease all the property of another company, can hold the property free from the claims of the general or unsecured creditors of the lessor company, is not entirely free from difficulty.[2] If the lessee acts in good faith, and the lease is such as the law authorizes it to take and its lessor to execute, it certainly does acquire valuable property rights. Where there is good faith, no liens, no notice, actual or constructive, and the lease is one the lessor has authority to execute and the lessee to accept, it is difficult to perceive any solid ground upon which the rights of the lessee can be subordinated to the claims of general or unsecured creditors. If the lessee company acts in bad faith, or if it secures property under such circumstances as to make it equitably chargeable as a trustee, then equity will so charge it, and will decree that the avails of property received under such circumstances may be applied to the payment of the claims of the creditors of the lessor company.[3] But we very

---

[1] Little Miami, etc., R. Co. v. Hambleton, 40 Ohio St. 496.

[2] Mr. Minor says that "A railroad company in debt can not transfer its entire property by lease so as to prevent the application of it, at its full value, to the debts of the company, and when such a transfer is made, a court of equity may decree a payment of a judgment debt of the lessor by the lessee." 19 Am. & Eng. Ency. 898. For the reasons given in the text, we respectfully suggest that Mr. Minor's statement is too broad. It may perhaps be true that a judgment debtor can reach the property in the hands of the lessee, for a judgment is notice, but where there is no judgment or lien of any kind it can not be justly said that the rights of the creditors are superior to those of the lessee.

[3] Chicago, etc., R. Co. v. Third National Bank, 134 U. S. 276, s. c. 10 Sup. Ct. R. 550, citing Central R., etc., Co. v. Pettus, 113 U. S. 116, 124, s. c. 5 Sup. Ct. R. 387; Mellen v. Moline, etc., Iron Works, 131 U. S. 352, 366, s. c. 9 Sup. Ct. R. 981. See, also, Chicago, etc., R. Co. v. Third National Bank, 26 Fed. R. 820. In the case first cited the question we are here dealing with was stated, but not decided. We quote from the opinion the following. "Can a corporation in debt transfer its entire property by lease, so as to prevent the application of the property at its full value, to the satisfaction of its debts? We do not care to pursue an

much doubt whether it can be deprived of the leased property in a case where it is entirely free from fault or wrong, and takes the property under an authorized lease. Doubtless a court of equity would make such a decree in the particular case as the principles of equity require, but it seems to us that it would not decree that the claims of unsecured creditors are in all cases paramount to the rights of the lessee. The rights of creditors should be protected, as far as it can be done, without depriving the lessee of its rights, but the rights of the lessee when it is entirely free from fault are entitled to protection.

§ 461. **Authorized lease, rights and duties to which lessee company succeeds.**—What are known as "prerogative franchises" do not pass to the lessee under an unauthorized lease, but such rights as are necessary to the operation of the road and the conduct of its affairs do pass to the lessee.[1] In other words, the lessee company, under such a lease, succeeds to the charter rights of the lessor company, so far as such rights are necessary to the operation of the road under the lease.[2] In granting the principal, that is, the right to lease, the incidental inquiry into this question at length, or consider what limitations would surround this doctrine as applied generally, preferring to notice a single matter which is significant and decisive."

[1] The execution of a lease does not, ordinarily, confer upon the lessee the franchise to be a corporation nor a franchise to take property under the power of eminent domain; but the legislature may, perhaps, by express and apt words confer such franchises. Such franchises do not pass under authority conferred in general terms to execute a lease. The general authority does not imply that the lessee shall take such high prerogative franchises, although it does imply that the lessee shall have power to do such things as are reasonably necessary to enable it to properly operate the road.

[2] Fisher v. New York Central R. Co., 46 N. Y. 644, where the lessee was held entitled to charge such rates as were legal for the company owning the leased line. But the right to appropriate property under the right of eminent domain does not pass to the lessee. Mayor v. Norwich, etc., R. Co., 109 Mass. 103; Chicago, etc., R. Co. v. Illinois Central R. Co., 113 Ill. 156. In Nebraska it is permitted to institute proceedings in the name of the lessor. Dietrichs v. Lincoln, etc., R. Co., 13 Neb. 361; Gottschalk v. Lincoln, etc., R. Co., 14 Neb. 389. See Kip v. New York, etc., R. Co., 67 N. Y. 227. See Chattanooga R. Co. v. Felton, 69 Fed. R. 273.

rights essential to the exercise of the principal right is also granted. As a general rule it is safe to say that the lessee is bound to perform all of the public duties imposed by law upon the lessor company. The lessee company takes the burdens with the benefits.[1]

§ 462. Contract obligations of lessor—Lessee not liable thereon.—It is obvious that it would be a violation of principle to hold that the lessee under an authorized lease is liable on the contracts of the lessor company in the absence of an express provision to that effect.[2] The legislative sanction protects the lessee from any imputation of wrong, and in taking possession of the road under the lease it does what it has a lawful right to do. It can not be held that by simply accepting a lease it binds itself by contracts made by the lessor before the execution of the lease. The legislature may make it a condition of the exercise of the power to take a lease that the lessee company shall perform the contracts of the lessor, but where the power is granted in general terms the duty to perform prior contracts entered into by the lessor does not necessarily devolve upon the lessee company.

[1] Pennsylvania R. Co. v. Sly, 65 Pa. St. 205; *In re* New York, etc., Co., 49 N. Y. 414; South Carolina, R. Co. v. Wilmington, etc., R. Co., 7 S. Car. 410. The lessee may be compelled to operate the road along such places as had extended aid to the lessor company. State v. Central Iowa R. Co., 71 Iowa 410. See Chicago, etc., R. Co. v. Crane, 113 U. S. 424. It must maintain all fences, cattle guards, etc., which the lessor company was required by law to maintain. Curry v. Chicago, etc., R. Co., 43 Wis. 665. It must give all statutory signals, etc., required of the lessor company. Linfield v. Old Colony, etc., R. Co., 10 Cush. (Mass.) 562. And it is bound to make alterations in a highway crossing required by statute. Town of Westbrook's Appeal, 57 Conn. 95. The corporation tax law of Vermont, 1882, imposes a tax upon the entire gross earnings of all railways operated in the state, and provides that when a railway is operated under a lease the tax shall be paid by the lessee. Where the lessee had paid the tax and deducted it from the rent, while such legislation was upheld by the decisions of the United States Supreme Court, the lessor was not permitted to recover from the lessee because of a later decision by that court that such tax was unconstitutional. Vermont & C. R. Co. v. Vermont Cent. R. Co., 63 Vt. 1.

[2] An agreement by the lessor company to give an annual pass to plaint-

§ 463. Recovery of rent under unauthorized lease.—The question of the right of the lessor to recover rent under an unauthorized lease, is one upon which there is a diversity of opinion. Some of the courts hold that rent may be recovered,[1] while others deny that there is a right of recovery on the lease. We think that there can be no recovery upon the lease for the reason that it is void, but it does not necessarily follow from the fact the lease is void that there can be no recovery of compensation for the reasonable rental value of the leased property. If it could be justly said that the lessee was estopped then there would be little difficulty in solving the question. But it is not easy to find any principle upon which a conclusion that the lessee is estopped can be rested.[2] Both parties do what they have no right to do, both parties have equal means of knowledge, and the question whether there was or was not power to execute the lease is one of law and not of fact. We are here speaking of cases where there is an entire absence of power, not simply a defective or improper exercise of power. Where there is power to lease, then, although the lease may be defectively executed, there may be an estoppel, but we do not think there can be an estoppel where there is an entire absence of power. There is an important distinction between a lease not properly executed and a lease executed where there is an utter and entire absence of power to execute a lease, but this distinction is often lost sight of and the result is confusion and error.

§ 464. Improvements of road by lessee operating under an unauthorized lease.—It has been held that a lessee operating

iff in consideration of a release of the right of way through his land is not binding upon another company to which that company leases the road. Pennsylvania Co. v. Erie, etc., R. Co., 108 Pa. St. 621.

[1] Woodruff v. Erie, etc., R. Co., 93 N. Y. 609, holding that although there is no power to execute a lease to an individual, yet if a lease is executed to an individual, he will be liable for the stipulated rent. The case of Abbott v. Johnstown, etc., R. Co., 80 N. Y. 27, s. c. 36 Am. R. 572, is distinguished, and the cases of Bissell v. Michigan, etc., R. Co., 22 N.Y. 258 and Whitney, etc., Co. v. Barlow, 63 N.Y. 62, s. c. 20 Am. R. 504, are followed. See Board v. Reynolds, 50 Ind. 85; Ogdensburg, etc., Co. v. Vermont, etc., R. Co., 4 Hun 268; Union Bridge Co. v. Troy, etc., Co., 7 Lans. 240; Farmers' Grain, etc., R. Co. v. St. Joseph, etc., Co., 2 Fed. R. 117.

[2] Ante, §§ 371, 372, 373.

a railroad under an unauthorized lease can not recover for improvements made while in possession of the road under the lease.[1] If such a lease is absolutely void then it can not confer any rights upon the lessee, and, unless there is some controlling element of estoppel or some protecting statute, the lessee can not recover money expended in improving the road. Whether the lessee company can be regarded as an occupying claimant under statutes protecting such claimants must depend upon whether the void lease confers color of title upon a company that was itself a wrong-doer in accepting the lease. The lease, being void, will not, of itself, give a right of action nor be sufficient foundation for an enforceable claim or demand. In the case referred to the court virtually held that the lessee was not "holding possession in good faith and under color of title."

§ 465. **Receiver's power to lease.**—The receiver of a railroad company can not execute a lease unless the statute grants permission.[2] If the railroad company has no power to execute a lease it seems clear that a receiver appointed by the court can not make a valid lease. We suppose that in the absence of a statute granting permission to execute a lease of a railroad the courts could not confer such a power upon a receiver of the corporation owning the road, for the power to lease is statutory.

§ 466. **Unauthorized lease—Liability of lessor—Generally.** The question whether a lease is or is not authorized is an important one in cases where claims for injury are sought to be enforced against the company which assumes to lease its railroad. If the lease is unauthorized, that is, made without legislative authority, it is, in our judgment, absolutely void, and if void, the lessor has not transferred any of its public duties or obligations. A transfer of a duty or obligation can not be made by a void act. If there is no transfer of duty it

---

[1] State v. McMinnville, etc., R. Co., 6 Lea 369, s. c. 4 Am. & Eng. R. Cas. 95. But see Mercantile T. Co. v. Missouri, etc., Ry. Co., 41 Fed. R. 8.

[2] State v. McMinnville, etc., R. Co.,

remains where the law cast it, and if there is a culpable breach of duty resulting in injury the fact that there was an attempt to transfer the duty will not relieve the party upon whom the law imposed the duty from liability. If the duty remains unaffected by a transfer, as it does where the transfer is void, the breach of duty is the wrong of the party upon whom the duty was imposed by law. It clearly and necessarily results from the principles stated that where the lease is unauthorized a wrongful breach resulting in injury imposes a liability upon the company that assumes, without power, to execute a lease. But while it is clear that there is a liability on the part of the lessor where the lease is unauthorized, that is, where there is no power to execute it, there is doubt whether this liability extends to the servants employed by the lessee in operating the road.[1] The weight of authority at present probably is that the lessor is liable to the servants of the lessee, but it is not clear that this doctrine is sound. It is elementary learning that there is no negligence where there is no duty, and that a party who bases an asserted right of action upon the negligence of the defendant must show the breach of a specific duty owing him,[2] and where the relation of master and servant exists the only

---

[1] Baltimore, etc., R. Co. v. Paul, 143 Ind. 23, s. c. 40 N. E. R. 519, denying the doctrine of East Line, etc., Railroad Co. v. Culberson, 72 Tex. 375, s. c. 10 S. W. R. 706, and distinguishing Macon, etc., Railroad Co. v. Mayes, 49 Ga. 355. Judge Cooley illustrates the general doctrine and says: "The general duty of a railroad company to run its trains with care becomes a particular duty to no one until he is in a position to have a right to complain of the neglect." Cooley on Torts, 660. In the case of Kahl v. Love, 37 N. J. Law 5, the rule was thus stated: "Actionable negligence exists only when the party whose negligence occasions the loss owes a duty, arising from contract or otherwise, to the person sustaining such loss." The court in Lary v. The Cleveland, etc., Co., 78 Ind. 323, 329, quoted a very similar statement of the rule with approval. The statement quoted is this: "Actionable negligence exists only where the one whose act causes or occasions the injury owed the injured person a duty created either by contract or by operation of law, which he has failed to discharge." Many cases are cited in the case from which we have quoted. Indianapolis, etc., R. Co. v. Pitzer, 109 Ind. 179, 182; Evansville, etc., R. Co. v. Griffin, 100 Ind. 221; Nave v. Flack, 90 Ind. 205, 207; The State, ex rel. Travelers' Ins. Co., v. Harris, 89 Ind. 363, 366.

[2] See *post*, § 472.

duty is that created by the contract of employment, so that it would seem that the employer is the only person liable.

§ 467. **Authorized lease—Liability of lessor for injuries caused by negligence of lessee—Cases holding lessor liable.**— There is a wide diversity of opinion upon the question whether a company that leases its railroad to another company under authority of law is liable for the negligence of the lessee in operating the road under the lease. Many of the courts and some of the text-writers affirm that the lessor is liable although the lease is executed under authority of law, unless the statute which grants the right to lease exempts the lessor from liability.[1] The theory of some of the cases which hold the lessor liable for the negligence of the lessee in operating the road is that a railroad company is never exonerated except where there is an express statutory provision relieving it from liability. The cases to which we refer deny that there can be exoneration by implication, and assert that the authority to lease does not protect the lessor.[2] Other courts hold that the lessor is exonerated from liability for the negligence of the lessee in

---

[1] In Logan v. North Carolina R. Co., 116 N. C. 940, s. c. 21 S. E. R. 959, the court referred to the cases of State v. Richmond, 72 N. C. 634; Gooch v. McGee, 83 N. C. 59; Hughes v. Commissioners, 107 N. C. 598, s. c. 12 S. E. R. 465, and other cases holding that express legislative authority is requisite to the validity of a lease and adjudged that even though there was legislative authority for the execution of the lease, the lessor company was liable for injuries caused by the negligence of the lessee. The court approved the case of Braslin v. Somerville, etc., Railroad Co., 145 Mass. 64, s. c. 13 N. E. R. 65. As sustaining the doctrine that the lessor was liable for an injury to a person employed by the lessee, the court cited National Bank, etc., v. Atlanta, etc., R. Co., 25 So. Car. 216; Harmon v. Columbia, etc., Railroad Co., 28 So. Car. 401, s. c. 5 S. E. R. 835; Naglee v. Alexandria, etc,. Railway Co., 83 Va. 707, s. c. 3 S. E. R. 369; Acker v. Alexandria, etc., Railroad Co., 84 Va. 648, s. c. 5 S. E. R. 688; Balsley v. St. Louis, etc., Railroad Co., 119 Ill. 68, 8 N. E. R. 859, 59 Am. R. 784; Singleton v. Southwestern Railroad Co., 70 Ga. 464, s. c. 21 Am. & Eng. R. Cas. 226; Beach Private Corp., § 366; Spelling Corp., § 135.

[2] Balsley v. St. Louis, etc., R. Co., 119 Ill. 68, s. c. 59 Am. R. 784; Wabash, etc., R. Co. v. Peyton, 106 Ill. 534, s. c. 18 Am. & Eng. R. Cas. 1; Chollette v. Omaha, etc., R. Co., 26 Neb. 159, s. c. 37 Am. & Eng. R. Cas. 16.

operating the road, but is liable for injuries resulting from a breach of duty owing to the public, as, for instance, negligence in the construction of tracks, station buildings and the like.[1]

§ 468. **Authorized lease—Liability of lessor for negligence of lessee in operating the road—Authorities denying liability.**—As said in the preceding section some of the cases make a distinction between negligence in the operation of the road and negligence in its construction, and adjudge that the lessor company is not liable for the negligence of the lessee in operating the road.[2] The text writers generally favor the doctrine that for negligence in operating the road the lessor is not liable.[3]

---

[1] Nugent v. Boston, etc., R. Co., 80 Me. 62, s. c. 38 Am. & Eng. R. Cas. 52; St. Louis, etc., R. Co. v. Curl, 28 Kan. 622, s. c. 11 Am. & Eng. R. Cas. 458; Bay City R. Co. v. Austin, 21 Mich. 390; Kearney v. Central, etc., R. Co., 167 Pa. St. 362, s. c. 31 Atl. R. 637; Kansas, etc., Railroad Co. v. Wood, 24 Kan. 619; Texas, etc., R. Co. v. Moore,(Texas Civ. App.) 27 S. W. R. 962; Central, etc., R. Co. v. Phinazee, 93 Ga. 488, s. c. 21 S. E. R. 66.

[2] Arrowsmith v. Nashville, etc., R. Co., 57 Fed. R. 165. In the case cited the court, after a very full review of the authorities, adopted the doctrine of the cases of Mahoney v. Atlantic, etc., Railroad Co., 63 Me. 68, and Nugent v. Boston, etc., Railroad Co., 80 Me. 62. s. c. 38 Am. & Eng. R. Cas. 52, and quoted from the latter case as expressive of the true rule the following: "And herein, as we think, lies the true distinction which marks the dividing line of the lessor's responsibility. In other words an authorized lease, without any exemption clause, absolves the lessor from the writs of the lessee resulting from the negligent operation and handling of trains and the general management of the leased road over which the lessor could have no control. But for an injury resulting from the negligent omission of some duty owed to the public, such as the proper construction of the road, station houses, etc., the charter company can not, in the absence of statutory authority, discharge itself of legal responsibility." The court in the case first named cited as supporting its conclusion the following authorities: Wood on Railroads, § 490; Ditchett v. Spuyten, etc., R. Co., 67 N. Y. 425; Miller v. New York, etc., R. Co., 125 N. Y. 118, s. c. 47 Am. & Eng. R. Cas. 369; St. Louis, etc., R. Co. v. Curl, 28 Kan. 622, s. c. 11 Am. & Eng. R. Cas. 458; Briscoe v. Southern, etc., R. Co., 40 Fed. R. 273; Virginia, etc., R. Co. v. Washington, 86 Va. 629, s. c. 43 Am. & Eng. R. Cas. 688.

[3] Mr. Hutchinson thus expresses his opinion: "An authorized lease, not otherwise providing, will absolve the lessor from the torts of the lessee, resulting from the negligent operation and handling of trains and the general management of the leased road over which the lessor has no control." Hutchinson on Carriers, § 575 B. Mr. Wood's views are expressed in this language: "But where the statute

§ 469. **Authorized lease—Liability of lessor for negligence of lessee in operating the road—Views of the authors.**—Our opinion is that where the lease is executed under the provisions of a statute, in accordance with its requirements, is made to a company having authority to accept it, and is made in good faith and not for the purpose of transferring duties or obligations to an irresponsible party, the lessor company is not liable for injuries caused by the negligence of the lessee and not attributable to a breach of any public duty of the company that executed the lease. It must be assumed that in granting the authority to execute a lease the legislature had in mind former statutes as well as the established rules of the common law.[1] When power to execute a lease is conferred upon a corporation the legislature must, in

authorizes the lease, the lessee assumes during the existence of the lease, all the duties and obligations of the lessor, and from the time that it enters into the possession of the road becomes solely liable for all injuries resulting from its management unless operating the road in the name of the lessor." Wood on Railroads, § 400. Mr. Pierce says: "The lease of a railroad under due authority of law effects a transfer of rights and liabilities in its management, so that the corporation owning the railroad is discharged from liability for the lessee's torts." Pierce on Railroads, § 283. Some of the courts say that the statements of the author quoted from are so coupled with conditions and qualifications as not to oppose the doctrine of the cases which hold that there is no exemption unless there is an express statutory provision granting it, but those courts are in error. As shown in Arrowsmith v. Nashville, etc., R. Co., 57 Fed 165, Mr. Pierce recognizes two classes of leases, authorized and unauthorized, and affirms of the former class that the lessor is not liable. The cases of Mahoney v. Atlantic, etc., R. Co., 63 Me. 68; Ditchett v. Spuyten, etc., R. Co., 67 N. Y. 425, s. c. 5 Hun 165, declare the doctrine he affirms so that there is no reason to doubt his meaning. Mr. Patterson's opinion is given in this language: "On the other hand where a railway under due authority of law has leased its line to another, the lessor railway is not liable for torts committed by the lessee railway in the operation of the line." Patterson's Ry. Acc. Law, §§ 130, 131. Some of the cases assert that Judge Redfield differs from the authors to whom we have referred, but, as is shown by Judge Linton in Arrowsmith v. Nashville, etc., R. Co., 57 Fed. R. 165, they are in error. Judge Rorer does not, as we understand him, express any opinion upon the direct question. He cites some of the opposing cases, so that it can not be determined what view he adopts. 1 Rorer on Railroads, §§ 605, 606.

[1] "The legislature are presumed to know existing statutes and the state of the law relating to the subjects with which they deal." Sutherland Stat. Const., § 287.

the absence of countervailing language, be deemed to intend to authorize the execution of such an instrument as the established law regards as a lease. The law enters as a silent factor into every contract, and hence of every lease it is an important element. The legal effect of a lease is to transfer for a prescribed period of time the possession and control of the property to the lessee. In authorizing the execution of a lease the legislature grants the right to execute and carry into effect such an instrument as divests the lessor of possession and control and places it in the lessee to the exclusion of the lessor. The possession of the one party is excluded and that of the other is made complete by the legislative sanction. If a sale is made under valid legislative authority the company that acquires the property acquires an exclusive right and interest, and the lessee by virtue of the lease acquires a similar right so far as possession, control and management are concerned, for the term for which the property was leased. It can not be doubted that a statute conferring general authority to sell means a complete and effective sale, and upon the same principle it must be concluded that the power to lease, unless qualified and limited by statute, is a power to make a complete and effective lease. A complete and effective lease certainly vests the right of possession, control and management in the lessee, since no other effect can be assigned such a lease without a direct and palpable violation of long and well established principles of law. The lessor company does no wrong in executing a lease which the law of the land gives it full power to execute, so that in executing the lease there is no improper motive, no illegal act, nor any wrongful attempt to escape a duty. In granting authority to lease, the legislature empowers the lessor company to transfer the duty of operating the road to the lessee, and in doing what the legislature authorizes no rule of public policy is violated. It is, indeed, inconceivable that there can be a violation of a rule of public policy where the act done by a party is done under a legislative enactment and in accordance with its provisions. The cases which hold the lessor liable, although the lease is an authorized one, upon the ground that there must be an express exemption from liability in order to exonerate the lessor, concede, what could not be denied without leaving the domain of reason, that the legislature may by express enactment exonerate the lessor, so that, even upon that theory (which we believe to be unsound) the question, at bottom, is one of statutory construction. The courts which assert the theory mentioned tacitly assume that in granting authority to lease, the legislature granted something less than an authority to lease. We believe that the only theory that can be defended on principle is that in granting authority to execute a lease the legislature conferred authority to execute an effective instrument with all the qualities and incidents with which the law invests a lease. If this be true then the lease does transfer possession and control from the one party to the other for the term of the lease, and the rights and obligations of the parties are such, and such only, as the law annexes to the relation of lessor and lessee. For negligence in managing and using the demised premises the lessor is not responsible. If it has performed its duty in constructing tracks and necessary structures it can not be held responsible for the negligence of the lessee in employing incompetent servants, or in negligently handling trains, or in negligently overloading cars, or in negligently failing to provide a sufficient number of persons to manage trains, or for any negligence which relates solely to the mode of operating the leased road.

§ 470. **Control reserved by lessor.**—Where the lessor company, in an authorized lease, retains control of the road, there is reason for holding it liable for the negligence of the lessee in operating the road. The fact that exclusive control is not transferred to the lessee is an influential factor, and may well be held to constitute the basis of an exception to what we conceive to be the general rule. If the lessor company does retain control its duty is to exercise that control as the law requires.[1]

[1] Driscoll *v.* Norwich, etc., R. Co., 65 Conn. 230, 32 Atl. R. 354. In the case cited the lessor reserved to itself the control of the road while in the

§ 471. Liability of lessee under authorized lease—Illustrative cases.—An authorized lease, that is, a lease executed under power granted by the legislature, imposes upon the lessee the duty of operating and conducting the road as the statute from which the lessor company derived its powers prescribes.[1] The lessee is under a duty to provide fences, as the charter of the company from which it acquired its title requires;[2] to exercise ordinary care and diligence to prevent the escape of fire, and to give signals at crossings, as provided in the statute governing the lessor company.[3] A lessee is liable for maintaining a nuisance after notice to abate, although the nuisance existed at the time the lease was executed.[4] The lessee is, as a rule, liable for injuries resulting from a failure to properly operate and maintain the road,[5] and for the negligent acts of its servants in the operation of the road.[6] It is liable for the failure to carry, safely and promptly, any persons or goods entrusted to it for carriage.[7] It may be safely asserted as a general rule that when a road is

hands of the lessee, so that there can be no doubt that the conclusion asserted by the court is sound.

[1] In re New York, etc., R. Co., 49 N. Y. 414; South Carolina, etc., R. Co. v. Wilmington, etc., R. Co., 7 S. Car. 410; Ogdensburg, etc., R. Co. v. 4 Hun 712; Penna. R. Co. v. Sly, 65 Pa. St. 205; State v. Central, etc., R. Co., 71 Iowa 410.

[2] Cook v. Milwaukee, etc., R. Co., 36 Wis. 45; McCall v. Chamberlain, 13 Wis. 637; Curry v. Chicago, etc., R. Co., 43 Wis. 665.

[3] Linfield v. Old Colony, etc., R. Co., 10 Cush. 562, s. c. 57 Am. Dec. 124.

[4] Western, etc., R. Co. v. Cox, 93 Ga. 561, s. c. 20 S. E. R. 68.

[5] St. Louis, etc., R. Co. v. Curl, 28 Kan. 622, 11 Am. & Eng. R. Cas. 458. The lessee has been held liable with the original owner or lessor for damages resulting from a permanent injury to property caused by the construction of the road. Stickley v. Chesapeake, etc., R. Co., 93 Ky. 323, 52 Am. & Eng. R. Cas. 56. The lessee is liable for the continuance of a nuisance erected by the lessor. Dickson v. Chicago, etc., R. Co., 71 Mo. 575. It is liable for injuries arising from a failure to fence the road. Missouri Pac. R. Co. v. Morrow, 32 Kan. 217; Cook v. Milwaukee, etc., R. Co., 36 Wis. 45; Ditchett v. Spuyten, etc., R. Co., 67 N. Y. 425; Illinois Central R. Co. v. Kanouse, 39 Ill. 272; Wabash R. Co. v. Williamson, 3 Ind. App. 190. See, Kearney v. Central, etc., R. Co., 31 Atl. R. 637.

[6] A company is liable for fires set by the engines of trains which it runs over a leased road. Cantlon v. Eastern R. Co., 45 Minn. 481.

[7] Feital v. Middlesex, etc., R. Co., 109 Mass. 398; Burroughs v. Norwich, etc., R. Co., 100 Mass. 26; Mahoney v. Atlantic, etc., R. Co., 63 Me. 68; Philadelphia, etc., R. Co. v. Anderson, 94 Pa. St. 351; Wabash, etc., R. Co. v. Peyton, 106 Ill. 534; Patterson, v. Wabash, etc., R. Co., 54 Mich. 91.

transferred by lease under legislative authority, the lessee company is liable as if it were operating the road as owner.[1]

472. **Unauthorized lease—Liability of lessor to employes of lessee—Generally.**—It is difficult without a departure from sound principle to support the doctrine of the cases which hold that the lessor is liable to the employes of the lessee for injuries caused by the negligence of the lessee in maintaining and operating the leased road. The case of an employe is in some important particulars essentially different from the case of persons using the road, or of persons whose goods are transported over it, or of persons who are themselves carried as passengers. The relations between the lessee company and its employes are contractual, and the duty which the contract creates is that of employer to employe. The person who takes service with the lessee company voluntarily accepts that company as its employer and out of this contract comes the duty which the contracting parties owe to each other. The employe of the lessee certainly owes no duty to the lessor, and it is difficult to conceive a tenable ground for the conclusion that the lessor owes a duty to the employe. The employer assumes to perform the duties imposed upon it by law, in its character of employer, and the employe voluntarily takes the lessee company as his employer. The employe does not contract with the lessee as the agent of the lessor, but contracts directly with the lessee as its own representative and not as the representative of some other person or corporation. There is in all that the term implies a direct and full privity of contract between the lessee and its employes. There is no privity of contract between the lessor and the employes of the lessee, and no implication that for breach of the duty of employer, the employe can look to the lessor for redress. In a recent case the ques-

[1] St. Louis, etc., R. Co. *v.* Curl, 28 Kan. 622; International, etc., R. Co. *v.* Dunham, 68 Tex. 231; Ditchett *v.* Spuyten, etc., R. Co., 67 N. Y. 425; Davis *v.* Providence, etc., R. Co., 121 Mass. 134; Philadelphia, etc., R. Co. *v.* Anderson, 94 Pa. St. 351; Patterson *v.* Wabash, etc., R. Co., 54 Mich. 91; Mahoney *v.* Atlantic, etc., R. Co., 63 Me. 68; Murch *v.* Concord R. Corp., 29 N. H. 9.

tion we are considering was discussed with signal ability, and it was held that, although the lease was not authorized by statute, the lessor was not liable to a servant of the lessee injured while engaged in performing the duties of his service by reason of defects in a locomotive used by the lessee in operating the road.[1] The theory of the court was that the lessor owed no duty to the servant of the lessee and as there was no duty there could not be actionable negligence. There is unquestionably much force in the reasoning of the court in the case under immediate mention for the settled rule is that where there is no duty there is no negligence, and a party can not have a right of action unless there is a breach of a specific duty owing to him. In the case of an employer and employe there is no consideration of public policy involved, such as there is in cases of third persons, for the employe by a voluntary contract creates the relation of employer and employe. His rights are such as his contract creates, the duty springs from the contract, and but for the contract he would really have no right on the road or any of its equipments. The difference between cases where third persons sue for injuries, and cases where the action is by an employe is so wide that cases deciding that there is a liability to third persons are hardly in point. We incline to the opinion that the lessor is not liable to the servants of the lessee for injuries received by them, in cases where the injuries are caused solely by the negligence of the lessee in operating the road, but the weight of authority is against our opinion. Whether the lessor can be held liable to an employe

---

[1] Baltimore, etc., R. Co. v. Paul, 143 Ind. 23, s. c. 40 N. E. R. 519. It was said by the court, speaking of the duty to third persons, that: "The law will not permit the owner of the road to shirk its duty to them by turning over its road to another company, nor will it be permitted to deny its liability where it has allowed such other company, without authority of law, negligently to injure wayfarers over the track or property along the line. There is no privity between the persons injured in such a case and the operating company. It is not so with an employe who voluntarily enters the service of the latter company with a knowledge of the facts and participates knowingly in the wrong, if wrong it be." In Missouri, etc., R. Co. v. Watts, 63 Texas 549, s. c. 22 Am. & Eng. R. Cas. 277, it was held that the lessor is not liable to the servant of the lessee for injuries received in the line of service required of him in operating the road.

of the lessee for negligence in the construction of the track or the like is a very different question from the question here considered, namely, the right of an employe of the lessee to hold the lessor liable for negligence in operating the road.

§ 473. **Unauthorized lease—Liability of lessor, general rule.** —The general rule as declared by the great weight of authority is this: Where the lease under which the road is transferred is unauthorized, even though a railroad company puts its road in the possession of a lessee, and surrenders the entire control and management of its road, it is liable for all damages caused by the lessee's negligence in the management and conduct of the railroad and its affairs.[1] There is, as we believe, and as we have more clearly pointed out in another place, an important difference between authorized leases and leases executed in cases where there is an entire want of power to execute them, and the rules which govern the one class of cases can not be justly held to govern the other class. The negligence of a lessee having actual possession and control of a railroad under a lease which the lessor had no power to execute, does not transfer liability from the lessor to the lessee; so the lessor remains liable for the wrongs of the lessee,[2] except in cases where by reason of contract relations, the specific duty which is violated is owing solely from the lessee to the injured person. The theory upon which many of the cases proceed is that the persons operating a road under an unauthorized lease are the agents of the lessor company.[3] But whatever may be the par-

---

[1] Arrowsmith v. Nashville, etc., R. Co., 57 Fed. R. 165, 171; Ricketts v. Birmingham, etc., Ry. Co., 85 Ala. 600, s. c. 5 So. R. 353; Rome, etc., Railroad Co. v. Chasteen, 88 Ala. 591, s. c. 7 So. R. 94; Galveston, etc., R. Co. v. Garterser, (Tex. Civ. App.) 29 S. W. R. 939; Parr v. Spartansburg, etc., Co., 43 S. C. 197, s. c. 20 S. W. R. 1009; Palmer v. Utah, etc., R. Co., 2 Idaho 350, 36 Am. & Eng. R. Cas. 443; Harmon v. Columbia, etc., 28 So. Car. 401; International, etc., R. Co. v. Moody, 71 Tex. 614; Briscoe v. Southern Kansas R. Co., 40 Fed. R. 273; Ricketts v. Chesapeake, etc., R. Co., 33 W. Va. 433.

[2] It is held that the lessor is liable for the lessee's refusal to carry freight offered for transportation. Central, etc., R. Co. v. Morris, 68 Tex. 49.

[3] Nelson v. Vermont, etc., R. Co., 26 Vt. 717; Briscoe v. Southern Kansas, etc., R. Co., 40 Fed. R. 273. In Van Dresser v. Oregon R., etc., Co., 48 Fed. R. 202, the court held that the

ticular theory adopted, the great weight of authority is that the company that executes such a lease still remains liable.[1]

§ 474. Liability of lessee for injuries resulting from negligence in operating the road.—The lessee is liable for all injuries occasioned by its negligent operation of a road under an unauthorized lease, inasmuch as its liability for its own torts is the same whether it is using its own property or that of another when the injury is done.[2] It is clear that principle requires the conclusion that a lessee operating under an unauthorized lease is liable for negligence in operating the road. To

lessee of a railroad, engaged in operating it under an unauthorized lease must be considered as the agent of the lessor company for the purpose of service of summons in a suit against such company. A contract for the shipment of freight over a railroad, made by a lessee of the road, does not bind the railroad company to do more than its lessee is bound to do. International, etc., R. Co. v. Thornton, 3 Tex. Civ. App. 197, s. c. 22 S. W. R. 67.

[1] Bouknight v. Chicago, etc., R. Co., 41 So. Car. 415, s. c. 19 S. R. 915; Fisher v. West Virginia, etc., Co., 39 W. Va. 366, s. c. 19 S. E. R. 578; Harmon v. Columbia, etc., R. Co., 28 So. Car. 401; Gulf, etc., Co. v. Morris, 67 Tex. 692, s. c. 35 Am. & Eng. R. Cas. 94; Hart v. Charlotte, etc., R. Co., 33 S. C. 427; Chollette v. Omaha, etc., R. Co., 26 Neb. 159, s. c. 37 Am. & Eng. R. Cas. 16; Ottawa, etc., R. Co. v. Black, 79 Ill. 262; Bower v. Burlington, etc., R. Co., 42 Iowa 546; Braslin v. Somerville, etc., R. Co., 145 Mass. 64; Freeman v. Minneapolis, etc., R. Co., 28 Minn. 443; Brown v. Hannibal, etc., R. Co., 27 Mo. App. 394; Abbott v. Johnstown, etc., R. Co., 80 N. Y. 27, s. c. 36 Am. R. 572; Aycock v. Raleigh, etc., R. Co., 89 N. C. 321; Lakin v. Willamette, etc., R. Co., 13 Ore. 436; Washington, etc., R. Co. v. Brown, 17 Wall. 445. See, generally, Chicago, etc., R. Co. v. Whipple, 22 Ill. 105; Palmer v. Utah, etc., R. Co., 2 Idaho 350, s. c. 36 Am. & Eng. R. Cas. 443; Penna. Co. v. Sellers, 127 Pa. St. 406; East Line, etc., R. Co. v. Culberson, 72 Tex. 375, s. c. 38 Am. & Eng. R. Cas. 225; Ohio, etc., R. Co. v. Dunbar, 20 Ill. 623; Sellers v. Richmond, etc., R. Co., 94 N. C. 654; Great Northern, etc., R. Co. v. Eastern, etc., R. Co., 12 Eng. L. & E. 224; Wasmer v. Delaware, etc., R. Co., 80 N. Y. 212.

[2] Cantlon v. Eastern R. Co., 45 Minn. 481, s. c. 48 N.W. R. 22; Wabash, etc., R. Co. v. Peyton, 106 Ill. 534; Philadelphia, etc., R. Co. v. Anderson, 94 Pa. St. 351. The lessee's liability is in nowise affected by the fact that the lease was without authority and therefore unlawful. Ricketts v. Chesapeake, etc., R. Co., 33 W. Va. 433, 41 Am. & Eng. R. Cas. 42; Hall v. Brown, 54 N. H. 495; Toledo, etc., Co. v. Rumbold, 40 Ill. 143; McCluer v. Manchester, etc., R. Co., 13 Gray 124, s. c. 74 Am. Dec. 624; Feital v. Middlesex, etc., R. Co., 109 Mass. 398, s. c. 12 Am. R. 720; Atlanta, etc., R. Co. v. Ray, 70 Ga. 674; McMillan v. Michigan, etc., R. Co., 16 Mich. 79; Sprague v. Smith, 29 Vt.

permit a mere intruder into the franchise of a railroad company to escape liability for his failure to perform the duties which he has assumed, upon the plea that he is acting under an invalid contract and is operating the road without right, would be to allow him to allege his own wrong in his defense.[1] If the lease is void the company operating a railroad under it can not, it is obvious, shield itself from liability for injuries caused by its culpable negligence. The person injured is in nowise to be prejudiced by the wrongful act of the corporation that causes him injury in assuming powers and duties it has no right to take upon itself. There is, however, such harmony among the authorities upon the general question that there is no necessity for extended discussion.

§ 475. **Contracts of the lessee.**—The case of one who founds his claim upon a contract with the lessee after the execution of the lease is essentially different from that of one who bases his right on the tort of the lessee. It is obvious that the lessor can not be held liable for a breach of the contracts entered into by the lessee. If the action is founded on the contract there is no privity between the lessor and the person with whom the lessee contracts. The contract gives the person with whom the lessee contracts no right of action against the lessor, for the latter has assumed no obligation whatever.[2]

§ 476. **Joint liability.**—The lessor and lessee are jointly liable for negligence in the management of the road where the lease under which it is operated is unauthorized.[3] There is a

---

421, s. c. 70 Am. Dec. 424; Cook v. Milwaukee, etc., R. Co., 36 Wis. 45; Haff v. Minneapolis, etc., R. Co., 4 McCrary 622; Missouri Pac. R. Co. v. Morrow, 32 Kan. 217.

[1] Sprague v. Smith, 29 Vt. 421.

[2] It has been held that under a lease transferring to the lessee all of the lessor's contracts, the lessor can not be held liable for goods delivered to the lessee under a contract between the owner of the goods and the lessor.

Pittsburg, etc., R. Co. v. Harbaugh, 4 Brewst. (Pa.) 115. But there is reason for doubting the soundness of this decision. See International, etc., Co. v. Thornton, 3 Tex. Civ. App. 197, 22 S. W. R. 67.

[3] Stickley v. Chesapeake, etc., R. Co., 93 Ky. 323, s.c. 52 Am. & Eng. R. Cas. 56; Little Miami, etc., R. Co. v. Hambleton, 40 Ohio St. 496, s. c. 14 Am. & Eng. R. Cas. 126. See Eaton v. Boston, etc., R. Co., 11 Allen 500; Lockhart

clear distinction between cases where the lease is authorized and cases where it is unauthorized. If the lease is unauthorized there is a joint wrong for both parties assume to do what the law forbids. The one attempts to escape obligations the law imposes upon it by making a contract which it has no power to make; the other attempts to assume powers it can not rightfully possess. The unauthorized lease being void the lessor has not transferred any duty, and the lessee in assuming rights and powers to which it is not entitled is really an intruder and an usurper.

§ 477. **Liability of company where it permits another company to use track in common with itself.**—It is held by the Supreme Court of the United States that a railroad company which permits another to make a joint use of its track is liable to a person injured by the negligence of the company to which the permission is granted.[1] The weight of authority supports the doctrine of the case referred to.[2] In the case to which we

v. Little Rock, etc., R. Co., 40 Fed. R. 631; Great Western, etc., R. Co. v. Blake, 7 H. & N. 987; Spangler v. Atchison, etc., R. Co., 42 Fed. R. 305; Buxton v. Northeastern, etc., R. Co., L. R. 3 Q. B. 548; Thomas v. Rhymney R. Co., L. R. 5 Q. B. 226, and L. R. 6 Q. B. 266; Muschamp v. Lancaster, etc., R. Co., 8 M. & W. 421; Readhead v. Midland, etc., R. Co., L. R. 2 Q. B. 412; Illidge v. Goodwin, 5 C. & P. 190; Skinner v. London, etc., R. Co., 15 Jur. 289; Wisconsin, etc., R. Co. v. Ross, 142 Ill. 1, s. c. 53 Am. & Eng. R. Cas. 73. It is held in Chicago, etc., R. Co. v. Darke, 148 Ill. 226, s. c. 57 Am. & Eng. R. Cas. 577, that the objection that the defendants are not jointly liable must be made in the trial court or it will not be considered on appeal.

[1] Railroad Co. v. Barron, 5 Wall. 90. In the course of the opinion it was said, "The question is not whether the Michigan company is responsible, but whether the defendants, by giving to that company the privilege of using the road have thereby, in the given case, relieved themselves from responsibility. The question has been settled, and we think rightly, in the courts of Illinois holding the company liable. The same principle has been affirmed in other states." The court cited the cases of Chicago, etc., R. Co. v. McCarthy, 20 Ill. 385; Chicago, etc., R. Co. v. Whipple, 20 Ill. 337; Chicago, etc., R. Co. v. Whipple, 22 Ill. 105; Nelson v. Vermont, etc., R. Co., 26 Vt. 717; McElroy v. Nashua, etc., R. Co., 4 Cush. 400.

[2] Delaware, etc., R. Co. v. Salmon, 39 N. J. Law 299, s. c. 23 Am. R. 214; Fort Wayne, etc., Co. v. Hinebaugh, 43 Ind. 354; Stetler v. Chicago, etc., R. Co., 49 Wis. 609; Lakin v. Willamette, etc., R. Co., 13 Oreg. 436; Peoria, etc., R. Co. v. Lane, 83 Ill. 448. See Harper v. Newport, etc., R. Co., 90 Ky. 359, s. c. 14 S. W. R. 346;

refer the question of the effect of an authorized lease was not considered, and, as we believe, there was no such question in the case. The case of a joint use by two companies is essentially different from a case where the lessor company by an authorized lease parts with possession and control of the road. If it be true, as the authorities declare,[1] that the lease transfers possession and control to the lessee to the exclusion of the lessor, the case is entirely different from one wherein one company grants a privilege of common use to another or suffers the latter company to operate the road in its name. Conceding the soundness of the conclusion in the case decided by the Supreme Court of the United States it can not be justly regarded as affirming that the lessor who executes a lease under due authority is liable for the negligence of the lessee in operating the road.[2] In the one class of cases there is a change of possession and control, in the other possession is not changed, nor is the right of control surrendered.

§ 478. **Fraudulent leases.**—A contract of lease, like any other contract, may be set aside for the fraud of the directors in executing it. Fraud, however, is not presumed but must be

Parker v. Rensselaer, etc., R. Co., 16 Barb. 315; Murch v. Concord, etc., R. Co., 29 N. H. 9, s. c. 61 Am. Dec. 631; Hanover R. Co. v. Coyle, 55 Pa. St. 396; Illinois, etc., R. Co. v. Kanouse, 39 Ill. 272, s. c. 89 Am. Dec. 307; Mills v. Orange, etc., R. Co., 1 McArthur 285; Webb v. Portland, etc., R. Co., 57 Me. 117; Sprague v. Smith, 29 Vt. 421, s. c. 70 Am. Dec. 424.

[1] In the Matter of New York, etc., R. Co., 49 N. Y. (4 Sickels) 414, 420; Pennsylvania, etc., Co. v. Sly, 65 Pa. St. 205; State v. Central, etc., R. Co., 71 Iowa 410; South Carolina, etc., R. Co. v. Wilmington, etc., R. Co., 7 So. Car. 410.

[2] The decision in Railroad Co. v. Brown, 17 Wall. 445, does not oppose this conclusion, for there was no consideration in that case of the effect of an authorized lease. The real point in the case cited was that as there was no change of possession the company granting the privilege to use still remained liable. The fact that there was no change of possession clearly discriminates the case from one where there is an authorized lease, for the central idea of a lease is that it does change possession. In the above named case the court said: "Besides, the company, having permitted the lessees and receiver to conduct the business of the road in this particular, as if there were no change of possession, is not in a position to raise any question as to its liability for their acts."

affirmatively proved. Circumstances may be established from which, under familiar rules, fraud may be inferred. The circumstances must be such that under the rules applicable to cases of a similar character, the court or jury may infer fraud. Fraud will not be presumed from the mere fact that a larger rent is reserved than the subsequent earnings of the road really justify, where it appears that the rent was fixed in accordance with the report of competent and disinterested experts, to whom the question was referred.[1] Nor will fraud be presumed from the fact that the directors failed to make the continuance of the lease dependent upon the construction of connecting roads, which were contemplated when the lease was executed, by which the leased road was expected to become part of an important through line.[2] It is held that a lease by a railroad company of a road constructed by a syndicate of its directors is presumed fraudulent and may be set aside at the suit of a person injured thereby.[3] But such a lease is voidable only and not void, and may be ratified by long acquiescence; and the lessee company can not dispute its liability to pay the rent reserved under such lease while holding and operating the leased property.[4] A lease fraudulently executed may be avoided, but it can not be justly said to be void.

§ 479. Unauthorized lease—Injunction.—A stockholder of a corporation, or other party having an interest entitled to protection, has a right to an injunction prohibiting the execution of an unauthorized lease.[5] It is true that such a lease is void,

---

[1] Jesup v. Illinois Cent. R. Co., 43 Fed. R. 483.

[2] Jesup v. Illinois Cent. R. Co., 43 Fed R. 483.

[3] Barr v. New York, etc., R. Co., 125 N. Y. 263. An application of stockholders to set aside a traffic contract for 99 years, entered into by one railroad company with another having only a proposed road 18 miles distant from the first, which has no present authority to build a connecting branch, even if the other had a road, said contract being entered into by the directors and officers for the personal profit and advantage of individual members, and known to be injurious to the company, will be granted. Bostwick v. Chapman, 24 Atl. R. 32; Starbuck v. Mercantile Trust Co., 24 Atl. R. 32; Shepaug Voting Trust Cases, 60 Conn. 553.

[4] Barr v. New York, etc., R. Co., 125 N. Y. 263.

[5] Pond v. Vermont, etc., R. Co., 12 Blatchf. 280; Board v. Lafayette, etc., R. Co., 50 Ind. 85.

§ 479	LEASES.	617

but as it may cloud titles and rights, an injunction is rightly held to be the appropriate remedy. The tendency of the modern cases is to extend the remedy by injunction,[1] and there is certainly no other remedy so effective or complete in such cases as those of which we are speaking as an injunction. The general doctrine is that where an act is entirely beyond and outside of the scope of the corporate powers, and is one which will injure the public or defeat public policy, an injunction will lie at the suit of the state or its representative.[2]

[1] Champ v. Kendrick, 130 Ind. 549; Pom. Eq., § 1357. See, generally, Morse v. Morse, 44 Vt. 84; Watson v. Sutherland, 5 Wall. 74; Boyce v. Grundy, 3 Pet. 210; Allen v. Hanks, 136 U. S. 300; Kilbour v. Sunderland, 130 U. S. 505; Gormley v. Clark, 134 U. S. 338; Kerr on Injunctions, 32.

[2] Attorney-General v. Delaware, etc., R. Co., 27 N. J. Eq. 631, 633; Attorney-General v. Chicago, etc., Railroad Co., 35 Wis. 425; Ware v. Regent's, etc., Co., 3 De Gex & J. 212; Fishmongers' Co. v. East India Co., 1 Dickens 163; Browne v. Monmouthshare R. Co., 13 Beav. 32; Attorney-General v. Johnson, 2 Wils. (Ch.) 87; Attorney-General v. Forbes, 2 Myl. & C. 123; Attorney-General v. Great Northern, etc., R. Co., 4 De Gex. & S. 75; Attorney-General v. Mid-Kent, etc., R. Co., L. R. 3 Ch. App. 100; 2 Redfield on Railroads, 307.

CHAPTER XIX.

RAILROAD SECURITIES.

§ 480. Power of railroad companies to issue notes and bonds.
481. Power to guaranty bonds.
482. Income bonds.
483. Convertible bonds.
484. Negotiability of bonds—*Bona fide* purchasers.
485. Form and manner of issuing bonds—Effect of irregularities.
486. Interest coupons.
487. Payment of bonds and interest.
488. No power to mortgage without legislative authority.
489. Legislative authority to mortgage.
490. Distinction between authority to mortgage franchises and authority to mortgage property.
491. Who may execute the mortgage.

§ 492. Ratification by stockholders of unauthorized or improperly executed mortgage.
493. When *ultra vires* mortgage may be made effective.
494. Recording mortgages.
495. Generally as to what property is covered by the mortgage.
496. What is covered by a mortgage of the undertaking.
497. Mortgage of after-acquired property.
498. Fixtures.
499. Reserved power to create prior lien or dispose of unnecessary property.
500. Priority of mortgages.
501. Trust deeds.
502. Equitable and defective mortgages.
503. Statutory mortgages.
504. Debentures.

§ 480. Power of railroad companies to issue notes and bonds.—In the absence of any provision upon the subject in the charter or statute, a railroad company has implied power to execute a promissory note in furtherance of its legitimate business.[1] It likewise has implied power to issue bonds.[2] As

---

[1] Olcott *v.* Tioga, etc., R. R. Co., 27 N. Y. 546; Richmond, etc., R. R. Co. *v.* Snead, 19 Gratt. (Va.) 354 (a due bill); Smead *v.* Indianapolis, etc., R. R. Co., 11 Ind. 104, 109; Hamilton *v.* Newcastle, etc., R. R. Co., 9 Ind. 359; Mitchell *v.* Rome R. R. Co., 17 Ga. 574. See, also, Louisville, etc., R. R. Co. *v.* Caldwell, 98 Ind. 245. The rule seems to be otherwise in England. Bateman *v.* Mid-Wales R. R. Co., L. R. 1 C. P. 499, s. c. 35 L. J. C. P. 205; Peruvian R. R. Co. *v.* Thames, etc., Co., L. R. 2 Ch. 617, s. c. 36 L. J. Ch. 864.

[2] Philadelphia, etc., R. R. Co. *v.* Lewis, 33 Pa. St. 33, s. c. 75 Am. Dec. 574; Kelly *v.* Alabama, etc., R. R. Co., 58 Ala. 489; Miller *v.* New York, etc., R. R. Co., 18 How. Pr. (N. Y.) 374;

§ 480   RAILROAD SECURITIES.   619

said in a leading case:[1] "There seems to be no reason why a railroad corporation should not be considered as having power to make a bond for any purpose for which it may lawfully contract a debt, without any special authority to that effect, unless restrained by some restriction, express or implied, in its charter, or in some other legislative act. A bond is merely an obligation under seal. A corporation having the capacity to sue and be sued, the right to make contracts, under which it may incur debts, and the right to make and use a common seal, a contract under seal is not only within the scope of its powers, but was originally the usual and peculiarly appropriate form of corporate agreement." So, as the corporation has power to issue such negotiable instruments in the first instance, it also has the power to indorse them when they have been received in the payment of debts due it, or the like, in the regular course of its business.[2] Bonds secured by a mortgage which is unauthorized, or otherwise invalid, may nevertheless be valid as unsecured obligations,[3] and, so, on the other hand, may bonds which are issued without any accompanying mortgage under a statute simply giving authority "to borrow money on mortgage."[4] Indeed, the power to mortgage is said to imply and include the power to borrow money and issue bonds.[5]

Olcott v. Tioga, etc., R. R. Co., 27 N. Y. 546; Commissioners of Craven v. Atlantic, etc., R. R. Co., 77 N. Car. 289.

[1] Commonwealth v. Smith, 10 Allen (Mass.) 448, s. c. 87 Am. Dec. 672.

[2] Olcott v. Tioga, etc., R. R. Co., 27 N. Y. 546. See, also, Bonner v. New Orleans, 2 Woods (U. S.) 135; Florida Cent. R. R. Co. v. Schutte, 103 U. S. 118; Tod v. Kentucky Union Land Co., 57 Fed. R. 47. The indorsement by the company of bonds issued by the state to aid in the construction of the road, although in the form of an express guaranty, gives no lien to the bondholders and in no way prevents the company from executing a mortgage to secure its own bonds which it is authorized to issue. McKittrick v. Arkansas Cent. Ry. Co., 152 U. S. 473, s. c. 14 Sup. Ct. R. 661.

[3] Philadelphia, etc., R. R. Co. v. Lewis, 33 Pa. St. 33, s. c. 75 Am. Dec. 574; Union Trust Co. v. N. Y., etc., R. R. Co., (Ohio Com. Pl.) 1 Ry. & Corp. L. J. 50.

[4] McMasters v. Reed, 1 Grant Cas. (Pa.) 36, approved and followed in Philadelphia, etc., R. R. Co. v. Lewis, *supra.*

[5] Gloninger v. Pittsburgh, etc. R. R. Co., 139 Pa. St. 13, 21 Atl. R. 211, s. c. 46 Am. & Eng. R. R. Cas. 276.

CORP. 40

§ 481. **Power to guaranty bonds.**—As a general rule, one corporation has no implied authority to lend its credit to another by guaranty of dividends, or the like, especially if they are engaged in different lines of business.[1] But, after much litigation, it now seems to be reasonably well settled that one railroad company may guaranty the bonds of another under certain circumstances. Thus, where it has power to issue bonds of its own it also has implied power to guaranty the bonds of another railroad company, properly taken in payment of a debt, in order to enable it to sell them for an adequate price or to use them in payment of its own debt.[2] And it may be safely stated, we think, as a general rule, that such a guaranty may be valid, without an express grant of authority to make it, if it is supported by a valuable consideration of a kind that the guarantor company has authority to receive or invest in.[3] Some courts have gone even further in upholding such a guaranty,[4] and by some the doctrine of estoppel has been applied in favor of those who had made investments and acted upon the faith of the guaranty.[5] A railroad company authorized by statute to make contracts for leasing and operating the

[1] Davis v. Old Colony R. R. Co., 131 Mass. 258; Central Bank v. Empire Stone Co., 26 Barb. (N. Y.) 23; Colman v. Eastern, etc., R. R. Co., 10 Beav. 1; Memphis, etc., Co. v. Memphis, etc., R. R. Co., 85 Tenn. 703, 5 S. W. R. 52; Stark Bank v. U. S. Pottery Co., 34 Vt. 144; Pennsylvania R. R. Co. v. St. Louis, etc., R. R. Co., 118 U. S. 290; Smead v. Indianapolis, etc., R. R. Co., 11 Ind. 104; Lucas v. White, etc., Co., 70 Iowa 541, 30 N.W. R. 771; Humbolt Min. Co. v. American, etc., Co., 62 Fed. R. 356.

[2] Rogers, etc., Works v. Southern R. R. Assn., 34 Fed. R. 278. See, also, McKittrick v. Arkansas Cent. Ry. Co., 152 U. S. 473, s. c. 14 Sup. Ct. R. 661 (guaranty of state railway aid bonds).

[3] Low v. Cent. Pac. R. R. Co., 52 Cal. 53; Arnot v. Erie Ry. Co., 67 N. Y. 315; Chicago, etc., R. R. Co. v. Howard, 7 Wall. (U. S.) 392; Green Bay, etc., R. Co. v. Union, etc., Co., 107 U. S. 98; Zabriskie v. Cleveland, etc., R. R. Co., 23 How. (U. S.) 381; Tod v. Kentucky Union Land Co., 57 Fed. R. 47; Marbury v. Kentucky Union Land Co., 62 Fed. R. 335. See, also, Ellerman v. Chicago, etc., Stock Yards Co., 49 N. J. Eq. 217, 23 Atl. R. 292.

[4] See Madison, etc., R. R. Co. v. Norwich Sav. Society, 24 Ind. 457; Harrison v. Union Pac. Ry. Co., 13 Fed. R. 522.

[5] See State Board of Agriculture v. Citizens St. Ry., 47 Ind. 407; Cozart v. Georgia, etc., R. R. Co, 54 Ga. 379; Arnot v. Erie, etc., R. R. Co., 67 N. Y. 315. But *contra*, see *ante*, §§ 371, 374.

road of another company has implied power to include in the lease a guaranty of the interest coupons of the latter as part of the rent to be paid.[1]

§ 482. **Income bonds.**—The right to issue income bonds seems to have been conceded or assumed in many cases. Such bonds, with interest payable out of the company's income or net earnings, are frequently issued; but the power to issue irredeemable bonds, the interest on which is to be paid only after a specified dividend has been declared on the common stock is not unquestioned. The existence of such a power, in the absence of an express grant of authority, has been both denied[2] and affirmed.[3] It has been held that the holder of the bonds of a railroad company "payable to bearer, with interest semi-annually, secured on the income from the sale of its lands and the operation of its road and line" is a creditor having a specific lien upon the income, which he has a right to pursue, and a bill in equity will lie to reach it in the hands of another company to which the road and property of the old company has passed by consolidation.[4] Income bonds are not, however, the most desirable investments, for practically, at

[1] Eastern Townships Bank v. St. Johnsbury, etc., R. R. Co., 40 Fed. R. 423, s. c. 40 Am. & Eng. R. R. Cas. 566. See, also, Opdyke v. Pacific R. R. Co., 3 Dill. (U. S.) 55.

[2] Taylor v. Philadelphia, etc., R. R. Co., 7 Fed. R. 386, reported together with McCalmont v. Philadelphia, etc., R. R. Co., s. c. 3 Am. & Eng. R. R. Cas. 163.

[3] Philadelphia & Reading R. R. Co.'s Appeal (Pa.) 4 A. & Eng. R. R. Cas. 118, 21 Am. L. Reg. 713. This case and those above cited grew out of the same transaction or scheme. The federal court conceded that the corporation had implied power to borrow money, but held that the scheme in question was not a loan because it was never to be paid back. A majority of the state court held that it was a loan, as it was a contract for the use of money and that it made no difference that it was perpetual. The scheme, however, contemplated the payment of six per cent. interest on the face value of each bond after the payment of a six per cent dividend on the stock, and that the bonds should then rank *pari passu* as to further interest with the common stock, although the bondholders were to pay for their bonds less than one-third of their face value, and a minority of the state court were of the opinion that this was unauthorized.

[4] Rutten v. Union Pac. Ry. Co., 17 Fed. R. 480. Compare, however, Thomas v. New York, etc., R. R. Co., 139 N. Y. 163.

least, it is largely within the power of the company to prevent any net income from being realized. Even where the bonds are secured by an income mortgage, as is usually the case, although it may pledge tangible property for the principal, the real security for the payment of interest is little more than the pledge of the good faith of the company in the management and operation of its road.[1] Much, of course, depends upon the provisions of the bonds and mortgage in any particular case, but, in the absence of any valid limitation upon their powers, the directors of the company, necessarily, have a wide discretion in determining what shall be treated as net income.[2] Thus, if it appears that the income contemplated is the profit of future transactions of the company arising from all sources, the bondholders can not complain if the profits which would have been realized by operating the original lines exclusively have been decreased by losses in the operation of new lines in conjunction therewith, deemed advisable because of competition or the demand for greater facilities.[3] Where, however, a specific lien is provided for upon the income from certain specified property or lines, to be ascertained by deducting specified expenses and liabilities from the gross earnings of such property or lines, a different rule applies and the directors have no right to deduct expenses, including interest charges, incurred in operating new lines acquired by the company out of the earnings of the original lines, from the spe-

---

[1] Spies v. Chicago, etc., R. Co., 40 Fed. R. 34, 38. In this case Judge Wallace, speaking of an income mortgage, says: "It necessarily contemplates such improvements as seem necessary to the efficient use and operation of such property, and such alterations in the *corpus* as appear desirable are to be made at the discretion of the directors; and, unless it contains some limitations upon the powers of the directors, express or implied, the right of the company to conduct its operations as it may see fit, subject only to the conditions of its organic law, is unqualified; and, consequently, the company can lawfully extend its lines, acquire new ones, discontinue old ones, and thus essentially change the earning capacity of the property."

[2] Day v. Ogdensburgh, etc., R. R. Co., 107 N. Y. 129; Spies v. Chicago, etc., R. R. Co., 40 Fed. R. 34, 39; Thomas v. New York, etc., R. R. Co., 54 N. Y. S. R. 498, s. c. 139 N. Y. 163.

[3] Day v. Ogdensburgh, etc., R. R. Co., 107 N. Y. 129; Buck v. Seymour, 46 Conn. 156; Spies v. Chicago, etc., R. Co., 40 Fed. R. 34, 38.

cific income fund to which the bondholders have a right to look under their contract.[1] It is the duty of the company to keep a proper account and make an honest effort to ascertain the net earnings or income out of which the bondholders are entitled to receive their interest.[2] In the case just cited an accounting was directed and it was held that upon such accounting the company should be disallowed any sums paid or charged on account of debts which it had contracted prior to the execution of the income mortgage, and that it should also be disallowed any charge against income arising from the sale of the income bonds at less than their face value, as well as interest, which it had not paid or become liable to pay, upon first mortgage bonds, which had been funded and was represented by the income bonds accepted by the first mortgage bondholders in lieu of interest. It was also held that the expenses defrayed or incurred in producing the earnings for a given interest period are the only charges which can enter into the income account for that period, except the payment of interest on prior incumbrances as stipulated, and that the holders of coupons for each separate interest period should be paid ratably out of the net income of that particular period.[3] It is sometimes provided that the coupons or interest shall be paid in money or in scrip at the option of the company, and, in such a case, if the company does not elect to pay in scrip when the interest becomes due, and the income is sufficient, the holder of the coupon may sue for the money.[4]

§ 483. Convertible bonds.—There seems to be no good reason why a corporation authorized to increase its stock may not lawfully receive its own bonds in payment for new shares which

---

[1] Spies v. Chicago, etc., R. R. Co., 40 Fed. R. 34.

[2] Barry v. Missouri, etc., Ry. Co., 27 Fed. R. 1, 34 Fed. R. 829.

[3] Barry v. Missouri, etc., Ry. Co., 27 Fed. R. 1. It has also been held that income bondholders are not entitled to make up a deficiency in the interest in one year out of a surplus in the next. Day v. Ogdensburgh, etc., R. R. Co., 107 N. Y. 129. Much, of course, depends upon the particular contract or statute involved in each case.

[4] Marlor v. Texas, etc., Ry. Co., 21 Fed. R. 383; Texas, etc., Ry. Co. v. Marlor, 123 U. S. 687, s. c. 8 Sup. Ct. R. 311.

it issues under such authority.[1] Bonds are sometimes issued which expressly provide that the holder may surrender them to the company and receive a certain number of shares of stock in exchange. Where the charter authorizes the issue of such bonds convertible into stock, it is held that the power to increase the capital stock by issuing shares in exchange for the bonds is given by necessary implication.[2] If they provide that they may be exchanged for stock at or before maturity the holder will waive or forfeit his right to exchange them for stock if he fails to present them until after maturity.[3] It is said, however, that he may demand the stock in exchange at any time before maturity, and that if he makes such demand just before a dividend is declared he is entitled to the dividend as well as the stock.[4] But, where he has received interest up to that time, it is said to be unreasonable to hold that he is also entitled to the dividend.[5] An agreement merely extending the time of payment of the bond, before maturity, does not give the holder

---

[1] Lohman v. New York, etc., R. R. Co., 2 Sandf. Super. Ct. (N. Y.) 39; Reed v. Hayt, 51 N. Y. Super. Ct. 121.

[2] Belmont v. Erie R. R. Co., 52 Barb. (N. Y.) 637; Ramsey v. Erie Ry. Co., 38 How. Pr. (N. Y.) 193. See, also, Pratt v. American Bell Tel. Co., 141 Mass. 225, s. c. 55 Am. R. 465. But compare Chaffee v. Middlesex R. R. Co., 146 Mass. 224, holding that damages may be given but that specific performance will not be decreed if the company has no stock. In the first case cited it was held that if it clearly appeared that the bonds were about to be issued for the purpose of fraudulently increasing the capital stock, and not to borrow money to complete and operate the road, which was the purpose for which their issue was authorized, an injunction would lie to prevent them from being issued, or to restrain their conversion into stock while in the hands of persons having notice of the fraud.

[3] Chaffee v. Middlesex R. R. Co., 146 Mass. 224, s. c. 16 N. E. R. 34. This case holds that where bonds were payable on the first day of February, 1895, which happened to be Sunday, it was too late to present them and demand stock in exchange on Monday, the second day of February, but that bonds which were presented a few minutes after three o'clock in the afternoon of Saturday, January 31, were presented in time, although the usual hour of closing the office of the company was three o'clock. The court said that the bonds could have been presented at "any reasonable time on that day."

[4] Jones v. Terre Haute, etc., R. R. Co., 57 N. Y. 196.

[5] See Sutliff v. Cleveland, etc., R. R. Co., 24 Ohio St. 147; 2 Beach Ry's, § 633. Certainly this is true as to past dividends.

any right to insist that it shall be converted into stock after the expiration of the time to which his option was originally limited, or, in other words, merely extending the time of payment, does not, of itself, extend the time within which stock must be demanded according to the terms of the bond.[1] So, where a decree of foreclosure provided that bondholders who purchased at the sale might, if they saw fit, exchange their bonds for stock, it was held that a bondholder who did not become a purchaser and had overlooked the fact that he owned bonds until after the conveyance of the property to the purchasers could not then insist upon receiving stock in exchange, although he was not aware of the foreclosure suit and proceedings.[2] It seems that as the issue of bonds convertible into stock amounts, in effect, to an issue of stock, they can not, ordinarily, be sold at a discount.[3] The right to demand a conversion of such a bond into stock can not be assigned without the bond, and a petition in an action against the corporation for refusal to allow the conversion must allege that the plaintiff is the holder of the bond.[4] A bondholder who has a right to exchange his bonds for stock can not be deprived of that right by a consolidation without being given an opportunity to exercise it,[5] and where a consolidation is effected by the new consolidated company assuming all the debts and liabilities of the old he may demand stock in the new company in exchange for his convertible bonds.[6]

§ 484. Negotiability of bonds—Bona fide purchasers.—
Railroad bonds, payable at a certain time and place, to bearer

[1] Muhlenberg v. Philadelphia, etc., R. R. Co., 47 Pa. St. 16.

[2] Landis v. Western Pa. R. R. Co., 133 Pa. St. 579, s. c. 19 Atl. R. 556. Where an option to exchange stock for bonds contains no express limitation it must nevertheless be exercised within some reasonable time. Catlin v. Green, 120 N. Y. 441.

[3] Cook on Stock and Stockholders, § 283; 2 Beach on Railways, § 633. Compare Van Allen v. Ill. Cent. R. R. Co., 7 Bosw. (N. Y.) 515.

[4] Denney v. Cleveland, etc., R. R. Co., 28 Ohio St. 108.

[5] Rosenkrans v. Lafayette, etc. R. R. Co., 18 Fed. R. 513.

[6] Day v. Worcester, etc., R. R. Co., 151 Mass. 302, 23 N. E. R. 824. See, also, Cayley v. Cobourg, etc., R. R. Co., 14 Grant Ch. (U. Can.) 571; John Hancock, etc., Co. v. Worcester, etc., R. R. Co., 149 Mass. 214, s. c. 21 N. E. R. 364.

or to order, are regarded as negotiable instruments whether under seal or not.[1] This is true, also, of convertible bonds giving the holder the option of exchanging them for stock,[2] and the negotiability of a bond is not destroyed by a provision that it may be registered and made payable by transfer only on the books of the company,[3] nor by a provision that it may be paid before maturity,[4] or that it shall be payable on or before a certain date,[5] nor by the fact that overdue coupons are attached to it.[6] Nor is a mere recital in a bond which purports to be the absolute obligation of the company and is negotiable on its face, that it is one of a series of bonds secured by a trust deed suf-

---

[1] White v. Vermont, etc., R. R. Co., 21 How (U. S.) 575; Kneeland v. Lawrence, 140 U. S. 209, s. c. 46 Am. & Eng. R. R. Cas. 319, and note; Connecticut, etc., Co. v. Cleveland, etc., R. R. Co., 41 Barb. (N. Y.) 9; Reid v. Bank, 70 Ala. 199, s. c. 14 Am. & Eng. R. R. Cas. 554, and note; Junction R. R. Co. v. Cleneay, 13 Ind. 161; Ide v. Passumpsic, etc., R. R. Co., 32 Vt. 297; Carr v. LeFevre, 27 Pa. St. 413. Many other authorities are referred to in subsequent notes herein, and most of the cases are cited in the note to McClelland v. Norfolk, etc., R. R. Co., 1 L. R. A. 299, and in Morris Canal, etc., Co. v. Fisher, 1 Stockt. Ch. (N. J.) 667, s. c. 64 Am. Dec. 423, and note. But coupons are not within a statute allowing days of grace on promissory notes. Chaffee v. Middlesex R. R. Co., 146 Mass. 224, s. c. 16 N. E. R. 34. In Evertson v. Nat. Bank, 66 N. Y. 14, it is held that the coupons are entitled to days of grace, while in Arents v. Commonwealth, 18 Gratt. (Va.) 750, it is held that they are not. It is generally held that "the mortgage follows and partakes of the negotiability of the bonds." Kenicott v. Supervisors, 16 Wall. (U. S.) 452; 2 Cook on Stock and Stockholders, § 770; authorities cited in Chicago Ry., etc., Co. v. Merchants' Nat. Bank, 136 U. S. 268, s. c 10 Super. Ct. R. 999, 1003. As shown in Spence v. Mobile, etc., Ry. Co., 79 Ala. 576, the only authorities to the contrary are in Ohio and Illinois.

[2] Hotchkiss v. Nat. Banks, 21 Wall. (U. S.) 354. See, also, Welch v. Sage, 47 N. Y. 143.

[3] Savannah, etc., R. R. Co. v. Lancaster, 62 Ala. 555.

[4] Union Cattle Co. v. International Trust Co., 149 Mass. 492, s. c. 21 N. E. R. 962.

[5] Union, etc., Co. v. Southern, etc., Co., 51 Fed. 840.

[6] Cromwell v. County of Sac, 96 U. S. 51; Indiana, etc., Ry. Co. v. Sprague, 103 U. S. 756; Morgan v. United States, 113 U. S. 476; Morton v. N. O., etc., R. R. Co., 79 Ala. 590; State v. Cobb, 64 Ala. 127; McElrath v. Pittsburg, etc., R. R. Co., 55 Pa. St. 189; Grand Rapids, etc., R. R. Co. v. Sanders, 54 How. Pr. (N. Y.) 214. But see First Nat. Bank v. Scott County Comrs., 14 Minn. 77; Parsons v. Jackson, 99 U. S. 434. While this is true as to the bond the purchaser is not a *bona fide* purchaser of the overdue coupons so as to be protected from defenses as to them. Gilbrough v. Norfolk, etc., R. R. Co., 1 Hughes (U. S.) 410.

ficient to destroy its negotiability or to put the purchaser in good faith upon inquiry as to the conditions in the deed qualifying the terms of the bond.[1] But if the conditions in the trust deed had been incorporated in the bond or so clearly referred to therein as to notify the bondholder of their existence, and, in legal effect, import them into the bonds, he would doubtless have taken the bond subject thereto, and it may be stated as a general rule that bonds which contain special stipulations making their payment subject to contingencies not within the control of the holders, lose the character of negotiable instruments and are subject in the hands of a transferee to defenses which would have been available if they were still in the hands of the original payee.[2] The fact that the name of the payee is omitted and that the bonds are payable in blank does not affect their negotiability, and the holder may fill in his own name and maintain suit upon them.[3] The purchaser of negotiable bonds issued by a railroad company in good faith, before maturity, without notice and for a valuable consideration, takes them free from all defenses short of an absolute want of power in the company to issue negotiable bonds.[4] Thus, he is en-

[1] Guilford v. Minneapolis, etc., R. R. Co., 48 Minn. 560, s. c. 51 N. W. R. 658, 51 Am. & Eng. R. R. Cas. 98. Distinguishing Manning v. Norfolk, etc., R. R. Co., 29 Fed. R. 838; Caylus v. New York, etc., R. R. Co., 10 Hun (N. Y.) 295, and McClelland v. Norfolk, etc., R. R. Co., 110 N. Y. 469. The correctness of this decision is not, perhaps, beyond question, but it seems to us that as the recital called attention to nothing unusual, as such bonds are nearly always secured by a trust deed and as they are intended to be' negotiable, the purchaser was not obliged to look for unusual conditions in the trust deed. As bonds are sold as negotiable instruments all over the world any other rule would be impracticable and disastrous. If there had been anything in the bonds calling attention to the unusual provisions of the trust deed the purchaser would doubtless have been bound thereby, but that is a different question.

[2] McClelland v. Norfolk, etc., R. R. Co., 110 N. Y. 469, s. c. 18 N. E. R. 237, 1 L. R. A. 299, 6 Am. St. Rep. 397. See, also, Reid v. Bank, 70 Ala. 199; Evertson v. Nat. Bank, 66 N. Y. 14.

[3] White v. Vermont, etc., R. R. Co., 21 How. (U. S.) 575; Chapin v. Vermont, etc., R. R. Co., 8 Gray (Mass.) 575; Hubbard v. New York, etc., R. R. Co., 14 Abb. Pr. (N. Y.) 275; note to Morris Canal, etc., Co. v. Fisher, 64 Am. Dec. 423; note to McClelland v. Norfolk, etc., R. R. Co., 1 L. R. A. 299. See, however, Evertson v. Nat. Bank, 66 N. Y. 14, s. c. 23 Am. R. 9; Augusta Bank v. Augusta, 49 Me. 507.

[4] Galveston, etc., R. R. Co. v. Cowdrey, 11 Wall. (U. S.) 459; McMurray

titled to enforce them against the company, although they may have been stolen,[1] or sold to a prior holder at less than par in violation of the charter or governing statute.[2] He is entitled to their full value no matter what he paid for them.[3] He is not affected in any way by a subsequent misapplication of the proceeds by the company to a purpose for which it is forbidden to issue bonds,[4] and it has been held that the fact that a merchant has taken bonds in payment for goods does not of itself prevent him from being a *bona fide* purchaser or holder of such bonds.[5] Good faith upon the part of the holder will usually be presumed and the burden of proving fraud or bad faith is upon the party charging it.[6] A *bona fide* pledgee of negotiable bonds, for value and before maturity, is entitled to the same protection as a *bona fide* purchaser to the extent of his loan.[7] The

v. Moran, 134 U. S. 150, s. c. 10 Sup. Ct. R. 427; Rouede *v.* Mayor, 18 Fed. R. 719; First. Nat. Bank *v.* Wheeler, 72 N. Y. 201; Stoney *v.* American Life Ins. Co., 11 Paige (N. Y.) 635; Webb *v.* Comrs., L. R. 5 Q. B. 642.

[1] Purchasers of stolen bonds were held to take a good title in the following cases: Carpenter *v.* Rommel, 5 Phila. (Pa.) 34; Dutchess, etc., Co. *v.* Hachfield, 73 N. Y. 226; Murray *v.* Lardner, 2 Wall. (U. S.) 110; Seybell *v.* Nat., etc., Bank, 2 Daly (N. Y.) 383; Raphael *v.* Governor, etc., 17 C. B. 161; Consolidated Assn. *v.* Avegno, 28 La. Ann. 552. Notice to trustee of defenses held not sufficient to destroy a *bona fide* holding of bonds under the trust deed. Comrs. of Johnson Co. *v.* Thayer, 94 U. S. 631.

[2] Ellsworth *v.* St. Louis, etc., R. R. Co., 98 N. Y. 553, approved in Gamble *v.* Queens, etc., Co., 9 L. R. A. 527; Tiedeman on Commercial Paper, § 116; Zabriskie *v.* Cleveland, etc., R. R. Co., 23 How. (U. S.) 381. But see Riggs *v.* Pennsylvania, etc., R. R. Co., 16 Fed. R. 804; Spence *v.* Mobile, etc., Ry. Co., 79 Ala. 576. See, generally, as tending to uphold such a transaction, Handley *v.* Stutz, 139 U. S. 417; Memphis, etc., R. R. Co. *v.* Dow, 120 U. S. 287; Nelson *v.* Hubbard, 96 Ala. 238, 17 L. R. A. 375.

[3] Cromwell *v.* County of Sac, 96 U. S. 51; Grand Rapids, etc., R. R. Co. *v.* Sanders, 17 Hun (N. Y.) 552.

[4] Peoria, etc., R. R. Co. *v.* Thompson, 103 Ill. 187; Philadelphia, etc., R. R. Co. *v.* Lewis, 33 Pa. St. 33.

[5] Kennicott *v.* Wayne Co., 6 Biss. (U. S.) 138. See, also, Mercantile Trust Co. *v.* Zanesville, etc., R. R. Co., 52 Fed. R. 342.

[6] Murray *v.* Lardner, 2 Wall. (U. S.) 110; Kneeland *v.* Lawrence, 140 U. S. 209, s. c. 46 Am. & Eng. R. R. Cas. 319, 322; Spence *v.* Mobile, etc., R. R. Co., 79 Ala. 576; Wickes *v.* Adirondack Co., 2 Hun (N. Y.) 112; Chicago, etc., Co. *v.* Peck, 112 Ill. 408; Jones on Corp. Bonds & Mort., § 200. But compare Simmons *v.* Taylor, 38 Fed. R. 682; Northampton Nat. Bank *v.* Kidder, 106 N. Y. 221, s. c. 60 Am. R. 443; Gilman *v.* New Orleans, etc., R. R. Co., 72. Ala. 566.

[7] Allen *v.* Dallas, etc., R. R. Co., 3 Woods (U. S.) 316; Claflin *v.* South Carolina R. R. Co., 8 Fed. R. 118;

pendency of a suit in which the validity of negotiable bonds, not yet due, is involved, is not constructive notice to one who subsequently purchases them in good faith before maturity.[1] But one who takes bonds after maturity or with notice of their illegality or other existing defenses is not protected as a *bona fide* purchaser of negotiable paper before maturity, unless he succeeds to the rights of such a purchaser. Thus, one who purchases stolen bonds after maturity is not a *bona fide* purchaser entitled to be protected in his purchase as against the true owner unless a *bona fide* purchaser has intervened before maturity.[2] So, a purchaser having knowledge of an equitable lien upon the bonds will usually be held to have taken them subject to such lien,[3] and if he has knowledge that they are issued or being disposed of for an unauthorized purpose or the like, he takes them at his peril;[4] but he may be protected as a *bona fide* purchaser of mortgage bonds notwithstanding the fact that he has knowledge of the claim of one who furnished material for the railroad if he bought them from a *bona fide* purchaser who had no such knowledge.[5]

Morton v. N. O., etc., R. R. Co., 79 Ala., 590, 621; Atwood v. Shenandoah Valley R. R. Co., 85 Va. 966, s. c. 9 S. E. R. 748, 38 Am. & Eng. R. R. Cas. 534; Jones on Pledges, §§ 89, 669; Hayden v. Lincoln, etc., R. Co., 43 Neb. 680, s. c. 62 N. W. R. 73. See Duncomb v. New York, etc., R. R. Co., 84 N. Y. 190; Tyrell v. Cairo, etc., R. R. Co., 7 Mo. App. 294.

[1] Town of Enfield v. Jordan, 119 U. S. 680, s. c. 7 Sup. Ct. R. 358; Marshal v. Town of Elgin, 8 Fed. R. 783; County of Warren v. Marcy, 97 U. S. 96; Farmers', etc., Co. v. Toledo, etc., Co., 54 Fed. R. 759.

[2] Northampton Nat. Bank v. Kidder, 106 N. Y. 221, holding also that there is no presumption that the thief negotiated the paper before it was due. See, also, Hinckley v. Merchants' Nat. Bank, 131 Mass. 147.

[3] Hervey v. Ill. Midland Ry. Co., 28 Fed. R. 169. So, where bonds are assigned after levy of execution. Hetherington v. Hayden, 11 Iowa 335.

[4] Chew v. Henrietta, etc., Co., 2 Fed. R. 5; City of Chicago v. Cameron, 120 Ill. 447. See, also, American L. & T. Co. v. St. Louis, etc., R. R. Co., 42 Fed. R. 819; Smith v. Florida, etc., R. R. Co., 43 Fed. R. 731; Silliman v. Fredericksburg, etc., R. R. Co., 27 Gratt. (Va.) 119; Trask v. Jacksonville, etc., R. R. Co., 124 U. S. 515, s. c. 8 Sup. Ct. R. 574; Mayor of Knoxville v. Knoxville, etc., R. R. Co., 22 Fed. R. 758; Garrard v. Pittsburgh, etc., R. R. Co., 29 Pa. St. 154, for instances in which the purchaser was chargeable with knowledge preventing him from being protected as a *bona fide* purchaser.

[5] Porter v. Pittsburg, etc., Co., 122 U. S. 267, s. c. 7 Sup. Ct. R. 1206. See, also, Commissioners v. Bolles, 94 U. S. 104, 109; Tiedeman on Commercial Paper, § 295.

§ 485. Form and manner of issuing bonds—Effect of irregularities.—Railroad bonds are generally issued with interest coupons attached, which are substantially in the form of promissory notes. They are usually signed by the president and attested or countersigned by the secretary or other proper officer according to the statute or by-laws.[1] These signatures may be either written or printed,[2] although it is better that they should be written, and it has been held that if the bonds have been properly executed and signed by both of such officers the coupons may be valid notwithstanding the fact that they are signed by only one of them.[3] The presence or absence of a seal is generally immaterial, so far as the negotiability of the instrument is concerned.[4] The amount and time and place of payment should be stated with certainty;[5] but the figures denoting the number of a particular bond in a series are not, ordinarily, an essential or material part of it, and an immaterial alteration in such numbers will not affect the rights of a *bona fide* holder.[6] Persons dealing in negotiable bonds of a corporation must take notice of any charter or statutory prohibition or want of power to issue instruments of that character, and so, if the bonds show upon their face that the provisions of the governing statute have not been complied with, the purchaser is chargeable with notice;[7] but, if the corporation has

[1] Of course the name of the corporation is in the body and should also, properly, be subscribed "by" the officers named.

[2] Lynde v. County, 16 Wall. (U. S.) 6; McKee v. Vernon County, 3 Dill. (U. S.) 210; Pennington v. Baehr, 48 Cal. 565.

[3] Thayer v. Montgomery Co., 3 Dill. (U. S.) 389. The coupons may be in almost any form creating an indebtedness. Tiedeman on Commercial Paper, § 475.

[4] Tiedeman on Commercial Paper, § 475; *ante*, § 484; 2 Cook on Stock and Stockholders, §§ 721, 768.

[5] Parsons v. Jackson, 99 U. S. 434; Jackson v. Vicksburg, etc., R. R. Co., 2 Woods (U. S.) 141; Maas v. Missouri, etc., R. R. Co., 83 N. Y. 223, s. c. 3 Am. & Eng. R. R. Cas. 30.

[6] Birdsall v. Russell, 29 N. Y. 220; City of Elizabeth v. Force, 29 N. J. Eq. 587; Commonwealth v. Emigrant, etc., Bank, 98 Mass. 12; Wylie v. Missouri Pac. Ry. Co., 41 Fed. R. 623.

[7] See Nesbit v. Riverside Independent Dist., 144 U. S. 610, s. c. 12 Sup. Ct. R. 746; Spence v. Mobile, etc., Ry. Co., 79 Ala. 576; Gilman v. New Orleans, etc., R. R. Co., 72 Ala. 566; Commonwealth v. Smith, 10 Allen (Mass.) 448, s. c. 87 Am. Dec. 672; Duke v. Brown, 96 N. Car. 127.

power to issue instruments of that class, and the particular bonds in question appear to be regular and in compliance with the law, a purchaser in good faith has a right to assume that all the preliminary proceedings were regular.[1] Thus, a requirement that the issue of bonds shall be authorized or ratified by the stockholders or by a resolution of the board of directors may be assumed to have been complied with.[2] So, generally, if the corporation has power under any circumstances to issue negotiable bonds, a *bona fide* holder has a right to presume, in the absence of anything to the contrary, that they were issued under those circumstances and that all conditions within the scope of the authority of the officers of the company have been fulfilled.[3] This is true, and a *bona fide* holder may enforce their payment, although the bonds may have been wrongfully put in circulation in the first instance[4] or issued in excess of the amount authorized or prescribed by statute.[5] But securities issued in a form materially different

[1] Ellsworth v. St. Louis, etc., R. R. Co., 98 N. Y. 553; Bank v. Dandridge, 12 Wheat. (U. S.) 64; Atwood v. Shenandoah, etc., R. R. Co., 85 Va. 966; Railway Co. v. McCarthy, 96 U. S. 258; Pearce v. Madison R. Co., 21 How. (U. S.) 441; Stewart v. Lansing, 104 U. S. 505; *In re* Land Credit Co., L. R. 4 Ch. 460; Fountaine v. Carmarthen Ry. Co., L. R. 5 Eq. 316.

[2] Connecticut Life Ins. Co. v. Cleveland, etc., R. R. Co., 41 Barb. (N.Y.) 9; Zabriskie v. Cleveland, etc., R. R. Co., 23 How. (U. S.) 381; Royal British Bank v. Turquand, 6 E. & B. 327; *In re* Tyson's Reef Co., 3 W. W. & A'B. (Vict. Sup. Ct.)Cas. at Law 162. Directors ordinarily have power to authorize the execution of bonds and mortgages. Thompson v. Natchez, etc., Co., 68 Miss. 423, 9 So. R. 821; Hodder v. Kentucky, etc., Ry. Co., 7 Fed. R. 793.

[3] Hackensack Water Co. v. DeKay, 36 N. J. Eq. 548; *In re* Athenæum Soc., 4 K. & J. 549.

[4] Grand Rapids, etc., R. R. Co. v. Sanders, 17 Hun (N.Y.) 552; Webb v. Comrs., L. R. 5 Q. B. 642; Long Island L. & T. Co. v. Columbus, etc., R. Co., 65 Fed. R. 455. But see Athenæum, etc., Ins. Soc. v. Pooley, 3 DeG. & J. 294.

[5] 2 Cook on Stock and Stockholders, § 760; Baker v. Guarantee, etc., Co., (N. J.) 31 Atl. R. 174; Fidelity, etc., Co. v. West Pa., etc., R. Co., 138 Pa. St. 494, s. c. 21 Atl. R. 21; Allis v. Jones, 45 Fed. R. 148; Warfield v. Marshall, etc., Co., 72 Iowa 666, s. c. 34 N.W. R. 467. But see Commonwealth v. Smith, 10 Allen (Mass.) 448, s. c. 87 Am. Dec. 672; Nesbit v. Riverside Independent Dist., 144 U. S. 610, s. c. 12 Sup. Ct. R. 746. All the *bona fide* bondholders participate in the mortgage security, notwithstanding some of the bonds are overissued. Stephens v. Benton, 1 Duv. (Ky.) 112; Stanton v. Alabama, etc., R. Co., 2 Woods (U. S.) 523.

from that prescribed by the statute giving the authority, or without compliance with a condition to be performed by some one other than the corporation, may generally be avoided even as against a so-called *bona fide* purchaser.[1] Thus, where the statute requires them to be certified on their face by a trust company and registered, and provides that no bond shall be valid until it is so certified and registered they will not be enforced even in the hands of a purchaser in good faith.[2]

§ 486. **Interest coupons.**—Interest coupons in the ordinary form, having the requisite certainty of negotiable instruments, may be severed from the bonds to which they are attached and pass by delivery from hand to hand so as to vest a complete title in the *bona fide* purchaser before maturity with all the rights of a holder of ordinary commercial paper.[3] Their negotiability is not affected by a statement that they represent interest upon certain bonds specified by their numbers.[4] They are in a sense independent securities and may be negotiated as such, yet their character as negotiable instruments and the rights of their holders are sometimes determined by the bonds to which the coupons are attached or to which they refer,[5] and a purchaser may be required to take notice of matters to which

---

[1] Hackensack Water Co. v. DeKay, 36 N. J. Eq. 548; Singer v. St. Louis, etc., R. R. Co., 6 Mo. App. 427.

[2] Morrison v. Inhabitants, etc., of Bernards, 36 N. J. L. 219; Maas v. Missouri, etc., R. R. Co., 83 N. Y. 223.

[3] Commonwealth v. Chesapeake, etc., Co., 32 Md. 501; Spooner v. Holmes, 102 Mass. 503, s. c. 3 Am. R. 491; Mercer County v. Hacket, 1 Wall. (U. S.) 83; Brainerd v. New York, etc., R. R. Co., 25 N. Y. 496; and numerous authorities cited in note to Morris Canal, etc., Co. v. Fisher. 64 Am. Dec. 423, 432, and in note McClelland v. Norfolk, etc., R. Co., 1 L. R. A. 299; also, Jones on Corp. Bonds & Mort., § 238.

[4] Evertson v. Nat. Bank, 66 N.Y. 14, s. c. 23 Am. R. 9.

[5] McCoy v. Washington Co., 3 Wall. Jr. (U. S.) 381, and Smith v. County of Clark, 54 Mo. 58, holding particular coupons negotiable because the bonds were negotiable; City of Lexington v. Butler, 14 Wall. (U. S.) 282; City of Kenosha v. Lamson, 9 Wall. 477; State v. Spartanburg, etc., R. R. Co., 8 So. Car. 129; Bailey v. County of Buchanan, 115 N. Y. 297. Though overdue they may still be negotiated like other overdue commercial paper so long as the bonds have not matured. Town of Thompson v. Perrine, 106 U. S. 589, s. c. 1 Sup. Ct. R. 564, 567; Grand Rapids, etc., R. R. Co. v. Sanders, 54 How. Pr. (N. Y.) 214.

they refer in the bonds or mortgage.[1] The peculiar relation of coupons to their bonds is further illustrated by the rules governing the application of the statute of limitations to such instruments. Thus, the period of limitation applicable to the bond is also applied to the coupon and if, for instance, the statute bars simple contract debts, such as the coupon would be except for its relation to the bond, in six years, while it does not bar debts in the nature of the bond short of twenty years, the coupon will not be barred until the expiration of the twenty years;[2] but the statute begins to run against a detached coupon from its own maturity and an action upon coupons may, therefore, be barred before an action upon the bonds which mature later, although the length of the period of limitation is the same.[3] Coupons are so far independent instruments, however, that when complete in themselves, with the requisite certainties of negotiable paper, they may be sued upon, and when severed from the bond before maturity a separate action may be maintained upon them,[4] even though the bond has been paid.[5] This rule has also been applied by some of the courts in favor of the holder of coupons that did not contain words of negotiability or any independent promise to pay the bearer or holder,[6]

[1] McClelland v. Norfolk, etc., R. R. Co., 110 N. Y. 469; McClure v. Township of Oxford, 94 U. S. 429; Silliman v. Fredericksburg, etc., R. R. Co., 27 Gratt (Va.) 119.

[2] City of Kenosha v. Lamson, 9 Wall. (U. S.) 477, 483; City of Lexington v. Butler, 14 Wall. (U. S.) 282; Huey v. Macon County, 35 Fed. R. 481. See, also, Meyer v. Porter, 65 Cal. 67, s. c. 1 West Coast R. 784.

[3] Clark v. Iowa City, 20 Wall. (U. S.) 583; Amy v. Dubuque, 98 U. S. 470; Huey v. Macon County, 35 Fed. R. 481; Koshkonong v. Burton, 104 U. S. 668. See, also, Griffin v. Macon County, 36 Fed. R. 885. Although the bondholders are given the option to sue for both principal and interest six months after default in the payment of interest, this does not, of itself, set the statute of limitations to running against the bonds. Nebraska, etc., Bank v. Nebraska, etc., Co., 14 Fed. R. 763.

[4] County of Beaver v. Armstrong, 44 Pa. St. 63; Commissioners of Knox County v. Aspinwall, 21 How. (U. S.) 539, 546; Thomson v. Lee County, 3 Wall. (U. S.) 327; Commonwealth v. State and Chesapeake, etc., R. Co., 32 Md. 501; North Penna. R. R. Co. v. Adams, 54 Pa St. 94.

[5] National Exch. Bank v. Hartford, etc., R. R. Co., 8 R. I. 375, s. c. 5 Am. R. 582. See, also, Walnut v. Wade, 103 U. S. 683, 696, quoting from Clark v. Iowa City, 20 Wall. (U. S.) 583.

[6] Mayor v. Potomac Ins. Co., 2 Baxt. 296; Town of Queensbury v. Culver, 19

but others have held that in such a case the coupon must be declared on in connection with the bond.[1] Coupons, although detached from the bond, do not lose their right to participate in the mortgage security,[2] but the fact that they are secured by mortgage does not deprive the holder of the right to sue on them at law when due;[3] nor is a suit on one coupon a bar to a subsequent suit on another which was also due at the time of such suit.[4] But neither a bondholder nor the holder of a coupon can enforce his judgment by levying an execution upon the mortgaged property and selling it to the disadvantage of the other bondholders.[5] Overdue coupons draw interest at the legal rate,[6] and it has been held that such interest is

Wall. (U. S.) 83; Smith v. County of Clark, 54 Mo. 58; Woods v. Lawrence County, 1 Black, (U. S.), 386; 2 Daniels' Negot. Instr., §§ 1511, 1512.

[1] Crosby v. New London, etc., R. Co., 26 Conn. 121; Jackson v. York, etc., R. Co., 48 Me. 147; Evertson v. Nat. Bank, 66 N. Y. 14. Approved in Jones on Corp. Bonds and Mortg., §§ 242, 262.

[2] Miller v. Rutland, etc., R. R. Co., 40 Vt. 399; Union Trust Co. v. Monticello, etc., R. R. Co., 63 N. Y. 311; Stevens v. New York, etc., R. R. Co., 13 Blatchf. (U. S.) 412; Haven v. Grand Junction R. R. Co., 109 Mass. 88; Champion v. Hartford, etc., Co., 45 Kan. 103, 10 L. R. A. 754.

[3] Manning v. Norfolk, etc., R. R. Co., 29 Fed. R. 838; Welsh v. First Division, etc., R. R., 25 Minn. 314; Montgomery, etc., Soc. v. Francis, 103 Pa. St. 378. Where the coupons are payable to bearer the holder is not necessarily an assignee and his right to sue in the United States courts does not depend upon the citizenship of any particular holder. Thompson v. Perrine, 106 U. S. 589, 103 U. S. 806.

[4] Butterfield v. Town of Ontario, 44 Fed. R. 171. See, also, Cromwell v. County of Sac, 94 U. S. 351; Stewart v. Lansing, 104 U. S. 505.

[5] Philadelphia, etc., R. R. Co. v. Woelpper, 64 Pa. St. 366; Butler v. Rahm, 46 Md. 541; Commonwealth v. Susquehanna, etc., R. R. Co., 122 Pa. St. 306; Fish v. New York Paper Co., 29 N. J. Eq. 16; Bowen v. Brecon Ry. L. R. 3 Eq. 541, and cases cited in Pugh v. Fairmount, etc., Co., 112 U. S. 238, s. c. 5 Sup. Ct. R. 131, 135. In the first two cases above cited it was held that injunction would lie at the suit of other bondholders.

[6] Aurora City v. West, 7 Wall. (U. S.) 82; Walnut v. Wade, 103 U. S. 683; Ashuelot R. R. Co. v. Elliott, 57 N. H. 397; Philadelphia, etc., R. R. Co. v. Smith, 105 Pa. St. 195; Langston v. South Carolina R. R. Co., 2 So. Car. 248; Rich v. Seneca Falls, 8 Fed. R. 852, and numerous authorities cited in note to Morris Canal, etc., Co. v. Fisher, 64 Am. Dec. 441. Even where the bonds continue to draw interest after maturity at the same rate they did before, which is greater than the rate fixed by statute in the absence of contract. Cromwell v. County of Sac, 96 U. S. 51; Langston v. South Carolina R. R. Co., 2 So. Car. 248; Spencer v. Pierce, 5 R. I. 63.

covered by the mortgage which secures the bonds and coupons.[1]

§ 487. **Payment of bonds and interest.**—The authorities are conflicting as to whether interest coupons are entitled to days of grace,[2] but, aside from this question, they are payable at the time fixed in the coupons and bond, and a provision in the bond that the interest shall be paid when the coupon is presented and surrendered does not change the rule as to the maturity of the coupon or require its presentment for payment at the time designated in order to hold the maker.[3] Coupons are usually paid in the order in which they fall due,[4] but, ordinarily, upon foreclosure of the mortgage mere priority of maturity gives no priority of satisfaction either over other coupons or over the bond, and the rule of distribution is that the bonds and coupons all share *pro rata* or *pari passu* in the proceeds.[5] Where, however, coupons have been presented for payment and cashed they are not entitled to share equally with the bondholders and coupon holders who had reason to sup-

[1] Gibert v. Washington City, etc., R. R. Co., 33 Gratt. (Va.) 586. It is generally held, as shown by the authorities cited in the preceding note, that a demand is unnecessary to start interest to running where the coupons are payable at a fixed time and place; but if no demand has been made interest may be defeated or abated by the mortgagor showing that he had the funds ready and was able and willing to pay at the time and place designated. North Penna. R. R. Co. v. Adams, 54 Pa. St. 94; Emlen v. Lehigh, etc., Co., 47 Pa. St. 76; Walnut v. Wade, 103 U. S. 683.

[2] Holding that they are not: Arents v. Commonwealth, 18 Gratt. (Va.) 750; 2 Daniels' Negot. Instr. (3d ed.), §§ 1490a, 1505. Holding that they are: Evertson v. Nat. Bank, 66 N. Y. 14; Jones on Corp. Bonds and Mort., § 245. In Massachusetts they are not, under the statute, and the soundness of the New York decision is questioned. Chaffee v. Middlesex R. R. Co., 146 Mass. 224.

[3] Arents v. Commonwealth, 18 Gratt. (Va.) 750, 776; City of Jeffersonville v. Patterson, 26 Ind. 15; County of Greene v. Daniel, 102 U. S. 187; Langston v. South Carolina R. R. Co., 2 So. Car. 248. See, also, Frank v. Wessels, 64 N. Y. 155.

[4] Jones on Corp. Bonds and Mort., § 247.

[5] Sewall v. Brainerd, 38 Vt. 364; State v. Spartanburg, etc., R. R. Co., 8 So. Car. 129; Ketchum v. Duncan, 96 U. S. 659, 671; Dunham v. Cincinnati, etc., Ry. Co., 1 Wall. (U. S.) 254. But compare Stevens v. New York, etc., R. R. Co., 13 Blatch. 412.

pose that they were paid and cancelled, and not merely purchased, although a third person advanced the money to take them up under an agreement with the company that they should be kept alive and delivered to him.[1] But, as against the corporation, they may exist as valid securities and be entitled to be paid out of any surplus remaining after the payment of the other bonds and coupons,[2] and where the persons who present the coupons for payment have knowledge at the time of facts showing that some one else is advancing the money and that the transaction is, in effect, a purchase rather than a final payment of the coupons, they can not complain if such third person is treated as a *bona fide* purchaser and permitted to share *pro rata* with them in the mortgage security.[3] The pledgee of bonds with coupons attached may collect the coupons as they fall due although the debt secured thereby has not yet matured.[4] In a proper case the payment of a lost bond will be enforced, and a court of chancery, it seems, may even compel the execution of a duplicate bond in place of a lost bond not yet due, upon proper indemnity being furnished.[5] Bondholders can not be compelled to accept payment and relinquish their lien before maturity,[6] and a clause in a bond payable at a certain time providing that it "will be redeemed, if desired," at an earlier date, is for the benefit of the holder rather than the maker.[7] Bonds may be made payable in

[1] Union Trust Co. v. Monticello, etc., R. R. Co., 63 N. Y. 311; Cameron v. Tome, 64 Md. 507; Commonwealth v. Chesapeake, etc., Co., 32 Md. 501; Lloyd v. Wagner, 93 Ky. 644, 21 S. W. R. 334; Bockes v. Hathorn, 20 Hun (N. Y.) 503; Fidelity, etc., Co. v. West, etc., R. R. Co., 138 Pa. 494, 21 Atl. R. 21; South Covington, etc., Ry. Co. Gest, 34 Fed. R. 628.

[2] Haven v. Grand Junction R.R., etc., Co., 109 Mass. 88; Union Trust Co. v. Monticello, etc., R. R. Co., 63 N. Y. 311.

[3] Ketchum v. Duncan, 96 U. S. 659. See, also, Claflin v. South Carolina R. R. Co., 8 Fed. R. 118; Wood v. Guarantee, etc., Co., 128 U. S. 416; Hand v. Savannah, etc., R. R. Co., 17 So. Car. 219.

[4] Warner v. Rising Fawn, etc., Co., 3 Woods (U. S.) 514.

[5] Rogers v. Chicago, etc., R. R. Co., 6 Abb. N. Cas. (N. Y.) 253; New Orleans, etc., R. R. Co. v. Mississippi College, 47 Miss. 560. See, also, Chesapeake, etc., Co. v. Blair, 45 Md. 102; Miller v. Rutland, etc., R. R. Co., 40 Vt. 399; Adams' Equity, 166, 168.

[6] Randolph v. Middleton, 26 N. J. Eq. 543.

[7] Allentown School Dist. v. Derr,

gold,[1] but this is not to be implied from the mere expectation of the holders where there is nothing in the contract to that effect or justifying such an implication.[2] The substitution of new bonds for the old ones does not, necessarily, operate as a payment nor prevent the holders from sharing to the same extent in the mortgage security;[3] but the rule is otherwise where a railroad company issues new bonds in order to fund its indebtedness and bondholders accept second mortgage bonds in exchange for first mortgage bonds knowing that the transaction is intended as a satisfaction of the first mortgage bonds.[4]

§ 488. **No power to mortgage without legislative authority.** —Railroad bonds are usually secured by mortgage or trust deed, and mortgages are frequently executed for other purposes as well. A railway company, inasmuch as it receives from the state special privileges because of its public purpose, and has public duties to perform in person, can not, without legislative authority, mortgage its franchises and property essential to their exercise.[5] This rule is not, however, applicable to

115 Pa. St. 439. See, also, Chicago, etc., R. R. Co. v. Pyne, 30 Fed. R. 86.

[1] Trebilcock v. Wilson, 12 Wall. (U. S.) 687; State v. Hays, 50 Mo. 34.

[2] Knox v. Lee, 12 Wall. (U. S.) 457.

[3] Gibert v. Washington City R. R. Co., 33 Gratt. (Va.) 586; Ames v. New Orleans, etc., R. R. Co., 2 Woods (U. U.) 206; Farmers', etc., Co. v. Green, etc., R. R. Co., 6 Fed. R. 100; Blair v. St. Louis, etc., R. R. Co., 23 Fed. R. 524; Stevens v. Mid-Hants, etc., R. R. Co., L. R. 8 Ch. 1064.

[4] Fidelity, etc., Co. v. Shenandoah, etc., R. R. Co., 86 Va. 1, s. c. 9 S. E. R. 759.

[5] Carpenter v. Black Hawk G. M. Co., 65 N. Y. 43, 50; Pullan v. Cincinnati & C. A. L. R. R. Co., 4 Biss. 35; Susquehanna C. Co. v. Bonham, 9 W. & S. (Pa.) 27; Pierce v. Emery, 32 N. H. 484; Coe v. Columbus, P. & I. R. R. Co., 10 Ohio St. 372, s. c. 75 Am. Dec. 518, and note; Atkinson v. Marietta, etc., R. R. Co., 15 Ohio St. 21; Stewart v. Jones, 40 Mo. 140; New Orleans, etc., R. R. Co. v. Harris, 27 Miss. 517; Hall v. Sullivan R. R., 21 Law R. 138; Wyatt v. St. Helen's, & R. G. Ry. Co., 2 Q. B. 364; Daniels v. Hart, 118 Mass. 543; Wood v. Bedford, etc., R. Co., 8 Phila. (Pa.) 94; Randolph v. Wilmington, etc., R. R. Co., 11 Phila. (Pa.) 502; State v. Mexican Gulf Ry. Co., 3 Rob. (La.) 513: Commonwealth v. Smith, 10 Allen (Mass.) 448, s. c. 87 Am. Dec. 672, and note; East Boston F. R. R. Co. v. Eastern R. R. Co., 13 Allen (Mass.) 422; Richardson v. Sibley, 11 Allen (Mass.) 65, s. c. 87 Am. Dec. 700, and note; Troy, etc., R. R. Co. v. Kerr, 17 Barb. (N. Y.) 581; Stewart's Appeal, 56 Pa. St. 413; Hays v. Ottawa, etc., R. R. Co., 61 Ill. 422;

property which is not essential to or of use in the fulfillment of the corporation's public purpose and not necessary to enable the company to perform its duties to the public.[1]

§ 489. **Legislative authority to mortgage.**—In almost all of the states general laws have been enacted authorizing railroad companies to mortgage their property and franchises.[2] The authority may, sometimes, be implied or inferred from the terms of the statute,[3] although not expressly mentioned; but, by expressly giving authority to mortgage to a certain amount the implication of an authority to mortgage beyond that amount may be forbidden.[4] Charter authority to mortgage real

Black v. Delaware, etc., Canal Co., 22 N. J. Eq. 130; Hart v. Eastern U. Ry. Co., 7 Exchq. 246. In a number of cases in the Supreme Court of the United States, most of which involved the question of the power to lease, it is stated in general terms that a railroad company has no implied power to alienate its franchises in any way, whether by sale, mortgage or lease. The most recent of these cases is Snell v. City of Chicago, 152 U. S. 191, s. c. 14 Sup. Ct. R. 489, 492, in which the others are cited. Some cases, however, hold that railroad companies may mortgage their property and franchises other than that of existing as a corporation, at least to secure indebtedness incurred for the legitimate purposes of construction or operation. Savannah & M. R. R. Co. v. Lancaster, 62 Ala. 555; Kelly v. Ala., etc., R. R. Co., 58 Ala. 489; Miller v. Rutland, etc., R. R. Co., 36 Vt. 452; Memphis, etc., R. R. Co. v. Dow, 22 Blatch. 48, 19 Fed. R. 388; Shepley v. Atlantic & S. L. R. R. Co., 55 Me. 395; Kennebec & P. R. R. Co. v. Portland & K. R. R. Co., 59 Me. 9, 23; Bickford v. Grand Junction Ry. Co., 1 Sup. Ct. of Canada 696, 738, reversing Grand Junction Ry. Co. v. Bickford, 23 Grant's Ch. (Ont.) 302; Bardstown & L. R. R. Co. v. Metcalfe, 4 Metc. (Ky.) 199; Commissioners v. Atlantic, etc., R. R. Co., 77 N. Car. 289. See, also, New Orleans, etc., R. Co. v. Delamore, 114 U. S. 501.

[1] Platt v. Union Pac. R. Co., 99 U. S. 48, 57; Tucker v. Ferguson, 22 Wall. 527, 572; Hendee v. Pinkerton, 14 Allen (Mass.) 381; Bickford v. Grand Junction Ry. Co., 1 Sup. Ct. of Canada 696, 735; Taber v. Cincinnati, etc., Ry. Co., 15 Ind. 459; Pierce v. Emery, 32 N. H. 484. See, also, Coe v. Columbus, etc., R. R. Co., 75 Am. Dec. 518, and note 550. This exception, it is said, includes surplus land acquired by eminent domain. Jones on Railroad Bonds and Mortgages, 12, citing Bickford v. Grand Junction R. Co., 1 Supreme Ct. of Canada, 696, 735.

[2] Jones on Corporate Bonds and Mort., § 27.

[3] East Boston F. R. R. Co. v. Eastern R. R. Co., 13 Allen (Mass.) 422. See, also, Branch v. Jesup, 106 U. S. 468, s. c. 1 Sup. Ct. R. 495; Willamette, etc., Co. v. Bank, 119 U. S. 191, s. c. 7 Sup. Ct. R. 187.

[4] Brice on Ultra Vires (2d Eng. ed.), 273. It is said, however, and rightly, as we think, that an express authority

estate refers to real estate acquired in whatsoever manner;[1] and a part of a railroad may be mortgaged under authority to mortgage the whole.[2] Power to pledge property also authorizes a mortgage of the property,[3] and so does a grant of power to borrow money and execute "such securities in amount and kind" as the company may deem expedient.[4] A mortgage, though made with charter authority, has been held not to be good against the state which has taken possession of the road under provisions of the charter entitling it to declare a forfeiture.[5]

§ 490. **Distinction between authority to mortgage franchises and authority to mortgage property.**—Authority to mortgage a prerogative franchise may not be inferred from a company's express right to sell and consequent[6] right to mortgage its property.[7] But, from the power to mortgage a corporation's to mortgage for certain purposes does not necessarily negative or qualify a general authority to borrow for other purposes for which the implied powers of a corporation are usually sufficient. Jones on Corporate Bonds and Mortgages, 7; Allen v. Montgomery R. R. Co., 11 Ala. 437; Mobile & C. P. R. R. Co. v. Talman, 15 Ala. 472; Phillips v. Winslow, 18 B. Mon. (Ky.) 431. See, In re Pooley Hall Colliery Co., 21 L. T. R. N. S. 690.

[1] Galveston, etc., R. Co. v. Cowdrey, 11 Wall. 459.

[2] Pullan v. Cincinnati, & C. A. L. R. R. Co., 4 Biss. 35, 45; Chartiers Ry. Co. v. Hodgens, 85 Pa. St. 501, 506; Bickford v. Grand Junction, etc., Ry., 1 Can. Sup. Ct. R. 696. But see East Boston, etc., R. R. Co. v. Hubbard, 10 Allen, (Mass.) 459, note.

[3] Mobile, etc., R. Co., v. Talman, 15 Ala. 472.

[4] Pierce v. Milwaukee, etc. R. Co., 24 Wis. 551, s. c. 1 Am. R. 203.

[5] Silliman v. Fredericksburg, O. & C. R. R. Co., 27 Gratt. (Va.) 119. See, also, Farnsworth v. Minnesota, etc., R. Co., 92 U. S. 49, 66. But see People v. O'Brien, 111 N. Y. 1; Mower v. Kemp, 42 La. Ann. 1007, 8 So. R. 830.

[6] Willamette M. Co. v. Bank of British Columbia, 119 U. S. 191, s. c. 7 Sup. Ct. R. 187.

[7] McAllister v. Plant, 54 Miss. 106; Branch v. Atlantic & G. R. R. Co., 3 Woods 481. Generally, it would seem that a statute authorizing a mortgage of corporation property does not by implication authorize a mortgage of franchises. Dunham v. Isett, 15 Iowa 284; Pollard v. Maddox, 28 Ala. 321; Pullan v. Cincinnati, & C. R. Co., 4 Biss. (U. S. C. C.) 35; Randolph v. Wilmington, etc., R. Co., 11 Phil. 502. A mortgage covering property and franchise, having been authorized by charter as to the former but not as to the latter, is not entirely void, but will operate to convey the corporation's property. Randolph v. W. & R. R. Co., 11 Phila. (Pa.) 502; Gloninger v. Pittsburg, etc., R. Co., 139 Pa. 13, 46 Am. & Eng. R. R. Cas. 276. See Butler v. Rahm, 46 Md. 541; Carpenter v. Black Hawk G. M. Co., 65 N. Y. 43; Central G. M. Co. v. Platt, 3 Daly (N. Y.) 263.

franchises may be implied the power to transfer both franchises and property to a purchaser at a foreclosure sale.[1] Authority to mortgage a railroad company's "means, property and effects," has been held sufficient to authorize a mortgage of all its franchises except that of being a corporation,[2] but the soundness of these decisions, in so far as they hold that a mortgage of any prerogative or true franchise was authorized, is not entirely beyond question. There must certainly be a very clear grant of power to authorize a mortgage of the franchise to be a corporation. But it has been held that the power to pledge the franchises and rights of a corporation implies, as incident thereto, the power to pledge everything necessary to the enjoyment of the franchise and upon which its real value depends.[3]

§ 491. Who may execute the mortgage.—The authority of a corporation to mortgage its property may, unless reserved to the stockholders, be exercised by its directors,[4] even outside the state of its creation,[5] or outside the state in which the railroad

---

[1] Galveston, etc., R. R. Co. v. Cowdrey, 11 Wall. 459; New Orleans, etc., R. R. Co. v. Delamore, 114 U. S. 501; Traer v. Clews, 115 U. S. 528; Phillips v. Winslow, 18 B. Mon. 431.

[2] Meyer v. Johnston, 53 Ala. 237; Bradstown, etc., R. R. Co. v. Metcalfe, 4 Met. (Ky.) 199. See, also, Wilmington R. Co. v. Reid, 13 Wall. (U. S.) 264; Pullan v. Cincinnati, etc., R. Co., 4 Biss. 35; McAllister v. Plant, 54 Miss. 106. So authority to mortgage "the entire road, fixtures, and equipments, with all the appurtenances, income and resources thereof," does not include the right to mortgage the franchise to be a corporation, but does include, according to another decision, the right to mortgage the franchise to maintain a railroad and take compensation as a carrier. Coe v. Columbus, P. & I. R. R. Co., 10 Ohio St. 372, s. c. 75 Am. Dec. 518.

[3] Phillips v. Winslow, 18 B. Mon. (Ky.) 431.

[4] Wood v. Whelen, 93 Ill. 153; Bank of Middlebury v. Rutland & W. R. R. Co., 30 Vt. 149; Hendee v. Pinkerton, 14 Allen 381; Tripp v. Swanzey Paper Co., 13 Pick. 291; Hodder v. Ky. & G. E. Ry. Co., 7 Fed. R. 793; Taylor v. Agricultural, etc., Assn., 68 Ala. 229; Burrill v. Nahant Bank, 2 Met. (Mass.) 163, 35 Am. Dec. 395; McCurdy's Appeal, 65 Pa. St. 290; Ohio, etc., R. R. Co. v. McPherson, 35 Mo. 13; Thompson v. Natchez, etc., Co., 68 Miss. 423, 9 So. R. 821.

[5] Arms v. Conant, 36 Vt. 744; Galveston R. R. v. Cowdrey, 11 Wall. 459; Ohio & M. R. R. Co. v. McPherson, 35 Mo. 13, 86 Am. Dec. 128; Wright v. Bundy, 11 Ind. 398; McCall v. Byram Mfg. Co., 6 Conn. 428; Bassett v. Monte Christo M. Co., 15 Nev. 293; Coe v. N. J. Midland Ry.

is situated.[1] Even where the authorization of the stockholders is required, it is held that the public has no interest in the requirement;[2] that it can not be pleaded by the corporation's creditors;[3] and that the stockholders can not complain after the issuance of bonds[4] to *bona fide* purchasers. The president of a railway company can not mortgage its property to secure its debt, even though he be authorized generally to act as its financial agent.[5] The use of the corporate seal in such a case only raises a rebuttable presumption that the mortgage has been authoritatively executed.[6] The individual signature of an executive officer, empowered to execute the mortgage, will, however, bind the corporation whose instrument it purports to be, though the corporate name be omitted.[7] Where the authority of the agent to execute the mortgage is in general terms he must include in it usual provisions only, and the company will

Co., 31 N. J. Eq. 105; Hodder v. Ky. & G. E. Ry. Co., 7 Fed. R. 793. In some of the states, however, charters and general laws prohibit the action of the directors without the authorization of the stockholders. Mass. Pub. Stat. Ch. 106, § 23. It has been held that this does not apply to a mortgage of property in Massachusetts owned by a corporation of Vermont. Saltmarsh v. Spaulding, 147 Mass. 224, 4 Ry. & Corp. Law J. 151; Tex. Rev. Stat., Art. 4220; 8 Vict. Ch. 16, § 38; *In re* Romford Canal, 24 Ch. Div. 85; Landowners', etc., Co. v. Ashford, 16 Ch. Div. 411; Fountaine v. Carmarthen Ry. Co., 5 Eq. 316; Hodges on Railways, 121.

[1] Hervey v. Illinois Midland Ry. Co., 28 Fed. R. 169.

[2] Thomas v. Citizens' Horse R. R. Co., 104 Ill. 462. See, also, Central Trust Co. v. Condon, 67 Fed. R. 84.

[3] Hervey v. Illinois Midland Ry. Co., 28 Fed. R. 169.

[4] Hodder v. Kentucky, etc., R. R. Co., 7 Fed. R. 793; Texas, etc., Ry. Co.

v. Gentry, 69 Tex. 625; McCurdy's Appeal, 65 Pa. St. 290.

[5] Despatch Line of Packets v. Bellamy Mfg. Co., 12 N. H. 205; Luse v. Isthmus Transit Ry. Co., 6 Ore. 125; Hoyt v. Thompson, 5 N.Y. 320; Whitwell v. Warner, 20 Vt. 425. But it might be otherwise if he were authorized to borrow the money. Hatch v. Coddington, 95 U. S. 48.

[6] Fidelity Ins. Co. v. Shenandoah Valley R. R. Co., 9 S. E. R. 180, 32 W. Va. 244; Wood v. Whelen, 93 Ill. 153; Gorder v. Plattsmouth Canning Co., 36 Neb. 548, s. c. 54 N. W. R. 830; Northern C. Railroad Co. v. Bastian, 15 Md. 494. See, also, Koehler v. Black River Falls Iron Co., 2 Black 715; Reed v. Bradley, 17 Ill. 321.

[7] Despatch Line of Packets v. Bellamy Mfg. Co., 12 N. H. 205; Haven v. Adams, 4 Allen (Mass.) 80; Savannah & M. R. R. Co. v. Lancaster, 62 Ala. 555. Of course this is not true when the instrument purports to be the officers'. Brinley v. Mann, 2 Cush. (Mass.) 337; Miller v. Rutland & W. R. R. Co., 36 Vt. 452.

not, ordinarily, be bound by any unusual provisions which may be included.[1]

§ 492. Ratification by stockholders of unauthorized or improperly executed mortgage. — An unauthorized mortgage, which the corporation has power to execute, may be ratified by the stockholders, either directly by vote or indirectly as by the payment of interest or the receipt and retention of the proceeds, or other acts recognizing the obligation.[2] The receipt of the proceeds of an unauthorized mortgage has been held to be such a ratification that a corporation may not thereafter repudiate it, even though executed in violation of a statute forbidding a mortgage without the approval of two-thirds of the stock.[3] So, where a corporation is authorized to increase its capital stock, and attempts to do so, but fails to give the statutory notice required in such a case, both the corporation and its stockholders who acquiesce therein, are estopped to question the validity of a mortgage executed to secure obligations greater in amount than the original capital, but less than the capital as increased, although the statute prohibits a mortgage

---

[1] Jesup v. City Bank of Racine, 14 Wis. 331; Pacific Rolling Mill v. Dayton, etc., R. Co., 5 Fed. R. 852. But see Coe v. New Jersey Midland Ry. Co., 31 N. J. Eq. 105.

[2] Ottawa, etc., R. Co. v. Murray, 15 Ill. 336; Farmers' L. & T. Co. v. Toledo, etc., R. Co., 67 Fed. R. 49; Thomas v. Citizens' Horse Ry. Co., 104 Ill. 462; McCurdy's Appeal, 65 Pa. St. 290; Harrison v. Annapolis, etc., R. R. Co., 50 Md. 490; Singer v. St. Louis, etc., Ry. Co., 6 Mo. App. 427; Trader v. Jarvis, 23 W. Va. 100; Lewis v. Hartford Silk Mfg. Co., 56 Conn. 25; Elwell v. Grand St., etc., R. R. Co., 67 Barb. (N. Y.) 83; Page v. Fall River, etc., R. R. Co., 31 Fed. R. 257; Lester v. Webb, 1 Allen (Mass.) 34; Kelley v. Newburyport, etc., R. Co., 141 Mass. 496; Merchants' Bank v. State Bank, 10 Wall. (U. S.) 604; Railway Co. v. McCarthy, 96 U. S. 258; National Bank v. Matthews, 98 U. S. 621; Mahoney Mining Co. v. Anglo-Californian Bank, 104 U. S. 192; Whitney Arms Co. v. Barlow, 63 N. Y. 62; Perkins v. Portland, etc., R. R. Co., 47 Me. 573; City F. Insurance Co. v. Carrugi, 41 Ga. 660; So. L. Ins. & T. Co. v. Lanier, 5 Fla. 110; Hays v. Galion Gas Light & C. Co., 29 Ohio St. 330; Foulke v. San Diego, etc., R. R. Co., 51 Cal. 365; Thompson v. Lambert, 44 Iowa 239.

[3] Texas W. Ry. Co. v. Gentry, 69 Texas 625; Forbes v. San Rafael T. Co., 50 Cal. 340. See, also, Gribble v. Columbus, etc., Co., 100 Cal. 67, s. c. 34 Pac. R. 527. But see Alta, etc., Co. v. Alta, etc., Co., 78 Cal. 629, 21 Pac. R. 373; Duke v. Markham, 105 N. Car. 131, 10 S. E. R. 1017.

exceeding the amount of the capital stock, and such a mortgage is ratified by the acquiescence of the stockholders for several years, although it was not originally authorized by them at a legally called meeting.[1]

§ 493. **When ultra vires mortgage may be made effective.**—An *ultra vires* mortgage may be ratified by the legislature either directly,[2] or indirectly, by an act authorizing the trustees to sell the road[3] or by other recognition of the obligation.[4] Where the want of power is not apparent in the charter, or in any statute, or in the instrument itself, the corporation may not plead *ultra vires* against an innocent holder for value.[5] An *ultra vires* mortgage may, however, be enjoined in a suit in equity brought by a stockholder.[6] But stockholders may estop themselves from questioning the validity of a mortgage either upon the ground that the corporation was not legally organized or upon the ground that the mortgage was not properly authorized, where they take part in an attempt to organize under a valid law and acquiesce in the mortgage.[7] A statutory

[1] Farmers' L. & T. Co. *v.* Toledo, etc., R. Co., 67 Fed. R. 49.

[2] Richards *v.* Merrimack & C. R. R. R., 44 N. H. 127; Kennebec & P. R. R. Co. *v.* Portland & K. R. R. Co., 54 Me. 173; Pierce *v.* Milwaukee & S. P. R. R. Co., 24 Wis. 551; St. Paul & P. R. R. Co. *v.* Parcher, 14 Minn. 297; White Water Valley Canal Co. *v.* Vallette, 21 How. (U. S.) 414; Gross *v.* United States, etc., Co., 108 U. S. 477; Shaw *v.* Norfolk Co. R. R. Co., 5 Gray (Mass.) 162; Shepley *v.* Atlantic, etc., R. R. Co., 55 Me. 395; Hatcher *v.* Toledo, etc., R. R. Co., 62 Ill. 477.

[3] Richards *v.* Merrimack & C. R. R. R., 44 N. H. 127.

[4] Troy, etc., R. R. Co. *v.* Boston, etc., R. R. Co., 86 N.Y. 107; Town of Ander *v.* Ely, 158 U. S. 312, 15 Sup. Ct. R. 954; Gardner *v.* London, etc., Ry. Co., Law R. 2 Ch. App. 201; Shrewsbury, etc., Ry. Co. *v.* Northwestern Ry. Co., 6 H. L. Cas. 113; East Anglian Ry. Co. *v.* Eastern Counties Ry. Co., 11 Com. B. 775; Winch *v.* Birkenhead, etc., Ry. Co., 5 DeGex & S. 562; Bagshaw *v.* Eastern Union Ry. Co., 7 Hare 114; Great Northern Ry. Co. *v.* Eastern Counties Ry. Co., 21 Law J. Ch. 837.

[5] Hays *v.* Galion Gas Light and Coal Co., 29 Ohio St. 330; Bissell *v.* Mich. S.& N. Ind. R. R. Co., 22 N.Y. 258; Monument National Bank *v.* Globe Works, 101 Mass. 57; Whitney Arms Co. *v.* Barlow, 63 N. Y. 62; Singer *v.* St. Louis, K. C. & N. Ry. Co., 6 Mo. App. 427. See Hackensack Water Co. *v.* DeKay, 36 N. J. Eq. 548.

[6] McCalmont *v.* Philadelphia, etc., R. R. Co., 27 Int. Rev. Rec. 162, 3 Am. & Eng. R. Cas. 163.

[7] Farmers' L. & T. Co. *v.* Toledo, etc., R. Co., 67 Fed. R. 49. See, also, Boyce *v.* Montauk Gas, etc., Co., 37 W.Va. 73, s. c. 16 S. E. R. 501.

provision requiring notice of a meeting to authorize a mortgage is for the benefit of the stockholders, and if they do not complain of the failure to give such notice no one else can do so.[1] Creditors holding debentures and standing in the same right as the mortgagee may, it has been held, by a bill in equity filed by any of them, secure an equal distribution of property mortgaged *ultra vires*.[2]

§ 494. Recording mortgages.—Railroad mortgages, like other mortgages—and in the case of real property subject ordinarily to the same laws and rules—must be recorded in order to charge third parties with constructive notice; but a mortgage expressly recognizing another unrecorded mortgage is entitled to no priority over it.[3] In some states railroad mortgages are recorded with the secretary of state. An unrecorded mortgage, drawn in the form of a lease, covering rolling stock to be paid for by annual rental, is not good against attachment and execution by creditors, nor against *bona fide* purchasers from the mortgagor.[4] A state's interests will not be prejudiced by the neglect of an agent to record a mortgage made by a railroad corporation in pursuance of a public statute.[5] An agreement to furnish supplies to a railroad company, the title remaining in the vendor while they are being paid for in installments, if not recorded in conformity with the Illinois chattel mortgage act, gives the vendor no lien against third persons.[6] Railroad mortgages covering the corporate franchises and realty, as well as the personalty connected therewith and used for railroad purposes, are not, ordinarily, subject to statutes regarding the acknowl-

---

[1] Central Trust Co. v. Condon, 67 Fed. R. 84.

[2] De Winton v. Brecon, 26 Beav. 533, 5 Jur. N. S. 882.

[3] Coe v. Columbus, P. & I. R. R. Co., 10 Ohio St. 372, 75 Am. Dec. 518. But see Cheesebrough v. Millard, 1 Johns. Ch. (N. Y.) 409, s. c. 7 Am. Dec. 494.

[4] Frank v. Denver, etc., Ry. Co., 23 Fed. R. 123; Heryford v. Davis, 102 U. S. 235, 2 Am. & Eng. R. R. Cas.

386; Hervey v. Rhode Island, etc., Works, 93 U. S. 664.

[5] Memphis and Little Rock R. R. Co. v. State, 37 Ark. 632.

[6] Ill. Rev. Stat. (1874), 711, 712; Murch v. Wright, 46 Ill. 487, 95 Am. Dec. 455; Fosdick v. Schall, 99 U. S. 235, 250; Hervey v. Rhode Island, etc., Works, 93 U. S. 664; Green v. Van Buskirk, 5 Wall. 307.

edgment and recording of chattel mortgages.[1] And so it has been held that a mortgage covering both the road and the rolling stock and recorded as a real estate mortgage need not be also recorded as a chattel mortgage;[2] but there is conflict among the authorities and it is generally safer to record it as both, unless, as in many of the states, the question is set at rest by legislative enactment. The institution of foreclosure proceedings will not interfere with the right of creditors, without actual notice of an unrecorded mortgage, to levy upon the corporate property.[3]

§ 495. **Generally as to what property is covered by the mortgage.**—The extent of property covered by a railroad mortgage is a matter of interpretation under the rules applicable to the interpretation of mortgages by individuals, reference, however, being had to the authorizing statute.[4] Nothing appearing to the contrary in a mortgage, whose terms are general, it will be held that all the property is included when the statute authorizes an encumbrance of the whole.[5] Of course, however,

---

[1] Peoria & Springfield R. R. Co. v. Thompson, 103 Ill. 187; Cooper v. Corbin, 105 Ill. 224; Hammock v. Loan & Trust Co., 105 U. S. 77. Thus they are not subject to statutes requiring record in the county where the property is situated. Metropolitan Trust Co. v. Pennsylvania, etc., R. R. Co., 25 Fed. R. 760. Nor, where a special statute provides that railroad companies may "mortgage their corporate property and franchises," is a mortgage of personal property in connection with the real estate and franchises subject to the provisions of a general chattel mortgage statute requiring an affidavit of good faith. Southern California, etc., Co. v. Union L. & T. Co., 64 Fed. R. 450.

[2] Farmers' Loan and Trust Co. v. St. Joseph & D. C. Ry. Co., 3 Dill. 412. But see Hoyle v. Plattsburg, etc., R. R. Co., 54 N. Y. 314; Williamson v. New Jersey S. R. R. Co., 29 N. J. Eq. 311; Radebaugh v. Tacoma, etc., R. Co., 8 Wash. 570; Palmer v. Forbes, 23 Ill. 301; Union, etc., Co. v. Southern, etc., Co., 51 Fed. R. 840; Jones on Corp. Bonds & Mort., Chapter V, where the question is discussed and the conflicting authorities are reviewed. See also ante, § 389.

[3] Coe v. New Jersey Midland R. R. Co , 31 N. J. Eq. 105.

[4] Wilson v. Gaines, 103 U. S. 417; Coe v. New Jersey Midland, etc., R. Co., 31 N. J. Eq. 105.

[5] Coe v. New Jersey Midland, etc., R. R. Co., 31 N. J. Eq. 105. In a recent case a railroad company chartered to build a road contracted with a construction company to pay for the construction of the road in specified bonds secured by mortgage. Part of the road was built, a proportionate part of the

general words can not extend the lien beyond the limitation of the statute.[1] Where a railroad company's property has been, without the execution of a formal instrument, mortgaged by the legislature, the statute itself interpreted with regard to the condition of the road will determine the extent of the lien.[2] Only such property as is helpful or essential in the operation of the road is, as a rule, included in a general mortgage of the railroad, and, therefore, it has been held not to cover property bought from a steamboat company for the purpose of stifling competition,[3] or unused land bought for shops and depots,[4] or a temporary track,[5] or woodland.[6] A specific enumeration of the property covered is generally exclusive of all other property.[7]

bonds delivered, and a mortgage executed and recorded covering all the property of the railroad company then owned or afterwards acquired. The contract was then cancelled and the chief promoter of the railroad company, who was also the president and only stockholder of the construction company, conveyed all the property of the construction company, including all rights of way acquired or contracted for on behalf of the railroad company, by deed duly recorded, to a firm which then conveyed it to a new railroad company chartered to build a road between two points on the same route, S. to L. A similar disposition was made of the remainder of the property of the construction company south of L., which passed into the hands of a third railway company, chartered to build the road over the remainder of the proposed route; and the two new companies completed the road on the line originally projected. The court held that they took with knowledge of the interest of the original company and that the mortgage executed by it secured to its bondholders a lien on the whole of the road as completed, prior to that of a mortgage executed by the new companies. Wade v. Chicago, etc., R. Co., 149 U. S. 327, s. c. 13 Sup. Ct. R. 892.

[1] Wilson v. Gaines, 103 U. S. 417.

[2] State v. Florida, etc., R. Co., 15 Fla. 690.

[3] Beach, Law of Railways, 763; Morgan v. Donovan, 58 Ala. 241.

[4] Youngman v. Elmira, etc., R. R. Co., 65 Pa. St. 278.

[5] Van Keuren v. Central R. R. Co., 38 N. J. L. 165.

[6] Dinsmore v. Racine, etc., R. R. Co., 12 Wis. 649.

[7] Smith v. McCullough, 104 U. S. 25; Brainerd v. Peck, 34 Vt. 496. Thus, in the case first cited *supra*, it was held that a mortgage of "all the present and in future to be acquired property" of a railroad company, containing a clause enumerating many articles having connection with the management and operation of the road after its construction, did not include municipal bonds issued in aid of the construction of the road. See, also, Wilkes v. Ferris, 5 Johns. (N.Y.) 335, s. c. 4 Am. Dec. 364, and note; Mims v. Armstrong, 31 Md. 87; Price v. Haynes, 37 Mich. 487; Bock v. Perkins, 28 Fed. R. 123; Driscoll v. Fiske, 21 Pick. (Mass.) 503.

Thus, the words "all other property" following a grant of "all lands granted by the United States" to the company do not include other lands not particularly described,[1] nor, it seems, do they include *choses in action* not specifically enumerated in a chattel mortgage.[2] Fuel purchased with the common earnings of a main line and its extension is not subject to the lien of a mortgage of all the property of the extension.[3] "All other corporate property * * * appertaining" or "appurtenant" to a railroad means only such property as is indispensable or at least useful in the exercise of the franchise;[4] and does not include town lots,[5] or an elevator[6] or canal boats used beyond the road's termini.[7] Land grants which the company can not accept,[8] or the conditions of which have not been realized,[9] are not included in such a mortgage. "All the real and personal property" has been held to include earnings and profits;[10] and necessary office furniture is subject to a mortgage of a road, its franchises and property.[11] A mortgage of a road and its fixtures, together with "all other property now owned and which may be hereafter owned by the railroad company," includes

[1] State of Alabama v. Montague, 117 U. S., 602, s. c. 6 Sup. Ct. R. 911. See, also Wilson v. Boyce, 92 U. S. 320; St. Louis, etc., R. R. Co. v. McGee, 115 U. S. 469.

[2] Milwaukee, etc., R. R. Co. v. Milwaukee, etc., R. Co., 20 Wis. 174.

[3] City of Bath v. Miller, 53 Me. 308. See Hunt v. Bullock, 23 Ill. 320.

[4] State v. Glenn, 18 Nev. 34; Morgan v. Donovan, 58 Ala. 241; Boston & N. Y. Air Line R. R. Co. v. Coffin, 50 Conn. 150; Mississippi Val. Co. v. Chicago, St. L. & N. O. R. R. Co., 58 Miss. 896; State of Alabama v. Montague, 117 U. S. 602; Millard v. Burley, 13 Neb. 259, 13 N. W. R. 278; New Orleans Pac. Ry. Co. v. Parker, 143 U. S. 42, s. c. 12 Sup. Ct. R. 364, 6 Lewis' Am. R. & Corp. R. 43.

[5] Calhoun v. Memphis, etc., R. R., 2 Flip. (U. S. C. C.) 442; Shamokin Valley R. R. Co. v. Livermore, 47 Pa. St. 465, 471, 86 Am. Dec. 552; Gardner v. London, etc., Ry. Co., L. R. 2 Ch. App. 201. But see Knevals v. Florida Cent., etc., R. Co., 66 Fed R. 224.

[6] Humphreys v. McKissock, 140 U. S. 304, s. c. 11 Sup. Ct. R. 779.

[7] Parish v. Wheeler, 22 N.Y. 494.

[8] Meyer v. Johnston, 53 Ala. 237.

[9] Campbell v. Texas, etc., R. R. Co., 2 Woods 263. See, also, New Orleans Pac. Ry. Co. v. Parker, 143 U. S. 42, 12 Sup. Ct. R. 364, 6 Lewis' Am. R. & Corp. R. 43, and authorities cited in the opinion of the court.

[10] Kelly v. Alabama, etc., R. R. Co., 58 Ala. 489.

[11] Wood v. Whelen, 93 Ill. 153; Ludlow v. Hurd, 1 Dis. (Ohio) 552; Raymond v. Clark, 46 Conn. 129. See Hunt v. Bullock, 23 Ill. 320.

cars, locomotives, and other rolling stock purchased by the company from time to time after the making of the mortgage.[1] And a mortgage of an entire line of railroad, "with all the revenue or tolls thereof," has been held to cover all the rolling stock and fixtures, whether movable or immovable, essential to the production of tolls and revenues.[2] Net earnings may be mortgaged, but so long as they are retained by the mortgagor are subject to trustee process in favor of the road's general creditors.[3] In a recent case,[4] a railroad company had leased its unfinished road to a company operating a connecting line and mortgaged its property, rights and franchises to secure certain bonds which were to be disposed of by the lessee, and the latter, in order to insure the prompt payment of interest and the ready sale of the bonds, being advised that it had no power to guarantee them, mortgaged to the lessor for that purpose all the net earnings of its own lines which might accrue to it "by reason of business coming to it from or over" the lines of the lessor. It was held that this included not only the profits of the business which came literally from off the lessor's road onto the lessee's road, but, also, the net earnings or business which came to the latter from both directions by reason of the fact that the leased road was an important feeder and brought new business to the lessee's road by opening up new markets and giving increased facilities. The court also held that, as there was nothing in the mortgage prescribing the method of ascertaining the net earnings, they must be determined in the usual way, that is, from the gross receipts

[1] Meyer v. Johnston, 53 Ala. 237, 332, 64 Ala. 603. See, also, Shaw v. Bill, 95 U. S. 10; Hamlin v. Jerrard, 72 Me. 62.

[2] State of Maryland v. Northern Central Ry. Co., 18 Md. 193. See, also, Pullan v. Cincinnati & C. A. L. R. R. Co., 4 Biss. 35, 43.

[3] Gilman v. Illinois, etc., R. R. Co., 91 U. S. 603; Galveston R. R. v. Cowdrey, 11 Wall. (U. S.) 459; Mississippi, etc., R. R. v. U. S. Express Co., 81 Ill. 534; Smith v. Eastern R. R. Co., 124 Mass. 154; Bath v. Miller, 51 Me. 341; Noyes v. Rich, 52 Me. 115; Galena, etc., R. R. Co. v. Menzies, 26 Ill. 121; Ellis v. Boston, etc., R. R. Co., 107 Mass. 1; Emerson v. European, etc., R. R. Co., 67 Me. 387; Dunham v. Isett, 15 Iowa 284; Clay v. East Tenn., etc., R. R. Co., 6 Heisk.(Tenn.) 421. Operating expenses must first be paid. Parkhurst v. Northern Central R. R. Co., 19 Md. 472.

[4] Schmidt v. Louisville, etc., R. Co., 95 Ky. 289, 61 Am. & Eng. R. Cas. 680.

must be deducted the cost of producing them, and that it knew of "no way to arrive at all this save, approximately, by a proportion distributing the total operating expense over the whole business," thus treating the business of the entire system as a unit.[1]

§ 496. **What is covered by a mortgage of the undertaking.**
—In England it is held that neither a mortgage of a railroad "undertaking"[2] nor one of the "undertaking, and all and singular the rates, tolls and other sums arising,"[3] includes the land on which the road is built; or the surplus lands;[4] or stock or property belonging to the company as a common carrier of passengers or goods for hire;[5] or future calls on the shareholders, they not being mortgageable without express legislative authority.[6] But it has been held that a mortgage of the undertaking may include the rails, stations, works and other buildings.[7] The undertaking is a going concern created by the incorporating act;[8] and it can not be broken up by the

[1] St. John v. Railway Co., 22 Wall. (U. S.) 136; Pullan v. Railroad Co., 5 Biss. (U. S. C. C.) 237; United States v. Kansas Pac. Ry. Co., 99 U. S. 455.

[2] Doe v. St. Helen's, etc., Ry. Co., 2 Eng. Ry. & Can. Cas. 756.

[3] Myatt v. St. Helen's, etc., Ry. Co., 2 Q. B. 364.

[4] Beach Railway Law, 763; Gardner v. London, C. & D. Ry. Co., L. R. 2 Ch. App. 201, 217, 36 L. J. Ch. 323; King v. Marshall, 33 Beav. 565; *Ex parte* Stanley, 33 Law J. Ch. 535; Moor v. Anglo-Italian Bank, L. R. 10 Ch. Div. 681; Wickham v. New Brunswick & C. Ry. Co., L. R. 1 P. C. 64; 1 Cox's Joint Stock Cas. 519.

[5] Hart v. Eastern Union Ry. Co., 7 Ex. 246.

[6] *In re* British Provident L. & F. Assn. Co., 4 DeG., J. & S. 407; *In re* Sankey Brook Coal Co., L. R. 10 Eq. 381; Companies Clauses Consolidation Act, 1845, 8 and 9 Vict. Ch. 16, § 43; Gardner v. London, C. & D. Ry. Co., L. R. 2 Ch. 201, 212; Browne & Theobald's Railway Law, 88; Lewis v. Glenn, 84 Va. 947. But see Pickering v. Ilfracombe Ry. Co., L. R. 3 Com. P. 235. A mortgage of "all the lands, tenements, and estates of the company, and all their undertakings," was held not to include calls, either future or existing, unpaid. King v. Marshall, 33 Beav. 565.

[7] Legg v. Mathieson, 2 Giff. 71. See Wickham v. New Brunswick, etc., Ry. Co., Law R. 1 P. C. 64.

[8] Gardner v. London, etc., Ry. Co., L. R. 2 Ch. 201. A mortgage of the undertaking is different from a mortgage of the company's property. Jones Corporate Bonds and Mortgages, 62; Perkins v. Pritchard, 3 Eng. Ry. & Can. Cas. 95; Hart v. Eastern Union Ry. Co., 6 Eng. Ry. & Can. Cas. 818, 7 Exch. 246, 265.

mortgagees, nor can they, by ejectment, take from the corporation property essential to the undertaking's continuance.[1] That which is pledged under a mortgage of the undertaking is rather the income of the property than the corpus of it.[2]

§ 497. **Mortgage of after-acquired property.**—It has been decided that, on the doctrine of accession, a railroad company will, in a mortgage of all its property, be held, even in the absence of express words of futurity, to have included essential property subsequently acquired under authority given before the execution of the mortgage. This doctrine, which is not well established,[3] is supported by the cases only when by virtue of some legislative authority the road's franchises and property may be treated as an indivisible entirety.[4] Unquestionably a railroad company having power to borrow money and secure it by mortgage on its property may by express terms mortgage property to be acquired subsequently.[5] In a recent

---

[1] Myatt v. St. Helen's Ry. Co., 2 Q. B. 364, 2 Eng. Ry. & Can. Cas. 756; 1 Hodges Railways, 124.

[2] In re Panama, N. Z. & A. Royal Mail Co., L. R. 5 Ch. 318, 321.

[3] See Dinsmore v. Racine, etc., R. R. Co., 12 Wis. 649; In re Panama, N. Z. & A. R. M. Co., L. R. 5 Ch. App. 318, 322; 4 Cox's Joint Stock Cas. 35; Ludlow v. Hurd, 1 Dis. (Ohio) 552, 560; Parker v. New Orleans, B. R. & V. R. Co., 33 Fed. R. 693; Shaw v. Bill, 95 U. S. 10; Phillips v. Winslow, 18 B. Mon. (Ky.) 431; Farmers' Loan & Trust Co. v. Commercial Bank, 11 Wis. 207, 212, 689; Calhoun v. Memphis & P. R. R. Co., 2 Flip. 442; Pierce v. Emery, 32 N. H. 484; Boston, C. & M. R. R. v. Gilmore, 37 N. H. 410. See, also, Galveston, etc., R. R. Co. v. Cowdrey, 11 Wall. 459; United States v. New Orleans R., 12 Wall. 362; Scott v. Clinton, etc., R. R. Co., 6 Biss. 529; Barnard v. Norwich, etc., R. K. Co., 4 Cliff. 351; Dillon v. Barnard, 1 Holmes 386. Of course, the rule applies with particular force to property acquired for a changed location of the road, the lien being discharged as to the abandoned route. Elwell v. Grand St., etc., R. R. Co., 67 Barb. (N. Y.) 83; Meyer v. Johnston, 53 Ala. 237. It is not applicable where mortgages are placed on separate divisions. Farmers' L. & T. Co. v. Commercial Bank, 11 Wis. 207.

[4] Pierce v. Emery, 32 N. H. 484; Phillips v. Winslow, 18 B. Mon. (Ky.) 431; Willink v. Morris Canal & Banking Co., 3 Green (N. J.) Ch. 377, 657.

[5] Dunham v. Cincinnati, etc., R. R. Co., 1 Wall. (U. S.) 254; Baker v. Guarantee, etc., Co., (N. J.) 31 Atl. R. 174; Coopers v. Wolf, 15 Ohio St. 523; Ludlow v. Hurd, 1 Dis. (Ohio) 552; Covey v. Pittsburg, etc., R. R. Co., 3 Phila. (Pa.) 173; In re General South American Co., L. R. 2 Ch. Div. 337; In re Panama, etc., Mail Co., L. R. 5 Ch. 318; Kelly v. Ala. & Cin. R. R. Co., 58 Ala. 489; Hamlin

§ 497 RAILROAD SECURITIES. 651

case,[1] this doctrine was applied to a *de facto* corporation, and it was held that, as a corporation created under the general railroad law of the state might mortgage after-acquired property, a mortgage or trust deed of such property by the *de facto* corporation, which was created by an unconstitutional special act but might have been organized under the general law, was valid not only as against the corporation but also as against creditors. The lien attaches to the property as soon as it is acquired;[2] and is superior to that of a subsequent mortgage or of a judgment.[3] A mortgage of "after-acquired" property has been held to include a lease of another road;[4] net earnings;[5] another company's capital stock purchased to effect a consolidation;[6] a hotel open to the general public as well as to passengers and employes;[7] land acquired for the location of car-houses

---

v. European & N. A. Ry. Co., 72 Me. 83; Buck *v.* Seymour, 46 Conn. 156; Parker *v.* New Orleans, B. R. & V. R. R. Co., 33 Fed. R. 693; Philadelphia, W. & B. R. R. Co. *v.* Woelpper, 64 Pa. St. 366; Campbell *v.* Texas & N. O. R. R. Co., 2 Woods (U. S. C. C.) 271; McGourkey *v.* Toledo, etc., R. Co., 146 U. S. 536.

[1] McTighe *v.* Macon Const. Co., 94 Ga. 306, 21 S. E. R. 701.

[2] Parker *v.* New Orleans, etc., R. R. Co., 33 Fed. R. 693; Seymour *v.* Canandaigua, etc., R. Co., 25 Barb. (N. Y.) 284. But see New Orleans, etc., R. Co. *v.* Parker, 143 U. S. 42, s. c. 12 Sup. Ct. R. 364, reversing the former case on the ground that the property (a land grant) was not appurtenant, and that it was not contemplated by the parties or definitely located.

[3] Dunham *v.* Cincinnati & P. Ry. Co., 1 Wall. 254, 266; Scott *v.* Clinton & S. R. R., 6 Biss. 529, 535; Michigan Central R. R. Co. *v.* Chicago & M. L. S. R. R. Co., 1 Brad. (Ill.) 399; Nichols *v.* Mase, 94 N. Y. 160; Coe *v.* Pennock, 6 Am. Law Reg. 27, 2 Redf. Am. Ry. Cas. 667; Pennock *v.* Coe, 23

How. 117, 127; Stevens *v.* Watson, 4 Abb. App. Dec. (N. Y.) 302.

[4] Buck *v.* Seymour, 46 Conn. 156; Barnard *v.* Norwich & W. R. R. Co., 4 Cliff. 351, 14 N. Bank R. 469, 3 Cent. L. J. 608; Hamlin *v.* European & N. A. Ry. Co., 72 Me. 83; Columbia Finance, etc., Co. *v.* Kentucky, etc., R. Co., 60 Fed. R. 794. But not a lease of the mortgaged road executed by the mortgagor to another company.

[5] Addison *v.* Lewis, 75 Va. 701; Tompkins *v.* Little Rock, etc., R. R. Co., 15 Fed. R. 6. *Contra*, Emerson *v.* European, etc., R. Co., 67 Me. 387; DeGraff *v.* Thompson, 24 Minn. 452; Pullan *v.* Cincinnati, etc., R. R. Co., 5 Biss. (U. S. C. C.) 237.

[6] Williamson *v.* N. J. Southern R. R. Co., 26 N. J. Eq. 398. But not unpaid subscriptions to the company's capital stock. Dean *v.* Biggs, 25 Hun (N. Y.) 122. It was held in Williamson *v.* New Jersey Southern R. R. Co., *supra*, that it was unnecessary to record the mortgage in accordance with the chattel mortgage act.

[7] United States Trust Co. *v.* Wabash, etc., Ry. Co., 32 Fed. R. 480; Omaha,

which were never built;[1] a completed road afterwards purchased which might have been constructed if it had not been purchased.[2] It does not extend to property acquired by fraud, so that the title thereto does not vest in the mortgagor;[3] nor does a mortgage of a road and its appurtenances existing or to be afterwards acquired extend to woodland seven miles from the road;[4] or to land acquired for a canal basin;[5] or to other property not properly appurtenant to the road.[6] But a mortgage of an entire road, "as said railroad now is or may be hereafter constructed, maintained, operated or acquired, together with all the privileges, rights, franchises, real estate, right of way, depots, depot grounds, side tracks, water tanks, engines, cars, and other appurtenances thereto belonging," has been held to include real estate separated from the right of way by a street, but of easy access to the station and side tracks, which real estate had been subsequently purchased by the company and upon which it had built a restaurant for the accommodation of its employes and passengers.[7] A lease by a mortgagor of the mortgaged road to another company has been held not to be included in

etc., R. Co. v. Wabash, etc., R. Co., 108 Mo. 298, s. c. 18 S.W. R. 1101. But not as an appurtenance unless it is used in connection with the road. Mississippi Valley Co. v. Chicago, etc., R. R. Co., 58 Miss. 896, 38 Am. R. 348.

[1] Hamlin v. European, etc., Ry. Co., 72 Me. 83, s. c. 4 Am. & Eng. R. Cas. 503.

[2] Branch v. Jesup, 106 U. S. 468.

[3] Williamson v. New Jersey Southern R. R. Co., 28 N. J. Eq. 277, 29 N. J. Eq. 311, 321; Field v. Post, 38 N. J. L. 346; Frazier v. Frederick, 24 N. J. L. 162.

[4] Dinsmore v. Racine, etc., R. R. Co., 12 Wis. 649.

[5] Shamokin Valley, etc., R. R. Co. v. Livermore, 47 Pa. St. 465, 86 Am. Dec. 552.

[6] Calhoun v. Memphis, etc., R. R. Co., 2 Flip. 442; Seymour v. Canandaigua, etc., R. R. Co., 25 Barb. 284; Mississippi Valley Co. v. Chicago, etc., R. R. Co., 58 Miss. 896, 38 Am. R. 348; Morgan v. Donovan, 58 Ala. 241; Shamokin Valley R. R. Co. v. Livermore, 47 Pa. St. 465, 86 Am. Dec. 552; Millard v. Burley, 13 Neb. 259; Calhoun v. Paducah, etc., R. R. Co., 9 Cent. L. J. 66; Walsh v. Barton, 24 Ohio St. 28; Farmers' L. & T. Co. v. Commercial Bank, 11 Wis. 207. Affirmed in Dinsmore v. Racine & M. R. R. Co., 12 Wis. 649; Farmers' L. & T. Co. v. Cary, 13 Wis. 110; Farmers' L. & T. Co. v. Commercial Bank, 15 Wis. 424; Brainerd v. Peck, 34 Vt. 496.

[7] Omaha, etc., R. Co. v. Wabash, etc., R. Co., 108 Mo. 298, s. c. 18 S. W. R. 1101.

the after-acquired property.[1] But, on the other hand, it has been held that a railroad mortgage of "all property, both real and personal, of every kind and description, which shall hereafter be acquired for use on said railroad, and all the corporate rights, privileges, franchises and immunities, and all things in action, contracts, claims, and demands, whether now owned or hereafter acquired in connection or relating to the said railroad," includes an after-acquired lease of terminal facilities to the mortgagor.[2] A branch road is held to be included if the authority to construct it antedates the mortgage;[3] otherwise, not.[4] Iron rails, though still at a distant port, have been held subject to the lien of a mortgage of "all materials whatsoever."[5] The specification of certain after-acquired articles which shall be subject to the lien excludes all others.[6] A mortgage of after-acquired property only attaches to such interest as the mortgagor acquires, and so does not displace a lien existing when the property was acquired by the mortgagor.[7] This rule, appli-

[1] Moran v. Pittsburgh, C. & St. L. Ry. Co., 32 Fed. R. 878; St. Paul & D. R. R. Co. v. United States, 112 U. S. 733.

[2] Columbia Finance, etc., Co. v. Kentucky, etc., R. Co., 60 Fed. R. 794, s. c. 61 Am. & Eng. R. Cas. 690, citing Central Trust Co. v. Kneeland, 138 U. S. 414; Toledo, etc., R. Co. v. Hamilton, 134 U. S. 296; Branch v. Jesup, 106 U. S. 468.

[3] Seymour v. Canandaigua, etc., R. R. Co., 25 Barb. (N.Y.) 284; Texas, etc., Ry. Co. v. Gentry, 69 Tex. 625; Parker v. New Orleans, B. R. & V. R. Co., 33 Fed. R. 693; Coe v. Del. L. & W. R.R. Co., 34 N. J. Eq. 266, 4 Am. & Eng. R. R. Cas. 513.

[4] Meyer v. Johnston, 53 Ala. 237, 331, 64 Ala. 603.

[5] Weetjen v. St. P. & P. R. R. Co., 4 Hun (N.Y.) 529. See Haven v. Emery, 33 N. H. 66.

[6] Hare v. Horton, 5 Barn. & Ad. 715; Raymond v. Clark, 46 Conn. 129; Buck v. Seymour, 46 Conn. 156; Brainerd v. Peck, 34 Vt. 496; Smith v. McCullough, 104 U. S. 25.

[7] Haven v. Emery, 33 N. H. 66; Williamson v. New Jersey Southern R. R. Co., 28 N. J. Eq. 277, 29 N. J. Eq. 311; Branch v. Atlantic, etc., R. R. Co., 3 Woods (U. S. C. C.) 481; Lake Erie, etc., R. Co. v. Priest, 131 Ind. 413, s. c. 31 N. E. R. 77; Dunham v. Cincinnati & P. Ry. Co., 1 Wall. 254; Galveston R. R. v. Cowdrey, 11 Wall 459; United States v. N. O. R. R., 12 Wall. 362; Willink v. Morris Canal & Banking Co., 3 Green (N. J.) Ch. 377; Boston Safe Deposit & T. Co. v. Bankers' & M. T. Co., 36 Fed. R. 288; Western Union Tel. Co. v. Burlington & S. W. Ry. Co., 3 McCrary 130; Fosdick v. Schall, 99 U. S. 235; Myer v. Car Co., 102 U. S. 1; Branch v. Jesup, 106 U. S. 468. It is subject to a vendor's lien for unpaid purchase-money on realty, the mortgagee not being considered a purchaser for value.

cable to all property capable of separate ownership, including real estate not used for railroad purposes, does not, however, apply to fixtures used in the operation of the road,[1] unless an agreement has been made as to their legal character.[2]

§ 498. **Fixtures.**—Fixtures, whether acquired before or after the execution of such a mortgage, are subject to its lien.[3] On the principle that fixtures, though subsequently severed, are subject to the lien of a mortgage of the freehold, worn-out rails replaced by new ones have been held to be included in a railroad mortgage; and so of new rails not yet laid.[4] A track laid merely for a temporary use has been held not to come under the lien as part of the realty;[5] so have repair tools,[6] fuel[7] and furniture.[8] A mortgage of a railroad, if its terms cover such future acquisitions, will, however, be held in equity to apply to after-acquired rolling stock[9] even if not specially

---

Loomis v. Davenport & St. P. R. R. Co., 17 Fed. R. 301. See Pierce v. Milwaukee & St. P. R. R. Co., 24 Wis. 551.

[1] Porter v. Pittsburg, etc., Co., 122 U. S. 267, s. c. 7 Sup. Ct. R. 1206, 30 Am. & Eng. R. R. Cas. 495; Wood v. Whelen, 93 Ill. 153; United States v. N. O. R. R. Co., 12 Wall. 362.

[2] Boston Safe Deposit & T. Co. v. Bankers' & M. T. Co., 36 Fed. R. 288; Western Union Tel. Co. v. Burlington & S. W. Ry. Co., 3 McCrary 130, 11 Fed. R. 1.

[3] Porter v. Pittsburgh, etc., Co., 122 U. S. 267, 283, 7 Sup. Ct. R. 1206; Wood v. Whelen, 93 Ill. 153.

[4] First Nat. Bank v. Anderson, 75 Va. 250. So held, if proper management requires that they be recast. Lehigh, etc., Co. v. Central R. R. Co., 35 N. J. Eq. 379; Weetjen v. St. Paul, etc., R. R. Co., 4 Hun (N. Y.) 529; Palmer v. Forbes, 23 Ill. 301. See Farmers' Loan & T. Co. v. Commercial Bank, 11 Wis. 207, 15 Wis. 424; Farmers' Loan & T. Co. v. Cary, 13 Wis. 110; Dins-

more v. Racine, etc., R. R. Co., 12 Wis. 649; Brainerd v. Peck, 34 Vt. 496.

[5] Van Keuren v. Central R. R. Co., 38 N. J. L. 165.

[6] Lehigh, etc., Co. v. Central R. R. Co., 35 N. J. Eq. 379; Williamson v. New Jersey, etc., R. R. Co., 29 N. J. Eq. 311, 28 N. J. Eq. 277; Brainerd v. Peck, 34 Vt. 496. But see Delaware, etc., R. Co. v. Oxford Iron Co., 36 N. J. Eq. 452.

[7] Hunt v. Bullock, 23 Ill. 320. But see Coe v. McBrown, 22 Ind. 252; Phillips v. Winslow, 18 B. Mon. (Ky.) 431, 448.

[8] Lehigh, etc., Co. v. Central R. R. Co., 35 N. J. Eq. 379; Hunt v. Bullock, 23 Ill. 320; Raymond v. Clark, 46 Conn. 129; Ludlow v. Hurd, 1 Disn. (O.) 552; Titus v. Mabee, 25 Ill. 257; Southbridge Savings Bank v. Mason, 147 Mass. 500. But see Wood v. Whelen, 93 Ill. 153.

[9] Jones Corp. Bonds and Mortgages, 120; Pennock v. Coe, 23 How. 117; Coe v. Pennock, 6 Am. Law Reg. 27.

mentioned; although it has been held that loose rolling stock, such as engines and cars, is, in such a case, subject to the liens on it[1] when it comes into the mortgagor's hands.[2]

§ 499. **Reserved power to create prior lien or to dispose of unnecessary property.**—A provision in a railroad mortgage permitting the company to sell, pledge, or otherwise dispose of any property not essential to the operation of the road, applying the proceeds in any manner not prejudicial to the interests of the mortgagee is not fraudulent or invalid.[3] Such provision does not, however, nullify the mortgage and withdraw the lien as unnecessary articles like broken rails, ties and wheels are cast aside.[4]

§ 500. **Priority of mortgages.**—We shall discuss the subject of preferred claims for operating expenses and the like in a subsequent chapter, but it may be well at this place to consider briefly the subject of the priority of one mortgage over another and over other claims and equities. As we have already shown, one of a series of bonds has no priority over others of the same series merely because it bears a smaller number.[5] It seems, however, that first mortgage bonds, although issued

---

[2] Redf. Am. Ry. Cas. 667; Galveston R. R. v. Cowdrey, 11 Wall. 459, 481; Dunham v. Cincinnati & P. Ry. Co., 1 Wall. 254, 266; Meyer v. Johnston, 53 Ala. 237, 64 Ala. 603; Scott v. Clinton & S. R. R. Co., 6 Biss. 529, 535; Michigan Central R. R. Co. v. Chicago & M. L. S. R. R. Co., 1 Brad. (Ill.) 399; Nichols v. Mase, 94 N.Y. 160; Morrill v. Noyes, 56 Me. 458, 471; Phillips v. Winslow, 18 B. Mon. (Ky.) 431, 448; Hamlin v. Jerrard, 72 Me. 62.

[1] Meyer v. Johnston, 53 Ala. 237, 332, 64 Ala. 603; State of Maryland v. Northern Central Ry. Co., 18 Md. 193; Pullan v. Cincinnati & C. A. L. R. R. Co., 4 Biss. 35, 43. But see Miller v. Rutland & W. R. R. Co., 36 Vt. 452.

[2] United States v. New Orleans R. R., 12 Wall. 362; Boston Safe Deposit & T. Co. v. Bankers' & M. Tel. Co., 36 Fed. R. 288; Myer v. Car Co., 102 U. S. 1 (subject to rights of vendor under conditional sale); Frank v. Denver, etc., R. Co., 23 Fed. R. 123.

[3] Butler v. Rahm, 46 Md. 541. See, also, Nickerson v. Atchison, T. & S. F. R. R. Co., 3 McCrary 455, 17 Fed. R. 408. As to reservation of power to create a prior lien, see Campbell v. Texas & New Orleans R. R. Co., 2 Woods 263.

[4] Coopers v. Wolf, 15 Ohio St. 523.

[5] Stanton v. Ala., etc., R. Co., 2 Woods 523; Commonwealth v. Susquehanna, etc., R. Co., 122 Pa. St. 306, 321.

after a second mortgage is executed, have priority over the second mortgage bonds, unless the second mortgage in terms limits the lien of the prior mortgage to bonds actually out, and provides against reissues.[1] One who purchases from a railroad company part of a series of bonds secured by mortgage on the road, under an agreement that no more bonds shall be issued, is entitled to be preferred over purchasers of the other bonds with notice of the agreement, but not over *bona fide* purchasers who have no notice of the agreement, either actual or constructive.[2] The general rule, of course, is that mortgages have priority in the order of their execution, but *bona fide* second mortgage bondholders may obtain priority over prior mortgagees if the prior mortgage is unrecorded and there is nothing charging them with notice of the prior mortgage. Where, however, a subsequent mortgage is expressly made subject to a former mortgage such former mortgage has priority, although not legally recorded.[3] So, a subsequent mortgage may be given priority over a former mortgage by agreement between the old bondholders and the mortgagor company.[4] This is sometimes done in order to enable the company to complete its road or to reorganize. A mortgage trustee, however, has no power to agree that an unsecured debt or a subsequent mortgage debt shall be paid in preference to the first mortgage bonds.[5] As a general rule, a fixed legal right under a mortgage can not be impaired by any equities subsequently arising,[6] although, as we shall hereafter see, there is an apparent exception to this rule in the case of operating expenses, and, by statute, employes are frequently given preferred claims.

---

[1] Claflin v. South Carolina R. Co., 4 Hughes (U. S. C. C.) 12.

[2] McMurray v. Moran, 134 U. S. 150, s. c. 10 Sup. Ct. R. 427.

[3] Coe v. Columbus, etc., R. Co., 10 Ohio St. 372, s. c. 75 Am. Dec. 518.

[4] Poland v. Lamoille Valley R. Co., 52 Vt. 144.

[5] Duncan v. Mobile, etc., R. Co., 2 Woods (U. S. C. C.) 542; Hollister v. Stewart, 111 N.Y. 644, s. c. 19 N. E. R. 782.

[6] Jones on Corp. Bonds and Mort., § 579. But see *ante*, §§ 496, 497. As to mechanics' liens, see Brooks v. Burlington, etc., R. Co., 101 U. S 443; Meyer v. Hornby, 101 U. S. 728, with which compare Bear v. Burlington, etc., R. Co., 48 Iowa 619; Tommey v. Spartanburg, etc., Co., 1 Am. & Eng R. Cas. 632, note.

Thus, the priority of a first mortgage is not effected by the fact that the road was completed or part of it wholly built by money obtained by means of a junior mortgage,[1] nor are unsecured claims of contractors or material men who have furnished money or material for building or repairing it entitled to priority over a prior mortgage.[2] Taxes may, of course, constitute a lien superior to a prior mortgage,[3] and it has also been held that a landholder's claim for damages for land condemned for the road is superior to a mortgage given before the damages have been assessed.[4] We have elsewhere considered the subject of the priority of liens in cases of consolidation,[5] but the question of priority sometimes arises in cases of mere succession or where separate mortgages are made on different divisions of a road. A mortgage on all property, materials, rights and privileges of a railroad company then or thereafter appertaining to the road, to secure bonds for money with which to construct it has priority over a subsequent mortgage of the earnings of a particular division or section of the road, executed to secure money used in constructing such section by a lessee who had agreed to construct it as part of the consideration for the lease, even though the lessor company which executed the first mortgage may have agreed to recognize the

---

[1] Galveston, etc., R. Co. v. Cowdrey, 11 Wall. (U. S.) 459; Dunham v. Cincinnati, etc., R. Co., 1 Wall. (U. S.) 254. See, also, McGourkey v. Toledo, etc., R. Co., 146 U. S. 536, s. c. 13 Sup. Ct. R. 170 (mortgage has priority over car trust certificates); Manhattan Trust Co. v. Sioux City, etc., Ry. Co., 68 Fed. R. 72.

[2] Dunham v. Cincinnati, etc., R. Co., 1 Wall. (U. S.) 254, and cases cited in last note *supra*. See, also, New Jersey Midland Ry. Co. v. Wortendyke, 27 N. J. Eq. 658; Denniston v. Chicago, etc., R. Co., 4 Biss. (U. S. C. C.) 414; Peninsular Iron Co. v. Eells, 68 Fed. R. 24.

[3] Farmers' L. & T. Co. v. Vicksburg, etc., R. Co., 33 Fed. R. 778; State of Georgia v. Atlantic, etc., R. Co., 3 Wood (U. S. C. C.) 434; Stevens v. New York, etc., R. Co., 13 Blatch. (U. S. C. C.) 104; Central Trust Co. v. New York, etc., R. Co., 110 N. Y. 250. But see Binkert v. Wabash, etc., R. Co., 98 Ill. 205, s. c. 5 Am. & Eng. R. Cas. 113.

[4] Western Penna R. Co. v. Johnston, 59 Pa. St. 290. See, also, Mercantile Trust Co. v. Pittsburgh, etc., R. Co., 29 Fed. R. 732; Buffalo, etc., R. Co. v. Harvey, 107 Pa. St. 319.

[5] *Ante*, § 336. See, also, Kneeland v. Lawrence, 140 U. S. 209, s. c. 11 Sup. Ct. R. 786; Wabash, etc., R. Co. v. Ham, 114 U. S. 587, s. c. 5 Sup. Ct. R. 1081.

subsequent mortgage as having priority.[1] And a mortgage on the property of a railroad company given by its successor has priority over claims for services and advances to the old company, by a creditor who did not obtain a judgment until after the execution of such mortgage, and whose services and advances were not such as to entitle him to a statutory lien.[2]

§ 501. Trust deeds.—A railroad mortgage is now generally made to trustees who take the mortgage title for the bondholders, thus securing to them all the benefits they would have had if named in the instrument.[3] The trustee may be an individual or a trust company.[4] It has also been held that a director or an officer of the mortgagor company may be a trustee,[5] and so may a non-resident.[6] Upon the death of one of two or more trustees, his interest vests according to the right of survivorship, notwithstanding a statute abolishing joint tenancies without expressly embracing trust estates.[7] Equity will not permit a trust to fail for want of a trustee.[8] A trust deed is regarded as in effect a mortgage,[9] and the right of possession remains in the grantor.[10] Authority to mortgage is authority

---

[1] Thompson v. White Water, etc., R. Co., 132 U. S. 68, s. c. 10 Sup. Ct. R. 29. The court held that this agreement as to priority could not affect the first mortgage bondholders. See, also, Wade v. Chicago, etc., R. Co., 149 U. S. 327, s. c. 13 Sup. Ct. R. 892.

[2] Fogg v. Blair, 133 U. S. 534, s. c. 10 Sup. Ct. R. 338.

[3] Butler v. Rahm, 46 Md. 541; McLane v. Placerville & S. V. R. R. Co., 66 Cal. 606; Chamberlain v. Conn. Cent. R. R. Co., 54 Conn. 472; Jones on Corporate Bonds and Mort., § 28. See "Trust Deeds," 26 Am. & Eng. Ency. of Law 860.

[4] Hervey v. Illinois, etc., Ry. Co., 28 Fed. R. 169; Farmers' L. & T. Co. v. Chicago, etc., Ry. Co., 27 Fed. R. 146.

[5] Bassett v. Monte, etc., Co., 15 Nev. 293; Ellis v. Boston, etc., R. Co., 107 Mass. 1.

[6] A statute prohibiting citizens of other states from acting as trustees is unconstitutional. Roby v. Smith, 131 Ind. 342, s. c. 30 N. E. R. 1093, 15 L. R. A. 792; Farmers' L. & T. Co. v. Chicago, etc., Ry. Co., 27 Fed. R. 146; Shirk v. La Fayette, 52 Fed. R. 857.

[7] McAllister v. Plant, 54 Miss. 106.

[8] See 27 Am. & Eng. Ency. of Law 16, 90, 91, and authorities there cited.

[9] Wisconsin Cent. R. R. Co. v. Wis. Riv. L. Co., 71 Wis. 94; WhiteWater, etc., Canal Co. v. Vallette, 21 How. 414; McLane v. Placerville, etc., R. R. Co., 66 Cal. 606; Coe v. Johnson, 18 Ind. 218; Coe v. McBrown, 22 Ind. 252.

[10] Southern Pacific R. R. Co. v. Doyle, 8 Sawyer 60, s. c. 11 Fed. R. 253.

to execute a deed of trust,[1] and statutes regulating the recording of mortgages embrace deeds of trust.[2] The power to sell without legal proceedings should be unequivocally and definitely expressed in the deed.[3] Foreclosure in an equity court is the more usual and the safer method.

§ 502. Equitable and defective mortgages.—An instrument which was intended to be the mortgage deed of a corporation, but which, not being executed by the corporation, or in its name, can not take effect as its deed, may nevertheless be regarded as an equitable mortgage and entitle the holders of it in equity to the full benefit of the security intended to be given.[4] An agreement, even by word of mouth as to personalty, to give a mortgage for certain sums, is enforceable in equity as a mortgage;[5] and so are bonds which recite that they are a lien;[6] and so is an agreement to place in a third person's hands certain earnings or property to meet specified obligations;[7] and so is a contract for the purchase of rolling stock by the payment of an annual rental with provision for forfeiture upon non-payment.[8] The holder of an old bond, to whom a

---

[1] Wright v. Bundy, 11 Ind. 398; Bennett v. Union Bank, 5 Humph. (Tenn.) 612; Turner v. Watkins, 31 Ark. 429.

[2] Woodruff v. Robb, 19 Ohio 212; Schultze v. Houfes, 96 Ill. 335; Magee v. Carpenter, 4 Ala. 469.

[3] Mason v.York, etc., R. R. Co., 52 Me. 82.

[4] Jones Corp. Bonds and Mortgages, 32; Miller v. Rutland & Washington R. R. Co., 36 Vt. 452; Randolph v. New Jersey, etc., R. R., 28 N. J. Eq. 49. A mortgage expressly recognizing another is subsequent thereto, notwithstanding the prior mortgage is not legally executed and recorded. Coe v. Columbus, P. & I. R. R. Co., 10 Ohio St. 372, 75 Am. Dec. 518.

[5] Waco Tap R. R. Co. v. Shirley, 45 Tex. 355, 13 Am. Ry. Rep. 233; Texas, etc., R. Co. v. Gentry, 69 Tex. 625; Ashton v. Corrigan, L. R. 13 Eq. 76; Peto v. Brighton, M. & T.W. Ry. Co., 1 H & Miller, 468.

[6] Poland v. Lamoille Val. R. R. Co., 52 Vt. 144, 171; White WaterValley Canal Co. v.Vallette, 21 How. 414; Town of Dundas v. Desjardins Canal Co., 17 Grant's Ch. (Upper Can.) 27.

[7] Ketchum v. Pacific Railroad, 4 Dill. 78, 86; Ketchum v. St. Louis, 101 U. S. 306, 317; Watson v. Wellington, 1 Rus. & Myl. 602; Yeates v. Groves, 1 Ves. Jr. 280; Lett v. Morris, 4 Sim. 607; *Ex parte* Alderson, 1 Madd. 39; Legard v. Hodges, 1 Ves. Jr. 477; Pinch v. Anthony, 8 Allen (Mass.) 536; Dillon v. Barnard, 1 Holmes 386.

[8] Hervey v. Rhode Island, etc., Works, 93 U. S. 664; Heryford v. Davis, 102 U. S. 235; Frank v. Denver, etc., Ry. Co., 23 Fed. R. 123; Fosdick

new bond can not be issued because the refunding scheme provides none so small, is entitled to a lien for the amount of the indebtedness to him equal to the other mortgage creditors' lien.[1] Where no words of inheritance appear in the mortgage but it is the evident intention that the trustees should take the fee, the instrument will be reformed by a court of equity.[2]

§ 503. **Statutory mortgages.**—A statute expressing its purpose in certain[3] terms may constitute a mortgage without the execution of any instrument of conveyance.[4] A statutory mortgage to the state may provide that it shall receive the income by way of interest, without foreclosure,[5] and may make such provision as will constitute an equitable assignment thereof to which subsequent mortgages will be subject.[6] State

v. Schall, 99 U. S. 235. But it is held that there is no mortgage where a railway company sells rolling-stock, contemporaneously hiring the same stock at an annual rental of one-fifth the selling price with provision for repurchase at the end of five years for a nominal price. Yorkshire Ry. Wagon Co. v. Maclure, 21 Ch. Div. 309; North Central Wagon Co. v. Manchester, etc., Ry. Co., 35 Ch. Div. 191.

[1] Blair v. St. Louis, etc., R. R. Co., 23 Fed. R. 524

[2] Coe v. New Jersey, etc., R. R. Co., 31 N. J. Eq. 105; Randolph v. New Jersey, etc., R. R. Co., 28 N. J. Eq. 49.

[3] Cincinnati City v. Morgan, 3 Wall. 275; Brunswick and Albany R. R. Co. v. Hughes, 52 Ga. 557; Collins v. Central Bank of Georgia, 1 Kelly (Ga.) 435; Whitehead v. Vineyard, 50 Mo. 30; Colt v. Barnes, 64 Ala. 108.

[4] United States v. Union Pacific R. R. Co., 91 U. S. 72; Wilson v. Boyce, 92 U. S. 320, 2 Dill. 539; Murdock v. Woodson, 2 Dill. 188; Woodson v. Murdock, 22 Wall. 351; State v. Florida, etc., R. R. Co., 15 Fla. 690;

Tompkins v. Little Rock & F. S. Ry. Co., 15 Fed. R. 6. An example is Act of July 1, 1862, 12 Stat. at Large, 489, mortgaging the Union Pacific Railroad. Such a mortgage may include after-acquired property. Whitehead v. Vineyard, 50 Mo. 30; Colt v. Barnes, 64 Ala. 108. The lien may be released by the legislature. Woodson v. Murdock, 22 Wall. 351; Darby v. Wright, 3 Blatchf. 170; Gibbes v. Greenville & C. R. R. Co., 13 So. Car. 228. By agreement a new lien-holder may be substituted. Ketchum v. St. Louis, 101 U. S. 306. It is not necessary that the bonds which are secured shall mention the lien of the mortgaging act. Dundas v. Desjardins, etc., Co., 17 Grant (U. S.) 27. The holder of bonds secured by statutory mortgage can avail himself of the security only by means of foreclosure instituted by the trustees in conformity with the statute. Florida v. Anderson, 91 U. S. 667.

[5] Macalester v. Maryland, 114 U. S. 598.

[6] Ketchum v. St. Louis, 101 U. S. 306.

aid bonds giving a lien in favor of the state do not entitle the purchasers to enforce the lien where it is waived or released by the state.[1] The bondholders can not enforce the lien either upon the principle of subrogation or under the claim that they have a specific lien as direct mortgage creditors.[2]

§ 504. Debentures.—Debentures, which are the commonest form of security issued by English corporations, are defined to be instruments under seal, creating a charge, according to their wording, upon the property of the corporation, and to that extent conferring a priority over subsequent creditors and over existing creditors not possessed of such a charge.[3] They are, in fact, equitable mortgages, being enforceable only in equity.[4] Their holder has no lien upon the corporation's traffic receipts and no right to a receiver of them.[5] The debenture is generally not accompanied by any separate instrument. Instead of securing the payment in one instrument of a debt which there is a promise to pay in another or others, each mortgage debenture ordinarily includes both the provisions in regard to the security and a covenant for the payment of the debt.[6] In England debentures are not required to be recorded, but in most of our states they would be very dangerous investments on this account, and the fact that an attachment of property in this country may take precedence over an unrecorded debenture, was admitted in a recent English case.[7] A so-called debenture is, however, coming into use in the United States, which is in effect a bond or note secured by pledge of collaterals deposited with a trustee.[8]

[1] Tennessee Bond Cases, 114 U. S. 663, s. c. 5 Sup. Ct. R. 974, 1098.
[2] Cunningham v. Macon, etc., R. R. Co., 156 U. S. 400, s. c. 15 Sup. Ct. R. 361. But see Railroad Co. v. Schutte, 103 U. S. 118.
[3] Brice on Ultra Vires (2d ed.), 279.
[4] Holroyd v. Marshall, 10 H. L. C. 191; In re General South American Co., L. R. 2 Ch. D. 337.
[5] Imperial Mercantile Credit Assn. v. Newry & A. Ry. Co., 2. Ir. Rep. Eq. 524; Preston v. Great Yarmouth, L.R. 7 Ch. 655. See, as bearing on rights of debenture-holders prior to the Railway Companies Act of 1867, Bowen v. Brecon Ry. Co., L. R. 3. Eq. 541; Russell v. East Anglian Ry. Co., 3 Mac. & G. 104, 151.
[6] Hart v. Eastern Union Ry. Co., 6 Eng. Ry. & Can. Cas. 818, 7 Exch. 246, 265; 2 Cook on Stock and Stockholders, § 776.
[7] In re Empire, etc., Co., 62 L. T. R. 493.
[8] 2 Cook on Stock and Stockholders, § 777.

CHAPTER XX.

FORECLOSURE.

§ 505. Foreclosure—Default.
506. Option to declare whole debt due—Election.
507. Foreclosure for default in payment of interest.
508. Parties to foreclosure suit—Plaintiffs.
509. Bondholders as plaintiffs.
510. Pledgees, assignees and others as plaintiffs.
511. Defendants in foreclosure suits—Generally.
§ 512. When other lien-holders should be made defendants.
513. Defenses to foreclosure suit.
514. Effect of provisions giving trustees the right to take possession and sell.
515. The decree.
516. Consent decree.
517. Deficiency decree.
518. Final and appealable decrees.

§ 505. **Foreclosure—Default.**—In order to maintain a suit for the foreclosure of a mortgage, the plaintiff must be able to show a default within its terms. An allegation that interest coupons are unpaid has been held insufficient, where it does not appear that any demand for payment has been made or that the company neglected or refused to pay at the place or in the manner provided.[1] But a demand is usually unnecessary

---

[1] Davies v. N.Y. Concert Co., 41 Hun (N. Y.) 492; Jones on Corp. Bonds and Mort., § 381. See, also, Doyle v. Phœnix Ins. Co., 44 Cal. 264; United States Rolling Stock Co. v. Atlantic, etc., Co., 34 Ohio St. 450, 467. But see Mayes v. Goldsmith, 58 Ind. 94; Douthit v. Mohr, 116 Ind. 482, and compare Carey v. Houston, 45 Fed. R. 438. In a recent case a railroad company alleged its insolvency, and prayed for a sale of its property and distribution of the proceeds among its creditors. A receiver was appointed. A mortgagee filed a cross-bill to foreclose two mortgages, on both of which default in the interest had been made, but the debt secured by the second only was due. The court held that both mortgages might be foreclosed, although by its terms the first was not subject to foreclosure until default in payment of the principal at maturity. McIlhenny v. Binz, 80 Tex. 1, 13 S. W. R. 655. Where the mortgage bonds have become the property of the railroad company's lessee, such lessee will be held to a strict account-

§ 505   FORECLOSURE.   663

before instituting a suit to foreclose a mortgage,[1] and the right to foreclose arises as soon as the condition of the defeasance is broken.[2] Railroad mortgages and trust deeds, however, generally provide that no suit to foreclose shall be instituted for failure to pay interest until after the default shall have continued for a specified period. A default may be waived,[3] but the

ing before it will be permitted to foreclose for an alleged default in the payment of interest, since there could be no default so long as the rent that was unaccounted for equaled the unpaid interest. Chamberlain v. Connecticut Cent. R. Co., 54 Conn. 472.

[1] Elliott's Gen. Pr., § 313; Union, etc., Co. v. Curtis, 35 Ohio St. 357; Gillett v. Balcom, 6 Barb. (N. Y.) 370; Clemens v. Luce, 101 Cal. 432, s. c. 35 Pac. R. 1032; Wiltsie on Mortgage Foreclosures, § 35. But the instrument may, of course, be so drawn as to require a demand. Potomac, etc., Co. v. Evans, 84 Va. 717, 6 S. E. R. 2; Bolman v. Lohman, 79 Ala. 63. Thus, there may be no default under the provisions of the particular instrument until demand and refusal or failure to comply with it. So a provision in bonds requiring a demand has been held to control the mortgage securing them. Railway Co. v. Sprague, 103 U. S. 756.

[2] Richards v. Holmes, 18 How. (U. S.) 143; Pomeroy v. Winship, 12 Mass. 513, s. c. 7 Am. Dec. 91; Central Trust Co. v. New York, etc., R. Co., 33 Hun (N. Y.) 513; Chicago, etc., R. Co. v. Fosdick, 106 U. S. 47.

[3] Dow v. Memphis, etc., R. Co., 20 Fed. R. 260; Nebraska City Bank v. Nebraska Gas, etc., Co., 14 Fed. R. 763; Randolph v. Middleton, 26 N. J. Eq. 543. Where a railroad trust deed provided that if the default occurred in payment of interest or principal of the bonds, the trustees were to act on the requisition of the holders of 25 per cent. of the bonds, and if "the default be in the omission of any act or thing required by article 12 of these presents for the further assurance of the title of the trustees to any property or franchise now possessed or hereafter acquired, or in any provisions herein contained to be performed by said company, then and in either of such cases the requisition shall be as aforesaid; but it shall be within the discretion of the trustees to enforce or waive the rights of the bondholders by reason of such default, subject to the power hereby declared of a majority in interest of such bondholders to instruct the said trustees to waive such default," it was held that the right of a majority to waive default extended only to failure to make further assurance, and not to failure to pay interest or principal of the bonds. Hollister v. Stewart, 111 N. Y. 644, s. c. 19 N. E. R. 782. Delay for three months in bringing suit after failure to pay installment of interest is not a waiver of a stipulation making the whole debt due at once upon such default. Atkinson v. Walton, 162 Pa. St. 219, s. c. 29 Atl. R. 898. See, also, Fletcher v. Dennison, 101 Cal. 292, s. c. 35 Pac. 868; Brown v. McKay, 151 Ill. 315, s. c. 37 N. E. R. 1037. But compare French v. Row, 77 Hun (N. Y.) 380, s. c. 28 N. Y. Supp. 849, where long delay, coupled with other circumstances, was held to be a waiver. Acceptance of the defaulted interest before instituting suit to foreclose is a waiver of the right of forfeiture on

waiver, if by parol and without consideration, may be revoked, and then, after a demand of payment, the payment waived will become due.[1] So, it has been held that an agreement not to exercise the option given in a trust deed to declare the entire debt due for default in payment of interest, when limited to a specified installment, although made in consideration of the assignment of rents accruing from the mortgaged premises, does not prevent the mortgagee from declaring the entire debt due upon default in the payment of a subsequent installment.[2] Failure to pay taxes or to perform other conditions may also be made a cause for declaring the entire debt due and justify a foreclosure for the whole amount,[3] but where there is no agreement by the mortgagor to pay taxes,[4] or where they are paid by him before the option is exercised by foreclosure or otherwise, the mortgagee can not foreclose merely because of such failure.[5]

§ 506. Option to declare whole debt due—Election.—Where an option is given to the mortgagee to declare the whole debt due, that is, the principal as well as the interest, upon the failure to pay the interest or any installment when due, he must, of course, in some way, indicate his election. There is some conflict among the authorities as to whether merely instituting suit to foreclose for the entire debt without giving any previ-

---

account of such default. Smalley v. Renken, 85 Iowa 612, s. c. 52 N.W. R. 507. But see Moore v. Sargent, 112 Ind. 484.

[1] Albert v. Grosvenor Investment Co., L. R. 3 Q. B. 123; Union Trust Co. v. St. Louis, etc., Co., 5 Dill. (U. S.) 1; Jones on Corp. Bonds and Mort., § 383. See, also, Sharpe v. Arnott, 51 Cal. 188; Gardner v. Watson, 13 Ill. 347; Massaker v. Mackerley, 9 N. J. Eq. 440.

[2] Martin v. Land, etc., Bank, 5 Tex. Civ. App. 167, s. c. 23 S. W. R. 1032. See, also, Malcolm v. Allen, 49 N. Y. 448.

[3] Martin v. Clover, 63 Hun (N. Y.) 628, 17 N. Y. S. 638; Williams v. Townsend, 31 N. Y. 411; Brickell v. Batchelder, 62 Cal. 623; Pope v. Durant, 26 Iowa 233; Wiltsie on Mortgage Foreclosures, § 45.

[4] Noble v. Greer, 48 Kan. 41, s. c. 28 Pac. R. 1004. A provision requiring the mortgagor company to pay taxes and assessments does not require it to pay an income tax upon the interest on the bonds.. Haight v. Railroad Co., 6 Wall. (U. S.) 15.

[5] Smalley v. Renken, 85 Iowa 612, s. c. 52 N.W. R. 507.

ous notice or otherwise showing an election to exercise the option, is sufficient. Much depends upon the provisions of the particular mortgage or trust deed in question. It may doubtless provide that notice shall be given or a declaration made of the mortgagee's intention to take advantage of the option before the institution of proceedings to foreclose. But, in the absence of any such provison, that is, where the mortgage merely provides that, upon failure to pay interest, or any installment, when due, the entire debt shall become due, or that the mortgagee shall have the option of declaring it due, the commencement of a suit to foreclose for the entire debt is, according to the better rule and the weight of authority, a sufficient election without a previous declaration thereof.[1] A written notice given by the holders of the notes or bonds secured by the trust deed to the trustee, requesting him to foreclose for the entire debt, has been held to be a sufficient declaration of an intention to exercise the option.[2] So, where a mortgage provided that until default in the payment of interest for six months after written demand by the trustee the mortgagor should remain in possession, but that after such default the trustee might take possession, it was held that this was a limitation merely upon the right of the trustee to take possession, and that he might institute proceedings to foreclose without giving notice and without waiting six months.[3] Decisions may be found which seem to go still further in this direction.[4] The

[1] Brown v. McKay, 151 Ill. 315, s.c. 37 N. E. R. 1037; New York Security, etc., Co. v. Saratoga, etc., Co., 34 N.Y. Supp. 890; Taylor v. Alliance Trust Co., 71 Miss. 694, s. c. 15 So. R. 121; Morling v. Bronson, 37 Neb. 608, s. c. 56 N. W. R. 205; Sichler v. Look, 93 Cal. 600, s. c. 29 Pac. R. 220, 223; Buchanan v. Berkshire Life Ins. Co., 96 Ind. 510; Young v. McLean, 63 N. Car. 576. *Contra*, Basse v. Gallegger, 7 Wis. 442, s. c. 76 Am. Dec. 225; Macloon v. Smith, 49 Wis. 200; Dean v. Applegarth, 65 Cal. 391, s. c. 4 Pac. R. 375 (distinguished in Hewitt v. Dean, 91 Cal. 5, s. c. 27 Pac. R. 423).

[2] Heffron v. Gage, 149 Ill. 182, s. c. 36 N. E. R. 569. See, also, Mallory v. West Shore, etc., R. Co., 3 J. & S. (N. Y. Super. Ct.) 174; Fellows v. Gilman, 4 Wend. (N. Y.) 414; American Tube, etc., Co. v. Kentucky, etc., Co., 51 Fed. R. 826.

[3] Farmers' L. & T. Co. v. Winona, etc., Ry. Co., 59 Fed. R. 957. To the same effect is Alabama, etc., Co. v. Robinson, 56 Fed. R. 690, affirming Robinson v. Alabama, etc., Co., 48 Fed. R. 12.

[4] See, for instance, Mercantile Trust Co. v. Chicago, etc., Ry. Co., 61 Fed. R. 372. But see *post*, § 507.

fact that the mortgaged property is in the possession of a receiver appointed at the suit of a third person will not prevent the mortgagee from exercising his option to declare the entire debt due, upon default in the payment of one installment, by instituting a suit to foreclose.[1] We doubt, however, if the mortgagee could sell the property, under a decree of foreclosure, while it is in the hands of the receiver.

§ 507. **Foreclosure for default in payment of interest.**— A foreclosure may be had for unpaid interest, although the principal debt is not due.[2] A railroad mortgage, providing that the bonds shall become due on default in the payment of interest, may be foreclosed on default, unless the statute authorizing the bonds states a minimum period, not yet elapsed, during which they must run, in which case the mortgage may be foreclosed for the default in the payment of interest, the decree directing a sale if payment is not made within a period appointed by the court, and the remainder of the proceeds, after the satisfaction of the defaulted interest and expenses, being held by the court subject to the mortgagee's lien for the payment of the subsequently maturing interest coupons and the principal.[3] But such a suit may generally be arrested

---

[1] Mulcahey v. Strauss, 151 Ill. 70, s. c. 37 N. E. R. 702. It was also held in this case that the failure to obtain leave to sue the receiver did not deprive the court of jurisdiction and that the objection was waived. Where the receiver is a party, however, leave should be obtained, for even if it is not jurisdictional, the failure to obtain it may be fatal where the question is properly raised.

[2] Union Trust Co. v. St. Louis, etc., R. Co., 5 Dill. U. S. 1; Howell v. Western, etc., R. Co., 94 U. S. 463; Chicago, etc., R. Co. v. Fosdick, 106 U. S. 47, 68; Central T. Co. v. New York, etc., R. Co., 33 Hun (N.Y.) 513. Where a railroad mortgage contains no provision making the principal due on default in the payment of interest, powers given to the trustee, after default in the payment of interest, to take possession of the mortgaged property and sell the same and apply the proceeds to the payment of interest and principal, do not accelerate the maturity of the principal so as to authorize foreclosure for the entire debt on such default. McFadden v. Mays Landing etc., R. Co., 49 N. J. 176, 22 Atl. R. 932.

[3] Howell v. Western R. R. Co., 94 U. S. 463; Wilmer v. Atlanta & Richmond Air Line R. Co., 2 Woods 409, 447; Macon & Augusta R. R. Co. v. Georgia R. R. Co., 63 Ga. 103; Central Trust Co. v. N.Y. City & N. R. R. Co., 33 Hun (N. Y.) 513; Wood v. Consolidated Electric L. Co., 36 Fed. R. 538.

by payment of the accrued interest and costs.[1] It is frequently provided in the mortgage or trust deed that upon default in the payment of interest the mortgage may be foreclosed for the entire debt. Such a provision is valid,[2] but it does not, at least unless it clearly makes the entire debt due for all purposes, authorize a personal judgment for any deficiency in the amount of the mortgaged property to pay the principal not yet due. Its effect is rather to make the principal due merely for the purposes of the foreclosure or entry and sale by the trustee under the provisions of the mortgage.[3] But, where the mortgaged property can not be sold in parcels, as is usually the case with railroads, the entire road may be sold even upon foreclosure for default in the interest alone, and the proceeds applied to the principal as well as the interest.[4] Practically

[1] See Tillinghast v. Troy, etc., R. Co., 48 Hun (N. Y.) 420; Philips v. Bailey, 82 Mo. 639. In Grape Creek Coal Co. v. Farmers' L. & T. Co., 63 Fed. R. 891, 895, it is said that such right doubtless exists "down to the entry of the decree," but it can not be exercised after a decree is entered declaring the whole debt due.

[2] McLean v. Presley, 56 Ala. 211; Pope v. Durant, 26 Iowa 233; Hoodless v. Reid, 112 Ill. 105; Richards v. Holmes, 18 How. (U. S.) 143; Marye v. Hart, 76 Cal. 291, 23 Am. & Eng. Corp. Cas. 506, and note; Wiltsie Mort. Foreclosure, § 37. In some jurisdictions this is the rule even in the absence of any express provision upon the subject: Farmers' L. & T. Co. v. Nova Scotia, etc., R. Co., 24 N. S. 542. Where the provision is that the entire debt may be declared due and collected by the trustee, after default in payment of interest, at the request of a certain number of bondholders, or the like, the condition must be performed before advantage can be taken of the provision. Chicago, etc., R. Co. v. Fosdick, 106 U. S. 47; Batchelder v. Council, etc., Co., 131 N.Y. 42; Farmers' L. & T. Co. v. Bankers', etc., Co., 44 Hun (N. Y.) 400.

[3] Morgan v. Martien, 32 Mo. 438; White v. Miller, 52 Minn. 367, 54 N. W. R. 736; McClelland v. Bishop, 42 Ohio St. 113; Railway Co. v. Sprague, 103 U. S. 756; Ohio Central R. Co. v. Central T. Co., 133 U. S. 83, s. c. 10 Sup. Ct. R. 235; Mallory v. West Shore, etc., R. Co., 35 N. Y. Super. Ct. 174; Grape Creek Coal Co. v. Farmers' L. & T. Co., 63 Fed. R. 891. (Provision held insufficient to authorize a decree declaring principal due and compelling its payment in order to redeem.) But see Wheeler, etc., Co. v. Howard, 28 Fed. R. 741; Noell v. Gaines, 68 Mo. 649.

[4] Olcott v. Bynum, 17 Wall. (U. S.) 44; Chicago, etc., R. Co. v. Fosdick, 106 U. S. 47, 68; Farmers' L. & T. Co. v. Oregon, etc., R. Co., 24 Fed. R. 407; Pennsylvania R. Co. v. Allegheny, etc., R. Co., 48 Fed. R. 139; McLean v. Presley, 56 Ala. 211; Bridges v. Bal-

therefore, to this extent a default in payment of interest may cause the entire debt to become due whether there is a provision in the mortgage to that effect or not. It is not to be inferred from this, however, that such a provision is unimportant. While it is proper, even in its absence, to direct the payment of the whole debt out of the proceeds of the sale of the property as an entirety, yet, in such a case, the amount of overdue interest should be stated in the decree and provision made for the mortgagor to redeem before the sale upon the payment of such interest and costs, whereas the presence of a provision expressly making the entire debt due upon default in payment of interest will authorize a decree declaring it all due and ordering a sale, unless the whole amount is paid within a reasonable time therein specified.[1]

§ 508. **Parties to foreclosure suit—Plaintiffs.**—Where the mortgage is made to trustees they may sue to foreclose it without joining the bondholders.[2] Where a bill in equity is filed by the trustees for the foreclosure of a mortgage, the individual bondholders are not necessary nor, as a rule, even proper parties to the suit.[3] They may be admitted as parties, however,

lard, 62 Miss. 237; McTighe v. Macon, etc., Const. Co., 94 Ga. 306, 21 S. E. R. 701, 706, 707.

[1] Grape Creek Coal Co. v. Farmers' L. & T. Co., 63 Fed. R. 891; Chicago, etc., R. Co. v. Fosdick, 106 U. S. 47, 75; Ohio Cent. R. Co. v. Central Trust Co., 133 U. S. 83, s. c. 10 Sup. Ct. R. 235.

[2] Chicago, etc., R. Land Co. v. Peck, 112 Ill. 408; Richter v. Jerome, 123 U. S. 233, s. c. 8 Sup. Ct. R. 106; Hale v. Nashua, etc., R. Co. v. Coffin, 50 Conn. 150; Coe v. Columbus, etc., R. Co., 10 Ohio St. 372, s. c. 75 Am. Dec. 518; Savannah, etc., R. Co. v. Lancaster, 62 Ala. 555.

[3] Shaw v. Norfolk Co. R. Co., 5 Gray (Mass.) 162; Wetmore v. St. Paul, etc., R. Co., 1 McCrary (U. S.) 466; Railroad Co. v. Howard, 7 Wall. (U. S.) 392; Shaw v. Little Rock, etc., R. Co., 100 U. S. 605. But see Wiltsie on Mortgage Foreclosures, § 110. In a railroad foreclosure suit the mortgage trustee represents the bondholders, and, if he acts in good faith, whatever binds him binds them, so that they have no right to be made parties, except when the trustee is not acting in good faith. Farmers' Loan & Trust Co. v. Kansas City, W. & N. W. R. Co., (C. C.) 53 Fed. R. 182; Beals v. Illinois, etc., R. R. Co., 133 U. S. 290, s. c. 10 Sup. Ct. Rep. 314; Elwell v. Fosdick, 134 U. S. 500, s. c. 10 Sup. Ct. R. 598; McElrath v. Pittsburg, etc., R. Co., 68 Pa. St. 37. This rule has been applied where the trustee was made defendant to a suit to cancel and satisfy the mortgage under a

where the trustee is guilty of misconduct or shows himself incompetent to properly execute the trust,[1] or where he is shown to have interests adverse to those of the bondholders.[2] If a part of the trustees refuse to act, the suit may be prosecuted by the remaining trustee or trustees, and those refusing to act may be made defendants.[3] So, where one of several trustees dies the surviving trustee or trustees may maintain the suit.[4]

§ 509. **Bondholders as plaintiffs.**—In case the trustees neglect or refuse to bring a foreclosure suit, or the trustee's office becomes vacant, and there is no provision in the mortgage forbidding such a course, one of the bondholders may bring a suit on behalf of himself and all others who choose to join him, to foreclose the mortgage for a default in the payment of the principal or interest of his bonds.[5] Such neglect, refusal,

reorganization agreement. Pollitz v. Farmers' L. & T. Co., 53 Fed. R. 210. But it is said that the trustee represents the bondholders only for the protection of their lien under the trust deed and not after he has denied their right. Moran v. Hagerman, 64 Fed. R. 499.

[1] Skiddy v. Atlantic, etc., R. Co., 3 Hughes (U. S.) 320. The simple fact that a single trust company is trustee under twelve mortgages given by different corporations which have united to form a single system, is not sufficient reason for admitting a committee of the bondholders of the principal corporation by which the other roads in the system are owned or controlled to become party plaintiffs in a suit to foreclose. Clyde v. Richmond, etc., R. Co., 55 Fed. R. 445.

[2] DeBetz's Petition, 9 Abb. N. C. (N. Y.) 246; Webb v. Vermont, etc., R. Co., 9 Fed. R. 793; American Tube, etc., Co. v. Kentucky, etc., Co., 51 Fed. R. 826.

[3] Tillinghast v. Troy, etc., R. Co., 48 Hun (N. Y.) 420; Robinson v. Alabama, etc., Co., 48 Fed. R. 12.

[4] Alabama, etc., Co. v. Robinson, 56 Fed. R. 690, affirming Robinson v. Alabama, etc., Co., 48 Fed. R. 12; Gibbes v. Greenville, etc., R. Co., 13 So. Car. 228.

[5] Van Benthuysen v. Central N. E., etc., R. Co., 17 N. Y. S. 709, 63 Hun (N. Y.) 627; Mason v. York, etc., R. Co., 52 Me. 82; Hotel Co. v. Wade, 97 U. S. 13; In re Chickering, 56 Vt. 82; March v. Eastern R. Co., 40 N. H. 548, 566; Seibert v. Minneapolis, etc., R. Co., 52 Minn, 148, 57 Am. & Eng. R. Cas. 208, s. c. 53 N. W. R. 1134, 20 L. R. A. 535, and note; Commonwealth v. Susquehanna, etc., R. Co., 122 Pa. St. 306; Wheelwright v. St. Louis, etc., Co., 56 Fed. R. 164; Brooks v. Vermont Central R. Co., 14 Blatchf. (U. S.) 463. In Alexander v. Central R. Co., 3 Dill. (U. S.) 487, the mortgage gave the trustee a power of sale to be exercised at the request of a majority of the stockholders, upon default in the payment of interest. It was held that

or vacancy must be alleged and proved or the court will refuse to grant relief.[1] Bondholders have also been permitted to maintain the suit where the only trustee has gone beyond the

this remedy was merely cumulative to the ordinary legal remedies, and that upon refusal of the trustee to bring a suit to foreclose the mortgage for a default in the payment of interest, any one of the bondholders could maintain a suit in equity for that purpose on behalf of himself and others, making the trustee a party defendant. Such a suit should usually be brought by the bondholder in behalf of himself and all other bondholders, but an averment to this effect is unnecessary when default has been made only on the bonds held by the complainant. McFadden v. Mays Landing, etc., R. Co., 49 N. J. Eq. 176, 22 Atl. R. 932. See, also, Tyler v. Yreka, etc., Co., 14 Cal. 212. In a recent case the Supreme Court of the United States held that a foreclosure was not invalid because one of the trustees was a director and the others stockholders in the company that procured the foreclosure; because one person was president of both companies; because a majority of the directors of one company were directors of the other; because the president of one company owned most of the other company's stock; or because the attorneys who instituted the foreclosure suit in the name of the trustees were in other matters attorneys for or directors of the company that procured it. Leavenworth County v. Chicago, etc., Ry. Co., 134 U. S. 688, 10 Sup. Ct. R. 708. The fact that the bondholder purchased his bonds at the request of the lessee of the mortgaged railroad, and that the suit was instituted as a means of relieving it from the inconvenience and loss attending the operation of the road does not deprive the bondholder of his remedy of foreclosure on default in the payment of the bonds. McFadden v. Mays Landing, etc., R. Co., supra.

[1] Clyde v. Richmond, etc., R. Co., 55 Fed. R. 445; Morgan v. Kansas Pac. R. Co., 15 Fed. R. 55; Hotel Co. v. Wade, 97 U. S. 13. In Chicago, etc., R. Co. v. Fosdick, 106 U. S. 47, where the terms of the mortgage gave the trustees the right, upon a default for six months in the payment of interest, and at the request of a majority of the bondholders, to take possession of the railroad property and sell the same, the court, by Mr. Justice Matthews, said: "But inasmuch as by the terms of the first article the conveyance is declared to be for the purpose of securing the payment of the interest as well as the principal of the bonds, and by the fourth article the mortgagor's right of possession terminates upon a default in the payment of interest as well as principal on the bonds, we are of opinion, independent of the provisions of the other articles, that the trustees, or on their failure to do so, any bondholder, on non-payment of any installment of interest on any bond, might file a bill for the enforcement of the security by a foreclosure of the mortgage, and sale of the mortgaged property. This right belongs to each bondholder separately, and its exercise is "not dependent upon the co-operation or consent of any others, or of the trustees. It is properly and strictly enforceable by and in the name of the latter, but if necessary may be prosecuted without and even against them."

jurisdiction of the court and it is shown that an emergency exists for immediate action and that great loss will result to the complainants before he can be reached.[1] Where a foreclosure suit has been commenced by bondholders on behalf of themselves and all others who desire to join them, the other bondholders may, upon petition, be permitted to become complainants.[2] But it is not necessary that they should do so, as the interests of all the bondholders are represented by the actual complainants, and by the trustees, who must, in such a suit, be made parties defendant.[3] The bondholder who brings the suit can not, by so doing, obtain an undue advantage over the other bondholders whose rights in the security are the same as his own; he is bound, in such a case, to act for all and not merely for himself.[4] In an action by a holder of bonds, suing on behalf of himself and others, to foreclose a mortgage securing the bonds, for a default in payment of interest thereon, a tender, unless of interest due on all the bonds, is insufficient to arrest the action.[5] Where a minority of the bondholders bring a foreclosure suit against the wishes of the majority, the court may grant a stay of proceedings upon application on condition that the bonds sued on shall be paid together with accrued costs.[6] It is competent for the bondholders to agree among themselves upon what conditions the right to sue may be exercised by an individual bondholder; and a provision in

---

[1] Ettlinger v. Persian, etc., Co., 142 N. Y. 189, s. c. 36 N. E. R. 1055.

[2] *In re* Chickering, 56 Vt. 82.

[3] First Nat. Ins. Co. v. Salisbury, 130 Mass. 303; Hackensack Water Co. v. DeKay, 36 N. J. Eq. 548; Jones on Mortgages, § 1385.

[4] Jackson v. Ludeling, 21 Wall. (U. S.) 616; New Orleans Pac. Ry. v. Parker, 143 U. S. 42, 58, s. c. 12 Sup. Ct. R. 364; 6 Lewis' Am. R. R. & Corp. R. 13; Commonwealth v. Susquehanna, etc., R. Co., 122 Pa. St. 306. See, also, Railroad Co. v. Orr, 18 Wall. (U. S.) 471, where it was held that a single bondholder could not maintain the suit without notice to others who were named in the mortgage. As he acts for all, he should be reimbursed out of the trust fund for expenses so incurred to the same extent as the trustee would have been entitled to be reimbursed. Seibert v. Minneapolis, etc., Ry. Co., 52 Minn. 246, 57 N. W. R. 1068. See Hobbs v. McLean, 117 U. S. 567.

[5] Van Benthuysen v. Central N. E. & W. R. Co., 17 N. Y. S. 709, 63 Hun 627.

[6] Tillinghast v. Troy, etc., R. Co., 48 Hun (N. Y.) 420.

the mortgage that no proceedings in law or equity shall be taken by any bondholder secured thereby, to foreclose the equity of redemption independently of the trustee, until after the refusal of the trustee to comply with a requisition first made upon him by the holders of a certain percentage of the bonds secured by such mortgage, is reasonable and valid. Such provisions are to be deemed *stricti juris*, but are, nevertheless, to be reasonably construed in view of the nature of the security, and the interest of the bondholders as a class. It is not the purpose or effect of such a stipulation to divest the bondholders of their rights to judicial remedies, or to oust the courts of their jurisdiction, but it is merely the imposition of certain conditions upon themselves in respect to the exercise of that right.[1] After suit is brought by individual bondhold-

[1] Seibert *v.* Minneapolis, etc., R. Co., 52 Minn. 148, 53 N. W. R. 1134. In this case the court said: "We are unable to see why the bondholders, subject to reasonable limitations, may not be bound by stipulations in the mortgage of this character, waiving a default, and providing, subject to the conditions named, for the foreclosure by the trustee exclusively. The interests of the bondholders as a class and the nature of the security are to be considered. They are agreements which the bondholders are at liberty to make, and there is nothing illegal or contrary to public policy in them. Chicago, etc., Railroad Co. *v.* Fosdick, 106 U. S. 47, 7 Am. & Eng. R. Cas. 427, 450. Each bondholder enters into contract relations with each and all of his co-bondholders. His right to appropriate the security in satisfaction of his bond in such lawful manner as he may choose is modified not only by the express provisions of the mortgage, but by the peculiar nature of the security. Gates *v.* Boston, etc., Railroad Co., 53 Conn. 333; Shaw *v.* Railroad Co., 100 U. S. 605; Canada, etc., Railroad Co. *v.* Gebhard, 109 U. S. 527, 537; Guilford *v.* Minneapolis, etc., Railroad Co., 48 Minn. 560, 51 N. W. R. 658. The legislature would have had an undoubted right to have incorporated in the enabling statute authorizing the execution of the mortgage and the issuance of the bonds secured thereby, a provision requiring the mortgage to contain similar stipulations. Howell *v.* Western Railroad Co., 94 U. S. 463. It is clear, then, that it would be competent for the bondholders themselves to agree to them. They are to be treated as *stricti juris*, but nevertheless are to be reasonably construed in view of the nature of the mortgage, which is the common security for all the bondholders, and the purposes to be subserved in making them. * * * * The trustee, as mortgagee, representing the interests of all the bondholders as beneficiaries, is the proper party to institute foreclosure proceedings, but if he unreasonably neglects or refuses to discharge his duty in the premises, doubtless any bondholder may bring an action to enforce the

ers to foreclose a mortgage, the trustees may ask leave to become complainants instead of defendants; and, unless they have been negligent and unfaithful, or have interests adverse to those of the bondholders, they will generally be allowed to do so. It has also been held that as soon as they are admitted as complainants, they have control of the suit, and may, upon leave of court, dismiss it, and pursue some other remedy.[1] A bondholder may bring an action at law for unpaid bonds or interest, but any judgment recovered in such an action will be subject to the prior lien of the mortgage.[2] Property of the company not covered by the mortgage may, however, be sold on execution for such a claim.[3] When a railroad company mortgages its property to the bondholders by name, all must join in or be made parties to a suit to foreclose the mortgage and no one can bring a suit on behalf of himself and all others who will come in and share the expenses of the suit.[4] In such

security for the common benefit. Chicago, etc , Railroad Co. v. Fosdick, 106 U. S. 47. The court said: "Why may not the mortgage in the common interest stipulate the conditions under which this right may be exercised by the bondholders, and in order to avoid the risk of rash or arbitrary proceedings which might result in great injury to the security, provide that no such proceedings should be instituted by an individual bondholder except upon the refusal of the trustee to obey the requisition of a reasonable number of the bondholders. It is not the intention or effect of such conditions or stipulations to divest the bondholders of their right to judicial remedies, or to oust the courts of their jurisdiction; it is merely the imposition of certain conditions upon themselves in respect to the exercise of that right. And this distinction is well recognized by the courts. Gasser v. Sun Fire Office, 42 Minn. 315, and cases; Guilford v. Minneapolis, etc,, Railroad Co., 48 Minn. 560, 51 N. W. R. 658. The provisions of this mortgage are not, we think, unreasonable or invalid." But see Guaranty Trust, etc., Co. v. Green Cove, etc., R. Co., 139 U. S. 137, s. c. 11 Sup. Ct. R. 512, for a provision held invalid as attempting to oust the jurisdiction of the court.

[1] Richards v. Chesapeake, etc., R. Co., 1 Hughes (U. S.) 28.

[2] Commonwealth v. Susquehanna, etc., R. Co., 122 Pa. St. 306; Philadelphia, etc., R. Co. v. Woelpper, 64 Pa. St. 366. Waiver of the right to foreclose a mortgage, on default in the payment of interest coupons on the bonds secured by it, does not affect the right to an action at law to recover on the coupons. Lyon v. New York, S. & W. R. Co., 14 Daly (N. Y.) 489.

[3] Carr v. LeFevre, 27 Pa. St. 413; Philadelphia, etc., R. Co. v. Johnson, 54 Pa. St. 127. See, also, Scott v. Farmers' L. & T. Co., 69 Fed. R. 17.

[4] Railroad Co. v. Orr, 18 Wall. (U. S.) 471.

a case, all parties should be before the court, because, if the mortgage should not prove an adequate security, it is the interest of each mortgagee to diminish the claim of every other mortgagee, and thereby add to his own security.[1]

§ 510. **Pledgees, assignees and others as plaintiffs.**—One who holds bonds as collateral may sue for a foreclosure by making his assignor a party.[2] Where the assignment is in writing it is unnecessary, in some jurisdictions, to make the assignor a party, but in others it is held that the assignment of the bonds or debt, passes merely the equitable and not the legal title to the security, and if there is any question as to the assignor having any interest it is advisable to make him a party.[3] But, in case the bonds have been pledged to secure a debt of the corporation, it has been held that the holder will be entitled to a decree for only the amount of the debt.[4] The bonds

[1] In Railroad Co. *v.* Orr, 18 Wall. (U. S.) 471, the court says: "In so far as he succeeds in doing that [diminishing the claims of his fellows], he adds to his own security. Each holder, therefore, should be present, both that he may defend his own claims and that he may attack the other claims should there be occasion for it. If, upon a fair adjustment of the amount of the debts, there should be a deficiency in the security, real or apprehended, every one interested should have notice in advance of the time, place, and mode of sale, that he may make timely arrangements to secure a sale of the property at its full value."

[2] Ackerson *v.* Lodi Branch R. Co., 28 N. J. Eq. 542; Morton *v.* New Orleans, etc., R. Co., 79 Ala. 590; Wiltsie on Mortgage Foreclosures, § 89. Where bonds were transferred as collateral to secure a loan with the condition that the pledgee, upon default in payment of the principal or interest of the note thus secured by the bonds, might sell the bonds without notice, and might become the purchaser thereof at any sale thus made, it was held that the pledgee, after having purchased the bonds at a sale held in accordance with the terms of the pledge, was entitled to a decree for the full amount of the face value of the bonds, with interest, and not merely the price paid therefor. Wade *v.* Chicago, etc., R. Co., 149 U. S. 327.

[3] See, Wiltsie on Mortgage Foreclosures, § 98. In Markel *v.* Evans, 47 Ind. 326, it is held that the assignor of a note secured by mortgage is neither a necessary nor a proper party to a suit to foreclose the mortgage. But see Nichol *v.* Henry, 89 Ind. 54.

[4] Jesup *v.* City Bank, 14 Wis. 331; Carpenter *v.* O'Dougherty, 67 Barb. (N. Y.) 397; Wiltsie on Mortgage Foreclosures, § 89. Where bonds are pledged by the corporation to secure its own debt under an agreement that the pledgee may purchase them at his own sale made upon default in payment of the notes secured, a purchase by the pledgee in accordance with the

are the principal and the mortgage the incident. It follows, therefore, that the assignee of the bonds or debt may foreclose even though he may have obtained no assignment of the mortgage,[1] while the mere assignment of a mortgage, which contains no promise to pay, without the debt, or bonds evidencing it, will not entitle the assignee to maintain a suit to foreclose.[2] It may be difficult, however, to apply these rules to trust deeds or railroad mortgages made to a trustee. We suppose that in such cases the assignee stands substantially in the position of his assignor and is represented in the same manner, and to the same extent, by the trustee. At all events the holder of bonds payable to bearer is to all intents and purposes an original payee, to whom the promise runs directly.[3] It has been held that a mortagee who has guaranteed payment of bonds and has taken up some of the overdue coupons attached thereto, may foreclose his mortgage subject to the rights of the holder of the bonds guaranteed,[4] and an assignee in bankruptcy[5] or a receiver[6] of a corporation may maintain a suit to foreclose in a proper case.

terms of the pledge is valid as against everybody, unless fraud or breach of trust is established. Third parties and strangers have no right to question the purchaser's title, but he may foreclose for the full amount of the bonds. Farmers' Loan & T. Co. v. Toledo, etc., R. Co., 54 Fed. R. 759. As a railroad is generally regarded as a unit and can not be sold in parcels so as to destroy its value and usefulness to the public, it may be that the decisions holding that the pledgee is entitled to a decree merely for the amount of his debt would not apply. The entire road may have to be sold and such a decree rendered as will fix the rights of all parties or hold the proceeds for future adjustment.

[1] Carpenter v. Longan, 16 Wall. (U. S.) 271; Converse v. Michigan, etc., Co., 45 Fed. R. 18; Ober v. Gallegher, 93 U. S. 199, 206; Parkhurst v. Watertown, etc., Co., 107 Ind. 594; Horn v. Bennett, 135 Ind. 158; Jackson v. Blodget, 5 Cow. (N. Y.) 202.

[2] Merritt v. Bartholick, 36 N. Y. 44; Hubbard v. Harrison, 38 Ind. 323; Lunt v. Lunt, 71 Me. 377; Nagle v. Macy, 9 Cal. 426; Hamilton v. Lubukee, 51 Ill. 415.

[3] Rutten v. Union Pac. Ry. Co., 17 Fed. R. 480; White v. Vermont, etc., R. Co., 21 How. (U. S.) 575. The first case just cited distinguishes Hayward v. Andrews, 106 U. S. 672, s. c. 1 Sup. Ct. R. 544, and New York Guaranty, etc., Co. v. Memphis, etc., Co., 107 U. S. 205, 2 Sup. Ct. R. 279.

[4] Burnett v. Hoffman, 40 Neb. 569, s. c. 58 N. W. R. 1134.

[5] Upton v. National Bank, 120 Mass. 153.

[6] Robinson v. Williams, 22 N. Y. 380; Iglehart v. Bierce, 36 Ill. 133.

§ 511. **Defendants in foreclosure suit—Generally.**—The indorsers of railroad bonds secured by mortgage are not necessary parties to a suit to foreclose the mortgage. Their interest in the proper application of the property to the extinguishment of the debt, however, it is said, gives them such an interest in the suit as makes them proper parties, and they should, if possible, be admitted as such. But where the indorser is a state which has made no provision for the institution of a suit against itself, it will not be permitted to intervene in the suit, and thereby oust the jurisdiction of the court.[1] It has also been held that a guarantor of the mortgage bonds of a railroad company, who afterwards joins the company in borrowing money with which to pay the interest coupons, is not thereby subrogated to the rights of the mortgagee so as to be a necessary or even a proper party to a subsequent suit to foreclose the mortgage, for there is no subrogation until the entire debt is paid.[2] It is doubtful whether the United States can be brought in as a party to a bill to foreclose against a railroad in which it is interested,[3] but it has been held that it may be bound by notice so that an effectual decree may be rendered foreclosing its interests in property not held for government purposes.[4] If the mortgagor has conveyed the property his grantee should be made a party,[5] and it may be said, in general, that no owner of an equity of redemption can be deprived of his right to redeem unless he is made a party to the foreclosure suit.[6] It is

---

[1] Young v. Montgomery, etc., R. Co., 2 Woods (U. S.) 606; Davis v. Gray, 16 Wall. (U. S.) 203. In deciding the first case Judge Woods said: "If the state has paid any interest on these bonds, and is thereby entitled to any part of the proceeds from the mortgaged property, she can propound her claim before the master, and it will be allowed."

[2] Columbia L. & T. Co. v. Kentucky Un. Ry. Co., 60 Fed. R. 794. But see cases cited in last note, *supra*, and Searles v. Jacksonville, etc., R. Co., 2 Woods (U. S.) 621.

[3] See Meier v. Kansas Pacific R. Co., 4 Dill. (U. S.) 378.

[4] Elliot v. Van Voorst, 3 Wall., Jr. (U. S. C. C.) 299; Jones on Corp. Bonds and Mort., § 400.

[5] Berlack v. Halle, 22 Fla. 236, s. c. 1 Am. St. R. 185, and numerous authorities cited in note; Wiltsie on Mortgage Foreclosures, § 126; Terrell v. Allison, 21 Wall. (U. S.) 289.

[6] Wiltsie on Mortgage Foreclosures, §§ 117, 126, 127; Gaskell v. Viquesney, 122 Ind. 244, s. c. 17 Am. St. R. 364, and note; Beekman v. Hudson, etc., Ry. Co., 35 Fed. R. 3.

a general rule, subject, however, to exception, that strangers to the cause can not be heard in it either by motion or petition. Thus unsecured general creditors[1] and individual stockholders[2] are not generally allowed to become parties to a foreclosure suit against the corporation. So, it has been held that the state has no right to intervene in a suit to foreclose a mortgage for the benefit of innocent bondholders for the purpose of having the mortgage declared invalid as in violation of the state law.[3] And prior mortgagees are not necessary parties unless the bill seeks the appointment of a receiver, or a sale of the entire property free from all liens or some other relief by which their interests will be affected.[4] Stockholders, however, may be ad-

---

[1] Bronson v. Railroad Co., 2 Black (U. S.) 524; Stout v. Lye, 103 U. S. 66; Thompson v. Huron Lumber Co., 4 Wash. 600, s. c. 30 Pac. R. 741; Farmers' Loan & T. Co. v. Chicago, etc., R. Co., 68 Fed. R. 412; Herring v. New York, etc., R. Co., 105 N. Y. 340. But see Hoffe v. Hoffe, 104 Cal. 94, 36 Pac. R. 389, 37 Pac. R. 894; Hollins v. Brierfield, etc., Co., 150 U. S. 371, s.c. 14 Sup. Ct. R. 127. The general creditors of a railroad company can not complain that a trustee in a mortgage executed to secure its bonds improperly released errors in a decree adjudicating that the rights of such company had passed to another corporation, under foreclosure proceedings, as the trustee represented the mortgage bondholders, and violated no duty to the company by giving the release. Loeb v. Chur, 6 N. Y. Sup. 296.

[2] Alexander v. Searcy, 81 Ga. 536, s. c. 36 Am. & Eng. R. Cas. 239; Foster v. Mansfield, etc., R. Co., 36 Fed. R. 627; Chicago, etc., Ry. Co. v. Howard, 7 Wall. (U. S.) 392.

[3] Farmers' Loan & T. Co. v. Chicago, etc., R. Co., 68 Fed. R. 412.

[4] Woodworth v. Blair, 112 U. S. 8; Wabash, etc., R. Co. v. Central Trust Co., 22 Fed. R. 138; Hagan v. Walker, 14 How. (U. S.) 29, 37; Ex parte McHenry, 9 Abb. (N. Y.) N. C. 256; Miltenberger v. Logansport Ry. Co., 106 U. S. 286, s. c. 1 Sup. Ct. R. 140. In the first case above cited the prior lien-holder was denied the right to intervene, and in the second, prior mortgagees who had been made parties were allowed their costs and the bill dismissed, as against them, upon the ground that they should not be put to the expense of litigation. There is sharp conflict among the authorities as to whether the prior incumbrancers are even proper parties so as to be bound by the decree. It seems desirable that all interests should be determined and adjusted in one suit, if possible, but the weight of authority is probably to the effect that in ordinary cases, they are not proper parties. The conflicting decisions are collected in notes to Woods v. Pittsburgh, etc., R. Co., 3 Am. & Eng. R. R. Cas. 525, 531, and Strobe v. Downer, 80 Am. Dec. 709, 714. See, also, post, § 512. The mortgagor can not complain, however, when the court adjudges that the junior mortgage is prior as to part of the property and the prior mortgagees, who were made parties, do not appeal. Seibert v. Minneapolis,

mitted as parties, where the directors refuse[1] to defend the corporation against unfounded and illegal claims, upon the same principle that bondholders are permitted to act when the trustees fail to do so.[2] And an assignee in bankruptcy[3] or a receiver of the mortgagor is generally a necessary party.[4]

§ 512. **When other lien-holders should be made defendants.** —Where a sale of the road is sought upon foreclosure of a junior mortgage, and it is desirable to quiet all outstanding titles, or to ascertain the validity or amount of prior liens about which there is substantial doubt, that the purchaser may know the value of the equity which he buys, the prior mortgagees should be joined as parties.[5] A failure to join the prior mortgagees as parties leaves them, generally speaking, with the same

---

etc., Ry. Co., 58 Minn. 39, 59 N. W. R. 822.

[1] A demand upon the directors to protect the interests of the corporation and a neglect or refusal by them to do so must usually be shown before the stockholders will be admitted to defend a foreclosure suit. Dimpfell v. Ohio, etc., R. Co., 110 U. S. 209; Alexander v. Searcy, 81 Ga. 536.

[2] Bronson v. La Crosse, etc., R. Co., 2 Wall. (U. S.) 524; Forbes v. Memphis, etc., R. Co., 2 Woods (U. S.) 323.

[3] Lenihan v. Hamann, 55 N. Y. 652; Bard v. Poole, 12 N. Y. 495; Griffin v. Hodshire, 119 Ind. 235.

[4] Raynor v. Selmes, 52 N. Y. 579. But see Herring v. New York, etc., R. Co., 105 N. Y. 340.

[5] Richards v. Chesapeake, etc., R. Co., 1 Hughes (U. S.) 28; Jerome v. McCarter, 94 U. S. 734; Hagan v. Walker, 14 How. (U. S.) 29; Dawson v. Danbury Bank, 15 Mich. 489. It is said, however, to be "well settled that in a foreclosure proceeding the complainant can not make a person who claims adversely to both the mortgagor and mortgagee a party, and litigate and settle his rights in that case." Dial v. Reynolds, 96 U. S. 340. See, also, "Trial of Adverse Title in Suit to Foreclose a Mortgage," 21 Cent. L. J. 223, and note to Strobe v. Downer, 80 Am. Dec. 709, 714. But compare the well-considered cases of Hefner v. Northwestern, etc., Co., 123 U. S. 747, s. c. 8 Sup. Ct. R. 337; Mendenhall v. Hall, 134 U. S. 559, s. c. 10 Sup. Ct. R. 616; Cohen v. Solomon, 66 Fed. R. 411; and in support of the well-settled rule in Indiana that an adverse claimant may be made a party and a conclusive adjudication rendered against him, see O'Brien v. Moffitt, 133 Ind. 660, s. c. 36 Am. St. R. 566; Craighead v. Dalton, 105 Ind. 72. See, generally, Wiltsie on Mortgage Foreclosures, Ch. IX; Farmers' L. & T. Co. v. Green Bay, etc., Co., 6 Fed. R. 100; Farmers' L. & T. Co. v. San Diego, etc., Co., 40 Fed. R. 105; Corcoran v. Chesapeake, etc., Co., 94 U. S. 741; Converse v. Michigan, etc., Co., 45 Fed. R. 18.

rights in the property that they had before the foreclosure.[1] Where the extent of the prior lien-holder's claim is definitely ascertained, and a foreclosure is sought subject to prior liens, he is not a necessary, nor as a rule, a proper party to the bill.[2] It is said that "the remedy of a junior incumbrancer, both before and after foreclosure, is to redeem the senior mortgage. Without the consent of the prior mortgagee, a junior lienor could not enforce a sale of more than the mortgagor's equity of redemption. If he wished a sale free from the prior lien, and the prior lienor will not consent, the decree should be that he redeem, and then foreclose for the enforcement of his own lien, and that he had redeemed.[3] A judicial foreclosure sale is not void because one interested in the equity of redemption, as a junior mortgagee, was not a party.'"[4] Where it is sought to cut off the right of a subsequent mortgagee, judgment creditor, or other lien-holder, to redeem, he must be made a party to the bill to foreclose.[5] And, in general, a junior lien-holder is entitled, on application, to be admitted as a party to contest the amount and validity of the claims preferred against the corporation.[6] But he

---

[1] Pittsburgh, etc., R. Co. v. Marshall, 85 Pa. St. 187; Wabash, etc., R. Co. v. Central Trust Co., 22 Fed. R. 138. A junior lien-holder can not compel the foreclosure of a mortgage constituting a prior lien upon the road. American Loan & T. Co. v. East & West R. Co., 37 Fed. R. 242; Seibert v. Minneapolis, etc., Ry. Co., 52 Minn. 246, s. c. 53 N. W. R. 1151. Where prior lien-holders have unnecessarily been made parties, the court may, of its own motion, dismiss the suit as to them, for they ought not to be put to the expense of making a defense where the amount and priority of their liens are undisputed. Wabash, etc., R. Co. v. Central Trust Co., 22 Fed. 138.

[2] Wabash, etc., R. Co. v. Central Trust Co., 22 Fed. R. 138; McMurtry v. Montgomery, etc., Co., 86 Ky. 206.

[3] Jones Mort., §§ 1394, 1396; Woodworth v. Blair, 112 U. S. 8, s. c. 5 Sup. Ct. R. 6; McKernan v. Neff, 43 Ind. 503; Spurgin v. Adamson, 62 Iowa 661, s. c. 18 N. W. R. 293.

[4] Compton v. Jesup, 68 Fed. R. 263, 311, citing Jones Mort., § 1395; Martin v. Noble, 29 Ind. 216; Frische v. Kramer, 16 Ohio 125; Rose v. Page, 2 Sim. 471; Fulghum v. Cotton, 3 Tenn. Ch. 296; Trayser v. Trustees, 39 Ind. 556; Emigrant, etc., Bank v. Goldman, 75 N. Y. 127.

[5] Searles v. Jacksonville, etc., R. Co., 2 Woods (U. S.) 621; Memphis, etc., R. Co. v. State, 37 Ark. 632; Beekman v. Hudson, etc., Ry. Co., 35 Fed. R. 3; Youngman v. Elmira, etc., R. Co., 65 Pa. St. 278; Hosford v. Johnson, 74 Ind. 479. But, otherwise, he is not, of course, a necessary party. Brooks v. Vermont Cent. R. Co., 14 Blatch. (U. S.) 463.

[6] Farmers' Loan & Trust Co. v. Texas Western R. Co., 32 Fed. R. 359.

is not a necessary party to a foreclosure against the mortgagor[1] although, as we have said, he may be a proper party in any case and his equity of redemption can not be cut off unless he is made a party. The original complainant in a foreclosure suit need not be made a party to an intervening petition, where it appears that he no longer has any interest in the fund in controversy, and no relief is asked against him.[2] The question whether or not a lien is prior to the mortgage sought to be foreclosed may properly be tried in a foreclosure suit if the bill contains proper averments that the defendant's title is subordinate to the title of the mortgagee.[3] A mortgagee should always be made a party where any doubt is entertained as to the priority of his lien; for a decree declaring a mortgage to be a first lien upon the property and franchises of a railroad company gives it no precedence over the prior lien of a party who had no notice of the proceedings, and was not a party or privy to the decree.[4] The title stands in the order in which conveyances were made, and can not be changed by any proceedings to which the holders of the title were not parties.[5]

Where a railroad extends into two states, in each of which the company is a domestic corporation, and the trustee in a mortgage on the whole road first brings a suit in one state to foreclose, and afterwards an ancillary suit in the other state for the same purpose, it has been held that he can not prevent a lien creditor of the company, who has not filed his claim in the first suit, from intervening in the second to establish his lien. Fidelity Ins. T. & S. D. Co. v. Shenandoah Val. R. Co., 32 W. Va. 244, s. c. 9 S. E. R. 180.

[1] Williams v. Kerr, 113 N. Car. 306, s. c. 18 S. E. R. 501; Pattison v. Shaw, 6 Ind. 377; Stockwell v. State, 101 Ind. 1.

[2] Central Trust Co. v. Sheffield, etc., R. Co., 44 Fed. R. 526.

[3] Harland v. Bankers', etc., Tel. Co., 33 Fed. R. 199; Converse v. Michigan, etc., Co., 45 Fed. R. 18; Corcoran v. Chesapeake, etc., Co., 94 U. S. 741; Lewis v. Smith, 9 N. Y. 502, 514, 515; Jones on Corp. Bonds and Mort., § 407.

[4] Pittsburgh, etc., R. Co. v. Marshall, 85 Pa. St. 187; Jones on Corp. Bonds and Mort., § 404. A decree rendered without proper notice to parties to be affected thereby is void. Central Trust Co. v. Florida R., etc., Co., 43 Fed. R. 751.

[5] Jerome v. McCarter, 94 U. S. 734. See Howard v. Milwaukee, etc., R. Co., 7 Biss. (U. S.) 73. But if one claiming to hold a prior lien is properly made a party to the bill, and appears, but fails to procure a dismissal as to himself, he will be bound by a decree and sale thereunder, and can not afterward assert any rights not saved to him by the decree. Woods v. Pittsburgh, etc., R. Co., 99 Pa. St. 101.

§ 513. **Defenses to foreclosure suit.**—As a general rule no defenses are allowed to a suit to foreclose in favor of *bona fide* purchasers of railroad mortgage bonds that would not be allowed in an action at law upon negotiable promissory notes.[1] The acts of the company subsequent to the execution of the mortgage can not be set up as a defense to a suit by the mortgagee to foreclose his lien,[2] and neither the company nor a purchaser who claims title by conveyance from it can deny the validity of its incorporation in a suit to foreclose a mortgage which it has executed.[3] The same principle applies where the mortgage is given by a consolidated company.[4] It is no defense that a construction company had agreed to pay the interest in default,[5] nor that the road has been leased,[6] although it may be a good defense to show that the mortgagee, who holds all the bonds, is the lessee and has been paid by way of rental all the interest alleged to be in default.[7] It has also been held that neither a misapplication of its earnings by the mortgagor company in order to cause a default, nor the fact that the largest bondholder was also a stockholder and had bought the bonds, after default in payment of interest, for the purpose of causing a foreclosure and purchasing at the sale, constituted a good defense either in favor of the mortgagor or another stockholder.[8] Where, however, a railroad company, executing a mortgage upon its road as contemplated, has no legal title to

[1] Kenicott v. Supervisors, 16 Wall. (U. S.) 452; Carpenter v. Longan, 16 Wall. (U. S.) 271; Swett v. Stark, 31 Fed. R. 858.

[2] Bronson v. La Crosse, etc., R. Co., 2 Wall. (U. S. 283; Hale v. Nashua, etc., R. Co., 60 N. H. 333.

[3] Beekman v. Hudson River, etc., R. Co., 35 Fed. R. 3. See, also, Williamson v. Kokomo, etc., Assn., 89 Ind. 389; Farmers' L. & T. Co. v. Toledo, etc., R. Co., 67 Fed. R. 49. A junior mortgagee can not deny the validity of a prior mortgage to which his mortgage is expressly made subject. Bronson v. La Crosse, etc., R. Co., 2 Wall.

(U. S.) 283; Jerome v. McCarter, 94 U. S. 734; Jones on Corp. Bonds and Mort., § 415.

[4] Coe v. New Jersey, etc., R. Co., 31 N. J. Eq. 105.

[5] Foster v. Mansfield, etc., R. Co., 36 Fed. R. 627.

[6] Hale v. Nashua, etc., R. Co., 60 N. H. 333.

[7] Chamberlain v. Connecticut, etc., R. Co., 54 Conn. 472.

[8] Farmers' L. & T. Co. v. New York, etc., Ry. Co., 78 Hun 213, s. c. 28 N. Y. Supp. 933. See, also, Coe v. East & W. R. Co., 52 Fed. R. 531.

the right of way, but merely holds contracts for a small portion thereof, to be conveyed on conditions which it never performs or has agreed to perform, and a new company is organized, which builds the road and acquires the legal title to most of the right of way and is equitably entitled to the remainder, no decree of foreclosure can be sustained under the mortgage, as against the new company, for the sale of its property. The mortgage creditors of the original company could have no rights superior to the company itself, and it had no such interest or title in the road as can be subjected to sale under the mortgage.[1]

§ 514. **Effect of provisions giving trustees the right to take possession and sell.**—It is usual, in mortgages of railroad property, to confer upon the mortgage trustee a right of possession and sale in case of a continuing default in the payment of the mortgage debt. In some instances this power can only be exercised by the trustees at the request of a majority of the bondholders, and it is generally provided that it shall only be exercised after the default in payment has continued for a specified time. Provisions of this character in restraint of the exercise of a power of summary foreclosure must be strictly complied with. Thus where it is provided that a power of sale may be exercised by the mortgage trustees in case of a continued default for sixty days after notice to the mortgagor of an intention to sell, but not until the sale has been previously advertised for sixty days, the sale must be advertised for sixty days from the close of the sixty days' notice to the corporation of an intention to sell.[2] It was also held in a recent case that a power of sale given to the mortgagee can be executed only by him, unless the debt has been assigned so as to pass the legal title, and that the assignee of the mortgage, without the debt, can

---

[1] Chicago, etc., R. R. Co. v. Loewenthal, 93 Ill. 433.

[2] Macon, etc., R. Co. v. Georgia R. Co., 63 Ga. 103; Gibbons v. McDougall, 26 Grant's Ch. (Ont.) 214. To same effect, see generally Jones on Corp. Bonds and Mort., § 384; Foster v. Boston, 133 Mass. 143; Shillabar v. Robinson, 97 U. S. 68; Equitable Trust Co. v. Fisher, 106 Ill. 189; Schanewerk v. Hoberecht, 117 Mo. 22, s. c. 38 Am. St. R. 631.

not execute the power of sale.[1] Where the trustees under a mortgage stipulating for possession of the mortgaged property are denied possession upon the happening of a default, they may maintain ejectment to recover the mortgaged real estate.[2] But since the corporate property usually includes personal property and choses in action for which ejectment will not lie, and since a judgment against an insolvent mortgagor for damages for the non-delivery of the property would be valueless, the remedy for the recovery of possession by an action at law is usually inadequate.[3] Equity will, in such a case, order the specific performance of a stipulation in a railroad mortgage authorizing the trustees to take possession.[4] The trustees may enforce their right to possession upon default even against a contractor engaged in constructing the road under a contract by which he is entitled to the possession of the road until his contract is completed.[5] A power to take possession, if exercised at all, must generally be exercised by the trustees as to the entire property. They can not take possession of a part of the property which has been seized on execution to satisfy the claim of a judgment creditor, while leaving the other mortgaged

---

[1] Sanford v. Kane, 133 Ill. 199, s. c. 23 Am. St. R. 602. See, also, Dameron v. Eskridge, 104 N. Car. 621. It has also been held that a sale and conveyance under a power, although defectively executed, passes the legal title to the purchaser, subject, however, to the right of redemption. Lanier v. McIntosh, 117 Mo. 508, s. c. 38 Am. St. R. 676. See notes in 31 Am. St. R. 328, 335, and 19 Am. St. R. 263, 266, 297.

[2] Rice v. St. Paul, etc., R. Co., 24 Minn. 464; Seibert v. Minneapolis, etc., R. Co., 52 Minn. 246, s. c. 53 N. W. R. 1151.

[3] Dow v. Memphis, etc., R. Co., 20 Fed. R. 260; First Nat. Ins. Co. v. Salisbury, 130 Mass. 303; North Carolina, etc., R. Co. v. Drew, 3 Woods (U. S.) 691, 713; Jones on Corp. Bonds and Mort., § 343.

[4] Dow v. Memphis, etc., R. Co., 20 Fed. R. 260; McLane v. Placerville, etc., R. Co., 66 Cal. 606; Sacramento, etc., R. Co. v. Superior Ct., 55 Cal. 453 (ordered over the objection of a majority of the bondholders); Shaw v. Norfolk County R. Co., 5 Gray (Mass.) 162; Shepley v. Atlantic, etc., R. Co., 55 Me. 395. The jurisdiction of the court is based upon its general equity jurisdiction to compel persons to keep and perform their lawful contracts, and not upon any rule of law authorizing a foreclosure of mortgage liens. Shepley v. Atlantic, etc., R. Co., *supra*, per Walton, J.

[5] Allan v. Dallas, etc., R. Co., 3 Woods (U. S.) 316.

property in the hands of the corporation.[1] The statutes of several of the states prescribe the duties of mortgage trustees as to taking possession of the mortgaged property of a railroad upon default in payment of its bonds or coupons, and operating it for the benefit of the parties interested. Where the statute provides for the rights and duties of trustees, it is unnecessary to provide therefor in each mortgage executed under the laws of the state, since those laws enter into and become a part of the mortgage.[2] But in the absence of such a statute the trustees have, in general, only those rights and powers conferred upon them by agreement of the parties.[3] The remedies by action at law to recover the debt, or by suit in equity to foreclose the mortgage lien are not taken away by a grant to the trustees of a power of entry and sale.[4] A suit at law by bondholders may be maintained for non-payment of the principal or interest of bonds secured by mortgage,[5] if the mortgage contains

[1] Coe v. Peacock, 14 Ohio St. 187.

[2] Mercantile Trust Co. v. Portland, etc., R. Co., (U. S. C. C. D. N. Hamp.) 10 Fed. R. 604.

[3] McLane v. Placerville, etc., R. Co., 66 Cal. 606; Macon, etc., R. Co. v. Georgia R. Co., 63 Ga. 103; Shepley v. Atlantic, etc., R. Co., 55 Me. 395. But see as to their right to sue to protect the trust, Mercantile T. Co. v. Texas, etc., Ry. Co., 51 Fed. R. 529; Clapp v. City of Spokane, 53 Fed. R. 515. As to the duties and liabilities of trustees in possession, see Jones v. Seligman, 81 N. Y. 190 (duty to fence); Daniels v. Hart, 118 Mass. 543; Sprague v. Smith, 29 Vt. 421, and Rogers v. Wheeler, 43 N. Y. 598 (liable in damages for injuries); Barter v. Wheeler, 49 N. H. 9 (liable for loss of freight); 2 Cook on Stock and Stockholders, § 823 (liable for deficiency in operating the road.) They are said to represent both the bondholders and the corporation. Ashuelot R. Co. v. Elliot, 57 N. H. 397, and owe an active duty to the former and to each and all of them to preserve the property and take care of their interests. Commonwealth v. Susquehanna, etc., R. Co., 122 Pa. St. 306, 320; Hollister v. Stewart, 111 N. Y. 644; Merrill v. Farmers' L. & T. Co., 24 Hun (N. Y.) 297; Sturges v. Knapp, 31 Vt. 1; Perry on Trusts, § 749.

[4] Mercantile Trust Co. v. Missouri, etc., R. Co., 36 Fed. R. 221; Williamson v. New Albany, etc., R. Co., 1 Biss. (U. S.) 198; Stewart v. Bardin, 113 N. Car. 277, s. c. 18 S. E. R. 320; Eaton, etc., R. Co. v. Hunt, 20 Ind. 457; Credit Foncier, etc., v. Andrew, 9 Manitoba R. 65; Utermehle v. McGreal, 1 App. Dist. Columbia 359; Martin v. Ward, 60 Ark. 510, 30 S. W. R. 1041.

[5] Philadelphia, etc., R. Co. v. Johnson, 54 Pa. St. 127; Commonwealth v. Susquehanna, etc., R. Co., 122 Pa. St. 306, s. c. 1 L. R. A. 225; Welsh v. First Division of St. Paul, etc., R. Co., 25 Minn. 314; Marlor v. Texas, etc., R. Co., 19 Fed. R. 867.

no agreement on the part of the mortgagee not to sue.[1] Indeed, it is held that a provision in a deed of trust to secure bonds of a railroad company, which prohibits foreclosure and judicial sale, by providing that the mode of sale by the trustee set forth in the deed shall be exclusive of all others, is of no effect.[2] Stipulations as to the time which must elapse between the happening of a default and an entry or a sale by the trustees under a power do not limit the right to bring an action to foreclose the mortgage, but such an action may be brought immediately upon default.[3] So, they may sue to foreclose the mortgage to recover interest due to a single bondholder, although the mortgage prohibits them from taking any steps to collect the principal of the bonds without the consent of a majority of the bondholders.[4] And, although the trustee is authorized at the request of a certain proportion of the bondholders to take possession of the mortgaged property and to operate or sell the same after default in payment of the mortgage debt, he may bring a suit to foreclose the mortgage without such request by the specified number of bondholders.[5]

[1] Manning v. Norfolk, etc., R. Co., 29 Fed. R. 838. The provision of a mortgage that holders of bonds secured by it shall not proceed at law or in equity to foreclose it, or procure a sale of the property independently of the trustee, does not defeat an action at law to recover on overdue interest coupons, although the mortgage provides for foreclosure on default in payment of the coupons. Lyon v. New York, S. & W. R. Co., 14 Daly (N. Y.) 489.

[2] Guaranty Trust & Safe Deposit Co. v. Green Cove Springs, etc., R. Co., 139 U. S. 137, s. c. 11 Sup. Ct. R. 512.

[3] Central Trust Co. v. New York City, etc., R. Co., 33 Hun (N. Y.) 513; Central Trust Co. v. Texas, etc., R. Co., 23 Fed. R. 846; Mercantile Trust Co. v. Missouri, etc., R. Co., 36 Fed. R. 221; Chicago, etc., R. Co. v. Fosdick, 106 U. S. 47; Farmers' L. & T. Co. v. Chicago, etc., R. Co., 61 Fed. R. 543; Mercantile T. Co. v. Chicago, etc., R. Co., 61 Fed. R. 372; Farmers' L. & T. Co. v. Winona, etc., R. Co., 59 Fed. R. 957; Farmers' L. & T. Co. v. Nova Scotia, etc., R. Co., 24 N. S. 542; Mercantile T. Co. v. Missouri, etc., R. Co., 36 Fed. R. 221, s. c. 1 L. R. A. 397.

[4] Farmers' Loan and Trust Co. v. Chicago, etc., R. Co., 27 Fed. R. 146.

[5] Guaranty Trust, etc., Co. v. Green Cove, etc., R. Co., 139 U. S. 137, 11 Sup. Ct. R. 512; Morgan's Louisiana, etc., R., Co. v. Texas Central R. Co., 137 U. S. 171, 11 Sup. Ct. R. 61, distinguishing Chicago, etc., R. Co. v. Fosdick, 106 U. S. 47. Such a limitation is to be strictly construed and applies to proceedings by the trustee *ex mero motu* without the intervention of the court. Authorities first above cited; also, Alexander v. Central R. Co., 3 Dill. (U. S.) 487; Credit Co. v. Arkansas Cent. R. Co., 15 Fed. R. 46.

§ 515. The decree.—A course of procedure prescribed by the mortgage to be pursued in case of sale by the trustee without foreclosure is not binding upon the court in proceedings to foreclose such mortgage, but such a decree may be entered as to the terms of payment and the manner of sale as the equities of the case demand.[1] The decree may provide that the sale shall be made subject to such claims as shall be finally adjudicated, where the amount of certain claims in dispute can only be known after a long course of litigation.[2] A decree in an action by a railroad bondholder to foreclose a mortgage securing bonds, which directs a sale of the mortgaged property, free of all liens and incumbrances, to satisfy plaintiff's claims, without making provision for other bondholders, subsequent mortgagees, or other creditors of the road, is fatally defective.[3] As a general rule the decree should declare the extent of the default, find the amount due and order the mortgaged property sold if payment is not made within a reasonable time, which should be specified therein.[4] It is customary, also, to fix an "upset" price[5] and direct that the fund be brought into court for distribution.[6] It may likewise provide that bonds may be

---

[1] Farmers' Loan & T. Co. v. Green Bay, etc., R. Co., 6 Fed. R. 100, 10 Biss. (U. S.) 203, 1 Am. & Eng. R. Cas. 622.

[2] Turner v. Indianapolis, etc., R. Co., 8 Biss. (U. S.) 380; Bound v. South Carolina R. Co., 58 Fed. R. 473; Sage v. Central R. Co., 99 U. S. 334. A consent decree in railroad foreclosure proceedings, provided that defendant, as purchaser, should "pay, satisfy, and fully discharge all debts and liabilities of such receivership of every kind now remaining unpaid." The defendant was held liable for an injury caused by the negligence of the receiver. Wabash R. Co. v. Stewart, 41 Ill. App. 640.

[3] New Orleans Pac. R. Co. v. Parker, 143 U. S. 42, 12 Sup. Ct. 364, 6 Lewis' Am. R. R. & Corp. R. 43.

[4] Blossom v. Milwaukee, etc., R. Co., 1 Wall. (U. S.) 655; Chicago, etc., R. Co. v. Fosdick, 106 U. S. 47. But it is often impracticable to determine and insert the exact amount of costs at the time the decree is drawn and the omission to do so is not fatal. Grape Creek Coal Co. v. Farmers', etc., Co., 63 Fed. R. 891. In Knevals v. Florida Central, etc., R. Co., 66 Fed. R. 224, it was held that a decree ordering the sale of a railroad, without describing the property, included all the property of the company covered by the mortgage and connected with the use and purpose of the road.

[5] Blair v. St. Louis, etc., R. Co., 25 Fed. R. 232. A form of decree is given in full in this case.

[6] Chicago, etc., Land Co. v. Peck, 112 Ill. 408.

received from the purchasers in payment of their bid.[1] The sale of a railroad extending into two states which have united in chartering the corporation by which it is owned, may, it has been held, be decreed by a court sitting in one of such states.[2] So, of course, if this be true, such a decree may be rendered by a Federal court sitting in one of the states.[3] Although the court can not send its process into another state nor deliver possession of property in another jurisdiction, it can command and enforce a transfer of the title to the purchaser.[4] A decree determining the rights of the parties to the suit is final and conclusive between them as to all matters which were or might have been litigated therein under the issues, and can only be questioned by appeal or in a direct proceeding for that purpose.[5] But it does not affect the rights and priorities of persons who had no notice of the proceedings and were neither parties nor privies thereto.[6]

§ 516. Consent decree.—A decree entered by consent of the parties has legal effect so long as it remains unreversed, and, after it has been executed, is binding, at least so far as it is embraced by the issues.[7] But it has been held that so long as they remain

[1] Ketchum v. Duncan, 96 U. S. 659; Kropholler v. St. Paul, etc., R. Co., 2 Fed. R. 302; Duncan v. Mobile, etc., R. Co., 3 Woods (U. S.) 597.

[2] McTighe v. Macon, etc., Co., 94 Ga. 306, s. c. 21 S. E. R. 701; McElrath v. Pittsburg, etc., R. Co., 55 Pa. St. 189. Subject, however, to existing liens in the other state. Hand v. Savannah, etc., R. Co., 12 So. Car. 314. Some of the courts refuse to recognize such a decree so far as it affects the road in their state which is subject to an underlying mortgage. See Eaton, etc., R. Co. v. Hunt, 20 Ind. 457; Pittsburgh, etc., R. Co.'s Appeal, (Pa.), 4 Atl. R. 385; Farmers' L. & T. Co. v Bankers', etc., Co., 44 Hun (N. Y.) 400.

[3] Wilmer v. Atlanta, etc., Co., 2 Woods (U. S. C. C.) 409, 447, 454;

Blackburn v. Selma, etc., R. Co., 2 Flip. 525; Muller v. Dows, 94 U. S. 444; Randolph v. Wilmington, etc., R. Co., 11 Phila. 502.

[4] Muller v. Dows, 94 U. S. 444; Jones on Corp. Bonds and Mort., § 417.

[5] Woods v. Pittsburgh, etc., R. Co., 99 Pa. St. 101; Brooks v. O'Hara, 2 McCrary (U. S.) 644; Indiana, etc., R. Co. v. Bird, 116 Ind. 217; Woolery v. Grayson, 110 Ind. 149; Herring v. New York, etc., R. Co., 105 U. S. 341.

[6] Pittsburgh, etc., R. Co. v. Marshall, 85 Pa. St. 187.

[7] Indiana, etc., R. Co. v. Bird, 116 Ind. 217; Wadhams v. Gay, 73 Ill. 415; Farmers' Loan & T. Co. v. Central R., 4 Dill (U. S.) 533; Pacific R. Co. v. Ketchum, 101 U. S. 289; 2 Beach Eq. Pr., §§ 792, 795. In Hutts v. Martin, 134 Ind. 587, 593, it is said that the

unexecuted, decrees entered by consent, like *ex parte* decrees, are subject to the control of the court.[1] A consent decree as to matters beyond the scope of the bill will bind the court in its future actions only so far as it is embraced by the bill. But it will, after it is executed by one of the parties, constitute a binding agreement upon the part of the other.[2]

§ 517. **Deficiency decree.**—It was formerly held by the Federal courts that, after a decree of foreclosure and sale, duly confirmed, it was erroneous to direct an execution for any deficiency, that is, for the balance of the debt in case the property did not sell for enough to pay it in full.[3] But, under the present equity rule,[4] "a decree may be rendered for any balance that may be found due to the complainant over and above the proceeds of the sale or sales, and execution may issue for the collection of the same." This rule, however, does not authorize such a decree unless the bill shows that the amount is actually due.[5] Thus, it is held in the case just cited that where there is no provision in the bonds or mortgage that the bonds

---

decree is based upon the agreement and not upon the pleadings and may, therefore, be binding upon the parties although not within the issues. See, also, Nashville, etc., Ry. Co. v. United States, 113 U. S. 261; Knobloch v. Mueller, 123 Ill. 554, s. c. 17 N. E. R. 696; Indianapolis, D. & W. Ry. Co. v. Sands, 133 Ind. 433, s.c. 32 N. E. R. 722; Schmidt v. Oregon, etc., Co., (Oreg.) 40 Pac. R. 406.

[1] Vermont, etc., R. Co. v. Vermont Central R. Co., 50 Vt. 500. "Consent decrees decide nothing. They merely authenticate private agreements, and render them executory between the parties." Union Bank v. Marin, 3 La. Ann. 34, 35, per Rost, J.

[2] Vermont, etc., R. Co. v. Vermont Central R. Co., 50 Vt. 500.

[3] Noonan v. Lee, 2 Black (U. S.) 499; Orchard v. Hughes, 1 Wall. (U. S.) 73. See, also, Libby v. Rennie, 31 N. J. Eq. 42. It is also held in some jurisdictions that there is no lien for the deficiency until after a sale has been made, the deficiency ascertained and a judgment entered therefor. Hibberd v. Smith, 50 Cal. 511; Linn v. Patton, 10 W. Va. 187. See, also, Myers v. Hewitt, 16 Ohio 449, 454. *Contra*, Fletcher v. Holmes, 25 Ind. 458.

[4] United States Equity Rule 92. See, also, Shepherd v. Pepper, 133 U. S. 626, s. c. 10 Sup. Ct. R. 438; Dodge v. Freedman's, etc., Trust Co., 106 U. S. 445, s. c. 1 Sup. Ct. R. 335.

[5] Ohio Cent. R. Co. v. Central Trust Co., 133 U. S. 83, s. c. 10 Sup. Ct. R. 235. Where proper facts are alleged, however, a personal decree for deficiency may be awarded under the prayer for general relief. Shepherd v. Pepper, 133 U. S. 626, s. c. 10 Sup. Ct. R. 438.

§ 518   FORECLOSURE.   689

shall become due, or may be declared due, upon any contingency before their maturity, it is error to find the unpaid balance due when it in fact has not matured and to enter a deficiency decree ordering execution therefor. So, in another recent case, it was held that on foreclosure of a mortgage for non-payment of interest, if the principal is not due and there is no provision in the bonds or mortgage that the principal shall become due on default in the payment of interest, no judgment can be rendered for any deficiency in the proceeds of the sale to pay the principal.[1] We suppose, also, that no deficiency decree, amounting to a personal judgment, can be rendered in any case against a party unless the court has jurisdiction of the person.[2]

§ 518. **Final and appealable decrees.**—A decree may be final although the case be referred to a master to execute the decree by a sale of the mortgaged property.[3] If, however, it leaves the amount due upon the debt to be determined, and the property to be sold is not ascertained and defined it is not final.[4] If it determines the whole controversy between the parties, leaving nothing to be done except to carry it into execution, it is appealable as a final decree notwithstanding the fact that the court retains the fund in controversy for the purpose of distributing it as decreed.[5] So, a decree of foreclosure, ascertaining the amount due, directing payment within a specified time

[1] Farmers' Loan & T. Co. v. Grape Creek, etc., Co., 65 Fed. R. 717. See, also, Danforth v. Coleman, 23 Wis. 528.

[2] See 1 Elliott's Gen. Pr., §§ 243, 244, 362. See, also, the extreme case of Bardwell v. Collins, 44 Minn. 97, s. c. 20 Am. St. R. 547.

[3] Bronson v. Railroad Co., 2 Black (U. S.) 524; Ray v. Law, 1 Cranch (U. S. C. C.) 349; Whiting v. United States Bank, 13 Peters (U. S.) 6; Elliott's App. Proc., § 92; 1 Freeman on Judgments, §§ 22, 24; 1 Black on Judgments, § 48.

[4] McGourkey v. Toledo, etc., Ry. Co., 146 U. S. 536, s. c. 13 Sup. Ct. R. 170, 172; Railroad Co. v. Swasey, 23 Wall. (U. S.) 405; Grant v. Phœnix Insurance Co., 106 U. S. 429, s. c. 1 Sup. Ct. R. 414; Burlington, etc., R. Co. v. Simmons, 123 U. S. 52, s. c. 8 Sup. Ct. R. 58; Parsons v. Robinson, 122 U. S. 112, s. c. 7 Sup. Ct. R. 1153; 1 Black on Judgments, § 48.

[5] Bank of Lewisburg v. Sheffey, 140 U. S. 445, s. c. 11 Sup. Ct. R. 755; Hoffman v. Knox, 50 Fed. R. 484. See, also, Stovall v. Banks, 10 Wall. (U. S.) 583.

and providing for an order of sale in case of default in such payment, is a final decree from which an appeal may be taken.[1] It is also "manifest that a substantial error, to the prejudice of one of the parties, may originate in a decree distributing the proceeds of a sale under a decree of foreclosure, and no question can be successfully raised against the right to appeal from such a decree."[2] There are also cases in which there are independent issues not affecting all parties, and in such cases an appeal may lie as to those whose interests are finally determined although the decree is not final as to all the issues between the other parties.[3] Thus, it has been held that a decree in a foreclosure suit awarding priority to a creditor who claims an interest in locomotives in the possession of the receiver and in use on the road is a final decree upon a distinct and independent issue.[4] And it may, perhaps, be stated as a general rule that where the parties are entirely dismissed from a case by the decree, it is so far final as to them that an immediate appeal may be taken, although other matters are retained in which they have no interest.[5] But where an intervener in a foreclosure suit claimed certain rolling stock in the possession of the receiver, as having been leased to the mortgagor, and, after sale of the property on foreclosure, a decree was made di-

---

[1] Milwaukee, etc., R. Co. v. Soutter, 2 Wall. (U. S.) 440.

[2] Chicago, etc., R. Co. v. Fosdick, 106 U. S. 47, 82, s. c. 1 Sup. Ct. R. 10, 12. See, also, Blossom v. Milwaukee, etc., R. Co., 1 Wall. (U. S.) 657; Louisville, etc., R. Co. v. Wilson, 138 U. S. 501, s. c. 11 Sup. Ct. R. 405; Kneeland v. American Loan & T. Co., 136 U. S. 89, s. c. 10 Sup. Ct. R. 950. But compare 1 Freeman on Judgments, § 22.

[3] Trustees v. Greenough, 105 U. S. 527; Hinckley v. Gilman, etc., R. Co., 94 U. S. 467; Fosdick v. Schall, 99 U. S. 235; Williams v. Morgan, 111 U. S. 684, s.c. 4 Sup. Ct. R. 638; Brush Electric Co. v. Electric Imp. Co., 51 Fed. R. 557.

[4] Central Trust Co. v. Grant Locomotive Works, 135 U. S. 207, s. c. 10 Sup. Ct. R. 736. See, also, *Ex parte* Farmers' Loan & Trust Co., 129 U. S. 206, s.c. 9 Sup. Ct. R. 265; *Ex parte* Jordan, 94 U. S. 248; Central Trust Co. v. Marietta, etc., Ry. Co., 48 Fed. R. 850 (holding decision in favor of an intervener a final decision under the Circuit Court of Appeals Act). That the term "final decision" in such act means final judgment or decree, see Duff v. Carrier, 55 Fed. R. 433; 2 Beach Mod. Eq. Pr., §§ 913, 941.

[5] Grant v. East & West R. Co., 50 Fed. R. 795; Hill v. Chicago, etc., R. Co., 140 U. S. 52, s. c. 11 Sup. Ct. R. 690. But see Keystone, etc., Iron Co. v. Martin, 132 U. S. 91, s. c. 10 Sup. Ct. R. 32.

recting the delivery of such property to the intervener, but referring the matter to a master to determine its rental value while used by the receiver, together with all questions between the receiver and the intervener growing out of its use and restoration, it was held that the decree directing the delivery of the property to the intervener was not such a final decree as to prevent the court from determining at a subsequent term that the title to such property had passed to the purchaser at the foreclosure sale.[1]

[1] McGourkey v. Toledo, etc., Ry. Co., 146 U. S. 536, s. c. 13 Sup. Ct. R. 170.

CHAPTER XXI.

SALE AND REORGANIZATION.

§ 519. Railroad company can not sell franchise and necessary property without statutory authority.
520. Execution sales.
521. Foreclosure sales — Authority —Purchasers.
522. Sale on default in payment of interest—Sale of road as an entirety.
523. Sale of consolidated road—Sale by receiver pending foreclosure.
524. Discretion of trustees and officers as to time and manner of sale.
525. Effect of sale—Purchaser's title.
526. When purchaser takes title free from liabilities and liens.

§ 527. Disposition of proceeds of sale.
528. Preferred claims—Six months' rule.
529. Setting sale aside.
530. Redemption.
531. Reorganization by purchasers at sale—Power of legislature to provide for.
532. Statutory reorganization—Liability of new corporation.
533. Reorganization by agreement —Rights of minority.
534. Rights and obligations of the parties—Laches and estoppel.
535. Fraud in the sale or reorganization.
536. Reorganization by the courts.

§ 519. Railroad company can not sell franchise and necessary property without statutory authority.—In the absence of legislative authority, a railroad company can not sell its road and franchises to another corporation, so as to prevent it from performing its duties to the public,[1] even though the latter cor-

---

[1] East Line, etc., R. Co. v. State, 75 Tex. 434; Gulf, etc., R. Co. v. Morris, 67 Tex. 692; Snell v. City of Chicago, 152 U. S. 191, 14 Sup. Ct. R. 489, 492; Oregon, etc., Nav. Co. v. Oregonian Ry. Co., 130 U. S. 1, s. c. 9 Sup. Ct. R. 409; Pennsylvania R. R. Co. v. St. Louis, etc., R. R. Co., 118 U. S. 290, s. c. 6 Sup. Ct. R. 1094; Fisher v. West Virginia, etc., R. R. Co., 39 W. Va. 366, 19 S. E. R. 578; Pierce on Railroads, 10; Taylor Corp., §§ 305, 131, 132; Morawetz Corp., 485, 490. See, also, elaborate note to Brunswick, etc., Co. v. United States Gas Co., 35 Am. St. R. 385, 390. In Central

poration should undertake to keep the road open at all times for the use of the public; for a corporation has no implied authority to delegate the performance of its public duties to another company.[1] An unauthorized attempt on the part of a

Transp. Co. v. Pullman, etc., Co., 139 U. S. 24, 11 Sup. Ct. R. 478, 484, Gray, J., states the reason for the rule as follows: "The charter of a corporation, read in the light of any general laws which are applicable, is the measure of its powers, and the enumeration of those powers implies the exclusion of all others not fairly incidental. All contracts made by a corporation beyond the scope of those powers are unlawful and void, and no action can be maintained upon them in the courts, and this upon three distinct grounds: The obligation of every one contracting with a corporation to take notice of the legal limits of its powers; the interest of the stockholders, not to be subjected to risks which they have never undertaken; and, above all, the interest of the public that the corporation shall not transcend the powers conferred upon it by law. A corporation can not, without the assent of the legislature, transfer its franchise to another corporation, and abnegate the performance of the duties to the public, imposed upon it by its charter as the consideration for the grant of its franchise. Neither the grant of a franchise to transport passengers, nor a general authority to sell and dispose of property, empowers the grantee, while it continues to exist as a corporation, to sell or to lease its entire property and franchise to another corporation. These principles apply equally to companies incorporated by special charter from the legislature, and to those formed by articles of association under general laws."

[1] Morawetz Priv. Corp. (2d ed.), § 1120, citing Beman v. Rufford, 1 Sim. N. S. 550; York, etc., R. Co. v. Winans, 17 How. (U. S.) 30, 39; Thomas v. West Jersey R. Co., 101 U. S. 71, 83; Great Northern R. Co. v. Eastern Counties R. Co., 21 L. J. Ch. 837; Cf. Rogers Locomotive, etc., Works. v. Erie R. Co., 20 N. J. Eq. 379; Clark v. City of Washington, 12 Wheat. (U. S.) 40, 54; Roper v McWhorter, 77 Va. 214. It has been held that by conveying its road and franchises, to trustees selected by itself, a railroad company can not evade its legal liability for injuries afterwards done to persons and property by the negligent operation of its road. Acker v. Alexandria & F. R. Co., 84 Va. 648, 5 S. E. 688; Naglee v. Alexandria & F. R. Co., 83 Va. 707, 3 S. E. 369. So, it has been held that a railroad company can not, without statutory authority, transfer the right to operate its road so as to absolve itself from its duties to the public, or its liability for the torts of the company which operates the road. East Line, etc., R. Co. v. Rushing, 69 Tex. 306, 6 S. W. R. 834; International, etc., R. Co. v. Eckford, 71 Tex. 274, 8 S. W. R. 679; International, etc., Co. v. Kuehn, 70 Tex. 582, 8 S. W. R. 484; Chollette v. Omaha & R. V. R. Co., 26 Neb. 159, 4 L. R. A. 135, 41 N. W. R. 1106; Anderson v. Cincinnati S. R. Co., 86 Ky. 44, 5 S. W. R. 49. In one of these cases it is said that legislative consent to the transfer is not sufficient of itself to relieve the company from such liabilities; there must be an exemption granted or a release from the

railroad company to dispose of its franchise may be ground for the forfeiture of its charter.[1] Nor can one railroad corporation purchase the property and franchises of another, without such authority.[2] A grant to a railroad corporation of power to sell its line will not be implied unless necessary to give effect to the language of the statute.[3] A provision in the charter of a railroad corporation prohibiting it from purchasing, selling, leasing, or consolidating with any other corporation owning a parallel or competing line does not carry implied power to sell to a company which does not own such a line. And it has been held that such a sale can not be legally made, although the two roads are expressly empowered by law to consolidate.[4] Neither does the grant of power to purchase other roads imply authority on the part of a corporation to sell its own.[5] A power to sell, except upon foreclosure, is not included in a power to mortgage,[6]

obligations of the company to the public. Chollette v. Omaha & R. V. R. Co., 26 Neb. 159, 4 L. R. A. 135, 41 N. W. R. 1106.

[1] Where a railroad company, having a land grant from the state, disposed of the entire interest in and control of the road to another company, reserving the granted land and certain corporate rights, but ceasing to do a railroad business, it was held that, as such separation of the franchises was not authorized by the legislative acts incorporating the companies, judgment of forfeiture and dissolution of both was authorized in *quo warranto* proceedings by the state. State v. Minnesota Cent. Ry. Co., 36 Minn. 246, 29 Am. & Eng. R. Cas. 440, 30 N. W. R. 816.

[2] Gulf, etc., R. Co. v. Morris, 67 Tex. 692. But it would seem that authority given to one corporation to purchase the franchise of another specified corporation gives the latter authority to sell. New York, etc., R. R. Co. v. New York, etc., R. R. Co., 52 Conn. 274.

[3] See Southern Pac. R. Co. v. Esquibel, 4 N. M. 337, 20 Pac. R. 109, 36 Am. & Eng. R. Cas. 410; East Line, etc., R. Co. v. State, 75 Tex. 434; Clarke v. Omaha, etc., R. R. Co., 4 Neb. 458; State v. Consolidation Coal Co., 46 Md. 1.

[4] East Line, etc., R. Co. v. State, 75 Tex. 434.

[5] Southern Pac. R. Co. v. Esquibel, 4 N. M. 337, 20 Pac. R. 109, 36 Am. & Eng. R. Cas. 410.

[6] Southern Pac. R. Co. v. Esquibel, 4 N. M. 337, 20 Pac. R. 109. In announcing the opinion of the court in this case, Reeves, J., said: "It was argued for the appellant that, if the land could be mortgaged for the means to construct, equip, and operate the road, it could be assigned, in the first place for the same object. The doctrine that a power to mortgage includes a power to sell is not supported by authority of law. A corporation must exercise its powers in the mode prescribed in its charter. The power to procure means to construct the road in question was not a general

or lease.[1] But railroads are empowered by general statute in many of the states to purchase the roads of connecting lines.[2] And this power is frequently granted by special charter. When the charter of one company authorizes it to purchase the property and franchise of another, this must be construed to be an implied authority to that other company to sell,[3] and where "any railroad company" is authorized to purchase the property and franchises of a certain corporation they may, it seems, be lawfully purchased by a railroad corporation of another state.[4]

§ 520. **Execution sales.**—The franchise of a railroad company, and corporate property essential to the enjoyment of the franchise, are not subject to sale on execution, unless the legislature authorizes or assents to the transfer.[5] But locomotives,

---

power, it was a particular power to be exercised for a specific object. The Texas & Pacific R. Co. was authorized to issue construction and land bonds, and to execute mortgages to secure the bonds on its land grant and other lands the company might acquire; the proceeds of the sale of the bonds to be applied to the construction, operation, and equipment of the road, and for the purchase, construction, completion, equipment, and operating of the other roads [which it was authorized to acquire] as contemplated and specified in the acts of congress. The acts require that the bonds and mortgages should contain an extract from the law authorizing them to be issued, and that the mortgages should be filed and recorded in the department of the interior. The appellant was not a mortgagee, nor a purchaser under a mortgage. No mortgage bond was given in aid of the construction of the road."

[1] Pittsburgh, etc., R. R. Co. v. Bedford, etc., R. Co., 81½ Pa. St. 104.

[2] Stimson's Am. Stat. (1892), § 8721.

In Michigan, the sale of an uncompleted road, begun in good faith, but which the company undertaking it has become unable to finish, is alone authorized. Young v. Toledo, etc., R. Co., 76 Mich. 485.

[3] New York, etc., R. Co. v. New York, etc., R. Co., 52 Conn. 274.

[4] Boston, etc., R. Co. v. Boston, etc., R. Co., 65 N. H. 393, 23 Atl. R. 529.

[5] Louisville, etc., R. Co. v. Boney, 117 Ind. 501; Indianapolis, etc., G. R. Co. v. State, 105 Ind. 37; Baxter v. Nashville, etc., Turnpike Co., 10 Lea (Tenn.) 488; Gue v. Tide Water Canal Co., 24 How. (U. S.) 257; East Alabama R. W. Co. v. Doe, 114 U. S. 340; Tippets v. Walker, 4 Mass. 595, 597, per Parsons, C. J.; Ludlow v. Hurd, 1 Disney (Ohio) 552; Oakland R. Co. v. Keenan, 56 Pa. St. 198; Ammant v. New Alexandria Turnpike Co., 13 Serg. & R. (Pa.) 210, s. c. 15 Am. Dec. 593, and note; Leedom v. Plymouth R. Co., 5 W. & S. (Pa.) 265; Stewart v. Jones, 40 Mo. 140; Brady v. Johnson, 75 Md. 445, s. c. 20 L. R. A. 737, and note; Wood v. Truckee Turnpike Co.,

cars and other personal property held by the corporation, if not in actual use in the operation of the road, are held by some authorities to be subject to sale on execution,[1] and there seems to be no reason why property of a railroad corporation not essential to the enjoyment of its franchise should not be subjected to the payment of its debts.[2] The general statutes of many of the states authorize a sale of the property and franchises of a railway corporation upon execution,[3] and it is said, perhaps too broadly, that "a general power to alienate franchises necessarily implies a liability to have them levied upon."[4] The statutory method of sale must be strictly pursued,[5] and, unless otherwise provided, a railroad can not be levied upon and sold in fragmentary parts although it may run into different counties.[6]

24 Cal. 474; Hatcher v. Toledo, etc., R. Co., 62 Ill. 477; Overton Bridge Co. v. Means, 33 Neb. 857, s. c. 29 Am. St. R. 514; Herman on Executions, § 361; Freeman on Executions, § 179.

[1] Louisville, etc., R. Co. v. Boney, 117 Ind. 501; Boston, etc., R. Co. v. Gilmore, 37 N. H. 410; Pierce v. Emery, 32 N. H. 484; Lathrop v. Middleton, 23 Cal. 257, s. c. 83 Am. Dec. 112. See, also, Williamson v. New Jersey, etc., R. R. Co., 29 N. J. Eq. 311; Stevens v. Buffalo, etc., R. R. Co., 31 Barb. 590. So, a portion of a railroad which the company has abandoned the use of and is proceeding to take up is subject to levy under execution. Benedict v. Heineberg, 43 Vt. 231; Gardner v. Mobile, etc., R. R. Co., 102 Ala. 635, 15 So. R. 271.

[2] Coe v. Columbus, etc., R. Co., 10 Ohio St. 372, s. c. 75 Am. Dec. 518; Louisville, etc., R. Co., v. Boney, 117 Ind. 501.

[3] Stimson's Am. Stat. (1892), § 8311; Commonwealth v. Susquehannah, etc., R. Co., 122 Pa. St. 306; Winchester, etc., R. Co. v. Colfelt, 27 Gratt. (Va.) 777; City of Atlanta v. Grant, etc., Co., 57 Ga. 340; State v. Rives, 5 Ired. Law (N. C.) 297.

[4] Note to Brunswick, etc., Co. v. United Gas, etc., Co., 35 Am. St. R. 385, 401, citing National Foundry Works v. Oconto, etc., Co., 52 Fed. R. 43, which, however, only inferentially sustains the proposition. So, in State v. Hare, 121 Ind. 308, 310, it is said that "the rule is that whatever the corporation might voluntarily alienate, its creditors may subject to sale by adverse process," citing Louisville, N. A. & C. Ry. Co. v. Boney, 117 Ind. 501; Coe v. Columbus, etc., R. R. Co., 10 Ohio St. 372, s. c. 75 Am. Dec. 518.

[5] James v. Pontiac, etc., Co., 8 Mich. 91; Taylor v. Jerkins, 6 Jones L. (N.C.), 316; Seymour v. Milford, etc., Co., 10 Ohio 476. See, also, Gregory v. Blanchard, 98 Cal. 311.

[6] Midland Ry. Co. v. Wilcox, 122 Ind. 84; Macon & Western R. R. Co. v. Parker, 9 Ga. 377; Noble v. State, 43 Ga. 466; Dayton, Xenia, etc., R. R. Co. v. Lewton, 20 Ohio St. 401. See,

§ 521. **Foreclosure sales — Authority — Purchasers. —** Authority to mortgage of course includes the power to enforce a sale of the mortgaged property upon foreclosure for default in payment of the mortgage debt.[1] And in many cases the charter authorizes the execution of a mortgage containing a power of sale.[2] A corporation may become the purchaser at a foreclosure sale, or obtain the property from the purchaser, if authorized by its charter to purchase and operate other lines of road.[3] So, mortgage bondholders and other creditors may lawfully combine to purchase a railroad at a foreclosure sale, if there is no intention of defrauding any party in interest by the use of an unfair advantage, or by preventing competition at the sale.[4]

also, National, etc., Works v. Oconto Water Co., 52 Fed. R. 43, 45; Brooks v. Railway Co., 101 U. S. 443, 451; Yellow River Improvement Co. v. Wood County, 81 Wis. 554, 51 N. W. R. 1004; Bound v. South Carolina Ry. Co., 46 Fed. R. 315, 316. So, where it is all mortgaged, it should be sold as an entirety although it runs into different states. Muller v. Dows, 94 U. S. 444.

[1] New Orleans, etc., R. R. Co. v. Delamore, 114 U. S. 501; Detroit v. Mutual Gas Light Co., 43 Mich. 594. Compare Savannah, etc., R. R. Co. v. Lancaster, 62 Ala. 555.

[2] McLane v. Placerville, etc., R. Co., 66 Cal. 606. An order that a railroad be sold as an entirety, together with all its franchises, on the foreclosure of a lien given by statute, which makes no express provision as to the mode of its enforcement, is in excess of the power of the court. In such a case payment must be enforced out of other property or funds, and the lien affords the basis for the exercise, by the court of chancery, of its flexible jurisdiction to coerce payment. Louisville, N. A. & C. R. Co. v. Boney, 117 Ind. 501, s. c. 20 N. E. 432.

[3] People v. Brooklyn, etc., Ry. Co., 89 N. Y. 75. It has been held in New Hampshire that a foreign corporation could lawfully become the purchaser of a railroad at foreclosure sale. Boston, etc., R. Co. v. Boston, etc., R. Co., 65 N. H. 393. There is nothing in the Michigan general railroad law of 1873 authorizing one railroad company to acquire the stock and franchises of another competing company, for the purpose of itself exercising such franchises, and such an acquisition is unlawful. Mackintosh v. Flint, etc., R. Co., 34 Fed. R. 582.

[4] Robinson v. Philadelphia, etc., R. Co., 28 Fed. R. 340; Kitchen v. St. Louis, etc., R. Co., 69 Mo. 224; Marie v. Garrison, 83 N. Y. 14, 13 Abb. N. C. 210; Jones on Corp. Bonds and Mort., § 687. A decree of foreclosure and sale of a railroad, entered by consent of creditors and the company, without fraud, and in pursuance of a plan of reorganization, will not be set aside at the suit of some of the stockholders merely because the principal of one mortgage was not yet due, when the sums due for interest thereon, for floating indebtedness, and on other mortgages then due, were so great as to render foreclosure inevitable, and when complainants do not offer to do

The bondholders for whom the road is purchased may also be permitted to apply their bonds in payment of the purchase-money, after satisfying the costs and charges of the litigation and trust[1] if there are no prior lienholders whose claims are unsatisfied.[2]

§ 522. **Sale on default in payment of interest—Sale of road as an entirety.**—Where a trust deed provides that the road and property shall be sold upon a default in the payment of principal or interest, but one sale is contemplated, and sufficient property should be sold to realize the debt, although default has been made in the payment of interest only. And if the property can not be sold in parts without injury to the whole, it may be sold as an entirety.[3] And even though the mortgage

---

[1] Duncan v. Mobile, etc., R. Co., 3 Woods (U. S.) 567; Farmers' L. & T. Co. v. Green, etc., R. R., 6 Fed. R. 100. And the mortgage may so provide. Child v. New York, etc., R. R., 129 Mass. 170. See, also, Easton v. German American Bank, 127 U. S. 532.

[2] Sanxey v. Iowa City Glass Co., 68 Iowa 542. Debts contracted in conserving the property and maintaining its value as a going concern are usually considered preferred claims and paid before the mortgage debt is satisfied. Farmers' Loan, etc., Co. v. Kansas City, etc., R. Co., 53 Fed. R. 182; Seibert v. Minneapolis, etc., R. Co., — Minn. —, 59 N. W. 879. See Finance Company v. Charleston, etc., R. Co., 61 Fed. R. 369; Bound v. South Carolina R. Co., 58 Fed. R. 473. Post, § 528. It has, however, been held erroneous to direct payment of claims for supplies furnished prior to the receivership first out of the proceeds of the sale, where no provision was made for such payment when the receiver was appointed, and it does not appear that current earnings, before or after his appointment, were diverted to paying interest on the bonded debt. Cutting v. Tavares, etc., R. Co., 61 Fed. R. 150. A claim for cutting and clearing away timber from the road for its original construction has also been refused preference on foreclosure of a prior mortgage on the road. Barstow v. Pine Bluff, M. & N. O. Ry. Co., 57 Ark. 334. Farmers' Loan, etc., Co. v. Candler, 81 Ga. 691, 18 S. E. R. 540.

[3] Wilmer v. Atlanta, etc., R. Co., 2 Woods (U.S.) 447; Chicago, etc., R. Co. v. Fosdick, 106 U. S. 47; Peoria, etc., R. Co. v. Thompson, 103 Ill. 187. This is the general rule as to the sale of mortgaged property, which can not readily be divided. Bound v. South Carolina R. Co., 50 Fed. R. 853; Farmers' Loan & T. Co. v. Oregon, etc., R. Co., 24 Fed. R. 407; Kneeland v. American Loan and Trust Co., 136 U. S. 89; 2 Jones on Mort., §§ 1181, 1459, 1478, 1616, 1619.

contains no provision making the whole debt due upon a default in the payment of interest, a sale of the whole property may be decreed by a court of equity, if it can not be divided without injury.[1] Or, it seems that the court may, in a proper case, direct that the property be leased for such a period as will secure the payment of the sum due and the interest accruing.[2] Where suit is brought to foreclose a railroad mortgage for default in payment of interest, the court may properly enter a decree *nisi*, ascertaining the amount of interest due, and giving the debtor a reasonable time to pay it; and directing that in case of non-payment, the property be sold, and the proceeds applied to the payment of both interest and principal. But under such a decree the debtor may redeem at any time before the sale is confirmed by payment of the unpaid interest and costs.[3] If the property is divisible, and interest only is due, no more should be sold than will pay the accrued interest, and then, upon a second default, a further order of sale may be made.[4]

---

[1] See McLane *v.* Placerville, etc., R. Co., 66 Cal. 606. In Peoria, etc., R. Co. *v.* Thompson, 103 Ill. 187, Mr. Justice Mulkey, in delivering the opinion of the court, said: "When a railway, its appurtenances, privileges, and franchises are mortgaged as a whole, there is, in our opinion, no power or authority to sell them separately. From the very nature of the property, one would be useless without the other. The franchise could not be used at all without the road, and the road could not lawfully be used, as against the state, without the franchise. Under such circumstances, to avoid the possibility of conflicting ownerships, the law has wisely determined that both must be sold as an entirety. Chicago, Danville and Vincennes R. Co. *v.* Loewenthal, 93 Ill. 433." As supporting the text, see Jones on Corporate Bonds and Mort., § 634. Some of the states have statutes providing for the sale of a mortgaged railroad upon foreclosure as an entirety. See Jones on Corp. Bonds & Mort., § 634, and note, citing laws of Indiana, New Jersey, Kansas, Kentucky and New York.

[2] Woods on Railroads (Minor's ed.), 2003, citing Bardstown, etc., R. Co. *v.* Metcalfe, 4 Met. (Ky.) 199. But compare Duncan *v.* Atlantic, etc., R. R. Co., 4 Hughes 125.

[3] Chicago, etc., R. Co. *v.* Fosdick, 106 U. S. 47. See, also, Howell *v.* Western R. R. Co., 94 U. S. 463.

[4] Jones on Corporate Bonds and Mort., § 634, citing Fleming *v.* Soutter, 6 Wall. (U. S.) 747; Tillinghast *v.* Troy, etc., R. Co., 48 Hun (N. Y.) 420, 425, per Learned, P. J. See, also, Farmers' Loan & Trust Co. *v.* Chicago, etc., Ry. Co., 27 Fed. R. 146; McFadden *v.* Mays Landing, etc., Co., 49 N. J. Eq. 176.

§ 523. Sale of consolidated road—Sale by receiver pending foreclosure.—A road formed by the consolidation of several roads, each of which was subject to a mortgage before consolidation, may properly be sold as an entirety upon foreclosure, where it will sell to better advantage as a whole than if sold in divisions, and the interest of the several mortgagees in the fund arising from the sale may be settled by a decree of the court.[1] But where the holders of a general mortgage elect to have the road sold in this manner, the holder of a prior lien upon one division of the road, is entitled to have his claim paid out of the aggregate proceeds of the sale of the entire property before any payment is made to the holders of the general mortgage.[2] In a proper case, where the property is of such a nature as to deteriorate rapidly in value, when not in use and is plainly insufficient in value to meet the company's indebtedness, and where the income from the property will not meet the expense of necessary repairs, the court may order the road and its franchise sold by the receiver pending a foreclosure suit.[3]

§ 524. Discretion of trustees and officers as to time and manner of sale.—After a decree of foreclosure has been obtained, the mortgage trustees are invested with discretion as to when they will sell the property under the decree, or whether they will sell it at all pending an appeal, subject, however, to the control which the court has over the execution of its own decrees, and when the trustees think it best for all the bondholders that the decree should not be executed pending the appeal the court will not order them to have it executed on the application of a portion of the bondholders.[4] When a sale is ordered it is made by the proper officer of the court, who must exercise a sound legal discretion as to the manner of conduct-

[1] Gibert v. Washington, etc., R. Co., 33 Gratt. (Va.) 586; Campbell v. Texas, etc., R. Co., 2 Woods (U. S.) 263.

[2] Farmers' Loan & T. Co. v. Newman, 127 U. S. 649, s. c. 8 Sup. Ct. R. 1364.

[3] Middleton v. New Jersey, etc., R. Co., 26 N. J. Eq. 269.

[4] Farmers' Loan & T. Co. v. Central R. Co., 4 Dill. (U. S.) 533. The supreme court will not interfere by mandamus to compel the execution of the decree of the lower court by a sale of the road. Jones on Corp. Bonds and Mort., § 640.

§ 525   SALE AND REORGANIZATION.   701

ing the sale, and as to whether he will strike off the property for such bids as are received, or will adjourn the sale until the attendance of bidders who will pay a reasonable value for it can be obtained.[1] And the court will decline to interfere with this discretion and order an immediate sale at the request of a part of the bondholders, where it does not clearly appear that their rights are prejudiced by the delay.[2] The rules above stated, of course, fully apply only in the absence of a governing statute, expressly, or impliedly, depriving the trustee or officer of any discretion as to the time and manner of the sale.

§ 525. Effect of sale—Purchaser's title.—The franchise of being a corporation, not being a part of the mortgaged security, does not pass upon a foreclosure sale.[3] The corporate existence of a company is not destroyed by the transfer of all its property to another corporation,[4] unless the statute so provides.[5] It continues in existence, until formally dissolved, for the purpose of collecting and paying debts, and performing such func-

[1] Blossom v. Railroad Co., 3 Wall. (U. S.) 196. In this case four separate adjournments were had extending over a period of seven months, although bids had been received in the meantime, and it was held that such adjournments were within the discretion of the officer. It was also held that, while it was customary for the officer to act under the advice of the complainant's solicitor, unreasonable directions of the solicitor were not obligatory and should not be followed.

[2] Farmers' Loan & T. Co. v. Central R. Co., 4 Dill. (U. S.) 533.

[3] Bank of Middlebury v. Edgerton, 30 Vt. 182, 190; Miller v. Rutland, etc., R. Co., 36 Vt. 452, 498; Atkinson v. Marietta, etc., R. R. Co., 15 Ohio St. 21; Western Penn. R. R. Co. v. Johnston, 59 Pa. St. 290; People v. Cook, 110 N. Y. 443, 449, s. c. 36 Am. & Eng. R. R. Cas. 256, 258. In Meyer v. Johnston, 53 Ala. 237, 325, Mr. Justice Manning, speaking for the court, said: "Strictly, 'the franchise to exist as a corporation' is not a corporate franchise, or 'franchise of the corporation' at all. It is a franchise of the individual corporators, of the natural persons who are shareholders of the capital stock, and pertains to them as such corporators, whereby they are endowed with the privilege and capacity of being constituted into and co-operating together, as a body politic, with power of succession, and without individual liability. And the corporation as such, in its collective capacity or by its board of directors, has no more power to sell this franchise thus pertaining to the corporators individually than it has to sell their paid-up shares of the capital stock."

[4] Wright v. Milwaukee, etc., R. Co., 25 Wis. 46; Arthur v. Commercial & R. Bank, 9 S. & M. (Miss.) 394; Bruffett v. Great Western R. R. Co., 25 Ill. 353.

[5] Even where the statute so provides, an illegal and fraudulent sale

tions as it may without the ownership of its property.[1] In the absence of any statute or agreement to the contrary, the foreclosure and sale, duly confirmed, cuts off all the interest of the corporation and stockholders or creditors claiming under it in the mortgaged property.[2] The purchaser at a foreclosure sale takes only the property which the decree ordered to be sold,[3] together with the accompanying rights and franchises necessary to its profitable use and lawfully included in the mortgage and sale.[4] In a very recent case it was held by the

---

does not work a dissolution. White Mountains R. Co. v. White Mountains R. Co., 50 N. H. 50.

[1] Smith v. Gower, 3 Met. (Ky.) 171, s. c. 2 Duv. (Ky.) 17; Wright v. Milwaukee, etc., R. Co., 25 Wis. 46.

[2] Vatable v. New York, etc., R. Co., 96 N.Y. 49; Thornton v. Wabash Ry. Co., 81 N. Y. 462; Carpenter v. Catlin, 44 Barb. (N. Y.) 75. See, also, Canada Southern Ry. Co. v. Gebhard, 109 U. S. 527.

[3] Jones on Corp. Bonds and Mort., § 694; Osterberg v. Union Trust Co., 93 U. S. 424.

[4] Wright v. Milwaukee, etc., R. Co., 25 Wis. 46; Memphis R. R. Co. v. Commissioners, 112 U. S. 609; New Orleans, etc., Co. v. Delamore, 114 U. S. 501; North Carolina, etc., R. R. Co. v. Carolina, etc., R. R. Co., 83 N. Car. 489. The question whether a right of exemption from taxation enjoyed by the old corporation passes to the purchaser or not has been much litigated. The answer to this question must depend upon the intent of the charter or statute by which such right was conferred. The supreme court of the United States has held in a number of cases that an exemption from taxation is not a franchise which will pass by a conveyance of the property and franchises. And that a statute authorizing the mortgage of the property and franchise of a corporation does not include a mere personal privilege like exemption from taxation. Trask v. Maguire, 18 Wall. (U. S.) 391; Morgan v. Louisiana, 93 U. S. 217; Wilson v. Gaines, 103 U. S. 417; Louisville, etc., R. Co. v. Palmes, 109 U. S. 244; Memphis, etc., R. Co. v. Railroad Commissioners, 112 U. S. 609; Chesapeake & Ohio Ry. Co. v. Miller, 114 U. S. 176, s. c. 5 Sup. Ct. R. 813. But where a sale is made by authority of the state, of all rights, privileges and immunities of the company, as well as its property and franchise, the state can not assert any rights against the purchaser which it did not have as against the old corporation. Knoxville, etc., R. Co. v. Hicks, 9 Baxt. (Tenn.) 442, commented on in Wilson v. Gaines, 103 U. S. 417; Wilmington, etc., Railroad Co. v. Alsbrook, 146 U. S. 279, 297, 13 Sup. Ct. R. 72; First Division of St. Paul, etc., R. Co. v. Parcher, 14 Minn. 297; Chicago, etc., R. Co. v. Pfaender, 23 Minn. 217; Hand v. Savannah, etc., R. Co., 17 So. Car. 219; Nichols v. New Haven, etc., R. Co., 42 Conn. 103; Atlantic, etc., R. Co. v. Allen, 15 Fla. 637; Gonzales v. Sullivan, 16 Fla. 791; Jones on Corp. Bonds and Mort., § 693. The privilege of regulating its charges conferred upon a railroad company does not pass to the purchasers under a mortgage foreclosure sale, and the reorganization by such

supreme court of the United States that an exemption from taxation, which was enjoyed by one of several companies afterwards consolidated, did not pass to the consolidated company because of the adoption of a new constitution, in the meantime, prohibiting such exemption, and that the purchaser at foreclosure sale obtains no exemption from taxation and could not successfully set up as a defense to an action for taxes a judgment rendered in favor of the company in a prior action by the county against it for taxes, nor a decree against the county in favor of certain stockholders enjoining the collection of taxes for other years. Neither the mortgage trustee, nor the bondholders were parties to these proceedings, and the court held that the purchaser could not avail himself of the judgment or decree because of the lack of privity between the parties.[1]

§ 526. **When purchaser takes title free from liabilities and liens.**—The purchaser generally takes the property freed from the debts[2] and contracts of the vendor,[3] except so far as purchasers is the formation of a new corporation, subject to the laws in force at the time of the reorganization. Dow v. Beidelman, 49 Ark. 325, 455, 5 S.W. 297, 125 U. S. 680.

[1] Keokuk & W. R. R. Co. v. State of Missouri, 152 U. S. 301, s. c. 14 Sup. Ct. R. 592, affirming 99 Mo. 30.

[2] Hopkins v. St. Paul, etc., R. Co., 2 Dill. (U. S.) 396; Cook v. Detroit, etc., R. Co., 43 Mich. 349, s. c. 9 Am. & Eng. R. R. Cas. 443; Cooper v. Corbin, 105 Ill. 224; Lake Erie, etc., R. Co. v. Griffin, 92 Ind. 487; Moyer v. Ft. Wayne, etc., R. R. Co., 132 Ind. 88, s. c. 31 N. E. R. 567; North Hudson County R. Co. v. Booraem, 28 N. J. Eq. 450; Vilas v. Page, 106 N. Y. 439; Ryan v. Hays, 62 Tex. 42; Gilman v. Sheboygan, etc., R. Co., 37 Wis. 317; Wellsborough, etc., Plank Road Co. v. Griffin, 57 Pa. St. 417; Pennsylvania Transp. Co.'s Appeal, 101 Pa. St. 576 (not liable on judgment against old company); Sullivan v. Portland, etc., R. Co., 94 U. S. 806; Vatable v. New York, etc., R. Co., 96 N. Y. 49. The purchaser of a railroad at foreclosure sale is not liable for damages occasioned by the acts of the old company, which had already accrued at the time of the purchase. Hammond v. Port Royal, etc., R. Co., 15 S. C. 10. (Injuries done to adjoining land.) Where one railroad company is sold to another, a person having a claim against the former for damages on account of personal injuries, can not maintain an action against the latter; and the old company having been dissolved by the sale, his only right of action remaining is against the stockholders of the old company, who received the purchase money. Chesapeake, O. & S. W. Co. v. Griest, 85 Ky. 619, 30 Am. & Eng. R. Cas. 149; Powell v. North Missouri R. Co., 42 Mo. 63; Louisville, etc., R. Co. v. Orr, 91 Ky. 109, 15 S. W. R. 8.

[3] City of Menasha v. Milwaukee, etc., R. Co., 52 Wis. 414; Hoard v. Chesa-

his title is made subject thereto by statute[1] or by the terms of the order of sale. The act providing for the reorganization of the purchasers into a new corporation may, however, require that it shall assume certain debts and liabilities of its predecessor, in which the acceptance of the act amounts to an as-

peake & Ohio Ry. Co., 123 U. S. 222, s. c. 8 Sup. Ct. R. 74; People v. Louisville, etc., R. Co., 120 Ill. 48, 10 N. E. R. 657, and see original opinion in same case reported in 5 N. E. R. 379, and 25 Am. & Eng. R. Cas. 235. See Houston, etc., R. Co. v. Shirley, 54 Tex. 125; Branson v. Oregonian R. Co., 11 Ore. 161; Lake Erie, etc., R. Co. v. Griffin, 92 Ind. 487. The purchaser at the foreclosure sale is not bound by a parol agreement made by the president of the railroad company to make a farm crossing and to maintain a fence of a certain description. Hunter v. Burlington, C. R. & N. R. Co., 76 Iowa 490, 41 N. W. R. 305. Nor is he bound by a contract of the corporation to maintain a depot at a certain place. Gulf, etc., R. Co. v. Newell, 73 Tex. 334. Even though the consideration of the contract was a large sum of money voted by the people of the county upon condition that the depot should be forever maintained, and the railroad was empowered by its charter to receive the aid and to make the contract. People v. Louisville, etc., R. Co., 120 Ill. 48, 10 N. E. R. 657. But it was held by the supreme court of Iowa that a railroad company that has purchased a line of road at a foreclosure sale of an insolvent company, part of which line was constructed and equipped with money raised by taxes voted to it by a town, assumes the obligations of the company whose line it purchased, and can not lease such line to another company, so as to surrender the exclusive use thereof, and, by ceasing to operate it, deprive the town of the benefits intended to be deprived therefrom. State v. Central Iowa Ry. Co., 71 Iowa 410, s. c. 32 N.W. R. 409. A contract between two railroad companies in relation to the carriage of freights and division of earnings, providing that this "contract, and any damages for the breach of the same, shall be a continuing lien upon the roads of the two contracting companies, their equipment and income, in whosesoever hands they may come," does not constitute a lien or obligation running with the land, so as to make it liable in the hands of a purchaser of one of them for earnings that would have accrued during the term of the contract. Des Moines & Ft. D. R. Co. v. Wabash, St. L. & P. R. Co., 135 U. S. 576, s. c. 10 Sup. Ct. R. 753.

[1] Statutory liens upon the property existing at the time of the sale continue to operate as liens upon it after the transfer. Hervey v. Illinois Midland R. Co., 28 Fed. R. 169. Where the statute declares judgments for personal injuries to be a prior lien upon the property of railroad companies, the purchasers of the property of such a company upon foreclosure of mortgage takes it subject to all unpaid judgments of this class. And it has been held that the purchasers were bound to perform a contract entered into by the old company for the payment of money in liquidation of a claim for personal injuries. Frazier v. East Tennessee, etc., R. Co., 88 Tenn. 138.

§ 526   SALE AND REORGANIZATION.   **705**

sumption of the payment of all claims.[1] Or the decree of the court may order the sale to be made subject to certain liabilities, in which case the purchaser's title is based upon the decree, and he can not question its validity, nor dispute the liability which it imposes upon him.[2] The purchaser also takes his title subject, of course, to all prior valid liens, of which he had or ought to have had notice, not cut off by the foreclosure proceedings.[3] But he may dispute the validity of any such liens except those which are adjudged in the order of sale to be superior to the title which he purchased.[4] The new company is also liable in equity upon the contracts of its predecessor in so far as it adopts them, and claims the benefit for itself.[5] Thus the purchasers at a foreclosure sale of the property of a railroad company are liable for unpaid damages for lands appropriated as the right of way by the railroad company and occupied and used as such by the purchasers.[6] The purchasers

---

[1] St. Louis, etc., R. Co. v. Miller, 43 Ill. 199. See, also, Welsh v. First Div. St. Paul, etc., R. R. Co., 25 Minn. 314; New Bedford R. R. Co. v. Old Colony R. R. Co., 120 Mass. 397.

[2] Wabash R. Co. v. Stewart, 41 Ill. App. 640; Brown v. Wabash R. Co., 96 Ill. 297; Farmers' Loan & T. Co. v. Central R. Co., 17 Fed. R. 758; Swann v. Wright, 110 U. S. 590. See, also, Vilas v. Page, 106 N. Y. 439; Williams v. Morgan, 111 U. S. 684; Olcott v. Headrick, 141 U. S. 543.

[3] Western Union Tel. Co. v. Burlington, etc., R. Co., 11 Fed. R. 1; Ketchum v. St. Louis, 101 U. S. 306; Brooks v. Railway Co., 101 U. S. 443; Morgan Co. v. Thomas, 76 Ill. 120. A vendor's lien for purchase-money may be enforced against the property in the hands of a corporation composed of the bondholders, by whom it was purchased. Western Division of Western North Carolina R. Co. v. Drew, 3 Woods (U. S) 691. An equitable lien for damages connected with the operation of the road by trustees can be enforced against the property in the hands of the new corporation when it is shown that funds from which the claim for damages should have been paid passed into the hands of the new corporation upon reorganization. Stratton v. European & N. A. R. Co., 76 Me. 269. See Houston, etc., Ry. Co. v. Keller (Tex.), 28 S. W. R. 724.

[4] Jones on Corp. Bonds and Mort., § 683, 685, citing Hackensack Water Co. v. DeKay, 36 N. J. Eq. 548, 555; Central National Bank v. Hazard, 30 Fed. R. 484; Swann v. Wright, 110 U. S. 590, 4 Sup. Ct. R. 235.

[5] Lake Erie, etc., R. Co. v. Griffin, 92 Ind. 487; Jacksonville, etc., Ry. Co. v. Louisville, etc., R. R. Co., 150 Ill. 480, s. c. 37 N. E. R. 924.

[6] Western Pennsylvania R. Co. v. Johnston, 59 Pa. St. 290; White v. Nashville, etc., R. Co., 7 Heisk. (Tenn.) 518; Gilman v. Sheboygan, etc., R. Co., 37 Wis. 317, 40 Wis. 653; Gillison v. Savannah, etc., R. Co., 7 So. Car. 173; Lake Erie, etc., R. Co. v.

may also, in a case where it is deemed advisable, assume the payment of the debts of the old corporation, and such an assumption will bind not only them but also their assignees with notice.[1]

§ 527. **Disposition of proceeds of sale.**—The proceeds of the sale, after the payment of costs and any other claims properly given preference, are applied first in satisfaction of bonds secured by the mortgage foreclosed, giving to each bond its *pro rata* share in case the proceeds are insufficient to satisfy the whole debt.[2] But overdue coupons may be given a preference over bonds which have not yet matured, especially when a part of the series to which they belong had been redeemed before the default occurred.[3] Where a bondholder received the bonds in pledge as collateral security for a loan, he is entitled to be repaid only the amount of his loan with interest.[4] Any surplus remaining after satisfying the mortgage indebtedness goes to the corporation as a trust fund for the payment of other creditors, and not first to the stockholders. And an agreement between the bondholders and the stockholders by which, in

---

Griffin, 92 Ind. 487; Rio Grande, etc., R. Co. *v.* Ortiz, 75 Tex. 602. Compare Moyer *v.* Ft. Wayne, etc., R. R. Co., 132 Ind. 88.

[1] Blair *v.* St. Louis, etc., R. Co., 24 Fed. R. 148, 25 Fed. R. 684. See, also, Island City Bank *v.* Sachtleben, 67 Tex. 420. But see Hervey *v.* Illinois Midland R. Co., 28 Fed. R. 169, holding that the assumption by the purchaser of debts of the old corporation creates a personal obligation only and not a lien upon the property.

[2] Hodge's Appeal, 84 Pa. St. 359; Barry *v.* Missouri, etc., Ry. Co., 34 Fed. R. 829; Pinkard *v.* Allen, 75 Ala. 73. See, also, Watkins *v.* Hill, 8 Pick. (Mass.) 522; Claflin *v.* South Carolina R. Co., 8 Fed. R. 118. All the bonds secured by the same mortgage are deemed to have been issued at the same time, and there is no priority in favor of any of them because they bear lower numbers than others. Stanton *v.* Alabama, etc., R. R. Co., 2 Woods (U. S.) 523. See, also, Mason *v.* York, etc., R. R. Co., 52 Me. 82; Commonwealth *v.* Susquehanna, etc., R. R. Co., 122 Pa. St. 306; Appeal of Reed, 122 Pa. St. 565.

[3] Stevens *v.* New York, etc., R. Co., 13 Blatchf. (U. S.) 412; Commonwealth of Virginia *v.* Chesapeake, etc., Canal Co., 32 Md. 501; Cutting *v.* Tavares, etc., R. R. Co., 61 Fed. R. 150. But see Ketchum *v.* Duncan, 96 U. S. 659.

[4] Rice's Appeal, 79 Pa. St. 168; Morton *v.* New Orleans, etc., R. Co., 79 Ala. 590; Peck *v.* New York, etc., R. Co., 59 How. (N. Y.) Pr. 419; Jesup *v.* City Bank, 14 Wis. 331. See, also, Duncomb *v.* New York, etc., R. R. Co., 84 N. Y. 190.

consideration of withdrawing opposition to the foreclosure suit, the stockholders are to be paid a portion of the purchase money, is fraudulent as against the general creditors.[1] On a sale for default in interest, the proceeds will usually be applied, "first, to the arrears of interest, then to the mortgage debt, then to the junior incumbrances, according to their respective priority of lien, and the surplus to the mortgagor."[2]

§ 528. **Preferred claims—Six months' rule.**—When a court of chancery is requested by the mortgagees to appoint a receiver of the railroad, pending proceedings for foreclosure, it may, and usually will, in the exercise of a sound discretion, impose such terms in reference to the payment from the income during the receivership of outstanding debts for labor, supplies, equipment, or permanent improvement of the mortgaged property as may, under the circumstances of the particular case, appear to be reasonable.[3] It is within the power of the court to use the income of the receivership to discharge such obligations, even where no such order is made at the time the receiver is appointed.[4] "He who seeks equity must

[1] Railroad Co. v. Howard, 7 Wall. (U. S.) 392.

[2] 2 Beach Priv. Corp., § 777, citing Chicago, etc., R. R. Co. v. Fosdick, 106 U. S. 47. See Chicago, etc., R. R. Co. v. Peck, 112 Ill. 408.

[3] Fosdick v. Schall, 99 U. S. 235; Huidekoper v. Locomotive Works, 99 U. S. 258; Miltenberger v. Logansport Ry. Co., 106 U. S. 256; Union Trust Co. v. Souther, 107 U. S. 591; Burnham v. Bowen, 111 U. S. 776; United States Trust Co. v. Wabash, etc., R. R. Co., 150 U. S. 287; Williamson v. Washington, etc., R. R. Co., 33 Gratt. (Va.) 624; Fidelity, etc., Co. v. Shenandoah Valley R. R. Co., 86 Va. 1; Douglass v. Cline, 12 Bush (Ky.) 608; McElhenny, etc., Co. v. Binz, 80 Tex. 1, s. c. 26 Am. St. R. 705; Litzenberger v. Jarvis, etc., Trust Co., 8 Utah 15, s. c. 28 Pac. R. 871, and authorities cited in following notes, *infra*. Contra, Coe v. N. J. Midland Ry. Co., 27 N. J. Eq. 37; Metropolitan Trust Co. v. Tonawanda, etc., R. R. Co., 103 N.Y. 245. As to apportionment among the several lines of one system, see Central Trust Co. v. Wabash, etc., R. Co., 30 Fed. R. 332.

[4] Farmers' L. & T. Co. v. Kansas City, etc., R. R. Co., 53 Fed. R. 182; Fosdick v. Schall, 99 U. S. 235; Central Trust Co. v. St. Louis, etc., Ry. Co., 41 Fed. R. 551. The mortgagor is not accountable to the mortgagee for earnings, while the property remains in his possession, until a demand is made, even though the mortgage covers income. Dow v. Memphis, etc., R. R. Co., 124 U. S. 652, s. c. 8 Sup. Ct. R. 673; Galveston Railroad Co. v. Cowdrey, 11 Wall. (U. S.) 459.

do equity." Such claims are usually paid out of the earnings of the road in the hands of the receiver, but where equity requires it, they may be paid out of the proceeds of the sale, or *corpus* of the property.[1] They may be preferred, not only where they have arisen during the receivership, but also where they arose a limited time before the appointment of the receiver, and it is the practice of the federal courts in most jurisdictions, upon the appointment of a receiver, to impose the condition that debts for materials, supplies, and labor furnished to the mortgagor within six months previous to the appointment shall be paid out of the net income or proceeds of the sale before the debt secured by the mortgage is paid.[2] This limitation is arbitrary, however, and in some cases it has been fixed at three months,[3] while in others such claims have been given a preference, although they arose more than six months prior to the appointment of the receiver.[4] Much depends upon the circumstances and equities of the particular case. But it is the exception and not the rule that priority of liens can be displaced in this way,[5] and such preference is usually confined to claims

[1] Finance Co. v. Charleston, etc., R. R. Co., 48 Fed. R. 188; Blair v. St. Louis, etc., Ry. Co., 22 Fed. R. 471; Thomas v. Peoria Ry. Co., 36 Fed. R. 808; Fosdick v. Schall, 99 U. S. 235; Farmers' L. & T. Co. v. Kansas City, etc., R. R. Co., 53 Fed. R. 182. But not ordinarily, where the suit is by stockholders or there is no diversion of income. St. Louis, etc., R. R. Co. v. Cleveland, etc., R. R. Co., 125 U. S. 658; Denniston v. Chicago, etc., R. R. Co., 4 Biss. 414; Cutting v. Tavares, etc., R. R. Co., 61 Fed. R. 150; Street v. Maryland Cent. Ry. Co., 59 Fed. R. 25; Farmers' L. & T. Co. v. Northern Pac. R. R. Co., 68 Fed. R. 36.

[2] Clark v. Central R. R., etc., Co., 66 Fed. R. 803; *In re* Kelly v. Receiver of Green Bay, etc., R. R. Co., 5 Fed. R. 846; Thomas v. Peoria, etc., R. R. Co., 36 Fed. R. 808; Putnam v. Jacksonville, etc., R. R. Co., 61 Fed. R. 440; Turner v. Indianapolis, etc., R. R. Co., 8 Biss. (U. S.) 315; Dow v. Memphis, etc., R. R. Co., 20 Fed. R. 260.

[3] Miltenberger v. Logansport, etc., Ry. Co., 106 U. S. 286; Finance Co. v. Charleston, etc., R. R. Co., 62 Fed. R. 205.

[4] Burnham v. Bowen, 111 U. S. 776; Farmers' L. & T. Co. v. Kansas City, etc., R. R. Co., 53 Fed. R. 182; Hale v. Frost, 99 U. S. 389; McIlhenny, etc., Co. v. Binz, 80 Tex. 1, s. c. 26 Am. St. R. 705; Atkins v. Petersburg Railroad Co., 3 Hughes 307; note to Blair v. Ry. Co., 22 Fed. R. 471; Central Trust Co. v. Wabash, etc., Ry. Co., 30 Fed. R. 332.

[5] Kneeland v. American Loan Co., 136 U. S. 89, 97; Thomas v. Western Car Co., 149 U. S. 95, s. c. 60 Am. & Eng. R. R. Cas. 443, 13 Sup. Ct. R. 824; Bound v. South Car. Ry. Co., 58

§ 528   SALE AND REORGANIZATION.   709

for current or operating expenses incurred in keeping up the railroad as a "going concern." Claims for work done in the original construction of the road are not included and are not entitled to a preference.[1] And it was held in a recent case, where a railroad went into the hands of a receiver without any funds, and the earnings under the receivership were barely sufficient to pay current operating expenses, that arrears of salary due the president should not be paid out of the proceeds of the sale in preference to the mortgage debt.[2] In a still later case it is held that sureties on an appeal bond executed solely for the accommodation of the company, and without pecuniary advantage to themselves, are not entitled to a preference over the mortgagors, although the judgment appealed from was obtained prior to the foreclosure and appointment of the receiver, and notwithstanding the fact that the assets of the company in the hands of the receiver had been preserved and increased, by virtue of such bond, to the extent of the judgment.[3] "It

Fed. R. 473. As to what are not "operating expenses," see Central Trust Co. v. Charlotte, etc., R. R. Co., 65 Fed. R. 264; Reyburn v. Consumers', etc., Co., 29 Fed. R. 561; Manchester Locomotive Works v. Truesdale, 44 Minn. 115, s. c. 9 L. R. A. 140. Claims for damages to persons or property arising from the operation of the road are classed as operating expenses. *Ex parte* Brown, 15 S. Car. 518; Klein v. Jewett, 26 N. J. Eq. 474; Mobile, etc., R. Co. v. Davis, 62 Miss. 271; Union Trust Co. v. Illinois, etc., R. Co., 117 U. S. 434, s. c. 6 Sup. Ct. R. 809.

[1] Toledo, etc., R. R. Co. v. Hamilton, 134 U. S. 296; Wood v. Guarantee, etc., Deposit Co., 128 U. S. 416, s. c. 9 Sup. Ct. R. 131; Addison v. Lewis, 75 Va. 701; Farmers' L & T. Co. v. Pine Bluff, etc., Ry. Co. 57 Ark. 334, 21 S. W. R. 652; Farmers' L. & T. Co. v. Candler, 92 Ga. 249, 18 S. E. R. 540. But compare McIlhenny, etc., Co. v. Binz, 80 Tex. 1, s. c. 26 Am. St. R. 705; *ante*, § 500.

[2] National Bank v. Carolina, etc., R. R. Co., 63 Fed. R. 25. See, also, Addison v. Lewis, 75 Va. 701; Wells v. Southern, etc., Ry. Co., 1 Fed. 270; and compare Blair v. St. Louis, etc., R. R. Co., 23 Fed. R. 521; Olyphant v. St. Louis, etc., Co., 22 Fed. R. 179 (salary of secretary preferred).

[3] Farmers' L. & T. Co. v. Northern Pac. R. R. Co., 68 Fed. R. 36. The court, in this case, insists that there must be a diversion of funds to the benefit of the bondholders and to the injury of the party seeking the preference before the priority of the mortgage lien will be displaced, and disapproves Farmers' L. & T. Co. v. Kansas City, etc., R. R. Co., 53 Fed. R. 182. These two cases seem to mark, in the *dicta* at least, the opposite extremes to which the federal courts have gone. Sureties have been reimbursed in other cases. Union T. Co. v. Morrison, 125 U. S. 591, s. c. 8 Sup. Ct. R. 1004; Rome & D. R. R. Co. v. Sibert, 97 Ala. 393; Dow v. Memphis, etc., Co., 124

must," however, says Chief Justice Fuller, "be regarded as settled that a court of equity may make it a condition of the issue of an order for the appointment of a receiver of a railroad company that certain outstanding debts of the company shall be paid from the income that may be collected by the receiver, or from the proceeds of sale; that preferential payments may be directed of unpaid debts for operating expenses, accrued within ninety days, and of limited amounts due to other and connecting lines of road for materials and repairs and for unpaid ticket and freight balances, in view of the interests both of the property and the public, that the property may be preserved and disposed of as a going concern, and the company's public duty discharged; and that such indebtedness may be given priority, notwithstanding there may have been no diversion of income, or that the order for payment was not made at the time, and as a condition, of the receiver's appointment, the necessity and propriety of making it depending upon the facts and circumstances of the particular case, and the character of the claims."[1]

§ 529. Setting sale aside.—Mortgagors may obtain relief from a fraudulent sale upon foreclosure if they apply for it

[1] Finance Co. v. Charleston, etc., R. Co., 62 Fed. R. 205, citing Miltenberger v. Logansport Railroad Co., 106 U. S. 286, 311, 1 Sup. Ct. R. 140; Union Trust Co. v. Souther, 107 U. S. 591, 594, 2 Sup. Ct. R. 295; Union Trust Co. v. Illinois M. Ry. Co., 117 U. S. 434, 6 Sup. Ct. R. 809; Morgan's, etc., Co. v. Texas Cent. Ry. Co., 137 U. S. 171, 11 Sup. Ct. R. 61; Kneeland v. Bass Foundry, etc., Works, 140 U. S. 592, 11 Sup. Ct. R. 857. See, also, Seibert v. Minn., etc., Co., (Minn.) 59 N. W. R. 829; Rome, etc., R. R. Co. v. Sibert, 97 Ala. 393. As to taxes and street assessments, see Clyde v. Richmond, etc., R. R. Co., 63 Fed. R. 21; Union L. & T. Co. v. Southern, U. S. 652. But compare Penn v. Calhoun, 121 U. S. 251.

etc., R. R. Co., 49 Fed. R. 267; Cutting v. Tavares, etc., R. R. Co., 61 Fed. R. 150; Ellis v. Boston, etc., Ry. Co., 107 Mass. 1; Central Trust Co. v. N. Y., etc., R. R. Co., 110 N. Y. 250, 1 L. R. A. 260. As to judgments, see Clyde v. Richmond, etc., R. R. Co., 56 Fed. R. 539; Chicago, etc., R. R. Co. v. McCammon, 61 Fed. R. 772; Phinizy v. Augusta, etc., R. R. Co., 63 Fed. R. 922; Penn Mutual Insurance Co. v. Heiss, 141 Ill. 35, 31 N. E. R. 138; Finance Co. v. Charleston, etc., R. R. Co., 61 Fed. R. 369; Texas, etc., R. R. Co. v. Bloom, 60 Fed. R. 979; Texas, etc., Railway Co. v. Johnson, 76 Tex. 421, and 151 U. S. 81, 14 Sup. Ct. R. 250; Central Trust Co. v. Charlotte, etc., R. R. Co., 65 Fed. R. 257.

§ 529   SALE AND REORGANIZATION.   711

within a reasonable time after discovering the fraud.[1] And a bill for this purpose may be maintained on behalf of the corporation by a single stockholder upon refusal of the corporation to ask that the sale be set aside.[2] But where dissenting stockholders and bondholders institute a suit to set aside a foreclosure sale on the ground of fraud and collusion upon the part of the majority, it is not sufficient to make the purchasing and selling companies parties defendants.[3] This right may be barred by laches,[4] and any considerable delay in bringing a bill for this purpose must be satisfactorily explained or a court of

[1] Harwood v. Railroad Co., 17 Wall. (U. S.) 78; Jones on Corp. Bonds and Mort., § 651. Suit on behalf of bondholders to set aside a foreclosure sale should usually be brought by their mortgage trustees. Meyer v. Utah, etc., R. R. Co., 3 Utah 280. See, also, Shaw v. Railroad Co., 100 U. S. 605; New Orleans, etc., Ry. Co. v. Parker, 143 U. S. 42. In Kent v. Lake Superior, etc., Co., 144 U. S. 75, it is held that bondholders must seek their remedy in the court which rendered the decree and confirmed the sale. See, generally, Wetmore v. St. Paul, etc., R. R. Co., 3 Fed. R. 177; Massachusetts, etc., Co. v. Chicago, etc., R. R. Co., 13 Fed. R. 857; Campbell v. Railroad Co., 1 Woods (U. S.) 368.

[2] Foster v. Mansfield, etc., R. Co., 36 Fed. 627. But where an insolvent railroad company had issued different series of mortgage bonds, some of the mortgages covering all of its property, and others only part, the principal of some of the mortgages being due, and the company having defaulted on the interest on all of them, and, in addition, it had a large floating debt, running into millions, with no fair prospect of its being able to pay the accrued interest on the bonds and the floating debt without a sale of all its property, it was held, that a decree foreclosing all the mortgages, entered by consent of the creditors, should not be set aside at the suit of some of the stockholders on the ground that the principal of some of the mortgages was not yet due, "as it was to the interest of the railroad company that the rights of all the mortgage bondholders should be cut off to enable the company to effect a reorganization which would secure and extend its bonded debt, and reduce the rate of interest thereon, and provide the necessary means to satisfy the floating debt." Carey v. Houston & T. C. Ry. Co., 45 Fed. R. 438.

[3] Ribon v. Railroad Companies, 16 Wall. (U. S.) 446. Trustees through whom the scheme was consummated should have been made parties, and so should the majority stockholders and bondholders, or a sufficient number of them, at least, if they had participated in the distribution of the proceeds and were required to refund.

[4] Foster v. Mansfield, etc., R. Co., 36 Fed. R. 627; Sullivan v. Portland, etc., R. Co., 4 Cliff. 212, 94 U. S. 806; Coddington v. Railroad Co., 103 U. S. 409; Graham v. Boston, etc., R. R. Co., 118 U. S. 161. See, also, Rabe v. Dunlap, 51 N. J. Eq. 40, 25 Atl. R. 959; Farmers' Loan & T. Co. v. Rockaway, etc., R. Co., 69 Fed. R. 9.

equity will deny relief.¹ The stockholders or other parties in interest can not wait until new equities arise or until they see that the purchasers, by improving the property, are likely to make it valuable, and then procure a return of the property with its added value, and discharged from the equities which have attached.² If the fraud is concealed from the mortgagor and its stockholders for a time, suit may be brought within a reasonable time after it is discovered.³ A sale of the property to pay the arrears due a single bondholder, at a grossly inadequate price and without notice to the other bondholders whose interests are affected, will be set aside at the suit of such bondholders, especially where it is shown that the bondholder who instituted the proceedings and the persons who became purchasers at the sale, several of whom were directors and officers of the road, had entered into a conspiracy to obtain the property at a sacrifice, and had prevented a reasonable competition at the sale.⁴ Where a sale is made under a notice setting forth that the amount of bonds secured by the mortgage foreclosed is ten times as great as it really is, and all competition in bidding is thereby destroyed and the property is purchased by the bondholders, such sale will be set aside at the suit of judgment creditors whose liens are thereby defeated.⁵ But the creditors who were defrauded by the sale can alone

---

¹ Credit Co. v. Arkansas Cent. R. Co., 15 Fed. R. 46, 5 McCrary 23; Farmers' Loan & T. Co. v. Green Bay, etc., R. Co., 6 Fed. R. 100; Harwood v. Railroad Co., 17 Wall. (U. S.) 78. The following periods of unexplained delay have been held fatal: Seven years, Sullivan v. Portland, etc., R. Co., 94 U. S. 806, 4 Cliff. 212; ten years, Foster v. Mansfield, etc., R. Co., 36 Fed. R. 627; eight years, Coddington v. Pensacola, etc., R. Co., 103 U. S. 409; five years, Harwood v. Railroad Co., 17 Wall. (U. S.) 78; eighteen months, Graham v. Birkenhead, etc., R. Co., 2 Mac. & G. (Eng. Ch.) 146.

² Twin Lick Oil Co. v. Marbury, 91 U. S. 587; Kitchen v. St. Louis, etc., R. Co., 69 Mo. 224.

³ Where the mortgagors remained ignorant for eight years of the fraud which had been practiced, they were permitted to bring suit to set aside the sale two years after the fraud was discovered. White Mountains R. Co. v. White Mountains R. Co., 50 N. H. 50.

⁴ Jackson v. Ludeling, 21 Wall. (U. S.) 616. A decree by which no provision is made for the interests of other bondholders beside the complainant, will be set aside on appeal. New Orleans, etc., R. Co. v. Parker, 143 U. S. 42, s. c. 12 Sup. Ct. R. 364.

⁵ James v. Railroad Co., 6 Wall. (U. S.) 752.

§ 529   SALE AND REORGANIZATION.   713

claim the benefit of a decree setting aside the sale, and neither the mortgage trustee by whom the property was sold on foreclosure, nor the bondholders at whose request the foreclosure and sale were had, can assert any rights under the mortgage; but they hold title to the property under the sale, subject to the equities of such creditors.[1] The parties in interest can not question the validity of a foreclosure sale, to which they have assented, on the ground that it was a fraud upon the rights of others.[2] A mortgage trustee in possession can not without express authority become a purchaser at his own sale.[3] And a director, or other person occupying a fiduciary relation toward the company, must act with perfect fairness, in purchasing its property at a sale under a trust deed to secure debts due to himself, or the sale will be set aside ; but the stockholders must act promptly in disaffirming a sale because of the fiduciary relations of the purchaser.[4] Where it is shown that the purchasers at a foreclosure sale have conspired with the directors of the corporation in effecting a fraudulent sale, they will be held as trustees for the benefit of the parties in interest to the full value of the property purchased.[5] It has been held that a fraudulent sale can not be validated by an act of the legislature, since the legislature has no power to transfer the property of one corporation to another without due process of law.[6]

[1] Railroad Co. v. Soutter, 13 Wall. (U. S.) 517; Barnes v. Chicago, etc., R. Co., 122 U. S. 1, s. c. 7 Sup. Ct. R. 1043.

[2] Barnes v. Chicago, etc., R. Co., 122 U. S. 1, affirming 8 Biss. 514; Symmes v. Union Trust Co., 60 Fed. R. 830. See, also, United States v. Union Pac. R. R. Co., 98 U. S. 569; Berry v. Broach, 65 Miss. 450, 4 So. R. 117; Matthews v. Murchison, 15 Fed. R. 691.

[3] Racine, etc., R. Co. v. Farmers' Loan, etc., R. Co., 49 Ill. 331; Ashhurst's Appeal, 60 Pa. St. 290; Kitchen v. St. Louis, etc., Co., 69 Mo. 224.

[4] Twin Lick Oil Co. v. Marbury, 91 U. S. 587. A director of a railroad corporation may honestly own its bonds secured by mortgage. Duncomb v. New York, etc., R. Co., 84 N. Y. 190, 88 N. Y. 1. And he can enforce them in the usual and ordinary way, and may purchase the mortgaged property at a sale which is fairly made in an effort to enforce the payment of his debt. Harpending v. Munson, 91 N. Y. 650. As to when director can not purchase, see post, § 535.

[5] Drury v. Cross, 7 Wall. (U. S.) 299; Merrill v. Farmers' Loan & T. Co., 24 Hun (N. Y.) 297; Jones on Corp. Bonds and Mort., § 663; post, § 535.

[6] White Mountains R. Co. v. White Mountains R. Co., 50 N. H. 50. See, also, Roche v. Waters, 72 Md. 264, s. c. 7 L. R. A. 533. This, we think,

A decree can only be avoided upon proceedings for that purpose, brought by a party in interest[1] and upon sufficient cause shown. Inadequacy of price alone is not sufficient grounds for setting aside a sale, where the sale was honestly and fairly made;[1] nor is mere increase in the value of the property sufficient cause for vacating the decree.[2] A purchase of the mortgaged property by a combination of the bondholders and other creditors is valid unless some unfair advantage is used to prevent competition and keep down the price, and such creditors have in general all the rights of *bona fide* purchasers.[4] The fact that the railroad company's solicitor acts for the creditors in making the purchase and that the title is taken in his name, does not invalidate the sale, if it was honestly conducted and no unfair advantage was taken.[5] The validity of the sale can not be attacked on the ground that the directors of the corporation were actuated by corrupt motives in suffering a default, and that this was known to the trustee, when there is no claim against him of collusion or fraud, and it appears that the default justifying foreclosure actually occurred, and the property was sold for an

would undoubtedly be true if the sale were absolutely void for want of jurisdiction, but a merely fraudulent sale would seem to be voidable only, and not necessarily void or beyond the power of the legislature to cure.

[1] One whose interest in the property expired before the final decree was entered can not maintain a suit to have the decree reopened. Ward v. Montclair R. Co., 26 N. J. Eq. 260; Graham v. Boston, etc., R. R. Co., 118 U. S. 161. See, also, *Ex parte* Fleming, 2 Wall. (U. S.) 759; Day v. Lyon, 11 N. J. Eq. 331; Symmes v. Union Trust Co., 60 Fed. R. 830; Hollins v. St. Paul, etc., R. Co., 9 N.Y. Supp. 909.

[2] Turner v. Indianapolis, etc., R. Co., 8 Biss. (U. S.) 380; Fidelity, etc., Co. v. Mobile, etc., Ry. Co., 54 Fed. R. 26; Jones on Corp. Bonds and Mort., § 662. See, also, Bethlehem Iron Co. v. Philadelphia, etc., Ry. Co., 49 N. J.Eq. 356, 23 Atl.R. 1077. Unless, perhaps, it is so great as to shock the conscience. Graffam v. Burgess, 117 U. S. 180; Fletcher v. McGill, 110 Ind. 395.

[3] County of Leavenworth v. Chicago, etc., Ry. Co., 25 Fed. R. 219.

[4] Thornton v. Wabash R. Co., 81 N. Y. 462; Vose v. Cowdrey, 49 N. Y. 336; Pennsylvania Trans. Co.'s Appeal, 101 Pa. St. 576; Wetmore v. St. Paul, etc., R. Co., 1 McCrary (U. S.) 466; *ante*, § 521. Holders of junior mortgage bonds can not have a sale to the first mortgage bondholders set aside where no fraud is shown. Their remedy is to redeem. Robinson v. Iron R. Co., 135 U. S. 522, 10 Sup. Ct. 907.

[5] Pacific R. Co. v. Ketchum, 101 U. S. 289.

adequate price.[1] In a suit to set aside a sale on foreclosure the validity and sufficiency of the proceedings in the foreclosure suit prior to the sale can not be questioned, since they were matters proper for adjudication in the foreclosure suit.[2]

§ 530. **Redemption.**—A valid foreclosure and sale, duly confirmed, cuts off the equity of redemption,[3] and the only remedy, if any, in such a case, is by suit to vacate the decree,[4] unless a statutory right to redeem is given.[5] Where, however, the mortgage trustee enters into possession, upon default, and manages the property for the bondholders, the corporation or stockholders may institute a suit to redeem and hold him to an accounting as trustee for the corporation as well as for the bondholders.[6] So, as we shall hereafter see,[7] where the transaction is voidable because a director or trustee has improperly purchased at the sale, the courts will usually allow a redemption. The right to redeem is a favorite equity and an opportunity to exercise it should be given before the sale is confirmed, that is, at least where the foreclosure is for failure to pay interest, a decree *nisi* should be entered declaring "the fact, nature, and extent of the default * * * and the amount due on account thereof, which, with any further sums subsequently accruing, and having become due, according to

[1] Harpending v. Munson, 91 N. Y. 650. Compare Symmes v. Union Trust Co., 60 Fed. R. 830.

[2] Robinson v. Iron R. Co., 135 U. S. 522, 10 Sup. Ct. 907.

[3] Parker v. Dacres, 130 U. S. 43, s. c. 9 Sup. Ct. R. 433; Turner v. Indianapolis, etc., R. R. Co., 8 Biss. (U. S.) 380; Eiceman v. Finch, 79 Ind. 511. As to who may redeem, see note to Horn v. Indianapolis, etc., Bank, 21 Am. St. R. 231, 245, *et seq.*

[4] Delaware, etc., R. R. Co. v. Scranton, 34 N. J. Eq. 429.

[5] See Stimson's Am. Stat. Law, §§ 1491, 1492; Brine v. Ins. Co., 96 U. S. 627; Parker v. Dacres, 130 U. S. 43, s. c. 9 Sup. Ct. R. 433; Jackson, etc.,

Co. v. Burlington, etc., R. R. Co.; 29 Fed. R. 474; Singer Mfg. Co. v. McCollock, 24 Fed. R. 667. In these cases the state statute was followed by the federal courts. See, also, Benedict v. St. Joseph, etc., R. Co., 19 Fed. R. 173. But a general statute applying in ordinary cases may not authorize or apply to a redemption in the case of a railroad. Peoria, etc., R. R. Co. v. Thompson, 103 Ill. 187; Hammock v. Farmers' L. & T. Co., 105 U. S. 77; Columbia Finance & T. Co. v. Kentucky Un. Ry. Co., 60 Fed. R. 794.

[6] Ashuelot R. R. Co. v. Elliott, 57 N. H. 397. See, also, Clark v. Reyburn, 8 Wall. (U. S.) 318.

[7] *Post*, § 535.

Corp. 46

the terms of the security, the mortgagor is required to pay within a reasonable time, to be fixed by the court, and which, if not paid, a sale of the mortgaged premises is directed."[1] Thus, in a recent foreclosure proceeding for default in payment of interest, it was held that, although the mortgage, as construed by the court, did not authorize a decree that the whole debt was due, it was proper to direct payment of the whole debt from the proceeds of the sale of the property as an entirety, but that the decree should also provide that the mortgagor might redeem before sale upon payment of the overdue interest and costs.[2] In another recent case[3] involving the right to redeem separate divisional mortgages on railroads afterwards consolidated the judges of the circuit court of appeals for the sixth circuit differed in opinion and each supported the position which he had taken by a very able argument. The mortgages on the separate divisions were made to the same trustee, and Judge Lurton held that the mortgagees were, therefore, to be regarded as the same, and that for this reason, as well as for the further reason that it is the settled policy of the courts to treat a railroad as an entirety and prevent its severance, if possible, there could be no separate redemption of the division covered by one of them, while Judge Taft held that they were separate mortgages and that, under the circumstances of the case, there could be a separate redemption. The case was complicated by a question of suretyship and a question as to the effect of prior decrees in the different states, in regard to both of which the judges disagreed. They also disagreed as to whether, in fixing the amount to be paid by the redemptioner he was entitled to have the principal and interest of the mortgages to be redeemed reduced by the net earnings received by

---

[1] Chicago, D. &. V. R. R. Co. *v.* Fosdick, 106 U. S. 47. See, also, to same effect, Clark *v.* Reyburn, 8 Wall. (U. S.) 318; Howell *v.* Western R. R. Co., 94 U. S. 463; Foster's Fed. Prac., § 322. For form of decree, see Blair *v.* St. Louis, etc., R. R. Co., 25 Fed. R. 132, 237. Four months has been held to be a reasonable time. Columbia Finance & T. Co. *v.* Kentucky Un. Ry. Co., 60 Fed. R. 794.

[2] Grape Creek, etc., Co. *v.* Farmers' L. & T. Co., 63 Fed. R. 891. See, also, Holden *v.* Gilbert, 7 Paige (N. Y.) 208; Olcott *v.* Bynum, 17 Wall. (U. S.) 44.

[3] Compton *v.* Jesup, 68 Fed. R. 263.

§ 531   SALE AND REORGANIZATION.   717

the purchaser. The case is one of great importance and merits careful study.[1]

§ 531. Reorganization by purchasers at sale—Power of legislature to provide for.—The purchaser of a railroad under a sale upon foreclosure, or otherwise, by legislative authority, does not, by reason of his purchase, take the place of the old corporation and become clothed with corporate powers,[2] unless the statute expressly so provides.[3] But the purchaser at a foreclosure sale takes with the property all franchises which are included and authorized to be included in the mortgage, and are necessary to the successful operation of the road, including, it seems, the franchise of eminent domain.[4] The same reasons which cause nearly all railroads to be built by corporations

[1] It is impossible to give an intelligent statement of all the facts of the case, with the reasoning and numerous authorities cited, without taking more space than we feel justified in giving to a review of any one case. The principal questions involved were certified to the supreme court, and it remains for that tribunal to settle the law upon the subject. In addition to the authorities cited in the case referred to, see Horn v. Indianapolis Nat. Bank, 125 Ind. 381, s. c. 21 Am. St. R. 231, and note.

[2] Dow v. Beidelman, 49 Ark. 325, 455, 125 U. S. 680; Atkinson v. Marietta, etc., R. Co., 15 Ohio St. 21; Memphis, etc., R. Co. v. Railroad Commissioners, 112 U. S. 609; Wellsborough, etc., Co. v. Griffin, 57 Pa. St. 417; ante, § 519.

[3] See Rev. Stat. Tex., § 4260.

[4] Lawrence v. Morgan's La. R., etc., Co., 39 La. Ann. 427, s. c. 4 Am. St. R. 265; Marshall v. Western, etc., R. R. Co., 92 N. Car. 322; New Orleans, etc., R. R. Co. v. Delamore, 114 U. S. 501. See, also, North Carolina, etc., R. R. Co. v. Carolina Central R. R. Co., 83 N. Car. 489. In the case of Morgan v. Louisiana, 93 U. S. 217, the supreme court of the United States, in defining what were the franchises which the purchaser of a railroad had acquired at marshal's sale, said: "The franchises of a railroad corporation are rights and privileges which are essential to the operations of a corporation, and without which its road and works would be of little value; such as the franchise to run cars, to take tolls, to appropriate earth and gravel for the bed of its road, or water for its engines and the like. They are positive rights and privileges, without the possession of which the road of the company could not be successfully worked. A conveyance by a railroad company of "all and singular the chartered rights, privileges, and franchises of every kind" belonging to, or which should thereafter belong to, it, does not include land grants which are not directly connected with the operation of the road. Shirley v. Waco Tap. R. Co., 78 Tex. 131. See, also, Little Rock, etc., R. R. Co. v. McGehee, 41 Ark. 202.

apply with equal force to urge the incorporation of the purchasers of a railroad at foreclosure sale.[1] The legislature has power to provide for the reorganization of the bondholders into a new corporation with the rights and duties of the old corporation, upon strict foreclosure of a railroad mortgage; and it has been held that when the majority effect an organization under legislative authority, a dissenting minority have no private rights that can be successfully asserted against such action.[2] It has also been held that the bondholders, under a trust deed of railroad property, acquire their rights subject to an obligation to execute the public trust cast upon the mortgaged property by devoting it to the public use for which it was created, and that no rights of any bondholder are violated by the action of the state in creating a new instrumentality to carry into effect the original design and to devote the property to the only use which the law of its creation permits, so long as he retains his original *pro rata* share of the trust property.[3] So, it is held that the legislature may constitute the purchasers at foreclosure sale a corporation under the charter of the old corporation.[4] Persons acquiring rights un-

[1] See Jones on Corp. Bonds and Mort., § 695.

[2] Gates v. Boston, etc., R. Co., 53 Conn. 333, s. c. 24 Am. & Eng. R. R. Cas. 143; Canada Southern R. R. Co. v. Gebhard, 109 U. S. 527, 534.

[3] Gates v. Boston, etc., R. Co., 53 Conn. 333. In this case Stoddard, J., said: "There is no reason why, subject to legislative and judicial control and direction, the majority in interest in common property, of an indivisible nature, consecrated to public use, should not so use that property as to advance the private interests in that property and secure the public welfare." In a case where the plaintiff, owning but one per cent. of the bonds, refused to accept a reorganization agreement, but sued to collect his bonds; and it appeared that all the other bondholders had accepted the plan of reorganization and had surrendered their bonds; that their interests demanded that the reorganization be confirmed, and that it had been substantially confirmed by a judgment of the United States Circuit Court in Oregon, the court held that plaintiff's bill must be dismissed and that he must surrender his old bonds and accept new ones, as provided in the agreement. Pollitz v. Farmers' Loan & T. Co., 53 Fed. R. 210.

[4] Witherspoon v. Texas Pacific R. Co., 48 Tex. 309; Acres v. Moyne, 59 Tex. 623; Gulf, etc., R. Co. v. Morris, 67 Tex. 692, 700. In Texas the statute provides as follows: "In case of the sale of the entire road-bed, track, franchise and chartered right of a railroad company, whether by virtue of an execution, order of sale, deed

der a mortgage upon the property of a railroad corporation must be held to have acquired them subject to the power of the legislature to provide for a continuous performance of all public duties imposed by law upon the corporation.[1] Statutes providing for the reorganization of the bondholders to form a new corporation may be altered at the pleasure of the legislature. A change in the law after the issue of the mortgage bonds does not impair the obligation of a contract, although the expense of reorganization is thereby increased.[2] So, as the franchise to be a corporation is deemed to be granted anew, the company formed upon reorganization may be made amenable to statutory or constitutional provisions enacted after the charter to the original company was granted and before the reorganization.[3]

§ 532. **Statutory reorganization—Liability of new corporation.**—Most of the states provide by general statutes for the incorporation of the purchasers of railroad property at foreclosure sale.[4] When they have complied with the statute they become a new and entirely different corporation from that whose property and franchises they obtained by purchase at the fore-

of trust, or any other power, the purchaser or purchasers at such sale, and their associates, shall be entitled to have and exercise all the powers, privileges and franchises granted to said company by its charter or by virtue of the general laws; and the said purchaser or purchasers and their associates shall be deemed and taken to be the true owners of said charter and corporators under the same, and vested with all the powers, rights, privileges and benefits thereof, in the same manner and to the same extent as if they were the original corporators of said company, and shall have power to construct, complete, equip and work the road upon the same terms and under the same conditions as are imposed by their charter and the general laws." Rev. Stat. Tex., § 4260; Pasch. Dig.,Vol. I, Art. 4912. Somewhat similar are How. Stat. Mich. (1882), § 4885, and Laws Tenn. 1885, Ch. 84.

[1] Gates v. Boston, etc., R. Co., 53 Conn. 333.

[2] People v. Cook, 148 U. S. 397, affirming s. c. 110 N.Y. 443, 18 N. E. R. 113.

[3] State v. Sherman, 22 Ohio St. 411; Trask v. Maguire, 18 Wall.(U. S.) 391; Railroad Co. v. Georgia, 98 U. S. 359; Keokuk & W. R. R. Co. v. State of Missouri, 152 U. S. 301, s. c. 14 Sup. Ct. R. 592. But see First Division of St. Paul, etc., R. R. Co. v. Parcher, 14 Minn. 297.

[4] 19 Am. & Eng. Encyc. of Law, 773.

closure sale, even though the statute expressly invests them with all the rights, franchises, powers and privileges possessed by the old corporation.[1] Under these and similar special acts it is customary to reorganize the persons having an interest in the road to form a new corporation for whom the property is purchased by a trustee chosen for that purpose. An agreement of this kind is legal and binding, and the trustee will be compelled to transfer the property to the corporation when organized.[2] But none of the creditors can claim an interest in a reorganized corporation without sharing in the expense of the sale and reorganization.[3] The statute providing for reorganization sometimes provides that the stockholders of the old corporation may become members of the new corporation upon certain terms.[4] And such provision is sometimes contained in the mortgage or in the reorganization agreement entered into by the purchasers.[5] A stockholder who would claim the benefit of an agreement or statutory provision by which the old stockholders are permitted to become members of the new corporation must show a strict compliance on his part with the terms of the agreement or statute.[6] The New York statute provides

[1] People v. Cook, 110 N.Y. 443, 449, s. c. 36 Am. & Eng. R. R. Cas. 256, 258; State v. Sherman, 22 Ohio St. 411; Smith v. Chicago, etc., R. R. Co., 18 Wis. 17.

[2] Marie v. Garrison, 83 N. Y. 14; Munson v. Syracuse, etc., R. Co., 103 N. Y. 58.

[3] Hancock v. Toledo, etc., R. Co., 11 Biss. (U. S.) 148; Jones on Corp. Bonds and Mort., § 691, citing Fidelity Insurance, etc., Co.'s Appeal, 106 Pa. St. 144. See, also, Huston's Appeal, 18 Atl. R. 419.

[4] See N. Y. Laws 1874, Ch. 430, as amended by Laws, 1876, Ch. 446.

[5] Unsecured creditors can not complain of the reorganization scheme as inequitable because the stockholders of the old company are to become stockholders of the new, while the unsecured bondholders are given second preferred income bonds at par in full for their claims. Hancock v. Toledo, etc., R. Co., 11 Biss. (U. S.) 148.

[6] The fact that he had no actual notice of the right accorded to stockholders to take stock until after the time allowed them for exercising the privilege had expired gives a stockholder no right to claim stock after the expiration of that time, where notice was given by publication as required by the agreement for reorganization. Thornton v. Wabash, etc., R. Co., 81 N. Y. 462; Vatable v. New York, etc., R. Co., 96 N. Y. 49. And where the bondholders purchased a railroad at foreclosure sale and entered into a reorganization scheme by which any stockholder should be entitled to exchange his stock for stock of the new company on payment of

that any old stockholder of a company whose property and franchises are purchased by trustees upon foreclosure sale for the purpose of reorganization "shall have the right to assent to the plan of readjustment and reorganization of interests pursuant to which such franchises and property shall have been purchased at any time within six months after the organization of said new company, and by complying with the terms and conditions of such plan become entitled to his *pro rata* benefits therein according to its terms."[1] Under this statute it is held that no notice at all to the stockholders need be provided for in a scheme for reorganization entered into in accordance with the terms of the statute, since all stockholders who are reasonably careful of their interests and vigilant in looking after their rights may be presumed to have notice of a protracted litigation to foreclose their interests in the corporation, and of a judicial sale made in pursuance thereto after due notice.[2] And a stockholder who fails to comply with the terms of the plan of reorganization within the time prescribed by it, that being not less than the statutory period of six months, has no right to come in after the expiration of such time and claim stock upon an offer to perform the conditions prescribed by the plan. And the fact that he had no actual notice of the adoption of the plan does not enlarge his rights.[3] Statutes providing for the reorganization of insolvent corporations do not ordinarily impose any additional liabilities upon the purchasers, but simply confer upon them and such persons as they choose to associate with them the power to exist as a corporation and to own and manage the property which they have acquired as a railroad corporation. The new corporation organized thereunder does not become liable for any debts or liabilities of the old company for which the purchasers would not be liable by the terms

---

fifteen dollars per share within a specified time, it was held that the administrator of a deceased stockholder could not demand new shares in exchange for old ones belonging to his decedent upon tender of that sum after the expiration of the time specified. Dow *v.* Iowa Central R. Co., 70 Hun 186, 24 N. Y. Supp. 292.

[1] N. Y. Laws 1874, Ch. 430, § 3.

[2] Vatable *v.* New York, etc., R. Co., 96 N. Y. 49.

[3] Vatable *v.* New York, etc., R. Co., 96 N. Y. 49.

of their purchase if incorporated.[1] But it does generally become liable to perform the public duties imposed by law upon the old corporation. Thus, the new company has been held liable for a failure to maintain and repair bridges forming a part of the highway over its road, where that duty was imposed by law upon its predecessor.[2]

§ 533. Reorganization by agreement—Rights of minority. —"In the absence of statutory authority, or some provision in the instrument which creates the trust, nothing can be done by a majority, however large, which will bind a minority without their consent,"[3] and a reorganization can not, therefore, be effected, without a foreclosure, by a majority of the bondholders in such a manner as to deprive dissenting bondholders of their rights under the mortgage.[4] But provisions may be, and often are, inserted in the mortgage or trust deed which enable a majority of the bondholders to modify the mortgage rights of all[5] and sometimes "go far towards organizing the bondholders into a body corporate to take the place and perform the functions of the original corporation upon

---

[1] Houston, etc., R. Co. v. Shirley, 54 Tex. 125; Lake Erie, etc., R. Co. v. Griffin, 92 Ind. 487; Vatable v. New York, etc., R. Co., 96 N. Y. 49. See ante, § 526. See, also, Brockert v. Iowa Cent. Ry. Co., (Iowa) 61 N. W. R. 405.

[2] New York, etc., R. Co. v. State, 50 N. J. L. 303, s. c. 32 Am. & Eng. R. R. Cas. 186. In announcing the opinion of the court in this case, Judge Reed said of the defendant company: "It proceeded to exercise all the powers with which the charter of the original company would invest it as a purchaser, so far as the new company wished to exert those powers and privileges. While it occupies this attitude it can not ignore those duties to the public which are coupled with the enjoyment of the corporate privileges." Montclair v. New York, etc., R. Co., 45 N. J. Eq. 436. See, also, State v. Central Iowa R. R. Co., 71 Iowa 410.

[3] Canada Southern R. R. Co. v. Gebhard, 109 U. S. 527, 534; Gilfillan v. Union Canal Co., 109 U. S. 401, 403.

[4] Hollister v. Stewart, 111 N.Y. 644; Taylor v. Atlantic, etc., Ry., 55 How. Pr. (N. Y.) 275; Poland v. Lamoille Valley R. R. Co., 52 Vt. 144; Bill v. New Albany, etc., R. R., 2 Biss. (U. S.) 390. See, also, Mason v. Pewabic Min. Co., 25 Fed. R. 882, s. c. 133 U. S. 50, 10 Sup. Ct. R. 224. And it has been held that the consent of a bondholder to a reorganization scheme is not implied from his silence. Philadelphia, etc., R. R. Co. v. Love, 125 Pa. St. 488, 17 Atl. R. 455.

[5] Follit v. Eddystone Granite Quarries, L. R. (1892) 3 Ch. 75; Sneath v. Valley Gold, L. R. (1893) 1 Ch. 477.

the insolvency of the latter."[1] And some of the courts have gone very far in upholding reorganization schemes adopted by the majority.[2] As a foreclosure cuts off or bars the rights of the stockholders and creditors against whom the decree is rendered, it is usually the safest way in which to prepare for a reorganization upon the insolvency of the corporation. Unsecured creditors and stockholders often have it in their power, however, to so embarrass and delay the foreclosure proceedings that it is found expedient for the mortgage creditors and other parties interested in the property to agree upon some scheme of reorganization whereby, after the foreclosure sale, all parties interested shall be allowed, upon equitable terms, to come into a new company which shall own the property and carry on the business. This may be necessary in order to preserve intact a system of railways, to obtain funds required in the reorganization, or to prevent the appointment of a receiver and the issuance of receiver's certificates, or the allowance of other preferred claims growing out of the operation of the road, which would lessen the value of the property or imperil the security of the bondholders, and it is, therefore, better for them to "give up something of their own security" in order to avoid the delay and danger of loss. Under such schemes of reorganization the old stockholders are usually allowed to become shareholders in the new corporation upon the payment of a certain sum for each share of stock held by them, or upon some other equitable basis, and the bondholders are generally permitted to exchange the old bonds for new ones issued by the new company. Of course, in the absence of any statutory provision upon the subject, no one who has not signed the agreement can be compelled to come into the new company, and where all the interested parties have agreed to the plan of reorganization their rights are measured by the

[1] Taylor Priv. Corp., § 816; Sage v. Central R. R. Co., 99 U. S. 334; Shaw v. Railroad Co., 100 U. S. 605.

[2] See Pollitz v. Farmers' L. & T. Co., 53 Fed. R. 210; Symmes v. Union Trust Co., 60 Fed. R. 830; Shaw v. Railroad Co., 100 U. S. 605; Gates v. Boston, etc., R. R. Co., 53 Conn. 333; Canada Southern R. R. Co. v. Gebhard, 109 U. S. 527.

agreement.[1] Such schemes of reorganization are legal and are encouraged by the courts in order to prevent loss and insure the operation of the road for the benefit of the public.[2]

§ 534. **Rights and obligations of the parties—Laches and estoppel.**—In the absence of a statute or provision in the mortgage giving the majority power to bind the minority, bondholders who refuse to participate in the reorganization are not bound to do so, but may usually insist on being paid in cash.[3] They are entitled to their proportion of the money realized from the sale, but nothing more, unless they come in within the time limited by the agreement.[4] Even in the absence of any specific limitation they should act within a reasonable time and may, by their own laches, lose their rights to come in,[5] or to set aside the sale.[6] So, of course, one who takes part in the reorganization may thereby estop himself from thereafter repudiating it.[7] The provisions of the reorgan-

---

[1] See generally, 2 Cook on Stock and Stockholders (3d ed.), § 886; Wait Insolv. Corp., § 451; Jones on Railroad Securities, § 614.

[2] Robinson v. Philadelphia, etc., R. R. Co., 28 Fed.R. 340; Riker v. Alsop, 27 Fed. R. 251; Gates v. Boston, etc., R. R. Co., 53 Conn. 333; Mackintosh v. Flint, etc., R. R., 34 Fed. R. 582; Shaw v. Railroad Co., 100 U. S. 605; Kropholler v. St. Paul, etc., Ry., 1 McCrary (U. S.) 299. The bondholders may combine to purchase at the sale. Terbell v. Lee, 40 Fed. R. 40. The stockholders may also combine with them. Pennsylvania Transportation Co.'s Appeal, 101 Pa. St. 576.

[3] Brooks v. Vermont, etc., R. R., 22 Fed. R. 211. Compare Pollitz v. Farmers' L. & T. Co., 53 Fed. R. 210, 213.

[4] Zuccani v. Nacupai, etc., Co., 61 L. T. R. 176; Vose v. Cowdrey, 49 N. Y. 336; Vatable v. New York, etc., R. R. Co., 96 N. Y. 49; Landis v. Western Pass. R. R. Co., 133 Pa. St. 579, 19 Atl. R. 556. Appeal of Huston, (Pa.) 18 Atl. R. 419. But minority bondholders have been permitted by the court to come in and participate in the purchase where they made their application before the sale. Duncan v. Mobile, etc., R. R., 3 Woods (U. S.) 597.

[5] Zebley v. Farmers', etc., Co., 63 Hun (N. Y.) 541; Carpenter v. Catlin, 44 Barb. (N. Y.) 75; Dow v. Iowa Central R. R. Co., 70 Hun, 186, 24 N. Y. Supp. 292; Holland v. Cheshire Ry., 151 Mass. 231, 24 N. E. R. 206.

[6] Wetmore v. St. Paul, etc., R. R., 1 McCrary (U. S.) 466; Carey v. Houston, etc., Ry. Co., 52 Fed. R. 671 Farmers', etc., Co. v. Bankers', etc., Co., 119 N. Y. 15.

[7] Symmes v. Union Trust Co., 60 Fed. R. 830; Matthews v. Murchison, 15 Fed. R. 691; Crawshay v. Soutter, 6 Wall. (U. S.) 739. See, also, St. Louis, etc., Co. v. Sandoval, etc., Co., 116 Ill. 770, 5 N. E. R. 370; United States v. Union Pac. R. R. Co., 98 U.

ization agreement must be duly complied with[1] and a change in the plan can not be made by the reorganization committee, unless the authority is clearly given.[2] But where the reorganization agreement makes the reorganization committee the agents of the signers, notice to the committee is notice to all the signers.[3] One who has signed and complied with the reorganization agreement and is wrongfully excluded may recover damages,[4] or, in other cases, equity will protect him and may even enforce the agreement.[5]

§ 535. **Fraud in the sale or reorganization.** — A secret agreement, whereby one of the parties seeks to obtain an undue advantage, will not be tolerated by the courts,[6] and a sale may be set aside where the mortgage trustee enters into a combination with part of the bondholders to purchase at the sale for a small price and reorganize in such a manner as to sacrifice the interests of the other bondholders.[7] But, as we have already seen, any number of stockholders or creditors may purchase for themselves so long as they do so in good faith without preventing competition or taking any undue advantage of the others.[8] It has been held that a purchase by a director[9] or a

S. 569; Hollins v. St. Paul, etc., R. Co., 9 N. Y. Sup. 909; Butterfield v. Cowing, 112 N. Y. 486.

[1] In order to hold a dissatisfied subscriber. Miller v. Rutland, etc., R. R. Co., 40 Vt. 399, s. c. 94 Am. Dec. 413; Martin v. Somerville, etc., Co., 27 How. Pr. 161. And by those who desire to come into the new company, in order to entitle them to do so. Thornton v. Wabash, etc., R. R. Co., 81 N. Y. 462; Van Alstyne v. Houston, etc., R. R. Co., 56 Tex. 377; Appeal of Fidelity, etc., Co., 106 Pa. St. 144.

[2] Dutenhofer v. Adirondack Ry. Co., 14 N. Y. Sup. 558.

[3] Cox v. Stokes, 78 Hun 331, s. c. 29 N. Y. Sup. 141.

[4] Reading, etc., Co. v. Reading, etc., Works, 137 Pa. St. 282, 21 Atl. R. 169; Harris v. Davis, 44 Fed. R. 172.

[5] May compel an accounting. Riker v. Alsop, 27 Fed. R. 251; Cushman v. Bonfield, 139 Ill. 219, 28 N. E. R. 937. May enforce agreement of purchaser to allow others to participate. Cornell v. Utica, etc., R. R. Co., 61 How. Pr. (N. Y.) 184; Marie v. Garrison, 83 N. Y. 14.

[6] *Ex parte* White, 2 So. Car. 469; Bliss v. Matteson, 45 N. Y. 22.

[7] Sahlgard v. Kennedy, 1 McCrary, U. S. 291.

[8] *Ante*, § 529. See, also, Carter v. Ford Plate Glass Co., 85 Ind. 180; Hayden v. Official, etc., Co., 42 Fed. R. 875; Osborne's Admx. v. Monks, (Ky.), 21 S. W. R. 101.

[9] 2 Cook on Stock and Stockholders, §§ 653, 886; Cumberland, etc., Co. v. Sherman, 30 Barb. (N. Y.) 553; Jones v. Arkansas, etc., Co., 38 Ark. 17;

trustee[1] at his own sale is constructively or *prima facie* fraudulent and voidable, but mortgage trustees are sometimes authorized by the courts to make a certain bid or purchase at the sale for the benefit of all the bondholders,[2] and in some cases purchases by directors in good faith have been upheld.[3] But the company, or mortgagor, may usually avoid the sale to a trustee by redeeming,[4] and a director who fraudulently purchases may be compelled to transfer the property or account as a trustee.[5] Property fraudulently transferred to a new company formed by the members of an old company, with the intention of cheating, hindering and delaying the creditors of the old corporation, may be reached by them on execution.[6] So, where a company was apparently properly incorporated and executed notes as a corporation, it was held that it could not escape liability upon the notes by attempting to dissolve on the ground that the incorporation was invalid and by reorgan-

Wilkinson v. Bauerle, 41 N. J. Eq. 635, s. c. 7 Atl. R. 514; European, etc., R. R. Co. v. Poor, 59 Me. 277; Re Iron, etc., Co., 19 Ont. R. 113, s. c. 33 Am. & Eng. Corp. Cas. 277. The company's attorney may purchase for the bondholders. Pacific R. R. v. Ketchum, 101 U. S. 289.

[1] Washington, etc., R. R. v. Alexandria, etc., R. R., 19 Gratt. (Va.) 592. But he may purchase at a sale brought about by other parties. Allan v. Gillette, 127 U. S. 589.

[2] 2 Cook on Stock and Stockholders, §§ 885; Sage v. Central R. R., 99 U. S. 334; Rogers v. Wheeler, 43 N. Y. 598.

[3] Saltmarsh v. Spaulding, 147 Mass. 224, s. c. 17 N. E. R. 316; Harpending v. Munson, 91 N. Y. 650; Twin Lick Oil Co. v. Marbury, 91 U. S. 587; Hill v. Nisbet, 100 Ind. 341; Hallam v. Indianola Hotel Co., 56 Iowa 178. See, also, for acts of officers in effecting reorganization held not to be fraudulent. Symmes v. Union Trust Co., 60 Fed. R. 830.

[4] Kitchen v. St. Louis, etc., Ry., 69 Mo. 224; Racine, etc., R. R. v. Farmers', etc., Co., 49 Ill. 331; Wasatch, etc., Co. v. Jennings, 5 Utah 243, 15 Pac. R. 65; Hoyle v. Plattsburgh, etc., R. R. Co., 54 N. Y. 314. See, also, James v. Cowing, 82 N. Y. 449.

[5] Harts v. Brown, 77 Ill. 226; Hope v. Valley City Salt Co., 25 W. Va. 789; Allen v. Jackson, 122 Ill. 567, 13 N. E. R. 840; Jackson v. Ludeling, 21 Wall. (U. S.) 616; Covington & L. R. R. Co. v. Bowler's Ex., 9 Bush (Ky.) 468; Bradbury v. Barnes, 19 Cal. 120; Tobin, etc., Co. v. Fraser, 81 Tex. 407, 17 S. W. R. 25; Raleigh v. Fitzpatrick, 43 N. J. Eq. 501.

[6] Booth v. Bunce, 33 N. Y. 139, s. c. 88 Am. Dec. 372. See, also, Blair v. St. Louis, etc., R. R. Co., 22 Fed. R. 36. A transfer of all the property of a railroad company to a new company formed by the members of the old with the same officers and a mere exchange of stock was held fraudulent as against creditors in San Francisco, etc., R. R. Co. v. Bee, 48 Cal. 398.

izing and reincorporating.[1] As a general rule it may, perhaps, be said that any sale or device by which all the assets of an insolvent corporation are to be parceled out among the stockholders, leaving creditors unpaid, is a fraud upon such creditors, and, in a proper case, they may follow the assets or the purchase-money in the hands of the stockholders. Thus, it has been held that a foreclosure sale made after the company had become insolvent, and expedited by an arrangement between the bondholders and the stockholders whereby the former received part of their debt and the latter the balance of the proceeds, is fraudulent as to the unsecured creditors, who may be allowed to intervene and obtain satisfaction of their debts out of the proceeds of the sale set apart for the stockholders.[2] In another case[3] an insolvent railroad company sold all its property to another company for bonds of the latter guarantied by a banking company, and the contract of sale provided that, in consideration for the guaranty, the banking company should become the owner of the stock and income bonds of the selling company, while the bonds of the buying company, instead of being held as assets by the officers of the selling company, were to be distributed among its shareholders and the owners of its income bonds. The court held that, as against unsecured creditors of the vendor company, its income bonds in the hands of the banking company should be treated as paid and canceled, saying that the device was "doubly fraudulent." It may be stated as a general rule, under these decisions, that a sale of all the property of an insolvent railroad company, under an arrangement whereby the stockholders of the selling company or such stockholders and the owners of its income bonds receive the entire purchase-price or proceeds of the sale, is fraudulent as against unsecured creditors known to exist by both parties at the time of the sale, and that, even in the ab-

[1] Empire Mfg. Co. v. Stuart, 46 Mich. 482.
[2] Railroad Co. v. Howard, 7 Wall. (U. S.) 392.
[3] Chattanooga, Rome & C. R. R. Co. v. Evans, 66 Fed. R. 809.

sence of express notice of their existence upon the part of the purchaser, the purchasing company, knowing that the purchase-price will be placed beyond their reach, is bound to inquire as to whether there are any unsecured creditors and is chargeable with the knowledge which an inquiry would disclose.[1]

§ 536. **Reorganization by the courts.**—It is, perhaps, not strictly correct to say that the courts will reorganize a corporation, but in many cases they have done what they could to further the reorganization of railroad companies in the interests of the public and of all parties concerned.[2] Thus, in a recent case,[3] the court approved a master's report wherein he laid down the rule that "a court of equity in foreclosure proceedings upon railroad mortgages, in view of the number and variety of persons and interests to be affected, and their probable sacrifice without combination for their protection, will facilitate combinations and schemes of reorganization to the end that a small minority of interests shall not enforce unreasonable and inequitable concessions from the majority, or the majority crush out or subject to disadvantage the rights of the minority."[4] The court also granted permission to the receiver to pay to a syndicate which had proposed to effect a reorganization by the advancement of funds for the purchase of overdue coupons, a commission of two and one-half per cent. on the money advanced in case the reorganization was perfected, stating that it would "regard with satisfaction any and every legitimate effort to terminate the receivership." It took care to observe, however, that receivers "should not enlist, on either side, in conflicts among those interested in the property," and that it would not pass upon the merits of rival schemes of reorganization nor coerce the judgment or control the action of

---

[1] See, also, Vance v. McNabb, etc., Coke Co., 92 Tenn. 47, s. c. 20 S. W. R. 424.

[2] See *ante*, § 533.

[3] Platt v. Philadelphia, etc., R. R. Co., 65 Fed. R. 872.

[4] Citing Sage v. Central R. Co., 99 U. S. 334; Carey v. Houston, etc., R. Co., 45 Fed. R. 438; Robinson v. Philadelphia, etc., R. Co., 28 Fed. R. 340; Cook on Stock and Stockholders (3d ed.), § 886.

the parties interested. So, in another case,[1] the court confirmed a plan of reorganization, over the objection of the minority, who were compelled to surrender their old bonds and accept new ones upon being duly secured.

[1] Pollitz *v.* Farmers' L. & T. Co., 53 Fed. R. 210.

CHAPTER XXII.

RECEIVERS.

§ 537. Receivers generally.
538. Jurisdiction of courts of equity—Statutory provisions.
539. Jurisdiction is sparingly exercised—Purpose of appointment.
540. General rules as to when receivers of railroads will be appointed.
541. Receivers will not be appointed merely because parties consent.
542. Extent to which jurisdiction has been exercised.
543. Insolvency as ground for appointment of receiver.
544. When insolvency is sufficient without default.
545. Default in payment of indebtedness as ground for appointment.
546. Appointment in foreclosure proceedings.
547. Other grounds for appointment.
548. Appointment upon application of unsecured creditor.
549. Appointment upon application of secured creditor.
550. Appointment upon application of stockholders.
551. Appointment upon application of corporation.
552. What court may appoint.
553. Court first obtaining jurisdiction retains it—Conflict of jurisdiction.

§ 554. Extra-territorial jurisdiction.
555. Ancillary appointment—Comity.
556. Procedure—*Ex parte* application.
557. Parties to proceedings for appointment of receiver.
558. Appointment upon motion or petition and notice—Affidavits.
559. Who may appoint—Appointment in vacation.
560. Suit must generally be pending.
561. Who may be appointed receiver.
562. Order appointing receiver.
563. Effect of appointment.
564. Collateral attack on appointment.
565. Title and possession of receiver.
566. Authority, rights and duties of receiver—Control by court.
567. Contracts of receiver.
568. Suits by receivers—Authority to sue.
569. When receiver may maintain suit—Defenses to receiver's suit.
570. Right of receiver to sue in other jurisdictions—Comity.
571. Suits against receivers—Leave to sue must be obtained.
572. Effect of failure to obtain leave to sue.
573. Effect of recent act of congress.

§ 537. RECEIVERS.

§574. Rule where suit has been commenced before appointment of receiver.	§ 579. Liability on contracts.
	580. Liability on claims arising from operation of the road.
575. Protection of receiver by the court.	581. Liability of corporation.
	582. Receivers of leased lines.
576. Liability of receivers—Generally.	583. Receiver's accounts.
	584. Compensation of receiver.
577. Liability for torts.	585. Attorney's fees.
578. Receiver is bound to perform public duties—Mandamus.	586. Removal and discharge.
	587. Effect of removal or discharge.

§ 537. **Receivers generally.**—A receiver is a person[1] appointed by the court to take charge of property pending litigation, or in pursuance thereof.[2] The appointment of a receiver is an auxiliary equitable remedy, devised, on account of the inadequacy of any remedy at law, to prevent loss or injury to property in litigation and preserve it, *pendente lite*, for the sake of all interested, to be finally disposed of as the court may decree.[3] A receiver stands indifferent between the parties, and occupies a fiduciary relation to all the creditors.[4] He is, in a sense, an officer of the court, and the court will protect the property in his hands.[5] In the absence of a statute authorizing it he can not be sued, ordinarily at least, without permission of the court by whom he was appointed.[6] So, as a rule,

---

[1] In many of the states provision is made for the appointment of corporations commonly called "trust companies."

[2] High on Receivers, § 1; Devendorf v. Dickinson, 21 How. Pr. (N. Y.) 275; Merritt v. Merritt, 16 Wend. (N. Y.) 405; Baker v. Backus, 32 Ill. 79; Foster's Fed. Pr., § 239; 3 Pom. Eq. Jur., § 1330.

[3] Stilwell v. Williams, 6 Madd. 38; Bank of Mississippi v. Duncan, 52 Miss. 740; Folsom v. Evans, 5 Minn. 418; Myers v. Estell, 48 Miss. 372. There are, however, cases where a receiver finally disposes of property as, for instance, under statutes authorizing a receiver to wind up the affairs of a corporation.

[4] Porter v. Williams, 9 N. Y. 142; Davis v. Gray, 16 Wall. 203, 217; Vermont, etc., R. Co. v. Vermont Cent. R. Co., 34 Vt. 1.

[5] 3 Pom. Eq. Jur., § 1336; Davis v. Gray, 16 Wall. 203, 218; Walling v. Miller, 108 N. Y. 173, s. c. 2 Am. St. R. 400.

[6] Barton v. Barbour, 104 U. S. 126; Keen v. Breckenridge, 96 Ind. 69; Wayne Pike Co. v. State, *ex rel.* Whittaker, 134 Ind. 672, 34 N. E. R. 440; De Graffenried v. Brunswick, etc., Co., 57 Ga. 22; Davis v. Ladoga Creamery Co., 128 Ind. 222, s. c. 27 N. E. R. 494; Matter of Christian Jensen Co., 128 N. Y. 550. See, however, Foster's Fed. Pr., § 251, for recent act of congress authorizing suit in some cases,

CORP. 47

he can only bring suit in his own name when authorized by statute or by the court.[1] As a general rule he derives his title from the debtor, and can only maintain suit where the debtor could have done so.[2] But there are exceptions to this general rule, for a receiver may sometimes bring suits which the debtor could not maintain. The paramount duty of a receiver is to secure assets for the payment of the debtor's liabilities, and he may for that purpose bring and sustain suits, such as a suit to set aside a fraudulent conveyance made by the debtor, that the latter could not successfully prosecute.[3]

§ 538. Jurisdiction of courts of equity—Statutory provisions.—The power to appoint a receiver is, we think, inherent in courts of equity, and in those code states in which the court of equity has lost its separate identity the power has descended to the courts having equitable jurisdiction.[4] It may

and Kinney v. Crocker, 18 Wis. 74; Allen v. Central R. R. Co., 42 Iowa 683; Lyman v. Central, etc., R. R. Co., 59 Vt. 167.

[1] Garver v. Kent, 70 Ind. 428; Green v. Winter, 1 Johns. Ch. (N. Y.) 60; Wilson v. Welch, 157 Mass. 77, 31 N. E. R. 712. See, also, Pendleton v. Russell, 144 U. S. 640, s. c. 12 Sup. Ct. R. 743. As to when the rule does not apply, see Pouder v. Catterson, 127 Ind. 434, s. c. 26 N. E. R. 66.

[2] Jacobson v. Allen, 12 Fed. R. 454, 457; LaFollett v. Akin, 36 Ind. 1; Republic, etc., Co. v. Swigert, 135 Ill. 150, s. c. 12 L. R. A. 328.

[3] Graham Button Co. v. Spielmann, 50 N. J. Eq. 120, 24 Atl. R. 571; Cole v. Satsop R. Co., 9 Wash. 487, 10 Lewis Am. R. R. & Corp. R. 604; Voorhees v. Indianapolis, etc., Co., 140 Ind. 220, 39 N. E. R. 738; National, etc., Bank v. Vigo Co. Nat'l Bank, 141 Ind. 352, 40 N. E. R. 799; Taylor Priv. Corp., §§ 274, 814; 2 Beach Eq. 905; Elliott's Gen. Pr., § 393. The receiver of a corporation may avoid a chattel mortgage on its property on the ground that it was not filed according to law. Farmers' L. & T. Co. v. Minneapolis, etc., Works, 35 Minn. 543. A receiver of a corporation may properly bring an action to set aside and vacate a judgment against the corporation on the ground that it was obtained in fraud of creditors, without consideration, and by collusion with the officers of the corporation. Whittlesey v. Delaney, 73 N. Y. 571. A receiver of a corporation may repudiate the illegal transfer of its securities by its officers and secure them as assets. Talmage v. Pell, 7 N. Y. 328. A receiver of an insolvent corporation appointed at the instance of creditors is clothed with all their rights and can sue to recover unpaid stock subscriptions in cases where the corporation can not sue. Cole v. Satsop R. Co., 9 Wash. 487, s. c. 43 Am. St. R. 858.

[4] Bitting v. Ten Eyck, 85 Ind. 357; McElwaine v. Hosey, 135 Ind. 481, 490; Folsom v. Evans, 5 Minn. 418; Hopkins v. Worcester, etc., Canal

§ 538   RECEIVERS.   733

be exercised in aid of their jurisdiction, as a general rule, whenever necessary in order to accomplish complete justice, but not, ordinarily, where the law affords any other safe or expedient remedy.[1] The appointment of receivers for railroad corporations is regulated largely by statute in many of the states,[2] and in England[3] as well. And it has been held

Prop., L. R. 6 Eq. 437; Williamson v. Wilson, 1 Bland (Md.) 420; U. S. Trust Co. v. New York, etc., R. Co., 101 N. Y. 478; High on Receivers, § 9; Beach on Law of Railways, § 708;note, 64 Am. Dec. 482. There is, however, considerable conflict as to whether the power to appoint receivers of railroad companies is inherent in courts of equity.

[1] Sollory v. Leaver, L. R. 9 Eq. 22; Cremen v. Hawkes, 2 Jones & La T. 674; Corey v. Long, 43 How. Pr. 492; Rice v. St. Paul, etc., R. Co., 24 Minn. 464; High on Receivers, § 10; Elliott's Gen. Pr., § 394.

[2] A receiver may be appointed at the request of a creditor or stockholder, upon the expiration of the corporate charter, in most of the states. Stimson's Am. Stat. (1892), §§ 8332, 8360. Or upon voluntary dissolution. Stimson's Am. Stat. (1892), citing laws of Massachusetts, New Jersey, Minnesota, Delaware, Alabama. Or upon dissolution by decree of court or otherwise. Stimson's Am. Stat. (1892), citing laws of Massachusetts, New York, Delaware, Montana, Ohio, West Virginia, North Carolina, Texas, California, Oregon, Washington, Idaho, Wyoming, Utah; § 8900, citing laws of New Jersey. So when the corporation is insolvent or in imminent danger of insolvency. Stimson's Am. Stat. (1892), §§ 8332, 8360, citing laws of North Carolina, Texas, Oregon, Washington, Idaho, Montana, Wyoming, Utah; § 8900, citing laws of New Jersey and Kentucky. A receiver may be appointed upon non-user or abuser or its corporate rights or the doing of any acts forfeiting such rights. Stimson's Am. Stat. (1892), §§ 8332, 8360, citing laws of North Carolina, Oregon, Washington, Idaho, Montana, Utah, R. S. Ind. 1894, § 1236. Neglect for sixty days to run trains regularly, R. S. 1883, Me. Ch. 51, § 47. Neglect for ten days to run daily trains, N. J. Supp. 1886, R. R.'s, § 42. The Indiana statute authorizes the appointment of a receiver where, in the discretion of the court or the judge thereof in vacation, it may be necessary to secure ample justice to the parties. R. S. Ind. 1894, § 1236. Under this statute it was held that a receiver of a turnpike company would be appointed at the suit of stockholders, upon a showing that the majority of the directors have converted and misappropriated the corporate revenues, tolls and earnings and suffered the road to become badly out of repair and wholly impassible for six weeks, although there is no prayer for a dissolution of the corporation. Wayne Pike Co. v. Hammons, 129 Ind. 368.

[3] 30 and 31 Vict. Ch. 127, § 4. Section 4 of this act, known as the Railway Companies act of 1867, provides that no part of the rolling stock or plant used or provided by a company for the purposes of the traffic on their railway, or of their stations or workshops, shall be liable to be taken on execution at law or in equity after the road is opened for traffic; but the per-

that specification by the legislature of the cases in which a receivership may be had excludes every other case and prohibits the appointment, except as authorized.[1] But it seems to us that the better rule is that the right is inherent in courts of equity, that such statutes are but declaratory of the common law and must be construed in the light of equity jurisprudence, and that they do not abridge the inherent power of the court of equity.[2] The inherent authority of a court of equity to take charge of and operate a railroad and control the extensive business interests therewith connected with a view to its continuance, has been denied in some jurisdictions on the grounds that a court of chancery will not assume the management of a business except with a view to its winding up or to keep it a going concern with a view to its sale, and that the public functions of the railroad corporation can not be delegated or transferred, but must be discharged by the company itself.[3] In such in-

son who has recovered a judgment against the corporation which remains unpaid may obtain the appointment of a receiver, and, if necessary, of a manager for the business of the company, on application to the court of chancery in England or Ireland, according to the situation of the railway owned by the company. Whenever the judgment creditor of a railway company is unpaid the appointment of a receiver or manager is a manner of right. *In re* Manchester, etc., R. Co., L. R. 14 Ch. Div. 645.

[1] Fellows *v.* Hermans, 13 Abb. Pr. N. S. (N. Y.) 1. The code of Georgia does not materially alter the equitable jurisdiction of the courts to appoint receivers. Skinner *v.* Maxwell, 66 N. Car. 45. In England it has been held that a court of chancery, in the absence of statute authority, has no power to appoint a manager for a railroad. Gardner *v.* London, etc., R. Co., L. R. 2 Ch. 201. But the weight of authority in the United States is overwhelmingly the other way.

[2] Beach on Rec., § 10; 20 Am. & Eng. Encyc. of Law 333, 339; 1 Elliott's General Practice, § 394; Bitting *v.* Ten Eyck, 85 Ind. 357; note to 64 Am. Dec. 482; Bispham's Prin. Eq. (4th ed.), § 576; Skinner *v.* Maxwell, 66 N. Car. 45; McElwaine *v.* Hosey, 135 Ind. 481, 490; U. S. Trust Co. *v.* New York, etc., R. Co., 101 N. Y. 478, 25 Am. & Eng. Ry. Cas. 601; Hollenbeck *v.* Donnell, 94 N. Y. 342. In Davis *v.* Gray, 16 Wall. 203, 220, Swayne, J., says: "As regards the statutes, we see no reason why a court of equity, in the exercise of its undoubted authority, may not accomplish all the best results intended to be secured by such legislation, without its aid."

[3] Gardner *v.* London, etc., R. Co., L. R. 2 Ch. 201; Attorney General *v.* Utica Ins. Co., 2 Johns. Ch. (N. Y.) 371; Second Ward Bank *v.* Upmann, 12 Wis. 499; East Line, etc., Co. *v.* State, 75 Tex. 434. Compare Attorney General *v.* Utica Ins. Co., 2 Johns. Ch. (N. Y.) 371; Attorney-General *v.* Bank

stances the defect of power has generally been supplied by statute,[1] and in some states the power of courts of equity has thus been greatly extended and enlarged. Such statutes are strictly construed.[2]

§ 539. **Jurisdiction is sparingly exercised—Purpose of appointment.**—The appointment of a receiver is a power to be somewhat sparingly exercised, and in America it is exercised reluctantly with regard to railroads, the courts proceeding cautiously with reference to the circumstances of each particular case and reserving a broad discretion[3] on account of the inability of a court of equity in all cases to properly care for the large business interests involved.[4] Courts of equity, however, will assume the management of railroads when a proper case presents itself, with a view to the winding up of insolvent companies, or the sale of their property for the benefit of creditors, and, if it is shown to be necessary, will continue

---

of Niagara, Hopk.Ch. (N.Y.) 354; Slee v. Bloom, 5 Johns. Ch. 366, 381; Howe v. Deuel, 43 Barb. 504; Belmont v. Erie R. R. Co., 52 Barb. 637; Baker v. Backus, 32 Ill. 79; Neall v. Hill, 16 Cal. 145. In Decker v. Gardner, 124 N. Y. 334, the court says: "The court of chancery * * * declined until the power was conferred by statute to sequestrate corporate property through the medium of a receiver, or to dissolve corporate bodies, or restrain the usurpation of corporate powers."

[1] See 30 and 31 Vict. Ch. 126, § 4; 36 and 37 Victoria, §§ 3, 27; Acts N. Y., 1825, Ch. 325, § 15; Acts Tex., 1887, p. 120, § 1, subd. 3; Connelly v. Dickson, 76 Ind. 440; Hellebush v. Blake, 119 Ind. 349, s. c. 21 N. E. R. 976.

[2] Bangs v. McIntosh, 23 Barb. 591; High on Receivers, § 289; 20 Am. & Eng. Encyc. of Law 271, and note; Chamberlain v. Rochester, etc., Co., 7 Hun (N. Y.) 557.

[3] Sage v. Memphis, etc., R. Co., 125 U. S. 361, and cases cited; Stevens v. Davison, 18 Gratt. (Va.) 819, s. c. 98 Am. Dec. 692. In Overton v. Memphis, etc., R. Co., 10 Fed. R. 866, Judge Caldwell said: "None of the prerogatives of a court of equity have been pushed to such extreme limits as this, and there is none so likely to lead to abuses. It is not the province of a court of equity to take possession of the property, and conduct the business of corporations or individuals, except where the exercise of such extraordinary jurisdiction is indispensably necessary to save or protect some clear right, of a suitor, which would otherwise be lost or greatly endangered, and which can not be saved or protected by any other action or mode of proceeding."

[4] Kelly v. Alabama, etc., R. Co., 58 Ala. 489. See Gardner v. London, etc., R. Co., L. R. 2 Ch. 201.

the operation of the roads by the intervention of receivers in order that they may be sold without depreciation of the property, and in order that the public interests shall not suffer. They are thus enabled to protect and enforce the rights of creditors and stockholders and to insure the discharge of the public function of the corporation.[1] Where the appointment of receivers to manage railroads is authorized by statute, the circumstances under which the appointment may be made and the manner of their appointment are often specifically set forth; but these statutes are largely declaratory of the common law as administered by the courts of other jurisdictions,[2] and, in the absence of such statutes, the jurisdiction of a court of equity may be said in general to extend to all cases where its interference is necessary to protect the property or to enforce the rights of persons interested in it, whether creditors or stockholders.[3]

§ 540. General rules as to when receivers of railroads will be appointed.—It is frequently said that the appointment of a receiver is within the sound discretion of the court.[4] This does not mean that the court can, without error, arbitrarily

---

[1] See post, § 542; In re Long Branch, etc., R. R. Co., 24 N. J. Eq. 398; Beach on Receivers, 329; Cook on Stock and Stockholders and Corporation Law, § 863.

[2] It is held in North Carolina that the code, which specifies certain cases in which a receiver may be appointed, "does not materially alter the equitable jurisdiction" of the courts of that state. Skinner v. Maxwell, 66 N. C. 45. In New Jersey the statute provides that a receiver may be appointed for any railroad which fails for ten days to run daily trains. N. J. Supp. Rep., p. 834, pl. 42. Delaware Bay, etc., R. Co. v. Markley, 45 N. J. Eq. 139.

[3] Stevens v. Davison, 18 Gratt. (Va.) 819; Meyer v. Johnston, 53 Ala. 237; Skinner v. Maxwell, 66 N. Car. 45; Sandford v. Sinclair, 8 Paige 373; Conro v. Port Henry Iron Co., 12 Barb. 27; Lawrence v. Greenwich Fire Ins. Co., 1 Paige 587; Conro v. Gray, 4 How. Pr. 166; Davis v. Gray, 16 Wall. (U. S.) 203, 219.

[4] Verplank v. Caines, 1 Johns. Ch. (N. Y.) 57; Ex parte Walker, 25 Ala. 81; Owen v. Homan, 4 H. L. Cas. 997, 1032; Oakley v. Paterson Bank, 2 N. J. Eq. 173; Simmons Hardware Co. v. Waibel, 1 So. Dak. 488, 11 L. R. A. 267, s. c. 47 N. W. R. 814; Smith v. Port Dover, etc., R. Co., 12 Ontario App. R. 288, 25 Am. & Eng. R. Cas. 639; Farmers' L. & T. Co. v. Chicago & A. R. Co., 27 Fed. R. 146; Mays v. Rose, Freem. Ch. (Miss.) 703, 718. See Elliott's Gen. Pr. 394, and cases cited.

appoint a receiver where such appointment is unauthorized and wholly uncalled for, or refuse the appointment where there is a clear, fixed and definite right to have a receiver appointed, but that a sound discretion is to be exercised according to well established principles of law.[1] It is only in clear cases that the power will be exercised, and as a general rule there must be a suit pending.[2] The English courts of chancery have always been averse to appointing receivers for railway property in operation,[3] and our courts have often expressed reluctance in exercising the power in the absence of statutory

[1] Mercantile Trust Co. v. Missouri, etc., R. Co., 36 Fed. R. 221; Orphan Asylum v. McCartee, 1 Hopk. Ch. (N. Y.) 423, (372); Milwaukee R. R. Co. v. Soutter, 5 Wall. 660; Lenox v. Notrebe, Hempst. (N. S.) 225; Vose v. Reed, 1 Woods (N. S.) 647; Daniels' Ch. Pr. (6th ed.) 1664. The action of the trial court is subject to review on appeal. Tysen v. Wabash R. R. Co., 8 Biss. 247; Winthrop Iron Co. v. Meeker, 109 U. S. 180; La Societe Francaise d'Epargnes, etc., v. District Court,53 Cal. 495; Smith v. Port Dover, etc., R. Co., 12 Ont. App. R. 288, 25 Am. & Eng. R. Cas. 639; Cook v. Detroit, etc., R. Co., 45 Mich. 453. Compare Dawson v. Parsons, 137 N. Y. 605.

[2] Pressley v. Harrison, 102 Ind. 14; Pressley v. Lamb,105 Ind.171;Crowder v. Moone, 52 Ala.220; National Bank v. Kent Circuit Judge,43 Mich. 292;Jones v. Bank, 10 Colo. 464; Wiltsie on Mortgage Foreclosures, § 630. Mr. Foster, in his Federal Practice, says: "Independently of statutory authority, a court of equity will ordinarily appoint a receiver of the property of a corporation in only seven cases: Firstly, at the suit of mortgagees or other holders of liens upon it; secondly, at the suit of judgment creditors seeking equitable assets; thirdly, at the suit of persons interested, whether as stockholders or creditors, in the property, where there is a breach of duty by the directors, and an actual or threatened loss; fourthly, where a corporation has been dissolved and has no officer to attend to its affairs; fifthly, where for a long time the corporation has ceased to transact business, and its officers have ceased to act; sixthly, where the governing body is so divided and engaged in such mutual contention that its members can not act together; and, seventhly, in one case a receiver was appointed at the application of the corporation itself, made before a default in the payment of interest upon bonds secured by mortgagees, where it was for the interest of the public that the business carried on by the corporation—a railroad company—should be continued without interruption, and the corporation was hopelessly insolvent, and there was danger of an attempt by creditors to gain a preference, by attachment or otherwise, in such a manner as would have prevented the continuance of the corporate business."

[3] Gardner v. London, etc., Ry. Co., L. R. 2 Ch. 201, 212; Latimer v. Aylesbury, etc., Ry. Co., L. R. 9 Ch. Div. 385.

authority.[1] Such reluctance is based upon the fact that the interests involved are generally large, the management intricate, and that the corporation is charged with a public duty of which it should not be divested, and its officers are charged with corporate duties which should not be delegated.[2] A receiver will not be appointed, as a rule, unless it clearly appears *prima facie* that the plaintiff is entitled to a final decree.[3] The remedy has been termed an equitable attachment,[4] and will not be employed to change the management of railroad property simply because stockholders or creditors are dissatisfied with the present existing management.[5] They must show that they have an equitable right and that it will be impaired unless the property available for its satisfaction is protected by the appointment of a receiver.[6] A court will not appoint a receiver upon slight grounds and merely because a receivership would do no harm;[7] nor upon good grounds where it would be useless, as, for instance, where there are no assets nor anything which could be

---

[1] Sage v. Memphis, etc., R. Co., 125 U. S. 361; Meyer v. Johnston, 53 Ala. 237; Kelly v. Alabama, etc., R. Co., 58 Ala. 489; American L. & T. Co. v. Toledo, etc., R. Co., 29 Fed. R. 416; Overton v. Memphis, etc., R. Co., 10 Fed. R. 866; Stevens v. Davison, 18 Gratt. (Va.) 819.

[2] Gardner v. London, etc., Ry. Co., L. R. 2 Ch. 201. See St. Louis, etc., R. R. Co. v. Dewees, 23 Fed. R. 519. Brewer and Treat, JJ.

[3] Mays v. Rose, Freem. Ch. (Miss.) 703, 718; Beecher v. Bininger, 7 Blatchf. (U. S.) 170; Wilkinson v. Dobbie, 12 Blatchf. (U. S.) 298; Cofer v. Ecberson, 6 Iowa 502; Gregory v. Gregory, 33 N. Y. Super. Ct. 1, 39; Owen v. Homan, 3 Macn. & G. 378, affir'd 4 H. L. Cas. 997; Lloyd v. Passingham, 16 Ves. 59. The plaintiff must show that he has a present existing right in the property in order to have a receiver appointed. Steele v. Aspy, 128 Ind. 367.

[4] Cincinnati, etc., R. Co. v. Sloan, 31 Ohio St. 1.

[5] American L. & T. Co. v Toledo, C. & S. Ry. Co., 29 Fed. R. 416, 420, 421; Fluker v. Emporia City Ry. Co., 48 Kan. 577, 30 Pac. R. 18. In the absence of gross abuse or fraud, the remedy of the stockholders is to elect new officers. Edison v. Edison, etc., Co., (N. J. Eq.) 29 Atl. R. 195.

[6] Cincinnati, etc., R. Co. v. Sloan, 31 Ohio St. 1; Union Mutual Life Ins. Co. v. Union Mills, etc., Co., 37 Fed. R. 286; Union Trust Co. v. St. Louis, etc., R. Co., 4 Dillon (N. S.) 114; Cheever v. Rutland, etc., R. Co., 39 Vt. 653; Woods' Railroads (Minor's edition) 2015.

[7] Smith v. Port Dover, etc., R. Co., 12 Ont. App. R. 288, 25 Am. & Eng. R. Cas. 639; Orphan Aslyum Soc. v. McCartee, 1 Hopk. (N. Y.) Ch. 429 (488); Blondheim v. Moore, 11 Md. 365.

made available to satisfy a judgment;[1] nor where it appears that in the latter case the plaintiff expects some of the defendants to pay his claim rather than suffer annoyance from a receiver.[2] Indeed, a court of equity will not interfere in any case where such interference would be a "vain and fruitless thing;"[3] nor where there is an adequate remedy at law.[4]

§ 541. **Receiver will not be appointed merely because parties consent.**—The mere fact that the parties consent to the appointment of a receiver is not sufficient,[5] especially where the rights of third persons are likely to be affected,[6] or the property is in the hands of a person not made a party to the suit.[7] If it appears that the consent was given for the mere purpose of preventing the seizure of the property of the corporation upon legal process, and without any intent to satisfy the plaintiff's demands against it, the receiver will be discharged.[8] Courts confine themselves strictly to the business of settling, according to the principles of law and equity, the real controversies which come within the "workshop of jurisprudence," and should never lend themselves to the schemes of those who wish to manipulate railroad securities for purposes of adventurous speculation.[9]

---

[1] Bigelow v. Union Freight R. Co., 137 Mass. 478. See *In re* Birmingham, etc., R. Co., L.R. 18 Ch. Div. 155, 3 Am. & Eng. R. Cas. 616. Where the company is shown to have no assets a receiver will not be appointed. Barton v. Enterprise Loan, etc., Assn., 114 Ind. 226.

[2] Smith v. Port Dover, etc., Co., 12 Ont. App. R. 288, 25 Am. & Eng. R. Cas. 639.

[3] Simpson v. Ottawa, etc., R. Co., 1 Ch. Chamb. R. 126. A receiver will only be appointed where the amount of the judgment warrants the expense. Weekly Notes (Eng., 1884), 63.

[4] Rice v. St. Paul, etc., R. Co., 24 Minn. 464; Pullan v. Cincinnati, etc., R. Co., 4 Biss. (U. S.) 35; Overton v. Memphis, etc., R. Co., 10 Fed. R. 866; Stevens v. Davison, 18 Gratt. (Va.) 819; Milwaukee, etc., R. Co. v. Soutter, 2 Wall. 510, 523.

[5] Whelpley v. Erie R. Co., 6 Blatchf. (U. S.) 271. See Sage v. Memphis, etc., R. Co., 18 Fed. R. 571.

[6] Whelpley v. Erie R. Co., 6 Blatchf. (U. S.) 271.

[7] Searles v. Jacksonville, etc., R. Co., 2 Woods (U. S.) 621; Einstein v. Rosenfeld, etc., Mills, 38 N. J. Eq. 309; Gluck & Becker on Rec. of Corp., 61.

[8] Sage v. Memphis, etc., R. Co., 18 Fed. R. 571.

[9] American Loan, etc., Co. v. Toledo, etc., R. Co., 29 Fed. R. 416.

§ 542. **Extent to which jurisdiction has been exercised.**—Courts of equity, by reason either of inherent power or statutory authority, in the United States, and in most of the states, have interposed with receivers for railway property to the extent necessary to accomplish the desired auxiliary aid, sometimes accompanying the dissolution of the corporation and winding up its affairs, sometimes operating the road until the income shall have discharged the primary obligation,[1] and at other times operating and improving the road with view to its advantageous sale. They have even interfered to complete a road in construction which had been retarded on account of the temporary lack of funds,[2] and in rare instances have taken charge of lines to compel them to properly perform their public duty.[3] But the right, in such cases, to divest the corporate officers of their powers and supersede them by receivers, when the court can command such officers by injunction or other process, has been questioned,[4] and, although the remedy has been extended in some cases, other courts have refused to appoint receivers on account of fraudulent mismanagement by corporate officers where such mismanagement is in itself ground for their removal.[5] While courts of equity are cautious in the exercise of this remedy, no rule can be laid down which would clearly define the grounds for its exercise or draw boundaries which would confine it, since the power of the equity court has been so enlarged by statute that its arm can be interposed in nearly every instance where complete justice would otherwise fail, and the railroad corporation[6] now enjoys

---

[1] Sage v. Memphis, etc., R. Co., 125 U. S. 361, and Sage v. Memphis, etc., R Co., 18 Fed. R. 571. See Barton v. Barbour, 104 U. S. 126, 137, 138.

[2] Allen v. Dallas, etc., R. Co., 3 Woods (U. S.) 316; Kennedy v. St. Paul, etc., R. Co., 2 Dillon (U. S.) 448.

[3] *In re* Long Branch, etc., R. R. Co., 24 N. J. Eq. 398; Beach on Receivers, 329; Fishback v. Citizens' St. Ry. Co., Nat. Corp. R. (Super. Ct. Marion Co., Ind.), March 4, 1892.

[4] See Cook on Stock and Stockholders, §§ 745 and 863, and cases cited *infra*; Waterbury v. Merchants', etc., Co., 50 Barb. 157; Featherstone v. Cooke, L. R. 16 Eq. 298.

[5] See preceding note; Edison v. Edison, etc., Co., 29 Atl. R. 195.

[6] See Barton v. Barbour, 104 U. S. 126, 137, 138, in dissenting opinion.

few exemptions from the rules which apply to the receivership of other corporations.

§ 543. **Insolvency as ground for appointment of receiver.** —Insolvency of a railway corporation is not of itself ground for the appointment of a receiver, unless made so by statute. Even if insolvency be shown the court will refuse to appoint a receiver, unless it can interfere usefully to prevent the impairment of some equitable right or of the value of some claim against the corporation.[1] Where insolvency is conceded or evident, with no probability of recovery, and there are dissensions among the parties in interest, or disagreements within the corporate management, which threaten dissipation of the assets and endanger the securities of parties in interest, a receiver will be appointed at the suit of the proper party.[2] But, ordinarily, if it be shown that it is for the best interest of all concerned to leave the directors in charge of affairs, a receiver will not be appointed;[3] nor will the remedy usually be exercised if the corporation, in obedience to a statute, is making the same disposition of the earnings of the road that a receiver would be required to make, and no assets would be available in his hands for payment of the plaintiff's debt.[4] Where, in addition to the insolvency of a railroad company, its property is in the hands of parties who deny the right of the stockholders to share in the management of the property, equity may, in order to afford relief to such stockholders, on their petition, appoint a receiver to take possession of the property.[5] So, if

[1] Denike v. N. Y., etc., Co., 80 N. Y. 599; Farmers' Loan, etc., Co. v. Chicago, etc., R. Co., 27 Fed. R. 146; McGeorge v. Big Stone, etc., Co., 57 Fed. R. 262. In absence of statute, a court of equity has no authority to sit as a court of insolvency to liquidate the affairs of an insolvent railway company. Pond v. Farmingham, etc., R. Co., 130 Mass. 194; Supreme Sitting, etc., v. Baker, 134 Ind. 293; Lawrence, etc., Co. v. Rockbridge Co., (Va.) 47 Fed. R. 755.

[2] Mercantile Trust Co. v. Missouri, etc., Ry. Co., 36 Fed. R. 221; Atlantic Trust Co. v. Consolidated, etc., Co., 49 N. J. Eq. 402, 11 R. & Corp. L. J. 223, 23 Atl. R. 934.

[3] Union T. Co. v. St. Louis, etc., R. Co., 4 Dillon 114; Tysen v. Wabash Ry. Co., 8 Biss. 247.

[4] Smith v. Port Dover, etc., R. Co., 12 Ont. App. R. 288, 25 Am. & Eng. R. Cas. 639.

[5] Bill v. New Albany, etc., R. Co., 2 Biss. (U. S.) 390.

742 THE CORPORATION. § 544

a corporation has been rendered insolvent by the fraudulent mismanagement of its officers, who remain in charge of its affairs, upon a proper application by the parties in interest, its property may be put into the hands of a receiver.[1] So, where the officers of an insolvent corporation resign their respective offices and abandon its property to the court,[2] it is proper to appoint a receiver to take charge of the effects of the corporation and to preserve them for the benefit of all the parties in interest.[3]

§ 544. When insolvency is sufficient without default.—As a general rule inadequacy of mortgage security, coupled with insolvency of the mortgagor, showing that a receiver is necessary, is sufficient ground for the relief.[4] Where the company is manifestly insolvent, is unable to meet its obligations to pay floating debts, and can not borrow money, and is in imminent peril of breaking up, although no default has yet occurred, a receiver may be appointed, at the suit of a bondholder, in order to preserve the corporate property,[5] but a receiver will not be appointed because of expected insolvency at some future time.[6] In all cases it must be shown that the insolvency will endanger or impair the plaintiff's rights unless the property is preserved by a receiver.[7] In general, it is only an extreme case that will move a court of equity to exercise this extraordinary power

---

[1] Forbes v. Memphis, etc., R. Co., 2 Woods (U. S.) 323. See Fisher v. Concord R. Co., 50 N. H. 200.

[2] Smith v. Danzig, 64 How. Pr. (N. Y.) 320.

[3] Gluck and Becker on Rec. of Corp., § 18.

[4] High on Receivers, § 376; Kelly v. Alabama, etc., R. Co., 58 Ala. 489; Ruggles v. Southern Minnesota Railroad, (U. S. Dist. of Minn.) 5 Chicago Legal News 110; Kerp v. Michigan, etc., R. Co., 6 Chicago Legal News 101; Dow v. Memphis, etc., R. Co., 20 Fed. R. 260, 17 Am. & Eng. R. Cas.

324; Cheever v. Rutland, etc., R. Co., 39 Vt. 653. A receiver will be appointed where the purchasers of the equity of redemption at an assignee's sale have diverted the use of the property and appropriated the income to which the mortgagee is entitled. Gest v. New Orleans, etc., R. Co., 30 La. Ann. 28; Ex parte Brown, 58 Ala. 536.

[5] Brassey v. N. Y., etc., R. Co., 19 Fed. R. 663, 17 Am. & Eng. R. Cas. 285.

[6] Edison v. Edison, etc., Co., (N. J. Ch.) 29 Atl. 195.

[7] Lawrence Iron Works v. Rock-

because of insolvency,[1] and it must appear to be necessary in order to preserve the best interests of all concerned.[2] Insolvency is sometimes, by statute, made a ground for the appointment of a receiver,[3] and in that case, when the fact of insolvency is established, the court grants the application as a matter of course.[4]

§ 545. **Default in payment of indebtedness as ground for appointment.**—Receivers are most frequently appointed over railway property in order to protect mortgagees and bondholders whose securities are a lien upon the road, in case of default in payment of the principal or interest upon obligations thus secured.[5] But default in itself is not necessarily ground for this extraordinary remedy;[6] it must be shown, in addition, that ultimate loss will result to the mortgagees or bondholders if the property is permitted to remain in the hands of the company,[7] or that the right of foreclosure exists and that a receiver is necessary to aid the foreclosure.[8] Even

---

bridge Co., 47 Fed. R. 755; McGeorge v. Big Stone Gap Imp. Co., 57 Fed. R. 262.

[1] Pullan v. Cincinnati, etc., R. Co., 4 Biss. (U. S.) 35.

[2] Stark v. Burke, 5 La. Ann. 740; People v. Northern R. R. Co., 42 N. Y. 217.

[3] Sewell v. Cape May, etc., R. Co., 30 Am. & Eng. R. Cas. 155. Failure to pay a judgment duly rendered is cause for the appointment of a receiver by the laws of England and of Kentucky. Eng. Railway Companies Act, § 4; Acts 1890, Ky. Ch. 1039, § 1. The appointment of a receiver or manager under this section is a matter of right whenever the judgment creditor of a railroad corporation is unpaid. *In re* Manchester, etc., R. Co., L. R. 14 Ch. Div. 645.

[4] Beach on Receivers, § 417; Attorney-General v. Bank of Columbia, 1 Paige 511. The facts showing insolvency should be specifically set forth as a mere general allegation is usually held insufficient. Newfoundland, etc., Co. v. Schack, 40 N. J. Eq. 222; Bank of Florence v. United States, etc., Co., 104 Ala. 297, 16 So. R. 110.

[5] High on Receivers, § 376.

[6] Sage v. Memphis, etc., R. Co., 125 U. S. 361; Morrison v. Buckner, 1 Hempst. (U. S.) 442; Whitehead v. Wooten, 43 Miss. 523; Am. Loan & Trust Co. v. Toledo, etc., R. Co., 29 Fed. R. 416; Tysen v. Wabash, etc., Ry. Co., 8 Bissell 247; Williamson v. New Albany R. Co., 1 Biss. 198; Beach on Receivers, § 330.

[7] Union Trust Co. v. St. Louis, etc., R. Co., 4 Dill. (U. S.) 114; Cheever v. Rutland, etc., R. Co., 39 Vt. 653.

[8] American Loan & Trust Co. v. Toledo, etc., R. Co., 29 Fed. R. 416; Beach on Receivers, § 331.

though possession has been refused upon a demand made by trustees under a mortgage after there has been a default in the payment of interest upon bonds secured thereby, a receiver will not be appointed unless it is shown to be necessary in order to prevent loss to the bondholders,[1] and it has been held that a receiver will not be appointed in a case where the default is waived by agreement for extension of time, but the directors afterward disagree and a portion of them rescind the agreement and petition for a receiver.[2] But where, in case of default, there is some other attendant circumstance or condition present which endangers the security of a bondholder, creditor or other party in interest, or where the default is evidence of, or accompanies, some fraudulent or unwise mismanagement by the officers or directors which threatens loss to stockholders or others, a receiver may be appointed, as, for instance, where there has been a default for ten years in the payment of interest on the company's bonds, and the officers refuse to permit an inspection of the company's books by the bondholders,[3] or where trustees fail to take possession of the trust property upon default, as required by the instrument creating the trust, and this without regard to any probable deficiency of the trust property to discharge the debts secured by the deed of trust.[4] Where the mortgage covers the tolls and income of a road and the earnings are diverted, causing default in payment of the mortgage debt, a receiver will ordinarily be appointed,[5] whether the default be followed by foreclosure or

[1] Union Trust Co. v. St. Louis, etc., Co., 4 Dill. (U. S.) 114; Cheever v. Rutland, etc., R. Co., 39 Vt. 653.

[2] Am. L. & T. Co. v. Toledo, etc., R. Co., 29 Fed. R. 416.

[3] Pullan v. Cincinnati, etc., R. Co., 4 Biss. (U. S.) 35.

[4] Wilmer v. Atlanta, etc., R. Co., 2 Woods 409; Shaw v. Norfolk Co. R. Co., 5 Gray (Mass.) 162. See Sacramento, etc., R. Co. v. Superior Court, 55 Cal. 453; Rice v. St. Paul, etc., R. Co., 24 Minn. 464. It has been held that where the deed of trust authorized trustees to take possession upon default, the default itself is sufficient ground for a receiver, without reference to the inadequacy of the mortgage security. Allen v. D. & W. R. Co., 3 Woods 316.

[5] Ruggles v. Southern Minnesota R. Co., 5 Chic. L. N. 110; Hopkins v. Worcester and Birmingham Canal Proprietors, L. R. 6 Eq. 437; De Winton v. Mayor of Brecon, 26 Beav. 533; Allen v. Dallas, etc., R. Co., 3

not. Default in the payment of taxes, the company allowing portions of its property to be sold for such taxes, has been held to be a strong indication of such hopeless insolvency as would justify the appointment of a receiver.¹ A receiver may be appointed before default where insolvency is manifest and it is shown that default is imminent and that the corporation is on the verge of dissolution.² So, a receiver was appointed at the suit of the corporation where it appeared that public interest required that the business be uninterrupted and default in payment of interest would have been followed by such a struggle among creditors as would have prevented continuance of the corporate business.³ As a general rule, however, the plaintiff must first pursue his remedy at law if an adequate remedy is open to him, or if he have a simpler equitable remedy he must pursue that before asking for the extraordinary aid of a receivership; and it has been held that the fact that the right of possession and sale is given to trustees does not change the rule⁴ in case possession is refused. In such cases a receiver will ordinarily be denied unless the trustee has first attempted to recover possession by other legal or equitable means available.⁵ It is held that the fact that the charter of a corporation specially authorizes the appointment of a receiver in a particular contingency does not oust the courts of jurisdiction to appoint one in a proper case.⁶

§ 546. **Appointment in foreclosure proceedings.**—The right to a receiver does not necessarily accompany the right to foreclose;⁷ but it is held to exist in foreclosure proceedings where

---

Woods (U. S.) 316; Whitehead v. Wooten, 43 Miss. 523; Morrison v. Buckner, 1 Hempst. (U. S.) 442.

¹ Putnam v. Jacksonville, etc., Co., 61 Fed. R. 440.

² Brassey v. N. Y., etc., R. Co., 19 Fed. R. 663, s. c. 22 Blatchf. 72; Long Dock Co. v. Mallery, 12 N. J. Eq. 431.

³ Wabash, etc., R. Co. v. Central, etc., Co., 22 Fed. R. 138, s. c. 22 Fed. R. 272, s. c. 23 Fed. R. 513, 515. But see Hugh v. McRae, Chase 466.

⁴ Dow v. Memphis, etc., R. Co., 20 Fed. R. 260; Kennedy v. St. Paul, etc., R. Co., 2 Dill. 448; McLane v. Placerville, etc., R. Co., 66 Cal. 606.

⁵ Rice v. St. Paul, etc., Ry. Co., 24 Minn. 464.

⁶ Fripp v. Chard Ry. Co., 11 Hare 241; Allen v. D. & W. R. Co., 3 Woods 316; Warner v. Rising Fawn Iron Co., 3 Woods 514; note, 64 Am. Dec. 486.

⁷ Mercantile Trust Co. v. Missouri,

for any reason "the complainant will not be in as good a position at the final decree as at present."[1] In the language of a judge who is now a member of the Supreme Court of the United States, "It should appear that there is some danger to the property; that its protection, its preservation, the interests of the various holders, require possession by the court before a receiver should be appointed. It does not go as a matter of course; and yet it is not a matter that a court can refuse simply because it is an annoyance."[2] Generally, insolvency of the mortgagor, coupled with inadequacy of the mortgage security, is sufficient ground for this relief,[3] and when the interest has long been unpaid and the value of the property is manifestly insufficient, a receiver will usually be appointed.[4] If the entire assets of an insolvent corporation are insufficient to afford security for the payment of the mortgage indebtedness, and the corporation is appropriating its earnings to its own use, a receiver will be appointed pending a suit to foreclose,[5] but where it is clear that upon foreclosure the property will bring enough to pay the debt, interest and costs, the court will usually decline to exercise that power on the ground that there

etc., R. Co., 36 Fed. R. 221, 36 Am. & Eng. R. Cas. 259; Am. L. & T. Co. v. Toledo, etc., R. Co., 29 Fed. R. 416; Williamson v. New Albany, etc., R. Co., 1 Biss. (U. S.) 198; Tysen v. Wabash, etc., Co., 8 Biss. 247.

[1] Ruggles v. South. Minn. R. Co., 5 Chic. L. N. 110; Kerp v. Michigan, etc., R. Co., 6 Chic. L. N. 101; U. S. Trust Co. v. N. Y., etc., R. Co., 101 N. Y. 478; Decker v. Gardner, 124 N. Y. 334; U. S. Trust Co. v. N. Y., etc., R. Co., 67 How. Pr. 390.

[2] Mercantile Trust Co. v. Missouri, etc., R. Co., 36 Fed. R. 221, 224, 36 Am. & Eng. R. Cas. 259.

[3] Kelly v. Trustees, 58 Ala. 489; Ruggles v. Southern Minn. R. Co., 5 Chic. L. N. 110; Kerp v. Michigan, etc., R. Co., 6 Chic. L. N. 101; Frelinghuysen v. Colden, 4 Paige Ch. (N. Y.) 204; Astor v. Turner, 2 Barb. (N. Y.) 444.

[4] Pullan v. Cincinnati, etc., R. Co., 4 Biss. 35. See Farmers' L. & T. Co. v. Winona, etc., R. Co., 59 Fed. R. 957.

[5] Dow v. Memphis, etc., R. Co., 20 Fed. R. 260; Cheever v. Rutland, etc., R. Co., 39 Vt. 653. See Brassey v. N. Y., etc., R. Co., 19 Fed. R. 663; Kerp v. Michigan, etc., R. Co., 6 Chic. L. N. 101. The court will never appoint a receiver, except where the right and necessity to do so are clear. Dow v. Memphis, etc., R. Co., *supra;* Overton v. Memphis, etc., R. Co., 10 Fed. R. 866; Texas, etc., R. Co. v. Rust, 17 Fed. R. 275; Sage v. Memphis, etc., R. Co., 18 Fed. R. 571; Credit Co. v. Arkansas Cent. R., 15 Fed. R. 46. See *ante,* § 545.

is another adequate remedy.[1] An application was refused on this ground in a case where mortgagees were seeking to foreclose a mortgage executed by authority of the legislature giving the mortgagees the right of possession.[2] The mere disagreement of mortgage creditors in a suit to foreclose is not sufficient ground for the appointment of a receiver, as equity will not interpose except to afford some incidental relief, and will not extend its arm simply to manage the property.[3] Where the mortgage covers the tolls and income of the road, which would otherwise be diverted from payment of the debt, a receiver will be appointed incidental to foreclosure.[4] So, where a road hopelessly insolvent is about to be foreclosed, and owing to dissensions among bondholders there is no other way to apply the rents and profits of the road to its debts, an application for a receiver may be granted.[5] And a receiver has been appointed, after decree, at the suit of bondholders entitled to the net income, when, according to statute, the sale must be delayed six months.[6] Where, in a suit to foreclose, the court directs the officers of the corporation to remain in possession, to conduct the business subject to its orders, and to account to the

---

[1] Pullan v. Cincinnati, etc., R. Co., 4 Biss. (U. S.) 35; Shotwell v. Smith, 3 Edw. Ch. (N. Y.) 588; Burlingame v. Parce, 12 Hun (N. Y.) 144. Where a railroad company has sublet a leased line contrary to the provisions of the lease, a receiver will not be appointed in a suit by the lessor to enforce a forfeiture of the lease when it appears that the lessor is responsible, and is operating the road. Boston, C. & M. R. R. v. Boston, etc., R., 65 N. H. 393.

[2] Rice v. St. Paul, etc., R. Co., 24 Minn. 464. See, also, Patten v. Accessory Transit Co., 4 Abb. Pr. (N.Y.) 235; Boston, etc., R. Co. v. New York, etc., R. Co., 12 R. I. 220.

[3] American L. & T. Co. v. Toledo, etc., R. Co., 29 Fed. R. 416. But the fact that the company is well managed does not always preclude the appointment of a receiver. Van Benthuysen v. Central, etc., R. Co., 63 Hun 627.

[4] De Winton v. Mayor of Brecon, 26 Beav. 533; Allen v. Dallas, etc., R. Co., 3 Woods (U. S.) 316. This follows the general doctrine that where the mortgage provides that the mortgagee shall have the rents, default in payment of the debt may be sufficient cause for appointment of a receiver to collect such rents. See Whitehead v. Wooten, 43 Miss. 523.

[5] Mercantile Trust Co. v. Missouri, etc., R. Co., 36 Fed. R. 221, 36 Am. & Eng. R. Cas. 259.

[6] Benedict v. St. J. & W. R. Co., 19 Fed. R. 173.

court, it has been held that these officers are thereby constituted receivers of the court.[1]

§ 547. **Other grounds for appointment.**—It is difficult to classify the cases in which a receiver will be appointed, for the reason that the grounds and purpose of the relief and the extent to which it may be pursued, lie so largely in the discretion of the court. There is a large number of cases in which receivers have been appointed which do not fall under the classes just discussed. Where there is no person authorized to hold the corporate property, the majority of the stockholders failing to elect directors,[2] or where the corporation has ceased to act and the officers have converted the property to their own use;[3] when the officers, owning a majority of the stock and controlling the road, fail to keep it in repair, thereby endangering the rights of stockholders and rendering the road unproductive,[4] or squander or embezzle its assets, with the connivance of the directors;[5] where the directors execute a lease, which works injury to the stockholders, in violation of a by-law forbidding contracts involving the franchises of the road;[6] where purchasers of an assignee in bankruptcy are operating the road for their exclusive benefit and appropriate the income to which the mortgage bondholders are entitled;[7] or where the governing body is so divided by dissension that it can not conduct the corporate business,[8] a receiver may be appointed upon

---

[1] *In re* Fifty-four First Mortgage Bonds, 15 S. C. 304; *Ex parte* Brown, 15 S. C. 518. See *Ex parte* Williams, 18 S. C. 299, as to rights of purchasers in such a case.

[2] Lawrence *v.* Greenwich Fire Ins. Co., 1 Paige (N. Y.) 587; Dobson *v.* Simonton, 78 N. C. 63; Edison *v.* Edison, etc., Co., 52 N. J. Eq. 620, 29 Atl. R. 195.

[3] Conro *v.* Gray, 4 How. Pr. (N. Y.) 166; Chicago, etc., R. Co. *v.* Cason, 133 Ind. 49.

[4] Wayne Pike Co. *v.* Hammons, 129 Ind. 368, 27 N. E. 487, 491.

[5] Forbes *v.* Memphis, etc., R. Co., 2 Woods (U. S.) 323; Fisher *v.* Concord R. Co., 50 N. H. 200. A receiver may be appointed to investigate the validity of sales made by a corporation, during and with knowledge of insolvency. Nichols *v.* Perry, 11 N. J. Eq. 126.

[6] Stevens *v.* Davidson, 18 Gratt. (Va.) 819.

[7] Gest *v.* New Orleans, etc., Ry. Co., 30 La. Ann. 28.

[8] Featherstone *v.* Cooke, L. R. 16 Eq. Cas. 298; Trade Auxiliary Co. *v.* Vickers, L. R. 16 Eq. Cas. 303; Edison *v.* Edison, etc., Co., 52 N. J. Eq. 620, 29 Atl. R. 195.

§ 547 RECEIVERS. 749

proper application. So, where several railroad companies, tenants in common of the right to pass through a tunnel or to use a railroad station erected for their joint use,[1] are engaged in a dispute as to their respective rights therein, the court may appoint a receiver to protect the rights of the injured party, if such rights can not readily be protected by other means. The dissolution of a corporation by decree of court is cause for the appointment of a statutory receiver in most, if not all, of the states.[2] It has been held that bondholders have a right to have a receiver appointed to complete a road, the construction of which has been stopped on account of lack of funds, when completion by a certain time is the condition of a valuable land grant which constitutes their principal security.[3] The fact that stockholders of a corporation disobey an injunction restraining them from voting to effect an illegal or unauthorized consolidation, is not a ground for the appointment of a receiver for the corporation, since, in the absence of any authority to consolidate, the original corporation would continue to exist in its integrity, with all its rights of property and franchises unaffected by such acts of the stockholders.[4] Where the application alleges that all the property of the company is mortgaged to one class of creditors; that it owes large amounts to other creditors, one of whom has attached all its property, and that it is proposing to lease its property to him for a long term

---

[1] Delaware, etc., R. Co. v. Erie R. Co., 21 N. J. Eq. 298; Russell v. East Anglican R. Co., 3 M. & G. 104; Fripp v. Chard R. Co., 11 Hare 239; Shrewsbury R. Co. v. Chester R. Co., 14 L. T. 217, 433; Midland R. Co. v. Ambergate R. Co., 10 Hare 359; Beach on Receivers, § 339.

[2] Stimson's Am. Stat. (1892), § 8335. See Texas Trunk R. Co. v. State, 83 Tex. 1, 18 S. W. 199, holding that a court declaring a forfeiture of the franchises of a railroad company, may appoint a receiver to operate the road in such a manner as to subserve the public interests.

[3] Allen v. Dallas, etc., R. Co., 3 Woods (U. S.) 316; Kennedy v. St. Paul, etc., R. Co., 2 Dillon (U. S.) 448.

[4] Railway Co. v. Jewett, 37 Ohio St. 649. Injunction, at the suit of the state, to prevent a corporation from misusing and abusing its corporate franchises and privileges and maintaining its property as a nuisance, though its acts also constitute a crime, may be aided, when necessary, by the more effective remedy of a receiver. Columbian Athletic Club v. State, 143 Ind. 98, s. c. 40 N. E. R. 914.

of years at a rental which is insufficient to pay the interest upon its indebtedness, but there is no allegation that the plaintiff has any lien upon, or any particular right in, any of the property, and there is no showing of any fraud or breach of trust on the part of those who are managing the corporate affairs, a receiver will not be appointed.[1] It has also been held that a receiver will not be appointed at the suit of one who has purchased stock alleged to have been illegally issued, and who claims the right to recover the purchase-price of such stock, when it appears that the money received for the sale of the stock has been mingled with the general funds of the corporation, so that it can not be traced nor identified.[2] Failure to perform a public duty has been held to be ground for the appointment of a receiver;[3] but the doctrine has not received any general application, and is of doubtful soundness. Indeed, we think it is clearly unsound as applied to ordinary cases in which there is nothing more than nonfeasance.

§ 548. Appointment upon application of unsecured creditors.—Ordinarily the application of unsecured creditors for the appointment of a receiver will be denied on the ground that there is a remedy at law;[4] but when the remedy at law has been found unavailing or is manifestly useless,[5] and the corporation has equitable assets which are not available upon execution,[6] or which are in danger of being dissi-

[1] Pond v. Farmingham, etc., R. Co., 130 Mass. 194.
[2] Whelpley v. Erie R. Co., 6 Blatchf. (U. S. C. C.) 271.
[3] In re Long Branch, etc., R. Co., 24 N. J. Eq. 398; Fishback v. Citizens' St. Ry. Co., Nat. Corp. Rep. (Ind. Super. Ct. of Marion county), March 4, 1892; Beach on Receivers, § 329.
[4] Putnam v. Jacksonville, etc., Ry. Co., 61 Fed. Rep. 440; Milwaukee, etc., R. Co. v. Soutter, 2 Wall. 510, 523; Parmly v. Tenth Ward Bank, 3 Edw. Ch. 395 (417); Beach Law of Railways, § 696; High on Receivers, § 10, and cases cited. The case must undoubtedly be exceptional to justify this relief in a suit by a simple creditor. Johnson v. Farnum, 56 Ga. 144; Ballin v. Ferst, 55 Ga. 546; Gregory v. Gregory, 1 J. & S. 1. See 3 Pom. Eq. Jur., § 1334.
[5] Sage v. Memphis, etc., R. Co., 125 U. S. 361; Conro v. Gray, 4 How. Pr. (N. Y.) 166; State v. Georgia Co., (N. C.) 54 Am. & Eng. R. Cas. 299.
[6] Covington Draw Bridge Co. v. Shepherd, 21 How. (U. S.) 112; Furness v. Caterham R. Co., 25 Beav. 614; Palmer v. Clark, 4 Abb. N. C.

pated[1] the equitable relief may be invoked; but courts have refused to interfere where the liability had not been liquidated or established,[2] where labor claims existed against several companies operating one road, but their accounts were in confusion, and the distribution of the debt was in doubt, such claims not having been reduced to judgment;[3] and in one case, where a receiver was about to be discharged, the court refused to continue him in order to settle claims which were in dispute, and which were comparatively small.[4] Where it appears that an execution issued upon a judgment against the corporation has been returned *nulla bona*, but that there are equitable assets which can not be reached by execution a court of equity will appoint a receiver.[5] And even though no execution has

(N.Y.) 25; Wood *v.* Dummer, 3 Mason 308; Ward *v.* Mfg. Co., 16 Conn. 593; Adler *v.* Milwaukee Mfg. Co., 13 Wis. 57 (63); Griffith *v.* Mangam, 73 N. Y. 611; Bartlett *v.* Drew, 57 N. Y. 587; Curling *v.* Marquis Townshend, 19 Ves. 628; Bloodgood *v.* Clark, 4 Paige 574; Osborn *v.* Heyer, 2 Paige 342; Johnson *v.* Tucker, 2 Tenn. Ch. 398.

[1] Turnbull *v.* Prentiss Lumber Co., 55 Mich. 387.

[2] Cook *v.* Detroit, etc., R. Co., 45 Mich. 453; Putnam *v.* Jacksonville, etc., R. Co., 61 Fed. Rep. 440.

[3] Putnam *v.* Jacksonville, etc., R. Co., 61 Fed. Rep. 440.

[4] Milwaukee, etc., R. Co. *v.* Soutter, 2 Wall. 510, 523.

[5] Covington Draw Bridge Co. *v.* Shepherd, 21 How. (U. S.) 112; Furness *v.* Caterham R. Co., 25 Beav. 614; Palmer *v.* Clark, 4 Abb. N. C. (N.Y.) 25; Wood *v.* Dummer, 3 Mason 308; Ward *v.* Mfg. Co., 16 Conn. 593; Adler *v.* Milwaukee, etc., Co., 13 Wis. 57 (63); Griffith *v.* Mangam, 73 N. Y. 611; Bartlett *v.* Drew, 57 N. Y. 587. In Union Trust Co. *v.* Illinois Midland R. Co., 117 U. S. 434, 458, the court said: "The coplaintiffs with Hervey were judgment creditors of the Paris and Decatur Co., with executions returned unsatisfied. The bill set out the precarious condition of all the property held and used by the Illinois Midland Co., and the necessity for a receiver in the interest of all the creditors of all four of the corporations [the Illinois Midland Co., and the three corporations of which it was composed, and whose debts it had assumed] to prevent the levy of executions upon such property; and it prayed for a judicial ascertainment and marshalling of all the debts of all the corporations, and their payment and adjustment as the respective rights and interests of the creditors might appear, and for general relief. The plaintiffs set forth that they represented a majority of the stock in all the corporations. This bill was quite sufficient to enable a court of equity to administer the property and marshal the debts, including those due the mortgage bondholders, making proper parties before adjudging the merits." Courts are sometimes required by statute to make an appointment under such circumstances. *In re* Manchester, etc., R. Co., L. R. 14 Ch. Div. 645. But it generally rests in the

been issued in the latter case circumstances may be present which call for the same remedy.[1] An application by a judgment creditor for the appointment of a receiver may be entertained where the bill alleges that the property is so heavily mortgaged that any attempt to enforce the plaintiff's debt by sale on execution would be unavailing, since no bids for more than a nominal amount would be received; while if the property were placed in the hands of a receiver and carefully operated for the transportation of passengers and freight there would be a large surplus each year for the payment of his debt.[2] The equitable aid formerly so frequently invoked to assist creditors at large,

---

discretion of the court, in view of all the circumstances. Plaintiff alleged that he had recovered a judgment against one of the defendant companies, and that it had transferred its road to the other defendant, that the grantee never operated the road, nor had the grantor any power to make the transfer, which was made for the sole purpose of defrauding plaintiff; and it prayed a receiver. A receiver was appointed. Louisville and St. L. Ry. Co. v. Southworth, 38 Ill. App. 225.

[1] Sage v. Memphis, etc., R. Co., 125 U. S. 361; Conro v. Gray, 4 How. Pr. (N. Y.) 166. A tax is a "debt" which the state and county may enforce against a corporation by creditors' bill for the appointment of a receiver. The state and county are not precluded from bringing such a suit because there is a specific remedy for the collection of taxes in the revenue act; nor because the state has the right to have the charter of the corporation declared forfeited when it fails to pay its taxes. State v. Georgia Co., (N. Car., 1893) 54 Am. & Eng. R. Cas. 299. In Kentucky the enforcement of judgments against railway companies, by an equitable suit for the appointment of a receiver to take possession of and operate the road until the debts against the company shall be paid is provided for by statute. Act April 24, 1890, (Pub. Acts 1889–90, c. 1039, p. 109).

[2] Sage v. Memphis, etc., R. Co., 125 U. S. 361. In announcing the opinion of the court in this case, Mr. Justice Harlan said: "We do not mean to say that a single judgment creditor or any number of such creditors of a railroad company are entitled, as matter of right, to have its property put in the hands of a receiver, merely because of its failure or refusal to pay its debts. Whether a receiver shall be appointed is always a matter of discretion, to be exercised sparingly and with great caution in the case of *quasi* public corporations operating a public highway, and always with reference to the special circumstances of each case as it arises. All that we say in this connection is that, under the circumstances presented in this case, the appointment of a receiver was within the power of the court. The order appointing him to operate and manage the property was not a nullity." See, also, Sage v. Memphis, etc., R. Co., 18 Fed. Rep. 571, where the receiver was discharged because appointed by collusion.

grew out of the narrowness of the legal remedy by execution, often useless because it could not reach equitable assets.[1] In many of the code states statutory provision has been made for the appointment of receivers in proceedings supplementary to execution, thus doing away in some cases with the "creditors' bill" of chancery practice;[2] and in addition the statutes have given wider scope to the writ of execution, extending legal relief to many cases where resort to equity was formerly necessary. Thus the instances in which the unsecured creditor has no other remedy are now less numerous than under the English chancery practice and the requirement that a strong, clear case must be made,[3] in connection with the reluctance of the courts to divest such large interests of the corporate management in order to satisfy claims which are generally comparatively small,[4] has resulted in a very rare and sparing exercise of this power of the court of equity in aid of the unsecured creditor of a railway corporation, although the appointment of a statutory receiver of the effects of a judgment debtor, on supplementary proceedings, is very frequent.[5]

§ 549. **Appointment upon application of secured creditors.**—It is to preserve the security of the mortgagee or bondholder that the control of the property and business of railway corporations is most often assumed by a court of equity.[6] Besides being available in connection with foreclosures[7] the remedy of a receivership is often employed at the suit of mortgagees or bondholders in cases of default,[8] insolvency,[9] fraud or mismanagement by officers, or the commission of some other act that endangers the mortgage security.[10] Exigencies may arise to threaten the destruction or depreciate the value of the property which would not

[1] 3 Pom. Eq. Jur., § 1415.
[2] High on Receivers, § 401.
[3] 3 Pom. Eq. Jur., § 1415.
[4] Milwaukee, etc., Co. v. Soutter, 2 Wall. 510, 523. Under N. Y. statute receiver will not be appointed at suit of a creditor at large. Lehigh, etc., Co. v. Central R. of N. J., 43 Hun 546.
[5] Heroy v. Gibson, 10 Bosw. 591; Coates v. Wilkes, 92 N. C. 376; Flint v. Webb, 25 Minn. 263.
[6] High on Receivers, § 376; *ante*, § 545, and cases cited.
[7] See *ante*, § 546.
[8] See *ante*, § 545.
[9] See *ante*, § 543.
[10] See *ante*, § 547.

justify foreclosure and which might, before cause for foreclosure could accrue, materially impair the petitioner's security,[1] and equity many times intervenes with a receiver in such cases; or in cases where the mortgage covers the tolls and income of the road, they may be so diverted as to give cause for the appointment of a receiver.[2] Where bonds are secured by a deed of trust in the nature of a mortgage, it is frequently provided that the mortgagee or trustee may take possession upon default. In that case, if the trustees, being denied possession, have a remedy at law or an ordinary remedy in equity to obtain possession, they must, as a rule, first pursue such remedy before a receiver will be appointed[3] unless such remedy be manifestly useless[4] or such a condition exist as would make a receiver necessary immediately after possession should be acquired.[5] Where there is a trust deed in the nature of a mortgage, the trustee must first have failed, refused or neglected to perform his duty under the trust deed before the individual bondholder can himself petition for a receiver, to act instead of the trustee, or in conjunction with him, but where the trustee has failed to do his duty the bondholder may invoke the aid of a receiver.[6] And it has been held that when the trustee, on being applied to in pursuance of the terms of the trust, refuses to sue, the bondholders may themselves sue, but must make

---

[1] Brassey v. New York, etc., R. Co., 19 Fed. R. 663, 17 Am. & Eng. R. Cas. 285; American L. & T. Co. v. Toledo, etc., R. Co., 29 Fed. R. 416, 417; Kennedy v. St. Paul, etc., Co., 2 Dill. 448; Whelpley v. Erie R. R. Co., 6 Blatch. 271; Long Dock Co. v. Mallery, 12 N. J. Eq. 431; Mercantile Trust Co. v. Missouri, etc., R. Co., 36 Fed. R. 221; Penn. Co.,etc., v. Jacksonville, etc., R. Co., 55 Fed. R. 131.

[2] Dumville v. Ashbrooke, 3 Russ. 99, note *; Hopkins v. Worcester, etc., Proprietors, L. R. 6 Eq.437; Ruggles v. Southern Minn. Railroad, 5 Chic. L. N. 110; Tysen v. Wabash Ry. Co., 8 Biss. 247; Allen v. Dallas, etc., R. Co., 3 Woods 316, 326.

[3] Rice v. St. Paul, etc., R. Co., 24 Minn. 464; High on Receivers, §379.

[4] Imperial Mercantile Credit Association v. Newry, etc., R. Co., Ir. Rep. 2 Eq. 1.

[5] Crewe v. Edleston, 1 DeG. & J. 93, 109, per Lord Justice Turner; Allen v. Dallas, etc., R. Co., 3 Woods (U. S.) 316; High on Receivers, §382.

[6] Shaw v. Norfolk, etc., R. Co., 5 Gray (Mass.) 162; Wilmer v. Atlanta, etc., R. Co., 2 Woods (U. S.) 409; Sacramento, etc., R. Co. v. Superior Ct., 55 Cal. 453; Rice v. St. Paul, etc., R. Co., 24 Minn. 464.

§ 549   RECEIVERS.   755

the trustee, the corporation and all other bondholders parties.[1] If one or more bondholders have a right to institute proceedings they necessarily act for all standing in a similar position and can not secure individual relief at the expense of others holding the same security;[2] and it has been held that where the sufficiency of the security is doubtful all other creditors similarly situated must have notice in order that they may protect their interests.[3] The rule laid down by Lord Eldon in the leading English case has been followed in some states as the fundamental law concerning the right of a junior mortgagee to invoke the appointment of a receiver, but it is based upon the common law theory of the mortgage. This rule is to the effect that while the first mortgagee is in possession and any portion of the mortgage debt remains unpaid,[4] the junior mortgagee can only secure the appointment of a receiver by paying off the balance of the first mortgage or offering to pay such claim, and in the general application of the rule it has been held that where the elder mortgagee has not asserted his right to possession or to the rents and income the junior mortgagee has a right to do so;[5] but a receivership on the application of the junior mortgagee will not operate to defeat the priority or the rights of the elder mortgagee,[6] except that in some cases it is held that his right of election to take possession is defeated,[7] the court

[1] Commonwealth v. Susquehanna, etc., R. Co., 122 Pa. St. 306.

[2] Jackson v. Ludeling, 21 Wall. 616; Vose v. Bronson, 6 Wall. 452; Stanton v. Alabama, etc., R. Co., 2 Woods 523; New Orleans, etc., R. Co. v. Parker, 143 U. S. 42, 58; Galveston Railway v. Cowdrey, 11 Wall. 459.

[3] Railway Co. v. Orr, 18 Wall. 471. See Overton v. Memphis, etc., R. Co., 10 Fed. R. 866; Pennock v. Coe, 23 How. 117; Taylor on Priv. Corp., § 815.

[4] Berney v. Sewell, 1 Jac. & W. 627.

[5] Ranney v. Peyser, 83 N. Y. 1; Howell v. Ripley, 10 Paige 43; Miltenberger v. Logansport, etc., R. Co., 106 U. S. 286, 1 Sup. Ct. R. 140.

[6] Berney v. Sewell, 1 Jac. & W. 627; Cortleyeu v. Hathaway, 11 N. J. Eq. 42, s. c. 64 Am. Dec. 478.

[7] Beverly v. Brooke, 4 Grattan 187; High on Receivers, § 689. Lord Eldon, in Berney v. Sewell, 1 Jac. & W. 627, held that the appointment of a receiver at the application of a junior mortgagee could not prejudice the right of the elder mortgagee to take possession at any time and thus dispossess the receiver. It seems, however, that this doctrine has yielded in Virginia to the generally accepted

having taken possession for all parties. The stringency of this rule has been relaxed in many of the states, in the federal courts and even in rare English cases, and where a clear case is made showing that the mortgagee in possession is irresponsible, is committing waste or material injury, endangering the security, or is fraudulently or carelessly mismanaging the property so as to impair the junior mortgage, a receiver may be appointed at the suit of the junior mortgagee.[1] As we have seen if the senior mortgagee be in possession and conduct the business so as to imperil the second mortgage security a receiver may be appointed, or if he have the right, by the terms of his mortgage, to take possession and refuses or neglects to do so, the junior mortgagee may sometimes invoke the aid of a receiver to secure the rents and profits. So, also, in cases where the mortgagor retains possession, the junior mortgagee may sometimes invoke the remedy to insure the proper management of the property and to compel the proper application of the revenues. It has been held that at the petition of the junior mortgagee a receiver may be directed to borrow money in order to pay the interest on first mortgage bonds where default would precipitate foreclosure and prove disastrous to the second mortgage security[2] and a receiver has been appointed on the application of a junior mortgagee to operate a road and apply the revenues where lack of harmony existed in the management, and without the rents and profits the security was wholly inadequate, and where, under the existing management, the junior mortgagee might be postponed indefinitely.[3] The interference of the court under such circumstances rests upon the

theory that a receiver, as an officer of the court, takes possession for all parties in interest and holds such possession until his function is discharged.

[1] Bolles v. Duff, 35 How. Pr. (N. Y.) 481; Williams v. Robinson, 16 Conn. 517; Beverly v. Brooke, 4 Gratt. (Va.) 187; Meaden v. Sealey, 6 Hare 620; Codrington v. Parker, 16 Ves. 469; Lloyd v. Passingham, 16 Ves. 59; Huguenin v. Baseley, 13 Ves. 105; Corcoran v. Doll, 35 Cal. 476; Rowe v. Wood, 2 Jac. & W. 553; Boston, etc., R. Co. v. New York, etc., R. Co., 12 R. I. 220; Wiltsie on Mortgage Foreclosures, § 680.

[2] Lloyd v. Chesapeake, etc., R. Co., 65 Fed. R. 351.

[3] Mercantile Trust Co. v. Missouri, etc., R. Co., 36 Fed. R. 221, s. c. 1 L. R. A. 397.

ground of necessity to compel a proper application of the revenues, and prevent dissipation of the property.[1] In case the mortgage security is inadequate, the debtor insolvent, and the property about to be sold for taxes, a junior mortgagee, whose debt is not due, may, pending foreclosure, have an interlocutory order appointing a receiver to collect rents.[2]

§ 550. **Appointment upon application of stockholders.**—As a general rule a receiver will not be appointed upon the application of a stockholder, because of mismanagement or internal dissensions, until after he has applied to the directors and officers of the corporation, and, in some cases, to the other stockholders.[3] But, as we have already seen,[4] where the directors and persons in charge are fraudulently depriving the minority stockholders of their rights, dissipating the property and the like, so that it would be useless to apply to them for relief, and especially if they have already brought about a state of insolvency, a receiver may generally be appointed on the application of stockholders.[5] So, where a controlling interest in the stock of one railroad company was purchased by another, which thus secured the election of a board of trustees consisting of its own officers and employes, and such board

---

[1] Hiles v. Moore, 15 Beav. 175; Bryan v. Cormick, 1 Cox 422; High on Receivers, § 682.

[2] Buchanan v. Berkshire, etc., Co., 96 Ind. 510, 531.

[3] Hand v. Dexter, 41 Ga. 454; Converse v. Dimock, 22 Fed. R. 573; Rathbone v. Parkersburg, etc., Co., 31 W. Va. 798; Strong v. McCagg, 55 Wis. 624; Pond v. Framingham, etc., R. Co., 130 Mass. 194; Hawes v. Oakland, 104 U. S. 450. See, also, Roman v. Woolfolk, 98 Ala. 219, s. c. 13 So. R. 212; Hardee v. Sunset Oil Co., 56 Fed. R. 51; Wheeler v. Pullman, etc., Co., 143 Ill. 197, s. c. 17 L. R. A. 818.

[4] *Ante*, §§ 543, 547.

[5] See 1 Morawetz Priv. Corp., §§ 242, 245, 273; Miner v. Belle Isle, etc., Co., 93 Mich. 97, s. c. 17 L. R. A. 412; State v. Second Judicial Dist. Ct., (Mont.) 27 L. R. A. 392; Featherstone v. Cooke, L. R. 16 Eq. 298; Albert v. State, 65 Ind. 413; Hall v. Astoria, etc., Co., 5 Ry. & Corp. L. J. 412; Wayne Pike Co. v. Hammons, 129 Ind. 368; Conro v. Gray, 4 How. Pr. (N. Y.) 166; Haywood v. Lincoln Lumber Co., 64 Wis. 639; Porter v. Industrial, etc., Co., 25 N. Y. Supp. 328; Towle v. American, etc., Society, 60 Fed. R. 131; *In re* Lewis, 52 Kan. 660, s. c. 35 Pac. R. 287. Several of these decisions are based on statutory provisions, but the others seem to have been decided on general principles of equity.

then executed an illegal traffic agreement or lease whereby the entire control of the franchises and property of the former company was surrendered to the latter, it was held that minority stockholders of the former could maintain a bill to annul such agreement without first applying to the board of trustees for relief, and the court appointed a receiver upon their application, which also showed that the company, as managed by the company owning the majority of its shares, could not pay operating expenses and was wholly insolvent.[1] But a receiver will not be appointed upon the application of a stockholder acting in the interest of persons hostile to the company;[2] and mere insolvency is generally insufficient to authorize the appointment of a receiver at the instance of a stockholder, in the absence of any statutory provision upon the subject.[3] In many of the states, however, there are statutory provisions authorizing the appointment of a receiver, in certain cases, at the suit of a stockholder.[4] A former shareholder is not entitled to a receiver, upon the ground of mismanagement by the officers and directors, after he has parted with all his interest in the corporation and its effects,[5] and in no case in which a stockholder seeks the appointment of a receiver upon the ground of a breach of trust or mismanagement by those in control will the court appoint a receiver if he has participated or acquiesced for a long time therein.[6]

§ 551. Appointment upon application of corporation.—A receiver may be appointed, in a proper case, upon the applica-

[1] Earle v. Seattle, etc., Ry. Co., 56 Fed. R. 909. See, also, Evans v. Union Pac. Ry. Co., 58 Fed. R. 497; Stevens v. Davison, 18 Gratt. (Va.) 819. In Putnam v. Ruch, 54 Fed. R. 216, a receiver was appointed upon the application of a stockholder because the charter had been repealed.

[2] Belmont v. Erie Ry. Co., 52 Barb. (N. Y.) 637.

[3] Merryman v. Carroll, etc., Co., 4 Ry. & Corp. L. J. 12; ante, § 543.

[4] See Supreme Sitting, etc., v. Baker, (Ind.) 20 L. R. A. 210, and note, where the statutes are referred to and the authorities reviewed.

[5] Smith v. Wells, 20 How. Pr. (N. Y.) 158. See, also, Dimpfell v. Ohio, etc., Ry. Co., 110 U. S. 209, s. c. 3 Sup. Ct. R. 573.

[6] Hyde Park, etc., Co. v. Kerber, 5 Bradw. (Ill.) 132; Gray v. Chaplin, 2 Russ. 126; Hager v. Stevens, 2 Halst. Ch. 374 (6 N. J. Eq. 374); Hood v. First Nat. Bank, 29 Fed. R. 55; Downing v. Dunlap, etc., Ry. Co., 93 Tenn. 221, s. c. 24 S. W. R. 122.

tion of the company itself. Thus, it has been held that a receiver may be appointed upon the application of a railroad company where it is shown that the company is hopelessly insolvent, that its property is likely to be seized by different courts and scattered abroad, its assets dissipated and its system disrupted and broken up into fragments to the irreparable injury and damage of all persons having an interest in the road.[1] It is said, however, that the court, in such a case, can not displace vested liens, but must require the property to be held and preserved by the receiver for the benefit of all concerned, as their interests may appear.[2] It undoubtedly requires a very strong showing to justify the appointment of a receiver upon the application of the corporation, but we think there are cases in which the court has the power to make the appointment, and is justified in exercising it. There are decisions, however, which seem to hold that a receiver can never be appointed upon the application of the corporation. In one of them it is said that a statutory provision that no receiver of a corporation shall ever be appointed upon its own petition is but a legislative declaration of the rule recognized by courts of equity.[3] In another case it is said: "That a court of equity has no inherent power, except in some few cases of particular jurisdiction, to appoint a receiver, except as an incident to and in a suit pending, has hitherto, with the exception of the Wabash Case,[4] been

[1] Wabash, etc., Ry. Co. v. Central T. Co., 22 Fed. R. 272; Quincy, etc., R. Co. v. Humphreys, 145 U. S. 82, s. c. 12 Sup. Ct. R. 787; Central Trust Co. v. Wabash, etc., Ry. Co., 29 Fed. R. 618, 623; Brassey v. New York, etc., R. Co., 19 Fed. R. 663.

[2] Quincy, etc., R. Co. v. Humphreys, 145 U. S. 82, s. c. 12 Sup. Ct. R. 787.

[3] Texas & P. R. Co. v. Gay, 86 Tex. 571, s. c. 25 L. R. A. 52, citing Robinson v. Hadley, 11 Beav. 614; Leddel v. Starr, 19 N. J. Eq. 159; Marr v. Littlewood, 2 Myl. & Cr. 455. See, also, Kimball v. Goodburn, 32 Mich. 10. In another case the same court suggests that the directors, as trustees for stockholders and creditors, would be the proper parties to institute the suit. McIlheny v. Binz, 80 Tex. 1, s. c. 26 Am. St. R. 705.

[4] Wabash, etc., Ry. Co. v. Central T. Co., 22 Fed. R. 269, and Central Trust Co. v. Wabash, etc., Ry. Co., 29 Fed. R. 618. These cases, which we have already cited, go further, perhaps, than the others heretofore cited in the same connection, and are criticised in one of the Texas cases cited in the preceding note, as well as in the case now under consideration.

a universally accepted doctrine; and outside of that case the doctrine that a court of equity, without statutory authority, has jurisdiction, upon the application of an insolvent corporation, to take charge and administer its affairs through a receiver, not only has no support, but whenever suggested has been repudiated."[1] It may be true that the "Wabash Case," in so far as it seems to authorize the appointment of a receiver, in the absence of a pending suit, violates the general rule, but it is said that there is no rule without exceptions, and, in any event, we think that where a suit is pending, as, for instance, where all interested persons are made parties and the company asks other relief in addition to the appointment of a receiver, the facts may be such and the emergency so great as to require the appointment upon the application of the company.

§ 552. What court may appoint.—The power of appointing a receiver is generally exercised only by courts having original jurisdiction.[2] But where an appellate court has jurisdiction of the suit by appeal, and of the parties, it may appoint a receiver of the property in controversy pending the appeal, if necessary in order to protect its appellate jurisdiction, or to make its decree effective.[3] On the other hand, it has been held that where a mortgage is foreclosed and an appeal taken from the decree of foreclosure, the suit may be considered as still pending for the purpose of an application for a receiver of the rents and profits, and that the court that rendered the decree is the proper

---

[1] State v. Ross, 122 Mo. 435, s. c. 23 L. R. A. 534. Citing Jones v. Bank of Leadville, 10 Colo. 464; French Bank Case, 53 Cal. 495; Smith v. Los Angeles Super. Ct., 97 Cal. 348, 32 Pac. R. 322; Hugh v. McRea, Chase, Dec. 466, Fed. Case No. 6,840; People v. St. Clair Circuit Judge, 31 Mich. 456; Kimball v. Goodburn, 32 Mich. 10; Neall v. Hill, 16 Cal. 145, 76 Am. Dec. 508; French v. Gifford, 30 Iowa 148; Whitehead v. Wooten, 43 Miss. 523; Attorney-General v. Utica Ins. Co., 2 Johns. Ch. 371; Ex parte Whitfield, 2 Atk. 315, 330; Wait Insolv. Corp., § 183; Gluck & B. Receivers, § 27.

[2] Pacific R. Co. v. Ketchum, 95 U. S. 1.

[3] West v. Weaver, 3 Heisk. (Tenn.) 589. See Kerr v. White, 7 Baxt. (Tenn.) 394. For a case where, under the circumstances, the Supreme Court of the United States declined to appoint a receiver, but without denying its jurisdiction to do so, see Pacific R. Co. v. Ketchum, 95 U. S. 1; Pacific R. Co. v. Missouri Pacific R. Co., 15 Am. R. W. R. 80; Allen v. Harris, 4 Lea 190.

court to hear and determine the application.[1] The general rule is that an appeal removes the entire case, or so much as is appealed to the appellate court, but there may be collateral or independent matters, distinct from the questions involved in the appeal, which are not taken from the jurisdiction of the trial court.[2] Owing to the fact that all long lines of railroad pass through many counties, and frequently through several states, and that the immediate jurisdiction of a circuit court of the United States is usually more extensive than that of the local courts, and because it is desirable to have the receiverships of the various parts of a railroad controlled by courts which administer a uniform system of laws and are governed by the same rules when sitting as courts of equity, applications for the appointment of receivers for railroad corporations are usually made to the federal courts. These courts are controlled by the principles of equity as developed in the high court of chancery of England, which principles, indeed, are followed in the interpretation and construction of the various statutes that have been enacted to regulate the appointment of receivers. In the states in which courts of law and courts of equity remain distinct, the power to appoint receivers is usually in the courts of chancery, while in the code states it is usually in the courts of general jurisdiction having both law and equity jurisdiction. The particular court having jurisdiction to appoint a statutory receiver of a corporation for insolvency, non-user or abuse of its corporate rights, or any other cause leading to its dissolution, is generally determined by the statutory law in the several states having statutes upon this subject.[3] It was formerly the practice, in many cases, to refer the matter to a master to select the receiver,[4] but this practice is seldom resorted to at the present time, and, in most

[1] Brinkman v. Ritzinger, 82 Ind. 358. See, also, Beard v. Arbuckle, 19 W. Va. 145; Grantham v. Lucas, 15 W. Va. 425, 431; Lottimer v. Lord, 4 E. D. Smith (N. Y.) 183; Penn Mut. Ins. Co. v. Semple, 38 N. J. Eq. 314. But compare Havemeyer v. Superior Court, 84 Cal. 327, s. c. 18 Am. St. R. 192.

[2] Elliott's App. Proc., §§ 541-546.

[3] Stimson's Am. St. (1892), §§ 8332, 8335, 8360, 8901.

[4] See Wiltsie on Mortg. Foreclosures, §§ 629, 640-644.

jurisdictions, the appointment must be made by the court. A court commissioner, it has been held, has no jurisdiction to appoint a receiver.[1] Where a suit is pending in a federal court for the foreclosure of a railroad mortgage and the appointment of a receiver, it will take jurisdiction of another bill filed by lienholders, without regard to the citizenship of the parties, on the ground that their right to enforce their liens in the state court will be cut off when the federal court takes possession of the property, and hence their suit may be regarded as an ancillary suit.[2]

§ 553. **Court first obtaining jurisdiction retains it—Conflict of jurisdiction.**—The court which first acquires jurisdiction of an action for the appointment of a receiver will retain it to the end of the litigation, to the exclusion of other courts of co-ordinate jurisdiction.[3] One court will not attempt, by a writ of mandamus, to control the action of receivers appointed by another court.[4] A state court will refuse to entertain a suit to foreclose against property in the hands of a federal court,[5] and a federal court will not entertain a bill to compel an accounting by a receiver who is acting under the order of a state court by which he was appointed.[6] Nor will a federal court enjoin a receiver in possession of a railroad under the appointment of a state court from issuing receiver's certificates, or restrain the parties from carrying out an agreement sanctioned by the state court.[7] But the pendency of an action in a state court to set

[1] Quiggle v. Trumbo, 56 Cal. 626.
[2] Central Trust Co. v. Bridges, 57 Fed. R. 753. See, also, Conwell v. White Water Canal Co., 4 Biss. (U. S. C. C.) 195; Krippendorf v. Hyde, 110 U. S. 276, s. c. 4 Sup. Ct. R. 27; Pacific Railroad v. Missouri Pac. Ry. Co., 1 McCrary, 647, s. c. 3 Fed. R. 772.
[3] Gaylord v. Fort Wayne, etc., R. Co., 6 Biss. (U. S.) 286; Bill v. New Albany, etc., R. Co., 2 Biss. (U. S.) 390; Ohio, etc., R. Co. v. Fitch, 20 Ind. 498; McCarthy v. Peake, 18 How. Pr. 138, s. c. 9 Abb. Pr. 164; O'Mahony v. Belmont, 37 N. Y. Super. Ct. 380; Pugh v. Brown, 19 Ohio 202, 211; Stearns v. Stearns, 16 Mass. 167; Judd v. Bankers', etc., Co., 31 Fed. R. 182; High on Receivers, §§ 49, 50.
[4] State v. Marietta, etc., R. Co., 35 Ohio St. 154.
[5] Milwaukee etc., R. Co. v. Milwaukee, etc., R. Co., 20 Wis. 165, (174).
[6] Conkling v. Butler, 4 Biss. (U. S.) 22.
[7] Reinach v. Atlantic, etc., R. Co., 58 Fed. R. 33.

aside an assignment as fraudulent and have a receiver appointed has been held to be no bar to a creditors' bill in a federal court by parties not before the state court.[1] Where a receiver has been regularly appointed and has obtained possession of the property, he can not be interfered with by the officers of another court in which a second suit has been begun.[2] Indeed it would seem to be the better law that it is not necessary that the court which first takes jurisdiction of the case, shall also first take, by its officers, actual possession of the property in controversy, and that it is sufficient that it shall have jurisdiction of the subject-matter and of the parties, and that its aid shall have been regularly invoked.[3] The fact

[1] Rejall v. Greenhood, 60 Fed. R. 784. But see Central Trust Co. v. South Atlantic, etc., R. Co., 57 Fed. R. 3.

[2] Young v. Montgomery, etc., R. Co., 2 Woods (U. S.) 606; Wilmer v. Atlanta, etc., R. Co., 2 Woods 409; Fort Wayne, etc., R. Co. v. Mellett, 92 Ind. 535; O'Mahony v. Belmont, 5 J. & S. (N. Y.) 380. Property in the hands of a receiver of a state court can not be levied upon by the United States marshal in behalf of a judgment creditor. Wiswall v. Sampson, 14 How. (U. S.) 52.

[3] Illinois Steel Co. v. Putnam, 68 Fed. R. 515; Adams v. Mercantile Trust Co., 66 Fed. R. 617; May v. Printup, 59 Ga. 128; Union Trust Co. v. Rockford, etc., R. Co., 6 Biss. (U. S.) 197, per Blodgett, J.; Kerp v. Michigan, etc., R. Co., 6 Chicago Leg. News 101; Sedgwick v. Menck, 6 Blatch. (U. S.) 156. But see Moran v. Sturges, 154 U. S. 256, s. c. 14 Sup. Ct. R. 1019. In Texas it is held that on an appeal from an order of a state court appointing a receiver of a railroad, where it appears that the federal court had already appointed a receiver for such road, but it does not appear when the suit in which he was appointed was instituted, the order of the state court will not be disturbed. Texas Trunk R. Co. v. State, 83 Tex. 1, 18 S. W. R. 199; Wilmer v. Atlanta, etc., Co., 2 Woods 409. (Woods, J.) In New York, under the code, the court has jurisdiction of a cause and all the subsequent proceedings from the time process is served or a provisional remedy is allowed, and a second court will decline to take jurisdiction or appoint a receiver where the first court has granted an injunction. McCarthy v. Peake, 18 How. Pr. 138; High on Receivers, § 49. In Gaylord v. Fort Wayne, etc., R. Co., 6 Biss. (U. S.) 286, Drummond, J., says: "The principle upon this subject is properly stated in the opinion of the circuit court of the northern district of Illinois, in the case of the U. T. Co. v. Rockford, Rock Island and St. Louis R. Co., reported in 7 Chicago Legal News 33: that the court which first takes cognizance of the controversy is entitled to retain jurisdiction to the end of the litigation, and incidentally to take the possession or control of the

that an action covering substantially the same issues is begun in a state court after the filing of a bill against a railroad company in the United States Circuit Court in which the appointment of a receiver is asked for, but before an appointment is made, and that the state court proceeds to appoint a receiver and to put him in possession of the property, will not affect the jurisdiction of the circuit court; but it will proceed in due course to appoint a receiver, if occasion for such action is shown, and will assert its jurisdiction.[1] And it is even held that after the technical but not necessarily final dismissal of a suit in the federal court, a suit in a state court for the appointment of a receiver will not supersede the jurisdiction of the federal court as to any further matters connected with the receivership in that court.[2] It has been held, however, that when the second suit relates to a different cause of action, this rule does not apply, although the thing which the litigation concerns is the same in both cases, and that, in such a case, priority of possession determines the priority of right to hold the property.[3] Where a receiver appointed by a state court in a

res, the subject matter of the controversy, to the exclusion of all interference from other courts of concurrent jurisdiction, and that the proper application of this principle does not require that the court which first takes jurisdiction of the controversy shall also first take the actual possession of the thing in controversy."

[1] Memphis v. Dean, 8 Wall. (U. S.) 64; Jones on Corp. Bonds, § 463. In Bill v. New Albany, etc., R. Co., 2 Biss. (U. S.) 390, it was held that such action on the part of the state court would, if justice required it, be treated as an interference, and the federal court would refuse to recognize a decree of foreclosure rendered in the state court in an action brought after suit was begun in the federal court, but before final adjudication.

[2] Union Trust Co. v. Rockford, etc., R. Co., 6 Biss. (U. S.) 197.

[3] Memphis v. Dean, 8 Wall. (U. S.) 64. In Wilmer v. Atlanta, etc., R. Co., 2 Woods 409, Woods, J., in taking the opposite view, says: "It is well settled that realty out of the state may be reached by acting on the person. Mitchell v. Bunch, 2 Paige Ch. 606; Ramsey v. Brailsford, 2 Des. 582, note. In the case in Paige it was held that if the person of the defendant is within its jurisdiction, the court has jurisdiction as to his property situated without such jurisdiction. When the property is situated outside the territorial jurisdiction of the court, the court may require assignments to be made by the defendant to the receiver. * * * Especial attention is called to the cases of Wiswall v. Sampson, 14 How. 52; Chittenden v. Brewster, 2 Wall. 191; Bill v. The New Albany R. Co., 2 Biss. 390. An examination of the cases cited will show

suit between the railroad company and a judgment creditor was in actual possession, it was held that the United States Circuit Court had no jurisdiction to compel such receiver to surrender possession to a receiver appointed by it in a suit between the mortgage creditors and the company, instituted before the suit in the state court was begun.[1] The soundness of that actual seizure of property has not been considered necessary to the jurisdiction of the court in a case where the possession of the property is necessary to the relief sought. The commencement of the action and service of process, or, according to some of the cases, the simple commencement of the suit by the filing of the bill, is sufficient to give the court jurisdiction to the exclusion of all other courts. * * * If this court, upon the bill filed in this case, has the power to take possession of the entire property granted by the trust deed, as we have already decided it has, then the filing of the bill asking this court to take possession of and administer the trust property, and the service of process excluded the jurisdiction of all other courts to take possession of and administer the same property or any part thereof." But see opinion of Bradley, J., in next note.

[1] Wilmer v. Atlanta, etc., R. Co., 2 Woods 409, 425, per Mr. Justice Bradley. In refusing a writ of assistance to put the receiver appointed by Judge Woods of the federal court in possession of the property, Mr. Justice Bradley said: "It is too well settled to admit of controversy that where two courts have concurrent jurisdiction of a subject of controversy the court which first assumes jurisdiction has it exclusive of the other. But where the objects of the suit are different, this rule does not apply, although the thing about or in reference to which the litigation is had is the same in both cases. * * * The controversy not being the same nor the parties the same, there is no conflict as to the question or cause. But * * * there has arisen a conflict of jurisdiction as to the thing or subject-matter. * * * The test, I think, is this: Not which action was first commenced, nor which cause of action has priority or superiority, but which court first acquired jurisdiction over the property. If the Fulton county court had the power to take possession when it did so, and did not invade the possession or jurisdiction of this court, its possession will not be interferred with by this court; the parties must either go to that court and pray for the removal of its hand, or, having procured an adjudication of their rights in this court must wait until the action of that court has been brought to a close, and judicial possession has ceased. Service of process gives jurisdiction over the person. Seizure gives jurisdiction over the property; and *until it is seized*, no matter when the suit was commenced, the court does not have jurisdiction. The alleged collusion and fraud of the parties can not alter the case. It is a question between the two courts; and we must respect the possession and jurisdiction of the sister court. We can not take the property out of its hands unless it has first wrongfully taken it out of our hands. This, as we have shown, has not been done. The application for a writ of assistance

this decision has many times been questioned,[1] although it has received recognition in some jurisdictions.[2] It has been held, however, that the general rule that the court which first takes cognizance of a suit has the exclusive right to decide every question arising therein, is subject to limitations, that it is only when property is in possession of the court, either actually or constructively that it can be protected from the process of other courts,[3] and that other courts may take any action which does not amount to an interference with the possession of the

and for an attachment must be denied." See, also, Barton v. Keyes, 1 Flippin 61; Levi v. Columbia, etc.,Ins. Co., 1 Fed. R. 206; Walker v. Flint, 7 Fed. R. 435; Erwin v. Lowry, 7 How. 172; Griswold v. Central, etc., R. Co., 9 Fed. R. 797; Covell v. Heyman, 111 U. S. 176, s. c. 4 Sup.Ct. R. 355; Heidritter v. Oilcloth Co., 112 U. S. 294, s. c. 5 Sup. Ct. R. 135; Beach Mod. Eq., § 723.

[1] See May v. Printup, 59 Ga. 128, where it was held that the filing of a bill is sufficient to give jurisdiction of the thing in controversy, in a case where the only recovery can be out of the property; and that a state court which takes possession of a railroad pending an application to the United States Circuit Court for the appointment of a receiver should surrender such possession when it is shown that the suit in the state court was filed by collusion of the parties after the suit in the federal court was begun. In Adams v. Mercantile Trust Co., 66 Fed. Rep. 617. (C. C. of App.) Pardee, J., says, concerning the opposing views of Judge Woods and Mr. Justice Bradley, Wilmer v. Atlanta, etc., Co., supra: "The views expressed by Judge Woods have been accepted and followed in this circuit, at least, and we fully concur therein, as a correct exposition of the law, and one particularly applicable to the present case; while the decision of Mr. Justice Bradley, doubted by himself, is open to the objection that thereby jurisdiction is frequently made to depend upon a race between marshals and sheriffs, likely to result in unseemly controversies between the state and federal courts." In Illinois Steel Co. v. Putnam, (C. C. of App.) 68 Fed. 515, 517, McCormick, J., says: "Where a bill in equity brings under the direct control of the court all the property and estate of the defendants, * * * * and the possession and control of the property are necessary to the exercise of the jurisdiction of the court, the filing of the bill and service of process is an equitable levy on the property, and pending the proceedings such property may properly be held to be in *gremio legis*. The actual seizure of the property is not necessary to produce this effect, where the possession of the property is necessary to the granting of the relief sought. In such cases the commencement of the suit is sufficient to give the court whose jurisdiction is invoked the exclusive right to control the property."

[2] Merchants', etc., Bank v. Trustees, 63 Ga. 549; East Tenn., etc., R. Co. v. Atlanta, etc., R. Co., 49 Fed. Rep. 608.

[3] Buck v. Colbath, 3 Wall. (U. S.) 334.

first court acquiring jurisdiction.[1] So, in a recent case,[2] it was held that the fact that a prior suit for foreclosure was pending in the state court, with no immediate purpose to ask for a receiver, did not prevent the federal court from taking jurisdiction and appointing a receiver, and that after such receiver had taken possession he could not be required to deliver possession to a receiver afterwards appointed by the state court in the prior suit.

§554. **Extra-territorial jurisdiction.**—A court of equity can not, as a rule at least, acquire extra-territorial jurisdiction by appointing receivers for property lying entirely outside of the state or district in which such court is organized.[3] Many cases are found, however, in which a receiver has been appointed over property lying within the jurisdiction and other property lying outside of the state or country where the parties interested in the property were personally before the court and subject to its orders, and the property in separate jurisdictions went to make up an

---

[1] Andrews v. Smith, 19 Blatchf. (U. S.) 100, 5 Fed. Rep. 833. The appointment of a receiver by one court will not be regarded as an interference with the jurisdiction of another court, which has granted an injunction concerning property without taking it into possession. San Antonio, etc., R. Co. v. Davis, (Tex. C. App.) 30 S.W. R. 693.

[2] East Tennessee, etc., R. Co. v. Atlanta, etc., R. Co., 49 Fed. R. 608. The court said: "The rule upon that subject in this state is deducible from the decision of the supreme court in Merchants', etc., Bank v. Trustees, 63 Ga.549, where the court uses this language: 'But it would seem here that the stockholders' bill has been pending here for a long time in the circuit court of the United States, and no receiver is yet appointed. Perhaps none ever will be. Is the judgment creditor to wait until one is to be appointed? He is not even in this case made a party to the bill in the United States court. If he were, and if the bill there filed was similar to this in review here, and could accomplish the same end, to-wit, the collection of this debt by the judgment creditor, having the final process of the state court in his hands, even then we should rule that neither law, nor equity, nor comity would require the equity court to wait upon the United States court in a case like this.' The application of that decision is that neither law, equity, nor comity will require the United States court to wait upon the state court in a case like this."

[3] Atkins v. Wabash, etc., R. Co., 29 Fed. R. 161; Booth v. Clark, 17 How. (U. S.) 321; Texas & P. R. Co. v. Gay, 86 Tex. 571, s. c. 25 L. R. A. 52, where the court carefully reviews the authorities bearing upon the question.

entity or belonged to the same corporate body.[1] Thus, where a single railroad corporation created by the concurrent legislation of several states owns a line extending into each of those states, a court having jurisdiction over the corporate body may acquire control of all its property by requiring it to execute assignments, or otherwise transfer the title to the receiver.[2] And it was held in one case that even though receivers had already been appointed by the state courts of Georgia, North Carolina and South Carolina to take charge of the several parts of a railroad incorporated by and extending across the three states, but having its principal office at Atlanta, in the state of Georgia, the circuit court for the northern district of Georgia, in which suit had been brought before any suit had been instituted in the state courts, had jurisdiction to appoint a receiver for the whole line.[3] On the other hand, it has been held that a federal

---

[1] Muller v. Dows, 94 U. S. 444; Ellis v. Boston, etc., R. Co., 107 Mass. 1; Mead v. New York, etc., R. Co., 45 Conn. 199, 223; State v. Northern Cent. R. Co., 18 Md. 193; ante, § 27. See, also, Blackburn v. Selma, etc., R. Co., 2 Flip. 525, s. c. 3 Fed. Cas. 526; Central Trust Co. v. Wabash, etc., R. Co., 29 Fed. R. 618. High on Receivers, § 42, and authorities cited.

[2] Muller v. Dows, 94 U. S. 444; Northern Indiana R. Co. v. Michigan Cent. R. Co., 15 How. (U. S.) 233; Port Royal, etc., R. Co. v. King, 93 Ga. 63, s. c. 24 L. R. A. 730.

[3] Wilmer v. Atlanta, etc., Co., 2 Woods (U. S.) 409. In announcing the opinion of the court appointing a receiver, Judge Woods said: "As the property of the defendant company is one entire and indivisible thing, and as it is all covered by one deed of trust, there seems to be no good reason why this court should not appoint a receiver for the whole, even though a part of the property may extend into another state. The court having jurisdiction of the defendant can compel it to do all in its power to put the receiver in possession of the entire property. If other persons outside of the territorial jurisdiction of this court have seized the property of the defendant the receiver may be compelled to ask the assistance of the courts of that jurisdiction to aid him in obtaining possession, but that is no reason why we should hesitate to appoint a receiver for the whole property. We think the courts of other jurisdictions would feel constrained, as a matter of comity, to afford all necessary aid in their power to put the receiver of this court in possession." But on a subsequent application to that court for a writ of assistance to enable the receiver to get possession of the property of the railroad company in Georgia, which the receiver appointed by the courts of that state refused to surrender, the application was refused by Judge Bradley. The reason upon which Judge Bradley based his refusal of the writ was that the state court had first acquired jurisdiction over

court in one state has no jurisdiction over a railroad in another state and can not appoint a receiver of such railroad, although it is the property of a consolidated corporation created by congress.[1] It is somewhat difficult to reconcile or distinguish the apparently conflicting decisions upon this subject, but we are inclined to think that the true distinction is this: Where the corporation is not within the jurisdiction of the court, or where no part of the property is within its jurisdiction, and it can not get possession or control of the property without sending its process to another state, it has no power to appoint a receiver of such property; but where the corporation is a corporation of the same state, consolidated or otherwise, although it may have lines extending into other states, if it is an indivisible entirety and the court has jurisdiction of all necessary parties, a receiver may be appointed for the entire road.

§ 555. Ancillary appointment—Comity.—Railroad receiverships are generally extended over the property of the company in other jurisdictions by ancillary appointment, for the rule of comity and the interests of all concerned require that the road should be operated as an entirety and under one management.[2] For this reason the question considered in the preceding section, as to the power of a court to appoint a receiver of an entire road extending into other jurisdictions, is not of such

the property by taking actual possession thereof, and such jurisdiction should not, therefore, be disturbed by a court of co-ordinate jurisdiction in a suit by other plaintiffs upon a different cause of action.

[1] Texas & P. R. Co. v. Gay, 86 Tex. 571, s. c. 25 L. R. A. 52. The court also held that the person so appointed, being permitted by the company to take possession and operate the road, was merely the agent of the company and that the company was liable for his negligence.

[2] New York, etc., R. Co. v. N. Y., etc., R. Co., 58 Fed. R. 268; Port Royal & Augusta R. Co. v. King, 93 Ga. 63, 19 S. E. R. 809, s. c. 24 L. R. A. 730; Dillon v. Oregon, etc., Ry. Co., 66 Fed. R. 622; Platt v. Philadelphia, etc., R. Co., 54 Fed. R. 569. But see Mercantile Trust Co. v. Kanawha, etc., R. Co., 39 Fed. R. 337, in which it was held, contrary to the ruling in some of the other cases above cited, that a United States circuit court would not take jurisdiction of a bill whose only purpose is to obtain an ancillary receivership.

vital importance as it would otherwise be. It is customary to appoint as ancillary receiver the same person that was originally appointed and to leave the management of the receivership very largely to the court in which the receiver was first appointed, to which court the receivers are usually required to account.[1] But it is held that these matters, so far as the appointment and control of the ancillary receiver are concerned, rest in the discretion of the court appointing him.[2] In a recent case[3] the court refused to appoint a separate receiver for a branch line of a street railway where a receiver had already been appointed for the entire railway. Where a new suit is brought in the same court concerning the same property, requiring the aid of a receiver, as, for instance, where creditors obtain the appointment of a receiver and a new suit is brought by the mortgage trustees to foreclose, the receivership will be extended so as to reach the subject-matter of the second suit, and independent receivers will not be appointed.[4] The appointment of a receiver by the courts in one jurisdiction will be recognized by the courts of other jurisdictions, and his title to the property of the insolvent corporation be enforced by those courts,[5] so long, at least, as his claims are not opposed to

---

[1] Jennings v. Philadelphia, etc., R. Co., 23 Fed. R. 569; Central Trust Co. v. Wabash, etc., Ry. Co., 29 Fed. R. 618; Port Royal, etc., R.Co. v. King, 93 Ga. 63, 19 S. E. R. 909, s. c. 24 L. R. A. 730; Chattanooga, etc., Ry. Co. v. Felton, 69 Fed. R. 273. See, also, Baldwin v. Hosmer, 101 Mich. 432, s. c. 59 N. W. R. 432; Ware v. Supreme Sitting, (N. J.) 28 Atl. R. 1041; Clyde v. Richmond R. Co., 56 Fed. R. 539.

[2] Atkins v. Wabash, etc., Ry. Co., 29 Fed. R. 161; Central Trust Co. v. Texas, etc., Ry. Co., 22 Fed. R. 135.

[3] Clap v. Interstate Ry. Co., 61 Fed. R. 537. The court said that the appointment of a separate receiver would do no good, but would simply complicate matters and cause additional expense.

[4] Lloyd v. Chesapeake, etc., R. Co., 65 Fed. R. 351; Mercantile Trust Co. v. Kanawha, etc., Ry. Co., 39 Fed. R. 337; Buswell v. Supreme Sitting, etc., 161 Mass. 224, 23 L. R. A. 846; Gilman v. Ketcham, 84 Wis. 60, 23 L. R. A. 52; State v. Jacksonville, etc., R. Co., 15 Fla. 201; Howell v. Ripley, 10 Paige (N. Y.) 43.

[5] Metzner v. Bauer, 98 Ind. 425; Patterson v. Lynde, 112 Ill. 196; Central Trust Co. v. Wabash, etc., R. Co., 29 Fed. R. 618; Buswell v. Supreme Sitting, etc., 161 Mass. 224, s. c. 23 L. R. A. 846; Failey v. Talbee, 55 Fed. R. 892; Boulware v. Davis, 90 Ala. 207, s. c. 9 L. R. A. 601. See, generally, as to the title and rights of a receiver in other jurisdictions than that in which he is appointed, Gilman v.

§ 555   RECEIVERS.   771

those of the citizens of the state in which he is compelled to sue.[1] The rule of comity between the courts of different states requires that a receiver appointed by a competent court of another state, with authority to sue, shall be permitted to maintain a suit in his own name,[2] but this courtesy will not, ordinarily, be extended so as to work detriment to citizens of the state in which the suit is brought.[3] Comity does not, as a rule, require that property should be turned over to a receiver appointed by the courts of another state if such action is opposed to the interests of local creditors, and courts will not, in such a case, enforce the claims of such a receiver in opposition to those of citizens of their own state.[4] It has also been held that a receiver appointed by a foreign court does not acquire, by such appointment, any title superior to that of a non-resident attaching creditor,[5] as the available legal remedy of a receiver is coextensive only with the jurisdiction of the court by which he was appointed when the right of precedence or priority of creditors is asserted in respect to property or funds of a non-resident debtor which the receiver has not yet reduced to possession.[6] But in regard to this question, as in regard to the

Hudson River, etc., Co., 23 L. R. A. 52, and note; Re Schuyler's, etc., Co., 136 N. Y. 169, s. c. 20 L. R. A. 391, and note; Actions by Foreign Receivers, 37 Cent. L. J. 315.

[1] Chandler v. Siddle, 3 Dill (U. S.) 477; Bagby v. Atlantic, etc., R. Co., 86 Pa. St. 291.

[2] Metzner v. Bauer, 98 Ind. 425; Bagby v. Atlantic, etc., R. Co., 86 Pa. St. 291; Hurd v. City of Elizabeth, 41 N. J. Law 1; Lycoming Fire Ins. Co. v. Wright, 55 Vt. 526; Peters v. Foster, 56 Hun (N. Y.) 607; Toronto, etc., Trust Co. v. Chicago, etc., R. Co., 123 N. Y. 37, 47. But see Booth v. Clark, 17 How. (U. S.) 322; Day v. Postal Telegraph Co., 66 Md. 354; Hazard v. Durant, 19 Fed. R. 471.

[3] Runk v. St. John, 29 Barb. (N. Y.) 585; Merchants' Nat. Bank v. McLeod, 38 Ohio St. 174.

[4] Hurd v. Columbus Ins. Co., 55 Me. 228; Day v. Postal Tel. Co., 66 Md. 354; Runk v. St. John, 29 Barb. (N. Y.) 585; Fawcett v. Supreme Sitting, etc., 64 Conn. 170, s. c. 24 L. R. A. 815 (a questionable decision); Lycoming, etc., Insurance Co. v. Wright, 55 Vt. 526; Thurston v. Rosenfield, 42 Mo. 474. "That the officer of a foreign court should not be permitted, as against the claims of creditors resident here, to remove from this state the assets of the debtor, is a proposition that seems to be asserted by all the decisions." Hurd v. City of Elizabeth, 41 N. J. L. 1.

[5] Patterson v. Lynde, 112 Ill. 196; Catlin v. Wilcox, etc., Co., 123 Ind. 477, s. c. 8 L. R. A. 62.

[6] Catlin v. Wilcox, etc., Co., 123 Ind. 477, s. c. 8 L. R. A. 62; State v. Jacksonville, etc., R. Co., 15 Fla. 201;

entire subject of the relative rights of a receiver in a foreign jurisdiction, and attaching or garnishing creditors, the authorities seem to be hopelessly in conflict. The solution of the problem depends so largely upon the idea of comity entertained in the particular jurisdiction in which the question arises, that it is impossible to lay down any rule that will be applied in all jurisdictions. We think, however, that one who is a resident of the same state in which the debtor resides and in which a receiver has been appointed should not be permitted to go into a foreign jurisdiction and there obtain relief which he could not obtain in his own state, by attachment or garnishment proceedings, securing a priority over the receiver appointed for the entire property.[1] But, as we have already seen, it is held by some courts, in accordance with what is probably the weight of authority, that a resident of a third state may obtain priority over a foreign receiver. It seems to us, however, that, to be consistent, the court ought, at least, to refuse to aid an attaching non-resident creditor to obtain priority over a receiver of the property, although he was appointed in a foreign jurisdiction.[2] There is more reason for holding, in accordance with the exception generally made in favor of domestic creditors, that the courts of one state may allow its own creditors to obtain priority, by attachment or garnishment of property therein, over a foreign receiver who has not yet taken actual possession of such property,[3] but the practical effect of such action

Farmers', etc., Ins. Co. v. Needles, 52 Me. 17; Hunt v. Columbian Ins. Co., 55 Me. 290.

[1] Gilman v. Ketcham, 84 Wis. 60, s. c. 23 L. R. A. 52, and note; Bagby v. Atlantic, etc., R. Co., 86 Pa. St. 291; Merchants' Nat. Bank v. McLeod, 38 Ohio St. 174. See, also, Cole v. Cunningham, 133 U. S. 107, s. c. 10 Sup. Ct. R. 269; Bacon v. Horne, 123 Pa. St. 452, s. c. 2 L. R. A. 355; Re Waite, 99 N. Y. 433; Woodward v. Brooks, 128 Ill. 222, s. c. 3 L. R. A. 702; Halsted v. Straus, 32 Fed. R. 279; Whipple v. Thayer, 16 Pick. (Mass.) 25, s. c. 26 Am. Dec. 626.

[2] See Long v. Girdwood, 150 Pa. St. 413, s. c. 23 L. R. A. 32, and note; May v. First Nat. Bank, 122 Ill. 551, s. c. 13 N. E. R. 806; Re Schuyler's, etc., Co., 136 N. Y. 169, s. c. 20 L. R. A. 391, and note; Hurd v. City of Elizabeth, 41 N. J. L. 1; Bockover v. Life Assn., 77 Va. 85.

[3] Taylor v. Columbian Ins. Co., 14 Allen (Mass.) 353; Warren v. Union Nat. Bank, 7 Phila. 156; Cleveland, etc., Co. v. Crawford, 9 Ry. & Corp. L. J. 171. See, also, Willits v. Waite, 25 N. Y. 577; Hunt v. Columbian Ins. Co., 55 Me. 290, s. c. 92 Am. Dec. 592; Lichtenstein v. Gillett, 37 La. Ann.

might sometimes be very disastrous to great interests and its justice may well be doubted. Some courts, however, have gone so far as to hold that after a receiver has taken actual possession of property and brought it in the course of his duty into another jurisdiction, domestic creditors therein may attach it and thus obtain a superior right to it.[1] This seems to us to be palpably erroneous and unsound.[2] Where a suit in which a state court has appointed a receiver is removed to the United States Circuit Court under the law for the removal of causes, the receiver is not thereby discharged, but remains in possession until removed by the federal court, and may be required to account to it for the manner in which he has discharged his trust.[3]

§ 556. Procedure—Ex parte application.—Courts of equity are very unwilling to appoint a receiver upon an *ex parte* application[4] since it would be unjust to condemn a man unheard

522; Rhawn v. Pearce, 110 Ill. 350, s. c. 51 Am. R. 691.

[1] Humphreys v. Hopkins, 81 Cal. 551, s. c. 6 L. R. A. 792, 15 Am. St. R. 76 (Thornton and McFarland, JJ., dissenting).

[2] Chicago, etc., Ry. Co. v. Keokuk, etc., Co., 108 Ill. 317, s. c. 48 Am. R. 557; Pond v. Cooke, 45 Conn. 126, s. c. 29 Am. R. 668; Cagill v. Wooldridge, 8 Baxt. 580, s. c. 35 Am. R. 716; Killmer v. Hobart, 58 How. Pr. (N. Y.) 452. See, also, the criticism of Mr. Freeman in 15 Am. St. R. 81. See further upon the general subject of attachment and garnishment of property over which a receiver has been appointed and protection of receivers by the courts, Schindelholz v. Cullum, 55 Fed. R. 885; Central Trust Co. v. Chattanooga, etc., R. Co., 68 Fed. R. 685; United States Trust Co. v. Omaha, etc., R. Co., 61 Fed. R. 531; Vermont, etc., R. Co. v. Vermont Cent. R. Co., 46 Vt. 792; Chafee v. Quidnick Co., 13 R. I. 442; Sercomb v. Catlin, 128 Ill. 556, s. c. 21 N. E. R. 606; Reynolds v. Adden, 136 U. S. 348, s. c. 10 Sup. Ct. R. 843; Barnett v. Kinney, 147 U. S. 476, s. c. 13 Sup. Ct. R. 403; Straughan v. Hallwood, 30 W. Va. 274, s. c. 8 Am. St. R. 29, and note; Parsons v. Charter Oak Ins. Co., 31 Fed. R. 305; McAlpin v. Jones, 10 La. Ann. 552; Relfe v. Rundle, 103 U. S. 222; Cole v. Oil Well, etc., Co., 57 Fed. R. 534; Ames v. Union, etc., Ry. Co., 60 Fed. R. 966.

[3] Hinckley v. Gilman, etc., Co., 100 U. S. 153; Mack v. Jones, 31 Fed. R. 189.

[4] Cleveland, etc., R. Co. v. Jewett, 37 Ohio St. 649; People v. Albany, etc., R. Co., 55 Barb. 344, 369; People v. Albany, etc., R. Co., 7 Abb. Pr. N. S. (N. Y.) 265; Devoe v. Ithaca, etc., R. Co., 5 Paige (N. Y.) 521; Whitehead v. Wooten, 43 Miss. 523; Bisson v. Curry, 35 Iowa 72; Blondheim v. Moore, 11 Md. 365; Cook v. Detroit, etc., R. Co., 45 Mich. 453; Young v. Rollins, 85 N. Car. 485. See,

and to dispossess him of property *prima facie* his, and hand over its enjoyment to another whose claim to it he has had no opportunity to contest.[1] But where it is shown that the defendant has left the state or can not be found,[2] or where, for some other reason, it becomes absolutely necessary for the court to interfere before there is time to give notice to the opposite party, in order to prevent the destruction or loss of property,[3]

also, as to the necessity for due notice to the opposing party, State *v.* Jacksonville, etc., R. Co., 15 Fla. 201; Fredenheim *v.* Rohr, 87 Va. 764, s.c.13 S. E.R. 193; Ruffner *v.* Mairs, 33 W. Va. 655; Turgeau *v.* Brady, 24 La. Ann.348; Meridian News, etc.,Co. *v.* Diem, etc.,Co., 70 Miss.695, s. c. 12 So. R.702;Crowder *v.* Moore, 52 Ala. 221; French *v.* Gifford, 30 Iowa 148; Johns *v.* Johns, 23 Ga. 31; Word *v.* Word, 90 Ala. 81; Howe *v.* Jones, 57 Iowa 130; Turnbull *v.* Prentiss Lumber Co., 55 Mich. 387. In Whitney *v.* Hanover Nat. Bank, 71 Miss. 1009, s. c. 15 So. R. 33, it was held that the appointment of a receiver for a bank on its own *ex parte* application was void and subject to collateral attack.

[1] Arnold *v.* Bright, 41 Mich. 207; Baker *v.* Backus, 32 Ill. 79. Notice is sometimes required by statute. May *v.* Greenhill, 80 Ind. 124; Moritz *v.* Miller, 87 Ala. 331; Whitehead *v.* Wooten, 43 Miss. 523.

[2] People *v.* Norton, 1 Paige (N. Y.) 17; Sandford *v.* Sinclair, 8 Paige (N. Y.) 373; Gibbons *v.* Mainwaring, 9 Sim. 77; Dowling *v.* Hudson, 14 Beav. 423. See Whitehead *v.* Wooten,43 Miss. 523; Pressley *v.* Harrison, 102 Ind. 14, 19. Thus, where no officer of the corporation can be found on whom service of notice can be made, the court may, in its discretion, appoint a receiver without notice to the corporation. Maish *v.* Bird, 59 Iowa 307; Dayton *v.* Borst, 31 N. Y. 435. So,

where a foreign corporation has discontinued its organization, and its officers have neglected to hold meetings, but have converted the corporate property to their own use, sold it, and retain the proceeds of the sale. De Bemer *v.* Drew, 57 Barb. (N. Y.) 438. But where it is shown that all the property of the defendant is in the hands and under the control of another railroad corporation which is operating the road, the non-residence of the defendant's officers will not excuse a failure to give notice to its lessee of an application for a receiver. Wabash R. Co. *v.* Dykeman, 133 Ind. 56, s. c. 32 N. E. R. 823.

[3] Platt *v.* Philadelphia, etc., R. Co., 54 Fed. R. 569; Cleveland, etc., R. Co. *v.* Jewett, 37 Ohio St. 649; Oil Run Petroleum Co. *v.* Gale, 6 W. Va. 525, 545; Gibson *v.* Martin, 8 Paige Ch. (N. Y.) 481; Sims *v.* Adams, 78 Ala. 395; Hardy *v.* McClellan, 53 Miss. 507; Ashurst *v.* Lehman, 86 Ala. 370; Olmstead *v.* Distilling, etc., Co., 67 Fed. R. 24. In a suit by judgment creditors against a railroad company for the appointment of a receiver, although the complaint alleged that executions had been levied on defendant's rolling stock, preventing its operation, that it and its predecessor were both insolvent, that there were large quantities of stock along the road under contract for immediate shipment, and a great quantity of grain to be threshed within the next ten days,

a receiver may be appointed without notice. The particular facts and circumstances which render such a summary proceeding proper should be set forth in the bill or petition on which the application is founded,[1] and the court should, it seems, in case a receiver is granted, save to the defendant the right thereafter to apply, upon meritorious grounds, for relief against the order.[2]

§ 557. **Parties to proceedings for appointment of receiver.** —If the property of the defendant corporation is in the possession of a lessee, such lessee should be made a party to the proceedings for the appointment of a receiver[3] and served with notice of the application.[4] But it seems that a receiver of the rents and profits may be appointed without making the lessee a party.[5] It has also been held that an insolvent stockholder is not a necessary party defendant to a proceeding for the ap-

---

which would be shipped over defendant's road if it was in operation, and that if trains were not running on the road at once, great damage would accrue both to citizens and to defendants, it was, nevertheless, held that the facts alleged did not justify the appointment of a receiver without notice to defendant. Chicago & S. E. Ry. Co. v. Cason, 133 Ind. 49, s. c. 32 N., E. R. 827. See Wabash, etc., R. Co. v. Dykeman, 133 Ind. 56.

[1] People v. Albany, etc., R. Co., 55 Barb. (N.Y.) 344, affirmed 57 N.Y. 161; Wabash R.Co.v.Dykeman,133 Ind.56; French v. Gifford, 30 Iowa 148; Moritz v. Miller, 87 Ala. 331; Verplanck v. Mercantile Ins. Co., 2 Paige(N.Y.)438. Affidavits of the belief of plaintiff or his attorneys that immediate action is necessary for the protection of complainants, and that the defendants would make use of the delay occasioned by giving notice to spirit away or dispose of their effects have been held insufficient. Moritz v. Miller, 87 Ala. 331; Thompson v. Tower Mfg. Co., 87 Ala. 733. In Wabash R. Co. v. Dykeman, 133 Ind. 56, the court said: "The statement in the verified complaint that there was an emergency for the immediate appointment of a receiver, without notice, was not a sufficient showing. This was a mere statement of an opinion. The facts on which the opinion was founded should have been pleaded in order to enable the court to judge of its correctness."

[2] People v. Norton, 1 Paige (N. Y.) 17.

[3] Kerp v. Michigan, etc., R. Co., 6 Chicago Leg. N. 101; Wabash R. Co. v. Dykeman, 133 Ind. 56, s. c. 32 N. E. R. 823; Wiltsie on Mort. Foreclosures, § 157. See, also, Searles v. Jacksonville, etc., R. Co., 2 Woods (U. S. C. C.) 621, 626.

[4] Wabash R. Co. v. Dykeman, 133 Ind. 56, s. c. 32 N. E. R. 823.

[5] Kerp v. Michigan, etc., R. Co., 6 Chicago Leg. N. 101.

pointment of a receiver and to compel individual stockholders to pay their subscriptions for the benefit of the corporate creditors.[1] Many of the states have laws providing that upon the dissolution of any corporation if a receiver is not appointed by some court of competent authority the directors or managers of the affairs of such corporation at the time of its dissolution, by whatever name they may be known in law, shall be the trustees of creditors and stockholders of the corporation dissolved, and shall have full power to settle the affairs of the corporation, collect and pay the outstanding debts and divide among the stockholders the moneys and other property that shall remain after the payment of debts and necessary expenses.[2] After the title to the corporate property has vested in the officers as trustees under such a statute, a receiver can afterward be appointed only in an action or proceeding to which they are parties.[3]

§ 558. Appointment upon motion or petition and notice—Affidavits.—Since the appointment of a receiver is generally regarded as an interlocutory order, and not as in any sense a decision upon the merits,[4] the appointment is usually made upon motion,[5] or petition supported by affidavit,[6] with notice

---

[1] Wilson v. California, etc., Co., 95 Mich. 117, s. c. 54 N.W. R. 643.

[2] Stimson's Am. St. (1892), § 8356, citing the laws of New York, New Jersey, Ohio, Wisconsin, Kansas, Nebraska, Maryland, Delaware, Tennessee, Missouri, Texas, California, Nevada, Colorado, Washington, Dakota, Montana, Idaho, Wyoming, Alabama, Florida, New Mexico, Oklahoma.

[3] People v. O'Brien, 111 N. Y. 1; Parker v. Browning, 8 Paige (N. Y.) 388.

[4] Cincinnati, etc., R. Co. v. Sloan, 31 Ohio St. 1; Chicago, etc., Min. Co. v. U. S. Petroleum Co., 57 Pa. St. 83; Hottenstein v. Conrad, 9 Kan. 435.

[5] Hursh v. Hursh, 99 Ind. 500; Hottenstein v. Conrad, 9 Kan. 435; Commercial, etc., Bank v. Corbett, 5 Sawy. (U. S.) 172; Blakeney v. Dufaur, 15 Beav. 40, 42; Cooke v. Gwyn, 3 Atk. 689 (653).

[6] An application for the appointment of a receiver pending litigation is made upon petition or motion. Affidavits and counter affidavits may be filed, or oral testimony heard as to the necessity for a receiver. Pouder v. Tate, 96 Ind. 330; Hursh v. Hursh, 99 Ind. 500. See Wiltsie on Mort. Foreclosures, § 633; 1 Elliott's Gen. Pr., § 395.

§ 558　　　　　　RECEIVERS.　　　　　　777

to the opposite party.[1] It is the better practice to pray for a receiver in the original bill,[2] but a receiver may be appointed on the final hearing, even after decree, although not prayed for in the original bill.[3] In passing upon the necessity for a receiver the court will consider the sworn answer of the defendant,[4] and affidavits offered in its support.[5] Under the modern practice affidavits may also be received in opposition to the answer.[6] A receiver may be appointed, in a proper case, before answer[7] and even before an appearance is en-

---

[1] See *ante*, § 556. It has been held unnecessary to serve notice on a trustee for bondholders, who is insane and confined in an aslyum in a foreign country. Ettlinger *v.* Persian, etc., Co., 66 Hun 94, s. c. 20 N. Y. Supp. 772. In Beck *v.* Ashkettle, 18 R. I. 374, 27 Atl. R. 505, it was held that personal notice was necessary under the statute, and that leaving a copy at the last and usual abode of the debtor, who had absconded, was insufficient. We doubt the soundness of this decision. See as to short notice being sufficient in an emergency, Miltenberger *v.* Logansport R. Co., 106 U. S. 286, s. c. 1 Sup. Ct. R. 140, 158; Haugan *v.* Netland, 51 Minn. 552, s. c. 53 N. W. R. 873.

[2] See Beach on Receivers, § 130; U. S. Equity Rule 21; 1 Elliott's Gen. Pr., § 395.

[3] Connelly *v.* Dickson, 76 Ind. 440; Bowman *v.* Bell, 14 Simons 392; Shannon *v.* Hanks, 88 Va. 338, s. c. 13 S. E. R. 437. See, also, Merritt *v.* Gibson, 129 Ind. 155, s. c. 15 L. R. A. 277.

[4] Rankin *v.* Rothschild, 78 Mich. 10; Goodman *v.* Whitcomb, 1 J. & W. 569; 1 Elliott's Gen. Pr., § 395. As a general rule the answer is to be taken as true in so far as it is responsive to the allegations of the bill, at least in the absence of sufficient evidence to the contrary. Thompsen *v.* Diffenderfer, 1 Md. Ch. 489; Voshell *v.* Hynson, 26 Md. 82 ; Buchanan *v.* Comstock, 57 Barb. (N. Y.) 568; Callanan *v.* Shaw, 19 Iowa 183. The answer of one defendant only, where a material co-defendant has not answered, must be regarded merely as an affidavit. Kershaw *v.* Mathews, 1 Russ. (Eng. Ch.) 362. Where affidavits are offered in support of the answer and to overcome the case made by the affidavits in support of the motion, counter affidavits may be admitted on the part of the plaintiff. There can be no just reason for excluding any facts material to the judgment of the court and which will enable it to act intelligently in the exercise of a sound discretion. Young *v.* Rollins, 85 N. Car. 485, 12 Am. & Eng. R. Cas. 455.

[5] Pouder *v.* Tate, 96 Ind. 330; Hursh *v.* Hursh, 99 Ind. 500; Ladd *v.* Harvey, 21 N. H. 514; Rhodes *v.* Lee, 32 Ga. 470.

[6] 2 Dan. Chanc. Pl. & Pr., 1736; 2 Beach Mod. Eq. Pr., § 729. See, also, Hayes *v.* Heyer, 4 Sandf. Ch. (N. Y.) 485 (517); Sobernheimer *v.* Wheeler, 45 N. J. Eq. 614.

[7] Vann *v.* Barnett, 2 Bro. Ch. 158; Williams *v.* Jenkins, 11 Ga. 595; Whitehead *v.* Wooten, 43 Miss. 523; Weis *v.* Goetter, 72 Ala. 259; 2 Beach Mod. Eq. Pr., § 724. But see Ranger *v.* Champion, etc., Co., 52 Fed. R. 609;

tered,[1] but the court will only act where a clear case of necessity for the appointment of a receiver at such a time is made out.[2]

§ 559. Who may appoint—Appointment in vacation.—In the absence of a statute specially authorizing such a proceeding, a receiver can not be appointed by a judge or judges of a court in vacation.[3] It is competent, however, for the legislature by statute to grant to a judge in vacation authority to appoint a receiver,[4] even upon an *ex parte* application.[5] It has been held by the supreme court of Georgia that the appointment of a receiver for a corporation is not necessarily the exercise of a judicial power, but that such an appointment might be made by the legislature, or authorized by it to be made by the executive department of the state.[6] The case referred to has been cited by several text writers,[7] apparently with ap-

Union Mut. L. Ins. Co. v. Union, etc., Co., 37 Fed. R. 286.

[1] Tanfield v. Irvine, 2 Russ. 149. See, also, Henshaw v. Wells, 9 Humph. (Tenn.) 568.

[2] Latham v. Chafee, 7 Fed. R. 525; Turnbull v. Prentiss Lumber Co., 55 Mich. 387; Micou v. Moses, 72 Ala. 439; Clark v. Ridgely, 1 Md. Ch. 70. Facts should be specifically stated and not merely upon information and belief. Cofer v. Echerson, 6 Iowa 502; Heavilon v. Farmers' Bank, 81 Ind. 249; Hanna v. Hanna, 89 N. Car. 68; Grandin v. LeBar, 3 N. Dak. 447, 50 N. W. R. 151.

[3] Newman v. Hammond, 46 Ind. 119; Hammock v. Loan & Trust Co., 105 U. S. 77; Hervey v. Illinois Midland R. Co., 28 Fed. Rep. 169. See, also, Chase v. Miller, 88 Va. 791, s. c. 14 S. E. R. 545; Conkling v. Ridgley, 112 Ill. 36, s. c. 54 Am. R. 204. But compare Walters v. Anglo-American, etc., Co., 50 Fed. R. 316; Greeley v. Provident Sav. Bank, 103 Mo. 212.

[4] Pressley v. Lamb, 105 Ind. 171, s. c. 4 N. E. R. 682. See, also, First

National Bank v. U. S. Encaustic Tile Co., 105 Ind. 227; Brewster v. Hartley, 37 Cal. 15, s. c. 99 Am. Dec. 237; Bitting v. Ten Eyck, 85 Ind. 357; McMurtry v. Tuttle, 13 Neb. 232, s. c. 13 N. W. R. 213; Morriss v. Virginia Insurance Co., 85 Va. 588, s. c. 8 S. E. R. 383. In Pressley v. Lamb, *supra*, the court held that a judge in vacation, acting under the statute authorizing the appointment of a receiver, is exercising *quod hoc* "the judicial power of the state."

[5] Real Estate Associates v. Superior Court, 60 Cal. 223. An appointment of a receiver can only be made in the absence of notice to the opposite party, in Indiana, upon sufficient cause shown by affidavit. R. S. Ind. 1894, § 1244. See Pressley v. Lamb, 102 Ind. 14; Hardy v. McClellan, 53 Miss. 507.

[6] Carey v. Giles, 9 Ga. 253. See, also, Foote v. Forbes, 25 Kan. 359; United States v. Ferreira, 13 How. (U. S.) 40; Toledo, etc., R. Co. v. Dunlap, 47 Mich. 456.

[7] High on Receivers, §§ 39, 343; Beach on Receivers, § 407.

proval, but we doubt its soundness. Other questions relating to the subject of this section have already been considered elsewhere.[1]

§ 560. **Suit must generally be pending.**—Since the appointment of a receiver by a court of equity is generally held to be merely an auxiliary proceeding in aid of a pending suit to determine the ultimate rights of the parties to the property for which a receiver is sought,[2] it is the general rule that a receiver can only be appointed for a corporation when there is a suit actually pending and that a court of chancery is not ordinarily justified in appointing a receiver before the filing of a complaint or bill.[3] Under the ancient practice of the court of chancery in England, a receiver was not appointed until after the coming in of the defendant's answer, but it is now settled, both in this country and in England, that the appointment may be made before answer, provided a special necessity therefor is shown to exist.[4] Except under extraordinary circumstances, as where the defendant had left the state to avoid process or the like, the rule seems to have been that a court could get no jurisdiction to appoint a receiver until after service of process and notice of the motion.[5] If an immediate necessity therefor is shown to exist, the application for a receiver may be entertained when the action is commenced, which, under the rule in Indiana, is when process is issued, or an appearance to the action entered, in the manner recognized.[6]

[1] See *ante*, § 552.
[2] Hottenstein *v*. Conrad, 9 Kan. 435; Cooke *v*. Gwyn, 3 Atk. 698 (653); Bufkin *v*. Boyce, 104 Ind.53; Chicago, etc., Min. Co. *v*. U. S. Petroleum Co., 57 Pa. St. 83; Cincinnati, etc., R. Co. *v*. Sloan, 31 Ohio St. 1.
[3] Dale *v*. Kent, 58 Ind. 584; Pressley *v*. Harrison, 102 Ind. 14; Merchants', etc., Bank *v*. Kent, 43 Mich. 292; Hardy *v*. McClellan, 53 Miss. 507; Guy *v*. Doak, 47 Kan. 236; Crowder *v*. Moone, 52 Ala. 220; *ante*, § 540.
[4] High on Receivers, §§ 105, 106.
[5] Whitehead *v*. Wooten, 43 Miss. 523; Edwards Receivers 13, 14.
[6] Pressley *v*. Harrison, 102 Ind. 14, 18, per Mitchell, J. See Pressley *v*. Lamb, 105 Ind. 171, and dissenting opinion of Judge Mitchell, on page 191, *et seq.*; Jones *v*. Bank of Leadville, 10 Colo. 464; Crowder *v*. Moone, 52 Ala. 220; Jones *v*. Schall, 45 Mich. 379.

CORP. 50

In a recent case where the service was defective and the defendant had entered a special appearance to quash the notice, it was held that a suit was pending so as to warrant the appointment of a receiver.[1]

§ 561. **Who may be appointed receiver.**—It is customary, where all the parties in interest are before the court and can agree upon a person to act as receiver, to appoint the receiver chosen by them.[2] Where this can not be done, two or more persons are often agreed upon, each of whom is expected to represent and look after the interests of one of the parties.[3] But the court is not necessarily controlled by the expressed wish of the parties, in making its selection of a receiver. Other interests may be affected by the action of the court besides those of the parties to the suit. It is also practically impossible in many cases to obtain the consent of the several holders of the capital stock of the corporation and of the different series of bonds secured by mortgage upon its property.[4] As was well said by Justice Miller, in pronouncing a judgment removing the receivers chosen by the parties, to make way for a receiver selected by the court: "A receiver is strictly and solely the officer of the court. It is his duty so to conduct the business that the lawful rights and legal interest of all persons in the property and in the business shall be protected, as far as possible, with equal and exact justice. This is much more likely to be done by a receiver who has no interest in the capital stock of the road, none in its debts, and no obligation to those who have. Such a person, acting under the control of the court, seeking its advice, and bound in a sufficient surety for the faithful performance of his duty, is the proper one for

---

[1] Hellebush v. Blake, 119 Ind. 349.

[2] In Mercantile Trust Co. v. Missouri, etc., R. Co., 36 Fed. Rep. 221, Judge Brewer said: "If parties agree upon a receiver, of course I shall appoint whoever you agree upon."

[3] Jones on Corp. Bonds and Mortg., § 459.

[4] In Sage v. Memphis, etc., R. Co., 18 Fed. Rep. 571, it appeared that a receiver had been appointed by collusion between the plaintiff and defendant, for the purpose of preventing unsecured creditors from recovering their claims by actions at law, and the court removed the receiver.

§ 561   RECEIVERS.   781

such an office. On the other hand, while it may be true that a large personal interest may stimulate the activity and direct the vigilance of the receiver, it is equally true that such vigilance, whenever occasion offered, will be directed unduly to advancing that personal interest, and that activity to securing personal advantages."[1] In accordance with this rule, a party to the cause should not, as a rule, be appointed receiver.[2] But a party whose interest extends only to a single claim is sometimes appointed receiver to wind up the business of the corporation.[3] Stockholders and directors of insolvent corporations should not be appointed unless the case is exceptional and urgent;[4] nor, as a general rule, should persons nearly related to a party or to the judge,[5] preferred or other creditors having hostile interests to the majority,[6] or others whose interests or relations are such that they can not well stand indifferent between the interested parties.[7] Where insolvency is due to the mismanagement of the officers, it would be clearly inadvisable to hand over the road to those whose administration has proved disastrous.[8] A person who can not, with the

[1] Meier v. Kansas Pac. R. Co., 5 Dill. (U. S.) 476. See, also, Wood v. Oregon, etc., Co., 55 Fed. R. 901; Shannon v. Hanks, 88 Va. 338, s. c. 13 S. E. R. 437.

[2] Young v. Rollins, 85 N. C. 485; Finance Co. v. Charleston, etc., R. Co., 45 Fed. R. 436. Neither the solicitor employed by complainant, nor his law partner, is such a disinterested person as may properly be appointed to act as receiver in a foreclosure suit. M. & M. Nat. Bank v. Kent Circuit Judge, 43 Mich. 292; Baker v. Backus, 32 Ill. 79. But see Shannon v. Hanks, 88 Va. 338, s. c. 13 S. E. R. 437. Special circumstances may justify the appointment of a party. Robinson v. Taylor, 42 Fed. R. 803, 812; Blakeney v. Dufaur, 15 Beav. 40.

[3] In the matter of Knickerbocker Bank, 19 Barb. (N. Y.) 602; Taylor v. Life Assn. of America, 3 Fed. Rep. 465.

[4] Atkins v. Wabash, etc., R. Co., 29 Fed. Rep. 161; Farmers' Loan & T. Co. v. Northern Pac. R. Co., 61 Fed. R. 546. See, also, McCullough v. Merchants', etc., Co., 29 N. J. Eq. 217; Attorney-General v. Bank, 1 Paige (N. Y.) 511. But compare In re Fifty-four First Mortgage Bonds, 15 S. Car. 304. Certainly an officer who is speculating in the stock of the corporation should not be appointed. Olmstead v. Distilling, etc., Co., 67 Fed. R. 24.

[5] Williamson v. Wilson, 1 Bland 418; 25 U. S. St. at Large, Ch. 373, § 7.

[6] People's Bank v. Fancher, 21 N. Y. Supp. 545.

[7] See Lupton v. Stephenson, 11 Ir. Eq. 484; New York, etc., R. Co. v. New York, etc., R. Co., 58 Fed. R. 268; Sutton v. Jones, 15 Ves. 584; Benneson v. Bill, 62 Ill. 408.

[8] Williamson v. New Albany, etc., R. Co., 1 Biss. (U. S.) 198; People v. Third Avenue Savings Bank, 50 How.

aid of others, manage a business successfully, is as a general rule regarded as unfit to wind it up alone.[1] But since it is necessary that the receiver of a railroad shall be some person who, by reason of his responsibility and business capacity and of his familiarity with the conduct of a business enterprise of this character is fully competent to have the management of the road, cases may arise in which it is proper that officers of the corporation, to whom no fault is imputed, should be made receivers.[2] The selection of the receiver is a matter resting very largely in the discretion of the court, and while the court will usually be guided by the rules already stated, the relationship of the receiver either to the parties or the cause will seldom constitute an absolute disqualification, in the absence of any statutory provision upon the subject. Thus, a party to the suit may be perfectly competent in some cases.[3] So may a relative of one of the parties,[4] or a non-resident.[5] And one corporation, having authority to act as

Pr..(N. Y.) 22; Wait on Insolv. Corp., §171.

[1] McCullough v. Merchants' Loan, etc., Co., 29 N. J. Eq. 217; Jones Corporate Bonds and Mortg., §459.

[2] Meyer v. Johnston, 53 Ala. 237. An order that the president and directors of a railroad corporation, under the order and subject to this court, shall continue in possession of the road, conduct and carry on its business, and make a report to the court of its condition, earnings, profits, and expenditures, was held to constitute such president and directors receivers of the road. But upon their failure to file accounts and perform the other duties required of them, they were removed and a single receiver appointed in order to place the property "more substantially in the hands and under the custody and order of this court." Gibbes v. Greenville, etc., R. Co., 15 S. Car. 304. The fact that one is an officer of a railroad company will not prevent his appointment as receiver thereof where he is familiar with the condition and necessities of the railway, is an efficient manager, and the insolvency of the company was not promoted by bad management on his part, and where the parties interested consent. Farmers' Loan & Trust Co. v. Northern Pac. R. Co., (C. C.) 61 Fed Rep. 546; Fowler v. Jarvis, etc., Co., 63 Fed. R. 888; Ralston v. Washington, etc., Ry. Co., 65 Fed. R. 557.

[3] Hubbard v. Guild, 1 Duer (N. Y.) 662.

[4] High on Receivers, §67. See Shainwald v. Lewis, 8 Fed. R. 878.

[5] Taylor v. Life Assn., 3 Fed. R. 465; Farmers' Loan & T. Co. v. Cape Fear, etc., R. Co., 62 Fed. R. 675; Wilmer v. Atlanta, etc., R. Co., 2 Woods (U. S. C. C.) 409. See, also, Roby v. Smith, 131 Ind. 342, s. c. 15 L. R. A. 792; Farmers' Loan & T. Co. v. Chicago, etc., R. Co., 27 Fed. R. 146.

trustee and receiver, may be appointed receiver of another corporation.[1]

§ 562. **Order appointing receiver.**—The order of appointment should clearly designate the property over which the receiver is appointed,[2] and the court may embody such directions and impose such conditions therein as are just and proper.[3] The penalty of the bond should usually be fixed and the general terms of the order prescribed at the time it is granted.[4] But it is customary, in most jurisdictions, for the attorney of the moving party to draw up and submit the form of order to the opposite party and to the court, after which it is filed with the clerk in the form approved by the court.[5] Copies are also required, in some jurisdictions, to be served upon all the interested parties.[6] If the mortgagor is in possession the order may direct him to deliver possession to the receiver,[7] and it is proper to direct the receiver therein to account from time to time and to keep down incumbrances out of the rents and profits.[8] It may also, in a proper case, reserve to other incumbrancers or parties the right to afterwards come in, and may state that the appointment is made without prejudice.[9] In short, the court

---

But, for obvious reasons, the appointment of a non-resident is not advisable. Meier v. Kansas Pac. Ry. Co., 5 Dill. (U. S. C. C.) 476.

[1] *In re* Knickerbocker Bank, 19 Barb. (N. Y.) 602.

[2] Crow v. Wood, 13 Beav. 271; O'Mahoney v. Belmont, 62 N. Y. 133; 2 Dan. Chanc. Pl. & Pr. 1737.

[3] United States Trust Co. v. New York, etc., R. Co., 25 Fed. R. 800; Central Trust Co. v. St. Louis, etc., R. Co., 41 Fed. R. 551; West v. Chasten, 12 Fla. 315. The order may provide that the company shall turn over to the receiver its books and papers. American Cont. Co. v. Jacksonville, etc., Ry. Co., 52 Fed. R. 937 (also its seal); Engel v. South, etc., Co., 66 L. T. R. 155.

[4] Wiltsie on Mortgage Foreclosures, § 644.

[5] Wiltsie on Mortgage Foreclosures, § 644.

[6] Whitney v. Belden, 4 Paige Ch. (N. Y.) 140; Rankin v. Pine, 4 Abb. Pr. (N. Y.) 309; Wiltsie on Mort. Foreclosures, § 644.

[7] Griffith v. Griffith, 2 Ves. Sen. 400; Everett v. Belding, 22 L. J. Ch. 75.

[8] 2 Dan. Chanc. Pl. & Pr. 1573.

[9] Smith v. Effingham, 2 Beav. 232; Wiltsie on Mort. Foreclosures, § 645. The court may withhold from the receiver a portion of the assets upon which there is a mortgage about to be enforced under power of sale. Weihl v. Atlanta, etc., Co., 89 Ga. 297, s. c. 15 S. E. R. 282.

may give therein all such directions as are just and proper to enable the receiver to perform his duties until the further order of the court and to preserve the rights of interested parties until the merits of the case can be fully determined. But the court has no power, ordinarily at least, to take into its custody or control, through a receiver, upon a bill to foreclose a mortgage, property not covered by the mortgage, nor to make any order which will delay and hinder creditors from subjecting property not covered by the mortgage to the payment of their debts.[1]

§ 563. **Effect of appointment.**—As already stated, the appointment of a receiver usually determines no rights and is not an adjudication upon the merits of the case.[2] It gives him the right to the possession and control of the property,[3] but it does not divest or retroactively affect existing liens or vested rights of third persons.[4] It has also been held that it does not deprive secured creditors of the right to possess and enforce their securities, and if the receiver has obtained possession of them he may be compelled to deliver them up.[5] But the lienholder may be compelled to go into the same court to enforce his lien where the entire estate is being administered.[6] The legal title is not transferred to the receiver by a mere inter-

---

[1] Scott v. Farmers' L. & T. Co., 69 Fed. R. 17; Hook v. Bosworth, 64 Fed. R. 443.

[2] *Ante*, § 558; In re Colvin, 3 Md. Ch. Dec. 278; Beverley v. Brooke, 4 Gratt. (Va.) 187; Tripp v. Chard Ry. Co., 11 Hare 264; 1 Elliott's Gen. Pr., § 194.

[3] *Post*, § 565. Property in his possession is *in custodia legis*. In re Merchants' Ins. Co., 3 Biss. (U. S. C. C.) 162; Robinson v. Atlantic, etc., Co., 66 Pa. St. 160; 1 Elliott's Gen. Pr., § 195. But see Illinois Steel Co. v. Putnam, 68 Fed. R. 515.

[4] Favorite v. Deardorff, 84 Ind. 555; Arnold v. Weimer, 40 Neb. 216, s. c. 58 N. W. R. 709; State v. Superior Court, 8 Wash. 210, s. c. 35 Pac. R. 1087; Artizan's Bank v. Treadwell, 34 Barb. (N. Y.) 553; Wilson v. Allen, 6 Barb. (N. Y.) 542; Lorch v. Aultman, etc., Co., 75 Ind. 162; Davenport v. Kelly, 42 N. Y. 193; Snow v. Winslow, 54 Iowa 200.

[5] Risk v. Kansas, etc., Co., 58 Fed. R. 45.

[6] Ellis v. Vernon Ice, etc., Co., 86 Tex. 109, s. c. 23 S. W. R. 858; Wiswall v. Sampson, 14 How. (U. S.) 52; Robinson v. Atlantic, etc., R. Co., 66 Pa. St. 160; Skinner v. Maxwell, 68 N. Car. 400.

locutory appointment,[1] but, at least after he has once taken possession, he has a possessory title or special property.[2] His rights to the property are superior to subsequent attachments, or executions[3] in the same jurisdiction, but not to prior valid attachments,[4] or executions already levied.[5] The appointment of a receiver for a corporation does not dissolve the corporation.[6] Pending suits against the corporation are not necessarily abated,[7] but the right of the corporation to sue is generally suspended by the appointment.[8] It may keep up its organization and still perform many acts as a corporation, notwithstanding the fact that the custody, control and manage-

[1] Foster v. Townshend, 2 Abb. N. Cas. (N. Y.) 29; Attorney-General v. Coventry, 1 P. Wms. 306; Fosdick v. Schall, 99 U. S. 235; Manlove v. Burger, 38 Ind. 211; Tillinghast v. Champlin, 4 R. I. 173, s. c. 67 Am. Dec. 510; St. Louis, etc., Co. v. Sandoval, etc., Co., 111 Ill. 32; Ellis v. Boston, etc., R. Co., 107 Mass. 1; Keeney v. Home Ins. Co., 71 N. Y. 396.

[2] Chicago, etc., Ry. Co. v. Keokuk, 108 Ill. 317, s. c. 48 Am. R. 557; Boyle v. Townes, 9 Leigh 158; Singerly v. Fox, 75 Pa. St. 112. His title dates back to the time of making the order. East Tenn., etc., R. Co. v. Atlanta, etc., R. Co., 49 Fed. R. 608; Steele v. Sturges, 5 Abb. Pr. (N. Y.) 442; Maynard v. Bond, 67 Mo. 315.

[3] McDonald v. Charleston, etc., R. Co., 93 Tenn. 281, s. c. 24 S. W. R. 252; State v. Ellis, 45 La. Ann. 1418, s. c. 14 So. R. 308; Harrison v. Waterberry, etc., Co. (Tex.), s. c. 27 S. W. R. 109; Skinner v. Maxwell, 68 N. Car. 400; Ames v. Trustees, 20 Beav. 332; Swift's, etc., Works v. Johnsen, 26 Fed. R. 828. But see as to real estate when there is no conveyance to the receiver, St. Louis, etc., Co. v. Sandoval, etc., Co., 111 Ill. 32.

[4] Jones v. Bank, 10 Col. 464, s. c. 20 Am. & Eng. Corp. Cas. 554; Kittredge v. Osgood, 161 Mass. 384, s. c. 37 N. E. R. 369.

[5] Chautauqua, etc., Bank v. Risley, 19 N. Y. 369; Becker v. Torrance, 31 N. Y. 631; Talladega, etc., Co. v. Jenifer, etc., Co., 102 Ala. 259, s. c. 14 So. R. 743.

[6] Kincaid v. Dwinelle, 59 N. Y. 548; State v. Railroad Comrs., 41 N. J. L. 235; Heath v. Missouri, etc., Ry. Co., 83 Mo. 617; Jones v. Bank, 10 Col. 464, s. c. 20 Am. & Eng. Corp. Cas. 554; National Bank v. Insurance Co., 104 U. S. 54; Taylor Priv. Corp., § 432.

[7] Mercantile Ins. Co. v. Jaynes, 87 Ill. 199; Toledo, etc., R. Co. v. Beggs, 85 Ill. 80, s. c. 28 Am. R. 613. So it is held that it may still be sued. Wyatt v. Ohio, etc., R. Co., 10 Ill. App. 289; Pringle v. Woolworth, 90 N. Y. 502; Allen v. Central R. Co., 42 Iowa 683; St. Joseph, etc., R. Co. v. Smith, 19 Kan. 225.

[8] *Post*, § 568. But see American Bank v. Cooper, 54 Me. 438; People v. Barnett, 91 Ill. 422. There are probably exceptions to this rule in regard to franchises or matters in which the receiver may have no interest.

ment of its property are in the hands of a receiver.[1] The subject of the liabilities of the corporation and of the receiver will be treated in another section.

§ 564. **Collateral attack on appointment.** — The order or judgment appointing a receiver is not open to collateral attack for any errors in the proceedings if the appointment was made by a court having jurisdiction of the case. It can only be assailed in a direct proceeding for that purpose.[2] Thus, where a receiver was appointed by the judge in vacation, under a statute authorizing such an appointment in certain actions, and a complaint was duly filed and both parties appeared before the judge, it was held that the appointment could not be collaterally attacked by a creditor for error of the judge in deciding that the complaint stated a cause of action of the kind designated, nor for any other mere irregularity or error in the order and proceedings.[3] So, where a complaint for the foreclosure of a mortgage prayed for the appointment of a receiver to collect the rents, it was held that it challenged the mortgagor to assert his right to the rent as well as to contest the appointment of a receiver, and that a decree adjudging that the mortgagee was entitled to the rents and appointing a receiver to collect them and apply them to the mortgage debt rendered the matter *res adjudicata* and could not be collaterally

---

[1] See McCalmont v. Philadelphia, etc., R. Co., 7 Fed. R. 386, s. c. 3 Am. & Eng. R. Cas. 163; State v. Merchant, 37 Ohio St. 251, s. c. 9 Am. & Eng. R. Cas. 516; Lehigh, etc., Co. v. Central, etc., R. Co., 35 N. J. Eq. 349; Louisville, etc., R. Co. v. Cauble, 46 Ind. 277; Ohio, etc., R. Co. v. Russell, 115 Ill. 52, s. c. 23 Am. & Eng. R. Cas. 149.

[2] Richards v. People, 81 Ill. 551; Attorney-General v. Guardian, etc., Ins. Co., 77 N. Y. 272; Jones v. Blun, 145 N. Y. 333, s. c. 39 N. E. R. 954; Davis v. Shearer, 90 Wis. 250, s. c. 62 N. W. R. 1050; Smith v. Hopkins, 10 Wash. 77, s. c. 38 Pac. R. 854; Keokuk, etc., Co. v. Davidson, 13 Mo. App. 561; Cook v. Citizens' Nat. Bank, 73 Ind. 256; Russell v. East Anglian Ry. Co., 3 Macn. & G. 104; Edrington v. Pridham, 65 Tex. 612; Greenawalt v. Wilson, 52 Kan. 109, s. c. 34 Pac. R. 403; Skinner v. Lucas, 68 Mich. 424; Comer v. Bray, 83 Ala. 217; Shields v. Coleman, 157 U. S. 168, s. c. 15 S. Ct. R. 570; Booher v. Perrill, 140 Ind. 529, s. c. 40 N. E. R. 36; Kerr on Receivers 166. But see State v. Ross, 122 Mo. 435, 25 S. W. R. 947, s. c. 23 L. R. A. 534; Edee v. Strunk, 35 Neb. 307, s. c. 53 N. W. R. 70.

[3] Pressley v. Lamb, 105 Ind. 171, 189.

attacked by the mortgagor.[1] But it has been held that a stockholder may show, in a suit by a receiver to collect an unpaid subscription, that the receiver was improperly appointed by a decree not binding upon the stockholder.[2] The soundness of this decision, however, is questionable.[3]

§ 565. **Title and possession of receiver.**—The appointment of a receiver gives him the right to immediate possession and control of the property over which he is appointed.[4] Where the defendants, or persons claiming under them, refuse to surrender possession, the court appointing him will assist the receiver by an order directing the surrender of the specific property to him[5] and will, if necessary, enforce its order by attachment.[6] In Iowa it is held that a receiver may call upon the sheriff to aid in enforcing his right to take possession of property committed to his charge by the court.[7] But where a third person holds property under claim of title the court will, in general, require the title of the receiver to be established by action before it will interfere.[8] The title of a receiver vests, by relation, at the date of his appointment, notwith-

---

[1] Storm v. Ermantrout, 89 Ind. 214.
[2] Chandler v. Brown, 77 Ill. 333.
[3] See Taylor Priv. Corp., § 542; Schoonover v. Hinckley, 48 Iowa 82; Burton v. Schildbach, 45 Mich. 504. The appointment of a receiver can not be attacked on the ground of mere irregularity or error, in a proceeding by him to enforce a mechanic's lien in favor of the corporation for which he is receiver. Florence, etc., Co. v. Hanby, 101 Ala. 15, s. c. 13 So. R.343.
[4] Fosdick v. Schall, 99 U. S. 235; Ellis v. Boston, etc., R. Co., 107 Mass. 1; Yeager v. Wallace, 44 Pa. St. 294; Union Trust Co. v. Weber, 96 Ill. 346, 3 Am. & Eng. R. Cas. 583. But see Illinois Steel Co. v. Putnam, 68 Fed. R. 515.
[5] Geisse v. Beall, 5 Wis. 224; Thornton v. Washington Savings Bank, 76 Va. 432; In re Cohen, 5 Cal. 494; People v. Central City Bank, 53 Barb. (N. Y.) 412.
[6] Miller v. Jones, 39 Ill. 54.
[7] State v. Rivers, 66 Iowa 653.
[8] Gelpeke v. Milwaukee, etc., R. Co., 11 Wis. 454; Coleman v. Salisbury, 52 Ga. 470; Levi v. Karrick, 13 Iowa 344; Parker v. Browning, 8 Paige (N. Y.) 388. In Gelpeke v. Milwaukee, etc., R. Co., 11 Wis. 454, Dixon, C. J., speaking for the court, said: "I know of no case where it has been adjudged that the possession of a stranger, who sets up a superior title, in pursuance of which he claims to have entered and to hold, might be thus disturbed. * * * Courts can only act in such cases, where the rights of the parties are obvious, and not the subject of doubts or serious controversy."

standing delay on his part in qualifying.[1] Indeed, it is held that even though the receiver does not qualify at all, but declines to act, the property is still in the custody of the court,[2] since a receiver is only the ministerial officer of the court which appoints him and his possession is the possession of the court.[3] This rule has even been applied as against the claim of a state for taxes, and it is held that property in the hands of a receiver of a federal court can not be reached by proceedings for the collection of state taxes without the consent of such court.[4] Where a person purchases property with notice that proceedings are pending for the appointment of a receiver, it has been held that he takes it subject to the rights of such receiver, if one is granted.[5]

§ 566. **Authority, rights and duties of receiver—Control** by court.—The term "receiver," as used in England, is employed to designate a person appointed by a court of chancery at the suit of some party in interest who receives rents, or other income, and pays ascertained outgoings with a view to conserving property until it can be sold for the payment of debts and liabilities of an insolvent person or corporation. If it is necessary to continue the business a "manager" is appointed.[6] But in the United States a receiver of a railroad is understood to be a ministerial officer of a court of chancery, appointed as an indifferent person between the parties to a suit, whose duty it is not only to preserve the tangible property of the corporation, but, also, its franchises and business, that the value of the railroad as a whole may not be impaired,[7] and that the

---

[1] Maynard v. Bond, 67 Mo. 315; Rutter v. Tallis, 5 Sandf. (N. Y.) 610; Hardwick v. Hook, 8 Ga. 354.

[2] Skinner v. Maxwell, 68 N. Car. 400.

[3] Robinson v. Atlantic, etc., R.Co.,66 Pa. St. 160; Ohio, etc., R. Co. v. Fitch, 20 Ind. 498; Skinner v. Maxwell, 68 N. Car. 400; In re Merchants' Ins. Co., 3 Biss. (U. S.) 165.

[4] Oakes v. Myers, 68 Fed. R. 807; In re Tyler, 149 U. S. 164, s. c. 13 Sup. Ct. R. 785.

[5] Weed v. Smull, 3 Sandf. Ch. (N. Y.) 273.

[6] In re Manchester, etc., R. Co., L. R. 14 Ch. D. 645. A manager of a railway company may be appointed at the suit of a judgment creditor. 38 & 39 Vict. Ch. 31; 30 & 31 Vict. Ch. 127.

[7] Barton v. Barbour, 104 U. S. 126; Wallace v. Loomis, 97 U. S. 146, 162; Milwaukee, etc., R. Co. v. Soutter, 2 Wall. (U.S.) 510; Mercantile Trust Co. v. Missouri, etc., R. Co., 36 Fed. R.

rights of the public to have it kept in operation as a public highway may not be infringed. To this end he is empowered to hire and pay workmen, agents, and all necessary assistants, to make contracts for the carriage of passengers and freight, and to do such other acts as are necessary in maintaining the railroad as a going concern.[1] In the management of such a complicated business as the operation of a railroad a large discretion is necessarily given to a receiver. It may, perhaps, be laid down as a general proposition that all outlays made by the receiver, in good faith, in the ordinary course, with a view to promote the business of the road and to render it profitable and successful, are fairly within the line of discretion which is necessarily allowed to a receiver intrusted with the management and operation of a railroad in his hands.[2] Thus, rebates of freight, paid in accordance with a customary practice necessary to secure business for the railway, the purchase-price of a truck and team of horses, and the expenses of drayage and wharfage have been held to be outlays properly within the discretion of the receiver.[3] So of counsel and witness fees in necessary litigation involving the receivership.[4] But the receiver should usually seek the advice of the court in advance, especially in case of any unusual expenditures,[5] and even then, if the hearing is *ex parte*, the judge may afterwards change his mind.[6]

221; State of Florida v. Jacksonville, etc., R. Co., 15 Fla. 201, 206.

[1] Ordinarily, the duties of a receiver only comprise the operation and management of the road, the payment of current expenses, and the application of the residue of the earnings and receipts to the extinguishment of the indebtedness, to secure which the receiver was appointed. Bank of Montreal v. Chicago, etc., R. Co., 48 Iowa 518. While a receiver may, of course, purchase material essential for the operation of the road, he can not bind the trust by a purchase of material not wanted, excessive in price and defective in quality. Lehigh Coal, etc., Co. v. Central R. Co. of N. J., 35 N. J. Eq. 426.

[2] Cowdrey v. Railroad Co., 1 Woods (U. S.) 334; Cowdrey v. Galveston, etc., R. Co., 93 U. S. 352; Martin v. New York, etc., R. Co., 36 N. J. Eq. 109. See, also, Continental Trust Co. v. Toledo, etc., R. Co., 59 Fed. R. 514.

[3] Cowdrey v. Railroad Co., 1 Woods (U. S. C. C.) 334, affirmed in 93 U. S. 352.

[4] Cowdrey v. Railroad Co., 1 Woods (U. S.) 334; Trustees of Internal, etc., Fund v. Greenough, 105 U. S. 527.

[5] Cowdrey v. Galveston, etc., R. Co., 93 U. S. 352.

[6] Missouri Pac. Ry. Co. v. Texas, etc.,

§ 567. **Contracts of receivers.**—A receiver may, in general, make binding contracts on any subject within the scope of his authority; and one who has, in good faith, executed such a contract, should not be denied compensation, even though the contract should appear to have been improvident and opposed to the best interests of the trust.[1] He may contract to carry freight at a specified rate even from points beyond the terminus of his road to a point on such road, and an order of court is not necessary to authorize him to do so.[2] So, he may effect insurance upon the property in his hands without special authority from the court.[3] But a receiver can not bind the company by a contract to perform duties of a personal nature through a long series of years,[4] nor bind the trust property by a lease involving a large expenditure of money and extending beyond the time of the receivership.[5] Where an executory contract can not, consistently with the interests of the trust, be enforced against the receiver, and the contractor has in good faith expended money in preparation for its performance, it is said that he should yet be made whole by an allowance of damages out of the fund, unless it appears that he has been guilty of collusion or bad faith.[6] For a court of equity can not revoke or annul

Ry. Co., 31 Fed. R. 862. See, also, *Ex parte* Chamberlain, 55 Fed. R. 704, 706.

[1] Vanderbilt *v.* Central R. Co., 43 N. J. Eq. 669. A receiver of a railroad who is operating the road and managing and controlling its business will be presumed to have authority to make contracts relative to the carriage of goods, until the authority conferred upon him by the court is shown. Bayles *v.* Kansas Pac. R. Co., 13 Colo. 181.

[2] Kansas Pac. Ry. Co. *v.* Bayles, 19 Col. 348, 35 Pac. R. 744.

[3] Thompson *v.* Phœnix Ins. Co., 136 U. S. 287, s. c. 3 Lewis' Am. R. & Corp. R. 119. See, also, Brown *v.* Hazlehurst, 54 Md. 26.

[4] Martin *v.* New York, etc., R. Co., 36 N. J. Eq. 109, 12 Am. & Eng. R. Cas. 448. In this case the receiver agreed with a landowner to give him a free annual pass for himself over the road during his life, in part consideration of the release of a right of way across his land, and the court held that the contract could not be enforced against the company.

[5] Chicago Vault Co. *v.* McNulta, 153 U. S. 554, s. c. 14 Sup. Ct. R. 915.

[6] Little *v.* Vanderbilt, 26 Atl. R. 1025, s. c. Vanderbilt *v.* Little, 51 N. J. Eq. 289. If the conduct of the receiver require it, the court might compel him to reimburse the fund for what would thus be taken from it. Vanderbilt *v.* Central R. Co., 43 N. J. Eq. 669. See Moran *v.* Lydecker, 27 Hun (N. Y.) 582.

at the pleasure of the chancellor the contracts of a receiver within the scope of the authority conferred by the order appointing him.[1] But one who contracts with a receiver must be assumed to know that, if he seeks to enforce his contract, it must come under the scrutiny of a court of equity; and no relief will be granted when it appears that the unreasonableness and improvidence of the contract were brought to his notice before he had taken any steps toward its performance.[2] And no contracts beyond such as are essential in order to the successful operation of the road may be made without the sanction of the court.[3] There are some contracts, of course, made by the corporation before the appointment of a receiver which remain binding after his appointment, but there are others which are not binding upon him unless he, in some way, ratifies them.[4] Where a receiver is appointed for a railroad which embraces leased lines he does not necessarily assume responsibility for the covenants of the leases, nor take the place of the lessees, but he is entitled to a reasonable time in which to determine whether to adopt or renounce them.[5] But in extraordinary cases, involving a large outlay of money, the receiver should apply to the court in advance and obtain its authority for the purchase or improvement proposed,[6] and this

---

[1] Vanderbilt v. Central R. Co., 43 N. J. Eq. 669.

[2] In Lehigh Coal, etc., Co. v. Central R. Co., 35 N. J. Eq. 426, the court, by Van Fleet, V. C., said: "All persons dealing with receivers do so at their peril, and are bound to take notice of their incapacity to conclude a binding contract without the sanction of the court."

[3] Lehigh Coal, etc., Co. v. Central R. of N. J., 35 N. J. Eq. 426; McMinnville, etc., R. Co. v. Huggins, 3 Baxt. (Tenn.) 177; Taylor v. Philadelphia, etc., R. Co., 9 Fed. R. 1.

[4] *In re* Seattle, etc., Ry. Co., 61 Fed. R. 541; Kansas Pac. Ry. Co. v. Bayles, 19 Col. 348, 35 Pac. R. 744; Girard, etc., Co. v. Cooper, 51 Fed. R. 332; Central Trust Co. v. Wabash, etc., Ry. Co., 52 Fed. R. 908; Ames v. Union Pac. R. Co., 60 Fed. R. 966; Howe v. Harding, 76 Tex. 17, s. c. 13 S. W. R. 41; 1 Lewis' Am. R. & Corp. R. 502.

[5] Clyde v. Richmond, etc., R. Co., 63 Fed. R. 21; Ames v. Union Pac. R. Co., 60 Fed. R. 966, citing numerous authorities; St. Joseph, etc., R. Co. v. Humphreys, 145 U. S. 105, s. c. 60 Am. & Eng. R. Cas. 431, and note; United States Trust Co. v. Wabash, etc., Ry. Co., 150 U. S. 287, s. c. 14 Sup. Ct. R. 86. But see New York, etc., R. Co. v. New York, etc., R. Co., 58 Fed. R. 268.

[6] Bradley, J., in Cowdrey v. Railroad Co., 1 Woods (U. S.) 331.

is always the safest course in case of doubt. In several cases the courts have refused to confirm the action of receivers in reducing wages of employes without notice to the employes.[1] A receiver, in a suit to foreclose a second mortgage, may be directed to pay interest on first mortgage bonds to prevent the foreclosure of the first mortgage, where it is to the interest of the second mortgage bondholders and the general creditors to prevent such foreclosure, although the application is opposed by the first mortgage bondholders and a majority of the second mortgage bondholders who are also interested in the first mortgage.[2] So, a receiver may be authorized to complete work already begun,[3] or to pledge collaterals to secure loans necessary for the operation of the road.[4]

§ 568. Suits by receivers—Authority to sue.—The right of a corporation to sue is generally suspended by the appointment of an acting receiver.[5] But the receiver, unless specially empowered by statute, can not maintain a suit upon any debt or claim accruing to the corporation which he represents without an order from the court appointing him, directing such suit to be brought.[6] A general permission to bring all necessary suits is usually given in the order making the appointment.[7]

---

[1] Ames v. Union Pac. Ry. Co., 60 Fed. R. 674; Ames v. Union Pac. Ry. Co., 62 Fed. R. 7, s. c. 4 Inters. Com. R. 619. As to controversies with employes, see, generally, Platt v. Philadelphia, etc., R. Co., 65 Fed. R. 660; Arthur v. Oakes, 63 Fed. R. 310; United States Trust Co. v. Omaha, etc., Ry. Co., 63 Fed. R. 737; Thomas v. Cincinnati, etc., R. Co., 62 Fed. R. 17; Continental Trust Co. v. Toledo, etc., R. Co., 59 Fed. R. 514; In re Seattle, etc., R. Co., 61 Fed. R. 541.

[2] Lloyd v. Chesapeake, etc., R. Co., 65 Fed. R. 351.

[3] Florence, etc., Co. v. Hanby, 101 Ala. 15, s. c. 13 So. R. 343.

[4] Clarke v. Central R., etc., Co., 54 Fed. R. 556.

[5] Davis v. Ladoga Creamery Co., 128 Ind. 222; Griffin v. Long Island R. Co., 102 N. Y. 449; Curtis v. McIlhenny, 5 Jones Eq. (N. C.) 290.

[6] Garver v. Kent, 70 Ind. 428; Davis v. Ladoga Creamery Co., 128 Ind. 222; Screven v. Clark, 48 Ga. 41; Davis v. Snead, 33 Gratt. (Va.) 705; Battle v. Davis, 66 N. C. 252; Merritt v. Merritt, 16 Wend. (N. Y.) 405; Coope v. Bowles, 28 How. Pr. (N. Y.) 10; Patrick v. Eells, 30 Kan. 680; State v. Games, 68 Mo. 289; Glenn v. Busey, 5 Mackey (D. C.) 233; Booth v. Clark, 17 How. (U. S.) 322; Ward v. Swift, 6 Hare (Eng.) 309. See, also, *ante*, § 537.

[7] Beach on Receivers, § 651. Such general authority may be given by an order made subsequent to the order

But authority to sue will extend only to causes of action embraced within the terms of the order.[1] The weight of authority is to the effect that even where leave to sue has been granted, a receiver can not, in the absence of statutory authority, institute and conduct actions in his own name, in matters concerning his receivership, unless specially authorized by the court from which he receives his appointment,[2] and that he must, unless so authorized, bring his action in the name of the corporation or party in whom was the right of action before the receiver was appointed.[3] The reason for this is that the legal title to choses in action or other property which he is authorized to reduce to possession, is ordinarily not transferred to the receiver, but remains in the owner. Neither the reason nor the rule, it seems, controls in case a receiver brings suit upon a contract made with him as such,[4] or seeks to recover damages for the seizure and conversion of property after it came into his possession,[5] since a receiver, being the instrument used by the court in accomplishing its purpose, or carrying into effect its decree, must be presumed to have the power to take all such steps as are essential to enforce the performance of contracts and agreements made with him in the course of his receivership,[6] and to protect the property in his possession.[7]

appointing the receiver. Lathrop v. Knapp, 37 Wis. 307.

[1] Beach on Receivers, § 651. An order authorizing the receiver to sue for all the assets of every kind and character does not give a right to maintain an action for injury to property not in the receiver's possession. Alexander v. Relfe, 9 Mo. App. 133. See Screven v. Clark, 48 Ga. 41.

[2] King v. Cutts, 24 Wis. 627; Yeager v. Wallace, 44 Pa. St. 294; Newell v. Fisher, 24 Miss. 392; Manlove v. Burger, 38 Ind. 211; High on Receivers, § 209.

[3] Cases in preceding note. Where statute authority is lacking, it must appear by the averments of the complaint that the court appointing the plaintiff as receiver authorized him to sue in his own name in matters concerning his receivership, or he can not recover in an action in his own name for a debt due the corporation. Garver v. Kent, 70 Ind. 428. But see Boyd v. Royal Ins. Co., 111 N. Car. 372, s. c. 16 S. E. R. 389.

[4] Pouder v. Catterson, 127 Ind. 434.

[5] Singerly v. Fox, 75 Pa. St. 112; Kehr v. Hall, 117 Ind. 405. A receiver may maintain replevin for property which has been wrongfully taken out of his possession. Boyle v. Townes, 9 Leigh (Va.) 158.

[6] Pouder v. Catterson, 127 Ind. 434.

[7] Kehr v. Hall, 117 Ind. 405.

That a court of equity may empower its receiver to bring all actions in his own name as receiver which may be necessary, instead of suing in the name of the corporation or joining it with him even in the absence of any statutory provisions on the subject is the settled doctrine of nearly all the modern cases.[1] And the courts of some of the states have gone to the extent of holding that the appointment of a receiver authorizes him, *virtute officii*, to bring all necessary suits in the discharge of his trust, and makes him so far the assignee of the legal title that he must sue in his own name.[2] Authority is given to the

---

[1] Davis *v.* Gray, 16 Wall. (U. S.) 203; Frank *v.* Morrison, 58 Md. 423; Inglehart *v.* Bierce, 36 Ill. 133; Lathrop *v.* Knapp, 27 Wis. 215; Hardwick *v.* Hook, 8 Ga. 354; Helme *v.* Littlejohn, 12 La. Ann. 298; Boyle *v.* Townes, 9 Leigh (Va.) 158; Henning *v.* Raymond, 35 Minn. 303; Wray *v.* Jamison, 10 Humph. (Tenn.) 185; High on Receivers, § 209; Beach on Receivers, § 688; Gluck & Becker on Rec. of Corp., pp. 155, 156. But in Pennsylvania and some other states, where the receiver is the mere custodian of the property, he is held to have no title upon which to maintain a suit in his own name, but, if authorized to bring suit, must sue in the name of the corporation. Dick *v.* Struthers, 25 Fed. R. 103; Yeager *v.* Wallace, 44 Pa. St. 294; Farmers', etc., Ins. Co. *v.* Needles, 52 Mo. 17; Comer *v.* Bray, 83 Ala. 217.

[2] Helme *v.* Littlejohn, 12 La. Ann. 298; Baker *v.* Cooper, 57 Me. 388; Wray *v.* Jamison, 10 Humph. (Tenn.) 185. In Wilkinson *v.* Rutherford, 49 N. J. L. 241, the court said: "It has already been shown that there is no statutory definition of the powers of the receiver. The question, consequently, that arises, is as to the inherent abilities of a receiver by force of the usual rules of jurisdiction. I can not agree to the doctrine that a receiver is a mere custodian of the property of the person whom, in certain cases, he is made to supplant, and it would seem he is an assignee of the assets within the scope of his office. There seems to be no reason why his powers should not be held to be co-extensive with his functions; and it is clear that he can not conveniently perform those functions unless upon the theory that some interest in the property, akin to that of an assignee's, passes to him. The receiver is to discharge the executory duty of collecting the debts, and taking into his possession, even against antagonistic claims, the tangible property; and after his appointment, a sale of such property by the insolvent would, it is presumed, be absolutely void; and yet, if the interest in the property was not vested in the receiver, it would be difficult to find ground on which to validate the transaction. * * * These embarrassments, as well as many others of a like kind, are obviated by the adoption of the doctrine that, *virtute officii*, a receiver becomes a provisional assignee of the property committed to him, and this doctrine is recognized in the case of Harrison *v.* Maxwell, 44 N. J. L. 316."

receiver by statute in many of the states to prosecute and defend actions in his own name as receiver.[1] Where this power is made absolute it is not necessary for him to show a special authority from the court appointing him to prosecute an action,[2] though he must set forth sufficient facts to show his character as receiver, and that he is the person authorized by the statute to act on behalf of the corporation.[3] Where, as is the case in Indiana, a receiver is given power to bring and defend actions, collect debts, etc., in his own name, "under the control of the court, * * * and generally to do such acts respecting the property, as the court or judge thereof may authorize," the complaint must allege that suit was brought by direction of the court appointing the receiver or it will be fatally defective.[4]

§ 569. When receiver may maintain suit—Defenses to receiver's suit.—The court may empower its receiver to sue upon any rights of action which belong to the person or corporation whose property has been put into the receiver's hands.[5] But a receiver usually has no power to maintain suits where the

[1] Stimson's Am. Stat. (1892), § 8362, citing laws of California, Idaho, Washington, Montana, Wyoming, Utah, Mississippi, Rhode Island, Ohio, Michigan, Maryland, North Carolina, Colorado. See Rev. Stat. Ind. 1894, § 1242.

[2] Miller v. Mackenzie, 29 N. J. Eq. 291.

[3] Miami Exporting Co. v. Gano, 13 Ohio 269; Asheville Division No. 15 v. Aston, 92 N.Car. 578; Gluck & Becker on Rec. of Corp., 156.

[4] Garver v. Kent, 70 Ind. 428; Moriarity v. Kent, 71 Ind. 601. See Davis v. Ladoga Creamery Co., 128 Ind. 222.

[5] Griffin v. Long Island R. Co., 102 N. Y. 449; Coope v. Bowles, 28 How. Pr. (N. Y.) 10, 42 Barb. 87; Litchfield Bank v. Peck, 29 Conn. 384; McIlrath v. Snure, 22 Minn. 391. As to suits against stockholders for unpaid subscriptions, see Cutting v. Damerel, 88 N. Y. 410; Sagory v. Dubois, 3 Sandf. Ch. (N. Y.) 466; Means' Appeal, 85 Pa. St. 75; Lathrop v. Knapp, 37 Wis. 307; Starke v. Burke, 5 La. Ann. 740; Schoonover v. Hinckley, 48 Iowa 82; Clarke v. Thomas, 34 Ohio St. 46; Stillman v. Dougherty, 44 Md. 380; Sawyer v. Hoag, 17 Wall. (U. S.) 610; Upton v. Tribilcock, 91 U. S. 45. In Illinois a suit can be maintained against the stockholders only when they were made parties to the suit in which a receiver was appointed. Chandler v. Brown, 77 Ill. 333. As to suits against corporate officers for breach of trust and for gross mismanagement and neglect of duty, see McCarty's Appeal, 110 Pa. St. 379; Ackerman v. Halsey, 37 N. J. Eq. 356.

CORP. 51

party whose effects he receives could not have sued, and the fact that an order of court directs him to bring the suit will not add to his right to maintain it.[1] This rule, however, as we have elsewhere shown,[2] is not without its exceptions, for there are cases in which a receiver may maintain a suit that the corporation could not have maintained. As a general rule, the same defenses may be interposed to an action by the receiver on a demand due the corporation that could have been set up in a suit by the corporation itself.[3] This rule is subject to the exception, however, that where the receiver is suing in the interest of the creditors, no defense is available against him which could not equitably be opposed to a suit by them. Thus, it has been held that a receiver appointed at the instance of creditors may recover dividends that were fraudulently paid by the corporation after it became insolvent,[4] or a subscription which the creditors themselves could enforce although the corporation could not,[5] and it has been held that a debtor can not interpose a judgment recovered upon a promissory note of the corporation as a set-off to an action by the receiver to enforce payment of his indebtedness due the corporation.[6]

§ 570. **Right of receiver to sue in other jurisdictions—Comity.**—Some authorities hold that a receiver owing his appoint-

---

[1] La Follett v. Akin, 36 Ind. 1; State, ex rel., v. Sullivan, 120 Ind. 197; Hyde v. Lynde, 4 N. Y. 387.

[2] Ante, § 537.

[3] Brooks v. Bigelow, 142 Mass. 6; Litchfield Bank v. Peck, 29 Conn. 384; Cox v. Volkert, 86 Mo. 505; Chase v. Petroleum Bank, 66 Pa. St. 169; Moise v. Chapman, 24 Ga. 249; Van Wagoner v. Paterson, etc., Co., 23 N. J. Law 283; Thomas v. Whallon, 31 Barb. (N. Y.) 172; Hade v. McVay, 31 Ohio St. 231.

[4] Osgood v. Ogden, 4 Keyes (N. Y.) 70.

[5] Cole v. Satsop R. Co., 9 Wash. 487, s. c. 43 Am. St. R. 858. See generally as to collection of subscriptions by receivers, note to Thompson v. Reno Sav. Bank, 3 Am. St. R. 797, 833.

[6] Where the effect of allowing a set-off would be to prefer one creditor over another, a set-off will not be allowed. Singerly v. Fox, 75 Pa. St. 112; Clark v. Brockway, 3 Keyes (N. Y.) 13; Litchfield Bank v. Church, 29 Conn. 137; Williams v. Traphagen, 38 N. J. Eq. 57. See, also, Lanier v. Gayoso, etc., Inst., 9 Heisk. (Tenn.) 506. But a set-off may sometimes be allowed. See High on Receivers, § 247; Cox v. Volkert, 86 Mo. 505; Colt v. Brown, 12 Gray (Mass.) 233; Hade v. McVay, 31 Ohio St. 231; Berry v. Brett, 6 Bosw. (N. Y.) 627.

§ 570   RECEIVERS.   797

ment to the common law jurisdiction of a court of equity can not sue outside of the jurisdiction of the court which appointed him.[1] This rule is generally followed, in the older cases, by the federal courts with regard to receivers appointed by the United States courts in other districts,[2] and is based upon the ground that a court of chancery has no authority to act beyond its jurisdiction, and that consequently a receiver at common law is not clothed with power to sue in a foreign jurisdiction.[3] But the better rule, as it seems to us, and one which is well sus-

---

[1] Farmers', etc., Ins. Co. v. Needles, 52 Mo. 17; Hope Mut. L. Ins. Co. v. Taylor, 2 Robt. (N. Y.) 278; Warren v. Union Nat. Bank, 7 Phila. (Pa.) 156; Moseby v. Burrow, 52 Tex. 396. See Bartlett v. Wilbur, 53 Md. 485; Graydon v. Church, 7 Mich. 36; Moreau v. Du Bellet, (Tex. Civ. App.) 27 S. W. R. 503. See, also, "Actions by Foreign Receivers," 37 Cent. L. J. 315.

[2] Booth v. Clark, 17 How. (U. S.) 322; Wilkinson v. Culver, 23 Blatchf. (U. S.) 416; Brigham v. Luddington, 12 Blatchf. (U. S.) 237; Holmes v. Sherwood, 3 McCrary (U. S.) 405; Hazard v. Durant, 19 Fed. R. 471. In Booth v. Clark, supra, the court said: "A receiver has no extra territorial power of official action; none which the court appointing him can confer, with authority to enable him to go into a foreign jurisdiction to take possession of the debtor's property; none which can give him, upon the principle of comity a privilege to sue in a foreign court or another jurisdiction, as the judgment creditor himself might have done, where his debtor may be amenable to the tribunal which the creditor may seek. * * * We think that a receiver could not be admitted to the comity extended to judgment creditors without an entire departure from chancery proceedings as to the manner of his appointment, the securities which are taken from him for the performance of his duties, and the direction which the court has over him in the collection of the assets of the debtor and the application and distribution of them." It may be that the act of March 3, 1887, as corrected August 13, 1888, found in 25 U. S. Stat. L. 433, may have some bearing upon this question, but so far as we know, the point has never been made.

[3] But where the receivers were appointed under statutory provisions existing at the organization of the corporation and entering into and forming part of its charter, by which the rights and duties of such receivers were defined, it was held that the shareholders and creditors of the corporation were charged with notice of the charter right of the corporation to have all of its property transferred to a receiver if it should become insolvent, and must be held to have impliedly agreed that, in such case, they would be bound by the laws of the state in which the corporation was organized, so far as they formed a part of the charter of the company. Parsons v. Charter Oak L. Ins. Co., 31 Fed. Rep. 305; Davis v. Life Association, 11 Fed. Rep. 781; Relfe v. Rundle, 103 U. S. 222; Bockover v. Life Association, 77 Va. 85.

tained by authority, is that, as a matter of comity, receivers duly appointed and qualified, and invested with authority to sue for and collect the corporate assets situated in other states, may, and usually will, be permitted to maintain suits in the courts of such other states.[1] This rule, however, is said to be subject to the exception that while a receiver may invoke the aid of a foreign court in obtaining possession of property or funds within its jurisdiction, aid will only be extended as against those who were parties to, or in some way in privity with, the proceedings in which his appointment was made, or who are in possession of the property or effects of the estate without right.[2] It is generally the policy of each state to retain within its control the property of a foreign debtor until all domestic claims have been satisfied, and in many of the states comity will not be extended by the courts to enable a receiver to take possession of, and withdraw from the state, property or funds which were already in such state and which resident creditors are seeking to subject to the payment of their debts, by proceedings duly instituted for that purpose.[3] After a receiver has reduced the property or effects of the corporation to possession he becomes vested with a special property therein, and is entitled to protect this special property, while it continues, by action, in like manner as if he was the absolute owner.[4] This property interest of the receiver will be recognized and enforced by the courts of other states, not alone upon

---

[1] Bagby v. Atlantic, etc., R. Co., 86 Pa. St. 291; Hurd v. City of Elizabeth, 41 N. J. L. 1; Metzner v. Bauer, 98 Ind. 425; Hoyt v. Thompson, 5 N. Y. 320; Sercomb v. Catlin, 128 Ill. 556; Lycoming Fire Ins. Co. v. Wright, 55 Vt. 526; High on Receivers, §§ 239, 244; ante, § 555. See also "Actions by Foreign Receivers," 37 Cent. L. J. 315, and authorities cited on page 318.

[2] Catlin v. Wilcox, etc., Co., 123 Ind. 477.

[3] Hurd v. City of Elizabeth, 41 N. J. L. 1; Lycoming Fire Insurance Co. v. Wright, 55 Vt. 526; Willitts v. Waite, 25 N. Y. 577. See State v. Jacksonville, etc., R. Co., 15 Fla. 201; Thurston v. Rosenfield, 42 Mo. 474. "We decline to extend our wonted courtesy so far as to work detriment to citizens of our own state who had been induced to give credit to the foreign insolvent." Runk v. St. John, 29 Barb. (N. Y.) 585. See ante, § 555.

[4] Pouder v. Catterson, 127 Ind. 434; Kehr v. Hall, 117 Ind. 405; Gluck and Becker on Rec. of Corp. 185.

principles of comity, but as a matter of right.[1] If he recovers judgment against a debtor in his own name as receiver, he may maintain an action against the debtor in another jurisdiction upon such judgment, as a judgment creditor.[2] So where he takes the debtor's note in payment of a claim due the corporation, the receiver may bring suit in a foreign state to collect the note.[3] A receiver may take property of which he has obtained legal possession into other jurisdictions without affecting his title thereto. And the citizens of other states into which the property is taken by the receiver in the performance of his duties, can not proceed against such property by attachment for the debts of the corporation.[4] So, if property is wrongfully and without the receiver's consent, taken out of his possession, he may follow it and reclaim it wherever found, and the courts of foreign states will aid him to recover it.[5]

§ 571. Suits against receivers—Leave to sue must be obtained.—In the absence of any statutory provisions on the subject, it is the general rule that a suit can not be maintained against a receiver without leave of the court appointing him,[6]

---

[1] See *ante*, §§ 555, 563.

[2] Wilkinson *v.* Culver, 25 Fed. Rep. 639.

[3] Inglehart *v.* Bierce, 36 Ill. 133.

[4] Crapo *v.* Kelly, 16 Wall. (U. S.) 610; Pond *v.* Cooke, 45 Conn. 126; Chicago, etc., R. Co. *v.* Keokuk, etc., Co., 108 Ill. 317; Cagill *v.* Wooldridge, 8 Baxter (Tenn.) 580. But it has been held in California that cars belonging to a railroad which is being operated by a receiver appointed by the United States Circuit Court in another state may be attached for a debt due a citizen of California, if they are sent into that state in the transaction of the business of the company. Humphreys *v.* Hopkins, 81 Cal. 551. See, however, comments on this case in note to § 555, *ante*. See Gluck and Becker on Rec. of Corp. 186.

[5] McAlpin *v.* Jones, 10 La. Ann. 552.

[6] Wiswall *v.* Sampson, 14 How. (U. S.) 52; Barton *v.* Barbour, 104 U. S. 126; St. Joseph, etc., Railroad Co. *v.* Smith, 19 Kan. 225; Rogers *v.* Mobile, etc., R. Co., (Tenn.) 12 Am. & Eng. R. Cas. 442; Martin *v.* Atchison, 2 Idaho 590, 33 Pac. Rep. 47; Keen *v.* Breckenridge, 96 Ind. 69; Melendy *v.* Barbour, 78 Va. 544; Little *v.* Dusenberry, 46 N. J. Law 614; De Graffenried *v.* Brunswick, etc., R. Co., 57 Ga. 22; Heath *v.* Missouri, etc., R. Co., 83 Mo. 617, 623; Miller *v.* Loeb, 64 Barb. (N. Y.) 454; Meredith, etc., Bank *v.* Simpson, 22 Kan. 414; Reed *v.* Richmond, etc., R. Co., (Va.) 33 Am. & Eng. R. Cas. 503; Reed *v.* Axtell & Myers, 84 Va. 231. A judgment in favor of a receiver in an ac-

but it has been held that where the suit is brought in such court, the fact that it entertains the suit is sufficient to establish the granting of leave to sue.[1] Since the receiver is but the "hand" of the court, it is held that any interference with his possession and control of the property by suit or otherwise is an interference with the process of the court, and not to be tolerated.[2] And it is argued that to permit the institution of such suits and the taking of judgments against the receiver would result in the creation of new liens upon the property in the hands of the receiver, over which the court would have no control, thereby clouding the title to the property, and that the whole purpose of the litigation in equity and of the taking possession of property through the receiver, would be defeated.[3] In accordance with this view it was held that a court had no jurisdiction to entertain a suit against the receiver of a railroad corporation, where it was shown that leave to sue had not been obtained, although the receiver was appointed by a court of the state of Virginia and was transacting business in the District of Columbia, where the suit was brought.[4] The court also held that the rule requiring leave to sue applies not only to cases where the pur-

---

tion against him begun without leave of court is, it seems, a nullity, and constitutes no defense to a subsequent action. Comer v. Felton, 61 Fed. R. 731.

[1] City of Ft. Dodge v. Minneapolis, etc., R. Co., 87 Iowa 389, 54 N. W. R. 243. In this case it was held that, where mandamus against a receiver is instituted in the court which appointed him, and the court entertains the action, he can not object that it is an improper remedy, or that the relief sought might have been obtained in a more summary and less formal manner.

[2] Thompson v. Scott, 4 Dillon (U.S.) 508; Barton v. Barbour, 104 U. S. 126.

[3] Thompson v. Scott, 4 Dillon (U.S.) 508.

[4] Barton v. Barbour, 104 U. S. 126.

But in this case the injury sued for was received while traveling on defendant's road in Virginia, and the fund from which payment was sought to be enforced was in Virginia, and the court declined to pass upon the general question as to the right to sue foreign receivers doing business outside of the jurisdiction by which they were appointed. In City of Fort Dodge v. Minneapolis, etc., R.Co., 87 Iowa 389, 55 Am. & Eng. R. Cas. 58, it was held that comity does not demand that the enforcement of a statute requiring the construction of railroad crossings should be deferred to await the action of the courts of another state, which appointed a receiver in reference to the property of the corporation situated in that state.

pose of the suit is to take from the receiver property which is actually in his possession, placed there by order of the court, but embraces as well any suit to recover judgment against a receiver for a money demand, even though the cause of action arose out of the operation of a railroad by the receiver.[1] In cases where leave to sue is essential, it may be given, in the case of a railroad operated by a receiver, by a general leave to all persons having demands against the receiver as such, for liabilities incurred by him in operating the road, without applying to the court for leave to do so, to bring suit thereon in any other court having jurisdiction.[2] An application for leave

[1] Barton v. Barbour, 104 U. S. 126. Mr. Justice Woods, in delivering the opinion of the court in this case, said: "The evident purpose of a suitor who brings his action against a receiver without leave, is to obtain some advantage over the other claimants, upon the assets in the receiver's hands. His judgment, if he recovered one, would be against the defendant in his capacity as receiver, and the execution would run against the property in his hands as such." See this case severely criticised in Lyman v. Central Vermont R. Co., 59 Vt. 167, and see also cases cited in notes 6, 2, *infra*, pages 803, 804.

[2] Dow v. Memphis, etc., R. Co., 20 Fed. R. 260. In this case the following order was made: That persons having demands or claims of any character against the receiver may, without applying to this court for leave to do so, bring suit thereon against the receiver in any court in this state having jurisdiction, or may file their petition and have their claim adjudicated in this court at their election. This clause shall not be construed as authorizing the levy of any writ or process on the property in the hands of the receiver, or taking the same from his custody or possession. Judge Caldwell said: "The general license to sue the receiver is given because it is desirable that the right of the citizen to sue in the local state courts on the line of the road should be interfered with as little as possible. It is doubtless convenient and a saving and protection to the railroad company and its mortgage bondholders, to have the litigation growing out of the operation of a long line of railroad concentrated in a single court, and on the equity side of that court, where justice is administered without the intervention of a jury. But, in proportion as the railroad and its bondholders profit by such an arrangement, the citizen dealing with the receiver is subjected to inconvenience and expense, and he is deprived of the forum, and the right of trial by jury, to which, in every other case of legal cognizance, he has the right to appeal for redress. It is not necessary, for the accomplishment of the purposes for which receivers of railroads are appointed, to impose such burdens and deprivations on citizens dealing with the receiver; and neither the railroad company nor its bondholders have any equity to ask it. Where property is in the hands of a receiver simply as a custodian, or

to sue is addressed to the sound discretion of the court,[1] and should not be granted unless the petition states a *prima facie* cause of action against the receiver; but the court should not, as a rule, undertake to decide the case in advance.[2]

§ 572. **Effect of failure to obtain leave to sue.**—It has been held that a complaint in such a suit which does not allege that leave to bring an action has been obtained is insufficient on demurrer.[3] But a complaint which does not aver that leave to sue has been obtained is sufficient to withstand a motion in arrest of judgment after verdict upon issue joined.[4] The objection that the action was begun without leave of court should be interposed by the receiver at the first opportunity, if he re-

for sale or distribution, it is proper that all persons having claims against it, or upon the fund arising from its sale, should be required to assert them in the court appointing a receiver. But a very different question is presented where the court assumes the operation of a railroad hundreds of miles in length, and advertises itself to the world as a common carrier. This brings it into constant and extensive business relations with the public. Out of the thousands of contracts it enters into daily as a common carrier, some are broken and property is damaged and destroyed, and passengers injured and killed by the negligent and tortious acts of its receiver and its agents. * * * When a court, through its receiver, becomes a common carrier, and enters the lists to compete with other common carriers for the carrying trade of the country, it ought not to claim or exercise any special privileges denied to its competitors and oppressive to the citizen. The court appointing a receiver can not, of course, permit any other jurisdiction to interfere with its possession of the property, or control its administration of the fund, but in the case of long lines of railroad, the question of the legal liability of its receiver to the demands of the citizen, growing out of the operation of the road, should be remitted to the tribunals that would have jurisdiction if the controversy had arisen between the citizen and the railroad company, giving to the citizen the option of seeking his redress in such tribunals, or in the court appointing the receiver."

[1] Meeker *v*. Sprague, 5 Wash. St. 242. But see Conwell *v*. Lawrance, 46 Kan. 83, s. c. 26 Pac. R. 461.

[2] Jordan *v*. Wells, 3 Woods (U. S. C. C.) 527. See Palys *v*. Jewett, 32 N. J. Eq. 302, to the effect that leave will usually be granted unless there is some good reason for not granting it.

[3] Keen *v*. Breckenridge, 96 Ind. 69; Wayne Pike Co. *v*. State, 134 Ind. 672, s. c. 34 N. E.R. 440; Barton *v*. Barbour, 104 U. S. 126. But see Kinney *v*. Crocker, 18 Wis. 74; St. Joseph, etc., R. Co. *v*. Smith, 19 Kan. 225; Allen *v*. Central R. Co., 42 Iowa 683.

[4] Elkhart Car Works Co. *v*. Ellis, 113 Ind. 215.

lies upon the protection of the court as a defense. After he has voluntarily submitted to the authority of the court and joined issue without objection, it has been held to be too late for him to urge that leave to sue him was not first obtained.[1] It has been held, however, that parties who bring such a suit without leave may be punished for contempt,[2] and that the proceedings may be restrained,[3] or stayed, or set aside on motion.[4] The constitutional right to sue in the federal courts in certain cases does not enable a litigant to maintain a suit without leave in one of those courts against a receiver appointed by a state court.[5] It has been held, however, that where the receiver, wrongfully or by mistake, takes possession of the property of a third person, such person may bring suit therefor against him personally as a matter of right; for, in such case, the receiver would be acting *ultra vires*, and can not be held to represent the court by which he was appointed.[6] A number of cases, also, while admitting the general doctrine that a court of equity may draw to itself all controversies to which the receiver is a party, hold that it is not bound to do so, but may properly leave the determination of actions at law for money demands, the

[1] Elkhart Car Works Co. v. Ellis, 113 Ind. 215; Hubbell v. Dana, 9 How. Pr. (N. Y.) 424; Town of Roxbury v. Central Vermont R. Co., 4 Ry. & Corp. L. J. 204; Naumburg v. Hyatt, 24 Fed. R. 898, 901; Mulcahey v. Strauss, 151 Ill. 70, s. c. 37 N. E. R. 702; Flentham v. Steward, 45 Neb. 640, s. c. 63 N. W. R. 924. See Jerome v. McCarter, 94 U. S. 734; Comer v. Felton, 61 Fed. R. 731; and see article in 25 Am. L. Reg. (N. S.) 289, in which the position is taken that the receiver can not give jurisdiction by waiving the objection.

[2] Kennedy v. Indianapolis, etc., R. Co., 3 Fed. R. 97; Wiswall v. Sampson, 14 How. (U. S.) 52, 67.

[3] Evelyn v. Lewis, 3 Hare 472; Tink v. Rundle, 10 Beav. 318.

[4] De Groot v. Jay, 30 Barb. (N. Y.) 483; Taylor v. Baldwin, 14 Abb. Pr. (N. Y.) 166.

[5] Reed v. Axtell, 84 Va. 231.

[6] Parker v. Browning, 8 Paige (N. Y.) 388; Paige v. Smith, 99 Mass. 395; Hills v. Parker, 111 Mass. 508. In this latter case the owner of a locomotive in use upon the road of an insolvent railroad corporation was permitted to maintain an action of replevin against the receiver of such corporation to recover his property, without having first obtained leave of court. In re Christian Jansen Co., 128 N. Y. 550, holds that even though property is wrongfully in the possession of a corporation, it can not be replevied without leave of court after it comes into the possession of a receiver appointed in voluntary proceedings to dissolve the corporation.

exact amount of which is uncertain, to be determined by other courts of competent jurisdiction,[1] and that the lack of leave to sue does not affect the jurisdiction of the court in which such a suit is brought,[2] and does not invalidate a judgment rendered by such court in case the proceedings are not stayed by the court which appointed the receiver.[3]

§ 573. **Effect of recent act of congress.** — It would seem highly proper that suits upon causes of action arising from the negligent operation of a railroad by a receiver, or from a breach of contracts made in the course of such operation,[4] should be tried in a court of law with the aid of a jury, and this is sometimes urged as a reason for denying that leave to

---

[1] St. Joseph, etc., R. Co. v. Smith, 19 Kan. 225; Kinney v. Crocker, 18 Wis. 74; Allen v. Cent. R., etc., 42 Iowa 683; Chautauqua County Bank v. Risley, 19 N. Y. 369; Blumenthal v. Brainerd, 38 Vt. 402.

[2] Lyman v. Central Vermont R.iCo., 59 Vt. 167; Blumenthal v. Brainerd, 38 Vt. 402; Nichols v. Smith, 115 Mass. 332; Kinney v. Crocker, 18 Wis. 74; Allen v. Central R. Co., 42 Iowa 683. In Kinney v. Crocker, *supra*, the court said: "A court of equity will, on proper application, protect its own receiver, when the possession which he holds under the order of the court is sought to be disturbed." And again: "But in all these cases it is not a question of jurisdiction in the courts of law, but only a question whether equity will exercise its own acknowledged jurisdiction of restraining suits at law, under such circumstances, and itself dispose of the matter involved. It follows that although a plaintiff in such case, desiring to prosecute a legal claim for damages against a receiver, might in order to relieve himself from the liability to have his proceeding arrested by an exercise of its equitable jurisdiction, very properly obtain leave to prosecute; yet his failure to do so is no bar to the jurisdiction of the court of law, and no defense to an otherwise legal action in the trial. There can be no room to question this conclusion in all cases where there is no attempt to interfere with the actual possession of property which the receiver holds under the order of the court of chancery, but only an attempt to obtain a judgment at law in a claim for damages."

[3] De Groot v. Jay, 30 Barb. (N. Y.) 483; Taylor v. Baldwin, 14 Abb. Pr. 166.

[4] For instances in which such suits have been maintained, see Allen v. Central R. Co., 42 Iowa 683; Blumenthal v. Brainerd, 38 Vt. 402; Newell v. Smith, 49 Vt. 255; Paige v. Smith, 99 Mass. 395; Nichols v. Smith, 115 Mass. 332; Barter v. Wheeler, 49 N. H. 9; Kain v. Smith, 80 N. Y. 458; Lyman v. Central Vermont R. Co., 59 Vt. 167; Lamphear v. Buckingham, 33 Conn. 237; Ballou v. Farnum, 9 Allen (Mass.) 47. See, also, Klein v. Jewett, 26 N. J.Eq. 474.

sue is jurisdictional.[1] The view that leave to sue in such a case ought not to be required has been taken by congress, and it is now provided[2] that every receiver or manager of any property appointed by any court of the United States may be sued in respect of any act or transaction of his in carrying on the business connected with such property, without the previous leave of the court in which such receiver or manager was appointed; but such suit shall be subject to the general equity jurisdiction of the court in which he was appointed, so far as the same shall be necessary to the ends of justice. It is held that this act gives an absolute right to sue a receiver appointed by a federal court in any court having jurisdiction of the subject-matter.[3] The judgment of the court trying such suit is as

---

[1] In a dissenting opinion in the case of Barton v. Barbour, 104 U. S. 126, Mr. Justice Miller said: "In the case before us the plaintiff sues to recover damages for a personal injury, caused by an act done by the receiver or his agents in the transaction of business as a common carrier, in which he was largely and continuously engaged. Why should the receiver not be sued like any one else on such a cause of action, in any court of competent jurisdiction? The reply is because he is a receiver of the road on which plaintiff was injured, and holds his appointment at the hands of a Virginia court of chancery. If this be a sufficient answer, then the railroad business of the entire country, amounting to many millions of dollars per annum, may be withdrawn from the jurisdiction of the ordinary courts having cognizance of such matters, and all the disputes arising out of these vast transactions must be tried alone in the court which appointed the receiver. Not only this, but the right of trial by jury, which has been regarded as secured to every man by the constitutions of the several states and of the United States, is denied to the person injured, and though his case has no element of equitable jurisdiction he is compelled to submit it to a court of chancery or to one of the masters of such court. In an action for a personal injury, which has always been considered as eminently fitted for a jury, and especially in the assessment of damages, this constitutional right is denied because the receiver of a railroad, and not its owners, committed the wrong." We fail to see, however, how these considerations meet the question. They may constitute forcible reasons against requiring a trial without a jury in the court which appointed the receiver, but they do not seem to be in point upon the mere question of the jurisdiction of another court where no leave to sue is granted. Leave will be given unless there is good reason for withholding it, and trial by jury may be had in any proper case.

[2] Act of Congress of March 3, 1887, as corrected by act of August 13, 1888, § 3, 24 U. S. St. 554, 25 U. S. St. 436.

[3] Texas, etc., R. Co. v. Gay, 86 Tex. 571; Dillingham v. Russell, 73 Tex. 47, s. c. 3 L. R. A. 634; Central Trust

final and conclusive against the receiver as against any other suitor, and will not be disturbed by the court appointing him because of any suggestion that he has not obtained justice in the other court.[1] The act applies to receivers appointed before it was passed as well as to those afterwards appointed, and they may be sued without leave in the same manner as those subsequently appointed.[2] And a receiver may be sued under the provisions of this act, in respect to an act of his predecessor in the office.[3] Actions for personal injuries caused by a station platform being out of repair are included,[4] as well as actions for injuries caused in the running of trains. But it has been held that such statute does not authorize a suit by a stockholder against the directors and receivers, without leave of court, upon a cause of action which accrued before the appointment of the receivers and upon which they have refused to bring suit.[5] Neither is a proceeding in garnishment a suit against the receiver for "any act or transaction of his," within the meaning of the statute.[6] The subjection of such suits to

Co. v. St. Louis, etc., R. Co., 40 Fed. Rep. 426; McNulta v. Lochridge, 141 U. S. 327, 332. Notwithstanding an order of court discharging the receiver and restoring the property to the receiver without foreclosure, and giving a limited time within which all claims must be presented, a suit may subsequently be brought against the receiver personally to recover damages for personal injuries due to the negligence of his employes. Texas, etc., R. Co. v. Johnson, 151 U. S. 81. But see Decker v. Gardner, 124 N. Y. 334.

[1] "This court will not entertain the suggestion that its receiver will not obtain justice in the state courts." Central Trust Co. v. St. Louis, etc., R. Co., 41 Fed. R. 551, 42 Am. & Eng. R. Cas. 26; Dillingham v. Hawk, 60 Fed. R. 494. The appointing court has no jurisdiction to enjoin the prosecution of an action against its receiver where authorized by the statute. Texas, etc., R. Co. v. Johnson, 151 U. S. 81; Central Trust Co. v. East Tennessee, etc., R. Co., 59 Fed. R. 523. But this statute does not limit nor destroy the right of the federal court to protect property in the hands of its receivers from external attack. Ex parte Tyler, 149 U. S. 164, 191, 13 Sup. Ct. 785, 793.

[2] See Texas & P. Ry. Co. v. Cox, 145 U. S. 593, s. c. 12 Sup. Ct. R. 905.

[3] McNulta v. Lockridge, 141 U. S. 327, s. c. 12 Sup. Ct. R. 11.

[4] Fullerton v. Fordyce, 121 Mo. 1, s. c. 25 S. W. R. 587. See, also, Central Trust Co. v. St. Louis, etc., Ry. Co., 40 Fed. R. 426; McNulta v. Lockridge, 137 Ill. 270, s. c. 31 Am St. R. 362; Texas, etc., Ry. Co. v. Cox, 145 U. S. 593, s. c. 12 Sup. Ct. R. 905.

[5] Swope v. Villard, 61 Fed. R. 417.

[6] Central Trust Co. v. Chattanooga, etc., R. Co., 68 Fed. R. 685; Central Trust Co. v. East Tennessee, etc., R.

the general equity jurisdiction of the court does not invest it with appellate or supervisory jurisdiction over state courts in which the suits may be brought, and it can not annul, vacate or modify their judgments. This provision merely gives the United States court a right to control suits which seek to deprive the receiver of possession of the property, and all process of execution which would have the effect, so far as may be necessary to the ends of justice, in preventing the road from being broken into parts, or deprived of its rolling stock, so as to impair the value as a going concern.[1] In other words, the time and mode of paying a judgment rendered by a state court remain under the control of the court appointing the receiver, although the amount of such judgment can not be changed. Some of the states have similar statutes, conferring a general authority upon all persons to sue receivers engaged in operating railroads under appointment by any court of equity.

§ 574. **Rule where suit has been commenced before appointment of receiver.**—Where suit has been commenced against the corporation before the appointment of a receiver such suit may be prosecuted to judgment, and such judgment will establish as against the receiver, the rightful amount of the claim.[2] In

Co., 59 Fed. R. 523. *Contra*, Irwin *v.* McKechnie, 58 Minn. 145, s. c. 59 N. W. R. 987, 26 L. R. A. 218. As to the general rule forbidding garnishment of property in the hands of a receiver, see Jackson *v.* Lahee, 114 Ill. 287; Columbian Book Co. *v.* De Golyer, 115 Mass. 67; Taylor *v.* Gillean, 23 Tex. 508; McGowan *v.* Myers, 66 Iowa 99; Smith *v.* McNamara, 15 Hun (N. Y.) 447.

[1] Eddy *v.* Lafayette, 49 Fed. R. 807; Central Trust Co. *v.* St. Louis, etc., R. Co., 41 Fed. R. 551; Dillingham *v.* Hawk, 60 Fed. R. 494.

[2] Pine Lake Iron Co. *v.* Lafayette Car Works, 53 Fed. R. 853. But such a judgment does not constitute a lien upon the property in the receiver's hands. Bell *v.* Chicago, etc., R. Co., 34 La. Ann. 785. The receiver of a railroad company may be substituted as defendant in an action for tort committed by the company before his appointment. Decker *v.* Gardner, 58 Hun 602, s. c. 11 N. Y. Supp. 388. But see Jones *v.* Pennsylvania R. Co., 19 D. C. (8 Mackey) 178, holding that the fact that a receiver of the property of a railroad company has been appointed will not affect the right of recovery against the company itself for personal injuries, where the receiver has allowed existing officers to manage the business, and received the net earnings of the road, without taking

some jurisdictions, however, the receiver should be substituted as a party defendant. The recovery of a judgment against the receiver appointed by a court of equity has no further effect than to fix the amount of the plaintiff's claim. An execution issued thereon can not be levied upon the property in the receiver's hands without leave from the court by which the receiver was appointed.[1] This rule is not changed as to the United States courts by the provisions of the "Federal Judiciary Act," but the levying of execution or other judicial process upon property in the hands of its receivers is, by that act, left under the control of the court which they represent.[2] Indeed, the very object of appointing a receiver would be defeated, if he could be stripped of the property piecemeal by process issued by rival courts at the suit of individual creditors. It has been held that a sale of property upon execution while it was in the possession of a receiver and without leave of court was illegal and void, although the levy was made before the receiver was appointed.[3]

§ 575. **Protection of receiver by the court.**—Not only in the matter of suits, but in all other respects, the court will protect its receiver in his possession and control of the property com-

---

[1] Coe v. Columbus, etc., R. Co., 10 Ohio St. 372; Skinner v. Maxwell, 68 N. C. 400; Russel v. East Anglian R. Co., 6 Eng. Railway & Canal Cases 501.

[2] See Central Trust Co. v. St. Louis, etc., R. Co., 41 Fed. R. 551.

[3] Walling v. Miller, 108 N. Y. 173. Earl, J., speaking for the court, says: "The lien of the execution was not destroyed by the appointment of the receiver, but the rights and interests of all parties in the property were thereafter to be adjusted by the court which appointed the receiver, and the property could not be taken out of the possession of the receiver, and sold upon any part in its management, the same remaining with the company. execution, without leave of court. The execution creditor could bring his lien to the attention of the court in the action in which the receiver was appointed, and ask to have the execution satisfied out of the proceeds of the property. But persons having liens upon the property had no right to interfere with its possession by the receiver and without any application to or adjudication of the court, sell and dispose of it, and thus dissipate it, and deprive the court of jurisdiction to administer it." It has been held otherwise where the sheriff retains actual possession under an attachment. State v. Superior Court, 8 Wash. 210, s. c. 35 Pac. R. 1087; State v. Graham, 9 Wash. 528, s. c. 36 Pac. R. 1085.

§ 575   RECEIVERS.   809

mitted to his care. An attempt to disturb him in the discharge of his duties with reference to such property may be a contempt of court.[1] The offender may be attached, and, if the circumstances justify it, punished by fine and imprisonment.[2] The wrongful seizure of property in the hands of a receiver upon process from another court is a contempt on the part of the officers executing the writ.[3] And it is also contempt of the court appointing the receiver to take property from his possession upon distraint for rent.[4] Actual violence offered to a receiver in the discharge of his duties or such threats of violence as to intimidate the receiver may amount to such an interference.[5] So may violence or threats by which the servants or employes of the receiver are prevented from carrying on the business as directed by the court. It is the duty of the court to see that property which is put into its hands, or in the hands of its receivers, is absolutely protected, and that nobody, directly or indirectly, wrongfully interferes with the management of that property.[6] Where the employes of another road who have struck, or any other persons, prevent the servants of a receiver from working and thereby interfere with the operation of the road as directed by the order of court, they are

[1] Secor v. Toledo, etc., R. Co., 7 Biss. (U. S.) 513; King v. Ohio, etc., R. Co., 7 Biss. (U. S.) 529; United States v. Kane, 23 Fed. R. 748; In re Wabash, etc., R. Co., 24 Fed. R. 217; In re Higgins, 27 Fed. R. 443; Chafee v. Quidnick Co., 13 R. I. 442; O'Mahoney v. Belmont, 62 N. Y. 133; Vermont & Canada R. Co. v. Vermont Cent. R. Co., 46 Vt. 792; Hazelrigg v. Bronaugh, 78 Ky. 62; Richards v. People, 81 Ill. 551; Helmore v. Smith, 56 L. J. Ch. Div. 145.

[2] See cases in preceding note. An interference with the possession and use of a street railway in the hands of a receiver may be enjoined. Fidelity Trust, etc., Co. v. Mobile St. R. Co., 53 Fed. R. 687. The rule that property in the hands of a receiver is in *custodia legis*, and that interference with such possession without leave of the court is a contempt, is as applicable in the case of seizure thereof to enforce payment of taxes due the state as in any other case. *Ex parte* Tyler, 149 U. S. 164, 191, 13 Sup. Ct. Rep. 785, 793.

[3] Commonwealth v. Young, 11 Phila. (Pa.) 606. See Albany City Bank v. Schermerhorn, 9 Paige (N. Y.) Ch. 373.

[4] Noe v. Gibson, 7 Paige (N. Y.) Ch. 513.

[5] Fitzpatrick v. Eyre, 1 Hogan (Irish Rolls) 171.

[6] United States v. Kane, 23 Fed. R. 748.

guilty of contempt of court.[1] The employes of a railroad operated by a receiver have the same right to quit work that other employes have, and it is not unlawful for them to use arguments and persuasion to induce their fellow-employes to do the same. But if a mere request, or mere advice to quit work, is accompanied by such a demonstration of force as is calculated to intimidate the receiver's employes, and induce them to abandon his service against their will, it will be punished as a contempt.[2] In case of a disagreement between the receiver and his employes, the proper course for them to pursue is to petition the court for an order directing a just and equitable settlement of the differences. The court will direct the receiver to enter into such agreements and contracts with his employes as may give them reasonable protection and at the same time guard the rights of creditors and others interested in the trust property.[3] Punishment for contempt is usually by fine and imprisonment which is largely within the discretion of the court against which the contempt was committed,[4] and while the court will not be tenacious of any mere prerogative to notice an unintentional interference,[5] or to visit severe punishment upon the offenders for a first or unpremeditated offense,[6] it is the duty of the court to see that property which is put into its hands, or in the hands of its receivers, is absolutely protected, and the punishment must be

[1] *In re* Higgins, 27 Fed. R. 443; *In re* Wabash R. Co., 24 Fed. R. 217; *In re* Doolittle, 23 Fed. R. 544; King v. Ohio, etc., R. Co., 7 Biss. (U. S.) 529; Secor v. Toledo, etc., R. Co., 7 Biss. (U. S.) 513.

[2] United States v. Kane, 23 Fed. R. 748; *In re* Higgins, 27 Fed. R. 443.

[3] Waterhouse v. Comer, 55 Fed. R. 149, s. c. 53 Am. & Eng. R. Cas. 329. In this case, Judge Speer granted the petition of the Brotherhood of Locomotive Engineers for an order directing the receiver to enter into a contract with them prescribing the terms of service, the qualifications necessary for promotion, and the rate of compensation. He required the petitioners, however, to waive rule 12 of the Brotherhood, by which it is provided that members shall refuse to handle the cars of roads with which the Brotherhood are at variance, since such rule is illegal, and a compliance with it would compel the engineers to violate the interstate commerce law.

[4] *In re* Higgins, 27 Fed. R. 443. There is said to be no appeal from the judgment of the court in such a case.

[5] *In re* Doolittle, 23 Fed. R. 544.

[6] *In re* Doolittle, 23 Fed. R. 544, and United States v. Kane, 23 Fed. R. 748.

made severe enough to restrain and prevent all interference with such property.[1] It is no defense to a proceeding for contempt in interfering with the receiver's possession of property placed in his hands by the court, to show that the order appointing him was erroneously or improvidently made.[2] An order of the court which is not void can not be assailed in a collateral proceeding,[3] and the court will not in a proceeding to punish a contempt review the questions which were passed upon when the receiver was appointed.[4] The fact that railroad companies are in some sense public agents presents an additional reason why judicial control should be extended as far as possible to prevent an interference with them in the exercise of their public functions.[5] An injunction will be granted, in a proper case, restraining unlawful interference by strikers or others, and its violation is punishable as a contempt of court. This matter, however, will be fully considered hereafter.

§ 576. Liability of receivers—Generally.—A receiver is the mere officer of the court by which he was appointed and can not question any order made by the court with reference to the control of the receivership property, but must implicitly obey all such orders.[6] It follows from this that the only personal liability which can attach to a receiver in the operation of a railroad is for some wrongful or unauthorized act of his own. His liability for acts done in the discharge of his duties is official only, and such acts bind only the trust estate.[7] It accords

---

[1] United States v. Kane, 23 Fed R. 748.
[2] Kerr on Receivers, 166.
[3] Cook v. Citizens' National Bank, 73 Ind. 256.
[4] Richards v. People, 81 Ill. 551; People v. Sturtevant, 9 N. Y. 263; Howard v. Palmer, Walk. (Mich.) 391; Russell v. East Anglian R. Co., 3 M. & G. 104.
[5] Delaware, etc., R. Co. v. Erie R. Co., 21 N. J. Eq. 298.

[6] Herrick v. Miller, 123 Ind. 304.
[7] A receiver is not personally liable for the torts of his employes. Kain v. Smith, 80 N. Y. 458; Cardot v. Barney, 63 N. Y. 281; Meara v. Holbrook, 20 Ohio St. 137; Klein v. Jewett, 26 N. J. Eq. 474; Erskine v. McIlrath, 60 Minn. 485, s. c. 62 N. W. R. 1130; Mersey Docks v. Gibbs, 11 H. L. Cas. 686. Nor on contracts properly made in his official capacity. Walsh v. Raymond, 58 Conn. 251;

with sound principle and reason that a receiver exercising the franchise of a railroad company shall be held amenable, in his official capacity, to substantially the same rules of liability that are applicable to the company while it exercises the same powers of operating the road.[1] And this is the rule established by the great weight of modern authority.[2] As has been seen, there is a conflict of authority as to whether this liability can be enforced by suit, or must be asserted by petition in the court by which the receiver was appointed, but the cases are practically unanimous in holding that a receiver who assumes to exercise the rights and powers of a common carrier becomes answerable in his official capacity for all injuries and losses sustained by persons dealing with him in that capacity to the same extent in general that the corporation would have been liable.[3]

§ 577. **Liability for torts.**—Upon the principle referred to in the preceding section receivers are held liable for damages

---

Livingston v. Pettigrew, 7 Lans. (N. Y.) 405. Nor for costs in actions which he prosecutes by direction of court. Columbian Ins. Co. v. Stevens, 37 N. Y. 536; Devendorf v. Dickinson, 21 How. Pr. (N. Y.) 275. But a receiver is personally liable upon unauthorized contracts entered into by him. Ryan v. Rand, 20 Abb. N. Cas. (N. Y.) 313. And for wrongful and negligent acts on his part by which loss is occasioned. Ricks v. Broyles, 78 Ga. 610; Carr v. Morris, 85 Va. 21; Brooks v. Miller, 29 W. Va. 499. See, also, Erwin v. Davenport, 9 Heisk. (Tenn.) 44; Kain v. Smith, 80 N. Y. 458. He is also liable like any other trustee for profits which he makes out of a use of the money or property belonging to the trust estate. Ryan v. Morrill, 83 Ky. 352; Schwartz v. Keystone Oil Co., 153 Pa. St. 283.

[1] Sprague v. Smith, 29 Vt. 421; Little v. Dusenberry, 46 N. J. L. 614.

[2] Blumenthal v. Brainard, 38 Vt. 402; Newell v. Smith, 49 Vt. 255; Lyman v. Central Vermont R. Co., 59 Vt. 167; Melendy v. Barbour, 78 Va. 544; Toledo, etc., R. Co. v. Beggs, 85 Ill. 80; Heath v. Missouri, etc., R. Co., 83 Mo. 617; Klein v. Jewett, 26 N. J. Eq. 474; Kinney v. Crocker, 18 Wis. 74; Paige v. Smith, 99 Mass. 395; Sloan v. Central Iowa R. Co., 62 Iowa 728; Farlow v. Kelly, 108 U. S. 288; Cowdrey v. Galveston, etc., R. Co., 93 U. S. 352; Ex parte Brown, 15 S. C. 518.

[3] Ohio, etc., R. Co. v. Anderson, 10 Ill. App. 313; Melendy v. Barbour, 78 Va. 544; Ex parte Brown, 15 S. C. 518; Lyman v. Central Vermont R. Co., 59 Vt. 167; Meara v. Holbrook, 20 Ohio St. 137; Klein v. Jewett, 26 N. J. Eq. 474; Sloan v. Central Iowa R. Co., 62 Iowa 728; Rogers v. Mobile, etc., R. Co., (Tenn.) 12 Am. & Eng. R. Cas. 442; McNulta v. Lockridge, 137 Ill. 270, s. c. 31 Am. St. R. 362.

for personal injuries sustained by passengers[1] and employes,[2] by reason of defects in the road or equipment,[3] or the negligence or misconduct of the receiver's servants.[4] Receivers as such have also been held liable for damage or loss of goods entrusted to them for carriage,[5] for injuries inflicted upon travelers,[6] for injuries to stock arising from a failure to fence

Note to Naglee v. Alexandria, etc., Ry. Co., 5 Am. St. R. 308, 315.

[1] Newell v. Smith, 49 Vt. 255; Mobile, etc., R. Co. v. Davis, 62 Miss. 271; Dillingham v. Russell, 73 Tex. 47, s. c. 3 L. R. A. 634; Bartlett v. Keim, 50 N. J. L. 260; Little v. Dusenberry, 40 N. J. L. 614, s. c. 50 Am. R. 445; Fullerton v. Fordyce, 121 Mo. 1, s. c. 42 Am. St. R. 516. But see Cardot v. Barney, 63 N. Y. 281.

[2] Rogers v. Mobile, etc., R. Co., 12 Am. & Eng. R. Cas. 442; Ex parte Brown, 15 S. Car. 518; Meara v. Holbrook, 20 Ohio St. 137; Sloan v. Central Iowa R. Co., 62 Iowa 728; Durkin v. Sharp, 88 N. Y. 225. The receiver of a railroad company, who is operating the road, can not escape liability for injuries to his employes owing to the insufficient number of trackmen employed to keep the track in good repair, on the ground that the lack of sufficient trackmen was due to the want of funds in his hands, as the road was not paying running expenses. Graham v. Chapman, 58 Hun 602, s. c. 11 N. Y. S. 318. It is held in Texas that the receiver is not liable for the death of an employe under a statute giving a right of action against the "proprietor, owner, charter, or hirer" of a railroad for injuries resulting in death caused by his negligence or that of his employes. Yoakum v. Selph, 83 Tex. 607, 19 S. W. R. 145; Houston, etc., R. Co. v. Roberts, (Tex. Sup.) 19 S. W. R. 512; Texas Pac. R. Co. v. Collins, 84 Tex. 121, 19 S. W. R. 365. In a joint action against a railroad company and its receiver for the death of a servant, caused by the negligence of the receiver, a recovery can not be had against the company, where the receiver was not primarily liable. Texas Pac. Ry. Co. v. Collins, 84 Tex. 121, 19 S. W. R. 365.

[3] The fact that the defect existed when the receiver took possession does not relieve him from liability for an injury, caused thereby while he is operating the road. A receiver is as much bound to remedy existing defects which render the operation of the road unsafe, as he is to discover and repair new defects as they arise. Texas, etc., R. Co. v. Geiger, 79 Tex. 13; Bonner v. Mayfield, 82 Tex. 234.

[4] A receiver, like any other common carrier, is liable for the damages occasioned by a malicious assault upon a passenger by the conductor in charge of a train, acting within the scope of his employment. Dillingham v. Russell, 73 Tex. 47, s. c. 3 L. R. A. 634.

[5] Kansas Pacific R. Co. v. Searle, 11 Col. 1; Paige v. Smith, 99 Mass. 395; Kinney v. Crocker, 18 Wis. 74; Newell v. Smith, 49 Vt. 255; Melendy v. Barbour, 78 Va. 544. See Mobile, etc., R. Co. v. Davis, 62 Miss. 271; Cowdrey v. Galveston, etc., R. Co., 93 U. S. 352.

[6] Lehigh Coal, etc., Co. v. Central R. Co., 42 N. J. Eq. 591; McNulta v. Lockridge, 137 Ill. 270, s. c. 31 Am. St. R. 362.

the road,[1] and, in general, for all damages for torts for which the corporation itself would be liable under similar circumstances.[2] Where the liability of a railroad company is merely statutory, however, it does not always follow that its receiver will also be liable to the same extent, for the statute may not embrace receivers within its terms or meaning. Thus, it has been held that a receiver is not a "proprietor, owner, charterer or hirer" of a railroad within the meaning of a statute giving a right of action for damages on account of injuries, resulting in death, caused by the negligence of any person of the class

---

[1] Central Trust Co. v. Wabash, etc., R. Co., 26 Fed. R. 12. See, also, Farrell v. Union Trust Co., 77 Mo. 475, s. c. 13 Am. & Eng. R. Cas. 552; Brockert v. Central Iowa R. Co., 82 Iowa 369, s. c. 47 N. W. R. 1026. It was held by the Supreme Court of Missouri in the case of Combs v. Smith, 78 Mo. 32, that an action may be maintained against the receiver of a corporation for a tort committed by the corporation or its servants before his appointment. And Judge Caldwell, in Dow v. Memphis, etc., R. Co., 20 Fed. R. 260, held that where the bill for foreclosure was filed more than a year after default in the payment of the mortgage debt, the receiver should be required to pay out of the earnings of the road, all debts due from the railroad company for operating expenses, including damages for injuries to persons or property, for a period of six months prior to the appointment of the receiver. See Miltenberger v. Logansport R. Co., 106 U. S. 286. And some states have statutes prohibiting any railway company from creating mortgage liens which shall be superior to judgments for injuries to persons or property. But the weight of authority holds that, in the absence of statutory provisions on the subject, the owner of a judgment in tort for injuries to person or property inflicted in the operation of the railroad before the receiver was appointed is merely a general creditor of the corporation, and, as such, is not entitled to any priority of payment over the mortgagees. Central Trust Co. v. East Tennessee, etc., R. Co., 30 Fed. R. 895; Farmers' Loan, etc., Co. v. Green Bay, etc., R. Co., 45 Fed. R. 664; In re Dexterville, etc., Mfg. Co., 4 Fed. R. 873. See Frazier v. East Tennessee, etc., R. Co., 88 Tenn. 138.

[2] In Klein v. Jewett, 26 N. J. Eq. 474, Van Fleet, V. C., speaking for the court, said: "A receiver operating a railroad under the order of a court of equity stands, in respect to duty and liability, just where the corporation would if it were operating the road. * * * Whether the receiver is regarded as the officer of the law or the representative of the proprietors of the corporation or its creditors, or as combining all these characters, he is entrusted with the powers of the corporation and must, therefore, necessarily be burdened with its duties and liabilities. There can be no such thing as an irresponsible power, exerting force or authority, without being subject to duty, under any sys-

designated or his servants or agents.[1] So, it has been held that a statute providing that certain persons engaged in the service of any railway corporation shall be deemed vice-principals and that certain other persons engaged in such service shall be deemed fellow-servants, does not apply to the employes of the receiver of such a corporation.[2] But, on the other hand, it has been held that a statute making railroad companies liable for injuries to an employe, caused by the negligence of co-employes of a certain class, applies to a receiver of such a company and his employes.[3] No general rule can be laid down upon this subject, but we think that, ordinarily, such a statute applying to railroad companies would also apply to their receivers engaged in the operation of the road. The question can only be determined, however, by a reference to the terms and purpose of the particular statute under consideration in each case.

§ 578. **Receiver is bound to perform duties to public—Mandamus.**—He is also bound, in general, to perform the public duties imposed by law upon the corporation whose franchises he is exercising. It has been held that he may be compelled, by mandamus, to construct a crossing which the railroad company has neglected or refused to build;[4] but the general rule is that a receiver will not be compelled to operate the road or perform a similar public duty by mandamus, both because the

tem of laws framed to do justice. It is an inseparable condition of every grant of power by the state, whether expressed or not, that it shall be properly exercised, and that the grantee shall be liable for injuries resulting directly and exclusively from his negligence."

[1] Turner v. Cross, 83 Tex. 218, s. c. 18 S. W. R. 578, 15 L. R. A. 262; Dillingham v. Blake, (Tex.) s. c. 32 S. W. R. 77; Allen v. Dillingham, 60 Fed. R. 176; Burke v. Dillingham, 60 Fed. R. 729. But see Murphy v. Holbrook, 20 Ohio St. 137.

[2] Campbell v. Cook, 86 Tex. 630, s. c. 59 Am. & Eng. R. Cas. 482, distinguishing Church of Holy Trinity v. United States, 143 U. S. 457.

[3] Hornsby v. Eddy, 56 Fed. R. 461; Rouse v. Harry, 55 Kan. 589, s.c. 40 Pac. R. 1007; Union Trust Co. v. Thomason, 25 Kan. 1. But see Beeson v. Busenbark, 44 Kan. 669; Henderson v. Walker, 55 Ga. 481. A statute of limitations in favor of the company has also been held applicable in an action against the receiver. Bartlett v. Keim, 50 N. J. L. 260, s. c. 13 Atl. R. 7.

[4] City of Fort Dodge v. Minneapolis, etc., R. Co., 87 Iowa 389, 55 Am. & Eng. R. Cas. 58.

court which appointed him may order and compel him to do so, and mandamus usually lies only when there is no other adequate and simple remedy, and because another court will not interfere with the court which appointed him.[1] The court which appointed him may compel him to perform such duty, and it has been held that the failure of the court to provide funds with which to perform it is not a good excuse for failing to obey the order of the court.[2] There may be public duties, however, not connected with the operation of the road, which the company, rather than the receiver, is still obliged to perform, and where the duties are statutory the terms of the statute may be such as not to include receivers, although they will generally be required to perform such public duties connected with the operation of the road as the company was obliged to perform. The fact that the receiver is empowered by statute to operate the railroad for the use of the public does not make him a public officer, so as to destroy this liability.[3] The duty of operating the road imposed on the receiver by such a statute is the same duty to the public which is imposed upon every railroad corporation acting under statutory authority. Its object is to secure the continued operation of the road as a common carrier with the same rights and subject to the same liabilities as before the railroad corporation became insolvent.

§ 579. Liability on contracts.—The receiver, as a general rule, can not be compelled to perform a contract of the corporation, where no lien was created in favor of the other contracting party.[4] Where, however, a receiver continued to use a right of way, which had been obtained by the company in con-

[1] State v. Marietta, etc., R. Co., 35 Ohio St. 154.
[2] Peckham v. Dutchess, etc., R. Co., 145 N. York 385, s. c. 40 N. E. R. 15.
[3] Little v. Dusenberry, 46 N. J. L. 614, 25 Am. & Eng. R. Cas. 632. But see Hopkins v. Connel, 2 Tenn. Ch. 323.
[4] Express Co. v. Railroad Co., 99 U. S. 191. The receiver of a railroad company is not liable for removing a switch, which the company had agreed to maintain, where he has not adopted the company's contract as his own, for his appointment and acts in managing the property, as an officer of the court, do not absolve the company from liability for consequent breaches of its contracts. Brown v. Warner, 78 Tex. 543.

sideration of an agreement by it to pay the owner a certain sum each month for the use of water from a spring upon his land, it was held that the receiver was bound to perform the contract so long as he used the right of way.[1] It is improper for a receiver to contract for supplies with a company composed of the superintendent and other officers of the railroad company for which he is the receiver, but he may give an unusually low rate of freight in order to introduce into general use a cheap and valuable article, which, if brought into general demand, would add greatly to the freight receipts of the road.[2] The liability of a receiver, as such, upon contracts made by him in the course of the receivership, depends, of course, very largely upon the nature and terms of the contract and his authority to make it, although there are cases in which the court will afford relief to one who has contracted with a receiver who had no authority to enter into the contract.[3] The receiver is not personally liable, under ordinary circumstances, to one who contracts with him as receiver in regard to matters connected with his trust.[4]

§ 580. **Liability on claims arising from operation of the road.**—The official liability of the receiver for claims arising from the operation of the road ceases with his final discharge.[5] But provision is usually made in the order discharging him, for the payment of such claims either by the railroad company

---

[1] Howe v. Harding, 76 Tex. 17, s. c. 13 S. W. R. 41, 1 Lewis Am. R. & Corp. R. 502.

[2] Clarke v. Central R., etc., Co., 66 Fed. R. 16.

[3] See *ante*, § 567.

[4] Livingston v. Pettigrew, 7 Lansing (N. Y. Sup. Ct.) 405; Newman v. Davenport, 9 Baxter (Tenn.) 538; Ellis v. Little, 27 Kan. 707.

[5] Davis v. Duncan, 19 Fed. Rep. 477; Ryan v. Hays, 62 Tex. 42; Mobile, etc., R. Co. v. Davis, 62 Miss. 271. An order of a federal court discharging the receiver, restoring the property to the company without foreclosure, and requiring that all claims against the receiver shall be presented to the court before a given date, in default whereof they shall be barred, does not, in view of the judiciary act of 1887–88, making receivers liable to suit in any competent court without leave of the appointing court, prevent the subsequent recovery in a state court of a judgment *in personam* for personal injuries, or its enforcement by the same court. Texas & P. Ry. Co. v. Johnson, 151 U. S. 81, s. c. 14 Sup. Ct. R. 250.

or by the purchasers of the property.[1] The expenses attending the operation of the road by the receiver properly constitute a first claim upon all moneys received from such operation, superior to the lien of mortgage creditors.[2] Claims for damages to persons or property arising from the operation of the road are classed as operating expenses, and are entitled as such to priority of payment over mortgage bonds.[3] So, also, are rents accruing during the receivership upon rolling stock held by the corporation under a conditional sale[4] together with the cost of necessary supplies[5] and the wages of employes.[6] Where the receiver undertakes the operation of another road than that over which he was appointed, under a lease, he assumes the same liability as any other lessee; and the fact that the contract of lease was entered into with the permission of the court

[1] See Farmers' Loan, etc., Co. v. Central R. Co., 7 Fed. Rep. 537; Texas, etc., R. Co. v. Adams, 78 Tex. 372.

[2] Mobile, etc., R. Co. v. Davis, 62 Miss. 271; Ex parte Brown, 15 S. Car. 518; Texas, etc., R. Co. v. Johnson, 76 Tex. 421; In re Eastern and Midland R. Co., L. R. 45 Ch. D. 367, 45 Am. & Eng. R. Cas. 71; Clark v. Central R., etc., Co., 66 Fed. R. 803; Wallace v. Loomis, 97 U. S. 146; Beach on Receivers, §§ 366, 367.

[3] Ex parte Brown, 15 S. Car. 518; Klein v. Jewett, 26 N. J. Eq. 474; Mobile, etc., R. Co. v. Davis, 62 Miss. 271; Cowdrey v. Galveston, etc., R. Co., 93 U. S. 352. Such claims must be paid, in the first instance, out of the income of the property. But if that prove insufficient, payment may be made out of the proceeds arising from a sale of the road. Union Trust Co. v. Illinois Midland R. Co., 117 U. S. 434.

[4] Kneeland v. American L. & T. Co., 136 U. S. 89; In re Eastern and Midland R. Co., L. R. 45 Ch. D. 367, 45 Am. & Eng. R. Cas. 71; Woodruff v. Erie Ry. Co., 93 N. Y. 609; Beach on Receivers, § 372. As to prior accrued installments due upon such rolling stock at the time the receiver was appointed, the vendors are simply general creditors. Fidelity Ins. Co. v. Shenandoah Valley R. Co., 86 Va. 1; Kneeland v. American L. & T. Co., supra; Thomas v. Peoria, etc., R. Co., 36 Fed. Rep. 808.

[5] Williamson v. Washington City, etc., R. Co., 33 Gratt. (Va.) 624; Poland v. Lamoille Valley R. Co., 52 Vt. 144; Kneeland v. Bass Foundry, etc., Works, 140 U. S. 592; Burnham v. Bowen, 111 U.S.776; see post, § 590.

[6] Hoover v. Montclair, etc., R. Co., 29 N. J. Eq. 4; Meyer v. Johnston, 53 Ala. 237; Langdon v. Vermont, etc., R. Co., 54 Vt. 593; McLane v. Placerville, etc., R. Co., 66 Cal. 606; Union Trust Co. v. Illinois Midland R. Co., 117 U. S. 434; Cowdrey v. Galveston, etc., R. Co., 93 U. S. 352; Stanton v. Alabama, etc., R. Co., 2 Woods (U. S.) 506; Kennedy v. St. Paul, etc., R. Co., 2 Dill. (U. S.) 448.

does not remove such liability, where the act of the receiver in making it was purely voluntary.[1]

§ 581. Liability of corporation.—The corporation itself is not ordinarily liable either civilly[2] or criminally[3] for any acts or upon any contracts of a receiver who has full possession of its property and entire charge of its affairs. Where, however, the receiver has used money which should have been applied to the payment of plaintiff's claim in the purchase of property which is afterward surrendered to the corporation upon the receiver's discharge, it seems that a court of equity will hold the corporation liable for such claim to the extent of the property so received by it.[4] The corporation continues liable for taxes imposed upon its property or business while managed

---

[1] Kain v. Smith, 80 N. Y. 458.

[2] Godfrey v. Ohio, etc., R. Co., 116 Ind. 30, s. c. 37 Am. &. Eng. R. Cas. 8; Memphis, etc., R. Co. v. Hoechner, 67 Fed. R. 456; Kansas Pac. R. Co. v. Wood, 24 Kan. 619; Turner v. Hannibal, etc., R. Co., 74 Mo. 602; Ohio, etc., R. Co. v. Russell, 115 Ill. 52; McNulta v. Lockridge, 137 Ill. 270, s. c. 31 Am. St. R. 362; Kansas Pac. R. Co. v. Searle, 11 Colo. 1; Kansas, etc., R. Co. v. Dorough, 72 Tex. 108; Thurman v. Cherokee R. Co., 56 Ga. 376; Memphis, etc., R. Co. v. Stringfellow, 44 Ark. 322; Erwin v. Davenport, 9 Heisk. (Tenn.) 44; Metz v. Buffalo, etc., R. Co., 58 N. Y. 61; Davis v. Duncan, 19 Fed. R. 477. But the possession of the receiver must usually be exclusive in order to exonerate the company and it should not hold itself out to the public as operating the road. Railroad Co. v. Brown, 17 Wall. (U. S.) 445.

[3] State v. Wabash, etc., R. Co., 115 Ind. 466.

[4] The net earnings of the road in the hands of the receiver are chargeable with the expenses of operating the road, including injuries to persons and property. And where such earnings have been diverted to the purchase of property and permanent improvements equity will follow them. Mobile, etc., R. Co. v. Davis, 62 Miss. 271; Texas, etc., R. Co. v. Johnson, 76 Tex. 421, s. c. 18 Am. St.R. 60, and note; Tex., etc., R. Co. v. White, 82 Tex. 543; Houston, etc., R. Co. v. Crawford, 88 Tex. 277, s. c. 31 S. W. R. 176; Garrison v. Texas, etc., R. Co., (Tex.) s. c. 30 S. W. R. 725; Texas, etc., R. Co. v. Bloom, 60 Fed. R. 979. See, also, Texas, etc., R. Co. v. Johnson, 151 U. S. 81, s. c. 60 Am. & Eng. R. Cas. 496, and note. But where there is no evidence that earnings have been diverted to the betterment of the road, an instruction that the company is not liable is proper. Texas, etc., R. Co. v. Hoffman, 83 Tex. 286, 18 S. W. Rep. 741. Rights of other parties may sometimes prevent the application of the doctrine stated in the text, and it is one not to be carelessly applied. It is possible that the court went too far in some of the cases cited, but we believe the doctrine is just and equitable.

by a receiver.[1] And where the duty of the railroad corporation to erect fences along its line is made absolute by statute, the corporation may be held liable for damages resulting from a failure to maintain such fences while a receiver is in charge of its property.[2] The appointment of a receiver does not relieve the corporation from the consequences of any neglect of duty in the original construction or subsequent maintenance of its road, but it may be held liable for damages directly traceable to its fault, even though they accrue during the receivership. Thus, a corporation is liable for damages resulting from the flooding of land caused by the negligent construction of one of its culverts, although the overflow occurred while the road was in the hands of a receiver.[3]

---

[1] Philadelphia, etc., R. Co. v. Commonwealth, 104 Pa. St. 80. In this case, the court held the defendant liable for a tax upon the gross receipts coming into the hands of the receiver. The court said: "If the owner of this property was not to bear the burden of the public charges against it, we are at a loss to determine upon whom they should fall. The receivers, the appointees of the United States Circuit Court, were owners neither of these receipts nor of the property whence they were derived, and they were not personally accountable for the taxes upon them. The decree of the circuit court made no change in the title to this property. * * * The commonwealth was entitled to her taxes, and that the owner of the property taxed should be made to pay the charges upon it is a conclusion that is but just and reasonable." In New York, where the property of an insolvent corporation has been sequestrated, and is in the hands of a receiver appointed in a foreclosure proceeding who has in his hands money derived from its gross earnings sufficient to pay the taxes, — a direct application for an order on him for payment may be made to the court in the foreclosure proceeding, by the attorney-general by petition, making the corporation and the receiver parties. Central Trust Co. v. New York City & N. R. Co., 110 N. Y. 250, 18 N. E. 92, 1, L R. A. 260, 13 Cent. 404, 18 N. Y. S. R. 30, 4 R. R. & Corp. L. J. 462.

[2] Louisville, etc., R. Co. v. Cauble, 46 Ind. 277; Ohio, etc., R. Co. v. Fitch, 20 Ind. 498; Kansas, etc., R. Co. v. Wood, 24 Kan. 619; Ohio, etc., R. Co. v. Russell, 115 Ill. 52. It seems to us, however, that where the receiver has possession and entire and exclusive control of the road and all its assets, the receiver rather than the corporation should be sued when the injury is caused by his own failure to fence, unless the terms of the statute are such as to require a different rule.

[3] Union Trust Co. v. Cuppy, 26 Kan. 754; Kansas Pacific R. Co. v. Wood, 24 Kan. 619. But the receiver is also liable for maintaining the nuisance erected by the corporation. Union Trust Co. v. Cuppy, *supra*.

§ 582. **Receivers of leased lines.**—A receiver may, with the consent of the lessors, continue in possession of leased lines operated by the insolvent corporation, but his appointment as receiver does not necessarily make him an assignee of the leases so as to give the rentals priority over the mortgages.[1] And where the road is operated under an order of court directing separate accounts to be kept with the leased lines, and expressly recognizing the right of the lessors to take possession of the leased lines for non-payment of rent upon making proper application therefor, the lessors can not assert such a lien against the earnings of the general system.[2] The fact that the leased line was held subject to resumption of control by the lessors at any time negatives the claim that the rental was a necessary expense originating in the course of the receiver's administration.[3] And where it appears that the earnings of the road did not suffice to pay for necessary labor and supplies used in operating the road, no equity can arise for the payment of rental on the theory of diverted earnings.[4] On the other hand, where the court appoints receivers for a company, for the benefit of that company and its creditors, no part of the expenses of the receivership are chargeable against the property of another road, leased by the insolvent company, the receivership not being for the benefit of the lessor or its

---

[1] Central Trust Co. v. Wabash, etc., R. Co., 34 Fed. R. 259; ante, § 567. Rent accrued under a railroad lease prior to the appointment of receivers for the lessee is an unsecured liability entitled to no priority. New York, etc., R. Co. v. New York, etc., R. Co., (C. C.) 58 Fed. R. 268. See, also, Thomas v. Western Car Co., 149 U. S. 95, s. c. 60 Am. & Eng. R. Cas. 443.

[2] Quincy, etc., R. Co. v. Humphreys, 145 U. S. 82, s. c. 12 Sup. Ct. R. 787. A railroad receiver, even though appointed on the petition of the company itself, and for the express purpose of preventing the disintegration of the system, does not become liable for rentals upon leased lines, eo instanti, by the mere act of taking possession, but is entitled to a reasonable time to ascertain the situation of affairs and determine what to do. United States Trust Co. v. Wabash W. Ry. Co., 150 U. S. 287, s. c. 14 Sup. Ct. R. 86; Seney v. Wabash W. Ry. Co., 150 U. S. 310, s. c. 14 Sup. Ct. R. 94; United States Trust Co. v. Wabash, etc., R. Co., 152 U. S. 287, s. c. 60 Am. & Eng. R. Cas. 480; ante, § 567.

[3] Quincy, etc., R. Co. v. Humphreys, 145 U. S. 82.

[4] Quincy, etc., R. Co. v. Humphreys, 145 U. S. 82; Park v. New York, etc., R. Co., 57 Fed. R. 799.

creditors.[1] In proceedings to compel a receiver in a foreclosure suit to pay rent for use of tracks and terminal facilities, where the amount of rent was left uncertain, a contract between other parties, oppressive in its terms, is not a test of the amount of rent which the receiver should pay; and it not being shown that the sum paid by the receiver was insufficient, the dismissal of the proceedings was proper.[2] It has been held, however, that receivers who take possession of cars held by an insolvent railroad company under a lease, with full authority to do so, and operate the cars with full knowledge of the lease and the burdens assumed by the company, are bound by the lease as assignees of the company.[3] It has also been held that the court has power, on consulting the receivers, and without notice to the mortgagees, to order the lease of another road which is found necessary to the profitable management of the mortgaged property, and to undertake the payment of rent for its use.[4]

§ 583. Receiver's accounts.—Since a receiver is only the ministerial officer of the court by which he was appointed, deriving his authority from its orders,[5] he is required to render to the court a strict account of his management of the trust.[6] These accounts must be made at such times as the court may direct,[7] and a failure to render an account when required may

[1] Brown v. Toledo, etc., R. Co., 35 Fed. R. 444.

[2] Peoria, etc., R. Co. v. Chicago, etc., R. Co., 127 U. S. 200.

[3] Easton v. Houston & T. C. R. Co., 38 Fed. R. 784; Sparhawk v. Yerkes, 142 U. S. 1, 13; Woodruff v. Erie Railway Co., 93 N. Y. 609; In re Otis, 101 N. Y. 580, 585.

[4] Mercantile Trust Co. v. Missouri, etc., R. Co., 41 Fed. R. 8, 43 Am. & Eng. R. Cas. 469. See United States Trust Co. v. Wabash, etc., R. Co., 152 U. S. 287, s. c. 60 Am. & Eng. R. Cas. 480.

[5] A receiver can not question the order of the court in reference to the trust property in his hands. Herrick v. Miller, 123 Ind. 304.

[6] Hooper v. Winston, 24 Ill. 353; Akers v. Veal, 66 Ga. 302. See, also, as to when an account should be approved. Heffron v. Rice, 149 Ill. 216, s. c. 36 N. E. R. 562. Provision for an accounting by receivers is made by statute in several states. Stimson's Am. Stat. (1892), citing laws of New York, Ohio, Michigan, Mississippi and Nebraska.

[7] Mabry v. Harrison, 44 Tex. 286.

be cause for the removal of the receiver.[1] The court, at the instance of a party interested, will compel the receiver to render an account at the appointed time.[2] The receiver's accounts are usually referred to a master,[3] whose action in passing them is held to be judicial rather than ministerial,[4] and renders the accounts so passed proof against collateral attack.[5] The books, contracts and accounts of a receiver are in the custody of the law, and bondholders, stockholders or creditors are entitled, upon reasonable application, to the privilege of inspecting them.[6] Although no appeal lies in favor of a receiver from an order of court made with reference to trust property in the receiver's hands,[7] he may appeal from a judgment of the court erroneously fixing the amount of property in his hands, and directing him to turn over more than he has in his custody, or from a final decree ascertaining the balance for which he is liable.[8]

[1] Bertie v. Lord Abingdon, 8 Beav. 53. So declared by statute in New York; Rev. Stat., Part 3, Ch. 4, Tit. 2, § 42.

[2] Adams v. Woods, 8 Cal. 306; Lowe v. Lowe, 1 Tenn. Ch. 515. An action at law for default of a receiver cannot be maintained against his sureties before an accounting. French v. Dauchy, 134 N. Y. 543.

[3] Foster's Federal Practice 383, § 257.

[4] Cowdrey v. Railroad Co., 1 Woods (U. S.) 331, affirmed in Galveston R. v. Cowdrey, 11 Wall. (U. S.) 459.

[5] Farmers' Loan & T. Co. v. Central R. Co., 1 McCrary (U. S.) 352, s. c. 2 Fed. R. 751. Unless exceptions to the receiver's account are first taken before the master, and the receiver is given an opportunity to sustain his report by any additional evidence at his command, the federal courts will decline to consider them when taken before the court. Cowdrey v. Railroad Co., 1 Woods (U. S.) 331, affirmed in Galveston R. v. Cowdrey, 11 Wall. (U. S.) 459. It has been held, however, that the receiver of a corporation to which lands were fraudulently conveyed may be compelled, in an action for fraud, to account for rents and profits received by him from such lands, after his accounts as receiver have been approved in court, and he has been discharged. Pondir v. New York, L. E. & W. R. Co., 72 Hun 384, 25 N. Y. S. 560, 31 Abb. N. C. 29.

[6] Jones on Corporate Bonds & Mortgages, § 531, citing Fowler's Petition, 9 Abb. N. C. (N. Y.) 268; Lafayette Co. v. Neely, 21 Fed. R. 738. In New York the statute provides that the receiver's accounts, statements, and all books and papers of the corporation in the hands of such receiver, shall, at all reasonable times, be open for the inspection of all persons having an interest therein. Rev. Stat., Part 3, Ch. 4, Tit. 2, § 42.

[7] Herrick v. Miller, 123 Ind. 304.

[8] Hinckley v. Gilman, etc., R. Co., 94 U. S. 467; Hovey v. McDonald, 109 U. S. 150; How v. Jones, 60 Iowa 70; Adair County v. Ownby, 75 Mo. 282.

§ 584. **Compensation of receiver.**—Receivers are allowed compensation for services rendered in the proper discharge of their duties as officers of the court, and it has been said that an order should not be made directing the receiver to pay over the entire fund in his hands without in some way providing for the payment of his commissions.[1] The receiver's compensation is payable out of the assets in his hands,[2] and it has been held that a receiver who has been legally and properly appointed can not be compelled to accept a judgment against the person procuring his appointment in payment for his services.[3] Where the funds in court are not sufficient to adequately compensate the receiver, the person procuring his appointment may be compelled to pay him.[4] The rate of compensation is fixed by statutes applying to certain classes of receiverships in some of the states,[5] and where it is so fixed that rate must be allowed, regardless of the value of the services rendered.[6] But the rule in England[7] and in the United States, in all cases in which the compensation is not definitely fixed by law,[8] is that

---

[1] Weston v. Watts, 45 Hun (N. Y.) 219.

[2] Hayes v. Ferguson, 15 Lea (Tenn.) 1; Jaffray v. Raab, 72 Iowa 335; Seligman v. Laussy, 60 Ga. 20; Beckwith v. Carroll, 56 Ala. 12; Ferguson v. Dent, 46 Fed. R. 88; *Ex parte* Izard, L. R. 23 Ch. Div. 75; High on Receivers (3d ed.), § 796.

[3] Radford v. Folsom, 55 Iowa 276, s. c. 7 N. W. R. 604. In Hoppensack v. Hoppensack, 61 How. Pr. (N. Y.) 498, it was held that the receiver, being an officer of the court, must be compensated out of the funds in the hands of the court, and that the owner thereof, in case they were wrongfully taken, must look to the person who procured the appointment of the receiver for redress. But the weight of authority favors the rule that a receiver who is improperly appointed and whose appointment is set aside, must look only to the plaintiff for remuneration. Weston v. Watts, 45 Hun (N. Y.) 219; French v. Gifford, 31 Iowa 428; Moyers v. Coiner, 22 Fla. 422.

[4] Tome v. King, 64 Md. 166.

[5] 20 Am. & Eng. Ency. of Law 169.

[6] Price v. White, 1 Bailey Eq. (S. Car.) 240. A court can not allow a greater compensation than the per cent. upon funds passing through the receiver's hands, which the statute fixes as his compensation. *In re* Orient Mut. Ins. Co., 21 N. Y. S. 237, 66 Hun (N. Y.) 633.

[7] High on Receivers (3d ed.), § 782; Beach on Receivers, § 760.

[8] United States Trust Co. v. New York, etc., R. Co., 101 N. Y. 478. Some states provide by statute that the court shall make a proper allowance to the receiver by way of compensation. Stimson's Am. Stat. (1892), § 8367, citing laws of Indiana, Mississippi, Ohio, Michigan; Rev. Stat. Me., 1883, Ch. 51, § 51; Gen. Stat. R. I. Ch. 140, § 46; Code Va. 1887, § 3411.

the amount of compensation to be allowed is a matter within the sound discretion of the court by whom the receiver was appointed, and is to be governed by the particular circumstances of the case.[1] Where the duties of the receiver are very slight,[2] or where one of the parties in interest serves as receiver to protect his own interests[3] the court may be justified in granting him little or no compensation. And in case the duties of a receiver prove more arduous than he or the court expected he may be allowed compensation in addition to that fixed by the order under which he was appointed.[4] If the receiver's duties are

---

[1] Cowdrey v. Railroad Co., 1 Woods (U. S.) 331; Jones v. Keen, 115 Mass. 170; Day v. Croft, 2 Beav. (Eng.) 488; Crumlish's Admr. v. Shenandoah, etc., R. Co., 40 W. Va. 627, s. c. 22 S. E. R. 90. Sometimes he is given the same compensation as the president of the road, and his duties and responsibilities may be such as to entitle him to even greater compensation. Central Trust Co. v. Wabash, etc., Ry. Co., 32 Fed. R. 187, 188. Receivers of railroads are frequently allowed as much as $10,000 a year. See 1 Foster's Fed. Pr., § 258; 2 Beach Mod. Eq. Pr., § 739.

[2] Marr v. Littlewood, 2 M. & Craig (Eng.) 454. A railroad receiver, residing at a distance from the property, who entrusts the active management to others, will not be allowed the full compensation usually paid to railroad presidents and receivers who are the active executive heads of going railroads. Central Trust Co. of New York v. Cincinnati, J. & M. Ry. Co., (C. C.) 58 Fed. R. 500. See, also, Boston, etc., Co. v. Chamberlain, 66 Fed. 847.

[3] Steel v. Holladay, 19 Ore. 517; Berry v. Jones, 11 Heisk. (Tenn.) 206; Blakeney v. Dufaur, 15 Beav. (Eng.) 40.

[4] Farmers' Loan & T. Co. v. Central R. Co., 8 Fed. R. 60; Adams v. Haskell, 6 Cal. 475; Stewart v. Boulware, 133 U. S. 78. In Farmers' Loan & T. Co. v. Central R. Co., *supra*, the opinion was expressed that a receiver should be allowed compensation in case he performs duties in addition to those ordinarily required of a receiver, and he was allowed a fee for services as counsel. But in other cases where claims have been made by receivers for compensation for legal services rendered while acting as such, the claims have been disallowed and the opinion expressed that a receiver acting also in other capacities should be paid for his services in the capacity of receiver only. This rule is based upon the public policy which forbids receivers and other trustees from entering into contracts by which they may make a personal profit from the management of the trust estate. It is said that the temptation to earn fees as counsel would be liable to warp the receiver's judgment as to what suits are proper and necessary. State v. Butler, 15 Lea (Tenn.) 113; Battaile v. Fisher, 36 Miss. 321. See as to the general rule that a receiver can not employ himself to perform services in addition to his duties as receiver. *In re* Bank of Niagara, 6 Paige (N. Y.) 213; Holcombe v. Holcombe, 13 N. J. Eq. 413, 417; Easton v. Houston, etc., R. Co., 40 Fed. R. 189; Martin v. Martin, 14 Ore. 165; Beach on Receivers, § 768.

imperfectly performed because of his negligence or misconduct, the court may reduce the amount of his compensation,[1] and, in a proper case, may even refuse him any compensation whatever.[2] It is the practice in most jurisdictions to fix the amount in a general order or to make allowances to the receiver for his own compensation and necessary counsel fees on his *ex parte* application, but it is said in a recent case that, in the absence of any well-settled rule of practice or general order, motions to fix the compensation of receivers or their counsel should not be heard *ex parte*, and that notice should be given to all parties in interest.[3] In case the compensation allowed is too large or too small, an appeal may be taken from the order.[4] But an appellate court will not interfere to correct the allowance made by the court appointing the receiver unless it has clearly abused the discretion with which it is vested.[5] And if the facts upon which the allowance was based are not before the appellate court, it will refuse to consider the question as to whether such allowance was excessive.[6]

§ 585. **Attorney's fees.**—The receiver is entitled to the benefit of legal counsel, and the court will upon application appoint one of the attorneys practicing before it to serve as his legal adviser.[7] The fees of such counsel for necessary services in connection with the management of the trust will be allowed by the court and paid out of the trust property.[8] The amount

In Kimmerle *v.* Dowagiac, etc., Co., (Mich.) s. c. 63 N. W. R. 529, it is held that a corporation appointed as a receiver is not entitled to additional compensation for its agent who performed the duties of the office.

[1] Beach on Receivers, § 758.
[2] Clapp *v.* Clapp, 49 Hun (N. Y.) 195.
[3] Merchants' Bank *v.* Crysler, 67 Fed. R. 388, citing Daniel Ch. Pl. & Pr. 1592, 1593.
[4] Russell *v.* First Nat. Bank, 65 Iowa 242; Herndon *v.* Hurter, 19 Fla. 397; Tompson *v.* Huron, etc., Co., 5 Wash.

527, s. c. 32 Pac. 536; Magee *v.* Cowperthwaite, 10 Ala. 966.

[5] Stuart *v.* Boulware, 133 U. S. 78; Greeley *v.* Provident Sav. Bank, 103 Mo. 212, s. c. 15 S. W. R. 429; Morgan *v.* Hardee, 71 Ga. 736; Heffron *v.* Rice, 149 Ill. 216, s. c. 36 N. E. R. 562.

[6] Greeley *v.* Provident Sav. Bank, 103 Mo. 212; Jones *v.* Keen, 115 Mass. 170.

[7] Blair *v.* St. Louis, etc., R. Co., 20 Fed. R. 348.

[8] Cowdrey *v.* Railroad Co., 1 Woods (U. S.) 331; Howes *v.* Davis, 4 Abb. Pr. (N. Y.) 71. Where there are no

must depend largely upon the circumstances of the particular case, and in fixing it, as in fixing the compensation of the receiver, the court is invested with a wide discretion.[1] Indeed, the receiver usually pays the counsel and the court makes the allowance to the receiver.[2] Not only the fees of the receiver's counsel but also those of counsel for complainant in the suit for the appointment of a receiver have been ordered paid out of the proceeds of a sale of the property. Such an allowance, if made with moderation and a jealous regard for the rights of those interested in the fund, is not only admissible but agreeable to the principles of equity and justice.[3] Where a receiver is appointed with the consent of all interested parties, and to the advantage of all, the services rendered by the complainant's attorneys, being for the common benefit, should be paid for from the assets of the company.[4] And even though the creditors do not all consent, if the litigation result in favor of the plaintiff and the fund be administered for the benefit of all the creditors, it is only fair that all should bear their ratable proportion of the expense of procuring the receiver's appointment. In many cases the claims of complainant's counsel have been allowed in whole or in part[5] before the litigation

surplus earnings, an attorney who recovers for a railroad, in the hands of a receiver, engines formerly leased by it to another road, and rent for their use, which recovery inures to the benefit of the security holders, is entitled to a reasonable compensation, to be paid out of the *corpus* of the property. Louisville, E. & St. L. R. Co. *v.* Wilson, 138 U. S. 501, s. c. 11 Sup. Ct. R. 405.

[1] Crumlish's Admr. *v.* Shenandoah, etc., R. Co., 40 W. Va. 625, s. c. 22 S. E. R. 90.

[2] Stuart *v.* Boulware, 133 U. S. 78.

[3] Trustees *v.* Greenough, 105 U. S. 527, 536, per Mr. Justice Bradley.

[4] Bound *v.* South Carolina R. Co., 43 Fed. R. 404.

[5] In Central Trust Co. *v.* Wabash, etc., R. Co., 23 Fed. R. 675, it was held that a partial allowance would be made for the fees of complainant's counsel upon application, leaving the balance to stand until the litigation should be disposed of, and it should become apparent whether the property in the receiver's hands were sufficient to pay all expenses. Though a receiver may, under certain circumstances, employ counsel to advise him with regard to the property in his charge, the necessity must be apparent, or a claim for attorney's fees will be disallowed. Terry *v.* Martin, (N. M.) 32 Pac. R. 157.

was ended, and while it still remained a matter of doubt whether the party who employed the attorney had any interest in the fund. But this practice is to be discouraged. The better course is to defer making any allowance to plaintiff's counsel until it shall have been demonstrated that his employment was necessary to protect the interests of the creditors.[1] If an opposite course is pursued, it may be found that the entire fund in the possession of the court has been consumed by expenses, and that nothing remains for the creditors in whose interest the litigation purported to have begun.[2]

§ 586. Removal and discharge.—The court appointing a receiver[3] has power to remove him at any time upon cause shown, and fill his place with some one who will discharge its

---

[1] In a dissenting opinion delivered in the case of Trustees v. Greenough, 105 U. S. 527, 538, Mr. Justice Miller said: "While I agree to the decree of the court in this case, I do not agree to the opinion, so far as it is an argument in favor of a principle on which is founded the grossest judicial abuse of the present day, namely, the absorption of a property or a fund which comes into the control of a court, by making allowances for attorney's fees and other expenses, pending the litigation, payable out of the common funds, when it may be finally decided that the party who employed the attorney, or incurred the cost, never had any interest in the property or fund in litigation. This system of paying out of a man's property some one else engaged in the effort to wrest that property from him, can never receive my approval."

[2] In Trustees v. Greenough, 105 U. S. 527, 536, Mr. Justice Bradley, speaking for the court, said: "Sometimes, no doubt, these allowances have been excessive and perhaps illegal; and we would be very far from expressing our approval of such large allowances to trustees, receivers, and counsel, as have sometimes been made, and which have justly excited severe criticism." In Cowdrey v. Galveston, etc., R. Co., 93 U. S. 352, the supreme court upheld an allowance of five thousand dollars in favor of counsel employed by certain bondholders to foreclose a mortgage, after the civil war had caused the discontinuance of a former suit in which the trustees agreed with their solicitor to pay him that sum for procuring a foreclosure.

[3] Another court to which the cause has been removed by due process of law has the same power in this respect as the court by which the receiver was appointed, and receivers appointed by a state court are as completely under the control of a federal court, to which the cause is afterward removed, as if originally appointed by the federal court. Texas, etc., R. Co. v. Rust, 17 Fed. R. 275; Hinckley v. Gilman, etc., R. Co., 100 U. S. 153; Dillon on Removal of Causes, § 80, p. 99. See Atkins v. Wabash, etc., R. Co., 29 Fed. R. 161. But see Young v. Montgomery, etc., R. Co., 2 Woods (U. S.) 606.

duties in a satisfactory manner. This power of removal is held to be a necessary incident of the power to appoint a receiver and to control his actions,[1] and its exercise rests in the sound discretion of the court.[2] A receiver may be removed and superseded for a failure to give bond with sufficient sureties,[3] if he becomes insolvent,[4] for physical or mental disability by which he is rendered incapable of discharging the duties of his office,[5] or for any misconduct[6] or negligence by which the interests of the trust estate are menaced or endangered.[7] Such a personal interest in the conduct of the business as might lead the receiver to sacrifice the interests of other claimants may also be cause for his removal.[8] And where it is shown that the receiver was appointed at the instance of the principal stockholder who has controlled the corporation, and who procured his appointment for a fraudulent purpose, the receiver will be removed and a new receiver appointed.[9] But a receiver whose management has been efficient and impartial will not be removed at the request of a controlling stockholder and his associates, when the litigation is not for the purpose of foreclosing

---

[1] Crawford v. Ross, 39 Ga. 44; Walters v. Anglo-American, etc., Co., 50 Fed. R. 316; *In re* Colvin, 3 Md. Ch. 278, 300; McCullough v. Merchants', etc., Co., 29 N. J. Eq. 217; Gluck & Becker on Rec. of Corp., § 114; 2 Beach Mod. Eq. Pr., § 749.

[2] High on Receivers (3d ed.), § 824.

[3] Where the bond becomes insufficient a receiver may be required to find additional sureties, and, upon his failure to do so, may be removed. Schakelford v. Schakelford, 32 Gratt. (Va.) 481.

[4] Crawford v. Ross, 39 Ga. 44; Bank of Monroe v. Schermerhorn, 1 Clarke Ch. (N. Y.) 366.

[5] Richardson v. Ward, 6 Mad. 266.

[6] An unlawful and unjust discrimination by the receiver of a railroad in favor of one shipper and against rival shippers is sufficient ground for his removal. Beers v. Wabash, etc., R. Co., 29 Fed. R. 161; Handy v. Cleveland, etc., R. Co., 31 Fed. R. 689. See Keeler v. Brooklyn El. R. Co., 9 Abb. N. Cas. (N. Y.) 166.

[7] *In re* St. George's Estate, 19 L. R. Ir. 566.

[8] Williamson v. Wilson, 1 Bland (Md.) 418; Etowah, etc., Co. v. Wills, etc., Co., (Ala.) 17 So. R. 522; Keeler v. Brooklyn El. R. Co., 9 Abb. N. Cas. (N. Y.) 166; Beers v. Wabash, etc., R. Co., 29 Fed. R. 161; Fripp v. Chard R. Co., 22 L. J. Ch. 1084, 11 Hare 241. Where two receivers, appointed to represent rival interests, are unable to agree as to the conduct of the business, the court should remove them and appoint a single disinterested person to act in their stead. Meier v. Kansas Pac. R. Co., 5 Dill. (U. S.) 476.

[9] Phinizy v. Augusta, etc., R. Co., 56 Fed. R. 273.

a mortgage, but is instituted by a minority stockholder on the ground that the indebtedness of the corporation was being wrongfully increased for the benefit of the controlling stockholders.[1] When the object for which the receiver was appointed has been attained[2] or the litigation in aid of which he was appointed has terminated by abatement or otherwise,[3] the receivership should be terminated and the receiver finally discharged.[4] And where it appears that the appointment of a receiver for the property of a railroad corporation was procured by collusion between the corporation and a creditor, for the purpose of putting the property beyond the reach of judicial process and without any intention of applying it in satisfaction of the petitioning creditor's claim, the court will discharge the receiver of its own motion.[5] A court of equity will not conduct the business of the corporation through a receiver unless the interests of the parties unmistakably require it.[6] It has been held that a receiver continues to be subject to the duties and possessed of the privileges annexed to his office, until discharged by a formal order of court, notwithstanding the litigation has ended, or other conditions have arisen which make it the duty of the court to discharge him.[7]

[1] Street v. Maryland Cent. Ry. Co., 58 Fed. R. 47.

[2] Sewell v. Cape May, etc., R. Co., (N. J.) 30 Am. & Eng. R. Cas. 155. Upon payment of the plaintiff's claim, and the receiver's lawful charges, the court is bound to discharge the receiver, even though some of the defendants desire that he be retained. Milwaukee, etc., R. Co. v. Soutter, 2 Wall. (U. S.) 510; Davis v. Duke of Marlborough, 2 Swanst. * p. 167, per Lord Eldon.

[3] National, etc., Assn. v. Mariposa Co., 60 Barb. (N. Y.) 423; Whiteside v. Prendergast, 2 Barb. Ch. (N. Y.) 472; Milwaukee, etc., R. Co. v. Soutter, 2 Wall. (U. S.) 510; Field v. Jones, 11 Ga. 413.

[4] But the discontinuance or abatement of the action does not of itself terminate the receivership. State v. Gibson, 21 Ark. 140; Newman v. Mills, 1 Hog. (Irish Rolls) 291; McCosker v. Brady, 1 Barb. Ch. (N. Y.) 329.

[5] Sage v. Memphis, etc., R. Co., 18 Fed. R. 571; Wood v. Oregon, etc., Co., 55 Fed. R. 901; Wilson v. Barney, 5 Hun (N. Y.) 257. The receiver will be discharged in any case where it is shown to the court that the order appointing a receiver was improvidently or wrongfully made. McHenry v. New York, etc., R. Co., 25 Fed. R. 114; Milwaukee, etc., R. Co. v. Soutter, 2 Wall. (U. S.) 510, 523; Copper Hill, etc., Co. v. Spencer, 25 Cal. 11, 16.

[6] Sage v. Memphis, etc., R. Co., 18 Fed. R. 571; Overton v. Memphis, etc., R. Co., 10 Fed. 866; Ferry v. Bank, 15 How. Pr. (N. Y.) 445.

[7] State v. Gibson, 21 Ark. 140.

§ 587. **Effect of removal or discharge.**—The removal of a receiver does not necessarily terminate the receivership. Since the receiver is a mere officer of the court, he may be superseded without affecting the trust which he is called upon to administer. The removal of a receiver to make way for a successor appointed by the court does not affect claims against the property arising from the operation of the railroad by the first receiver. The management of the court is one even if it becomes necessary to change the receiver more than once.[1] After the receiver has been discharged by the court he is no longer liable either for the debts of the corporation or for any debts or liabilities incurred during his receivership.[2] Nor is the corporation, as a general rule, personally liable for the latter.[3] The corporation may, however, be held liable for the acts and defaults of the receiver's servants to the extent that earnings of the road have been used in the purchase of property surrendered to the corporation by the receiver upon his final discharge.[4] But after the discharge of the receiver and the restoration of the property to the corporation, the jurisdiction of the court over the receivership is ended, and it has even been held that a provision in the decree relieving the property from liability for claims not filed within a specified time, in the suit in which the receiver was appointed, is void.[5]

[1] Gibbes v. Greenville, etc., R. Co., 15 S. Car. 304; Bond v. State, 68 Miss. 648, s. c. 9 So. R. 353.

[2] Lehman v. McQuown, 31 Fed. Rep. 138; Farmers' L. & T. Co. v. Central R. Co., 7 Fed. Rep. 537; New York, etc., Tel. Co. v. Jewett, 115 N. Y. 166; Ryan v. Hays, 62 Tex. 42; Bond v. State, 68 Miss. 648, s. c. 9 So. R. 353. A judgment against an ancillary receiver after his discharge is not binding, even though the court did not know of his discharge. Reynolds v. Stockton, 140 U. S. 254, s. c. 11 Sup. Ct. R. 773.

[3] Godfrey v. Ohio, etc., R. Co., 116 Ind. 30; Davis v. Duncan, 19 Fed. Rep. 477, 17 Am. & Eng. R. Cas. 295. But it has been held that the company is liable for injuries caused by the negligence of a receiver appointed through collusion, whether the court had jurisdiction to appoint or not. Texas, etc., Ry. Co. v. Gay, 86 Tex. 571, s. c. 26 S. W. R. 599. The court regarded the receiver as the agent of the company.

[4] Mobile, etc., R. Co. v. Davis, 62 Miss. 271; Texas, etc., R. Co. v. Johnson, 76 Tex. 421, s. c. 13 S. W. R. 463. See Texas, etc., R. Co. v. Griffin, 76 Tex. 441.

[5] Missouri, etc., Ry. Co. v. Chilton, (Tex.) s. c. 27 S. W. R. 272; Texas, etc., Ry. Co. v. Watts, (Tex.) 18 S. W. R. 312, following Texas, etc., R. Co. v. Johnson, *supra*.

CHAPTER XXIII.

RECEIVER'S CERTIFICATES.

§ 588. Definition and nature of receiver's certificates.
589. Power of courts to authorize.
590. Purposes for which receiver's certificates may be issued—Extent of power.
591. Order giving authority to issue.
592. Lien created by receiver's certificates.
§ 593. Statutory provisions as to lien.
594. Negotiability of receiver's certificates.
595. Rights of holders of receiver's certificates.
596. Who may question validity of receiver's certificates.
597. Payment and redemption of certificates.

§ 588. Definition and nature of receiver's certificates.—A receiver's certificate has been defined as "a non-negotiable evidence of debt, or debenture, issued by authority of a court of chancery as a first lien upon the property of a debtor corporation in the hands of a receiver."[1] It frequently becomes necessary that a receiver of a railroad should borrow money in order to keep the road in repair and operate it for the good of the public, to prevent the loss of business and good will, and to preserve it as a "going concern" for the benefit of all parties interested. Unless good security can be given it would be impossible to borrow the money, and it is to the interest, both of the public and of the parties, that some just means of obtaining the money and giving security should be devised. This is accomplished by the issue of certificates of indebtedness, negotiable in form, for the payment of which, out of the proceeds of the property in its hands, the faith of the court is pledged.[2]

---

[1] Beach on Receivers, § 379.

[2] Taylor v. Philadelphia, etc., R. Co., 14 Phila. (Pa.) 451, 461. "The certificates are not debts of the company, but of the receivers, backed by the pledged faith of the court, that the property, on the proceeds of which they are charged, is in its possession, subject to be, and that it will be, disposed of by it for the payment of

§ 589. Power of courts to authorize.—Since the best and cheapest mode of conserving a railroad is by operating trains thereon, and keeping it in repair for their use, and since this is the only way in which the public duties and obligations of the railroad can be discharged and a forfeiture of its charter prevented, power to raise money for the repair and operation of the road necessarily accompanies the power to assume control of it for the benefit of the corporate creditors.[1] This power is a part of the jurisdiction, exercised by a court of equity, by which it undertakes to protect and preserve the trust funds in its hands.[2] It may be stated as a general rule, there-

them. This results from the fact that they are but a substitute for common methods by which money is raised for the use of a receiver in a particular case, a mode of appropriating, in advance, a portion of the value of the property, in order to enable the court to save a greater value thereof from destruction." Meyer v. Johnston, 53 Ala. 237.

[1] Meyer v. Johnston, 53 Ala. 237.

[2] Wallace v. Loomis, 97 U. S. 146. In some states the issue of receiver's certificates in certain cases is authorized by statute. In announcing the opinion of the court in the case of Meyer v. Johnston, 53 Ala. 237, Judge Manning said: "It was not necessary that the question of the power of a court to authorize the issue of first lien certificates of indebtedness to enable a receiver to raise the money he might need, should be decided before the introduction of railroads. But these properties, with their appurtenances, vast in extent and value, yet very perishable if unused and neglected, existing as the estates of private individuals associated into corporations, but essentially public works, in whose operations the public at large and the state are concerned, when drawn into litigation, must be dealt with by the courts according to the nature and circumstances of the subject. And any one can understand that the best and cheapest mode of conserving a railroad may be by operating trains thereon and keeping it in repair for their use. To preserve its value, it must generally be continued in operation, and be sold as a going concern." The court also said that if the road were permitted to become a useless wreck, "the inconvenience and loss which this would inflict on the population of large districts, coupled with the benefit to parties who are powerless to take care of themselves, of preventing the rapid diminution of value, and derangement and disorganization that would otherwise result, seem to require—not for the completion of an unfinished work, or the improvement, beyond what is necessary for its preservation, of an existing one—but to keep it up, to conserve it as a railroad property, if the court has been obliged to take possession of it, that the court should borrow money for that purpose, if it can not otherwise do so in sufficiently large sums, by causing negotiable certificates of indebtedness to be issued constituting a first lien on the proceeds of the property, and redeemable when it is sold or disposed of by the court."

fore, that where it is necessary that a receiver should expend money for the repair of a railroad in his hands, in order to keep it in operation, the court by which he was appointed has power to authorize him to borrow money necessary to make such repairs, and to make the indebtedness so incurred a first lien upon the property in its hands. And it is equally well settled that the court may authorize the receiver to issue receiver's certificates as evidence of such indebtedness.[1]

§ 590. **Purposes for which receiver's certificates may be issued—Extent of power.**—Where a portion of the road has been built in a hasty manner with materials which answer only a temporary use,[2] or where valuable property rights will be lost by a failure to complete unfinished portions of the road within a limited time,[3] it may be necessary for the receiver to borrow money with which to build such parts of the road, and the court may authorize him to issue certificates therefor.[4] But this jurisdiction must not be exercised to the extent of improving the owners and lienholders out of their property. The whole power of the court, when exercised to its fullest extent, without the consent of the lienholders express or implied, is usually confined to making necessary repairs and protecting the property as it is.[5] The propriety of every expenditure is to

[1] Meyer v. Johnston, 53 Ala. 237; Turner v. Peoria, etc., R. Co., 95 Ill. 134; Wallace v. Loomis, 97 U. S. 146; Miltenberger v. Logansport, etc., R. Co., 106 U. S. 286; Union Trust Co. v. Illinois Midland R. Co., 117 U. S. 434.

[2] Stanton v. Alabama, etc., R. Co., 2 Woods (U. S.) 506.

[3] Kennedy v. St. Paul, etc., R. Co., 2 Dill.(U. S.) 448, 5 Dill. (U. S.) 519. The receiver can not bind the company by an oral contract to give a land owner an annual pass during life in consideration of a grant of necessary land for a right of way. Martin v. New York, etc., R. Co., 36 N. J. Eq. 109, 12 Am. & Eng. R. Cas. 448.

[4] Jerome v. McCarter, 94 U.S.734. In this case, the United States had made a large grant of land to a company engaged in digging a canal, conditioned upon the completion of the canal within a certain time. The receiver was authorized to borrow the money necessary for its completion by the issue of receiver's certificates, and, upon appeal, the supreme court approved their issue. See, also, Kennedy v. St. Paul, etc., R. Co., 2 Dill. (U. S. C. C.) 448; Bank of Montreal v. Chicago, etc., R. Co., 48 Iowa 518.

[5] Jones on Corporation Bonds and

be judged by the necessity of making it in order to preserve the value of the trust estate.¹ This power extends, as a general rule, only to such expenditures as are necessary for the protection of the property.² And the court will not, ordinarily, authorize expenditures for the completion of a road unless it is morally certain that the property in consequence will sell for a higher price.³ A receiver should not be permitted to expend money

Mortgages, § 543, citing Snow v. Winslow, 54 Iowa 200; Taylor v. Philadelphia, etc., R. Co., 9 Fed. R. 1; Credit Co. v. Arkansas Cent. R. Co., 5 McCrary (U. S.) 23; Metropolitan Trust Co. v. Tonawanda Valley, etc., R. Co., 103 N. Y. 245, per Danforth, J.

¹ Shaw v. Railroad Co., 100 U. S. 605. "Aside from any consideration of the mortgagor and others having the right to redeem, against whom a court of equity has power analogous to that of a mortgagee in possession to incur charges for the preservation and repair of the property it has taken possession of through its receiver, a court of equity has no power to impair the obligation of a mortgage contract, by creating a superior lien without the mortgagee's consent, unless it be in the exercise of a like equitable power of preserving and protecting the property. The law does not permit the obligation of contracts to be impaired. The constitution of the United States inhibits even a state from doing an act which shall have that effect. And, certainly, a court, which is a portion of the government of the state, can not have a power which is denied to the state in convention assembled. If, therefore, the action of a chancellor in this cause goes to the extent of taking the property of the defendant corporation into its hands for the purpose, through his appointees, of completing an unfinished work, or of enlarging or improving a finished one, beyond what is necessary for its preservation, and to that end raising money, by charging the railroad and its appurtenances with liens which are to supersede older ones, without the consent of the holders of these, he has inadvertently passed beyond the boundaries of a chancellor's jurisdiction. In our opinion no such power is vested or resides in any judicial tribunal." Jones on Corporate Bonds and Mortgages, § 551, quoting from the opinion of Manning, J., in Meyer v. Johnston, 53 Ala. 237, 345.

² Jones on Corporate Bonds and Mortgages, § 559, citing Hand v. Savannah, etc., R. Co., 17 S. Car. 219, 270, per McGowan; Metropolitan Trust Co. v. Tonawanda Valley, etc., R. Co., 103 N. Y. 245, 249, per Danforth, J. The certificates of a receiver of an insolvent railroad company, issued under an order of court to obtain money to operate the road, are paramount liens. Central Trust Co. v. Tappan, 6 N. Y. Supp. 918.

³ Jones on Corporate Bonds and Mortgages, § 545, citing Investment Co. v. Ohio, etc., R. Co., 36 Fed. R., p. 48. In this case the circumstances were as follows: The petition of a receiver of an insolvent railroad for authority to borrow a large sum of money and issue his certificates therefor, showed that part of the amount was to be used in completing a portion of the road and widening its gauge;

or incur obligations to secure mere speculative advantages. A greater latitude is permitted to receivers of railroads than to receivers of other corporations in the matter of incurring debts for management and operation, because of the public rights which are involved and of the consequences of a failure on the part of the railroad to discharge its public duties.[1] Accordingly the courts have authorized the issue of certificates to construct the unfinished portions of an incomplete railroad, and to purchase the necessary rolling stock, machinery and supplies for its operation,[2] and even to pay debts of the company for taxes, labor, and materials due prior to the appointment of the re-

---

$35,000 for purchasing and laying track over another portion already graded and bridged at an expense of $49,000; $47,243.18 to pay claims for material furnished, which were not a lien on the road; $20,000 to reimburse bondholders for advances to meet arrearages of wages and avert a strike; $100,000 to purchase leased rolling stock, for which the company paid an annual rental of $28,000, the lessors cancelling a claim for $7,000 unpaid rent, if the purchase was made; $4,000 to relay a line of track on a connecting road, and thus cancel a debt of $8,000 due that road, and secure enough additional business to pay the cost in three months, and $29,430 to make final payment on valuable real estate. A majority of the holders of both the first and second mortgage bonds consented to the certificates being issued; the remaining holders of first and second mortgage bonds not consenting, and a number of them, together with other lienholders, objecting. The court held that, as it was doubtful whether the improvements would add to the selling price of the road, the petition should be denied absolutely as to the items of $35,000 and of $20,000, and as to the item of $47,243.18, unless all lienholders consented; but that certificates should be issued for the other items, if desired by the consenting bondholders, with leave thereafter to petition to have them made a charge on the non-consenting bondholders. Investment Co. v. Ohio, etc., R. Co., 36 Fed. R. 48.

[1] Jones on Corporate Bonds and Mortgages, § 555. See, also, Farmers' L. & T. Co. v. Grape Creek, etc., Co., 50 Fed. R. 481, s. c. 16 L. R. A. 603, and note; Wood v. Guarantee Trust Co., 128 U. S. 416, s. c. 9 Sup. Ct. R. 131; Morgan's, etc., Co. v. Texas, etc., Ry. Co., 137 U. S. 171, s. c. 11 Sup. Ct. R. 61; Fidelity, etc., Co. v. Roanoke, etc., Co., 68 Fed. R. 623; Snively v. Loomis Coal Co., 11 Nat. Corp. Rep. 207.

[2] Wallace v. Loomis, 97 U. S. 146; Smith v. McCullough, 104 U. S. 25; Miltenberger v. Logansport R. Co., 106 U. S. 286; Swann v. Clark, 110 U. S. 602; Bank of Montreal v. Thayer, 7 Fed. R. 622; Meyer v. Johnston, 53 Ala. 237; Bank of Montreal v. Chicago, etc., R. Co., 48 Iowa 518; Turner v. Peoria, etc., R. Co., 95 Ill. 134; Gibert v. Washington City, etc., R. Co., 33 Gratt. (Va.) 586; Mercantile Trust Co. v. Kanawha, etc., R. Co., 50 Fed. R. 874.

ceiver.[1] But it was held in a recent case that where a receiver is appointed at the suit of a stockholder and not upon the application of a bondholder, and no earnings have been diverted to pay interest on the bonds, there is no lien or equity requiring the issuance of receiver's certificates for money to pay labor or material claims, existing before the appointment of the receiver, out of the corpus of the property.[2] The power to issue receiver's certificates, however, is one which should be sparingly exercised.[3] It is liable to great abuse; and while it is usually resorted to under the pretext that it will enhance the security of the bondholders, it not unfrequently results in taking from them the security they already have, and appropriating it to pay debts contracted by the court.[4]

[1] Union Trust Co. v. Illinois Midland R. Co., 117 U. S. 434; Taylor v. Philadelphia, etc., R. Co., 7 Fed. R. 377; Langdon v. Vermont, etc., R. Co., 53 Vt. 228; Humphreys v. Allen, 101 Ill. 490.

[2] Street v. Maryland, etc., Ry. Co., 59 Fed. R. 25. See, also, Cutting v. Tavares, etc., R. Co., 61 Fed. R. 150; Farmers' Loan & T. Co. v. Northern Pac. R. Co., 68 Fed. R. 36. But compare Farmers' Loan & T. Co. v. Kansas City, etc., R. Co., 53 Fed. R. 182, and note. See, generally, § 528, *ante*.

[3] Credit Co. v. Arkansas Cent. R. Co., 5 McCrary (U. S.) 23; Investment Co. v. Ohio, etc., R. Co., 36 Fed. R. 48; Kneeland v. American, etc., Co., 136 U. S. 89.

[4] Caldwell, J., in Credit Co. v. Arkansas Cent. R. R. Co., 5 McCrary (U. S.) 23. He adds: "The history of Wallace v. Loomis, 97 U. S. 146, 162, 2 Woods 506, under the title of Stanton v. Alabama, etc., R. Co., furnishes an instructive lesson on this subject." Mr. Beach, in his work on receivers, § 379, says: "Within the past twelve or fifteen years these certificates, to the amount of many millions of dollars, have been issued, and the courts are constantly authorizing the further issue of them, ostensibly for the preservation of the property and in the interest of the bondholders, but, it is believed, in a majority of cases in which they are issued, to the hindrance and delay of a prompt foreclosure, to the impairment of the bondholder's security and to the scandal of the courts of equity." Mr. Jones, in his work on Corporate Bonds and Mortgages, § 541, says: "Complaint as to the management of railroad receivers has generally come, not from the stockholders, because it is seldom they care to redeem, but from mortgage bondholders; and as often, perhaps, from those at whose solicitation the receiver was appointed as from others who may hold under junior mortgages, and who, therefore, have a right to redeem. The history of such management in this country shows that the bondholders chiefly interested have sometimes found themselves improved out of their interest in the property." And, in a note which he appends, he adds: Judge Baxter is reported to have expressed himself strongly, in a recent case before the Circuit Court of the

§ 591. **Order giving authority to issue.**—Certificates can only be issued in strict conformity to the order of court authorizing them,[1] and may be issued only for the purposes mentioned in such order,[2] and upon a valid consideration.[3] Notice United States, against the practice of placing railroads in the hands of receivers. He cited the case of a railroad in Georgia which cost $15,000,000. The receiver, who was in charge for three years, issued certificates to the value of $1,500,000, and when the road was sold, the proceeds were not sufficient to pay the certificates. In another case, in Detroit, a road cost over $8,000,000. When the road came to be sold, eminent counsel requested the judge to fix the minimum price for the sale, suggesting that such price should be a sum sufficient to cover the charges of the receiver and his counsel. 11 Chicago Legal News 8.

[1] State v. Edgefield, etc., R. Co., 6 Lea (Tenn.) 353; Newbold v. Peoria, etc., R. Co., 5 Ill. App. 367.

[2] Newbold v. Peoria, etc., R. Co., 5 Ill. App. 367; Fidelity Ins. Co. v. Shenandoah, etc., Co., 42 Fed. R. 372.

[3] Certificates issued without consideration are held absolutely void. Union Trust Co. v. Chicago, etc., R. Co., 7 Fed. Rep. 513; Turner v. Peoria, etc., R. Co., 95 Ill. 134. In Bank of Montreal v. Chicago, etc., R. Co., 48 Iowa 518, the court says: "The receiver, being an officer of the court, has no implied powers other than those derived from the order of the court. Such being true, we think it clear he could not issue certificates which would constitute a first lien on the road except for money borrowed, material furnished, or labor performed. When the material was furnished or labor performed, he was authorized to issue the certificates therefor, and not until then. And if he made a contract for the construction of the road, he might issue certificates as the material was furnished or the labor performed, and on the completion of the road he could issue his certificates in final payment. But the power is not conferred to issue certificates in payment for material not furnished or labor not performed. On the contrary, we are of the opinion, it fairly appears he was prohibited from so doing. If the necessity existed for enlarged powers, they should have been applied for. * * * *
As the certificates on their face state they were 'issued under and by virtue of certain provisions of an order duly entered by the District Court of Clinton County, Iowa, on July 27, 1876,' the plaintiff is chargeable with notice of all such order contains. Whether under the order the receiver had the power to issue negotiable securities, or for property agreed to be delivered at a future day, were legal questions which the plaintiff was bound to determine at his peril. The receiver's authority was bounded and limited by the order. He had no general powers, except such as could be derived therefrom. It is true he had power to issue certificates but this was not unlimited. It was only in certain cases he could do so. And being an officer of the court and vested with the care of property in his charge as such officer, we think the plaintiff was bound to know whether these certificates were issued in accordance with the terms and contingencies contemplated by the order."

should usually be required to be given to the parties in interest before an order should be made authorizing the receiver to issue certificates.[1] But a full opportunity to be heard as to the propriety of the expenditures and the right to make them a first lien has been held equivalent to prior notice,[2] and, as a matter of fact, such orders are frequently made without prior notice. When it is desirable to incur expenses in building or repairing the railroad, beyond what is essential for its preservation, the consent, express or implied, of those whose rights of property will be affected, should be had.[3] It has been held that when a receiver contracts debts under a consent order, such debts are not binding upon bondholders who refused their consent, but they may insist upon the enforcement against the property of such liens as they held prior to the granting of the order.[4] Cases in which the right of the court to authorize the issue of certificates constituting a lien upon the property superior to that of mortgage bondholders has been called in question, have not often arisen, since the consent, express or implied, of those interested in the fund has usually been obtained.[5] Prior lien-holders who have not consented and who were not parties to the suit in which the issue of receiver's certificates was authorized are entitled to come into court to dispute the necessity of the expenditures which the certificates were issued to meet, and to assert the superiority of their liens.[6] Joining with the

[1] *Ex parte* Mitchell, 12 S. Car. 83.
[2] Union Trust Co. *v.* Illinois, etc., R. Co., 117 U. S. 434, s. c. 25 Am. & Eng. R. Cas. 560.
[3] Jones on Corporate Bonds and Mortgages, § 559.
[4] Hand *v.* Savannah, etc., R. Co., 17 S. Car. 219. The court may, in a proper case, authorize the issue of certificates constituting a lien upon the interest of such of the bondholders as have asked for them, leaving the interests of the non-consenting bondholders unaffected by the order. Investment Co. *v.* Ohio, etc., R. Co., 36 Fed. Rep. 48.

[5] Jones on Corporate Bonds and Mortgages, § 551, citing Central Trust Co. *v.* Seasongood, 130 U. S. 482; Kennedy *v.* St. Paul, etc., R. Co., 2 Dill. (U. S.) 448, 5 Dill. 519; Stanton *v.* Alabama, etc., R. Co., 2 Woods (U. S.) 506; Hoover *v.* Montclair, etc., R. Co., 29 N. J. Eq. 4; Vermont, etc., R. Co. *v.* Vermont Central R. Co., 50 Vt. 500.
[6] While the court, under some circumstances, and for some purposes, and in advance of the prior lienholders being made parties, may have jurisdiction to charge the property with the amount of receiver's certifi-

receiver in a petition for authority to borrow money on the credit of the property, or acquiescing without opposition in an order conferring such authority, is sufficient consent to bind a party to the suit in which the order was made.[1]

§ 592. Lien created by receiver's certificates.—Receiver's certificates are usually made a first lien upon the income and entire property in the hands of the receiver. The nature or extent of the lien, in the absence of any statute upon the subject, depends upon the terms of the order of the court authorizing the certificates to be issued. It is not to be understood by this, however, that the lien will hold good if the order is

cates issued by its authority, it can not, it is said, without giving such parties their day in court, deprive them of their priority of lien. When such prior lienholders are brought before the court, they become entitled, upon the plainest principles of justice and equity, to contest the necessity, validity, effect and amount of all such certificates, as fully as if such questions were then for the first time presented for determination. If it appears that they ought not to have been made a charge upon the property superior to the lien created by the mortgages, then the contract rights of the prior lienholders must be protected. On the other hand, if it appears that the court did what ought to have been done, even had the trustees and the bondholders been before it at the time the certificates were authorized to be issued, the property should not be relieved from the charge made upon it for its protection and preservation. Hervey v. Illinois Midland R. Co., 28 Fed. Rep. 169, 176, affirmed in Union Trust Co. v. Illinois Midland R. Co., 117 U. S. 434. An appeal lies from an order authorizing receiver's certificates. Farmers' L. & T. Co., Petitioner, 129 U. S. 206. "The lien of receiver's certificates continues as long as the order authorizing their issuance remains in force, though such order was made without notice to parties interested; and the fact that a reference is had to determine all claims against the receiver, and a report is confirmed which makes no allusion to the certificates, is not an adjudication against them, when it appears that they were not presented or considered, and that their holder had no notice of the reference." Mercantile Trust Co. v. Kanawha & O. Ry. Co., 50 Fed. Rep. 874.

[1] Jones on Corporate Bonds and Mortgages, § 552, citing Humphreys v. Allen, 101 Ill. 490; Metropolitan Trust Co. v. Tonawanda Valley, etc., R. Co., 103 N. Y. 245, reversing 40 Hun 80. Receiver's certificates issued under an order made after a decree of foreclosure and sale of property, containing a provision authorized by the order making them a lien on the property, will constitute a first lien thereon, if the order is not appealed from. In re Farmers' Loan & Trust Co., 129 U. S. 206, s. c. 9 Sup. Ct. Rep. 265.

improperly made and unauthorized, nor that the lien can be made superior to that of the state for taxes or the like. But certificates issued to raise money for the repair and preservation of the road may be made a superior lien upon the property in the hands of the court to that of the first mortgage, although issued at the suit of junior mortgagees and without the consent of the holders of a senior mortgage.[1] Parties who have acquiesced with knowledge that the receivers have obtained loans upon the credit of the property are estopped to deny that such loans constitute a prior and first lien upon such property.[2] The court may order the property in its hands to be sold subject to the lien of the certificates which have been issued by its receiver,[3] or the lien may be transferred to the proceeds of the sale.[4] If the property is sold subject to the lien of the certificates, it seems that such lien may be enforced by the holder in an independent suit.[5]

§ 593. **Statutory provisions as to lien.**—In some of the states statutory provisions are found which authorize receivers to borrow money and create liens upon the mortgaged property in certain cases.[6] Such statutes, in the main, simply declare the rule followed by chancery courts, and especially by the federal courts, which we have already stated. Sometimes, however, they extend that rule to private business corporations and authorize liens to be created for money borrowed for some purposes other than those generally authorized by the courts in the absence of such a statute. It may be that the legislature has no power to impair the obligation of existing contracts in

[1] Meyer v. Johnston, 53 Ala. 237, 348; Union Trust Co. v. Illinois Midland R. Co., 117 U. S. 434; Wallace v. Loomis, 97 U. S. 146.
[2] Jones on Corp. Bonds and Mortg., § 553.
[3] Mercantile Trust Co. v. Kanawha, etc., R. Co., 50 Fed. R. 874.
[4] Mercantile Trust Co. v. Kanawha, etc., R. Co., 58 Fed. 6, s. c. 60 Am. & Eng. R. Cas. 513.

[5] Swann v. Clark, 110 U. S. 602, s. c. 4 Sup. Ct. R. 241; Mercantile Trust Co. v. Kanawha, etc., R. Co., 58 Fed. R. 6, s. c. 60 Am. & Eng. R. Cas. 513, 526. But see Turner v. Peoria, etc., R. Co., 95 Ill. 134, s. c. 35 Am. R. 144.
[6] See 19 Am. & Eng. Ency. of Law 752; Beach on Receivers, § 395.

this way, but, as the public statutory law enters into every contract, such legislation is doubtless constitutional as to future contracts. The authority of the court to create superior liens by receiver's certificates may, doubtless, be limited as well as extended by such statutes, but whether this is the effect in any particular instance must depend largely upon the particular statute in question. It may also be a matter of doubt as to how far, if at all, such statutes can bind the federal courts.

§ 594. **Negotiability of receiver's certificates.**—It is sometimes said that receiver's certificates are negotiable, and it is true that they are usually negotiable in form, that is, they are made payable to order or bearer, and may be transferred from hand to hand by assignment or delivery. But they are not negotiable, in the strict sense of that term, like bills of exchange or promissory notes. In other words, receiver's certificates are not commercial paper, whatever the form that may be given to them, and a second or subsequent holder can assert no greater rights than were acquired by the first taker.[1] An assignee, therefore, can only recover to the extent that the original payee or holder could have recovered.[2] The transfer of such a certificate by written indorsement does not render the transferer liable as an indorser of commercial paper, or as a guarantor,

---

[1] Union Trust Co. v. Chicago, etc., R. Co., 7 Fed. R. 513; Central Nat. Bank v. Hazard, 30 Fed. R. 484; Stanton v. Alabama, etc., R. Co., 31 Fed. R. 585; Turner v. Peoria, etc., R. Co., 95 Ill. 134; Tiedeman Commerc. Paper, § 498. A receiver's certificate has none of the elements of a negotiable instrument; it is the mere acknowledgment that a debt is due the payee, payable out of a specific fund. There is entire harmony upon this point in the adjudged cases. All agree in holding that such certificates are not promissory notes or bills of exchange. McCurdy v. Bowes, 88 Ind. 583, citing above cases, and Baird v. Underwood, 74 Ill. 176; Newbold v. Peoria, etc., R. Co., 5 Bradwell (Ill.) 367; Dawkes v. Lord De Lorane, 3 Wils. 207; Mechanics' Bank v. New York, etc., R. Co., 13 N. Y. 599, 623. "A receiver's certificates, which are ordered to be paid out of the income of the road from time to time, are in the nature of a call loan, and the holder has a right to presume that the receiver will notify him when the loan is to be called or the money paid." Mercantile Trust Co. v. Kanawha & O. Ry. Co., 50 Fed. R. 874.

[2] Turner v. Peoria, etc., R. R. Co., 95 Ill. 134, s. c. 35 Am. R. 144.

nor does such an indorsement imply a warranty that the certificate is collectible and will be paid.[1]

§ 595. **Rights of holders of receiver's certificates.**—Receiver's certificates are usually drawn upon an uncertain fund and do not create against any one an absolute and unconditional liability.[2] As a general rule, the fund alone is liable for their payment and their validity depends upon the order of court, and such order can be sustained only when the certificates are issued for certain limited purposes and may sometimes be modified, in effect at least, by further action adjusting the rights of parties who have not had their day in court. It may readily be seen, therefore, that the rights of the holders of such certificates are somewhat precarious, and that even a *bona fide* purchaser from the original holder occupies a very different position from the *bona fide* holder of commercial paper under the law merchant. Holders of such certificates must take notice of the terms of the order under which they were issued and are bound to know whether they were issued in accordance with such terms and for an authorized purpose.[3] Certificates issued in excess of the receiver's authority are void even in the hands of a *bona fide* holder for value,[4] and, where the certificates were disposed of by the receivers at much less than their face value, the holders have been permitted to claim only the sum actually advanced with interest upon surrendering the certificates.[5]

[1] McCurdy v. Bowes, 88 Ind. 583.

[2] Credit Co. v. Arkansas, etc., R. Co., 15 Fed. R. 46; Tiedeman Commerc. Paper, §498; Beach on Receivers, § 396.

[3] Bank of Montreal v. Chicago, etc., R. Co., 48 Iowa 518; Mercantile Trust Co. v. Kanawha, etc., R. Co., 58 Fed. R. 6, s. c. 60 Am. & Eng. R. Cas. 513:

[4] Newbold v. Peoria, etc., R. Co., 5 Ill. App. 367.

[5] Stanton v. Alabama, etc., R. Co., 2 Woods (U. S.) 506. See, also, Union Trust Co. v. Illinois, etc., R. Co., 117 U. S. 434, s. c. 6 Sup. Ct. R. 809; Central Nat. Bank v. Hazard, 30 Fed R. 484. But the purchaser of receiver's certificates is not bound to oversee the application of the money which he advances. Where a purchaser of receiver's certificates has paid their par value to the receiver, without notice of any facts to put him upon inquiry, his lien is not affected by the fact that the receiver appropriates the money to his own use. Mercantile Trust Co. v. Kanawha & O. Ry. Co., (Cir. Ct.) 50 Fed. R. 874.

CORP. 54

Where, however, the court authorizes them to be sold at a certain discount, and they are sold within the limit fixed by the court, it has been held that the purchasers thereof are entitled to their face value, as established by the order of the court.[1] If the certificates are issued without consideration they are invalid, even in the hands of an innocent holder for value.[2] Certificates may be exchanged directly for material furnished or labor performed if the exchange is made for an adequate consideration.[3] But they are valid only to the extent of the consideration actually received.[4]

§ 596. **Who may question validity of receiver's certificates.**—Although receiver's certificates are not negotiable instruments under the law merchant, yet, when they are regularly issued under the order of court, bondholders and purchasers of the property at foreclosure sale may be estopped from questioning their validity and priority of lien after they have been sold to good faith purchasers. As we have already seen, prior lienholders and bondholders, where no notice has been given to them or their trustees and no hearing has been afforded them as to the propriety of the expenditures and the right to make the certificates a prior lien, will generally be allowed to question their validity or right to priority, at least before they are issued to *bona fide* purchasers.[5] But those who consent or are

---

[1] Union Trust Co. *v.* Illinois, etc., R. Co., 117 U. S. 434, s. c. 6 Sup. Ct. R. 809.

[2] Jones on Corp. Bonds and Mortg., § 566, citing Turner *v.* Peoria, etc., R. Co., 95 Ill. 134; Bank of Montreal *v.* Chicago, etc., R. Co., 48 Iowa 518; Union Trust Co. *v.* Chicago, etc., R. Co., 7 Fed. R. 513. See, also, Beach on Receivers, § 397. If the certificates are issued for an inadequate consideration, a subsequent *bona fide* holder for value will be protected only to the amount actually advanced by the first purchaser. Central Nat. Bank *v.* Hazard, 30 Fed. R. 484.

[3] Jones on Corporate Bonds and Mortgages, § 550, citing Taylor *v.* Philadelphia, etc., R. Co., 14 Phila. (Pa.) 451, 461; People *v.* Erie R. Co., 54 How. (N. Y.) Pr. 59. See Coe *v.* N. J. Midland R. Co., 27 N. J. Eq. 37.

[4] Bank of Montreal *v.* Chicago, etc., R. Co., 48 Iowa 518.

[5] See *Ex parte* Mitchell, 12 S. Car. 83; Hand *v.* Savannah, etc., R. Co., 17 S. Car. 219; Hervey *v.* Illinois Midland R. Co., 28 Fed. R. 169; Coe *v.* New Jersey, etc., R. Co., 27 N. J. Eq. 37; *In re* United States Rolling Stock Co., 55 How. Pr. (N. Y.) 286; article in 12 Am. L. Rev. 660, and 13 Am. L. Rev. 40. In Snow *v.* Winslow, 54 Iowa 200, it was held that where the road was

given due notice and an opportunity to be heard can not afterwards question their validity or priority.[1] Nor can bondholders who, with knowledge of the facts, permit certificates to be issued without objection under the order of the court, question their validity or priority of lien after they have been issued and sold to *bona fide* purchasers.[2] Especially is this true where the bondholders appoint a committee of their own number to represent them all and such committee consents to the issuance of the certificates.[3] So, where the road is sold under a decree of foreclosure which makes it subject to the lien of the receiver's certificates, the purchaser at the foreclosure sale is estopped from questioning the validity of the lien.[4] The receiver who obtained the order and issued the certificates thereunder can

---

sold to satisfy the certificates it must be regarded as sold subject to a mechanic's lien, to enforce which suit had been instituted before the receiver was appointed, and that such lien was not divested or affected as the holder thereof was not made a party and did not consent to the appointment of the receiver or the order or decree of the court.

[1] *Ante*, § 591.

[2] Humphreys v. Allen, 101 Ill. 490, s. c. 4 Am. & Eng. R. Cas. 14; Langdon v. Vermont, etc., R. Co., 53 Vt. 228, s. c. 4 Am. & Eng. R. Cas. 33. See, also, Union Gold Mining Co. v. Rocky Mountain Nat. Bank, 96 U. S. 640; Lovett v. German Reformed Church, 12 Barb (N. Y.) 67. In the Vermont case cited in this note it was held that although the purpose for which the receiver was appointed had been accomplished so that he might have been discharged, yet if he continued to act as receiver and issued obligations as such, with the knowledge and assent of all parties interested, they were estopped to deny, as against *bona fide* holders, that the obligations were what they purported to be, namely, receiver's obligations entitled to priority of payment out of the assets of the trust.

[3] Langdon v. Vermont, etc., R. Co., 53 Vt. 228, s. c. 4 Am. & Eng. R. Cas. 33.

[4] Swann v. Clark, 110 U. S. 602, s. c. 4 Sup. Ct. R. 241; Mercantile Trust Co. v. Kanawha, etc., R. Co., 58 Fed. R. 6, s. c. 60 Am. & Eng. R. Cas. 513, 526. See, also, Central Trust Co. v. Sheffield, etc., Ry. Co., 44 Fed. R. 526. In this last case it appeared that, by consent of all parties, the receiver of a railroad company, though not engaged in operating the road, was authorized by order of court to issue certificates which should constitute a lien on the company's property superior to certain prior mortgages, and that the money obtained on such certificates was used in preserving and improving the property. It was held that the purchasers of the property, who purchased with the understanding that the receiver's certificates, under the order of the court, constituted a prior lien on the property, which they were to pay, at a subsequent sale to foreclose such mortgages, were estopped from denying the validity of the certificates.

not, it is obvious, object to their priority of lien nor can the mortgagor nor his assignees.[1] And a property owner along the line of the road can not restrain the completion of the road by questioning the validity of the receiver's certificates.[2]

§ 597. **Payment and redemption of certificates.**—As we have seen, receiver's certificates are not promises to pay money absolutely, creating a personal liability, but are rather to be considered as acknowledgments of indebtedness for the payment of which out of some specific fund usually to be ascertained thereafter the faith of the court is said to be pledged. As a general rule, therefore, an independent action will not lie to enforce them, but the application for their payment or redemption should be made to the court which authorized them to be issued.[3] The court may, doubtless, in a proper case, order them to be paid out of the fund in the hands of the receiver, but as the income or assets in the hands of the receiver will seldom be found sufficient to redeem the certificates and pay necessary expenses, and as the courts can not often tell in advance just what will be the condition of the trust or what questions may arise, certificates are seldom redeemed in advance of the foreclosure sale, and it is customary, therefore, to provide in the order authorizing their issue that they shall be a lien on the proceeds of the sale and payable out of the purchase-money.[4] Instead of this, however, the court may order that the lien shall remain upon the property which the purchaser shall take subject to such lien.[5] In such a case, as elsewhere stated, it has been held that the lien may be enforced against the property in the hands of the purchaser or his grantees in an independent action.[6] It has also been held that,

---

[1] Jerome v. McCarter, 94 U. S. 734. See, also, Central Trust Co. v. Seasongood, 130 U. S. 482, s. c. 9 Sup. Ct. R. 575; Vilas v. Page, 106 N. Y. 439, 452.

[2] Moran v. Lydecker, 11 Abb. N. Cas. (N. Y.) 298.

[3] Turner v. Peoria, etc., R. Co., 95 Ill. 134, s. c. 35 Am. R. 144. For cases in which an independent suit may be brought, see *ante*, § 592.

[4] Beach on Receivers, § 401.

[5] Mercantile Trust Co. v. Kanawha, etc., R. Co., 58 Fed. R. 6.

[6] *Ante*, § 592.

although the order authorizing the certificates provided that they should be a first and paramount lien upon the property, a final decree vesting in the purchaser of the property a title free from all liens operated *pro tanto* to set the order aside and transferred the lien, if any, to the proceeds of the sale.[1] It was further held, in the same case, that the holder of the receiver's certificates who was guilty of laches in not acting before the final decree, could not follow the proceeds of the sale into the hands of bondholders who received the same on distribution by final decree, notwithstanding the fact that the court had failed to redeem its pledge to make the certificates a paramount lien by providing on distribution for their payment. If the fund or property is insufficient to redeem or pay all the certificates in full, the holders must usually share *pro rata* in the proceeds.[2] But the rights of the holders of a portion of the certificates may, of course, be waived or made subordinate to those of others by agreement, and if the proceeds are insufficient to pay the latter, the former may get nothing.[3]

[1] Mercantile Trust Co. *v.* Kanawha, etc., R. Co., 58 Fed. R. 6, distinguishing Vilas *v.* Page, 106 N. Y. 439.

[2] Turner *v.* Peoria, etc., R. Co., 95 Ill. 134, s. c. 35 Am. R. 144.

[3] Fletcher *v.* Waring, 137 Ind. 159, s. c. 36 N. E. R. 896. Under the agreement in this case it was held that the party in whose favor the waiver was made and whose certificates were not paid in full, might even recover from the other party the amount paid for a right of way for which the certificates were issued to the latter.

CHAPTER XXIV.

INSOLVENCY AND DISSOLUTION.

§ 598. Scope of the chapter.
599. Railroad company is subject to state insolvency law.
600. Trust fund doctrine.
601. When a corporation is deemed insolvent—Effect of insolvency.
602. Assignments by corporations.
603. Preferences by corporations.
604. Preference of stockholders and officers.
605. Statutory preference of employes.
606. What constitutes a dissolution.
607. Judicial determination of dissolution.

§ 608. Voluntary dissolution — Surrender of charter.
609. Proceedings to dissolve.
610. Dissolution in case of consolidated company.
611. Effect of dissolution.
612. Corporation may have a qualified existence after dissolution.
613. Disposition of property on dissolution.
614. Rights of creditors upon dissolution.

§ 598. **Scope of the chapter.**—We have already considered in a general way the subject of the dissolution of a corporation by forfeiture or repeal of its charter and by expiration of the time to which its charter life is limited. But we have not considered what becomes of the property after dissolution, nor have we treated specifically of insolvency and the relations and rights of the various parties when a corporation becomes insolvent, except as incidentally connected with the subjects of foreclosure sales and receivers. In this chapter we shall treat briefly of these matters, including assignments and preferences.

§ 599. **Railroad company is subject to state insolvency law.**—Domestic railroad corporations, like all other corporations, are subject to the insolvency laws of the states wherein they are respectively incorporated and may be proceeded against

§ 600   INSOLVENCY AND DISSOLUTION.   849

under those laws.[1] But such laws, as a general rule at least, have no extra-territorial effect.[2] A voluntary assignment of personal property, however, if valid where it is made, will usually be treated as valid everywhere and may operate to transfer personal property of the assignor wherever it is found,[3] unless, perhaps, where it is contrary to good morals or repugnant to the policy or positive institutions of the state in which it is found.[4] But this rule does not apply to the same extent to assignments of real estate.[5] The effect of state insolvency laws upon consolidated corporations will be discussed elsewhere.

§ 600. **Trust fund doctrine.**—When a company becomes insolvent its capital stock with all its other property is said to become assets or to constitute a trust fund for the payment of its debts.[6] This is the well known "trust fund" doctrine to which we have elsewhere referred. It is usually stated substantially as we have stated it, but the statement, perhaps, needs explanation. It does not mean that there is any direct trust or lien upon the property of the corporation in favor of creditors, nor that the corporation may not manage or dispose

---

[1] Central Nat. Bank v. Worcester Horse R. Co., 13 Allen (Mass.) 105; Platt v. New York, etc., R. Co., 26 Conn. 544. The Maryland Act of 1888 providing for the payment of wages and salaries due employes of insolvent employers does not subject corporations to the insolvent laws of the state. Ellicott Machine Co. v. Speed & Co., 72 Md. 72, 18 Atl. 863.

[2] Glenn v. Clabaugh, 65 Md. 65; Warren v. First Nat. Bank, 149 Ill. 9, s. c. 25 L. R. A. 746; Franzen v. Hutchinson, (Iowa) 62 N. W. R. 698. But see as to the effect of insolvent laws on non-residents. Brown v. Smart, 145 U. S. 454, s. c. 12 Sup. Ct. R. 958; Macdonald v. First Nat. Bank, 47 Minn. 67, s. c. 49 N. W. R. 395.

[3] Baltimore, etc., R. Co. v. Glenn, 28 Md. 287; Caskie v. Webster, 2 Wall. Jr. (U. S. C. C.) 131; Burrill on Assignments, § 275; Story Confl. L., § 423, a. Many courts refuse to enforce foreign assignments to the prejudice of the citizens of their own state, holding that the rule of comity does not require them to do so in such a case.

[4] Burrill on Assignments,§§ 275, 279; Weider v. Maddox, 66 Tex. 372, s. c. 1 S. W. R. 168; Blake v. Williams, 6 Pick. (Mass.) 286; Herver v. Rhode Island, etc., Works, 93 U. S. 664; Ex parte Dickinson, 29 S. Car. 453, s. c. 7 S. E. R. 593.

[5] Burrill on Assignments, § 277; Osborn v. Adams, 18 Pick. (Mass.) 245.

[6] Wabash, etc., R. Co. v. Ham, 114 U. S. 587, 594; Graham v. LaCrosse, etc., R. Co., 102 U. S. 148, 161.

of it in the usual course of business while the corporation is "a going concern" with a reasonable prospect of continuing and there is no intention of suspending, although it may be insolvent in the sense that its liabilities are greater than its assets, or in the sense that it may not be able to fully meet its obligations as they become due. It simply means, according to recent decisions, that when the corporation is insolvent and a court of equity has possession of its assets for administration, they must be appropriated to the payment of its debts before any distribution to the stockholders.[1] In such a case equity will compel the payment of a balance due on unpaid stock.[2] The history of the evolution of the "trust fund" doctrine is an interesting one, but it would not be profitable to pursue it here. Some of the courts have undoubtedly misapplied and unduly extended it, but it may well be questioned if others, in the present reaction, are not inclined to unduly limit it. We have stated the doctrine as explained in the latest decisions of the supreme court of the United States, but it may be somewhat difficult to reconcile the rule thus stated with other statements of the rule made by the federal, as well as the state, courts, although we are inclined to think there is no real conflict. Thus, it is said that "when a corporation is dissolved or becomes insolvent and determines to discontinue the prosecution of business its property is thereafter affected by an equitable lien or trust for the benefit of creditors," and that the directors then hold a fiduciary relation to creditors and can not prefer themselves in view of expected suspension on account of insolvency, although the corporation might, while still "a going concern," secure them for advancements

---

[1] Hollins v. Brierfield, etc., Co., 150 U. S. 371, s. c. 14 Sup. Ct. R. 127; Fogg v. Blair, 133 U. S. 534, 541, s. c. 10 Sup. Ct. R. 338; Henderson v. Indiana Trust Co., 143 Ind. 561, s. c. 40 N. E. R. 516; First Nat. Bank v. Dovetail, etc., Co., 143 Ind. 550, s. c. 40 N. E. R. 810; Worthen v. Griffith, 59 Ark. 562, s. c. 28 S. W. R. 286; O'Bear, etc., Co. v. Volfer, (Ala.) 17 So. R. 525; Thomson-Houston, etc., Co. v. Henderson, etc., Co., 116 N. Car. 112, 21 S. E. R. 951; Alberger v. Nat. Bank, 123 Mo. 313, s. c. 27 S. W. R. 657; Chattanooga, etc., R. Co. v. Evans, 66 Fed. R. 809.

[2] Richardson v. Green, 133 U. S. 30; Morgan v. New York, etc., R. Co., 10 Paige Ch. Rep. 290; Barcalow v. Totten, (N. J.) 32 Atl. R. 2.

made to carry on the business with the reasonable expectation of successfully overcoming financial embarrassment.[1] This is a much more reasonable doctrine than that which forbids any preference after the company has become insolvent even though it is "a going concern" and has reasonable expectation of overcoming its financial embarrassment, and the only question is as to whether the "trust fund" doctrine should have been applied at all so long as the corporation had not quit business and its property had not been taken charge of by the court. The capital stock and properties of a corporation, however, constitute a trust fund for the payment of its debts in such a sense that when there is a misappropriation of the funds of a corporation, equity, on behalf of the creditors of such corporation, will follow the fund so diverted,[2] unless it has passed into the hands of a *bona fide* purchaser.[3]

§ 601. When a corporation is deemed insolvent—Effect of insolvency.—It is extremely difficult to formulate any general rule for determining just when a corporation is to be deemed

[1] Sutton Mfg. Co. v. Hutchinson, 63 Fed. R. 496; Sabin v. Columbia Fuel Co., 25 Ore. 15, s. c. 42 Am. St. R. 756. But compare Sanford Fork, etc., Co. v. Howe, etc., Co., 157 U. S. 312, s. c. 15 Sup. Ct. R. 621. See further on this subject, §§ 603, 604.

[2] Chicago, etc., R. Co. v. Chicago Third Nat. Bank, 134 U. S. 276; Wabash, etc., R. R. Co. v. Ham, 114 U. S. 587; Railroad Co. v. Howard, 7 Wall. (U. S.) 392, 409; Bish v. Bradford, 17 Ind. 490; Rorke v. Thomas, 56 N. Y. 559; Chattanooga, etc., R. Co. v. Evans, 66 Fed. R. 809; Chicago, etc., Bridge Co. v. Fowler, 55 Kan. 17, s. c. 39 Pac. R. 727; Hastings v. Drew, 76 N. Y. 9; Wait Insolv. Corp., §§ 150, 156; Taylor Priv. Corp., § 656. When one corporation transfers all its assets to another corporation without having paid its debts, the latter takes the property as a trustee subject to a lien in favor of the creditors of the old company. National Bank of Jefferson v. Texas Invest. Co., 74 Tex. 421, 12 S. W. 101; Montgomery, etc., Co. v. Dienelt, 133 Pa. St. 585. It has also been held that when a corporation has sold all its property, franchises, etc., and thus in effect has been dissolved, its creditors may enforce their demands in a court of equity against the former stockholders, the proceeds of the property being considered assets in the hands of stockholders for the payment of debts. But no action can be maintained against the purchasing company if the purchase was made in good faith. Chesapeake, etc., R. Co. v. Griest, 85 Ky. 619.

[3] Fisk v. Union Pac. R. R. Co., 10 Blatchf. (U. S.) 518; Sanger v. Upton, 91 U. S. 56, 60.

insolvent. It has been said that a corporation is insolvent when it is not able to pay its debts, as they become due in the usual course of business,[1] or when it has not property or assets sufficient to pay its debts.[2] But it frequently happens that a corporation or an individual may not be able to pay all debts as they mature, and may yet have assets far in excess of the liabilities. So, a corporation or an individual may not at some particular time have assets equal to the liabilities and yet may be able to meet all debts as they fall due or make such arrangements as will prevent financial embarrassment. It seems to us, therefore, that a corporation should not be deemed insolvent merely because its assets are insufficient to meet all its liabilities at any particular time, if it is still prosecuting business with the prospect and expectation of continuing to do so successfully. It is certainly not insolvent in such a sense as to justify the application of the "trust fund" doctrine, even if that can be applied in any case of mere insolvency, although it may, perhaps, be insolvent within the meaning of some statute. The mere insolvency of a corporation, however, does not *per se* work its dissolution, although it may be cause for a judgment dissolving it.[3] A corporation may exist without property,[4] and mere insolvency or impairment of capital, without surrender or forfeiture of the charter, does not prevent the members of the corporation from furnishing "renewed capital, and then proceeding to use the corporate powers."[5] So long, at least, as the corporation proceeds in good faith, with the reasonable expectation of paying its debts and successfully carrying on its business, it would seem that it is not insolvent in such a sense as to prevent the corporation from continuing the management

---

[1] Atwater v. American, etc., Bank, 152 Ill. 605, s. c. 38 N. E. R. 1017; Mish v. Main, 81 Md. 36, s. c. 31 Atl. R. 799; People v. Excelsior, etc., Co., 3 How. Pr. N. S. (N. Y.) 137.

[2] Wait Insolv. Corp., §§ 28, 29. See, also, Chicago Life Ins. Co. v. Auditor, 101 Ill. 82; Toof v. Martin, 13 Wall. (U. S.) 40; In re European, etc., Society, L. R. 9 Eq. 122.

[3] Angell & Ames on Corp., § 775; Shenandoah Valley R. R. Co. v. Griffith, 76 Va. 913; Moseby v. Burrow, 52 Tex. 396.

[4] Bruffett v. Great Western R. R. Co., 25 Ill. 353; Boston Glass Mfg. Co. v. Langdon, 24 Pick. (Mass.) 49; Wait Insolv. Corp., § 356.

[5] Coburn v. Boston, etc., Co., 10 Gray (Mass.) 243.

§ 602   INSOLVENCY AND DISSOLUTION.   853

of its assets in the regular course of business or to authorize creditors to interfere.[1]

§ 602. **Assignments by corporations.**—At common law, and under the statutes of most of the states, an insolvent corporation may make a general assignment in trust for the benefit of its creditors.[2] In the absence of any provision to the contrary, the assignment may be made by the directors without any action upon the part of the stockholders,[3] and it has also been held that this power may be exercised by a quorum of the board of directors at a regularly called meeting at which a bare quorum is present.[4] The president of the corporation, however, has no implied authority to do so by virtue of his office.[5] Such an assignment does not carry with it the prerogative franchises, such as that of being a corporation, and does not operate as a dissolution.[6] Owing to the peculiar nature of

---

[1] 2 Morawetz Priv. Corp., §786; Wait Insolv. Corp., § 34; Paulding v. Chrome Steel Co., 94 N. Y. 334, 338; Pond v. Framingham, etc., R. R. Co., 130 Mass. 194; Baker v. Louisiana, etc., R.R.Co.,34 La. Ann. 754;Warren v. First. Nat. Bank, 149 Ill. 9, s. c. 25 L. R. A. 746.

[2] Vanderpoel v. Gorman, 140 N. Y. 563, s. c. 24 L. R. A. 548; De Ruyter v. Trustees, 3 Barb. Ch. (N. Y.) 119, citing authorities from many states; Shockley v. Fisher, 75 Mo. 498; Wilkinson v. Bauerle, 41 N. J. Eq. 635; Lamb v. Cecil, 25 W. Va. 288; Tripp v. Northwestern Nat. Bank, 41 Minn. 400, 43 N. W. R. 60; Warner v. Mower, 11 Vt. 385; McCallie & Jones v. Walton, 37 Ga. 611, s. c. 95 Am. Dec. 369; State v. Bank, 6 Gill & J. 205, s. c. 26 Am. Dec. 561; Burrill on Assignments (6th ed.), § 45, and numerous authorities there cited. But see Meloy v. Central Nat. Bank, 17 Wash. L. R. 68.

[3] De Camp v. Alward, 52 Ind. 468; Ardesco Oil Co. v. North American, etc., Co., 66 Pa. St. 375, 382; Hutchinson v. Green, 91 Mo. 367, 1 S. W. R. 853; Wright v. Lee, 2 S. Dak. 596, 51 N. W. R. 706, s. c. 4 S. Dak. 237, 55 N. W. R. 931; Descombes v. Wood, 91 Mo. 196. Compare Chew v. Ellingwood, 86 Mo. 260, 273, s. c. 56 Am. R. 429, and Eppright v. Nickerson, 78 Mo. 482.

[4] Buell v. Buckingham, 16 Iowa 284; Chase v. Tuttle, 55 Conn. 455, s. c. 12 Atl. R. 874; Simon v. Sevier Assn., 54 Ark. 58.

[5] Richardson v. Rogers, 45 Mich. 591,s.c. 8 N. W. R. 526. And an assignment to himself is void. Rogers v. Pell, 35 N. Y. Sup. 17.

[6] Germantown Pass. Ry. Co. v. Fitler, 60 Pa. St. 124, s. c. 100 Am. Dec. 546, and note; Town v. Bank, 2 Doug. (Mich.) 530; Arthur v. Commercial & R. R. Bank, 9 Sm. & M. (Miss.) 394, s. c. 48 Am. Dec. 719; Parsons v. Eureka Powder Works, 48 N. H. 66; Hurlbut v. Carter, 21 Barb. (N. Y.) 221; State v. Bank, 6 Gill. & J. (Md.) 205, s. c. 26 Am. Dec. 561;

a railroad company, however, it may be that the rules applicable to assignments and preferences by ordinary business corporations do not all apply with full force to railroad companies.

§ 603. **Preferences by corporations.**—As a general rule, in the absence of any charter or statutory provision to the contrary, a corporation may exercise the right to make an assignment to the same extent and in the same manner as a natural person. Preferences in general assignments are prohibited in many of the states, but where they are permitted they may be made, in the absence of any provision to the contrary, by corporations as well as by individuals.[1] And even where preferences in general assignments are forbidden, they may usually be made by mortgage, securing particular creditors, or by transfer of property to them in good faith before a general assignment is made.[2]

§ 604. **Preference of stockholders and officers.**—It is generally held that stockholders, who are also creditors, may be preferred in good faith as such creditors.[3] It is also held, in

Shryock v. Bashore, 82 Pa. St. 159; Ohio L. & T. Co. v. Merchants', etc., Co., 11 Humph. (Tenn.) 1. But see State v. Real Estate Bank, 5 Ark. 595, s. c. 41 Am. Dec. 109; Smith v. New York, etc., Co., 18 Abb. Pr. (N. Y.) 419, and dissenting opinion of Story, J., in Beaston v. Farmers' Bank, 12 Pet. (U. S.) 102, 138.

[1] Gould v. Little Rock, etc., Ry. Co., 52 Fed. R. 680; Bier v. Gorrell, 30 W. Va. 95, s. c. 3 S. E. R. 30; Coats v. Donnell, 94 N. Y. 168; Bissell v. Besson, 47 N. J. Eq. 580, s. c. 22 Atl. R. 1077; Ringo v. Biscoe et al., 13 Ark. 563; Rollins v. Shaver, etc., Co., 80 Iowa 380, s. c. 45 N. W. R. 1037; Catlin v. Eagle Bank, 6 Conn. 233; Knoxville Iron Co. v. Wilkins, etc., Co., 74 Ga. 493; note to Lyons-Thomas Hardware Co. v. Perry Stove Co., 86 Tex. 143, 22 L. R. A. 802; Burrill on Assignments, § 45. Contra, Rouse v. Merchants' Nat. Bank, 46 Ohio St. 493, s. c. 22 N. E. R. 293, 5 L. R. A. 378, followed, as the law of Ohio, in Smith, etc., Purifier Co. v. McGroarty, 136 U. S. 237, s. c. 10 Sup. Ct. R. 1017; Lyons-Thomas Hardware Co. v. Perry Stove Co., supra; Kankakee Woolen Mill Co. v. Kampe, 38 Mo. App. 229.

[2] Bank of Montreal v. Potts, etc., Co., 90 Mich. 345; Warner v. Littlefield, 89 Mich. 329; Rollins v. Shaver, etc., Co., 80 Iowa 380, s. c. 45 N. W. R. 1037; Ragland v. McFall, 137 Ill. 81; Henderson v. Indiana Trust Co., (Ind.) 40 N. E. R. 516, and authorities cited in last note, supra.

[3] Burr v. McDonald, 3 Gratt. (Va.) 215; Lexington, etc., Co. v. Page, 17

§ 604   INSOLVENCY AND DISSOLUTION.   855

some jurisdictions, that directors and officers may likewise be preferred;[1] but there are other authorities to the effect that, after a corporation has become clearly insolvent, directors and officers can not take advantage of their position to obtain a preference for unsecured debts which there was no agreement to secure while the corporation was solvent or at the time the debts were created.[2] A corporation may, however, in good faith, and while solvent, borrow money from a director, or officer, for use in its business, and give a mortgage to him to secure its payment, and the fact that the corporation afterwards becomes insolvent does not impair the validity of his security.[3]

B. Mon. (Ky.) 412, s. c. 66 Am. Dec. 165; Reichwald v. Commercial Hotel Co., 106 Ill. 439; Warfield, etc., Co. v. Marshall, etc., Co., 72 Iowa 666; Garrett v. Burlington, etc., Co., 70 Iowa 697, s. c. 59 Am. R. 461. Contra, Swepson v. Exchange, etc., Bank, 9 Lea (Tenn.) 713.

[1] Planters' Bank v. Whittle, 78 Va. 737; Brown v. Grand Rapids, etc., Co., 58 Fed. R. 286, s. c. 22 L. R. A. 817; Gould v. Little Rock, etc., Ry. Co., 52 Fed. R. 680; Bank of Montreal v. Potts, etc., Co., 90 Mich. 345, s. c. 51 N. W. R. 512; Buell v. Buckingham, 16 Iowa 284, s. c. 85 Am. Dec. 516; Garrett v. Burlington, etc., Co., 70 Iowa 697, s. c. 59 Am. R. 461; Smith v. Skeary, 47 Conn. 47; Duncomb v. New York, etc., R. R. Co., 84 N. Y. 190; Hospes v. Car Co., 48 Minn. 174, s. c. 50 N. W. R. 1117; Schufeldt v. Smith, 131 Mo. 280, s. c. 31 S. W. R. 1039; Blaloch v. Kernersville, etc., Co., 110 N. Car. 99, s. c. 14 S. E. R. 501.

[2] Corey v. Wadsworth, 99 Ala. 68, 42 Am. St. R. 29, s. c. 11 So. R. 350 (overruled in O'Bear, etc., Co. v. Volfer, 17 So. R. 525); Olney v. Conanicut, etc., Co., 16 R. I. 597, s.c. 5 L. R. A. 361, 27 Am. St. R. 767, and note; Haywood v. Lincoln Lumber Co., 64 Wis. 639; Sicardi v. Keystone Oil Co., 149 Pa. St. 148; Consolidated Tank Line Co. v. Kansas City, etc., Co., 45 Fed. R. 7; Beach v. Miller, 130 Ill. 162, s. c. 17 Am. St. R. 291, and note; Roseboom v. Whittaker, 132 Ill. 81, s. c. 23 N. E. R. 339; Smith v. Putnam, 61 N. H. 632; Adams v. Kehlor, etc., Co., 35 Fed. R. 433; Sweeney v. Grape Sugar Co., 30 W. Va. 443, s. c. 8 Am. St. R. 88; Howe, etc., Co. v. Sanford, etc., Co., 44 Fed. R. 231 (reversed in Sanford Fork, etc., Co. v. Howe, etc., Co., 157 U. S. 312); Farmers' L. & T. Co. v. San Diego, etc., Ry. Co., 45 Fed. R. 518; Stratton v. Allen, 16 N. J. Eq. 229; Bradley v. Farwell, 1 Holmes 433; Hill v. Pioneer Lumber Co., 113 N. Car. 173, s. c. 21 L. R. A. 560; Gaslight, etc., Co. v. Terrell, L. R. 10 Eq. 168; Montgomery v. Phillips, (N. J.) 31 Atl. R. 622; Bosworth v. Jacksonville, etc., Bank, 64 Fed. R. 615; Ingwersen v. Edgecombe, 42 Neb. 740, s. c. 60 N. W. R. 1032. See, also, Sawyer v. Hoag, 17 Wall. (U. S.) 610.

[3] O'Conner, etc., Co. v. Coosa, etc., Co., 95 Ala. 614, s. c. 36 Am. St. R. 251; Twin Lick Oil Co. v. Marbury, 91 U. S. 587; Hotel Co. v. Wade, 97 U. S. 13; Paulding v. Chrome Steel Co., 94 N. Y. 334; Mullanphy Bank v. Schott, 135 Ill. 655, 26 N. E. R. 640;

Indeed, according to the better reason and the later authorities a corporation may, in good faith, secure its directors who have lent their credit to it, "to induce a continuance of the loan of that credit, and obtain renewals of maturing paper at a time when the corporation, though not in fact possessed of assets equal to its indebtedness, is a going concern, and is intending and expecting to continue its business."[1] And where advancements are made by directors under an agreement, made at the time, that they are to have securities, the mere fact that such securities are not given to them until after the corporation becomes insolvent will not affect their validity where the entire transaction is in good faith.[2] Such transactions will, however, be closely scrutinized,[3] and the rule announced in the later decisions of the federal courts would not, perhaps, be extended by them to cases in which a general assignment is made or a

---

Neal's Appeal, 129 Pa. St. 64, 18 Atl. R. 564; Re Pyle Works, 63 L. T. R. 628; Saltmarsh v. Spaulding, 147 Mass. 224.

[1] Per Brewer, J., in Sanford Fork, etc., Co., v. Howe, Browne & Co., 157 U. S. 312, 15 Sup. Ct. R. 620; see, also, Sabin v. Columbia Fuel Co., 25 Oreg. 15, s. c. 42 Am. St. R. 756; Holt v. Bennett, 146 Mass. 437, s. c. 16 N. E. R. 5; Gould v. Little Rock, etc., Ry. Co. 52 Fed. R. 680; Henderson v. Indiana Trust Co., (Ind.) 40 N. E. R. 516; County Court v. Baltimore, etc., R. R. Co., 35 Fed. R. 161; Hopson v. Ætna, etc., Co., 50 Conn. 597; Illinois Steel Co. v. O'Donnell, 156 Ill. 624, s. c. 41 N. E. R. 185. "So a mortgage executed by a corporation whose debts exceed its assets, to secure a liability incurred by it or on its behalf, will be sustained, if it appears to have been given in good faith to keep the corporation upon its feet and enable it to continue the prosecution of its business. A corporation is not required by any duty it owes to creditors to suspend operations the moment it becomes financially embarrassed, or because it may be doubtful whether the objects of its creation can be attained by further effort upon its part. It is in the line of right and of duty, when attempting, in good faith, by the exercise of its lawful powers and by the use of all legitimate means, to preserve its active existence, and thereby accomplish the objects for which it was created. In such a crisis in its affairs, and to those ends, it may accept financial assistance from one of its directors, and by a mortgage upon its property secure the payment of money then loaned or advanced by him, or in that mode protect him against liability then incurred in its behalf by him." Per Harlan, J., in Sutton Mfg. Co. v. Hutchinson, 63 Fed. R. 496, 501.

[2] See Stout v. Yaeger Mill Co., 13 Fed. R. 802; Baker v. Harpster, 42 Kan. 511, s. c. 22 Pac. R. 415.

[3] Richardson's Exr. v. Green, 133 U. S. 30, 43, s. c. 10 Sup. Ct. R. 280; Twin Lick Oil Co. v. Marbury, 91 U. S. 587, 588.

mortgage executed to secure a director after the corporation has become hopelessly insolvent and has no intention of continuing business. Under such circumstances "entirely different considerations come into view," says Justice Harlan in a recent case,[1] from which we have already quoted. "In our judgment, when a corporation becomes insolvent and intends not to prosecute its business, or does not expect to make further effort to accomplish the objects of its creation, its managing officers or directors come under a duty to distribute its property or its proceeds ratably among all creditors, having regard, of course, to valid liens or charges previously placed upon it. Their duty is 'to act up to the end or design' for which the corporation was created,[2] and when they can no longer do so their function is to hold or distribute the property in their hands for the equal benefit of those entitled to it. Because of the existence of this duty in respect to a common fund in their hands to be administered, the law will not permit them, although creditors, to obtain any peculiar advantage for themselves to the prejudice of other creditors."[3] It is not, however, altogether safe to predict that this decision will be followed without question.

§ 605. **Statutory preference of employes.**—Statutes exist in many of the states giving laborers and employes a lien or preference upon the insolvency or dissolution of a corporation. It is generally held that such statutes are to be liberally construed;[4] but different courts have not always reached the same conclusion as to what persons are entitled to the benefit of the

[1] Sutton Mfg. Co. v. Hutchinson, 63 Fed. R. 496, 502. See, also, Bosworth v. Jacksonville Nat. Bank, 64 Fed. R. 615.
[2] 1 Bl. Comm. 480.
[3] Sutton Mfg. Co. v. Hutchinson, supra. The court cites Lippincott v. Shaw Carriage Co., 25 Fed. R. 577, and cases following it. The authority of that case and of some of the others cited is weakened, if not destroyed, by the decision in Sanford Fork, etc., Co. v. Howe, Browne & Co., 157 U. S. 312, but this does not necessarily impair the force of Judge Harlan's decision, for the Lippincott case was an extreme case and went much further than Judge Harlan did.
[4] Pendergast v. Yandes, 124 Ind. 159, s. c. 24 N. E. R. 724, 3 Lewis Am. R. R. & Corp. R. 645; Mining Co. v. Cullins, 104 U. S. 176; Bass v. Doerman, 112 Ind. 390, s. c. 14 N. E. R. 377.

statute, although the provisions of many of the statutes are very similar. An independent contractor is clearly not a laborer or an employe within the meaning of such a statute.[1] Nor are the regular officers of a corporation ordinarily included,[2] although it has been held that a head miller,[3] the superintendent of a gas company,[4] and the foreman or "boss" of a mine[5] are entitled to the benefit of the statute.[6] An attorney, employed for a special purpose, is not entitled to a preference under a statute preferring "wages or salaries to clerks, servants or employes.'"[7]

§ 606. What constitutes a dissolution.—As elsewhere stated, a dissolution may result from the expiration of the time to which the corporate life was limited, or by repeal of the charter under the reserved power of repeal; but, with these and one or two other exceptions, the general rule is that a corporation remains *in esse* until dissolved by judicial decree. Many acts and omissions may be cause for dissolution without operating

---

[1] Vane v. Newcombe, 132 U. S. 220; Tod v. Kentucky Union R. R. Co., 52 Fed. R. 241, s. c. 18 L. R. A. 305; Delaware, L. & W. R. R. Co. v. Oxford Iron Co., 33 N. J. Eq. 192. Nor a sub-contractor, although he personally works with the men employed by him to work on part of a railroad, which he has contracted to construct at a fixed price. Rogers v. Dexter, etc., R. R. Co., 85 Me. 372, 21 L. R. A. 528. See, also, Lehigh Coal, etc., Co. v. Central R. R. Co., 29 N. J. Eq. 252.

[2] Appeal of Black, 83 Mich. 513.

[3] England v. Beatty Organ, etc., Co., 41 N. J. Eq. 470; Wells v. Southern, etc., R. R. Co., 1 Fed. R. 270.

[4] Pendergast v. Yandes, 124 Ind. 159, s. c. 24 N. E. R. 724, 3 Lewis Am. R. R. & Corp. R. 645. It appeared, however, that he was not an officer or general manager, but merely superintended the digging of trenches and laying of pipes.

[5] Capron v. Strout, 11 Nev. 304; Mining Co. v. Cullins, 104 U. S. 176.

[6] But compare Seventh Nat. Bank v. Shenandoah Iron Co., 35 Fed. R. 436; Missouri, K. & T. R. R. Co. v. Baker, 14 Kan. 563; Pennsylvania & D. R. R. Co. v. Leuffer, 84 Pa. St. 168; People v. Remington, 45 Hun (N. Y.) 329. See, also, notes to Pendergast v. Yandes, 3 Lewis Am. R. R. & Corp. Cas. 645, 650, and Tod v. Kentucky Union R. R. Co., 18 L. R. A. 305, where the various statutes are referred to and the conflicting authorities collected. Also *ante*, § 186.

[7] Lewis v. Fisher, 80 Md. 139, 26 L. R. A. 278; Louisville, E. & St. L. R. Co. v. Wilson, 138 U. S. 501. See, also, *In re* Manchester, etc., Co., L. R. (1893), 2 Ch. Div. 638, s. c. 60 Am. & Eng. R. R. Cas. 541. But compare Gurney v. Atlantic, etc., R. R. Co., 58 N. Y. 358.

of themselves to dissolve the corporation. Thus, as we have seen, insolvency does not work a dissolution;[1] nor does suspension of business,[2] omission to elect officers,[3] failure to exercise corporate powers,[4] lease or sale of all the corporate property,[5] the assignment of such property for the benefit of creditors,[6] or the appointment of a receiver.[7] The acquisition of all the stock by a single member does not necessarily work a dissolution;[8] nor does a consolidation necessarily operate as

[1] Nor does a judicial decree of insolvency, together with an injunction against continuing business, and the appointment of a receiver. Second Nat. Bank v. New York, etc., Co., 11 Fed. Rep. 532; Coburn v. Boston, etc., Co., 10 Gray (Mass.) 243.

[2] Nimmons v. Tappan, 2 Sweeny (32 N. Y. Super.) 652; Mickles v. Rochester City Bank, 11 Paige (N. Y.) 118, s. c. 42 Am. Dec. 103; State v. Barron, 58 N. H. 370; Kansas City Hotel Co. v. Sauer, 65 Mo. 278; Valley Bank v. Ladies', etc., Sewing Society, 28 Kan. 423.

[3] Allen v. New Jersey Southern R. R. Co., 49 How. Pr. (N. Y.) 14; Boston Glass Manufactory v. Langdon, 24 Pick. (Mass.) 49; Harris v. Mississippi Valley, etc., R. R. Co., 51 Miss. 602; Wait on Insolv. Corp., § 372.

[4] Rollins v. Clay, 33 Me. 132; Swan Land, etc., Co. v. Frank, 39 Fed. Rep. 456; Russell v. McLellan, 14 Pick. (Mass.) 63; Brandon Iron Co. v. Gleason, 24 Vt. 228; Slee v. Bloom, 5 Johns. Ch. 366, reversed in Slee v. Bloom, 19 Johns. 456, s. c. 10 Am. Dec. 273.

[5] Hill v. Fogg, 41 Mo. 563; Bruffett v. Great Western, etc., R. R. Co., 25 Ill. 353; Swan Land, etc., Co. v. Frank, 39 Fed. Rep. 456; State v. Western, etc., Co., 40 Kan. 96, s. c. 10 Am. St. Rep. 166; Troy, etc., R. R. Co. v. Kerr, 17 Barb. (N. Y.) 581; Commonwealth v. Cent. Pass. R. R. Co., 52 Pa. St. 506; Sewell v. East Cape, etc., Co., 50 N. J. 717, 25 Atl. Rep. 929.

[6] Boston Glass Manufactory v. Langdon, 24 Pick. (Mass.) 49; De-Camp v. Alward, 52 Ind. 468; State v. Bank, 6 Gill & J. (Md.) 205. *Ante*, § 602.

[7] Moseby v. Burrow, 52 Tex. 396; Kincaid v. Dwinelle, 59 N. Y. 548; Heath v. Missouri, etc., Ry. Co., 83 Mo. 617; State v. Railroad Commissioners, 41 N. J. L. 235; National Bank v. Insurance Co., 104 U. S. 54; Dewey v. St. Albans, etc., Co., 56 Vt. 476, s. c. 48 Am. Rep. 803; Ohio, etc., R. R. Co. v. Russell, 115 Ill. 52; Rosenblatt v. Johnston, 104 U. S. 462; Kirkpatrick v. State Board, (N. J.) 29 Atl. Rep. 442.

[8] Newton Mfg. Co. v. White, 42 Ga. 148; Louisville Banking Co. v. Eisenman, 94 Ky. 83, s. c. 21 S. W. Rep. 531 and 1049; Russell v. McLellan, 14 Pick. (Mass.) 63. See also, Hopkins v. Roseclare, etc., Co., 72 Ill. 373; Swift v. Smith, 65 Md. 428, s. c. 57 Am. Rep. 336; Button v. Hoffman, 61 Wis. 20, s. c. 50 Am. Rep. 131; Wilde v. Jenkins, 4 Paige (N. Y.) 481; Sharpe v. Dawes, 46 L. J. Q. B. 104. But see *contra*, Bellona Company's Case, 3 Bland (Md.) 442.

a complete dissolution of the old companies in all cases,[1] although it may do so.[2] The question is generally one of intent to be determined from the statute and agreement of consolidation.[3] So, where the statute provides for a dissolution upon the failure to perform certain conditions or upon the happening of some contingency, it is largely a question of legislative intent as to whether the corporation is dissolved upon such failure or the happening of such contingency. As a general rule it is not dissolved by the mere failure to perform conditions subsequent[4] nor by the happening of a contingency made by the statute a ground of forfeiture.[5]

§ 607. **Judicial determination of dissolution.**—A judicial determination of the existence of such grounds in the particular instance and decree of forfeiture or dissolution is usually essential. But it is held that the legislature, in the charter or governing statute, may provide for a dissolution in certain cases of the kind specified without judicial decree.[6] This doctrine,

[1] Lightner v. Boston and Albany R. R. Co., 1 Lowell (U. S.)338, 340; Central R. R., etc., Co. v. Georgia, 92 U. S. 665; Boardman v. Lake Shore, etc., Ry. Co., 84 N. Y. 157, 181; Meyer v. Johnston, 64 Ala. 603; Philadelphia, etc., R. R. Co. v. Maryland, 10 How. (U. S.) 376.

[2] McMahan v. Morrison, 16 Ind. 172, s. c. 79 Am. Dec. 418; Clearwater v. Meredith, 1 Wall. (U. S.) 25, 40; Shields v. Ohio, 95 U. S. 319; Bishop v. Brainerd, 28 Conn. 289; Pullman Palace Car Co. v. Missouri Pac. Ry. Co., 115 U. S. 587, 594. See, also, Cheraw, etc., R. R. Co. v. Commissioners, 88 N. Car. 519; Kansas, etc., Ry. Co. v. Smith, 40 Kan. 192; Fee v. New Orleans, etc., Co., 35 La. Ann. 413.

[3] Wabash, St. L. & P. Ry. Co. v. Ham, 114 U.' S. 587, 595; Central R. R., etc., Co. v. Georgia, 92 U. S. 665, 670.

[4] Brooklyn Cent. R. R. Co. v. Brooklyn City R. R. Co., 32 Barb. (N. Y.) 358; In re New York Elevated R. R. Co., 70 N. Y. 327, 338; State v. Fagan, 22 La. Ann. 545; Chesapeake, etc., Co. v. Baltimore, etc., R. R. Co., 4 G. & J. (Md.) 1, 121, 127; Briggs v. Cape Cod, etc., Canal Co., 137 Mass. 71; Santa Rosa, etc., R. Co. v. Central St. Ry. Co., (Cal.) s. c. 38 Pac. R. 986.

[5] La Grange, etc., R. R. Co. v. Rainey, 7 Coldw. (Tenn.) 420; Taylor Priv. Corp., § 432; 2 Morawetz Priv. Corp., § 1006. So, where the statute provides that a corporation shall be dissolved by a mortgage sale of its franchise and property, it is not dissolved by an illegal and fraudulent sale. White Mts. R. R. Co. v. White Mts. R. R. Co., 50 N. H. 50.

[6] Matter of Brooklyn, W., etc., R. R. Co., 75 N. Y. 335; Brooklyn Steam, etc., Co. v. Brooklyn, 78 N. Y. 524; Oakland R. R. Co. v. Oakland, etc., R. R. Co., 45 Cal. 365. See review of cases in Bybee v. Oregon, etc., R. R.

however, should not be unduly extended, and, in order to justify its application in any case, it should clearly appear that the legislature intended that the matters specified should *per se* work a dissolution, and not merely that they should be sufficient cause for dissolution.[1]

§ 608. Voluntary dissolution—Surrender of charter.—Ordinary business corporations, where the rights of the state or the public do not intervene, may cease to do business and surrender their charters by a unanimous vote of the stockholders,[2] although some authorities hold that the surrender of a charter must be accepted by the state.[3] But most of the cases holding that an acceptance on the part of the state is necessary were decided under special charters or under the old doctrine that the dissolution of a corporation extinguished all its debts. There seems to be no valid reason why a purely private corporation, incorporated under general laws and charged with no public duties, should not be allowed to voluntarily cease business and dissolve or surrender its charter without an express acceptance on the part of the state.[4] Nor is a unanimous vote of the stockholders always essential. A private business corporation should not be compelled to continue a losing business, which is certain to result in financial catastrophe or the failure of the object for which the company was incorporated, and, in such a case,

Co., 139 U. S. 663, s. c. 11 Sup. Ct. R. 641.

[1] See La Grange, etc., R. R. Co. v. Rainey, 7 Coldw. (Tenn.) 420; Flint, etc., Co. v. Woodhull, 25 Mich. 99; Vermont, etc., R. R. Co. v. Vermont Cent. R. R. Co., 34 Vt. 1; People v. Manhattan Co., 9 Wend. (N. Y.) 351, 382; Galveston, etc., Ry. v. State, 81 Tex. 572, 17 S. W. R. 67; Santa Rosa, etc., R. Co. v. Central St. Ry. Co., (Cal.) s. c. 38 Pac. R. 986.

[2] Mumma v. Potomac Co., 8 Peters (U. S.) 281; Read v. Frankfort Bank, 23 Me. 318; Houston v. Jefferson College, 63 Pa. St. 428; Slee v. Bloom, 19 Johns. 456, s. c. 10 Am. Dec. 273; Mobile, etc., R. R. Co. v. State, 29 Ala. 573; Webster v. Turner, 12 Hun (N. Y.) 264; Bruce v. Platt, 80 N. Y. 379; 1 Beach Priv. Corp., § 781; 1 Cook on Stock and Stockholders, § 629.

[3] Kincaid v. Dwinelle, 59 N. Y. 448; Moseby v. Burrow, 52 Tex. 396; Boston Glass Manufactory v. Langdon, 24 Pick. (Mass.) 49; Town v. Bank, 2 Doug. (Mich.) 530, and 2 Beach Priv. Corp., § 781, where other authorities are cited *pro* and *con*.

[4] Taylor Priv. Corp., § 434; 2 Beach Priv. Corp., § 781; Holmes, etc., Co. v. Holmes, etc., Co., 127 N. Y. 252; Merchants' and Planters' Line v. Waganer, 71 Ala. 581.

a majority of the stockholders may surrender the charter and take steps to wind up the business.[1] And there are cases of this kind in which even the minority may compel the corporation to wind up its business.[2] But a charter can not be voluntarily surrendered and the corporation dissolved in such a manner and under such circumstances as to escape liability for debts or preclude suits therefor.[3] For this purpose the corporation still has a qualified existence,[4] which is generally provided for by statute. Railroad companies, unlike strictly private corporations, owe a duty to the public, and they can not, therefore, voluntarily cease to do business and dissolve without the consent of the state, no matter what may be the true rule in regard to strictly private corporations. No matter whether all the stockholders consent or not, the corporation can not evade its duties to the public by a voluntary dissolution and surrender or transfer of its charter and franchises without the consent of the state,[5] except, perhaps, where it is clearly insolv-

[1] Treadwell v. Salisbury Mfg. Co., 7 Gray (Mass.) 393, s. c. 66 Am. Dec. 490; Black v. Delaware, etc., Co., 22 N. J. Eq. 130; Hancock v. Holbrook, 9 Fed. R. 353; Price v. Holcomb, 89 Iowa 123, 56 N. W. R. 407; Lauman v. Lebanon, etc., R. R. Co., 30 Pa. St. 42, s. c. 72 Am. Dec. 685; McCurdy v. Myers, 44 Pa. St. 535; Trisconi v. Winship, 43 La. Ann. 45, s. c. 26 Am. St. R. 175; 1 Morawetz Priv. Corp., § 413; 1 Beach Priv. Corp., § 781; Taylor Priv. Corp., § 610. But see Polar Star Lodge v. Polar Star Lodge, 16 La. Ann. 53; Berry v. Broach, 65 Miss. 450.

[2] Marr v. Bank, 4 Coldw. (Tenn.) 471; O'Connor v. Knoxville etc., Co., 93 Tenn. 708, s. c. 28 S. W. R. 308; Masters v. Electric, etc., Co., 6 Daly (N. Y.) 455; In re Bristol, etc., Bank, L.R. 44 Ch. Div. 703; Miner v. Belle Isle Ice Co., 93 Mich. 97. But not ordinarily, Denike v. New York, etc., Co., 80 N. Y. 599; Matter of Pyrolusite, etc., Co., 29 Hun (N. Y.) 429; Hardon v. Newton, 14 Blatchf. (U. S.) 376; In re Suburban Hotel Co., L. R. 2 Ch. 737; Pratt v. Jewett, 9 Gray (Mass.) 34; Curien v. Santini, 16 La. Ann. 27.

[3] Portland, etc., Co. v. Portland, 12 B. Mon. (Ky.) 77; Kincaid v. Dwinelle, 59 N. Y. 548, 552; Baptist Meeting House v. Webb, 66 Me. 398; In re Directors of Binghamton, etc., Co., 143 N. Y. 261, s. c. 38 N. E. R. 297; Taylor Priv. Corp., § 431.

[4] 1 Morawetz Priv. Corp., § 411.

[5] Lauman v. Lebanon Valley R. R. Co., 30 Pa. St. 42, s. c. 72 Am. Dec. 685; Central R. R., etc., Co. v. Collins, 40 Ga. 582; Wilson v. Central Bridge Co., 9 R. I. 590; Treadwell v. Salisbury Mfg. Co., 7 Gray (Mass.) 393, s. c. 66 Am. Dec. 490. See, also, State v. Western, etc., R. R. Co., 95 N. Car. 602; New Orleans, etc., Ry. Co. v. State 112 U. S. 12.

ent and incapable of performing such duties.[1] But it has been held that where a railroad company has lost all its property by judicial sale, has done no business for a great many years, and has neither elected new officers nor had any old officers within the state during such period, a surrender of its charter and acceptance of such surrender by the state will be presumed.[2]

§ 609. **Proceedings to dissolve.**—The dissolution of a corporation will not be decreed in a foreign jurisdiction,[3] but a valid decree of dissolution in the state in which the charter was granted is generally binding everywhere.[4] Notwithstanding such a decree, however, it has been held that, for the protection of home creditors, the corporation may be treated in another state in which it does business and in which such creditors reside, as still in existence in a certain sense for the purpose of enabling them to reach its effects in that state,[5] at least where an action has been commenced against it therein before the decree of dissolution in the state of its birth.[6] Statutes exist in most of the states providing more or less specifically the mode of dissolving and winding up a corporation, and keeping it alive for that purpose after it has surrendered its charter or is so far dissolved as to be unable to carry on its regular business.[7] In the absence of a statute giving courts of

[1] Boston, etc., R. R. Co. v. New York, etc., R. R. Co., 13 R. I. 260.

[2] Combes v. Keyes, 89 Wis. 297, s. c. 62 N. W. R. 89.

[3] Wilkins v. Thorne, 60 Md. 253; Importing, etc., Co. v. Locke, 50 Ala. 332; Society v. New Haven, 8 Wheat. (U. S.) 464; Merrick v. Van Santvoord, 34 N. Y. 208; Folger v. Columbian, etc., Co., 99 Mass. 267, s. c. 96 Am. Dec. 747, and note. A federal court, sitting as a court of equity, has no power, in the absence of any statute conferring it, to dissolve a foreign corporation and wind up its affairs. Republican, etc., Mines v. Brown, 58 Fed. R. 644, s. c. 48 Am. & Eng. Corp. Cas. 28.

[4] Remington v. Samana Bay Co., 140 Mass. 494, s. c. 5 N. E. R. 292.

[5] Life Assn. v. Fassett, 102 Ill. 315.

[6] Hunt v. Columbian, etc., Co., 55 Me. 290; Henry v. Stuart, 14 Phila. (Pa.) 110; 2 Morawetz Priv. Corp., § 988.

[7] See St. Louis, etc., Coal Co. v. Sandoval Coal Co., 111 Ill. 32; Mariners' Bank v. Sewall, 50 Me. 220; Herron v. Vance, 17 Ind. 595; Stetson v. City Bank, 12 Ohio St. 577; Von Glahn v. De Rosset, 81 N. Car. 467; Folger v. Chase, 18 Pick. (Mass.) 63; Tusca-

equity jurisdiction it is generally, although not uniformly, held that proceedings for the forfeiture of a charter must be had in a court of law, usually by *quo warranto*, at the suit of the state or its proper representative.[1] But the right of the state to have the charter forfeited and the right of creditors and stockholders to the protection of a court of equity are two different things. On the one hand, it is true that there are many grounds or circumstances which would be cause for forfeiture at the suit of the state without giving the stockholders or creditors any right to interfere, no matter whether the state enforces the forfeiture or waives it. So, on the other hand, there may be circumstances under which creditors or stockholders may obtain relief even to the extent of winding up the affairs of the corporation and virtually dissolving it, although there might not be sufficient ground for forfeiture by the state; and insolvency, which may be cause for forfeiture, may also, under certain circumstances, as, for instance, where it is impossible to accomplish the purpose of the incorporation, be cause for winding up the corporate affairs at the suit of creditors or shareholders, at least under the statutes of many of the states.[2]

loosa, etc., Assn. *v.* Green, 48 Ala. 346. For New York and other statutes, see 2 Beach Priv. Corp., §§ 779, 780; 2 Morawetz Priv. Corp., §§ 1036, 1037; Marstaller *v.* Mills, 143 N. Y. 398, s. c. 38 N. E. R. 370.

[1] See *ante,* §§ 53, 54; Folger *v.* Columbian, etc., Co., 99 Mass. 267, s. c. 96 Am. Dec. 747, and note in which many authorities are cited. Republican M. S. Mines *v.* Brown, 58 Fed. R. 645, s. c. 24 L. R. A. 776; Strong *v.* McCagg, 55 Wis. 624; Wheeler *v.* Pullman, etc., Co., 143 Ill. 197, 32 N. E. R. 420; Decker *v.* Gardner, 124 N. Y. 334; Hinckley *v.* Pfister, 83 Wis. 64, s. c. 53 N. W. R. 21; People *v.* Weigley, 155 Ill. 491, s. c. 40 N. E. R. 300.

[2] See Mickles *v.* Rochester, etc., Bank, 11 Paige (N. Y.) 118, 126, s. c. 42 Am. Dec. 103; Ward *v.* Sea Ins. Co., 7 Paige (N. Y.) 294; Hitch *v.* Hawley, 132 N. Y. 212; Hurst *v.* Coe, 30 W. Va. 158, 3 S. E. R. 564; Merchants' & Planters' Line *v.* Waganer, 71 Ala. 581; O'Connor *v.* Knoxville, etc., Co., 93 Tenn. 708, 28 S. W. R. 308; Baker *v.* Backus, 32 Ill. 79; Hunt *v.* Le Grand, etc., Co., 143 Ill. 118, 32 N. E. R. 525; Newfoundland R. R. Co. *v.* Schack, 40 N. J. Eq. 222; Miner *v.* Belle Isle Ice Co., 93 Mich. 97, s. c. 6 Lewis' Am. R. R. & Corp. R. 660; 2 Beach Priv. Corp., §§ 782, 783; 1 Pom. Eq. Jur., § 171; 1 Morawetz Priv. Corp., § 284. In New York it seems that creditors must be judgment creditors before they can maintain such a suit. Cole *v.* Knickerbocker, etc., Co., 23 Hun 255. But see Alling *v.* Ward, (Ill.) 24 N. E. R. 551, s. c. 2 Lewis' Am. R. R. &

§ 610. Dissolution in case of consolidated company.—Where by the consolidation of corporations of several states a new corporation is formed, which exists under the laws of two or more states it has been held that each of the original companies remains liable to be proceeded against under the insolvent laws of the state by which it was created on account of its separate indebtedness.[1] In case it has maintained no distinct place of business and has chosen no new officers in the state, the original place of business of the defendant corporation will be regarded as continuing to be such for the purposes of the suit; and its former officers, for purposes of service and place of suit, will be regarded as the officers of the company.[2] It has also been held that the new corporation formed by such consolidation is liable to be proceeded against in bankruptcy in either of the states under whose laws it was formed,[3] and it may be wound up and dissolved in one state without its franchise in the other states being affected.[4] Each state usually retains jurisdiction over the portion of the road within its borders,[5] but the effect of the consolidation upon the old companies depends, as we have elsewhere stated, very largely upon the statute and agreement of consolidation in the particular case.

§ 611. Effect of dissolution.—It was formerly held that, upon the dissolution of a corporation, its real estate reverted to the grantor and its personal property to the state or sovereign, and that the debts due to it and from it were forgiven and extinguished, but this is no longer the rule.[6] The modern

Corp. R., 727 (see Alling v. Wenzel, 133 Ill. 264); White v. University Land Co., 49 Mo. App. 450.

[1] Platt v. New York, etc., R. Co., 26 Conn. 544.

[2] Platt v. New York, etc., R. Co., 26 Conn. 544.

[3] *In re* Boston, etc., R. Co., 9 Blatch. (U. S.) 101.

[4] Hart v. Boston, etc., R. Co., 40 Conn. 524. Compare Graham v. Boston, etc., R. R. Co., 118 U. S. 162; Covington, etc., Bridge Co. v. Mayer, 31 Ohio St. 317.

[5] Wait on Insolv. Corp., § 445.

[6] Taylor Priv. Corp., § 437; 1 Cook on Stock and Stockholders, § 641; notes to State Bank v. State, 12 Am. Dec. 234, 239; Miners' Ditch Co. v. Zellerbach, 99 Am. Dec. 300, 336; People v. O'Brien, 7 Am. St. R. 684, 717. Debts are not extinguished. Blake v. Portsmouth, etc., R. R. Co., 39 N. H. 435; Howe v. Robinson, 20 Fla. 352; McCoy v. Farmer,

doctrine is well stated by Justice Miller in a recent case.[1] Speaking of the effect of the repeal of a charter, he says: "In short, whatever power is dependent solely upon the grant of the charter, and which could not be exercised by unincorporated private persons under the general laws of the state, is abrogated by repeal of the law which granted these special rights. Personal and real property acquired by the corporation during its lawful existence, rights of contract or choses in action so acquired, and which do not, in their nature, depend upon the general powers conferred by the charter, are not destroyed by such repeal; and the courts may, if the legislature does not provide some special remedy, enforce such rights by the means within their power. The rights of the shareholders of such a corporation to their interest in its property are not annihilated by such a repeal, and there must remain in the courts the power to protect those rights."[2]

§ 612. **Corporation may have a qualified existence after dissolution.**—The corporation may be, and is, by statute in many of the states, kept alive in a qualified sense for a certain period in order to wind up its affairs, but it can not carry on new business under its charter. Thus, where such a statute provided that it should continue to be a body corporate for three years for the purpose of closing up its business and disposing of its property, it was held that the minority stockholders were entitled to have the property sold and the proceeds, after paying debts, distributed as in case of the termination of a partnership; that the majority had no right to transfer the assets to a new corporation designed to continue the business of the old, at a valuation fixed by themselves, and to compel the minority to accept a *pro rata* amount of stock in the new company

---

65 Mo. 244. Nor are contract obligations generally. Mumma *v.* Potomac Co., 8 Peters (U. S.) 281; Wait Insolv. Corp., § 382. Nor a covenant in a lease to pay rent. People *v.* National Trust Co., 82 N. Y. 283. But it is held that stock can not be transferred after dissolution so as to pass the legal title. James *v.* Woodruff, 2 Denio (N. Y.) 574.

[1] Greenwood *v.* Freight Co., 105 U. S. 13, 18.

[2] See, also, International, etc., R. Co. *v.* State, 75 Tex. 356, 378; People *v.* O'Brien, 111 N. Y. 1.

or a *pro rata* amount in cash at such valuation, and that the directors could be compelled to account to the stockholders for their acts and doings where they continued the business of the corporation for a year after its dissolution.[1] As a general rule, in the absence of any provision to the contrary, a corporation can neither sue nor be sued after its dissolution,[2] and suits already commenced against it are abated.[3] In many of the states, however, the statutes to which we have already referred keep the corporation alive for the purpose of suing and being sued in winding up its affairs.[4] In other states receivers or trustees are appointed for this purpose.[5] It has also been held, in a state in which corporations are kept alive by statute for the purpose of suing and being sued, that a corporation which con-

---

[1] Mason *v.* Pewabic Mining Co., 133 U. S. 50, s. c. 10 Sup. Ct. R. 224, 1 Lewis Am. R. R. & Corp. R. 227. See, also, to same effect, Frothingham *v.* Barney, 6 Hun (N. Y.) 366. But the court will not always appoint a receiver and order a sale, for, where the valuation is just, a company may, prior to its dissolution, transfer its assets to a new company to discharge its liabilities and carry on the business and give the stockholders the option of taking cash or stock in such new company, where there is no question of its ability to carry out the arrangement. Baltimore, etc., R. R. Co. *v.* Cannon, 72 Md. 493, 20 Atl. R. 123, s. c. 3 Lewis Am. R. R. & Corp. Cas. 202; Sawyer *v.* Dubuque, etc., Co., 77 Iowa 242; Treadwell *v.* Salisbury, etc., Co., 7 Gray (Mass.) 393; Buford *v.* Keokuk Northern Line, etc., Co., 3 Mo. App. 159.

[2] Dobson *v.* Simonton, 86 N. Car. 492; Merrill *v.* Suffolk Bank, 31 Me. 57, s. c. 50 Am. Dec. 649; Miami, etc., Co. *v.* Gano, 13 Ohio 269; Gold *v.* Clyne, 58 Hun (N. Y.) 419; Logan *v.* Western, etc., R. R. Co., 87 Ga. 533, 13 S. E. R. 516; City Ins. Co. *v.* Commercial Bank, 68 Ill. 348; Bank of Louisiana *v.* Wilson, 19 La. Ann. 1; Nelson *v.* Hubbard, 96 Ala. 238, 11 So. R. 428, s. c. 17 L. R. A. 375.

[3] National Bank *v.* Colby, 21 Wall. (U. S.) 609; Saltmarsh *v.* Planters', etc., Bank, 17 Ala. 761; Thornton *v.* Marginal Freight Ry. Co., 123 Mass. 32; *In re* New York, etc., Co., 33 N. Y. Supp. 726; McCulloch *v.* Norwood, 58 N. Y. 562; Ingraham *v.* Terry, 11 Humph. (Tenn.) 572; Terry *v.* Merchants', etc., Bank, 66 Ga. 177; note to May *v.* State Bank, 40 Am. Dec. 726, 737. But compare Giles *v.* Stanton, 86 Tex. 620; Lindell *v.* Benton, 6 Mo. 361; Platt *v.* Archer, 9 Blatchf. (U. S.) 559.

[4] Stetson *v.* City Bank, 2 Ohio St. 167; Foster *v.* Essex Bank, 16 Mass. 245; Greenbrier Lumber Co. *v.* Ward, 30 W. Va. 43, 3 S. E. Rep. 227; Herron *v.* Vance, 17 Ind. 595; Kansas City Hotel Co. *v.* Sauer, 65 Mo. 279; and authorities cited in 1 Beach Priv. Corp., § 785; Angell & Ames on Corp., § 779 *a*.

[5] 1 Beach Priv. Corp., §§ 785, 786; Taylor Priv. Corp., § 436.

tinued to do business, without winding up, after its charter had expired, could be sued in the corporate name for a tort committed by it while carrying on such business;[1] but it has been held in Indiana that stockholders are not bound by a contract made by the officers of a corporation after the repeal or forfeiture of its charter.[2]

§ 613. **Disposition of property on dissolution.**—Creditors do not lose their rights nor do stockholders lose their interest in the property upon the dissolution of a corporation. The assets of the corporation become a trust fund for the payment of corporate creditors, and the surplus belongs to the stockholders.[3] Debts due the corporation, choses in action,[4] and certain so-called franchises or rights and powers,[5] which may be regarded as property survive the dissolution, and may be treated and disposed of as other property for the benefit of creditors and shareholders. But the franchise to be a corporation does not survive,[6] and it would seem that all such franchises or powers as are "dependent solely upon the grant of the charter, and which could not be exercised by unincorporated private persons under the general laws of the state" are abrogated by the

[1] Miller v. Newberg, etc., Co., 31 W. Va. 836.

[2] Wilson v. Tesson, 12 Ind. 285.

[3] Commercial Fire Ins. Co. v. Board, 99 Ala. 1, s. c. 42 Am. St. R. 1; People v. National Trust Co., 82 N. Y. 283; Heman v. Britton, 88 Mo. 549; Bacon v. Robertson, 18 How. (U. S.) 480, 486; Lum v. Robertson, 6 Wall. (U. S.) 277; Lothrop v. Stedman, 42 Conn. 583, s. c. 13 Blatchf. (U. S.) 134; Montgomery, etc., R. R. Co. v. Branch, 59 Ala. 139; Western, etc., R. R. Co. v. Rollins, 82 N. Car. 523. See ante, § 600. The authorities above cited show that it is virtually a trust fund for shareholders, after creditors are paid, as well as for the creditors themselves.

[4] Mumma v. Potomac Co., 8 Pet. (U. S.) 281; New Jersey v. Yard, 95 U. S. 104; Read v. Frankfort Bank, 23 Me. 318; Thornton v. Marginal Freight Ry. Co., 123 Mass. 32.

[5] International, etc., Ry. Co. v. State, 75 Tex. 356, 378; Hall v. Sullivan R. R. Co., 1 Brunner's C. C. 613; New Orleans, etc., R. R. Co. v. Delamore, 114 U. S. 501; People v. O'Brien, 111 N. Y. 1, s. c. 7 Am. St. R. 684, and note. See, also, County of Scotland v. Thomas, 94 U. S. 682; Hannibal, etc., R. R. Co. v. Marion County, 36 Mo. 294.

[6] See Memphis, etc., R. R. Co. v. Railroad Commissioners, 112 U. S. 609; Willamette Mfg. Co. v. Bank, 119 U. S. 191; Southern, etc., Co. v. Orton, 32 Fed. R. 457; Coe v. Columbus, etc., R. R. Co., 10 Ohio St. 372, s. c. 75 Am. Dec. 518, **and note.**

repeal of the law which granted them, under the reserved power of repeal.[1] So, it has been held that the special privilege of immunity from taxation does not ordinarily survive the dissolution of the corporation.[2] If the legislature has failed to make provision for the collection of debts, the distribution of the assets and the protection of creditors and shareholders, equity will provide the means.[3] After the claims of creditors are satisfied the stockholders are entitled to share in the surplus in proportion to the amount of their respective interests.[4] Common and preferred stockholders share alike,[5] unless otherwise provided by statute or contract. If, however, a dividend has been properly declared out of surplus profits, leaving the capital of the company unimpaired, a shareholder entitled thereto may have it preferred to the claims of creditors, even though he may not have demanded it until after the company has become insolvent.[6]

§ 614. **Rights of creditors upon dissolution.**—As we have

---

[1] Greenwood v. Freight Co., 105 U. S. 13; Tomlinson v. Jessup, 15 Wall. (U. S.) 454; Railroad Co. v. Maine, 96 U. S. 499; Sinking Fund Cases, 99 U. S. 700; Erie, etc., R. R. Co. v. Casey, 26 Pa. St. 287; International, etc., Ry. Co. v. State, 75 Tex. 356, 378; Shields v. Ohio, 95 U. S. 319. See, also, Grand Rapids Bridge Co. v. Prange, 35 Mich. 400; Commonwealth v. Smith, 10 Allen (Mass.) 448, s. c. 87 Am. Dec. 672; Snell v. City of Chicago, 133 Ill. 413, 24 N. E. R. 532; St. Louis R. R. Co. v. Gill, 156 U. S. 649, s. c. 15 Sup. Ct. R. 484, 11 Lewis Am. R. & Corp. R. 709.

[2] Morgan v. Louisiana, 93 U. S. 217; Railroad Co. v. Georgia, 98 U. S. 359; Railroad Co. v. County of Hamblen, 102 U. S. 273. But see Tomlinson v. Branch, 15 Wall. (U. S.) 460; Humphrey v. Pegues, 16 Wall. (U. S.) 244.

[3] Greenwood v. Freight Co., 105 U. S. 13; Howe v. Robinson, 20 Fla. 352; McCoy v. Farmer, 65 Mo. 244; Van Glahn v. De Rosset, 81 N. Car. 467; Curran v. Arkansas, 15 How. (U. S.) 304; Moore v. Schoppert, 22 W. Va. 282; Hightower v. Thornton, 8 Ga. 486, s. c. 52 Am. Dec. 412.

[4] Krebs v. Carlisle Bank, 2 Wall. C. C. 33; Heath v. Barmore, 50 N. Y. 302; Shorb v. Beaudry, 56 Cal. 446; Wood v. Dummer, 3 Mason (U. S.) 308; Dudley v. Price, 10 B. Mon. (Ky.) 84; In re Bridgewater Nav. Co., 3 Ry. & Corp. L. J. 591; Hartman v. Ins. Co., 32 Gratt. (Va.) 242 (in proportion to their "in-put"); 2 Beach Priv. Corp., § 789.

[5] McGregor v. Home Ins. Co., 33 N. J. Eq. 181; In re London, etc., Co., L. R. 5 Eq. 519.

[6] Le Roy v. Globe Ins. Co., 2 Edw. Ch. (N. Y.) 657. See, also, Van Dyck v. McQuade, 86 N. Y. 38; In re Petition of Le Blanc, 14 Hun (N. Y.) 8.

already seen, the law protects, as far as possible, the interests of creditors upon the dissolution of a corporation. As a general rule the rights of creditors are such as they have at the time of the dissolution, and can not be enlarged by subsequent proceedings after the corporate assets have passed into the hands of an assignee or receiver.[1] And shareholders or directors who are also lawful creditors are generally entitled, as such creditors, to share *pro rata* with the other creditors.[2] Unsecured creditors usually share *pro rata*, as do creditors of the same class with each other, but those who have taken a valid mortgage or similar security, or have otherwise obtained a lawful priority, will usually have the preference.[3] It is held, however, in a recent case, that the holders of railroad bonds guaranteed by another corporation are not entitled, upon the insolvency of such corporation, to have a dividend declared in their favor, or to have money retained in court to meet a possible future liability on the guaranty, as against other creditors whose claims are past due, where the railroad company is solvent and the bonds are not due.[4]

---

[1] Marr *v.* Bank, 4 Coldw. (Tenn.) 471; Dean & Son's Appeal, 98 Pa. St. 101; Roseboom *v.* Whittaker, 132 Ill. 81; Clinksales *v.* Pendleton, etc., Co., 9 S. Car. 318.

[2] Bristol Milling, etc., Co. *v.* Probasco, 64 Ind. 406.

[3] See Taylor Priv. Corp., Ch. XVII; Florsheim, etc., Co. *v.* Wettermark, (Tex.) 30 S. W. R. 505.

[4] Gay Mfg. Co. *v.* Gittings, 53 Fed. R. 45. The court held that the bondholders had no standing in court; that their claim was not a provable claim as it was not yet due and the liability was not fixed; and that they had no right to share as creditors in the present distribution of assets.

CHAPTER XXV.

ACTIONS BY AND AGAINST CORPORATIONS.

§ 615. Generally — Suits by corporations.
616. When incorporation must be alleged.
617. Actions and suits against corporations.
618. Power of corporation over litigation — Power to compromise and arbitrate.
619. Estoppel to deny corporate existence.
620. When stockholders may sue.
621. Service of process.
622. Return of service.
623. Venue of actions against corporations.
624. Attachment and garnishment.
625. Duty and liability of garnishee.
626. What may be reached in garnishment.
627. Garnishment of employes' wages.
628. Injunction—Generally.
629. Injunction where the company seeks to take or condemn lands.
§ 630. Injunction where railroad is laid in a street.
631. Enjoining a nuisance.
632. Injunction at suit of the company.
633. Enjoining strikers.
634. Injunction at suit of stockholder.
635. Mandatory injunction—English cases.
636. Rule in the United States—Illustrative cases.
637. Mandamus—Generally.
638. Mandamus to compel completion and operation of road.
639. Mandamus to compel restoration of highway and construction of crossings or viaducts.
640. Mandamus to compel carriage of freight.
641. Mandamus to compel the company to maintain stations and furnish increased facilities.
642. When mandamus will not lie.
643. Who may be relator.
644. *Quo warranto.*

§ 615. **Generally—Suits by corporations.** — The power to sue and be sued is one of the necessary incidents of a corporation,[1] since to be recognized by law as a collective body with

---

[1] In several of the states it is provided by the state constitutions that all corporations may sue and be sued in the courts like natural persons. Stimson's Am. Stat., citing constitutions of New York, Michigan, Minnesota, Kansas, Nebraska, North Carolina, California, Nevada, Ala-

(871)

enforceable rights is essential to its legal existence.[1] It has been held that the consent of a majority of the directors or trustees of a corporation is necessary to entitle it to sue,[2] but it is certainly not the general rule that the directors must take action before a suit can be instituted, and, in any event, in the absence of proof to the contrary, the court will presume that the suit was properly authorized.[3] A corporation may, in general, avail itself of any legal remedies which would be available to an individual under similar circumstances. It may bring an action at law upon a contract,[4] and may by the usual remedies recover damages for any kind of wrong which it suffers.[5] It may sue in trespass for an injury to its business,[6] and in equity, in a proper case, for an injunction to prevent injuries to its property.[7] It may have a writ of mandamus to compel the performance by others of legal duties owed to it.[8] In a proper case it may also maintain a bill of interpleader.[9]

§ 616. When incorporation must be alleged.—It is frequently

bama; 4 A. & E. Enc. of Law 189. In Colorado a corporation may sue and be sued as an individual, and its insolvency does not change the rule. Breene v. Merchants' & M. Bank, 11 Colo. 97, 17 Pac. 280.

[1] 1 Morawetz on Priv. Corp. (2d ed.), 356. This power existed at common law. 1 Blackstone's Com. 475. See, also, Bangor, etc., R. R. Co. v. Smith, 47 Me. 34; Baltimore, etc., R. R. Co. v. Gallahue, 12 Gratt. (Va.) 655; Heaston v. Cincinnati, etc., R. R. Co., 16 Ind. 275; Wilder v. Chicago, etc., R. R. Co., 70 Mich. 382, 38 N. W. 289, 35 Am. & Eng. R. Cas. 162.

[2] Dart v. Huston, 22 Ga. 506. But see American Ins. Co. v. Oakley, 9 Paige (N. Y.) 496; Colman v. West Va. etc., Co., 25 W. Va. 148; Trustees of Smith Charities v. Connolly, 157 Mass. 272, s. c. 31 N. E. R. 1058; Davis v. Memphis, etc., R. Co., 22 Fed. R. 883.

[3] Bangor R. Co. v. Smith, 47 Me. 34; Angell & Ames on Corp., § 370. The affidavit in support of an application by a corporation for change of venue on account of local prejudice may be made by the secretary of the corporation. St. Louis, O. H. & C. Ry. Co. v. Fowler, 113 Mo. 458, 20 S. W. 1069.

[4] Eakright v. Logansport, etc., R. Co., 13 Ind. 404.

[5] Morawetz on Priv. Corp., § 358.

[6] A corporation may sue to recover damages for a libel against it in its business. Metropolitan etc., Co. v. Hawkins, 4 H. & N. 87; Hahnemannian Life Ins. Co. v. Beebe, 48 Ill. 87; Knickerbocker Life Ins. Co. v. Ecclesine, 42 How. Pr. (N. Y.) 201; Trenton Mut. Life Ins. Co. v. Perrine, 23 N. J. L. 402.

[7] See post, 628.

[8] See post, 637.

[9] Salisbury Mills v. Townsend, 109 Mass. 115.

§ 616   ACTIONS BY AND AGAINST CORPORATIONS.   873

required by statute that a plaintiff corporation shall allege the fact of its incorporation,[1] and to do so is always the better practice. A failure to aver corporate existence in an action by or against a corporation can not, however, be taken advantage of by a demurrer for want of facts.[2] Pleading the general issue,[3] or going to trial on the merits[4] generally amounts to an admission of the plaintiff's corporate existence and capacity to sue. In some states, as apparently at common law, it is not necessary to allege the incorporation of a plaintiff corporation.[5] The theory of the cases so holding is that the

[1] Texas, etc., R. Co. v. Virginia, etc., Co., (Tex.) 7 S. W. R. 341; Adams v. Lamson, etc., Co., 59 Hun (N. Y.) 127; Miller v. Pine Min. Co., 2 Idaho 1206. See, also, Bliss Code Pl. (3d ed.), § 246, et seq.

[2] John T. Noye Mfg. Co. v. Raymond, (Super. Ct. Buff.), 8 Misc. R. 353, 28 N. Y. Supp. 693; Fulton Fire Ins. Co. v. Baldwin, 37 N. Y. 648; Bliss Code Pl. (3d ed.), § 408, a. See, also, Stanly v. Richmond, etc., R. Co., 89 N. Car. 331; Cone Export, etc., Co. v. Poole, 41 S. Car. 70, 24 L. R. A. 289; Wiles v. Trustees of Phillipi Church, 63 Ind. 206; Nolte v. Lebbert, 34 Ind. 163; Seymour v. Thomas Harrow Co., 81 Ala. 250; Bliss on Code Pl., § 408.

[3] Mississippi, etc., R. Co. v. Cross, 20 Ark. 443; Cicero, etc., D. Co. v. Craighead, 28 Ind. 274; Heaston v. Cincinnati, etc., R. Co., 16 Ind. 275; Rockland, etc., Co. v. Sewall, 78 Me. 167; Beatty v. Bartholomew, etc., Society, 76 Ind. 91; Litchfield Bank v. Church, 29 Conn. 137; Bailey v. Valley, etc., Bank, 127 Ill. 332, s. c. 19 N. E. R. 695; Rembert v. South Carolina Ry. Co., 31 S. Car. 309, 9 S. E. R. 968. The rule is different in England and some of the states. Henriquez v. Dutch West Indies Co., 2 Ld. Raym. 1532; Holloway v. Memphis R. Co., 23 Texas 465; Jackson v. Bank of Marietta, 9 Leigh (Va.) 240; Williams v. Bank of Michigan, 7 Wend. (N. Y.) 540; Oregonian Ry. Co. v. Oregon, etc., Co., 23 Fed. R. 232; Bank of Jamaica v. Jefferson, 92 Tenn. 537, 22 S. W. R. 211. As to plea of nul tiel corporation, see Johnson v. Hanover, etc., Bank, 88 Ala. 271, s. c. 6 So. R. 909; Michigan Ins. Bank v. Eldred, 143 U. S. 293; Excelsior Draining Co. v. Brown, 47 Ind. 19; Schloss v. Montgomery Trade Co., 87 Ala. 411, s. c. 13 Am. St. R. 51.

[4] United States v. Insurance Companies, 22 Wall. 99; Lehigh Bridge Co. v. Lehigh Coal Co., 4 Rawle (Pa.) 9. See St. Cecilia Academy v. Hardin, 78 Ga. 39, 3 S. E. 305; Sengfelder v. Mut. L. Ins. Co., 5 Wash. St. 121; Wright v. Fire Ins. Co., 12 Mont. 474. Corporate capacity need not be proved unless it be challenged by an affirmative allegation of no corporation. Dry Dock, E. B. & B. R. Co. v. North & East River Ry. Co., (Com. Pl. N. Y.) 22 N. Y. S. 556, 3 Misc. Rep. 61.

[5] German Reformed Church v. Von Puechelstein, 27 N. J. Eq. 30; Union Cement Co. v. Noble, 15 Fed. R. 502. See Baltimore, etc., R. Co. v. Sherman, 30 Gratt. (Va.) 602; Maxwell on Code Pl. 161; Bliss on Code Pl., § 247. Many of the states provide by statute that in suits where a corporation is a party, no evidence of its corporate

874   THE CORPORATION.   § 617

"name carries with it the assertion of a fact," and it is sufficient if the name of the plaintiff imports a corporation.[1]

§ 617. Actions and suits against corporations.—Suits may, in general, be brought against a corporation upon any cause of action on which an individual would be liable under similar circumstances,[2] and two or more corporations may become jointly liable in the same manner as individuals.[3] It is sufficient at common law to sue a corporation by its corporate name, without an averment of the act of incorporation.[4] But

existence need be offered unless the same is denied by verified plea. Rosenberg v. Claflin Co., 95 Ala. 249, 10 So. R. 521; Michigan Ins. Bank v. Eldred, 143 U. S. 293, construing Code Wis., § 4199; Jones v. Ross, 48 Kan. 474, 29 Pac. R. 680; Swift & Co. v. Crawford, 34 Neb. 450, 51 N. W. 1034; Vulcan v. Myers, 58 Hun (N. Y.) 161; Canal St. Gravel R. Co. v. Paas, 95 Mich. 372, 54 N. W. R. 907; McElwee Mfg. Co. v. Trowbridge, 68 Hun (N. Y.) 28. But it has been held that this does not dispense with an allegation that the defendant is a corporation. State v. Chicago, etc., P. Co., 4 S. D. 261, 56 N. W. R. 894.

[1] Smythe v. Scott, 124 Ind. 183. See Cincinnati, etc., R. Co. v. McDougall, 108 Ind. 179; Shearer v. R. S. Peele & Co., 9 Ind. App. 282, 36 N. E. R. 455; Bliss Code Pl. (3d ed.), § 251.

[2] A corporation is liable for the torts of its servants committed in the course of their employment. Chestnut Hill T. Co. v. Rutter, 4 Serg. & R. (Pa.) 6. See, *ante*, §§ 213, 214. The corporation is liable, generally, to the same extent and in the same manner that a natural individual would be liable under like circumstances. First Baptist Church v. Schenectady R. Co., 5 Barb. (N. Y.) 79. A corporation may be liable for malicious prosecution. Springfield Engine & T. Co. v. Green, 25 Ill. App. 106; Gulf, etc., R.Co. v. James, 73 Tex. 12, 10 S. W. R. 744. A corporation may become civilly responsible for libel. Missouri Pac. R. Co. v. Richmond, 73 Tex. 568, 11 S. W. R. 555, 29 Cent. L. J. 69; Fogg v. Boston, etc., R. Co., 148 Mass. 513.

[3] An action may be maintained jointly against two railroad companies for injuries received in a collison caused by the concurrent wrongful acts or negligence of both defendants. Flaherty v. Minneapolis, etc., R. Co., 39 Minn. 328, s. c. 40 N. W. R. 160, 1 L. R. A. 680. One of them, however, in a proper case, may ask judgment over against its codefendant, if judgment is rendered against it. Gulf C. & S. F. R. Co. v. Hathaway, 75 Tex. 557, 41 Am. & Eng. R. Cas. 219.

[4] Exchange Nat. Bank v. Capps, 32 Neb. 242, 49 N. W. R. 223; Maxwell on Code Pl. 161. Designating the defendant by a name which imports a corporation is a sufficient allegation of its corporate existence. Cincinnati, etc., R. Co. v. McDougall, 108 Ind. 179; Adams Express Co. v. Harris, 120 Ind. 73, s. c. 21 N. E. R. 340. In an action on a note signed by a company in its corporate name, it is not necessary to aver its corporate existence, as it is estopped by such signature to deny it. Griffin v. Asheville Light & Power Co., 111 N. C. 434.

§ 618   ACTIONS BY AND AGAINST CORPORATIONS.   875

in several of the states an allegation of the defendant's corporate existence must be contained in the complaint in such a suit.[1] Proof of the facts so averred, however, in most states, is not required unless they are denied under oath.[2] Where a corporation formed by the consolidation of several corporations is sued for the debt of one of the constituent companies, it has been held that the declaration should show against which company it arose, and the facts necessary to fix liability upon the new corporation.[3]

§ 618. Power of corporation over litigation—Power to compromise and arbitrate.—The expediency or inexpediency of litigation is a matter for the corporation, or the directors, acting in good faith within the scope of their powers, to determine, and their action in bringing and defending suits affecting the rights and obligations of the corporation is usually binding upon the stockholders.[4] A corporation may, therefore, compromise a pending lawsuit when the directors believe it to be to the best interests of the corporation to do so.[5] It may also refer matters to arbitration,[6] and has implied power to execute a bond in a judicial proceeding in which it is interested.[7] So, it may appeal or refuse to appeal a case, and not

[1] Rothschild v. Grand Trunk R. Co., 14 N. Y. Supp. 807; Saunders v. Sioux City, etc., Co., 6 Utah 431, 24 Pac. R. 532; People v. Central Pac. R. Co., 83 Cal. 393; Miller v. Pin Mining Co., 2 Idaho 1206, 31 Pac. R. 803; State v. Chicago, etc., R. Co., 4 S. Dak. 261, 56 N. W. R. 894. See Bliss Code Pl. (3d ed.), § 260.

[2] Calumet Paper Co. v. Knight, etc., Co., 43 Ill. App. 566; Hummel v. First Nat. Bank, 2 Colo. App. 571, 32 Pac. R. 72; Dry Dock, etc., Co. v. North, etc., R. Co., 22 N. Y. Supp. 556, 3 Misc. R. 61. But proof is required in some states of the due incorporation of a foreign corporation. Bank of Jamaica v. Jefferson, 92 Tenn. 537, 22 S. W. R. 211. See Hummel v. First Nat. Bank, 2 Colo. App. 571, 32 Pac. R. 72.

[3] Langhorne v. Richmond City R. Co., (Va.) 19 S. E. R. 122.

[4] Farnum v. Ballard, etc., Shop, 12 Cush. (Mass.) 507; Graham v. Boston, etc., R. Co., 14 Fed. R. 753, affirmed in 118 U. S. 161; MacDougall v. Gardiner, L. R. 1 Ch. D. 13; note to Bissit v. Kentucky, etc., Co., 15 Fed. R. 353, 361.

[5] Donohoe v. Mariposa, etc., Co., 66 Cal. 317; Stewart v. Hoyt, 111 U. S. 373; New Albany v. Burke, 11 Wall. (U. S.) 96.

[6] Boston, etc., R. Co. v. Nashua, etc., R. Co., 139 Mass. 463; Alexandria Canal Co. v. Swann, 5 How. (U. S.) 83.

[7] Collins v. Hammock, 59 Ala. 448.

CORP. 56

even a majority of the stockholders can have an appeal dismissed which the directors, acting in good faith, have ordered to be taken and prosecuted to final determination in the appellate court.[1]

§ 619. **Estoppel to deny corporate existence.**—In suits against a body of persons as a corporation where they assume to act as a corporation under color of an apparent organization, in pursuance of a law authorizing it, they are generally estopped to set up the irregularity of the corporate organization as a defense to the corporate liability which would otherwise have attended their actions.[2] And a person who enters into a contract with such a *de facto* corporation is usually estopped to deny its corporate existence in a suit upon that contract.[3] Thus, while it is true that persons can not dispute the corporate liability on such a contract because of the unauthorized or irregular organization of the company, on the other hand, those who deal with them as a corporation may be estopped from treating them as partners. If the corporation was organized under authority of law, persons seeking to enforce contracts into which they have entered with it can not, as a rule, take advantage of any failure to observe the legal formalities necessary to a valid organization, in order to charge the

---

[1] Railway Co. v. Alling, 99 U. S. 463. See, also, Silk Mfg. Co. v. Campbell, 27 N. J. L. 539. Under the Ohio statute stockholders may appeal in certain cases. Henry v. Jennes, 47 Ohio St. 116, 24 N. E. R. 1077.

[2] Kelley v. Newburyport Horse R. Co., 141 Mass. 496; Blackburn v. Selma, etc., R. Co., 2 Flippin (U. S.) 525; Georgia Ice Co. v. Porter, 70 Ga. 637; Empire Mfg. Co. v. Stuart, 46 Mich. 482; Griffin v. Asheville, etc., Co., 111 N. C. 434. See *ante*, § 190.

[3] Swartwout v. Michigan, etc., R. Co., 24 Mich. 389; Imboden v. Etowah, etc., Mfg. Co ,. 70 Ga. 86; Smelser v. Wayne, etc., Turnpike Co., 82 Ind. 417; Cravens v. Eagle, etc., Co., 120 Ind. 6; Keene v. Van Reuth, 48 Md. 184; McCord, etc., Co. v. Glenn, 6 Utah 139, 21 Pac. R. 500; French v. Donohue, 29 Minn. 111; Beekman v. Hudson River, etc., Co., 35 Fed. R. 3; Butchers', etc., Bank v. McDonald, 130 Mass. 264; Cahall v. Citizens', etc., Assn., 61 Ala. 232; Griffin v. Asheville, etc., Co., 111 N. C. 434. One who deals with a corporation as existing in fact, is estopped to deny as against the corporation that it has been legally organized. Close v. Glenwood Cemetery, 107 U. S. 466, per Mr. Justice Gray; Bliss Code Pl. (3d ed.), § 252, *et seq*. *Ante*, § 190.

shareholders as partners.¹ But where the organization was without any authority of law for its existence, the fact that the persons called themselves a corporation will not enable them to escape from personal liability for their acts.²

§ 620. When stockholders may sue.—As already intimated, suits to enforce corporate rights or to avert threatened wrongs to the corporate interests should be brought by the officers of the corporation in its name, and a stockholder, as such, has generally no right to sue.³ But where the directors refuse to enforce the corporate rights,⁴ and are proceeding *ultra vires,* or are fraudulently combining with others to despoil the corporation,⁵ a stockholder may maintain a suit in his own name to enforce those rights,⁶ especially if he can show that irremediable loss will accrue if he is not allowed to bring suit.⁷ But it has been

---

¹ Stout *v.* Zulick, 48 N. J. L. 599; Humphreys *v.* Mooney, 5 Colo. 282; First Nat. Bank *v.* Almy, 117 Mass. 476; Planters', etc., Bank *v.* Padgett, 69 Ga. 159; Second Nat. Bank *v.* Hall, 35 Ohio St. 158. *Ante,* § 190.

² Hill *v.* Beach, 12 N. J. Eq. 31; Lewis *v.* Tilton, 64 Iowa 220; Methodist Episcopal Church *v.* Pickett, 19 N. Y. 482. But see Winget *v.* Quincy, etc., Assn., 128 Ill. 67.

³ Waterman on Corp., § 138; 2 Beach Priv. Corp., § 878.

⁴ Morgan *v.* Railroad Co., 1 Woods (U. S.) 15; Detroit *v.* Dean, 106 U. S. 537; Shawhan *v.* Zinn, 79 Ky. 300; Dodge *v.* Woolsey, 18 How. (U. S.) 331. It must appear that their refusal is a breach of trust on their part and not a mere error of judgment in a matter properly within their discretion. Pacific R. Co. *v.* Missouri Pac. R. Co., 2 McCrary (U. S.) 227; Dempfell *v.* Ohio, etc., R. Co., 110 U. S. 209.

⁵ Where such a state of facts is shown as to clearly indicate that the corporate management is adverse or indifferent to the interests of the corporation and that it would be useless to request the corporation to sue, a stockholder may sue in the first instance. Barr *v.* New York, etc., R. Co., 96 N. Y. 444; Crumlish *v.* Shenandoah Valley Railroad Co., 28 W. Va. 623; Wilcox *v.* Bickel, 11 Neb. 154; Doud *v.* Wisconsin, etc., Ry. Co., 65 Wis. 108; Davis *v.* Gemmel, 70 Md. 356, s. c. 17 Atl. R. 259; Barr *v.* Pittsburgh, etc., Co., 40 Fed. R. 412. But, unless this is true, a request should precede suit and an earnest effort should first be made to have the corporation sue. Taylor *v.* Holmes, 127 U. S. 489; Dempfell *v.* Ohio, etc., Ry. Co., 110 U. S. 209; Foote *v.* Cunard, etc., Co., 17 Fed. R. 46; City of Chicago *v.* Cameron, 120 Ill. 447. See *ante,* §§ 165, 167.

⁶ Hawes *v.* Oakland, 104 U. S. 450, where the court states in the form of distinct propositions what must be shown in order to enable a stockholder to sue.

⁷ Detroit *v.* Dean, 106 U. S. 537, 542. It is suggested that each probable loss from a failure to permit the bringing

held that the corporation should, in such a case, be made a party defendant,[1] although the relief prayed is really in its favor.[2]

§ 621. Service of process.—Process can not, of course, be served upon a corporation aggregate directly. At common law service was required to be made upon some agent bearing the relation to the corporation of a head officer, whose knowledge would be that of the corporation.[3] The statutes of the various states prescribe the agents of the company upon whom service of process shall be made in order to be valid as service upon the company itself. These statutes resemble each other though they vary much in detail.[4] Where the method of serving process upon a corporation is prescribed by statute that method is generally, but not always, held to be exclusive of any other.[5] The statute of Indiana provides that service may be made upon the president or other chief officer, or if its chief officer is not found in the county, then upon its cashier, treasurer, director,

of a suit against an outsider, to recover damages for past injuries, would be very difficult to show in almost all cases. Waterman on Corp., § 142. But see City of Chicago v. Cameron, 120 Ill. 447, 458, where the stockholders were permitted to sue to cancel bonds wrongfully issued twelve years before.

[1] Shawhan v. Zinn, 79 Ky. 300; Hawes v. Oakland, 104 U. S. 450; Slattery v. St. Louis, etc., Co., 91 Mo. 217, 4 S. W. 79; Byers v. Rollins, 13 Colo. 22.

[2] Jones v. Bolles, 9 Wall. (U. S.) 364. Relief can not be granted unless the corporation is brought before the court so that the decree may conclude it. Shawhan v. Zinn, 79 Ky. 300.

[3] Heltzell v. Chicago, etc., R. Co., 77 Mo. 315; Newell v. Great Western R. Co., 19 Mich. 336; Glaize v. South Carolina R. Co., 1 Strobh. Law (S. C.) 70; Boyd v. Chesapeake, etc., Canal Co., 17 Md. 195; Newby v. Van Oppen, L. R. 7 Q. B. 293. Service on the officers of a domestic corporation was held to be service upon the corporation, but it seems that jurisdiction over a foreign corporation could not be thus acquired under the early common law. 1 Elliott's Gen. Pr., § 359.

[4] Stimson's Am. Stat., Vol. 3.

[5] Cosgrove v. Tebo, etc., R. Co., 54 Mo. 495; Union Pac. R. Co. v. Pillsbury, 29 Kan. 652; North v. Cleveland, etc., R. Co., 10 Ohio St. 548; Congar v. Galena, etc., R. Co., 17 Wis. 477; Hartford Fire Ins. Co. v. Owen, 30 Mich. 441. And the method prescribed in a special statute is held to be exclusive of the methods prescribed in a prior general statute. In re St. Paul, etc., R. Co., 36 Minn. 85. Contra, State v. Hannibal, etc., R. Co., 51 Mo. 532; Jeffersonville, etc., R. Co. v. Dunlap, 29 Ind. 426; Fowler v. Detroit, etc., R. Co., 7 Mich. 79.

secretary, clerk, general or special agent. If none of these officers is to be found in the county, process may be served upon any person authorized to transact business in the name of such corporation.[1] Under this statute it is held that service upon the conductor of a passenger train,[2] or a freight train,[3] or upon a local freight agent,[4] is valid and effective as service upon the railroad company by which he is employed;[5] since the term "special agent" must be held to include persons holding such a special authority.[6] But it has been held by the Supreme Court of Michigan that the "general or special agent" of a corporation upon whom a summons in garnishment may be served under a similar statute, is an agent having a general or special controlling authority, either generally or in respect to some department of corporate business, and that a ticket agent is not such an agent.[7] Service must usually be made upon the *de facto* officers, or agents, or persons in possession of the offices under claim of right, who, having control of the business and property of the company, are in a position to care for and protect its rights. Service upon persons claiming to be officers *de jure*, but not having possession of the offices they claim, is not sufficient.[8] In the case of foreign corporations conducting business within the jurisdiction, the head officer or managing

[1] R. S. Ind. 1894, § 318.

[2] New Albany, etc., R. Co. v. Grooms, 9 Ind. 243; New Albany, etc., R. Co. v. Tilton, 12 Ind. 3.

[3] Ohio, etc., R. Co. v. Quier, 16 Ind. 440.

[4] And this is true even though there be a superintendent and director of the company residing in the same county. Toledo, etc., R. Co. v. Owen, 43 Ind. 405. For other cases holding service of process upon a local depot or station agent valid, see *Ex parte* St. Louis, etc., R. Co., 40 Ark. 141; Hudson v. St. Louis, etc., R. Co., 53 Mo. 525; Ruthe v. Green Bay, etc., R. Co., 37 Wis. 344; Smith v. Chicago, etc., R. Co., 60 Iowa 512; Missouri Pac. R. Co. v. Collier, 62 Tex. 318. In St. Louis, etc., R. Co. v. De Ford, 38 Kan. 299, it was held that service of a summons upon a section foreman, as "a local superintendent of repairs" of a railroad company, was a valid service upon the company. *Contra*, Richardson v. Burlington, etc., R. Co., 8 Iowa 260.

[5] The return must state the agency held by the person upon whom service was made or it will be held insufficient. Dickerson v. Burlington, etc., R. Co., 43 Kan. 702.

[6] New Albany, etc., R. Co. v. Grooms, 9 Ind. 243.

[7] Lake Shore, etc., R. Co. v. Hunt, 39 Mich. 469.

[8] Berrian v. Methodist Soc. in New York, 4 Abb. Pr. (N. Y.) 424.

agent in charge of such business is the proper person upon whom to serve process, in the absence of any statutory provision designating the officer or agent upon whom service may be made.[1] But where there is a general statute providing for the service of process upon corporate agents, and there are no special provisions relative to service upon foreign corporations, such corporations are within the operation of the general statute.[2] Most of the states have statutes regulating the method of serving foreign corporations with process. These statutes usually require that foreign railroad or other corporations acting within their jurisdiction shall keep specified agents therein who are fully authorized to accept service of process.[3] If no agent is designated to receive service of process, as required by law, service may be made upon a managing agent as at common law.[4] Where foreign corporations engaged in busi-

[1] St. Clair v. Cox, 106 U. S. 350, 355; Newby v. Van Oppen, L. R. 7 Q. B. 293; Weight v. Liverpool, etc., Ins. Co., 30 La. Ann. 1186; New York, etc., R. Co. v. Purdy, 18 Barb. (N. Y.) 574.

[2] Hannibal, etc., R. Co. v. Crane, 102 Ill. 249; Midland Pac. R. Co. v. McDermid, 91 Ill. 170; Chicago, etc., R. Co. v. Manning, 23 Neb. 552.

[3] Such a regulation is within the constitutional power of a state. Lafayette Ins. Co. v. French, 18 How. (U. S.) 404; Hannibal, etc., R. Co. v. Crane, 102 Ill. 249; Gibson v. Manufacturers', etc., Co., 144 Mass. 81; 1 Elliott's Gen. Pr., § 359, and numerous authorities there cited. See, also, *ante*, § 24. A corporation which does business in a state whose general laws prescribe a certain method of serving process upon foreign corporations will be held to have submitted to the provisions of the law. Weymouth v. Washington, etc., R. Co., 1 McArthur (D. C.) 19; Morawetz on Priv. Corp. (2d ed.), § 982.

[4] State v. Pennsylvania R. Co., 42 N. J. L. 490; New York, etc., R. Co. v. Purdy, 18 Barb. (N. Y.) 574; Thomas v. Placerville, etc., Mining Co., 65 Cal. 600. The statutes of some of the states require service upon a "managing agent" within the jurisdiction. There is considerable conflict in the cases as to what constitutes a managing agent. The superintendent and general manager of a foreign corporation owning a road within the state are held to be such agents. Bank of Commerce v. Rutland, etc., R. Co., 10 How. Pr. (N. Y.) 1. So of the vice-president and general superintendent. Norfolk, etc., R. Co. v. Cottrell, 83 Va. 512. Or, a general passenger agent or other person having general control of a particular department or branch of the business. Tuchband v. Chicago, etc., R. Co., 115 N. Y. 437. But see Maxwell v. Atchison, etc., R. Co., 34 Fed. R. 286. In Ohio it seems that a suit *in personam* can not be maintained against a foreign corporation unless it has a managing agent within the state. Barney v. New Albany, etc., R. Co., 1 Handy (Ohio) 571. Ticket sellers have been held not to be managing

§ 621   ACTIONS BY AND AGAINST CORPORATIONS.   881

ness in a state whose law provides that they may be summoned by process served upon an agent in charge of their business, it was held that they were "found" in the district in which such agent is doing business within the meaning of a former act of congress, and that service of process upon such an agent would confer jurisdiction upon the United States courts, to the same extent that the state courts would acquire jurisdiction by a similar service of process.[1] But the act of August 13, 1888, has changed this rule by providing that "where the jurisdiction is founded only on the fact that the action is between citizens of different states, suit shall be brought only in the district of the residence of either the plaintiff or defendant."[2] It is not necessary that the officer or agent upon whom process is served shall reside within the jurisdiction, if he has the control of the business of the corporation at a particular place therein, at which his official residence as an officer of the corporation is established.[3] On the other hand, service upon an officer or agent casually within the state, when he is not there in the performance of the duties of his office, and is not authorized in any way to submit the corporation to the jurisdiction of the courts, is not such service as will bind a foreign corpo-

agents. Doty v. Michigan Cent. R. Co., 8 Abb. Pr. (N.Y.) 427; Mackereth v. Glasgow, etc., R. Co., L. R. 8 Exch. 149. But see Smith v. Chicago, etc., R. Co., 60 Iowa 512; Missouri Pac. R. Co. v. Collier, 62 Tex. 318, and a baggage-master is not. Flynn v. Hudson River R. Co., 6 How. Pr. (N. Y.) 308. See further on this subject, 1 Elliott's Gen. Pr., § 359, and note to Hampson v. Weare, 66 Am. Dec. 116, 120.

[1] Block v. Atchison, etc., R. Co., 21 Fed. R. 529; McCoy v. Cincinnati, etc., R. Co., 13 Fed. R. 3; Lung Chung v. Northern Pac Ry. Co., 19 Fed. R. 254; Ex parte Schollenberger, 96 U. S. 369; Morawetz Priv. Corp. (2d ed.), § 982; Van Dresser v. Oregon R., etc., Co., 48 Fed. R. 202. In this latter case it was held that a foreign railroad company which had formed a combination with other lines extending into the state of Oregon, and which, through its agents, was engaged in making contracts in that state for the carriage of passengers and freight over such connecting lines and its own road was bound by a service of summons upon the agent through whom such contracts were made. But see St. Clair v. Cox, 106 U. S. 350.

[2] Construed in Southern Pac. R. Co. v. Denton, 146 U. S. 202; Shaw v. Quincy Mining Co., 145 U. S. 444; McCormick, etc., Co. v. Walthers, 134 U. S. 41.

[3] Porter v. Chicago, etc., R. Co., 1 Neb. 14; Governor v. Raleigh, etc., R. Co., 3 Ired. Eq. (N. Car.) 471.

ration, which has no office and transacts no business within the state.[1]

§ 622. Return of service.—The return of service upon an officer of a corporation should show his official position in such a manner as to make it clear that the service was upon the officer or agent designated by the statute, and that he was served in his official or representative character.[2] So, where the statute permits service upon a subordinate officer only when the president or highest officer is absent or a non-resident, the return of service upon the subordinate should show the absence or non-residence of the president or chief officer.[3] A

[1] Latimer v. Union Pac. R. Co., 43 Mo. 105; Fitzgerald, etc., Construction Co. v. Fitzgerald, 137 U. S. 98, s. c. 11 Sup. Ct. R. 36, 39; Newell v. Great Western R. Co., 19 Mich. 336; Goldey v. Morning News, 42 Fed. R. 112, 156 U. S. 518, (on appeal); Midland Pac. R. Co. v. McDermid, 91 Ill. 170; Dallas v. Atlantic, etc., R. Co., 2 McArthur (D. C.) 146; Phillips v. Burlington Library Co., 141 Pa. St. 462; Barnes v. Mobile, etc., R. Co., 12 Hun (N. Y.) 126. But see Shickle, etc., Co. v. Wiley, etc., Co., 61 Mich. 226, s. c. 1 Am. St. R. 571; Klopp v. Creston, etc., Co., 34 Neb. 808, 52 N.W. R. 819; Pope v. Terre Haute, etc., Co., 87 N. Y. 137. In Chicago, etc., R. Co. v. Walker, 9 Lea (Tenn.) 475, it was held that service upon the "Southern passenger agent" of defendant company, in an action for breach of a contract entered into with him, was invalid because of his lack of authority to receive service of process. The agent had no authority to sell tickets for his principal, and had no regular place of business. His business was to travel over the territory south of the Ohio river, and over Virginia, Arkansas and Texas, and induce travelers to take a route which led over his road, to assist them in checking their baggage and to conduct them to the nearest ticket office where a ticket over his road could be purchased. But see Van Dresser v. Oregon R., etc., Co., 48 Fed. R. 202. In United States Graphite Co. v. Pacific, etc., Co., 68 Fed. R. 442, the rule stated in the text was held applicable although the officer served was in the state on business of the corporation, which, however, had no office or agency there. See, also, Goldey v. Morning News, 156 U. S. 518, s. c. 15 Sup. Ct. R. 559; Fidelity Trust, etc., Co. v. Mobile St. Ry. Co., 53 Fed. R. 850. *Contra*, Gravely v. Southern, etc., Co., (La.) 16 So. R. 866; Shickle, etc., Co. v. Wiley Const. Co., 61 Mich. 226, s. c. 28 N. W. R. 77; Pope v. Terre Haute, etc., Co., 87 N. Y. 137. A thorough review of the authorities will be found in 2 Am. L. Reg. & Rev. (N. S.) 680.

[2] Jones v. Hartford Ins. Co., 88 N. Car. 499; Oxford Iron Co. v. Spradley, 42 Ala. 24; O'Brien v. Shaw's Flat, etc., Co., 10 Cal. 343; Powder Co. v. Oakdale, etc., Co., 14 Phila. (Pa.) 166; 1 Elliott's Gen. Pr., § 359.

[3] St. Louis, A. & T. H. R. Co. v. Dorsey, 47 Ill. 288; Miller v. Norfolk, etc., R. Co., 41 Fed. R. 431; Toledo, etc., R. Co. v. Owen, 43 Ind. 405; Hoen v. Atlantic, etc., R. Co., 64 Mo.

return that the summons was served on the "general manager" of the defendant corporation, naming him, was held insufficient where the statute required that the service should be upon its "president or other principal officer."[1] But a service may be good when the return shows that the proper officer was served, although the writ merely names the defendant company without designating the officer upon whom it should be served.[2]

§ 623. **Venue of actions against corporations.**—An action against a corporation for personal injuries or other trespass of a personal nature,[3] being of a transitory character, may usually be brought in any county in which service upon the corporation can be obtained.[4] But a statute which provides that an action shall be brought and tried in the county in which the defendant resides or is found applies to corporations as well as to natural persons.[5] As elsewhere shown, railroad companies are usually required to have an agent upon whom process can be served in each state, and are sometimes made, in effect,

---

561. But see Kansas City, etc., R. Co. v. Daughtry, 138 U. S. 298, s. c. 11 Sup. Ct. R. 306.

[1] Dale v. Blue Mountain, etc., Co., 15 Pa. Co. Ct. R. 513, affirmed in 167 Pa. St. R. 402, s. c. 31 Atl. R. 633.

[2] Illinois Steel Co. v. San Antonio, etc., Ry. Co., 67 Fed. R. 561.

[3] South Florida R. Co. v. Weese, 32 Fla. 212; Dave v. Morgan's Louisiana, etc., R. Co., 46 La. Ann. 273, 14 So. R. 911; Atchison, etc., R. Co. v. Worley, (Tex. Civ. App.) 25 S. W. R. 478; Heiter v. East St. Louis Connecting R. Co., 53 Mo. App. 331; Williams v. East Tennessee, etc., R. Co., 90 Ga. 519.

[4] The statutes of several of the states expressly provide that railroads may be sued in ordinary actions in any county of the state through which the road runs. Williams v. East Tennessee, etc., R. Co., 90 Ga. 519, 16 S. E. R. 303; South Florida R. Co. v. Weese, 32 Fla. 212, s. c. 13 So. R. 436. Wherever the company has an agent. Schoch v. Winona, etc., R. Co., 55 Minn. 479, 57 N.W. R. 208; Atchison, etc., R. Co. v. Worley, (Tex.) 25 S.W. R. 478; Red River, etc., R. Co. v. Blount, 3 Tex. Civ. App. 282. A declaration against a railroad company which alleges that the defendant damaged plaintiffs by constructing a railroad upon their land in the county in which suit is brought, sufficiently shows that the railroad lies wholly or partly in that county to withstand a general demurrer for want of facts to constitute a cause of action. East Georgia, etc., R. Co. v. King, 91 Ga. 519. As to what actions are transitory, see, also, Hanna v. Grand Trunk R. Co., 41 Ill. App. 116; Nonce v. Richmond, etc., R. Co., 33 Fed. R. 429; Heiter v. East St. Louis, etc., Ry. Co., 53 Mo. App. 331; 1 Elliott Gen. Pr., § 253.

[5] Holgate v. Oregon Pac. Ry. Co., 16 Ore. 123.

residents of each county through which their line runs and in which they have an agent for the purpose of suing or being sued,[1] although, when citizens of a foreign state they can not be prohibited from removing a cause to the federal courts under proper circumstances. But such a company, incorporated in one state only, although it has a place of business in another state, can not be sued in a United States circuit court of the latter state, which is in a different district from that in which the company is incorporated, by a citizen of a third state,[2] although a suit between corporations organized in different states may be brought in the district in which the plaintiff is incorporated as well as that in which the defendant is incorporated, when the jurisdiction is founded solely on diverse citizenship under the act of congress of August 13, 1888.[3] A state statute which provides that suits against a railroad company may be brought in any county into which its line extends is subordinate, in so far as the federal courts are concerned, to the act of congress above referred to, and where another statute of the state declares that "the public office of a railroad corporation shall be considered the domicile of such corporation," a domestic railroad company of such state is an "inhabitant" of the district in which such public office is located, and can not be sued in a circuit court of the United

[1] See *ante*, § 24; St. Louis, etc., R. Co. *v.* Traweek, 84 Tex. 65; Bristol *v.* Chicago, etc., Railroad Co., 15 Ill. 436; Slavens *v.* South Pac. Railroad Co., 51 Mo. 308, 310; Schoch *v.* Winona, etc., R. Co., 55 Minn. 479, 57 N. W. R. 208; Newberry *v.* Arkansas, etc., R. Co., 52 Kan. 613, 35 Pac. R. 210; Louisville, etc., R. Co. *v.* Saucier, (Miss.) 1 So. R. 511.

[2] Shaw *v.* Quincy Mining Co., 145 U. S. 444, s. c. 12 Sup. Ct. R. 935, 6 Lewis' Am. R. R. & Corp. R. 357; Campbell *v.* Duluth, etc., R. Co., 50 Fed. R. 241; Southern Pac. Co. *v.* Denton, 146 U. S. 202. There are cases in the federal circuit courts to the contrary, but the first decision of the supreme court, *supra*, has settled the law upon the subject. But see *In re* Hohorst, 150 U. S. 653, s. c. 14 Sup. Ct. R. 221, holding that a foreign corporation might be sued by a citizen of a state in any district thereof in which valid service could be had.

[3] N. K. Fairbank & Co. *v.* Cincinnati, etc., R. Co., 54 Fed. R. 420; St. Louis, etc., Ry. Co. *v.* McBride, 141 U. S. 127, s. c. 11 Sup. Ct. R. 982, holding also that the objection to jurisdiction on this ground may be waived.

§ 623   ACTIONS BY AND AGAINST CORPORATIONS.   885

States in another district through which its road extends.[1] In some jurisdictions, where the statute does not, in effect, make railroad companies residents of the different counties through which their lines run and in which they have agents, it is held that the residence of a railroad company will be presumed to be in the county in which its principal office is located, and that the venue should be laid in that county.[2] It was also held, in a recent case, that an action for personal injuries might be brought in the county in which the company had its principal office, although the injury was inflicted in another county in the same state, and although the statute provided that the company might be sued in the county in which the injury was inflicted.[3] Local actions, such as those involving the title or possession of land, or for injuries thereto, must generally be brought in the county or district in which the land is situated,[4]

[1] Galveston, etc., R. Co. v. Gonzales, 151 U. S. 496, s. c. 14 Sup. Ct. R. 401, 57 Am. & Eng. R. Cas. 71.

[2] Thorn v. Railroad Co., 26 N. J. L. 121; Transportation Co. v. Scheu, 19 N. Y. 408; Railroad Co. v. Cooper, 30 Vt. 476; Pelton v. Transportation Co., 37 Ohio St. 450; Jenkins v. Stage Co., 22 Cal. 537. But, as a general rule, a transitory action against a non-resident may be brought in any county in which process can be served upon him. 1 Elliott's Gen. Pr., § 254, and authorities there cited in note 3, p. 313.

[3] The court regarded the statute as permissive and cumulative and not exclusive. Williams v. East Tennessee, etc., R. Co., 90 Ga. 519.

[4] See 1 Elliott's Gen. Pr., § 252, and authorities there cited. Unless otherwise provided by statute, the general rule is that an action is transitory "when the transaction out of which it grows, or the occurrence upon which it is founded, is one that might have taken place anywhere." 1 Elliott's Gen. Pr., § 253, citing Mostyn v. Fabrigas, 1 Cowp. 161, s. c. 1 Smith's Lead.

Cases 652. "Actions are deemed transitory when the transactions on which they are founded might have taken place anywhere, but are local where their cause is in its nature necessarily local." Nonce v. Richmond, etc., R. Co., 33 Fed. R. 429, 433, 434. For actions held local, see East Tennessee, etc., R. Co. v. Atlanta, etc., R. Co., 49 Fed. R. 608, (bill for appointment of receiver held of a "local nature" within meaning of U. S. Rev. Stat., §§ 740, 742); Cox v. St. Louis, etc., R. Co., 55 Ark. 454, s. c. 18 S. W. R. 630 (suit to restrain company from removing earth from plaintiff's land); Morris v. Missouri Pac. R. Co., 78 Tex. 17, s. c. 14 S. W. R. 228 (action for flooding lands, but the contrary is held in Archibald v. Mississippi, etc., R. Co., 66 Miss. 424, s. c. 6 So. R. 238); Indiana, etc., R. Co. v. Foster, 107 Ind. 430 (action for damages to land by fire from locomotive); Atkins v. Wabash, etc., R. Co., 29 Fed. R. 161 (suit to foreclose mortgage); Postal, etc., Co. v. Norfolk, etc., Co., 88 Va. 920, s. c. 14 S. E. R. 803; Drinkbut this subject is largely regulated by legislative enactments. Other questions as to the venue in actions against consolidated corporations and in different kinds of suits and actions are discussed elsewhere, in connection with the particular cases in which they arise.[1]

§ 624. **Attachment and garnishment.**—Jurisdiction over a corporation, to a limited extent at least, may sometimes be obtained by attachment or garnishment. These remedies or proceedings, however, are creatures of statute, and, as the statutory provisions vary in different states, we shall not attempt to treat the subject in detail, but it may be well to call attention to some rules of a general nature that are peculiarly applicable to railroad companies. Attachment and garnishment are usually auxiliary or provisional remedies and can only be pursued when authorized by statute and in conformity with the statutory provisions as to the procedure.[2] If personal service upon the company is properly obtained in the main action a personal judgment may be rendered against it in a proper case,[3] but if it is a non-resident and does not appear or otherwise waive service, no personal judgment can be rendered against it.[4] So far as the property itself is concerned, however, jurisdiction is generally obtained, in case of a non-resident, by its seizure and by giving notice by publication in com-

house v. Spring Valley, etc., Co., 80 Cal. 308, s. c. 22 Pac. R. 252; Mississippi, etc., R. Co. v. Ward, 2 Black (U. S.) 485; Du Breuil v. Pennsylvania Co., 130 Ind. 137.

[1] See, generally, Chapter III, Legal Status.

[2] For instances in which attachment was held to lie against railroad companies, see Seeley v. Missouri, etc., R. Co., 39 Fed. R. 252; Curtis v. Bradford, 33 Wis. 190; South Carolina R. Co. v. People's Sav. Inst., 64 Ga. 18, s. c. 12 Am. & Eng. R. Cas. 432; Kitchen v. Chatham, etc , R. Co., 17 New Bruns. 215; Breed v. Mitchell, 48 Ga. 533; Fithian v. New York, etc., R. Co., 31 Pa. St. 114. For instances in which it was held that attachment would not lie, see Central R., etc.,Co. v. Georgia, etc., Co., 32 S. Car. 319, s. c. 11 S. E. R. 192; Phillipsburgh Bank v. Lackawanna R. Co., 27 N. J. L. 206; Farnsworth v. Terre Haute, etc., R. Co., 29 Mo. 75; Martin v. Mobile, etc., R. Co., 7 Bush (Ky.) 116.

[3] Mahany v. Kephart, 15 W. Va. 609; Drake on Attachment, § 5.

[4] 1 Elliott's Gen. Pr., §§ 243, 378; Eastman v. Wadleigh, 65 Me. 251, s. c. 20 Am. R. 695; Elliot v. McCormick, 144 Mass. 10; Cooper v. Reynolds, 10 Wall. (U. S.) 308; Wade on Attachment, § 267.

§ 624   ACTIONS BY AND AGAINST CORPORATIONS.   887

pliance with the statute.[1] But if no property is found and no personal service is had, no judgment can be rendered against a non-resident defendant who does not appear or waive service.[2] As a general rule any property subject to execution may be attached, and engines and cars not in actual use are usually regarded as personal property liable to attachment.[3] A railroad company may be subject to garnishment the same as a natural person, although not specially mentioned in the statute,[4] but it has been held in Michigan that a statutory provision for the service of process in suits against foreign corporations does not apply to the service of a writ of garnishment.[5] One or two courts have held that the same considerations of public policy which exempt public officers in the discharge of their duties from garnishment apply to common carriers,[6] and possibly there may be cases in which the garnishment would so interfere with the duties of the company to the public that the courts should refuse to permit the garnishment to be enforced, but such a case is hardly conceivable, and, if the statute authorizing the garnishment applies to the case, it would seem to be the duty of the courts to enforce it. But a non-resident corporation can not, ordinarily, be held ac-

[1] Neufelder v. German American Ins. Co., 6 Wash. 336, s. c. 22 L. R. A. 287, 290; Cooper v. Reynolds, 10 Wall. (U. S.) 308; King v. Vance, 46 Ind. 246; 1 Elliott's Gen. Pr., §§ 243, 378.

[2] Pennoyer v. Neff, 95 U. S. 714; Cooper v. Smith, 25 Iowa 269; Bruce v. Cloutman, 45 N. H. 37; Clymore v. Williams, 77 Ill. 618.

[3] Hall v. Carney, 140 Mass. 131, s. c. 3 N. E. R. 14; Boston, etc., R. Co. v. Gilmore R. Co., 37 N. H. 410; Dinsmore v. Racine, etc., R. Co., 12 Wis. 725.

[4] Pennsylvania R. Co. v. Peoples, 31 Ohio St. 537; Baltimore, etc., R. Co. v. Gallahue, 12 Gratt. (Va.) 655, s. c. 65 Am. Dec. 254; Taylor v. Burlington, etc., R. Co., 5 Iowa 114; Hannibal, etc., R. Co. v. Crane, 102 Ill. 249, s. c. 40 Am. R. 581; Hughes v. Oregonian Ry. Co., 11 Ore. 158. A foreign corporation doing business in the state was held subject to garnishment in the first case above cited. So, in Weed Sewing Machine Co. v. Boutelle, 56 Vt. 570; Barr v. King, 96 Pa. St. 485; Burlington, etc., R. Co. v. Thompson, 31 Kan. 180, s. c. 16 Am. & Eng. R. Cas. 480; Carson v. Memphis, etc., R. Co., 88 Tenn. 646; Fairbank v. Cincinnati, etc., R. Co., 54 Fed. R. 420.

[5] Milwaukee, etc., R. Co. v. Brevoort, 73 Mich. 155; First Nat. Bank v. Burch, 76 Mich. 608.

[6] Michigan Cent. R. Co. v. Chicago, etc., R. Co., 1 Ill. App. 399. See, also, Holland v. Leslie, 2 Harr. (Del.) 306.

countable as garnishee unless it has property of the defendant within the state in which the proceedings are had, or is bound to pay him money or deliver him goods in that state.[1] Thus, it has been held that a company of one state operating a road running into another state as lessee can not be charged as garnishee in the latter state in an action for a debt payable in the former state, in which the plaintiff and defendant both reside.[2] But we shall not attempt to reconcile or review the conflicting authorities upon this general subject as to the *situs* of the debt or the jurisdiction of the court. It is held in Illinois that a railroad company doing business in that and another state may be garnished in Illinois by a resident in the other state for a debt owing by the company to another resident of that state, and that the motives of the plaintiff are immaterial.[3] In Tennessee it has been held that a company which owns and operates a continuous line through that and several other states, having a separate charter from each of them, is a resident and domestic corporation of Tennessee, and subject as such to garnishment therein, by a citizen thereof, although the claim sought to be reached was contracted in one of the other states and is due to a non-resident.[4]

[1] Wright v. Chicago, etc., R. Co., 19 Neb. 175, s. c. 27 N. W. R. 90; Missouri Pac. R. Co. v. Sharitt, 43 Kan. 375, s. c. 44 Am. & Eng. R. R. Cas. 657, and authorities cited by Valentine, J.; Cronin v. Foster, 13 R. I. 196; Louisville, etc., R. Co. v. Dooley, 78 Ala. 524; Young v. Ross, 31 N. H. 201; Todd v. Missouri Pac. R. Co., 33 Mo. App. 110; Buchanan v. Hunt, 98 N. Y. 560; Schmidlapp v. LaConfiance Ins. Co., 71 Ga. 246; Wade on Attachment, § 344. See, generally, to the effect that the court must have jurisdiction both of the garnishee and the property as well, 8 Am. & Eng. Ency. of Law 1129, 1150, and authorities there cited; Bates v. Chicago, etc., R. Co., 60 Wis. 296, s. c. 19 N. W. R. 72, 50 Am. R. 369; Pennsylvania R. Co. v. Pennock, 51 Pa. St. 244; Douglass v. Phenix Ins. Co., 138 N. Y. 209, s. c. 20 L. R. A. 118; see, also, note to Illinois Cent. R. Co. v. Smith, 19 L. R. A. 577; Central Trust Co. v. Chattanooga, etc., R. Co., 68 Fed. R. 685.

[2] Towle v. Wilder, 57 Vt. 622; Gold v. Housatonic R. Co., 1 Gray (Mass.) 424. But see *supra*, note 1.

[3] Wabash R. Co. v. Dougan, 142 Ill. 248, s. c. 31 N. E. R. 594. See, also, Drake v. Lake Shore, etc., R. Co., 69 Mich. 168; Stevens v. Brown, 20 W. Va. 450. But see *post*, § 627, notes 2, 3, on p. 895.

[4] Mobile, etc., R. Co. v. Barnhill, 91 Tenn. 395, s. c. 19 S. W. R. 21, 50 Am. & Eng. R. Cas. 646. But see Wells v. East Tenn., etc., R. Co., 74 Ga. 548.

§ 625		ACTIONS BY AND AGAINST CORPORATIONS.		889

§ 625. **Duty and liability of garnishee.**—If the corporation is properly served as garnishee it must appear and answer, disclosing the facts. It answers, ordinarily, under its corporate seal, by its proper officer or agent.[1] If the principal defendant has not been personally served and does not appear it is generally the duty of the garnishee, which it owes to the defendant, to question the jurisdiction of the court, if it has none, and this it should always do, in case of doubt, for its own protection.[2] It has also been held that the garnishee must present the question of the defendant's right to exemption,[3] and this, we think, is the true rule where wages are garnished, which are expressly exempted therefrom by statute, and, possibly, in all cases where the garnishee has knowledge of the right of the defendant to exemption, but, in the absence of knowledge, where such a statute does not exist or does not apply, we think the garnishee is not necessarily bound to raise the question. Indeed, as the right to exemption is generally considered a mere personal privilege, it would seem that, upon principle, the garnishee can neither insist upon such a defense, where the principal defendant waives it, nor be held liable for not making it, in the absence of a special statute.[4]

---

[1] Oliver v. Chicago, etc., R. Co., 17 Ill. 587; Baltimore, etc., R. Co. v. Gallahue, 12 Gratt.(Va.) 655, s. c. 65 Am. Dec. 254. The answer must usually be verified by the proper officer. Chicago, R. I., etc., R. Co. v. Mason, 11 Ill. App. 525; Memphis, etc., R. Co. v. Whorley, 74 Ala. 264. But the affidavit need not be made by the same officer upon whom the writ was served, and it has been held that it may be made by any officer having knowledge of the facts. Duke v. Rhode Island, etc., Works, 11 R. I. 599; Whitworth v. Pelton, 81 Mich. 98, s. c. 45 N. W. R. 500 (affidavit by assistant treasurer). It has also been held that the court may permit the garnishee to file an amended answer in furtherance of justice. Crerar v. Milwaukee, etc., R. Co., 35 Wis. 67.

[2] Debs v. Dalton, 7 Ind. App. 84, s. c. 34 N. E. R. 236; Emery v. Royal, 117 Ind. 299, s. c. 20 N. E. R. 150; Pierce v. Carleton, 12 Ill. 358, s.c. 54 Am. Dec. 405; Laidlaw v. Morrow, 44 Mich. 547; Kellogg v. Freeman, 50 Miss. 127; Thayer v. Tyler, 10 Gray (Mass.) 164; Drake on Attachment, § 965.

[3] Mineral Point R. Co. v. Barron, 83 Ill. 365; Terre Haute, etc., R. Co. v. Baker, 122 Ind. 433, s. c. 24 N. E. R! 83; Clark v. Averill, 31 Vt. 512, s. c. 76 Am. Dec. 131; Davis v. Meredith, 48 Mo. 263; Mull v. Jones, 33 Kan. 112; Smith v. Dickson, 58 Iowa 444.

[4] See 1 Elliott's Gen. Pr., § 388, and notes, where the subject is fully considered.

The garnishment usually binds the garnishee, as to the debt or property in his hands, from the date of the service of the writ,[1] and his liability is ordinarily determined by his accountability to the defendant at that time.[2] But where the writ is served on one agent of a corporation while the property is in the actual possession of another agent, and the latter delivers it to the owner before the first agent can, in the exercise of reasonable diligence, notify the other, it has been held that the corporation is not liable.[3] The garnishee may, in general, set up any defense that he would have had if sued by the defendant,[4] and if he has been garnished in a prior proceeding for the same matter he may set up that fact.[5]

§ 626. **What may be reached in garnishment.**—Real estate is not subject to garnishment unless the statute so provides;[6] nor, it seems, is money set apart for the payment of interest

---

[1] First Nat. Bank v. Armstrong, 101 Ind. 244; Brashear v. West, 7 Pet. (U. S.) 608; Emanuel v. Bridger, L. R. 9 Q. B. 286; Holmes v. Tutton, 5 El. & B. 65. But in Smith v. Boston, etc., R. Co., 33 N. H. 337, it is said that his liability is determined by the state of facts existing at the time of his disclosure and set forth therein.

[2] Baltimore, etc., R. Co. v. Wheeler, 18 Md. 372; Huntington v. Risdon, 43 Iowa 517; Getchell v. Chase, 124 Mass. 366; Lieberman v. Hoffman, 102 Pa. St. 590; Cleanay v. Junction R. Co., 26 Ind. 375; Reagan v. Pacific R. Co., 21 Mo. 30.

[3] Bates v. Chicago, etc., R. Co., 60 Wis. 296, s. c. 19 N. W. R. 72, 50 Am. R. 369. This seems to us a just decision.

[4] 1 Elliott's Gen. Pr., § 388; Drake on Attachment, § 458; Hazen v. Emerson, 9 Pick. (Mass.) 144 (statute of limitations); Benton v. Lindell, 10 Mo. 557; Pennell v. Grubb, 13 Pa. St. 552 (Set-off); Cox v. Russell, 44 Iowa 556, 562; Wheeler v. Emerson, 45 N. H. 526. See, generally, Center v. McQueston, 24 Kan. 480; Schuler v. Israel, 120 U. S. 506; Sauer v. Nevadaville, 14 Col. 54; North Chicago, etc., Co. v. St. Louis, etc., Co., 152 U. S. 596, s. c. 14 Sup. Ct. R. 710. But see, as to property fraudulently transferred, Lamb v. Stone, 11 Pick. (Mass.) 527; Cummings v. Fearey, 44 Mich. 39.

[5] Wade on Attachment, § 382; Houston v. Walcott, 7 Iowa 173; Royer v. Fleming, 58 Mo. 438; Everdell v. Sheboygan, etc., Co., 41 Wis. 395; Dealing v. New York, etc., R. Co., 8 N. Y. St. R. 386; Robarge v. Central Vt. R. Co., 18 Abb. N. Cas. (N. Y.) 363. But see Alabama, etc., R. Co. v. Chumley, 92 Ala. 317, s. c. 9 So. R. 286.

[6] How v. Field, 5 Mass. 390; Stedman v. Vickery, 42 Me. 132; Hunter v. Case, 20 Vt. 195; Risley v. Welles, 5 Conn. 431; National, etc., Bank v. Brainerd, 65 Vt. 291, s. c. 26 Atl. R. 723.

on railroad mortgage bonds,[1] nor are funds in the hands of an officer or agent of the company garnishable in an ordinary action against the company itself,[2] for the possession by an agent of money collected for his principal is usually deemed to be the possession of the principal.[3] It is said, with what appears to be good reason, that stock can not be garnished in the hands of a railroad company for the debts of the stockholders, as the corporation, while a "going concern," is not required to pay the stockholders anything but proper dividends and they are not its creditors.[4] But provision is usually made for reaching shares of stock, or the stockholder's interest, by attachment,[5] and an unpaid subscription for which a call has been made is subject to garnishment at the instance of the corporate creditors,[6] although it is held otherwise where no call has been made.[7] It has been held that property in transit, in another county, in the hands of a railroad company, can not be garnished,[8] but property may be garnished, after it has reached

[1] Galena, etc., R. Co. v. Menzies, 26 Ill. 122. But see Smith v. Eastern R. Co., 124 Mass. 154; Mississippi, etc., R. Co. v. United States Exp. Co., 81 Ill. 534.

[2] Wilder v. Shea, 13 Bush. (Ky.) 128; Fowler v. Pittsburgh, etc., R. Co., 35 Pa. St. 22; First Nat. Bank v. Davenport, etc., Railroad Co., 45 Iowa 120; Pettingill v. Androscoggin R. Co., 51 Me. 370; McGraw v. Memphis, etc., R. Co., 5 Coldw. (Tenn.) 434. *Contra*, Littleton Nat. Bank v. Portland, etc., Co., 58 N. H. 104; Everdell v. Sheboygan, etc., R. Co., 41 Wis. 395.

[3] Flanagan v. Wood, 33 Vt. 332; Hall v. Filter Mfg. Co., 10 Phila. (Pa.) 370; Neuer v. O'Fallon, 18 Mo. 277, s. c. 59 Am. Dec. 313.

[4] Ross v. Ross, 25 Ga. 297; Planters', etc., Bank v. Leavens, 4 Ala. 753; Mooar v. Walker, 46 Iowa 164; Younkin v. Collier, 47 Fed. R. 571. See, also, Smith v. Downey, 8 Ind. App. 175, 34 N. E. R. 823. But see Harrell v. Mexico, etc., Co., 73 Tex. 612, 11 S. W. R. 863; Baker v. Wasson, 53 Tex. 150.

[5] Chesapeake, etc., R. Co. v. Paine, 29 Gratt. (Va.) 502; Shenandoah Valley R. Co. v. Griffith, 76 Va. 913, s. c. 13 Am. & Eng. R. R. Cas. 120, and note; 1 Cook on Stock and Stockholders, § 404. But only, as a rule, in the state in which the company is incorporated. Winslow v. Fletcher, 53 Conn. 390, 55 Am. R. 122, 13 Am. & Eng. Corp. Cas. 39; 1 Cook on Stock and Stockholders, § 485.

[6] Kern v. Chicago, etc., Assn., 140 Ill. 371, s. c. 29 N. E. R. 1035; Joseph v. Davis, (Ala.) s. c. 10 So. R. 830; Hannah v. Moberly Bank, 67 Mo. 678.

[7] Teague v. Le Grand, 85 Ala. 493, s. c. 5 So. R. 287; Bunn's Appeal, 105 Pa. St. 49; Brown v. Union Ins. Co., 3 La. Ann. 177; McKelvey v. Crockett, 18 Nev. 238.

[8] Bates v. Chicago, etc., R. Co., 60 Wis. 296, s. c. 19 N. W. R. 72, 50 Am.

its destination, while held by the company as a warehouseman.[1] Property *in custodia legis* is, as a general rule, exempt from attachment or garnishment in the hands of the officer,[2] but there are some cases in which the earnings or other property of a railroad company have been permitted,by the courts to be attached or garnished in the hands of a receiver,[3] and such earnings, although subject to a mortgage, are generally liable to garnishment until a foreclosure is had or possession is taken by the trustee.[4] Bonds of a foreign corporation in the hands of an agent for sale have been held in New York not to be liable to attachment against the company.[5] And it has

R. 369; Illinois C. R. Co. *v.* Cobb, 48 Ill. 402; Bingham *v.* Lamping, 26 Pa. St. 240; Pennsylvania R. Co. *v.* Pennock, 51 Pa. St. 244, 254; Western R. Co. *v.* Thornton, 60 Ga. 300. See, also, Chicago, B. & Q. R. Co. *v.* Painter, 15 Neb. 394. *Contra*, Adams *v.* Scott, 104 Mass. 164, and compare Walker *v.* Detroit, etc., R. Co., 49 Mich. 446. In several of the cases first cited there were peculiar circumstances, and in none of them, perhaps, was it necessary to decide that this is an invariable rule. There are forcible reasons, however, for affirming that this is the general rule where the property is actually in transit at a distant point. As to when goods *in transitu* may be attached, see note in 14 Am. & Eng. R. R. Cas. 700, 709; Locke on Foreign Attachment 32.

[1] Cooley *v.* Minnesota, etc., Co., 53 Minn. 327, s. c. 55 N. W. R. 141, 55 Am. & Eng. R. Cas. 616.

[2] Drake on Attachment, § 281; Hill *v.* La Crosse, etc., Railroad Co., 14 Wis. 291, s. c. 80 Am. Dec. 783; Taylor *v.* Carryl, 24 Pa. St. 259; Averill *v.* Tucker, 2 Cranch. C. C. (U. S.) 544; People, *ex rel.* Tremper, *v.* Brooks, 40 Mich. 333; Field *v.* Jones, 11 Ga. 413; Beach on Receivers, § 228; High on Receivers, § 151.

[3] Phelan *v.* Ganebin, 5 Col. 14; First Nat. Bank *v.* Portland, etc., R. Co., 2 Fed. R. 831; Humphreys *v.* Hopkins, 81 Cal. 551, s. c. 22 Pac. R. 892. And see Conover *v.* Ruckman, 33 N. J. Eq. 303; Gaither *v.* Ballew, 4 Jones L. (N. Car.) 488, s. c. 69 Am. Dec. 763; Hurlburt *v.* Hicks, 17 Vt. 193, s. c. 44 Am. Dec. 329; Wehle *v.* Conner, 83 N. Y. 231; Warren *v.* Booth, 51 Iowa 215.

[4] Smith *v.* Eastern, etc., R. Co., 124 Mass. 154; Mississippi, etc., R. Co. *v.* United States Express Co., 81 Ill. 534; De Graff *v.* Thompson, 24 Minn. 452; Galveston, etc., R. Co. *v.* Cowdrey, 11 Wall. (U. S.) 459; Gilman *v.* Illinois, etc., Co., 91 U. S. 603; Noyes *v.* Rich, 52 Me. 115. But see Dunham *v.* Isett, 15 Iowa 284. In Milwaukee, etc., R. Co. *v.* Brooks, etc., Works, 121 U. S. 430, s. c. 7 Sup. Ct. R. 1094, 30 Am. & Eng. R. R. Cas. 499, it was held that funds belonging to a leased road operated temporarily by the mortgage trustee of the lessor road could be garnished in his hands by a creditor of the lessee company. See, also, Root, etc., *v.* Davis, 51 Ohio St. 29, 36 N. E. R. 669, s. c. 23 L. R. A. 445.

[5] Coddington *v.* Gilbert, 17 N. Y. 489. See, also, as to bonds pledged as collateral or in the hands of third persons, Tweedy *v.* Bogart, 56 Conn.

been held in Massachusetts that a railroad company, which has an arrangement with other companies having lines that form a continuous connection, to make monthly settlements with the company whose road joins its own, including therein amounts due the other connecting roads beyond, is not liable, as trustee in foreign attachment, to the first connecting carrier for money due the other companies under the agreement.[1]

§ 627. **Garnishment of employes' wages.**—Railroad companies are frequently garnished in actions against their employes, but in most of the states there are statutes providing that the wages of employes for a specified period, or to a specified amount, shall be exempt. It has been held that a foreign railroad company, doing business in another state, may be garnished in the latter state for the debt of a non-resident employe contracted out of such state,[2] and that a corporation organized under the laws of the United States, where the wages are earned in a state in which both the employe and the creditor reside, may be garnished in another state in which the company is personally served.[3] But, on the other hand, it has been held by another court that wages due from a company incorporated in one state to an employe in that state can not be reached by a creditor in another state by attachment against the debtor and garnishment of the corporation.[4] In any event, the garnishee

419, s. c. 15 Atl. R. 374; Galena, etc., R. Co. v. Stahl, 103 Ill. 67, with which compare Warren v. Booth, 53 Iowa 742.

[1] Chapin v. Connecticut, etc., R. Co., 16 Gray (Mass.) 69. So, where goods are shipped over several roads it is held that the consignee is not liable as garnishee to the road delivering the goods for freight due the others. Gould v. Newburyport R. Co., 14 Gray (Mass.) 472.

[2] Burlington, etc., R. Co. v. Thompson, 31 Kan. 180, s. c. 1 Pac. R. 622, 47 Am. R. 497; Carson v. Memphis, etc., R. Co., 88 Tenn. 646, s. c. 13 S. W. R. 588. See, also, Bolton v. Pennsylvania R. Co., 88 Pa. St. 261; Neufelder v. German American Ins. Co., 6 Wash. 336, s. c. 22 L. R. A. 287. But compare Central Trust Co. v. Chattanooga, etc., R. Co., 68 Fed. R. 685, and numerous authorities there cited.

[3] Mooney v. Union Pac. R. Co., 60 Iowa 346. Followed in Oberfelder v. Union Pac. R. Co., 60 Iowa 755, and approved in Carson v. Memphis etc., R. Co., 88 Tenn. 646.

[4] Louisville, etc., R. Co. v. Dooley, 78 Ala. 524. See, also, Drake v. Lake Shore, etc., R. Co., 69 Mich. 168, s. c. 37 N. W. R. 70. But it will generally be found in these cases that the garnishee had no property of the defend-

proceedings bind only the amount due at the date of the service of the writ, and do not reach wages subsequently earned.[1] So, under statutes providing that the debt must be due "absolutely and without contingency," it is held that where the contract of employment provides that the amount of work done during one month and the wages to be paid therefor shall be estimated and determined after the end of the month, such earnings can not be garnished in the hands of the company before the end of the month.[2] Exemption laws have no extraterritorial effect,[3] and, as a general rule, neither a debtor nor his garnishee can obtain the benefit of the exemption laws of the state in which they reside when sued in another state;[4] but, where wages are exempt in both states, it has been held that the debtor will be entitled to the exemption, and that it is the duty of the garnishee to claim it for him.[5] The law upon this subject, however, is not well settled, and the question is not

ant, or did not owe him a debt in the state in which the suit was brought.

[1] Burlington, etc., R. Co. v. Thompson, 31 Kan. 180, s. c. 1 Pac. R. 622, 47 Am. R. 497.

[2] Williams v. Androscoggin, etc., R. Co., 36 Me. 201; Fellows v. Smith, 131 Mass. 363. See, also, Dawson v. Iron Range, etc., R. Co., 97 Mich. 33, s. c. 56 N. W. R. 106. But compare Ware v. Gowen, 65 Me. 534.

[3] Freeman on Executions, § 209. See, also, Central Trust Co. v. Chattanooga, etc., R. Co., 68 Fed. R. 685. But see Drake v. Lake Shore, etc., R. Co., 69 Mich. 168, s. c. 37 N. W. R. 70; Missouri Pac. R. Co. v. Sharitt, 43 Kan. 375, and authorities there cited.

[4] The garnishee is not bound, therefore, to claim any exemption for the debtor. Burlington, etc., R. Co. v. Thompson, 31 Kan. 180; East Tennessee, etc., R. Co. v. Kennedy, 83 Ala. 462; Morgan v. Neville, 74 Pa. St. 52; Carson v. Memphis, etc., R. Co., 88 Tenn. 646, s. c. 13 S. W. R. 588; Mooney v. Union Pac. R. Co., 60 Iowa 346, s. c. 9 Am. & Eng. R. Cas. 131; Eichelburger v. Pittsburgh, etc., R. Co., (Ohio), 9 Am. & Eng. R. Cas. 158; Lieber v. Union Pac. R. Co., 49 Iowa 688; Broadstreet v. Clark, 65 Iowa 670. But see Pierce v. Chicago, etc., R. Co., 36 Wis. 283.

[5] Mineral Point R. Co. v. Barron, 83 Ill. 365; Chicago & A. R. Co. v. Ragland, 84 Ill. 375; Wabash R. Co. v. Dougan, 142 Ill. 248, s. c. 31 N. E. R. 594; Terre Haute, etc., R. Co. v. Baker, 122 Ind. 433, s. c. 24 N. E. R. 83; Wright v. Chicago, etc., R. Co., 19 Neb. 175, s. c. 27 N. W. R. 90; Missouri Pac. R. Co. v. Maltby, 34 Kan. 125, s. c. 8 Pac. R. 235; Missouri Pac. R. Co. v. Whipsker, 77 Tex. 14, s. c. 13 S. W. R. 639; Kansas City, etc., R. Co. v. Gough, 35 Kan. 1, s. c. 10 Pac. R. 89. In several of these cases, however, the statute of the state in which the suit was brought was construed as exempting wages attached or garnished in the state, no matter whether the employe is a resident or a non-resident.

entirely free from doubt.[1] Indeed, it has been held that a resident of a state, in which the debt is contracted and payable, is not subject to attachment or garnishment in another state.[2] Thus, where the statute made it a criminal offense for any person to send a claim against a resident debtor out of the state for collection, in order to evade the exemption laws, it was held that injunction would lie to restrain a resident of the state from sending the claim to another state and there prosecuting attachment proceedings for the purpose of evading the exemption law.[3] In another case it was held that a railroad company was liable to an employe for wages earned and due in the state in which suit was brought and in which all parties resided, notwithstanding the pendency of garnishment proceedings against the company in another state to reach the same wages.[4] The court took the ground that it had sole jurisdiction; that it would not presume that the foreign court, upon being duly advised, would proceed to judgment against the garnishee, and that, in any event, it would protect and enforce the exemption laws of its own state.

§ 628. Injunction—Generally.—A railroad company is subject in general in a court of equity to the same remedies as an individual. In other words, the jurisdiction of equity is the same in its general nature over corporations as it is over natural

---

[1] See Moore v. Chicago, etc., R. Co., 43 Iowa 385; Carson v. Memphis, etc., R. Co., 88 Tenn. 646, s. c. 13 S. W. R. 588; Chicago, etc., R. Co. v. Meyer, 117 Ind. 563, s. c. 19 N. E. R. 320; Baltimore, etc., R. Co. v. May, 25 Ohio St. 347.

[2] Bush v. Nance, 61 Miss. 237; Wilson v. Joseph, 107 Ind. 490; Kestler v. Kern, 2 Ind. App. Ct. R. 488; Illinois Cent. R. Co. v. Smith, 70 Miss. 344, 12 So. R. 461.

[3] Wilson v. Joseph, 107 Ind. 490; Cole v. Cunningham, 133 U. S. 107, s. c. 10 Sup. Ct. R. 269; Keyser v. Rice, 47 Md. 203, s. c. 28 Am. R. 448; Engel v. Scheuerman, 40 Ga. 206, s. c. 2 Am. R. 573; Snook v. Snetzer, 25 Ohio St. 516; Dehon v. Foster, 4 Allen (Mass.) 545; Mumper v. Wilson, 72 Iowa 163; Zimmerman v. Franke, 34 Kan. 650; Missouri Pac. R. Co. v. Maltby, 34 Kan. 125, s. c. 8 Pac. R. 235; Mason v. Beebee, 44 Fed. 556.

[4] Illinois Cent. R. Co. v. Smith, 70 Miss. 344, s. c. 12 So. R. 461. See, also, Missouri Pac. R. Co. v. Sharitt, 43 Kan. 375, s. c. 44 Am. & Eng. R. R. Cas. 657. For a review of the conflicting decisions upon the general subject, see note to the first case above cited in 19 L. R. A. 577.

persons. As a general rule any wrongful invasion by it of the rights of others may be prevented by injunction,[1] provided a complete remedy at law is not available.[2] Equity will refuse to interfere where an injunction would work great injury to the defendant[3] and the plaintiff will suffer but a slight injury for

[1] Wrongs of a repeated and continuous character which occasion damages estimable only by conjecture and not by any accurate standard may be enjoined. Such damages are irreparable within the meaning of the United States statute providing for an injunction where the party does not have a plain, adequate and complete remedy at law. Payne v. Kansas, etc., R. Co., 46 Fed. Rep. 546. The prosecution of an action at law may be enjoined in a proper case. Chicago, etc., R. Co. v. Pullman Palace Car Co., 49 Fed. 409.

[2] Planet, etc., Co. v. St. Louis, etc., R. Co., 115 Mo. 613. Condemnation proceedings will not be enjoined on the ground that there has been a previous condemnation of the same land for the same purpose, resulting in a verdict assessing compensation, since that fact is in itself an adequate legal defense, which can be pursued by motion in the second condemnation suit. Chicago, R. I. & P. R. Co. v. City of Chicago, 143 Ill. 641; Northern Pac. R. Co. v. Cannon, 49 Fed. Rep. 517. Where the plaintiffs all have different interests, the fact that a number of actions at law arise out of the same transaction and depend upon the same matters of fact and law is not sufficient warrant for enjoining the prosecution of such actions, and the joinder of the different parties interested in a single suit in chancery as defendants to prevent a multiplicity of suits. Tribbette v. Illinois Central R. Co., 70 Miss. 182. Where proceedings by a city to open a boulevard across a railway company's tracks are pending on appeal, a bill to enjoin the city from such proceedings, on the ground that irreparable injury will be done to the company, will not lie, as the question is a legal one, which will be disposed of in the condemnation proceedings. Detroit, G. H. & M. Ry. Co. v. City of Detriot, 91 Mich. 444. One holding land under a judgment of condemnation may maintain suit to restrain ejectment proceedings and to quiet title, although such judgment is a perfect defense to the action of ejectment. Foltz v. St. Louis, etc., R. Co., 60 Fed. Rep. 316. An action of ejectment to recover land upon which it has, with the consent of plaintiff and his grantor, built its tracks, cattle sheds, and warehouse, may be enjoined at the suit of a railroad company, although it has no title. South, etc., R. Co. v. Alabama, etc., R. Co., (Ala.) 14 So. Rep. 747.

[3] City of Scranton v. Delaware, etc., Canal Co., 12 Pa. Co. Ct. Rep. 283. A preliminary injunction will not be granted to restrain a company "from the further operation and management" of a leased railroad on the allegation, among others, that the roads are "parallel and competing," and the lease *ultra vires*, and contrary to the provision of the constitution where all the grounds for equitable relief are denied; since it would involve difficult questions of law and fact, and would, if granted, work incalculable injury to defendant and the public. Gummere v. Lehigh Val. R. Co., (Pa. Com. Pl.) 12 Pa. Co. Ct. R. 106.

§ 629   ACTIONS BY AND AGAINST CORPORATIONS.   897

which he can readily be compensated by damages.[1] The courts may, it seems, take into consideration the fact that companies are common carriers and *quasi* public in their nature, and refuse to grant an injunction for slight cause where it would prevent or obstruct the operation of the road and not only cause great injury to it, but also inconvenience the public.[2] This is particularly true in regard to preliminary injunctions before the case can be heard upon its merits. With this possible exception, however, the rules governing injunctions generally are applicable, in the main, at least, where an injunction is sought against a railroad company. We need not, therefore, further consider the elementary rules, but will refer to the specific classes of cases in which injunctions are usually sought against railroad companies.

§ 629. **Injunction where the company seeks to take or condemn lands.**—Where a railroad company that is so imperfectly incorporated as not to possess the power of eminent domain, is seeking to condemn property of another corporation necessary for its use in carrying on its business, it has been held that such condemnation proceedings may be enjoined.[3] But it is the general rule that the existence of a corporation, acting as such under a law authorizing it and with which it has attempted to comply, can not be collaterally attacked, and the fact that there may be cause for forfeiting its charter will not support ejectment or an injunction at the suit of a landowner whose property it has condemned or is about to condemn.[4] A

---

[1] Savannah, etc., Canal Co. v. Suburban, etc., R. Co., 93 Ga. 240, 18 S. E. Rep. 824; Abraham v. Meyers, (N. Y. Sup. Ct.) 29 Abb. N. C. 384.

[2] Torrey v. Camden, etc., R. Co., 3 C. E. Green Ch. (N. J.) 293; Cook v. North, etc., R. Co., 46 Ga. 618; Gammage v. Georgia, etc., R. Co., 65 Ga. 614. See, also, Indiana, etc., R. Co. v. Allen, 113 Ind. 581; Gray v. Manhattan, etc., R. Co., 128 N. Y. 499.

[3] Hoke v. Georgia R., etc., Co., 89 Ga. 215. And the abuse of its eminent domain powers by a railroad corporation may always be enjoined, without reference to insufficiency of legal remedies or irreparable damages. Western R., etc., v. Alabama, etc., R. Co., 96 Ala. 272.

[4] In the matter of the application of Brooklyn, etc., R. Co., 125 N. Y. 434; Cincinnati, etc., R. Co. v. Clifford, 113 Ind. 460; Bravard v. Cincinnati, etc., R. Co., 115 Ind. 1; New York, etc., R. Co. v. New York, etc., R. Co., 52 Conn. 274; Briggs v. Cape Cod

railroad company may be enjoined at the suit of a party injured thereby from appropriating land for which it has failed to make compensation as required by law,[1] but an injunction will not be granted against the use of land by a railroad company which has taken without right, where the owner has acquiesced in the appropriation until the company has expended money thereon, and the public interest has become involved.[2] Where the corporation is given power to take lands for the use of its road, it may, within the statutory limits, exercise its discretion as to what shall be taken; and the fact that it owns[3] or could

Canal, 137 Mass. 71. See, also, Rafferty v. Central Traction Co., 147 Pa. St. 579, s. c. 23 Atl. R. 884, 6 Lewis' Am. R. & Corp. R. 287.

[1] Lake Erie, etc., R. Co. v. Michener, 117 Ind. 465; Ray v. Atchison, etc., R. Co., 4 Neb. 439; Spencer v. Point Pleasant, etc., R. Co., 23 W. Va. 406, s. c. 20 Am. & Eng. R. Cas. 125; Kansas City, etc., R. Co. v. St. Joseph, etc., R. Co., 97 Mo. 457; Chattanooga, etc., R. Co. v. Jones, 80 Ga. 264; Elliott on Roads and Streets 185; 10 Am. & Eng. Ency. of Law 969, and numerous authorities there cited. But it has been held that an injunction will not be granted where the land has been condemned in a court of competent jurisdiction, but the landowner has appealed therefrom, and the case is pending on appeal. Traverse City, etc., R. Co. v. Seymour, 81 Mich. 378. See Dillon v. Kansas City, etc., R. Co., 43 Fed. R. 109. The construction of a railroad over condemned land will not be restrained for errors of law in the condemnation proceedings. Cooper v. Anniston & A. R. Co., 85 Ala. 106, 4 So. R. 689. The fact that the right to immediate possession is in another who has purchased the right to use and occupy the land for a term of twenty years at a sale thereof for non-payment of taxes, does not deprive the landowner of the right to an injunction to prevent a railroad from occupying the land until compensation is made. Pratt v. Roseland R. Co., 50 N. J. Eq. 150. Even in states where an injunction is only granted to restrain *irreparable* injuries, a railroad company may be enjoined from making excavations upon land which they have not condemned. Baltimore, etc., R. Co. v. Lee, 75 Md. 596.

[2] Roberts v. Northern Pacific R. Co., 158 U. S. 1, s.c. 15 Sup.Ct. R.756; Organ v. Memphis, etc., R. Co., 51 Ark. 235; Osborne v. Missouri Pac. R. Co., (C. C. E. D. Mo.) 35 Fed. R. 84, 37 Fed. R. 830; Denver & S. F. R. Co. v. Domke, 11 Colo. 247, 17 Pac. 777; Chambers v. Baltimore & O. R. Co., 139 Pa. St. 347; Midland, etc., R. Co. v. Smith, 113 Ind. 233; Indiana, etc., R. Co. v. Allen, 113 Ind. 581, and authorities there cited; Pettibone v. Railroad Co., 14 Wis. 479; Chicago, etc., Railroad Co. v. Goodwin, 111 Ill. 273; Lexington, etc., Railroad Co. v. Ormsby, 7 Dana 276; Harlow v. Marquette, etc., Railroad Co., 41 Mich. 336, s. c. 2 N. W. R. 48; Western, etc., R. Co. v. Johnston, 59 Pa. St. 290. *Contra*, Louisville, etc., R. Co. v. Liebfried, 92 Ky. 407, s. c. 17 S. W. R. 870.

[3] Stark v. Sioux City, etc., R. Co., 43 Iowa 501; Dougherty v. Wabash, etc., R. Co., 19 Mo. App. 419.

acquire by purchase[1] adjoining lands which would answer its purpose will not entitle the landowners to an injunction where the company acts in good faith. Where the company is acting in bad faith with the purpose of securing lands which it is not empowered to hold, equity may interfere.[2] In the case of a suit for an injunction by one having only a remote or indirect interest in lands, which are subject to condemnation, and in which all other interests have been secured by the company, it has been held that the court may dissolve the injunction upon a bond being filed by the company to pay all damages awarded to the complainant in an action at law.[3] A railroad company may be enjoined from shutting up a private right of way which furnishes the only convenient egress from the plaintiff's land to the public highway, even after the acts complained of have actually been committed.[4] Where the railroad company has obtained possession of land for its right of way under contract to construct its road in a particular manner, it has been held that it may be enjoined from violating the contract. Thus a contract by a railroad company to maintain and keep open two existing passage ways for stock under its road through a certain farm is sufficiently certain to entitle the owner of the farm to an injunction against its violation, although the size, nature, and location of the ways are not stated in the contract.[5]

§ 630. **Injunction where railroad is laid in a street.**—An abutting owner may enjoin it from occupying a street or other

[1] Lodge v. Philadelphia, etc., R. Co., 8 Phila. (Pa.) 345; Ford v. Chicago, etc., R. Co., 14 Wis. 609; New York, etc., R. Co. v. Kip, 46 N. Y. 546; Eldridge v. Smith, 34 Vt. 484.

[2] Flower v. London, etc., R. Co., 2 Dr. & Sm. 330; Great Western R. Co. v. May, L. R. 7 H. L. 283; Eversfield v. Mid Sussex R. Co., 3 De G. & J. 286.

[3] Columbus, etc., R. Co. v. Witherow, 82 Ala. 190.

[4] Lakenan v. Hannibal, etc., R. Co., 36 Mo. App. 363. And an injunction will be granted to prevent the closing of a private right of way under the railroad track reserved by the landowner at the time of the conveyance of the railroad right of way, by which communication between two parts of the same farm are established. Rock Island, etc., R. Co. v. Dimick, 55 Am. & Eng. R. Cas. 65. See, also, Lake Erie, etc., R. Co. v. Young, 135 Ind. 426, s. c. 58 Am. & Eng. R. Cas. 665.

[5] Rock Island, etc., R. Co. v. Dimick, 144 Ill. 628.

public highway, and operating its road therein without authority, upon proof of special damage,[1] at least where he owns the fee to the center of the street.[2] Indeed, where his easement of access will be destroyed, we think he is entitled to pursue this remedy whether he owns the fee or not.[3] The fact that the

[1] Hart v. Buckner, 54 Fed. R. 925; Ward v. Ohio River R. Co., 35 W. Va. 481; Georgia, etc., R. Co. v. Ray, 84 Ga. 376, 43 Am. & Eng. R. Cas. 95; Riedinger v. Marquette, etc., R. Co., 62 Mich. 29; Kavanagh v. Mobile, etc., R. Co., 78 Ga. 271; Metropolitan City R. Co. v. City of Chicago, 96 Ill. 620; State v. Dayton, etc., R. Co., 36 Ohio St. 434; Barker v. Hartman Steel Co., 129 Pa. St. 551; Columbus, etc., R. Co. v. Witherow, 82 Ala. 190; Bell v. Edwards, 37 La. Ann. 475; Cornwall v. Louisville, etc., R. Co., 87 Ky. 72; Charles H. Heer, etc., Co. v. Citizens' R. Co., 41 Mo. App. 63; Story v. New York El. R. Co., 90 N. Y. 122; Conner v. Covington, etc., R. Co., (Ky.) 19 S. W. R. 597. Where a railroad has been laid in a street by authority of the legislature, an injured party who has a complete remedy by way of damages for any direct injury will not be granted an injunction. Hyland v. Short Route R. Transfer Co., (Ky.) 10 Ky. L. R. 900, 11 S. W. R. 79. But see Georgia, etc., R. Co. v. Ray, 84 Ga. 376, 43 Am. & Eng. R. Cas. 95. Where a company is authorized to construct and operate a railroad track in a street, a court can not restrict the number of trains to be operated as a condition precedent to the construction of the road. Kentucky & I. Bridge Co. v. Krieger, 93 Ky. 243, 19 S. W. R. 738. In Colorado an abutter whose fee is not sought to be taken can not enjoin the construction and operation of a railroad merely because he does not receive in advance compensation for the damage suffered or to be suffered by him. Denver & S. F. R. Co. v. Domke, 11 Colo. 247, 17 Pac. R. 777. In West Virginia the abutting owners on a street, part of which is occupied by a railroad, whether they own the fee in the land covered by the street or not, are not entitled to enjoin excavation and construction along the street in a careful and proper manner, unless the consequent injury to them will be such as will entirely destroy the value of their property, and therefore be equivalent to a virtual taking of it by the railroad company. Arbenz v. Wheeling & H. R. Co., 33 W. Va. 1, 40 Am. & Eng. R. Cas. 284. See Paquet v. Mt. Tabor St. R. Co., 18 Ore. 233; Van Horn v. Newark, etc., R. Co., 48 N. J. Eq. 332, 21 Atl. R. 1034.

[2] Where the fee is in the municipality some authorities hold that an abutting owner has only an action at law for his damages. Mills v. Parlin, 106 Ill. 60; Osborne v. Missouri Pac. R. Co., 147 U. S. 248. It has also been held that the fact that the street has been declared vacated by an invalid ordinance gives an abutting owner no right to an injunction, since the ordinance, being invalid, does not operate to revest the title to the street in the abutting owners. Corcoran v. Chicago, etc., R. Co., 149 Ill. 291, 37 N. E. R. 68.

[3] See Elliott on Roads and Streets, 526–529, 536; Railroads as Additional Servitude to Streets, 1 Am. & Eng. R. Cas. (N. S.) 1; Lockwood v. Wabash R. Co., 122 Mo. 86, s. c. 1 Am. & Eng. R. Cas. (N. S.) 16, and note; Dooly Block v. Salt Lake, etc., Co., 9 Utah

time allowed by the charter in which to build the road has expired has been held sufficient to show that the building of the road is illegal and unauthorized.[1] It is held in some states that even where the consent of the legislature and of the municipal authorities has been obtained the abutting owner may enjoin the construction or operation of the railroad until his damages are assessed and paid.[2] Where the right to lay a railroad track in a street is prohibited, until the damage is ascertained and paid to abutting owners, it has been held that the company may be enjoined from operation of the road until payment of the damages, although a prior judgment for the damages has been obtained in an action at law, but remains unpaid.[3] But the right to an injunction for this cause may be lost by the abutting owner's acquiescence in the construction of the road,[4] or in its use for a length of time after construction.[5] The public may enjoin an unauthorized use of a public street or other

---

31, s. c. 33 Pac. R. 229, 8 Lewis' Am. R. & Corp. R. 327; Abendroth v. Manhattan R. Co., 122 N. Y. 1; Field v. Barling, 149 Ill. 556, s. c. 41 Am. St. R. 311, and note; 2 Dillon Munic. Corp. (4th ed.), §§ 704, 704 a, 726, 923 c; 1 Hare Const. L. 370, 375; Theobold v. Louisville, etc., R. Co., 66 Miss. 279, s. c. 6 So. R. 230, 14 Am. St. R. 564; Adams v. Chicago, etc., R. Co., 39 Minn. 286, s. c. 12 Am. St. R. 644; White v. Northwestern, etc., R. Co., 113 N. Car. 610, s. c. 22 L. R. A. 627.

[1] Bonaparte v. Baltimore, etc., R. Co., 75 Md. 340, 49 Am. & Eng. R. Cas. 198.

[2] Cox v. Louisville, etc., R. Co., 48 Ind. 178; Georgia, etc., R. Co. v. Ray, 84 Ga. 376; Barber v. Saginaw Union R. Co., 83 Mich. 299; Pennsylvania R. Co. v. Angel, 41 N. J. Eq. 316; Imlay v. Union Branch R. Co., 26 Conn. 249; Wager v. Troy, etc., R. Co., 25 N. Y. 526; Stroub v. Manhattan R. Co., 15 N. Y. Supp. 135. See Appeal of Kemble, 140 Pa. 14, 21 Atl. R. 225.

Contra, Paquet v. Mt. Tabor St. R. Co., 18 Ore. 233; Ohio River R. Co. v. Gibbens, 35 W. Va. 57, 12 S. E. R. 1093; O'Brien v. Baltimore Belt R. Co., 74 Md. 363, 22 Atl. R. 141; Randall v. Jacksonville St. R. Co., 19 Fla. 409. See Western R. Co. v. Alabama, etc., R. Co., 96 Ala. 272. Abutting owners will not be granted an injunction against a railroad company to prevent its entering into a contract with the county commissioners whereby it is permitted to maintain its tracks in a street at a grade alleged to be illegal; the proper remedy is mandamus requiring the county commissioners to perform their duties under the law. Dyer v. Cincinnati, P. & V. Ry. Co., 7 Ohio Cir. Ct. R. 255.

[3] Harbach v. Des Moines, etc., R. Co., 80 Iowa 593.

[4] Merchants', etc., Co. v. Chicago, etc., R. Co., 79 Iowa 613; Burkam v. Ohio, etc., R. Co., 122 Ind. 344.

[5] Merchants', etc., Co. v. Chicago, etc., R. Co., 79 Iowa 613.

highway by an action on behalf of the state in the name of the attorney-general or other proper officer,[1] or the suit for an injunction may be maintained in the name of the town or city,[2] or other municipality to which the state has confided the care and control of such highway.[3]

§ 631. **Enjoining a nuisance.**—An injunction may generally be had at the suit of the state to restrain unauthorized acts by which the public has been or will be injured.[4] As a public nuisance is a criminal offense which may be reached by indictment or information in the ordinary course of a prosecution for crime, it has been doubted whether an injunction will lie to restrain it at the suit of the state, or its proper representative. But the jurisdiction of equity in such cases is well established in England, as is shown by the authorities already cited, and we think the authorities, both in that country and in this, justify us in stating that the proper public officer may, in a proper case, by a suit in the name of the state, enjoin a railroad company from maintaining a public nuisance.[5] This is cer-

---

[1] Attorney-General v. Delaware, etc., R. Co., 27 N. J. Eq. 631; Attorney-General v. Metropolitan R. Co., 125 Mass. 515; Commonwealth v. Railroad Co., 24 Pa. St. 159.

[2] Rio Grande R. Co. v. Brownsville, 45 Tex. 88; Philadelphia v. Friday, 6 Phila. 275; Philadelphia v. Railway Co., 8 Phila. 648; Greenwich v. Easton, etc., R. Co., 24 N. J. Eq. 217; Springfield v. Connecticut River R. Co., 4 Cush. (Mass.) 63. And a removal of tracks already laid may be compelled by a company which afterward obtains authority to lay its tracks in the street, although the first company improved and reclaimed the street. Galveston Wharf Co. v. Gulf, etc., R. Co., 81 Tex. 494. Unless expressly authorized, a railroad company is not presumed to have the right to condemn and appropriate to its use land already dedicated to the public for streets; and either the municipal corporation or the owner of the fee may enjoin such use. Cornwall v. Louisville & N. R. Co., 87 Ky. 72.

[3] Commissioners v. Long, 1 Pars. Eq. Cas. (Pa.) 143. Appeal of Township of North Manheim, (Pa.) 14 Atl. R. 137, 36 Am. & Eng. R. Cas. 194.

[4] Attorney-General v. Chicago, etc., Railroad Co., 35 Wis. 425; Stockton v. Central, etc., Co., 50 N. J. Eq. 52, 17 L. R. A. 97; Ware v. Regent's Canal Co., 3 De Gex & J. 212; Attorney-General v. Great Northern Ry. Co., 4 De Gex & S. 75; Taylor v. Salmon, 4 Mylne & C. 134, 141; Brice's *Ultra Vires*, 506-509. See United States v. Union Pac. R. Co., 98 U. S. 569.

[5] District Attorney v. Lynn, etc., R. Co., 16 Gray (Mass.) 242; People v. Sturtevant, 9 N.Y. 263; Attorney-General v. Chicago, etc., Railroad Co., 35

tainly true where the relief sought is not merely to prevent the commission of a crime, but to prevent the abuse of corporate powers and privileges to the injury of the public. A prosecution for the crime or a suit to dissolve the corporation or forfeit its charter will not afford adequate relief in such a case, because, in the meantime, the corporation, unless restrained by the courts, may persist in its course of crime and its abuse of corporate privileges. An injunction is, therefore, necessary to accomplish complete justice and prevent continued injury to the public. So, of course, injunction will lie, in a proper case, at the suit of an individual who is specially injured by a public nuisance.[1] But where no nuisance yet exists and it is merely claimed that injury will arise from the use to which property is proposed to be devoted, and not from the character of the property or structure, an injunction will not be awarded if the structure and the use to which it is to be put are authorized and lawful in themselves and the apprehended injury is merely contingent or uncertain.[2] Indeed, we think it may be safely affirmed that where a structure, such as a coal chute, a

Wis. 425; Georgetown v. Alexandria Canal Co., 12 Pet. (U. S.) 91; People's Gas Co. v. Tyner, 131 Ind. 277, 283, s. c. 31 N. E. R. 59; State v. Saline Co., 51 Mo. 350; Carleton v. Rugg, 149 Mass. 550, s. c. 22 N. E. R. 55; State v. Crawford, 28 Kan. 726; Mayor v. Jacques, 30 Ga. 506; People v. City of St.Louis,5 Gil.(Ill.)351, 357; Attorney-General v. Hunter, 1 Dev. Eq. (N. Car.) 12; State v. Saunders, (N. H.) 18 L. R. A. 646; Littleton v. Fritz, 65 Iowa 488, s. c. 54 Am. R. 19; Columbian Athletic Club v. State, 143 Ind. 98, 40 N. E. R. 914. In the last case just cited it was held, after a careful review of many of the authorities, that injunction would lie and that a receiver might also be appointed in aid of the injunction.

[1] Elliott on Roads and Streets 496, et seq.; Pennsylvania R. Co. v. Angel, 41 N. J. Eq. 316, s. c. 56 Am. R. 1; Cogswell v. New York, etc., R. Co., 103 N. Y. 10; note to South Carolina, etc., Co. v. South Carolina R. Co., 4 L. R. A. 209; Wylie v. Elwood, 134 Ill. 281, s. c. 23 Am. St. R. 673, and note Field v. Barling, 149 Ill. 556, 37 N. E. R. 850; Innis v. Cedar Rapids, etc., R. Co., 76 Iowa 165; Gold v. Philadelphia, 115 Pa. St. 184.

[2] Rouse v. Martin, 75 Ala. 510, s. c. 51 Am. R. 463; Duncan v. Hayes, 22 N. J. Eq. 25; Rhodes v. Dunbar, 57 Pa. St. 274, s. c. 98 Am. Dec. 221; Powell v. Macon,etc., R.Co.,92 Ga. 209, 17 S. E. R. 1027; Keiser v. Lovett, 85 Ind. 240; Pfingst v. Senn, 94 Ky. 556, 23 S. W. R. 358; Dumesnil v. Dupont, 18 B. Mon. (Ky.) 800, s. c. 68 Am. Dec. 750; Earl of Ripon v. Hobart, 1 Cooper (Temp. Brougham) 333; 1 High Inj., §§ 743, 788; 2 Wood on Nuisances (3d ed.), §§796, 797.

water-tank, or the like, essential to the operation of the railroad, is properly constructed, the remedy of an individual inconvenienced by its use, if any he has, must, ordinarily, be an action for damages.[1] And even this remedy is not open to him where the structure is properly constructed in a proper place and the inconvenience is such only as necessarily results from its authorized use.[2]

§ 632. Injunction at suit of the company.—A railroad company may have an injunction, in a proper case, to protect its rights from a threatened invasion. It may enjoin an interference with its roadbed by piling obstructions thereon,[3] or by tearing up its track or placing obstacles in the way of constructing its road upon a proposed route which it has located according to law.[4] If the former owner wrongfully threatens to resist the occupancy by the railroad company of lands which it has acquired by regular condemnation proceedings, he may be re-

[1] See Gilbert v. Showerman, 23 Mich. 448; Owen v. Phillips, 73 Ind. 284; Barnard v. Sherley, 135 Ind. 547, 558, and authorities there cited; Robb v. Carnegie Bros. & Co., 145 Pa. St. 324, s. c. 14 L. R. A. 329; Huckenstine's Appeal, 70 Pa. St. 102; Goodall v. Crofton, 33 Ohio St. 271, s. c. 31 Am. R. 535. Of course we do not mean to say that an individual who is specially injured may not have an injunction, in a proper case, where this remedy at law is inadequate, against a nuisance caused by the use of a thing as well as against the thing itself. See note 1, *supra*, p. 903.

[2] Dunsmore v. Central, etc. R. Co., 72 Iowa 182, s. c. 33 N. W. R. 456; Pennsylvania Co. v. Lippincott, 116 Pa. St. 472; Pennsylvania Co. v. Marchant, 119 Pa. St. 541; Barnard v. Sherley, 135 Ind. 547, 553, s. c. 34 N. E. R. 600; Booth v. Rome, etc., R. Co., 140 N. Y. 267, s. c. 35 N. E. R. 592 (railroad company held not liable for incidental injury caused by blasting on its own land a place to lay its tracks); Randle v. Pacific, etc., Co., 65 Mo. 325; Parrott v. Cincinnati, etc., Railway Co., 10 Ohio St. 624; Cosby v. Owensboro, etc., Railway Co., 10 Bush (Ky.) 288.

[3] Henderson v. Ogden City R. Co., 7 Utah 199, 26 Pac. R. 286. But it has been held that a preliminary injunction will not be granted to restrain the erection of buildings on land claimed by the railroad company as its right of way, where it appears that the defendant also claims title to the land. Delaware, etc., R. Co. v. Newton, etc., Co., 137 Pa. St. 314.

[4] Rochester, etc., R. Co. v. New York, etc., R. Co., 110 N. Y. 128; Easton, etc., Ry. Co. v. Easton, 133 Pa. St. 505 (city enjoined); Asheville St. Ry. Co. v. City of Asheville, 109 N. Car. 688, s. c. 14 S. E. R. 316 (chief of police enjoined from tearing up track). See, also, Millville, etc., Co, v. Goodwin, (N. J.) 32 Atl. R. 263.

§ 632   ACTIONS BY AND AGAINST CORPORATIONS.   905

strained by injunction.[1] So, where a riparian proprietor had conveyed to a railroad company a right of way, with "such exclusive interest and estate in said strip of land" as the company could have acquired by condemnation under the statute, it was held that a subsequent grantee of the fee from such original proprietor had no right to construct along the river bank, and upon such right of way, a levee which would raise the water flowing in the stream at times of ordinary flood, although in some places beyond the low-water banks, so as to endanger the bridge, trestlework and track of the railroad, and that the company was entitled to have the same enjoined.[2] While there is conflict among the decisions upon the question as to what constitutes surface water, the authorities cited by the court fully sustain the ruling upon that branch of the case, and, as the railroad company had not only a dominant estate, to which that of the defendant was servient,[3] but also had the right, at least as against the defendant, to the exclusive possession and control of the land within its right of way or location, for railroad purposes,[4] it seems clear that the construction of the levee, as proposed, would have been a very material invasion of the plaintiff's rights, and that the decision of the court was undoubtedly sound. The grantees of land who purchased it with knowledge that a railroad company had laid

---

[1] Montgomery R. Co. v. Walton, 14 Ala. 207. Any interference with the easement of the company by the owner of the fee may be enjoined. Chance v. East Texas R. Co., 63 Tex. 152.

[2] Cairo, etc., Ry. Co. v. Brevoort, 62 Fed. R. 129. The river referred to in this case is a navigable river forming the boundary between two states, and the court also held that the question involved was not, therefore, a local question, but was one depending on the general principles of law, so that the decisions of the courts of one of the states were not binding on the federal court.

[3] Davidson v. Nicholson, 59 Ind. 411; Robinson v. Thrailkill, 110 Ind. 117, s. c. 10 N. E. R. 647; Herman v. Roberts, 119 N. Y. 37, s. c. 7 L. R. A. 226; Hayden v. Skillings, 78 Me. 413, 6 Atl. R. 830.

[4] Jackson v. Rutland, etc., R. Co., 25 Vt. 150; Brainard v. Clapp, 10 Cush. (Mass.) 6; Proprietors, etc., v. Nashua, etc., R. Co., 104 Mass. 1; Hayden v. Skillings, 78 Me. 413, 6 Atl. R. 830; St. Louis, etc., R. Co. v. Clark, 119 Mo. 357, 25 S. W. R. 192; Chicago, etc., R. Co. v. McGrew, 104 Mo. 282, 297; Shelby v. Chicago, etc., R. Co., 143 Ill. 385, 32 N. E. R. 438; Atlantic, etc., Tel. Co. v. Chicago, etc., R. Co., 6 Biss. 158.

pipes across it from a certain spring to a tank, under a contract with a former owner of the land, may be enjoined from interfering with such pipes; and the fact that the tank is not located in the exact place specified in the contract is immaterial, where the change does not affect the position of the pipes, which, owing to the topography of the country, are necessarily laid just where they are.[1] A railroad company may enjoin another company having a right of way across its land from interfering with its use of its own property as a freight yard as permitted by the contract granting the easement even though some uncertain damages would result to the grantee company from such use because of its interference with the grantee's use of its tracks.[2] So, a street railway company which has laid its track in a street under a grant from a city may enjoin another company, to which the city afterward grants similar rights, from tearing up the plaintiff's track or placing its own track over that of the plaintiff in derogation of the latter's rights.[3] A threatened invasion of an exclusive right granted to a street railway company to build a road over the lands of a railroad company to its depot may also be enjoined.[4] Where a shipper threatened to bring a great number of separate actions for damages against a railroad company for the

---

[1] Diffendal v. Virginia Midland R. Co., 86 Va. 459.

[2] Chicago, etc., R. Co. v. Lake Shore, etc., R. Co., 30 Ill. App. 129.

[3] See Hamilton St. R., etc., Co. v. Hamilton, etc., Co., 5 Ohio Cir. Ct. R. 319; Kansas City, etc., Ry. Co. v. Kansas City, etc., Ry. Co., 129 Mo. 62, s. c. 31 S. W. R. 451; Indianapolis Cable St. Ry. Co. v. Citizens' St. Ry. Co., 127 Ind. 369, s. c. 24 N. E. R. 1054, and 26 N. E. R. 893; Citizens' Coach Co. v. Camden, etc., R. Co., 33 N. J. Eq. 267. See, generally, as to joint use of streets and tracks, Booth on Street Railways, Ch. V.; Elliott on Roads and Streets 566, *et seq.* Where the grant to use a street is not exclusive—and the rule against monopolies will generally prevent an exclusive grant—the company can not enjoin another company from using another portion of the street under a subsequent grant. Pennsylvania, etc., R. Co. v. Philadelphia, etc., R. Co., 157 Pa. St. 42, s. c. 56 Am. & Eng. R. Cas. 610. See, also, West Jersey R. Co. v. Camden, etc., R. Co., 52 N. J. Eq. 31, 29 Atl. R. 423, s. c. 2 Am. L. Reg. & Rev. (N. S.) 38, and note; Chicago, etc., R. Co. v. Whiting, etc., R. Co., 139 Ind. 297, s. c. 38 N. E. R. 604 (holding that injunction would not lie to restrain a street railway company from crossing a steam railroad company's tracks in a street).

[4] Fort Worth St. R. Co. v. Queen City R. Co., 71 Tex. 165.

separate cars as to which he alleged he was entitled to recover under the state law prohibiting a charge for carriage above a certain rate, it was held that he could be enjoined from suing separately for the overcharge on each car.[1] An injunction may also be granted to prevent a railroad company from violating its contract by which it has agreed to stop trains within a certain distance of the other company's road, and not to cross until signaled to do so by the flagman.[2] Where it is shown that the extension of a city street so as to cross the tracks and yards or depot grounds of a railroad company would render them useless to the railroad company, or, in other words, where the two public uses can not co-exist, the city may be enjoined, in the absence of an express statute conferring the right, from so extending the street.[3] Until a railroad company has complied with the requirements of the statute giving it authority to cross another railroad, it has no right to enter upon that company's premises to build its road,[4] and an injunction may be granted to restrain it from so doing.[5] An injunction will

[1] Texas, etc., R. Co. v. Kuteman, 54 Fed. R. 547. As to when an injunction may be granted to restrain the bringing of a multiplicity of suits, and the plaintiffs compelled to submit to the jurisdiction of a court of equity, see Tribette v. Illinois Central R. Co., 70 Miss. 182; Western Union Tel. Co. v. Poe, 61 Fed. R. 449; Lake Erie, etc., R. Co. v. Young, 135 Ind. 426, 35 N. E. R. 177; Carney v. Hadley, 32 Fla. 344. It has been held that the federal courts have no jurisdiction to restrain by injunction a criminal prosecution by a state under an unconstitutional law of such state. Minneapolis, etc., R. Co. v. Milner, 57 Fed. R. 276.

[2] Cornwall, etc., R. Co.'s Appeal, 125 Pa. St. 232.

[3] Cincinnati, etc., R. Co. v. City of Anderson, 139 Ind. 490, s. c. 38 N. E. R. 167; City of Fort Wayne v. Lake Shore, etc., R. Co., 132 Ind. 558, s. c. 32 N. E. R. 215; Baltimore, etc., R. Co. v. North, 103 Ind. 486; Winona, etc., R. Co. v. City of Watertown, 4 S. Dak. 323, 56 N. W. R. 1077; New Jersey, etc., R. Co. v. Long Branch, 39 N. J. L. 28; Milwaukee, etc., R. Co. v. City of Faribault, 23 Minn. 167; Prospect Park, etc., Co. v. Williamson, 91 N. Y. 552; Housatonic R. Co. v. Lee, etc., R. Co., 118 Mass. 391; Elliott on Roads and Streets 167, 168. But see Illinois Cent. R. Co. v. Chicago, 141 Ill. 586, s. c. 30 N. E. R. 1044; Little Miami, etc., R. Co. v. Dayton, 23 Ohio St. 510; Detroit, etc., R. Co. v. Detroit, 91 Mich. 444, s. c. 52 N. W. R. 52.

[4] Lake Shore, etc., R. Co. v. Cincinnati, etc., R. Co., 116 Ind. 578.

[5] Northern Pac. R. Co. v. St. Paul, etc., R. Co., 1 McCrary (U. S.) 302; 3 Fed. R. 702; Pennsylvania R. Co. v.

not lie, however, for a naked trespass without irreparable injury, and upon this ground it has been held that it will not lie where one railroad company enters upon the roadbed of another and constructs its tracks without first making compensation as required by law,[1] and the same court has held that where two street railway companies are operating their respective roads under legal authority, their roads crossing each other at the intersection of two streets, the mere fact that one of them is proceeding to lay a double track at the crossing will not entitle the other to an injunction, where no irreparable injury is shown and the company is solvent and able to respond in damages.[2] But the general rule is that injunction will lie where compensation is not paid or tendered,[3] and it seems to us that an entry under claim and color of right, which may ripen into a title, is not a mere fugitive trespass that can cause no irreparable injury.[4]

§ 633. Enjoining "strikers."—The great strike of the members of the American Railway Union in 1894, and other strikes about the same time, gave rise to a number of decisions in which old principles were applied to a comparatively new state of facts by the courts of equity, thus illustrating the rule that equity will keep pace with the needs of society and accommodate its methods of procedure to the development of the public interests by applying its remedies to the varying demands for

---

Consolidation Coal Co., 55 Md. 158. But in cases where the interests of the public demand it the injunction may be dissolved upon the filing of a bond to pay damages and costs adjudged against it in the condemnation proceedings by which it is authorized to acquire title. Northern Pac. R. Co. v. St. Paul, etc., R. Co, 2 McCrary (U. S.) 260, 4 Fed. R. 688.

[1] Mobile, etc., R. Co. v. Alabama, etc., R. Co., 87 Ala. 520, s. c. 6 So. R. 407, and cases cited.

[2] Highland Ave., etc., R. Co. v. Birmingham Union R. Co., 93 Ala. 505. See, also, Chicago, etc., R. Co. v. Illinois, etc., R. Co., 113 Ill. 156; Pennsylvania R. Co. v. National Docks, etc., R. Co., 56 Fed. R. 697.

[3] Evans v. Missouri, etc., R. Co., 64 Mo. 453; Gardner v. Newburgh, 2 Johns Ch. (N. Y.) 162; Georgia Midland, etc., R. Co. v. Columbus, etc., R. Co., 89 Ga. 205, s. c. 15 S. E. R. 305, 51 Am. & Eng. R. R. Cas. 538; High on Inj., § 391; Elliott on Roads and Streets, 185; ante, § 629.

[4] See Webb v. Portland, etc., Co., 3 Sumner (U. S.) 189.

§ 633   ACTIONS BY AND AGAINST CORPORATIONS.   909

equitable relief.¹ It has been said that there is no such thing as a peaceable and lawful strike,² but a United States court of appeals has taken a different view, holding that a strike is not unlawful if it is merely a combination of employes to withdraw from the service of their employer for the purpose of accomplishing some lawful purpose.³ Combinations of workmen for their common benefit, to develop skill in their trade, to prevent the overcrowding thereof, to obtain better wages than they might be able to obtain individually, and to accumulate a fund for these purposes, are not necessarily unlawful. Nor, as a general rule, is it unlawful—except in so far as it involves a breach of contract, for which an injunction will seldom, if ever, be granted—for a man to quit the service of his employer and bestow his labor where he will.⁴ But where employes endeavor to enforce their demands by forcibly preventing others from working in their places, or by destroying property or preventing its use, a court of equity has power to enjoin them and may enforce its order by punishing the violators for contempt. Conspiracies to obstruct or interfere with the business and management of railroad companies, especially when the carriage of mail is obstructed, by threats, intimidation and violence, have often been enjoined as a violation of the interstate commerce law,⁵ and also as constituting

¹ See Toledo, etc., R. Co. v. Pennsylvania Co., 54 Fed. R. 746; Southern Cal. R. Co. v. Rutherford, 62 Fed. R. 796; Joy v. St. Louis, 138 U. S. 1, 50, s. c. 11 Sup. Ct. R. 243.

² See Farmers' Loan & T. Co. v. Northern Pac. R. Co., 60 Fed. R. 803; The Legal Side of the Strike Question, 33 Am. L. Reg. (N. S. 1894) 609, 614.

³ Arthur v. Oakes, 63 Fed. R. 310, s. c. 25 L. R. A. 414. See, also, Longshore, etc., Co. v. Howell, 26 Ore. 527, s. c. 28 L. R. A. 464, and note.

⁴ See Longshore, etc., Co. v. Howell, 26 Ore. 527, s. c. 28 L. R. A. 464; Carew v. Rutherford, 106 Mass. 1, s. c. 8 Am. R. 287; Reynolds v. Everett, 144 N. Y. 189, s. c. 39 N. E. R. 72 (not unlawful to use persuasion to induce others to leave); Arthur v. Oakes, 63 Fed. R. 310; Bohn Mfg. Co. v. Hollis, 54 Minn. 223, s. c. 21 L. R. A. 337.

⁵ United States v. Debs, 64 Fed. R. 724; Toledo, etc., R. Co. v. Pennsylvania Co., 54 Fed. R. 746, s. c. 19 L. R. A. 395; Southern Cal. R. Co. v. Rutherford, 62 Fed. R. 796; United States v. Agler, 62 Fed. R. 824; United States v. Elliott, 62 Fed. R. 801; United States v. Workingmen's Amalgamated Council, 54 Fed. R. 994, affirmed in Workingmen's, etc., Council v. United States, 57 Fed. R. 85; Waterhouse v. Comer, 55 Fed. R. 149, s. c. 19 L. R. A. 403.

an obstruction of the highways of interstate commerce.[1] But these are not the only grounds upon which strikers may be enjoined. An injunction may be granted at the suit of a railroad company upon the ground of irreparable injury and in order to prevent a multiplicity of actions.[2] So, in a proper case, the court may even grant a mandatory injunction. Thus, where the chief officer of the Brotherhood of Locomotive Engineers had issued an order requiring the members thereof who were in the employ of certain railroad companies to refuse to handle and deliver cars or freight in course of transportation from one state to another, the court granted a mandatory injunction compelling him to rescind it.[3] As we have already stated, and as most of the authorities we have cited hold, the violation of an injunction against strikers may be punished as a contempt. It has been held that an injunction against strikers who are named as defendants and all others who aid and abet them is binding not only upon all who are served although they are not made parties to the suit,[4] but also upon others of the class designated who have notice of the injunction, although they are not served with a copy of the order.[5] It is also well

---

[1] *In re* Debs, 158 U. S. 564, s. c. 15 Sup. Ct. R. 900.

[2] "The Legal Side of the Strike Question," 33 Am. L. Reg. (N. S. 1894) 609; Blindell v. Hagan, 54 Fed. R. 40, affirmed in Hagan v. Blindell, 56 Fed. R. 696; Cœur D'Alene, etc., Co. v. Miners' Union, 51 Fed. R. 260; Lake Erie, etc., R. Co. v. Bailey, 61 Fed. R. 494; Wick China Co. v. Brown, 164 Pa. St. 449; Murdock v. Walker, 152 Pa. St. 595; Sherry v. Perkins, 147 Mass. 212, s. c. 17 N. E. R. 307.

[3] Toledo, etc., R. Co. v. Pennsylvania Co., 54 Fed. R. 730, s. c. 19 L. R. A. 387. See, also, Chicago, etc., R. Co. v. Burlington, etc., R. Co., 34 Fed. R. 481; Coe v. Louisville, etc., R. Co., 3 Fed. R. 775; High on Inj., § 2; Toledo, etc., R. Co. v. Pennsylvania Co., 54 Fed. R. 746, s. c. 19 L. R. A. 395; Beadel v. Perry, 3 L. R. Eq. 465; Broome v. New York, etc., Co., 42 N. J. Eq. 141, s. c. 7 Atl. R. 851.

[4] Toledo, etc., R. Co. v. Pennsylvania Co., 54 Fed. R. 746; United States v. Agler, 62 Fed. R. 824. See, also, United States v. Elliott, 64 Fed. R. 27.

[5] *Ex parte* Lennon, 64 Fed. R. 320, affirmed in *In re* Lennon, 150 U. S. 393; Rapalje on Contempt, 46; Ewing v. Johnson, 34 How. Pr. (N. Y.) 202; Waffle v. Vanderheyden, 8 Paige (N. Y.) 45. See, also, United States v. Debs, 64 Fed. R. 724; 2 Beach Mod. Eq., § 894.

settled that any unlawful interference with a railroad in the hands of a receiver is punishable as a contempt.[1]

§ 634. **Injunction at suit of stockholders.**—A stockholder may enjoin the corporation and those in control of it from acts by which a forfeiture of the charter will be incurred, or from other acts amounting to a breach of the trust reposed in them by the stockholders.[2] He may enjoin the making of material and fundamental changes in the original contract of association,[3] the diversion of corporate funds to purposes not authorized by the charter and outside of the objects for which the corporation was organized,[4] and *ultra vires* acts generally, such as unauthorized consolidations, leases, or the like.[5] He may prevent the payment of dividends where no money has in fact been earned from which to pay them,[6] or where losses have consumed the surplus earnings set apart to pay them,[7] or

---

[1] Thomas v. Cincinnati, etc., R. Co., 62 Fed. R. 803; United States v. Debs, 64 Fed. R. 724; Secor v. Toledo, etc., R. Co., 7 Biss. (U. S. C. C.) 513; *In re* Higgins, 27 Fed. R. 443; United States v. Kane, 23 Fed. R. 748; Frank v. Denver, etc., R. Co., 23 Fed. R. 757. See, also, Arthur v. Oakes, 63 Fed. R. 310; *In re* Acker, 66 Fed. R. 290.

[2] Wilcox v. Bickel, 11 Neb. 154; Bagshaw v. Eastern, etc., R. Co., 7 Hare 114; Gamble v. Queens County, etc., Co., 123 N. Y. 91, s. c. 25 N. E. R. 201; Pond v. Vermont Valley R. Co., 12 Blatchf. (U. S.) 280; March v. Eastern R. Co., 40 N. H. 548, s. c. 77 Am. Dec. 732. But in order to warrant such interference there must be a gross abuse of its powers, which will result in injury to the complainant, or the acts complained of must be clearly in excess thereof. Union Pac., etc., R. Co. v. Lincoln County, 3 Dill. (U. S.) 300; Jones v. Mayor, etc., of Little Rock, 25 Ark. 301.

[3] Zabriskie v. Hackensack, etc., R. Co., 18 N. J. Eq. 178, s. c. 90 Am. Dec. 617; Stevens v. Rutland, etc., R. Co., 29 Va. 545; 4 Thomp. Corp., § 4517.

[4] Marseilles Land Co. v. Aldrich, 86 Ill. 504; Kean v. Johnson, 9 N. J. Eq. 401; Baltimore, etc., R. Co. v. Wheeling, 13 Gratt. (Va.) 40; Dodge v. Woolsey, 18 How. (U. S.) 331; Central R. Co. v. Collins, 40 Ga. 582; Cherokee, etc., Co. v. Jones, 52 Ga. 276.

[5] Young v. Rondout, etc., Co., 15 N. Y. Supp. 443; Botts v. Simpsonville, etc., Co., 88 Ky. 54, s. c. 10 S. W. R. 134, 2 L. R. A. 594; Small v. Minneapolis, etc., Co., 45 Minn. 264, s. c. 47 N. W. R. 797; see *ante*, §§ 376, 328.

[6] Painesville, etc., R. Co. v. King, 17 Ohio St. 534; Carpenter v. New York, etc., R. Co., 5 Abb. Pr. (N. Y.) 277; Burnes v. Pennell, 2 H. L. Cas. 497; *ante*, § 317.

[7] Fawcett v. Laurie, 1 Dr. & Sm. 192. Where a specific fund has been set apart to pay dividends, and money belonging to other funds is lost the dividends must be paid. LeRoy v. Globe Ins. Co., 2 Edw. Ch. (N. Y.) 657.

where the stock upon which dividends are claimed is spurious.[1] He may also restrain the holding of a corporate election, if great and irreparable injury to him would result therefrom,[2] and the illegal voting of shares in furtherance of a conspiracy to get control of the corporation,[3] or the illegal forfeiture of his own shares.[4] So, a stockholder of a railroad company which has located and partially constructed its lines may maintain a bill to enjoin a rival company from appropriating the partially completed work to its own use, through the collusion of the directors of his own company.[5] But a court of equity will not interfere by injunction to control the discretion of the officers in matters which come fairly within their powers, where the contemplated acts do not amount to a breach of trust but it appears that the real ground of complaint is a difference of opinion as to what the interests of the corporation require.[6] And the alleged invalidity of their title has been held not to be sufficient ground for restraining *de facto* directors from acting as such.[7] The interest of the stockholder does not extend to the acts of third persons with reference to the corporate property, and a stockholder is not entitled to an injunction to restrain slander of the title of property belonging to the corporation.[8] And even where a stockholder might have been entitled to an injunction if he had acted in time or if he had not taken part or acquiesced in the act of which he complains, his acquiescence or laches may estop him from afterwards maintaining the suit.

[1] Underwood v. New York, etc., R. Co., 17 How. Pr. (N. Y.) 537.

[2] Walker v. Devereaux, 4 Paige (N. Y.) 229; Webb v. Ridgely, 38 Md. 364; Wright v. Bundy, 11 Ind. 404; Hilles v. Parrish, 14 N. J. Eq. 380.

[3] Moses v. Tompkins, 84 Ala. 613, s. c. 4 So. R. 763; Memphis, etc., R. Co. v. Woods, 88 Ala. 630, s. c. 16 Am. St. R. 81.

[4] Moore v. New Jersey, etc., Co., 5 N. Y. Supp. 192; Moses v. Tompkins, 84 Ala. 613, s. c. 4 So. R. 763.

[5] Weidenfeld v. Sugar Run R. Co., 48 Fed. Rep. 615, 51 Am. & Eng. R. Cas. 505.

[6] Ellerman v. Chicago Junction R., etc., Co., 49 N. J. Eq. 217, s. c. 23 Atl. Rep. 287; Hunter v. Roberts, etc., Co., 83 Mich. 63; McWhorter v. Pensacola, 24 Fla. 417. See, also, Converse v. Hood, 149 Mass. 471, s. c. 21 N. E. R. 878, 4 L. R. A. 521; Woodruff v. Dubuque, etc., R. Co., 30 Fed. R. 91.

[7] Mozley v. Alston, 1 Phill. 790.

[8] Langdon v. Hillside, etc., Co., (C. C. S. D. N. Y.) 41 Fed. Rep. 609.

§ 635. **Mandatory injunctions — English cases.** — Where the prevention of threatened acts by injunction is sought, together with the continuance of certain other acts, a court of equity, having acquired jurisdiction for one purpose, will retain the suit for all purposes of relief, and may compel by mandatory injunction the permanent or continuous performance of affirmative acts, notwithstanding there might be no right to a mandamus.[1] In suits against railroad companies, the English courts of equity have not only enjoined the further commission of acts complained of in the several cases, but have also required the company to do many affirmative acts, such as to construct and maintain at a specific point a first-class depot building,[2] to stop all its trains at a certain station,[3] to build a side track,[4] and to so run its trains as to furnish convenient facilities for passengers and shippers of goods,[5] all this upon the ground that these were common law duties of the railroad company as a common carrier. It is doubtful if the courts of this country would go so far in this direction as some of the English courts.[6]

§ 636. **Rule in the United States—Illustrative cases.**—All the authorities agree, however, that where a specific duty is prescribed by statute and the railroad company not only threatens to perpetrate wrongs for which it may be enjoined, but also at the same time neglects such duty, it may be compelled to perform its duty by mandatory injunction. Acting

---

[1] City of Wheeling v. Mayor, 1 Hughes (U. S.) 90. See, also, Central Trust Co. v. Moran, 56 Minn. 188, s. c. 57 N. W. R. 471; City of Moundsville v. Ohio River R. Co., (W. Va.) 20 L. R. A. 161, and note.

[2] Hood v. North Eastern Co., L. R. 8 Eq. 666. See, also, Railroad Comrs. v. Portland, etc., R. Co., 63 Me. 269.

[3] Earl of Lindsey v. Great Northern R. Co., 10 Hare 664.

[4] Greene v. West C. Co., L. R. 13 Eq. 44.

[5] Great Northern R. Co. v. Manchester R. Co., 5 DeG. & S. 138.

[6] The weight of authority in America is against extending the powers of a court of equity to enforce many duties which are not imposed by the charter or by statute or by necessary implication therefrom upon a railroad company. Northern Pac. R. Co. v. Washington, 142 U. S. 492. But see, as to enforcement of public duties, Rogers, etc., Co. v. Erie, etc., Co., 20 N. J. Eq. 379; American, etc., Co. v. Consolidation Co., 46 Md. 15.

under the authority of particular statutes, courts of equity have by injunction compelled the defendant railroad company to deliver cattle at the plaintiff's stock-yard,[1] to deliver carloads of grain consigned to him upon his private side track without extra charge,[2] to carry for plaintiff on equal terms with others,[3] to restore a stream of water to its natural channel,[4] and to remove a wall which it had unlawfully erected.[5] A railroad company may also be compelled to receive and handle freight delivered to it by a connecting carrier as required by the interstate commerce act,[6] and such an injunction will bind the agents and employes of the company, and takes effect as to them as soon as they are notified thereof without the necessity of making them parties.[7] A railroad company may also seek relief by a mandatory injunction, and where persons were engaged in laying a railroad track upon the line of plaintiff's road so as to obstruct and prevent the operation thereof, an injunction was awarded not only forbidding the further obstruction of plaintiff's track, but also commanding the removal of the track, already laid.[8] So, in many other cases parties have been compelled not only to cease unlawful acts, but also to undo what they had already wrongfully done or to restore the plaintiff to his original situation or condition.[9] Mandatory injunctions, as we

[1] McCoy v. Cincinnati, etc., Railroad, 22 Am. Law Reg. (N. S.) 725.
[2] Vincent v. Chicago, etc., R. Co., 49 Ill. 33.
[3] *In re* Harris, etc., R. Co., 3 C. B. N. S. 693. But see Express Cases, 117 U. S. 1.
[4] Corning v. Troy, etc., Factory, 40 N. Y. 191.
[5] Great North, etc., R. Co. v. Clarence R. Co., 1 Collier 507.
[6] Toledo, etc., R. Co. v. Pennsylvania Co., 54 Fed. R. 730, 746, s. c. 53 Am. & Eng. R. Cas. 293. See, also, Interstate, etc., Com. v. Lehigh Valley R. Co., 49 Fed. R. 177; Chicago, etc., Co. v. Burlington, etc., Co., 34 Fed. R. 481; Chicago, etc., R. Co. v. New York, etc., Co., 24 Fed. R. 516. But, see, Atchison, etc., R. Co. v. Denver, etc., R. Co., 110 U. S. 667.
[7] Toledo, etc., R. Co. v. Pennsylvania Co., 53 Am. & Eng. R. Cas. 293.
[8] Henderson v. Ogden City R. Co., 7 Utah 199, s. c. 46 Am. & Eng. R. Cas. 95, 26 Pac. R. 286.
[9] *Ex parte* Chamberlain, 55 Fed. R. 704; Tucker v. Howard, 128 Mass. 361; Town of Jamestown v. Chicago, etc., R. Co., 69 Wis. 648; Toledo, etc., R. Co. v. Pennsylvania Co., 54 Fed. R. 730; White v. Tidewater, etc., Co., 50 N. J. Eq. 1, s. c. 25 Atl. R. 199; Atchison, etc., R. Co. v. Long, (Kan.) 27 Pac. R. 182; Chattanooga, etc., R. Co. v. Felton, 69 Fed. 273.

have already seen,[1] have likewise been issued against "strikers." An injunction which is preventive in form is frequently mandatory in effect and it is common practice to so draw the order and thus to compel an act to be done by enjoining the defendant from refusing to do it.[2]

§ 637. Mandamus—Generally.—A writ of mandamus to compel a railroad corporation to do a particular act in constructing its road or buildings or in running its trains can be issued when there is a specific legal duty on its part to do that act, and clear proof of a breach of that duty;[3] but not otherwise.[4] Mandamus is an extraordinary remedy and is resorted to, as a general rule, only where there is no ordinary remedy which will afford adequate relief. It has therefore been held that laws extending its operation should be strictly construed,[5]

[1] Ante, § 633. So, in California R. Co. v. Rutherford, 62 Fed. R. 796.

[2] See Delaware, etc., R. Co. v. Central, etc., Co., 43 N. J. Eq. 71; Lane v. Newdigate, 10 Ves. 192 (in which the practice is said to have originated); Rogers Locomotive, etc., Works v. Erie R. Co., 20 N. J. Eq. 379; 2 Beach Mod. Eq., § 753.

[3] State v. Minneapolis, etc., R. Co., 39 Minn. 219; City of Oshkosh v. Milwaukee, etc., R. Co., 74 Wis. 534; State v. Chicago, etc., R. Co., 29 Neb. 412; Cummins v. Evansville, etc., R. Co., 115 Ind. 417; Chicago, etc., R. Co. v. Suffern, 129 Ill. 274; State v. New Orleans, etc., R. Co., 42 La. Ann. 138, 43 Am. & Eng. R. Cas. 258. It is irregular to proceed by rule to compel a legal organization to perform a duty, however clearly imposed upon it. ' Such a proceeding ought to be by mandamus. Oliver v. Board of Liquidation, 40 La. Ann. 321. Where a clear legal right to a writ of mandamus is shown the court has no discretion to refuse the writ. Illinois Central R. Co. v. People, 143 Ill. 434.

[4] Northern Pac. R. Co. v. Washington Territory, 142 U. S. 492; Crane v. Chicago, etc., R. Co., 74 Iowa 330, 37 N. W. R. 397; State v. Pensacola, etc., R. Co., 27 Fla. 403. In absence of a written assignment mandamus can not be employed to compel a corporation to transfer shares of stock to a person to whom they have been delivered by the former owner. Burnsville Turnp. Co. v. State, ex rel. McCalla, 119 Ind. 382. The right of a writ of mandamus to compel a corporation to allow stockholders to inspect its books is in the discretion of the court. Lyon v. American Screw Co., 16 R. I. 472, 17 Atl. 61. Two things must concur, a specific legal right, and the absence of an effectual legal remedy, to warrant the issuance of a mandamus on the relation of any private person. State v. Patterson, etc., R. Co., 43 N. J. Law 505. Mandamus will not lie to enforce the performance of private contracts. Florida Cent., etc., R. Co. v. State, 31 Fla. 482.

[5] State v. New Orleans, etc., R. Co., 42 La. Ann. 138.

although the general rule is that remedial statutes should receive a liberal construction so as to "advance the remedy."[1] Mandamus is frequently resorted to as against corporations, and is a peculiarly apt remedy in the case of railroad companies on account of their public or *quasi* public character. Indeed, it is a general rule that when a corporation devotes its property to a public use, and for that reason, obtains unusual rights and powers, it, in effect, grants to the public an interest in that use and must submit, so far at least, to the control of the public for the common good.[2]

§ 638. **Mandamus to compel completion and operation of road.**—The writ of mandamus has been awarded to compel a company to operate its road as one continuous line,[3] to compel the completion of the road which the corporation was chartered to build,[4] to prevent the abandonment of a part of its road after its completion,[5] to compel the company to run daily

---

[1] Tousey v. Bell, 23 Ind. 423; Smith v. Wilcox, 24 N. Y. 353; Haydon's Case, 3 Rep. (Coke) 7; Broom's Leg. Max. 59; Sutherland Stat. Constr., § 207. For this reason we incline to the opinion that where there is a clear legal right and no means of enforcing it except by mandamus, a statute providing for that remedy should be liberally construed.

[2] Chicago, etc., R. Co. v. Iowa, 94 U. S. 155; Peik v. Chicago, etc., R. Co., 94 U. S. 164; Munn v. Illinois, 94 U. S. 113; Pensacola Tel. Co. v. Western Union Tel. Co., 96 U. S. 1; Hockett v. State, 105 Ind. 250; Chesapeake, etc., Co. v. Baltimore, etc., Co., 66 Md. 399; Nash v. Page, 80 Ky. 539; People v. Budd, 117 N. Y. 1; Chicago, etc., R. Co. v. People, 56 Ill. 365; People v. Rome, etc., R. Co., 103 N. Y. 95; Merrill on Mandamus, §§ 15, 25, 27a.

[3] Union Pac. R. Co. v. Hall, 91 U. S. 343.

[4] Farmers' Loan, etc., Co. v. Henning, 17 Am. L. Reg. (N. S.) 266; People v. Rome, etc., R. Co., 103 N. Y. 95.

[5] Where a railroad company has abandoned a portion of its line which it is under a duty to maintain, mandamus will lie to compel the maintenance and operation of such portion of its road. Chicago, etc., R. Co. v. Crane, 113 U. S. 424; Talcott v. Township of Pine Grove, 1 Flipp. 145. But where a railroad company, by consolidation with another company, became the owner of two lines of road between certain points, it was held that it could not be compelled by mandamus to maintain and operate both lines if it appears that all public needs are served by the operation of a single line. People v. Rome, etc., R. Co., 103 N. Y. 95. Where the company, owning a short line of railroad, is wholly insolvent, has neither rolling stock nor funds with which to operate its road, the use of which has been abandoned for several months, and can not be re-

§ 638   ACTIONS BY AND AGAINST CORPORATIONS.   917

trains,[1] to stop all regular trains at county towns as required by statute,[2] to run passenger trains to the terminus of the road,[3] to compel the erection of a bridge,[4] and the building of fences and cattle-guards where required by law,[5] and to compel the construction of the road across streams so as not to interfere with navigation.[6] It has also been granted to compel a railroad company to finish its track to the terminus specified in the charter and run cars thereon,[7] notwithstanding it had agreed with another common carrier not to do so,[8] to compel a street railway company to operate its road in accordance with the provisions of the ordinance under which it was constructed,[9] to compel a railroad company to deliver grain to all elevators alike on its road where it was in the habit of delivering grain to some of them and there was no reason why it should not treat all alike,[10] and, in general, to compel the company to operate its road and exercise its franchises.[11]

sumed, except at a great loss, the company will not be compelled by mandamus to replace or repair its track, a part of which has been torn up, as such an order would be of no public benefit. State v. Dodge City, M. & T. Ry. Co., 53 Kan. 329, 36 Pac. R. 755.

[1] In re New Brunswick, etc., R. Co., 17 New Brunswick (1 P. & B.) 667.

[2] Illinois Central R. Co. v. People, 143 Ill. 434.

[3] Union Pac. R. Co. v. Hall, 91 U. S. 343; State v. Hartford, etc., R. Co., 29 Conn. 538. But where the state charters a parallel line for some distance from one terminus for the carriage of passengers exclusively, and such company absorbs the business along that part of the route so that the receipts from passenger traffic over that part of the road will not pay expenses of operation, the railroad company is under no obligation to run passenger trains thereon. Commonwealth v. Fitchburg R. Co., 12 Gray (Mass.) 180.

[4] People v. Boston, etc., R. Co., 70 N. Y. 569; State v. Savannah, etc., Co., 26 Ga. 665; State v. Wilmington B. Co., 3 Harr. (Del.) 312; New Orleans, etc., R. Co. v. Mississippi, 112 U. S. 12. Mandamus will not lie to compel a railroad company to locate its station at a particular point within the limits of a town. Florida Central, etc., R. Co. v. State, 31 Fla. 482.

[5] People v. Rochester, etc., R. Co., 76 N. Y. 294.

[6] State v. Northeastern R. Co., 9 Rich. L. (S. C.) 247, s. c. 67 Am. Dec. 551.

[7] People v. Albany, etc., R. Co., 24 N. Y. 261, s. c. 82 Am. Dec. 295.

[8] State v. Hartford, etc., R. Co., 29 Conn. 538.

[9] City of Potwin Place v. Topeka R. Co., 51 Kan. 609, s. c. 37 Am. St. R. 312, and note.

[10] People v. Chicago, etc., R. Co., 55 Ill. 95, s. c. 8 Am. R. 631.

[11] See People v. Albany, etc., R. Co., 24 N. Y. 261; King v. Severn, etc., Rail-

§ 639. **Mandamus to compel restoration of highway and construction of crossings or viaducts.**—The constitution of Illinois prescribes that "all railroad companies shall permit connections to be made with their track, so that any * * * public ware-house, coal-bank, or coal-yard, may be reached by the cars on said railroad." Where the switch connection to which the owners of a coal mine or other specified business are entitled under this provision is improperly disconnected, they are entitled to a mandamus to compel its restoration.[1] Where the statute provides that railroads may construct their roadbeds along, across, or upon streets or other highways, on condition that they restore such highways to their former state of usefulness, a railroad may be compelled by mandamus to restore a highway[2] upon or across which it has constructed its road, if

way Co., 2 Barn. & Ald. 646. Under the New Hampshire statute prohibiting the operation of a railroad by a rival and competing company, and providing that any citizen may apply for an injunction to prevent it, a citizen, as such, can not maintain a suit for a writ of mandamus to compel one of two rival and competing companies to operate its own road. State, ex rel. Chandler, v. Manchester & L. R. Co., 62 N. H. 29. The supreme court of a state has no jurisdiction to compel an interstate railroad company to operate its road within the state, during a general strike, on the allegation that enough competent men are willing to work "for reasonable compensation." State v. Great Northern Ry. Co., 14 Mont. 381, 36 Pac. Rep. 458; People v. Colorado Central R. Co., 42 Fed. R. 638; State v. Republican Valley R. Co., 17 Neb. 647, s. c. 52 Am. R. 424; State v. Paterson, etc., R. Co., 43 N. J. L. 505; People v. New York, etc., R. Co., 104 N. Y. 58, s. c. 58 Am. R. 484; Railroad Comrs. v. Portland, etc., R. Co., 63 Me. 269, s. c. 18 Am. R. 208; State v. Jacksonville, etc., R. Co., 29 Fla. 590; People v. Chicago, etc., R. Co., 130 Ill. 175. For an extreme case in which mandamus was awarded against a railroad company to compel it to operate its road notwithstanding a strike, see "Mandamus as a means of settling strikes," 34 Am. L. Reg. & Rev. (2 N. S., 1895) 102.

[1] Chicago, etc., R. Co. v. Suffern, 129 Ill. 274. Mandamus will issue to compel the replacement of a track taken up in violation of the company's charter. Rex v. Severn, etc., R. Co., 2 B. & Ald. 646.

[2] Town of Jamestown v. Chicago, etc., R. Co., 69 Wis. 648. A simple permission to the railroad company to lay its track in the street gives it no authority to destroy the street, and the company may be compelled by mandamus to restore the highway to its former condition without regard to any statute expressly imposing such duty. A failure to build and maintain suitable crossings will render the company liable for maintaining a nuisance. City of Moundsville v. Ohio Riv. R. Co., 37 W. Va. 92, s. c. 54 Am. & Eng. R. Cas. 538.

it neglects to do so within a reasonable length of time;[1] and this is so notwithstanding the street sought to be restored lies within a city which has power to do the work and recover the expense thereof from the company,[2] and notwithstanding an action to compel the construction of crossings is given by statute.[3] So where the statute imposes upon a railroad the absolute duty to construct farm crossings their construction may be compelled by mandamus, unless a valid excuse for neglecting to build them can be shown.[4] And the fact that the statute gives the occupant of a farm the right to recover a penalty from the company upon its failure to construct proper crossings will not deprive him of the benefit of the writ.[5] Mandamus has been held proper to determine the mode in which a railroad company shall be required to restore a street and to compel it to perform its duty, although the city council has not yet changed the established grade of the street to conform to the lawful change which the relator claims should be adopted.[6] The writ has also been awarded to compel a railroad company to construct a bridge or viaduct where its tracks cross a street.[7]

§ 640. **Mandamus to compel carriage of freight.**—Where a railroad company wrongfully refuses to receive and carry freight, to the injury of the public generally, a writ of mandamus may be issued at the suit of the proper public officer commanding the company to resume the discharge of its duties, by promptly receiving, transporting, and delivering all such freight as is offered for transportation, on the usual and

[1] Cummins v. Evansville, etc., R. Co., 115 Ind. 417; Indianapolis, etc., R. Co. v. State, 37 Ind. 489; People v. Chicago, etc., R. Co., 67 Ill. 118; State v. Hannibal, etc., R. Co., 86 Mo. 13. See People v. Dutchess, etc., R. Co., 58 N. Y. 152; People v. New York, etc., R. Co., 74 N. Y. 302.

[2] City of Oshkosh v. Milwaukee, etc., R. Co., 74 Wis. 534.

[3] State v. Chicago, etc., R. Co., 29 Neb. 412.

[4] State v. Chicago, etc., R. Co., 79 Wis. 259.

[5] State v. Chicago, etc., R. Co., 79 Wis. 259.

[6] State v. Minneapolis, etc., R. Co., 39 Minn. 219.

[7] State v. St. Paul, etc., Ry. Co., 35 Minn. 131, s. c. 59 Am. R. 313; State v. Missouri, etc., Ry. Co., 33 Kan. 176.

reasonable terms and charges.[1] The writ has been awarded to compel the company to treat all shippers alike,[2] and to deliver grain to all elevators similarly situated upon its line.[3] But in England it has been held that it will not be granted to compel a railroad company to extend equal facilities to all upon similar terms.[4] And where a person has an adequate remedy at law by an action for damages it would seem that he ought not to be aided by the extraordinary remedy of mandamus to redress his own private grievances caused by the failure of the company to carry his freight upon the same terms as those upon which it carries the freight of others.[5] It may be, however, where the company refuses to perform its duty as a common carrier and continually discriminates against him unjustly and oppressively, that an action for damages will not afford him adequate relief, and, in such a case, he might, in some jurisdictions, apply for a writ of mandamus. The entire matter is now very largely regulated by congressional and state legislation.

§ 641. **Mandamus to compel the company to maintain stations and furnish increased facilities.**—The question as to whether mandamus will issue to compel the re-establishment of an abandoned station, or the erection and maintenance of new stations at points where they are demanded for the convenience of the public has been much discussed. That such a writ may be issued if the statute imposes the duty of maintaining a station at that point admits of no question,[6] and the

---

[1] People v. New York, etc., R. Co., 28 Hun (N. Y.) 543.

[2] State v. Delaware, etc., R. Co., 48 N. J. L. 55, s. c. 57 Am. R. 543. See, also, State v. Fremont, etc., R. Co., 22 Neb. 313; Central Un. Tel. Co. v. State, 118 Ind. 194, s. c. 10 Am. St. R. 114; Central Un. Tel. Co. v. State, 123 Ind. 113; Price v. Riverside, etc., Co., 56 Cal. 431.

[3] Chicago, etc., R. Co. v. People, 56 Ill. 365, s. c. 8 Am. R. 690. In Mobile, etc., R. Co. v. Wisdom, 5 Heisk. 125, the company was compelled by mandamus to accept tax receipts, under a statute in payment of fare and freight charges.

[4] *Ex parte* Robins, 3 Jur. 103.

[5] People v. New York, etc., R. Co., 22 Hun 533. See, also, Crane v. Chicago, etc., R. Co., 74 Iowa 330, s. c 37 N. W. R. 397.

[6] Commonwealth v. Eastern R. Co., 103 Mass. 254; People v. Louisville, etc., R.Co., 120 Ill.48; Northern Pac. R Co. v. Washington Ter., 142 U. S. 492;

courts have gone far in construing statutes to raise such an obligation. In a Maine case, the company's charter provided "that said corporation * * * shall be bound at all times to have said road in good repair, and a sufficient number of engines, carriages, and vehicles for the transportation of persons and articles, and be obliged to receive at all proper times *and places*, and convey the same." The supreme court held that a mandamus should issue for the establishment of a station at a point designated by the railroad commissioners as a proper and necessary place for the receipt and discharge of passengers and freight.[1] The doctrine has been advanced that the common law under the principle that it is the duty of a railway company to furnish reasonably sufficient and equal facilities to the public whose servant it is, authorizes courts, by mandamus, to compel the erection and maintenance of new stations in proper cases.[2] In a case before the supreme court of Washington Territory it appeared that the defendant railroad company refused to stop its trains at Yakima City at any time or for any purpose, although the place contained at the time of the trial a resident population of one hundred and fifty persons, and maintained a flouring mill, two hotels, twenty-seven dwelling houses, and both public and private schools, and had been, until injured by unjust discrimination after the advent of the railroad, three times as large, and transacting a business of

State *v.* New Haven, etc., R. Co., 37 Conn. 153; State *v.* New Haven, etc., R. Co., 43 Conn. 351. In the two latter cases the statute forbade the abandonment of a railway station established for 12 years. So in State *v.* New Haven, etc., R. Co., 41 Conn. 134, the company was compelled by mandamus to resume an abandoned station.

[1] Railroad Commissioners *v.* Portland, etc., R. Co., 63 Me. 269, s. c. 18 Am. R. 208.

[2] People *v.* Chicago, etc., R. Co., 130 Ill. 175; State *v.* Republican Valley R. Co., 17 Neb. 647. In McCoy *v.* Cincinnati, etc., R. Co., 13 Fed. R. 3, the United States Circuit Court in Ohio issued an order to compel the defendant to receive and deliver stock at the plaintiff's stockyard, although the defendant had a contract with the proprietor of an adjoining stockyard for the use of his yard for all business transacted at that point. In giving his decision, Judge Baxter remarked that by accepting its charter, a railroad undertakes to erect depots, and designates stopping places wherever the public necessities require them. See, also, Commonwealth *v.* Eastern R. Co., 103 Mass. 254.

more than $200,000 per year. The only facilities provided for the receipt and discharge of either passengers or freight were at the town of North Yakima, four miles distant, to and from which point all traffic had to pass by private conveyance. The court granted a writ of mandamus to compel the railway company to construct a depot and give other railroad facilities at the town.[1] But upon appeal to the supreme court of the United States this decision was reversed, Justices Brewer, Field and Harlan dissenting,[2] and the court held that mandamus to compel a railroad company to do a particular act in constructing its road or buildings, or in running its trains, will lie only where there is a specific duty on its part to do that act, and clear proof of a breach of that duty; and that no common law duty exists on the part of a railroad to stop its trains at any particular point.[3] Under the Illinois statute it

[1] Northern Pac. R. Co. v. Territory, 3 Wash. Ter. 303, s. c. 29 Am. & Eng. R. Cas. 82. The court says: "In the absence of legislation providing other means for regulating and controlling the matter, we have no doubt of the power of a court of general jurisdiction, in a proper case, to compel a railroad to extend to the public proper facilities for the transaction of business."

[2] Northern Pacific R. Co. v. Washington Ter., 142 U.S. 492. See, also, People v. New York, etc., R. Co., 104 N. Y. 58. In his dissenting opinion in the former case, Justice Brewer says: "A railroad corporation has a public duty to perform as well as a private interest to subserve, and I never before believed that the courts would permit it to abandon the one to promote the other. Nowhere in its charter is in terms expressed the duty of carrying passengers and freight. Are the courts impotent to compel the performance of this duty? Is the duty of carrying passengers and freight any more of a public duty than that of placing its depots and stopping its trains at those places which will best accommodate the public? If the State of Indiana incorporates a railroad to build a road from New Albany through Indianapolis to South Bend, and that road is built, can it be that the courts may compel the road to receive passengers and transport freight, but in the absence of a specific direction from the legislature are powerless to compel the road to stop its trains and build a depot at Indianapolis? I do not so belittle the power or duty of the courts."

[3] Northern Pac. R. Co. v. Washington Ter., 142 U. S. 492. To the same effect see People v. Chicago, etc., R. Co., 35 Am.& Eng. R.Cas. 462, reversed,130 Ill. 175; People v. New York, etc., R. Co., 104 N. Y. 58, 66; Mobile, etc., R. Co. v. People, 132 Ill. 559; State v. New Orleans, etc., R. Co., 42 La. Ann. 138, 43 Am. & Eng. R. Cas. 258. In the absence of a law or a rule of the railroad commission prescribing the type to be used in printing schedules of rates to be posted by railroad com-

§ 642   ACTIONS BY AND AGAINST CORPORATIONS.   923

has been held that a railroad company may be compelled by mandamus to stop all regular trains at certain stations to discharge and receive passengers and freight.[1] But, in the absence of any statutory provision upon the subject, it has been held that a railroad company will not be compelled by mandamus to furnish increased passenger facilities by running any particular number of trains, especially if the amount of travel will not support an additional train.[2]

§ 642. **When mandamus will not lie.**—Mandamus will not issue to compel the performance of acts which are not clearly within the legal duties of those against whom the writ is directed, and it must appear in the application for a writ of mandamus that the defendant is under legal obligation to perform such acts, and that the petitioner has a legal right to demand their performance.[3] And even where the duty seems clear the court will not issue a mandamus when, if issued, it would prove unavailing,[4] as in a case of the performance of duties involving the exercise of a large measure of good faith and discretion on the part of the corporation and its agents.

panies in their stations, the supreme court can not by mandamus direct in what size type they shall be printed. State v. Pensacola & A. R. Co., 27 Fla. 403, 9 So. R. 89. Mandamus will lie to compel a railway company to pay into the county court the amount of damages assessed by reason of the location and operation of its railway across the petitioner's premises, on a showing that the right of way has been lawfully condemned, the damages duly awarded, and no appeal taken therefrom. State v. Grand Island & W. C. R. Co., 27 Neb. 694, 43 N. W. 419.

[1] Illinois, etc., R. Co. v. People, 143 Ill. 434. See, also, New Haven, etc., R. Co. v. State, 44 Conn. 376, 384.

[2] Ohio, etc., R. Co. v. People, 120 Ill. 200; People v. Long Island R. Co., 31 Hun (N. Y.) 125; Commonwealth v. Fitchburg R. Co., 12 Gray (Mass.) 180. See, also, People v. Rome, etc., R. Co., 103 N. Y. 95; People v. New York, etc., R. Co., 104 N. Y. 58, s. c. 58 Am. R. 484.

[3] People v. Colorado Cent. R. Co., 42 Fed. R. 638. In this case the petitioner appeared "on behalf of the people of the state of Colorado," but failed to show that he was one of them.

[4] High on Mandamus, § 14; Merrill on Mandamus, § 75. The court will deny an application for a writ of mandamus to compel the operation of a road to a point beyond its jurisdiction. People v. Colorado Central R. Co., 42 Fed. R. 638.

CORP. 59

For this reason courts of equity hesitate to undertake to compel a railroad corporation to construct or to complete its road, since the proper construction of a railroad would necessarily involve the exercise of much technical skill and judgment, and depend largely upon the good faith of the parties directing the work.[1] So, where the company is utterly unable, by reason of insolvency or the like, to perform its duties to the public, the courts will not, as a rule, attempt to compel it to do so by mandamus, as this would be "a vain and fruitless thing."[2] Some courts, however, have issued the writ notwithstanding the return of the company that it had no funds and no means of obtaining any.[3] There is some reason for the latter practice, especially when the company, by its own fault, has placed itself in such a position, for circumstances may change, and, in any event, it may be well to thus compel the company to make a *bona fide* effort to perform its duties and comply with the order. If it is then found to be impossible the court can see that no injustice is done to the company and will refuse to punish it for contempt. Mandamus will not lie, ordinarily, at least, to enforce private contracts with a railroad company,[4] nor, as a general

---

[1] Ohio, etc., R. Co. v. People, 120 Ill. 200; Morawetz on Priv. Corp. (2d ed.), § 1136, citing Ross v. Union Pac. R. Co., 1 Woolw. 26; Fallon v. Railroad Co., 1 Dill (U. S.C. C.) 121; Danforth v.Philadelphia, etc., R. Co., 30 N. J. E. 12, and cases in reporter's note; Heathcote v. North Staffordshire R. Co., 20 L. J. Ch. 82; South Wales R. Co. v. Wythes, 5 De G., M. & G. 880; Ranger v. Great Western R. Co., 1 Eng. R. & Canal Cas. 1, 51; Wheatley v. Westminster, etc., Coal Co., L. R. 9 Eq. 538.

[2] State v. Dodge City, etc., Ry. Co., 53 Kan. 329, s. c. 36 Pac. R. 755, 24 L. R. A. 564, and note; Ohio, etc., Ry. Co. v. People, 120 Ill. 200; Queen v. Ambergate, etc., R. Co., 1 El. & Bl. 372; *In re* Bristol, etc., R. Co., L. R. 3 Q. B. D. 10; Queen v. London, etc., R. Co., 16 Ad. & E. (N. S.) 864.

[3] Savannah, etc., Co. v. Shuman, 91 Ga. 400, s. c. 17 S. E. R. 937, 44 Am. St. R. 43; Silverthorne v. Warren R. Co., 33 N. J. L. 173; People v. Dutchess, etc., R. Co., 58 N. Y. 152; Queen v. Birmingham, etc., R. Co., 2 Ad. & E. (N. S.) 47; Queen v. Trustees, etc., 1 Ad. & E. (N. S.) 860. See, also, City of Fort Dodge v.Minneapolis, etc., R. Co., 87 Ia. 389, s. c.55 Am. & Eng. R. Cas. 58 (holding lack of funds no reason for refusing to compel a receiver to perform a legal duty, such as constructing a crossing).

[4] State v. New Orleans, etc., R. Co., 37 La. Ann. 589; Florida Cent. R. Co. v. State, 31 Fla. 482, s. c. 34 Am.St. R. 30; State v. Paterson, etc., R. Co., 43 N. J. L. 505.

§ 643   ACTIONS BY AND AGAINST CORPORATIONS.   925

rule, in any case where there is an adequate remedy at law.[1] It will not lie to prevent the exercise of a lawful discretion with which the company is vested,[2] nor to compel a judge to decide in a particular way an application by the receivers of a railroad company for authority to enter into an agreement for the partial readjustment of its affairs.[3] A railroad company may be estopped by its acts to claim the benefit of a writ of mandamus. The fact that a railroad company agreed to the entry of a judicial order as to a crossing by it over the track of another company and has acted under it is a sufficient reason for denying a writ of mandamus to set aside and vacate the order.[4]

§ 643. **Who may be relator.**—There is considerable conflict among the authorities as to whether a private party may be a relator in a proceeding for a mandamus to enforce a public right. The attorney-general, or other proper public officer, may doubtless apply for the writ in all such cases,[5] but not, ordinarily, unless he seeks to protect some public right or to secure some public interest.[6] Some of the courts also hold that a private party can not be a relator unless he has some private interest to be protected or some particular right to be enforced independent of that which he has merely as one of the general public.[7] But the weight of authority is to the effect that a private citizen may, as one of the general public, be relator and apply for a mandamus to enforce a public right or duty, due to the public at large and not merely to the government, without showing any special and peculiar interest.[8]

[1] State v. Mobile, etc., R. Co., 59 Ala. 321.
[2] People v. New York, etc., R. Co., 104 N. Y. 58, s. c. 58 Am. R. 484; Florida, etc., R. Co. v. State, 31 Fla. 482, s. c. 34 Am. St. R. 30; State v. Canal, etc., R. Co., 23 La. Ann. 333.
[3] *In re* Rice, 155 U. S. 396, s. c. 15 Sup. Ct. R. 149.
[4] Fort Street Union Depot Co. v. State R., etc., Co., 81 Mich. 248.
[5] Merrill on Mandamus, § 229.
[6] Attorney-General v. Albion, etc., Inst., 52 Wis. 469; People v. Rome, etc., R. Co., 103 N. Y. 95.
[7] Mitchell v. Boardman, 79 Me. 469; Bobbett v. State, 10 Kan. 9; Smith v. Mayor, etc., of Saginaw, 81 Mich. 123; Heffner v. Com., 28 Pa. St. 108; Merrill on Mandamus, § 229.
[8] Union Pac. R. Co. v. Hall, 91 U. S. 343; Attorney-General v. Boston, 123 Mass. 460, 469; State v. Board, etc., 92 Ind. 133; Village of Glencoe v. People, 78 Ill. 382; State v. Gracey, 11 Nev. 223; Chumasero v.

He must, however, show that he is one of the general public to whom the duty is due or whose rights are injuriously affected.[1]

§ 644. Quo warranto.—We have elsewhere considered the subject of *quo warranto* as a means of forfeiting the charter of a corporation and as a remedy for abuse of powers as well as the usurpation of franchises.[2] In that connection we also considered, to some extent, the general nature of the proceeding, the jurisdiction of the courts and the proper parties to the proceeding. Little, therefore, remains to be said, as the practice is so far regulated by different statutory provisions in the various states that few general rules can be laid down. At common law, the writ of *quo warranto* was a writ of right, but in modern practice it has been, almost everywhere, superseded by an information in the nature of a *quo warranto*, which is a civil proceeding and is governed by the rules of civil practice[3] rather than those relating to criminal prosecutions, although it is, in a sense, an extraordinary remedy and is usually regulated very largely by statute. The proceeding will not lie to forfeit the charter of a corporation in a foreign court,[4] but, although actions to recover possession of real estate must be brought in the county in which it is located, *quo warranto* proceedings for usurping the franchise of being a corporation and owning and using land in one county for railroad purposes, need not necessarily be instituted in such county.[5] Such pro-

Potts, 2 Mont. 242; State *v.* Francis, 95 Mo. 44; State *v.* Brown, 38 Ohio St. 344; State *v.* VanDuyn, 24 Neb. 586; State *v.* Ware, 13 Ore. 380; State *v.* Dayton, etc., R. Co., 36 Ohio St. 434; Savannah, etc., Co. *v.* Shuman, 91 Ga. 400, s. c. 44 Am. St. R. 43; Wise *v.* Bigger, 79 Va. 269; State *v.* Hannibal, etc., R. Co., 86 Mo. 13; State *v.* Weld, 39 Minn. 426; Chicago, etc., R. Co. *v.* Suffern, 129 Ill. 274; Merrill on Mandamus, § 23. See Crane *v.* Chicago, etc., Ry. Co., 74 Iowa 330, s. c. 7 Am. St. R. 479, and note.

[1] People *v.* Colorado, etc., R. Co., 42 Fed. R. 638.

[2] See *ante*, §§ 53, 54, 55.

[3] People *v.* Cook, 8 N. Y. 67, s. c. 59 Am. Dec. 451; State *v.* Kupferle, 44 Mo. 154, s. c. 100 Am. Dec. 565; Attorney-General *v.* Sullivan, 163 Mass. 446, s. c. 40 N. E. R. 843; Atchison, etc., R. Co. *v.* People, 5 Col. 60; Ames *v.* Kansas, 111 U. S. 449. *Contra*, Donnelly *v.* People, 11 Ill. 552; Territory *v.* Lockwood, 3 Wall. (U. S.) 236.

[4] *Ante*, § 55.

[5] Smith *v.* State, 140 Ind. 343, s. c. 39 N. E. R. 1060.

ceedings have been held proper both to determine the rights of individuals to corporate franchises and to determine whether franchises properly granted have been misused and forfeited,[1] to try the right of a foreign corporation to do business in the state,[2] and to determine the right of a company duly incorporated to exercise a particular franchise.[3] So, under a statute providing that *quo warranto* proceedings may be instituted against a corporation "when it claims a franchise privilege or right in contravention of law, such proceedings will lie against a railroad company to contest its claim to exercise a right or privilege in state canal lands.[4] Other decisions showing when *quo warranto* will or will not lie are reviewed elsewhere.[5] As we have seen the proceedings are usually instituted on behalf of the state by the attorney-general, or, in some jurisdictions, by the prosecuting attorney, but in most jurisdictions, private persons having an interest in the matter, may file the information, with leave of the court.[6] In some jurisdictions the defendant must either disclaim or justify, and it is held that a plea of not guilty or *non usurpavit* is not good,[7] but in others he may set forth as many defenses as he may have.[8] The entire matter is largely regulated by statute. If the information is insufficient a demurrer would seem to be proper.[9]

---

[1] People v. Utica Ins. Co., 15 Johns. (N. Y.) 353, s. c. 8 Am. Dec. 243; Petty v. Tooker, 21 N. Y. 267; State v. Milwaukee, etc., Railroad Co., 45 Wis. 579; State v. Barron, 57 N. H. 498.

[2] State v. Fidelity, etc., Co., 39 Minn. 538, s. c. 41 N. W. R. 108; State v. Western, etc., Society, 47 Ohio St. 167, s. c. 24 N. E. R. 392.

[3] People v. Utica Ins. Co., 15 Johns. (N. Y.) 353, s. c. 8 Am. Dec. 243; State v. Citizens', etc., Asso., 6 Mo. App. 163.

[4] State v. Pittsburgh, etc., Ry. Co., (Ohio St.) s. c. 41 N. E. R. 205.

[5] See *ante*, §§ 48-51.

[6] 19 Am. & Eng. Ency. of Law 675, 676; 7 Lawson Rights, Rem. & Pr., §§ 40, 42, 43.

[7] Illinois, etc., R. Co. v. People, 84 Ill. 426; Distilling, etc., Co. v. People, 156 Ill. 448, s. c. 41 N. E. R. 188; Attorney-General v. Foote, 11 Wis. 14, s. c. 78 Am. Dec. 689; State v. Utter, 14 N. J. L. 84; State v. Barron, 57 N. H. 498; Buckman v. State, 34 Fla. 48, s. c. 15 So. R. 697.

[8] State v. Brown, 34 Miss. 688; People v. Stratton, 28 Cal. 382; State v. McDaniel, 22 Ohio St. 354; People, *ex rel.* Coon, v. Plymouth, etc., Co., 31 Mich. 178; Rex v. Autridge, 8 T.R.467.

[9] State v. Boal, 46 Mo. 528; Commonwealth v. Commercial Bank, 28 Pa. St. 383; People, *ex rel.* Palmer v. Woodbury, 14 Cal. 43; Territory v. Lockwood, 3 Wall. (U. S.) 236.

CHAPTER XXVI.

REMOVAL OF CAUSES.

§ 645. When removal is authorized—Statutes now in force.
646. What are suits of a civil nature under the removal acts.
647. Parties.
648. Rights of removal as affected by amount in controversy.
649. Diverse citizenship as a ground for removal.
650. Separate controversy.
651. Prejudice or local influence as a ground for removal.

§ 652. Removal where federal question is involved.
653. Time and manner of making application for removal.
654. Effect of application on jurisdiction of state and federal court.
655. Remanding and dismissing cause.
656. Pleading and practice in federal court after removal.

§ 645. When removal is authorized—Statutes now in force. —The act of congress of March 3, 1887, as corrected by the act of August 13, 1888,[1] defines the jurisdiction of the circuit courts of the United States, requiring the amount or value of the matter in dispute to exceed two thousand dollars, and provides for the removal from any state court to the circuit court of the United States for the proper district of "any suit of a civil nature, at law or in equity, arising under the constitution or laws of the United States, or treaties made, or which shall be made, under their authority, of which the circuit courts of the United States are given original jurisdiction" by the first section of such act; that any other suit of a civil nature, of which the circuit courts are so given jurisdiction, may be removed from any state court to the proper circuit court by the defendant or defendants therein, being non-residents of that state; that when in any suit of any of the classes specified there shall be a controversy which is wholly

---

[1] 25 U. S. St. at L. 433.

between citizens of different states, and which can be fully determined as between them, then either one or more of the defendants actually interested in such controversy may remove the suit; that suits may be removed, under specified circumstances, on account of prejudice or local influence, and that suits between citizens of the same state may also be removed, under certain circumstances, where the title to land is concerned and they claim under grants from different states. This act tends to restrict[1] rather than to extend the right of removal, as given by previous acts, and repeals several of the older acts, although it leaves some of them still in force.[2] The only provisions of former acts still in force which seem to be applicable in any case in which a railroad company is interested are those found in sections 641 and 642 of the Revised Statutes of the United States relating to suits or criminal prosecutions "against any person who is denied or can not enforce in the judicial tribunals of the state, or in the part of the state where such suit or prosecution is pending, any right secured to him by any law providing for the equal civil rights of citizens of the United States or of all persons within the jurisdiction of the United States." This law is intended to carry out the provisions of the Fourteenth Amendment to the United States Constitution,[3] and is directed against state action denying civil rights.[4]

§ 646. **What are suits of a civil nature under the removal acts.**—As most of the provisions for the removal of causes

[1] Hanrick v. Hanrick, 153 U. S. 192, 197, s. c. 14 Sup. Ct. R. 835; Smith v. Lyon, 133 U. S. 315, s. c. 10 Sup. Ct. R. 303; In re Pennsylvania Co., 137 U. S. 451, 454, s. c. 11 Sup. Ct. R. 141.

[2] It expressly repeals § 640 Rev. St. U. S., and the last paragraph of § 5 of the act of March 3, 1874, and all laws or parts of laws in conflict with its provisions, but expressly provides that it shall not be deemed to repeal §§ 641, 642, 643, or 722, of title 24, Rev. St. U. S., or § 8 of the act of March 3, 1875. It has been held that it repeals by implication the act of March 2, 1867. Short v. Chicago, etc., R. Co., 33 Fed. R. 114; Whelan v. New York, etc., R. Co., 35 Fed. R. 849; Minnick v. Union Ins. Co., 40 Fed. R. 369. But see Hills v. Richmond, etc., R. Co., 33 Fed. R. 81; Fisk v. Henarie, 32 Fed. R. 417, reversed in 142 U. S. 459, s. c. 12 Sup. Ct. R. 207.

[3] Strauder v. West Virginia, 100 U. S. 303; Virginia v. Rives, 100 U. S. 313.

[4] Ex parte Alabama, 71 Ala. 363; Virginia v. Rives, 100 U. S. 313; Neal

authorize the removal only where the suit is of a civil nature, it is important to determine what is meant by the term "suit of a civil nature." It has been held that an action to recover a penalty for the violation of a state statute, although the statute expressly provides that the penalty shall be recovered in a civil action, is essentially criminal in its nature and can not be removed.[1] So, it has been held that a special assessment proceeding under the Illinois law, involving the exercise of the taxing power, is not a "suit" within the meaning of the removal act;[2] nor is a claim for a right of way pending before the board of county commissioners.[3] But it seems to be well settled that proceedings to determine the value of land condemned or affected by a taking under the power of eminent domain may be removed in a proper case.[4] So mandamus,[5] *habeas corpus*,[6] and *quo warranto*[7] proceedings have been held to come within the meaning of the removal acts. Actions in

---

v. Delaware, 103 U. S. 370; State v. Chue Fan, 42 Fed. R. 865; Cooper v. State, 64 Md. 40.

[1] State of Iowa v. Chicago, etc., R. Co., 37 Fed. R. 497; Ferguson v. Ross, 38 Fed. R. 161; United States v. Mexican, etc., Ry. Co., 40 Fed.R.769; State of Texas v. Day, etc., Co., 41 Fed. R. 228. See, also, Ames v. Kansas, 111 U. S. 449, s. c. 4 Sup. Ct. R. 437; Boyd v. United States, 116 U. S. 616, s. c. 6 Sup. Ct. R. 524; Herriman v. Burlington, etc., Railroad Co., 57 Iowa 187, s. c. 9 N. W. R. 378, and 10 N. W. R. 340; Wisconsin v. Pelican Insurance Co., 127 U. S. 265, s. c. 8 Sup. Ct. R. 1370.

[2] *In re* City of Chicago, 64 Fed. R. 897. See and compare Union Pacific R. Co. v. Myers, 115 U. S. 1, s. c. 5 Sup. Ct. R. 1113; Upshur Co. v. Rich, 135 U. S. 467, and *In re* Jarnecke Ditch, 69 Fed. R. 161.

[3] Fuller v. County of Colfax, 14 Fed. R. 177.

[4] Mississippi, etc., Boom Co. v. Patterson, 98 U. S. 403; Searl v. School Dist., 124 U. S. 197, s. c. 8 Sup. Ct. R. 460; Union Pacific R. Co. v. Myers, 115 U. S. 1, s. c. 5 Sup. Ct. R. 1113; Mineral Range R. Co. v. Detroit, etc., Co., 25 Fed. R. 515; Kansas City, etc., R. Co. v. Interstate Lumber Co., 37 Fed. R. 3; City of Chicago v. Hutchinson, 11 Biss. 484, s. c. 15 Fed. R. 129.

[5] Kendall v. United States, 12 Pet. (U. S.) 524; Washington Imp. Co. v. Kansas Pac. R. Co., 5 Dill. (U. S. C. C.) 489. See, also, People v. Colorado Cent. R. Co., 42 Fed. R. 638. But compare Rosenbaum v. Bauer, 120 U. S. 450.

[6] Holmes v. Jannison, 14 Pet. (U. S.) 540; *Ex parte* Milligan, 4 Wall. (U. S.) 2. But not, it seems, under the later acts, where the jurisdiction depends on the value of the matter in dispute. Kurtz v. Moffitt, 115 U. S. 487; Snow v. United States, 118 U. S. 346, 354.

[7] Ames v. Kansas, 111 U. S. 449; State of Illinois v. Illinois Cent. R. Co., 33 Fed. R. 721.

ejectment,[1] and replevin,[2] and those begun by attachment[3] have been removed under former acts; but it has been held that a suit begun by foreign attachment, without personal service, can not be removed under the last act.[4] It is said, however, in another case, that the court in the decision just referred to erroneously assumed that there was no distinction in this regard between cases originally brought in the circuit court and cases removed thereto, and that the circuit court had jurisdiction of the suit removed after the state court had acquired jurisdiction by foreign attachment, although there was no personal service.[5] Many years ago in a case in which it was held that a proceeding for a writ of prohibition was a "suit" within the meaning of another statute, Chief Justice Marshall said: "The term is certainly a very comprehensive one, and is understood to apply to any proceeding in a court of justice by which an individual pursues that remedy in a court of justice which the law affords him. The modes of proceeding may be various, but, if a right is litigated between parties in a court of justice, the proceeding by which the decision of the court is sought is a suit."[6] The mere fact that a bill or petition is filed, however, without having any process issued or giving any notice, and without any appearance by the adverse party, does not make the proceeding a "suit" within the meaning of the removal acts.[7] Neither is a mere auxiliary proceeding a "suit" within the meaning of such

[1] Torrey v. Beardsly, 4 Wash. (U. S. C. C.) 242; Ex parte Girard, 3 Wall. Jr. (U. S. C. C.) 263.

[2] Beecher v. Gillett, 1 Dill. (U. S. C. C.) 308; Dennistoun v. Draper, 5 Blatchf. (U. S. C. C.) 336.

[3] Sayles v. Northwestern Ins. Co., 2 Curtis (U. S. C. C.) 212; Barney v. Globe Bank, 5 Blatchf. (U. S. C. C.) 107; Keith v. Levi, 2 Fed. R. 743. But see Bentlif v. London, etc., Corp., 44 Fed. R. 667, and authorities there cited.

[4] Perkins v. Hendryx, 40 Fed. R. 657.

[5] Crocker Nat. Bank v. Pagenstecher, 44 Fed. R. 705. See, also, Amsinck v. Balderston, 41 Fed. R. 641; Fales v. Chicago, etc., R. Co., 32 Fed. R. 673; American Finance Co. v. Bostwick, 151 Mass. 19. But compare Bentlif v. London, etc., Corp., 44 Fed. R. 667, and authorities there cited.

[6] Weston v. City of Charleston, 2 Pet. (U. S.) 449, 464.

[7] See West v. Aurora City, 6 Wall. (U. S.) 139; In re Iowa, etc., Co., 2 McCrary (U. S. C. C.) 178.

acts.[1] But a proceeding against stockholders to obtain an execution for the amount of their unpaid stock, under the Missouri statute, after a return of *nulla bona* on an execution against the corporation, has been held to be a "suit" which can be removed by the stockholders on the ground of diverse citizenship, and not merely a proceeding auxiliary to the suit against the corporation.[2]

§ 647. Parties.—One who is not a party to a cause and refuses to become a party of record is not entitled to have the cause removed, although he may be interested in the controversy.[3] But it has been held, under former acts, that parties properly required to interplead, or having a statutory right to intervene, which they have attempted to exercise, may have the cause removed, in a proper case, although the state court refused to permit them to intervene.[4] Substituted parties generally stand in the same position, with regard to the right of removal, as those whose place they take.[5] It is well settled that the right of removal can neither be obtained nor refused by joining merely nominal or improper parties for that purpose.[6]

---

[1] Barrow v. Hunton, 99 U. S. 80; First Nat. Bank v. Turnbull, 16 Wall. (U. S.) 190; Smith v. St. Louis, etc., Co., 3 Tenn. Ch. 350; Weeks v. Billings, 55 N. H. 371; Poole v. Thatcherdeft, 19 Fed. R. 49; Jackson v. Gould, 74 Me. 564; Goodrich v. Hunton, 29 La. Ann. 372; Hockstadter v. Harrison, 71 Ga. 21. See, also, Lawrence v. Morgans, etc., R. Co., 121 U. S. 634.

[2] Lackawanna, etc., Co. v. Bates, 56 Fed. R. 737, overruling Webber v. Humphreys, 5 Dill. (U. S. C. C.) 223. See, also, Bondurant v. Watson, 103 U. S. 281; Pettus v. Georgia R., etc., Co., 3 Woods (U. S. C. C.) 620; Kalamazoo, etc., Co. v. Snavely, 34 Fed. R. 823; Pelzer, etc., Co. v. Hamburg, etc., Ins. Co., 62 Fed. R. 1.

[3] Bertha Zinc, etc., Co. v. Carico, 61 Fed. R. 132; Dill Remov. Causes (5th ed.), § 101.

[4] Snow v. Texas, etc., R. Co., 16 Fed. R. 1; Hack v. Chicago, etc., R. Co., 23 Fed. R. 356; Healy v. Prevost, 8 The Rep. 103. See, also, Burdick v. Peterson, 2 McCrary (U. S. C. C.) 135. *Contra*, Williams v. Williams, 24 La. Ann. 55. See, also, Olds Wagon Works v. Benedict, 67 Fed. R. 1.

[5] Richmond, etc., R. Co. v. Findley, 32 Fed. R. 641; Cable v. Ellis, 110 U. S. 389; Jefferson v. Driver, 117 U. S. 272; Houston, etc., R. Co. v. Shirley, 111 U. S. 358; Grand Trunk Ry. Co. v. Twitchell, 59 Fed. R. 727.

[6] United States v. Douglas, 113 N. Car. 190, s. c. 18 S. E. R. 202; Bates v. New Orleans, etc., R. Co., 16 Fed. R. 294; Hatch v. Chicago, etc., R. Co., 6 Blatchf. (U. S. C. C.) 105; Carneal v. Banks, 10 Wheat. (U. S.) 181; Barney v. Latham, 103 U. S. 205; Chattanooga, etc., R. Co. v. Cincinnati, etc.,

It is not always easy to determine, however, who are merely nominal parties and who are necessary parties actually interested as such in the controversy.[1] It has been held that the voluntary joinder of a number of complainants to enforce a common liability of the defendants has the same effect on the right of removal on the ground of diverse citizenship as if they had been compelled to unite.[2] But the court, for the purpose of determining the right of removal, will arrange the parties as plaintiffs or defendants according to their actual interest in the controversy,[3] and if parties are collusively joined for the mere purpose of effecting a removal, the petition may be refused,[4] or if the cause has already been removed the court may remand it.[5] So, on the other hand, it has been held that where a plaintiff makes a party a co-defendant for the purpose of preventing a removal, and, after the time for removal is past, dismisses as to such party, the cause may, nevertheless, be re-

R. Co., 44 Fed. R. 456; Wortsman v. Wade, 77 Ga. 651; Danvers Sav. Bank v. Thompson, 133 Mass. 182; Powers v. Chesapeake, etc., R. Co., 65 Fed. R. 129. See and compare Merchants', etc., Co. v. Ins. Co., 151 U. S. 368, s. c. 14 Sup. Ct. R. 367; Arrowsmith v. Nashville, etc., R. Co., 57 Fed. R. 165; Springer v. Sheets, 115 N. Car. 370, s. c. 20 S. E. R. 469.

[1] As to who are actually interested and not mere nominal parties, see Knapp v. Railroad Co., 20 Wall. (U. S.) 117; Myers v. Swann, 107 U. S. 546; Thayer v. Life Assn., 112 U. S. 717; St. Louis, etc., R. Co. v. Wilson, 114 U. S. 60; Miller v. Sharp, 37 Fed. R. 161; Central R. Co. v. Mills, 113 U. S. 249; Chicago, etc., R. Co. v. Crane, 113 U. S. 424; Douglas v. Richmond, etc., R. Co., 106 N. Car. 65; Fox v. Mackay, 60 Fed. R. 4; Wilson v. Oswego Twp., 151 U. S. 56, s. c. 14 Sup. Ct. R. 259; Merchants', etc., Co. v. Insurance Co., 151 U. S. 368, s. c. 14 Sup. Ct. R. 367. As to who are merely nominal parties, see Hatch v. Chicago, etc., R. Co., 6 Blatchf. (U. S. C. C.) 105; Arapahoe Co. v. Kansas Pac. R. Co., 4 Dill. (U. S. C. C.) 277; Bates v. New Orleans, etc., R. Co., 16 Fed. R. 294; Bacon v. Rives, 106 U. S. 99; County Court of Taylor Co. v. Baltimore, etc., R. Co., 35 Fed. R. 161; Over v. Lake Erie, etc., R. Co., 63 Fed. R. 34; Shattuck v. North British, etc., Ins. Co., 58 Fed. R. 609.

[2] Merchants', etc., Co. v. Insurance Co., 151 U. S. 368, s. c. 14 Sup. Ct. R. 367; Corporation v. Winter, 1 Wheat. (U. S.) 91.

[3] Harter v. Kernochan, 103 U. S. 562; Ayres v. Chicago, 101 U. S. 184; Anderson v. Bowers, 40 Fed. R. 708. But see Springer v. Sheets, 115 N. Car. 370, s. c. 20 S. E. R. 469.

[4] Cushman v. Amador, etc., Co., 118 U. S. 58; Sachse v. Citizens' Bank, 37 La. Ann. 364.

[5] Williams v. Nottowa, 104 U. S. 209; Little v. Giles, 118 U. S. 596. But see Deputron v. Young, 134 U. S. 241.

moved upon proper application by a party entitled to such removal.[1]

§ 648. **Right of removal as affected by amount in controversy.**—The value of the matter in dispute must exceed two thousand dollars, exclusive of interest and costs. It is not sufficient that its value is exactly two thousand dollars.[2] Thus, where the prayer for relief in the complaint asked for "two thousand dollars and all other proper relief," and, under the pleadings, no other proper relief could be obtained, it was held that the cause could not be removed.[3] The amount is to be determined from the complaint, declaration or bill,[4] and it seems that if the amount, as so determined, is insufficient, the filing of a counterclaim by the defendant exceeding that amount does not entitle him to remove the suit.[5] This rule, if it can be sustained at all as a general rule, must be placed upon the ground that the defendant, having voluntarily submitted his claim to the state court as a plaintiff in the cross-complaint, can not for that reason take advantage of his own act and remove the suit which could not otherwise have been removed by him.

[1] Powers v. Chesapeake, etc., R. Co., 65 Fed. R. 129; Arrowsmith v. Nashville, etc., R. Co., 57 Fed. R. 165. But see Provident, etc., Society v. Ford, 114 U. S. 635; Vimont v. Chicago, etc., R. Co., 64 Iowa 513.

[2] Tod v. Cleveland, etc., R. Co., 65 Fed. R. 145; Mayor of Baltimore v. Postal Tel. Co., 62 Fed. R. 500; Pittsburgh, etc., R. Co. v. Ramsey, 22 Wall. (U. S.) 322; Walker v. United States, 4 Wall. (U. S.) 163. See Weber v. Travelers' Ins. Co., 45 Fed. R. 657.

[3] Baltimore, etc., R. Co. v. Worman, 12 Ind. App. 494, 40 N. E. R. 751. But where other relief may be obtained and the value of the matter in dispute exceeds two thousand dollars the cause may be removed although the money judgment demanded is less than that sum. Dickinson v. Union, etc., Co., 64 Fed. R. 895.

[4] Yarde v. Baltimore, etc., R. Co., 57 Fed. R. 913; Gordon v. Longest, 16 Pet. (U. S.) 97; Western Un. Tel. Co. v. Levi, 47 Ind. 552. In an action in tort the amount of damages claimed by the plaintiff is the value of the matter in dispute. Gordon v. Longest, *supra*; Western Un. Tel. Co. v. Levi, *supra*; Louisville, etc., R. Co. v. Roehling, 11 Ill. App. 264.

[5] Bennett v. Devine, 45 Fed. R. 705; La Montagne v. T. W. Harvey Lumber Co., 44 Fed. R. 645; Falls Wire, etc., Co. v. Broderick, 2 McCrary (U. S. C. C.) 489. *Contra*, Clarkson v. Manson, 18 Blatchf. (U. S. C. C.) 443; Carson, etc., Lumber Co. v. Holtzclaw, 39 Fed. R. 578.

The jurisdictional amount may be made up of several distinct claims exceeding two thousand dollars in the aggregate.[1]

§ 649. **Diverse citizenship as a ground for removal.**—We have already called attention to the provisions of the removal acts in regard to removals on the ground of diverse citizenship.[2] A corporation, as we have elsewhere shown,[3] is regarded as a citizen of the state in which it was incorporated, within the meaning of these acts.[4] The citizenship of the stockholders is immaterial.[5] We have also shown that no state can deprive a foreign corporation of the right of removal given by congress.[6] But a corporation may be adopted so as to become a domestic corporation and a citizen of the state adopting it,[7] or it may be formed by concurrent legislation of two or more states or consolidated under their laws so as to become a citizen of each.[8] The mere fact, however, that it carries on business, or is authorized to carry on business or hold property in another state than that in which it is incorporated, does not

[1] Marshall v. Holmes, 141 U. S. 589, s. c. 12 Sup. Ct. R. 62; Bernheim v. Birnbaum, 30 Fed. R. 885. See, also, Brown v. Trousdale, 138 U. S. 389, s. c. 11 Sup. Ct. R. 308.

[2] Ante, § 645.

[3] Ante, § 23.

[4] "Federal Jurisdiction of Corporations as Citizens," 36 Cent. L. J. 333; Marshall v. Baltimore, etc., R. Co., 16 How. (U. S.) 314; Rundle v. Delaware, etc., Canal Co., 14 How. (U. S.) 80; Railway Co. v. Whitton, 13 Wall. (U. S.) 270; Bonaparte v. Camden, etc., R. Co., Bald. (U. S.) 205; Stanley v. Chicago, etc., R. Co., 62 Mo. 508; W. U. Tel. Co. v. Dickinson, 40 Ind. 444; Louisville, etc., R. Co. v. Letson, 2 How. 497; Ohio & M. R. Co. v. Wheeler, 1 Black 286; Boom Co. v. Patterson, 98 U. S. 403; Quigley v. Cent. Pacific R. Co., 11 Nev. 350. The citizenship of a corporation is sufficiently disclosed by an allegation that it is a corporation duly organized under the laws of New York. Dodge v. Tulleys, 144 U. S. 451, s. c. 12 Sup. Ct. R. 728. See, also, Robertson v. Scottish, etc., Ins. Co., 68 Fed. R. 173.

[5] Baltimore, etc., R. Co. v. Cary, 28 Ohio St. 208; Quigley v. Central R. Co., 11 Nev. 350; Pomeroy v. New York, etc., R. Co., 4 Blatch. (U. S.) 120; Hatch v. Chicago, etc., R. Co., 6 Blatch. (U. S.) 105; Minnett v. Milwaukee, etc., R. Co., 3 Dill. (U. S.) 460.

[6] Ante, § 23; "Federal Jurisdiction of Corporation as Citizens," 36 Cent. L. J. 333; Southern Pac. Co. v. Denton, 146 U. S. 202, s. c. 13 Sup. Ct. R. 44.

[7] Ante, § 23.

[8] Ante, §§ 26, 28. See Colglazier v. Louisville, etc., R. Co., 22 Fed. R. 568; Uphoff v. Chicago, etc., R. Co.,

make it a citizen of such other state.[1] Neither does a state statute requiring a foreign corporation to have an agent in the state, upon whom process can be served, make it a citizen of that state.[2] As the jurisdictional clause of the removal act refers to citizens and not merely to residents of different states, the petition for removal on the ground of diverse citizenship should show that the controversy is between citizens of different states, and not merely that the defendant is a non-resident or a resident of a different state from the plaintiff.[3] It has been strongly urged that, within the meaning of the last removal act, a corporation can only remove a cause to the federal court where it is a resident as well as a citizen of another state.[4] But it is now well settled by judicial decision that in order to be a "non-resident of the state" in which suit is brought within the meaning of this act, the defendant need only be a corporation created by the laws of another state.[5] Although there is considerable conflict among the decisions of the different circuit courts of the United States, as well as among the decisions of the various state courts, it now seems

---

[5] Fed. R. 545, and compare Nashua, etc., R. Co. v. Boston, etc., R. Co., 136 U. S. 356, with Pacific R. Co. v. Missouri Pac. R. Co., 23 Fed. R. 565, s. c. 20 Am. & Eng. R. Cas. 590. See, also, Fitzgerald v. Missouri Pac. R. Co., 45 Fed. R. 812; Paul v. Baltimore, etc., R. Co., 44 Fed. R. 513.

[1] Martin v. Baltimore, etc., R. Co., 151 U. S. 673, s. c. 14 Sup. Ct. R. 533; Guinn v. Iowa Cent. R. Co., 14 Fed. R. 323; Holden v. Putnam, etc., Ins. Co., 46 N. Y. 1, s. c. 7 Am. R. 287; Baltimore, etc., R. Co. v. Kountz, 104 U. S. 5; Conn v. Chicago, etc., R. Co., 48 Fed. R. 177; Pennsylvania Co. v. St. Louis, etc., R. Co., 118 U. S. 290, s. c. 6 Sup. Ct. R. 1094; Alleghaney Co. v. Cleveland, etc., R. Co., 51 Pa. St. 228; Baltimore, etc., R. Co. v. Cary, 28 Ohio St. 208; Baltimore, etc., R. Co. v. Wightman, 29 Gratt. (Va.) 431.

[2] Chicago, etc., R. Co. v. Minnesota, etc., R. Co., 29 Fed. R. 337; Amsden v. Norwich, etc., Ins. Co., 44 Fed. R. 515; Fales v. Chicago, etc., R. Co., 32 Fed. R. 673; Martin v. Baltimore, etc., R. Co., 151 U. S. 673, s. c. 14 Sup. Ct. R. 533; Western Un. Tel. Co. v. Dickinson, 40 Ind. 444, s. c. 13 Am. R. 295; Morton v. Mutual, etc., Ins. Co., 105 Mass. 141. But see Scott v. Texas, etc., Co., 41 Fed. R. 225.

[3] Pennsylvania Co. v. Bender, 148 U. S. 255, s. c. 13 Sup. Ct. R. 591; Chicago, etc., R. Co. v. Ohle, 117 U. S. 123; Mansfield, etc., R. Co. v. Swan, 111 U. S. 379; Brown v. Keene, 8 Pet. (U. S.) 112; Neel v. Pennsylvania Co., 157 U. S. 153, s. c. 15 Sup. Ct. R. 589.

[4] Residence of corporations under the removal act, by Charles R. Pence, 35 Cent. Law J. 285.

[5] Fales v. Chicago, etc., Co., 32 Fed. R. 673; Henning v. Western U. Tel.

to be well settled by the decisions of the supreme court of the United States, as well as by the weight of authority generally, that the requisite diversity of citizenship must exist not only at the time the petition for removal is filed, but also at the time the suit is commenced.[1] But it has been held in a recent case, contrary to the rule which prevails where the removal is sought upon the ground of a federal question or where the question is as to a separable controversy, that the diverse citizenship may be shown in the petition for removal and that it need not appear in the complaint.[2]

§ 650. Separable controversy.—The latest act upon the subject of the removal of causes restricts the right of removal where there is a separable controversy, which was formerly given to one or more of the plaintiffs or defendants, to "one or more of the defendants actually interested in such controversy;" but the decisions as to what is a separable controversy apply equally well to both acts. This separable controversy must be wholly between citizens of different states and must also be such as can be fully determined as between them;[3] but it need not be the principal controversy in the case, and the number of controversies is immaterial.[4] In an action in tort against a railroad company and one of its employes, where each was charged with a different negligent act causing the in-

---

Co., 43 Fed. R. 97; Martin v. Baltimore, etc., R. Co., 151 U. S. 673, 676, s. c. 14 Sup. Ct. R. 533; Robertson v. Scottish, etc., Ins. Co., 68 Fed. R. 173. The receiver of a railroad company, being a citizen of another state, may remove an action brought against him in his official capacity for death by wrongful act, though the railroad company is a citizen of the state in which the action is brought. Brisenden v. Chamberlain, 53 Fed. R. 307.

[1] La Confiance, etc., v. Hall, 137 U. S. 61, s. c. 11 Sup. Ct. R. 5; Crehore v. Railroad Co., 131 U. S. 240, s. c. 9 Sup. Ct. R. 692; Stevens v. Nichols, 130 U. S. 230, s. c. 9 Sup. Ct. R. 518; Indianapolis, etc., R. Co. v. Risley, 50 Ind. 60; Blackwell v. Lynchburg, etc., R. Co., 107 N. Car. 217. See, also, Laird v. Connecticut, etc., R. Co., 55 N. H. 375, s. c. 20 Am. R. 215.

[2] City of Ysleta v. Canda, 67 Fed. R. 6.

[3] Corbin v. Van Brunt, 105 U. S. 576; Shainwald v. Lewis, 108 U. S. 158; Capital City Bank v. Hodgin, 22 Fed. R. 209; In re The Jarnecke Ditch, 69 Fed. R. 161, and numerous authorities there cited; National Docks, etc., R. Co. v. Pennsylvania R. Co., 52 N. J. Eq. 58, 28 Atl. R. 71; Torrence v. Shedd, 144 U. S. 527, 530, s. c. 12 Sup. Ct. R. 726.

[4] Farmers' L. & T. Co. v. Chicago, etc., R. Co., 9 Biss. (U. S.) 133; Snow

jury to the plaintiff, it has been held that a separable controversy was presented and that the suit might be removed.[1] But it has been held, on the other hand, that there is no separable controversy where the only question is as to the priority of different liens on the same property,[2] even though each defendant makes a separate defense,[3] or where land is sought to be condemned as against both the lessor and lessee,[4] or where two corporations are jointly charged with trespassing on the plaintiff's land, even though one of the defendants claims that the other did not have a corporate existence and that it alone committed the alleged trespass,[5] or where a sub-contractor sues both a railroad company and the principal contractor under a statute giving contractors and material men a lien on the railroad.[6] The question whether there is a separable controversy authorizing a removal is to be determined by the state of the pleadings or record at the time of the application, and not from the allegations of the petition for removal or the subsequent proceedings.[7] Indeed, it is held that it must be determined from the declaration or pleadings of the plaintiff, and that a defendant can not, by answer, raise a separable controversy.[8]

v. Smith, 4 Hughes (U. S. C. C.) 204. See, also, for cases in which it was held that there was a separable controversy, County Court of Taylor Co. v. Baltimore, etc., R. Co., 35 Fed. R. 161; Foster v. Chesapeake, etc., R. Co., 47 Fed. R. 369.

[1] Fergason v. Chicago, etc., R. Co., 63 Fed. R. 177; Beuttel v. Chicago, etc., R. Co., 26 Fed. R. 50.

[2] Bissell v. Canada, etc., R. Co., 39 Fed. R. 225.

[3] Fidelity Ins. Co. v. Huntington, 117 U. S. 280, s. c. 6 Sup. Ct. R. 733; Young v. Parker, 132 U. S. 267, s. c. 10 Sup. Ct. R. 75.

[4] Bellaire v. Baltimore, etc., Railroad Co., 146 U. S. 117, s. c. 13 Sup. Ct. R. 16; Kohl v. United States, 91 U. S. 367.

[5] Louisville, etc., Railroad Co. v. Wangelin, 132 U. S. 599, s. c. 10 Sup. Ct. R. 203.

[6] Ames v. Chicago, etc., R. Co., 39 Fed. R. 881. See, generally, Merchants', etc., Co. v. Insurance Co., 151 U. S. 368, s. c. 14 Sup. Ct. R. 367; St. Louis, etc., Railway Co. v. Wilson, 114 U. S. 60, s. c. 5 Sup. Ct. R. 738; Thurber v. Miller, 67 Fed. R. 371; Haire v. Rome R. Co., 57 Fed. R. 321; Sweeney v. Grand Island, etc., R. Co., 61 Fed. R. 3; Fox v. Mackay, 60 Fed. R. 4.

[7] Barney v. Latham, 103 U. S. 205; Graves v. Corbin, 132 U. S. 571, s. c. 10 Sup. Ct. R. 196; In re The Jarnecke Ditch, 69 Fed. R. 161; Grand Trunk R. Co. v. Twitchell, 59 Fed. R. 727.

[8] Ayres v. Wiswall, 112 U. S. 187, s. c. 5 Sup. R. 90; Louisville, etc., R. Co. v. Ide, 114 U. S. 52, s. c. 5 Sup. Ct. R. 735; Thurber v. Miller, 67 Fed. R. 371; National Docks, etc., R. Co. v. Pennsylvania R. Co., 52 N.J. Eq. 58, 28 Atl. R. 71; Arrowsmith v. Nashville, etc., R. Co., 57 Fed. R. 165.

The rule is thus stated in a recent case.[1] "As this court has repeatedly affirmed, not only in cases of joint contracts, but in actions for torts, which might have been brought against all or against any one of the defendants, separate answers by the several defendants sued on joint causes of action may present different questions for determination, but they do not necessarily divide the suit into separate controversies. A defendant has no right to say that an action shall be several which a plaintiff elects to be joint. A separate defense may defeat a joint recovery, but it can not deprive a plaintiff of his right to prosecute his own suit to final determination in his own way. The cause of action is the subject-matter of the controversy, and that is, for all the purposes of the suit, whatever the plaintiff declares it to be in his pleadings."[2] The fact that one of two joint defendants fails to answer or suffers a default does not make the controversy a separable one between the plaintiff and the other defendant.[3]

§ 651. Prejudice or local influence as a ground for removal. —The provisions for removal where there is a separate controversy are not applicable where the removal is sought upon the ground of prejudice or local influence.[4] The act of March 3, 1887, as corrected by the act of August 13, 1888, unlike the earlier acts, gives the plaintiff no right of removal upon the ground of prejudice or local influence, but it permits one of several defendants, where the requirements as to citizenship and the amount in controversy are satisfied, to obtain a re-

[1] Torrence v. Shedd, 144 U. S. 527, 530, s. c. 12 Sup. Ct. R. 726.

[2] Citing Louisville, etc., Railroad Co. v. Ide, 114 U. S. 52, 56, 5 Sup. Ct. R. 735; Pirie v. Tvedt, 115 U. S. 41, 43, 5 Sup. Ct. 1034, 1161; Sloane v. Anderson, 117 U. S. 275, 6 Sup. Ct. 730; Little v. Giles, 118 U. S. 596, 601, 602, 7 Sup. Ct. 32; Thorne Wire Hedge Co. v. Fuller, 122 U. S. 535, 7 Sup. Ct. 1265.

[3] Wilson v. Oswego Twp., 151 U. S. 56, s. c. 14 Sup. Ct. R. 259; Putnam v. Ingraham, 114 U. S. 57; Feison v. Hardy, 114 N. Car. 58, 429, 19 S. E. R. 91, 701. So held, even where no process was served against one of the defendants and he did not appear. Patchin v. Hunter, 38 Fed. R. 51; Ames v. Chicago, etc., R. Co., 39 Fed. R. 881.

[4] Jefferson v. Driver, 117 U. S. 272; Young v. Parker, 132 U. S. 267, s. c. 10 Sup. Ct. R. 75.

moval,[1] whereas the act of 1867 required all the defendants to join in the petition. He must, however, be a citizen of a different state from that in which the suit is brought,[2] and it has been held that the plaintiffs must all be citizens of the state in which the suit is brought.[3] A defendant who is a citizen of the same state as some of the plaintiffs can not have the suit removed merely upon the ground of prejudice or local influence as between himself and other defendants.[4] It is now settled, after some conflict among the authorities, that the value of the matter in dispute, exclusive of interest and costs, must exceed two thousand dollars.[5] The application should be made to the proper circuit court of the United States and not to the state court.[6] The act provides for a removal to the proper circuit court by a defendant "when it shall be made to appear to said circuit court that from prejudice or local influence he will not be able to obtain justice in the state court in which the suit is pending, or in any other state court to which the said defendant may, under the laws of the state, have the right, on account of such prejudice or local influence, to remove it;" but it does not prescribe the method for making this appear to

---

[1] Haire v. Rome R. Co., 57 Fed. R. 321; Fisk v. Henarie, 32 Fed. R. 417; Whelan v. New York, etc., R. Co., 35 Fed. R. 849. See, also, Campbell v. Collins, 62 Fed. R. 849. It makes no difference that some of the other defendants are residents of the state in which the suit is brought. Jackson, etc., Co. v. Pearson, 60 Fed. R. 113.

[2] The clause authorizing a removal upon the ground of prejudice or local influence does not apply where one party is an alien. Cohn v. Louisville, etc., R. Co., 39 Fed. R. 227; Grand Trunk R. Co. v. Twitchell, 59 Fed. R. 727.

[3] Thouron v. East Tenn., etc., R. Co., 38 Fed. R. 673; Niblock v. Alexander, 44 Fed. R. 306; Rike v. Floyd, 42 Fed. R. 247. This is true at least where the plaintiffs are all jointly interested against the non-resident defendant who seeks the removal. Young v. Parker, 132 U. S. 267, s. c. 10 Sup. Ct. R. 75; Gann v. Northeastern R. Co., 57 Fed. R. 417.

[4] Hanrick v. Hanrick, 153 U. S. 192, s. c. 14 Sup. Ct. R. 835.

[5] *Ex parte* Pennsylvania Co., 137 U. S. 451, s. c. 11 Sup. Ct. R. 141; Carson, etc., Lumber Co. v. Holtzclaw, 39 Fed. R. 578; Malone v. Richmond, etc., R. Co., 35 Fed. R. 625; Roraback v. Pennsylvania Co., 42 Fed. R. 420.

[6] Williams v. Southern, etc., R. Co., 116 N. Car. 558, s. c. 21 S. E. R. 298; Southworth v. Reid, 36 Fed. R. 451; Huskins v. Cincinnati, etc., R. Co., 37 Fed. R. 504; Rome, etc., R. Co. v. Smith, 84 Ga. 238; Beyer v. Soper Lumber Co., 76 Wis. 145. But see Short v. Chicago, etc., R. Co., 34 Fed. R. 225.

the circuit court. This is usually accomplished by the affidavit of the party seeking the removal. It is the better and safer practice to state the facts showing the prejudice or local influence,[1] but in a few of the circuits it has been held sufficient to follow the language of the statute.[2] It is also held in some circuits that the defendant's affidavit is conclusive and can not be controverted,[3] but we think the better rule is that the court may receive counter-affidavits or other evidence as to the existence of prejudice or local influence.[4]

§ 652. Removal where federal question is involved.—As we have seen, provision is made for the removal of suits "of a civil nature, at law or in equity, arising under the constitution or laws of the United States, or treaties made under their authority." It is not always easy, however, to determine when a suit is one arising under the constitution or laws of the United States. It was said by Chief Justice Marshall that "a case in law or equity consists of the right of the one party as well as the other, and may truly be said to arise under the constitution or a law of the United States whenever its correct decision depends on the right construction of either."[5] But the suit must actually arise out of the operation, construction or application of some provision of the constitution or laws of the United States, and it is not sufficient that during its progress a

---

[1] *Ex parte* Pennsylvania Co., 137 U. S. 451, s. c. 11 Sup. Ct. R. 141; P. Schwenk & Co. *v.* Strang, 59 Fed. R. 209; Goldworthy *v.* Chicago, etc., R. Co., 38 Fed. R. 769; Amy *v.* Manning, 38 Fed. R. 536. It is insufficient to state that affiant believes and has reason to believe that prejudice and local influence exist. Collins *v.* Campbell, 62 Fed. R. 850; Short *v.* Chicago, etc., R. Co., 33 Fed R. 114. See, also, Niblock *v.* Alexander, 44 Fed. R. 306.

[2] Whelan *v.* New York, etc., R. Co., 35 Fed. R. 849; Cooper *v.* Richmond, etc., R. Co., 42 Fed. R. 697.

[3] Cases cited in last note, *supra;* also, Huskins *v.* Cincinnati, etc., R. Co., 37 Fed. R. 504; Brodhead *v.* Shoemaker, 44 Fed. R. 518; Hills *v.* Richmond, etc., R. Co., 33 Fed. R. 81.

[4] Malone *v.* Richmond, etc., R. Co., 35 Fed. R. 625; Short *v.* Chicago, etc., R. Co., 34 Fed. R. 225; Carson, etc., Lumber Co. *v.* Holtzclaw, 39 Fed. R. 578; Robison *v.* Hardy, 38 Fed. R. 49. See, also, Walcott *v.* Watson, 46 Fed. R.529; *Ex parte* Pennsylvania Co., 137 U. S. 457, s. c. 11 Sup. Ct. R. 143.

[5] Cohens *v.* Virginia, 6 Wheat. (U. S.) 264, 379. See, also, Germania Ins. Co. *v.* Wisconsin, 119 U. S. 473; New Orleans, etc., R. Co. *v.* Mississippi, 102 U. S. 135.

construction of the constitution or some law of the United States may become necessary.[1] If the only right claimed by the plaintiff is under a state law, a mere suggestion in his bill that the defendant will claim that such law is void because in contravention of the constitution of the United States will not entitle the defendant to remove the suit upon the ground that a federal question is involved.[2] Among the suits that have been held removable as arising under the constitution or laws of the United States are those in which the question as to whether a state law impairs the obligation of a contract is involved;[3] suits by or against a corporation created by congress;[4] suits against receivers appointed by a federal court;[5] and suits against interstate carriers of goods for unjust discrimination and excessive charges contrary to the interstate commerce law.[6] On the other hand, an application, by a commissioner appointed to abolish grade crossings, for a mandamus to compel a railroad company to obey its order changing the location of the company's tracks has been held not to be removable on the ground that a federal question was involved.[7] So, a suit does

[1] Gold, etc., Water Co. v. Keyes, 96 U. S. 199; Carson v. Dunham, 121 U. S. 421, s. c. 7 Sup. Ct. R. 1030; Fitzgerald v. Missouri Pac. R. Co., 45 Fed. R. 812; State of Iowa v. Chicago, etc., R. Co., 33 Fed. R. 391; Illinois Central R. Co. v. Chicago, etc., R. Co., 122 Ill. 473; Dowell v. Griswold, 5 Sawy. (U. S. C. C.) 39; Starin v. New York, 115 U. S. 248.

[2] State of Tennessee v. Union, etc., Bank, 152 U. S. 454, s. c. 14 Sup. Ct. R. 654.

[3] Smith v. Greenhow, 109 U. S. 669; People v. Chicago, etc., R. Co., 16 Fed. R. 706; Illinois v. Illinois Cent. R. Co., 33 Fed. R. 721; State v. Port Royal, etc., R. Co., 56 Fed. R. 333. But see Hamilton Gaslight, etc., Co. v. City of Hamilton, 146 U. S. 258, s. c. 13 Sup. Ct. R. 90; Stein v. Bienville Water Co., 141 U. S. 67, s. c. 11 Sup. Ct. R. 892.

[4] Pacific Railroad Removal Cases, 115 U. S. 1; Ames v. Kansas, 111 U. S. 449; Union Pac. R. v. McComb, 1 Fed. R. 799.

[5] Jewett v. Whitcomb, 69 Fed. R. 417; Evans v. Dillingham, 43 Fed. R. 177; Texas, etc., Railway Co. v. Cox, 145 U. S. 593, s. c. 12 Sup. Ct. R. 905; Central Trust Co. v. East Tennessee, etc., R. Co., 59 Fed. R. 523; Hardwick v. Kean, 95 Ky. 563, 26 S. W. R. 589.

[6] Lowry v. Chicago, etc., R. Co., 46 Fed. R. 83. See, also, State v. Port Royal, etc., R. Co., 56 Fed. R. 333; Ex parte Lennon, 64 Fed. R. 320. For other cases removable on this ground, see Kansas Pac. R. Co. v. Atchison R. Co., 112 U. S. 414; Southern Pac. R. Co. v. California, 118 U. S. 109, s. c. 6 Sup. Ct. R. 993.

[7] Woodruff v. New York, etc., R. Co., 59 Conn. 63; Dey v. Chicago, etc., R. Co., 45 Fed. R. 82.

not arise under the constitution or laws of the United States, and is not removable on that ground, merely because it requires the statutes of one state to be construed by a court of another state.[1] Nor does a bill in equity to set aside a lease by a corporation of one state to a corporation of another state as *ultra vires* and void and obtain an accounting, assert or raise any federal question.[2] It has also been held that a proceeding to prevent a bridge company from using a franchise to operate a railroad in a public street does not involve a federal question.[3] A suit is not removable as arising under the laws of the United States merely because the supreme court or some other federal court has, in another case, decided the questions of law involved;[4] but, on the other hand, it has been held that a proposition of law which has once been decided by the supreme court of the United States can no longer be treated as a federal question.[5] The fact that a federal question is involved must appear from the plaintiff's own statement of his claim, and where it is not so made to appear it can not be supplied by any allegation in the petition for removal or the subsequent pleadings.[6]

§ 653. Time and manner of making application for removal.

—Under the act of March 3, 1887, as corrected by the act of August 13, 1888, the application for removal upon any other ground than that of prejudice or local influence should be made by filing a petition in the state court "before the defendant is

---

[1] Chicago, etc., R. Co. v. Wiggins Ferry Co., 108 U. S. 18, s. c. 1 Sup. Ct. R. 614.

[2] Central R. Co. v. Mills, 113 U. S. 249, s. c. 5 Sup. Ct. R. 456.

[3] Commonwealth v. Louisville Bridge Co., 42 Fed. R. 241.

[4] Leather Manufacturers' Nat. Bank v. Cooper, 120 U. S. 778, s. c. 7 Sup. Ct. R. 777.

[5] State of Kansas v. Bradley, 26 Fed. R. 289. This decision, however, seems to us to be erroneous and in conflict with the case cited in the last preceding note. The federal courts do not make the laws of the United States.

[6] State of Tennessee v. Union, etc., Bank, 152 U. S. 454, s. c. 14 Sup. Ct. R. 654; Chappell v. Waterworth, 155 U. S. 102, s. c. 15 Sup. Ct. R. 34; East Lake Land Co. v. Brown, 155 U. S. 488, s. c. 15 Sup. Ct. R. 357; Postal Tel., etc., Co. v. State of Alabama, 155 U. S. 482, s. c. 15 Sup. Ct. R. 192; Haggin v. Lewis, 66 Fed. R. 199; Caples v. Texas, etc., R. Co., 67 Fed. R. 9.

required by the laws of the state or the rule of the state court in which such suit is brought to answer or plead to the declaration or complaint of the plaintiff." If no application is filed within that time the right of removal is lost.[1] But it is held that the petitioner has the full time allowed the defendant in which to answer or plead, although the latter may demur or answer before it has expired,[2] and that where an amended complaint is filed which states an entirely different cause of action in which the original suit is merged the time begins to run from the filing of such amended complaint.[3] The application comes too late, however, if not filed before the time at which the defendant is required to plead to the jurisdiction or in abatement, even though it is filed before the time at which he is required to plead to the merits.[4] A defendant who makes no application for removal himself can not assign as error the action of the court in denying a removal upon the application of other defendants.[5] So, on the other hand, it is held that objection to the jurisdiction of a United States circuit court over a suit, otherwise removable, because the application for removal was not made in time, is waived where it is not made until the case is taken to the supreme court on writ of error.[6] The application for removal upon the ground of prejudice or local influence may be made at any time before the trial. It is held, however, that it can not be made after one trial has been had and a reversal obtained, and it is intimated that the right of removal must be exercised before or at the term at which

[1] Price v. Lehigh, etc., R. Co., 65 Fed. R. 825; Font v. Gulf, etc., Co., 47 La. Ann. 272, s. c. 16 So. R. 828; Williams v. Southern, etc., 116 N. Car. 558, 21 S. E. R. 298; Woolf v. Chisholm, 30 Fed. R. 881; Beyer v. Soper Lumber Co., 76 Wis. 145. See, also, Houston, etc., R. Co. v. Shirley, 111 U. S. 358; Fletcher v. Hamlet, 116 U. S. 408.

[2] Tennessee, etc., Co. v. Waller, 37 Fed. R. 545; Gavin v. Vance, 33 Fed. R. 84; Conner v. Skagit, etc., Coal Co., 45 Fed. R. 802.

[3] Mattoon v. Reynolds, 62 Fed. R. 417; Evans v. Dillingham, 43 Fed. R. 177.

[4] Martin v. Baltimore, etc., R. Co., 151 U. S. 673, s. c. 14 Sup. Ct. R. 533.

[5] Merchants', etc., Co. v. Insurance Co., 151 U. S. 368, s. c. 14 Sup. Ct. R. 367; Rand v. Walker, 117 U. S. 340, s. c. 6 Sup. Ct. R. 769.

[6] Martin v. Baltimore, etc., R. Co., 151 U. S. 673, s. c. 14 Sup. Ct. R. 533. See, also, Tod v. Cleveland, etc., R. Co., 65 Fed. R. 145.

the cause "could be first tried, and before the trial thereof," as under the act of 1875.[1] Provision is also made in the removal act for the filing of a bond in certain cases and a copy of the record.[2] It has been held that the petition for removal forms part of the record, and if the record, including the petition, shows that the case is one of federal jurisdiction it is sufficient.[3] But it is said that an additional petition presented to the federal court with the removal papers, alleging facts not presented to the state court, will not confer jurisdiction on the federal court,[4] although a petition may be amended in the latter court so as to more fully state the facts which appear in the record or upon which the statements in the original petition were based.[5]

§ 654. Effect of application on jurisdiction of state and federal court.—When a proper petition and bond have been filed in the state court, it is the duty of that court to accept the same, and all further proceedings therein are *coram non judice*.[6] It has been held that the filing of a petition for re-

---

[1] Fisk v. Henarie, 142 U. S. 459, s. c. 12 Sup. Ct. R. 207. See, also, Lookout Mountain R. Co. v. Houston, 32 Fed. R. 711; Davis v. Chicago, etc., R. Co., 46 Fed. R. 307. But compare Huskins v. Cincinnati, etc., R. Co., 37 Fed. R. 504; Brodhead v. Shoemaker, 44 Fed. R. 518; Stix v. Keith, 90 Ala. 121.

[2] 1 Suppl. U. S. Rev. St. 613. See Hayes v. Todd, 34 Fla. 233, s. c. 15 So. R. 752; Lucker v. Phœnix, etc., Co., 66 Fed. R. 161; Waite v. Phœnix Ins. Co., 62 Fed. R. 769; Austin v. Gagan, 39 Fed. R. 626; Foster's Fed. Pr., § 385.

[3] Supreme Lodge v. Wilson, 66 Fed. R. 785. See, also, Security Co. v. Pratt, 65 Conn. 161, s. c. 32 Atl. R. 396; Crehore v. Ohio, etc., R. Co., 131 U. S. 240, s. c. 9 Sup. Ct. R. 692.

[4] Waite v. Phœnix Ins. Co., 62 Fed. R. 769.

[5] Powers v. Chesapeake, etc., R. Co., 65 Fed. R. 129; Carson v. Dunham, 121 U. S. 421, s. c. 7 Sup. Ct. R. 1030. See, also, Hardwick v. Kean, 95 Ky. 563, 26 S. W. R. 589.

[6] Gordon v. Longest, 16 Pet. (U. S.) 97; National Steamship Co. v. Tugman, 106 U. S. 118; Hatch v. Chicago, etc., R. Co., 6 Blatchf. (U. S. C. C.) 105; Stevens v. Phœnix Ins. Co., 41 N. Y. 149; Southern Pac. R. Co. v. Harrison, 73 Tex. 103; New Orleans, etc., R. Co. v. Mississippi, 102 U. S. 135; Parker's Admr. v. Clarkson, 39 W. Va. 184, s. c. 19 S. E. R. 431; Northern Pac. R. Co. v. McMullen, 86 Wis. 501, s. c. 56 N. W. R. 629. Participating in proceeding in the state court which persists in detaining jurisdiction after removal, is not necessarily a waiver of the removal. Home, etc., Ins. Co. v. Dunn, 19 Wall. (U. S.) 214; McMullen v. Northern Pac.

moval, without objecting to the jurisdiction of the state court, constitutes a general appearance and operates as a waiver of defects in the summons or service thereof,[1] but we think the better rule is that a special appearance for the purpose of obtaining a removal does not operate as a general appearance and waiver of such defects.[2] The state courts have generally claimed and been conceded the right to examine the petition and record and determine whether the statutory requirements have been complied with;[3] but the federal courts are the final judges of their own jurisdiction, and the decision of a state court is not conclusive as to such jurisdiction.[4] The jurisdiction of the federal court attaches where the suit is removable, as soon as the statutory requirements are complied with, whether the state court makes an order for the removal or not.[5] An order for the removal of a suit, where it may be remanded, merely suspends the jurisdiction of the state court, and, if the federal court remands the case, that jurisdiction will be resumed.[6]

R. Co., 57 Fed. R. 16; Northern Pac. R. Co. v. McMullen, 86 Wis. 501, s. c. 56 N. W. R. 629; Waite v. Phœnix Ins. Co., 62 Fed. R. 769; Stanley v. Chicago, etc., R. Co., 62 Mo. 508; Little Rock, etc., R. Co. v. Iredell, 50 Ark. 388.

[1] Wabash Western Ry. Co. v. Brow, 65 Fed. R. 941; O'Donnell v. Atchison, etc., R. Co., 49 Fed. R. 689; Farmer v. National, etc., Assn., 138 N. Y. 265.

[2] 2 Elliott's Gen. Pr., § 474; Garner v. Second Nat. Bank, 66 Fed. R. 369; Goldey v. Morning News, 156 U. S. 518, s. c. 15 Sup. Ct. R. 559; Ahlhauser v. Butler, 50 Fed. R. 705; Perkins v. Hendryx, 40 Fed. R. 657.

[3] Baltimore, etc., R. Co. v. New Albany, etc., R. Co., 53 Ind. 597; Carswell v. Schley, 59 Ga. 17; Burch v. Davenport, etc., R. Co., 46 Iowa 449, s. c. 26 Am. R. 150; Larson v. Cox, 39 Kan. 631; Broadway Nat. Bank v. Adams, 130 Mass. 431; Burlington, etc., R. Co. v. Dunn, 122 U. S. 513, s. c. 7 Sup. Ct. R. 1262; Beadleston v. Harpending, 32 Fed. R. 644; Roberts v. Chicago, etc., R. Co., 45 Fed. R. 433.

[4] Wilson v. Western Union Tel. Co., 34 Fed. R. 561; Baltimore, etc., R. Co. v. Koontz, 104 U. S. 5; Marshall v. Holmes, 141 U. S. 589, s. c. 12 Sup. Ct. R. 62; Barrow v. Hunton, 99 U. S. 80; Home, etc., Ins. Co. v. Dunn, 19 Wall. (U. S.) 214; Knahtla v. Oregon, etc., R. Co., 21 Ore. 136, s. c. 27 Pac. R. 91.

[5] Wills v. Baltimore, etc., R. Co., 65 Fed. R. 532; Shepherd v. Bradstreet Co., 65 Fed. R. 142; Hayes v. Todd, 34 Fla. 233, s. c. 15 So. R. 752; Kern v. Huidekoper, 103 U. S. 485; Fisk v. Union Pac. R. Co., 6 Blatchf. (U. S. C. C.) 362; Chattanooga, etc., R. Co. v. Cincinnati, etc., R. Co., 44 Fed. R. 456; St. Anthony, etc., Co. v. King, etc., Co., 23 Minn. 186; McNeal, etc., Co. v. Howland, etc., Co., 99 N. Car. 202.

[6] Young v. Parker, 132 U. S. 267, s. c.

§ 655. **Remanding and dismissing cause.**—The last removal act specifically provides for remanding suits removed on the ground of prejudice or local influence as to defendants not affected thereby, where such suits can be fully and justly determined as to them in the state court.[1] It is also provided generally in that portion of section 5, of the act of March 3, 1875, which still remains in force, that, "if in any suit commenced in a circuit court, or removed from a state court to a circuit court of the United States, it shall appear to the satisfaction of said circuit court, at any time after such suit has been brought or removed thereto, that such suit does not really and substantially involve a dispute or controversy properly within the jurisdiction of said circuit court, or that the parties to said suit have been improperly or collusively made or joined, either as plaintiffs or defendants, for the purpose of creating a case cognizable or removable under this act, the said circuit court shall proceed no further therein, but shall dismiss the suit or remand it to the court from which it was removed as justice may require, and shall make such order as to costs as shall be just.'"[2] Objections appearing upon the face of the record should be taken advantage of by motion to remand,[3] and a party by going to trial without objection, or even by undue delay, may waive his right to have the cause remanded on account of mere irregularities, such as the failure to file the petition for removal in

[1] 1 U. S. Supp. Rev. St. 612.
[2] 18 U. S. Stat. at L. 470; 1 Supp. U. S. Rev. St. 83. See, also, Ayres v. Wiswall, 112 U. S. 187, s. c. 5 Sup. Ct. R. 90; Williams v. Nottawa, 104 U. S. 209; Graves v. Corbin, 132 U. S. 571, s. c. 10 Sup. Ct. R. 196; Shepherd v. Bradstreet, 65 Fed R. 142; Hamblin v. Chicago, etc., R. Co., 43 Fed. R. 401; Texas, etc., Co. v. Seeligson, 122 U. S. 519, s. c. 7 Sup. Ct. R. 1261; Pennsylvania R. Co. v. Allegheny, etc., R. Co., 25 Fed. R. 113. The court may also remand the suit for failure to file a transcript of the record in time, but this seems to be largely discretionary with the court. St. Paul, etc., R. Co. v. McLean, 108 U. S. 212, s. c. 2 Sup. Ct. R. 498; Lucker v. Phœnix, etc., Co., 66 Fed. R. 161; Removal Cases, 100 U. S. 457; Jackson v. Mutual L. Ins. Co., 3 Woods (U. S. C. C.) 413.
[3] Hoyt v. Wright, 4 Fed. R. 168; Martin v. Baltimore, etc., R. Co., 151 U. S. 673, s. c. 14 Sup. Ct. R. 533; Tod v. Cleveland, etc., R. Co., 65 Fed. R. 145; Newman v. Schwerin, 61 Fed. R. 865.

10 Sup. Ct. R. 75; Southern Pac. R. Co. v. Superior Court, 63 Cal. 607.

time, or the like.¹ But it is said that when the record on its face shows that the court has jurisdiction, the want of jurisdiction should be shown by plea in abatement.² The court, of its own motion, should remand the cause where it appears that it has no jurisdiction because the case is not one of federal cognizance, and this objection, unlike that based upon a mere irregularity, is not, therefore, waived by the failure to make it in the first instance.³ It has been held that a case which has been properly removed can not be remanded by consent.⁴ The state court can not review the action of the federal court in remanding the suit,⁵ and no appeal or writ of error lies from the order of the circuit court remanding the suit.⁶

¹ French v. Hay, 22 Wall. (U. S.) 238; Ayres v. Watson, 113 U. S. 594, s. c. 5 Sup. Ct. R. 641; Carrington v. Florida, etc., R. Co., 9 Blatchf. (U. S. C. C.) 467; Baltimore, etc., R. Co. v. Ford, 35 Fed. R. 170; Wyly v. Richmond, etc., R. Co., 63 Fed. R. 487; Martin v. Baltimore, etc., R. Co., 151 U. S. 673, s. c. 14 Sup. Ct. R. 533.

² Hoyt v. Wright, 1 McCrary (U. S. C. C.) 130; Clarkhuff v. Wisconsin, etc., R. Co., 26 Fed. R. 465; Rumsey v. Call, 28 Fed. R. 769. See, also, Coal Co. v. Blatchford, 11 Wall. (U. S.) 172. The burden of proof is upon the petitioner, and if it does not clearly appear that the federal court has jurisdiction, the cause should be remanded. Carson v. Durham, 121 U. S. 421; Fitzgerald v. Missouri Pac. R. Co., 45 Fed. R. 812; Wolff v. Archibald, 14 Fed. R. 369.

³ Cameron v. Hodges, 127 U. S. 322, s. c. 8 Sup. Ct. R. 1154, 1156; Brice v. Sommers, 8 Chicago Leg. News 290; Mansfield, etc., R. Co. v. Swan, 111 U. S. 379, s. c. 4 Sup. Ct. R. 510; Ferguson v. Ross, 38 Fed. R. 161; Jackson v. Allen, 132 U. S. 27, s. c. 10 Sup. Ct. R. 9; Frisbie v. Chesapeake, etc., R. Co., 57 Fed. R. 1; Bronson v. St. Croix Lumber Co., 35 Fed. R. 634. The supreme court, on reversal of a suit because the circuit court did not have jurisdiction on removal, will direct the circuit court to remand it to the state court, without allowing any amendment of the petition for removal in the circuit court. Crehore v. Ohio, etc., R. Co., 131 U. S. 240, s. c. 9 Sup. Ct. R. 692; Hancock v. Holbrook, 112 U. S. 229, s. c. 5 Sup. Ct. R. 115; Jackson v. Allen, *supra*.

⁴ Lawton v. Blitch, 30 Fed. R. 641. But see Wadleigh v. Standard, etc., Ins. Co., 76 Wis. 439.

⁵ Tilley v. Cobb, 56 Minn. 295, s. c. 57 N. W. R. 799; Fitzgerald v. Fitzgerald, etc., Co., 44 Neb. 463, s. c. 62 N. W. R. 899.

⁶ Morey v. Lockhart, 123 U. S. 56, s. c. 8 Sup. Ct. R. 65; Burlington, etc., R. Co. v. Dunn, 122 U. S. 513, s. c. 7 Sup. Ct. R. 1262; May v. State Nat. Bank, 59 Ark. 614, s. c. 28 S. W. R. 431; Chicago, etc., R. Co. v. Gray, 131 U. S. 396, s. c. 9 Sup. Ct. R. 793; Birdseye v. Schaeffer, 140 U. S. 117, s. c. 11 Sup. Ct. R. 885; Richmond, etc., R. Co. v. Thouron, 134 U. S. 45, s. c. 10 Sup. Ct. R. 517.

§ 656. **Pleading and practice in federal court after removal.**—It is not necessary to file new pleadings in the circuit court after removal, if the pleadings filed in the state court are in proper condition for the trial of the issue between the parties.[1] The general rule is that no repleader is necessary if the action is, in its nature, a common law action;[2] but if legal and equitable causes of action or defenses are united under the state practice a suit may be recast or separated into an action at law and a suit in equity,[3] and a repleader is usually necessary.[4] The rules of practice in the federal court govern the case, in general, after its removal;[5] but the federal circuit courts, on the law side, are bound to follow the state practice "as near as may be" in most respects, and it has been held that where a receiver, appointed by a federal court, on being sued in a state court as authorized by the recent act of congress, removes the suit to the federal court, the plaintiff is entitled to a trial by jury if he would have been entitled to such a trial in the state court.[6] So, as a general rule, the federal circuit court will follow the rulings of the state court made in the case before its removal.[7]

---

[1] 20 Am. & Eng. Ency. of Law 1021; Gridley v. Westbrook, 23 How. (U.S.) 503; Merchants', etc., Nat. Bank v. Wheeler, 13 Blatchf. (U. S. C. C.) 218, s. c. 3 Cent. L. J. 13; City of Detroit v. Detroit City R. Co., 55 Fed. R. 569.

[2] Thompson v. Railroad Companies, 6 Wall. (U. S.) 134; Dart v. McKinney, 9 Blatchf. (U. S. C. C.) 359; Bills v. New Orleans, etc., R. Co., 13 Blatchf. (U. S. C. C.) 227; Partridge v. Phœnix, etc., Ins. Co., 15 Wall. (U. S.) 573.

[3] Fisk v. Union Pac. R. Co., 8 Blatchf. (U. S. C. C.) 299; Perkins v. Hendryx, 23 Fed. R. 418; Lacroix v. Lyons, 27 Fed. R. 403; Foster's Fed. Pr., § 391. See Northern Pac. R. Co. v. Paine, 119 U. S. 561.

[4] Hurt v. Hollingsworth, 100 U. S. 100; Whittenton, etc., Co. v. Memphis, etc., R. Co., 19 Fed. R. 273; La Mothe, etc., Co. v. National Tube Works, 15 Blatchf. (U. S. C. C.) 432.

[5] Henning v. Western Un. Tel. Co., 40 Fed. R. 658.

[6] Vany v. Receiver of Toledo, etc., R. Co., 67 Fed. R. 379. See, also, North Alabama, etc., Co. v. Orman, 55 Fed. R. 18.

[7] Bryant v. Thompson, 27 Fed. R. 881; Davis v. St. Louis, etc., R. Co., 25 Fed. R. 786; Duncan v. Gegan, 101 U. S. 810. But see Spring Co. v. Knowlton, 103 U. S. 49.

CHAPTER XXVII.

GOVERNMENTAL CONTROL.

§ 657. Introductory.
658. Effect of the commerce clause of the federal constitution upon the power of the states.
659. Legislative power over private rights of railroad companies—Nature of.
660. Constitutional protection.
661. The limits of legislative power unduly extended.
662. Regulations affecting acts and duties of a public nature.
663. Corporate rights are subject to the police power.
664. The police power is fettered by limitations.
665. The subject must be one over which the police power extends – Cases adjudging statutes invalid.
§ 666. Police power—Legislative and judicial questions.
667. The police power and the commerce clause of the federal constitution.
668. Regulations that have been held valid.
669. The power to impose penalties in favor of private persons—Constitutional questions.
670. Regulating speed of trains.
671. Grade crossings.
672. Requiring services and denying compensation.
673. Federal corporations—State can not transform into a domestic corporation.

§ 657. **Introductory.**—The question as to the limitations that may be imposed upon railroad corporations, or as to the burdens which may be laid upon them, or as to the duties exacted of them, by legislative enactments passed prior to the organization or adopted at the time of the creation of the corporation, is very different from that which arises where the legislative enactments are passed subsequent to the creation of the corporation. The familiar doctrine, heretofore discussed, that the charter of a corporation protects it because the charter is a contract, materially limits the legislative power, but does not, by any means, carry corporations beyond the domain over which that power extends. The legislature may effectively prescribe many regulations for the government of railway companies although the statutes prescribing the regulations may be enacted subsequent to the organization of the company. It is our purpose in this chapter to consider the nature and extent of the legislative power to enact such statutes. We shall, however, treat incidentally only of the influence of the commerce clause of the federal constitution, and of regulations operating upon railroads in their capacity of common carriers we shall do little else than make mention. The subjects just named will be considered in another part of our work, but it is necessary to speak of them—incidentally, at least,—in this chapter, since in some phases they are intimately connected with the topics to the discussion of which this chapter is devoted.

§ 658. **Effect of the commerce clause of the federal constitution upon the power of the states.**—It is not our purpose at this place to do more than direct attention to the commerce clause of the federal constitution, and, in general terms, to say that it materially limits the power of the states. A state can not, in any form, enact a statute which constitutes a regulation of interstate commerce, but it may effectively regulate intrastate commerce.[1] There can be no doubt that the states

[1] Robbins v. Shelby County Taxing District, 120 U. S. 489, and cases cited; Western Union Tel. Co. v. Pendleton, 122 U. S. 347; Telegraph Co. v. Texas, 105 U. S. 460; Norfolk, etc., R. Co. v. Commonwealth, 136 U. S. 114; Wabash, etc., R. Co. v. Illinois, 118 U. S. 557; Swift v. Philadelphia, etc., Railroad Co., 58 Fed. R. 858; Fitzgerald v. Fitzgerald, etc., R. Co., 41 Neb. 374, s. c. 59 N. W. R. 838; State v. Woodruff, etc., Co., 114 Ind. 155; United States v. Michigan, etc., R.Co. 43 Fed.R. 26; Hardy v.Atchison, etc., R. Co., 32 Kan. 698; Carton v. Illinois, etc., R. Co., 59 Iowa 148; Commonwealth v. Housatonic, etc., R. Co., 143 Mass. 264; State v. Chicago, etc., R. Co., 70 Iowa 262, s. c. 30 N. W. R. 398; State v. Indiana, etc., Co., 120 Ind. 575; City of Bangor v. Smith, 83 Me. 422. See, upon the general subject, Louisville,etc.,Co.v.Railroad Commissioners, 19 Fed.R. 679; Illinois, etc., R. Co.v.Stone, 20 Fed. 468; Leloup v. Port of Mobile, 127 U. S. 640; Fargo v. Michigan, 121 U. S. 230. In the case of Chicago, etc., R. Co. v. Wolcott, 141 Ind. 267, s. c. 39 N. E. R. 451, the court seems to make the question of the power of the state to legislate turn upon the question whether the statute is in "conflict with the right of congress to legislate upon interstate commerce," but we respectfully affirm that this view is erroneous, for

are prohibited from regulating interstate commerce, but there is some doubt as to what shall be considered a regulation of commerce between the states for it is not every legislative enactment which bears upon the subject that can be regarded as a regulation of interstate commerce. But as this chapter is directed to a consideration of the power of the states and the purpose is to only touch the question of the rights and powers of the federal government, we do not here, except incidentally, consider the extent or scope of the national power.

§ 659. [Legislative power over private rights of railroad companies—Nature of.—It is true that railroad corporations are in a sense public corporations, but this is true only in a qualified and limited sense.[1] They are not, as elsewhere said, governmental corporations or governmental subdivisions, and the power of the legislature over them falls far short of that which it has over governmental corporations. But, as a railroad corporation is in a sense public, the legislative power over it is greater than its power over strictly private corporations or individuals. Yet, the legislative power is only greater in so far as a railroad corporation is public, and, on principle, it is not greater over private rights, such, for instance, as contract and property rights, than is its power over strictly private corporations or natural persons. There is reason for affirm-

the states have no power at all to enact statutes that are regulations of commerce between the states. The conclusion we affirm is strongly supported by the decision in Gulf, etc., R. Co. v. Hefley, 158 U. S. 98, s. c. 15 Sup. Ct. R. 802, in which it was held that a provision of a state statute prohibiting the collection of any greater rate of freight than that specified in the bill of lading was in conflict with the commerce clause of the federal constitution and void. The court cited, among others, the cases of Railroad Co. v. Fuller, 17 Wall. 560; Henderson v. Mayor, 92 U. S. 259; Morgan's, etc., Co. v. Louisiana, etc., 118 U. S. 455, s. c. 6 Sup. Ct. R. 1114; Pound v. Truck, 95 U. S. 459; Packet Co. v. Catlettsburg, 105 U. S. 559; Escanaba, etc., Co. v. Chicago, 107 U. S. 678, s. c. 2 Sup. Ct. R. 185; James Gray v. John Fraser, 12 How. 184; Cooley v. Board, 12 How. (U. S.) 299; Willson v. Black-bird, etc., Co., 2 Pet. 245; Gilman v. Philadelphia, 3 Wall. 713; *Ex parte* McNiel, 13 Wall. 236.

[1] *Ante,* §§ 2, 33. In considering the legal status of a railroad corporation we have discussed questions closely allied to some of the questions of which this chapter treats. *Ante,* Chapter III.

ing that in so far as a railroad corporation is public the legislative power is much greater than over natural persons or strictly private corporations, but there is no valid reason for affirming that as to purely private rights the legislative power is greater than over strictly private corporations or individuals. Thus, for illustration, a railroad corporation in so far as concerns its rights and duties as a common carrier is, in a qualified sense, a public corporation, while as to its strictly private rights and duties it is a private corporation. But even as to its public rights the legislative power is limited, for under guise of controlling such rights the legislature can not destroy private corporate rights. For instance, the legislature may regulate charges for transporting freight and passengers but it can not deprive the corporation of the right to compensation, nor can it fix the charges at such a low rate that the corporation can not make a fair and reasonable profit.[1] The element of private right is so strong that it limits the legislative control over the public element which enters into the corporate being. While it is within the legislative power to regulate public rights and duties it is beyond that power to make a regulation that will destroy property or contract rights of a private nature. In other words, the public element can not be used as a weapon to destroy vested private rights. There is, as it seems to us, no reason to doubt that the nature of the legislative power over railroad companies, in so far as their private rights are concerned, is substantially the same as that which it possesses over similar rights possessed by private corporations, or, indeed, individuals, and no greater, but that as to public rights, or matters in which the corporation is "affected by the public interest," its legislative power is much

[1] Chicago, etc., R. Co. v. Dey, 35 Fed. R. 866; Chicago, etc., R. Co. v. Becker, 35 Fed. R. 883; Dow v. Beidelman, 125 U. S. 680, s. c. 8 Sup. Ct. R. 1028; Chicago, etc., Railway Co. v. Minnesota, 134 U. S. 418; Chicago, etc., Railway Co. v. Wellman, 143 U. S. 339, s. c. 12 Sup. Ct. R. 400; Reagan v. Farmers' Loan & Trust Co., 154 U. S. 362, s. c. 14 Sup. Ct. R. 1047; Stone v. Farmers', etc., Co., 116 U. S. 307, s. c. 6 Sup. Ct. R. 334; Railroad Commission Cases, 116 U. S. 307; St. Louis, etc., v. Gill, 156 U. S. 649, s. c. 15 Sup. Ct. R. 484.

more extensive, and that, although the power over public matters is the greater, it is not extensive enough to justify the destruction of private rights vested in the corporation.

§ 660. **Constitutional protection.**—It is evident from what has been said, that so far as concerns property or contract rights railroad corporations are protected by the provisions of the state and federal constitution. The legislature can not take from them any right guaranteed to them by the constitution, except in some mode not forbidden by the constitution. The principle that railroad corporations are within the protection given to property, property rights and contract rights is recognized in many cases and in a variety of forms. Thus, it is held that even where the power to amend or repeal the charter is reserved the legislature can not authorize a seizure of the property of a railroad company for a highway without compensation, nor compel it to devote its property to the use of the public and fit it for that use.[1] So, a corporation is a person and entitled to protection as such under the fourteenth amendment to the federal constitution.[2] So, also, railroad corporations are protected by constitutional provisions against unequal or double taxation. It is not within the legislative power to pass special or local laws affecting railroad companies where the constitution prohibits the enactment of such laws.[3] There is, in truth, no diversity of opinion upon

---

[1] Miller v. New York, etc., R. Co., 21 Barb. 513; People v. Lake Shore, etc., R. Co., 52 Mich. 277; Chicago, etc., R. Co. v. Hough, 61 Mich. 507; City of Detroit v. Detroit Plank Road Co., 43 Mich. 140. But see Portland, etc., R. Co. v. Deering, 78 Me. 61; Boston, etc., R. Co. v. Commissioners, 79 Me. 386; Illinois Central, etc., R. Co. v. Willenborg, 117 Ill. 203; Montclair v. New York, etc., R. Co., 45 N. J. Eq. 436.

[2] Pembina, etc., Co. v. Pennsylvania, 125 U. S. 181; Santa Clara County v. Southern Pacific, etc., R. Co., 118 U. S. 394, s. c. 24 Am. & Eng. R. Cas. 523; Minneapolis, etc., Co. v. Beckwith, 129 U. S. 26.

[3] Indiana, etc., R. Co. v. Gapen, 10 Ind. 292; Madison, etc., R. Co. v. Whiteneck, 8 Ind. 217; Chicago, etc., R. Co. v. Moss, 60 Miss. 641; South, etc., R. Co. v. Morris, 65 Ala. 193; Wilder v. Chicago, etc., Railroad Co., 70 Mich. 382, 384, 385; Brown v. Alabama, etc., R. Co., 87 Ala. 370, s. c. 6 So. R. 259. See, generally, Lafferty v. Chicago, etc., Railroad Co., 71 Mich. 35; Schut v. Chicago, etc., Railway Co., 70 Mich. 433; Grand Rapids, etc., R. Co. v. Runnels, 77 Mich. 104; Smith

the general question, but there is much diversity of opinion in the application of the principles to actual cases.

§ 661. **The limits of legislative power sometimes unduly extended.**—Theoretically all the courts act upon the principle that railroad corporations as to similar property and contract rights are entitled to substantially the same constitutional protection as natural persons,[1] but many of the courts, while professing to adopt the true theory, practically deny the same measure of protection to railroad corporations in respect to such rights that they yield to individual citizens. There are cases wherein statutes directed against corporations are upheld which would be overthrown if the persons against whom the statutes are directed were natural instead of artificial persons. The tendency is to strip corporations of constitutional protection, and, as it seems to us, many of the cases go too far in that direction. Differences between corporations and natural persons are often assumed to exist which are purely imaginary. This unjust assumption is made for the purpose of sustaining legislation directed against corporations, which, if directed against individuals, would be promptly condemned as unconstitutional. Burdens are frequently imposed upon railroad companies, which, in effect, constitute a taking of property without compensation. This course is generally defended upon the ground that statutes imposing such burdens are enacted in the exercise of the police power. The constitutional inhibitions directed against local and special legislation are sometimes evaded by holding that the peculiar nature of a railroad corporation justifies particular legislation. By indirection that is done in many instances which would be unhesitatingly overthrown if done directly. So, too, unconstitutional statutes are frequently so

---

v. Louisville, etc., Railroad Co., 75 Ala. 449; Zeigler *v.* South and N. R. Co., 58 Ala. 594; South and N. R. Co. *v.* Morris, 65 Ala. 193.

[1] We do not mean, of course, that corporate rights are as free from limitation as the rights of natural persons. Corporate rights, as elsewhere said and as is well known, are derivative, and are limited by the charter of the corporation. But as to contract and property rights conferred by the charter the constitutional protection extends.

disguised by the form they are made to assume, that, although in their practical effect and operation they invade private rights, yet the courts, misled by form, lose sight of substance and sustain them.

§ 662. **Regulations affecting acts and duties of a public nature.**—Some of the cases seem to place the power of the legislature to regulate the public acts and duties of railroad companies entirely upon the police power, losing sight of the fact that as to matters wherein corporate property rights and duties are "affected by a public interest" the legislature possesses the power to enact reasonable regulations for the comfort, welfare and safety of the public, although such regulations may not be strictly police regulations. Where the rights and property of a railroad company are "affected by a public interest," the company in accepting a special charter or availing itself of the benefit of a general act of incorporation submits its rights and property to public control, and this control extends far beyond that to which private property is subject.[1] Where the subject of the legislation is the public part, or element, of a corporation the legislative authority does not, as we have elsewhere indicated, rest entirely upon the police power, but rather upon the right to regulate the acts, business and duties of a public corporation. The power of the legislature to make regulations concerning the public rights, duties and acts of railroad companies is analogous to that which it possesses over municipal or governmental corporations, but is by no means so broad or comprehensive as that power. It is to be observed that, as heretofore shown, no state regulation can be valid, whether rested on the police power or in the power to control public

---

[1] Munn v. Illinois, 94 U. S. 113; Chicago, etc., R. Co. v. Iowa, 94 U. S. 155; Chicago, etc., R. Co. v. Ackley, 94 U. S. 179; Winona, etc., R. Co. v. Blake, 94 U. S. 180; Railroad Co. v. Richmond, 96 U. S. 521; Railroad Co. v. Fuller, 17 Wall. 560; Ruggles v. Illinois, 108 U. S. 526; Illinois Central R. Co. v. People, 108 U. S. 541, s. c. 1 Am. & Eng. R. Cas. 188; Commonwealth v. Duane, 98 Mass. 1; Sharpless v. Mayor, 21 Pa. St. 147; Hockett v. State, 105 Ind. 250; City of Rushville v. Rushville, etc., Co., 132 Ind. 575; City of Zanesville v. Zanesville, etc., Co., 47 Ohio St. 1, s. c. 23 N. E. R. 55.

corporations, if it is, in fact, a regulation of commerce between the states in the constitutional sense of the term. Under the power to control the public part, or element, of a railroad company, many important duties may be imposed upon it and many requirements be made that could not be made or imposed in matters of strictly private right. It has been held that under the general power to control matters of a public nature the state may require railroad companies to place in their stations blackboards, and note thereon the time of the arrival of trains, "and if late how much."[1] There are decisions adjudging that it is competent for the legislature to require railroad companies to erect and maintain suitable stations for the accommodation of passengers[2] and to provide reasonable facilities for the interchange of freight.[3] Statutes requiring railroad companies to provide station agents with certificates of authority and requiring such companies to redeem unused tickets have been adjudged to be valid.[4] It is held competent for the legislature to compel railroad companies to provide waiting rooms,[5] to properly light and heat them,[6] to provide water closets,[7] to require

[1] State v. Indiana, etc., R. Co., 133 Ind. 69. The questions decided in the case are close and it may be doubted whether there is not error in some of the conclusions asserted. In the course of the opinion the court said: "While this statute may be on the border of legislative authority, yet we do not think it is an attempt to regulate commerce or to interfere with it." In State v. Kentucky, etc., R. Co., 136 Ind. 195, s. c. 35 N. E. R. 991, it was held that the statute did not apply to cases where the time occupied in running over the entire route was less than twenty minutes. See, also, Pennsylvania, etc., Co. v. State, 142 Ind. 428, s. c. 41 N. E. R. 937.

[2] San Antonio, etc., R. Co. v. State, 79 Texas 264, s. c. 14 S. W. R. 1063.

[3] State v. Kansas City, etc., R. Co., 32 Fed. R. 722.

[4] Burdick v. People, 149 Ill. 600, s. c. 36 N. E. R. 948, 10 Am. R. & Corp. R. 451; Fry v. State, 63 Ind. 552; State v. Fry, 81 Ind. 7; Commonwealth v. Wilson, 14 Phila. 384, s. c. 56 Am. & Eng. R. Cas. 230; State v. Corbett, 57 Minn. 345, s. c. 59 N. W. R. 317. See State v. Ray, 109 N. Car. 736, s. c. 14 S. E. R. 83; State v. Clark, 14 S. E. R. 84.

[5] State v. St. Paul, etc., R. Co., 40 Minn. 353; State v. Wabash, etc., R. Co., 83 Mo. 144, s. c. 25 Am. & Eng. R. Cas. 133; San Antonio, etc., R. Co. v. State, 79 Texas 264, s. c. 45 Am. & Eng. R. Cas. 586; State v. Kansas City, etc., R. Co., 32 Fed. R. 722. See Kinealy v. St. Louis, etc., R. Co., 69 Mo. 658; Baltimore, etc., R. Co. v. Compton, 2 Gill 20.

[6] Texas, etc., Co. v. Mayes, (Texas) 15 S. W. R 43. See State v. Cleveland, etc., R. Co., 137 Ind. 75, s. c. 36 N. E. R. 713.

[7] Louisville, etc., R. Co. v. Commonwealth, (Ky.) 30 S. W. R. 616.

rules and schedules to be posted in stations or depots,[1] and to require its ticket office to be kept open a specified length of time before the departure of trains.[2] Some of the cases seem to hold that, independent of statute, there is an absolute duty to erect and maintain depots or stations, which performance may be coerced by mandamus,[3] but there are well reasoned cases limiting and qualifying this broad doctrine.[4]

§ 663. **Corporate rights are subject to the police power.**—All corporate rights are taken subject to the great power reserved in every state and commonly known as the police power.[5] This power is governmental in the strictest sense of the term and can neither be surrendered nor bargained away

---

[1] Chicago, etc., R. Co. v. Fuller, 17 Wall. 560; Fuller v. Chicago, etc., R. Co., 31 Iowa 187.

[2] Brady v. State, 15 Lea 628.

[3] State v. Republican Valley, etc., R. Co., 17 Neb. 647, s. c. 52 Am. R. 424; Railroad Commissioners v. Portland, etc., R. Co., 63 Me. 269; State v. New Haven, etc., R. Co., 43 Conn. 351; North Pacific, etc., R. Co. v. Territory, 3 Wash. Ter. 303. The case last cited was reversed on appeal.

[4] Chicago, etc., R. Co. v. People, 152 Ill. 230, s. c. 38 N. E. R. 562; Ohio, etc., R. Co. v. People, 120 Ill. 200, s. c. 11 N. E. R. 347; People v. Chicago, etc., R. Co., 130 Ill. 175, s. c. 22 N. E. R. 857; Mobile, etc., R. Co. v. People, 132 Ill. 559, s. c. 24 N. E. R. 643; Northern Pacific, etc., R. Co. v. Territory, 142 U. S. 492, s. c. 48 Am. & Eng. R. Cas. 475. See York, etc., R. Co. v. Regina, 1 El. & B. 858; Commonwealth v. Fitchburg, etc., R. Co., 12 Gray 180; State v. Southern, etc., R. Co., 18 Minn. 40; People v. New York, etc., R. Co., 104 N. Y. 58, s. c. 58 Am. R. 484; Atchison, etc., R. Co. v. Denver, 110 U. S. 667, s. c. 16 Am. & Eng. R. Cas. 57.

[5] The principle is so familiar and so firmly established that it is hardly necessary to cite authorities, but we cite a few of the multitude of cases: Boston, etc., Co. v. Massachusetts, 97 U. S. 25; Railroad Co. v. City of Richmond, 96 U. S. 521; Jamieson v. Indiana, etc., Co., 128 Ind. 555; State v. Hoskins, 58 Minn. 35, s. c. 61 Am. & Eng. R. Cas. 571; Thorpe v. Rutland, etc., R. Co., 27 Vt. 140, s. c. 62 Am. Dec. 625; Indianapolis, etc., R. Co. v. Kercheval, 16 Ind. 84; Pennsylvania Co. v. Riblet, 66 Pa. St. 164, s. c. 5 Am. R. 360; Buckley v. New York, etc., R. Co., 27 Conn. 479; Toledo, etc., R. Co. v. Jacksonville, 67 Ill. 37, s. c. 16 Am. R. 611; Boston, etc., R. Co. v. County Commissioners, 79 Me. 386; Kansas Pacific R. Co. v. Mower, 16 Kan. 573; Sloan v. Pacific R. Co., 61 Mo. 24, s. c. 21 Am. R. 397; Wilder v. Maine, etc., R. Co., 65 Me. 332, s. c. 20 Am. R. 698; Horn v. Atlantic, etc., Co., 35 N. H. 169; Jones v. Galena etc., Co., 16 Iowa 6; Cincinnati, etc., R. Co. v. Cole, 29 Ohio St. 126; Sawyer v. Vermont, etc., R. Co., 105 Mass. 196. See, also, Cooley Const. Lim. (6th ed.), 707; Tiedeman's Limitations of Police Power 593-602; Elliott on Roads and Streets 564, 573, 598.

by contract. All property is subject to this power whether it belongs to natural or artificial persons. The legislature could not, if it would, grant a charter which would place corporate rights above this power. There is no contrariety of opinion, nor can there be, upon the proposition that corporate rights, no matter what their nature, are subject to the proper exercise of this high power, but there is often difficulty in determining what is or is not a valid exercise of the power. Statutes have been upheld on the ground that in enacting them the legislature exercised this power when, in truth, the subject of the statutes was not a subject over which the police power extends. So, too, statutes have been upheld upon the theory that the legislature is the sole judge of what subjects are or are not within the police power. The courts have sometimes surrendered the power it was their clear duty to exercise and assumed without just reason that the legislative judgment was conclusive and closed all inquiry and forbade all investigation. So they have in some instances adjudged the subject to be within the police power when it was not, and, again, in other instances, they have tacitly conceded that the police power is without limit. These unsound theories and undue assumptions have led to unjust results and have given force to unconstitutional measures oppressive and tyrannical in their nature and effect.

§ 664. **The police power is fettered by limitations.**—There are limitations upon the police power. The legislative judgment is not always conclusive. The courts are not bound to inactivity because the legislature assumes to decide that a regulation it prescribes is a valid exercise of the police power, nor are the courts invariably concluded by the legislative judgment that the subject upon which it legislates is one which falls within the scope of the police power.[1] When the question

[1] The doctrine we assert is illustrated by the cases which declare and enforce the rule that the legislature can not make that a nuisance which is not, in fact, a nuisance. City of Janesville v. Carpenter, 77 Wis. 288, s. c. 20 Am. St. R. 123; Hutton v. City of Camden, 10 Vroom (N. J.) 122, s. c. 23 Am. R. 203; *Ex parte* O'Leary, 65 Miss. 180, s. c. 7 Am. St. R. 640; Coe

is one of power or no power, as, for instance, whether the subject is one over which the police power extends, or whether there was power to enact the particular statute, the question is

v. Schultz, 47 Barb. 64. Judge Cooley thus lays down the law: "The limit to the exercise of the police power in these cases must be this: the regulations must have reference to the comfort, safety and welfare of society; they must not be in conflict with any of the provisions of the charter, and they must not, under pretense of regulation, take from the corporation any of the essential rights and privileges which the charter confers. In short, they must be police regulations in fact, and not amendments of the charter in curtailment of the corporate franchises." Cooley's Const. Lim. (6th ed.), 710. Judge Dillon says: "All embracing and penetrating as the police power of the state is, and of necessity must be, it is nevertheless subject, like all other legislative powers, to the paramount authority of the state and federal constitutions. A right conferred or protected by the constitution can not be overthrown or impaired by any authority derived from the police power." 1 Dillon's Munic. Corp. (4th ed.), § 142. Mr. Tiedeman says: "And it is a judicial question whether a particular regulation is a reasonable exercise of the police power or not." Tiedeman Lim. Police Power, § 194. The Court of Appeals of New York, in Matter of Jacobs, 98 N. Y. 98, s. c. 50 Am. R. 636, 643, after citing many cases, said: "These citations are sufficient to show that the police power is not without its limitations, and that in its exercise the legislature must respect the great fundamental rights guaranteed by the constitution. If this were otherwise, the power of the legislature would be practically without limitation. In the assumed exercise of the police power in the interest of health, the welfare or safety of the public, every right of the citizen might be invaded and every constitutional barrier swept away." The doctrine asserted in the case last cited was approved and enforced in People *v.* Gillson, 109 N. Y. 389, s. c. 4 Am. St. R. 465. In the case of Toledo, etc., R. Co. *v.* City of Jacksonville, 67 Ill. 37, s. c. 16 Am. R. 611, the court thus stated the rule, "What are reasonable regulations, and what are subjects of police powers, must necessarily be judicial questions. The law-making power is the sole judge when the necessity exists, and when, if at all, it will exercise that right to enact such laws. Like other powers of government, there are constitutional limitations to its exercise. It is not within the power of the general assembly, under the pretense of exercising the police power of the state, to enact laws not necessary to the preservation of the health and safety of the cummunity that will be oppressive and burdensome upon the citizen. If it should prohibit that which is harmless in itself, or command that to be done which does not tend to promote the health, safety or welfare of society, it would be an unauthorized exercise of power, and it would be the duty of the courts to declare such legislation void." In the case of Town of Lake View *v.* Rose Hill Cemetery Co., 70 Ill. 191, s. c. 22 Am. R. 71, it was said: "As a general proposition, it may be stated, it is the province of the law-making power to determine when the exigency exists, calling into exercise this power. What are the subjects of a judicial one and is for the courts. It is always the duty of the courts to decide whether the statute is in truth a police regulation or an invasion of substantial rights under the guise of a police regulation. An arbitrary assumption that a subject is one over which the police power extends or that the regulation is valid as an exercise of that power will not remove the question from the domain of the judiciary.[1] To affirm that the legislature may by an arbitrary decision of its own foreclose controversy upon such a question is to affirm that upon questions concerning the highest rights of property the legislative power is unlimited. Such a doctrine is directly opposed to the foundation theory of our government.[2] The question whether there is a reasonable necessity for the exercise of the police power or not,[3] and the question whether the subject is

its exercise is clearly a judicial question. There must necessarily be constitutional limitations upon this power. It is essential that such regulations must have reference to the comfort, safety or welfare of society, and, when applied to corporations, they must not be in conflict with any of the provisions of the charter. It is not lawful, under the pretense of police regulations, to take from a corporation any of the essential rights and privileges conferred by the charter."

[1] A writer of acknowledged ability says: "It is at the same time clear that a state can not, by arbitrarily assuming that a trade or commodity is injurious to the common weal, justify the breach of a contract or impair the rights of a corporation or individual. The police power is, like all others, subject to the constitution, and can not be used as a color for the disregard of the restrictions which that imposes. Convenience, utility or profit will not alone sustain such a plea, nor can it rest on the recitals of a statute where there is no substantial basis."

1 Hare's Am. Const. Law 618. In the Slaughter House Cases, 16 Wall. 36, 87, the court said: "But under the pretense of prescribing a police regulation, the state can not be permitted to encroach upon any of the just rights of the citizen which the constitution intended to secure against abridgment."

[2] In the case of Loan Association v. Topeka, 20 Wall. 655, 663, it was said: "The theory of our governments, state and national, is opposed to the deposit of unlimited power anywhere. The executive, the legislative, and the judicial branches of these governments are all of limited and defined powers. There are limitations on such power which grow out of the essential nature of all free governments." Cases decided by some of the courts tacitly disregard or are unmindful of this fundamental principle. Some of the expressions in State v. Hoskins, 58 Minn. 35, s. c. 61 Am. & Eng. R. Cas. 571, are opposed to this doctrine.

[3] Mr. Tiedeman, speaking of railroad companies, says: "But there is no more need for a judicial determina-

one within the field of the police power are judicial questions or else the system of distributed power and checks and balances is an empty, impotent abstraction.

§ 665. **The subject must be one over which the police power extends—Cases adjudging statutes invalid.**—A statute professing to make a police regulation and assuming to be based upon that power is invalid, if it be clear that the subject is not one within the scope of that power.[1] In an Illinois case the statute assumed to require railroad companies to bear the expense of coroner's inquests held upon persons who died on their trains and also the expense of the burial of such persons, but the court rightly declared the statute unconstitutional.[2] The police power will not authorize the enactment of a statute declaring a railway depot or the like to be a nuisance,[3] for such a structure of itself is not injurious to the public welfare. It is held that a statute which assumes to make a railroad company liable for stock killed by its trains where there is no negligence on the part of the company is unconstitutional.[4] It was held in a

---

tion of the limitations of the police power in this phase of its exercise than in any other. The same principles govern its exercise in every case." Tiedeman's Lim. Police Power, § 194. See, generally, Sloan v. Pacific R. Co., 61 Mo. 24, s. c. 21 Am. R. 397; Philadelphia, etc., R. Co. v. Bowers, 4 Houst.(Del.) 506; Mayor v. Radecke, 49 Md. 217, s. c. 33 Am. R. 239; State v. Noyes, 47 Me. 189; Washington, etc., Co. v. State, 18 Conn. 53; Commonwealth v. Pennsylvania, etc., Co., 66 Pa. St. 41; Bailey v. Philadelphia, etc., R. Co., 4 Harr. 389; People v. Jackson, etc., Co., 9 Mich. 284; White's Creek, etc., Co. v. Davidson County, 3 Tenn. Ch. 396.

[1] The authorities referred to in a preceding section sustain the statement of the text, and our immediate purpose is to show the application of the general doctrine.

[2] Ohio, etc., R. Co. v. Lackey, 78 Ill. 55, s. c. 20 Am. R. 259. The court, it is proper to say, does not discuss the question whether the statute could be upheld upon the ground that it was a valid exercise of the police power, but it is evident that the court did not regard the subject of the statute as within the scope of that power.

[3] State v. City of Jersey City, 29 N. J. Law 170. See Yates v. Milwaukee, 10 Wall. 497.

[4] Schenck v. Union Pacific R. Co., (Wyo.) s. c. 40 Pac. R. 840. In the case cited the court said: "The principles upon which such statutes are held to be unconstitutional have been so often discussed that a new consideration of them would be unprofitable and tedious." The court cited Jensen v. Union Pacfic R. Co., 6 Utah 253, s. c. 21 Pac. R. 994; Denver, etc., Railway v. Outcalt, 2 Colo. App.

well reasoned case that a statute assuming to compel a railroad company to pay its employes in full upon discharging them although such employes by their wrongful acts may have caused injury to the company is not a valid exercise of the police powers and is unconstitutional.[1] A statute providing

395, s. c. 31 Pac. R. 177; Parsons v. Russell, 11 Mich.113; Taylor v. Porter, 4 Hill 140; Zeigler v. South, etc., R. Co., 58 Ala. 594; Oregon, etc., Railway Co. v. Smally, 1 Wash. 206, 23 Pac. R. 108; Atchison, etc., Railway Co. v. Baty, 6 Neb. 37. See, also, Bielenberg v. Montana, etc., R. Co., 8 Mont. 271, s. c. 38 Am. & Eng. R. Cas. 275; Cottrel v. Union Pac. R. Co., 2 Idaho 540, s. c. 21 Pac. R. 416; Birmingham, etc., R. Co. v. Parsons, 100 Ala. 662, s. c. 27 L. R. A. 263; East Kingston v. Towle, 48 N. H. 57; People v. Tighe, 30 N. Y. S. (9 Misc. R. 607) 368; City of Sioux Falls v. Kirby, (So. Dak.) s. c. 60 N. W. R. 156. Some of the cases cited bear directly upon the point that where there is a right to notice, a statute which is professedly enacted in the exercise of the police power is invalid, if it deprives the party of notice, but they serve to show that the exercise of the police power is not beyond judicial investigation as well as to show that a police regulation can not override constitutional limitations. It seems difficult to reconcile the cases holding invalid statutes assuming to make railroad companies absolutely liable with Mathews v. St. Louis, etc., R. Co., 121 Mo. 298, s. c. 25 L. R. A. 161; Union, etc., R. Co. v. De Busk, 12 Colo. 294, s. c. 3 L. R. A. 350, and other cases in which statutes making railroad companies absolutely liable for injuries caused by fires from their locomotives were upheld. There is, we venture to say, notwithstanding the array of authority, reason for affirming that in the class of cases just referred to the doctrine has been pressed too far. In authorizing the construction and operation of railroads the legislature necessarily authorizes the use of fire and we can not perceive how a lawful and proper use of that which is lawful can be made the basis of a statute inflicting a penalty, in the form of damages upon a party whether that party be a corporation or a citizen, for doing in a lawful mode what the party is authorized by law to do. See *post*, § 1222, 1223.

[1] Leep v. St. Louis, etc., R. Co., 58 Ark. 407. In the opinion in the case cited the court referred with approval to the cases of the State v. Goodwill, 33 W. Va. 179, 6 L. R. A. 621; State v. Loomis, 115 Mo. 307, s. c. 21 L. R. A. 789; Godcharles v. Wigeman, 113 Pa. St. 431; State v. Fore Creek, etc., Co., 33 W. Va. 188, 6 L. R. A. 359; Ramsey v. People, 142 Ill. 380, s. c. 17 L. R. A. 853; Braceville, etc., Co. v. People, 147 Ill. 66, s. c. 22 L. R. A. 340; Commonwealth v. Perry, 155 Mass. 117, s. c. 14 L. R. A. 325; San Antonio, etc., R. Co. v. Wilson, (Texas) s. c. 19 S. W. R. 910, and disapproved the cases of State v. Peel, etc., Co., 36 W. Va. 802, s. c. 17 L. R. A. 385, and Hancock v. Yaden, 121 Ind. 366, s. c. 6 L.R. A. 576. The court justly discriminated the decision in Hancock v. Yaden, and said that the "statute was held to be constitutional" on the ground that "it protected and maintained the medium of payment established by the sovereign power of the nation." The holding in Hancock v. Yaden as cited

that upon filing a sworn statement showing that the company is indebted for work and labor performed or for services rendered it, the court should issue an injunction restraining the company from operating its road, was held unconstitutional upon the ground that it made it obligatory upon the courts to grant the injunction and deprived the company of a hearing, and, in effect, was a taking of the property without due process of law.[1]

§ 666. Police power—Legislative and judicial questions.— It is clear that if the question which the legislature is required to decide is a legislative one the decision of the legislature is conclusive.[2] The difficulty is to determine what are and what are not legislative questions. So far as concerns matters of policy and expediency there is no doubt that the legislative decision is final.[3] But it is by no means within the legislative power to shut out judicial investigation and judgment. It is true that judicial investigation very often ends with the discovery that the question is one of policy or expediency. This is far from being true, however, in all cases. It often becomes necessary for the courts to ascertain and decide whether a constitutional provision is violated under the pretense of exercising the police power. The legislature can not make that a legislative question which is a judicial one. If, for instance,

in Leep v. St. Louis, etc., R. Co., *supra*, proceeds upon the theory that the state may protect the money of the national government by interdicting parties from contracting in advance that some other thing than money shall be taken as payment. See, generally, State v. Brown, etc., Co., 18 R. I. 16, s. c. 25 Atl. R. 246, 17 L. R. A. 856.

[1] Creech v. Pittsburgh, etc., R. Co., 29 W. L. Bull. 112.

[2] State v. Wiley, 109 Mo. 439, s. c. 19 S. W. R. 197; Stockton v. Powell, 29 Fla. 1, s. c. 15 L. R. A. 42, 50; Elliott's Gen. Prac., § 148.

[3] The principle to which we refer is a familiar one and was thus stated in the License Tax Cases, 5 Wall. 462: "This court can know nothing of public policy except from the constitution and the laws, and the course of administration and decision. It has no legislative powers. It can not modify or amend any legislative acts. It can not examine any questions as expedient or inexpedient, as politic or impolitic. Considerations of that sort must be addressed to the legislature. Questions of policy there are concluded here."

§ 666   GOVERNMENTAL CONTROL.   965

a trade or occupation is not injurious to the community the legislature can not arbitrarily decide that it is injurious and by that decision exclude the interference of the judiciary.[1] If the case is one wherein due process of law requires notice then the legislature can not arbitrarily decide, without providing for notice, that an act shall or shall not be done.[2] "Due process of law" and the "law of the land" are terms of great force, and the requirements made by such terms are not satisfied by a legislative enactment which denies a hearing where a hearing is provided for by the organic law.[3] The power to adjudicate where adjudication is necessary is judicial and not legislative.[4] If, therefore, an adjudication is essential, the legislature, while it may prescribe regulations, can not make an adjudication, that is, it can not adjudicate in the sense that a court of justice does when it pronounces judgment. If the case be one in which the organic law secures to the party a hearing, then the legislature can not abridge that right by arrogating to itself the power to decide arbitrarily and conclusively. The duty of the courts is to ascertain if the case is one in which the party is entitled to a hearing, and, in the event that it be found that he is entitled to a hearing, overthrow the statute if it denies the right to a hearing. So it is often necessary for the courts to ascertain and decide whether,

[1] State v. Moore, 113 N. C. 697, s. c. 22 L. R. A. 472; Bertholf v. O'Reilly, 74 N. Y. 509, s. c. 30 Am. R. 323; People v. Marx, 99 N. Y. 377; ante, § 664.

[2] The principle considered in the text is illustrated by the cases which hold that although the legislature may confer authority to summarily seize property it can not authorize a destruction of the property without giving the owner a hearing. Lowry v. Rainwater, 70 Mo. 152, s. c. 35 Am. R. 420; Attorney-Gen. v. Justices, etc., 103 Mass. 456; State v. Robbins, 124 Ind. 308. See Lincoln v. Smith, 27 Vt. 328; Wynehamer v. People, 13 N. Y. 378; People v. Haug, (Mich.) 37 N. W. R. 21; Robison v. Miner, 68 Mich. 549. See, also, authorities cited in note to the preceding section.

[3] Taylor v. Porter, 4 Hill 140; Norman v. Heist, 5 Watts & S. 171; Hoke v. Henderson, 4 Dev. (N. C.) 1; Dash v. Van Kleeck, 7 Johns. 477; Goshen v. Stonington, 4 Conn. 209; Fletcher v. Peck, 6 Cranch 87; Ervine's Appeal, 16 Pa. St. 256, 266; Trustees, etc., v. Bailey, 10 Fla. 238.

[4] Taylor v. Place, 4 R. I. 324; Greenough v. Greenough, 11 Pa. St. 489; People v. Board of Supervisors, 16 N.Y. 424; Cincinnati, etc., R. Co. v. Commissioners, 1 Ohio St. 77; Merrill v. Sherburne, 1 N. H. 199, 203.

under the pretense of a police regulation, there is, in fact, an attempt to authorize the taking of property without compensation. It has been adjudged that the legislature can not arbitrarily fix the value of animals killed by the trains of a railroad company, for the question of value is one upon which there is a right to "a day in court."[1]

§ 667. **The police power and the commerce clause of the federal constitution.**—The police power is resident in the states[2] and may be exercised by them upon interstate railroads, but not in such a way as to interfere with commerce between the states.[3] The commerce clause of the federal constitution is, as we have seen, a limitation upon the police power of the states but it does not destroy that power. Where, however, the power of the federal government and the power of the state to enact police regulations come in conflict the federal power will prevail. It follows from the rule just stated that, if under pretense of prescribing a police regulation, the legislature in fact assumes to regulate interstate commerce the statute will be void.[4] But police regulations may be valid although they do

---

[1] Wadsworth v. Union Pacific R. Co., 18 Colo. 600, s. c. 56 Am. & Eng. R. Cas. 145. In the case referred to the court quoted the well known statement of Webster, "By the law of the land is most clearly intended the general law; a law which hears before it condemns, which proceeds upon inquiry and renders judgment only after trial."

[2] Mugler v. Kansas, 123 U. S. 623, s. c. 8 Sup. Ct. R. 273; Prigg v. Pennsylvania, 16 Pet. 539; United States v. De Witt, 9 Wall. 41; Patterson v. Kentucky, 97 U. S. 501; Jamieson v. Indiana, etc., Co., 128 Ind. 555, s. c. 12 L. R. A. 652; Cooley's Const. Lim. 574.

[3] Leisy v. Hardin, 135 U. S. 100, s. c. 10 Sup. Ct. R. 681; Bowman v. Chicago, etc., Railway Co., 125 U. S. 465, 8 Sup. Ct. R. 689; Chicago Railway Co. v. Minnesota, 134 U. S. 418, s. c. 10 Sup. Ct.R.462; Wilkerson v.Rahrer, 140 U. S. 545, s. c. 11 Sup. Ct. R. 865, s. c. In re Rohrer, 140 U. S. 545; State v. Gooch, 44 Fed. R. 276; Western Union Tel. Co. v. Pendleton, 122 U. S. 347, s. c. 7 Sup. Ct. R. 1126; Lyng v. Michigan, 135 U. S. 161, s. c. 10 Sup. Ct. R. 725; In re Beine, 42 Fed. R. 545; In re Spickler, 43 Fed. R. 653, 659; Spellman v. City of New Orleans, 45 Fed. R. 3; United States v. Fiscus, 42 Fed. R. 395; American, etc., Co. v. Board, etc., 43 Fed. R. 609; Cuban, etc., Co. v. Fitzpatrick, 66 Fed. R. 63; Ex parte Scott, 66 Fed. R. 45; Plumley v. Commonwealth, 155 U. S. 461, s. c. 15 Sup. Ct. R. 154.

[4] Chy Lung v. Freeman, 92 U. S. 275; Henderson v. Mayor, etc., of New York, 92 U. S. 259; Hannibal, etc., R. Co. v. Husen, 95 U. S. 465; Kimmish

affect interstate commerce, provided they are not in fact regulations of commerce between the states.[1]

§ 668. Regulations that have been held valid.—It is now firmly settled that statutes requiring railroad companies to fence their tracks are valid.[2] Railroad companies may be compelled to conduct examinations to ascertain the qualifications of their employes.[3] It has been held that a statute prohibit-

---

v. Ball, 129 U. S. 217; Minnesota v. Barber, 136 U. S. 313. See Telegraph Co. v. Texas, 105 U. S. 460; Pensacola Tel. Co. v. Western Union Tel. Co., 96 U. S. 1.

[1] Western Union Tel. Co. v. Pendleton, 122 U. S. 347. The court said in the case cited that: "Undoubtedly, under the reserved powers of the state, which are designated under that somewhat ambiguous term of 'police powers,' regulations may be prescribed for the good order, peace, and protection of the community." In Hannibal, etc., R. Co. v. Husen, 95 U. S. 465, the court said: "Many acts of a state may, indeed, affect commerce without amounting to any regulation of it in the constitutional sense of the term." See Smith v. Alabama, etc., R. Co., 124 U. S. 465; Nashville, etc., R. Co. v. Alabama, 128 U. S. 96; Sherlock v. Alling, 93 U. S. 99; Ex parte Siebold, 100 U. S. 371; Wilson v. McNamee, 102 U. S. 572; State v. Penny, 19 So. Car. 218; Pittsburg, etc., Co. v. Bates, 156 U. S. 577, s. c. 15 Sup. Ct. R. 415.

[2] The decisions upon this question are very numerous, but the rule is so well established that it is only necessary to cite a few of the many cases: Thorpe v. Rutland, etc., R. Co., 27 Vt. 140; Gorman v. Pacific, etc., R. Co., 26 Mo. 441; New Albany, etc., R. Co. v. Tilton, 12 Ind. 3; Wilder v. Maine, etc., R. Co., 65 Me. 332; Corwin v. New York, etc., R. Co., 13 N. Y. 42; Horn v. Atlantic, etc., R. Co., 35 N. H. 169; Bulkley v. New York, etc., R. Co., 27 Conn. 479; Jones v. Galena, etc., R. Co., 16 Iowa 6; Winona, etc., R. Co. v. Waldron, 11 Minn. 515; Sawyer v. Vermont, etc., R. Co., 105 Mass. 196; Pennsylvania Co. v. Riblet, 66 Pa. St. 164, s. c. 5 Am. R. 360; Kansas, etc., R. Co. v. Mower, 16 Kan. 573; Illinois Central R. Co. v. Arnold, 47 Ill. 173; Quackenbush v. Wisconsin, etc., R. Co., 62 Wis. 411; O'Bannon v. Louisville, etc., R. Co., 8 Bush (Ky.) 348; Burlington, etc., R. Co. v. Webb, 18 Neb. 215; Owensboro, etc., R. Co. v. Todd, 91 Ky. 175, s. c. 11 L. R. A. 285. In the case of the Birmingham, etc., R. Co. v. Parsons, 100 Ala. 662, s. c. 27 L. R. A. 263, a different view of the question is taken, the court holding that as the legislature may make the duty to build fences absolute it may leave the question whether a fence shall be built to the decision of the land-owner. In that case the court sanctions the doctrine that land-owners may release the company from the duty to fence, but we suppose that a release by a land-owner would not avail the company if the breach of duty to fence was the proximate cause of an injury to a passenger or other person having a right of action against the damages for injuries resulting from negligence.

[3] Nashville, etc., R. Co. v. State, 83

ing railroad companies from making "flying" or "running switches," and making them liable to a person injured although such person is guilty of contributory negligence, is a valid exercise of the police power.[1] There are cases affirming that railroad companies may be compelled to heat their cars in some other mode than by stoves.[2] So, too, there are decisions that it is competent for the legislature to enact a law applicable exclusively to railroad companies, prescribing who shall and who shall not be deemed fellow-servants of a common master.[3] It has been held that a statute making railroad companies absolutely liable to persons injured on their trains, except where the injury is attributable to the criminal negligence of the person injured or to a violation of a rule or regulation of the company, is constitutional.[4] Statutes requiring trains to stop at crossings of other roads, at county seats and the like, have been held valid.[5] A statute requiring railroad companies to

Ala. 71; Nashville, etc., R. Co. v. Alabama, 128 U. S. 96; Smith v. Alabama, 124 U. S. 465; McDonald v. State, 81 Ala. 279. In Nashville, etc., R. Co. v. Alabama, 128 U. S. 96, it was said in the course of the opinion that the company could be compelled to bear the expense of such examinations. Louisville, etc., R. Co. v. Baldwin, 85 Ala. 619, s. c. 38 Am. & Eng. R. Cas. 5.

[1] Jones v. Alabama, etc., R. Co., 72 Miss. 32, s. c. 16 So. R. 379. That such a statute as the one under consideration in the case cited is valid where the switches are made entirely on the exclusive private property of the company is not so clear on principle, but the general trend of the decisions seems to warrant the conclusion that such a statute is valid, although there is conflict upon the general question.

[2] People v. New York, etc., R. Co., 55 Hun 409; People v. Clark, 14 N. Y. Supp. 642. It has also been held that a railroad company may be required to light and heat its station buildings. Texas, etc., R. Co. v. Mayes, (Tex.) 15 S. W. R. 43.

[3] Campbell v. Cook, 86 Texas 630, s. c. 26 S. W. R. 486; Georgia, etc., R. Co. v. Miller, 90 Ga. 571, s. c. 16 S. E. R. 939; Missouri Pac. Railroad Co. v. Mackey, 127 U. S. 205, s. c. 8 Sup. Ct. R. 1161; Missouri Pacific R. Co. v. Mackey, 33 Kan. 298, s. c. 6 Pac. R. 291; Herrick v. Minneapolis, etc., R. Co., 31 Minn. 11, s. c. 11 Am. & Eng. R. Cas. 256; Georgia R. Co. v. Ivey, 73 Ga. 499, s. c. 28 Am. & Eng. R. Cas. 392; Austin Rapid Transit Co. v. Groethe, (Texas Civil App.) 31 S. W. R. 197.

[4] Union Pacific R. Co. v. Porter, 38 Neb. 226, s. c. 56 N. W. R. 808.

[5] Illinois Central R. Co. v. People, 143 Ill. 434, s. c. 33 N. E. R. 173, 19 L. R. A. 119; People v. Louisville, etc., R. Co., 120 Ill. 48; Chicago, etc., R. Co. v. Suffern, 129 Ill. 274; Chicago, etc., R. Co. v. People, 105 Ill. 657; Ohio, etc., R. Co. v. People, 29 Ill. App. 561; St. Louis, etc., R. Co. v.

stop their trains for five minutes at each station on the line of their roads has been upheld,[1] but it seems to us that the decisions upholding the statute are of doubtful soundness. The supreme court of Illinois holds that under the police power the construction of farm crossings may be compelled,[2] but this seems to us a very great stretch of the police power, at least as to cases where the right of way was secured prior to the enactment of the statute. In Texas it is correctly held that where the right of way was obtained prior to the enactment of the statute there is no power to compel the construction of farm crossings.[3] It is held by the supreme court of Ohio that rail-

---

B'Shears, 59 Ark. 237, s. c. 61 Am. & Eng. R. Cas. 556. The English cases hold that an agreement to stop trains at a particular station for a designated length of time is valid and enforceable. Rigby v. Great Western, etc., R. Co., 14 M. & W. 811. See Phillips v. Great Western, etc., R. Co., L. R. 7 Ch. 409; Greene v. West Cheshire Lines, etc., L. R. 13 Eq. 44, 41 L. J. Ch. 17; Raphael v. Thames Valley, etc., R. Co., L. R. 2 Ch. 147; Turner v. London and South Western, etc., R. Co., L. R. 17 Eq. 561; Burnett v. Great North, etc., R. Co., L. R. 10 App. 147; Price v. Bala, etc., R .Co., 50 L. T. R. 787; Flood v. North Eastern. etc., R.Co., 21 L.T. R. 258. As the first and highest duty of a railroad company is to discharge its duties to the public there is, at least, fair reason for the conclusion that such contracts must yield to the public necessity. The rapid progress and the great changes wrought by time in this country must, as it seems to us, be influential considerations in cases such as are here under immediate mention, and these matters must be regarded as matters of which parties must take notice when they enter into contracts.

[1] Galveston, etc., R. Co. v. La Gierse, 51 Texas 189.

[2] Illinois Central R. Co. v. Willenborg, 117 Ill. 203, s. c. 26 Am. & Eng. R. Cas. 358.

[3] Gulf, etc., R. Co. v. Rowland, 70 Texas 298, s. c. 35 Am. & Eng. R. Cas. 286. In the case cited the court said: "The main case relied upon by the appellee, in order to sustain the constitutionality of the act in question is Thorpe v. Rutland, etc., R. Co., 27 Vt. 140. That case maintained the validity of an act of the legislature requiring railroad companies to put in cattle-guards at farm crossings. It seems to us that requirements for fence and cattle-guards stand upon the same principle. They are necessary for the protection of such domestic animals as are likely to stray upon the track, and more especially for the safety of passengers and employes of the railroad companies. Farm crossings are for the sole convenience of the owners of the land, and stand upon a different ground. Besides it does not appear in that case that the owner of the farm had been in any manner compensated for the expense of constructing his own crossings or cattle-guards. That decision, though it extends, as we think, the doctrine of the police power to its extreme limits, is not in conflict with the views expressed in this

road companies may be compelled to light their tracks situated within the limits of incorporated villages and cities,[1] and if this decision is to be understood as holding that companies may be compelled to light crossings and places to which the public have a right of access we think it is correct, but if it is to be understood as holding that railroad companies may be compelled to maintain lights at places where the members of the community have no right to go, that is, places owned by the companies and to which they have an exclusive right, we can not regard the decision as sound, for, while we believe that the legislature has power to provide for the safety and welfare of the public, we do not believe that the power extends to the control of private property, where no rights of the public are involved, although it is owned by a railroad company, nor do we believe that the legislature can prescribe the particular or specific kind of light that shall be used,[2] for, as we believe,

opinion. We think it would have been competent for the legislature, in providing for fences, to have required the companies to put in farm crossings, as a regulation of its undoubted power to require such fences. All subsequent rights of way would be presumed to have been acquired with reference to that law, and the landowner would not have been presumed to have assumed the burden of their construction. We, therefore, think that, as in all subsequent acquisition of rights of way, in the absence of some express or implied agreement to the contrary, the railroad companies will be charged with the duty imposed by the statute, and the measure of the compensation will be regulated accordingly; therefore, as to such future cases, in our opinion, the statute should be constitutional in so far as it applies to crossings without enclosures. Smith v. New York, etc., Railroad Co., 63 N. Y. 58." The opinion from which we have quoted justly discriminates between matters affecting public interest and matters of private concern. The distinction drawn in the opinion referred to is often lost sight of, and the result of losing sight of it is confusion and error. An exercise of the police power for purely private benefit can no more be defended than can the exercise of the right of eminent domain for a private purpose.

[1] Cincinnati, etc., R. Co. v. Sullivan, 32 Ohio St. 152. In the case cited the court held that under the police power railroad companies may be compelled to light their tracks situated within the limits of incorporated villages and cities, and that in the event of the failure of a company to provide lights the municipality might do so at the expense of the company, but that the expense could not be regarded as an assessment or a tax, but must be enforced by an action against the company.

[2] To hold that the legislature may arbitrarily and conclusively determine exactly what kind of a light

the legislative power extends no further than the enactment of a statute requiring tracks to be so lighted as to afford protection to the members of the community. The speed of trains through towns and cities may be regulated. The authorities are agreed that where the trains move upon or across highways their speed may be regulated, but there is a contrariety of opinion as to whether the speed of trains operating exclusively upon the private property of the company can be limited.[1] It is competent for the legislature to require railroad companies to keep tracks clear of weeds and other combustible materials.[2] Railroad companies may also be compelled to keep flagmen at crossings where the public safety or welfare requires the presence of flagmen.[3]

---

should be used would be to confer upon it the absolute power to choose between different kinds of light, and this would make the legislature the absolute arbiter of all questions of fact, such as the sufficiency of the light, its suitableness for the purpose and like questions, thus denying a hearing upon such questions. We do not mean to say that the legislature may not provide that a general kind of light may be used, as, for instance, electric lights or gas lights, but what we mean is that the legislature can not arbitrarily require the use of a lamp or lamps of a particular pattern or description.

[1] Gratiot v. Missouri Pacific R. Co., 116 Mo. 450, s. c. 21 S. W. R. 1094, 16 S. W. R. 384; Mobile, etc., R. Co. v. State, 51 Miss. 157; Whitson v. City of Franklin, 34 Ind. 892; Penna R. Co. v. Lewis, 79 Pa. St. 33; Chicago, etc., R. Co. v. Reidy, 66 Ill. 43; Merz v. Missouri Pac. R. Co., 88 Mo. 672; State v. Jersey City, 29 N. J. L. 170; Crowley v. Burlington, etc., R. Co., 65 Iowa 658; Haas v. Chicago, etc., R. Co., 41 Wis. 44; Horn v. Chicago, etc.,

R. Co., 38 Wis. 463; Cleveland, etc., R. Co. v. Harrington, 131 Ind. 426; Clark v. Boston, etc., R. Co., 64 N. H. 823, s. c. 81 Am. & Eng. R. Cas. 548; Toledo, etc., R. Co. v. Deacon, 63 Ill. 91.

[2] Diamond v. Northern Pac. R. Co., 6 Mont. 580. See, upon the general subject, State v. Nelson, (Ohio St.) s. c. 39 N. E. R. 22, 10 Lewis' Am. & Corp. R. 771; State v. Hoskins, 58 Minn. 35, s. c. 59 N. W. R. 545; Ditberner v. Chicago, etc., R. Co., 47 Wis. 138; Kent v. New York Central R. Co., 12 N. Y. 628; Pratt v. Atlantic, etc., R. Co., 42 Me. 579; Sioux City, etc., Co. v. Sioux City, 138 U. S. 98; American Rapid Tel. Co. v. Hess, 125 N. Y. 641, s. c. 4 Lewis' Am. R. & Corp. R. 199, 26 N.E.R. 919; City, etc., R. Co. v. Mayor, etc., of Savannah, 77 Ga. 731; Nelson v. Vermont, etc., R. Co., 26 Vt. 717; Tombs v. Rochester, etc., R. Co., 18 Barb. 583.

[3] Toledo, etc., R. Co. v. Jacksonville, 67 Ill. 37; Lake Shore, etc., R. Co. v. Cincinnati, etc., R. Co., 30 Ohio St. 604; City of Erie v. Erie Canal Co., 59 Pa. St. 174.

§ 669. The power to impose penalties in favor of private persons—Constitutional questions.—There is a stubborn conflict of authority upon the question of the power of the legislature to impose penalties, in the form of double damages and the like, upon railroad companies for the benefit of persons who have a cause of action against such companies. Many statutes give individuals a right to double damages and the like against railroad companies and in so doing enact a law that can only apply to a single class and a particular kind of actions, namely, civil actions against railroad companies. It seems to us that many of the courts in sustaining such statutes have disregarded the constitutional provisions prohibiting special and local legislation. Where there are no constitutional provisions inhibiting the enactment of local and special laws there is less difficulty in sustaining such statutes, but where there are such prohibitions it seems to us that statutes making special rules for the government of railroad companies can not be upheld except where the subject of the statute is peculiar to railroad companies. It has been held by the supreme court of the United States that a statute which gives a land-owner a right of action against railroad companies which fail to fence their roads for consequential damages does not conflict with the provisions of the federal constitutional though consequential damages are not recoverable under the laws of the state against any other persons or corporations except railway companies.[1] The weight of au-

[1] Minneapolis, etc., R. Co. v. Emmons, 149 U. S. 364, s. c. 13 Sup. Ct. R. 870. In the course of the opinion the court answering the contention of counsel that the statute denied to railroad companies the equal protection of the laws, said: "The answer to this is that there is no inhibition upon a state to impose such penalties for disregard of its police regulations as will insure prompt obedience to their requirements. For what injuries the party violating their requirements shall be liable, whether immediate or remote, is a matter of legislative discretion. The operating of railroads without fences and cattle-guards undoubtedly increases the danger which attends the operation of all railroads. It is only by such fences and guards that the straying of cattle running at large upon tracks can be prevented, and security had against accidents from that source; and the extent of the penalties which should be imposed by the state for any disregard of its legislation in that respect is a matter entirely within its control. It was not essential that the penalty should be confined to damages for the actual

thority is that legislation directed against railroad companies and not against any other corporations or persons is not local or special, but on this point there is conflict of authority.[1] The reasoning of many of the cases is, we venture to say, not entirely satisfactory. It may be true that as to matters peculiar to railroad companies which are not characteristics of any other corporation, a law applying to such companies exclusively is not special, but surely this is not true where the matter is a general one not peculiar to railroad companies. That some of the cases go too far is, as we believe, unquestionably true, but it must be said that it is not easy to draw a line between general and special statutes. So far as concerns the public duties of railroad companies there can, of course, be no reasonable controversy, for it is clear that as to such matters the legislature has power to enforce police regulations by imposing penalties for violations of law, but where the right exercised by railroad companies is a private right and in its general character the same as that exercised by corporations generally, there is very great, if not insurmountable, difficulty in sustaining statutes which apply exclusively to railroad companies.

loss to the owner of cattle injured by the want of fences and guards. It was entirely competent for the legislature to subject the company to any incidental or consequential damages, such as loss of rent, the expenses of keeping watch to guard cattle from straying upon the tracks, or any other expenditure to which the adjoining owner was subjected in consequence of failure of the company to construct the required fences and cattle-guards. No discrimination is made against any particular railroad companies or corporations. All are treated alike and required to perform the same duty; and, therefore, no invasion was attempted of the equality of protection ordained by the fourteenth amendment."

[1] Affirming the validity of such statutes, Gulf, etc., R., Co. v. Ellis, 87 Texas 19, s. c. 61 Am. & Eng. R. Cas. 357; Peoria, etc., R. Co. v. Duggan, 109 Ill. 537, s. c. 20 Am. & Eng. R. Cas. 489; Perkins v. St. Louis, etc., Ry. Co., 103 Mo. 52; Dow v. Beidelman, 49 Ark. 455, s. c. 31 Am. & Eng. R. Cas. 14; Burlington. etc., R. R. Co. v. Dey, 82 Iowa 312, s. c. 45 Am. & Eng. R. Cas. 391; Wortman v. Kleinschmidt, 12 Mont. 316; Jacksonville, etc., R. Co. v. Prior, 34 Fla. 271, s. c. 15 So. R. 760; Missouri Pac. Ry. Co. v. Humes, 115 U. S. 512; Kansas Pac. R. R. Co. v. Mower, 16 Kan. 573; Illinois Central R. Co. v. Crider, 91 Tenn. 489, s. c. 56 Am. & Eng. R. Cas. 157. Denying the validity of such statutes, Chicago, etc., R. Co. v. Moss, 60 Miss. 641; South, etc., R. Co. v. Morris, 65 Ala. 193; Wilder v. Chica-

§ 670. **Regulating speed of trains.**—There is no doubt that the legislature has power to make reasonable regulations as to the speed at which railroad trains shall run, and that it may confer power upon the municipalities of the state to make and enforce such regulations. We think that municipal ordinances may be so unreasonable as to authorize the courts to adjudge them ineffective.[1] Upon the same principle on which schedules of rates fixed by railroad commissioners are held unreasonable and ineffective ordinances of municipal corporations may be adjudged invalid if their effect is clearly and surely to practically disable a railroad company from properly discharging its public duties.

§ 671. **Grade crossings.**—The legislature of a state in the exercise of the police power may compel a railroad company to change a grade crossing.[2] It has been adjudged that a crossing

---

go, etc., R. R. Co., 70 Mich. 382; Schut v. Chicago, etc., R. R. Co., 70 Mich. 433; Zeigler v. South, etc., R. R. Co., 58 Ala. 594; Smith v. Louisville, etc., R. R. Co., 75 Ala. 449; State v. Divine, 98 N. Car. 778; Indiana, etc., R. Co. v. Gapen, 10 Ind. 292; Madison, etc., R. Co. v. Whiteneck, 8 Ind. 217; St. Louis, etc., R. R. Co. v. Williams, 49 Ark. 492. See, generally, Van Zant v. Waddel, 2 Yerg. 260; Janes v. Reynolds, 2 Texas 250; Durkee v. City of Janesville, 28 Wis. 464; Gordon v. Winchester, 12 Bush. 110; Wally's Heirs v. Kennedy, 2 Yerg. 554; Bull v. Conroe, 13 Wis. 233, 244; Calder v. Bull, 3 Dall. 386, 388.

[1] Evison v. Chicago, etc., R. Co., 45 Minn. 370; Meyers v. Chicago, etc., R. Co., 57 Iowa 555, s. c. 7 Am. & Eng. R. Cas. 406; Burg v. Chicago, etc., R. Co., 90 Iowa 106, s. c. 60 Am. & Eng. R. Cas. 159, 57 N. W. R. 680.

[2] New York, etc., R. Co. v. Town of Bristol, 151 U. S. 556, s. c. 14 Sup. Ct. R. 437, citing Woodruff v. Catlin, 54 Conn. 277, s. c. 6 Atl. R. 849; Town of Westbrook's Appeal, 57 Conn. 95, s. c. 17 Atl. R. 368; Woodruff v. New York, etc., R. R. Co., 59 Conn. 63, s. c. 20 Atl. R. 17; Doolittle v. Selectmen, 59 Conn. 402, s. c. 22 Atl. R. 336; New York, etc., R. Co. v. City of Waterbury, 60 Conn. 1, s. c. 22 Atl. R. 439; City of Middletown v. New York, etc., R. Co., 62 Conn. 492, s. c. 27 Atl. R. 119. In the first of the cases cited the court said: "It is likewise thoroughly established in this court that the inhibitions of the constitution of the United States upon the impairment of the obligation of contracts, or the deprivation of property without due process of law, or of the equal protection of the laws, by the states, are not violated by the legitimate exercise of legislative power in securing the public safety, health and morals. The governmental power of self-protection can not be contracted away, nor can the exercise of rights granted, nor the use of property be withdrawn from the implied governmental regulation in particulars essential to the preservation of the com-

at grade may be deemed a nuisance and as such be subject to change or removal.[1] The cases to which we refer lay down the doctrine in very broad terms, but we suppose that as it was not necessary in those cases to determine what limitations there are upon the power, these cases can not be regarded as adjudging that the legislative judgment is conclusive in all cases and entirely precludes the courts from deciding upon the validity of the statutory requirement.

§ 672. **Requiring services and denying compensation.**—It is quite clear that the legislature can not compel a railroad company to render services without compensation. This is decided in the Railroad Commission cases and other cases referred to in the preceding section. The conclusion we affirm rests on elementary principles of constitutional law and is strongly fortified by decisions of analogous cases.[2] Under the form of regulating the compensation for transporting freight and passengers the legislature can not compel a railroad corporation

munity from injury. Beer Co. v. Massachusetts, 97 U. S. 25; Fertilizing Co. v. Hyde Park, 97 U. S. 659; Barbier v. Connolly, 113 U. S. 27; New Orleans Gas Co. v. Louisiana, etc., Co., 115 U. S. 650, s. c. 6 Sup. Ct. R. 252; Budd v. New York, 143 U. S. 517, s. c. 12 Sup. Ct. R. 468." See, also, upon the subject of the power to compel change of crossings, Elliott on Roads and Streets, 166, 334, 598; In re Mayor, etc., of City of Northampton, 158 Mass. 299, s. c. 55 Am. & Eng. R. Cas. 31; City of Roxbury v. Boston, etc., R. Co., 6 Cush. 424; Commonwealth v. Eastern R. Co., 103 Mass. 254; Mayor, etc., of Worcester v. Norwich, etc., R. Co., 109 Mass. 103; In re City of Northampton, 158 Mass. 299; Boston, etc., Co. v. County Commissioners, 79 Me. 386; State v. Wabash, etc., R. Co., 83 Mo. 144, s. c. 25 Am. & Eng. R. Cas. 133.

[1] New York, etc., R. Co.'s Appeal, 58 Conn. 532, s. c. 20 Atl. R. 670.

[2] Georgia, etc., R. Co. v. Smith, 128 U. S. 174; Ruggles v. Illinois, 108 U. S. 526; Connecticut, etc., R. Co. v. County Commissioners, 127 Mass. 50, s. c. 34 Am. R. 338; Drury v. Midland, etc., R. Co., 127 Mass. 571; Mercantile Trust Co. v. Texas, etc., R. Co., 51 Fed. R. 529; Wynehamer v. People, 13 N. Y. 378; Roberts v. Northern Pacific, etc., R. Co., 158 U. S. 1, s. c. 15 Sup. Ct. R. 756. See Rippe v. Becker, 56 Minn. 100, s. c. 22 L. R. A. 857; State v. Billings, 55 Minn. 467; Evison v. Chicago, etc., R. Co., 45 Minn. 370, s. c. 11 L. R. A. 434; Eaton v. Boston, etc., R. Co., 51 N. H. 504, s. c. 12 Am. R. 147; Thompson v. Androscoggin, etc., R. Co., 54 N. H. 545; State v. Beackmo, 8 Blckf. 246; State v. Ravine, etc., Com., 39 N. J. Law. 665; Vanhorne v. Dorrance, 2 Dall. (U. S.) 304.

to carry freight and passengers unless compensation is adequately provided. In our opinion the legislature has no power to require a railroad company to carry freight or passengers without compensation in money, and can not substitute for money property or claims against some other company or person.[1] There may be and probably is an exception to the general rule that compensation must be made in money, and that is where the sovereign requires the services, for there is authority for holding that where the sovereign takes property it need not pay the compensation at the time.

§ 673. **Federal corporation—State can not transform into a domestic corporation.**—It is beyond the power of a state to transform a corporation created by the federal congress into a state corporation.[2] In the cases referred to in the note the state of Wisconsin had given its consent to a railroad company created by the United States to enter its territory and it was held that the state had no power to enact a statute making the corporation a domestic one, and that, notwithstanding such a statute, it remained a federal corporation, and, as such, derived its rights from the general government.[3] The supreme court of the United States, while professing to distinguish the decisions of the state court, practically denied their authority.[4]

---

[1] The conclusion we affirm is fully sustained by the reasoning in Attorney-General v. Old Colony R. Co., 160 Mass. 62, s. c. 22 L. R. A. 112. It certainly rests on solid principle. The decision in the case of Reagan v. Farmers' Loan, etc., Co., 154 U. S. 362, s. c. 14 Sup. Ct. R. 1047, as it seems to us, declares the principle which we have asserted. In the case last cited the court adjudged that the decision in Budd v. New York, 143 U. S. 517, s. c. 12 Sup. Ct. R. 468, did not assert a contrary doctrine.

[2] Roberts v. Northern Pacific R. Co., 158 U. S. 1, s. c. 15 Sup. Ct. R. 756.

[3] See Pacific Railroad Removal Cases, 115 U. S. 1, s. c. 5 Sup. Ct. R. 1113; Olcott v. Supervisors, 16 Wall. 678; Osborn v. Bank, 9 Wheat. 737, 817; Cromwell v. County of Sac, 94 U. S. 351; Johnson Co. v. Wharton, 152 U. S. 252, s. c. 14 Sup. Ct. R. 608.

[4] The case of Ellis v. Northern Pac. Railroad Co., 77 Wis. 114, s. c. 45 N. W. R. 811, was practically overruled. So, also, was Whiting v. Sheboygan, etc., Railroad Co., 25 Wis. 167.

CHAPTER XXVIII.

STATE RAILROAD COMMISSIONERS.

§ 674. Introductory.
675. Nature of state railroad commissions.
676. The power to create railroad commissions.
677. Strictly judicial powers can not be conferred upon administrative or ministerial officers.
678. Granting authority to make regulations not a delegation of legislative power.
679. Legislature can not authorize a railroad commission to make unjust discriminations.
680. Members of railroad commission are public officers.
681. Qualifications of commissioners.
682. Powers of railroad commissioners—Illustrative cases.
683. Jurisdiction of railroad commissioners.
684. Jurisdiction of commission not extended by implication—General rule.
685. Incidental powers of a railroad commission.
686. Right of railroad companies to a hearing.
687. Orders of commissioners not contracts.
688. Certificates of commissioners that rates are reasonable—Effect of.
689. Regulation of charges for transporting property and passengers.
690. Domestic commerce.

§ 691. Reasonableness of freight and fare tariff of rates—How far a judicial question.
692. Regulation of charges—Test of reasonableness.
693. Tariff of rates—Test of reasonableness.
694. Stations—Power to order company to provide.
695. Procedure before the commissioners.
696. Effect of the decision of the commissioners that a company has not committed an act authorizing a forfeiture.
697. Enforcing the orders of the commissioners—Generally.
698. Enforcing the orders of the commissioners—Mandamus.
699. Mandamus enforcing orders of commissioners—Illustrative cases.
700. Suits against railroad commissioners are not ordinarily suits against the state.
701. Remedies for illegal acts of railroad commissioners.
702. Specific statutory remedy.
703. Parties to suits against railroad commissioners.
704. Review by *certiorari*.
705. Injunction against commissioners—Generally.
706. Where commissioners exceed their jurisdiction injunction will lie.
707. Vacating orders of commissioners on the ground of fraud.
708. Federal question—Removal of causes from state courts.

(977)

§ 674. **Introductory.**—The system of governing and regulating railroads by commissions is in most of the states borrowed in the main from the English statutes.[1] The statutes enacted by the states are essentially different in matters of detail,[2] but all are directed to the attainment of the same general object, namely, the regulation of the duties of railroads as common carriers and the regulation of the management and control of railroads, so far as they are affected by a public interest. The power to establish such commissions is rested upon the general principle that the state has control over property and pursuits of a public nature.[3] It has been said that the statutes create no new or additional duties,[4] but this statement as applied to some of the state statutes requires qualification. The principal and leading purpose of most of the statutes is to control and regulate the charges for the transportation of freight and passengers, but the provisions of the statutes generally go far beyond the regulation of charges for transportation and confer comprehensive powers over the maintenance, management and operation of railroads. It is not our purpose in this chapter to treat very fully of the power of state railroad commissions to regulate the charges made by railroad companies in perform-

---

[1] For the principal features of the English system see 1 Hodges on Railways (7th ed.), pp. 175, 348, 308. See 2 Redfield on Railways 606; 1 Woods on Railroads, p. 658.

[2] In some of the states the commissioners are little else than mere advisory officers, while in other states they have power to make orders which in their nature closely resemble judgments and to invoke the aid of the courts to compel obedience to their orders. People v. New York, etc., R. Co., 104 N. Y. 58, s. c. 29 Am. & Eng. R. Cas. 480; Interstate Commerce Commission v. Brimson, 154 U. S. 447, s. c. 14 Sup. Ct. R. 1125; State v. Fremont, etc., R. Co., 22 Neb. 313; McWhorter v. Pensacola, etc., R. Co., 24 Fla. 417, s. c. 37 Am. & Eng. R. Cas.

566; State v. Chicago, etc., Railroad Co., 38 Minn. 281; Board of Railway Commissioners v. Oregon, etc., R. Co., 17 Ore. 65.

[3] Chicago, etc., R. Co. v. Iowa, 94 U. S. 155; Peik v. Chicago, etc., R. Co., 94 U. S. 164; Stone v. Farmers', etc., Trust Co., 116 U. S. 307; Ruggles v. Illinois, 108 U. S. 526; Stone v. Natches, etc., R. Co., 62 Miss. 646. See *post*, § 676. In Wellman v. Chicago, etc., R. Co., 83 Mich. 592, s. c. 45 Am. & Eng. R. Cas. 249, the question of the power of a state to establish a railroad commission received careful consideration.

[4] Atchison, etc., R. Co. v. Denver, etc., R. Co., 110 U. S. 667, s. c. 16 Am. & Eng. R. Cas. 57.

ing services and duties as common carriers, nor to treat of the power of the states to enact statutes relating to interstate railroads, although we shall incidentally discuss those subjects, since they naturally fall within the general scope of this chapter, but as those subjects will be considered in the part of our work devoted to a discussion of the rights, duties and liabilities of railroads as common carriers, we pass them without an extended or elaborate consideration.

§ 675. **Nature of state railroad commissions.**—Governmental control of railroads in many of the states is exercised through the instrumentality of officers generally called railroad commissioners. These officers, of course, derive all their powers from the statute which creates the commission, and a railroad commission is a tribunal possessing naked statutory powers. It is not a court, although it may exercise powers of a judicial nature.[1] The fact that powers in their nature judicial are exercised by an officer, a board of officers, or by a body of officers, does not make the officer a judge nor does it constitute the body or board a court.[2] The truth is that all officers

---

[1] Interstate Commerce Com. v. Cincinnati, etc., Co., 64 Fed. R. 981; Kentucky, etc., Bridge Co. v. Louisville, etc., R. Co., 37 Fed. R. 567, 612. The principle asserted in the text is laid down in the cases which hold that state tax boards and similar tribunals are not courts, although they are invested with *quasi* judicial power. Langenberg v. Decker, 131 Ind. 471; State v. Wood, 110 Ind. 82; Kuntz v. Sumption, 117 Ind. 1.

[2] Flournoy v. City of Jeffersonville, 17 Ind. 169, s. c. 79 Am. Dec. 468; Wilkins v. State, 113 Ind. 514, 519; Betts v. Dimon, 3 Conn. 107; Crane v. Camp, 12 Conn. 463. The decisions recognize the constitutionality of the act of congress creating the federal interstate commerce commission and affirm that the powers of that tribunal are not judicial in the proper sense of the term. Interstate Commerce Commission v. Brimson, 154 U.S. 447, s. c. 14 Sup. Ct. R. 1125. In the case last cited the decision in Re Interstate Commerce Commission, 53 Fed. R. 476, was reversed, and it was held that the provision of the act of congress authorizing the commission to apply to the courts to punish a witness who refused to give testimony or produce documents was constitutional. The court cited the cases of Smith v. Adams, 130 U. S. 167, s. c. 9 Sup. Ct. R. 566; Osborn v. Bank, 9 Wheat. 738; Cherokee Nation v. Southern Kans., etc., R. Co., 135 U. S. 641, s. c. 10 Sup. Ct. R. 965; Gordon v. United States, 117 U. S. 697; In re Sanborn, 148 U. S. 222, s. c. 13 Sup. Ct. R. 577; De Groot v. United States, 5 Wall. 419; Anderson v. Dunn, 6 Wheat. 204; Kilbourn v. Thompson, 103 U. S. 168,

who have discretionary duties to perform exercise *quasi* judicial power. A constable who takes a bond, a sheriff who levies a writ, or a governor who decides upon the validity of a requisition for a fugitive from justice exercises a power that is in its nature judicial, but it is not a judicial power in the same sense as the power of a court or judge. The functions and duties of railroad commissioners are administrative or ministerial and neither legislative nor judicial. Their powers can not be legislative, for legislative powers can not be delegated,[1] nor can their powers be judicial in the proper sense of the term, for the judicial power can only be exercised by courts and judges.[2]

§ 676. The power to create railroad commissions.—The power to create a board of railroad commissioners rests, as we believe, upon the principle that where rights or property are "affected with a public interest," they are subject to legislative control. Many of the cases which uphold statutes creating

190; Whitcomb's Case, 120 Mass. 118, and after commenting on those cases, said that "The views we have expressed in the present case are not inconsistent with anything said or decided in those cases. They do not in any manner infringe upon the salutary principle that congress, excluding the special cases provided for in the constitution—as, for instance—in section 2 of article 2, may not impose upon the courts of the United States any duties that are not strictly judicial." The court asserted by its line of reasoning that the commission was not a court nor its duties judicial in the proper sense of the term. See *Re* Pacific R.Com'n.,32 Fed. R. 241; Interstate Commerce Com. *v.* Cincinnati, etc., Co., 64 Fed. R. 981.

[1] Cooley's Const. Lim. (6th ed.), 137. In Chicago, etc., R. Co. *v.* Dey, 35 Fed. R. 866, the court adjudged that in creating a board of railroad commissioners and investing it with authority to regulate freight tariffs and the like the legislature did not delegate legislative powers. It is difficult to define with precision the line between legislative and ministerial power, but it is clear that where a law is enacted providing general rules for the government of officers charged with the administration of the law there is no delegation of legislative power although the officers may be invested with authority to make rules and regulations.

[2] Interstate Commerce Commission *v.* Brimson, 154 U. S. 447, s. c. 14 Sup. Ct. R. 1125; Hayburn's Case, 2 Dall. 409; United States *v.* Ferreira, 13 How. (U. S.) 40, note; Gans, *Ex parte*, 17 Fed. R. 471; Burgoyne *v.* Board of Supervisors, 5 Cal. 9; *In re* Allen, 19 Fed. R. 809; State *v.* Noble, 118 Ind. 350; Van Slyke *v.* Trempealeau, etc., Co., 39 Wis. 390; Vandercook *v.* Williams, 106 Ind. 345.

such boards, however, proceed upon the theory that such statutes rest upon the police power. But whatever may be the true theory as to the principle on which such statutes rest, there can be no doubt as to their validity. There is practically no diversity of judicial opinion upon the general question.[1]

[1] The federal courts have affirmed the validity of the act of congress establishing the interstate commerce commission, and the principle asserted applies to state railroad commissions. Interstate Commerce Commission v. Brimson, 154 U. S. 447, s. c. 14 Sup. Ct. R. 1125; Kentucky, etc., Co. v. Louisville, etc., Co., 37 Fed. R. 567; Fargo v. Michigan, 121 U. S. 230, 239; Interstate Commerce Com. v. Cincinnati, etc., Co., 64 Fed. R. 981. The federal courts have also upheld state statutes creating boards of railroad commissioners. Stone v. Farmers' Loan and Trust Co., 116 U. S. 307, s. c. 6 Sup. Ct. 334; Chicago, etc., Co. v. Dey, 35 Fed. R. 866, 875; Tilley v. Savannah, etc., Railroad Co., 5 Fed. R. 641. In the case of Reagan v. Farmers', etc., Co., 154 U. S. 362, s. c. 14 Sup. Ct. R. 1047, the court said: "Passing from the question of jurisdiction to the act itself there can be no doubt of the general power of the statute to regulate the fares and freights which may be charged by railroads or other carriers, and that this regulation can be carried on by means of a commission. Such a commission is merely an administrative board created by the state for the purpose of carrying into effect the will of the state as expressed by its legislation. Railroad Commission Cases, 116 U. S. 307, s. c. 6 Sup. Ct. R. 334. No valid objection, therefore, can be made on account of the general features of this act—those by which the state has created a railroad commission, and intrusted it with the duty of prescribing rates of freights and fares, as well as other regulations for the management of the railroads of the state." In the case of the Charlotte, etc., R. Co. v. Gibbes, 142 U. S. 386, s. c. 12 Sup. Ct. R. 255, the court upheld a state statute creating a board of railroad commissioners, and, in the course of the opinion, in speaking of railroad companies, said: "Being the recipients of special privileges from the state to be exercised in the interest of the public, and assuming the obligations thus mentioned, their business is deemed affected with a public use, and to the extent of that use is subject to legislative regulation. Georgia, etc., Banking Co. v. Smith, 128 U. S. 174, 179, s. c. 9 Sup. Ct. R. 47." The state courts have uniformly adjudged such statutes to be valid. State v. Chicago, etc., R. Co., 38 Minn. 281, s. c. 37 N. W. R. 782; State v. Fremont, etc., R. Co., 22 Neb. 313, s. c. 35 N. W. R. 118, and 23 Neb. 117, s. c. 36 N. W. R. 308; Charlotte, etc., R. Co. v. Gibbes, 27 So. Car. 385, s. c. 31 Am. & Eng. R. Cas. 464; Stone v. Natchez, etc., R. Co., 62 Miss. 646, s. c. 21 Am. & Eng. R. Cas. 6; Georgia, etc., R. Co. v. Smith, 70 Ga. 694, s. c. 9 Am. & Eng. R. Cas. 385; Stone v. Yazoo, etc., R. Co., 62 Miss. 607, s. c. 21 Am. & Eng. R. Cas. 6, 52 Am. R. 193; Board of R. Com. v. Oregon R., etc., Co., 17 Ore. 65, s. c. 35 Am. & Eng. R. Cas. 542; Chicago, etc., R. Co. v. Jones, 149 Ill. 361, s. c. 24 L. R. A. 141, 37 N. E. R. 247.

§ 677. **Strictly judicial powers can not be conferred upon administrative or ministerial officers.**—We have elsewhere suggested that purely or strictly judicial power can not be conferred upon railway commissioners, for they are administrative or ministerial officers. The constitutional provision relative to the separation of the departments of government is not a mere empty declaration but is a part of the organic law, and is of great force and vigor. It forbids the blending of judicial duties and functions with those that are ministerial or administrative. In accordance with this fundamental principle it is held that the legislature has no power to invest railway commissioners with authority to define offenses and prescribe punishment.[1] It has, however, been held that a railroad commission may be constituted a court and as such invested with judicial power.[2] The attention of the court in the case to which we refer does not seem to have been directed to the principle that the departments of government are separate and that judicial power and administrative power can not be blended and bestowed upon a board of public officers. It may possibly be that where the constitution of the state does not provide that the departments shall be separate, judicial and ministerial powers may be blended and bestowed upon a board or commission, but we believe that the principle that the departments of government are separate is fundamental and essential to the existence of a republican government,[3] and that no statute can be valid which violates that

---

[1] State v. Gaster, 45 La. Ann. 636. The reasoning of Baxter, J., in Louisville, etc., R. Co. v. Railroad Commission, 19 Fed. R. 679, supports the doctrine of the text.

[2] Atlantic Express Co. v. Wilmington, etc., R. Co., 111 N. C. 463, s. c. 32 Am. St. R. 805, citing Durham, etc., R. Co. v. Richmond, etc., R. Co., 104 N. C. 673; Georgia R., etc., Co. v. Smith, 70 Ga. 694. The cases cited do not, however, go to the question of the power to make a board of railroad commissioners a court, but to the general question of the right to regulate railroads because a public use is impressed upon them.

[3] Cooley's Principles of Const. Law 41, 44; Black's Constitutional Law 72; Montesquieu's Spirit of the Laws, book II, ch. 6; 1 Bryce's Am. Com. 3; Wilson Congressional Government 12, 36; Sill v. Village of Corning, 15 N. Y. 297, 303; Calder v. Bull, 3 Dall. 386; Greenough v. Greenough, 11 Pa. St. 489; Alexander v. Bennett, 60 N. Y. 204; State v. Noble, 118 Ind. 350.

principle. It is, at all events, quite clear that where the state constitution requires that the departments shall be kept separate the legislature can not unite the powers and bestow them upon a single tribunal.[1]

§ 678. Granting authority to make regulations not a delegation of legislative power.—It is sometimes difficult to clearly define the line between a delegation of legislative power and a grant of authority to perform acts which are in their nature *quasi* legislative but not strictly so. The constitutional inhibition which prevents the delegation of legislative power does not prevent the grant of authority to make rules and regulations for the government of a particular subject. In creating a board of railroad commissioners and investing it with authority to make rules and regulations for the government of railroads the legislature really enacts the law which governs the subject but intrusts to the board the execution of the law. For the law the statute must be looked to, as the commissioners can not enact laws, although they may make reasonable rules and regulations where the authority to make such rules and regulations is expressly or impliedly conferred upon them by the statute.[2]

§ 679. Legislature can not authorize a railroad commission to make unjust discriminations.—The decisions which declare

[1] Perkins v. Corbin, 45 Ala. 103; People v. Albertson, 55 N. Y. 50; Missouri, etc., Co. v. First National Bank, 74 Ill. 217; *In re* Pacific Railway Com., 32 Fed. R. 241, 267; Turner v. Althaus, 6 Neb. 54; Kilbourn v. Thompson, 103 U. S. 168; People v. Keeler, 99 N. Y. 463, s. c. 52 Am. R. 49; Wright v. Defrees, 8 Ind. 298; Smythe v. Boswell, 117 Ind. 365, and authorities cited; Houston v. Williams, 13 Calf. 24; Hawkins v. The Governor, 1 Ark. 570; *Ex parte* Randolp, 2 Brock. 447; Vaughn v. Harp, 49 Ark. 160.

[2] In Atlantic, etc., Co. v. Wilmington, etc., R. Co., 111 N. C. 463, s. c. 32 Am. St. R. 805, the court quoted with approval from the opinion in Georgia R. Co. v. Smith, 70 Ga. 694, the following: "The difference between the power to pass a law and the power to adopt rules and regulations to carry the law into effect is apparent and great, and this we understand to be the distinction recognized strikingly by all the courts as the true rule in determining whether or not in such cases a legislative power is granted. The former would be unconstitutional whilst the latter would not." See Storrs v. Pensacola R. Co., 29 Fla. 617; Woodruff v. New York, etc., R. Co., 59 Conn. 63.

that statutes are valid although they enact rules that apply only to the class of corporations known as railroad companies carry the doctrine quite as far as it can be done with reason, and, indeed, it may well be doubted if some of those decisions do not go too far. If they can be defended upon principle at all it must be upon the ground that railroad companies constitute a general distinctive class of corporations and that for this reason there is a sufficient basis of classification. If there be no such basis of classification and a mere naked arbitrary singling out of railway corporations and the imposition upon them of special burdens and penalties, there is, as it seems to us, an infraction of the federal constitution forbidding the denial to any person of the equal protection of the laws. For illustration, if a statute should provide that all contracts of railroad companies for the purchase or sale of lands should be stamped with a government stamp of a particular value, and should not require such a stamp from other persons, it seems to us that the constitutional provision would be violated. So, too, such a statute would, as we believe, transgress the constitutional provisions incorporated in the constitution of most of the states prohibiting the enactment of special or local laws. All things being equal, a railroad commission must, as we suppose, place all railroad companies upon an equality and not unjustly discriminate between them.[1] Doubtless there may be cases where the commission may make a difference between railroad companies,[2] but to authorize such a course there must, in our opinion, be some substantial basis for the discrimination, for surely neither the caprices of the commissioners nor their mere arbitrary conclusions can be permitted to control where to permit such a thing would result in an unjust and groundless discrimination. In a strongly reasoned case it is held that the legislature can not delegate to a railroad commission the power to prescribe penalties for acts not defined and de-

[1] Dow v. Beidelman, 125 U. S. 680; Dow v. Beidelman, 49 Ark. 325; Little Rock, etc., R. Co. v. Hanniford, 49 Ark. 291; Chicago, etc., R. Co. v. Iowa, 94 U. S. 155.

[2] Louisville, etc., R. Co. v. Railroad Commission, 19 Fed. R. 679.

clared offenses by the legislature,[1] nor can the power be committed to the unlimited discretion of a jury.

§ 680. Members of railroad commission are public officers. —A member of a railroad commission created by the state, whether elected by the voters of the state, or by the legislature, or appointed by the governor, is a public officer. The general rules which apply to the term, tenure, and duties of public officers apply to members of a state board of railway commissioners so far as the statute does not otherwise provide. Thus it is held that where there is a failure to elect a railroad commissioner at the time prescribed by statute the incumbent under a prior election will hold over under the general law providing that officers shall hold until their successors are elected and qualified.[2] The statute, it is barely necessary to

[1] Louisville, etc., R. Co. v. Railroad Commission, 19 Fed. R. 679, 683. It was said by Baxter, J., that: "We think the property of a citizen—and a railroad corporation is, in legal contemplation, a citizen—can not be thus imperiled by such vague, uncertain, and indefinite enactments. The corporations and persons against whom this act is directed can do nothing under it with reasonable safety. They may take counsel of the commission, act upon their advice, and honestly endeavor to conform to the statute. But if a jury before whom they may be subsequently arraigned shall, in their judgment and upon such arbitrary basis as they are at liberty to adopt, conclude that the commissioners misadvised or that the managers of the accused railroad corporation made a mistake in regulating their charges upon a 5 per cent., instead of a 4 per cent., basis, the honesty and good faith of the accused will go for nothing, and penalty upon penalty may be added until the defendants' property shall be gradually transferred to the public. This can not be permitted. Penalties can not be thus inflicted at the discretion of a jury. Before the property of a citizen, natural or corporate, can be thus confiscated, the crime for which the penalty is inflicted must be defined by the law-making power. The legislature can not delegate this power to a jury. If it can declare it a criminal act for a railroad corporation to take more than a 'fair and just return' on its investments, it must, in order to the validity of the law, define with reasonable certainty what would constitute such 'fair and just return.' The act under review does not do this, but leaves it to the jury to supply the omission."

[2] Eddy v. Kincaid, (Ore.) s. c. 41 Pac. R. 156, citing State v. Simon, 20 Ore. 365, s. c. 26 Pac. R. 170; Gosman v. State, 106 Ind. 203, s. c. 6 N. E. R. 349; State v. Harrison, 113 Ind. 434, s. c. 16 N. E. R. 384; State v. Howe, 25 Ohio St. 588; People v. Tilton, 37 Cal. 614; Badger v. United States, 93 U. S. 599; Scott County v. Ring, 29 Minn. 398, s. c. 13 N. W. R. 181; State v. Wells, 8 Nev. 105; Mayor

suggest, governs, and to the statute recourse must be had to ascertain what are the particular rights, powers and duties of railway commissioners, but where there is no statutory provision to the contrary the general rules of law are of controlling influence.[1]

§ 681. **Qualification of commissioners.**—The legislature, within constitutional limits, may prescribe the qualifications of the members of railway commissions. It is to the statute that recourse must be had to determine what qualifications are made requisite. The constitutional principle that no man can be a judge in his own case forbids a person who has a substantial and direct interest in questions before the commissior from sitting as a member when those questions are under consideration.[2]

§ 682. **Powers of railroad commissioners — Illustrative cases.**—As the powers of railroad commissioners are statutory it is not possible to determine what effect a given decision may have in any other state than that in which it is rendered except when general principles are involved. But while the effect of a given decision can not be accurately ascertained without an examination of the statute upon which it is based, still, the decisions almost always illustrate some general principle or enforce some rule of statutory construction. With these prefatory suggestions we direct attention to some of the

v. Horn, 2 Harr. (Del.) 190; State v. Kurtzeborn, 78 Mo. 98; Charman v. Daniel, 6 Jones (N. C.) 444.

[1] Where the statute creating a board of railroad commissioners expressly provides that the executive council may remove members of the board from office and appoint others to fill their places and does not provide for assigning causes for the removal, the executive council may, at its discretion, remove a commissioner from office. The discretion so vested in the council can not be controlled by the courts. State v. Mitchell, 50 Kan. 289, s. c. 33 Pac. R. 104, 20 L. R. A. 306.

[2] Dimes v. Grand Junction, etc., Co., 3 H. L. C. 759; Cooley's Const. Lim., 175; Elliott's Gen. Pr., § 210. As to the nature of the interest which will disqualify, see Sauls v. Freeman, 24 Fla. 209, s. c. 12 Am. St. R. 190, 4 So. R. 525; Inhabitants of Northampton v. Smith, 11 Metc. 390; Gregory v. Cleveland, etc., R. Co., 4 Ohio St. 675; Sjoberg v. Nordin, 26 Minn. 501; Elliott's Gen. Pr., § 212.

decided cases. It has been held that where there is statutory power to order a relocation of tracks near a station as the public interest may require, the board has authority in ordering one company to take the tracks of another to make it a condition of the taking of such tracks that the company taking the track shall permit the company from which they are taken to use its tracks.[1] The statutes usually grant to the board of commissioners power to order the location and relocation of stations,[2] and the decision of the board in such matters can not be overthrown unless it is affirmatively shown that it proceeded in violation of some provision of the constitution or the statute, or grossly abused the power conferred upon it. Very important powers in relation to the matter of requiring railroad companies to construct and maintain crossings are generally granted to the commissioners.[3] It is held that jurisdiction of applications to condemn lands may be conferred upon railroad commissioners in cases where the land is required for

---

[1] Providence, etc., R. Co. v. Norwich, etc., R. Co., 138 Mass. 277, s. c. 22 Am. & Eng. R. Cas. 493.

[2] State v. Chicago, etc., R. Co., 19 Neb. 476; State v. Alabama, etc., R. Co., 67 Miss. 647; State v. Des Moines, etc., R. Co., 84 Iowa 419, s. c. 49 Am. & Eng. R. Cas. 186; State v. Kansas, etc., R. Co., 47 Kan. 497, s. c. 49 Am. & Eng. R. Cas. 176; State v. Fremont, etc., R. Co., 22 Neb. 313, s. c. 32 Am. & Eng. R. Cas. 426; Board of Railroad Commissioners v. Oregon, etc., R. Co., 17 Ore. 65, s. c. 35 Am. & Eng. R. Cas. 542. The Minnesota court has held the orders of the board conclusive. State v. Chicago, etc., R. Co., 38 Minn. 281; Railroad, etc., Co. v. Railroad, etc., Commission, 39 Minn. 231; State v. Minneapolis, etc., R. Co., 40 Minn. 156. But in so holding the court was in error. See State v. Chicago, etc., R. Co., 86 Iowa 304, s. c. 53 N. W. R. 253; State v. Alabama, etc., R. Co., 68 Miss. 653.

[3] State v. Des Moines, etc., R. Co., 84 Iowa 419, s. c. 49 Am. & Eng. R. Cas. 186; Doolittle v. Selectmen, 59 Conn. 402, s. c. 22 Atl. R. 336; New York, etc., R. Company's Appeal, 62 Conn. 527, s. c. 26 Atl. R. 122; Smith v. New Haven, etc., R. Co., 59 Conn. 203, s. c. 22 Atl. R. 146; In re Railroad Commissioners, 83 Me. 273, s. c. 22 Atl. R. 168; State v. Chicago, etc., R. Co., 29 Neb. 412, s. c. 45 N. W. R. 469; State v. Shardlow, 43 Minn. 524, s. c. 46 N. W. R. 74; Detroit, etc., R. Co. v. Probate Judge, 63 Mich. 676, s. c. 28 Am. & Eng. R. Cas. 285. See City of Cambridge v. Railroad Commissioners, 153 Mass. 161, s. c. 26 N. E. R. 241; Fort Street, etc., Co. v. State, etc., Board, 81 Mich. 248, s. c. 45 N. W. R. 973; Guggenheim v. Lake Shore, etc., R. Co., 66 Mich. 150, s. c. 32 Am. & Eng. R. Cas. 89.

a depot.¹ Jurisdiction to compel companies to resume or continue operation of lines of railroad may be conferred upon the commissioners.² But it is held that the commissioners can not make a palpably unreasonable requirement of a railroad company in respect to change of stations or tracks.³ Commissioners are authorized in some of the states to make and enforce orders requiring railroad companies to place flagmen at crossings,⁴ and to require railroad companies to fence their tracks.⁵ Authority conferred upon a board of commissioners to regulate rates does not empower it to compel the opening of offices for public accommodation.⁶

§ 683. Jurisdiction of railroad commissioners.—A board of railroad commissioners is, as we have said, a tribunal invested with *quasi* judicial power, so that it is not improper to apply to it the term jurisdiction. In ascertaining the jurisdiction of such a tribunal the statute creating it must always, it is obvious, be consulted, since the only jurisdiction it possesses is such as the statute confers. We suppose that the ordinary rules which govern *quasi* judicial tribunals created by statute and invested with naked statutory powers govern boards of railroad commissioners, and that nothing can be intended to be within their jurisdiction which is not placed there by the statute. It is not necessary, as we believe, that the statute should expressly and explicitly define the jurisdiction of the commissioners, but it is sufficient if jurisdiction is conferred in general terms. If jurisdiction over a general subject is conferred then authority over branches and details of that subject is conferred by necessary implication. Statutes creating railroad commissions are to be construed according to

---

[1] Jager v. Dey, 80 Iowa 23, s. c. 42 Am. & Eng. R. Cas. 683.

[2] See Winsford, etc., Board v. Cheshire, etc., L. R. 24 Q. B. D. 456; Dickson v. Great Northern, etc., R. Co., L. R. 18 Q. B. D. 176.

[3] State v. Des Moines, etc., R. Co., 87 Iowa 644, s. c. 54 N. W. R. 461; State v. Chicago, etc., R. Co., 86 Iowa 304, s. c. 53 N. W. R. 253.

[4] Guggenheim v. Lake Shore, etc., R. Co., 66 Mich. 150, s. c. 32 Am. & Eng. R. Cas. 89.

[5] Davidson v. Michigan, etc., R. Co., 49 Mich. 428, s. c. 13 Am. & Eng. R. Cas. 650.

[6] State v. Western Union Tel. Co., 113 N. C. 213, s. c. 18 S. E. R. 389, 22 L. R. A. 570.

the general rules laid down for the construction of statutes, and the cardinal rule that the intention of the legislature is to be sought and enforced prevails in cases where such statutes are under consideration.[1] The courts will not, if their assistance is properly invoked, permit a railroad commission to deal with matters not within its jurisdiction, for such tribunals are not above the law nor beyond judicial control.[2] Where, however, the matter is one entirely within the jurisdiction of the commission and it is invested with discretionary powers in relation to the subject, the courts will not control the exercise of such powers although they will interfere where there is a clear abuse of those powers resulting in injury to the complainant.

[1] This general rule was applied to a statute, creating a board of railroad commissioners by the supreme court of Maine in *In re* Canadian Pacific R. Co., 32 Atl. R. 863. In the course of the opinion there given it was said: "To place all railroad crossings within the limits of the state under the control of the railroad commissioners has manifestly been the paramount object of the legislation on this subject since the enactment of 1878. The several provisions in regard to the right of application, and the apportionment of the expense, enacted in different years, are of a subordinate character, and of secondary importance. They are not all conditions precedent to the jurisdiction of the railroad commissioners in unincorporated places. The fact that all the provisions of the statute respecting the right of application, and the adjustment of the expense in the case of cities and towns, are not also applicable to unincorporated places, can not take away the jurisdiction of the railroad commissioners over the latter while there is an express provision, applicable to all crossings, authorizing an application by the railroad company, and also placing upon the company the burden of the expense. In the case of cities or towns, either the municipal officers or the railroad company may invoke the jurisdiction of the railroad commissioners; and thereupon the expense of building the way within the limits of the railroad may all be imposed on the railroad company, or be apportioned between the railroad company and the town, as the commissioners may determine. But with respect to ways in unincorporated places, where there are no municipal officers, the application can only be made by the parties owning or operating the railroad; and inasmuch as there is no provision for the payment or apportionment of the expense applicable to such a case, except that which places this burden on the railroad company, 'the expense of building and maintaining so much thereof as is within the limits of such railroad shall be borne by such railroad company.'"

[2] Toomer v. London, etc., R. Co., L. R. 2 Exch. Div. 450; Southeastern R. Co. v. Railway Commissioners, L. R. 6 Q. B. D. 586. See Hall v. London, etc., Co., L. R. 17 Q. B. D. 230. In Georgia R. Co. v. Smith, 70 Ga. 694, the court said: "While we hold the

§ 684. Jurisdiction of commission not extended by implication—General rule.—The general rule is that the jurisdiction of a statutory tribunal will not be extended by implication except in cases where the implication necessarily arises from a consideration of the objects or language of the statute.[1] The rule that, where new rights are created and new remedies prescribed the construction of the statute creating such rights and prescribing such remedies shall be strict, is an influential one.[2] The supreme court of Oregon adjudged that the jurisdiction of the commission could not be extended by implication, but must be confined to the cases clearly placed within its jurisdiction by the statute.[3]

act of October 14, 1879, constitutional and the orders of the commission valid and binding, yet we are not to be understood as holding that their powers are unlimited or beyond the legal control by the proper authorities of the state. On the contrary, we hold that the powers which have been conferred upon them are to be exercised within the legal and constitutional limitations and in such a way as not to invade the rights of others."

[1] Matter of Beekman Street, 20 Johns. 269; Thatcher v. Powell, 6 Wheat. 119; Kansas City, etc., R. Co. v. Campbell, 62 Mo. 585; Shivers v. Wilson, 5 Harr. & John. 130; Ryan v. Commonwealth, 80 Va. 385; Beebe v. Scheidt, 13 Ohio St. 406; Keitler v. State, 4 Greene (Iowa) 291; School Inspectors v. People, 20 Ill. 525; Pringle v. Carter, 1 Hill L. (S. Car.) 53; Thompson v. Cox, 8 Jones L. (N. Car.) 311. See authorities cited Elliott's Gen. Pr., § 256, note.

[2] Keller v. Corpus Christi, 50 Texas 614; Willard v. Fralick, 31 Mich. 431; Dent v. Ross, 52 Miss. 188; Bloom v. Burdick, 1 Hill 130; Staples v. Fox, 45 Miss. 667; Anness v. Providence, 13 R. I. 17; Walker v. Burt, 57 Ga. 20; Monk v. Jenkins, 2 Hill Ch. 9.

[3] Board of Railroad Commissioners v. Oregon, etc., Co., 17 Ore. 65, s. c. 2 L. R. A. 195. It was said by the court that, "It has for a very longtime been considered the safer and better rule, in determining questions of jurisdiction of boards and officers exercising powers delegated to them by the legislature, to hold that their authority must affirmatively appear from the commission under which they claim to act. There is too strong a desire in the human heart to exercise authority, and too much of a disposition on the part of those intrusted with it to extend it beyond the design for which, and the scope within which, it was intended it should be exercised, to leave the question of its extent to inference. Should it be so left serious disturbances might arise, involving a conflict of jurisdiction, which would be highly detrimental to the community. It is not, it seems to me, requiring too much of the legislative branch of the government to exact that when it creates a commission and clothes it with important functions, it shall define and specify the authority given it so clearly that no doubt can reasonably arise in the mind of the public as to its extent." See, gener-

§ 685. **Incidental powers of a railroad commission.**—A railroad commission, although it is a statutory tribunal, with naked statutory powers, necessarily possesses some incidental or implied powers. The implied powers are such as by necessary implication result from the principal powers granted by the statute creating the commission. It is held in accordance with this general principle that the power to make rates carries, by necessary implication, the power to ascertain what corporation is in control of the line.[1]

§ 686. **Right of railroad companies to a hearing.**—The fundamental rule is that there is not due process of law unless a party is given an opportunity to be heard before he is subjected to a burden or deprived of property rights, and this principle applies to the proceedings of a state railroad commission. The right of a railroad company to receive reasonably remunerative compensation for carrying property and passengers is a property right of which it can not be deprived, and hence it is entitled to a hearing upon the question whether rates fixed by the commission are reasonable. If there is no opportunity for a hearing before the final decision of that question there is not due process of law.[2]

---

ally, *In re* Railroad Commissioners, 83 Me. 273, s. c. 22 Atl. R. 168; City of Cambridge v. Railroad Commissioners, 153 Mass. 161, s. c. 26 N. E. R. 241.

[1] State v. Western Union, etc., Co., 113 N. C. 213, s. c. 22 L. R. A. 570; State v. Mason City, etc., R. Co., 85 Iowa 516, s. c. 52 N. W. R. 490. In the case first cited the court held, citing Mayo v. Western, etc., Co., 112 N. C. 342, and Atlantic Express Co. v. Wilmington, etc., R. Co., 111 N. C. 463, s. c. 18 L. R. A. 393, that the commission is a court, but we very much doubt the soundness of this conclusion. We do not believe that ministerial and strictly judicial duties can be conferred upon a single tribunal, nor do we believe that the legislature can make such a board or body of officers as a railroad commission a court of record, although it may confer upon such a board, as upon any board, *quasi* judicial powers. See, *ante*, § 677.

[2] Chicago, etc., R. Co. v. State, 134 U. S. 418, s. c. 10 Sup. Ct. R. 462, reversing State v. Chicago, etc., R. Co., 37 N. W. R. 782, citing Stone v. Farmers' Loan & Trust Co., 116 U. S. 307, s. c. 6 Sup. Ct. 334, 388, 1191; Minneapolis, etc., R. Co. v. State, 134 U. S. 467, s. c. 10 Sup. Ct. R. 473, 134 U. S. 418, s. c. 10 Sup. Ct. R. 702, reversing State v. Minneapolis, etc., R. Co., 41 N. W. R. 465; Richmond, etc., R. Co. v. Trammel, 53 Fed. R. 196.

§ 687. Orders of commissioners not contracts.—The orders of a board of railroad commissioners are not contracts within the meaning of the provisions of the federal constitution prohibiting the states from enacting laws impairing the obligation of a contract. In accordance with the doctrine stated it was held by the supreme court of the United States that the approval of the board of commissioners of the application of a railroad company to discontinue a station did not constitute a contract although the statute authorized the company to discontinue stations in cases where the board directed it.[1] Where, however, the legislature authorizes the board of commissioners to enter into a contract with a railroad company, and a contract is entered into, a consideration being yielded by the company, the state can not by a subsequent statute impair the obligation of the contract. The state may, it seems clear, authorize a board of commissioners to make contracts, but by simply authorizing a board to make orders regulating charges for transporting freight and passengers or regulating the operation of the road, the legislature does not empower the board to enter into contracts with railroad companies.

§ 688. Certificates of commissioners that rates are reasonable—Effect of.—It has been held that the provisions of a statute making the certificate of the commissioners *prima facie* evidence that the maximum rate fixed by them is reasonable are valid.[2] It was also held in the case referred to that as the

---

[1] New Haven, etc., R. Co. v. Hammersely, 104 U. S. 1, s. c. 2 Am. & Eng. R. Cas. 418.

[2] Chicago, etc., Co. v. Jones, 149 Ill. 361, s. c. 24 L. R. A. 141, 146. In the course of the opinion the court said: "It is argued that the provision of the statute making the schedule of the commissioners *prima facie* evidence that the rates therein fixed are reasonable maximum rates of charges is unconstitutional and void, not only as depriving the carriers of their property without due process of law, but as infringing upon the right of trial by jury. We do not think that this objection should be sustained. In the first place the act does not deprive the railroad corporations of the right to have a judicial determination of the reasonableness of the rates, if they are not satisfied with the schedule made by the commission. The courts are open to them for a review of the acts of the commissioners in fixing the rates of charges. In the next place, the provision is an exercise by the legislature of its undoubted power

statute related to matters of procedure it took effect immediately and governed pending cases. But, as the authorities referred to in the preceding section show, the legislature can not confer upon the commission power to finally fix the charges to be made for carrying freight and passengers without giving the parties a right to be heard.[1]

§ 689. Regulation of charges for transporting property and passengers.—The field in which the power of railroad commissioners is best displayed and most strongly developed is that of regulating charges of railroad companies in their capacity of

to prescribe the rules of evidence. 2 Rice Ev., pp. 806, 807; Com. v. Williams, 6 Gray 1; State v. Hurley, 54 Me. 562. Such provisions are not unusual. Cases have arisen in this state under a statute making the fact of injury caused by sparks from a locomotive passing along the road *prima facie* evidence of negligence, and no question has ever been raised as to the validity of the statute. Pittsburg, C. & St. L. R. Co. v. Campbell, 86 Ill. 443; Saint Louis, V. & T. H. R. Co. v. Funk, 85 Ill. 460; Toledo, W. & W. R. Co. v. Larmon, 67 Ill. 68; Rockford, R. I. & St. L. R. Co. v. Rogers, 62 Ill. 346; Chicago & A. R. Co. v. Clampit, 63 Ill. 95; Chicago & A. R. Co. v. Quaintance, 58 Ill. 389. Acts making tax deeds *prima facie* evidence of the regularity of the proceedings antecedent to the deed have been held to be valid. 2 Rice Ev., p. 607; Hand v. Ballou, 12 N. Y. 541; Delaplaine v. Cook, 7 Wis. 44; Allen v. Armstrong, 16 Iowa 508; Wright v. Dunham, 13 Mich. 414; Gage v. Caraher, 125 Ill. 447. See, also, Williams v. German Mut. F. Ins. Co., 68 Ill. 387. Cases referred to by counsel, which involve the validity of acts providing for references to auditors or referees, and making the finding of facts by them in their reports *prima facie* evidence of the facts in trials before juries, will be found to be clearly distinguishable from the case at bar. The supreme court of Iowa has decided that a provision making the schedule of the commission *prima facie* evidence of the reasonableness of the rates of charges, as contained in the statute of that state similar to the said act of 1873, was not obnoxious to the objections here urged against it, saying: 'The provision of the statute that the rates fixed by the commissioners shall be regarded as *prima facie* reasonable is not of an unusual character, and was enacted in the exercise of the undoubted power of the state to prescribe rules of evidence in all proceeding under the laws of the state. The law presumes the acts of officers of the state to be rightfully done, and gives them faith accordingly. This rule is not unlike the provision of the statute complained of by the plaintiff.' Burlington, C. R. & N. R. Co. v. Dey, 82 Iowa 312, 12 L. R. A. 436. See, also, Chicago & A. R. Co. v. People, 67 Ill. 11, 16 Am. R. 599." See, also, Richmond, etc., R. Co. v. Trammel, 53 Fed. R. 196.

[1] Richmond, etc., R. Co. v. Trammel, 53 Fed. R. 196.

common carriers. Over the matter of regulating charges for the transportation of passengers and property the powers of railway commissioners are very broad and full.[1] The principal restraint upon their power over that subject is that imposed by the commerce clause of the federal constitution, for that firmly prohibits any regulation of commerce between the states.[2] There are, of course, other constitutional restraints, some of which have already been considered and others that will be hereafter discussed. But, as we have said, we do not intend in this chapter to do much more than incidentally treat of the power to regulate charges for transporting property and passengers, and we pass the subject without further comment except in so far as we may touch upon the subject in speaking of domestic or interstate commerce and matters therewith connected.

§ 690. Domestic commerce.—The power to regulate domestic or intrastate commerce resides in the states. The states may make such regulations as they deem expedient or politic for the government of commerce within their own borders, provided that the regulations do not violate some constitutional provision. If the places from which the passengers or property are transported are within the state and the places to which they are carried are also within the limits of the same state, the commerce is domestic and not interstate commerce, and, as

---

[1] Georgia, etc., R. Co. v. Smith, 128 U. S. 174, s. c. 9 Sup. Ct. R. 47; Winsor Coal Co. v. Chicago, etc.. Co., 52 Fed. R. 716; Chicago, etc., R. Co. v. Dey, 38 Fed. R. 656; Reagan v. Trust Co., 154 U. S. 413, s. c. 14 Sup. Ct. R. 1060, and cases cited; Burlington, etc., R. Co. v. Dey, 82 Iowa 312, s. c. 48 N. W. R. 98.

[2] Among the great number of cases bearing upon this question are the following: Cunningham v. Macon, etc., Railroad Co., 190 U. S. 446, s. c. 3 Sup. Ct. R. 292; Reagan v. Farmers' L. & Trust Co., 154 U. S. 362, s. c. 14 Sup. Ct. R. 1047; Gloucester, etc., Co. v. Pennsylvania, 114 U. S. 196, s. c. 5 Sup. Ct. R. 826; Cuban, etc., Co. v. Fitzpatrick, 66 Fed. R. 63; Cutting v. Florida, etc., Co., 46 Fed. R. 641; Lord v. Steamship Co., 102 U. S. 541; Pacific, etc., Co. v. Board of Railroad Com., 18 Fed. R. 10; Sternberger v. Cape Fear, etc., R. Co., 29 S. Car. 510, s. c. 2 L. R. A. 105; Railroad Commissioners v. Railroad Co., 22 S. Car. 220; City of Bangor v. Smith, 83 Me. 422, s. c. 22 Atl. R. 379; City of Council Bluffs v. Kansas City, etc., R. Co., 45 Iowa 338.

domestic commerce, is subject to state control.[1] If the place from which passengers and property are transported, and the place to which they are carried, are both within the territorial limits of the state and the carriage is continuous, then the transportation is intrastate commerce, although in course of carriage passengers or property may on the line of transportation pass beyond the borders of the state.[2] To the rule that where both the place where the passengers or property are received and the place of destination are within the territorial limits of the same state the commerce is intrastate and subject to state regulation, there is an exception, and that exception is this,—if the carriage is over the high seas, although from place to place in the same state, it is interstate commerce and can not be regulated by the state.[3] If the property has begun to move

[1] Interstate commerce is "commerce which concerns more states than one." Gibbons v. Ogden, 9 Wheat. 1; Reagan v. Mercantile Trust Co., 154 U. S. 413, s. c. 14 Sup. Ct. R. 1060; Interstate Commerce Commission v. Cincinnati, etc., R. Co., 4 Int. Com. R. 582; Louisville, etc., v. Mississippi, 133 U. S. 587, s. c. 10 Sup. Ct. R. 348; Georgia, etc., Co. v. Smith, 128 U. S. 174, s. c. 9 Sup. Ct. R. 47; Pacific, etc., Co. v. Seibert, 142 U. S. 339, s. c. 12 Sup. Ct. R. 250.

[2] Campbell v. Chicago, etc., R. Co., 86 Iowa 587, s. c. 17 L. R. A. 443; Lehigh Valley R. Co. v. Pennsylvania, 145 U. S. 192; Seawell v. Kansas City, etc., R. Co., 119 Mo. 224, s.c. 24 S.W.R. 1002. See State v. Chicago, etc., R. Co., 40 Minn. 267, s. c. 41 N. W. R. 1047; Commonwealth v. Lehigh Valley, etc., R. Co., (Pa. St.) s. c. 17 Atl. R. 179; State v. Western, etc., Co., 113 N. C. 213, s. c. 44 Am. & Eng. Corp. Cas. 377, 18 S. E. Rep. 389; Scammon v. Kansas City, etc., R. Co., 41 Mo. App. 194; Chicago, etc., R. Co. v. Jones, 149 Ill. 361, s. c. 37 N. E. R. 247, 24 L. R. A. 141; Pacific, etc., R. Co. v. Board of Railroad Commissioners, 9 Sawyer 253; Fort Worth, etc., R. Co. v. Whitehead, 6 Texas Civil App. 595, s. c. 26 S. W. R. 172; Harmon v. City of Chicago, 140 Ill. 374, s. c. 26 N. E. R. 697, 29 N. E. R. 732, 43 Alb. L. J. 375; Ex parte Kieffer, 40 Fed. R. 399; State v. Stilsing, 52 N. J. L. 517, s. c. 20 Atl. R. 65. The business of soliciting freight and passengers for interstate railroads is interstate commerce. McCall v. California, 136 U. S. 104, s. c. 10 Sup. Ct. R. 881, 42 Alb. L. J. 42. The case of Sternberger v. Cape Fear, etc., R. Co., 29 So. Car. 510, s. c. 7 S. E. R. 836, 2 L. R. A. 105, is overruled by the decision in Lehigh Valley Co. v. Pennsylvania, supra, in so far at least as it holds that where there is continuous carriage from point to point within the same state, the commerce is interstate if in course of transit the goods or passengers are temporarily on the soil of another state.

[3] Lord v. Steamship Co., 102 U. S. 541. See The City of Salem, 37 Fed. R. 846.

from one state to another, then commerce between the states as to that property has commenced.[1] The time and place of making transfers of articles of commerce from one interstate carrier to another can not be regulated by a state.[2]

§ 691. Reasonableness of freight and fare tariff of rates— How far a judicial question.—The question as to the power of the courts to set aside a schedule of charges for the transportation of property and passengers framed either by a state legislature directly or by a board of commissioners acting under authority of a state statute can no longer be regarded as an open one, for the power has been adjudged to exist by many decisions of the court of last resort. The question may be presented in opposing an application to enforce an order of the board, by an injunction to restrain the enforcement of an order, and in other modes. In a very recent case the supreme court of the United States held that a railroad company in defending an action to recover a penalty might show that the rate fixed by the commissioners was an unreasonable one.[3] In the case

[1] The Daniel Ball, 10 Wall. 557; State v. Indiana, etc., Co., 120 Ind. 575, s. c. 30 Cent. L. J. 179, 41 Alb. L. J. 187, 22 N. E. R. 778. See Coe v. Errol, 116 U. S. 517; Corson v. Maryland, 120 U. S. 502; Railroad Co. v. Husen, 95 U. S. 465; Western Union Co. v. Massachusetts, 125 U. S. 530; In re Greene, 52 Fed. R. 104; Woodruff, etc., Co. v. State, 114 Ind. 155; Kidd v. Pearson, 128 U. S. 1; Delaware, etc., Co. v. Commonwealth, (Pa.) 17 Atl. R. 175.

[2] City of Council Bluffs v. Kansas City, etc., R. Co., 45 Iowa 338. See State v. Chicago, etc., R. Co., 33 Fed. R. 391; Hart v. Chicago, etc., R. Co., 69 Iowa 485.

[3] St. Louis, etc., R. Co. v. Gill, 156 U. S. 649, s. c. 15 Sup. Ct. R. 484. In that case it was said: "This court has declared in several cases that there is a remedy in the courts for relief against legislation establishing a tariff of rates, which is so unreasonable as to practically destroy the value of property of companies engaged in the carrying business, especially may the courts of the United States treat such a question as a judicial one and hold such acts of legislation to be in conflict with the constitution of the United States, as depriving them of the equal protection of the laws." The court referred to the fact that in some of the states commissions were established, and said: "But there are other cases, and the present is one, where the legislatures choose to act directly on the subject by themselves establishing a tariff of rates, and prescribing penalties. In such cases there is no opportunity of resorting to a compendious remedy, such as a proceeding in equity, because there is no public functionary or commission, which can be made to respond, and,

to which we refer the railroad company was defeated, not, however, because the defense that the rate fixed was an unreasonable one might not be interposed, but because the company did not satisfactorily prove that the rate was unreasonable. The courts will decide whether the rate prescribed is or is not a reasonable one,[1] but they will not fix the rate.[2] The question as to how far the courts can go is not free from difficulty, but it is quite clear that they have no power to make a tariff of rates. For this conclusion there are, at least, two reasons: (1) The power to fix rates is by law conferred upon a tribunal composed of administrative or ministerial officers; (2) The power to fix rates is a ministerial and not a judicial power and hence can not be exercised by the courts. The legislature can not directly or through the medium of commissioners make rates so low as to deprive a railroad company of a fair and reasonable remuneration, for while there is power to regulate there is no power to deprive the company of the right to tolls, freights or fares.[3] It is to be understood, of course, that a state can not enact a statute, which, within the meaning of the constitution, is a regulation of interstate commerce.

therefore, if the companies are to have any relief, it must be found in a right to raise the question of the reasonableness of the statutory rates by way of defense to an action for the collection of the penalties."

[1] Dow v. Beidelman, 125 U. S. 680, s. c. 8 Sup. Ct. R. 1028; Dow v. Beidelman, 49 Ark. 325, s. c. 31 Am.& Eng. R. Cas. 14; Railroad Commission Cases, 116 U. S. 307, s. c. 6 Sup. Ct. R. 334; Chicago,etc.,Railway Co.v.Minnesota, 134 U. S. 418, s. c. 10 Sup. Ct. R. 462; Railway Co. v. Wellman, 143 U. S. 339, s. c. 12 Sup. Ct. R. 400; Reagan v. Farmers' L. and Trust Co., 154 U. S. 362, s. c. 14 Sup. Ct. R. 1047; St. Louis, etc., R. v. Gill, 156 U. S. 649, s. c. 15 Sup. Ct. R. 484.

[2] In St. Louis, etc., Co. v. Gill, 156 U. S. 649, s. c. 15 Sup. Ct. R. 484, the court, after reviewing the cases, said of the case of Reagan v. Trust Co., 154 U. S. 362, that: "The opinion of this court on appeal was that while it was within the power of the court of equity in such case to decree that the rates so established by the commission were unreasonable and unjust, and to restrain their enforcement it was not within its power to establish rates itself, or to restrain the commission from again establishing rates."

[3] Stone v. Farmers' Loan, etc., Co., 116 U. S. 307; Attorney-General v. Germantown, etc., Road, 55 Pa. St. 466; Miller v. New York, etc., R. Co., 21 Barb. 513; Ex parte Koehler, 30 Fed. R. 867, s. c. 21 Am. & Eng. R. Cas. 52. See Stone v. Natchez, etc., R. Co., 62 Miss. 646; Tilley v. Savannah, etc., Co., 5 Fed. R. 641.

§ 692. Regulation of charges—Test of reasonableness.—
The courts have, as is evident from their opinions, been perplexed by the question as to the tests which shall be employed in determining whether tariffs of rates established by a state legislature directly, or through the instrumentality of a board of railroad commissioners, are so unreasonable as to require judicial condemnation. The question can not, as yet, be regarded as settled.[1] That a tariff of rates so unreasonable as to deprive a company of fair and just remuneration is invalid, has been clearly and unequivocally adjudged, but we can find no case which satisfactorily defines what constitutes an unreasonable rate. In our opinion no precise definitions can be framed, nor can any rules be formulated that will fitly apply to or govern all cases. Outlines may be sketched and general directions given, but exact rules or precise definitions can not be safely stated. Some tests have been suggested, and so far as concerns the particular case, they are well enough, but when it is attempted to carry the tests beyond particular cases confusion arises and error is almost certain to result. It is safe to say that the general test is that if the rates established are such as to prevent a company from making any net earnings, the act establishing such rates is invalid.

§ 693. Tariff of rates—Tests of reasonableness.—In the preceding section we said that as yet no satisfactory test by which the question of the reasonableness of a tariff of rates can be solved has yet been constructed or formulated by the courts, but there are cases which directly bear upon the general question. It has been adjudged by the supreme court of the United States that whether a tariff of rates is or is not a reasonable one, is to be ascertained by its effect upon the line of road and not merely upon part of it.[2] The language em-

[1] In the case of Ames *v.* Union Pacific R. Co., 64 Fed. R. 165, Mr. Justice Brewer said: "What is the test by which the reasonableness of rates is determined? This has not yet been fully settled. Indeed, it is doubtful whether any single rule can be laid down applicable to all cases."

[2] In St. Louis, etc., R. Co. *v.* Gill, 154 U. S. 649, s. c. 15 Sup. Ct. R. 484, the court said: "It, therefore, appears that the allegations made and

ployed in the opinion given in the case referred to is very
broad and seems to deny that the effect of a tariff of rates upon
part of a road can be considered as unreasonable in any case,
if the entire line within the state can, under the tariff, earn
remunerative freights and fares. We venture to suggest that
there may be cases where a tariff although affecting part only
of a road might be so palpably unjust and unreasonable as to
make it the duty of the courts to adjudge it ineffective. If the
traffic between two towns of the same state is the principal
intrastate traffic, we do not believe that the state legislature
could fix the rate for transporting passengers and property so
low that the company must suffer a serious loss on every passenger and all freight that it transports, even though the rates
fixed for carriage on other parts of the road should be such as
to leave the company reasonable net earnings. If, for illustration, the companies should adopt a schedule, providing that
from the station of Buffalo, in New York, to the station of
Utica in the same state, the company should charge each
passenger one penny for carriage and charge half penny a ton
for transporting property, of which the actual cost of carriage
was more than tenfold the rates fixed, would the action of the
commissioners in establishing such a tariff be sustained even

the evidence offered did not cover the company's railroad as an entirety, even in the state of Arkansas, but were made in reference to that portion of the road originally belonging to the St. Louis, Arkansas and Texas Railway Company and extending from the northern boundary of Arkansas to Fayetteville in said state. In this state of facts, we agree with the supreme court of Arkansas, as disclosed in the opinion contained in the record, and which was to the effect that the correct test was the effect of the act on the defendant's entire line, and not upon that part which was formerly a part of one of the consolidating roads; that the company can not claim the right to earn a net profit from every mile, section or other part into which the road might be divided, nor attack as unjust a regulation which fixed a rate at which some part would be unremunerative; that it would be practically impossible to ascertain in what proportion the several parts would share with others in the expenses and receipts in which they participated; and, finally, that to the extent that injustice is to be determined by the effect of the act of the earnings of the company, the earnings of the entire line must be estimated as against all its legitimate expenses under the operation of the act within the limits of the state of Arkansas."

though taking the entire line, say from Buffalo to the City of New York, the tariff would yield fair remuneration? It seems to us that it could not. We believe that reasonable remuneration must be provided for carriage from station to station where the distance is considerable, but we do not believe that it is necessary that it should be such as will make every "mile or section" of the road yield net earnings. To us it seems that the question must be determined upon the facts of each particular case and that broad general rules can not be safely laid down. The court can not say that in every instance a rate which deprives investors of profit is necessarily an unreasonable one. There can not be a rigid general rule making the fact that no profits can be realized the universal or, indeed, even the uniform test.[1] It has always been the rule that common carriers can not make unreasonable charges,[2] and to permit them to make such charges would be to depart from long settled law and enable such carriers to injure others; on the other hand, to compel them to do business without reaping a profit seems palpably unjust. It is no easy matter to escape from the dilemma which naturally arises from a consideration of the conflicting rights and interests. There may be, as pointed out by a distinguished federal judge,[3] changes of such a radical

[1] In Reagan v. Trust Co., 154 U. S. 413, 14 Sup. Ct. R. 1060, the court said: "It is unnecessary to decide, and we do not wish to be understood as laying down an absolute rule, that in every case a failure to produce some profit, to those who have invested their money in the building of a road is conclusive that the tariff is unjust and unreasonable. And yet justice demands that every one should receive some compensation for the use of his money or property, if it be possible without injury to others."

[2] Chicago, etc., Railway Co. v. Osborne, 52 Fed. R. 912, s. c. 3 C. C. A. 347.

[3] In Ames v. Union Pacific R. Co., 64 Fed. R. 165, 177, Mr. Justice Brewer used this language: "If it be said that the rates be such as to secure to the owners a reasonable per cent. on the money invested, it will be remembered that many things have happened to make the investment far in excess of the actual value of the property, injudicious contracts, poor engineering, unusually high cost of material, rascality on the part of those engaged in the construction or management of the property. These and many other things, as is well known, are factors which have largely entered into the investments with which many railroad properties stand charged. Now, if the public was seeking to take title to the railroad by condemnation, the present value of

character as to make it unsafe and unjust to take as a test the right to reap profits from the business conducted by a railroad company. It is safe to say that a rate which is not sufficient to pay the costs of service is an unreasonable one.[1] The state can not require any person, artificial or natural, to render service without receiving in return the cost of the service, since that would be to deprive such person of property without compensation, but we suppose that if the company by its own fault or wrong increases the costs of service beyond that which, if there were no wrong, would be the actual cost, it can not be heard to say that the rate established is unreasonable because the property and not the cost is that which they would have to pay. In like manner, it may be argued that, when the legislature assumes the right to reduce, the rates so reduced can not be adjudged unreasonable if, under them, there is earned by the railroad company a fair interest on the actual value of the property. It is not easy to always determine the value of railroad property, and if there is no other testimony in respect thereto, than the amount of stock and bonds outstanding, or the construction account, it may be fairly assumed that one or the other of these represents it, and computation as to the compensatory quality of rates may be based on such amounts. In the cases before us, however, there is abundant testimony that the cost of reproducing these roads is less than the amount of the stock and bond account, or the cost of construction and that the present value of the property is not accurately represented by either the stocks and bonds, or the original construction account. Nevertheless, the amount of money that has gone into the railroad property—the actual investment, as expressed, theoretically, at least, by the amount of stocks and bonds—is not to be ignored, even though such sum is far in excess of the present value."

[1] In the case of Clyde v. Richmond, etc., R. Co., 57 Fed. R. 436, 440, this language was used: "The question under discussion in this case is, is this rate recently established by the respondents, be it a change of rate or a new classification, just and reasonable? Mr. Justice Brewer, while on the circuit bench, defines what are just and reasonable rates, or rather states what rates are not just and reasonable. 'A schedule of rates, when the rates prescribed do not pay the costs of service, can not be enforced.' Chicago, etc., Railroad Co. v. Becker, 35 Fed. R. 883. In another case (Chicago, etc., Railway v. Dey, 35 Fed. R. 866) he enters into an elaborate illustration of those terms. 'When the rates prescribed will not pay some compensation to the owners, then it is the duty of the courts to interfere, and protect the companies from such rates.' He defines 'compensation' to mean, enough to pay costs of service, fixed charges of interest, and a dividend however small." See Mercantile, etc., Co. v. Texas, etc., R. Co., 51 Fed. R. 529; Chicago, etc., R. Co. v. Dey, 38 Fed. R. 656; Tilley v. Savannah, etc., Railroad Co., 5 Fed. R. 641.

less than the costs of service. We think that when the courts speak of the costs of the service they must mean such costs as are incurred in the good faith, conduct and management of the business. If, for instance, extravagant and unreasonable salaries are paid to officers they could not, as we conceive, be justly considered in determining the costs of service, but if the salaries were paid in good faith and were not palpably beyond reason they may justly be regarded as part of such costs. Here, again, we come to the point where general rules can not be safely laid down, for it is manifest that what is or is not a palpably unreasonable salary must be determined from the facts of the particular case.

§ 694. Stations—Power to order company to provide.—The question as to the power of a railroad commission to order a railroad company to provide new or additional stations is not free from difficulty. We suppose that it is within the power of the legislature to authorize the commission to require railroad companies to provide reasonable facilities for receiving or discharging traffic, as well as reasonable accommodations for passengers.[1] But we do not believe that the commission can be invested with power to arbitrarily require a company to provide stations wherever the commission may deem necessary. We believe that the decisions which adjudge that the legislature can not fix rates so low as to deprive railroad companies of reasonable remuneration for carrying freight and passengers support our

[1] Southeastern, etc., R. Co. v. Railway Commissioners, 3 Nev. & Mac. 464, L. R. 6 Q. B. D. 586; Commonwealth v. Eastern R. Co., 103 Mass. 254, s. c. 4 Am. R. 555; Railroad Commissioners v. Portland, etc., R. Co., 63 Me. 269, s. c. 18 Am. R. 208; State v. Kansas City, etc., R. Co., 32 Fed. R. 722. See Northern Pacific, etc., R. Co. v. Territory, 142 U. S. 492, s. c. 12 Sup. Ct. R. 283, 48 Am. & Eng. R. Cas. 475; People v. Chicago, etc., R. Co., 130 Ill. 175; Mobile, etc., R. Co. v. People, 132 Ill. 559, s. c. 42 Am. & Eng. R. Cas. 671; Texas, etc., Railroad Co. v. Marshall, 136 U. S. 393, s. c. 42 Am. & Eng. R. Cas. 637; State v. Alabama, etc., Co., 68 Miss. 653, s. c. 50 Am. & Eng. R. Cas. 14. See State v. Wabash, etc., R. Co., 83 Mo. 144, s. c. 25 Am. & Eng. R. Cas. 133; State v. New Hayen, etc., R. Co., 43 Conn. 351; State v. Kansas City, etc., R. Co., 32 Fed. R. 722; Cunningham v. Board of Railroad Commissioners, 158 Mass. 104, s. c. 56 Am. & Eng. R. Cas. 301; Florida, etc., Co. v. State, 31 Fla. 482, s. c. 56 Am. & Eng. Cas. 306.

conclusion. We do not believe that railway commissioners can rightfully be invested with the control of a railroad, and this would be the practical effect of holding that railroad commissioners may compel railroad companies to provide stations at all points the commissioners might select. Our judgment is that the only power that the legislature can bestow upon a commission is the power to regulate, and that it can not, under the guise of conferring power to regulate, take the control of a railroad from its owner and vest it in a board of commissioners. If it be affirmed that a railway commission may, at its own uncontrolled pleasure, order a company to provide stations, the result will be that the commission may so burden a company as to destroy its ability to earn reasonable compensation for the duties and services it performs. We do not mean to be understood as affirming that broad and comprehensive powers may not be conferred upon a railway commission, nor that such a body may not be empowered to compel railroad companies to provide stations where they are required by the public interest, but we do believe that an arbitrary power to compel railroad companies to establish stations wherever it may be the pleasure of the commissioners to locate them can not be rightfully conferred upon a railway commission. It seems to us that there is a limit to the right to regulate, and that this limit can not be passed without violating the constitution. It seems to us, also, that there must be a reasonable necessity for the establishment of a station in order to warrant the commission in compelling a railroad company to establish it. Whether there is such a necessity is a matter to be determined after a hearing and not summarily or arbitrarily. Doubtless the courts would be reluctant to overthrow the decision of the commission as to the necessity for a station, but, nevertheless, if it clearly and satisfactorily appears that there was no such necessity, the courts would not hesitate to review, and, if need be, reverse the decision of the commissioners.[1]

[1] State v. Des Moines, etc., R. Co., 87 Iowa 644, s. c. 54 N. W. R. 461. In the case cited the court reversed the order of the commissioners, saying, among

§ 695. **Procedure before the commissioners.**—The procedure in matters brought before a board of commissioners is so much a matter of statutory regulation that general rules can not be safely stated. It seems to us that even in the absence of statutory provisions requiring it the board must make a record of its proceedings, since it is implied in the manner of its organization and the object for which it was organized that it shall act as a board and put its proceedings on record.[1] It is probably not necessary unless so required by statute, to keep a regular and formal record such as is kept by a court, but there must be such a written record of the proceedings as can be used as an instrument of evidence. It has been held that the commissioners may proceed without a petition or complaint and this, we suppose, is true where there is no statute requiring the filing of a written petition, application, or complaint.[2] It is competent for the commissioners to make reasonable rules and regulations governing matters of procedure, but they can not, of course, rightfully adopt rules or regulations which are in conflict with the rules of law.[3] Authority to adopt and enforce rules and regulations is implied from the grant of power to hear and determine. The object and purpose being specified the authority to effect that object and carry

---

other things: "There is nothing in the case which tends to show that the managers of the road had any intention to deprive any one of proper facilities for transacting business with the company. The income of the road did not warrant the maintenance of extensive stations, but demanded the strictest economy. It was thought by the management that, by establishing two stations at points nearer the junction of the other roads named, the defendant would be able to control more traffic, by being nearer to the inhabitants residing in the vicinity of Osceola and Van Wert. It appears to us that the owners of the road should not be interfered with in the management of their property, including the location of their stations, where, as in this case, there is no competent evidence that any patron of the road has been deprived of reasonable facilities for transacting business with the defendant."

[1] State v. Chicago, etc., R. Co., 86 Iowa 642, s. c. 53 N. W. R. 323; Boston, etc., Co. v. Nashua, etc., Co., 157 Mass. 258, s. c. 31 N. E. R. 1067.

[2] State v. Chicago, etc., R. Co., 86 Iowa 642, s. c. 55 Am. & Eng. R. Cas. 487. But see Boston, etc., Co. v. Nashua, etc., Co., 157 Mass. 258, s. c. 31 N. E. R. 1067.

[3] Atlantic, etc., Co. v. Wilmington, etc., R. Co., 111 N. C. 463, s. c. 55 Am. & Eng. R. Cas. 498.

into effect that purpose necessarily carries the incidental authority to adopt appropriate and reasonable means for accomplishing the object for which the board was created. It seems to us that there must be notice, for without notice the interested parties are deprived of their right without such a hearing as due process of law requires that they should have. It has been held that notice of the official action of the board of commissioners given by its secretary in response to a telegram of a party interested in and affected by its decision, is binding upon the board.[1] We suppose, however, that as a rule the board is not bound by the action of its secretary or by any individual action, but that it is bound where the facts or circumstances are sufficient to authorize the inference that he acted as its representative. It is held in an English case that commissioners have no authority to compel a railroad company to pay costs of a petitioner whose petition is denied.[2]

§ 696. **Effect of the decision of the commissioners that a company has not committed an act authorizing a forfeiture.**— It has been held by the court of appeals of New York that, as against the state, the certificate of the board of railroad commissioners that the public interests do not require the extension of a road is conclusive against the state and constitutes a complete defense to an action to forfeit the charter for failure to build the road.[3] The decision goes very far and seems to

---

[1] Chicago, etc., R. Co. v. Dey, 35 Fed. R. 866, s. c. 1 L. R. A. 744. In the case cited it was said: "It is insisted by the defendants that this action was taken, not by the board, but by one commissioner acting independently, the others not consenting or being aware of the action. Upon this matter there was considerable discussion, both as to the sufficiency of the notice, the number of times publication was required, the fact of the two publications of the notice, the power of one commissioner to make the change, etc. I deem it unnecessary to consider these, nor do I express any opinion upon the rights of any other corporations than the four who united in the telegram to defendants. An official board acts through its secretary. This complainant, with others, addressed an official communication to the board. It received an answer in the regular way, one signed by the secretary as secretary. Equity and good faith forbid going behind such notification."

[2] Foster v. Great Western, etc., R. Co., L. R. 8 Q. B. D. 515.

[3] People v. Ulster, etc., R. Co., 128

trench upon the rule that ministerial officers can not be clothed with judicial power. There is, however, force and vigor in the reasoning of the court.

§ 697. **Enforcing the orders of the commissioners—Generally.**—Where the commissioners have jurisdiction to make an order and they do make a valid order upon due process of law, the courts will, upon proper application, compel compliance with it. The legislature in conferring authority upon railroad commissioners impliedly grants, as we believe, a right to successfully invoke the aid of the courts to make the order effective. To hold otherwise would be, in effect, to adjudge that the orders of the commissioners are mere empty declarations without force or effect. If the statute gives a right there must be a remedy, for the existence of a right implies the existence of a remedy. If a right is given and no specific remedy is provided, then the courts will enforce the right by the appropriate

N. Y. 240. The court said in the course of the opinion that, " By this enactment the state has indicated in the most imperative form its will in respect to such actions. It thereby declared that the certificate of the railroad commissioners to the effect that no public interests were involved should thereafter be a conclusive answer to any attempt to annul the existence of a reorganized railroad corporation for a failure to make an extension of its road. By this act the state devolved upon the railroad comsioners the duty, previously performed by its attorney-general, of inquiring whether the public interests required it to enforce an alleged forfeiture against a reorganized railroad corporation, and necessarily thereby deprived other departments of the government of the power of determining the preliminary question upon which the action of the state in instituting and prosecuting such actions must be founded. By leaving to another department of the state the determination of a question upon which its own action was thereafter to be controlled, it neither delegated legislative power to, or conferred judicial functions upon, such department. It simply institutes an *ex parte* inquiry to determine its own future action, as had been the uniform practice of the state government for many previous years. The question whether the public interests are involved is always a condition precedent to the right of maintaining any action by the attorney-general for the forfeiture of corporate rights, and the state by this act says that it will hereafter leave this question in certain cases to railroad commissioners to determine, instead of to the attorney-general, by whom it had theretofore been decided. In other words it has made the railroad commissioners' certificate conclusive evidence of the non-existence of any sufficient ground of forfeiture."

remedy. A statute does not stand alone, detached and isolated from other statutes, or other rules of law, but takes its place as part of a uniform system of law.[1] It is aided by other statutes and by the recognized rules of law, and to give it force and effect other statutes and the general rules of law may be considered and applied. The general rule is that where a new right is created and no new remedy provided the courts will enforce the right by means of the appropriate remedy. If the remedy be in equity, then the right may be enforced by the appropriate suit in equity; if the remedy be at law, then by the proper action.[2]

§ 698. Enforcing the orders of the commissioners—Mandamus.—Where there is no other remedy provided by statute and no other adequate common law remedy, we can see no reason why the valid and imperative orders of a board of railroad commissioners may not be enforced by mandamus. The grant of authority to the commissioners to make orders gives to their orders a legal force and effect sufficient to impose upon the railroad company a specific and imperative duty. There must, of course, be jurisdiction, the order must be made in due course of law and must be specific and mandatory.[3] It has

[1] Humphries v. Davis, 100 Ind. 274; Rushville, etc., Co. v. City of Rushville, 121 Ind. 206, 213, and cases cited; Hyland v. Brazil, etc., Co., 128 Ind. 335, 341; Bishop Written Laws, §§ 86, 113a.

[2] This principle is strikingly illustrated by the cases which hold that where a state statute creates a right the federal courts will enforce it by means of the remedy which, by the rules of those courts, is the appropriate one. Fitch v. Creighton, 24 How. (U. S.) 159; Clark v. Smith, 13 Pet. 195; Holland v. Challen, 110 U. S. 15.

[3] Mandamus will lie to enforce obedience to the requirements of the ordinances of the governing bodies of municipal corporations, county supervisors or commissioners, and the like, and it seems to us that the principles which are declared in cases of the class mentioned require the conclusion that mandamus will lie to compel obedience to the orders of railroad commissioners. State v. Janesville, etc., R. Co., 87 Wis. 72, s. c. 41 Am. St. R. 23; Union Pacific R. Co. v. Hall, 91 U. S. 343; People v. Chicago, etc., R. Co., 130 Ill. 175; State v. Northeastern, etc., R. Co., 9 Rich. 247, s. c. 67 Am. Dec. 551; People v. Chicago, etc., R. Co., 67 Ill. 118; Indianapolis, etc., R. Co. v. State, 37 Ind. 489; People v. Boston, etc., R. Co., 70 N. Y. 569. In granting power to a board of railroad commissioners to make orders, the legislature authorizes the

been held that where the railroad commissioners have jurisdiction to order the location of a station, and an imperative order is made locating a station, the order may be enforced by mandamus.[1] So, upon the same general principle, it has been held that where the commissioners have authority to order a railroad company to construct a crossing, mandamus will lie to enforce obedience to the order.[2] The enforcement of an order made by a board of commissioners requiring a railroad company to conform to a schedule of rates established by the commissioners, is a matter of public interest, and hence an action is properly brought in the name of the state.[3]

§ 699. Mandamus—Enforcing orders of commissioners—Illustrative cases.—In addition to the cases referred to in discussing the general question of enforcing the orders of railroad commissioners, we refer to other cases which illustrate the general doctrine. In a Florida case it was held that mandamus was the appropriate remedy to compel a railroad company to comply with the order of the commissioners requiring schedules to be posted, but it was held that the court could not, in the absence of an order of the commissioners specifically prescribing the kind and size of type that should be used, specifically direct what kind and size of type the company should use.[4] In one of the reported cases the relator asked for a writ to compel the railroad company to locate a station at a place where by contract it had agreed with the relator that it should be located, but the court denied the writ, holding that a pri-

---

board to do what the legislature had it so elected might have directly done, so that the orders of the board have all the force and effect that a statute could put into the orders of any board of public officers.

[1] Railroad Commissioners v. Portland R. Co., 63 Me. 269. The statute involved in the case cited provided that the commissioners might apply to the courts for the enforcement of its orders.

[2] State v. Chicago, etc., R. Co., 29 Neb. 412, s. c. 45 N. W. R. 469, 42 Am. & Eng. R. Cas. 248.

[3] Campbell v. Chicago, etc., R. Co., 86 Iowa 587, s. c. 17 L. R. A. 443, 53 N. W. R. 351.

[4] State v. Pensacola, etc., R. Co., 27 Fla. 403, s. c. 46 Am. & Eng R. Cas. 704. In this case the court decided that schedules "must be kept continuously posted."

vate obligation of the nature of the one relied upon by the relator could not be enforced by mandamus.[1] If the duties required are discretionary, performance can not be coerced by mandate.[2] Where the charter of a railroad company expressly requires it to build and maintain its line to a designated point, the duty created is a specific and imperative one, and its performance may be coerced by mandamus,[3] and we can see no reason why the rule laid down does not apply to specific and imperative orders made by railroad commissioners under legislative authority. It was held that, under the Iowa statute, which conferred authority upon the courts to enforce the orders of the board of commissioners by "equitable actions" in the "name of the state," mandamus is not the exclusive remedy.[4] We do not, however, understand the case referred to as deciding that mandamus is not an appropriate remedy, but we understand it as simply deciding that mandamus is not the only remedy, although it is an appropriate one.[5] It is held that

---

[1] Florida Central, etc., R. Co. v. State, 31 Fla. 482, s. c. 56 Am. & Eng. R. Cas. 306, citing State v. Paterson, etc., R. Co., 43 N. J. Law 505; Parrott v. City, 44 Conn. 180.

[2] People v. New York, etc., R. Co., 104 N. Y. 58; Northern Pacific R. Co. v. Territory, 142 U. S. 492, s. c. 12 Sup. Ct. R. 283, 48 Am. & Eng. R. Cas. 475, overruling Northern Pacific, etc., R. Co. v. Territory, 3 Wash. Ter. 303, s. c. 13 Pac. R. 604.

[3] Union Pac. Railroad Co. v. Hall, 91 U. S. 343. See State v. Hartford, etc., Railroad, 29 Conn. 538; New Orleans, etc., Railway Co. v. Mississippi, 112 U. S. 12; People v. Boston, etc., Railroad Co., 70 N. Y. 569. In Northern Pacific, etc., R. Co., 142 U. S. 492, s. c. 12 Sup. Ct. R. 283; 48 Am. & Eng. R. Cas. 475, the court approves the cases of York, etc., Railway Co. v. Queen, 1 El. & Bl. 858; Commonwealth v. Fitchburg Railroad, 12 Gray 180; State v. Southern, etc., Railroad, 18 Minn. 40; Atchison, etc., R. Co. v. Denver, etc., R., 110 U. S. 667, s. c. 4 Sup. Ct. R. 185; South Eastern Railway Co. v. Commissioners, 6 Q. B. Div. 586, and denied the doctrine of State v. Republican, etc., Railroad Co., 17 Neb. 647, s. c. 24 N. W. R. 329.

[4] State v. Mason City R. Co., 85 Iowa 516, s. c. 55 Am. & Eng. R. Cas. 73.

[5] In the case referred to the court said: "It was held in Boggs v. Chicago, etc., Railway Co., 54 Iowa 435, that mandamus was a proper remedy to such a right, and other cases have been prosecuted by such a proceeding, but it is not held that such a remedy is exclusive. It should not be claimed that but a single remedy can be available to a party. The doctrine of the election of remedies is old and familiar." But the rule is that where there is another adequate remedy parties can not resort to the extraordinary remedy of mandamus.

although a penalty is prescribed for disobeying the orders of the commissioners, mandamus will lie,[1] but other cases assert a different doctrine.[2] We think that the mere fact that a penalty is prescribed is not sufficient to defeat an application for mandamus, for the recovery of a penalty may not afford adequate relief.[3]

§ 700. Suits against railroad commissioners are ordinarily not suits against the state.—The settled general rule is that a suit can not be successfully prosecuted against a state except by its consent. This rule applies to actions against officers if the result will be to create a claim against the state. If the action is actually against the state, although nominally against its officers, the suit can not be maintained.[4] In one of the reported cases it was held that so far as the suit against the commissioners sought to enjoin them from formulating a schedule it was not a suit against the state, but that so far as it sought to enjoin the commissioners from bringing a suit in the name of the state to collect penalties it was a suit against the state.[5] The general rule as affirmed by the federal courts, and it is one

---

[1] State v. Chicago, etc., R. Co., 79 Wis. 259. The same court has held that a mandatory injunction will be awarded. Town of Jamestown v. Chicago, etc., R. Co., 69 Wis. 648; City of Oshkosh v. Milwaukee, etc., R. Co., 74 Wis. 534. See People v. Mayor, etc., 10 Wend. 393. Objection to the remedy must be taken by answer or demurrer, or on the trial, or it will be unavailing. Buffalo, etc., Co. v. Delaware, etc., R. Co., 130 N. Y. 152, s. c. 29 N. E. R. 121, Elliott's Appellate Procedure, §§ 658, 679.

[2] State v. Mobile, etc., R. Co., 59 Ala. 321; Railroad Commissioners v. Railroad Co., 26 S. Car. 353, s. c. 2 S. E. R. 127. To authorize recovery of penalty, order must be specific in directing what the company shall do. State v. Alabama, etc., R. Co., 67 Miss. 647, s. c. 7 So. R. 502. See, generally, United States v. Delaware, etc., R. Co., 40 Fed. R. 101.

[3] Rex v. Barker, 3 Burr. 1265.

[4] Louisiana v. Jumel, 107 U. S. 711; Cunningham v. Macon, etc., R. Co., 109 U. S. 446; Hagood v. Southern, 117 U. S. 52; In re Ayers, 123 U. S. 443; Virginia Coupon Cases, 114 U. S. 270; State v. Burke, 33 La. Ann. 498; Weston v. Dane, 51 Me. 461; Marshall v. Clark, 22 Texas 23; Houston, etc., R. Co. v. Randolph, 24 Texas 317; Printup v. Cherokee R. Co., 45 Ga. 365; Moore v. Tate, 87 Tenn. 725, s. c. 10 Am. St. R. 712. See, generally, Baltzer v. State, 104 N. Car. 265, s. c. 10 S. E. R. 153; Lincoln County v. Luning, 133 U. S. 529, s. c. 10 Sup. Ct. R. 363.

[5] McWhorter v. Pensacola, etc., R. Co., 24 Fla. 417, s. c. 5 So. R. 129, 12 Am. St. R. 220, 2 L. R. A. 504.

resting on sound principle, is that suits against railroad commissioners are not suits against the state.[1]

§ 701. **Remedies for illegal acts of railroad commissioners.**—It seems to us to be clear, on principle, that where railroad commissioners exceed their jurisdiction, or by wrongful acts invade the rights of others, the parties may resort to the appropriate remedies for a vindication of their rights, whether those remedies be legal or equitable. If a right be established and its wrongful invasion shown the courts will apply the appropriate remedy.[2] The proper remedy is, of course, to be determined from the nature of the case and the character of the relief sought; but, given a case where remediable rights are shown, the courts will find a remedy. If an exclusive statutory remedy is given, that remedy must be pursued.[3] The complainant who seeks to recover under the statute must plead such facts as bring his case fully within the statutory provisions.[4]

§ 702. **Specific statutory remedy—Federal rule.**—The general rule is that where a statute creates a new right the remedy specifically provided must be pursued.[5] The federal courts do

[1] Reagan *v.* Farmer's L. and Trust Co., 154 U. S. 362, s. c. 14 Sup. Ct. R. 1047, 9 Am. R. & Corp. Cas. (Lewis), 641.

[2] Murray *v.* Chicago, etc., R. Co., 62 Fed. R. 24; Chicago, etc., Railway Co. *v.* Osborne, 52 Fed. R. 912, s. c. 3 C. C. A. 347.

[3] Winsor, etc., Co. *v.* Chicago, etc., R. Co., 52 Fed. R. 716; Young *v.* Kansas City, etc., Railroad Co., 33 Mo. App. 509. It is held in the first of the cases cited that the remedy given by statute to recover extortionate charges supersedes the common law remedy. It was also held that unless the carrier charges more than the maximum rate fixed by statute, no action will lie, citing Burlington, etc., Railroad Co. *v.* Dey, 82 Iowa 312, s. c. 48 N. W. R. 98; State *v.* Fremont, etc., R. Co., 22 Neb. 313, s. c. 35 N. W. R. 118; Sorrell *v.* Central Railroad Co., 75 Ga. 509; Chicago, etc., R. Co. *v.* People, 77 Ill. 443. But see Little Rock, etc., R. Co. *v.* East Tennessee, etc., R. Co., 47 Fed. R. 771, where it is held that the statutory remedy is cumulative.

[4] Winsor, etc., Co. *v.* Chicago, etc., R. Co., 52 Fed. R. 716, citing Kennayde *v.* Railroad Co., 45 Mo. 255; King *v.* Dickenson, 1 Saund. 135; Bayard *v.* Smith, 17 Wend. 88.

[5] Chandler *v.* Hanna, 73 Ala. 390; Janney *v.* Buell, 55 Ala. 408; Dudley *v.* Mayhew, 3 N. Y. 9; Hollister *v.* Hollister Bank, 2 Keyes (N. Y.) 245; Dickinson *v.* Van Wormer, 39 Mich. 141; Carolina, etc., Railroad *v.* McKaskill, 94 N. C. 746; McIntire *v.* Western, etc., R. Co., 67 N. C. 278;

not, however, give full effect to this rule, but maintain that the procedure of the federal tribunals can not be regulated by state statutes.[1] We do not understand the federal courts to hold that rights given by state statutes will not be enforced; on the contrary, our understanding is that such rights will be enforced, but the remedy and procedure will be such as prevail in the courts of the nation. In a case in one of the United States circuit courts the railroad commissioners had made an order classifying the railroads of the state and fixing a tariff of charges. The railroad company insisted that the rates fixed by the commissioners were unreasonable and sued for an injunction, the commissioners contended that the federal court had no jurisdiction because there existed an adequate remedy by petition to the supreme court of the state, but the court denied the contention of the commissioners and held that it had jurisdiction.[2]

Indiana, etc., R. Co. v. Oakes, 20 Ind. 9.

[1] Clark v. Smith, 13 Pet. 195; Fitch v. Creighton, 24 How. (U. S.) 159; Mills v. Scott, 99 U. S. 25; Van Norden v. Morton, 99 U. S. 378; Cummings v. National Bank, 101 U. S. 153; Holland v. Challen, 110 U. S. 15; Reynolds v. Crawfordsville, etc., Bank, 112 U. S. 405; Orvis v. Powell, 98 U. S. 176, 178; Connecticut, etc., Co. v. Cushman, 108 U. S. 51; Flash v. Wilkerson, 22 Fed. R. 689; Borland v. Haven, 37 Fed. R. 394; Davis v. Jones, 2 Fed. R. 618; Fechheimer v. Baum, 37 Fed. R. 167.

[2] Ames v. Union Pacific R. Co., 64 Fed. R. 165, 172. In the course of the opinion of the court prepared by Mr. Justice Brewer, it was said: "It is further insisted by defendants that this court has no jurisdiction over these actions. First, because, in the act itself, an adequate legal remedy is provided by petition to the supreme court of the state, and courts of equity may not interfere when adequate legal remedies are provided; secondly, because the rates are prescribed by a direct act of the legislature, and not fixed by any commission. I am unable to assent to either of these contentions. The remedy referred to is found in section 5, which authorizes any railroad company, believing the rates prescribed to be unreasonable and unjust, to bring an action in the supreme court of the state, and if that court is satisfied that the rates are, as claimed, unjust and unreasonable to such company, it may make an order directing the board of transportation to permit the railroad to raise its rates to any sum in the discretion of the board, provided that the rates so raised shall not be higher than were those charged by such railroad on the first day of January, 1893. But this comes very far short of being an adequate legal remedy." The court also said: "An adequate legal remedy is one which secures, absolutely and of right, to the injured party relief from the wrong done. But even if it were a full and complete legal remedy, it is

§ 703. **Parties to suits against railroad commissioners.—** The complainant in a suit to enjoin a board of' railroad commissioners from establishing a schedule of rates can not, it has been held, succeed unless he shows an interest in the controversy peculiar to himself and not common to the public.[1] The fact that a state ships goods over a railroad does not make it a party to a suit to determine the validity of rates of freight established by the commissioners.[2] Railroad commissioners who grant authority to one railroad company to cross the tracks of another are held to be mere nominal parties to a suit to enjoin the commissioners from rehearing the case upon the application of the company whose road the other company was granted a right to cross.[3]

[1] Board of Railroad Commissioners v. Symns, etc., Co., 53 Kan. 207, s. c. 9 Am. & Corp. Cas. (Lewis) 676, citing Scofield v. Railway Co., 43 Ohio St. 571, s. c. 3 N. E. R. 907; Commissioners v. Smith, 48 Kan. 331, s. c. 29 Pac. R. 565. The court discriminated the case before it from the cases of Chicago, etc., R. Co. v. Dey, 35 Fed. R. 866; Chicago, etc., R. Co. v. Minnesota, 134 U. S. 418, s. c. 10 Sup. Ct. R. 462; Budd v. People, 143 U. S. 517, s. c. 12 Sup. Ct. R. 468, saying: "We are cited to cases where injunction was maintained by the railroad company against the enforcement of the order of such a board, but in these cases it was held to be maintainable because the rates proposed to be put in force were so unreasonable as to be confiscatory. The railroad company, being a public carrier and obliged to transport commodities offered for shipment, and use their property in so doing, it was held that a provision requiring the carriage of a person or property without reward amounted to the taking of private property for a public use without just compensation, or without due process of law, and hence a court of equity might prevent the enforcement of such a provision." See State v. Chicago, etc., R. Co., 86 Iowa 304, s. c. 53 N. W. R. 253. one which can be secured only in a single court, and that a court of the state. And, as was held in the case of Reagan v. Farmers' L. and Trust Co., 154 U. S. 362, 14 Sup. Ct. 1047, it is not within the power of the state to tie up citizens of other states to the courts of that state for the redress of their rights, and for the protection against wrong. The laws of congress, passed under the authority of the constitution of the United States, open the doors of the federal courts to citizens of other states to suits and actions for the prevention or redress of wrong, and the state can not close those doors. Whatever the effect such legislation may have upon the courts of the state, the courts of the United States are as open now as they were to actions for the protection of citizens of other states in their property rights within the state of Nebraska."

[2] Clyde v. Richmond, etc., R. Co., 57 Fed. R. 436.

[3] Union, etc., R. Co. v. Board of Railroad Commissioners, 52 Kan. 680, s. c. 35 Pac. R. 224.

§ 704. Review by certiorari.—In jurisdictions where the practice of bringing before the court for review the proceedings, "of an inferior court tribunal, or officer exercising judicial authority, whose proceedings are summary or in a course different from the common law,"[1] by a writ of *certiorari* prevails, we suppose that in many instances the appropriate mode of reviewing the proceedings of a board of railroad commissioners would be by *certiorari*. The board of commissioners is an inferior tribunal invested with powers in their nature judicial, so that it would seem that in the proper case their proceedings are reviewable by *certiorari*. In a Massachusetts case it was assumed that *certiorari* was a proper remedy, but it was held that the petition must be dismissed for the reason among others that the petitioners were not parties to the proceedings.[2]

§ 705. Injunction against commissioners—Generally.—The illegal and unauthorized acts of a board of railroad commissioners may be restrained by injunction. Where a state statute is unconstitutional, the board of commissioners will be enjoined from enforcing orders assumed to be made by authority of such statute.[3] The earlier English statute recognized the power of the courts to enjoin the proceedings of railway commissioners in cases where they assumed powers they did not possess or violated settled rules of law,[4] but the courts of England reluctantly interfere with the decisions of the commissioners, and will do so only in clear cases.[5] In this country courts have jurisdiction over the

---

[1] Farmingham, etc., Co. *v.* County Commissioners, 112 Mass. 206. Elliott on Roads and Streets, 271.

[2] Cunningham *v.* Board of Railroad Commissioners, 158 Mass. 104, s. c. 56 Am. & Eng. R. Cas. 301.

[3] Chicago, etc., R. Co. *v.* Dey, 35 Fed. R. 866, s. c. 1 L. R. A. 744, Piek *v.* Chicago, etc., R. Co, 6 Biss. 177; Louisville, etc., R. Co. *v.* Railroad Commission, 19 Fed. R. 679; Farmers' L. and Trust Co. *v.* Stone, 20 Fed. R. 270; Reagan *v.* Farmers' L. and Trust Co., 154 U. S. 362, s. c. 14 Sup. Ct. R. 1047; Chicago, etc., R. Co. *v.* Dey, 35 Fed. R. 866, overruling Chicago, etc., R. Co. *v.* Becker, 32 Fed. R. 883; McWhorter *v.* Pensacola, etc., R. Co., 24 Fla. 417, s. c. 12 Am. St. R. 220; Seawell *v.* Kansas City, etc., R. Co., 119 Mo. 224, s. c. 9 Am. R. & Corp. Cas. (Lewis) 606.

[4] 1 Hodges on Railways, 431, note f.

[5] Barret *v.* Great Northern, etc., R. Co., 1 C. B. (N. S.) 423, s. c. 28 L. T. 254, 38 Eng. Law & Eq. 218.

proceedings of railroad commissioners, although there may be no statute specifically or expressly conferring it. Granting to railroad commissioners power to make orders does not necessarily take away the jurisdiction of the courts. The general rule is that jurisdiction once granted is not divested unless there is a clear statutory provision divesting it.[1] But the power of the courts rests on higher grounds. The legislature does not create or vest the judicial power of the commonwealth; that is done by the constitution; the legislature simply distributes the power. The legislature has no judicial power, for its power is exclusively legislative, and as it has no judicial power, it can not, in the proper sense, delegate such power.[2]

§ 706. **Where commissioners exceed their jurisdiction, injunction will lie.**—If railway commissioners exceed their jurisdiction, and their acts are more than mere fugitive or transient trespasses, injunction will lie. The rule that where a tribunal, such as a board of railroad commissioners, transcends its powers, injunction is the appropriate remedy, is a familiar one. The difficulty in practically applying the rule stated is in determining whether the commissioners have exceeded their jurisdiction. As their jurisdiction is wholly statutory, they exceed it whenever they do an act not authorized by the statute from which they derive their powers.[3]

[1] Sutherland Stat. Const., § 395.
[2] Greenough v. Greenough, 11 Pa. St. 489; Perkins v. Corbin, 45 Ala. 103; Vandercook v. Williams, 106 Ind. 345; Smythe v. Boswell, 117 Ind. 365. Authorities cited, Elliott's Appellate Proc., §§ 1, 2, 3 and notes. Mr. Bryce says: "But in America a legislature is a legislature and nothing more. The same instrument which creates it creates also the executive, governor and the judges. They hold by a title as good as its own. If the legislature should pass a law depriving the governor of an executive function conferred by the constitution, that law would be void. If the legislature attempted to interfere with the courts, their action would be even more palpably illegal and ineffectual." Bryce Am. Com. 429. It is not to be understood, however, that the legislature may not interfere with the courts, so far as concerns matters of procedure, but judicial powers resident in courts legislative action is ineffective to take away or bestow upon administrative or ministerial officers.
[3] South Eastern, etc., R. Co. v. Railway Commissioners, 6 L. R. Q. B. D. 586, per Lord Selborne *vide*, p. 591; Great Western R. Co. v. Railroad Commissioners, L. R. 7 Q. B. D. 182; South Eastern R. Co. v. Railway Com-

§ 707. Vacating orders of commissioners on the ground of fraud.—A board of railroad commissioners is subject to the equity jurisdiction of the courts.[1] If it makes an order which is fraudulent in its nature, the order may be vacated by a decree of a court of chancery.[2] To entitle a party to a decree vacating or annulling an order upon the ground of fraud it must be made to appear that there was actual fraud in obtaining the order, and if there be no fraud the order will not be vacated although the parties who obtained it were influenced by corrupt motives.

§ 708. Federal question—Removal of causes from state courts.—It has been held that where a state board of railroad commissioners brings an action to enforce obedience to its orders the case can not be removed to the federal court, although it appears that a federal question is involved.[3] The court suggested that the proper course was to put in a pleading presenting the federal question, and in the event of an adverse decision by the highest court of the state, carry the case to the supreme court of the United States by a writ of error. In another case,[4] however, the doctrine of the case referred to is denied, and it is asserted that the case may be removed. The case last referred to holds that if the petition for removal[5]

---

missioners, L. R. 5 Q.B. D. 217; Regina v. Railway Commissioners, L. R. 22 Q. B. D. 642. See, Caterham, etc., R. Co. v. London, etc., Ry. Co., 1 C. B. (N. S.) 410; Bennett v. Manchester, etc., R. Co., 6 C. B. (N. S.) 707, 714; Pelsall, etc., R. Co. v. London, etc., R. Co., L. R. 23 Q. B. D. 536.

[1] Clyde v. Richmond, etc., R. Co., 57 Fed. R. 436.

[2] Coe v. Aiken, 61 Fed. R. 24. In the case cited the court said: "With reference to the second objection there is no doubt in my mind that a court of equity may set aside the action of a tribunal of this character, if it is fraudulent in its nature or essence, or was fraudulently obtained. It may even go further, and for the same reasons, set aside the judgments of a judicial tribunal. This is a fundamental principle of law."

[3] Dey v. Chicago, etc., R. Co., 45 Fed. R. 82.

[4] State v. Coosaw, etc., Co., 45 Fed. 804.

[5] The court, in the case referred to, State v. Coosaw, etc., Co., 45 Fed. R. 804, 811, cited in support of its conclusion, Metcalf v. City of Watertown, 128 U. S. 589, 9 Sup. Ct. R. 173; State v. Illinois, etc., Railroad Co., 33 Fed. R. 721; Austin v. Gagan, 39 Fed. R. 626; McDonald v. Salem, etc., Co., 31 Fed. R. 577; Johnson v. Accident Insurance Co., 35 Fed. R. 374, but as

shows that a federal question is involved, a removal will be ordered, but in so holding the court was in error. The law as declared by the supreme court of the United States is, that a cause is not removable as involving a federal question unless the facts making it removable appear from the plaintiff's statement of his claim.[1]

appears from the cases referred to in the following note those cases were wrongly decided.

[1] Chappell v. Waterworth, 155 U. S. 102, s. c. 15 Sup. Ct. R. 34; East Lake, etc., Co. v. Brown, 155 U. S. 488, 15 Sup. Ct. R. 357; Tennessee v. Union, etc., Bank, 152 U. S. 454, s. c. 14 Sup. Ct. R. 654.

CHAPTER XXIX.

PENAL OFFENSES BY AND AGAINST RAILROAD COMPANIES.

§ 709. Penal offenses by railroad companies—Generally.
710. Penal statutes strictly construed—No extra-territorial effect.
711. Right of action as affected by penal statutes—Effect of violation as proof of negligence.
712. Action for enforcement of penal statutes.
713. The informer's rights—Parties.
714. The penalty—Computation.
715. When "penalty" and when "liquidated damages."
716. Indictment of railroad companies for causing death.
717. Violation of Sunday laws.
718. Indictment of railroad company for maintaining a nuisance.
719. Obstruction of highways.
720. Failure to maintain accommodations at stations.
721. Statutory signals — Stops at crossings.
§ 722. Blackboards and bulletins at stations.
723. Unlawful speed.
724. Other penal regulations.
725. Violation of federal regulations.
726. Penalty for confinement of live stock.
727. Offenses against railroads—Obstructing mails and interfering with interstate commerce.
728. Sale of tickets without authority—Scalpers.
729. Climbing on cars — Evading payment of fare.
730. Placing obstruction on track.
731. Shooting or throwing missiles at car.
732. Breaking into depot or car—Burglary.
733. Injury to railroad property—Malicious trespass.
734. Other crimes against railroad companies.

§ 709. **Penal offenses by railroad companies—Generally.**—Railroad corporations are the subject of much legislation by congress, legislatures and municipalities, within their respective spheres. Regulations arising from the power to regulate commerce are usually such as apply to common carriers generally, but many statutes and ordinances enacted in the exercise of the police power look particularly to the peculiar nature of the operation of railroads and often apply to steam railroads exclusively. It is thoroughly established that legislatures, within

§ 709   PENAL OFFENSES.   1019

their spheres, have power to compel railroad companies to discharge their duties and obligation to shippers and the public by reasonable statutory regulations, which may be enforced by fines and penalties.[1] Some courts have held that corporations are not included in general penal statutes forbidding the commission of particular acts unless included in express language,[2] and base their decisions upon the rule that penal statutes must be strictly construed, maintaining that the term "person" under such strict construction can not apply to a corporation,[3] but it seems to be the sound rule, supported by the weight of authority, that corporations are amenable to penal statutes forbidding the commission of offenses by "persons," when the circumstances in which they are placed are identical with those of a natural person expressly included in the statute, and where the statute can be applied equally well to them as corporations.[4] It is generally held that corporations are indict-

[1] McGowan v. Wilmington, etc., R. Co., 95 N. C. 417, s. c. 27 Am. & Eng. R. Cas. 64; Branch v. Wilmington, etc., R. Co., 77 N. Car. 347; Missouri Pacific R. Co. v. Humes, 115 U. S. 512, 22 Am. & Eng. R. Cas. 557. See chapter on governmental control.

[2] In Benson v. Monson, etc., R. Co., 9 Met. (Mass.) 562, it was held that a statute imposing a penalty upon "the owner, agent, or superintendent of any manufacturing establishment" did not apply to a "manufacturing corporation." See 5 Thomp. Corp., § 6285.

[3] In Cumberland, etc., Co. v. Portland, 56 Me. 77, the court held that an action for penalty could not be maintained against a municipal corporation which had violated a statute imposing a penalty upon "any person or persons." Another Maine decision asserts that an action can not be maintained against a corporation for the commission of an offense forbidden by a penal statute applying in terms to "any person," and which, in another section, provided that the offense should constitute larceny, for the double reason that criminal intent can not be imputed to a corporation, and that such statutes are not to be enlarged by construction. Androscoggin, etc., Co. v. Bethel, etc., Co., 64 Me. 441. See, also, Commonwealth v. Swift Run Gap Turnpike, 2 Va. Cas. 362; State v. Ohio, etc., R. Co., 23 Ind. 362; Indianapolis & C. R. Co. v. State, 37 Ind. 489, 493.

[4] 5 Thomp. Corp., § 6285; State v. Morris, etc., R. Co., 23 N. J. L. 360; State v. Vermont Cent. R. Co., 27 Vt. 103; Stewart v. Waterloo Turn Verein, 71 Iowa 226, s. c. 60 Am. Rep. 786; South Carolina R. Co. v. McDonald, 5 Ga. 531; Wales v. Muscatine, 4 Iowa 302; State v. Security Bank, 2 S. Dak. 538, s. c. 51 N. W. R. 337; State v. First Nat. Bank, 2 S. Dak. 568, s. c. 51 N. W. R. 587. See

CORP. 65

able for non-feasance in the cases in which a natural person would be indictable,[1] but there is conflict as to whether they are thus indictable for acts of misfeasance. It is maintained by some courts, and it seems with good reason, that a corporation may be indicted for misfeasance, or the doing of an act unlawful in itself and injurious to the rights of others, as well as for an omission of duty,[2] but it is said that they can not be indicted for offenses which derive their criminality from evil intent, or which are simply violations of the social duties peculiar to natural persons.[3] Lord Coke early laid down the rule that corporations are persons within the purview of penal statutes, and Mr. Justice Story, "finding, therefore, no authority at common law, which overthrows the doctrine of Lord Coke," refused to "engraft any such constructive exception upon the text of the statute."[4] The act, to be punishable by penalty, must come within the scope of the duty or power of the corporation,[5] otherwise the penalty can only be inflicted upon the members and officers or representatives of the corporation,[6] who may be presumed to have acted as individuals.

State v. Baltimore, etc., R. Co., 15 W. Va. 362, s. c. 36 Am. R. 803, for a review of the authorities.

[1] 1 Bishop Crim. Law, § 503; Gillett on Criminal Law, § 4; Angell and Ames on Corp., § 394; Texas, etc., R. Co. v. State, 41 Ark. 498, 20 Am. & Eng. R.Cas. 626; People v. Albany, 11 Wend. 539; Waterford, etc., v. People, 9 Barb. 161; Queen v. Birmingham, etc., R. Co., 2 Gale & D. 236; Commonwealth v. Central Bridge Corp., 12 Cush. 242; Louisville, etc., R. Co. v. Commonwealth, 13 Bush (Ky.) 388; Boston, etc., R. Co. v. State, 32 N. H. 215.

[2] Commonwealth v. Prop. of New Bedford Bridge, 2 Gray (Mass.) 339; Queen v. Great, etc., R. Co., 9 Q. B. 315, 10 Jur. 755; State v. Morris, etc., R. Co., 23 N. J. L. 360; State v. Vermont Cent. R. Co., 27 Vt. 103; State v. Baltimore, etc., Co., 15 W. Va. 362, s. c. 36 Am. R. 803, citing authorities. See, also, Commonwealth v. Lehigh Valley R. Co., 165 Pa. St. 162, s. c. 30 Atl. R. 836.

[3] It has been held that an action of trespass for false imprisonment will lie against a corporation, but an action on the case for malicious prosecution will not lie for the reason that malicious intent can not be imputed to a corporation. Owsley v. Montgomery, etc., R. Co., 37 Ala. 560.

[4] United States v. Amedy, 11 Wheat. 393, 412; Queen v. Great, etc., R. Co., 9 Q. B. 315, 10 Jur. 755; Louisville, etc., R. Co. v. State, 3 Head (Tenn.) 523.

[5] Reg. v. Great North of England Railway, 9 Q. B. 315, 326; Bishop Crim. Law., § 506.

[6] Kane v. People, 3 Wend. 363; Edge v. Commonwealth, 7 Pa. St. 275.

But the members and officers are not always criminally liable when the corporation is.¹ Where a railroad is in the hands of a receiver the corporation can not be prosecuted for crimes or misdemeanors committed by the agents or servants of the receiver.² Under the rule of strict construction it has been held that a penalty denounced against a "railway company" is not recoverable against a "receiver."³ But it has been held that receivers appointed by the federal courts do not fall under this rule as they are required by a federal statute to operate the roads under and in compliance with the laws governing railway companies in the states respectively in which the property is situated.⁴

§ 710. Penal statutes strictly construed—No extra-territorial effect.—The rigid rules of the common law with reference to the liability of common carriers should not be applied in cases involving the violation of a penal statute, for a penal statute is to be construed strictly in favor of one charged with violating it,⁵ but it has been held that "this rule is not violated by adopting the sense of the words which best harmonize with the object and intent of the legislature, and the whole context of the statute must be construed together."⁶ The dec-

---

¹ State v. Barksdale, 5 Humph. 154; 1 Bishop Crim. Law § 507.

² State v. Wabash R. Co., 115 Ind. 466, 35 Am. & Eng. R. Cas. 1, 17 N. E. R. 909.

³ Bonner v. Franklin Co-op. Assn., 4 Tex. Civil App. 166, 23 S. W. R. 317; Turner v. Cross, 83 Tex. 218, 18 S. W. R. 578; Texas, etc., R. Co. v. Barnhart, 5 Tex. Civil App. 601, 23 S. W. R. 801; Missouri, etc., R. Co. v. Stoner, 5 Tex. Civil App. 50, 23 S. W. R. 1020.

⁴ Bonner v. Franklin Co-op. Assn., 4 Tex. Civil App. 166, 23 S. W. R. 317.

⁵ Whitehead v. Wilmington, etc., R. Co., 87 N. C. 255, 9 Am. & Eng. R. Cas. 168; Bond v. Wabash, etc., R. Co., 67 Iowa 712, 23 Am. & Eng. R. Cas. 608; Omaha, etc., R. Co. v. Hale, (Neb.) 63 N. W. R. 849.

⁶ State v. Indiana, etc., R. Co., 133 Ind. 69; State v. Hirsch, 125 Ind. 207, 24 N. E. Rep. 1062. In United States v. Wiltberger, 5 Wheaton (U. S.) 76, Marshall, C. J., said, "Though penal laws are to be construed strictly, they are not to be construed so strictly as to defeat the obvious intention of the legislature. The maxim is not to be so applied as to narrow the words of the statute to the exclusion of cases which those words in their ordinary acceptation, or in that sense in which the legislature has obviously used them, would comprehend. The intention of the legislature is to be collected from the words they employ. Where there is no ambiguity in the words, there is no room for construction." In United States v. Hartwell, 6 Wall.

laration or complaint must present a case strictly within the provisions of the statute, not leaving any essential facts to be gathered by argument or inference.[1] Besides being strictly construed, these statutes carry no extra-territorial effect, whether the penalty be to the public or to persons, and they can not be enforced in the courts of another state, either by force of the statute or upon the principles of comity.[2] The supreme court of the United States has held, however, that a statute making directors personally liable to creditors of a corporation for making false reports may be enforced anywhere, deciding that while such a statute is penal in the sense that it should receive a strict construction, it is not penal in the sense that it can not be enforced in a foreign state, for it gives a civil remedy at the suit of the creditor only, measured by the amount of the debt.[3] It has also been held by the supreme court of the United States that the question whether a statute is penal in such a sense as to forbid its enforcement in a foreign jurisdiction, "depends upon the question whether its pur-

(U. S.) 385, Swayne, J., said: "The object in construing penal as well as other statutes is to ascertain the legislative intent. That constitutes the law. If the language be clear it is conclusive. There can be no construction where there is nothing to construe. The words must not be narrowed to the exclusion of what the legislature intended to embrace; but that intention must be gathered from the words and they must be such as to leave no room for a reasonable doubt upon the subject. It must not be defeated by a forced and overstrict construction."

[1] State v. Androscoggin R. Co., 76 Me. 411, s. c. 20 Am. & Eng. R. Cas. 624; Barter v. Martin, 5 Me. 76; Western U. Tel. Co. v. Wilson, 108 Ind. 308, 16 Am. & Eng. Corp. Cas. 257; Whitecraft v. Vanderver, 12 Ill. 235. Where the statute says that the action shall be brought in the name of the people of the state of Michigan, an action in the name of the prosecuting attorney for and on behalf of the people of the state of Michigan will lie. People v. Brady, 90 Mich. 459.

[2] Blaine v. Curtis, 59 Vt. 120, 59 Am. Rep. 702; Ogden v. Folliott, 3 T. R. 726; Scoville v. Canfield, 14 Johns. 338, 7 Am. Dec. 467; First National Bank v. Price, 33 Md. 487; Derrickson v. Smith, 27 N. J. L. 166; Carnahan v. W. U. Tel. Co., 89 Ind. 526; Taylor Priv. Corp., § 393; Story, Confl. of Laws, §§ 620, 621. See Western U. Tel. Co. v. Hamilton, 50 Ind. 181; Henry v. Sargeant, 13 N. H. 321, 40 Am. Dec. 146.

[3] Huntington v. Attrill, 146 U. S. 657, per Gray, J. See Boyce v. Wabash, etc., Co., 63 Iowa 70, 23 Am. & Eng. R. Cas. 172, in which an Iowa court allowed an action for double damages provided by an Illinois statute.

state, or to a a private remedy to a person injured by the wrongful act."[1]

§ 711. Right of action as affected by penal statutes—Effect of violation as proof of negligence.—Unless the common law right of action is thereby taken away in express terms or by necessary implication, the penalty imposed by a penal statute is cumulative only, and the common law right of action continues to exist unimpaired.[2] It may, perhaps, be laid down as a general rule that the enactment of a penal statute does not establish a new liability aside from the penalty denounced by the statute itself. In other words, a penal statute can not ordinarily be regarded as the foundation of a new right of action in addition to that prescribed, and the best reasoned cases hold that the only new liability arising from the neglect of such purely statutory duty is for the prescribed penalty,[3]

[1] Huntington v. Attrill, 146 U. S. 657, s. c. 13 Sup. R. 224, per Gray, J.; Dennick v. Railroad Co., 103 U. S. 11; Herrick v. Minneapolis, etc., Ry. Co., 31 Minn. 11, 16 N. W. R. 413; Chicago, etc., R. Co. v. Doyle, 60 Miss. 977; Knight v. West Jersey R. Co., 108 Pa. St. 250; Morris v. Chicago, etc., Ry. Co., 65 Iowa 727, 23 N. W. Rep. 143; Higgins v. Central, etc., R. Co., 155 Mass. 176, 29 N. E. Rep. 534. In Mexican Natl. R. Co. v. Jackson, (Tex. Civil App.) 32 S. W. Rep. 230, it was held that a law of Mexico making negligence resulting in injury to another a penal offense, and also giving a right of action civil in nature, was not penal in the sense that the civil remedy could not be enforced in the courts of Texas, and the Texas court awarded damages, although the injury occurred in Mexico. See, also, 2 Am. L. Reg. & Rev. (N. S.) 725.

[2] See post, § 712; United States v. Howard, 17 Fed. R. 638; Caswell v. Worth, 5 El. & Bl. 848, per Coleridge, J.; Couch v. Steel, 3 El. & Bl. 402; Aldrich v. Howard, 7 R. I. 199; Tyler v. W. U. Tel. Co., 54 Fed. R. 634.

[3] Flynn v. Canton Co., 40 Md. 312; Taylor v. Lake Shore, etc., R. Co., 45 Mich. 74, per Cooley, J.; City of Hartford v. Talcott, 48 Conn. 525; Heeney v. Sprague, 11 R. I. 456; Vandyke v. Cincinnati, 1 Disney (Ohio) 532; Kirby v. Boylston Market Asso., 14 Gray (Mass.) 249; Philadelphia R. Co. v. Ervin, 89 Pa. St. 71. But see Bott v. Pratt, 33 Minn. 323, s. c. 53 Am. R. 47, 53 n.; Jetter v. N. Y., etc., R. Co., 2 Abb. Dec. 458. In his opinion in the Michigan case, supra, Judge Cooley said: "If it was only a public duty it can not be pretended that a private action can be maintained for a breach thereof. * * * Nevertheless, the burden that individuals are required to bear for the public protection or benefit may in part be imposed for the protection or benefit of some particular individual or class of individuals also, and then

except, perhaps, where the statute prescribes that the duty shall be to particular persons or to a particular class of persons, and not purely a public duty.[1] In one instance, however, the supreme court of the United States held in the case of the death of a boy resulting from a violation of an ordinance requiring railroad companies to fence their right of way in a prescribed manner, that "the duty is due, not to the city as a municipal body, but to the public, considered as composed of individual persons; and each person specially injured by the breach of the obligation is entitled to his individual compensation, and to an action for its recovery."[2] It is also well settled that where the statute prescribes a duty which is owing to an individual or class of individuals, the fact of its violation may constitute negligence, or at least *prima facie* evidence thereof, and contribute an important element of the injured person's cause of action,[3] even though the omission of the duty may not have constituted negligence before the passage of the law. It has been held that non-performance of such statutory duty, resulting in injury to another, may be pronounced to be negligence as a conclusion of law.[4] There is, however, much conflict among the

there may be an individual right of action as well as a public prosecution of a breach of duty which causes individual injury. * * * The nature of the duty and the benefits to be accomplished through its performances must generally determine whether it is a duty to the public in part or exclusively, or whether individuals may claim that it is a duty imposed wholly or in part for their especial benefit." In Aldrich *v.* Tripp, 11 R. I. 141, the plaintiff sought to recover damages for an injury arising from a violation of an ordinance which created a *new* duty. The court said: "We do not suppose that the creation of new civil liabilities between individuals was any part of the object for which the power to enact ordinances was granted." On the other hand, in Jetter *v.* N. Y., etc., R. Co., 2 Abb. Dec. 458, the court, taking an extreme view and overruling some previous decisions, said: "It is an axiomatic truth that every person, while violating an express statute, is a wrong-doer, and as such is *ex necessitate* negligent in the eye of the law, and every innocent party whose person is injured by the act which constitutes the violation of the statute is entitled to a civil remedy for such injury, notwithstanding any redress the public may also have."

[1] Taylor *v.* Lake Shore, etc., R. Co., 45 Mich. 74.

[2] Hayes *v.* Mich. Cent. R. Co., 111 U. S. 228, 4 Sup. Ct. R. 369, per Matthews, J.

[3] Hayes *v.* Mich. Cent. R. Co., 111 U. S. 228, 4 Sup. Ct. R. 369.

[4] Terre Haute & Indianapolis R. Co.

§ 711   PENAL OFFENSES.   1025

authorities as to how far the violation of these statutory duties should be deemed to constitute negligence. In some states the statutes themselves provide that where injury follows violation, the violation shall constitute a *prima facie* case of negligence,[1] and in one of these states where violation of the statute is followed by injury, the element of proximate cause has been conclusively presumed by the courts.[2] These last decisions are, as it seems to us, unsound, and the rule, supported by the weight of authority, is that while one who violates a statute or an ordinance[3] may be regarded as a wrong-doer, and the act regarded as negligence, still it may or may not be the proximate cause of the injury complained of according to the facts of the particular case. In some courts, however, it is held that the mere violation of a municipal ordinance is not negligence *per se*, but merely evidence of it.[4] It is generally held, and this we regard

v. Voelker, 129 Ill. 540, 39 Am. & Eng. R. Cas. 615; Central R., etc., Co. v. Smith, 78 Ga. 694, 34 Am. & Eng. R. Cas 1.

[1] In Mississippi, Georgia and Tennessee. See Chicago, etc., R. Co. v. Trotter, 60 Miss. 442; Mobile, etc., R. Co. v. Dale, 61 Miss. 206, 20 Am. & Eng. R Cas. 651; Columbus, etc., R. Co. v. Kennedy, 78 Ga. 646, 31 Am. & Eng. R. Cas. 92; Tennessee R. Co. v. Walker, 11 Heisk. (Tenn.) 383.

[2] Tennessee R. Co. v. Walker, 11 Heisk. (Tenn.) 383; Hill v. Louisville, etc,. R.Co.,9 Heisk.(Tenn.) 823; Nashville, etc., R. Co. v. Thomas, 5 Heisk. (Tenn.) 262. But see Louisville, etc., R. Co. v. Connor, 9 Heisk. (Tenn.) 19.

[3] Wesley City Coal Co. v. Healer, 84 Ill. 126; Pennsylvania R. Co. v. Hensil, 70 Ind. 569, s. c. 36 Am. R. 188, 6 Am. & Eng. R. C. 79; Chicago, etc., R. Co. v. Boggs, 101 Ind. 522, s. c. 51 Am. R. 761; Pennsylvania R.Co.v.Stegemeier, 118 Ind. 305, 309; Indiana, etc., R. Co.v. Barnhart, 115 Ind. 399, 410; Pennsylvania R. Co. v. Horton, 132 Ind. 189; Wanless v. N. E. R. W. Co., L. R. 6 Q. B. 481 (L. R. 7 H. L. Cas. 12); Railway Co. v. Schneider, 45 Ohio St. 678;Baker v. Pendergast, 32 Ohio St. 494; St. Louis, etc., R. Co. v. Dunn, 78 Ill. 197; Correll v. B., C. R. & N. R. Co., 38 Iowa 120; San Antonio, etc., Ry. Co. v. Bowles, 88 Tex. 634, 32 S. W. R. 880. See, also, Salisbury v. Herchenroder, 106 Mass. 458; Baltimore City Ry. Co. v. McDonnell, 43 Md. 552.

[4] Lane v. Atlantic Works, 111 Mass. 136; Hanlon v. South Boston, etc., R. Co., 129 Mass. 310; Liddy v. St. Louis R. R. Co., 40 Mo. 506; Kelley v. Hannibal, etc., R. Co., 75 Mo. 138; Baltimore, etc., R. Co. v. McDonnell, 43 Md. 534; Philadelphia, etc., R. Co. v. Boyer, 97 Pa. St. 91, 2 Am. & Eng. R. Cas. 172; Van Horn v. Burlington, etc., R. Co., 59 Iowa 33, s. c. 7 Am. & Eng. R. Cas. 591; Faber v. St. Paul, etc., R. Co., 29 Minn. 465, s. c. 8 Am. & Eng. R. Cas. 277; Knupfle v. Knickerbocker, etc., Co., 84 N. Y. 491; Hayes v. Mich. Cent. R. Co., 111 U. S. 228, s. c. 4 Sup. Ct. R. 369; Meek v. Pennsylvania R. Co., 38 Ohio St. 632, s. c. 13 Am. & Eng. R. Cas. 643, and

as the true doctrine, that the element of proximate cause must be established, and that it will not necessarily be presumed from the fact that an ordinance or statute has been violated.[1] Negligence, no matter in what it consists, can not create a right of action unless it is the proximate cause of the injury complained of by the plaintiff.

§ 712. Action for enforcement of penal statutes.—Actions for the enforcement of statutory penalties against corporations are generally held to be civil actions.[2] In jurisdictions in which corporations are held to be included in the term "persons" in general statutes, the action should conform to the usual or prescribed action under such statutes, be it civil or criminal. It is held in some jurisdictions which still recognize common law crimes and actions, that the statutory penalty may be recovered by indictment or information unless such mode is excluded by the statute, and that the prescribed remedy is only cumulative to the one given by the common law.[3] In some other jurisdictions it has been held that both

note. Upon principle this seems to us to be a better rule than that which makes the violation of an ordinance, or even a statute, conclusive proof of negligence or negligence *per se.*

[1] Hayes v. Mich. Cent. R. Co., 111 U. S. 228, s. c. 4 Sup. Ct. R. 369, 15 Am. & Eng. R. Cas. 394; Pennsylvania R. Co. v. Hensil, 70 Ind. 569; Philadelphia, etc., R. Co. v. Stebbing, 62 Md. 504, 19 Am. & Eng. R. Cas. 36; Cooley on Torts, 657, 658; Patterson's Ry. Accident Law, 40; Kelley v. Hannibal, etc., R. Co., 75 Mo. 138, s. c. 13 Am. & Eng. R. Cas. 638.

[2] Katzenstein v. Raleigh, etc., R. Co., 84 N. Car. 688, 6 Am. & Eng. R. Cas. 464; Rockwell v. State, 11 Ohio 130; Edenton v. Wool, 65 N. Car. 379. 3 Blacks. Com. 160. See, also, McCoun v. New York Central, etc., R. Co., 50 N. Y. 176; Durham v. State, 117 Ind. 477; Western Union Tel. Co. v. Scircle, 103 Ind. 227; Corporation, etc., v. Eaton, 4 Cranch C.C. 352; Davis v.State, 119 Ind. 555; Chaffee v. United States, 18 Wall. 516. As elsewhere stated, however, it is held that an action to recover a penalty, although civil in form, is essentially criminal in its nature. *Ante,* § 646, p. 930, note 1.

[3] United States v. Howard, 17 Fed. R. 638; State v. Wabash, etc., R. Co., 89 Mo. 562; State v. Corwin, 4 Mo. 609; Hodgman v. People, 4 Den. (N. Y.) 235; State v. Helgen, 1 Speer (S. Car.) 310; State v. Meyer, 1 Speer (S. Car.) 305; State v. Maze, 6 Humph. (Tenn.) 17. It is held that the Missouri statute permits one bringing a *qui tam* action to bring the action either civilly or criminally by information. State v. Hannibal, etc., Co., 30 Mo. App. 494.

the statutory penalty and the actual damages may be recovered in one action where both arise from the same transaction.[1]

§ 713. The informer's rights—Parties.—The informer can not maintain an action in his own name unless plainly authorized by statute, nor can he control such action, without such authority, when brought.[2] It is held that the penalty is a forfeiture to the sovereign for the violation of the law and the share accorded the informer is simply an inducement to the citizen to apprise the public officer of violations.[3] It has also been held that a complaint is defective, on demurrer, if the informer is made plaintiff when only the state can sue, and in one case leave to amend by making the state plaintiff was refused,[4] but other courts have permitted amendments.[5] It is said that the same strict construction precludes the state from prosecuting an action where the statute gives that right to the informer,[6] but to exclude the state, the right in the informer must be plainly conferred by the statute, although not necessarily in express words,[7] and it has been held that where one moiety goes to the state, the state may prosecute for the whole, unless the informer has commenced a *qui tam* action.[8] It

[1] Kansas City, etc., R. Co. v. Spencer, 72 Miss. 491, 17 So. R. 168; Hodges v. Wilmington, etc., Railroad Co., 105 N. C. 170, 10 S. E. 917; Wells v. New Haven, etc., Co., 151 Mass. 46, 44 Am. & Eng. R. Cas. 491, n., 23 N. E. R. 724.

[2] Omaha, etc., R. Co. v. Hale, 45 Neb. 418, 63 N. W. R. 849; Colburn v. Swett, 1 Metc. (Mass.) 232; Fleming v. Bailey, 5 East 313; Barnard v. Gostling, 2 East 569; Drew v. Hilliker, 56 Vt. 641; Nye v. Lamphere, 2 Gray (Mass.) 297; Seward v. Beach, 29 Barb. (N. Y.) 239. But see Chicago, etc., Co. v. Howard, 38 Ill. 414.

[3] Omaha, etc., R. Co. v. Hale, 45 Neb. 418, 63 N. W. R. 849.

[4] St. Louis, etc., R. Co. v. State, 56 Ark. 166, 19 S. W. 572.

[5] See Maggett v. Roberts, 108 N. Car. 174, 12 S. E. 890.

[6] Higby v. People, 5 Ill. 165; United States v. Laescki, 29 Fed. R. 699.

[7] The clause "who may prosecute" or "who prosecutes" has been held sufficient to show the legislative intent. Drew v. Hilliker, 56 Vt. 641. A common informer has the right to sue under a statute giving the penalty "to any person who may prosecute therefor." Nye v. Lamphere, 2 Gray (Mass.) 297. In United States v. Laescki, 29 Fed. R. 699; the use of the language "recoverable, one-half to the use of the informer" in the statute was held to authorize the informer to sue. See, also, Lynch v. The Economy, 27 Wis. 69.

[8] Commonwealth v. Howard, 13 Mass. 221; State v. Bishop, 7 Conn. 181; Rex v. Hymen, 7 T. R. 532.

would seem that the offense should not go unpunished and the state thereby lose its portion of the penalty, simply because no citizen elected to prosecute an action in the role of informer. It has also been held that where the state prosecutes a civil action for the penalty or when the grand jury returns an indictment it must appear of record that the informer complained in the prescribed manner, under the statute,[1] or the whole penalty will go to the state. No acts can render one an informer unless he actually gave the information leading to conviction,[2] nor can a person claim an informer's share of the penalty simply because he is the sole witness in the case.[3] Some of the courts hold that if the party injured is authorized to sue for the penalty, any one of several parties jointly injured by the same offense may sue and recover the penalty,[4] but it has been held, on the other hand, that a penal action can not be maintained by several persons jointly as common informers unless the statute authorizes such a proceeding,[5] although it seems that if the penalty is specific and does not rest in computation, only one action can be brought, and the parties injured must join in a single action in order that all may secure their respective shares.[6] The party who first commences a *qui tam* action thereby acquires an interest in the penalty of which he can not be divested by a subsequent suit by another informer, even though judgment first be awarded in the latter suit,[7] but while the informer, by first instituting suit or, perhaps by giving the necessary information to the prosecutor, acquires a right superior to any other informer of the same offense, he does not acquire a vested right to the penalty until after judgment,[8] and his right to a share of a for-

---

[1] Commonwealth v. Frost, 5 Mass. 53; Commonwealth v. Davenger, 10 Phila. (Pa.) 478; State v. Smith, 49 N. H. 155.

[2] Brewster v. Gelston, 1 Paine (U. S.) 426.

[3] Williamson v. State, 16 Ala. 431. See United States v. Conner, 138 U. S. 61, s. c. 11 Sup. Ct. R. 229.

[4] Phillips v. Bevans, 23 N. J. L. 373.

[5] Commonwealth v. Winchester, 3 Pa. L. J. Rep. 34.

[6] Edwards v. Hill, 11 Ill. 22.

[7] Beadleston v. Sprague, 6 Johns. (N. Y.) 101; Pike v. Madbury, 12 N. H. 262.

[8] Bank of St. Mary's v. State, 12 Ga. 475; Chicago, etc., R. Co. v. Adler, 56 Ill. 344; Confiscation Cases, 7 Wall. (U. S.) 454.

feiture does not vest until the money is ready for distribution. Accordingly, his share of the penalty will be determined by the law in force at the time of the final decree directing distribution.[1] By some of the statutes a private citizen is given the right to sue in his own name to recover the penalty, where, after a certain time, the proper officers, having had notice of the offense, fail to sue for the state, and in such a case it is no defense that the suit is brought without authority of such officers or without notice to them.[2] Upon recovery, the informer properly designated on the record as such may secure his share of the penalty by motion to have it paid to him.[3] It has been held that the fact that the informer rode on trains repeatedly for the sole purpose of accumulating penalties accruing by reason of overcharges in fare will not constitute a defense, and the penalties may be collected.[4] In one instance it was held that in case of the compromise of an action for a penalty the informer was entitled to his share of the amount the same as if it had been prosecuted to judgment.[5] But, ordinarily, penal actions brought *qui tam* can not be compromised without leave of the court,[6] and as a general rule it will require that the portion due the state be paid.[7]

§714. The penalty—Computation.—Where the statute simply prescribes a maximum and minimum penalty, and does

[1] United States v. About Twenty-five Thousand Gallons, etc., 1 Ben. (U. S.) 367; United States v. Twenty-five Thousand Segars, 5 Blatchf. (U. S.) 500; United States v. Eight Barrels Distilled Spirits, 1 Ben. (U. S.) 472; United States v. Connor, 138 U. S. 61, 11 Sup. Ct. R. 229. But in Indiana, Missouri, Kentucky and elsewhere this common law rule has been altered somewhat by statute and it is only necessary that the penalty should have accrued before the repeal of the statute imposing it.

[2] Commissioners v. Purdy, 13 Abb. Pr. (N. Y.) 434, 36 Barb. 266; Root v. Alexander, 63 Hun 557, 18 N. Y. S. 632. See Pomroy v. Sperry, 16 How. Pr. (N. Y.) 211.

[3] Hull v. Welsh, 82 Iowa 117, 47 N. W. 982.

[4] St. Louis, etc., R. Co. v. Gill, 54 Ark. 101, 11 L. R. A. 452, 15 S. W. Rep. 18; Fisher v. N. Y. Cent. and H. R. Co., 46 N. Y. 644; Parks v. Nashville, etc., R. Co., 13 Lea 1, 18 Am. & Eng. R. Cas. 404.

[5] Hull v. Welsh, 82 Iowa 117, 47 N. W. 982.

[6] Middleton v. Wilmington, etc., R. Co., 95 N. Car. 167; Caswell v. Allen, 10 Johns. (N. Y.) 118; Raynham v. Rounseville, 9 Pick. (Mass.) 44.

[7] Wardens v. Cope, 2 Ired. (N.

not specify who shall fix the amount, it has been held that the question is for the jury.[1] And if the statute directs that the penalty shall equal double the value of certain goods, the jury may determine the value of the goods by verdict, and the court may double the amount;[2] but if, after proper instructions, the jury find for a specific sum, that sum is presumed to be twice the value of the goods, unless otherwise shown in the verdict.[3] If the offense is single and continuous and it is plain that the statute only contemplates one offense, it is held that only one penalty will have accrued up to the time the action is brought;[4] but where a specific penalty is declared for each separate offense, or for each day or week of its continuance, the amount of the judgment may be a matter of computation for the court, after conviction for each offense.[5] In some cases, however, it has been maintained that it was not the legislative intent that an informer be allowed to open a book account of penalties earned, and, delaying suit a year, bring an action for an enormous sum, and that but one penalty could be recovered for all delin-

---

Car.) 44. See Bradway v. LeWorthy, 9 Johns. (N. Y.) 251; Haskins v. Newcomb, 2 Johns. (N. Y.) 405.

[1] McDaniel v. Gate City Co., 79 Ga. 58; Hines v. Darling, 99 Mich. 47, 57 N. W. R. 1081. It seems to us that a statute which does not designate the penalty, or give some rule for ascertaining it, should be held invalid.

[2] Dygert v. Schenck, 23 Wend. (N. Y.) 446.

[3] Cross v. U. S., 1 Gall (U. S.) 26.

[4] It has also been held that if the offense was committed by several persons, only one penalty can be recovered, and the offense will not be regarded a distinct offense by each. Palmer v. Conly, 4 Den. (N. Y.) 374; Conley v. Palmer, 2 N. Y. 182; Ingersoll v. Skinner, 1 Den. (N. Y.) 540. Held, under Ohio statute providing that railway companies shall provide a blackboard and register the time of arrival, lateness, etc., of each train, and providing a penalty of $10 for "each violation of the provisions of the act," that failure to provide a blackboard renders the company liable to only one penalty, although a large number of trains were unregistered. State v. Cleveland, etc., R. Co., 8 Ohio C. C. R. 604. Under the differently worded Indiana statute it was held that one penalty could be collected for each train not registered, no blackboard having been erected. State v. Indiana, etc., R. Co., 133 Ind. 69.

[5] Where the penalty was for each day's continuance, it was held unnecessary to declare in separate counts, but all were properly grouped together. Toledo, etc., R. Co. v. Stephenson, 131 Ind. 203, 30 N. E. R. 1082. But the second offense must be of the same nature as the first, and there must be conviction. Scot v. Turner, 1 Root (Conn.) 163.

quencies prior to each action,[1] and this is on the additional ground that the penalty is not for the satisfaction of the injured party, for he still has his action for damages. But where the language of the statute is plain, courts, although sometimes reluctant, have felt bound to award a penalty for each violation, where the sum amounted to many thousands of dollars.[2] Following the rule of strict construction, it has been held that only one penalty can be assessed where the plaintiff has paid, in one payment, an account covering a large number of overcharges, where the statute provided a penalty for each "collection or demand."[3] In enforcing the federal statute relating to confinement of animals, the courts have refused to construe the law so as to make the confinement of each animal a separate offense, where a large shipment was made.[4] We have elsewhere discussed the constitutionality of statutes giving double damages.[5] Such statutes are in their nature penal,[6] but are construed by some courts as remedial. Statutes giving the party injured by overcharges a right of action for an amount equal to three and even five times the legal amount of freight have been upheld.[7]

§ 715. When "penalty" and when "liquidated damages."—It is often a close question whether the statute in prescribing

[1] Fisher v. N. Y., etc., R. Co., 46 N. Y. 644; Parks v. Nashville, etc., R. Co., 13 Lea 1; Murray v. Galveston, etc., R. Co., 63 Tex. 407. This seems to us the true doctrine. But the statute may so plainly provide for separate prosecutions that nothing remains for the courts but to enforce it as it is written.

[2] See State v. Kansas City R. Co., 32 Fed. R. 722, per Brewer, J.

[3] Porter v. Dawson Bridge Co., 157 Pa. St. 367. The practice of giving penalties to informers has been condemned by able jurists, and certainly statutes giving such penalties should not be extended by construction.

[4] United States v. Boston, etc., R. Co., 15 Fed. R. 209.

[5] See *ante*, § 669.

[6] Bettys v. Milwaukee, etc., R. Co., 37 Wis. 323; Missouri Pac. R. Co. v. Humes, 115 U. S. 512, 22 Am. & Eng. R. Cas. 557.

[7] Burkholder v. Union Trust Co., 82 Mo. 572, 23 Am. & Eng. R. Cas. 656; Mo. Pac. R. Co. v. Humes, 22 Am. & Eng. R. Cas. 557, and authorities cited; Spealman v. Mo. Pac. R. Co., 71 Mo. 434. A statute awarding five times the legal freight rate to the victim of overcharges was upheld in Herriman v. Burlington, etc., R. Co., 57 Iowa 187, 9 Am. & Eng. R. Cas. 339.

an amount to be paid to the person injured by its disregard contemplates the enforcement of a penalty or the liquidation of damages. It arises when the court proceeds to give effect to the widely different rules of construction which apply respectively to penal statutes and to statutes creating or defining a civil liability. It has been held in condemnation proceedings where by the terms of the inquisition the company is required to pay a fixed sum to the owner in case it fails to perform specified conditions that such sum is not a penalty but liquidated damages.[1] And the rule was held to be substantially the same as that which prevails in cases of contracts. Where it is stated in "clear and unambiguous terms that a certain sum shall be paid by way of compensation upon a breach of the contract, or where the covenant is to do several acts the damages arising from the breach of which are uncertain, and incapable of being ascertained by any fixed pecuniary standard," the sum so fixed will be considered as liquidated damages and not as a penalty.[2] On the other hand it has been as clearly laid down that where the breach is capable of accurate valuation and the parties have agreed on a different sum to be paid in default, such sum is to be regarded as a penalty and not as liquidated damages.[3] The reasoning in these cases has been applied to statutes, in regard to which the same distinction has been drawn, and it has been held that laws prescribing the amount to be paid upon a violation, where without reference to the statute the person injured has a cause of action, simply prescribe the measure of damages and do not denounce a penalty;[4] in other words, that such statutes are not penal but remedial.[5] In some states it is held that the "forfeiture" as designated by the statute is a penalty

---

[1] Pennsylvania R.Co. v. Reichert, 58 Md. 261, s. c. 10 Am. & Eng. R. Cas. 429.

[2] Geiger v. The Western Maryland R. Co., 41 Md. 4.

[3] St. Louis, etc., R. Co. v. Shoemaker, 27 Kan. 677, s. c. 11 Am. & Eng. R. Cas. 379.

[4] Houston, etc., R. Co. v. Harry, 63 Tex. 256, 18 Am. & Eng. R. Cas. 502.

[5] Frohock v. Pattee, 38 Me. 103; Quimby v. Carter, 20 Me. 218; Reed v. Inhabitants of Northfield, 13 Pick. 94.

§ 715   PENAL OFFENSES.   1033

as is also the attorney's fee allowed,[1] but while the attorney's fees may be allowed in addition to the statutory amount prescribed, it is said that it can not be maintained that they constitute a "penalty for exercising the right of defense."[2] The Connecticut statute providing that railroad companies shall be liable for fires kindled by sparks from their locomotives, although they are free from negligence, is held not to be penal but remedial,[3] and statutes allowing treble the usurious interest collected, double damages for fraudulently removing property, and double damages for injuries resulting from defects in highways have respectively been held to be remedial statutes which should be liberally construed.[4] Even revenue laws imposing forfeitures for fraud were held by the supreme court of the United States not to be technically penal in such a sense as to require strict construction.[5] On the other hand, it is held that statutes relating to criminal offenses and all statutes which impose as punishment any penalties, pecuniary or otherwise, or forfeitures of money or other property, or which provide for the recovery of damages beyond just compensation to the party injured, whether recovered in a suit by the state or by a private individual, are penal in the sense that they fall under the rule of strict construction.[6] This is the only doctrine that can be defended on principle. The question must, however,

---

[1] Dow v. Beidelman, 49 Ark. 455, s. c. 31 Am. & Eng. R. Cas. 14; Kan. Pac. R. Co. v. Mower, 16 Kan. 573; Kan. Pac. R. Co. v. Yanz, 16 Kan. 583.

[2] Burlington, etc., R. Co. v. Dey, 82 Iowa 312.

[3] Newton v. N. Y., etc., R. Co., 56 Conn. 21, 32 Am. & Eng. R. Cas. 347. In our opinion this doctrine is of doubtful soundness.

[4] Gray v. Bennett, 3 Met. (Mass.) 522; Stanley v. Wharton, 9 Price 301; Reed v. Northfield, 13 Pick. (Mass.) 94, s. c. 23 Am. Dec. 662. But see, contra, Hines v. Wilmington, etc., R. Co., 95 N. Car. 434; Coble v. Shoffner, 75 N. Car. 42; Bay City, etc., R. Co. v. Austin, 21 Mich. 390; Cohn v. Neeves, 40 Wis. 393.

[5] Taylor v. United States, 3 How. (U. S.) 197.

[6] Henderson v. Sherborne, 2 M. & W. 236; Nicholson v. Fields, 7 H. & N. 810; Brooks v. Western Union Tel. Co., 56 Ark. 224; Cumberland, etc., Canal Corp. v. Hitchings, 57 Me. 146; Bay City, etc., R. Co. v. Austin, 21 Mich. 390; Camden, etc., R. Co. v. Briggs, 22 N. J. L. 623; Schooner Bolina, 1 Gall. (U. S.) 75; Hines v. Wilmington, etc., R. Co., 95 N. Car. 434. See 23 Am. & Eng. Cyc. of Law, 374, 378, 379.

necessarily depend largely upon the language of the particular statute and is to be determined, in part, by the apparent intention that the statute carries of providing for redress or for punishment.

§ 716. **Indictment of railroad companies for causing death.** —In some of the states railroad companies are by statute made subject to indictment and fine in case the death of any person is caused by their negligence or that of their servants. Such statutes have been held constitutional and valid.[1] It has been held under the old New Hampshire statute that the form of the indictment is governed, in the main at least, by the principles of the criminal law,[2] but as the fine or penalty is recoverable, under most of the statutes, for the widow, children, next of kin, heirs or other designated person more or less dependent upon the deceased, it is said that such statutes are designed to take the place of Lord Campbell's act,[3] and it is held that the indictment must show the existence of some person of the class designated.[4] It is also held, for the same reason, that the same rules of evidence and principles of law are to be applied on the trial as in analogous civil actions for damages.[5] Thus, under the Maine statute, it has been held that the deceased must be shown to have been free from contributory negligence.[6] But the contrary has been held as to passengers in Massachusetts.[7] In Maine, but not in Massachusetts, it seems

[1] Boston, etc., R. Co. v. State, 32 N. H. 215, and authorities cited in following notes *infra*. But see Smith v. Louisville, etc., R. Co., 75 Ala. 449, s. c. 21 Am. & Eng. R. Cas. 157.

[2] State v. Manchester, etc., R. Co., 52 N. H. 528; State v. Wentworth, 37 N. H. 196. For the history of the New Hampshire legislation and the present statute in that state, see French v. Maconia, etc., Co., 20 Atl. 363; Tiffany on Death by Wrongful Act, § 47.

[3] State v. Grand Trunk R. Co., 58 Me. 176.

[4] State v. Grand Trunk, etc., R. Co., 60 Me. 145; Commonwealth v. Eastern R. Co., 5 Gray (Mass.) 473; State v. Gilmore, 24 N. H. 461. Compare Commonwealth v. Boston, etc., R. Co., 11 Cush. (Mass.) 517.

[5] State v. Grand Trunk R. Co., 58 Me. 176; State v. Maine Cent. R. Co., 77 Me. 490, s. c. 21 Am. & Eng. R. Cas. 216; State v. Manchester, etc., R. Co., 52 N. H. 528.

[6] State v. Maine Cent. R. Co., 76 Me. 357, s. c. 19 Am. & Eng. R. Cas. 312.

[7] Commonwealth v. Boston, etc., R. Co., 134 Mass. 211; Merrill v. Eastern R. Co., 139 Mass. 252. As to one not

§ 717   PENAL OFFENSES.   1035

that the remedy by indictment is limited to cases where the injured person dies immediately, and is not an employe of the company.[1] The proof should support the theory of the indictment, and a material variance may be fatal to a recovery.[2]

§ 717. **Violation of Sunday laws.**—It has been held in some instances that a railroad company is a person within the purview of general penal statutes against "persons" requiring the observance of Sunday.[3] Many states have regulations looking particularly to the operation of railroads on that day. Some prohibit the running of freight or excursion trains, and the loading or unloading of freight. Some designate the hours during which trains may run or the emergency which shall excuse their running during the prohibited hours.[4] These statutes are upheld as falling properly within the police power, and they are enforced by penalty recoverable sometimes by civil action and in some states by indictment. The weight of authority, however, is to the effect that the running of trains is excluded from the statute on the ground of its being "a work of necessity," where such exception is made,[5] but some well reasoned decisions have held it not to be so.[6]

a passenger the same ruling was made as in Maine. Commonwealth v. Boston, etc., R. Co., 126 Mass. 61.

[1] State v. Maine Cent. R. Co., 60 Me. 490; State v. Grand Trunk, etc., R. Co., 61 Me. 114. But see Commonwealth v. Metropolitan, etc., R. Co., 107 Mass. 236; Daley v. Boston, etc., R. Co., 147 Mass. 101, s. c. 33 Am. & Eng. R. Cas. 298; Commonwealth v. Boston, etc., R. Co., 8 Am. & Eng. R. Cas. 297. The Massachusetts statute has been changed several times, and under some of the acts death need not result, and special provision is also made for recovery where a servant is killed.

[2] See Commonwealth v. Fitchburg R. Co., 120 Mass. 372; Commonwealth v. Fitchburg R. Co., 126 Mass. 472; State v. Maine Cent. R. Co., 81 Me. 84, s. c. 16 Atl. R. 368; Commonwealth v. Boston, etc., R. Co., 133 Mass. 383, s. c. 8 Am. & Eng. R. Cas. 297.

[3] State v. Baltimore, etc., R. Co., 15 W. Va. 362, 36 Am. R. 803; Sparhawk v. Union, etc., R. Co., 54 Pa. St. 401, 439. In West Virginia the law has since been changed by statute. State v. Norfolk, etc., R. Co., 33 W. Va. 440, 43 Am. & Eng. R. Cas. 330.

[4] 2 Stimson's Am. Stat., § 8824.

[5] Com. v. Louisville, etc., R. Co., 80 Ky. 291, 44 Am. R. 475; Augusta R. Co. v. Renz, 55 Ga. 126; Smith v. New York, etc., R. Co., 46 N. J. L. 7, 18 Am. & Eng. R. Cas. 399. Carrying forward of trains loaded with stock is a work of necessity and not illegal. Philadelphia, etc., R. Co. v. Lehman, 56 Md. 209, 40 Am. R. 415.

[6] Sparhawk v. Union, etc., R. Co., 54 Pa. St. 401; Com. v. Jeandell, 2

CORP. 66

§ 718. **Indictment of railroad company for maintaining a nuisance.**—A railroad company may be indicted for maintaining a nuisance.[1] Thus, railroad companies have been indicted for placing and leaving cars in a public highway,[2] for failing to keep a crossing in repair,[3] for failure to give warnings or signals at crossings,[4] for unlawfully cutting through and obstructing a public highway,[5] and for permitting pools of water to form on their land and become stagnant.[6] So, they are liable for maintaining a private nuisance to those who are specially injured thereby.[7] But there are many acts that might constitute a nuisance if performed by an individual which will not constitute a nuisance by a railroad company. This is especially true

---

Grant's Cas. (Pa.) 506; Johnston v. Com., 22 Pa. St. 102. This rule has been changed by statute in Pennsylvania. The decision of Strong, J., in Sparhawk v. Union, etc., R. Co., *supra*, is a valuable contribution to the law on this subject.

[1] Northern Cent. R. Co. v. Commonwealth, 90 Pa. St. 300, s. c. 5 Am. & Eng. R. Cas. 318; State v. Vermont Cent. R. Co., 27 Vt. 103; Commonwealth v. New Bedford, etc., Co., 2 Gray (Mass.) 339; Reg. v. Great North, etc., R. Co., 9 Q. B. 315; Louisville, etc., R. Co. v. State, 3 Head (Tenn.) 523; note in 14 Am. & Eng. R. Cas. 152, and authorities in following notes, *infra*.

[2] State v. Morris, etc., R. Co., 23 N. J. L. 360; Cincinnati R. Co. v. Com., 80 Ky. 137; State v. Western, etc., R. Co., 95 N. Car. 602; State v. Troy, etc., R. Co., 57 Vt. 144; *post*, § 719.

[3] State v. Morris, etc., R. Co., 23 N. J. L. 360, and authorities cited; Paducah, etc., R. Co. v. Com., 80 Ky. 147, s. c. 10 Am. & Eng. R. Cas. 318; Memphis, etc., R. Co. v. State, 87 Tenn. 746, s. c. 11 S. W. R. 946; People v. New York, etc., R. Co., 74 N. Y. 302; *post*, § 719.

[4] Louisville, etc., R. Co. v. Commonwealth, 13 Bush (Ky.) 388; Louisville, etc., R. Co. v. Com., 80 Ky. 143, s. c. 44 Am. R. 468.

[5] Reg. v. Longton Gas. Co., 2 El. & E. 651; Commonwealth v. Nashua, etc., R. Co., 2 Gray (Mass.) 54; Pittsburgh, etc., R. Co. v. Reich, 101 Ill. 157; Fanning v. Osborne, 102 N. Y. 441; Elliott on Roads and Streets 479; *post*, § 719.

[6] City of Salem v. Eastern R. Co., 98 Mass. 431, s. c. 96 Am. Dec. 650. This, however, was not a prosecution by indictment, but was an action by a city, under a statute, to recover the expense of removing the nuisance.

[7] Baltimore, etc., R. Co. v. Fifth Baptist Church, 108 U. S. 317, s. c. 11 Am. & Eng. R. Cas. 15; Little Rock R. Co. v. Brooks, 39 Ark. 403, s. c. 17 Am. & Eng. R. Cas. 152; Pennsylvania R. Co. v. Angel, 41 N. J. Eq. 316, s. c. 56 Am. R. 1; Cogswell v. New York, etc., R. Co., 103 N. Y. 10, s. c. 56 Am. R. 6, and note; Brown v. Eastern, etc., R. Co., 22 Q. B. 391, s. c. 37 Am. & Eng. R. Cas. 558; Jones v. Railroad Co., 107 Mass. 261.

where the alleged nuisance merely affects the public. A railroad company authorized by the legislature to construct and operate a road for the public use is thereby relieved from many of the consequences attending the construction and operation of a road by an individual without such authority, and it may, perhaps, be stated as a general rule that, so long as it keeps within the scope of the powers and authority granted, a railroad company is not liable either civilly or criminally for a nuisance which is the necessary result of the construction and operation of its road, in accordance with its charter,[1] although it may be made liable for many acts of commission or omission by express legislation under the police power. It has been

---

[1] State v. Louisville, etc., R. Co., 86 Ind. 114, s. c. 10 Am. & Eng. R. Cas., 286; Uline v. New York Cent., etc., R. Co., 101 N. Y. 98; Danville, etc., R. Co. v. Com., 73 Pa. St. 29; Randall v. Jacksonville, etc., R. Co., 19 Fla. 409, s. c. 17 Am. & Eng. R. Cas. 184; Chope v. Detroit, etc., R. Co., 37 Mich. 195, s. c. 26 Am. R. 512; Eaton v. Boston, etc., R. Co., 51 N. H. 504; Rogers v. Kennebec, etc., R. Co., 35 Me. 319; Rex v. Pease, 4 B. & Ad. 30. Certainly this is true as to the state, but it is frequently said that the legislature can not authorize a private nuisance, and it can not take away or destroy individual rights, such as the right of access by authorizing additional burdens upon a highway. Elliott on Roads and Streets, 484, 485, and authorities cited. Where property has been taken, however, under the right of eminent domain the property-owners are presumed to have been compensated at the time it was taken, for the inconvenience arising from the ordinary operation of the road. Clark v. Hannibal, etc., R. Co., 36 Mo. 202; Porterfield v. Bond, 38 Fed. R. 391; Dearborn v. Boston, etc., R. Co., 24 N. H. 179; Chicago, etc., Co. v. Loeb, 118 Ill. 203, s. c. 8 N. E. R. 460, and numerous authorities cited; Lafayette, etc., Co. v. New Albany, etc., Co., 13 Ind. 90; Swinney v. Fort Wayne, etc., Co., 59 Ind. 205; Lafayette, etc., Co. v. Murdock, 68 Ind. 137; Indiana, etc., Co. v. Allen, 113 Ind. 308; White v. Chicago, etc., Co., 122 Ind. 317. "Railroads can not be operated without fuel, and proper structures for supplying engines therewith at convenient points for that purpose. They are necessarily incidental to the operation of the road. The owners of property near a railroad necessarily suffer inconvenience, such as detention by trains upon the track, the noise of passing trains, the smoke emitted from engines and the like, for which they can not recover in a suit for damages." Pierce on Railroads, 210; Rorer on Railroads, 457; Randle v. Pacific, etc., Co., 65 Mo. 325; Parrot v. Cincinnati, etc., Railway Co., 10 Ohio St. 624; Cosby v. Owensboro Railway Co., 10 Bush 288; Struthers v. Dunkirk, etc., Railway Co., 87 Pa. St. 282; Dunsmore v. Central, etc., R. Co., 72 Iowa 182, s. c. 33 N. W. R. 456. See, also, Pennsylvania Co. v. Lippincott, 116 Pa. St. 472; Pennsylvania Co. v. Marchant, 119 Pa. St. 541.

held that a provision in the charter of a turnpike company imposing a penalty for failing to keep its road in repair does not, *ipso facto*, take away its liability to indictment,[1] and it has also been held, on the other hand, that a corporation can not be indicted for maintaining a nuisance while in the hands of a receiver.[2] But, while this is doubtless true when the nuisance is created and maintained by the receiver, we think there may be cases where the company remains in existence, in which the company might be held liable for a nuisance caused by itself and not connected with the operation of the road by the receiver.

§ 719. **Obstruction of highways.**—Railroad companies, in many jurisdictions, are liable to indictment for the obstruction of public highways, sometimes under general statutes and sometimes under statutes directed specifically against them.[3] In Tennessee it is held that a railroad company is indictable, under the common law, for obstructing highways while constructing their road, if they can prevent obstruction of the highway by building bridges or substituting a road, which must be done within a reasonable time, and that this is the rule, whether the charter prohibits the obstruction or not.[4] In most of the states the matter is regulated by statutes which prescribe the penalty and the mode of collecting it,[5] but in the absence of statutes the railroad company is amenable to the common law. In Indiana the statute imposes a

---

[1] Susquehanna, etc., Turnpike Co. v. People, 15 Wend. (N. Y.) 267; President, etc., v. People, 9 Barb. (N. Y.) 161.

[2] State v. Vermont Cent. R. Co., 30 Vt. 108; State v. Wabash Ry., 115 Ind. 466, s. c. 17 N. E. R. 909, 1 L. R. A. 179.

[3] State v. Morris, etc., R. Co., 23 N. J. L. 360; State v. Vermont Cent. R. Co., 27 Vt. 103, 107; Louisville, etc., R. Co. v. State, 3 Head (Tenn.) 523, s. c. 75 Am. Dec. 778; Northern Cent. R. Co. v. Com., 90 Pa. St. 300.

[4] Louisville, etc., R. Co. v. State, 3 Head (Tenn.) 523, s. c. 75 Am. Dec. 778, citing Redfield on Railways, 515–518; Commonwealth v. Erie, etc., R. Co., 27 Pa. St. 339, s. c. 67 Am. Dec. 471.

[5] See Northern Cent. R.Co. v.Comm., 90 Pa. St. 300; Pittsburgh, etc., R. Co. v. Comm., 101 Pa. St. 192; Illinois, etc., R. Co. v. State, 71 Miss. 253; State v. Floyd, 39 S. Car. 23; State v. Dubuque, etc., Railroad Co., 88 Iowa 508; Town of Corning v. Head, 33 N. Y. S. 360, 86 Hun 12.

penalty upon "any person" who shall, "unnecessarily and to the hindrance of passengers," obstruct any highway, and declares that the word "persons" shall here include corporations. Strictly construing this statute, the court held that an action seeking to recover the penalty for failure to restore a highway, after construction of the railroad, would not lie, but said that the company could be compelled, by mandate, to restore the highway to its original condition.[1] Under the same statute the company was required to pay the penalty for each day of the continuance of obstruction, where the road was constructed at such a grade as to make the highway passing under it impassable.[2] Railroad companies, in most states, are made liable to penalties for obstructing passage over a highway by allowing their trains to stand on crossings beyond a reasonable or necessary time.[3] It has been held that the simple stopping of trains on the highway does not constitute the offense unless it has actually obstructed travel.[4] A railroad company has been held not to be liable to a fine for obstructing a street in a town having no ordinance on the subject where the statute provides for a fine for obstructing a street for a longer time "than the ordinance shall prescribe."[5] Railroad companies necessarily have the right to construct their road upon their right of way over highways, but the common law, and, in many states, special laws relating to highways, require that they shall do so without unnecessary inconvenience to the public. The right of way over public highways is generally obtained on the condition, either implied or specified in the grant or condemnation proceedings, that after construction the highway shall be restored to a condition at least as good as the original, and upon failure of such

---

[1] Cummins v. Evansville, etc., R. Co., 115 Ind. 417, citing Indianapolis, etc., R. Co. v. State, 37 Ind. 489; State v. Demaree, 80 Ind. 519; Clawson v. Chicago, etc., R. Co., 95 Ind. 152.

[2] Toledo, etc., R. Co. v. Stephenson, 131 Ind. 203, 30 N. E. R. 1082.

[3] See Com. v. Boston, etc., R. Co., 135 Mass. 550; Illinois, etc., R. Co. v. State, 71 Miss. 253, 14 So. R. 459; ante, § 718.

[4] Illinois, etc., R. Co. v. People, 49 Ill. App. 538, 540, 542. But this must depend upon the particular statute involved.

[5] Illinois, etc., R. Co. v. State, 71 Miss. 253, 14 So. R. 459.

restoration prosecution may follow,[1] and it is not necessary that a demand first be made upon the defendant to restore the highway.[2] Where the company claims to have constructed a sufficient substitute for the highway impaired the question is for the jury.[3]

§ 720. **Failure to maintain accommodations at station.**—It is generally conceded that railroad companies may, by statute, be required to maintain such station-houses as will accommodate their passengers, and it has even been held by a few courts, in the absence of express statutory requirement, that mandamus will lie to compel the construction of a station at a proper and necessary place.[4] But in some states there are statutes prescribing penalties for such omission, which may be enforced by suit;[5] and it has been held, in the absence of a penal statute, that where the station is poorly kept and is unsuitable for its purpose, the company may be liable to indictment and fine for criminal negligence in the performance of its public duties.[6] Where two companies had both violated a statute by not providing waiting-rooms at the crossing of their roads, it was held that either was liable separately, and that they need not be joined as defendants, and one com-

---

[1] State v. Ohio River R. Co., 38 W. Va. 242, 18 S. E. R. 582; State v. Monongahela R. Co., 37 W. Va. 108, 16 S. E. R. 519; Chicago, etc., R. Co. v. People, 44 Ill. App. 632; People v. New York, etc., R. Co., 89 N. Y. 266, 10 Am. & Eng. R. Cas. 266; People v. Chicago & Alton R. Co., 67 Ill. 118; Paducah, etc., R. Co. v. Commonwealth, 80 Ky. 147, 10 Am. & Eng. R. Cas. 318; Pittsburgh, etc., R. Co. v. Commonwealth, 101 Pa. St. 192, 10 Am. & Eng. R. Cas. 321. See Louisville, etc., R. Co. v. Commonwealth, (Ky.) 26 S. W. R. 536.

[2] Town of Corning v. Head, 33 N. Y. S. 360, 86 Hun 12.

[3] State v. Monongahela R. Co., 37 W. Va. 108, 16 S. E. R. 519; Roberts v. Chicago, etc., R. Co., 35 Wis. 679.

[4] State, ex rel. Mattoon, v. Republican, etc., R. Co., 17 Neb. 647, s. c. 22 Am. & Eng. R. Cas. 500; State, ex rel. Moore, v. Chicago, etc., R. Co., 19 Neb. 476, s. c. 27 N. W. R. 434. But see ante, § 641.

[5] Bonham v. Columbia, etc., R. Co., 26 S. Car. 353, 30 Am. & Eng. R. Cas. 177; State v. Wabash, etc., R. Co., 83 Mo. 144, 25 Am. & Eng. R. Cas. 133; State v. Concord, etc., R. Co., 59 N. H. 85; State v. Alabama, etc., Co., 67 Miss. 647, 42 Am. & Eng. R. Cas. 681; State v. Kansas City, etc., R. Co., (Mo.) 32 Fed. R. 722.

[6] McKinney v. I. C. R. Co., 6 Iowa Ry. Com. 557.

pany was compelled to pay the penalty for each day of the continuance of the violation.[1] Where it was made the duty of the railroad commission to direct the building of station-houses and to prescribe their dimensions, the company was held not liable to the penalty for each day of a violation of the order of the commission, as the commissioners had failed to prescribe the dimensions.[2] In most of the states there are statutes requiring railway companies to maintain stations and freight depots either under the order of railway commissioners or where some prescribed population or amount of business exists to demand them, and in some cases the offices and waiting-rooms are required to be open and in condition to receive the public for a designated time before the arrival of trains. In some instances the neglect to follow the statute constitutes a misdemeanor on the part of the officer or servant, and in other cases the statute denounces a penalty against the corporation.[3]

§ 721. Statutory signals—Stops at Crossings.—The legislatures of the different states possess and freely exercise the power to prescribe regulations for the moving and operation of trains with safety both to the passengers and to the public. In most cases they require that each locomotive shall carry a bell and whistle and prescribe the signals which shall be given upon approaching crossings, upon starting trains, or while moving through populous neighborhoods. Most cities exercise the power through ordinances.[4] These regulations are enforced sometimes by penalty against the corporation and sometimes by fine or even imprisonment of the servant who disregards them.[5] Where the statute imposes a penalty for each failure

[1] State v. Kansas City, etc., R. Co., 32 Fed. R. 722, per Brewer, J.
[2] State v. Alabama, etc., R. Co., 67 Miss. 647, 42 Am. & Eng. R. Cas. 681. As to extent of power of railroad commissions, see chapter on State Railroad Commissions, ante.
[3] 2 Stimson's Am. Stat., § 8803.
[4] Pittsburgh, etc., Co. v. Brown, 67 Ind. 45, 33 Am. Rep. 73; Galena, etc., R. Co. v. Loomis, 13 Ill. 548; Com. v. Eastern R. Co., 103 Mass. 254, 4 Am. Rep. 555; Kaminitsky v. Northeastern R. Co., 25 S. Car. 53; Galena, etc., R. Co. v. Appleby, 28 Ill. 283. See 2 Stimson's American Statutes, §§ 8814, 8822.
[5] People v. N. Y.,etc.,R. Co.,25 Barb. (N. Y.) 199; State v. Kansas City, etc., Railroad Co., 54 Ark. 546, 16 S.W. Rep.

to give the statutory signals, the penalty may be collected once for each time a crossing is passed without the giving of the signals,[1] and it has been held that the regulation applies whether the crossing be at grade or not.[2] While, ordinarily, an action for damages will lie where injury results from failure to observe these regulations, there are instances in which the only liability is the penalty.[3] Statutes requiring signals are mandatory and there is ordinarily no question for the jury where the facts showing a failure to give the signals are undisputed.[4] The enforcement is often by indictment.[5] In many states trains are required to come to a full stop at the crossing with other railroads, except where safety appliances are used or where watchmen are kept constantly, and failure to stop is punishable, under some of the statutes, by indictment.[6]

§ 722. Blackboards and bulletins at stations.—In Indiana and Ohio railroad companies are required to erect at each station having a telegraph office a blackboard, upon which it is the duty of the agent to record the time of the arrival of trains, and "if late, how much." Both statutes have been upheld as constitutional, and the language of the Ohio statute has been construed to impose but one penalty where no blackboard was

---

567; St. Louis, etc., R. Co. v. State, 58 Ark. 39, 22 S. W. Rep. 918; Missouri, etc., R. Co. v. Reynolds, (Tex.) 26 S. W. Rep. 879; Beck v. Portland, etc., R. Co., 25 Ore. 32, 34 Pac. Rep. 753; Western Union R.Co.v.Fulton, 64 Ill. 271; St. Louis, etc., R. Co. v. State, 55 Ark. 200, 17 S. W. R. 806. An ordinance imposing imprisonment upon the person in charge of train who crosses a street, upon which street cars run, without being signaled by the watchman required to be at the crossing is held valid as within the grant of powers of the city. State v. Cozzens, 42 La. Ann. 1069, 8 So. Rep. 268.

[1] People v. N. Y., etc., R. Co., 25 Barb. (N. Y.) 199.

[2] People v. New York, etc., Railroad Co., 13 N. Y. 78. *Contra*, Jenson v. Chicago, etc., R. Co., 86 Wis. 589, 57 N. W. R. 359.

[3] Chicago, etc., R. Co. v. McDaniels, 63 Ill. 122.

[4] Havens v. Erie R. Co., 53 Barb. (N. Y.) 328; Semel v. N. Y., etc., R. Co., 9 Daly (N. Y.) 321. We suppose, however, that there may be cases where necessity will excuse or justify the failure to give the prescribed signals.

[5] Commonwealth v. Boston, etc., R. Co., 133 Mass. 383, 8 Am. & Eng. R. Co. 297, and note citing authorities.

[6] Commonwealth v. Chesapeake, etc., R. Co., (Ky.) 29 S. W. Rep. 136.

erected at all, on the ground that the failure to erect the board was a necessary part of each violation.[1] The more explicit language of the Indiana statute has been held to authorize a penalty for each train not recorded after a reasonable time being allowed for the erection of the blackboard, and a large accumulation of penalties has several times been allowed,[2] but it is held not to apply to a company operating a line, the regular time of passage from one end to the other of which is less than the time required to elapse between the posting of the bulletin and the arrival of the train, for the reason that it would be useless, impracticable, and not within the implication of the statute.[3] It has been held that the owner of a railway not operating it is not within the letter or spirit of the act, and that a railway company created by the consolidation of two companies is not liable for a failure of the lessee of one of the extinguished companies to give the blackboard notices.[4] It is also held a valid exercise of the police power to require a railroad company to annually fix its passenger and freight rates and post a schedule in each of its depots or stations, and such a requirement is not a regulation of interstate commerce.[5]

§ 723. **Unlawful speed.**—The speed of trains moving through cities and towns where not regulated by statute is usually governed by ordinances enacted within the local exercise of the police power. The statutory limitations upon the rate of speed of trains at highway crossings are held to be limitations upon the company's franchises, and a violation may be prosecuted

[1] State v. Cleveland, etc., R. Co., 8 Ohio C. C. R. 604. It is doubtful whether these statutes referred to in the text are constitutional, but they have been upheld. Pennsylvania Co. v. State, 142 Ind. 428, s. c. 41 N. E. R. 937.

[2] State v. Indiana, etc., R. Co., 133 Ind. 69, 32 N. E. R. 817; State v. Penn. R. Co., 133 Ind. 700, 32 N. E. R. 822; Pennsylvania Co. v. State, 142 Ind. 428, 41 N. E. R. 937. It has been held that the statute does not apply to night trains at stations where there is no night telegraph operator. Terre Haute, etc., R. Co. v. State, 142 Ind. 428, s. c. 41 N. E. R. 952.

[3] State v. Kentucky, etc., Bridge Co., 136 Ind. 195, 35 N. E. R. 991.

[4] State v. Pittsburgh, etc., R. Co., 135 Ind. 578.

[5] Chicago, etc., R. Co. v. Fuller, 17 Wall. (U. S.) 560, affirming Fuller v. Chicago, etc., R. Co., 31 Iowa 187.

by indictment or otherwise.[1] Where the penalty is awarded to "the person aggrieved," it has been held to be collectible at the suit of one who suffered injury resulting from the frightening of his horse because of the illegal rate of speed, although no actual collision occurred.[2]

§ 724. Other penal regulations.—There are many penal regulations applying to the operation of railroads which are not easily classified. In some states railroad commissioners have jurisdiction to require gates, flagmen, or electric signals at railroad crossings.[3] In other states this power is to a limited extent conferred upon the county commissioners, and may be exercised by the towns and cities through ordinances, and in most of the states the municipal corporations are granted the power to make reasonable regulations.[4] Railroads are usually required to provide large signs at road crossings to warn travelers of the proximity of the track and its danger, and to maintain and keep in repair proper crossings.[5] In Indiana cities and towns have power to require railroad intersection with streets to be lighted at night.[6] Different states make it a penal offense to place a freight car in the rear of a passenger coach in mixed trains.[7] And most states have regulations requiring that cars shall be rendered comfortable and safe, that tools shall be carried to be available in case of accident, that certain combustibles be not carried, and in several states automatic

[1] Horn v. Chicago, etc., R. Co., 38 Wis. 463; Mobile, etc., R. Co. v. State, 51 Miss. 137; Merz v. Missouri Pac. R. Co., 88 Mo. 672; Haas v. Chicago, etc., R. Co., 41 Wis. 44; People v. Boston, etc., R. Co., 70 N. Y. 569; Buffalo, etc., R. Co. v. Buffalo, 5 Hill (N. Y.) 209; Chicago, etc., R. Co. v. Haggerty, 67 Ill. 113; Whitson v. Franklin, 34 Ind. 393; Clark v. Boston, etc., R. Co., 64 N. H. 323, 31 Am. & Eng. R. Cas. 548; Penn., etc., R. Co. v. Lewis, 79 Pa. St. 33.

[2] Chicago, etc., R. Co. v. People, 120 Ill. 667, 12 N. E. R. 207; Grand Trunk R. Co. v. Rosenberger, 9 Can. S. C. 311, s. c. 19 Am. & Eng. R. Cas. 8.

[3] Massachusetts, Vermont, Connecticut, Ohio, Michigan, South Carolina. See People v. Long Island R. Co., 58 Hun 412, s. c. 34 N. Y. S. R. 715.

[4] See 2 Stimson's Am. Stat., § 8814; R. S. Ind. 1894, § 5174.

[5] 2 Stimson's Am. Stat., § 8814.

[6] R. S. Ind. 1894, § 5173. Also Ohio. See Cincinnati, etc., R. Co. v. Sullivan, 32 Ohio St. 152.

[7] R. S. Ind. 1894, § 5191; Cook's Penal Code (N. Y.), § 422; 2 Stimson's Am. Stat., § 8823.

§ 724   PENAL OFFENSES.   1045

couplers are required on all freight and passenger cars.[1] Penalties are exacted of railroads in some jurisdictions where employes are retained who are color blind, or in the habit of becoming intoxicated, and in a number of states the law designates the number of brakeman to accompany a train, and prescribes the use of air brakes or others equally as good.[2] Railroad companies are generally required to fence their right of way, and to maintain cattle-guards at public crossings. Failure to do so is sometimes punished by specific penalties, but in many cases by imposing an absolute liability for stock killed by reason of the neglect.[3] Sometimes the kind of switch to be used is prescribed by law, and the company is required to construct switches, frogs, guard rails, and the like, in such a manner as to insure the minimum danger to employes or others walking over them.[4] In many states the laws regulate the stopping of trains at stations, designating the length of time a train must stop and the frequency of stopping to be observed at stations of certain descriptions.[5] It is sometimes made a penal offense to fail to announce the stopping place previous to arrival at each station.[6] In a number of states it is provided that upon demand of the federal authorities any or all trains must carry mail or transport troops in time of war, and a heavy penalty is denounced for refusal.[7] There are many other penal regulations in the different states, which we will not enumerate here, but which will be treated under the subject of carriers, and the discussion of the operation of the road.

---

[1] 2 Stimson's Am. Stat., § 8821. As to heating cars, see People v. Clark, 14 N. Y. Supp. 642; People v. N. Y., etc., R. Co., 55 Hun (N. Y.) 409.

[2] 2 Stimson's Am. Stat., §§ 8820, 8825, 8826. Regulation as to color blindness held valid and violation punishable by indictment. Nashville, etc., R. Co. v. State, 83 Ala. 71, affirmed 128 U. S. 96, s. c. 38 Am. & Eng. R. Cas. 1. See also Baldwin v. Kouns, 81 Ala. 272, 31 Am. & Eng. R. Cas. 347. Legislative requirements as to qualifications of employes are valid. Smith v. Alabama, 124 U. S. 465, 33 Am. & Eng. R. Cas. 425.

[3] Stimson's Am. Stat., § 8815.

[4] Stimson's Am. Stat., § 8811.

[5] See Davidson v. State, 4 Tex. App. 545, s. c. 30 Am. R. 166; Galveston, etc., R. Co. v. La Gierse, 51 Tex. 189; Davis v. State, 6 Tex. App. 166. Compare State v. Noyes, 47 Me. 189; 2 Stimson's Am. Stat., § 8803.

[6] Parks v. Nashville, etc., R. Co., 13 Lea (Tenn.) 1, 18 Am. & Eng. R. Cas. 404.

[7] 2 Stimson's Am. Stat., §§ 8804, 8805.

§ 725. Violations of federal regulations.—Under the constitutional power to regulate commerce congress has enacted federal statutes, which, for the most part, relate to the duties of the railroad as a common carrier, and sometimes extend to legislation for the safety of passengers, and the expeditious and safe carriage of livestock. It has been held that the power to regulate commerce includes that of punishing all offenses against commerce, such as larceny, where it does not thereby interfere with the internal police regulations of a state.[1] These statutes being penal are strictly construed, yet the construction must be fair and reasonable so as to give effect to the legislative will. Thus it was held that a statute forbidding the shipment of nitroglycerine on passenger trains extended to a shipment of dynamite and the statutory penalty was exacted.[2]

§ 726. Penalty for confinement of live stock.—Outside of the interstate commerce act of 1887, with its later amendments, there has been little affirmative federal legislation affecting railroad traffic, the most important act looking to the humane treatment of live stock, and requiring that animals shall not be confined in shipment more than twenty-eight hours continuously without unloading for food, rest and water, and providing a penalty for its violation to be recovered in a civil action in the name of the United States.[3] The statute requires that the time of confinement, immediately prior to delivery to the particular carrier, shall be included in estimating the period, and it is held that the carrier who has possession at the time the period expires is alone liable, although the first carrier may have contracted for through carriage,[4] and the statute has been held to apply only to shipments from one state to another.[5]

---

[1] United States v. Coombs, 12 Pet. (U. S.) 72; K. & I. Br. Co. v. L. & N. R. Co., 37 Fed. R. 567; and see penal clauses of various statutes.

[2] United States v. Saul, 58 Fed. R. 763; Rev. St. U. S., § 5353, and following.

[3] Rev. Stat. U. S., §§ 4386–4389; 5 Thomp. Corp., § 6435. Upheld as constitutional in U. S. v. Boston, etc., Co., 15 Fed. R. 209.

[4] Rev. Stat. U. S., § 4386; United States v. Louisville & N. R. Co., 18 Fed. R. 480.

[5] United States v. East Tennessee, etc., R. Co., 13 Fed. R. 642.

The liability of the company on account of omission of the duty imposed by this statute has been held to be avoided by a special contract by which the shipper agrees to feed and water the stock himself, but this doctrine has been questioned although followed in many states which have their own regulations.[1] Non-compliance with the statute is not excused by an accident resulting from negligence of the company.[2] In addition to the penalty, the carrier is liable to the owner in actual damages, but it has been held that the owner must affirmatively plead that the failure to feed, water and provide rest did not fall within the exceptions named in the statute.[3] The courts have refused to construe the statute so as to make the unlawful confinement of each animal a separate offense and thus multiply the penalty.[4]

§ 727. Offenses against railroads—Obstructing mails and interfering with interstate commerce.—Obstructing the United States mails,[5] or unlawfully conspiring and interfering with the passage of trains engaged in interstate commerce,[6] is indictable as a crime under the United States statutes. This has been announced as the law, not only in the cases to which we have just referred, but also in many other cases, elsewhere referred to, growing out of railroad strikes. In one of them, boys only twelve years old, who obstructed a mail car during a strike, were held liable to indictment and punishment for obstructing the mails.[7]

§ 728. Sale of tickets without authority—"Scalpers."—Some of the states prohibit "ticket scalping," or the sale, by

[1] Mo. Pac. R. Co. v. Texas & P. R. Co., 41 Fed. R. 913.
[2] Newport, etc., Co. v. U. S., 61 Fed. R. 488.
[3] Hale v. Mo., etc., Co., 36 Neb. 266, 54 N. W. R. 517.
[4] United States v. Boston, etc., R. Co., 15 Fed. R. 209.
[5] In re Charge to Grand Jury, 62 Fed. R. 828; United States v. Thomas, 55 Fed. R. 380; United States v. Clark, Fed. Cas. 14805; United States v. Kirby, 7 Wall. (U. S.) 482; United States v. Kane, 9 Sawy. (U. S. C. C.) 614.
[6] In re Grand Jury, 62 Fed. R. 834, 840; Thomas v. Cincinnati, etc., R. Co., 62 Fed. R. 803; United States v. Debs, 64 Fed. R. 724; United States v. Elliott, 62 Fed. R. 801.
[7] United States v. Thomas, 55 Fed. R. 380.

others than ticket agents of the respective roads, of railroad tickets. Such a statute being in the nature of a police regulation, it is held not to be a regulation of interstate commerce, and does not violate the constitution of the United States, nor does it violate the provision of a state constitution that "no person shall be deprived of life, liberty or property without due process of law."[1] But this regulation is generally held not to apply to the sale by a traveler of an unused portion of a ticket purchased for his own use.[2]

§ 729. **Climbing on cars—Evading payment of fare.**— Numerous special provisions for the protection of railroad companies in the operation of their roads and of the public patronizing them have been made by law in the various states. In many of the states, clinging to or climbing upon railroad engines or cars by one not a passenger or employe is made a misdemeanor.[3] So, in some states a penalty is prescribed for riding upon freight trains without lawful authority, and for entering passenger trains furtively, with the intention of riding thereon, and evading the payment of fare.[4]

§ 730. **Placing obstruction on track.**—It is made a penal offense in nearly all the states to place any obstruction upon the track of a railroad, or to willfully or maliciously commit any other act in order to throw from the track the engine and

[1] Fry v. State, 63 Ind. 552; Burdick v. People, 149 Ill. 600, s. c. 36 N. E. R. 948; Commonwealth v. Wilson, 37 Legal Intelligencer (Pa.) 484, 56 Am. & Eng. R. Cas. 230.

[2] In North Carolina the statute provides that "it shall be unlawful for any person to sell or deal in tickets issued by any railroad company unless he is a duly authorized agent of said railroad company." It was held that the prohibition does not extend to the simple sale of a ticket an individual may happen to have that he can not use, since such a sale is not "dealing in tickets," and is not within the reason for the statute. State v. Ray, 109 N. Car. 736, s. c. 52 Am. & Eng. R. Cas. 157; State v. Clarke, 109 N. Car. 739, note. In Indiana the statute does not apply to special, half-fare, or excursion tickets; and the sale of a ticket marked with the word "special" is *prima facie* not unlawful. State v. Fry, 81 Ind. 7.

[3] R. S. Ind., 1894, § 2290; Laws Md., 1892, Ch. 397, p. 543; Moore's & Elliott's Ind. Crim. L., § 670 (form of indictment, § 1190).

[4] Laws Md., 1892, Ch. 17, p. 17; Dyer v. County of Placer, 90 Cal. 276, s. c. 27 Pac. R. 197. See Reg. v. Frere, 4 El. & Bl. 598; Queen v. Paget, L. R. 8 Q. B. D. 151.

§ 730   PENAL OFFENSES.   1049

cars.¹ It is not material, in making out an offense under such a statute, to show that the railroad company whose track was obstructed was duly incorporated. The offense may be committed by obstructing the track of a railroad operated by private individuals.² It is not necessary to show that any engine or car was actually stopped or impeded.³ The principal element of criminality in the offense is the endangering of life or property, and it is sufficient to show that the act tended to render dangerous the passage of trains over the road.⁴ No in-

---

¹ Clifton v. State, 73 Ala. 473; Riley v. State, 95 Ind. 446; Coghill v. State, 37 Ind. 111; State v. Beckman, 57 N. H. 174; State v. Kilty, 28 Minn. 421; State v. Douglass, 44 Kan. 618, 26 Pac. R. 476; Barton v. State, 28 Tex. App. 483; Commonwealth v. Bakeman, 105 Mass. 53; Hodge v. State, 82 Ga. 643; Crawford v. State, 15 Lea (Tenn.) 343; People v. Adams, 16 Hun (N. Y.) 549; State v. Hessenkamp, 17 Iowa 25; People v. Dunkel, 39 Mich. 255; State v. Kluseman, 53 Minn. 541; Moores & Elliott's Ind. Crim. L., §§ 398, 989 (form of indictment). The word "railroad" in such an act includes street railroads. Commonwealth v. McCaully, 2 Pa. Dist. R. 63.

² Hodge v. State, 82 Ga. 643. See, also, Walker v. State, (Ga.) s. c. 22 S. E. R. 528. Under the California penal code the malicious destruction of a railroad track is a felony; and this applies to a track which is used for the running of cable street cars. People v. Stites, 75 Cal. 570, 17 Pac. R. 693; Commonwealth v. McCaully, 2 Pa. Dist. R. 63.

³ State v. Kilty, 28 Minn. 421; State v. Clemens, 38 Iowa 257. To sustain a conviction under the Texas statute, the evidence must show that the obstruction was such as might have endangered human life. Bullion v. State, 7 Tex. App. 462. But the persons whose lives were endangered need not be specified. Barton v. State, 28 Tex. App. 483.

⁴ State v. Wentworth, 37 N. H. 196. As to sufficiency of indictment, see State v. Oliver, 55 Kan. 711, s. c. 41 Pac. R. 954. In Riley v. State, 95 Ind. 446, the court says: "We suppose that if the obstruction was apparently sufficient to endanger the passage of trains, or to throw the engine or cars from the track, the offender ought not to be acquitted merely because, through a lack of judgment, he did not provide sufficient means to accomplish his criminal purpose. Under 3 and 4 Vict. Ch. 97, § 15, it is a crime to place an obstruction upon a railway track, even though the road has not yet been opened up for traffic. Regina v. Bradford, 8 Cox C. C. 309. But in Tennessee, the statute provided a punishment for the obstruction of a railroad track, whereby cars are thrown off the track. It was held that to make out the offense, some vehicle mentioned in the statute must be shown to have been thrown from the track, and that where it appeared that a handcar only had been derailed by the obstruction, a conviction could not be sustained, since the statute did not mention handcars. Harris v. State, 14 Lea (Tenn.) 485. It is not necessary to prove that all the obstructions named in the indictment were placed upon the road. It is suf-

tent to injure any particular person need be shown;[1] nor need a specific intent to do an injury to life or property be shown.[2] Evidence that the road was so obstructed as to endanger the passage of trains, and that the person obstructing it knew at the time that it was being used and operated as a railroad, will raise the presumption of malicious intent.[3] And this presumption can not be overcome by proof that the intention was merely to stop the train and claim a reward, or to do some other mischievous act by which no injury should be permitted to accrue to life or property.[4] The fact that the railroad has never become the legal owner of its right of way across defendant's land, or has been guilty of a breach of the contract by which such right was acquired, is no defense to an indictment against a land-owner for obstructing a railroad track where it crosses his land.[5] Evidence that the defendant placed a similar obstruction on another part of the track a short time after the offense under consideration has been held competent in trying an indictment for a crime of this character, as tending to raise the presumption of the defendant's guilt[6] and as part

ficient, in making out the crime, to show that the road was obstructed by any one of the articles alleged to have been placed thereon. Allison v. State, 42 Ind. 354.

[1] Commonwealth v. Bakeman, 105 Mass. 53. It is sufficient to charge the crime in the language of the statute, without setting out in the indictment the names of the persons whose lives were endangered. Barton v. State, 28 Tex. App. 483. As to indictment, see Riley v. State, 95 Ind. 446; State v. Kluseman, 53 Minn. 541, 55 N. W. R. 741; Commonwealth v. Hicks, 7 Allen (Mass.) 573; State v. Wentworth, 37 N. H. 196; McCarty v. State, 37 Miss. 411.

[2] Clifton v. State, 73 Ala. 473; People v. Adams, 16 Hun (N. Y.) 549.

[3] State v. Hessenkamp, 17 Iowa 25. Evidence of the probable consequences of the act is sufficient to warrant the jury in inferring a criminal purpose. Commonwealth v. Bakeman, 105 Mass. 53.

[4] State v. Beckman, 57 N. H. 174; State v. Johns, 124 Mo. 379, s. c. 27 S. W. R. 1115; Crawford v. State, 15 Lea (Tenn.) 343, s. c. 54 Am. R. 423. But advising and encouraging another to place an obstruction on the track, believing that it is so placed with malicious intent, is not sufficient to constitute a crime under such a statute where the person placing the obstruction on the track is a detective seeking evidence against the accused, and only places the obstruction for the purpose of obtaining such evidence. State v. Douglass, 44 Kan. 618, 26 Pac. R. 476. See, also, Nowell v. State, 94 Ga. 588, s. c. 21 S. E. R. 591.

[5] State v. Hessenkamp, 17 Iowa 25.

[6] State v. Wentworth, 37 N. H. 196.

of the *res gestæ*.[1] The English statute is designed to prevent any and all interference with the operation of railroads, and is much more general in its prohibition than the statutes of most of the states.[2] Under this statute it has been held a crime to place an obstruction on the track of a railroad which had not yet been opened up for traffic.[3] And one who piles rubbish on the track of a railroad,[4] or alters signals,[5] or stands upon the railroad right of way and makes gestures with his hands and arms,[6] thereby causing trains to stop, or otherwise interfering with the operation of the road, is guilty of obstructing the road within the meaning of the statute.

§ 731. **Shooting or throwing missile at car.**—Many states prescribe a penalty for shooting at or throwing any missile at a railroad car.[7] Under the North Carolina statute the indictment must charge that the car was in motion or stopped merely for a temporary purpose at the time the alleged offense was committed.[8] The court, in the case referred to, construed the statute as intended to secure the safety of persons upon the train and protect the cars while in use and not when in the round-house or in the yards of the company with no one upon them. But, under the Massachusetts statute, throwing a missile at a car is a penal offense, whether the car is in use at the time or not.[9] Where the offense denounced by the statute

[1] Barton v. State, 28 Tex. App. 483, s. c. 13 S. W. R. 783.
[2] 24 and 25 Vict. Ch. 97, § 15.
[3] Regina v. Bradford, 8 Cox C. C. 309.
[4] Roberts v. Preston, 9 C. B. N. S. 206.
[5] Regina v. Hadfield, 11 Cox C. C. 574, L. R. 1 Cr. Cas. Res. 253.
[6] Regina v. Hardy, 11 Cox C. C. 656.
[7] Under the Indiana statute it is murder to kill any human being by shooting or throwing at a car. R. S. Ind., 1894, §§ 2036, 2037. An indictment for shooting at and injuring a car under the Georgia statute must aver that the car belonged to a "chartered" railway company. Kiser v. State, 89 Ga. 421. An indictment under the Florida statute must set forth the facts and circumstances which constitute the offense. Hamilton v. State, 30 Fla. 229, s. c. 11 So. R. 523.
[8] State v. Boyd, 86 N. Car. 634, s. c. 9 Am. & Eng. R. Cas. 155. See, also, State v. Hinson, 82 N. Car. 597.
[9] Commonwealth v. Carroll, 145 Mass. 403, s. c. 14 N. E. R. 618.

consists in merely shooting or throwing at a car, it is, of course, unnecessary to prove that the car was struck.[1]

§ 732. Breaking into depot or car—Burglary.—Breaking and entering a railroad depot,[2] or station-house,[3] or a railroad car,[4] with intent to commit a felony, is made burglary by the statutes of most of the states. Breaking into a ticket office in the day-time, with intent to steal, is merely a misdemeanor in Massachusetts.[5] This is the general rule. In the absence of a statute changing the rule, the breaking and entering must be in the night-time in order to constitute burglary.[6]

§ 733. Injury to railroad property—Malicious trespass.—Injury to or interference with railroad property is made an offense by special statute in many states.[7] Even in the absence

---

[1] State v. Hinson, 82 N. Car. 597.

[2] State v. Scripture, 42 N. H. 485. If the depot was jointly used or occupied by two railroad corporations, it may be so charged in the indictment. State v. Edwards, 109 Mo. 315, s. c. 19 S. W. R. 91; State v. Bishop, 51 Vt. 287.

[3] Norton v. State, 74 Ind. 337. This case holds that it is sufficient to designate the railroad company by its corporate name in the indictment without averring its corporate existence, since that will be implied. In deciding this case the court said: "No innocent man can ever be put in peril by the adoption of this rule, and many guilty ones may by its operation, be prevented from escaping merited punishment." Burke v. State, 34 Ohio St. 79.

[4] Boyer v. Commonwealth, (Ky.) 19 S. W. 845; Lyons v. People, 68 Ill. 271; Nicholls v. State, 68 Wis. 416, s. c. 32 N. W. R. 543; State v. Parker, 16 Nev. 79. On a trial under the Alabama statute for breaking into a railroad car "upon or connected with a railroad in this state," it is not necessary to prove that the car was "standing on" the tracks of the railroad company. Johnson v. State, 98 Ala. 57, s. c. 13 So. R. 503.

[5] Commonwealth v. Carey, 12 Cush. (Mass.) 246.

[6] 2 Bish. Crim. L., § 106; 2 Am. & Eng. Ency of L. 659, 686.

[7] Clifton v. State, 73 Ala. 473. Offenses against property of steam-boats, railroads and other carriers made punishable. Act July 1, 1890 (Acts La. 1890, No. 47, p. 40). Malicious injury to railroad tracks, bridges, etc., punished by imprisonment at hard labor. Act March 2, 1891 (Laws Wash. 1891, c. 69, § 4, p. 120). The willful injury to or interference with railroad property made a misdemeanor. Act March 19, 1891 (St. Nev. 1891, c. 67, p. 78). The Minnesota statute declares that "any person who displaces, removes, injures or destroys a rail, sleeper,

of such a special statute an injury to the property of a railroad company, if committed with a malicious intent, would doubtless be punishable as malicious mischief or malicious trespass in most of the states.[1] But employes of a railroad company who remove a fence from real estate claimed by the company are not guilty of malicious trespass in the absence of any malicious intent.[2]

§ 734. Other crimes against railroad companies.—We have treated at some length many of the offenses against railroad companies which are specifically denounced by statute in most of the states; but there are many other crimes from which railroad companies as well as individuals may suffer, even though they are not expressly named in the statute defining the offense. We shall mention some of the most common offenses of this character, without considering them in detail. Railroad officers and employes have often been held guilty of embezzlement under general statutes,[3] and third persons have been held indictable for obtaining goods or money from railroad companies by false pretenses.[4] So, it has been held that the fraudulent and unlawful counterfeiting of a railroad ticket is forgery

switch, bridge, viaduct, culvert, embankment, or structure, or any part thereof attached to or appertaining to or connected with a railway" shall be punished. It was held that this did not apply to a fence or other structure not constituting a part of the railroad proper. State v. Walsh, 43 Minn. 444. Those structures forming parts of railway beds by which they span streams, chasms, ditches, etc., are "bridges," the willful and malicious burning of which is prohibited by the Florida statute. Duncan v. State, 29 Fla. 439, s. c. 10 So. R. 815.

[1] See State v. Simpson, 2 Hawks (N. Car.) 460; Rex v. Bowry, 10 Jur. 211; 1 Bish. Crim. L., § 1004; 2 Bish. Crim. L., § 955, et seq.

[2] Hughes v. State, 103 Ind. 344, s. c. 2 N. E. R. 956.

[3] See Ex parte Ricord, 11 Nev. 287; Calkins v. State, 18 Ohio St. 366; Commonwealth v. Tuckerman, 10 Gray (Mass.) 173; State v. Goode, 68 Iowa 593, s. c. 27 N. W. R. 772; State v. Porter, 26 Mo. 201. Compare Panama R. Co. v. Johnson, 63 Hun 629, s. c. 17 N. Y. Sup. 777; State v. Mims, 26 Minn. 191, s. c. 2 N. W. R. 492.

[4] Reg. v. Boulton, 2 C. & K. 917, s. c. 13 Jur. 1034, distinguished in Reg. v. Kilham, 11 Cox C. C. 561, s. c. 22 L. T. 625. See, also, White v. State, 86 Ala. 69, s. c. 5 So. R. 674; State v. Haven, 59 Vt. 399, s. c. 9 Atl. R. 841.

at common law.[1] Stealing a railroad ticket may also constitute larceny,[2] and so, of course, may the stealing of grain or other property from a car.[3] An interesting question arose in a recent case in which the defendant was charged with feloniously breaking and entering a freight car in the night-time with intent to commit larceny. The entry was made in one county, while the car was moving, and the defendant continued in the car, with the same felonious intent, until after the car had passed into another county, in which the defendant was indicted. The court held that there was, in law, a fresh entry in the latter county, and that the defendant was indictable therein.[4]

[1] Commonwealth v. Ray, 3 Gray (Mass.) 441. See, also, State v. Weaver, 94 N. Car. 836, s. c. 55 Am. R. 647, and note; Reg. v. Boult, 2 C. & K. 604, s. c. 61 Eng. C. L. 603.

[2] Eaton v. Farmer, 46 N. H. 200; McDaniels v. People, 118 Ill. 301, s. c. 8 N. E. R. 687; State v. Brin, 30 Minn. 522, s. c. 16 N. W. R. 406. But see State v. Hill, 1 Houst. Crim. (Del.) 421; State v. Musgang, 51 Minn. 556, s. c. 53 N. W. R. 874.

[3] Price v. State, 41 Tex. 215; Manson v. State, 24 Ohio St. 590; State v. Poynier, 36 La. Ann. 572; State v. Sharp, 106 Mo. 106, s. c. 17 S. W. R. 225; Smith v. State, 28 Ind. 321; Lucas v. State, 96 Ala. 51, s. c. 11 So. R. 216; Rogers v. State, 90 Ga. 463, s. c. 16 S. E. R. 205; Sikes v. State, (Tex. Crim. App.) 28 S. W. R. 688.

[4] Powell v. State, 52 Wis. 217, s. c. 9 N. W. R. 17, 9 Am. & Eng. R. Cas. 156.

CHAPTER XXX.

TAXATION OF RAILROAD PROPERTY.

§ 735. Taxation of railroads—Preliminary.
736. Legislative power.
737. Appropriate method of assessing.
738. Methods of taxation.
739. Statutory method of assessment exclusive.
740. Legislative discretion—Classification.
741. Equality and uniformity.
742. Duties of corporation—Rights of stockholders.
743. Failure of the corporation to make return — Effect on stockholder.

§ 744. Discrimination.
745. Lien of assessment.
746. Relinquishment of the power of taxation.
747. Exemption from taxation—Consolidation.
748. Right of exemption non-assignable.
749. Immunity from taxation not a franchise.
750. Exemption of property used in operating railroad.
751. Remedies—Injunction.
752. Tender of amount of taxes owing is required.

§ 735. **Taxation of railroads—Preliminary.**—The power of a state to tax railroad property of every description is a sovereign power, and over purely domestic or intrastate railroad companies the power of the state is supreme, but over railroad companies engaged in interstate commerce the power of the state is necessarily abridged by the commerce clause of the federal constitution. The property of a railroad company engaged in interstate commerce which is not used in its business of conducting commerce between the states is, of course, subject to taxation by the state to the same extent as the like property of any artificial or natural person. If, for instance, a railroad company is the owner of lots which are not used in connection with its business as a carrier of articles of interstate commerce the lots are subject to taxation by the state to the same extent as similar property of natural persons, and the power to tax such property is not affected by the commerce clause of the federal constitution. As the federal constitution exerts such an important influence upon the subject of taxation the subject can be more clearly presented by treating the class of railroad companies which may be denominated interstate railroads in a separate chapter, and accordingly we have adopted that method.

§ 736. **Legislative power.**—The legislature is invested with supreme power over the subject of taxation, except in so far as the constitution limits and abridges the power. Taxes must be levied by the legislature and the mode of assessing property must be prescribed by statute.[1] We do not mean, of course, that the exact sum shall be designated by statute, but we do mean that the tax shall be provided for by statute and due authority conferred upon state, county or municipal officers to designate the amount of the tax that shall be assessed. All taxation must rest upon legislation, and the law making department must provide the mode of assessment. Defects in the mode can not be remedied by the judiciary, but where a mode is provided and an exemption is made which the legislature had no power to make, the provision making the exemption will fall and the other part of the statute will stand.[2] Of

[1] Wisconsin Cent. Ry. v. Taylor Co., 52 Wis. 37; State v. Central, etc., Co., 21 Nev. 260; Porter v. Rockford, etc., Co., 76 Ill. 561; Louisville, etc., Co. v. Commonwealth, 10 Bush 43; City of Dubuque v. Chicago, etc., Co., 47 Iowa 201; Railroad Co. v. Pennsylvania, 15 Wall. 300; North Missouri, etc., Co. v. Maguire, 20 Wall. 46; Bragg v. Tufts, 49 Ark. 554; State Railroad Tax Cases, 15 Wall. 284; Delaware Railroad Tax Case, 18 Wall. 206; State v. Bentley, 23 N. J. L. 532; State v. Flavell, 24 N. J. L. 370; State Railroad Tax Cases, 92 U. S. 575; Turner v. Althaus, 6 Neb. 54; Union Pacific, etc., Co. v. Peniston, 18 Wall. 5; Ottawa v. McCaleb, 81 Ill. 559; Meriwether v. Garrett, 102 U. S. 472, 515; Rees v. City of Watertown, 19 Wall. 107, 116; Heine v. Levee Commissioners, 19 Wall. 655; Hyland v. Brazil, 128 Ind. 335. Judge Cooley again and again emphasizes the rule that the whole subject belongs to the legislative department. Cooley Taxation, 200, 378; Cooley Const. Lim. (5th ed.), 637. In Meriwether v. Garrett, *supra*, it was said, "The levying of taxes is not a judicial act. It has no elements of one. It is a high act of sovereignty, to be performed only by the legislature."

[2] Little Rock, etc., Co. v. Worthen, 46 Ark. 312; Huntington v. Worthen, 120 U. S. 97; Norris v. Boston, 4 Met. (Mass.) 282.

§ 737   TAXATION OF RAILROAD PROPERTY.   1057

all matters of policy and expediency, the legislature is the exclusive judge and its determination is final and conclusive.[1] The policy of the law is to compel all property held or used for purposes of gain or profit to bear its burden of taxation, but as there can be no effective assessment of taxes without legislative authority, it is evident that the failure to include all property may have the effect to relieve it from taxation. A *casus omissus* can not be supplied by the courts,[2] and where the legislature omits to subject property to taxation it may escape, for the courts have no power to lay taxes upon property. It has been held that where a method is not specifically prescribed for taxing corporate property, the tax must be paid by the owner of the shares of stock, but we suppose that this can be true only in cases where provision is made for taxing the stock in the hands of the stockholder.[3]

§ 737. **Appropriate method of assessing.**—The best method of taxing the property of a railroad company forming part of its line and used in the operation of its road is by regarding it as a unit and assessing the property as an entirety, since any other method would dissect the property into fragmentary parts and lead to confusion and injustice. Some of the courts hold that the property can only be taxed as an entirety,[4] but in our opinion the legislature is, in the absence of constitutional provisions prescribing the method of assessing the property, the sole judge of the method that shall be pursued. The power of the legislature is so broad and comprehensive that it is difficult to conceive upon what principle it can be correctly held that the only method that it can provide is that of assessing the property as an entirety.[5]

[1] Spinney, *Ex parte*, 10 Nev. 323; Cooley on Taxation, 165, 324, 378; Cooley Const. Lim. (5th ed.), 637, 638.
[2] Gwynne *v.* Burnell, 7 Cl. & F. 572, 696; Jones *v.* Smart, 1 T. R. 44.
[3] Conwell *v.* Town of Connersville, 15 Ind. 150; King *v.* City of Madison, 17 Ind. 48.
[4] Applegate *v.* Ernst, 3 Bush 648, s. c. 96 Am. Dec. 272. See, generally, Graham *v.* Mt. Sterling Coal Co., 14 Bush 425; Franklin County *v.* Nashville, etc., Co., 12 Lea 521, s. c. 17 Am. & Eng. R. Cas. 445; *In re* Railroad School Tax, 78 Mo. 596, s. c. 17 Am. & Eng. R. Cas. 491.
[5] There are many cases recognizing the validity of assessments by

§ 738. Methods of taxation.—The four principal methods of taxation are, (1) on the capital stock, (2) on the corporate property, (3) on the franchises, (4) on the business done by the corporation.[1] As the levying of taxes and the mode of assessment are matters for legislative consideration and determination the legislature may, where no constitutional provision forbids a choice of methods, select the method, and the method selected is exclusive. While the courts may declare invalid a statute which is in conflict with the constitution, they can not supervise or control legislative discretion nor can they dictate the policy to be pursued.[2]

counties. Huntington v. Central Pacific, etc., Co., 2 Sawy.(U. S. Cir.) 503; People v. Placerville, etc., Co., 34 Cal. 656; People v. McCreey, 34 Cal. 432; Orange, etc., Co. v. Alexandria, 17 Gratt. 176; Albany, etc.,Co.v. Canaan, 16 Barb. 244; Albany, etc., Co. v. Osborn, 12 Barb. 223; Mohawk, etc., Co. v. Clute, 4 Paige 384; Wilson v. Weber, 96 Ill. 454, s. c. 5 Am. & Eng. R. Cas. 112; State v. Illinois Central R. Co., 27 Ill. 64, s. c. 79 Am. Dec. 396; Sangamon, etc., Co. v. Morgan, 14 Ill. 163, s. c. 56 Am. Dec. 497; Providence, etc., Co. v. Wright, 2 R. I. 459. See, generally, Missouri River, etc., Co. v. Morris, 7 Kan. 210; State v. Severance, 55 Mo. 378; Richmond, etc., Co. v. Alamance County, 84 N. Car. 504; Chicago, etc., Co. v. Davenport, 51 Iowa 451; The Tax Cases, 12 Gill & J. 117.

[1] Tennessee v. Whitworth, 117 U. S. 129; Louisville, etc., Co. v. State, 8 Heisk. (Tenn.) 663, 795. See Cleveland, etc., Co. v. Backus, 133 Ind. 513; State v. Hamilton, 5 Ind. 310; King v. City of Madison, 17 Ind. 48; Whitney v. City of Madison, 23 Ind. 331, 335. There is reason for saying that there is a fifth method, namely a tax on the profits of the business, but we have followed the usual course in naming the methods of taxation. Beach on Corp., § 798; Cook on Stockholders (3d ed.), § 562; Pierce on Railroads, 474. The reason given for not making a separate division of profits of the business is that it is included in the third method of tax on the franchise, but the reason is hardly satisfactory.

[2] Mr. Justice Bradley forcibly expressed the general rule in Legal Tender Cases, 12 Wall. 457, 561. "The legislative department," said that able judge, "being the nation itself speaking by its representatives, has a choice of methods and is the master of its own discretion." The State v. Haworth, 122 Ind. 462, 467; Carr v. State, 127 Ind. 204, 208; City of Dubuque v. Chicago, etc., Co., 47 Iowa 196; City of Davenport v. Chicago, etc., Co., 38 Iowa 633; City of Dubuque v. Illinois, etc., Co., 39 Iowa 56. In State v. Kolsem, 130 Ind. 434, 440, it was said: "Where the principal subject belongs, there the incidents belong. Means, methods and the like belong to the department that is invested with power over the general subject. It is for that department to make choice of modes and

§ 739. **Statutory method of assessment exclusive.**—Where the statute prescribes a specific method for assessing or valuing the property of railroad companies the method prescribed excludes all others and must be pursued.[1] The legislative method is always exclusive. The rule is settled that where the legislature classifies property and prescribes the mode in which it shall be taxed, neither the taxing officers nor the courts can prescribe any other.

§ 740. **Legislative discretion—Classification.**—The legislature may, in its discretion, provide different methods for assessing corporations of different classes, and a statute can not be successfully assailed upon the ground that it prescribes a method of assessing railroad corporations different from that prescribed for assessing other corporations.[2] Classifications may be made and railroad corporations may constitute a distinct and separate class of corporations, and a mode of assessing and valuing their property may be prescribed different from that prescribed for taxing and valuing the property of other corporations. The legislative discretion is broad, and no matter how unjustly or capriciously it may be exercised the courts are powerless to interfere, but they may interfere in cases where the legislature transcends its constitutional powers. The question is power or no power; if there be power the judiciary can not alter, amend or annul the statute, if there be no power the courts may annul the statute by adjudging it to be void.

means." Cooley Const. Lim. (4th ed.), 129, 637; Cook on Stockholders, § 562; Cooley Taxation, 378, 324; Desty on Taxation, 83, 84.

[1] Louisville, etc., Co. v. Warren County, 5 Bush 243.

[2] Chamberlain v. Walter, 60 Fed. R. 788; St. Louis, etc., Co. v. Worthen, 52 Ark. 529, s. c. 7 L. R. A. 374; Cincinnati, etc., Co. v. Kentucky, 115 U.S. 321; Kentucky Railroad Tax Cases, 92 U. S. 663; Bell's Gap Railroad Co. v. Pennsylvania, 134 U. S. 232; Pacific Express Co. v. Seibert, 142 U. S. 339; Ancona v. Becker, 14 Pa. Co. Ct. 73; Western Union, etc., Co. v. Poe, 64 Fed. R. 9, overruling Western Union, etc., Co. v. Poe, 61 Fed. 449; State v. Jones, 51 Ohio St. 492, s. c. 37 N. E. R. 945; Cummings v. Merchants', etc., Bank, 101 U. S. 160; San Francisco, etc., Co. v. State Board, 60 Cal. 12; Central Iowa Co. v. Board, etc., 67 Iowa 199; Pulaski County, etc., Cases, 49 Ark. 518; Missouri v. Lewis, 101 U. S. 22; Home, etc., Co. v. New York, 134 U. S. 594; Missouri, etc., Co. v. Mackey, 127 U. S. 205, s. c. 33 Am. & Eng. R. Cas. 390; Minneapolis, etc., Co. v. Beckwith, 129 U. S. 26.

§ 741. **Equality and uniformity.**—Where the constitution requires that taxes shall be equal and uniform the mode of assessing railroad companies must be uniform, that is, one company of the same class and character can not be assessed in one method and another company of precisely the same kind and character in a materially different method.[1] Corporations of different classes may be assessed in different methods, but corporations of the same class can not be assessed in different methods. The general rule is as we have stated it, but it is possible that in very rare instances there may be some peculiar elements that will carry the case out of the operation of the general rule. Where the constitution of the state requires equality and uniformity of taxation the tax upon railroad property can not rightfully be materially or essentially greater than that imposed upon other property, although, as we have seen, the mode of assessment may be different. This is so independently of the influence of the federal constitution.[2]

§ 742. **Duties of corporation—Rights of stockholders.**—Where the tax is laid upon the corporation the corporate officers must make the required returns and pay the taxes. The tax in such a case is laid upon the legal entity and must be paid out of the corporate revenues. If the tax is unauthorized and not enforceable the resistance to its enforcement is properly made by the corporation and not its members. Where there are errors or irregularities prejudicial to the interests of the corporation it is incumbent upon the corporate officers to take

---

[1] Worth v. Wilmington, etc., Co., 89 N. Car. 291, s. c. 45 Am. R. 679; Illinois Tax Cases, 92 U. S. 575; Durach's Appeal, 62 Pa. St. 491; State v. Lathrop, 10 La. Ann. 398; Kneeland v. Milwaukee, 15 Wis. 454; City of New Orleans v. Kaufman, 29 La. Ann. 283, s. c. 29 Am. R. 328; Pittsburg, etc., R. Co. v. State, 49 Ohio St. 189, s. c. 16 L. R. A. 380. But see Chicago, etc., Co. v. Siders, 88 Ill. 320.

[2] Board of Assessment v. Alabama, etc., R. Co., 59 Ala. 551; Schmidt v. Galveston, etc., Co., (Tex. Civ. App.) 24 S. W. R. 547; Board, etc., v. Chicago, etc., R. Co., 44 Ill. 229; Chicago, etc., Co. v. Board, etc., 44 Ill. 244; Cumberland, etc., Co. v. City of Portland, 37 Me. 444; State Treas., etc., v. Auditor, etc., 46 Mich. 224, 13 Am. & Eng. R. Cas. 296. See, however, City of Dubuque v. Illinois Cent. Co., 39 Iowa 56; Mississippi Mills v. Cook, 56 Miss. 40; Williams v. Rees, 9 Biss. 405; Francis v. Atchison, etc., Co., 19 Kan. 303.

measures to secure the proper correction or appropriate relief. The shareholders, however, have an interest in preventing the enforcement of illegal taxes against the corporation and in having errors corrected, and this enables them to invoke judicial assistance in the event that the corporate officers refuse to perform their duty.[1] To entitle a stockholder to relief he must show, in addition to the other essential facts, that the corporate officers have been guilty of fraud, or, upon proper request, have refused to take proper steps to protect the corporate interests.

§ 743. **Failure of the corporation to make return—Effect on stockholder.**—Corporations may be made the instrumentalities for collecting from the stockholders the tax, or the tax may be laid directly on the shares of stock in the hands of the shareholders or it may be laid upon the corporation. Where the tax is laid on the shares of stock in the hands of the stockholders it can not be accurately said that the tax is laid on the corporation, for, where the tax is placed upon the stock in the hands of the shareholders, the tax is really laid upon individual and not upon corporate property. If the tax is laid on the corporation and not on the members the breach of duty in failing to make returns is that of the corporation, and the members can not be in fault for failing or refusing to return the property for taxation. The corporation may, if guilty of a culpable breach of duty, be liable to such penalties as may be provided, but the stockholder can not be.[2]

[1] Bailey v. Atlantic, etc., Co., 3 Dill. 22; Parmley v. St. Louis, etc., R. Co., 3 Dill. 13; Greenwood v. Freight Co., 105 U. S. 13; Davenport v. Dows, 18 Wall. 626; City of Louisville v. Louisville, etc., 90 Ky. 409, 14 S. W. R. 408; Lenawee, etc., Bank v. City of Adrian, 66 Mich. 273; Dodge v. Woolsey, 18 How. (U. S.) 331; Foote v. Linck, 5 McLean 616; Paine v. Wright, 6 McLean 395; State Bank, etc., v. Knoop, 16 How. U. S. 369; Wilmington, etc., Co. v. Reed, 13 Wall. 264; Davenport v. Dows, 18 Wall. 626. The corporation is a necessary party to such a suit, and the suit should be brought in behalf of all the stockholders.

[2] Whitaker v. Brooks, 90 Ky. 68, 13 S. W. R. 355; Gillespie v. Gaston, 67 Texas 599, 4 S. W. R. 248. In the first of the cases cited it was said: "It seems to us it is a sufficient answer by the stockholder when called upon to assess his stock to say the law requires the corporation to assess

§ 744. **Discrimination.**—Where the constitution of the state requires equality and uniformity, there can not be a material and unjust discrimination against railroad property.[1] This is so, independently of any federal questions or rules. The requirement of equality and uniformity is violated by imposing a burden upon railroad companies heavier than that imposed upon other persons or corporations. We suppose, however, that the burden imposed must be palpably and materially greater than that imposed upon other property, since in all systems of taxation there is some inequality.[2]

its corporate property and declares that the stock of the shareholder shall be exempt. It matters not to him whether the corporation has done so or not. If not, it should be made to do so. The grant of exemption to the stockholder has not been made to depend upon this being done. If it can not be done under existing law, then resort must be had to additional legislation, instead of a court attempting to annul a plain legislative grant of exemption to one because another has failed to perform what is perhaps a legal duty. If the statute declares without condition (as it does) that the corporation, and not the stockholder, shall answer for the tax, then it is immaterial to him in the present condition of the law whether the corporation has or has not listed its property and paid the tax. He need only show that the law places the burden upon the corporation."

[1] In Chicago, etc., Co. v. Board, 54 Kan. 781, 39 Pac. R. 1039, the court said: "While exact uniformity and equality can not be had, and while mistakes and omissions by assessors may not, in all cases, be the subject of adequate remedy in the courts, yet for the gross injustice and violation of the law complained of, there ought to be some remedy." At another place it was said: "We do not think the courts are powerless to prevent such a gross discrimination in the assessment and taxation of property as is shown in this case, where one class of property is assessed and taxed at its actual value, and all other property in the same county is assessed and taxed at only twenty-five per cent. of its value.' See Stanley v. Supervisors, 121 U. S. 535, s. c. 7 Sup. Ct. R. 1234.

[2] If property of other persons and corporations is taxed only once, double taxation of railway property would be a discrimination, against which the courts should interpose their power. Cumberland Marine, etc., Co. v. City of Portland, 37 Me. 444; New York, etc., R. Co. v. Sabin, 26 Pa. St. 242; Osborn v. New York, etc., 40 Conn. 491; Hannibal, etc., Co. v. Shacklett, 30 Mo. 550; State v. Hannibal, etc., Co., 37 Mo. 265. But see Dunleith, etc., Co. v. City of Dubuque, 32 Iowa 427; Orange, etc., Co. v. City of Alexandria, 17 Gratt. 176. This general doctrine obtains where there is a constitutional limitation requiring equality and uniformity, but some of the decisions hold that it does not prevail where there is no such limitation. United States, etc., Co. v. State, 79 Md. 63, 28 Atl. R. 768.

§ 745.   TAXATION OF RAILROAD PROPERTY.   1063

§ 745. Lien of assessment.—The principle that railroad property is assessed as a unit requires the conclusion that the lien for the taxes assessed attaches to the entire property.[1] The question may, of course, be controlled by statutory provisions, but where there are no statutory provisions prescribing a different rule the lien will fasten upon the entire property within the state. We suppose, however, that taxing officers could not sell the property lying outside of the limits of the state for the reason that a state law can have no extra-territorial effect.

§ 746. Relinquishment of the power of taxation.—The general rule is that where there is no constitutional prohibition interdicting it, the power of taxation may be relinquished in particular instances.[2] It may well be doubted whether the cases which hold this doctrine have not departed from principle since the power of taxation, being a sovereign one, is incapable of abdication or surrender, but the decisions have settled the question. The presumption is that there has been no relinquishment of the power, and the party who insists that it has been relinquished must clearly and fully establish his assertion, otherwise it will be adjudged that there was no relinquishment.[3]

[1] Maricopa, etc., R. Co. v. Arizona, 156 U. S. 347, s. c. 15 Sup. Ct. R. 391.

[2] New Jersey v. Wilson, 7 Cranch 164; Tomlinson v. Branch, 15 Wall. 460; Tomlinson v. Jessup, 15 Wall. 454; Home of Friendless v. Rouse, 8 Wall. 430; Ohio, etc., Co. v. Debolt, 16 How. (U. S.) 416; Humphrey v. Pegues, 16 Wall. 244; Pacific, etc., Co. v. Maguire, 20 Wall. 36; McGee v. Mathis, 4 Wall. 143; Railroad Co. v. Loftin, 105 U.S. 258; Dodge v. Woolsey, 18 How. (U. S.) 331; Mobile, etc., Co. v. Tennessee, 153 U. S. 486; Franklin Branch Bank v. State, 1 Black (U. S.) 474; Wright v. Sill, 2 Black (U.S.) 544; Piqua Bank v. Knoop, 16 How. (U. S.) 369; Columbia, etc., Co. v. Chilberg, 6 Wash. 612, s. c. 34 Pac. R. 163; State v. Wright, 41 N. J. L. 478; Natchez, etc., Co. v. Lambert, 70 Miss. 779; Commonwealth v. Philadelphia, etc., Co., 164 Pa. 252, 30 Atl. R. 145; Barnes v. Kornegay, 62 Fed. R. 671; Louisville, etc., v. Gaines, 3 Fed. R. 266; South Pacific Co. v. Laclede County, 57 Mo. 147; Gardner v. State, 21 N. J. L. 557; LeRoy v. East-Saginaw Railroad Co., 18 Mich. 233; State Bank v. People, 5 Ill. 303; City of St. Louis v. Manufacturers' Savings Bank, 49 Mo. 574; Farmers' Bank v. Commonwealth, 6 Bush 127; Mayor of Mobile v. Stonewall Insurance Co., 53 Ala. 570.

[3] Keokuk, etc., Co. v. State, 152 U. S. 301, s. c. 14 Sup. Ct. R. 592; Mobile, etc., Co. v. Tennessee, 153 U. S.

§ 747. **Exemption from taxation—Consolidation.**—The rule that exemption from taxation does not exist unless the exemption is conferred by clear statutory provisions would seem to require the conclusion that where two railroad corporations are consolidated, the right to exemption is lost unless expressly or impliedly saved by the statute authorizing the consolidation. The theory of the adjudged cases, however, is that where the consolidated corporation becomes essentially a new corporation, the right of exemption is lost, but if the identity of the two corporations is preserved the right of exemption is not destroyed.[1] Whether the right of exemption is lost must depend

486, s. c. 14 Sup. Ct. R. 986; People v. Cook, 148 U. S. 397, s. c. 13 Sup. Ct. R. 645; Wells v. Hyattsville, 77 Md. 125, 26 Atl. R. 357, s. c. 20 L. R. A. 89; Vicksburg Railroad Co. v. Dennis, 116 U.S.665; City of Richmond v. Richmond, etc., Co., 21 Gratt. 604; Louisville, etc., Co. v. Gaines, 3 Fed. R. 266; Cook v. State, 33 N. J. Eq. 474; Wisconsin, etc., Co. v. Taylor County, 52 Wis.37, s. c. 1 Am. & Eng. R. Cases 532; Railroad Co. v. Maine, 96 U. S. 499; City of Portland v. Portland, etc., Co., 67 Me. 135; State v. Baltimore, etc., Co., 48 Md. 49; Illinois, etc., Co. v. Goodwin, 94 Ill. 262; Mobile, etc., Co. v. Moseley, 52 Miss. 127; Grand Gulf, etc., Co. v. Buck, 53 Miss. 246; Scotland County v. Missouri, etc., Co., 65 Mo. 123; Atlantic, etc., Co. v. Allen, 15 Fla. 637; Oliver v. Memphis, etc., Co., 30 Ark. 128.

[1] In the case of Shields v. Ohio, 95 U. S. 319, 323, the court said, speaking of the consolidation: "It could not occur without their consent. The consolidated company had then no existence. It could have none while the original corporation subsisted. All the old and the new could not co-exist. It was a condition precedent to the existence of the new corporation that the old ones should first surrender their vitality and submit to a dissolution. This being done, *eo instante* the new corporation came into existence." In Keokuk, etc., Co. v. State, 152 U. S. 301, s. c. 14 Sup.Ct.R. 592, the court held that the consolidated corporation was a new corporation and did not acquire a right of exemption conferred upon one of the constituent companies. The court said: "It follows that when the new corporation came into existence it came precisely as if it had been organized under a charter granted at the date of the consolidation and subject to the constitutional provisions then existing, which required (Art. 11, § 16) that no property, real or personal, should be exempted from taxation, except such as was used exclusively for public purposes; in other words, that the exemption from taxation contained in section 9 of the original charter of the Alexandria and Bloomfield Railway Company did not pass to the Missouri, Iowa and Nebraska Company. As was said of an Arkansas corporation in St. Louis, etc., Railway Co. v. Berry, 113 U. S. 465, 475, 5 Sup. Ct. 529: 'It came into existence as a corporation of the state of Arkansas, in pursuance of its constitution and laws, and subject in all respects to their re-

almost entirely upon the statutes under which the consolidation is effected, but in construing the statutes, the court should, we venture to affirm, keep in mind the general principle forbidding the bargaining away of the powers of government as well as the salutary rule that justice requires that the burden of taxation shall fall equally and uniformly upon all property and that exemptions can not exist except when clearly granted by constitutional statutes. The right of exemption does not extend to lines of railroad leased to the corporation to which the exemption is granted.[1] There is no consolidation in such cases and there can not be any implication or presumption that leased property is exempt, for the presumption in the absence of countervailing facts is always against exemptions and in favor of equality and uniformity.

strictions and limitations. Among these was that one which declared that the property of corporations, now existing, or hereafter created, shall forever be subject to taxation the same as property of individuals. This rendered it impossible for the consolidated corporation to receive by transfer from the Cairo and Fulton Railway Company, or otherwise, the exemption sought to be enforced in this suit.' See, also, Memphis & L. R. R. Co. v. Railroad Com'rs, 112 U. S. 609, 5 Sup. Ct. 299; Shields v. Ohio, 95 U. S. 319; Railroad Co. v. Palmes, 109 U. S. 244, 3 Sup. Ct. 193. Nor was the exemption saved by section 3 of article 11, providing that 'all statute laws of this state now in force, not inconsistent with this constitution, shall continue in force until they shall expire by their own limitation, or be amended or repealed by the general assembly.' This referred to statutes in force at the time the constitution was adopted, the operation of which is continued, notwithstanding the constitution. In this case, however, the exemption contained in section 9 of the charter of the Alexandria and Bloomfield Railway Company ceased to exist, not by the operation of the constitution, but by the dissolution of the corporation to which it was attached." See, also, Tomlinson v. Branch, 15 Wall. 460; Philadelphia, etc., Co. v. State, 10 How. (U. S.) 376; Delaware Railroad Tax, 18 Wall. 206; Central, etc., Co. v. Georgia, 92 U. S. 665; Chesapeake, etc., Co. v. Virginia, 94 U. S. 718; Green Co. v. Conness, 109 U. S. 104, s. c. 3 Sup. Ct. R. 69; Tennessee v. Whitworth, 117 U. S. 139, s. c. 6 Sup. Ct. R. 649; Railroad Co. v. Maine, 96 U. S. 499; Railroad Co. v. Georgia, 98 U. S. 359; St. Louis, etc., Railway Co. v. Berry, 113 U. S. 465, s. c. 5 Sup. Ct. R. 529; McMahan v. Morrison, 16 Ind. 172; Scovill v. Thayer, 105 U. S. 143; Railroad Co. v. Gaines, 97 U. S. 697; State v. Keokuk, etc., Co., 99 Mo. 30, s. c. 6 L. R. A. 222.

[1] Lake Shore, etc., Co. v. City of Grand Rapids, 102 Mich. 374, 60 N.W. R. 767.

§ 748. Right of exemption non-assignable.—The courts have generally manifested a reluctance to extend the doctrine that the power of taxation can be relinquished, and, wherever possible without denying the doctrine of the earlier cases, have limited the rule. The rule is, in our judgment, not only unwise, but is also opposed to the principle that the powers of government can not be bargained away, abrogated, or surrendered, and there is, therefore, strong reason for confining its operation within narrow limits. The cases which hold that the right can not be assigned assert a wise doctrine, but, it must be confessed, that it is difficult to see how this result can be logically reached if it be true that the right of exemption is one created by contract, and as such protected by the constitution, since it would seem to necessarily follow that if the right is one of contract, it may be sold and assigned. The decisions of the court of final resort, however, have settled the question by adjudging that the right is not assignable.[1]

§ 749. Immunity from taxation not a franchise.—There is conflict in the cases upon the question whether immunity

[1] The question was considered in Louisville, etc., Co. v. Palmes, 109 U. S. 244, s. c. 3 Sup. Ct. R. 193, and the court, referring to the case of Morgan v. Louisiana, 93 U. S. 217, held the right to be not assignable. In the case first named it was said, "The exemption from taxation, created by the eighteenth section of the internal improvement act of 1855, is in every respect similar to that which was declared in Morgan v. Louisiana, 93 U. S. 217, to be not assignable. No words of assignability are used by the legislature of the state in the language creating it, and from its nature and context it is to be inferred that the exemption of the property of the company was intended to be of the same character as that declared in reference to its capital stock and to its officers, servants and employes, and that all alike were privileges personal to the corporation, or to individuals connected with it, entitled to them by the terms of the law. This exemption, therefore, did not pass from the Alabama and Florida Railroad Company to the Pensacola and Louisville Railroad Company by the conveyances which passed the title to the railroad itself, and to the franchises connected with and necessary in its construction and operation." See, also, Wilmington, etc., Co. v. Alsbrook, 146 U. S. 279, s. c. 13 Sup. Ct. R. 72; Wilmington, etc., Co. v. Alsbrook, 110 N. Car. 137, citing Southwestern Railroad Co. v. Wright, 116 U. S. 231; Chicago, etc., Railroad Co. v. Guffey, 120 U. S. 569; State v. Mercantile Bank, 95 Tenn. 212, s. c. 31 S. W. R. 989; Bloxam v. Florida, etc., R. Co., 35 Fla. 625, s. c. 17 So. R. 902.

§ 750   TAXATION OF RAILROAD PROPERTY.   1067

from taxation is a franchise,[1] and it is unsafe to assume, to express an opinion upon the question. We think that the rule should be that. the immunity can not be regarded as a franchise passing by assignment, unless that conclusion is imperatively required by the provisions of the statute, and if there be doubt it must be resolved against the claim that the immunity is a franchise. It is bad enough to permit the immunity to be granted as a contract right, and to extend the erroneous rule beyond what a rigid adherence to the earlier cases require would be to give to a pernicious doctrine a very wide and evil influence.

§ 750. **Exemption of property used in operating railroad.**—The cardinal and well known rule of construction is that a statute exempting property from taxation is to be strictly construed. The general rule is settled and familiar, but its practical application is not always free from difficulty. It would not be profitable to comment upon the cases in which the rule has been applied, for they are numerous, and the statutes to

[1] In Keokuk, etc., Co. v. Missouri, 152 U. S. 301, s. c. 14 Sup. Ct. R. 592, the court said: "Whether under the name franchises and privileges an immunity from taxation would pass to the new company may admit of some doubt in view of the decisions of this court, which upon this point are not easy to be reconciled. In Chesapeake, etc., Railway Co. v. Miller, 114 U. S. 176, 5 Sup. Ct. 813, it was held that an immunity from taxation enjoyed by the Covington and Ohio Railway Company did not pass to a purchaser of such road under foreclosure of a mortgage, although the act provided that 'said purchaser shall forthwith be a corporation' and 'shall succeed to all such franchises, rights and privileges * * * as would have been had * * * by the first company but for such sale and conveyance.' It was held, following in this particular Morgan v. Louisiana, 93 U. S. 217, that the words 'franchises, rights and privileges' did not necessarily embrace a grant of an exemption or immunity. See, also, Picard v. East Tenn. Railroad Co., 130 U. S. 637, 9 Sup. Ct. 640. Upon the other hand, it was held in Tennessee v. Whitworth, 117 U. S. 139, 6 Sup. Ct. 649, that the right to have shares in its capital stock exempted from taxation within the state is conferred upon a railroad corporation by state statutes granting to it 'all the rights, powers and privileges' conferred upon another corporation named, if the latter corporation possesses by law such right of exemption; citing in support of this principle a number of prior cases. See, also, Wilmington, etc., Railroad Co. v. Alsbrook, 146 U. S. 279, 297, 13 Sup. Ct. 72." See, also, Detroit R. Co. v. Guthard, 51 Mich. 180.

which it has been applied differ in many material particulars.[1] The courts are often called upon to determine the meaning of such phrases, as "all property used by a railroad company," or "all property used for railroad purposes." In such cases the decisions have generally been that it is only such property as is actually used or required in operating the railroad that is exempt. There is, however, difficulty in determining what is such use as will bring the particular case within the exemption, and there is some confusion among the authorities upon the question.[2] A great diversity of opinion prevails although all the cases profess adherence to the cardinal rule. Some of the courts enforce the rule with rigid strictness, holding that there must be actual use for railroad purposes and not merely a use for a purpose indirectly connected with the operation of the railroad, while other courts extend the exemption to property incidentally connected with the operation of the railroad.[3] As much as can be safely said is that in each par-

[1] See, generally, State v. Receiver, etc., 38 N. J. L. 299, s. c. 13 Am. Ry. Rep'ts 50; Schuylkill, etc., Co. v. Commissioners, 11 Pa. St. 202; Mayor of Baltimore v. Baltimore, etc., Co., 6 Gill 288; State v. Branin, 23 N. J. L. 484; County Comrs. v. Farmers' National Bank, 48 Md. 117; Hope Mining Co. v. Kennon, 3 Mont. 35; Atlantic, etc., Co. v. Allen, 15 Fla. 637; Vicksburg, etc., Co. v. Bradley, 66 Miss. 518; Atlantic, etc., Co. v. Lesueur, 1 L. R. A. 244, 2 Inter. Com. R. 189.

[2] Wilmington, etc., Co. v. Reid, 13 Wall. 264; Milwaukee, etc., Co. v. City of Milwaukee, 34 Wis. 271; County of Erie v. Erie, etc., Co., 87 Pa. St. 434; De Soto Bank v. City of Memphis, 6 Baxt. 415; Day v. Joiner, 6 Baxter 441; St. Louis, etc., Co. v. Loftin, 30 Ark. 693; State v. Woodruff, 36 N. J. L. 94; State v. Haight, 35 N. J. L. 40; State v. Wetherill, 41 N. J. L. 147; State v. Collector, etc., 38 N. J. L. 270; Railroad Co. v. Berks County, 6 Pa. St. 70; Wayne County v. Delaware, etc., Co., 15 Pa. St. 351; Milwaukee, etc., Co. v. Board of Supervisors, 29 Wis. 116; Chicago, etc., Co. v. Board of Supervisors, 48 Wis. 666; State v. Baltimore, etc., Co., 48 Md. 49; New York, etc., Co. v. Sabin, 26 Pa. St. 242; Lackawanna, etc., Co. v. Luzerne County, 42 Pa. St. 424; Atlanta, etc., Co. v. City of Atlanta, 66 Ga. 104; Detroit, etc., Co. v. Detroit, 88 Mich. 347; State v. Nashville, etc., Co., 86 Tenn. 438; *In re* Swigert, 119 Ill. 83, s. c. 59 Am. R. 789; Milwaukee, etc., Co. v. Milwaukee, 34 Wis. 271; Northampton, etc., Co. v. Lehigh, etc., Co., 75 Pa. St. 461; Northern Pacific Co. v. Carland, 5 Mont. 146; Portland, etc., R. Co. v. Saco, 60 Me. 196; Todd County v. St. Paul, etc., Co., 38 Minn. 163; Illinois Central Co. v. Irvin, 72 Ill. 452; Osborn v. Hartford, etc., Co., 40 Conn. 498; State v. Haight, 34 N. J. L. 319; State v. Newark, 26 N. J. L. 520.

[3] It has been held that an inn used exclusively by passengers and em-

ticular case the question is one of legislative intention, that intention being gathered from the particular statute strictly construed against the corporation which claims that its property is exempt from taxation, and it appearing clearly that the property claimed as exempt is essential and not barely convenient to the operation of the railroad.[1] The statement made does not advance us very far, for the question of importance and difficulty which must be solved is as to what property is reasonably necessary to the proper operation of the railroad, but it is not possible to give any general rule which will enable the investigator to work out a solution of the legal problem.

§ 751. Remedies—Injunction.—We believe the true rule to be that where the tax sought to be enforced is illegal and void its enforcement will be restrained by injunction except in cases where an adequate remedy is provided by statute. The rule we have stated is, as we believe, supported by sound principle, and it is well fortified by authority.[2] We can see

ployes traveling on railroad trains comes within the exemption of "property necessarily used in operating the railroad." Milwaukee, etc., Co. v. Board of Supervisors, 29 Wis. 116.

[1] Property not used for railroad purposes is taxable as provided for taxing property of like character, in the hands of ordinary corporations or of individuals. Osborn v. Hartford, etc., Co., 40 Conn. 498; United, etc., Co. v. Jersey City, 53 N. J. L. 547, s. c. 22 Atl. R. 59; State v. Hancock, 33 N. J. L. 315; Toledo, etc., Co. v. City of Lafayette, 22 Ind. 262; Chicago, etc., Co. v. Paddock, 75 Ill. 616; Applegate v. Ernst, 3 Bush (Ky.) 648, s. c. 96 Am. Dec. 272; Pfaff v. Terre Haute, etc., Co., 108 Ind. 144, 153; People v. Chicago, etc., Co., 116 Ill. 181, s. c. 24 Am. & Eng. R. Cases 612; Santa Clara County v. Southern, etc., Co., 118 U. S. 394.

[2] Illinois Cent., etc., Co. v. McLean County, 17 Ill. 291; Small v. Lawrenceburg, etc., Co., 128 Ind. 231, s. c. 27 N. E. R. 500; Topeka, etc., Co. v. Roberts, 45 Kan. 360, s. c. 25 Pac. R. 854; Pelton v. Bank, 101 U. S. 143; Cummings v. Bank, 101 U. S. 153; Lefferts v. Board, 21 Wis. 697; People v. Weaver, 100 U.S. 539; Chicago, etc., Co. v. Board, 54 Kan. 781, 39 Pac. R. 1039; Schmidt v. Galveston, etc., Co., 24 Texas Civ. App. 547, 24 S. W. R. 547; Cook v. Galveston, etc., Co., 5 Texas Civ. App. 644, 24 S. W. R. 544; Railroad Co. v. Hodges, 113 Ill. 323; Crim v. Town of Philippi, 38 W. Va. 122, s. c. 18 S. E. R. 466; Bramwell v. Gukeen, 2 Idaho 1069, 29 Pac. R. 110; Stewart v. Hovey, 45 Kan. 708, 26 Pac. R. 683; Kerr v. Woolly, 3 Utah 456, s. c. 24 Pac. R. 831; Woodruff v. Perry, 103 Cal. 611, 37 Pac. R. 526; McTwiggan v. Hunter, 18 R. I. 776, 30 Atl. R. 362; Arthur v. School District, 164 Pa. St. 410, 30 Atl. R. 299; Board of Assessors of Parish of New Orleans v. Pullman Co., 60 Fed. 37. If the statute expressly provides a remedy for relief

no reason for holding that the enforcement of an illegal tax may not be enjoined, although it may be void. Even a void proceeding may cloud title and do injury to a property owner and there is no remedy, except that of injunction, which will effectively prevent or redress the injury. It seems to us that where the entire controversy can be settled by the comprehensive equity remedy, and all complications prevented, the remedy should be applied rather than drive the taxpayer to an action for damages. There is certainly no objection to the employment of the equitable remedy except that which grows out of the old doctrine established when the strife between courts of law and courts of equity was bitter, and as that doctrine is now of comparatively little practical importance there is reason for extending, as many courts are doing, the remedy of injunction. We think it wiser to restrain by injunction than to compel an action against the officer whose duty it is to collect the tax. There is, however, conflict of authority upon this question.[1] If there is nothing more than a mere irregularity in the proceedings injunction will not lie.[2]

against taxes illegally assessed and the remedy is adequate injunction will not lie. Albuquerque National Bank v. Perea, 147 U. S. 87, s. c. 13 Sup. Ct. R. 194; Bellevue, etc., Co. v. Bellevue, 39 Neb. 876, s. c. 58 N. W. R. 446; Thatcher v. Adams, 19 Neb. 485; Caldwell v. Lincoln City, 19 Neb. 569; Price v. Lancaster County, 18 Neb. 199; Stanley v. Supervisors, 121 U. S. 535, s. c. 7 Sup. Ct. R. 1234; Robinson v. City of Wilmington, 65 Fed. R. 856, citing Kirtland v. Hotchkiss, 100 U. S. 491; Shelton v. Platt, 139 U. S. 591; In re Tyler, 149 U. S. 164.

[1] United States Co. v. Grant, 137 N. Y. 7; Mayor, etc., v. Davenport, 92 N. Y. 604; Delaware, etc., Co. v. Atkins, 121 N. Y. 246; Dusenbury v. Mayor, etc., 25 N. J. Eq. 295; Hannewinkle v. Georgetown, 15 Wall. 547, 548; McClung v. Livesay, 7 W. Va. 329; Bull v. Read, 13 Gratt. (Va.) 78; Cook County v. Chicago, etc., 35 Ill. 460; Lucas County v. Hunt, 5 Ohio St. 488; Williams v. Mayor, 2 Gibbs. (Mich.) 560; Clarke v. Ganz, 21 Minn. 387; City Council v. Sayre, 65 Ala. 564; Sayre v. Tompkins, 23 Mo. 443; Barrow v. Davis, 46 Mo. 394; Harkness v. District, 1 McArthur (D. C.) 121; Warden v. Board, 14 Wis. 672; Mills v. Gleason, 11 Wis. 493; Greene v. Mumford, 5 R. I. 472; Dodd v. Hartford, 25 Conn. 232; Hixon v. Oneida County, 82 Wis. 515; Odlin v. Woodruff, 31 Fla. 160, 22 L. R. A. 699.

[2] Ricketts v. Spraker, 77 Ind. 371; Delphi v. Bowen, 61 Ind. 29; Alexander v. Dennison, 2 McArthur 562; Montgomery v. Sayre, 65 Ala. 564; Simmons v. Mumford, 5 R. I. 472, s. c. 73 Am. Dec. 79; Sherman v. Leonard, 10 R. I. 469; Porter v. Milwaukee,

§ 752. **Tender of amount of taxes owing is required.**—Upon the principle that he who asks equity must do equity, a tender of the amount of the tax owing from the plaintiff is invariably required.[1] Considerations of policy are sometimes urged, and with force, in support of the general rule we have stated,[2] but its chief support is the elementary principle referred to by us. Where no part of the tax is due, the reason of the rule fails and no tender is required.[3]

19 Wis. 625, s. c. 88 Am. Dec. 711; Youngblood v. Sexton, 32 Mich. 406, s. c. 20 Am. R. 654; Loud v. Charlestown, 99 Mass. 208; Whiting v. Mayor, etc., Boston, 106 Mass. 350; Rockingham, etc., v. Portsmouth, 52 N. H. 17; Deane v. Todd, 22 Mo. 90; Sayre v. Tompkins, 23 Mo. 443; Mayor, etc., v. Baltimore, etc., Co., 21 Md. 50; Douglass v. Harrisville, 9 W. Va. 162, s. c. 27 Am. R. 548; Jones v. Sumner, 27 Ind. 510; Litchfield v. Polk Co., 18 Iowa 70; Smith v. Osburn, 53 Iowa 474; Gates v. Barrett, 79 Ky. 295; Darling v. Gunn, 50 Ill. 424; Iowa, etc., Co. v. Carroll County, 39 Iowa 151; Robinson v. City of Wilmington, 65 Fed. R. 856.

[1] Albuquerque National Bank v. Perea, 147 U. S. 87, s. c. 13 Sup. Ct. R. 194; State Railroad Tax Cases, 92 U. S. 575; Morrison v. Jacoby, 114 Ind. 84; Baily v. Atlantic, etc., Co., 1 Cent. L. J. 502; Hagaman v. Commissioners, 19 Kan. 394; Smith v. Humphrey, 20 Mich. 398.

[2] In State Railroad Tax Cases, 92 U. S. 575, 616, it was said: "It is a profitable thing for corporations or individuals whose taxes are very large to obtain a preliminary injunction as to all their taxes, contest the case through several years' litigation, and when, in the end, it is found that but a small part of the tax should be permanently enjoined, submit to pay the balance. This is not equity. It is in direct violation of the first principles of equity jurisdiction. It is not sufficient to say in the bill that they are ready and willing to pay whatever may be found due. They must first pay what is conceded to be due, or what can be seen to be due on the face of the bill, or be shown by affidavits, whether conceded or not, before the preliminary injunction should be granted.

[3] Walla Walla, etc., Bank v. Hungate, 62 Fed. R. 548; Guidry v. Broussard, 32 La. Ann. 924.

CHAPTER XXXI.

TAXATION AS AFFECTED BY THE FEDERAL CONSTITUTION.

§ 753. Taxing interstate commerce railroads.
754. Interstate commerce—Obstruction of.
755. Railroad property used in interstate commerce is taxable by the states.
756. Interstate commerce — Taxation of property brought from one state into another.
757. Railroad in more than one state.
758. Mileage basis of valuation.
759. License tax.
760. Privilege tax on interstate railroads.
761. Privilege tax discriminated from a property tax.
762. Excise tax.
763. Tax on passengers carried.
764. Tax on interstate freight.
765. Tax on gross receipts of interstate commerce corporations.
766. Fees for the right to be a corporation not taxes.
767. Municipal tax as compensation for use of streets.
§ 768. Impairing obligation of a contract.
769. Impairing obligation of contracts—Tax on bonds.
770. Exemption of railroad property—Contract alteration of charter.
771. Due process of law in tax proceedings.
772. Equal protection of the laws.
773. Equal protection of the laws—Corporations are persons.
774. Equal protection of the laws—What is a denial of.
775. Fourteenth amendment—Unequal protection generally.
776. Classification not a denial of equal protection.
777. Fourteenth amendment—Tax for salaries of railroad commissioners.
778. Corporations deriving rights from the United States.
779. Land grants.
780. Domestic commerce.

§ 753. Taxing interstate commerce railroads.—The power of a state to tax property of all kinds and classes within its territorial limits is broad and comprehensive, but this power, great as it is, is not unlimited. The commerce clause of the federal constitution restrains this power and limits its exercise. It is not easy to define the extent of the limitation imposed by the federal constitution. It is safe, however, to say that the power can not be so exercised as to obstruct commerce between the states, or to restrain or defeat the power of the federal congress to regulate commerce.[1]

§ 754. Interstate commerce—Obstruction of.—It is settled law that under the guise of taxing railroads a state can neither obstruct nor regulate commerce between the states. The power to regulate interstate commerce is in the federal government, not in any state, so that if the tax so operates as to regulate interstate commerce there is an invasion of the domain of the federal government. If a state tax operates so as to obstruct such commerce then the statute providing for levying the tax is void since no state can impede or obstruct commerce between the states. The mere form of the statute is of no importance, for its validity depends upon its operation and effect.[2] The general principle is easily understood, but there is difficulty in ap-

---

[1] In the case of Brown v. Maryland, 12 Wheat. 419, Chief Justice. Marshall, speaking of the taxing power, said: "We admit this power to be sacred, but can not admit that it may be so used as to obstruct the free exercise of a power given to congress. We can not admit that it may be used so as to obstruct or defeat the power to regulate commerce. It has been observed that the power remaining with the states may be so exercised as to come in conflict with those vested in congress. When this happens, that which is not supreme must yield to that which is supreme. This great and universal truth is inseparable from the nature of things, and the constitution has applied it to the often interfering powers of the general and state governments, as a vital principle of perpetual operation. It results, necessarily, from this principle, that the taxing power of the state must have some limits." In the State Freight Tax Case, 15 Wall. 232, Mr. Justice Wayne expressed the same general doctrine in this language:" While on the one hand it is of the utmost importance that the states should possess the power to raise revenue for all the purposes of a state government, by any means and in any manner not inconsistent with the powers which the people of the state have conferred upon the general government, it is equally important that the domain of the latter should be preserved from invasion and that no state legislation should be sustained which defeats the avowed purpose of the federal constitution, or which assumes to regulate or control subjects committed by the constitution exclusively to the regulation of congress." See, also, Osborne v. State, 33 Fla. 162, s. c. 25 L. R. A. 120, 39 Am. St. R. 99, 14 So. R. 588.

'[2] State Freight Tax, 15 Wall. 232, 272; Bank of Commerce v. New York City, 2 Black 620; The Bank Tax Case, 2 Wall. 200; Society for Savings v. Coite, 6 Wall. 594; Provident Bank v. Massachusetts, 6 Wall. 611.

plying it. Each particular case stands, in a great measure, upon its own facts, and whether in the particular case the statute obstructs or regulates commerce is a question which is not always easy of solution.

§ 755. **Railroad property used in interstate commerce is taxable by the states.**—The fact that property is used in the business of interstate commerce does not exonerate it from taxation by the states.[1] Property within the state may be taxed, although it may be employed exclusively in interstate traffic, but the business of interstate commerce itself can not be burdened by state taxes. There is a difference between taxing the business done by the company and taxing the property of which it is the owner.[2] But to authorize the taxing of property employed in interstate commerce, it is necessary that it should have its *situs* in the state which imposes the tax. Property merely passing through the state, or temporarily there while in actual use for interstate commerce purposes, can not be taxed.[3] The doctrine we have stated is peculiarly applicable

[1] Delaware Railroad Tax, 18 Wall. 206, 232; Telegraph Co. *v.* Texas, 105 U. S. 460, 464; Gloucester Ferry Co. *v.* Pennsylvania, 114 U. S. 196, 206, s. c. 5 Sup. Ct. R. 826; Western Union Telegraph Co. *v.* Attorney-General, 125 U. S. 530, 549, s. c. 8 Sup. Ct. R. 961; Marye *v.* Railroad Co., 127 U. S. 117, 124, s. c. 8 Sup. Ct. R. 1037; Leloup *v.* Mobile, 127 U. S. 640, 649, s. c. 8 Sup. Ct. R. 1380.

[2] Pullman Palace Car Co. *v.* Pennsylvania, 141 U. S. 18, s. c. 46 Am. & Eng. R. R. Cas. 236; Pullman, etc., Co. *v.* Commonwealth, 107 Pa. St. 156; Pittsburgh, etc., Co. *v.* Backus, 154 U. S. 421, s. c. 14 Sup. Ct. R. 1114; Denver, etc., Co. *v.* Church, 17 Colo. 1. See, generally, Bain *v.* Richmond, etc., Co., 105 N. C. 363; Pullman, etc., Co. *v.* Gaines, 3 Tenn. Ch. 587; Pittsburg, etc., Co. *v.* Commonwealth, 66 Pa. St. 73; Dubuque *v.* Illinois Cent. R. Co., 39 Iowa 56; Western Un. Tel. Co. *v.* Taggart, 141 Ind. 281, s. c. 40 N. E. R. 1051.

[3] Hays *v.* Pacific Mail Steamship Co., 17 How. (U. S.) 596; St. Louis *v.* Ferry Co., 11 Wall. 423; Wiggins Ferry Co. *v.* East St. Louis, 107 U. S. 365, s. c. 2 Sup. Ct. R. 257; Gloucester Ferry Co. *v.* Pennsylvania, 114 U. S. 196, s. c. 5 Sup. Ct. R. 826. In Pullman's Palace Car Co. *v.* Pennsylvania, 141 U. S. 18, s. c. 11 Sup. Ct. R. 676, the court said: "The cars of this company within the state of Pennsylvania are employed in interstate commerce, but their being so employed does not exempt them from taxation by the state; and the state has not taxed them because of their being so employed, but because of their being within its territory and jurisdiction. The cars were continuously and permanently

§ 755   TAXATION UNDER THE FEDERAL CONSTITUTION.   1075

to vessels traversing navigable waters, but we suppose it must apply to all the agencies of interstate commerce where it is clear that such agencies are temporarily in the state and have a fixed and known *situs* elsewhere. We do not mean, of course, that a mileage basis of valuation and assessment may not be adopted where the corporation owning the property regularly or generally uses it in the state; what we mean is that where a car or locomotive is brought into a state for a purely temporary purpose, and is owned by a railroad company which does not regularly or generally conduct business in that state, it is not subject to taxation. A different rule would probably obtain if the car or locomotive were generally, habitually or reg- employed in going to and fro upon certain routes of travel. If they had never passed beyond the limits of Pennsylvania it could not be doubted that the state could tax them, like other property within its borders, notwithstanding they were employed in interstate commerce. The fact that, instead of stopping at the state boundary, they cross that boundary in going out and coming back, can not affect the power of the state to levy a tax upon them. The state having the right, for the purposes of taxation, to tax any personal property found within its jurisdiction, without regard to the place of the owner's domicile, could tax the specific cars which at a given moment were in its borders. The route over which the cars travel extending beyond the limits of the state, particular cars may not remain within the state; but the company has at all times substantially the same number of cars within the state, and continuously and constantly uses there a portion of its property; and it is distinctly found, as matter of fact, that the c o m p a n y continuously, throughout the periods for w h i c h these taxes were levied, carried on business in Pennsylvania, and had about one hundred cars within the state. The mode which the state of Pennsylvania adopted to ascertain the proportion of the company's property upon which it should be taxed in that state was by taking as a basis of assessment such proportion of the capital stock of the company as the number of miles over which it ran cars within the state bore to the whole number of miles in that and other states over which its cars were run. This was a just and equitable method of assessment; and, if it were adopted by all the states through which these cars ran, the company would be assessed upon the whole value of its capital stock, and no more. The validity of this mode of appropriating such a tax is sustained by several decisions of this court in cases which came up from the circuit courts of the United States, and in which, therefore, the jurisdiction of this court extends to the determination of the whole case, and was not limited, as upon writs of error to the state courts, to questions under the constitution and laws of the United States."

ularly used in the state, although it might not permanently be kept or used therein.

§ 756. Interstate commerce—Taxation of property brought from one state into another.—Where property is brought from one state into another, the latter state being its destination, it may be there taxed.[1] This must be the rule, otherwise property might entirely escape taxation. The doctrine, as declared by the supreme court of the United States, is a broad one, since it authorizes taxation of property by the state into which it is brought, although taxes were paid upon it in the state from which it came.[2] It is, as we suppose, always to be understood that taxes can not be so levied as to restrict interstate commerce.[3]

§ 757. Railroad in more than one state.—The decisions affirm that in valuing railway property for taxation the taxing officers may take into consideration the part lying in an adjoining state for the purpose of determining the value of the entire line.

---

[1] Brown v. Houston, 114 U. S. 622, s. c. 5 Sup. Ct. R. 1091. Citing Woodruff v. Parham, 8 Wall. 123; Brown v. Maryland, 12 Wheat. 419; Cooley v. Board of Wardens, 12 How. 299; Welton v. State, 91 U. S. 275; Pittsburgh, etc., Co. v. Bates, 156 U. S. 577, 15 Sup. Ct. R. 415.

[2] In Brown v. Houston, 114 U. S. 622, s. c. 5 Sup. Ct. R. 1091, the court said: "Of course the assessment should be a general one, and not discriminative of goods between different states. The taxing of goods coming from other states, as such or by reason of their so coming, would be a discriminating tax against them as imports, and would be a regulation of interstate commerce, inconsistent with that perfect freedom which congress has seen fit should remain undisputed. But if, after their arrival in the state, that being their destination for use or trade—if after this they are subjected to a general tax laid on all alike, we fail to see how such a tax can be deemed a regulation of commerce which would have the objectionable feature referred to." The court discriminated the case from that of Woodruff v. Parham, 8 Wall. 123, and marked, in a general way, the line of difference.

[3] Moran v. New Orleans, 112 U. S. 69, s. c. 5 Sup. Ct. R. 38, citing Sinnot v. Davenport, 22 How. 227; Telegraph Co. v. Texas, 105 U. S. 460; Case of State Freight Tax, 15 Wall. 232; Crandall v. Nevada, 6 Wall. 35; Osborne v. Mobile, 16 Wall. 479; Transportation Co. v. Wheeling, 99 U. S. 273; Morgan v. Parham, 16 Wall. 471; Hays v. Pacific Mail Steamship Co., 17 How. 596; Wiggins Ferry Co. v. East St. Louis, 107 U. S. 365, s. c. 2 Sup. Ct. R. 257.

§ 758   TAXATION UNDER THE FEDERAL CONSTITUTION.   1077

This seems to us very much like an unjust discrimination. It is difficult to conceive why it is not unequal taxation and an unwarrantable burden upon instrumentalities of interstate commerce. The owner of a large manufacturing establishment situated in one state can only be taxed in that state, although the principal part of his business may be done in another state, and yet according to the decisions, a railway company may be taxed in two or more states. The question is, however, settled by the adjudged cases.[1]

§ 758. **Mileage basis of valuation.**—The doctrine of the court of last resort is that the taxing officers may make a valuation upon a mileage basis although the property assessed is used as an instrumentality of commerce between the states.[2] A distinction is made between the cases which deny the right of a state to lay a tax upon the business of interstate commerce itself and those which affirm that a tax may be laid on property within the limits of the state. The doctrine is, indeed, extended, as we have elsewhere shown, to property beyond the state boundaries.[3]

[1] Pittsburg, etc., Co. v. Backus, 154 U. S. 421, s. c. 14 Sup. Ct. R. 1114, citing State Railroad Tax Cases, 92 U. S. 575; Columbus, etc., Ry. Co. v. Wright, 151 U. S. 470, s. c. 14 Sup. Ct. R. 396; Delaware Railroad Tax, 18 Wall. 206; Erie R. Co. v. Pennsylvania, 21 Wall. 492; Western Union Tel. Co. v. Attorney-General, 125 U. S. 530, s. c. 8 Sup. Ct. R. 961; Pullman, etc., Co. v. Pennsylvania, 141 U. S. 18, s. c. 12 Sup. Ct. R. 121; Charlotte, etc., R. Co. v. Gibbes, 142 U. S.. 386, s. c. 12 Sup. Ct. R. 255; Franklin County v. Nashville, etc., Ry. Co., 12 Lea 521. To the same effect is the decision in Cleveland, etc., Co. v. Backus, 154 U. S. 439, s. c. 14 Sup. Ct. R. 1122. It is evident that the rule sanctioned by the supreme court must lead to confusion and that under it double taxation of a vicious character is almost unavoidable. In Pittsburg, etc., Co. v. Backus, *supra*, the court says that "there may be exceptional cases," and granting this it seems difficult to see how double and unequal taxation can be avoided, since so much is left to the judgment or discretion of the taxing officers of the different states through which the railroad runs.

[2] Western Union Tel. Co. v. Massachusetts, 125 U. S. 530, s. c. 8 Sup. Ct. R. 961; Pullman, etc., Co. v. Pennsylvania, 141 U. S. 18, s. c. 11 Sup. Ct. R. 876; Maine v. Grand Trunk, etc., Co., 142 U. S. 217, s. c. 12 Sup. Ct. R. 121, 163; Railroad Co. v. Gibbs, 142 U. S. 386; Pittsburgh, etc., Co. v. Backus, 154 U. S. 421, s. c. 14 Sup. Ct. R. 1114.

[3] In the case of Pullman, etc., Co. v. Pennsylvania, 141 U. S. 18, s. c. 11

§ 759. **License tax.**—A license tax imposed upon an interstate railroad is invalid. Such a tax is not a tax upon property, nor is it the exaction of a fee for the privilege of becoming a corporation, or of effecting a consolidation under the laws of the state.[1] As we shall presently show, a privilege tax can not

Sup. Ct. R. 876, it was said: "Much reliance is also placed by the plaintiff in error upon the cases in which this court has decided that citizens or corporations of one state can not be taxed by another state for a license or privilege to carry on interstate or foreign commerce within its limits. But in each of those cases the tax was not upon the property employed in the business, but upon the right to carry on the business at all, and was therefore held to impose a direct burden upon the commerce itself. Moran v. New Orleans, 112 U. S. 69, 74, 5 Sup. Ct. R. 38; Pickard v. Car Co., 117 U. S. 34, 43, 6 Sup. Ct. R. 635; Robbins v. Shelby County Taxing Dist., 120 U. S. 489, 497, 7 Sup. Ct. R. 592; Leloup v. Port of Mobile, 127 U. S. 640, 644, 8 Sup. Ct. R. 1380. For the same reason, a tax upon the gross receipts derived from the transportation of passengers and goods between one state and other states or foreign nations has been held to be invalid. Fargo v. Michigan, 121 U. S. 230, 7 Sup. Ct. R. 857; Philadelphia, etc., Steamship Co. v. Pennsylvania, 122 U. S. 326, 7 Sup. Ct. R. 1118. The tax now in question is not a license tax or a privilege tax; it is not a tax on business or occupation; it is not a tax on or because of the transportation or the right of transit of persons or property through the state to other states or countries. The tax is imposed equally on corporations doing business within the state, whether domestic or foreign, and whether engaged in interstate commerce or not. The tax on the capital of the corporation on account of its property within the state is, in substance and effect, a tax on that property. Gloucester Ferry Co. v. Pennsylvania, 114 U. S. 196, 209, 5 Sup. Ct. R. 826; Western Union Telegraph Co. v. Attorney-General, 125 U. S. 530, 552, 8 Sup. Ct. R. 961. This is not only admitted, but insisted on by the plaintiff in error."

[1] McCall v. California, 136 U. S. 104; Norfolk, etc., Co. v. Pennsylvania, 136 U. S. 114; Leloup v. Port of Mobile, 127 U. S. 640; Crutcher v. Kentucky, 141 U. S. 47, s. c. 11 Sup. Ct. R. 851; Inman Steamship Co. v. Tinker, 94 U. S. 238; Telegraph Co. v. Texas, 105 U. S. 460; Norfolk, etc., Company v. Pennsylvania, 136 U. S. 114; Brennan v. City of Titusville, 153 U. S. 289; Robbins v. Shelby County Taxing Dist., 120 U. S. 489, s.c.7 Sup.Ct.R.592; Lyng v. Michigan, 135 U. S. 161, s. c. 10 Sup. Ct. R. 725; Asher v. Texas, 128 U. S. 129; Stoutenburg v. Hennick, 129 U. S. 141. In the case of Cutcher v. Commonwealth, *supra*, the court said: " We have repeatedly decided that a state law is unconstitutional which requires a party to take out a license for carrying on interstate commerce, no matter how specious the pretext may be for imposing it." In the case of Brennan v. City of Titusville, 153 U. S. 289, the court said: "The case of Ficklen v. Shelby County Taxing Dist., 145 U. S. 1, is no departure from the rule of decision so firmly settled by the prior decisions."

be imposed, and we regard a license tax as substantially the same as a privilege tax, but a decision in regard to what is called an excise tax has produced some confusion.[1] A license tax, assigning to the term license tax the meaning generally given by the authorities, and this is the meaning in which we employ the term, is a tax imposed as a condition of permitting business to be conducted within the state, and hence is a tax upon commerce between the states.

§ 760. Privilege tax on interstate railroads.—The settled rule that a state has no power to regulate or burden interstate commerce precludes a state from taxing a railroad company for the privilege of conducting the business of interstate commerce within its territorial limits. Exacting a license from such companies, as a condition precedent to the right to do business in the state, is substantially the same thing as imposing a tax upon the privilege of doing business in the state, but there is a shade of difference between the two classes of cases. The attempt to restrict or regulate interstate commerce is always abortive no matter in what form it is made, but the difficulty is to determine what is a restriction or regulation and what is a property tax.[2]

§ 761. Privilege tax discriminated from a property tax.— A statute laying a tax on property as property where the property is within the state does not violate the federal constitution,

---

[1] Maine v. Grand Trunk, etc., Co., 142 U. S. 217, s. c. 12 Sup. Ct. R. 163.

[2] Pickard v. Pullman, etc., Co., 117 U. S. 34, s. c. 6 Sup. Ct. R. 635, citing Almy v. State, 24 How. (U. S.) 169; Woodruff v. Parham, 8 Wall. 123, 138; Crandall v. Nevada, 6 Wall. 35; State Freight Case, 15 Wall. 232; Railroad Co. v. Maryland, 21 Wall. 456; Head Money Cases, 112 U. S. 580, s. c. 5 Sup. Ct. R. 247; Guy v. Baltimore, 100 U. S. 434; Moran v. New Orleans, 112 U. S. 69, s. c. 5 Sup. Ct. R. 38. See Tennessee v. Pullman, etc., Co., 117 U. S. 51, s. c. 6 Sup. Ct. R. 643. The decision in the case of Pullman, etc., Co. v. Gaines, 3 Tenn. Ch. 587, was overruled or rather reversed in the case of Tennessee v. Pullman Co., supra. See, also, Pullman, etc., Co. v. Nolan, 22 Fed. R. 276. In the paragraph which follows we have referred to a case which discriminates between a property tax and a privilege tax, and it must be confessed that the distinction made in that case is a very fine one, and much that is there said is not easily harmonized with rulings in other cases.

but a privilege tax is not, as we have seen in the preceding section, a property tax. Whether the tax is laid upon property or imposed upon a corporation for the privilege of conducting business in the state is to be determined from the operation and practical effect of the state statute and not from its mere form. The distinction between a privilege tax and a property tax is a subtle one, and it is not easy to plainly mark the line which separates them.[1]

[1] The question received consideration in the case of the Postal, etc., Co. v. Adam, 155 U. S. 688, s. c. 15 Sup. Ct. R. 268, where it was held that a tax of a designated sum per mile of telegraph wire in the state was a tax on property and not a mere privilege tax. The court used this language: "As pointed out by Mr. Justice Field in Horn Silver Min. Co. v. New York, 143 U. S. 305, 12 Sup. Ct. R. 403, the right of a state to tax the franchise or privilege of being a corporation as personal property has been repeatedly recognized by this court, and this, whether the corporation be domestic or a foreign corporation, doing business by its permission within the state. But a state can not exclude from its limits a corporation engaged in interstate or foreign commerce, or a corporation in the employment of the general government, either directly in terms or indirectly by the imposition of inadmissible conditions. Nevertheless the state may subject it to such property taxation as only incidentally affects its occupation, as all business, whether of individuals or corporations, is affected by common governmental burdens. Ashley v. Ryan, 153 U. S. 436, 14 Sup. Ct. R. 865, and cases cited. Doubtless no state could add to the taxation of property according to the rule of ordinary property taxation, the burden of a license or other tax or the privilege of using, constructing or operating an instrumentality of interstate or international commerce or for the carrying on of such commerce; but the value of property results from the use to which it is put and varies with the profitableness of that use, and by whatever name the exaction may be called, if it amounts to no more than the ordinary tax upon property, or a just equivalent therefor, ascertained by reference thereto, it is not open to attack as inconsistent with the constitution. Cleveland, etc., R. Co. v. Backus, 154 U. S. 439, 445, 14 Sup.Ct. R. 1122. The method of taxation by 'a tax on privileges' has been determined by the supreme court of Mississippi to be in harmony with the constitution of that state, and that 'where the particular arrangement of taxation, provided by legislative wisdom, may be accounted for on the assumption of compromising or commuting for a just equivalent, according to the determination of the legislature, in the general scheme of taxation, it will not be condemned by the courts as violative of the (state) constitution.' Vicksburg Bank v. Worrell, 67 Miss. 47, 7 So. R. 219. In that case privilege taxes imposed on bank of deposit or discount, which varied with the amount of capital stock or assets, and were declared to be 'in lieu of all other taxes, state, county or municipal, upon the shares and assets of said bank,' came under review, and it was decided that

§ 762. **Excise tax.**—The court of last resort has adjudged that an excise tax may be imposed upon an interstate railroad company. The cases denying the power to levy a privilege tax are not expressly denied, but it is held that a state is not precluded from levying an excise tax.[1] We suppose that if a state, under the guise of imposing an excise tax, should levy a direct privilege tax, the statute providing for such a tax would be ineffective. The difference between an excise tax of the character contained in the case referred to in the note, is not

the privilege tax, to be effectual as a release from liability for all other taxes, must be measured by the capital stock, and entire assets or wealth of the bank, and that real estate bought with funds of the bank was exempt from the ordinary *ad valorem* taxes, but was part of the assets of the bank to be considered in fixing the basis of its privilege tax."

[1] In the case of Maine *v.* Grand Trunk, etc., Co., 142 U. S. 217, s. c. 12 Sup. Ct. R. 163, the court said: "The tax, for the collection of which this action is brought, is an excise tax upon the defendant corporation for the privilege of exercising its franchises within the state of Maine. It is so declared in the statute which imposes it; and that a tax of this character is within the power of the state to levy there can be no question. The designation does not always indicate merely an inland imposition or duty on the consumption of commodities, but often denotes an impost for a license to pursue certain callings, or to deal in special commodities, or to exercise particular franchises. It is used more frequently, in this country, in the latter sense than in any other. The privilege of exercising the franchises of a corporation within a state is generally one of value, and often of great value, and the subject of earnest contention. It is natural, therefore, that the corporation should be made to bear some proportion of the burdens of government. As the granting of the privilege rests entirely in the discretion of the state, whether the corporation be of domestic or foreign origin, it may be conferred upon such conditions, pecuniary or otherwise, as the state, in its judgment, may deem most conducive to its interest or policy. It may require the payment into its treasury, each year, of a specific sum, or may apportion the amount exacted according to the value of the business permitted, as disclosed by its gains or receipts of the present or past years. The character of the tax, or its validity, is not determined by the mode adopted in fixing its amount for any specific period, or the times of its payment. The whole field of inquiry into the extent of revenue from sources at the command of the corporation is open to the consideration of the state in determining what may be justly exacted for the privilege. The rule of apportioning the charge to the receipts of the business would seem to be eminently reasonable, and likely to produce the most satisfactory results, both to the state and the corporation taxed."

a very plain one, and there is, it seems to us, great difficulty in giving the doctrine of the majority, in the case mentioned, practical effect. We venture to say, and with utmost deference, that the doctrine of the minority opinion is the sounder and better one.[1]

---

[1] Mr. Justice Bradley, who wrote the minority opinion (concurred in by Harlan, Lamar and Brown, JJ.), said: "But passing this by, the decisions of this court for a number of years past have settled the principle that taxation (which is a mode of regulation) of interstate commerce, or of the revenues derived therefrom (which is the same thing), is contrary to the constitution. Going no further back than Pickard v. Pullman, etc., Car Co., 117 U. S. 34, 6 Sup. Ct. R. 635, we find that principle laid down. There a privilege tax was imposed upon Pullman's Palace Car Company by general legislation, it is true, but applied to the company, of $50 per annum on every sleeping car going through the state. It was well known, and appears by the record, that every sleeping car going through the state carried passengers from Ohio and other northern states to Alabama, and vice versa, and we held that Tennessee had no right to tax those cars. It was the same thing as if they had taxed the amount derived from the passengers in the cars. So, also, in the case of Leloup v. Port of Mobile, 127 U. S. 640, 8 Sup.Ct. R. 1380, we held that the receipts derived by the telegraph company from messages sent from one state to another could not be taxed. So in the case of Norfolk, etc., R. Co. v. Pennsylvania, 136 U. S. 114, 10 Sup. Ct. R. 958, where the railroad was a link in a through line by which passengers and freight were carried into other states, the company was held to be engaged in the business of interstate commerce, and could not be taxed for the privilege of keeping an office in the state. And in the case of Crutcher v. Kentucky, 141 U. S. 47, 11 Sup. Ct. R. 851, we held that the taxation of an express company for doing an express business between different states was unconstitutional and void. And in the case of Philadelphia, etc., Steamship Co. v. Pennsylvania, 122 U. S. 326, 7 Sup. Ct. R. 1118, we held that a tax upon the gross receipts of the company was void, because they were derived from interstate and foreign commerce. A great many other cases might be referred to showing that in the decisions and opinions of this court this kind of taxation is unconstitutional and void. We think that the present decision is a departure from the line of these decisions. The tax, it is true, is called a 'tax on a franchise.' It is so called, but what is it in fact? It is a tax on the receipts of the company derived from international transportation. This court and some of the state courts have gone a great length in sustaining various forms of taxes upon corporations. The train of reasoning upon which it is founded may be questionable. A corporation, according to this class of decisions, may be taxed several times over. It may be taxed for its charter, for its franchises, for the privilege of carrying on its business; it may be taxed on its capital, and it may be taxed on its property. Each of these taxations may be carried to the full amount of the property of the company."

§ 763. **Tax on passengers carried.**—It results from the doctrine of the cases that a tax can not be levied upon each passenger carried by an interstate railroad through a state.[1] To permit this to be done would be to authorize a tax upon commerce itself. The carriage of passengers is commerce and to impose a tax upon each passenger would be just as much a restriction or regulation of commerce as a tax upon each ton of freight carried through the state would be.

§ 764. **Tax on interstate freight.**—It has been held in numerous cases that a state can not lay a tax on freight transported in interstate commerce traffic.[2] Such a tax is regarded

---

[1] Head Money Cases, 112 U. S. 580, s. c. 5 Sup. Ct. R. 247; The Passenger Cases, 7 How. (U. S.) 282; Henderson v. Mayor, 92 U. S. 259; Commissioners, etc., v. North German Lloyd, etc., Co., 92 U. S. 259; People v. Compaignie, etc., 107 U. S. 59, s. c. 2 Sup. Ct. R. 87; Tennessee v. Pullman Co., 117 U. S. 51; State v. Woodruff, etc., Co., 114 Ind. 155. In the case last cited the court quoted with approval from the State Freight Tax Case, 15 Wall. 232, the statement that "a tax upon freights and fares is a tax upon the transportation itself." In Tennessee v. Pullman, etc., Co., supra, the court said, "The principles which governed the decisions in Welton v. Missouri, 91 U. S. 275; Guy v. Baltimore, 100 U. S. 434; Moran v. New Orleans, 112 U. S. 69, holding unlawful the state taxes on interstate commerce in merchandise, are equally applicable to the tax in this case on the transit of passengers." See, also, Brown v. Houston, 114 U. S. 622; Chy Lung v. Freeman, 92 U. S. 275; State v. Steamship, etc., 42 Cal. 578, s. c. 10 Am. R. 303; Clarke v. Philadelphia, etc., Co., 4 Houst. (Del.) 158; Piek v. Chicago, etc., Co., 6 Biss. 177; Council Bluffs v. Kansas City, etc., R. Co., 45 Iowa 338, s. c. 24 Am. R. 773; Crandall v. Nevada, 6 Wall. 35; Sweatt v. Boston, etc., Co., 3 Cliff. (U. S. Cir.) 339; People v. Raymond, 34 Cal. 492; People v. Pacific Co., 16 Fed. R. 344; People v. Downer, 7 Cal. 169, Pullman, etc., Co. v. Nolan, 22 Fed. R. 276.

[2] State Freight Tax Case, 15 Wall. 232; Railroad Co. v. Maryland, 21 Wall. 456, 472; Head Money Cases, 112 U. S. 580, s. c. 5 Sup. Ct. R. 247; Welton v. Missouri, 91 U. S. 275; Moran v. New Orleans, 112 U. S. 69, s. c. 5 Sup. Ct. R. 826; Woodruff v. Parham, 8 Wall. 123; Hall v. DeCuir, 95 U. S. 485; Erie Co. v. State, 31 N. J. L. 531, s. c. 86 Am. Dec. 226; Wabash, etc., Co. v. Illinois, 118 U. S. 557; Baird v. St. Louis, etc., Co., 41 Fed. R. 592; United States, etc., Co. v. Hemmingway, 39 Fed.R.60; Brumagin v. Tillinghast, 18 Cal. 265; Howe, etc., Co. v. Gage, 100 U. S. 676; State v. Engle, 34 N. J. L. 425; The Daniel Ball v. United States, 10 Wall. 557; Koehler Ex parte, 30 Fed. R. 867; Ogilvie v. Crawford County, 7 Fed. R. 745; Osborne v. Mobile, 16 Wall. 479; Fargo v. Michigan, 121 U. S. 230; State v. Carrigan, 39 N. J. L. 35; State v. Cumberland, etc., Co., 40 Md. 22.

as laid upon interstate commerce itself, and in some of the cases it is said that where such a tax is enforced it falls upon those for whom the property is carried. But whatever doubt there may be as to the true reason for the rule there is no doubt as to its existence and effect. Freight destined to a point within the state and placed on the cars at a point in the same state is not interstate freight although in the course of continuous transit it may pass through parts of another state.[1]

§ 765. **Tax on gross receipts of interstate commerce corporations.**—The decisions are uniformly to the effect that a tax can not be laid on the business of interstate commerce. There is, however, some difficulty in giving practical effect to the general rule. Taxes may be assessed upon a mileage basis and upon tangible property having its *situs* within the state, since these methods of taxation are not regarded as a tax upon the business of interstate commerce itself. A tax can not, however, be laid upon the gross receipts of an interstate company for the reason that such a method is a tax upon interstate commerce.[2]

---

[1] Lehigh Valley R. Co. *v.* Pennsylvania, 145 U. S. 192, 205, s. c. 12 Sup. Ct. R. 806; Campbell *v.* Chicago, etc., Co., 86 Iowa 641, s. c. 53 N. W. R. 351. Citing the above case and the cases of Welton *v.* Missouri, 91 U. S. 275; Mobile County *v.* Kimball, 102 U. S. 691; Gibbons *v.* Ogden, 9 Wheat. 189.

[2] State Freight Tax, 15 Wall. 232; Telegraph Co. *v.* Texas, 105 U. S. 460; Philadelphia, etc., Co. *v.* Pennsylvania, 122 U. S. 326; Fargo *v.* Michigan, 121 U. S. 230; Ratterman *v.* Western Union, etc., Co.,127 U. S. 411; Gloucester Ferry Co. *v.* Pennsylvania Co.,114 U. S. 196; McCall *v.*California, 136 U. S. 104; Norfolk, etc., Co. *v.* Pennsylvania, 136 U. S. 114. The decisions are not harmonious. State Tax on Gross Receipts, 15 Wall. 284, is opposed to the later decisions, and there are some expressions in other cases which seem to indicate that gross receipts may be taxed. We do not understand that the cases which declare that a mileage basis is valid authorize the conclusion that a state may tax gross receipts. We think the court intended to make a distinction between the two methods, and that it has done so. We can see no escape from the conclusion that a tax upon gross receipts is a tax upon interstate commerce itself, and if it be, it is certainly levied in violation of the commerce clause of the constitution. In the case of Philadelphia, etc., Co. *v.* Pennsylvania, 122 U. S. 326, s. c. 7 Sup. Ct. R. 1118, 1123, the court said: "A review of the question convinces us that the first ground on which State Tax on Railway Gross Receipts was placed is not tenable, that it is not supported by anything decided in Brown *v.*

§ 766. **Fees for the right to be a corporation not taxes.**—A state has power to exact fees of an association which asks the right or privilege of being a corporation, and the exaction of such fees is not the imposition of a tax upon interstate commerce.[1] The court concedes that the exaction of such fees may incidentally affect interstate commerce, but denies that such an exaction is a regulation of commerce between the states, in such a sense as to be within the inhibition of the constitution. The theory of the court is that the state has power to grant or refuse a charter, and hence may prescribe the terms upon which it will grant the corporate privileges and franchises asked by the persons who desire to organize a corporation under its laws.

§ 767. **Municipal tax as compensation for use of streets.**—The right of a municipal corporation to impose a tax as compensation for the use of its streets was asserted in a recent case.[2] The court adjudged that such a tax was neither a

[1] Ashley v. Ryan, 153 U. S. 436, s. c. 14 Sup. Ct. R. 865, citing California v. Central Pacific Co., 127 U. S. 1, 40, s. c. 8 Sup. Ct. 1073; Home Ins. Co. v. New York, 134 U. S. 594, s. c. 10 Sup. Ct. R. 593; Bank v. Earle, 13 Pet. 517; Lafayette Insurance Co.v.French, 18 How.(U. S.) 404; Paul v.Virginia, 8 Wall. 168; Ducat v. Chicago, 10 Wall. 410; Railroad Co. v. Maryland, 21 Wall. 456; Philadelphia, etc., Co. v. New York, 119 U. S. 110. The court marks the distinction between a tax imposed upon the privilege of doing business in the state and the exaction of a fee for the privilege of becoming a corporation, saying: "The question here is not the power of the state of Ohio to lay a charge on interstate commerce, or to prevent a foreign corporation from engaging in interstate commerce within its confines, but simply the right of the state to determine upon what conditions its laws as to the consolidation of corporations may be availed of."

[2] City of St. Louis v. Western Union Tel. Co., 148 U. S. 92, s. c. 13 Sup. Ct. R. 485. In the course of the opinion in that case, it was said: "And first with reference to the ruling that this charge was a privilege or license tax. To determine this question, we must refer to the language of the ordinance itself, and by that we find that the charge is imposed for the privilege of using the streets, alleys and public places, and is graduated by the amount of such use. Clearly, this is no privilege or license tax. The amount to be paid is not graduated by the amount of the business, nor is it a sum fixed for the privilege of doing business. It is more in the nature of a charge for the use of property belonging to the city—that which may properly be

Maryland, but, on the contrary, that the reasoning in that case is decidedly against it."

license tax nor a privilege tax. There is reason for discriminating between a privilege or license tax and a requirement that compensation be paid for the use of city streets, but the difference between such cases is somewhat indistinct and shadowy. Unless restrained by clearly defined rules there is danger of great abuses flowing from the doctrine of the case referred to in the note. It is always a delicate thing for courts to interfere in cases where the existence of the power asserted is conceded and the suitor seeks assistance solely upon the ground that the power has been abused or transcended, and it is so in dealing with municipal taxation of the character of that under consideration in the case cited.

§ 768. **Impairing obligation of a contract.**—We have elsewhere discussed the question of the effect of a provision in the charter of a railroad corporation exempting it from taxation, and have said that under the federal decisions it is to be regarded as a contract right protected by the clause of the federal constitution forbidding the impairment of the obligation of a contract.[1] The question is, of course, a federal one and the

called rental. 'A tax is a demand of sovereignty; a toll is a demand of proprietorship.' State Freight Tax Case, 15 Wall. 232, 278. If, instead of occupying the streets and public places with its telegraph poles, the company should do what it may rightfully do, purchase ground in the various blocks from private individuals, and to such ground remove its poles, the section would no longer have any application to it. That by it the city receives something which it may use as revenue does not determine the character of the charge or make it a tax. The revenues of a municipality may come from rentals as legitimately and as properly as from taxes. Supposing the city of St. Louis should find its city hall too small for its purposes, or too far removed from the center of business, and should purchase or build another more satisfactory in this respect, it would not therefore be forced to let the old remain vacant or to immediately sell it, but might derive revenue by renting its various rooms. Would an ordinance fixing the price at which those rooms could be occupied be in any sense one imposing a tax? Nor is the character of the charge changed by reason of the fact that it is not imposed upon such telegraph companies as by ordinances are taxed on their gross income for city purposes. In the illustration just made in respect to a city hall, suppose that the city, in its ordinance fixing a price for the use of rooms, should permit persons who pay a certain amount of taxes to occupy a portion of the building free of rent, that would not make the charge upon others for their use of rooms a tax."

[1] Pacific, etc., Co. *v.* Maguire, 20

§ 768   TAXATION UNDER THE FEDERAL CONSTITUTION.   1087

decisions of the supreme court of the United States are final and conclusive. It is true that so far as concerns purely local questions and matters involving the construction of state constitutions and statutes the federal courts follow the decisions of the state courts.[1] Those decisions, indeed, become part of the statutes much to the same extent as if written in the text.[2] But the statute or charter must contain a contract in all that the term implies.[3] There must, of course, be a consideration for the contract, but it is held that no consideration beyond that which is to be expected to result from the formation of the corporation is required.[4] It is not every charter which provides for exemption that can be considered as a contract, since the exemption may be in the nature of a mere donation, or bounty, and if there is nothing more than a gift or a provision for a bounty there is no contract upon which the constitution can operate.[5] Federal courts do not accept the decision of the state tribunals as to what is or is not a contract. That is a question which the federal court will determine for

Wall. 36; State v. Miller, 1 Vroom 368; State v. Winona, etc., Co., 21 Minn. 315.

[1] Nesmith v. Sheddon, 7 How. (U. S.) 812; Green v. Neal, 6 Peters 289; Suydam v. Williamson, 24 How. (U. S.) 427; Cross v. Allen, 141 U. S. 528; Shelly v. Guy, 11 Wheat. 361; Stutsman County v. Wallace, 142 U. S. 293; Detroit v. Osborne, 135 U. S. 492, s. c. 10 Sup. Ct. R. 1012; Bucher v. Railroad Co., 125 U. S. 555, s. c. 8 Sup. Ct. R. 974; Burgess v. Seligman, 107 U. S. 20, s. c. 2 Sup. Ct. R. 10; Claiborne v. Brooks, 111 U. S. 400, s. c. 4 Sup. Ct. R. 489; Chicago, etc., Co. v. Stahley, 62 Fed. R. 363, and cases cited.

[2] Douglas v. County of Pike, 101 U. S. 677; Anderson v. Santa Ana, 116 U. S. 356; Ohio, etc., Insurance Co. v. Debolt, 16 How. (U. S.) 115; Gelpecke v. Dubuque, 1 Wall. 175; Olcott v. Supervisors, 16 Wall. 678; Taylor v. Ypsilanti, 105 U. S. 60.

[3] "It is to be kept in mind that it is not the charter which is protected, but any contract which the charter may contain. If there is no contract there is nothing on which the constitution can act." Per Waite, C. J., in Stone v. Mississippi, 101 U. S. 814.

[4] Home of the Friendless v. Rouse, 8 Wall. 430.

[5] Christ's Church v. Philadelphia, 24 How. (U. S.) 300; East Saginaw, etc., Co. v. East Saginaw, 19 Mich. 259; East Saginaw, etc., Co. v. East Saginaw, 13 Wall. 373; Detroit v. Plankroad Co., 43 Mich. 140; Welch v. Cook[1] 97 U. S. 541. In the case last cited the court, in speaking of the act of congress under consideration, said: "This is a bounty law, which is good as long as it remains unrepealed, but there is no pledge that it shall not be repealed at any time."

itself.[1] The federal court must, therefore, determine whether the particular statute granting the exemption does or does not constitute an inviolable contract in every case where the state court has denied that it does constitute a contract between the state and the corporation.

§ 769. **Impairing obligation of contracts—Tax on bonds.**— A state has no power to compel an interstate railroad company

---

[1] This question received careful consideration in the case of Mobile, etc., Co. v. Tennessee, 153 U. S. 486. In that case it was said: "It is well settled that the decision of a state court holding that, as a matter of construction, a particular charter or a charter provision does not constitute a contract, is not binding on this court. The question of the existence or non-existence of a contract in cases like the present is one which this court will determine for itself, the established rule being that where the judgment of the highest court of a state, by its terms or necessary operation, gives effect of some provision of the state law which is claimed by the unsuccessful party to impair the contract set out and relied on, this court has jurisdiction to determine the question whether such a contract exists as claimed, and whether the state law complained of impairs its obligation. A brief reference to some of the authorities is sufficient to show this: In Bank v. Shelby, 1 Black 436, 443, it was said by this court: 'Its (the supreme court) rule of interpretation has invariably been that the constructions given by courts of the states to state legislation and to state constitutions have been conclusive upon this court, with a single exception, and that is when it has been called upon to interpret the contracts of states, though they had been made in the forms of law, or by the instrumentality of a state's authorized functionaries, in conformity with state legislation. It has never been denied, nor is it now, that the supreme court of the United States has an appellate power to revise the judgment of the supreme court of a state whenever such court shall adjudge that not to be a contract which has been alleged, in the forms of legal proceedings, by a litigant, to be one within the meaning of that clause of the constitution of the United States which inhibits the states from passing laws impairing the obligation of contracts. Of what use would the appellate power be to a litigant who feels himself aggrieved by some particular state legislation, if this court could not decide, independently of all adjudication by the supreme court of a state, whether or not the phraseology of an instrument in controversy was expressive of a contract, and within the protection of the constitution of the United States, and that its obligation should be enforced notwithstanding a contrary decision by the supreme court of a state?'" See, also, New Orleans, etc., Co. v. Louisiana, etc., Co., 125 U. S. 18, 38; Railroad Co. v. Alsbrook, 146 U. S. 279; Huntington v. Attril, 146 U. S. 657; Town of East Hartford v. Hartford, etc., Co., 10 How. (U. S.) 536; University v. People, 99 U. S. 309, 321; Louisville, etc., Co. v. Citizens', etc., Co., 115 U. S. 683; Railroad Co. v. Dennis, 116 U. S. 665; Railroad Co. v. Thomas, 132 U. S. 174; Bryan v. Board, 151 U. S. 639.

doing business within the state boundaries, by permission granted by statute, to deduct from the interest on its bonds, issued prior to the enactment of the statute, the tax levied by the state and pay such tax to the state. The court held that the statute assuming to require the company to assess and collect the tax impaired the obligation of the contract between the state and the company. The statute under which the company obtained the right to enter and do business in the state was held to be a contract and to preclude the state from imposing any additional burdens on the corporation.[1]

§ 770. Exemption of railroad property—Contract—Alteration of charter.—As we have elsewhere shown the exemption of the property of a railroad company may constitute a part of the contract and be within the provision of the federal constitution forbidding the states from impairing the obligation of contracts. The rule which protects an exemption clause as part of the contract does not preclude a state from enacting a statute subjecting the property of the railroad company to taxation in cases where the power to alter or amend the charter or act of incorporation is expressly reserved. The reservation of the right to alter, amend or repeal invests the state with ample power to withdraw the exemption,[2] but where the rights of third

---

[1] New York, etc., Co. v. Pennsylvania, 153 U. S. 628, s. c. 14 Sup. Ct. R. 952, citing Crutcher v. Commonwealth, 141 U. S. 47, s. c. 11 Sup. Ct. R. 851; Clark v. Iowa City, 20 Wall. 583; Hartman v. Greenhow, 102 U. S. 672, 684; Koshkonong v. Benton, 104 U. S. 668; State Tax on Foreign Held Bonds, 15 Wall. 300; Railroad Co. v. Jackson, 7 Wall. 262; St. Louis v. Ferry Co., 11 Wall. 423; Delaware Railroad Tax Case, 18 Wall. 206. The cases of Bell's Gap R. Co. v. Pennsylvania, 134 U. S. 232, s. c. 10 Sup. Ct. R. 533; Jennings v. Coal Co., 147 U. S. 147, s. c. 13 Sup. Ct. R. 282, were distinguished.

[2] Tomlinson v. Jessup, 15 Wall. 454, cited with approval in New York, etc., Co. v. Town of Bristol, 151 U. S. 556, s. c. 14 Sup. Ct. R. 437; Holyoke, etc., Co. v. Lyman, 15 Wall. 500; State v. Atlantic, etc., Co., 60 Ga. 268; Hoge v. Richmond, etc., Co., 99 U. S. 348; New York, etc., Co. v. City of Waterbury, 60 Conn. 1, s. c. 22 Atl. R. 439; State v. Miller, 1 Vroom 368; State v. Miller, 2 Vroom 561; State v. Collectors of Chambersburg, 8 Vroom 228; West, etc., Co. v. Supervisors, 35 Wis. 257. See, generally, Close v. Glenwood Cemetery, 107 U. S. 466, s. c. 2 Sup. Ct. R. 267; Waterworks v. Schottler, 110 U. S. 347; Pennsylvania College Cases, 13 Wall. 190; City of St. Paul v.

persons intervene and the alteration, amendment or repeal would destroy those rights the power to withdraw the exemption can not, as it has been held, be exercised.[1] We suppose, however, that the rights of third persons must be property rights and in the nature of vested rights in order to preclude a state from withdrawing or annulling the exemption granted by the corporate charter.[2]

St. Paul, etc., Co., 23 Minn. 469; State v. Maine, etc., Co., 66 Me. 488; Maine etc., v. Maine, 96 U. S. 499; State v. Northern, etc., Co., 44 Md. 131; Roxbury v. Boston, etc., Co., 6 Cush. 424.

[1] In Tomlinson v. Jessup, 15 Wall. 454, 458, the court said: "There is no subject over which it is of greater moment for the state to preserve its power than that of taxation. It has nevertheless been held by this court, not, however, without occasional earnest dissent from a minority, that the power of taxation over particular parcels of property, or over property of particular persons or corporations, may be surrendered by one legislative body, so as to bind its successors and the state. It was so adjudged at an early day in New Jersey v. Wilson, 7 Cranch 164; the adjudication was affirmed in Jefferson Bank v. Skelly, 1 Black 436, and has been repeated in several cases within the past few years, and notably so in the cases of The Home of the Friendless v. Rouse, 8 Wall. 430, and Wilmington Railroad v. Reid, 13 Wall. 264. In these cases, and in others of a similar character, the exemption is upheld as being made upon considerations moving to the state which give to the transaction the character of a contract. It is thus that it is brought within the protection of the federal constitution. In the case of a corporation the exemption, if originally made in the act of incorporation, is supported upon the consideration of the duties and liabilities which the corporators assume by accepting the charter. When made, as in the present case, by an amendment of the charter, it is supported upon the consideration of the greater efficiency with which the corporation will thus be enabled to discharge the duties originally assumed by the corporators to the public, or of the greater facility with which it will support its liabilities and carry out the purposes of its creation. Immunity from taxation constituting in these cases a part of the contract with the government, is by the reservation of power such as is contained in the law of 1841, subject to be revoked equally with any other provision of the charter whenever the legislature may deem it expedient for the public interests that the revocation shall be made. The reservation affects the entire relation between the state and the corporation, and places under legislative control all rights, privileges, and immunities derived by its charter directly from the state. Rights acquired by third parties, and which have become vested, under the charter, in the legitimate exercise of its powers stand upon a different footing."

[2] Brightman v. Kirner, 22 Wis. 54.

§ 771. **Due process of law in tax proceedings.**—The federal constitution requires due process of law in tax proceedings, as well as in other proceedings where property rights are involved. The requirement of due process of law does not demand that the person upon whose property a tax is imposed shall be present when the assessment is made. Notice of some kind is necessary, but it need not be personal notice.[1] Where provision is made for the establishment of a board or tribunal to value and assess property, and the tax-payer is by law required to report or return his property to such board or tribunal, the sittings of which are designated by law, the requirements of the constitution as to notice are satisfied.[2]

§ 772. **Equal protection of the laws.**—The fourteenth amendment to the federal constitution prohibits the states from denying to citizens the equal protection of the laws, and a state statute which violates the provisions of the amendment is, of

---

[1] County of San Mateo v. Southern Pac. R. Co., 13 Fed. R. 722; County of Santa Clara v. Southern Pacific R. Co., 18 Fed. R. 385; Hagar v. Reclamation Dist., 111 U. S. 701; Garvin v. Daussman, 114 Ind. 429; Kentucky Tax Cases, 115 U. S. 321; Stuart v. Palmer, 74 N. Y. 183; Kuntz v. Sumption, 117 Ind. 1; Johnson v. Joliet, etc., Co., 23 Ill. 124; Scott v. City of Toledo, 36 Fed. R. 385; Palmer v. McMahon, 133 U. S. 660; Spencer v. Merchant, 125 U. S. 345, 356; Paulsen v. Portland, 149 U. S. 30; Matter of Ford, 6 Lans. 92; Minard v. Douglas Co., 9 Oregon 206; Weimer v. Bunbury, 30 Mich. 201; Matter of Trustees, 31 N. Y. 574; Cooper v. Board, 108 Eng. C. L. R. 181; Davidson v. New Orleans, 96 U. S. 97; Hurtado v. California, 110 U. S. 535, 536; Desty on Taxation, § 114, p. 601; Cooley on Taxation 51. Judge Cooley says: "It has been decided that the revenue laws of a state may be in harmony with the fourteenth amendment, though they do not provide for giving a party an opportunity to be present when the tax is assessed against him, and to be then heard, if they give him the right to be heard afterwards in a suit to enjoin the collection, in which both the validity of the tax and the amount of it may be contested."

[2] Pittsburg, etc., Co. v. Backus, 154 U. S. 421, s. c. 14 Sup. Ct. R. 1114; Kentucky Railroad Tax Cases, 115 U. S. 321, 331; State Railroad Tax Cases, 92 U. S. 609; Railway Co. v. Wright, 151 U. S. 470, s. c. 14 Sup. Ct. R. 396; Smith v. Rude, etc., Co., 131 Ind. 150; Hyland v. Brazil, etc., Co., 128 Ind. 335; Neal v. Delaware, 103 U. S. 370; Bell's Gap, etc., Co. v. Pennsylvania, 134 U. S. 232; Adsit v. Lieb, 76 Ill. 198; Porter v. Railroad Co., 76 Ill. 561; Railroad Co. v. Commonwealth, 81 Ky. 492; St. Louis, etc., Co. v. Worthen, 52 Ark. 529; State v. Runyon, 41 N. J. L. 98; Hannibal, etc., Co. v. State Board, 64 Mo. 294.

course, invalid. There is no difficulty in declaring the general rule, and in asserting that there may be a denial of the equal protection of the laws by a statute subjecting railroad property to taxation,[1] but there is real difficulty in determining what constitutes a denial of the equal protection guaranteed by the federal constitution. It may be said, generally, that where there is a palpably unjust and arbitrary discrimination against railroad companies, the result of which is to put upon them an oppressive burden much greater and essentially different from that placed upon other property subject to taxation there is a violation of the constitutional provision, but merely providing different methods of assessing railroad corporations or providing different boards or tribunals from those provided for assessing the property of other corporations or persons is not a violation of the constitutional provision under consideration.[2]

§ 773. Equal protection of the laws—Corporations are persons.—Railroad corporations are persons within the meaning of the constitution and can not be denied the equal protection of the laws.[3] Corporations are not within the constitutional

---

[1] In County of Santa Barbara v. Southern Pacific R. Co., 18 Fed. R. 385, 399, the question was ably discussed by Mr. Justice Field, who said *inter alia:* "It is a matter of history that unequal and discriminating taxation, leveled against special classes, has been the fruitful means of oppression, and the cause of more commotions and disturbances in society, of insurrections and revolutions than any other cause in the world. It would indeed be a charming spectacle to present to the civilized world, as counsel in the San Mateo ironically observed, if the amendment were to read, as contended it does in law, 'Nor shall any state deprive any person of his property without due process of law, except it be in the form of taxation, nor deny to any person within its jurisdiction the equal protection of the law, except it be by taxation.'"

[2] Cincinnati, etc., Co. v. Commonwealth, 115 U. S. 321; Missouri v. Lewis, 101 U. S. 22, 30; Columbus, etc., Co. v. Wright, 151 U. S. 470, s. c. 14 Sup. Ct. R. 396; State Railroad Tax Cases, 92 U. S. 575; Charlotte, etc., Railroad v. Gibbes. 42 U. S. 386, s. c. 12 Sup. Ct. R. 255; Railroad Co. v. Beckwith, 129 U. S. 26, s. c. 9 Sup. Ct. R. 207; Columbus, etc., Co. v. Wright, 89 Ga. 574, s. c. 15 S. E. R. 293; Cincinnati, etc., Co. v. Commonwealth, 81 Ky. 492; Cleveland, etc., Co. v. Backus, 133 Ind. 513, s. c. 18 L. R. A. 729.

[3] Pembina, etc., Co. v. Commonwealth, 125 U. S. 181, s. c. 8 Sup. Ct. R. 737; Santa Clara County v. Southern Pacific R. Co., 118 U. S. 396; Minneapolis, etc., Co. v. Beckwith, 129 U. S. 27; Cleveland, etc., Co. v. Backus, 133 Ind. 513, s. c. 18 L. R. A. 729.

provision which declares that "citizens of each state shall be entitled to all privileges and immunities of citizens of the several states."[1] The distinction made between the two clauses of the federal constitution is an important one, but does not exert a direct influence upon the subject under immediate discussion, yet it seems necessary to refer to it in order to prevent possible confusion.

§ 774. Equal protection of the laws—What is a denial of.—We suppose that a tax designedly made unequal and intended to impose upon a special class a burden clearly unjust and plainly beyond that imposed upon other classes of persons would come within the prohibition of the fourteenth amendment, for a tax which would burden a special class grossly more than other classes would be a denial of the fundamental principle of law that the burden of taxation shall be equalized as nearly as practicable. We do not mean, of course, that there must be absolute equality, nor, indeed, that there must be substantial equality or uniformity. There probably never was a tax levied that was truly uniform and equal, and, certainly, the federal tribunals would not interfere where nothing more than inequality was shown, even though the inequality be manifest and material. It can not be justly said that there is a denial of the equal protection of the laws where there is a simple error of judgment or an unwise or even unjust exercise of legislative discretion, but there may be a denial of the equal protection of the laws where there is a design and purpose to relieve from taxation many classes by placing an unjust, oppressive and unequal burden upon a special class.[2] It may possibly

---

[1] Paul v. Virginia, 8 Wall. 168; Railroad Co. v. Koontz, 104 U. S. 5; Pensacola, etc., Co. v. Western Union Tel. Co., 96 U. S 1, 19; Ducat v. Chicago, 10 Wall. 410; Lafayette Ins. Co. v. French, 18 How. (U. S.) 404; Doyle v. Continental Ins. Co., 94 U.S. 535,539; Elston v. Piggott, 94 Ind. 14, 17; People v. Fire Association, 92 N. Y. 311.

[2] In the case of Bells Gap R. Co. v. Commonwealth, 134 U. S. 232, s. c. 10 Sup. Ct. R. 533, the court said: "The provision in the fourteenth amendment that no state shall deny to any person within its jurisdiction the equal protection of the laws, was not intended to prevent a state from adjusting its system of taxation in all proper and reasonable ways." It was also said: "It may impose different spe-

be true that where the statute so operates as to place an unjust and oppressive burden upon a special class it will be held invalid, although it can not be said that there was a formed design or purpose to make an unjust discrimination,[1] but this could be true only in an extreme case, where, to permit the statute to stand, would be to practically authorize confiscation of property or to uphold an enforced and unequal contribution to the revenues of the state.

§ 775. **Fourteenth amendment—Unequal taxation—Generally.**—It is difficult to precisely define the line which separates the rightful domain of a state from the domain of the federal government in the field of taxation for general revenue purposes and declare when the federal judiciary may rightfully interfere. That a tax levied by a state legislature may be so grossly unequal and so palpably unjust that the federal tribunals will overthrow the statute which levies the tax seems clear, but what will constitute the inequality or unjust discrimination that will authorize the exercise of the federal jurisdiction is as yet clouded by confusion and doubt. There must be inequality great enough to be justly characterized as a denial of the equal protection of the laws, for, manifestly, if all persons are treated alike, although the burdens imposed may be cific taxes upon different trades and professions, and may vary the rates of excise upon various products; it may tax real estate and personal property in a different manner; it may tax visible property only, and not tax securities for the payment of money; it may allow deductions for indebtedness or not allow them. All such regulations, and those of like character, so long as they proceed within reasonable limits and general usage, are within the discretion of the state legislature or the people of the state in framing their constitution. But clear and hostile discriminations against particular persons and classes, especially such as are of an unusual character and unknown to the practice of our governments, might be obnoxious to the constitutional prohibition. It would, however, be unwise and impracticable to lay down any general rule or definition on the subject that would include all cases. They must be decided as they arise." The court adopted the rule stated in Barbier *v.* Connelly, 113 U. S. 27, 31, s. c. 5 Sup. Ct. R. 357.

[1] The operation of a statute, rather than its form, determines its character. Yick Wo *v.* Hopkins, 118 U. S. 356; State *v.* The Judges, 21 Ohio St. 1; *Ex parte* Westerfield, 55 Cal. 550; State *v.* Herrmann, 75 Mo. 340; Nichols *v.* Walters, 37 Minn. 270.

unjust and oppressive, the jurisdiction of the federal tribunals can not be successfully invoked.[1] It is not a question of hardship or oppression, but of unjust discrimination against a class of persons or property resulting in an inequality of taxation, constituting a denial of the equal protection of the laws.

§ 776. **Classification not a denial of equal protection.**—A state is not bound to provide the same method of taxing all classes of property, but, as we have elsewhere shown, the legislature has a choice of methods, so that in classifying property for taxation and prescribing modes for valuing and assessing it there is no transgression of the fourteenth amendment, provided there is no hostile and unjust discrimination. It is possible to prescribe a method that necessarily discriminates against a special class to such an extent as to deprive it of the equal protection of the laws, but this result does not follow simply because the method adopted is unwise or leads to some inequality.[2] It is not enough, as we believe, to bring a case within the constitutional prohibition that there be some discrimination, for mere discrimination can not be said to be, of itself, a denial of the equal protection of the laws.

§ 777. **Fourteenth amendment—Tax for salaries of railroad commissioners.**—The extent to which a state may go without violating the provisions of the fourteenth amendment is strikingly illustrated by the cases which adjudge that railroad companies may be taxed to pay the salaries of the members of a railroad

---

[1] In the case of San Mateo County v. Southern Pacific R. Co., 13 Fed. R. 722, Mr. Justice Field said: "It is undoubtedly true that the hardship and injustice of a tax levied by the state, considered with reference to its amount, are not subjects of federal cognizance."

[2] Home Ins. Co. v. New York, 134 U. S. 594; Pacific Express Co. v. Seibert, 142 U. S. 339; Charlotte, etc., Railroad Co. v. Gibbes, 142 U. S. 386; Missouri, etc., Railway Co. v. Mackey, 127 U. S. 205. See, generally, Kentucky Railroad Tax Cases, 115 U. S. 321; State Railroad Tax Cases, 92 U. S. 575; Cleveland, etc., Co. v. Backus, 133 Ind. 513; Pittsburgh, etc., Co. v. Backus, 154 U. S. 421, s. c. 14 Sup. Ct. R. 1114; Cleveland, etc., Co. v. Backus, 154 U. S. 439, s. c. 14 Sup. Ct. R. 1122; Dow v. Beidelman, 125 U. S. 680.

commission.[1] This seems to us a very strong assertion of the power of the states, and, with all deference to the great tribunal which asserted the doctrine, a very dangerous and doubtful rule. The reasoning of the court necessarily leads to the conclusion that like commissions may be created for all classes of corporations having duties and powers of a public nature, and the business of maintaining them imposed on such corporations, and this would be to put upon them a much heavier and essentially different burden from that imposed upon other bodies politic and corporate. It is to be noted, we may properly say in passing, that the decisions of the supreme court go only to the federal side of the question and have no direct influence upon a question arising under a state constitution forbidding special legislation and requiring equality and uniformity of taxation.

§ 778. Corporations deriving rights from the United States.—The property of a private corporation having its *situs* in a state may be taxed by the state, although the corporation may derive privileges and franchises from the United States. It is the property that is the subject of taxation, for in the case of an interstate corporation the business or operations can not be taxed by the state, since that would be to tax interstate commerce itself. It is important, in all phases of the subject, to keep in mind the distinction between taxing the property of an interstate corporation situated within the boundaries of a state and taxing the business or operation of the corporation engaged in carrying articles of commerce from state to state, for confusion will result if this distinction is not observed.[2]

§ 779. Land grants.—Land granted to a railroad company

[1] Charlotte, etc., Co. v. Gibbes, 142 U. S. 386, s. c. 12 Sup. Ct. R. 255, citing Georgia, etc., Banking Co. v. Smith, 128 U. S. 174, s. c. 9 Sup. Ct. R. 47; New York v. Squire, 145 U. S. 175, s. c. 12 Sup. Ct. R. 880.

[2] Railroad Co. v. Peniston, 18 Wall. 5; Thomson v. Pacific Railroad, 9 Wall. 579; Reagan v. Mercantile Trust Co., 154 U. S. 413, s. c. 14 Sup. Ct. R. 1060; Western Union Tel. Co. v. Att'y-Gen'l, 125 U. S. 530, s. c. 8 Sup. Ct. R. 961; City of St. Louis v. Western Union Tel. Co., 148 U. S. 92, s. c. 13 Sup. Ct. R. 485.

§ 780   TAXATION UNDER THE FEDERAL CONSTITUTION.   1097

by the United States is subject to taxation by the state in which the land is situated, and this is true, although the railroad company transports freight and passengers for the government.[1] The conclusion stated seems to us the just one, but there was stubborn conflict of opinion upon the question when it was before the court. If land becomes the property of a private corporation, yielding to that corporation revenues and profits, it is justly taxable, no matter from what grantor the land was derived, nor is the question, as we believe, changed by the fact that use is made of the railroad by the general government, for, after all, the corporation exists, and its business is conducted for the private benefit of its stockholders.

§ 780. **Domestic commerce.**—Intrastate or domestic commerce is under the dominion of the state, for it is only commerce between the states upon which the commerce clause of the federal constitution operates.[2] The state may regulate

---

[1] Railroad Company v. Peniston, 18 Wall. 5; Lane County v. Oregon, 7 Wall. 71; Thomson v. Pacific Railroad, 9 Wall. 579; Reagan v. Mercantile Trust Co., 154 U. S. 413, s. c. 14 Sup. Ct. 1060; Reagan v. Farmers', etc., Co., 154 U. S. 362, s. c. 14 Sup. Ct. R. 1047, citing Railroad Commission Cases, 116 U.S. 307, s. c. 6 Sup. Ct. R. 334; Mercantile Trust Co. v. Texas R. Co., 51 Fed. R. 529. See, generally, Chicago, etc., Co. v. Davenport, 51 Iowa 451; West., etc., R. Co. v. Supervisors, 35 Wis. 257. But where land is granted by the United States, it is not taxable by the state until the title vests in the grantee. Railway Co. v. Prescott, 16 Wall. 603; County of Cass v. Morrison, 28 Minn. 257; Wheeler v. Merriman, 30 Minn. 372. See, upon the general subject, McGregor, etc., Co. v. Brown, 39 Iowa 655; Grant v. Iowa, etc., Railroad Co., 54 Iowa 673; Doe v. Iowa, etc., Railroad Co., 54 Iowa 657; Central, etc.,Co. v. Howard, 52 Cal. 227; Hunnewell v. Cass County, 22 Wall. 464; Colorado Company v. Commissioners, 95 U. S. 259; Litchfield v. County of Webster, 101 U. S. 773.

[2] Postal Tel. Co. v. City Council of Charleston, 153 U. S. 692, s. c. 14 Sup. Ct. R. 1094; Home Ins. Co. v. City of Augusta, 93 U. S. 116; Ratterman v. Western Union, etc., Co., 127 U. S. 411, s. c. 8 Sup. Ct. R. 1127; Western Union, etc., Co. v. Alabama State Board, 132 U. S. 472, s. c. 10 Sup. Ct. R. 161; Pacific Express Co. v. Seibert, 142 U. S. 339, s. c. 12 Sup. Ct. R. 250; Western Union Tel. Co. v. City Council of Charleston, 56 Fed. 419, citing Western Union Tel. Co. v. Attorney-General, 125 U. S. 530, s. c. 8 Sup. Ct. R. 961. In the case of Western Union Tel. Co. v. Texas, 105 U. S. 460, a distinction between interstate and domestic commerce was drawn and it was held that property within the state was subject to taxation. The question was considered in the case of Lehigh, etc., Co. v.

domestic commerce as it deems proper unaffected by the clause of the national constitution which governs the subject of interstate commerce, but a state can not, of course, enact any statute in reference to domestic commerce which will impair the obligation of a contract, deny the equal protection of the laws, or violate any other provision of the federal constitution.

Pennsylvania, 145 U. S. 192, where it was said: "Taxation is undoubtedly one of the forms of regulation, but the power of each state to tax its own commerce, and the franchises, property or business of its own corporations engaged in such commerce has always been recognized, and the particular mode of taxation in this instance is conceded to be in itself not open to objection, and while interstate commerce can not be regulated by a state by the laying of taxes thereon in any form, yet whenever the subject of taxation can be separated, so that that which arises from interstate commerce can be distinguished from that which arises from commerce wholly within the state, the distinction will be acted upon by the courts, and the state permitted to collect that arising upon commerce solely within its own territory."

CHAPTER XXXII.

LOCAL ASSESSMENTS.

§ 781. Assessments and taxes—Distinction.
782. Local assessments—Power to levy.
783. Statute must be complied with.
784. Property subject to local assessment—General rule.
785. Property of railroad companies.
786. Right of way—Whether subject to assessment.
§ 787. Abutting property — Right of way is not.
788. Right of way—Mode of assessing.
789. Lien of the assessment.
790. Assessment of right of way—Enforcing assessment.
791. Procedure.

§ 781. **Assessments and taxes—Distinction.**—There is a broad distinction between a local assessment and a tax levied for the purpose of raising governmental revenue.[1] The principal ground for the distinction is that local assessments are founded upon the theory that there is a special benefit resulting from the expenditure of the money derived from the assessment, while in the case of ordinary taxes there is a common benefit. Taxes proper, or ordinary taxes, are levied upon all property except certain classes specially exempted, such as property used for religious, charitable and kindred purposes in order to secure revenue to defray the expenses of the general government.[2] No special benefit accrues to any one from

[1] Roosevelt Hospital v. Mayor, 84 N. Y. 108. In Mix v. Ross, 57 Ill. 121, it is said: "There is a plain distinction between taxes, which are burdens or charges imposed upon persons or property to raise money for public purposes, and assessments for city or village improvements, which are not regarded as burdens, but as an equivalent or compensation for the enhanced value which the property of the person assessed has derived from the improvement."

[2] Loan Association v. Topeka, 20 Wall. 655, 664; Illinois Central, etc., Co. v. City of Decatur, 147 U. S. 190, s. c. 13 Sup. Ct. R. 293; Rich v. City of Chicago, 152 Ill. 18, 38 N. E. R. 255;

the payment of taxes; the benefit is general and accrues to all citizens and property alike, and consists in the general benefits which the government guarantees in the protection and enjoyment of life and property, and the promotion of those institutions which have for their object the welfare of all. Local assessments are not levied in order to raise general revenue for the purposes of government, but are charges assessed against the property of some particular locality because that property derives some special benefit from the expenditure of the money collected by the assessment in addition to the general benefit accruing to all property or citizens of the commonwealth.[1] The distinction is very clearly pointed out in

Elliott on Roads and Streets, 369-370.

[1] Chicago, etc., Co. v. City of Joliet, 154 Ill. 522, 39 N. E. R. 1077; Palmer v. Stumph, 29 Ind. 329; Cleveland v. Tripp, 13 R. I. 50; Richmond, etc., Co. v. City of Lynchburg, 81 Va. 473; McGehee v. Mathis, 21 Ark. 40; King v. City of Portland, 2 Ore. 146; Palmyra v. Morton, 25 Mo. 593; People v. Mayor, 4 N. Y. 419; City of Lexington v. McQuillan, 9 Dana (Ky.) 514; Moale v. Baltimore, 5 Md. 314; Hurford v. Omaha, 4 Neb. 336; Charnock v. Levee Co., 38 La. Ann. 323; Norfolk City v. Ellis, 26 Gratt. 224; Emery v. San Francisco, etc., Co., 28 Cal. 345; Willard v. Presbury, 14 Wall. 676; Commonwealth v. Woods, 44 Pa. St. 113; State v. Dean, 23 N. J. L. 335; Hines v. Leavenworth, 3 Kan. 186; Sewall v. St. Paul, 20 Minn. 511; City of New Albany v. McCulloch, 127 Ind. 500; Sheehan v. Good Samaritan, etc., 50 Mo. 155; Illinois, etc., Co. v. City of Decatur, 147 U. S. 190; City of Denver v. Knowles, 17 Colo. 204, 17 L. R. A. 135; Farrar v. St. Louis, 80 Mo. 379; Hammett v. Philadelphia, 65 Pa. 146; Speer v. Athens, 85 Ga. 49; Hoyt v. East Saginaw, 19 Mich. 39; Cain v. Commissioners, 86 N. Car. 8; Allen v. Galveston, 51 Tex. 302; Hale v. Kenosha, 29 Wis. 599; Cooley on Taxation, (2d ed.) 606, 607; Winona, etc., Co. v. City of Watertown, 1 S. Dak. 46, 44 N. W. R. 1072; Rich v. City of Chicago, 152 Ill. 18, 38 N. E. R. 255. "Taxes are impositions for purposes of general revenue; assessments are special and local impositions upon property in the immediate vicinity for an improvement for the public welfare, which are necessary to pay for the improvement, and laid with reference to the special benefit which such property derives from such expenditure." Reeves v. Treasurer, 8 Ohio St. 333. The distinction between a tax and a local assessment is very clearly pointed out by Chief Justice George in the case of Town of Macon v. Patty, 57 Miss. 378, 386, as follows: "A local assessment can only be levied on land; it can not, as a tax can, be made a personal liability of the tax-payer; it is an assessment on the thing supposed to be benefited. A tax is levied on the whole state or a known political subdivision, as a county or a town. A local assessment is levied on property situated in a district created for the express purpose of the levy, and possessing no other function, or

those cases which hold that a statute exempting property from taxation does not exempt it from local assessments,[1] and also in those which hold that the levy of a local assessment does not violate constitutional provisions requiring uniformity of taxation.[2]

§ 782. Local assessments—Power to levy.—The authority or power to levy local assessments has for its foundation the general taxing power of the commonwealth.[3] The power to levy general taxes and local assessments comes from the same source. The power is usually conferred through legislative enactments upon local governmental instrumentalities, such as counties, cities, towns and the like. For a time there was much doubt as to the validity of statutes conferring upon mu-

even existence, than to be the thing on which the levy is made. A tax is a continuing burden, and must be collected at stated short intervals for all times, and without it government can not exist. A local assessment is exceptional, both as to time and locality —it is brought into being for a particular occasion, and to accomplish a particular purpose, and dies with the passing of the occasion and the accomplishment of the purpose. A tax is levied, collected and administered by a public agency, elected by and responsible to the community upon which it is imposed; a local assessment is made by an authority *ab extra*, yet it is like a tax in that it is imposed under an authority derived from the legislature, and is an enforced contribution to the public welfare, and its payment may be enforced by the summary method allowed for the collection of taxes. It is like a tax in that it must be levied for a public purpose, and must be apportioned by some reasonable rule among those upon whose property it is levied. It is unlike a tax in that the proceeds of the assessment must be expended in an improvement from which a benefit clearly exceptive and plainly perceived must inure to the property upon which it is imposed."

[1] Roosevelt Hospital v. Mayor, 84 N. Y. 108; First Presbyterian Church v. City of Fort Wayne, 36 Ind. 338; Illinois, etc., Co. v. Decatur, 126 Ill. 92; Chicago, etc., Co. v. People, 120 Ill. 104; Buffalo Cemetery v. Buffalo, 46 N. Y. 506; Olive Cemetery v. Philadelphia, 93 Pa. St. 129; Mayor, etc., of Baltimore v. Greenmount Cemetery, 7 Md. 517; City of Bridgeport v. New York, etc., R. Co., 36 Conn. 255. See, also, State v. Binninger, 42 N. J. 528, 1 Am. & Eng. R. R. Cas. 410; Cooley on Taxation, (2d. ed.) 207; Winona, etc., Co. v. City of Watertown, 1 S. Dak. 46, 44 N. W. R. 1072; Illinois Cent. Co. v. City of Decatur, 154 Ill. 173, 38 N. E. R. 626.

[2] Chamberlain v. Cleveland, 34 Ohio St. 551; City of Zanesville v. Richards, 5 Ohio St. 589; City of Denver v. Knowles, 17 Colo. 204, 17 L. R. A. 135; Mayor of Birmingham v. Klein, 89 Ala. 461, 8 L. R. A. 369; Reeves v. Treasurer, 8 Ohio St. 333.

[3] Winona, etc., Co. v. City of Water-

nicipalities the power to levy assessments to pay for local improvements, but the validity of such statutes is now so firmly established by judicial decisions as to be no longer considered an open question.[1] The right to levy a local assessment proceeds, and is justified, upon the theory that the property against which the assessment is placed is enhanced in value by the construction of the improvement to an amount equal to the assessment exacted.[2] It has been held that if the property against which an assessment has been levied has not been benefited by the improvement, the collection of the assessment may be

town, 1 S. Dak. 46, 44 N. W. R. 1072; McComb v. Bell, 2 Minn. 256; Pray v. Northern Liberties, 31 Pa. St. 69; Walsh v. Mathews, 29 Cal. 123; New Orleans Praying for Opening of Streets, 20 La. Ann. 497; Reeves v. Treasurer, 8 Ohio St. 333; Hines v. Leavenworth, 3 Kan. 186; Van Antwerp, In re, 56 N. Y. 261; People v. Mayor, 4 N. Y. 419; Keith v. Bingham, 100 Mo. 300, s. c. 13 S. W. R. 683; City of St. Louis v. Allen, 53 Mo. 44; Sheehan v. Good Samaritan, etc., 50 Mo. 155; City of Austin v. Austin, etc., Co., 69 Tex. 180; Town of Monticello v. Banks, 48 Ark. 251; Allen v. Drew, 44 Vt. 174; Adams County v. Quincy, (Ill.) 6 L. R. A. 155; State v. Fuller, 34 N. J. L. 227; State v. Newark, 35 N. J. L. 168; Weeks v. Milwaukee, 10 Wis. 242; Motz v. Detroit, 18 Mich. 494; Mayor, etc., of Baltimore v. Greenmount Cemetery, 7 Md. 517; Beach on Pub. Corp., § 1072; Glasgow v. Rowse, 43 Mo. 479. In the case of In re Vacation of Centre Street, 115 Pa. St. 247, s. c. 8 Atl. R. 56, it is said: "Municipal assessments for grading, paving, opening, widening or vacating streets, and other purposes for which, within proper limits, they may be authorized, are referable solely to the taxing power. Indeed, there is nothing else upon which they can be sustained."

[1] Raleigh v. Peace, 110 N. Car. 32, 17 L. R. A. 330; Stroud v. Philadelphia, 61 Pa. St. 255; City of Wilmington v. Yopp, 71 N. C. 76; Cooley Const. Lim., 506; Elliott Roads and Streets, 370; Tiedeman, Munic. Corp., § 259a. "The subject has been thoroughly discussed and every principle bearing upon it severely analyzed in almost every state of the Union where the power has been exercised; and it is now as firmly established as any other doctrine of American law." Palmyra v. Morton, 25 Mo. 593.

[2] Lockwood v. St. Louis, 24 Mo. 20; Wright v. Boston, 9 Cush. 233; McGonigle v. Allegheny City, 44 Pa. St. 118; Litchfield v. Vernon, 41 N. Y. 123; New Orleans Praying for Opening of Streets, 20 La. Ann. 497; Allen v. Drew, 44 Vt. 174; City of Paterson v. Society, 24 N. J. L. 385; City of Auburn v. Paul, 84 Me. 212, 24 Atl. R. 817; Municipality No. 2 v. Dunn, 10 La. Ann. 57; City of Philadelphia v. Tryon, 35 Pa. St. 401; State v. Judges, 51 Minn. 539, 53 N. W. R. 800; Preston v. Rudd, 84 Ky. 150; City of Fort Wayne v. Shoaff, 106 Ind. 66; Mock v. Muncie, 9 Ind. App. 536, 37 N. E. R. 281, 32 N. E. R. 718; Davies v. Los Angeles,

§ 783   LOCAL ASSESSMENTS.   1103

enjoined,[1] but this doctrine is to be taken with careful qualification, for it is only in very clear cases that the courts can interfere.[2] Since the power to levy a local assessment depends upon a statutory enactment, it can have no existence unless there be a valid statute conferring it upon the municipality which claims the right to exercise it.[3] The general authority to levy taxes for municipal purposes is not broad enough to confer the right to levy assessments for local improvements.[4] A statute conferring such a power upon a municipality must be strictly construed in favor of the person against whom the assessment is levied.[5]

§ 783. **Statute must be complied with.**—Where the statute prescribes the mode in which the improvement shall be made

86 Cal. 37; Illinois Central Railroad Co. v. City of Decatur, 147 U. S. 190, 13 Sup. Ct. R. 293; Oregon, etc., Co. v. City of Portland, 25 Ore. 229, 35 Pac. R. 452; Mt. Pleasant v. Baltimore, etc., Railroad Co., 138 Pa. St. 365. "The principle upon which rests that numerous class of statutes which charge lots of ground with the expense of grading and paving the streets in front of them is, that the value of the lots is enhanced by the public expenditure." Schenley v. Commonwealth, 36 Pa. St. 29.

[1] Oregon, etc., Co. v. City of Portland, 25 Ore. 229, 35 Pac. R. 452. See City of Bloomington v. Chicago, etc., R. Co., 134 Ill. 451; Mount Pleasant v. Baltimore, etc., Co., 138 Pa. St. 365, 11 L. R. A. 520; New York, etc., R. Co. v. New Haven, 42 Conn. 279.

[2] Where the question of the amount of the benefit is committed to the judgment of the municipal officers, the courts can not control the assessment in that respect. Motz v. City of Detroit, 18 Mich. 494; LeRoy v. Mayor, 20 Johns. 430; Ex parte Mayor, etc., 23 Wend. 277; Mooers v. Smedley, 6 Johns. Ch. 28; Commonwealth v. Woods, 44 Pa. St. 113; Mayor of Brooklyn v. Meserole, 26 Wend. 132; Lyon v. City of Brooklyn, 28 Barb. 609; City of Ft. Wayne v. Cody, 43 Ind. 197.

[3] Griswold v. Pelton, 34 Ohio St. 482; Matter of Second Ave. Church, 66 N. Y. 395; Niklaus v. Conkling, 118 Ind. 289.

[4] Drake v. Phillips, 40 Ill. 388; Minn., etc., Co. v. Palmer, 20 Minn. 468; Mayor, etc., of Savannah v. Hartridge, 8 Ga. 23; Lott v. Ross, 38 Ala. 156; Hare v. Kennerly, 83 Ala. 608, s. c. 3 So. R. 683; Mays v. Cincinnati, 1 Ohio St. 268; City of Cincinnati v. Bryson, 15 Ohio 625; City of Chicago v. Wright, 32 Ill. 192; City of Leavenworth v. Norton, 1 Kan. 432; City of Richmond v. Daniel, 14 Gratt. (Va.) 385; Kyle v. Malin, 8 Ind. 34; Green v. Ward, 82 Va. 324; Com'rs of Asheville v. Means, 7 Ired. (Law) 406; City of Fairfield v. Ratcliff, 20 Iowa 396; Mayor, etc., of Annapolis v. Harwood, 32 Md. 471; Board of Com'rs of Winston v. Taylor, 99 N. C. 210, s. c. 6 S. E. R. 114.

[5] Matter of Second Avenue Church, 66 N. Y. 395; Niklaus v. Conkling,

and the assessment levied, that mode must be strictly pursued by the municipal authorities in making the levy.[1] "The mode constitutes the measure of power."[2] But the rule of construction is not so strict that a literal compliance with the statute in immaterial matters is necessary in every case. If there is a substantial compliance with the mode prescribed the assessment will usually be held valid.[3] So where the statute does not prescribe in detail the manner or mode in which an improvement shall be made and the assessment to pay for the same levied, but does in general terms grant the principal power to levy the assessment, the courts have held that all subordinate and incidental powers necessary to a valid exercise of the rights conferred by the statute pass with the grant of the principal power.[4] As the power to improve streets and the like is a continuing one, it has been held that the levy of one local

---

118 Ind. 289; Griswold v. Pelton, 34 Ohio St. 482; Allentown v. Henry, 73 Pa. St. 404; Reed v. Toledo, 18 Ohio 161; City Council of Augusta v. Murphey, 79 Ga. 101, 3 S. E. R. 326; Walker v. District of Columbia, 6 Mackey 352, 12 Cent. Rep. 408.

[1] Taylor v. Downer, 31 Cal. 480; Smith v. Davis, 30 Cal. 536; Merritt v. Portchester, 71 N. Y. 309; White v. City of Saginaw, 67 Mich. 33, 34 N. W. R. 255; Massing v. Ames, 37 Wis. 645; State v. Bayonne, 44 N. J. L. 114; Newman v. City, 32 Kan. 456; City of St. Louis v. Ranken, 96 Mo. 497, 9 S. W. R. 910; Bouldin v. Baltimore, 15 Md. 18; Sewall v. St. Paul, 20 Minn. 511; City of Chicago v. Wright, 32 Ill. 192; Brophy v. Landman, 28 Ohio St. 542; Butler v. Nevin, 88 Ill. 575; Leach v. Cargill, 60 Mo. 316; Hager v. Burlington, 42 Iowa 661; Allen v. Galveston, 51 Tex. 302; Hurford v. Omaha, 4 Neb. 336; In re Cambria Street, 75 Pa. St. 357; City of Lexington v. Headley, 5 Bush (Ky.) 508; Fayssoux v. Succession of Baroness De Chaurand, 36 La. Ann. 547. The provisions of the statute conferring the power to levy assessments should be construed as mandatory rather than directory. Merritt v. Village of Portchester, 71 N. Y. 309; Starr v. Burlington, 45 Iowa 87; State v. Mayor, etc., of Jersey City, 38 N. J. L. 85; Cambria Street, 75 Pa. St. 357.

[2] Zottman v. San Francisco, 20 Cal. 96. See, also, Murphy v. Louisville, 9 Bush (Ky.) 189; Nicolson Paving Co. v. Painter, 35 Cal. 699.

[3] State v. South Orange, 46 N. J. L. 317; Stebbins v. Kay, 4 N. Y. Sup. 566; Lynam v. Anderson, 9 Neb. 367; City of Springfield v. Sale, 127 Ill. 359, 20 N. E. R. 86; Jenkins v. Stetler, 118 Ind. 275; Parish v. Golden, 35 N. Y. 462.

[4] Schenley v. Com., 36 Pa. St. 29; Bigelow v. Perth Amboy, 26 N. J. L. 297; McNamara v. Estes, 22 Iowa 246; Smith v. City of Madison, 7 Ind. 86; Smith v. City of Newbern, 70 N. C. 14, s. c. 16 Am. Rep. 766; Spaulding v. Lowell, 23 Pick. 71; Cook County v. McCrea, 93 Ill. 236; State v. Jersey City, 30 N. J. L. 148.

assessment does not exhaust the power of the municipality, and second and subsequent assessments may be levied against the same property to pay for repairs, repaving, additional improvements and the like.[1] It is obvious that if this power were not a continuing one it would be impossible to repair, replace or extend an improvement when the same becomes out of repair, or inadequate for the purposes for which it was made.

§ 784. Property subject to local assessment—General rule.—The general rule is that all lands lying within the designated limits of the district or locality for which a local improvement is made, by whomsoever held or owned, are subject and liable to an assessment to aid in paying the cost of constructing such improvement,[2] and this rule is enforced, even though there be a statute exempting particular property from taxation. Thus it has been held that statutes exempting cemeteries, churches, charitable institutions and the like from taxation does not relieve them from assessments to pay for local improvements from which they derive a special benefit.[3] Stat-

[1] Wilkins v. Detroit, 46 Mich. 120; Sheley v. Detroit, 45 Mich. 431; State v. Hotaling, 44 N. J. L. 347; Board of Commissioners v. Fullen, 111 Ind. 410; In re Burmeister, 76 N. Y. 174; Farrar v. St. Louis, 80 Mo. 379; Estes v. Owen, 90 Mo. 113; Goszler v. Corporation of Georgetown, 6 Wheat. 593; Chicago, etc., Co. v. City of Quincy, 136 Ill. 563, 27 N. E. R. 192.

[2] Elliott on Roads and Streets, 376. See Broadway Church v. McAtee, 8 Bush (Ky.) 508, s. c. 8 Am. Rep. 480. In Louisville Transfer Co. v. Obst, (Ky.) February, 1875, the court said: "Real property held by railroad companies within the corporate limits of the city of Louisville is not exempt from street taxation. The terms of the grant of the power to tax for such purposes includes all real estate, and that held by railroad companies, like that held by churches, colleges, hospitals, and other institutions of like character, must bear its proportion of the local burden. There is no constitutional restriction to impose local taxation upon railroad companies. It is merely a question of local policy."

[3] Authorities, *ante*, § 781; Chicago, etc., Co. v. People, 120 Ill. 104, 11 N. E. R. 418; City of Paterson v. Society, 24 N. J. L. 385; State v. Newark, 27 N. J. 185; Sheehan v. Good Samaritan, 50 Mo. 155; Beals v. Providence Rubber Co., 11 R. I. 381; Worcester Agricultural Society v. Worcester, 116 Mass. 189; Harvey v. South Chester, 99 Pa. St. 565; Sewickley, etc., Church's Appeal, 165 Pa. St. 475, s. c. 30 Atl. R. 1007; Allen v. Galveston, 51 Tex. 302; Illinois Central Co. v. City of Decatur, 147 U. S. 190, 13 Sup. Ct. R. 293; Chicago, etc.,

utes under which an exemption from local assessment is asserted must be strictly construed against the person claiming the exemption, and liberally in favor of the assessment.[1] The enforcement of such assessment is placed on the ground that the statutes are intended only to relieve from the burdens of general taxation, and that local assessments are a species of special taxation not included in the general term taxation. But where the statutes provide that the property shall be exempt from taxation and assessments of every kind, it has been held that local assessments can not be levied against such property.[2]

§ 785. **Property of railroad companies.**—As to the liability of lands owned by railroad companies as part of their right of way or as necessary to the operation of their roads to local assessments there is some conflict among the authorities.[3] Some of the authorities make a distinction on the ground of the nature of the uses to which the lands are put. For the purposes of our discussion we will divide the lands owned by railroads into two classes, viz., that occupied by and used as a right of way, and that used for other purposes, such as shops, warehouses, depots, depot grounds and the like. The liability of the right of way to local assessments will be considered in the next and succeeding sections. While there may be some conflict in the decisions the overwhelming weight of authority is that depots, depot grounds and other lands owned by railway companies

---

R. Co. v. Milwaukee, 89 Wis. 506, s. c. 28 L. R. A. 249, 62 N. W. R. 417. And it has been held that a railway is not a "public highway" within a statute exempting public highways from local assessments. City of Nevada v. Eddy, 123 Mo. 546, 27 S. W. R. 471.

[1] Roosevelt Hospital v. Mayor, 84 N. Y. 108.

[2] Brightman v. Kirner, 22 Wis. 54; First Division St. Paul, etc., Co. v. City of St. Paul, 21 Minn. 526. A statute providing that "no tax or impost" shall be levied does not exempt from local assessments. State v. Jersey City, 42 N. J. L. 97, 1 Am. & Eng. R. R. Cas. 406; State v. Elizabeth, 37 N. J. L. 330.

[3] There can be no doubt that property held by a railroad company for purposes not connected with the operation of the road is subject to assessment. Where the property is not used in operating the road the company holds it substantially as property is held by individuals or strictly private corporations.

and not occupied as a right of way are subject to local assessments the same as the lands owned by any individual.[1]

§ 786. **Right of way—Whether subject to assessment.**—As said in the preceding section, there is a conflict in the adjudicated cases as to whether or not the right of way of a railroad company is subject to local assessments. The question has been discussed in a great number of instances, and different conclusions reached in apparently similar cases. The latest authorities on the subject, however, recognize what we believe to be the true rule, and that is, that where the right of way receives a benefit from the improvement for which the assessment is levied, and there is no statute exempting the railroad company from local assessments in clear and unequivocal terms, it is subject to assessment.[2] Some of the authorities

[1] City of Ludlow v. Cincinnati Southern, 78 Ky. 357, 7 Am. & Eng. Ry. Cas. 231; New York, etc., R. Co. v. New Britian, 49 Conn. 40; Nevada v. Eddy, 123 Mo. 546; Reopening of Berks St., 12 W. N. C. 10; Burlington, etc., Co. v. Spearman, 12 Iowa 112; Borough of Mt. Pleasant v. Baltimore, etc., Co., 138 Pa. 365, 20 Atl. R. 1052; In re Alexander Avenue, 17 N. Y. Supp. 933; Chicago, etc., Co. v. People, 120 Ill. 104; New Jersey, etc., Co. v. Mayor, 42 N. J. L. 97; City of Nevada v. Gilfillan, 123 Mo. 546, 27 S. W. R. 471; Bradley v. New York, etc., Co., 21 Conn. 294; Chicago, etc., Co. v. City of Chicago, 139 Ill. 573, 28 N. E. R. 1108; Chicago, etc., R. Co. v. Milwaukee, 89 Wis. 506, 28 L. R. A. 249. In the case of Chicago, etc., Co. v. People, 120 Ill. 667, s. c. 31 Am. & Eng. R. R. Cas. 487, the court said: "Whatever may be said in regard to the mere track of the railway, it is impossible to see why depot grounds, and other real estate used by the company, may not be benefited by improvements of the character here contemplated, at least, as much as may be the public square occupied by the county court-house, the canal lands, and the lot occupied by the church, by like improvements; and since the question of jurisdiction turns upon the right of inquiry, and not upon the correctness of decision, it is enough that railroad property may sometimes, under certain circumstances, be specially benefited by improvements of the general character of the present." "We are of the opinion that, while the road-bed or right of way of a railroad company is not the subject of the claim for paving, it does not follow that a passenger depot or freight depot, the ground belonging to the company and used as a lumber yard, or other purpose, may not be subject to such a charge." Borough v. Baltimore, etc., Co., *supra*. *Contra*, New York, etc., Co. v. New Haven, 42 Conn. 279. The decision in this case, it seems, was placed on the ground that it was not shown that the railway company reaped any advantage from the improvement.

[2] Ludlow v. Cincinnati, etc., R. Co., 78 Ky. 357; State v. Passaic, 54 N. J.

hold that the making of a local improvement, such as a street, along or near a railway right of way, can not possibly be a benefit to the company; that it can run its trains as well without the improvement as with it, and therefore that no assessment can be levied.[1] Thus, where a street crosses a railway

L. 340; Jacksonville Ry. Co. v. City of Jacksonville, 114 Ill. 562, 2 N. E. R. 478; Chicago, etc., Co. v. People, 120 Ill. 104; Lightner v. City of Peoria, 150 Ill. 80; Illinois, etc., Co. v. City of Mattoon, 141 Ill. 32; Illinois Central Co. v. City of Decatur, 13 Sup. Ct. R. 293, s. c. 54 Am. & Eng. R. R. Cas. 282; Illinois Central v. City of Mattoon, 141 Ill. 32, 30 N. E. R. 773; Illinois Central v. Decatur, 126 Ill. 92; City of Chicago v. Baer, 41 Ill. 306; Northern, etc., Co. v. Connelly, 10 Ohio St. 159; Burlington, etc., Co. v. Spearman, 12 Iowa 112; Peru, etc., Co. v. Hanna, 68 Ind. 562; Kuehner v. City of Freeport, 143 Ill. 92, 32 N. E. R. 372; Little v. Chicago, 46 Ill. App. 534; State v. City of Passaic, 54 N.J. 340, 23 Atl. R. 945; Transportation Co. v. City of Elizabeth, 37 N. J. L. 330; Railroad Co. v. Jersey City, 42 N. J. L. 97; Rich v. City of Chicago, 152 Ill. 18, 38 N. E. R. 255; Muscatine v. Chicago, etc., R. Co., 79 Iowa 645. See Trustees v. City of Chicago, 12 Ill. 403. In Northern, etc., R. Co. v. Connelly, *supra*, it was said: "If railroad tracks are taxable, for general purposes, it is difficult to perceive why they should not be subject also to special taxes or assessments. The company, to advance its own interests, has seen fit to appropriate to its use grounds within the corporate limits of the city of Toledo, and over which the city had the power of making assessments to defray the expense of local improvements, and why should not the company be held to have taken it *cum* onere? A citizen would scarcely claim exemption, because he had devoted his lot to uses which the improvement could not in any way advance, and we see no good reason why a railroad company should be permitted to do so. The company have the exclusive right to the possession, so long as it is used for the road, and if the road-bed was exempt from taxation for general purposes, it would by no means follow that it was not liable for such special assessments." In Chicago, etc., Co. v. City of Joliet, 153 Ill. 649, 39 N.E. R. 1079, it was said: "Where a railway is contiguous to a proposed street improvement, it falls within the designation of property that may be specially taxed for the making of the local improvement." *Contra*, Allegheny, etc., Co. v. Western, etc., Co., 138 Pa. St. 375.

[1] Philadelphia v. Philadelphia, etc., Co., 33 Pa. St. 41; Bridgeport v. New York, etc., Co., 36 Conn. 255; Matter of Public Parks, 47 Hun 302; Detroit, etc., R. Co. v. Grand Rapids, (Mich.) 28 L. R. A. 793; Chicago, etc., R. Co. v. Milwaukee, 89 Wis. 506, s. c. 28 L. R. A. 249. In Borough of Mt. Pleasant v. Baltimore, etc., Co., 138 Pa. St. 365, 20 Atl. R. 1052, the court said: "It requires no argument to show that the paving of a footway by the side of a railroad track can confer no possible benefit upon the property known as the right of way, hence the whole theory which justifies such charges fails in this instance. But this reason does not apply to a railroad station where passengers assemble to take a

§ 786　　　　　　LOCAL ASSESSMENTS.　　　　　　1109

right of way at right angles, it has been held that no benefit accrues to the railway company from the improvement of the street, and that no assessment can be levied.[1] And where a

train; much less does it apply to ground used as a freight station or lumber yard."

[1] Junction, etc., Co. v. City, 88 Pa. St. 424; New York, etc., Co. v. Morrisania, 7 Hun 652; State v. City of Elizabeth, 37 N. J. L. 330; Great Eastern, etc., Co. v. Hackney District, L. R. 8 App. Cas. 687. See Town of Salem v. Henderson, 13 Ind. App. 563, s. c. 41 N. E. R. 1062. If the right of way is broader than necessary for the track, the surplus may be assessed. New York, etc., Co. v. Morrisania, *supra*. Compare Northern, etc., Co. v. Connelly, 10 Ohio St. 159; Chicago, etc., Co. v. City of Chicago, 139 Ill. 573, 28 N. E. R. 1108. The doctrine of the text was declared and enforced in the recent case of Detroit, etc., R. Co. v. Grand Rapids, (Mich.) 28 L. R. A. 793, where it was said: "The right of way so assessed contains the main track and one side track. It has nothing else upon it, and is used for no other purpose. It has already been dedicated to a public use, and the question is presented whether a railroad right of way can be assessed by municipal corporations for public improvements. So far from being any benefit, it is established by the evidence that the opening and paving of the street were a damage to the complainant. A right of way can not be benefited by the opening and paving of a street across it. None of the buildings of the complainant are within two blocks of this crossing. We can see no benefits, immediate or prospective, to the complainant. The division of the right of way into three parcels was arbitrary, as were also the valuations and supposed benefits. The point is so clearly and concisely stated by the court of Pennsylvania, that we quote the opinion in Philadelphia v. Philadelphia W. & B. R. Co., 33 Pa. St. 41: 'The municipal authorities paved the Gray's Ferry road for a considerable distance, at a place where it lies side by side with the defendants' railroad, and now seek to charge them with the half of the cost of it; but they can not do it. Their claim has no foundation, either in the letter of the law or in its spirit, or in the form of the remedy. Not in the letter, because the defendants do not own the land sought to be charged, and have only their right of way over it. Not in the spirit, because the paving laws are means of compulsory contribution among the common sharers in a common benefit, and as a railroad can not, from its very nature, derive any benefit from the paving, while all the rest of the neighborhood may, we can not presume that the compulsion was intended to be applied to them. Not in the form of the remedy, because the execution of this sort of claim is, *levari facias*, a writ not commonly allowed against corporations, and which would hardly produce much when directed against a public right of way. It would be strange legislation that would authorize the soil of one public road to be taxed in order to raise funds to make or improve a neighboring one.' The same doctrine is held in Junction R. Co. v. Philadelphia, 88 Pa. 424; State v. Elizabeth, 37 N. J. L. 331; New York & H. R. R. Co. v. Morrisania Trustees, 7 Hun 652; Bloomington v. Chicago & A. R. Co., 134 Ill. 451; Bridgeport v. New York

railway company has a mere right of way across a lot to which it does not hold title, it can not be assessed for the construction of an improvement adjoining the lot.[1] In many of the cases in which it was held that the right of way could not be assessed, the improvement, to pay for which the assessment was sought to be levied, was a street, and it clearly appeared that no benefit resulted to the right of way, but where it clearly appears that a benefit results from the improvement, such as the benefit derived from the construction of a street drain, sewer, or the like, the levy of the assessment may be proper and valid.[2]

§ 787. Abutting property — Right of way is not. — Where a railway company has its track or right of way in a street, it has been held that the right of way is not assessable as property "abutting on the street,"[3] or as property "bordering on or touching the street."[4] It is held that where the only interest a railway company has in a right of way laid in a street is the right to run its trains over the track, it can not be assessed for a local improvement.[5] But where the tracks of a company are laid in a street, the company is liable to assessment for keeping the street in repair.[6] And it has also been

& N. H. R. Co., 36 Conn. 255, 4 Am. Rep. 63; South Park Comrs. v. Chicago, B. & Q. R. Co., 107 Ill. 105; New York & N. H. R. Co. v. New Haven, 42 Conn. 279, 19 Am. R. 534."

[1] City of Muscatine v. Chicago, etc., Co., 88 Iowa 291, 55 N. W. R. 100.

[2] City of Bloomington v. Railroad Co., 134 Ill. 451, 26 N. E. R. 366; Troy, etc., Co. v. Kane, 9 Hun (N.Y.) 506; Louisville, etc., Co. v. Beckman, 122 Ind. 443; Louisville, etc., Co. v. Boney, 117 Ind. 501; Appeal of North Beach, etc., Co., 32 Cal. 499. Thus a street railway has been held liable to an assessment for the widening of a street. Appeal of North Beach, etc., R. Co., 32 Cal. 499.

[3] South Park Commissioners v. Chicago, etc., Co., 13 Am. & Eng. R. R. Cas. 415. See also Oshkosh City R. Co. v. Winnebago County, 89 Wis. 435, s. c. 61 N. W. R. 1107. But see post, § 788.

[4] O'Reilly v. Kingston, 114 N. Y. 439. Statutes conferring authority to levy and enforce are, as we have seen, to be strictly construed, and it is difficult to perceive any valid reason for holding a right of way on which tracks are laid to be property or lots fronting, abutting or bordering on a street.

[5] Louisville, etc., Co. v. East St. Louis, 134 Ill. 656.

[6] Chicago v. Baer, 41 Ill. 306; Fair Haven, etc., Co. v. New Haven, 38 Conn. 422, s. c. 9 Am. R. 399. See, also, Page v. Chicago, 60 Ill. 441; Peo-

held that a railroad right of way located in a public street is liable to assessment for a local improvement under the Illinois statute, providing for local improvements by special assessment of "contiguous property."[1]

§ 788. Right of way—Mode of assessing.—Where the right of way of a railroad company is liable to an assessment to pay for a local improvement there seems to be no distinction between the mode of assessing it and other lands subject to the assessment for the same improvement, where the right of way bears the same relation to the street as other lands adjoining the street. But where the railway runs longitudinally along the street a special rule usually applies. The different modes of assessment which have been held valid in assessing local charges against the lands of individuals and lands not occupied as a right of way by a railway company seem to be equally applicable to lands occupied as a railway right of way. Thus where the mode of assessment to pay for the improvement of a street was by assessments levied in proportion to the front feet abutting on the improvement, it was held that a railway right of way abutting on the improvement was subject to assessment as abutting property, the same as other lands or lots.[2]

ple v. Chicago, etc., R. Co., 67 Ill. 118; Louisville, etc., R. Co. v. State, 3 Head. (Tenn.) 524; Memphis, etc., Ry. v. State, 87 Tenn. 746, s. c. 11 S. W. R. 946; Eyler v. Allegheny Co., 49 Md. 257; Elliott on Roads and Streets, 591, 592. *Contra*, Mayor v. Royal, etc., Co., 45 Ala. 322.

[1] Rich v. Chicago, 152 Ill. 18, s. c. 38 N. E. R. 255. See, also, Chicago, etc., R. Co. v. Joliet, 153 Ill. 649, s. c. 39 N. E. R. 1077, 1079.

[2] Northern, etc., Co. v. Connelly, 10 Ohio St. 159; City of Chicago v. Baer, 41 Ill. 306; Burlington, etc., Co. v. Spearman, 12 Iowa 112; Illinois Cent. Co. v. City of Decatur, 126 Ill. 92, 18 N. E. R. 315; Lake Erie, etc., Co. v. Walters, 9 Ind. App. 684, 37 N. E. R. 295; Chicago, etc., Co. v. City of Joliet, 153 Ill. 655, 39 N. E. R. 1077. But it seems to us that there is reason to doubt the soundness of the doctrine of some of the cases cited. In Peru, etc., Co. v. Hanna, 68 Ind. 562, it was said by the court: "We are of the opinion that the track of a railroad company, when it borders on a street, is properly assessable for its due proportion of the cost of the improvement of such street under an ordinance of the city." Much depends upon the particular statute under which the assessment is levied, and it is unsafe to accept as indicative of a general rule cases decided upon particular statutes.

Where a railroad track ran longitudinally through a street, a statute making the company liable to local assessment for improving the street for the proportional amount of the street occupied by the track was held to be valid.[1]

§ 789. **Lien of the assessment.**—The statutes conferring upon municipalities the power to levy local assessments to pay for local improvements usually, if not always, provide that the amount of the assessment shall be a lien upon the lots or lands against which the assessment is levied. These liens are purely statutory, and their existence, force and extent depend upon the terms of the statute creating them.[2] Such liens are ordinarily superior to all liens except general taxes, and the authority of the legislature to make them such is firmly established. The assessments being made on the theory that the property is benefited and enhanced in value in a sum equal to the amount of the assessment, no injury can result to other lien holders such as mortgagees, mechanic lien holders and the like. In addition to the lien given against the property benefited some of the statutes make the property owner personally liable for the assessment. This personal liability, however, can not exist in any event, unless there is a valid statute creating it. There is very grave doubt as to the constitutionality of such a statute.[3] Imposing such a liability on the owner would in many cases be a great hardship, for it is easy to conceive of cases where the assessment might be so heavy that the property would not sell for enough to pay it. The weight of authority, if numerical superiority controls, seems to be in favor of the constitutionality of such statutes,[4]

---

[1] Lake Shore, etc., Co. v. Dunkirk, 20 N. Y. Supp. 596.

[2] Gause v. Bullard, 16 La. Ann. 197; Philadelphia v. Greble, 38 Pa. St. 339; State, ex rel., v. Ætna Life Ins. Co., 117 Ind. 251; Kiphart v. Pittsburgh, etc., Co., 7 Ind. App. 122, 34 N. E. R. 375.

[3] In our opinion there can, upon principle, be no personal liability since the whole right to levy a local assessment rests upon the ground that the property is benefited to the extent of the assessment.

[4] City of Muscatine v. Chicago, etc., Co., 79 Iowa 645; Lake Shore, etc., Co. v. City of Dunkirk, 65 Hun 494, 20 N. Y. Supp. 596; Nichols v. Bridgeport, 23 Conn. 189; City of New Orleans v. Wire, 20 La. Ann. 500.

but there is very great conflict.[1] The statutes creating a lien for local assessments being remedial in their nature and intended to secure the person constructing the improvement for his outlay should be liberally construed to accomplish that purpose.[2] A statute which provides for the recovery of a reasonable attorney's fee in actions to foreclose the lien of an assessment for a local improvement is constitutional.[3]

[1] City of Seattle v. Yesler, 1 Wash. Ter. 571; Higgins v. Ausmuss, 77 Mo. 351; Taylor v. Palmer, 31 Cal. 240; City of Burlington v. Quick, 47 Iowa 222; City of Virginia v. Hall, 96 Ill. 278; Town of Macon v. Patty, 57 Miss. 378; Cooley on Taxation, 674; Sweaney v. Kansas City, etc., Co., 54 Mo. App. 265. In Neenan v. Smith, 50 Mo. 525, 528, it is said: "All taxation is supposed to be for the benefit of the person taxed. That for raising a general revenue is imposed primarily for his protection as a member of society, both in his person and his property in general and hence the amount assessed is against him to be charged against his property, and may be collected of him personally. But on the other hand, local taxes for local improvements are merely assessments upon the property benefited by such improvements, and to pay for the benefits which they are supposed to confer; the lots are increased in value, or better adapted to the uses of town lots, by the improvement. Upon no other ground will such partial taxation for a moment stand. Other property held by the owner is affected by this improvement precisely and only as is the property of all other members of the community, and there is no reason why it should be made to contribute, that does not equally apply to that of all others. The sole object, then, of a local tax being to benefit local property, it should be a charge upon that property only, and not a general one upon the owner. The latter, indeed, is not what is understood by local or special assessment, but the very term would confine it to the property in the locality; for if the owner be personally liable, it is not only a local assessment but also a general one as against the owner. The reasonableness of this restriction will appear when we reflect that there is no call for a general execution until the property charged is exhausted. If that is all sold to pay the assessment, leaving a balance to be collected otherwise, we should have the legal anomaly—the monstrous injustice— of not only wholly absorbing the property supposed to be benefited and rendered more valuable by the improvement, but also of entailing upon the owner the loss of his other property. I greatly doubt whether the legislature has the power to authorize a general charge upon the owner of local property which may be assessed for its especial benefit, unless the owners of all taxable property within the municipality are equally charged. As to all property not to be so specially benefited, he stands upon the same footing with others; he has precisely the same interests, and should be subject to no greater burdens."

[2] Chaney v. State, 118 Ind. 494.

[3] Lake Erie, etc., R. Co. v. Walters, (Ind. App.) 41 N. E. R. 465.

§ 790. **Assessment of right of way—Enforcing assessment.**
—While it is probably true that there may be a lien on the right of way of a railroad for a local assessment, where such assessment is authorized by statute, the manner of enforcing such assessment is not clearly settled. The right of way of a railway company is a part of the company's property, without which it could not perform the duties it owes to the public. To subject a portion of the right of way to a sale to enforce a local improvement would greatly embarrass, if not entirely destroy, the ability of the company to perform its public functions.[1] The rights of the public are regarded as superior to the rights of any individual, or group of individuals. Local assessments are usually levied on a small portion of a railway right of way, varying from a few feet in length to miles in length. To permit such portion to be sold would prevent the operation of the road, and, on grounds of public policy, it is held that the ordinary remedy of enforcing the collection of a local assessment by a sale of the property benefited does not apply to the enforcement of an assessment against the right of way of a railway company. While there is a conflict of authority on this subject, the decided weight is that the right of way, if sold to pay the assessment, must be sold as a whole and not in broken fragments.[2] "The public have a right to have a rail-

[1] Chicago, etc., R. Co. v. Milwaukee, 89 Wis. 506, s. c. 28 L. R. A. 249; Detroit, etc., R. Co. v. Grand Rapids, (Mich.) 63 N. W. R. 1007, s. c. 28 L. R. A. 793. As we have elsewhere shown the rule is that a railroad is to be treated as a unity, and this rule would forbid the sale of a part, as a few hundred feet, or the like, to pay a local assessment.

[2] Lake Shore, etc., R. Co. v. Grand Rapids, 102 Mich. 374; Detroit, etc., R. Co. v. Grand Rapids, (Mich.) 28 L. R. A. 793; Louisville, etc., Railway Co. v. State, 122 Ind. 443, s. c. 24 N. E. R. 350; Midland Railway Co. v. Wilcox, 122 Ind. 84; Muller v. Dows, 94 U. S. 444; Dano v. Mississippi, etc., Railroad Co., 27 Ark. 564; Cox v. Western Pacific R. R. Co., 44 Cal. 18; Cox v. Western Pacific R. R. Co., 47 Cal. 87; Knapp v. St. Louis, etc., R. Co., 74 Mo. 374; Cranston v. Union Trust Co., 75 Mo. 29; Louisville, etc., Co. v. State, 122 Ind. 443; Indianapolis, etc., Co. v. State, 105 Ind. 37; Ammant v. President, etc., 13 S. & R. 210; Dunn v. North, etc., Co., 24 Mo. 493; Macon, etc., Co. v. Parker, 9 Ga. 377. "We fully agree with appellant's counsel that a continuous line of railroad is to be treated as an entirety, and we adjudge that as such it must be sold, for it would be unjust to lien holders, as well as to the railroad company, to sell a bridge, a

way remain an entirety, and it would be destructive to public interest to permit it to be broken up into disjointed and practically useless fragments."[1] Even if it be conceded that a personal judgment for the amount of the assessment can be rendered,[2] still it does not follow that a railroad can be sold in fragments.

culvert or a few rods, or even a mile of a railroad." Farmers', etc., Co. v. Canada, etc., R. Co., 127 Ind. 250. "For the sake of the public whatever is essential to the corporate functions shall be retained by the corporation. The only remedy which the law allows to creditors against property so held is sequestration, and that remedy is consistent with corporate existence, whilst a power to alien, or liability to levy and sale on execution, would hang the existence of the corporation on the caprices of the managers or on the mercy of its creditors." Plymouth R. R. Co. v. Colwell, 39 Pa. St. 337, s. c. 80 Am. Dec. 526. But in Illinois it was held that the portion of the right of way of a railway company lying within a drainage district might be sold to pay the assessment for constructing the drain. In Wabash, etc., Co. v. East Lake Fork District, 134 Ill. 384, 10 L. R. A. 285, it is said, "Again, it is urged that the decree is erroneous in directing a sale of a portion of the railroad for the satisfaction of the lien. This proposition was presented and considered in Illinois Cent. R. Co. v. Commissioners of, etc., 129 Ill. 417, and it was there held that an order for the sale of the track and right of way of the railroad company within the district for the payment of the assessment was proper. We are still inclined to adhere to the conclusion to which we arrived in that case." See, also, Little v. City of Chicago, 46 Ill. App. 534.

[1] Farmers', etc., Co. v. Canada, etc., Co., 127 Ind. 250. See, also, the following authorities, which declare and enforce the same doctrine: Indiana, etc., Co. v. Allen, 113 Ind. 581; Black v. Delaware, etc., Co., 22 N. J. Eq. 130; Thomas v. West Jersey Railroad Co., 101 U. S. 71; East Alabama, etc., Co. v. Doe, 114 U. S. 340; Stewart's Appeal, 56 Pa. St. 413; Richardson v. Sibley, 11 Allen 65; Foster v. Fowler, 60 Pa. St. 27.

[2] Louisville, etc., Co. v. State, 8 Ind. App. 377, 35 N. E. R. 916; Lake Shore, etc., v. City of Dunkirk, 65 Hun 494, 20 N. Y. Sup. 596; Louisville, etc., v. State, 122 Ind. 443; Lake Erie, etc., Railroad Co. v. Bowker, 9 Ind. App. 428, 36 N. E. R. 864. "The proceeding to enforce a lien for an assessment on account of street improvements is *in rem*, and ordinarily no personal judgment may be rendered against the owner in such proceedings. The only reason why a personal judgment may become a proper and available remedy in certain cases of this character, where the proceeding is against a railway company to enforce a lien upon its railroad property and franchises, is that it would be contrary to public policy to decree the sale of the specific property to which the lien has attached, and as the lessor might otherwise be left without any remedy whatever, equity will, in a proper case, award such lienor the right of collecting the amount due him by

§ 791. **Procedure.**—The matter of procedure is so much a matter of statutory regulation that we shall not attempt to give the subject much consideration. It may be said that direct proof of the assessment must be made and a county tax list is incompetent for that purpose.[1] And where the statute so provides an attorney's fee may be recovered.[2] The lien, it has been held, may be enforced against the property-owner whether the work was completed according to the original plans and specifications or not if it appear that the contractor performed his work as far as it was in his power to do, or where the municipality waived a strict compliance with the ordinance directing the improvement.[3] Where the statute prescribes what steps shall be taken in order to the existence of a valid assessment there must be a substantial compliance with its provisions. The general rule is that where the statute specifically provides a remedy for the enforcement of the assessment that remedy must be pursued, but if a right be given and no remedy prescribed the courts will usually provide the appropriate remedy.

virtue of the lien, in the way of such personal judgment." Lake Erie, etc., Co. v. Walters, 9 Ind. App. 684, 37 N. E. R. 295.

[1] City of Muscatine v. Chicago, etc., Co., 88 Iowa 291, 55 N. W. R. 100.

[2] Lake Erie, etc., R. Co. v. Walters, 13 Ind. App. 275, 41 N. E. R. 465.

[3] Lake Erie, etc., R. Co. v. Walters, 13 Ind. App. 275, 41 N. E. R. 465.

CHAPTER XXXIII.

LAND GRANTS.

§ 792. The ground upon which public aid to railroads rests.
793. Land grants.
794. Construction of land grants.
795. Construction of land grants—Illustrative cases.
796. Effect of grant.
797. Effect of grant—Illustrative cases.
798. Reserved lands.
799. Indemnity lands.
800. Priority of rights.
801. Breach of condition—Forfeiture.
802. Legislative declaration of forfeiture.
803. Cancellation of grants and entries.
§ 804. Staking and surveying line does not conclude the company.
805. Aid to two companies by same grant.
806. Grants by the government—Estoppel.
807. Where state renders performance of condition impossible grant is not defeated.
808. Partial failure to perform conditions.
809. Notice by possession.
810. Injunction on the application of company.
811. Effect of reservation of right to use railroad as a highway.

§ 792. **The grounds upon which public aid to railroads rests.**—The public nature of railroads authorizes the use of public money or property in aid of their construction and maintenance. Even in jurisdictions where the legislature has no power to appropriate money or property to private individuals aid may be given or granted to railroad companies because they are not strictly private corporations. Burdens may be placed upon them because they are "affected with a public interest," and for the same reason benefits may be bestowed upon them that can not be rightfully bestowed on strictly private corporations. The construction and maintenance of railroads has been generally considered a matter of public concern, and the machinery of government, local, state, and national, has been liberally employed in aiding to build new lines of road, not only between centers of trade, but far out into unsettled portions of the country where the operation of a railroad can prove a profitable business only after settlers have developed the resources of the country. It will be found upon examination of the cases decided by the federal courts hereafter referred to that the policy of the government in granting land to railroad companies exerts an important influence upon the construction of such grants for the construction given them is a very liberal one, the courts assuming that by making such grants congress intended to encourage the building of railroads.

§ 793. **Land grants.**—The term "land grants," when used in the branch of the law relating to railroads, has a peculiar meaning. It does not, as ordinarily used, mean a grant by an individual, but means a grant by the nation or by a state. Aid has been given to railroads in many instances by a direct grant of land by the federal government, and in other cases the grant is made to a state for the benefit of the railroad company. Where the grant is made to the state for the benefit of a company the position of the state is that of a trustee for the company.[1]

§ 794. **Construction of land grants.**—A congressional grant of land is a peculiar one, for there is both a statute and a conveyance, so that the rules for construing conveyances made by individuals do not fully apply to land grants.[2] A land grant has the effect of a legislative enactment and the intention of the legislature is to be sought and enforced.[3] The statute

---

[1] Rice v. Minnesota, etc., R. Co., 1 Black 358; Kansas City, etc., R. Co. v. Attorney-General, 118 U. S. 682; Leavenworth, etc., R. Co. v. United States, 92 U. S. 733; Litchfield v. Webster Co., 101 U. S. 773; Wolsey v. Chapman, 101 U. S. 755; Van Wyck v. Knevals, 106 U. S. 360; Hannibal, etc., R. Co. v. Smith, 9 Wall. 95; Schulenberg v. Harriman, 21 Wall. 44; Grinnell v. Chicago, etc., R. Co , 103 U. S. 739; Railroad Land Co. v. Courtright, 21 Wall. 310; Miller v. Swann, 89 Ala. 631. The term "land grants," as we here use it, means a grant of lands by the federal government or by a state.

[2] Missouri, etc., R. Co. v. Kansas Pacific R. Co., 97 U. S. 491; Hall v. Russell, 101 U. S. 503.

[3] Winona, etc., R. Co. v. Barney, 113 U. S. 618, s. c. 5 Sup. Ct. R. 606;

§ 794　　　　　LAND GRANTS.　　　　　1119

making the grant abrogates common law rules so far as they conflict with its provisions.[1] Statutes granting lands to aid in building railroads are liberally construed in favor of the grantees, to enable them to carry out the purposes of the grant. Thus a grant to a railroad "of every alternate section of public land designated by odd numbers, to the amount of five alternate sections per mile on each side of said railroad on the line thereof," was held not to be limited to lands situated on lines at right angles to the general line of the road, where, in consequence of turns or changes of direction in the road, such a rule of selection would cause an overlapping on one side, and leave a vacancy on the other.[2] As we have said, land grants are usually construed to pass the land at once but to convey it upon condition subsequent, although, of course, a grant may be upon condition precedent.[3] Whether the grant is

United States v. Denver, etc., R. Co., 150 U. S. 1, s. c. 14 Sup. Ct. R. 11; Bradley v. New York, etc., Railroad Co., 21 Conn. 294; Pierce on Railroads, 491. See Brewster v. Kansas City, etc., R. Co., 25 Fed. R. 243.

[1] St. Paul, etc., R. Co. v. Greenhalgh, 26 Fed. R. 563; Kansas, etc., R. Co. v. Dunmeyer, 113 U. S. 629.

[2] United States v. Union Pac. R. Co., (C. C. D. Colo.) 2 Denver Leg. News, 83, 37 Fed. R. 551. But it was held that the acts of congress granting to the state of Alabama, in aid of the construction of railroads in that state every alternate section of land designated by odd numbers, and within six miles of either side of the projected line of said roads, does not embrace, by implication, land within six miles of that portion of the roads constructed through the state of Georgia. Swann v. Jenkins, 82 Ala. 478, 2 So. 136. The Joint Resolution of Congress of May 31, 1870, giving the Northern Pacific Railroad Company, in the event of there not being within the limits prescribed by its charter the amount of lands per mile which had been granted to it, the right to make up the deficiency from sections designated by odd numbers within ten miles "on each side of the said road beyond the limits prescribed in said charter," was held to give the company an additional ten-mile indemnity limit, and not to restrict it to a loss of land occurring subsequent to the grant, nor does it restrict it to the state or territory where such deficiency occurs. Northern Pac. R. Co. v. United States, 36 Fed. R. 282.

[3] United States v. Southern Pacific R. Co., 39 Fed. R. 132; Shepard v. Northwestern Life Ins. Co., 40 Fed. R. 341; New Orleans, etc., R. Co. v. United States, 124 U. S. 124; Farnsworth v. Minnesota, etc., R. Co., 92 U. S. 49; Cedar Rapids, etc., R. Co. v. Herring, 110 U. S. 27; Chamberlain v. St. Paul, etc., R. Co., 92 U. S. 299; Vicksburg, etc., R. Co. v. Sledge, 41 La. Ann. 896. See United States v. Southern Pacific R. Co., 62 Fed. R. 531; Buttz v. Northern Pac. Railroad Co., 119 U. S. 55, s. c. 7 Sup. Ct. R.

upon condition precedent or upon condition subsequent must, it is obvious, be determined from the language of the statute making the grant.[1] In other words, the grant is usually regarded as conveying a present title but upon condition subsequent. It is upon this principle that it is held that possession under the grant for the statutory period will give title by limitation.[2] The rule is that where a railway company fails to comply with the provisions of the act of congress granting the right of way to railroads through the public lands of the United States it has no right to run its road through the land of a homesteader who has complied with the terms of the homestead law, although he has not at the time received his patent, as, in such case, his claim is superior to that of the company.[3]

§ 795. Construction of land grants—Illustrative cases.— Under acts granting a right of way over all government lands along certain routes, the railroad has been held to acquire a right of way over sections numbered sixteen and thirty-six, although such sections have been, before the grants were made, designated generally as school sections, but have not been definitely disposed of.[4] Grants to railroads by congress can not be construed to include routes not contemplated by the charters of the companies at the time of the grant.[5] Where the act of congress authorized the Northern Pacific Railroad Company to construct a road from Lake Superior westerly by the most eligi-

100; St. Paul, etc., R. Co. v. Northern Pac. R. Co., 139 U. S. 1.

[1] State v. Rusk, 55 Wis. 465, s. c. 10 Am. & Eng. R. Cas. 642; Rogers v. Port Huron, etc., R. Co., 45 Mich. 460, s. c. 10 Am. & Eng. R. Cas. 635; United States v. Southern Pacific R. Co., 62 Fed. R. 531.

[2] Wheeler v. City of Chicago, 68 Fed. R. 526.

[3] Savannah, F. & W. R. Co. v. Davis, 25 Fla. 917, s. c. 43 Am. & Eng. R. Cas. 542, 7 So. 29.

[4] Coleman v. St. Paul, etc., R. Co., 38 Minn. 260; Union Pac. R. Co. v. Douglas County, 31 Fed. R. 540. The grant of a right of way over the school sections of the public domain, acquired by a railroad company under an act of congress and a subsequent territorial statute, was not a grant *in præsenti*, but *in futuro*; and must be used under the statutes referred to, if at all, before the sale of the land by the state. Radke v. Winona & St. P. R. Co., 39 Minn. 262.

[5] Jackson v. Dines, 13 Colo. 90, 21 Pac. R. 918.

ble route within the United States north of 45 degrees of latitude, to Puget's Sound, with a branch via the valley of the Columbia river to Portland, Oregon, it was held that the company, upon finding a more eligible route, could follow down the Columbia river to and past Portland, cross over and go north to Puget's Sound, thereby dispensing with its branch to Portland.[1] And where the title of the Indians and their right of occupation of certain lands in Michigan had been fully extinguished, they were held to pass under the act of congress of June 3, 1856, notwithstanding they were held by the United States in trust to sell them for the benefit of the Indians.[2] To the extent of such claims, when the grant was for lands with specific boundaries, or known by a particular name, and also to the extent of the quantity named within boundaries containing a greater area, Mexican claims are excluded from a grant to a railroad company.[3] And lands "claimed to be included in a Mexican grant of a specific boundary, which grant was *sub judice* at the time of the grant of March 3, 1871, were not public land at that date, and did not pass by the grant, though they were afterwards held not to be embraced by the Mexican grant."[4] But a railroad land grant embracing within its boundaries Mexican floating grants takes effect except as to the quantity of land granted in the Mexican grant; and the railroad company is entitled to patents for the odd sections of the remainder.[5] Where lands had been granted to the state to

---

[1] United States v. Northern Pac. R. Co., (C. C. D. Ore.) 41 Fed. R. 842. At all events the resolution of congress of May 31, 1870, recognized and approved this location. United States v. Northern Pac. R. Co., (C. C. D. Ore.) 41 Fed. R. 842.

[2] Shepard v. Northwestern Life Ins. Co., (C. C. E. D. Mich.) 40 Fed. R. 341.

[3] Foss v. Hinkell, 78 Cal. 158, 20 Pac. R. 393; Doolan v. Carr, 125 U. S. 618.

[4] United States v. Southern Pac. R. Co., 39 Fed. R. 132, construing Southern Pac. R. Land Grants; Southern Pacific R. Co. v. Brown, 68 Fed R. 333. And the same is true as to a floating Mexican grant, to the extent of the lands embraced by it. United States v. McLaughlin, 30 Fed. R. 147, construing the Central Pacific R. Land Grant with reference to the fraudulent Mosquelamos grant; United States v. McLaughlin, 127 U. S. 428. Carr v. Quigley, 79 Cal. 130, 21 Pac. R. 607, construing the Western Pac. R. Land Grant with reference to a valid Mexican grant.

[5] State v. McLaughlin, 127 U. S. 428; United States v. Curtner, (C. C. N. D. Cal.) 38 Fed. R. 1.

aid in building railroads under certain restrictions, the legislature was held, in a Michigan case, to have authority to accept a surrender of the grant and to regrant the lands to another company; and a transfer of the lands, which was in form a sale to another company of the lands granted, upon condition that it would complete the first company's road, made by authority of the legislature, was construed to be such a surrender and regrant.[1] But where there is no authority to execute a certificate of surrender, the certificate is ineffective and the filing of it in the general land office does not transfer title to the United States.[2] The courts will not presume that the officers of the land department erred in carrying out the provisions of such an act, but will uphold their acts done in pursuance of the construction which they have given it, unless a very clear case of error is presented; especially where the actions of the officers have been acquiesced in until the lands have in large part been sold by the company.[3] The ruling in the cases decided by the supreme court of the United States is that where the grant is to be satisfied out of sections along the line of the road the implication, in the absence of a specific designation or of some provision to the contrary, is that the grant conveys the land in sections of the character specified nearest the line of the road, but, of course, does not convey lands previously disposed of.[4] Where there is a conflict between two companies, both claiming, under the same grant, they take in undivided moieties.[5]

[1] Jackson, etc., R. Co. v. Davison, 65 Mich. 416.

[2] Lake Superior, etc., R. Co. v. Cunningham, 155 U. S. 354, s. c. 15 Sup. Ct. R. 103. In Lake Superior, etc., R. Co. v. Finan, 155 U. S. 385, s. c. 15 Sup. Ct. R. 115, it was held that an entry upon land granted to a railroad company gave no title to person entering, and the case was distinguished from the first of the cases cited in this note.

[3] United States v. Union Pac. R. Co., 37 Fed. R. 551; United States v. Missouri, etc., R. Co., 37 Fed. R. 68. A patent to the S. P. R. Co., for land which, at the time of its grants, was within the exterior limits of a Mexican or Spanish grant then *sub judice*, is void from the beginning. Foss v. Hinkell, 78 Cal. 158.

[4] Wood v. Burlington, etc., R. Co., 104 U. S. 329; Ryan v. Central, etc., R. Co., 99 U. S. 382.

[5] St. Paul, etc., R. Co. v. Winona, etc., R. Co., 112 U. S. 720. See, generally, Verdier v. Port Royal, etc., R. Co., 15 So. Car. 476; Sams v. Port

§ 796. **Effect of grant.**—Where a grant of land to a railroad company becomes effective it relates back to the time of the enactment of the statute.[1] The general rule as to the time such grants become effective is that they take effect when the road is located and the sections thereby identified.[2] It is generally held that congress, by a grant of land to a railroad to aid in its construction, confers a present title to the designated sections along its route, with such restrictions upon their use and disposal as to secure them for the purposes of the grant, subject to be defeated, however, on non-compliance with the terms of the grant.[3] In other words the grant is regarded as immediately conveying title but conveying it upon condition subsequent. It is upon this principle that it has been held that no one but the grantor can take advantage of a breach of

Royal, etc., R. Co., 15 So. Car. 484; United States *v.* Union Pacific R. Co., 37 Fed. R. 551; Farmers', etc., Co. *v.* Chicago, etc., R. Co., 39 Fed. R. 143; Southern Pacific R. Co. *v.* Esquibel, 4 New Mex. 337; Eldred *v.* Sexton, 30 Wis. 193; Platt *v.* Union Pacific R. Co., 99 U. S. 48; Wood *v.* Burlington, etc., R. Co., 104 U. S. 329; Bullard *v.* Des Moines, etc., R. Co., 122 U. S. 167; St. Louis, etc., R. Co. *v.* McGee, 115 U. S. 469.

[1] Winona, etc., Co. *v.* Barney, 113 U. S. 618; Van Wyck *v.* Knevals, 106 U. S. 360; Schulenberg *v.* Harriman, 21 Wall. 44; Railroad Co. *v.* Baldwin, 103 U. S. 426; Broder *v.* Natoma Water Works Co., 101 U. S. 274; St. Paul, etc., Co. *v.* Winona, etc., Co., 112 U. S. 720.

[2] St. Paul, etc., R. Co. *v.* Northern Pacific, etc., R. Co., 139 U. S. 1, s. c. 11 Sup. Ct. R. 389; United States *v.* Southern Pacific R. Co., 146 U. S. 570; Northern Pacific R. Co. *v.* Musser, etc., Co., 68 Fed. 993.

[3] Wisconsin C. R. Co. *v.* Price County, 133 U. S. 4^6, 10 Sup. Ct. Rep. 341, 41 Am. & Eng. R. Cas. 669;

Washington, etc., R. Co. *v.* Northern Pac. R. Co., 2 Idaho 513, 21 Pac. Rep. 658; United States *v.* Curtner, 38 Fed. Rep. 1; Southern Pac. R. Co. *v.* Orton, 32 Fed. Rep. 457; California, etc., Land Co. *v.* Munz, 29 Fed. Rep. 837; United States *v.* Northern Pac. R. Co., 6 Mont. 351, 12 Pac. Rep. 769; Coleman *v.* St. Paul, etc., R. Co., 38 Minn. 260; United States *v.* Northern Pac. R. Co., 41 Fed. Rep. 842; Jackson, etc., R. Co. *v.* Davison, 65 Mich. 416. Among the many cases holding the grant to be *in præsenti* may be cited in addition to those already cited the following: Summers *v.* Dickinson, 9 Cal. 554; Lee *v.* Summers, 2 Ore. 260; Blakesly *v.* Caywood, 4 Ore. 279; Hall *v.* Russell, 101 U. S. 503; Fremont *v.* United States, 17 How. 542. The words "shall be and are hereby granted," are held to always import a grant *in præsenti*. Wright *v.* Roseberry, 121 U. S. 488; Martin *v.* Marks, 97 U. S. 345; Hannibal, etc., R. Co. *v.* Smith, 9 Wall. 95; Winona, etc., R. Co. *v.* Barney, 113 U. S. 618.

1124   THE CORPORATION.   § 796

the condition.[1] Under the various acts by which such grants have been made, the title has been held in most instances to vest in the railroad when a map of the proposed route has been duly filed;[2] but the filing of the map does not preclude a change of route where the rights of third persons have not intervened.[3] No notice of the filing of such a map or of the withdrawal from entry of the lands granted need be given by the United States officers in order to vest the title in the railroad company, unless the act specially requires it.[4] The secretary of the interior has no authority to suspend or modify a statute withdrawing lands from pre-emption and any orders he may make as to lands within the limits of the grant will not affect the rights of the railroad company.[5] The rule is that all claims which subsequently attach, either by homestead or pre-emption, or claims of right of way by other roads under grants subsequently made by the government, are ineffective as against a railroad company, holding an effective grant.[6] It is not necessary that a patent should be issued to the company,[7]

[1] Wheeler v. City of Chicago, 68 Fed. R. 526.

[2] Coleman v. St. Paul, etc., R. Co., 38 Minn. 260; Southern Pac. R. Co. v. Poole, 32 Fed. Rep. 451; United States v. Curtner, 38 Fed. Rep. 1; United States v. McLaughlin, 30 Fed. Rep. 147; Sioux City, etc., Co. v. Griffey, 72 Iowa 505, 34 N. W. 304; Southern Pac. R. Co. v. Orton, 32 Fed. Rep. 457. But in some cases the right of the railroad company to lands is suspended until a certain portion of the road is built and the lands are selected. The sale by the railroad of any specific parcels of lands not exceeding the quantity earned, and lying within the limits specified in the grant, would, to that extent, be an effectual selection. Jackson, etc., R. Co. v. Davison, 65 Mich. 416; Shepard v. Northwestern Life Ins. Co., 40 Fed. Rep. 341.

[3] Washington, etc., R. Co. v. Coeur D'Alene, etc., Co., 60 Fed. R. 981.

[4] The neglect of the secretary of the interior to file a map furnished by a railroad company showing the route of its road can not impair the company's rights. United States v. Northern Pac. R. Co., 41 Fed. Rep. 842.

[5] Northern Pac. R. Co. v. Orton, 32 Fed. Rep. 457.

[6] Washington, etc., R. Co. v. Northern Pac. R. Co., 2 Idaho 513, 21 Pac. Rep. 658; United States v. Curtner, 38 Fed. Rep. 1; Southern Pac. R. Co. v. Orton, 32 Fed. Rep. 457; United States v. Northern Pacific R. Co., 41 Fed. Rep. 842.

[7] Whitehead v. Plummer, 76 Iowa 181; Minnesota, etc., Co. v. Davis, 40 Minn. 455. The failure to pay the expense of surveying as required by the act of congress only prevents the issue of the patent. It does not prevent the title attaching under the congressional grant. Francoeur v. Newhouse, (C. C. N. D. Cal.) 40 Am. & Eng. R. Cas. 439, 40 Fed. Rep. 618.

§ 797   LAND GRANTS.   1125

since the effect of a patent to lands granted by such an act is not to vest title to them, but to afford record evidence thereof.[1] By operation of the act itself, the conditions having been fully complied with as to a portion of the road, the railroad company's title to lands given along that portion becomes perfect and indefeasible.[2] The general rule is that until a survey and definite location of the road have been made, and a map of the proposed route has been filed, the railroad acquires no rights adverse to those of others taking claims under general laws.[3]

§ 797. Effect of grant—Illustrative cases.—It has been held that where the condition of the grant is that two roads shall be built, the grant is not fully effective, unless the two roads are built and that it is not satisfied by the building of one.[4] If the state holds lands as a trustee for a railroad company, congress can at any time before the execution of the

[1] Pengra v. Munz, 29 Fed. Rep. 830; California, etc., Co. v. Munz, 29 Fed. Rep. 837. The title which vests under the congressional grant of lands to the Central Pacific Railroad Company, and the performance of the prescribed conditions, is a legal title, and an action of ejectment may be maintained upon it before the patent issues. Francoeur v. Newhouse, (C. C. N. D. Cal.) 40 Fed. Rep. 618, 40 Am. & Eng. R. Cas. 439.

[2] United States v. Northern P. R. Co., (C. C. D. Ore.) 41 Fed. Rep. 842. Under an act of congress granting the odd-numbered sections for a prescribed width on each side of a railroad, with a right of selection, when the line of road should be definitely fixed, to make up any deficiencies the title to specific lands between the two limits does not vest until selection and approval. Musser v. McRae, 38 Minn. 409; Elling v. Thexton, 7 Mont. 330.

[3] Sioux City, etc., Co. v. Griffey, 72 Iowa 505, 34 N. W. 304; Weeks v. Bridgman, 41 Minn. 352; Larsen v. Oregon R., etc., Co., 19 Ore. 240, 23 Pac. 974, 44 Am. & Eng. R. Cas. 92. See Southern Pac. R. Co. v. Orton, 32 Fed. Rep. 457, in which it is held that where lands had been set apart by act of congress to aid in the construction of a railroad, and unconditionally withdrawn from pre-emption, no pre-emption right could be acquired in them even if the grantee at the time of an attempted pre-emption was not authorized to take title. After settlement on public lands and properly filing of the homestead claim, it ceases to be public land through which a railroad can acquire the right of way by complying with the act of congress of March 3, 1875. Larsen v. Oregon R. and Nav. Co., 19 Ore. 240, 44 Am. & Eng. R. Cas. 92, 23 Pac. 974.

[4] Brewster v. Kansas City, etc., R. Co., 25 Fed. R. 243.

trust annul the power of the state by repealing the statute.[1] The state may impose conditions [2] upon its own grant, but if it does not impose conditions, the grantee company will take all the title the state could convey.[3] A patent from the state conveys whatever title was vested in the state by the act of congress, but it does not prove that the state had title,[4] and we suppose the same rule must apply to a land grant by the state. The effect of a grant of a right of way over the public lands is to confer upon the railroad company a right to construct and operate a railroad upon lands not previously pre-empted or in some other mode disposed of by the government.[5] Where the grant provided that the company should take on the line of the road, and in equal quantities on each side thereof, it was held that the company could not take more land on the one side of the road than on the other.[6] Where lands are granted by a joint resolution of congress, and its effect made contingent upon the favorable action of the president thereon, the resolution becomes effective as a land grant upon the issuing of an order declaring the executive judgment and setting apart the land.[7]

§ 798. **Reserved lands.**—A grant of lands by the federal congress does not operate upon lands theretofore reserved.[8]

---

[1] Rice v. Minnesota, etc., R. Co., 1 Black 358. But see Nash v. Sullivan, 29 Minn. 206, s. c. 10 Am. & Eng. R. Cas. 552.

[2] State v. Rusk, 55 Wis. 465, s. c. 10 Am. & Eng. R. Cas. 642; Rogers v. Port Huron, etc., R. Co., 45 Mich. 460, s. c. 10 Am. & Eng. R. Cas. 635.

[3] Railroad Land Co. v. Courtright, 21 Wall. 310; Miller v. Iowa, etc., Co., 56 Iowa 374, s. c. 3 Am. & Eng. R. Cas. 27.

[4] Musser v. McRae, 38 Minn. 409.

[5] Tuttle v. Chicago, etc., R. Co., (Minn.) s. c. 63 N. W. R. 618; Missouri, etc., R. Co. v. Kansas, etc., R. Co., 97 U. S. 491; St. Joseph, etc., R. Co. v. Baldwin, 103 U. S. 426, s. c. 2 Am. & Eng. R. Cas. 510. See Simonson v. Thompson, 25 Minn. 450; Wilkinson v. Northern Pacific R. Co., 5 Mont. 538, s. c. 10 Am. & Eng. R. Cas. 320; Flint, etc., R. Co. v. Gordon, 41 Mich. 420; Rider v. Burlington, etc., R. Co., 14 Neb. 120, s. c. 10 Am. & Eng. R. Cas. 688. See Oregon, etc., R. Co. v. United States, 67 Fed. R. 650.

[6] United States v. Burlington, etc., R. Co., 98 U. S. 334. See Neer v. Williams, 27 Kan. 1, s. c. 10 Am. & Eng. R. Cas. 561; Brown v. Carson, 16 Ore. 388, s. c. 19 Pac. R. 66, 21 Pac. R. 47.

[7] Republican, etc., Co. v. Kansas Pacific R. Co., 12 Kan. 409.

[8] Northern Pacific R. Co. v. Musser, etc., Co., 68 Fed. R. 993; Kansas, etc.,

Lands withdrawn from sale are reserved.[1] It follows from these settled rules that where lands are reserved they do not vest in a railroad company receiving a grant. Until the road is located or the route determined, the grant is "in the nature of a float;" "the title does not attach to any specific sections" until they are capable of identification, but "when once identified the title attaches to them as of the date of the grant."[2] Where there is a grant to a railroad company of land the effect of the grant to the extent and purposes thereof is to withdraw the land granted from the operation of a prior act of reservation. When the land is so withdrawn the effect of the withdrawal so far as concerns the property and rights withdrawn is to re-establish the dominion of the state or territory.[3]

§ 799. Indemnity lands.—In order to secure to the company the quantity of land granted to it and prevent a deficiency by reason of some of the land being pre-empted or taken up, it is usually provided that the company may take lands from other

R. Co. v. Atchison, etc., R. Co., 112 U. S. 414, s. c. 5 Sup. Ct. R. 208; United States v. McLaughlin, 127 U. S. 428, s. c. 8 Sup. Ct. R. 1177; Wisconsin, etc., R. Co. v. Price Co., 133 U. S. 496, s.c. 10 Sup. Ct. R. 341; United States v. Missouri, etc., R. Co., 141 U. S. 358, s. c. 12 Sup. Ct. R. 13. See Oregon, etc., R. Co. v. United States, 67 Fed. R. 650; McIntyre v. Roeschlaub, 37 Fed. R. 556; United States v. Northern Pacific R. Co., 152 U. S. 284, s. c. 14 Sup. Ct. R. 598.

[1] Wisconsin, etc., Railroad Co. v. Forsythe, 159 U. S. 46. See Kansas City, etc., R. Co. v. Attorney-General, 118 U. S. 682, s. c. 7 Sup. Ct. R. 66; Johnson v. Towsley, 13 Wall. 72; Shepley v. Cowan, 91 U. S. 330; Doolan v. Carr, 125 U. S. 618; United States v. Missouri, etc., R. Co., 141 U. S. 358, s. c. 12 Sup. Ct. R. 13; Oakes v. Myers, 68 Fed. 807.

[2] St. Paul, etc., R. Co. v. Northern Pacific R. Co., 139 U. S. 1, s. c. 11 Sup. Ct. R. 389; United States v. Southern Pacific R. Co., 146 U. S. 570; Northern Pacific R. Co. v. Musser, etc., Co., 68 Fed. R. 993; Schulenberg v. Harriman, 21 Wall. 44; Leavenworth, etc., R. Co. v. United States, 92 U. S. 733; Railroad Co. v. Baldwin, 103 U. S. 426; Wolcott v. Des Moines Company, 5 Wall. 681; Dubuque, etc., Railroad Co. v. Litchfield, 23 How. 66; Southern, etc., R. Co. v. Groeck, 68 Fed. R. 609.

[3] Maricopa, etc., R. Co. v. Arizona Territory, 156 U. S. 347, s. c. 15 Sup. Ct. R. 391, citing Utah, etc., Railway Co. v. Fisher, 116 U. S. 28, s. c. 6 Sup. Ct. R. 246; Harkness v. Hyde, 98 U. S. 476. See, generally, Wolcott v. Des Moines Co., 5 Wall. 681; Riley v. Welles, 154 U. S. 578, s. c. 14 Sup. Ct. R. 1166. See Hamblin v. Western, etc., Co., 147 U. S. 531.

parts of the public domain. The loss of land covered by the grant is made good to the company where the land is taken up as homesteads out of the lands designated in the statute. As appears from what has been elsewhere said and from the authorities referred to, the government is careful to encourage and protect the settlers who pre-empt land and also to preserve the rights of the railroad under the grant, so that a liberal construction is given to the statutes providing indemnity lands.[1] While it is well settled that what are called "place lands" pass *in præsenti* there is conflict upon the question whether indemnity lands pass *in præsenti*.[2] "The ordinary rule with respect to indemnity lands is that no title passes until after selection."[3] But as between two companies claiming under grants it is not necessary in order to give priority to the company claiming under the earlier grant that there should have been a formal selection.[4]

§ 800. **Priority of rights.**—If there are two conflicting grants the first in point of time has priority.[5] If the company having the priority of right locates its road, files the proper map, and the map is approved by the secretary of the interior, its rights are vested subject to be divested if conditions subsequent are not performed. If a forfeiture is declared because of a breach of conditions the land reverts to the United States,

---

[1] Kansas, etc., R. Co. v. Atchison, etc., R. Co., 112 U. S. 414; Wisconsin Central R. Co. v. Price County, 133 U. S. 496; Barney v. Winona, etc., R. Co., 117 U. S. 228; Southern Pacific, etc., R. Co. v. Tilley, 41 Fed. R. 729.

[2] Railroad Co. v. Barnes, 2 N. Dak. 310, s. c. 51 N. W. R. 386. But in Grandin v. La Bar, 3 N. Dak. 447, s. c. 57 N. W. R. 241, a different doctrine was declared. The court in the latter case discussed the decisions in Railroad Co. v. Wiggs, 43 Fed. R. 333; St. Paul, etc., R. Co. v. Northern Pacific R. Co., 139 U. S. 1, s. c. 11 Sup. Ct. R. 389, and held that they did not decide that indemnity lands passed *in præsenti*. In the case of Railroad Co. v. Barnes, *supra*, C. J. Corliss, in a very vigorous opinion, dissented, and we think his opinion expresses the law.

[3] United States v. Colton, etc., Co., 146 U. S. 615; United States v. Southern Pac. Railroad Co., 146 U. S. 570.

[4] St. Paul, etc., R. Co. v. Northern Pacific R. Co., 139 U. S. 1. See Smith v. Northern Pacific R. Co., 58 Fed. R. 513.

[5] United States v. Southern Pacific R. Co., 146 U. S. 570.

and does not pass to the company having a grant junior to the company which secured the prior right.[1]

§ 801. Breach of condition—Forfeiture.—The railroad company may, of course, lose the benefit of a grant by failure to perform the conditions imposed upon it, but in order to constitute a forfeiture action must be taken by the government.[2] It is held that when a grant has once vested, it can only be defeated by breach of conditions, and divestiture of title thereupon by proper proceedings on behalf of the United States,[3] but while a judicial proceeding is the usual and appropriate one, it has been held that a forfeiture may be declared by congress. A third person will not be heard to question the title of the corporation on the ground that it had no authority to take the land, for this is a question between the government and the corporation.[4] Where a statute assumes to convey the

[1] United States v. Southern Pacific R. Co., 146 U. S. 570; United States v. Northern Pacific R. Co., 152 U. S. 284, s. c. 57 Am. & Eng. R. Cas. 362; Sioux City, etc., R. Co. v. Countryman, 159 U. S. 377, s. c. 16 Sup. Ct. R. 28. See Chicago, etc., R. Co. v. United States, 159 U. S. 372, s.c.16 Sup. Ct.R.26; Sioux City, etc., R. Co. v. United States, 159 U. S. 349, 16 Sup. Ct. R. 17.

[2] Bybee v. Oregon, etc., R. Co., 139 U. S. 663.

[3] United States v. Curtner, (C. C.) 38 Fed. 1. If the company conveys any of the lands before constructing its road, and the grant is subsequently revoked for a failure to comply with the conditions subsequent upon which it was made, the title of the company's grantees will fail. Shepard v. Northwestern Life Ins. Co., 40 Fed. Rep. 341; Southern Pac. R. Co. v. Esquibel, 4 N. M. 337, 20 Pac. Rep. 109. It has been held that sales made in excess of the amount earned by a railroad company which is entitled, by the terms of the grant, to a certain quantity of land upon the completion of a stated number of miles of its road, are absolutely void, even though the road afterward earns the lands sold. Jackson, etc., R. Co. v. Davison, 65 Mich. 416; Swann v. Miller, 82 Ala. 530, 1 So. Rep. 65. See Lake Superior, etc., Co. v. Cunningham, 44 Fed. R. 587; Grinnell v. Chicago, etc., R. Co., 103 U. S. 739; St. Paul, etc., R. Co. v. St. Paul, etc., R. Co., 68 Fed. R. 2; Sioux City, etc., R. Co. v. Countryman, 159 U. S. 377, s. c. 16 Sup. Ct. R. 28. In Bybee v. Oregon, etc., R. Co., 139 U. S. 663, the court distinguished the cases of Union Hotel Co. v. Hersee, 79 N. Y. 454; Farnham v. Benedict, 107 N. Y. 159; Brooklyn, etc., Co. v. City of Brooklyn, 78 N. Y. 524, holding that the legislative act did not avoid the grant by forfeiture upon the non-performance of the conditions, but because the corporate existence had expired.

[4] Schulenberg v. Harriman, 21 Wall. 44; United States v. Repentigny, 5 Wall. 211, 268; Southern Pac. R. Co.

title to lands adjoining the right of way of a railroad, its effect in passing the title to particular tracts can not be questioned by a third person.[1] In Louisiana it was held that the United States government is the only claimant that can dispute the validity of rights to such lands acquired with the sanction and authority of the state legislature, and that parties who have acquired title through a sale under a mortgage authorized by the legislature have the legal title to the lands, as against a party claiming no title except by possession, and who went on the land, expecting it to be thrown open to public sale and entry.[2] All the cases agree, however, that the state has no power to sanction any disposition of the lands which will tend to defeat or to render impossible the performance of conditions upon which the grant was made by congress.[3]

§ 802. Legislative declaration of forfeiture.—It is held by the supreme court of the United States that where the statute containing the grant provides for a forfeiture within a specified time, the legislature may effectively declare a forfeiture, and that it is not necessary to obtain a declaration of forfeiture by judicial proceedings.[4] It is said that where the declaration is made by congress it must be "direct, positive and free from all doubt and ambiguity."[5] It is, of course, compe-

---

v. Orton, 32 Fed. Rep. 457. See Kennett v. Plummer, 28 Mo. 142; Cowell v. Springs Co., 100 U. S. 55; American, etc., Christian Union v. Yount, 101 U. S. 352, 361; Cole, etc., Mining Co. v. Virginia, etc., Co., 1 Sawyer 478; Rutland, etc., Railroad Co. v. Proctor, 29 Vt. 93; Bissell v. Michigan, etc., Railroad Co., 22 N. Y. 258; Natoma, etc., Mining Co. v. Clarkin, 14 Cal. 544.

[1] Minnesota Land, etc., Co. v. Davis, 40 Minn. 455. See Vicksburg, etc., R. Co. v. Sledge, 41 La. Ann. 896.

[2] Vicksburg, S. & P. R. Co. v. Sledge, 41 La. Ann. 896.

[3] Miller v. Swann, 89 Ala. 631, 7 So. Rep. 771; Vicksburg, etc., R. Co. v. Sledge, 41 La. Ann. 896; Jackson, etc., R. Co. v. Davison, 65 Mich. 416.

[4] Farnsworth v. Minnesota, etc., R. Co., 92 U. S. 49; Bybee v. Oregon, etc., R. Co., 139 U. S. 663; United States v. Repentigny, 5 Wall. 211, 267; McMicken v. United States, 97 U. S. 204; Atlantic, etc., R. Co. v. Mingus, (N. Mex.) s. c. 34 Pac. R. 492.

[5] St. Louis, etc., Railway Co. v. McGee, 115 U. S. 469, 473, s. c. 6 Sup. Ct. R. 123.

tent for the legislature to avert a forfeiture by dispensing with performance of the conditions.[1]

§ 803. Cancellation of grants and entries.—The cancellation of a homestead entry after a subsequent grant to a railroad and the definite location of its line of road does not inure to the benefit of the railroad company, but the land reverts to the government, and becomes a part of the domain, subject to appropriation by the first legal applicant.[2] The voluntary filing of an amended pre-emption claim operates as a cancellation of a previous claim or entry, although there is no formal record of cancellation.[3] The federal courts will entertain a suit by the United States to cancel patents erroneously issued by its officers in derogation of rights previously acquired by homestead or pre-emption or otherwise under existing laws.[4] A *bona fide* purchaser of lands conveyed to a railroad company by patent, but which were in fact not included in the grant, because held under prior pre-emption claims, may successfully defend against a suit to cancel the patent.[5] Where a pre-emption claim was filed but canceled because the claimant had not lived on the land, the land was held to be exempted from the grant.[6] A company, by laches, may lose its right to have a patent canceled.[7]

[1] United States v. Denver, etc., R. Co., 150 U. S. 1.
[2] Hastings & Des Moines R. Co. v. Whitney, 132 U. S. 357, 363, s. c. 40 Am. & Eng. R. Cas. 426, 10 Sup. Ct. R. 112. A homestead entry made before the definite location of a railroad, but voluntarily abandoned before location, although the filing was not canceled until after the location, will not except the land from the grant to the company, under an act of congress donating lands to aid in the construction of railroads. Young v. Goss, 42 Kan. 502, s. c. 40 Am. & Eng. R. Cas. 435, 22 Pac. R. 572.
[3] Amacker v. Northern Pac. R. Co., 58 Fed. R. 850. See Bardon v. Northern Pac. Railroad Co., 145 U. S. 535, s. c. 12 Sup. Ct. R. 856; Hastings, etc., Railroad Co. v. Whitney, 132 U. S. 357, s. c. 10 Sup. Ct. R. 112; Kansas Pac. Railway Co. v. Dunmeyer, 113 U. S. 629, s. c. 5 Sup. Ct. R. 566; Galliher v. Cadwell, 145 U. S. 368, s. c. 12 Sup. Ct. R. 873. See Northern Pacific R. Co. v. De Lacy, 66 Fed. R. 450.
[4] United States v. Missouri, etc., R. Co., 141 U.S. 358, reversing 37 Fed. R. 68.
[5] United States v. Winona, etc., R. Co., 67 Fed. R. 969.
[6] Whitney v. Taylor, 158 U. S. 85, s. c. 15 Sup. Ct. R. 796, citing Bardon v. Northern Pac. Railroad Co., 145 U. S. 535, s. c. 12 Sup. Ct. R. 856; Newhall v. Sanger, 92 U. S. 761; Hastings, etc., Railroad Co. v. Whitney, 132 U. S. 357, s. c. 10 Sup. Ct. R. 112. See Wood v. Beach, 156 U. S. 548, s. c. 15 Sup. Ct. R. 410.
[7] Curtner v. United States, 149 U. S. 662; Sage v. Winona, etc., R. Co., 58

§ 804. **Staking and surveying line does not conclude the company.**—A railroad company is not concluded by surveying and staking a line of road. For purposes concerning the land grant it is not concluded until a map is made and filed. It has a right to survey and stake many lines, since that course is necessary in order to enable it to finally decide upon the line on which it will construct its road.[1] The doctrine of the cases referred to in the note was applied to the decision of commissioners appointed to decide and report upon the construction of the road.[2]

§ 805. **Aid to two companies by same grant.**—The rule is that where two lines of road are aided by land grants made by the same act, and the lines of the roads cross or intersect the lands within the "place" limits of both, the lands do not pass to either company in preference to the other, no matter which road may be first located and built, but pass in equal undivided moieties.[3] Where the lands are granted to the state for the accomplishment of specific purposes those purposes can not be defeated by the state or by any corporations which are beneficiaries under the grant, so that where the state attempts to release the land to one of the companies and the release is effective only in part, the state and the United States will hold the land not effectively released in undivided portions.[4]

§ 806. **Grants by the government—Estoppel.**—The general rule is that a state is not bound by the unauthorized acts of its officers and that an estoppel arising from such acts will not

---

Fed. R. 297; Southern, etc., R. Co. v. St. Paul, etc., R. Co., 55 Fed. R. 690.

[1] Sioux City, etc., Land Co. v. Griffey, 143 U. S. 32, 39, s. c. 12 Sup. Ct. R. 362; Kansas Pac. Railroad Co. v. Dunmeyer, 113 U. S. 629, s. c. 5 Sup. Ct. R. 566; Van Wyck v. Knevals, 106 U. S. 360, 366, s. c. 1 Sup. Ct. R. 336.

[2] Smith v. Northern Pacific R. Co., 58 Fed. R. 513. See, generally, Blum v. Houston, etc., R. Co., (Tex. Civ. App.) 31 S. W. R. 526.

[3] Donahue v. Lake Superior, etc., R. Co., 155 U. S. 386, s. c. 15 Sup. Ct. R. 115, citing St. Paul, etc., R. Co. v. Winona, etc., R. Co., 112 U. S. 720, s. c. 5 Sup. Ct. R. 334; Sioux City, etc., R. Co. v. Chicago, etc., R. Co., 117 U. S. 406, s. c. 6 Sup. Ct. R. 790.

[4] Donahue v. Lake Superior, etc., R. Co., 155 U. S. 386, s. c. 15 Sup. Ct. R. 115.

§ 806   LAND GRANTS.   1133

operate against it.[1] But this general rule has its limitations and exceptions.[2] A state as the owner of property and as a party to a contract is not always, by any means, entitled to assert its rights as a sovereign, for, in relation to property and to contracts, there are cases in which it may be regarded substantially as a private corporation or an individual citizen.[3] It does not follow because a state can not be sued[4] that it can not be estopped, for there is an essential difference between its exemption as a sovereign from suit and its right to enforce a contract or assert a cause of action where equity and good conscience forbid. Upon sound principle it is held that where the officers of the state assuming to act for the state and under its authority grant lands to a railroad company to aid it in constructing its road, and there is long acquiescence and all the elements of estoppel exist, the state can not maintain a suit to avoid the grant although the officers exceeded their

[1] Crane v. Reeder, 25 Mich. 303; Ellsworth v. Grand Rapids, 27 Mich. 250; Rogers v. Port Huron, etc., Railroad Co., 45 Mich. 460, s. c. 8 N. W. R. 46; Lake Shore, etc., R. Co. v. People, 46 Mich. 193, s. c. 9 N. W. R. 249; Plumb v. City of Grand Rapids, 81 Mich. 381, s. c. 45 N. W. R. 1024; Hull et al. v. Marshall County, 12 Iowa 142; Whiteside v. United States, 93 U. S. 247; McCaslin v. State, 99 Ind. 428; Brown v. Ogg, 85 Ind. 234; Vail v. McKernan, 21 Ind. 421; Ferris v. Cravens, 65 Ind. 262; Skelton v. Bliss, 7 Ind. 77; Reid v. State, 74 Ind. 252; Bigelow on Estoppel, 246.

[2] State v. Flint, etc., R. Co., 89 Mich. 481, s. c. 51 N. W. R. 103; Attorney-General v. Ruggles, 59 Mich. 123, s. c. 26 N. W. R. 419; United States v. McLaughlin, 30 Fed. R. 147; State v. Milk, 11 Fed. R. 389; Cahn v. Barnes, 5 Fed. R. 326; Hough v. Buchanan, 27 Fed. R. 328; Pengra v. Munz, 29 Fed. R. 830; United States v. Missouri, etc., R. Co., 37 Fed. R. 68; United States v. Willamette, etc., Co., 54 Fed. R. 807; Bigelow on Estoppel, (4th ed.) 131. See United States v. Alabama, etc., R. Co., 142 U. S. 615 s. c. 12 Sup. Ct. R. 306; United States v. Hill, 120 U. S. 169, s. c. 7 Sup. Ct. R. 510.

[3] Carr v. State, 127 Ind. 204, s. c. 11 L. R. A. 370; Hartman v. Greenhow, 102 U. S. 672; Poindexter v. Greenhow, 114 U. S. 270; Keith v. Clark, 97 U. S. 454; Murray v. Charleston, 96 U. S. 432; Fletcher v. Peck, 6 Cranch 87; Terrett v. Taylor, 9 Cranch 43; Wabash, etc., Co. v. Beers, 2 Black 448; Davis v. Gray, 16 Wall. 203; Hall v. Wisconsin, 103 U. S. 5; State v. Cardozo, 8 S. Car. 71; People v. Canal Commissioner, 5 Denio 401; Georgia, etc., Co. v. Nelms, 71 Ga. 301; Lowry v. Francis, 2 Yerg. 534; Grogan v. San Francisco, 18 Cal. 590.

[4] Hans v. Louisiana, 134 U. S. 1; State v. Lazarus, 40 La. Ann. 856; Commonwealth v. Weller, 82 Va. 721; In re Ayers, 123 U. S. 443; Murdock, etc., Co. v. Commonwealth, 152 Mass. 28, s. c. 8 L. R. A. 399, and notes.

authority.[1] The doctrine of estoppel has been applied to the case of a county granting land to a railroad company, and the reasoning by which the court reached its conclusion would seem to support the conclusion that a state may be estopped.[2] In one of the cases it is held that the United States is not estopped by a failure to promptly take measures to set aside the certification of land to the state.[3]

§ 807. **Where state renders performance of condition impossible, grant is not defeated.**—The well-known general rule that if the grantee by his own act renders the performance of a condition subsequent impossible, he can not enforce a forfeiture of the estate for non-performance of the condition, applies to land grants. A state can not defeat the estate of the grantee by a wrongful act of its own which disables or prevents a railroad company, the beneficiary in a grant, from performing the conditions of the grant. This doctrine was applied to a state which, by seceding from the Union, rendered it impossible for the railroad company to perform the conditions subsequent embodied in the grant of land to it.[4]

§ 808. **Partial failure to perform conditions.**—In some of the grants provision is made that in the event that a certain

---

[1] State v. Jackson, etc., R. Co., 69 Fed. R. 116, citing United States v. Alabama, etc., R. Co., 142 U. S. 615; United States v. Macdaniel, 7 Pet. 1; United States v. Union Pacific R. Co., 37 Fed. R. 551; Michigan, etc., Co. v. Rust, 68 Fed. R. 155.

[2] Roberts v. Northern Pacific R. Co., 158 U. S. 1, s. c. 15 Sup. Ct. R. 756.

[3] United States v. Winona, etc., R. Co., 67 Fed. R. 969, citing Lea v. Polk County Copper Co., 21 How. 493, 498; Noyes v. Hall, 97 U. S. 34; Siebert v. Rosser, 24 Minn. 155; Lindsey v. Miller, 6 Pet. 666; United States v. Knight, 14 Pet. 301; Gilson v. Chouteau, 13 Wall. 92; United States v. Thompson, 98 U. S. 486; Fink v. O'Neil, 106 U. S. 272, s. c. 1 Sup. Ct. R. 325; United States v. Nashville, etc., R. Co., 118 U. S. 120, s. c. 6 Sup. Ct. R. 1006; United States v. Beebe, 127 U. S. 338, s. c. 8 Sup. Ct. R. 1083. It is not easy to reconcile the decision in the first of the cases cited in this note with that in State v. Jackson, etc., R. Co., 69 Fed. R. 116. We think that the rule laid down in the latter case is the correct one, and that it is probable that there may be a distinction between the two cases, but there is conflict in the statements of the opinions in those cases. See, generally, St. Paul, etc., Railroad Co. v. Sage, 49 Fed. R. 315, s. c. 1 C. C. A. 256.

[4] Davis v. Gray, 16 Wall. 203.

part of the road is completed within a designated time, title to a specified quantity of land shall vest in the company, and another designated part shall vest when another or other parts of the road are completed, and under such grants it is held that upon the completion of a part of the road entitling it to a designated quantity of land, title to that quantity will vest although the other part of the road may not be completed within the time limited.[1] As we have elsewhere shown a trespasser or intruder can not successfully raise the question whether there has or has not been either part or full performance of the condition subsequent.[2]

§ 809. **Notice by possession.**—The general rule that a party is bound to take notice of the rights of a person in possession of land, has been applied to a railroad company under a land grant. It was held that where the claimant was in possession under "a pre-emption filing," his possession was notice to the company claiming title under a grant made by statute.[3] The fact that the claimant was in possession under his pre-emption claim was said to be "a decisive fact." It is the province of the courts to determine who are purchasers without notice and to protect the rights of *bona fide* purchasers of public lands.[4]

§ 810. **Injunction on the application of company.**—There can, of course, be no doubt that, after the location of the road

[1] Courtright v. Cedar Rapids, etc., R. Co., 35 Iowa 386; Iowa, etc., Co. v. Courtright, 21 Wall. 310. See, generally, Sioux City, etc., R. Co. v. Osceola Co., 43 Iowa 318; Dubuque, etc., R. Co. v. Des Moines, etc., R. Co., 54 Iowa 89, s. c. 6 N. W. R. 157.

[2] Hannibal, etc., R. Co. v. Moore, 45 Mo. 443; Leavenworth, etc., R. Co. v. United States, 92 U. S. 733; Grinter v. Kansas Pacific R. Co., 23 Kan. 642. See Cooper v. Roberts, 18 How. 173.

[3] United States v. Winona, etc., R. Co., 67 Fed. R. 969, citing Lea v. Polk County Copper Co., 21 How. 493, 498; Noyes v. Hall, 97 U. S. 34, 37; Siebert v. Rosser, 24 Minn. 155, 16 Am. & Eng. Ency. of Law, 800. The court discriminated the case before it from United States v. Winona, etc., R. Co., 67 Fed. R. 948; Spokane Falls, etc., R. Co. v. Ziegler, 61 Fed. R. 392.

[4] Bogan v. Edinburgh, etc., Co., 63 Fed. R. 192; Cunningham v. Ashley, 14 How. 377; Garland v. Wynn, 20 How. 6; Lytle v. State, 22 How. 193; Lindsey v. Hawes, 2 Black 554; Johnson v. Towsley, 13 Wall. 72; Bernier v. Bernier, 147 U. S. 242, s. c. 13 Sup. Ct. R. 244.

and the identification of the land, a company receiving a grant may maintain injunction to prevent the destruction of timber, where the destruction of timber would work irreparable injury.[1] The question as to the right to an injunction is not so clear where there has been no location, and, consequently, no identification of the land. But it has been held, and with reason, that the company, even before the location of the road, may maintain a suit to enjoin the destruction of timber.[2]

§ 811. **Effect of reservation of right to use railroad as a highway.**—In some of the land grants congress incorporated a provision reading as follows: "The said railroad shall be and remain a public highway for the use of the government of the United States, free from all toll or other charge for the transportation of any property or troops," and it has been held that this provision secures to the government the free use of the road, but does not entitle it to have troops or property transported free of charge.[3] The reasoning of the court was that reference should be had to the conditions existing at the time the act was passed and that congress in adopting the act was influenced by the mode in which railroads were then used. Cases were cited holding that persons or corporations might run cars over the tracks of the company.[4]

---

[1] Erhardt *v.* Boaro, 113 U. S. 537, s. c. 5 Sup. Ct. R. 565.

[2] Northern Pacific R. Co. *v.* Hussey, 61 Fed. R. 231, citing Frasher *v.* O'Connor, 115 U. S. 102, s. c. 5 Sup. Ct. R. 1141; Doe *v.* Wilson, 23 How. 457; Dubuque, etc., Railroad Co. *v.* Litchfield, 23 How. 66; Ross *v.* McJunkin, 14 Sergt. & R. 364; Toledo, etc., R. Co. *v.* Pennsylvania Co., 54 Fed. R. 746. An incipient location of land gives the person making the location an equitable interest in the land which he can sell. Kingman *v.* Holthaus, 59 Fed. R. 305, distinguishing Lessieur *v.* Price, 12 How. 59; Rector *v.* Ashley, 6 Wall. 142; Gilson *v.* Chouteau, 13 Wall. 92; Shepley *v.* Cowan, 91 U. S. 330, citing Bush. *v.* Marshall, 6 How. 285; Landes *v.* Brant, 10 How. 348; Levi *v.* Thompson, 4 How. 17; Callahan *v.* Davis, 90 Mo. 78, s. c. 2 S. W. R. 216; Massey *v.* Papin, 24 How. 362.

[3] Lake Superior, etc., R. Co. *v.* United States, 93 U. S. 442; Boyle *v.* Philadelphia, etc., R. Co., 54 Pa. St. 310.

[4] King *v.* Severn R. Co., 2 B. & A. 646; Queen *v.* Grand Junction, etc., R. Co., 4 Q. B. 18; 2 Redfield Ry. § 249; Pierce on Railroads 519.

CHAPTER XXXIV.

PUBLIC AID.

§ 812. State aid.
813. State aid—Lien of state.
814. Constitutionality of statutes authorizing municipal aid to railroads.
815. Construction of constitutional provisions.
816. Corporate power—Constitutional limitation.
817. Constitutional prohibitions.
818. Direct limitations upon the state not limitations upon power to authorize municipalities to grant aid.
819. Constitutional restrictions operate prospectively.
820. Limitation upon the power of municipalities to incur debts.
821. Constitutional questions—Delegation of legislative power.
822. Submission to vote.
823. Submission to popular vote—Constitutional requirements.
824. Constitutional power—Compelling public corporations to aid railway companies.
825. Scope of the legislative power.
826. Scope of the legislative power—Illustrative cases.
827. Power to aid railroads—Statutory authority.
828. Power to grant aid is continuous.
829. Railroad aid laws not restricted to new companies.
830. Taxing the property of one railroad company to aid in the construction of the road of another company.

§ 831. Construction of statutes conferring authority to aid railroad companies.
832. Impairment of contract rights.
833. Impairment of contract rights—Illustrative cases.
834. Construction of statutes—Implied powers.
835. Construction of statutes conferring authority to aid railroad companies—Illustrative instances.
836. Construction of enabling acts—Adjudged cases.
837. Means and methods.
838. Requirements of statute—Classes of cases.
839. Power to aid by subscription does not authorize the execution of bonds.
840. Levy of taxes—Withdrawal of power—Time.
841. Donations and subscriptions.
842. Repeal of enabling act—Withdrawal of authority.
843. Validating proceedings—Retrospective laws.
844. Legislative power to authorize ratification.
845. Curative statutes—Requisites of.
846. Division of municipality for purpose of voting.
847. What corporations may be authorized to grant aid.
848. Subscription to unorganized company.
849. Votes—Voters—Majority of votes.

§ 850. Failure to conform to the requirements of the enabling act—Illustrative cases.
851. Conditions—Performance of—Excuse for non-performance—Illustrative cases.
852. Conditions—Power of municipality to prescribe.
853. Change of municipality.
854. Limitations upon the amount.
855. Valuation of property.
856. Conditions must be performed.
857. Preliminary survey.
858. Petition—Requisites of—Petitioners—Qualifications of.
859. Notice of election.
860. Influencing voters.
861. Vote does not of itself constitute a contract.
862. Aid authorized by popular vote—Duty of local officers.

§ 863. Contract granting aid—Subscription—Enforcement.
864. Power of municipal officers where statute requires submission to popular vote.
865. Decision of local officers as to jurisdictional facts.
866. Acceptance of aid.
867. Ratification of subscription.
868. Stock subscribed by municipality—Legislative control of.
869. Rights and liabilities of municipal corporations as stockholders.
870. Defenses to municipal [subscriptions.
871. Estoppel of tax-payers.
872. Remedies of tax-payers.
873. Remedies of municipalities.
874. Remedies of railroad companies.

§ 812. **State aid.**—Where there is no constitutional provision prohibiting it a state may aid in the construction of a railroad although the railroad is owned by a railroad corporation.[1] Where a change in the constitution withdraws power from the legislature or makes the right to grant aid depend upon a popular vote the legislature can not grant aid after the change in the constitution where the change operates as a withdrawal of the power, or, where the constitution so requires, without submitting the matter to a vote of the people.[2] The statute granting the aid and the acceptance of the company constitute the contract, and if the statute does not expressly or by fair implication provide that the stockholders of the company shall be personally liable then no such liability exists.[3]

[1] Cooley on Taxation, 132. If, as held in the cases hereafter cited, the state may authorize municipalities to grant such aid, it necessarily follows that the state may grant it directly. See *post*, § 814,

[2] McKittrick *v.* Arkansas Central R. Co., 152 U. S. 473, s. c. 14 Sup. Ct. R. 661, citing Aspinwall *v.* Daviess County, 22 How. 364; Wadsworth *v.* Supervisors, 102 U. S. 534; State *v.* Little Rock, etc., R. Co., 31 Ark. 701.

[3] United States *v.* Stanford, 69 Fed. R. 25, citing United States *v.* Union Pac. R. Co., 91 U. S. 72; Sinking Fund Cases, 99 U. S. 700; Union Pac. R.

§ 813. State aid—Lien of state.—A state by guarantying the bonds of a railway company, or by issuing its own bonds in aid of a railway company, does not secure a lien on the property of the company or on any specific fund, unless the statute expressly and clearly provides that the state shall have a lien.[1] It has, however, been held that a statute may be so framed as to give the state a lien on the property, or a right to a specific fund.[2] The rule that a state when it enters into a contract is to be regarded substantially as any other contracting party, requires the conclusion that unless a lien is provided for by the statute or contract, none exists. Where a lien exists in favor of the state, it can not be divested except by the state, or by a valid decree.[3]

§ 814. Constitutionality of statutes authorizing municipal aid to railroads.—The question as to the power of the legislature to authorize municipal corporations to aid railroad companies by donations or subscriptions can not now be regarded as an open one. The question has been much debated but the overwhelming weight of authority sustains the validity of statutes authorizing public corporations to aid in building railroads.[4] The prevailing doctrine has met with opposition,

Co. v. United States, 104 U. S. 662; Hudson Canal Co. v. Pennsylvania, etc., Co., 8 Wall. 276; Hale v. Finch, 104 U. S. 261, 269; Carrol v. Green, 92 U. S. 509.

[1] Tompkins v. Little Rock, etc., R. Co., 125 U. S. 109, s. c. 8 Sup. Ct. R. 762; McKittridge v. Arkansas, etc., R. Co., 152 U. S. 473, s. c. 14 Sup. Ct. R. 661.

[2] Ketchum v. St. Louis, 101 U. S. 306; Knevals v. Florida, etc., R. Co., 66 Fed. R. 224, 13 C. C. A. 410; Wilson v. Ward, etc., Co., 67 Fed. R. 674.

[3] Wilson v. Boyce, 92 U. S. 320; Whitehead v. Vineyard, 50 Mo. 30; Chouteau v. Allen, 70 Mo. 290, 327, 328. See Wilson v. Beckwith, 117 Mo.

61, s. c. 22 S. W. 639; Hawkins v. Mitchell, 34 Fla. 405, 16 So. R. 311.

[4] Of the great number of cases upon this subject we cite: Railroad Company v. Otoe County, 16 Wall. 667; Olcott v. Supervisors, 16 Wall. 678; Rogers v. City of Keokuk, 154 U. S. 546, s. c. 14 Sup. Ct. R. 1162; Sharpless v. Mayor, etc., 21 Pa. St. 147, s. c. 59 Am. Dec. 759; City of Opelika v. Daniel, 59 Ala. 211; Stockton, etc., Co. v. Stockton, 41 Cal. 147; Harney v. Indianapolis R. Co., 32 Ind. 244; Pitzman v. Freeburg, 92 Ill. 111; Hawkins v. Carroll County, 50 Miss. 735; Reineman v. Covington, etc., R. Co., 7 Neb. 310; City of Bridgeport v. Housatonic Co., 15 Conn. 475; Winn v. Macon, 21 Ga. 275; Powers v. In-

but it is now too thoroughly settled to be successfully assailed. It is true that money can not be raised by taxation for the benefit of private persons or purely private corporations,[1] but a railroad is, as we have elswhere shown, a public enterprise, and, theoretically, if not always practically, does promote the public welfare. Because of its public nature it is subjected to many burdens from which private corporations and individual citizens are free.[2] There is, therefore, reason supporting the accepted doctrine, although, as often happens, there are reasons supporting a different view. It is to be remarked that it is solely upon the ground that a railroad is a matter of public concern that the power to lay a tax upon the inhabitants of a municipality can be sustained.[3] So that if a corporation

ferior Court, etc., 23 Ga. 65; Quincy, etc., R. Co. v. Morris, 84 Ill. 410; Douglas v. Chatham, 41 Conn. 211; Cotton v. County Commissioners, 6 Fla. 610; Leavenworth County v. Miller, 7 Kan. 479; Courtney v. Louisville, 12 Bush (Ky.) 419; State v. Linn County Court, 44 Mo. 504; Augusta Bank v. Augusta, 49 Me. 507; Perry v. Keene, 56 N. H. 514; Louisville, etc., Co. v. Davidson County, etc., 1 Sneed (Tenn.) 637; People v. Mitchell, 35 N. Y. 551; Walker v. Cincinnati, 21 Ohio St. 14; Lamville, etc., Co. v. Fairfield, 51 Vt. 257; Hill v. Commissioners, 67 N.C. 368; Harcourt v. Good, 39 Texas 455; Longhorne v. Robinson, 20 Gratt. 661; State v. Charleston, 10 Rich. (S. Car.) L. 491. See Cooley's Const. Lim. (6th ed.), 263; Elliott on Roads and Streets, 63; Dillon Municipal Corp. (4th ed.), §§ 153–160.

[1] Loan Association v. Topeka, 20 Wall. 655; Lowell v. Boston, 111 Mass. 454, s. c. 15 Am. R. 39; Feldman v. Charleston, 23 S. Car. 57; Parkersburg v. Brown, 106 U. S. 487, s. c. 2 Am. & Eng. Corp. Cas. 263; Curtis v. Whipple, 24 Wis. 350, s. c. 1 Am. R. 187; Blair v. 'Cuming County, 111 U. S. 363; Cole v. La Grange 113 U. S. 1, s. c. 7 Am. & Eng. Corp. Cas. 379; State v. Osawkee Township, 14 Kan. 418, s. c. 19 Am. R. 99; Weismer v. Village of Douglas, 64 N. Y. 91; Brewer Brick Co. v. Brewer, 62 Me. 62, s. c. 16 Am. R. 395; Coates v. Campbell, 37 Minn. 498.

[2] Northern Pacific R. Co. v. Roberts, 42 Fed. R. 734. In this case the court denied the doctrine of Whiting v. Sheboygan, etc., R. Co., 25 Wis. 167, and declared that it was opposed to the doctrine asserted in Pratt v. Brown, 3 Wis. 603; Hasbrouck v. Milwaukee, 13 Wis. 37; Robbins v. Milwaukee, etc., R. Co., 6 Wis. 636; Soens v. Racine, 10 Wis. 271; Brodhead v. Milwaukee, 19 Wis. 624; Roberts v. Northern Pacific R. Co., 158 U. S. 1.

[3] In the case of Northern Pacific R. Co. v. Roberts, 42 Fed. R. 734, the court treats a railroad as a public highway. The question is well considered in the case referred to, and many cases are cited, some already referred to by us, and others, among them, Beekman v. Saratoga, etc., R. Co., 3 Paige 45; Brocaw v. Board, 73 Ind. 543; Town of Bennington v. Park,

has, if we may use the term, a public and a private side, it is only to the public side that municipal aid can be given.[1]

§ 815. Construction of constitutional provisions.—It seems to us where the constitution provides that specified acts shall be done, before aid can be given, that such provisions should be regarded as mandatory, for, in our judgment, all the provisions of the constitution should be regarded as mandatory unless the context clearly shows that they were intended to be directory,[2] but, as will be presently shown, some of the adjudged cases do not adhere very closely to this principle. So, where specific things are enumerated, it seems to us that the enumeration should be held to exclude things not enumerated, for, as we believe, the rule that the express mention of one thing excludes others applies with even greater force to written constitutions than to any other instruments.[3] In accordance with what we believe to be the true rule it has been held that a provision requiring publication for a designated length of time prior to the enactment of a statute is mandatory.[4]

§ 816. Corporate purpose—Constitutional limitation.—The question has arisen in some jurisdictions as to whether the

50 Vt. 178; Hallenbeck v. Hahn, 2 Neb. 377; Ex parte Selma, etc., R. Co., 45 Ala. 696.

[1] It has been held that although a private corporation is organized for the double purpose of building and operating a railroad and erecting a cotton compress, the former a public improvement, and the latter a private enterprise, a special tax which is voted by a municipal corporation in its behalf, in aid of the construction of the former alone, is valid. McKenzie v. Wooley, 39 La. Ann. 944, s. c. 3 So. 128.

[2] Varney v. Justice, 86 Ky. 596; May v. Rice, 91 Ind. 546; State v. Johnson, 26 Ark. 281; Cannon v. Mathes, 8 Heisk. 504; Cooley's Const. Lim. (6th ed.) 94. See, also, Gulf, etc., R. Co. v. Miami County, 12 Kan. 230; Portland R. R. Co. v. Standish, 65 Me. 63; Leavenworth R. R. Co. v. Platte County, 42 Mo. 171.

[3] Page v. Allen, 58 Pa. St. 338, s. c. 98 Am. Dec. 272; State v. Blend, 118 Ind. 426.

[4] The constitution of Maryland contains a provision wherein it is declared that no county shall contract any debt or obligation in the construction of a railroad, nor give or loan its credit to a corporation, unless authorized by an act of the assembly, "which shall be published for two months before the next election for members of the house of delegates in the newspapers published in said counties," and this was held to be mandatory. Baltimore & D. R. Co. v. Pumphrey, 74 Md. 86.

grant of aid can be justly regarded as a "corporate purpose." The power to grant aid, as we have seen, is not an ordinary or incidental corporate power, and exists only by virtue of legislative enactment. But it does not follow because the power to grant aid is not an ordinary corporate power, that granting aid is not a "corporate purpose." No constitutional provision forbidding, any public purpose not palpably foreign to the object of a municipal corporation may be regarded as " a corporate purpose," where the legislature so enacts. We should very much doubt whether a statute assuming to make that a corporate purpose which palpably and unmistakably could not be a corporate purpose would be valid, since such a rule would make the provisions of the constitution limiting the power to tax to corporate purposes practically inoperative.[1] But

---

[1] In the case of Atlantic Trust Co. v. Town of Darlington, 63 Fed. R. 76, it was said: "The constitution permits the legislature to authorize municipal corporations to assess and collect taxes for corporate purposes (Séction 8, Article 9), and none other. A municipal corporation is not only a representative of the state, but a portion of its governmental power. It is one of its creatures, made for a specific purpose, to exercise within a limited sphere the powers of the state. United States v. Railroad Co., 17 Wall. 322. The powers of a municipal corporation, dependent wholly upon the source whence they are derived, may be enlarged at any time by the legislature. Rogers v. Burlington, 3 Wall. 654. The legislature then determines the purpose for which they have been created, and clothes them with the means of attaining them. These purposes are their corporate purposes. The legislature may declare that corporate purposes may be promoted by affording aid to a railroad. The unchanging course of legislation shows that this is a public purpose, as well as a corporate purpose; and, without question, cities, towns, villages, and counties, have again and again been clothed with this power. It is true that in Floyd v. Perrin, 30 S. C. 1, 8 S. E. 14, arguendo, the court says that counties have the right to aid in such construction, because they have jurisdiction over highways, and a railroad is a highway. But streets in cities, towns and villages are also highways; and, although the authority of the county over its highways ends at its boundaries, a county has the right to aid a railroad whose termini are in other counties,—perhaps in other states. Floyd v. Perrin, relied on in argument, does not decide that aid to a railroad can not be a corporate purpose." The doctrine is broadly stated in the opinion from which we have quoted, but there can be no doubt that the power of the legislature to determine what are corporate purposes is very broad and comprehensive. Railroad aid bonds can not be issued where the statute prohibits the municipality from incurring any indebtedness, except such as shall be

whatever may be the extent to which the legislature can go, there can be no doubt that the legislature may confer the right to aid railroad companies, although the power to levy taxes is limited to taxes for "corporate purpose."[1]

§ 817. Constitutional prohibitions.—A provision in a state constitution forbidding municipal corporations from becoming stockholders in railroad corporations, and from raising money for such a corporation, or loaning their credit thereto, is violated by a statute which assumes to empower a township to construct a railroad within the limits of the township, which road is designated to form part of a line of road owned by a railroad company.[2] Bonds issued under such a statute are void in the hands of *bona fide* holders.[3] It was also held in the first of the cases referred to in the note that the township might prove the facts averred in its answer, which tended to establish the unconstitutionality of the statute.

§ 818. Direct limitations upon the state not limitations upon power to authorize municipalities to grant aid.—The adjudged cases favor the doctrine that constitutional provisions prohibiting the state from taking stock in a corporation, lend-

"necessary to the administration of its internal affairs." Lewis v. Pima County, 155 U. S. 54, s. c. 15 Sup. Ct. R. 22; Town of Darlington v. Atlantic Trust Co., 68 Fed. R. 849.

[1] Johnson v. County of Stark, 24 Ill. 75; Perkins v. Lewis, 24 Ill. 208; Chicago, etc., Co. v. Smith, 62 Ill. 268; Butler v. Dunham, 27 Ill. 473; Town of Keithsburg v. Frick, 34 Ill. 405; County of Livingston v. Darlington, 101 U. S. 407, 411. Analogous cases fully support the statement of the text. Taylor v. Thompson, 42 Ill. 9; Henderson v. Lagow, 42 Ill. 360; Briscoe v. Allison, 43 Ill. 291; Johnson v. Campbell, 49 Ill. 316; Town of Middleport v. Ætna Life Ins. Co., 82 Ill. 562.

[2] Ætna Life Ins. Co. v. Pleasant Township, 53 Fed. R. 214; Ætna Life Ins. Co. v. Pleasant Township, 62 Fed. R. 718; Pleasant Township v. Ætna Life Ins. Co., 138 U. S. 67, s. c. 11 Sup. Ct. R. 215; Wyscaver v. Atkinson, 37 Ohio St. 80; Counterman v. Dublin Township, 38 Ohio St. 515. The case of Walker v. City of Cincinnati, 21 Ohio St. 14, was distinguished, and it was held not to be inconsistent with the decisions in the cases last cited. We do not believe, we may say, by the way, that townships can embark in the business of building and operating railroads.

[3] The conclusion stated in the text is clearly right. The statute being void there was no power to issue the bonds, and the entire absence of power is always a defense.

ing its credit to a corporation, and incurring an indebtedness in aid of a corporation do not restrain the legislature from empowering public corporations to grant aid to railroad companies.[1] Thus a constitutional provision that the state shall not subscribe for the stock of a railroad has been held not to affect the right of the legislature to authorize a municipal corporation to do so.[2] So, it has been held, limitations upon the power of the state to incur indebtedness to aid in internal improvements do not prevent the legislature from granting power to municipalities to issue railroad aid bonds.[3] Indeed, so far has judicial construction been carried in support of the system of aiding railroads by public funds, that an article in the constitution of Ohio declaring that, "The general assembly shall never authorize any county, city, town, or township, by vote of its citizens or otherwise, to *become a stockholder* in any joint stock company, corporation, or association whatever; or to *raise money* or loan its credit to, or in aid of, any such company, corporation, or association," was held not to prohibit the legislature from authorizing a city to issue its bonds in payment of a loan of ten million dollars, to be expended in the construction of a railroad lying almost entirely outside the state.[4] But where there is an express limitation upon the power of a public corporation the legislature can not confer upon it authority to grant aid to railroad companies.[5]

---

[1] The tendency of the decisions is to support statutes authorizing municipalities to grant aid to railroad companies.

[2] Prettyman v. Supervisors, 19 Ill. 406, s. c. 71 Am. Dec. 230; Dubuque County v. Dubuque, etc., R. Co., 4 G. Greene (Iowa) 1; Leavenworth County v. Miller, 7 Kan. 479; City of Aurora v. West, 9 Ind. 74; Slack v. Maysville, etc., R. Co., 13 B. Monr. 1; Robertson v. Rockford, 21 Ill. 451; Clark v. Janesville, 10 Wis. 136. But see Griffith v. Commissioners of Crawford County, 20 Ohio 609; People v. State Treas., 23 Mich. 499. See, generally, Cass v. Dillon, 2 Ohio St. 607; Clark v. Janesville, 10 Wis. 136; City of Sioux City v. Weare, 59 Iowa 95.

[3] Thompson v. City of Peru, 29 Ind. 305; Slack v. Maysville, etc., R. Co., 13 B. Mon. (Ky.) 9; Prettyman v. Supervisors, 19 Ill. 406; Police Jury v. McDonogh, 8 La. Ann. 341.

[4] Walker v. Cincinnati, 21 Ohio St. 14.

[5] A statute of Ohio which authorized a certain township to construct a few miles of railroad within its limits, intended to ultimately form part of a continuous line of road to be operated

§ 819. **Constitutional restrictions operate prospectively.—** The general rule is that constitutional provisions operate prospectively and not retroactively. Under this rule it is held that where there is a statute in force, a constitutional provision adopted after proceedings resulting in a contract were had under the statute, does not invalidate or impair the validity of such proceedings.[1] If, however, a constitutional provision is adopted before proceedings are taken under the statute, the proceedings are not effective.[2] Constitutional or statutory provisions may, however, be so worded as to affect prior proceedings,[3] but contract rights can not be impaired.

and equipped by private capital, was held to violate a constitutional provision, which prohibits the general assembly from authorizing any county, city, town, or township to become a stockholder in any private corporation, or to raise money for or loan its credit to or in aid of such corporation. Pleasant Tp. v. Ætna Life Ins. Co., 138 U. S. 67, s. c. 11 Sup. Ct. R. 215.

[1] Norton v. Board, etc., 129 U. S. 479, s. c. 26 Am. & Eng. Corp. Cas. 583; Aspinwall v. Commissioners, 22 How. 364; Wadsworth v. Supervisors, 102 U. S. 534; Scotland County v. Hill, 132 U. S. 107; County of Callaway v. Foster, 93 U. S. 567; County of Henry v. Nicolay, 95 U. S. 619; County of Schuyler v. Thomas, 98 U. S. 169; County of Cass v. Gillett, 100 U. S. 585; County of Ralls v. Douglass, 105 U. S. 728. See Green County v. Conners, 109 U. S. 104; Livingston County v. First Nat. Bank, 128 U. S. 102. Contra, State v. Dallas County, etc., 72 Mo. 329; State v. County Court, 51 Mo. 522; State v. Gurroutte, 67 Mo. 445. See, also, Decker v. Hughes, 68 Ill. 33; Maxcy v. Williamson County, 72 Ill. 207; Board v. Bolton, 104 Ill. 220; Mason v. Shawneetown, 77 Ill. 533; Knox County v. Ninth Nat. Bank, 147 U. S. 91, s. c. 13 Sup. Ct. R. 267.

[2] Town of Concord v. Robinson, 121 U. S. 165, s. c. 7 Sup. Ct. R. 937; Citizens', etc, Asso. v. Perry County, 156 U. S. 692, s. c. 15 Sup. Ct. R. 547.

[3] Wadsworth v. Supervisors, 102 U. S. 534; Railroad Company v. Falconer, 103 U. S. 821. Upon the general subject, see Supervisors v. Galbraith, 99 U. S. 214; Fairfield v. Gallatin Co., 100 U. S. 47; Dodge v. County of Platte, 16 Hun (N. Y.) 285; State v. Green Co., 54 Mo. 540; State v. Clark, 23 Minn. 422; Fosdick v. Perrysburg, 14 Ohio St. 472; Slack v. Maysville, etc., R. Co., 13 B. Mon. (Ky.) 1. It was held, in Louisville v. Savings Bank, 104 U. S. 469, that the constitution of Illinois, adopted on July 8, 1870, did not invalidate bonds issued in pursuance to a vote of the township on the same day that the constitution was adopted, although it provides that "no county, city, township or other municipality shall ever become a subscriber to the capital of any railroad or private corporation, or make donation to or loan its credit in aid of such corporation," unless the subscription shall "have been authorized under existing laws, by a vote of the people prior to such adoption." The courts say that they will presume the vote upon the question of levying the tax to have been

§ 820. **Limitation upon the power of municipalities to incur debts.**—A constitutional provision prohibiting a municipal corporation from aiding a railroad by subscriptions or donations would, it is hardly necessary to say, place it beyond the power of the legislature to empower municipal corporations to grant such aid.[1] But a provision of the constitution prohibiting municipal corporations from incurring a debt in aid of a corporation does not necessarily prohibit the municipalities from giving aid to railroad companies. The effect of such a provision is to preclude the municipalities from incurring a debt, but it does not preclude them from raising money by taxation in aid of railroad companies. There can be no debt created, but a donation or subscription may be authorized.[2] In jurisdictions where municipalities are forbidden to incur an indebtedness the railroad company is not, as it is held, entitled to the money until it is collected.[3]

completed before the close of the day, since the meeting for an election was called for nine o'clock in the morning and only fifty-two votes were cast. But the supreme court of Illinois holds that where the issuance of railroad aid bonds is authorized by a vote at the same election at which this amendment to the constitution was adopted, the issue is unconstitutional. People v. Town of Bishop, 111 Ill. 124. The party asserting the validity of bonds issued after this provision referred to in the above case took effect is held to have the burden of proof to show that they come within the exception. Williams v. People, 132 Ill. 574.

[1] Norton v. Board of Commissioners, 129 U. S. 479; Wadsworth v. Supervisors, 102 U. S. 534; Buffalo, etc., R. Co. v. Falconer, 103 U. S. 821; Kelley v. Town of Milan, 127 U. S. 139, 154; Mayor, etc., v. Gilmore, 21 Fed. R. 870; Taxpayers, etc., v. Tennessee, etc., R. Co., 11 Lea 329; List v. Wheeling, 7 W. Va. 501.

[2] Lafayette, etc., R. Co. v. Geiger, 34 Ind. 185; Harney v. Indianapolis, etc., R. Co., 32 Ind. 244; City of Aurora v. West, 9 Ind. 74; Dronberger v. Reed, 11 Ind. 420; Evansville, etc., Co. v. City of Evansville, 15 Ind. 395; Board v. Bright, 18 Ind. 93; Aspinwall v. Commissioners, 22 How. (U. S.) 364; Town of Concord v. Portsmouth Savings Bank, 92 U. S. 625; Falconer v. Buffalo, etc., R. Co., 69 N. Y. 491.

[3] Bittinger v. Bell, 65 Ind. 445; Board v. Louisville, etc., R. Co., 39 Ind. 192; Sankey v. Terre Haute, etc., R. Co., 42 Ind. 402; Petty v. Myers, 49 Ind. 1; Jager v. Doherty, 61 Ind. 528; Pope v. Board, 51 Fed. R. 769; Board v. State, 115 Ind. 64, s. c. 4 N. E. R. .589, 17 N. E. R. 855. Where aid is voted and an additional levy is required a tax-payer may have mandamus to compel the proper officers to make the additional levy of taxes. Board v. State, 86 Ind. 8. See, also, Board v. Montgomery, 106 Ind. 517; Board v. State, 109 Ind. 596. It is held, that where a

§ 821. **Constitutional questions—Delegation of legislative power.**—It is a well known principle of constitutional law that legislative power can neither be surrendered nor delegated. This principle, however, does not forbid the legislature from enacting a law authorizing the inhabitants of a locality to determine by ballot, petition or otherwise, whether they will lay a tax upon themselves to aid a railroad company by donation or subscription.[1] In enacting a general law authorizing public corporations to aid railroad companies, there is no delegation of legislative power, nor is the taking effect of the law made to depend upon the act or authority of any other persons or bodies than that of the lawmakers. The law is effective when it leaves the hands of the law-making power, and all that is left to the inhabitants of a locality is to determine whether they will avail themselves of the provisions of the law.[2] If, however, the legislature should provide that a law should take effect only in the event that the people should vote in favor of its taking effect the enactment would not be valid,[3] but this is a very different thing from enacting a general law and simply leaving it to localities to take action under it.

§ 822. **Submission to vote.**—The general legislative practice is to provide for submitting the question of granting aid to a railroad to the people and allowing them to determine,

tax is levied the railroad company acquires such an interest therein as will pass to a company with which it consolidates. Scott *v.* Hansheer, 94 Ind. 1; Pope *v.* Board, 51 Fed. R. 760.

[1] Cincinnati, etc., R. Co. *v.* Commissioners of Clinton Co., 1 Ohio St. 77; Lafayette, etc., R. Co. *v.* Geiger, 34 Ind. 185, 220; Baltimore, etc., R. Co. *v.* County of Jefferson, 29 Fed. R. 305; Clarke *v.* Rochester, 24 Barb. (N. Y.) 446; Starin *v.* Genoa, 23 N. Y. 439; Louisville, etc., R. Co. *v.* County Court, 1 Sneed (Tenn.) 637; Lafayette, etc., R. Co. *v.* Geiger, 34 Ind. 185; Hobart *v.* Supervisors, 17 Cal. 23;

Stein *v.* Mobile, 24 Ala. 591; Cotton *v.* Leon County, 6 Fla. 610; Slack *v.* Maysville, etc., R. Co., 13 B. Mon. (Ky.) 1; Police Jury *v.* McDonogh, 8 La. Ann. 341; Cincinnati, etc., R. Co. *v.* Comrs. of Clinton County, 1 Ohio St. 77; Moers *v.* Reading, 21 Pa. St. 188.

[2] Aspinwall *v.* Commissioners of Daviess County, 22 How. (U. S.) 364; Board *v.* Spitler, 13 Ind. 235; Thompson *v.* City of Peru, 29 Ind. 305; Robinson *v.* Schenck, 102 Ind. 307.

[3] State *v.* Young, 26 Iowa 122, s. c. 2 Am. & Eng. R. Cas. 348.

either by ballot or by petition, whether aid shall be granted, but where there is no constitutional provision requiring it the legislature may authorize a municipality to grant aid without submitting the matter to the people. The subject is essentially legislative and the legislature is not bound to provide for a vote or petition by the inhabitants of the municipality, except where a provision of the constitution so requires.[1] If the legislature does provide for a submission to vote or petition then there must be an election held as the enabling act requires or such a petition as the act prescribes.

§ 823. Submission to popular vote—Constitutional requirements.—Where the constitution requires the question of granting aid to a railroad company to be submitted to a vote of the tax-payers or inhabitants of the municipality, the requirement is mandatory and must be obeyed. The legislature in such a case has no power to authorize the grant of aid without submitting the question to the people of the locality. Where a specified number of votes in favor of the aid is required by the constitution in order to authorize the municipality to grant the aid it is not in the power of the legislature to provide that aid may be granted unless the vote prescribed is given in favor of granting the aid.[2] There is a difference between cases where the statute assumes to authorize municipal officers to grant aid

[1] County of Ralls v. Douglass, 105 U. S.728; Thomson v. Lee County, 3 Wall. 327; McCallie v. Chattanooga, 3 Head (Tenn.) 317; Long v. New London, 9 Biss. 539; County of Livingston v. Darlington, 101 U. S. 407, 415; Town of Keithsburg v. Frick, 34 Ill. 405; Marshall v. Silliman, 61 Ill. 218; Quincy, etc., R. Co. v. Morris, 84 Ill. 410. But see Union Bank v. Board Comrs., 116 N. Car. 339, s. c. 21 S. E. R. 410.

[2] Hill v. City of Memphis, 134 U. S. 198, s. c. 10 Sup. Ct. R. 562; Hill v. City of Memphis, 23 Fed. R. 872. In the case of Hill v. City of Memphis, 134 U. S. 198, s. c. 10 Sup. Ct. R. 562, the court held that a vote of two-thirds of the electors in favor of subscribing for the stock of a railroad company did not authorize the municipal authorities to issue bonds of the municipality. The principles declared by the cases below cited were applied. Police Jury v. Britton, 15 Wall. 566; Kelley v. Milan, 127 U. S. 139, s. c. 8 Sup. Ct. R. 1101; Young v. Clarendon Township, 132 U. S. 340, s. c. 10 Sup. Ct. R. 107; Claiborne County v. Brooks, 111 U. S. 400, s. c. 4 Sup. Ct. R. 489.

without submitting the question to a vote and cases where the statute provides for a submission, but the municipal officers do not submit the question to the voters as the statute requires. If it appears on the face of the statute that the legislature has assumed to confer authority upon the municipal officers to grant aid without submitting the matter to the voters of the locality there can be no power, since if the statute be in conflict with the constitution it is void and a void statute can not confer authority or right. In such a case there can be no estoppel, for when the constitution is consulted and the statute tested by it the absence of legislative power is at once revealed. No person can be heard to say that he was ignorant of the constitution or the statute under which public corporations are organized so that there is no ground upon which an estoppel can be founded. Where, however, the legislature obeys the constitutional mandate and provides for a submission of the question to the voters of the municipality and the municipal officers do not follow the provisions of the statute, then there is reason for holding that there may be an estoppel in cases where the other elements essential to the existence of an estoppel are present.

§ 824. **Constitutional power—Compelling public corporations to aid railroad companies.**—The power of the legislature over public corporations is, as we have seen, very great. It seems to be a necessary conclusion from the rule asserted by the weight of authority that the legislature may, without consulting the citizens of a locality, compel them to tax themselves to aid public enterprises.[1] Accordingly it has been held that it may compel the various municipalities through which

[1] This is the general rule. Martin v. Dix, 52 Miss. 53, s. c. 24 Am. R. 661; United States v. Memphis, 97 U. S. 284; New Orleans v. Clark, 95 U. S. 644, 654; Gordon v. Cornes, 47 N. Y. 608; In re Madera, etc., Dist., 92 Cal. 296; Walker v. Tarrant County, 20 Tex. 16; Marks v. Purdue University, 37 Ind. 155; Jewell v. Weed, 18 Minn. 272; Bass v. Fountleroy, 11 Tex. 698; County of Livingston v. Darlington, 101 U. S. 407. Although it seems to be an arbitrary rule to compel taxpayers to burden themselves in order to aid railroad companies, it is difficult to perceive why it is not a necessary conclusion from the settled principle.

the railroad passes to take stock in the enterprise, even against the will of the inhabitants,[1] though this right is denied by some authorities,[2] and but few attempts have been made to exercise it.

§ 825. Scope of the legislative power.—The scope of the legislative power, when not fenced about by constitutional limitations, is very wide and far reaching. The subject of taxation is a legislative one and where it is not restricted by constitutional provisions the legislature may authorize a tax for almost any strictly public purpose. The power to tax has, however, inherent limitations, since it is always implied that the power to raise revenues by taxation is limited by the subject itself, insomuch as taxes can only be levied for public or governmental purposes. As it is settled that using money to aid in building a railroad is devoting it to a public purpose it necessarily follows that the legislature has very great and extensive power over the subject of granting aid to railroad companies. So great and extensive is this power that it is competent for the legislature to authorize a municipality to give aid to a railroad, although the railroad may not be located within the territorial limits of the municipality. The legislature, where no constitutional limitation prohibits, may doubtless group counties and townships together, or may separate them into districts for the purpose of authorizing them to

[1] Napa Valley R. Co. v. Napa County, 30 Cal. 435. Permitting the authorities to subscribe without a submission of the question to the people may amount to a compulsory assessment of taxes, but the right of the legislature to do this has been upheld. Thompson v. Perrine, 106 U. S. 589; County of Ralls v. Douglass, 105 U. S. 728; Thomson v. Lee County, 3 Wall. (U. S.) 327; McCallie v. Chattanooga, 3 Head (Tenn.) 317; Long v. New London, 9 Biss. (U. S.) 539. And even where the state constitution prohibits the passage of laws for the benefit of individuals, the legislature may enact a valid law permitting certain counties to grant aid without a preliminary vote of the inhabitants, when the general law requires such a vote. County of Tipton v. Rogers L. & M. Works, 103 U. S. 523.

[2] People v. Batchellor, 53 N. Y. 128; Horton v. Thompson, 71 N. Y. 513; Cairo, etc., R. Co. v. Sparta, 77 Ill. 505; Williams v. Town of Roberts, 88 Ill. 11; Sykes v. Columbus, 55 Miss. 115. See Choisser v. People, 140 Ill. 21, 29 N. E. R. 546; Post v. Pulaski County, 49 Fed. R. 628, 1 C. C. A. 405.

grant aid to railroad companies.[1] The decisions which lay down the rule that the legislature may create taxing or assessment districts support the rule we have stated.[2]

§ 826. Scope of the legislative power—Illustrative cases.— The power of the legislature to authorize a municipal corporation to aid in the construction of a railroad was recognized in a case wherein it was held that the action of the municipality granting aid to a railroad company, under a statute providing that townships might subscribe to the stock of any railway company, "building or proposing to build a railroad into, through or near such township," was conclusive upon the courts, although the railroad was nine miles distant from the township.[3] Where the building of a road will tend to increase the business of other roads leading to the municipality, it is held that aid may be given, although the road aided lies at a distance from the municipality authorized to aid it.[4] It has also been held that where counties through which a proposed road will run are authorized to aid the construction of it or its connecting lines, aid in the construction of the latter may lawfully be extended, as soon as the construction of such a connecting line has been duly authorized by charter, and a

[1] McFerron v. Alloway, 14 Bush. (Ky.) 580. See, also, Breckenridge County v. McCracken, 61 Fed. R. 191.

[2] Howell v. Buffalo, 37 N. Y. 267, 273; Challiss v. Parker, 11 Kan. 394; Langhorne v. Robinson, 20 Gratt. 661; Hingham, etc., Turnpike Corp. v. County of Norfolk, 6 Allen 353; Gilson v. Board, 128 Ind. 65; Scovill v. Cleveland, 1 Ohio St. 126; Hill v. Higdon, 5 Ohio St. 243, 245; City of Philadelphia v. Field, 58 Pa. St. 320. See, generally, Merrick v. Amherst, 12 Allen 500; Burr v. Carbondale, 76 Ill. 455; Hensley Township v. People, 84 Ill. 544; County of Livingston v. Darlington, 101 U. S. 407; Town of Waterville v. Kennebec Co., 59 Me. 80; Litchfield v. Vernon, 41 N. Y. 123; Shaw v. Dennis, 10 Ill. 405.

[3] Kirkbride v. Lafayette County, 108 U. S. 208, s. c. 2 Sup. Ct. R. 501. See, also, Brocaw v. Board, 73 Ind. 543; Nixon v. Campbell, 106 Ind. 47; Walker v. City of Cincinnati, 21 Ohio St. 14, s. c. 8 Am. R. 24.

[4] In the case of Van Hostrup v. Madison City, 1 Wall. (U. S.) 291, it was held that authority "to take stock in any chartered company for making a road, or roads, to said city," empowered the city of Madison to take stock in the Columbus and Shelby Railroad, which approached no nearer to Madison than forty-six miles distant, at which point it connected with another road running to that city.

contract for its construction has been entered into.[1] Municipalities may exercise the same privilege of taking stock to aid in building branches of a railroad that they may exercise in aid of the main road, in case the company is chartered to build the road with branches.[2] It has been held that a railroad may be lawfully aided by a subscription to its stock, although it lies outside the state,[3] and, indeed, even if it lies outside the country.[4] There are also cases holding that the legislature may confer the power to subscribe to a corporation not in existence, but to be subsequently created.[5] A provision in the charter of a railroad company, authorizing any town or village along the line of its route to extend aid to it, will, as it has been held, confer such power upon a village which comes into existence after the charter is granted.[6] The legislature may authorize subscriptions to aid a railroad company whose charter empowers it to carry on some other business in connection with the operation of its road, as dealing in coal, or mining,[7] but we suppose that it is only in so far as the busi-

[1] Kenicott v. Supervisors, 16 Wall. (U. S.) 452.

[2] Tyler v. Elizabethtown, etc., R. Co., 9 Bush (Ky.) 510.

[3] Railroad Company v. County of Otoe, 16 Wall. (U. S.) 667; Quincy, etc., R. Co. v. Morris, 84 Ill. 410; State v. Charleston, 10 Rich. L. (S. Car.) 491. See Falconer v. Buffalo, etc., R. Co., 69 N. Y. 491; Walker v. Cincinnati, etc., R. Co., 21 Ohio St. 14. In Moulton v. Evansville, 25 Fed. Rep. 382, it was held that the constitution of Indiana presents no obstacle to a grant by the legislature to a city in that state of power to aid a railroad corporation whose road lies entirely in other states, and which connects with such city by means of a line of boats running from its terminus.

[4] In White v. Syracuse, etc., R. Co., 14 Barb. (N. Y.) 559, it is held that the statute of New York, authorizing railway companies of that state to subscribe for stock in the Great Western Railway, Canada West, is constitutional.

[5] James v. Milwaukee, 16 Wall. (U. S.) 159. It is held that the provisions of a general act, conferring on counties, cities, and towns, generally, power to make donations to railroad companies, practically become a part of all subsequent charters of cities and towns. Madry v. Cox, 73 Tex. 538. See, also, MacKenzie v. Wooley, 39 La. Ann. 944.

[6] Perrin v. New London, 67 Wis. 416.

[7] Kentucky Improvement Co. v. Slack, 100 U. S. 648; County of Randolph v. Post, 93 U. S. 502; MacKenzie v. Wooley, 39 La. Ann. 944, where the railroad company was also to erect and operate a cotton compress. But the subscription must be used only to aid in constructing the *railroad*. MacKenzie v. Wooley, 39 La. Ann. 944.

§ 827   PUBLIC AID.   1153

ness is of a public nature that aid can be given by public corporations. It has been expressly held that a general power to subscribe aid to a railroad may be exercised by making a subscription to the stock of a company chartered to build and operate a railroad, even though it also engaged in the business of mining, and in other transactions expressly authorized by its charter. And bonds issued in pursuance of such subscriptions were held valid.[1]

§ 827. **Power to aid railroads — Statutory authority.** — Statutory authority is essential to the existence of power in a municipal or governmental corporation to aid railroad companies by donations or subscriptions. Upon this point there is no diversity of opinion.[2] In the absence of express legislative enactment the power can not exist inasmuch as the power to aid a railroad company by donations or subscriptions is not an inherent or incidental corporate power. Statutory authority to manage or control the affairs and business of a public or governmental corporation is not sufficient to authorize aid to a railroad company.[3] The power to aid railroad com-

[1] County of Randolph v. Post, 93 U. S. 502.

[2] Kelley v. Milan, 127 U. S. 139; Norton v. Dyersberg, 127 U. S. 160; Young v. Clarendon Township, 132 U. S. 340; Concord v. Robinson, 121 U. S. 165; Daviess County v. Dickinson, 117 U. S. 657; Lewis v. Shreveport, 108 U. S. 282; Claiborne County v. Brooks, 111 U. S. 400; Town of South Ottawa v. Perkins, 94 U. S. 260; Wells v. Supervisors, 102 U. S. 625; Weightman v. Clark, 103 U. S. 256; Town of Coloma v. Eaves, 92 U. S. 484; St. Joseph Township v. Rogers, 16 Wall. 644; Kenicott v. Supervisors, 16 Wall. 453; Thomson v. Lee County, 3 Wall. 327; Marsh v. Fulton County, 10 Wall. 676; Commercial Nat. Bank v. Iola, 2 Dillon (U. S. C. C.) 353; Katzenberger v. Aberdeen, 16 Fed. R. 745; New Orleans, etc., R. Co. v. Dunn, 51 Ala. 128; City of Aurora v. West, 22 Ind. 88; Starin v. Genoa, 23 N.Y. 439; City of Bridgeport v. Housatonic, etc., R. Co., 15 Conn. 475; Cook v. Sumner, etc., Manufacturing Co., 1 Sneed 698; McCoy v. Briant, 53 Cal. 247; City, etc., of St. Louis v. Alexander, 23 Mo. 483; Board, etc. v. McClintock, etc., 51 Ind. 325; Jeffries v. Lawrence, 42 Iowa 498; City of Atchison v. Butcher, 3 Kan. 104; Clay v. Nicholas County, 4 Bush 154; Hawkins v. Board, etc., 50 Miss. 735; Reineman v. Covington, etc., Co., 7 Neb. 310; Welch v. Post, 99 Ill. 471; Gaddis v. Richland County, 92 Ill. 119, 36 Central L. J. 133; Fisk v. Kenosha, 26 Wis. 23; Pennsylvania R. Co. v. Philadelphia Co., 47 Pa. St. 189.

[3] In the case of Lewis v. Pima County, 155 U. S. 54, s. c. 15 Sup. Ct. R. 22, the statute of the United States provided, *inter alia*, that the general

panies is said by some of the authorities to be an extraordinary power,[1] and this is true. But while the power is not an ordinary one yet it is one that is often essential to the interests of municipalities and to the exercise of which many counties, towns and cities owe their development and prosperity. If it be the object of law to promote the public welfare, as unquestionably it is, statutes conferring authority to aid in constructing improvements of a public character are wise and politic. Because a power may be abused is not, as it seems to us, a sufficient reason for condemning legislative action in granting it to municipalities. The danger of abuse may be, and doubtless is, sufficient reason to call for great care in guarding and limiting the grant of the power. The power is so far an extraordinary one as to require that it be not held to exist in municipal corporations unless conferred by clear statutory provisions, and to require, also, that the construction of statutes conferring such power be strict, as against railroad companies claiming aid.

§ 828. Power to grant aid is continuous.—Where power is conferred upon a municipal corporation to aid a railroad company, it is a continuous power, and is not exhausted by a single exercise.[2] Where a limit is fixed by the enabling act, the municipality may repeatedly exercise the power, provided it does not go beyond the limit fixed by the statute. A failure at one meeting or at one election to order the granting of aid does not preclude the municipality from holding other meet-

assembly of the territory should have power to create towns, cities or other municipal corporations and to confer upon them corporate powers and privileges necessary to their local administration, but also provided that the corporations should not be invested with power to incur any debt or obligation "other than such as shall be necessary to the administration of its internal affairs," and the court held that municipal corporations could not incur any debt to aid a railroad company. The court, in the course of the opinion, said: "It could never have been contemplated, however, that this power would be used to incur obligations in favor of a railroad operated by a private corporation for private gain, though also subserving a public purpose."

[1] 1 Dillon Municipal Corp. (4th ed.) 153.

[2] Empire Township v. Darlington, 101 U. S. 87; Brocaw v. Board, 73 Ind. 543, 548.

§ 828   PUBLIC AID.   1155

ings or elections.[1] It has been held that a general authority to accept by a two-thirds vote a power conferred upon the municipality to subscribe in aid of a railroad, is not exhausted by a single vote, and that the power will survive repeated rejections, and that a two-thirds vote at a subsequent meeting will be a valid acceptance of the power to extend the desired aid.[2] The common council of a city can not, however, two years after having rejected a petition presented by the stockholders, asking that aid be given to a certain railroad, reconsider such petition and extend the aid for which it asks.[3] But the doctrine of the case cited in the note can not be understood as preventing a second or subsequent petition from being presented to and acted upon by the common council. A general authority to subscribe to the capital stock of any railroad does not fail with a single exercise, but subscriptions may be made to the stock of any number of companies, so long as the terms of the statute are followed in each case.[4] And a municipality

---

[1] Society for Savings v. City of New London, 29 Conn. 174.

[2] Society for Savings v. City of New London, 29 Conn. 174. See Woodward v. Calhoun County, (U. S. D. C. N. D. Miss.) 2 Cent. L. Jour. 396. In the absence of any prohibition in the statutes against submitting the question to the electors more than once, a second vote may be taken. Supervisors v. Galbraith, 99 U. S. 214. A township subscribed to the stock of a railroad, on the condition, among others, that a depot should be built at a certain place. By mistake this place, as set out in the petition and notices of election, was different from that intended, and from that where the depot was built. Upon discovery of this mistake, it was attempted to hold another election, in which the true route of the road and place for the depot should be set out, relying on the provisions of the statute that a second election should be held "for the same purpose" as the first, under certain circumstances. In the preliminaries for the second election a different amount for the subscription, and a different route and time of completion of the road, were specified. The court held that the election was not for the same purpose as the first, and the subscription was invalid. Kansas City and Pac. R. Co. v. Rich Tp., 45 Kan. 275, s. c. 25 Pac. R. 595.

[3] City of Madison v. Smith, 83 Ind. 502.

[4] County of Chicot v. Lewis, 103 U. S. 164. Provided, of course, that the total of the subscriptions does not exceed the amount that the municipality has power to subscribe. It is held, under the provisions of the Kansas statute limiting the amount of subscription or loan to a railroad by a county, city or township, that such limit is not confined to the subscription or loan to any one railroad, but restricts indebtedness for railroad

may make several subscriptions to the same company if their sum does not exceed the amount which it is empowered to subscribe in aid of such company.[1]

§ 829. **Railroad aid laws not restricted to new companies.**—It is obvious that the welfare of a community may be promoted by the extension of an existing railroad and hence there is no reason for denying that a statute authorizing in general terms the grant of aid to railroad companies may apply to the extension of the road of an existing company. The theory upon which railroad aid laws principally rests is that the construction of the road is a benefit to the municipality, and as the extension of an old road into a municipality is a benefit to the municipality there is no just ground upon which it can be held that aid may not be granted in order to secure an extension.[2] It may, perhaps, be competent for the legislature to limit the power to grant aid to new roads, but where there is no provision limiting the authority conferred upon the municipal corporation to grant aid to corporations newly created the courts can not make such a limitation, since that would be to legislate.

§ 830. **Taxing the property of one railroad company to aid in the construction of the road of another company.**—The property of a railroad company within the limits of a municipality which has voted aid to a competing railroad is subject to taxation to pay the aid voted.[3] It is affirmed in the case referred to in the note that all property subject to taxation must

purposes generally, whether the aid be extended to one or more corporations. Chicago, K. & W. Ry. Co. v. Freeman, 38 Kan. 597, 16 Pac. R. 828. Under the New Mexico statute, authorizing any county to issue county bonds to assist in the construction of any railroad passing through the county, "not exceeding five per centum of the assessed value of the property of the county," bonds to the extent of five per centum may be issued to each road passing through the county, when so ordered by a vote of the people. Coler v. Board County Com'rs Santa Fe County, (N. M.) 27 Pac. R. 619.

[1] Empire Township v. Darlington, 101 U. S. 87; Brocaw v. Board of Commissioners, 73 Ind. 543.

[2] Pittsburgh, etc., R. Co. v. Harden, 137 Ind. 486.

[3] Pittsburgh, etc., R. Co. v. Harden, 137 Ind. 486.

be made to bear its share of the burden, otherwise the tax would not be equal and uniform.[1] The court refused assent to the argument of counsel that as the existing company could not be benefited by the construction of a rival road there was no power to levy the tax.[2] The good of the local public is to be regarded, not that of particular corporations or persons, and it is for the majority to determine what is for the good of the municipality. It is evident that if particular corporations or persons could defeat a tax because they were not benefited the public good might be sacrificed to private interests. Such a result is always to be avoided, since it is opposed to fundamental principles of government.

§ 831. **Construction of statutes conferring authority to aid railroad companies.**—As the power to aid railroad companies is not an ordinary corporate power but exists only by virtue of express statutory grant,[3] it necessarily follows that statutes conferring power to aid railroad companies must be strictly construed. The cardinal rule that the legislative intention is to be ascertained and carried into effect controls, but neverthe-

---

[1] Citing Cooley on Taxation, 130, 134.

[2] On this point it was said: "There may always be found one or more persons who might make the claim that the tax imposed is of no benefit to them; and there are many more persons who, by reason of absence, sex, infancy or other disability, are denied a voice in the imposition of the tax. Yet, when a majority have determined in favor of the burden, it is taken as the voice of the whole community; and not only those who do not or can not vote upon the proposition, but even those who vote against it are equally bound by the result. The majority of the voters proceeding under the forms and by the authority sanctioned by the legislature, speaks for the general good. Even the rival railroad company participates in the increased prosperity caused by the construction of the new road."

[3] *Ante*, § 827; City of Lynchburg v. Slaughter, 75 Va. 57; Brodie v. McCabe, 33 Ark. 690; Barnes v. Lacon, 84 Ill. 461; Campbell v. Paris, etc., R. Co., 71 Ill. 611; Lamoille, etc., R. Co. v. Fairfield, 51 Vt. 237; Northern Bank v. Porter Township, 110 U. S. 608; Bissell v. Kankakee, 64 Ill. 249, s. c. 16 Am. R. 554. See, also, Mellen v. Town of Lansing, 11 Fed. R. 820, 829; Purdy v. Lansing, 128 U. S. 557, s. c. 9 Sup. Ct. R. 172; Sutherland Stat. Constr., §§ 362, 365, 378. There must, in every instance, be a valid statute. Amoskeag Bank v. Town of Ottawa, 105 U. S. 667; Turner v. Commissioners. 27 Kan. 314; Gilson v. Town of Dayton, 123 U. S. 59.

less, the construction is to be strict as against the company, and liberal in favor of the public. The construction, to be sure, is not to be so strict as to defeat the intention of the framers of the statute, but the statute can not be construed as granting authority that is not conferred either expressly or by clear and necessary implication.[1]

§ 832. Impairment of contract rights.—The obligation of a contract is protected by the federal constitution against the people of a state, as well as against a state legislature. A contract right can not, therefore, be impaired by an amendment to a state constitution, nor by a change thereof.[2] It is quite clear that the rights of a railroad company, when vested by virtue of an effective contract, can not be impaired, but the difficulty is in determining when there is an effective contract. It can not be held that a mere vote or order declaring that aid be granted constitutes a contract, but if the railroad company should accept the proffered aid, and especially if it should in reliance on the offer of aid actually undertake the work of constructing the road, and should expend money in the work, there would, as we believe, be a contract within the protection of the constitution.[3] If, however, the offer of aid should be

[1] Pitzman v. Freesburg, 92 Ill. 111; Lewis v. Shreveport, 3 Woods 205; Lewis v. City of Shreveport, 108 U. S. 282; Allen v. Louisiana, 103 U. S. 80; Marsh v. Fulton Co., 10 Wall. 676; Leavenworth County v. Miller, 7 Kan. 479, s. c. 12 Am. R. 425. See State v. Charleston, 10 Rich. L. (S. C.) 491; City Council v. Wentworth, etc., Baptist Church, 4 Strob. 306, 308; Singer, etc., Co. v. Elizabeth, 42 N. J. L. 249. In the case of Meyer v. Muscatine, 1 Wall. 384, a broader doctrine than that stated in the text was announced, but we think that the decision in that case is greatly modified if not entirely overruled by later and better considered cases. Kelley v. Milan, 127 U. S. 139, s. c. 22 Am. & Eng. R. Cas. 1; Merrill v. Monticello, 138 U. S. 673, s. c. 11 Sup. Ct. R. 441; Brenham v. German Am. Bank, 144 U. S. 173; Claiborne Co. v. Brooks, 111 U. S. 400; State v. Glover, 155 U. S. 513, s. c. 15 Sup. Ct. R. 186; Coffin v. City of Indianapolis, 59 Fed. R. 221, and cases cited.

[2] Gunn v. Barry, 15 Wall. 610; United States v. Jefferson County, 1 McCrary (U. S.) 356.

[3] Even in those jurisdictions where the rule is that the railroad company is not entitled to the money until it is collected, it is held that it has such an interest as will pass to the consolidated corporation, of which it forms part. Scott v. Hansheer, 94 Ind. 1; Pope v. Board, 51 Fed. R. 769. See ante, § 329, and authorities cited in note 1.

withdrawn before acceptance, there would be no contract. It has been held that the contract is not complete until the subcription is actually placed upon the books of the railroad company,[1] but this seems to us a doctrine that can not justly be extended to cases where the railroad company, acting upon the order granting aid and influenced thereby, has expended money in the construction of the road. Where there is a failure to perform the acts required, in order to entitle the railroad company to the aid ordered or voted it, there is no contract,[2] for until those acts are performed, the agreement is not complete. If, however, there is a complete agreement, the failure to do what is required will not, as we believe, destroy or annul the contract, but may be cause for defeating a claim to the aid, or for adjudging the contract to be ineffective. Where the constitution declares that its provisions shall not apply to prior proceedings, they are not, it is obvious, affected by such provisions.[3] Where bonds are issued and sold, there can be no question as to the existence of a contract within the protection of the federal constitution, although there may be a question as to the validity of such bonds, as, for instance, where the conditions essential to the existence of power to issue them were not complied with by the municipal officers.

§ 833. **Impairment of contract rights—Illustrative cases.**—Where rights become contract obligations they will not be affected by constitutional amendments adopted after the date of their acquisition.[4] But it has been held that where a rail-

[1] Aspinwall v. Commissioners, etc., 22 How. (U. S.) 364; List v. Wheeling, 7 W. Va. 501; Cumberland, etc., R. Co. v. Barren County, etc., 10 Bush. (Ky.) 604; Land Grant, etc., Co. v. Davis County, 6 Kan. 256.

[2] Jeffries v. Lawrence, 42 Iowa 498; Falconer v. Buffalo R. Co., 69 N. Y. 491.

[3] Fairfield v. County of Gallatin, 100 U. S. 47; Louisville v. Portsmouth, etc., Bank, 104 U. S. 589; Lippincott v. Pana, 92 Ill. 24; Town of Middleport v. Ætna, etc., Co., 82 Ill. 562; County of Clay v. Society, etc., 104 U. S. 579; People v. Hamill, 134 Ill. 666, s. c. 22 Am. & Eng. Corp. Cas. 39; County of Moultrie v. Fairfield, 105 U. S. 370, s. c. 7 Am. & Eng. R. Cas. 194.

[4] Kansas City, etc., R. Co. v. Justices of Nodaway County, 47 Mo. 349; Slack v. Maysville, etc., R. Co., 13 B. Mon. 1; County of Henry v. Nicolay, 95 U. S. 619.

road company, after the adoption of a new constitution, accepts an amendment to its charter, authorizing its extension through other counties not included in the route designated in the original charter, all subscriptions by counties along such extension will be controlled by the provisions of the new constitution. A repeal of the act authorizing the issue of municipal bonds in aid of a railroad will not affect the liability of the municipality upon bonds issued under authority of such act before its repeal, and the municipality may be compelled by mandamus to raise a tax with which to pay them.[2]

§ 834. **Construction of statutes—Implied powers.**—Statutes conferring power upon municipalities to aid railroad companies usually prescribe the nature of the aid that may be given and provide what means shall be adopted for paying the donations or subscriptions, but in many cases no provision is made as to the mode for paying the subscriptions or the bonds, so that resort must be had to other statutes or to the general rules of law. A statute is not to be considered as an isolated or detached fragment of law, but as a part of one uniform system of laws,[3] hence a statute providing for giving aid to a railroad company, not fully effective in itself, may be made entirely effective by the help of other statutes or the general rules of the unwritten law. It may happen, it is true, that a statute may be so vague and indefinite as to be incapable of enforcement, but this can very seldom occur. A rule which often aids in giving effect to statutes is this: the grant of a principal power carries with it such incidental powers as are necessary to effectuate it. By force of this rule statutes empowering a municipal corporation to grant aid to a railroad, give power to levy a tax to raise the money necessary to pay the donation or subscription, or, if bonds are lawfully issued, to

---

[1] State v. Saline County Court, 51 Mo. 350.

[2] St. Joseph, etc., R. Co. v. Buchanan County Ct., 39 Mo. 485; People v. County of Tazewell, 22 Ill. 147; Sibley v. City of Mobile, 3 Woods 535, s. c. 4 Am. L. Times (N. S.) 226; Von Hoffman v. Quincy, 4 Wall. (U. S.) 535.

[3] Humphries v. Davis, 100 Ind. 274; Bishop's Written Laws, §§ 86, 113a, 242b.

pay the bonds.[1] Where a tax is provided for, and no specific provision is made for collecting it, the implication is that it is to be collected as taxes are ordinarily collected, with the usual interest and penalties for delinquencies.[2] The rule that a statute forms part of a uniform system authorizes the conclusion we have stated. It may be noted, also, that the rule is that statutes will not be suffered to fail if, by considering them in connection with other statutes or with principles of the common law, they can be given effect. Reference may be had to other statutes to determine whether delinquents can be charged with a penalty.[3]

§ 835. **Construction of statutes conferring authority to aid railroad companies—Illustrative instances.**—Authority conferred upon a county to aid a company which constructs a road through the county does not empower the county to vote aid to a company that locates and builds its road entirely outside of the county.[4] Where authority is conferred to grant aid to a designated road and to a certain other road, aid may be given to either.[5] Power conferred by the charter of a municipal corporation to "borrow money and issue bonds therefor" does not confer authority to aid railroad companies.[6] While the later cases must be regarded as settling the law and as adjudging that authority to aid a railroad company by subscriptions does not carry with it power to execute negotiable instruments, still the language of the statute may be such as to carry

---

[1] Nelson v. Haywood Co., 87 Tenn. 781; Nichol v. Mayor, etc., 9 Humph. (Tenn.) 251; Ralls County v. United States, 105 U. S. 735, 736.

[2] Bothwell v. Millikan, 104 Ind. 162.

[3] Although the statute specifically limits the tax that may be assessed to a designated per centum, a penalty may be charged against delinquent tax-payers. Chicago, etc., Co. v. Hartshorn, 30 Fed. R. 541; Tobin v. Hartshorn, 69 Iowa 648, s. c. 29 N. W. R. 764. See Snell v. Campbell, 24 Fed. R. 880. In the case last cited it was held that the state might remit the penalties, but this was denied in Tobin v. Hartshorn, *supra*, and in Chicago, etc., Co. v. Hartshorn, *supra*, the court followed Tobin v. Hartshorn.

[4] State v. Hancock County, 11 Ohio St. 183.

[5] First National Bank v. Concord, 50 Vt. 257.

[6] City of Jonesboro City v. Cairo, etc., R. Co., 110 U. S. 192, s. c. 4 Sup. Ct. R. 67; Lewis v. Shreveport, 108 U. S. 282, s. c. 2 Sup. Ct. R. 634.

such authority.[1] A statute conferring authority to subscribe for stock and issue bonds does not empower the municipality to make a donation of property.[2] A sale of stock back to the company and a nominal consideration paid in bonds does not, it has been held, render the bonds invalid in the hands of a *bona fide* holder, although the statute requires stock to be subscribed and does not provide for a donation,[3] but on this point there is a conflict of authority.[4] Where cities are authorized to aid railroad companies they may exercise the power, although they form part of townships to which a like power is given.[5] It was held under a statute authorizing "any village, city, county or township" to aid a railroad company that aid might be given by an incorporated town, as towns were included in the term any village,[6] but upon this point there is some conflict of authority.[7] So, upon a somewhat similar line of reasoning to that pursued by the supreme court of the United States in one of the cases referred to,[8] it was held that a city incorporated by a special charter might grant aid, although one of the state statutes provided that "no general laws as to the powers of cities shall be construed to extend to cities organized under a special charter."[9]

---

[1] Ashley v. Board, 60 Fed. R. 55; Commonwealth v. Milliamston, 156 Mass. 70, s. c. 30 N. E. R. 472; City of Evansville v. Woodbury, 60 Fed. R. 718. See, generally, Nolan County v. State, 83 Texas 182, s. c. 17 S. W. R. 823; City of Brenham v. German Am. Bank, 144 U. S. 173, s. c. 12 Sup. Ct. R. 555; Coffin v. Board, 57 Fed. R. 137; Dodge v. Memphis, 51 Fed. R. 165.

[2] Choisser v. People, 140 Ill. 21, s. c. 29 N. E. R. 546. See Sampson v. People, 140 Ill. 466, s. c. 30 N. E. R. 689; Post v. Pulaski County, 49 Fed. R. 628.

[3] City of Cairo v. Zane, 149 U. S. 122, s. c. 13 Sup. Ct. R. 803; Enfield v. Jordan, 119 U. S. 680.

[4] Board v. State, 115 Ind. 67; Choisser v. People, 140 Ill. 21, s. c. 29 N. E. R. 546; Post v. Pulaski County, 49 Fed. 628. See Olcott v. Supervisors, 16 Wall. 678; Town of Queensbury v. Culver, 19 Wall. 83.

[5] Bard v. Augusta, 30 Fed. R. 906; City of Iola v. Merriman, 46 Kan. 49. But we suppose that if the language of the statute conferred power upon the townships only it could not be exercised by cities.

[6] Enfield v. Jordan, 119 U. S. 680; Martin v. People, 87 Ill. 524.

[7] Welch v. Post, 99 Ill. 471. See Sampson v. People, 141 Ill. 17, s. c. 30 N. E. R. 781.

[8] Town of Enfield v. Jordan, 119 U. S. 680.

[9] Bartemeyer v. Rohlfs, 71 Iowa 582, 32 N. W. R. 673.

§ 836. Construction of enabling acts—Adjudged cases.—
Questions of construction present themselves in different forms and it is very difficult to state rules. Not only is it true that it is difficult to state rules, but it is also true that a better practical conception of the prevailing doctrines can be obtained by a reference to the adjudged cases, and for that reason we refer to cases in addition to those to which we have already directed attention. The statute which confers the power must be reasonably construed to carry into effect the purposes of its enactment,[1] and such of its provisions as are merely directory need not always be strictly complied with.[2] The authority by

[1] Curtis v. Butler County, 24 How. (U. S.) 435; Woods v. Lawrence County, 1 Black (U. S.) 386. The term "village," in the Illinois act amending the charter of the Illinois Southeastern Railway Company, authorizing "any village, city, county or township" along the route of the road to subscribe or make donations to the stock of the company, and to issue bonds therefor, includes "towns," and the bonds of an incorporated town issued thereunder are valid. Town of Enfield v. Jordan, 119 U. S. 680, 7 Sup. Ct. R. 358. The notice provided that "one-half of the tax should be levied and collected in the year 1887, and the other half in the year 1888." As the board of supervisors had no power to levy taxes and collect them the same year, but taxes levied in one year were not collectible until the next, the clause of the notice was held to mean that the levy should be made within such time as that the tax would be collectible in the year 1887, and a levy made in 1886 was proper. Bartemeyer v. Rohlfs, 71 Iowa 582, 32 N. W. 673.

[2] As to what provisions are merely directory and what are mandatory, see the following cases: Wood v. Lawrence Co., 1 Black 386; McPherson v. Foster, 43 Iowa 48; Wilmington, etc., R. Co. v. Commissioners, 116 N. Car. 563, s. c. 21 S. E. R. 205; Redd v. Commissioners, 31 Gratt. (Va.) 695; Board v. Texas, etc., R. Co., 46 Tex. 316; City of Vicksburg v. Lombard, 51 Miss. 111; State v. Saline Co. Ct., 48 Mo. 390; City of Mt. Vernon v. Hovey, 52 Ind. 568; Town of Eagle v. Kohn, 84 Ill. 292; Society for Saving v. New London, 29 Conn. 174; Deming v. Houlton, 64 Me. 254; Hardenbergh v. Van Keuren, 16 Hun (N. Y.) 17; Draper v. Springport, 104 U. S. 501; Stanton v. Alabama, etc., R. Co., 2 Woods (U. S.) 523; Town of Roberts v. Bolles, 101 U. S. 119; County of Cass v. Gillett, 100 U. S. 585; Supervisors v. Galbraith, 99 U. S. 214; Town of Coloma v. Eaves, 92 U. S. 484. But it must be borne in mind that the interpretation of the statute is very much more liberal when the validity of bonds actually issued is in question than when the question arises between the original parties before the aid has been given. A statute provided that the clerk of the election should certify the result of the election, together with the time, terms, and conditions upon which the tax, when collected, should be paid to the railroad

CORP. 74

which a municipality is enabled to subscribe aid to a railroad may be contained in the charter of the railroad company, and such a grant will generally carry with it by necessary implication the power to levy taxes to meet the subscription.[1] If the power to subscribe be granted to all the towns and villages along the line of the road, which is undetermined, a town will have no authority to subscribe until the road is finally and definitely located with reference to it.[2] Such a subscription can be voted only to a corporation authorized to receive it, and it can be made only to the corporation designated in the vote.[3] A

---

company, and also provided that the order of the board of supervisors making the levy should indicate upon what conditions the tax should be paid over to the railroad company. The clerk made out his certificate, as required, and the supervisors, in making the levy, had this certificate before them, but failed to direct in their order upon what terms the railroad should be entitled to the tax. The court held that this was a mere omission, not of the essence of the thing done, and that it did not affect the validity of the levy, especially as the certificate of the clerk had made all the stipulations and conditions of record. Meriwether v. Muhlenburg County Court, 120 U. S. 354, 7 Sup. Ct. R. 563.

[1] Peoria, etc., R. Co. v. People, 116 Ill. 401. See, also, Loan Assn. v. Topeka, 20 Wall. (U. S.) 655; Nelson v. Haywood Co., 87 Tenn. 781. But we think that the rule that the authority of the municipality to subscribe may be given in the charter of the company can not apply under constitutions forbidding special or local laws, and requiring legislative acts to embrace only one subject.

[2] Purdy v. Town of Lansing, 128 U. S. 557.

[3] County of Bates v. Winters, 97 U. S. 83; Marsh v. Fulton County, 10 Wall. (U. S.) 676; Bell v. Mobile, etc., R. Co., 4 Wall. (U. S.) 598; Town of Big Grove v. Wells, 65 Ill. 263; Board, etc., Fulton County v. Mississippi, etc., R. Co., 21 Ill. 338. But compare Denison v. City of Columbus, 62 Fed. R. 775. A proposition submitted to the voters of a county, in which it is proposed to vote the bonds of such county to a railroad company, must specifically designate the donee. A proposition in the alternative, to issue to a certain corporation named or to another designated corporation, is not sufficient to authorize the bonds, although adopted by the legal voters. State v. Roggen, 22 Neb. 118, 34 N. W. R. 108. An order submitting to the voters of a county a proposition to subscribe stock in aid of a railroad under the general railroad law of Missouri, need not specify the name of the corporation, where the proposition describes the proposed route of the road with the requisite certainty. Ninth Nat. Bank v. Knox County, 37 Fed. R. 75. See, also, MacKenzie v. Wooley, 39 La. Ann. 944; Kentucky Union Ry. Co. v. Bourbon County, 85 Ky. 98; Young v. Webster City, etc., R. Co., 75 Iowa 140; State v. Harris, 96 Mo. 29; Onstott v. People, 123 Ill. 489.

grant to a railroad of power to *receive* aid from certain classes of municipalities will not necessarily authorize such municipalities to grant the aid. Such a grant has been construed to be made with reference to an existing general statute by which only a portion of the municipalities were empowered to make subscriptions of this character, and it was held that the charter did not extend the powers contained in the general act to other municipalities not embraced by its terms.[1] But the general rule is that a special act will be construed to be independent of a prior general act and in addition thereto, if it makes no reference to the general act. And the powers conferred by the different acts may be separately exercised.[2] So, where a charter authorized the railroad to receive subscriptions from a county upon certain terms, it was held that the validity of bonds issued in accordance therewith was not affected by a prior special act of the legislature requiring the question of issuing such bonds to be submitted to a vote of the tax-payers.[3] Where a special act refers to a prior general act as fixing the limits of the authority conferred by it and defining the mode of its exercise, the court will construe the special act as conferring the powers enumerated in the general act.[4] A general act forbidding municipal subscriptions in aid of railroads has been construed to repeal special acts authorizing them.[5] But it has been held that the facts which would authorize a writ of mandamus to compel a subscription do not necessarily establish a binding contract. And the repeal of a statute under

---

[1] Pitzman v. Freeburg, 92 Ill. 111. See, also, Campbell v. Paris, etc., R. Co., 71 Ill. 611; Township of East Oakland v. Skinner, 94 U. S. 255.

[2] See Stevens v. Anson, 73 Me. 489, where two several subscriptions were made under a general and a special act, and both were held valid. The Kansas act for the organization of cities of the third class, providing that such cities shall remain a part of the corporate limits of the townships in which they are situated, for various purposes, including that of subscribing stock in aid of constructing railroads, is held not to exclude such cities from the power to issue railroad aid bonds. Bard v. City of Augusta, 30 Fed. R. 906.

[3] Burr v. Chariton County, 2 McCrary (U. S.) 603. But the bonds in this case were in the hands of innocent purchasers. See Butz v. Muscatine, 8 Wall. (U. S.) 575; Quincy v. Jackson, 113 U. S. 332.

[4] Henderson v. Jackson County, 2 McCrary (U. S.) 615.

[5] Jeffries v. Lawrence, 42 Iowa 498.

which a subscription was made, and to enforce the provisions of which the proceedings in mandamus were pending, was held to defeat the proceedings.[1]

§ 837. **Means and methods.**—Where there are no limiting constitutional provisions the legislature has a choice of means and methods, and may provide how and upon what terms and conditions donations or subscriptions in aid of railroads may be made. The subject is legislative, and, in the absence of constitutional limitations, the general rule is that it is for the legislature to determine the means and methods that shall be employed.[2] Municipal corporations are creatures of legislation and subject to legislative control, so that it is within the power of the legislature, except where limitations are imposed by the constitution, to control the action of such corporations.[3] The general doctrines to which we have referred give to the legislature very extensive dominion over the subject of aiding railroads, for the subject lies within the legislative domain, and the legislative decision upon questions of policy and expediency is conclusive. It is only where some constitutional provision is violated that the courts can interfere.

§ 838. **Requirements of statute—Classes of cases.**—It seems to us that there are two general classes of cases, namely, those in which tax-payers bring suit before the acquisition of rights by third persons, and those in which the rights of third persons are acquired before suit is brought. There is an essential difference between the two classes, and there should be, as we believe, different rules for each class. If interested persons

---

[1] Covington, etc., R. Co. v. Kenton County Court, 12 B. Mon. (Ky.) 144, 152. See State v. Garroutte, 67 Mo. 445; People v. Pueblo County, 2 Col. 360.

[2] Legal Tender Cases, 110 U. S. 421; State v. Haworth, 122 Ind. 462; Hancock v. Yaden, 121 Ind. 366; State v. Kolsem, 130 Ind. 434, 442; Cooley's Const. Lim. (6th ed.), 102, 106.

[3] Laramie County v. Albany County, 92 U. S. 307, 308; People v. Morris, 13 Wend. 325; Meriwether v. Garrett, 102 U. S. 472, 511; Cheaney v. Hooser, 9 B. Monr. 330; Mobile v. Watson, 116 U. S. 289; State v. Jennings, 27 Ark. 419; City of Clinton v. Cedar Rapids, etc., Railroad Co., 24 Iowa 455; Demarest v. New York, 74 N. Y. 161; David v. Portland, etc., Co., 14 Ore. 98.

have an opportunity to test the proceedings of municipal officers and negligently fail to make use of it until third persons acquire rights, they should not be allowed to avail themselves of irregularities or errors to defeat the proceedings unless the errors go to the question of power or jurisdiction. The distinction between the two classes of cases is lost sight of or disregarded by some of the courts for they apply quite as strict rules in cases where the rights of third persons have intervened as in cases where suit is brought before the acquisition of rights by third persons. It is true that the power is purely statutory, and that where a power is statutory the provisions of the statute conferring it must be strictly pursued, but statutory provisions may be waived either by words or conduct, and persons who stand by until third persons acquire rights should be held to have waived a compliance with the requirements of the statute except where the failure to comply affects the question of power or jurisdiction.

§ 839. **Power to aid by subscription does not authorize the execution of bonds.**—Power conferred upon a municipal corporation to aid a railroad company, by subscribing for stock, does not empower the municipality to issue bonds. The power to issue municipal bonds, whether aid bonds or any other class of bonds, is not, as a rule, to be implied from the mere grant of authority to aid railroad companies by donations or subscriptions.[1] The later decisions very much, and, as we believe, very wisely, restrict the earlier decisions.[2] It seems to us that as

[1] Kelley v. Milan, 127 U. S. 139, s. c. 22 Am. & Eng. Corp. Cas. 1; Daviess County v. Dickinson, 117 U. S. 657; Marsh v. Fulton County, 10 Wall. 676; Wells v. Supervisors, 102 U. S. 625, s. c. 2 Am. & Eng. R. Cas. 605; Ottawa v. Carey, 108 U. S. 110; Mayor, etc., of Pulaski v. Gilmore, 21 Fed. R. 870; Tax-payers v. Tennessee, etc., Railroad Co., 11 Lea (Tenn.) 330; Norton v. Town of Dyersburg, 127 U. S. 160, s. c. 8 Sup. Ct. R. 1111; Hill v. City of Memphis, 134 U. S. 198, s. c. 10 Sup. Ct. R. 562; Town of Scipio v. Wright 101 U. S. 655; Barnum v. Town of Okolona, 148 U. S. 393, s. c. 13 Sup. Ct. R. 638; Sheboygan Co. v. Parker, 3 Wall. 93; Claiborne Co. v. Brooks, 111 U. S. 400, s. c. 4 Sup. Ct. R. 489; Young v. Township of Clarendon, 132 U. S. 340, s. c. 10 Sup. Ct. R. 107.

[2] City of Brenham v. German Am. Bank, 144 U. S. 173, s. c. 12 Sup. Ct. R. 559; Merrill v. Monticello, 138 U. S. 673; City of Jonesboro City v. Cairo, etc., R. Co., 110 U. S. 192, s. c.

municipal corporations are not business or trading corporations, but instrumentalities of government,[1] it should be held that there is no power to issue negotiable bonds or promissory notes, unless the power is conferred by statute. Persons who deal in municipal bonds ought to be made to understand that municipal corporations have only such powers as are clearly conferred by statute, so that in dealing with municipal corporations, they must ascertain whether power to issue the bonds exist, and where they are fully put upon inquiry and there is no element of estoppel, determine for themselves whether the bonds are valid.

§ 840. Levy of taxes—Withdrawal of power—Time.—Where power is expressly conferred upon a municipal corporation to incur an indebtedness the power to provide for its payment by taxation is implied.[2] The power to tax can not be withdrawn until the debt is satisfied.[3] The failure, neglect or refusal of

---

4 Sup. Ct. 67; Town of Concord v. Robinson, 121 U. S. 165, s. c. 7 Sup. Ct. R. 937; Katzenberger v. City of Aberdeen, 121 U. S. 172, s. c. 7 Sup. Ct. R. 947; Norton v. Town of Dyersberg, 127 U. S. 160, s. c. 8 Sup. Ct. R. 1111. In Barnum v. Town of Okolona, 148 U. S. 393, s. c. 13 Sup. Ct. R. 638, it was said, in speaking of authority to aid railroad companies: "* * * * that such legislative permission does not carry with it authority to execute negotiable securities except subject to the conditions and restrictions of the enabling act, are propositions so well settled by frequent decisions that we do not pause to consider them." Such cases as Rogers v. Burlington, 3 Wall. 654, and Mitchell v. Burlington, 4 Wall. 270, can not be regarded as authority, for the doctrine they assert has been repeatedly denied.

[1] White v. Board, 129 Ind. 396; Claiborne Co. v. Brooks, 111 U. S. 400; Elliott Roads and Streets, 317.

[2] United States v. Jefferson County, 5 Dill. 310; Riggs v. Johnson, 6 Wall. 166, 194; Loan Association v. Topeka, 20 Wall. 655; United States v. New Orleans, 98 U. S. 381, 393; Ralls County Ct. v. United States, 105 U. S. 733, 735; Parkersburg v. Brown, 106 U. S. 487; United States v. Macon, 99 U. S. 582; Quincy v. Jackson, 113 U. S. 332, s. c. 7 Am. & Eng. Corp. Cas. 368.

[3] Ralls County Ct. v. United States, 105 U.S. 733; Louisiana v. Pilsbury, 105 U. S. 278; Von Hoffman v. Quincy, 4 Wall. 535; Edwards v. Kearzey, 96 U. S. 595; State v. Mayor, 109 U. S. 285; City of Galena v. Amy, 5 Wall. 705; Rees v. Watertown, 19 Wall. 107; Mobile v. Watson, 116 U. S. 289; Cape Girardeau Co. Ct. v. Hill, 118 U. S. 68; People v. Common Council, 140 N. Y. 300, s.c. 37 Am. St. R. 563; McGahey v. Virginia, 135 U. S. 662; Lansing v. County Treasurer, 1 Dill. 522; United States v. Jefferson County, 1 McCreary (C.C.) 356; State v. Milwaukee, 25 Wis. 122; Western Saving Fund Society v.

the municipal officers to levy the tax at the time designated by the statute does not impair the authority to make the levy,[1] nor does one levy exhaust the power.

§ 841. **Donations and subscriptions.**—If the legislature has authority over the general subject, then upon the principle that it has a choice of means and methods and is "master of its own discretion," it may determine whether the aid shall be given by way of donation or by subscription to the capital stock of the company. The legislature may, if no constitutional provision forbids, determine the mode in which the aid shall be granted. If it deems proper the legislature may leave it to the inhabitants of the local governmental subdivision to determine whether they will aid by subscription or donation.[2]

Philadelphia, 31 Pa. St. 175, s. c. 72 Am. Dec. 730; Beckwith v. English, 51 Ill. 147; Commissioners v. Rather, 48 Ala. 433; Edwards v. Williamson, 70 Ala. 145; Vance v. Little Rock, 30 Ark. 435, 440; Trustees v. Bailey, 10 Fla. 112, s. c. 81 Am. Dec. 194; Coffin v. Rich, 45 Me. 507, s. c. 71 Am. Dec. 559; Henderson, etc., R. Co. v. Dickerson, 17 B. Monr. 173, s. c. 66 Am. Dec. 148; Williams v. Johnson, 30 Md. 500, s. c. 96 Am. Dec. 613.

[1] Commissioners v. Rather, 48 Ala. 433; Town of Darlington v. Atlantic Trust Co., 68 Fed. R. 849.

[2] The legislature has the same right to authorize a donation of money or property to a railway company by a municipal corporation that it has to authorize a subscription to the capital stock of such a company. Scott v. Hansheer, 94 Ind. 1; Converse v. Fort Scott, 92 U. S. 503. The court will not presume, in the absence of proof, that a donation was intended, although the consideration is grossly inadequate to a sale of bonds, as where fifty thousand dollars of municipal bonds were sold to the railroad company for one dollar. County Court of Madison County v. People, 58 Ill. 456. See, also, Roberts v. Northern Pac. R. Co., 158 U. S. 1, s. c. 15 Sup. Ct. R. 756, distinguishing Whiting v. Sheboygan, etc., Railroad Co., 25 Wis. 167. Where a county agreed, by popular vote, to subscribe for $100,000 of stock in a railroad company, and to issue bonds therefor, but, before delivery of the bonds, the county authorities agreed to sell and did sell the stock back to the company in exchange for $30,000 in said bonds, which were returned to the county, the court held that the $70,000 of bonds delivered to the company were void, since the transaction, being in effect a gift instead of a subscription, was not authorized by the popular vote. Sampson v. People, 140 Ill. 466, 30 N. E. R. 689; Choisser v. People, 140 Ill. 21, 29 N. E. R. 546; Post v. Pulaski County, 49 Fed. R. 628, 9 U. S. App. 1. But see City of Cairo v. Zane, 149 U. S. 122, s. c. 13 Sup. Ct. R. 893. In the case of the Board, etc., v. Center Township, 105 Ind. 422, it appeared that a donation of money was voted in aid of a railroad in 1870, that the money was collected in 1871 and 1873 and placed

§ 842. Repeal of the enabling act—Withdrawal of authority.—It is obvious that if an enabling act is repealed before a subscription is made the authority of the municipal corporation is taken away. It is equally clear that if rights in the nature of a contract have been acquired prior to the repeal of the act under which they were acquired the repeal does not destroy those rights.[1] The question of difficulty, as suggested in another connection, is as to when the rights of a railroad company can be regarded as so far fixed by contract as to be within the protection of the constitution. If there is a complete right to the aid, then, as we believe, the right can not be rendered nugatory by a refusal to levy the necessary tax or issue the proper bonds.[2] In one of the cases it was held that although there was no binding contract between the town and the railroad company, but the company had done work on the faith of the action of the town authorities, the court would so construe the statute as to preserve the rights of the company and relieve the legislature from the imputation of bad faith.[3] It was also held in the case referred to that after the company

in the county treasury, and that the road was not completed until 1880, and the court held it entitled to the donation.

[1] Nelson v. Haywood County, 87 Tenn. 781; Murfreesboro Railroad v. Commissioners, 108 N. C. 56; Scotland County Ct. v. Hill, 140 U. S. 41; Von Hoffman v. Quincy, 4 Wall. 535; Wolff v. New Orleans, 103 U. S. 358. See, generally, State v. Commissioners, 38 Kan. 317; Barthel v. Meader, 72 Iowa 125; Richeson v. People, 115 Ill. 450; Louisville v. Savings Bank, 104 U. S. 469; Louisiana v. Taylor, 105 U. S. 454; County of Henry v. Nicolay, 95 U. S. 619; State v. Greene County, 54 Mo. 540; City of East St. Louis v. Maxwell, 99 Ill. 439; List v. Wheeling, 7 W. Va. 501; Jeffries v. Lawrence, 42 Iowa 498; United States v. Norton, 97 U. S. 164; County of Ray v. Vansycle, 96 U. S. 675; People v. Logan County, 63 Ill. 374; Kennedy v. Palmer, 6 Gray 316; People v. Clark, 1 Cal. 406; Hays v. Dowes, 75 Mo. 250; Edwards v. Williamsom, 70 Ala. 145; Fairfield v. County of Gallatin, 100 U. S. 47; County of Randolph v. Post, 93 U. S. 502.

[2] Babcock v. Helena, 34 Ark. 499; State v. Lancaster County, 6 Neb. 214. See Callaway County v. Foster, 93 U. S. 567; County of Macon v. Shores, 97 U. S. 272; Huidekoper v. Dallas County, 3 Dill. (U. S.) 171; Louisiana v. Taylor, 105 U. S. 454; County of Schuyler v. Thomas, 98 U. S. 169; County of Henry v. Nicolay, 95 U. S. 619; Nicolay v. St. Clair County, 3 Dill. (U. S.) 163; Moultrie County v. Rockingham, etc., Bank, 92 U. S. 631; Supervisors v. Galbraith, 99 U. S. 214.

[3] Town of Red Rock v. Henry, 106 U. S. 596, s. c. 1 Sup. Ct. R. 434, citing Broughton v. Pensacola, 93 U. S. 266.

had done all that it was required to do, a repeal of the statute under which the town officers acted would not impair the rights of the railroad company.[1] In order to entitle the railroad company to the aid ordered to be given it by a popular vote it must show, it has been held, that the company acted upon the belief that it would receive the aid, and in that belief expended money in the construction of the road prior to the repeal of the statute under which the aid was voted.[2] But it was held by the same court that if the company does act on the faith of the vote and does expend money in the construction of its road the repeal of the statute will not sweep away its rights,[3] and this seems to us to be the sound doctrine, notwithstanding the decisions to which we have elsewhere referred.[4]

§ 843. **Validating proceedings—Retrospective laws.—** Where there is no constitutional provision interdicting it the legislature has power to pass laws curing or healing defects in proceedings had in aid of railroad companies.[5] The plenary

---

[1] Town of Red Rock v. Henry, 106 U. S. 596, s. c. 1 Sup. Ct. R. 434. In the course of the opinion it was said: "The amendatory act of March 2, 1871, with its repealing clause, can have no effect on this controversy. That act was passed more than six months after the railroad had fully complied with all the conditions upon which the town of Red Rock had agreed to issue its bonds. It was too late then for the legislature to interfere. The railroad company was entitled to the bonds, and any attempt by the legislature to forbid their issue would be unconstitutional."

[2] Barthel v. Meader, 72 Iowa 125, s. c. 33 N. W. R. 446.

[3] Burges v. Mabin, 70 Iowa 633; Cantillon v. Dubuque, etc., R. Co., 78 Iowa 48.

[4] Wadsworth v. Supervisors, 102 U. S. 534; Railroad Co. v. Falconer, 103 U. S. 821.

[5] Rogers v. City of Keokuk, 154 U. S. 546, s. c. 14 Sup. Ct. R. 1152; Bolles v. Brimfield, 120 U. S. 759; City of Jonesboro City v. Cairo, etc., R. Co., 110 U. S. 192; Quincy v. Cooke, 107 U. S. 549; Township of Elmwood v. Marcy, 92 U. S. 289; Supervisors v. Schenck, 5 Wall. 772; Anderson v. Santa Anna, 116 U. S. 356; Pompton v. Cooper Union, 101 U.S. 196; Grenada County Supervisors v. Brogden, 112 U. S. 261, s. c. 5 Sup. Ct. R. 125; Katzenberger v. Aberdeen, 121 U. S. 178, s. c. 7 Sup. Ct. R. 947; Dennison v. Mayor, etc., 62 Fed. R. 775; Board v. Bright, 18 Ind. 93; Brown v. Mayor, 63 N. Y. 239; Knapp v. Grant, 27 Wis. 147; Cairo, etc., R. Co. v. Sparta, 77 Ill. 505; Steines v. Franklin County, 48 Mo. 167; Otoe County v. Baldwin, 111 U. S. 1.

nature of the legislative power, the fact that the subject of aiding railroads is essentially legislative, and the fact that the power of the legislature over municipal corporations is so broad and comprehensive, require the conclusion we have stated. If vested rights have intervened or if constitutional limitations forbid, then, of course, defects can not be remedied by retroactive statutes.[1] In illustration of the principle stated we may refer to the cases which hold that the legislature has power to pass retrospective statutes confirming the validity of railroad bonds that have been illegally issued.[2] A validation by competent legislative power is in effect equivalent to precedent legislative authority.[3] The question is always one of power, and if the legislature had no power to authorize the proceedings or the issue of bonds in the first instance, it can not validate them by a curative act.[4] There is, however, some apparent, if

[1] Where the subject is one upon which the legislature is prohibited from enacting special laws a special curative statute will be invalid, but a general statute may be effective. Atchison, etc., R. Co. v. Commissioners, 17 Kan. 29. See, generally, upon the subject of curative statutes, State v. Saline County Court, 48 Mo. 390, s. c. 8 Am. R. 108; Kunkle v. Town of Franklin, 13 Minn. 127, s. c. 97 Am. Dec. 226; Wilson v. Hardesty, 1 Md. Ch. 66; New Orleans v. Poutz, 14 La. Ann. 853; Williams v. Roberts, 88 Ill. 11.

[2] City of Kenosha v. Lamson, 9 Wall. (U. S.) 477; Bissell v. Jeffersonville, 24 How. (U. S.) 287; Kimball v. Rosendale, 42 Wis. 407; Town of Duanesburgh v. Jenkins, 57 N. Y. 177; People v. Mitchell, 35 N. Y. 551; Black v. Cohen, 52 Ga. 621; Knapp v. Grant, 27 Wis. 147; Steines v. Franklin Co., 48 Mo. 167. This doctrine is announced in many cases where the bonds passed into the hands of bona fide holders, and the ratifying act protects their interests. The legislature had a right to assume, from the fact that the townships had voted aid to the railroads, that a public purpose existed, warranting the exercise of the taxing power. State v. Whitesides, 30 S. Car. 579, s. c. 9 S. E. R. 661; State v. Harper, 30 S. Car. 586, s. c. 9 S. E. R. 664; State v. Neely, 30 So. Car. 587, s. c. 9 S. E. R. 664. See Hayes v. Holly Spring, 114 U. S. 120; Otoe County v. Baldwin, 111 U. S. 1; Gardner v. Haney, 86 Ind. 17; Dows v. Town of Elmwood, 34 Fed. R. 114; Thompson v. Perrine, 103 U. S. 806; Bolles v. Brimfield, 120 U. S. 750; Kimball v. Rosendale, 42 Wis. 407, s. c. 24 Am. R. 421; Bissell v. Jeffersonville, 24 How. 287; City of Kenosha v. Lamson, 9 Wall. 477; Black v. Cohen, 52 Ga. 621; Town of Duanesburgh v. Jenkins, 57 N.Y. 177.

[3] County of Jasper v. Ballou, 103 U. S. 745; Shaw v. Norfolk, etc., R. Co., 5 Gray 180; Wilson v. Hardesty, 1 Md. Ch. 66.

[4] Single v. Supervisors, 38 Wis. 364; Hardenbergh v. Van Keuren, 4 Abb. (N. Y. N. Cas.) 43; Katzenberger

§ 843   PUBLIC AID.   1173

not actual, conflict of authority upon this question, for the existence of such a power is denied by some of the cases.[1] An emphatic assertion of the general rule is found in the cases which hold that the legislature may confirm and make valid bonds issued by the municipality, although no authority whatever existed in the municipality at the time the bonds were issued,[2] unless prohibited by the state constitution.[3] Upon the

v. Aberdeen, 121 U. S. 172; Sykes v. Columbus, 55 Miss. 115; Katzenberger v. Aberdeen, 16 Fed. R. 745; People v. Batchellor, 53 N. Y. 128; Horton v. Thompson, 71 N. Y. 513; Marshall v. Silliman, 61 Ill. 218; Township of Elmwood v. Marcy, 92 U. S. 289. If there is an entire absence of power to authorize the proceedings in aid of railroad companies, then no validating or curative act can be effective, but some of the cases referred to in the note seem to go further and deny the power to validate where there was original power to authorize the proceedings. So far as the cases can be regarded as holding the doctrine stated we believe them to be wrongly decided. The decision in Horton v. Thompson, 71 N. Y. 513, was denied by the supreme court of the United States in Thompson v. Perrine, 103 U. S. 806.

[1] Horton v. Town of Thompson, 71 N. Y. 513; People v. Batchellor, 53 N. Y. 128. In Thompson v. Perrine, 103 U. S. 806, the court refused to follow Horton v. Town of Thompson, supra, and referred to Bank of Rome v. Village of Rome, 18 N. Y. 38; People v. Mitchell, 35 N. Y. 551, and Williams v. Town of Duanesburgh, 66 N. Y. 129, as declaring a different doctrine. See County of Richland v. People, 3 Brad. (Ill.) 210; Marshall v. Silliman, 61 Ill. 218; Williams v. Roberts, 88 Ill. 11; Gaddis v. Richland County, 92 Ill. 119; Choisser v. People, 140 Ill. 21, 29 N. E. R. 546; Post

v. Pulaski County, 49 Fed. R. 628, 9 U. S. App. 1. The power may exist and yet not be effectively exercised. Thus, for example, a special act may be void if enacted in cases where only general laws are valid. But it does not follow that because special laws are not effective there is no power to enact general curative statutes.

[2] Supervisors of Cumberland Co. v. Randolph, 89 Va. 614; Thompson v. Perrine, 103 U. S. 806; First National Bank v. County of Yankton, 101 U. S. 129. See Napa Valley R. Co. v. Napa County, 30 Cal. 435; State v. Charleston, 10 Rich. L. (S. Car.) 491; Shelby County Ct. v. Cumberland, etc., R. Co., 8 Bush (Ky.) 209; City of Bridgeport v. Housatonic R. Co., 15 Conn. 475; Bouknight v. Davis, 33 S. Car. 410. The South Carolina act, declaring all township bonds theretofore issued in aid of a railroad to be a debt of the township, authorizing the levy of a tax to pay it, and providing that the bonds might be used as evidence of the amount and character of such debt, was held to impress such debt on the township, *proprio vigore*, and it was bound therefor, although the act authorizing the issue of the bonds was unconstitutional and the bonds void. Granniss v. Cherokee Township of York County, 47 Fed. R. 427.

[3] See Gaddis v. Richland County, 92 Ill. 119; People v. Batchellor, 53 N. Y. 128; Horton v. Thompson, 71 N.

same general principle it is held that congress may ratify and render valid an unauthorized subscription in aid of a railroad made by a municipal corporation in one of the territories.[1] But if the legislature could not, at the time the bonds were issued, give authority to issue them in the way they were issued, it can not afterward confirm and make valid the bonds so issued.[2] It has been held that an act purporting only to cure irregularities will not validate bonds which were issued without legal authority.[3] It may be remarked, in passing, that where the local officers have no authority whatever to grant aid, their proceedings are not simply irregular, but are acts performed where no jurisdiction exists, so that a statute assuming to do no more than cure irregularities can not be extended to a case where there was an entire absence of authority. If, however, the terms of the statute clearly embrace unauthorized acts, then it will, as a rule, validate them.[4] Where a constitutional provision forbidding the grant of aid has taken effect before the ratifying act is passed, the legislature can not validate a prior subscription made without authority.[5]

§ 844. Legislative power to authorize ratification.—Where the legislature has power in the first instance to impose or dispense with conditions at its discretion, it may authorize a ratification, although conditions prescribed by the enabling act were not complied with in granting the aid. It has been held, in New York, that conditions imposed by the enabling act

Y. 513. Such an act will be construed to affect only aid voted before its passage, and will not be held to validate acts subsequently done. Town of Concord v. Robinson, 121 U. S. 165, s. c. 7 Sup. Ct. R. 937; Post v. County of Pulaski, 47 Fed. R. 282.

[1] First National Bank v. Yankton County, 101 U. S. 129.

[2] Township of Elmwood v. Marcy, 92 U. S. 289. Such, for example, as a subscription made without a preliminary vote, where the constitution permits the legislature to confer the power of subscribing only after the proposition has been accepted by a popular vote.

[3] Williamson v. Keokuk, 44 Iowa 88.

[4] It is to be understood, of course, that no curative statute can be valid if the provisions of the constitution are infringed, but a curative act, although retrospective, is not from that fact alone to be always regarded as void.

[5] Sykes v. Columbus, 55 Miss. 115; People v. Jackson County, 92 Ill. 441.

§ 844   PUBLIC AID.   1175

may be waived and acts done in disregard of its requirements may be ratified by the legislature, even during litigation.[1] There is a difference, as appears from what has been elsewhere said, between cases where there has been some irregularity and cases where there is an entire absence of power. There is however some diversity of opinion, for it has been held, erroneously, as we are inclined to think, that irregularities may prevent legislative ratification.[2]

---

[1] Town of Duanesburgh v. Jenkins, 57 N. Y. 177. The Wisconsin act providing that all proceedings on the part of a certain county, heretofore had, in subscribing and paying for any stock of a designated railway company, "are hereby legalized and declared to be of the same legal force and effect as though the law governing the mode and procedure" in such cases "had been in all respects complied with," was held to cure any defects in such proceedings, although it was enacted after the commencement of a suit based on alleged defects in the proceedings. Hall v. Baker, 74 Wis. 118, s. c. 42 N. W. R. 104.

[2] Where an act was passed by the legislature legalizing a special election to vote aid to a railroad, and certain acts of the board of county commissioners in levying the tax so voted, such note and subsequent acts having been so irregularly performed that a suit was even then pending to set the whole proceedings aside, the supreme court of Indiana held the act to be unconstitutional. The court said: "It seems very clear, we think, that in the enactment and approval of the statute now under consideration, the legislative and executive departments of our state government have exercised, or attempted to exercise, judicial functions. * * * The powers of the general assembly are almost unlimited; but they can not, as a rule, try and determine the rights of parties to a pending law suit." Columbus, etc., R. Co. v. Board of Commissioners, 65 Ind. 427. See, also, Allison v. Louisville, etc., R. Co., 9 Bush (Ky.) 247. As we have elsewhere shown, it is well settled that municipalities have no inherent or implied right to subscribe stock or issue bonds in aid of a railroad company, although the purpose may be to enable such company to construct its road by or through such municipality, and that where the claim of authority rests upon mere inference it will not be sustained. Town of South Ottawa v. Perkins, 94 U. S. 260; Ogden v. County of Daviess, 102 U. S. 634; Cagwin v. Town of Hancock, 84 N. Y. 532; Welch v. Post, 99 Ill. 471; Goddard v. Stockman, 74 Ind. 400; Pennsylvania R. Co. v. Philadelphia, 47 Pa. St. 189; Lamoille Valley R. Co. v. Fairfield, 51 Vt. 257; Board, etc., of Delaware County v. McClintock, 51 Ind. 325; Jeffries v. Lawrence, 42 Iowa 498; French v. Teschemaker, 24 Cal. 518; Brodie v. McCabe, 33 Ark. 690; Young v. Clarendon Township, 132 U. S. 340; Campbell v. Paris, etc., R. Co., 71 Ill. 611; Township of East Oakland v. Skinner, 94 U. S. 255; Macon, etc., R. Co. v. Gibson, 85 Ga. 1, s. c. 43 Am. & Eng. R. Cas. 318. But it does not follow from this settled principle that ratification of proceedings granting aid may not be authorized by subsequent

§ 845. Curative statutes—Requisites of.—The constitutional power of the legislature to validate proceedings granting aid to railroad companies must be exercised by a valid statute. In jurisdictions where special laws are prohibited and general laws required, a special curative statute would not be effective.[1] The intention of the legislature to validate prior proceedings must be expressed with reasonable clearness and precision. The intention to validate the proceedings must not be left to conjecture in cases where the aid was granted in the first instance without complying with conditions which the constitution made it the duty of the legislature to impose.[2] It seems, indeed, a little difficult to sustain the conclusion that proceedings not taken in conformity to the provisions of the constitution can be cured since it would seem that where there is a failure to comply with constitutional requirements there is an absence of power, and where power is absent the proceedings are void.[3] The legislature has no power to validate a debt incurred in violation of a constitutional provision, and hence can not validate bonds issued in excess of the amount designated by the constitution.[4]

statutes. Whether ratification may be authorized does not depend upon the principle that express statutory authority is essential to the existence of authority to grant aid, but upon entirely different principles.

[1] State v. Riordan, 24 Wis. 484; State v. Supervisors, 25 Wis. 339; Zeigler v. Gaddis, 44 N. J. L. 363; Hodges v. Baltimore, etc., Co., 58 Md. 603; Davis v. Woolnough, 9 Iowa 104; Brown v. Denver, 7 Col. 305. The legislature may enact special laws where there is no constitutional provision prohibiting it.

[2] Hayes v. Holly Springs, 114 U. S. 120; Beloit v. Morgan, 7 Wall. 619; Brown v. New York, 63 N. Y. 239; Grenada County v. Brogden, 112 U. S. 261; Erskine v. Nelson County, 4 N. Dak. 66, s. c. 27 L. R. A. 696.

[3] St. Joseph Township v. Rogers, 16 Wall. 644; Buchanan v. Litchfield, 102 U. S. 278; Dixon County v. Field, 111 U. S. 83; Doon Township v. Cummins, 142 U. S. 366. See Beard v. City of Hopkinsville, 95 Ky. 215, s. c. 44 Am. St. R. 222; Sutro v. Pettit, 74 Cal. 332, s. c. 5 Am. St. R. 442; First National Bank v. District Township, 86 Iowa 330, s. c. 41 Am. St. R. 489; Citizens' Bank v. City of Terrell, 78 Texas 450; McPherson v. Foster, 43 Iowa 48, s. c. 22 Am. R. 215; State v. Mayor, etc., 32 Neb. 568; Dunn v. Great Falls, 13 Mont. 58.

[4] Mosher v. Independent, etc., District, 44 Iowa 122; State v. Stoll, 17 Wall. 425; Erskine v. Nelson County, 4 S. Dak. 66, s. c. 27 L. R. A. 696. See McBryde v. Montesano, 7 Wash. 69; Massachusetts, etc., Co. v. Cane Creek Tp., 45 Fed. Rep. 336.

§ 846. **Division of municipal corporations for purpose of voting.**—The principle laid down in the cases which hold that the general power of the legislature over the subject of taxation authorizes it to create taxing districts, supports the conclusion that the legislature may divide townships or other municipal corporations into districts for the purpose of voting aid to railroad companies unless there is some provision in the constitution forbidding such a division. The whole subject of aid to railroad companies is so essentially a legislative one that it is not easy to set bounds to the legislative power, except, of course, in those jurisdictions where the power is limited and defined by the constitution. The adjudged cases show that the legislative power is one of wide sweep. The general rule is that the legislature is not confined to fixed limits of municipal bodies in laying taxation for local purposes, but may authorize their imposition upon such particular districts as are to be benefited thereby.[1] It has been held that a portion only of a county may be authorized to subscribe aid, where its interests are more immediately dependent upon the success of the enterprise than are those of other portions.[2] So, it has been held, that contiguous territory may be added to a city for the purpose of subscribing.[3]

[1] City of Lexington v. McQuillan's Heirs, 9 Dana (Ky.) 513; People v. Mayor, etc., of Brooklyn, 4 N. Y. 419.

[2] County Judge of Shelby County v. Shelby R. Co., 5 Bush (Ky.) 225, 229. See Deland v. Platte County, 54 Fed. Rep. 823; Ogden v. County of Daviess, 102 U. S. 634. The New York bonding act of 1869 transformed towns from mere divisions of the state into municipal corporations, with power to borrow money to aid railroads, upon the consent of the tax-payers, after the requisite statutory proceedings and the proper adjudication by the county judge. Brownell v. Greenwich, 114 N. Y. 518, s. c. 4 L. R. A. 685, 22 N. E. R. 24.

[3] Henderson v. Jackson County, 12 Fed. Rep. 676. Authority given to a city to tax property outside its corporate limits to pay bonds issued in aid of a railroad was sustained in Langhorne v. Robinson, 20 Gratt. (Va.) 661. *Contra*, Wells v. Weston, 22 Mo. 384; Town of Cameron v. Stephenson, 69 Mo. 372. The trustees of a township within which a city is located, and which embraces territory not within the city limits, are the proper persons to order an election to determine whether aid should be voted to a railroad company. Young v. Webster City & S. W. R. Co., 75 Iowa 140. For such a city forms a part of the township for the purposes of voting aid and of taxation to pay the aid voted. Young v.

§ 847. **What corporations may be authorized to grant aid.**—The general rule is that counties, townships, cities and incorporated towns and villages which are invested with taxing power may be empowered by express statute to grant aid to railroad companies.[1] Much, of course, depends upon the constitution of the state, for it is obvious that a tax can not be authorized where it is forbidden by constitutional provisions. It is generally held that aid can not be granted where the construction of a railroad is foreign to the purpose for which the public corporation was created.[2] "Taxation by municipal or public corporations must be for a corporate purpose. It is not always easy to decide whether a certain tax is within or without this limitation; but it may be safely said that, as a general rule, a corporate purpose must be some purpose which is germane to the general scope of the object for which the corporation was created."[3] This principle would preclude corporations formed for educational purposes and the like from making subscriptions or donations to railroad companies, since aiding in the construction of railroads can not be regarded as a corporate purpose in such a case.

§ 848. **Subscription to unorganized company.**—It has been held where the statute makes it a prerequisite to the right

Webster City & S. W. R. Co., 75 Iowa 140; Scott v. Hansheer, 94 Ind. 1. See, also, Town of Waterville v. County Commissioners, 59 Me. 80.

[1] Folsom v. Ninety-six, 159 U. S. 611, s. c. 16 Sup. Ct. R. 174, 179; Livingstone County v. Darlington, 101 U. S. 407; Harter v. Kernochan, 103 U. S. 562, 571; Anderson v. Santa Anna Township, 116 U. S. 356, s. c. 6 Sup. Ct. Rep. 413; Bolles v. Brimfield, 120 U. S. 759, s. c. 7 Sup. Ct. R. 736; Johnson v. County of Stark, 24 Ill. 75; Chicago, etc., Railroad Co. v. Smith, 62 Ill. 268; Nichol v. Mayor, etc., 9 Humph. 252; Brown v. Commissioners, 100 N. Car. 92, s. c. 5 S. E. R. 178; Hackett v. Ottawa, 99 U. S. 86; State v. Chester, etc., R. Co., 13 So. Car. 290; Floyd v. Perrin, 30 So. Car. 1, s. c. 8 S. E. R. 14; State v. Whitesides, 30 So. Car. 579, 584, s. c. 9 S. E. R. 661; State v. Neely, 30 So. Car. 587, s. c. 9 S. E. R. 664; Atlantic, etc., Co. v. Darlington, 63 Fed. R. 76, affirmed by Town of Darlington v. Atlantic, etc., Co., 68 Fed. R. 849, 16 C. C. A. 28.

[2] Johnson v. Campbell, 49 Ill. 316; Harvard v. St. Clair, etc., Dist., 51 Ill. 130; Madison County v. People, 58 Ill. 456; Trustees v. People, 63 Ill. 299; People v. Dupuyt, 71 Ill. 651; People v. Trustees, etc., 78 Ill. 136.

[3] Weightman v. Clark, 103 U. S. 256, 260.

to do corporate business, that a designated amount of stock shall be subscribed, and the designated amount has not been subscribed, a municipality can not make a valid subscription to such corporation.[1] The decision in the case referred to may, perhaps, be sustained upon the ground that there was not even a *de facto* corporation, but if the decision is to be regarded as going to the extent that there can not be an effective municipal subscription to a *de facto* corporation, we think that it must be regarded as unsound. If there be a *de facto* corporation, that is, a corporation assumed to be formed under a valid statute, authorizing the formation of such a corporation, and also acts performed as a corporation, then, as we believe, there may be an effective municipal subscription. It is probably true, however, that if it should be shown by a tax-payer, or other party having a right to complain, that the corporation had not even a *de facto* existence, or that having a bare *de facto* existence, cause existed for a *quo warranto*, and there is a likelihood that the state will proceed by *quo warranto*, the courts would enjoin the granting of aid, or if the rights of third persons had not intervened, enjoin the enforcement of the order or vote granting the aid.

§ 849. **Votes—Voters—Majority of votes.**—In construing statutes empowering municipal corporations to aid railroad companies, it often becomes important to determine the meaning of the terms employed in the statutes. Ordinary rules of construction applicable to statutes granting a right not possessed by the public generally, are, of course, to be applied to aid statutes, but there are some applications of those rules which it is important to consider. The phrase, a "majority of the voters," in such a statute, is held to mean a majority of those depositing ballots,[2] unless so qualified as to show dis-

---

[1] Allison v. Louisville, etc., R. Co., 9 Bush (Ky.) 247. But see *ante*, §§ 102, 826, note 5, p. 1152.

[2] County of Cass v. Johnston, 95 U. S. 360; Douglass v. Pike County, 101 U. S. 677; Melvin v. Lisenby, 72 Ill. 63; Reiger v. Commissioners, 70 N. Car. 319; Louisville, etc., R. Co. v. State, 8 Heisk. (Tenn.) 663. But see the reasoning in McWhorter v. People, 65 Ill. 290; Hawkins v. Carroll County, 50 Miss. 735; Webb v. Lafayette County,

tinctly that another meaning is intended.¹ It is generally held that all the voters who do not exercise the right to vote will be presumed to assent to the expressed will of a majority of those voting.² It is held, under the Minnesota statute, that the question of giving aid must be submitted to the legal voters of the town, and can not be voted upon by all resident tax-payers without regard to whether they are legal voters or not.³ Where it appears that some of those voting for the subscription are aliens, and that a majority of the legal voters have not authorized it, the company can not compel a subscription.⁴ But it

67 Mo. 353. In State *v.* Harris, 96 Mo. 29, it is held, that in order that a county court may subscribe to the stock of a railroad company, it must appear that two thirds of the qualified voters of the county, at an election held thereon, assented to the subscription by voting in favor of it; and the fact that a voter does not vote does not express his assent, within the Missouri constitution. In another case it was held that where a statute provides for an election, and requires that a majority of the qualified voters of a county assent to a county subscription to the capital stock of a railway construction company, it is necessary to look to the whole number of registered "qualified voters" in the county in order to determine the result of the election; and a majority of the votes actually cast is not sufficient to give validity to a subscription under such statute when such majority is not a majority of the whole number of registered qualified voters. McDowell *v.* Rutherford Ry. Const. Co., 96 N. Car. 514, s. c. 2 S. E. R. 351.

¹Where the statute required a majority of the legal voters living in the county, and the result of the election showed that by the county record a majority of the voters had voted for the subscription, and the order of the county court recited that all the conditions prescribed for the election had been complied with, the court held that the number of legal voters living in the county was a matter *dehors* the record which the county court could only determine by investigation, and that its finding was conclusive, and the county was estopped to show the contrary. Citizens', etc., Assn. *v.* Perry County, 156 U. S. 692, 15 Sup. Ct. R. 547.

²County of Cass *v.* Johnston, 95 U. S. 360. See, also, Hawkins *v.* Carroll County, 50 Miss. 735; Milner *v.* Pensacola, 2 Woods (U. S.) 632.

³Harrington *v.* Plainview, 27 Minn. 224. In the contemplation of the constitution and laws of Louisiana, the property tax-payers who are entitled to vote on the levy of a special tax, for the purposes therein mentioned, are only those who are entitled to vote at a general election under the election laws of the state. MacKenzie *v.* Wooley, 39 La. Ann. 944, 3 So. R. 128.

⁴People, *ex rel., v.* Cline, 63 Ill. 394. But where it does not appear how many illegal votes were cast for the subscription nor that a majority of the legal votes cast were against the subscription, and it is shown that the exact number of such votes could be

has been held that the fact that a portion of the voters are absent in military service, and the question has not been submitted to them, is not a valid objection to the making of a subscription authorized by the voters who cast ballots at a properly conducted election.[1] A mere majority vote can not dispense with conditions annexed to a resolution to extend aid, adopted by a two-thirds vote.[2] It is the doctrine of some of the cases that where a majority vote is obtained by means of bribery, the election will be vitiated, and the vote will confer no authority.[3] But we think that this doctrine can not apply where the rights of third persons, who have acted in good faith, have intervened. Doubtless a railroad company that should directly or indirectly take part in bribing voters or in corrupting election officers could not take any benefit from the election, but if rights were acquired by it in good faith, the wrongs of others should not be allowed to prejudice those rights.

§ 850. **Failure to conform to the requirements of the enabling act—Illustrative cases.**—Some of the courts lay down a very strict rule and hold that they will not undertake to say that any of the requirements of the statute are immaterial,[4] but this we regard as an extreme doctrine. We think that there may be provisions a departure from which the courts may well adjudge of such little importance as not to invalidate the proceedings.[5] Statutes empowering municipalities to grant aid to railroad

ascertained with judicial certainty, the court will presume in favor of the legality of the proceedings. Woolley v. Louisville, etc., R. Co., 93 Ky. 223, 19 S. W. 595.

[1] Cedar Rapids, etc., R. Co. v. Boone County, 34 Iowa 45.

[2] Portland, etc., R. Co. v. Inhabitants of Hartford, 58 Me. 23. It has been held that a subsequent vote can not change the conditions, either directly or indirectly. People v. Waynesville, 88 Ill. 469. But we think this doctrine of doubtful soundness.

[3] People v. Supervisors, 27 Cal. 655; Butler v. Dunham, 27 Ill. 473; Chicago, etc., R. Co. v. Shea, 67 Iowa 728. See Woolley v. Louisville, etc., R. Co., 93 Ky. 223, 19 S. W. R. 595.

[4] Merritt v. Portchester, 71 N. Y. 309.

[5] A substantial compliance with the law by county commissioners is, in the absence of fraud, sufficient. Wilmington, etc., R. Co. v. Comrs., 116 N. C. 563, s. c. 21 S. E. R. 205.

companies are, unquestionably, to receive a strict construction, but not such a construction as will make matters important that are clearly immaterial. It has been held that the fact that the meeting for an election was not called by the particular officer designated for that duty,[1] or that notice of such meeting was not given for the requisite number of days,[2] or that a vote *viva voce* was taken when the statute required a vote by ballot, will be sufficient grounds for setting aside any action of the municipal officers based thereon.[3] So, it is held, that where the town is authorized to vote an appropriation in aid of a railroad at any "regular" town meeting, it can not pass a valid vote to that effect at a special meeting called for that purpose,[4] but we do not believe that this doctrine can apply where the rights of persons acting in good faith have intervened or where there are effective elements of an estoppel. It has been held that a failure of the commissioners of estimate to take the prescribed oath

[1] Supervisor v. Schenck, 5 Wall. (U. S.) 772; County of Richland v. People, 3 Brad. (Ill.) 210. See Bowling Green, etc., R. Co. v. Warren County Ct., 10 Bush (Ky.) 711. But it is held in Iowa that the majority of the board of township trustees may order an election to determine whether aid shall be voted to a railroad company, where a petition therefor is signed by a majority of resident freeholders of the township, although the other trustees are not notified, being absent from the township and inaccessible for notice. Young v. Webster City, etc., R. Co., 75 Iowa 140.

[2] Harding v. Rockford, etc., R. Co., 65 Ill. 90; Williams v. Roberts, 88 Ill. 11. So, where a proposition to vote bonds was so modified just before the election as to become a new proposition, a vote upon such new proposition without again giving notice for the required time will confer upon the municipal authorities no right to extend aid of any kind. Packard v. Jefferson County, 2 Col. 338. Where thirty days' notice is required, the fact that the order calling the election was entered less than thirty days before the election was held, is sufficient evidence that no legal notice of the election was given. Williams v. People, 132 Ill. 574.

[3] New Haven, etc., R. Co. v. Chatham, 42 Conn. 465. If it plainly appears by the pleadings that a majority of the legal voters did not vote for the subscription the court will not hesitate to set aside all the acts of the municipal officers based thereon. People v. Logan County, 63 Ill. 374.

[4] Pana v. Lippincott, 2 Brad. (Ill.) 466. In Indiana a petition may be presented to the board of county commissioners at any regular or special meeting, and no restrictions are placed upon the calling of a special meeting for any purpose which the auditor may think a public interest requires. Jussen v. Board, etc., 95 Ind. 567; Oliver v. Keightley, 24 Ind. 514.

will render the assessment void, but we can not believe this doctrine to be sound, although it may be that under the particular statute such a conclusion is the only admissible one.[1] Where counties are authorized to submit the question of giving aid at some general or special election, authority to hold a special election for that purpose will be implied.[2] The laws of Nebraska[3] authorize a city to issue bonds in aid of a railroad, provided the city council "shall first submit the question of the issuing of such bonds to a vote of the legal voters" of said city; and provide that "the proposition of the question must be accompanied by a provision to levy a tax annually for the payment of the interest on said bonds as it becomes due," and "shall state the rate of interest such bonds shall draw, and when the principal and interest shall be made payable." In an action to enjoin the issuing of certain bonds of a city under this statute in aid of a railway, it appeared that the whole question had not been submitted to the electors of the city and of that no vote had been submitted or adopted for the payment of the principal at any time. The court held that an injunction should be granted.[4]

§ 851. Conditions, performance of—Excuses for non-performance—Illustrative cases.—The general rule is, as elsewhere shown, that conditions prescribed by the statute must be complied with, but there may be cases in which the doctrine of estoppel will preclude the tax-payers and the municipalities from successfully insisting upon non-performance as a defense, and so, it seems, there may be cases where performance will be excused. It has been held that a condition which can not lawfully be fulfilled may be annexed to a subscription, although

[1] Merritt v. Portchester, 71 N. Y. 309.
[2] Cedar Rapids, etc., R. Co. v. Boone County, 34 Iowa 45.
[3] Comp. Stat. Neb. Ch. 45.
[4] Cook v. City of Beatrice, 32 Neb. 80, 48 N. W. R. 828. See State v. Babcock, 21 Neb. 599; Williams v. People, 132 Ill. 574. Where an act authorizing the issuance of aid bonds fails to provide for an election on the question, the election by necessary implication should be conducted under the existing laws relating to the borrowing of money by municipalities; and bonds issued pursuant to such an order are valid in the hands of *bona fide* holders. Union Bank v. Board of Comrs. of Oxford, 116 N. Car. 339, 21 S. E. R. 410.

the impossibility of a performance of such condition might render the subscription void.[1] Thus, in the case cited, a city, under legislative authority, issued bonds as a donation to a railroad, conditioned that they should be paid out of money to be raised by a special tax upon property in a certain part of the city. The court held that the city had a right to impose the condition, although the constitution of the state forbade the collection of such a tax; and since the condition could not be complied with, it was held that the bonds could not be enforced.[2] There is a conflict in the authorities as to whether time is of the essence of the contract where the subscription of a town is conditioned upon the completion of the road to a certain point within a limited time.[3] But the better opinion seems to be that the failure of a railway company to comply with a condition that it shall construct its road from a certain point to a certain other point within a certain time will defeat the subscription[4] unless there is some element of waiver, or estoppel, or some legal excuse. It has been held that this is so even though the company is prevented by rains and floods from completing its line within the time specified, but afterward completes it.[5] It has also been held that an agreement of a railroad company to refund to a municipal corporation the money received for bonds of the latter issued in payment for stock of the company, in case of a failure to construct the road within a certain time, may be strictly enforced against the railroad company upon its failure to complete its line before the expiration of the time

---

[1] Chicago, etc., R. Co. v. Aurora, 99 Ill. 205.

[2] Chicago, etc., R. Co. v. Aurora, 99 Ill. 205.

[3] In the case of Kansas City, etc., R. Co. v. Alderman, 47 Mo. 349, it is said by the court that a failure to complete the road within the time limited may entitle the county to an abatement in the shape of damages, but not to an entire release from payment of bonds issued to pay a subscription, where it is shown that the road has, in fact, been built.

[4] Memphis, etc., R. Co. v. Thompson, 24 Kan. 170; Chicago, etc., R. Co. v. Town of Marseilles, 84 Ill. 145; McManus v. Duluth, etc., R. Co., 51 Minn. 30; Clark v. Town of Rosedale, 70 Miss. 542. See *ante*, § 111.

[5] Memphis, etc., R. Co. v. Thompson, 24 Kan. 170. See McManus v. Duluth, etc., R. Co., 51 Minn. 30.

specified in the agreement.[1] Where a subscription was made by a town upon condition that the railroad company should locate its machine shops at a certain point, which was accordingly done, and the subscription was paid, it was held that the town could not recover against a good faith purchaser of the property and franchise of the railroad company for removing the machine shops to another town. The contract was personal and gave the town no lien upon the property of the railroad company.[2]

§ 852. **Conditions—Power of municipality to prescribe.**— Where the statute specifically and definitely prescribes the terms or conditions upon which aid may be granted to railroad companies it impliedly excludes authority to dispense with such terms or conditions or to impose any others. Where, however, there are no specific provisions as to terms and conditions a different rule applies. It may be laid down as a general rule that a subscription may be made by a municipal corporation upon conditions annexed by the legislature, by the municipal officers who are given discretion in the matter, by the voters in their petition or vote, or by an agent appointed to make the subscription.[3] It is implied, it may be said, to

---

[1] Chicago, etc., R. Co. v. Town of Marseilles, 84 Ill. 145.

[2] Board of Trustees Elizabethtown v. Chesapeake, etc., R. Co., 94 Ky. 377, 22 S. W. R. 609.

[3] Merrill v. Welsher, 50 Iowa 61; Bittinger v. Bell, 65 Ind. 445; People v. Waynesville, 88 Ill. 469; Falconer v. Buffalo, etc , R. Co., 69 N. Y. 491; Cooper v. Sullivan County, 65 Mo. 542; Justices of Campbell County v. Knoxville, etc., R. Co., 6 Coldw. (Tenn.) 598; Virginia, etc., R. Co. v. Lyon County, 6 Nev. 68; Bucksport, etc., R. Co. v. Brewer, 67 Me. 295; Brocaw v. Board, 73 Ind. 543; State v. County Court, 51 Mo. 522; Port Clinton, etc., R. Co. v. Cleveland, etc., R., 13 Ohio St. 544, 549; People v. Dutcher, 56 Ill. 144. Where an act provides for a town meeting, "to see what sum the town will vote to raise and appropriate as a gratuity to" a railroad, "said road to be completed on or before" a day named, the town is empowered to vote a gratuity upon condition that the road be completed in a reasonable time, but where the town voted aid to a railroad, provided that it completed the road before January 1, 1878, but the clerk failed to record the provision as to time, and the road was completed in August, 1878, an amendment of the record in September, 1878, by inserting the condition as to time within which the road was required to have been completed, will not be

prevent misunderstanding, that the general power of a public corporation to prescribe conditions does not authorize it to prescribe illegal conditions or such as are antagonistic to the general rules of law. The enabling act must take its place in the great system of law as part thereof, and can not be regarded as an isolated fragment standing by itself and apart from other laws. It has been held that specifications in the proposition submitted to the township by the railroad to be voted upon may amount to conditions precedent to the payment of the subscription.[1]

§ 853. Change of municipality.—The plenary power of the legislature over municipal corporations empowers it to make changes in the boundaries and organizations of such corporations, but where private contract rights have been acquired by third persons, such rights can not be impaired. But while such rights can not be impaired, there may be a change in the boundaries of public corporations if such rights are protected. The division of a county or other municipal corporation after a subscription has been made will not affect its liability to pay the stock taken or bonds issued in exchange therefor.[2] But the

---

allowed to defeat the railroad's claim. Sawyer v. Manchester and K. Railroad, 62 N. H. 135, 13 Am. St. Rep. 541.

[1] Town of Platteville v. Galena, etc., R. Co., 43 Wis. 493. Bonds were voted by a county to a railroad company in payment of subscription to its capital stock, on the condition, among others, that the bonds should be delivered when the road was "built of standard gauge, and completed as first-class, and in operation by lease or otherwise." The court held that, to entitle plaintiff to receive the bonds of the county, its road, if constructed according to the terms of the contract, need not have been perfect in every respect at the prescribed date for its completion, but it should have been completed and in operation at that date in such a manner that it might be properly and regularly used for the purpose of transporting freight and passengers. Southern Kan. and P. R. Co. v. Towner, 41 Kan. 72.

[2] County Commissioners of Columbia County v. King, 13 Fla. 451. It is said in Hurt v. Hamilton, 25 Kan. 76, that if a town or county is divided after aid has been voted, and the legislature provides that both parts shall remain liable for its debts as before, only the proportion of a debt created in extending such aid may be collected from each part which its valuation bears to the whole valuation at the time the aid was voted. But a more reasonable and logical rule, in case bonds have been issued, would be that

portion so detached will not be relieved from liability by such a division, but may be compelled, at the suit of the original county, to contribute to such payment.[1] And where, after the division of a county, funding bonds were issued by the original county to take up bonds issued before the division, on terms more favorable to the county than those upon which the loan was first made, the court held the detached territory liable on such funding bonds to the same extent that it had been liable on the railroad bonds.[2] In case of the extinction of a municipality by legislative action after it has incurred obligations in aid of such an enterprise, they will survive against the corporation into which it is merged, to the extent to which it succeeds to the property of the extinct corporation.[3]

§ 854. **Limitations upon the amount.**—The usual course is to prescribe in the enabling act the amount of aid that may be granted, and where the amount is fixed the municipality has no power to go beyond it. But the amount is not always fixed by the statute nor is there always a constitutional limitation upon the power of municipalities to incur debts. Where the discretionary power of fixing the amount is vested in the voters,[4] or in certain designated officers,[5] it should be exercised by fix-

---

stated in the text; since the holder's right to enforce payment can not be defeated nor apportioned by subsequent legislation, but is a matter of arrangement between the counties. County Commissioners of Columbia County v. King, *supra*.

[1] Commissioners of Sedgwick County v. Bailey, 11 Kan. 631. *Contra*, State v. Lake City, 25 Minn. 404.

[2] Marion County v. Harvey County, 26 Kan. 181.

[3] Mount Pleasant v. Beckwith, 100 U. S. 514.

[4] Cincinnati, etc., R. Co. v. Wells, 39 Ind. 539.

[5] Mercer County v. Pittsburgh, etc., R. Co., 27 Pa. St. 389. An act amending an act incorporating the Pittsburgh & Erie Railroad Company, provides that subscriptions to the stock of said railroad company by certain counties "shall be made by the county commissioners after, and not before, the amount of such subscriptions shall have been designated, advised, and recommended by the grand jury." Bonds of Mercer county given for stock subscribed for by the commissioners, on the mere recommendation of the grand jury that they subscribe for an amount not exceeding $150,000, were held to be illegal, on the ground that all the discretionary power was vested in the grand jury by said act and could be exercised by no one else. Frick v. Mercer County, 138 Pa. St. 523, 27 W. N. C. 352. Failure to state the maxi-

ing the amount before a subscription can lawfully be made. It has been held that a vote that an amount not exceeding a certain sum shall be subscribed will not confer authority to make the subscription. We suppose, however, that where a discretionary power respecting the amount of aid that shall be granted is vested in the municipality a failure to designate the amount prior to making the final contract would not make the proceedings void as against third persons who had acquired rights in good faith and upon the belief that the proceedings were regular. If the proceedings were void in the proper sense of the term and not simply irregular, then, as we believe, the principle of estoppel would be applied for the protection of third persons who had acquired rights in good faith, but if the proceedings were absolutely void then an estoppel could not arise. There is difficulty in some instances in determining when the proceedings are void and when only voidable.[1] Where a statutory requirement is violated in designating the amount then the proceedings may usually be regarded as void, since the question is one of power to be determined from an examination of a public statute. If the statute specifically limits the amount and the municipality assumes to grant aid in violation of the statutory provisions, there is no foundation for the proceedings, for the reason that it is established law that a municipality can not aid in the construction of a railroad except by virtue of a valid statute expressly conferring upon it authority to grant such aid.

§ 855. **Valuation of property.**—It is often provided in the enabling acts that the limit shall not exceed a designated per

mum amount proposed to be subscribed will not invalidate an order directing the submission to the voters of the question of a subscription to aid a railroad, under a charter providing for subscriptions according to the forms prescribed by the Virginia code of 1873. Taylor v. Board of Supervisors, 86 Va. 506, 13 Va. L. J. 802, 29 Am. & Eng. Corp. Cas. 187, 10 S. E. 433.

[1] The general rule is that objections, because of formalities and irregularities in the proceedings, must be made before the rights of innocent third persons have intervened. Johnson v. County of Stark, 24 Ill. 75; County of Jasper v. Ballou, 103 U. S. 745.

centum upon the value of property subject to taxation, and it is sometimes difficult to determine the valuation intended. The valuation must, of course, be that referred to by the statute, but it is not always easy to determine what that valuation is. It has been held that where the statute confers authority to vote aid in a sum not exceeding a certain per cent. of the valuation of property in the municipality, the valuation in force at the time the vote is taken will control, although another valuation is even then in process of completion, and takes effect before the subscription is made.[1] It is obvious that, unless the words of the statute clearly require a different construction, the natural construction is that an existing valuation is meant since it can not be presumed that the action of the municipal voters or officers was based on a valuation not known at the time the action was taken.

§ 856. **Conditions must be performed.**—Where the question is not affected by the doctrine of estoppel the conditions prescribed in granting the aid must, as a general rule, be performed. A railroad company or one claiming through it, there being no estoppel, must perform the conditions prescribed or else there can be no effective claim to the aid. The conditions relating to a vote of the people of the municipality to a preliminary petition, or the like, must, as a rule, be substantially complied with, or the proceedings will not be effective. The construction of the road substantially upon the route as chartered by the legislature is generally a condition precedent to the payment of the subscription. But in all such matters the statute governs and regard must always be had to its provisions. It has been held that a tax voted by a town in aid of a railroad whose charter stated that its object was to construct, operate, and maintain a railroad from Dubuque, in a western and northwestern direction in Iowa, Minnesota, and Dakota, to a junction with the Northern Pacific, was not invalidated by the fact that the company sold and merged its line with that of another company after it had completed

[1] Hurt v. Hamilton, 25 Kan. 76.

fifty miles of road in Iowa, where the road of such consolidated company extended from Dubuque to St. Paul in Minnesota, and where the tax was not conditioned upon the construction of the original road as specified by its charter.[1]

§ 857. **Preliminary survey.**—In some of the states a survey is required as a condition precedent to the exercise of the power to vote aid. If such a survey is not made the proceedings will fall before a direct attack. It is held, however, that a popular election held in pursuance of the provisions of such a statute to determine the question of subscription to the stock, is not invalid for lack of a final and definite survey and location of the entire line of the company's road, and that a substantial location, defining the general direction and route, and specifying the termini of the road, with an estimate of the cost

---

[1] Cantillon v. Dubuque & N. W. R. Co., 78 Iowa 48, 35 N. W. R. 620, 42 N. W. R. 613; Lamb v. Anderson, 54 Iowa 190; Noesen v. Port Washington, 37 Wis. 168. See Town of Platteville v. Galena, etc., R. Co., 43 Wis. 493. Where the county commissioners were authorized to subscribe to the capital stock of any railway company which might locate its road through the county, and to issue its bonds in payment thereof, it was held that the fact that the road had never been located through or in the county was a sufficient defense to a suit upon bonds purporting to have been issued in aid of a railway company, even though they were in the hands of a *bona fide* holder. State v. Hancock County, 11 Ohio St. 183. In Indiana the statute suspends the company's right to aid voted by townships until the road is completed and a train of cars is run over the same. Board, etc., v. Louisville, etc., R. Co., 39 Ind. 192. Where an interest coupon covers a period before and after the completion and acceptance of the road, only so much of the interest thereon as was earned after such completion can be recovered under the act providing that no tax shall be levied to pay any interest which may have accrued on railroad aid bonds prior to completion and acceptance of the road. Granniss v. Cherokee Township of York County, 47 Fed. Rep. 427. Where the petition did not designate the time within which the road should be completed, an injunction will not lie against the collection of the tax before the completion of the road, since the commissioners may withhold the money until the road is completed. Pittsburgh, C. C. & St L. Ry. Co. v. Harden, 137 Ind. 486, 37 N. E. 324. A donation may be made for the completion of a railroad already so far laid as to admit of running cars over it, by the construction of grades, digging ditches, and furnishing and laying ties and iron. Barner v. Bayless, 134 Ind. 600.

of construction, is sufficient.[1] Much, it is obvious, depends upon the statute governing the particular case, and where the statute requires a survey it must be made as the statute requires. As the power to aid a railroad enterprise comes from the enabling act, the authority conferred by it must be exercised in substantial conformity to the letter and spirit of the statute; and the preliminary conditions imposed by it must be substantially performed in order to sustain the subscription.[2] Where the rights of third persons have not intervened and there is no element of estoppel, a tax-payer of the municipality may have an injunction to restrain the levy of a tax in pursuance of such a vote or subscription, if all the substantial requirements of the statute have not been met.[3]

§ 858. Petition—Requisites of—Petitioners—Qualifications of.—In many of the states a petition of a designated number of the tax-payers is made necessary to confer authority upon the county officials to extend aid or to order an election for the purpose of determining whether aid shall be extended.[4] There is much diversity of opinion as to the rules which govern such petitions. Some of the courts lay down very strict rules,[5]

[1] County of Wilson v. National Bank, 103 U. S. 770. This, however, was an action to enforce payment of bonds by *bona fide* holders, and the rule might be different in a direct proceeding to test the validity of the election before the rights of third parties had intervened.

[2] People v. Smith, 45 N. Y. 772. Commissioners appointed under the statute have no power to bind the town by an act not done in strict compliance with the authority conferred by vote of the tax-payers. Horton v. Thompson, 71 N. Y. 513.

[3] Peed v. Millikan, 79 Ind. 86; Alvis v. Whitney, 43 Ind. 83. See People v. Waynesville, 88 Ill. 469; People v. Spencer, 55 N. Y. 1; Daviess County v. Howard, 13 Bush (Ky.) 101; Lawson v. Schnellen, 33 Wis. 288.

[4] R. S. N. Y. 1880, Ch. 1869, title 907, §§ 1–6; Ch. 1872, title 883; R. S. Ind. 1894, § 3612, § 3613, § 5340; Laws Iowa 1884, Ch. 159, § 6; Laws Iowa 1890, Ch. 19, Laws Iowa 1882, Ch. 133; Gen. Stat. Kan. 1889, Ch. 23, §§ 126, 149.

[5] Where a verification is required it should always be made. It has been held, pressing the doctrine very far, that the verification must cover all the essential allegations of the petition or it will be held fatally defective. Angel v. Hume, 17 Hun (N. Y.) 374. We can not believe that the doctrine of the case cited can be correct, if sound in any case, where the attack upon the proceedings is collateral. Where the assault is a direct one and made before rights are acquired by third persons a different rule prevails from that which

while others, with more reason, as it seems to us, adopt more liberal rules. It may be said that the authorities generally affirm that the petition must conform, in all substantial respects, to the requirements of the statute. In such a case the requisite number of signers must be procured before any steps can legally be taken toward granting the aid.[1] Where such a petition is required, several petitions may be circulated at once and presented at different times.[2] The term "tax-payers" will be given a liberal construction; persons representing property in the payment of taxes should be counted, even though they do not own the property.[3] Joint owners of property and part-

---

obtains where the proceedings of the municipality are assailed in a collateral proceeding. Loesnitz v. Seelinger, 127 Ind. 422, s. c. 26 N. E. R. 887; Jones v. Cullen, 142 Ind. 335, s. c. 40 N. E. R. 124. See, upon the general question, Longfellow v. Quimby, 29 Me. 196; State v. Prince, 45 Wis. 610; Parks v. Boston, 8 Pick. 218; Dwight v. Springfield, 4 Gray 107; Gay v. Bradstreet, 49 Me. 580; Ballard v. Thomas, 19 Gratt. 14; Maxwell v. Board, 119 Ind. 20, s. c. 19 N. E. R. 617.

[1] People v. Hughitt, 5 Lans. (N. Y.) 89. Under the New York statute providing that a majority of the tax-payers, other than those only taxed for dogs and highways, of any municipal corporation, may petition the county judge for the issue of railroad aid bonds by their municipality, the petition must aver that its signers are a majority of tax-payers, excluding those taxed for dogs and highways only, though the act itself defines the word "tax-payers" as used therein as excluding that class. Town of Mentz v. Cook, 108 N. Y. 504; Rich v. Mentz Township, 134 U. S. 632; Strang v. Cook, 47 Hun (N. Y.) 46.

[2] People v. Hughitt, 5 Lans. (N. Y.) 89.

[3] People v. Hulbert, 59 Barb. (N.Y.) 446. The petition for an election to authorize a township to subscribe to the capital stock of a railroad company was in all respects in conformity with the provisions of the statute, save that it purported to be signed by two-fifths of the "legal voters" of the township, instead of "tax-payers," as required by the statute. The voting at the election was general, and a majority of the votes being for the subscription, the subscription was treated as valid by all parties, and the railroad company, on the faith of it, changed the location of the road to conform to its conditions, at an additional expense, and constructed the road, ready for operation. The township brought suit to enjoin the issue of bonds in payment of the railroad company's stock, as contemplated by the subscription, on the ground that the petition was defective as purporting to be signed by "legal voters" instead of "tax-payers." The railroad was allowed to show that the petition was signed by tax-payers, as required by the statute. Kansas City & Pac. R. Co. v. Rich Township, 45 Kan. 275, 25 Pac. R. 595.

ners must be counted separately.[1] And non-residents who pay taxes must be counted like other tax-payers,[2] unless the statute restricts the right of petition to residents of the municipality.[3] But the agent of a tax-payer is not a proper party to such a petition.[4] Where there is a direct attack upon the proceedings the petitioners must be identified as the tax-payers of the county. The fact that the names are the same as those on the assessment roll is *prima facie* evidence that the persons are the same as those paying taxes.[5] It is held that where the petition is required to be signed by "legal voters," proof that they are "citizens" of the municipality is insufficient,[6] but this doctrine can not, as we believe, be justly applied where there is a collateral and not a direct attack. It has been held that a town is not bound by the decision of its assessor that a majority of the tax-payers have signed the petition,[7] but the question must depend very largely upon the provisions of the statute involved in the particular case. If the officer is invested with power to decide, then as against a collateral attack his decision is conclusive. Where there is a direct attack upon the proceedings, they will fail if the petition be insufficient. If, however, facts sufficient to confer jurisdiction over the general subject are alleged, a collateral attack will not prevail, although the petition may be defective. Strictly speaking, all of the matters required by statute should be fully set out in the petition, but a failure to set them out will not always invalidate the proceedings. It has been held essential that the petition should direct whether the money raised by an issue of bonds

---

[1] People v. Franklin, 5 Lans. (N. Y.) 129; People v. Hughitt, 5 Lans. (N. Y.) 89.

[2] People v. Oliver, 1 T. & C. (N. Y.) 570.

[3] In Indiana, the right is given to resident freeholders in cities, (R. S. 1895, §§ 3612, 3613), and to freeholders in townships (R. S. 1894, § 5340). In Iowa resident freehold tax-payers (Laws Iowa, 1884, Ch. 159, § 2), and in Kansas resident tax-payers (Gen. Stat. 1889, Ch. 23, § 149) may petition for a submission to the voters of the question of giving aid.

[4] People v. Smith, 45 N. Y. 772.

[5] People v. Smith, 45 N. Y. 772.

[6] People v. Supervisor of Oldtown, 88 Ill. 202.

[7] People v. Barrett, 18 Hun (N. Y.) 206.

should be invested in stock or in bonds of the railroad;[1] and this ruling is correct where there is a direct attack, but we think that it can not be the law where the attack is collateral. So it has been held that the petition should specify the amount proposed to be appropriated;[2] and that it must designate with certainty the road to which the aid shall be given, where the municipality is authorized to aid either of two or more roads.[3]

§ 859. Notice of election.—Where, as is usually the case, notice of an election is required by the enabling act the notice required must be given. Here, again, it is necessary to direct attention to the doctrine of estoppel and to the difference between a direct and a collateral attack. The doctrine of estoppel may often so operate as to preclude tax-payers from taking advantage of defects in a notice, and defects may be available in a direct attack which would be unavailing if the attack were a collateral one.[4] Formal defects in a notice or defects that are not of any materiality ought not to be held to render the election ineffective. In Wisconsin it is held that the requirement that notices of an election to determine whether aid shall be granted shall be posted by the town clerk or supervisors need not be literally complied with; but it is sufficient if others post the notices for them.[5] Other cases hold that a notice of

[1] People v. Van Valkenburgh, 63 Barb. (N. Y.) 105. But under the Indiana statute it is held unnecessary to state in the petition whether the money is to be donated or used for the purchase of stock. Jussen v. Board, 95 Ind. 567; Petty v. Myers, 49 Ind. 1. It is held in Indiana that the levy of a tax to aid in the construction of a railroad is not vitiated by any uncertainty or ambiguity in the language of the petition for the appropriation, when it appears that no one was deceived thereby, nor in fact could be, since the intention of the petitioners could not be misapprehended. Jussen v. Board, etc., 95 Ind. 567. See, also, Scott v. Hansheer, 94 Ind. 1; Goddard v. Stockman, 74 Ind. 400.

[2] Wilson v. Board, 68 Ind. 507; Detroit, etc., R. Co. v. Bearss, 39 Ind. 598.

[3] Monadnock R. Co. v. Peterborough, 49 N. H. 281.

[4] It is held by some of the courts that the decision of the local officers, such as the board of county commissioners, board of supervisors or the like is conclusive as against a collateral assault where there is some notice, although it may be defective. Hilton v. Mason, 92 Ind. 157; Faris v. Reynolds, 70 Ind. 359; Reynolds v. Faris, 80 Ind. 14.

[5] Phillips v. Albany, 28 Wis. 340; Lawson v. Milwaukee, etc., R. Co., 30 Wis. 597.

§ 860   PUBLIC AID.   1195

such an election will be held sufficient if it sets forth with reasonable certainty the matters to be acted upon.[1]

§ 860. **Influencing voters.**—Some of the courts hold that oral misrepresentations made to voters to induce them to vote for furnishing aid will not affect the validity of the tax[2] if voted without conditions, although such misrepresentations are made by the agents of the company,[3] but there is conflict among the authorities.[4] So it has been held that the fact that the officers of the municipality were induced by means of false and fraudulent promises to submit the question to a popular vote, will not be sufficient grounds for setting aside the proceedings.[5] It

---

[1] Belfast, etc., R. Co. v. Brooks, 60 Me. 568, where the meeting was called "to see if the town will loan its credit to aid in the construction" of the railroad. An order of the county court submitting to the voters of the county a proposition to subscribe for stock in aid of a railroad, under the laws of Missouri in force March 4, 1867, was not defective because it failed to specify the name of the corporation, where it had described the proposed route with requisite certainty. Ninth Nat. Bank v. Knox County, (C. C. E. D. Mo.) 37 Fed. Rep. 75. Under the general law of Iowa, requiring that the notice of a railroad aid tax to be voted shall specify the line of railroad to be aided, it was held that a notice naming the railroad, and giving location of line in direction and terminal points, meets the requirements of the statute. Yarish v. Cedar Rapids, I. F. & N. W. Ry. Co., 72 Iowa 556, 34 N. W. 417; Burges v. Mabin, 70 Iowa 633, 27 N. W. Rep. 464.

[2] Cedar Rapids, etc., R. Co. v. Boone County, 34 Iowa 45; Platteville v. Galena, etc., R. Co., 43 Wis. 493.

[3] Illinois Midland R. Co. v. Barnett, 85 Ill. 313, where the proposed route was misrepresented. State v. Lake City, 25 Minn. 404, where the alleged misrepresentations related to the location of car and machine shops, etc.

[4] Many who signed a petition for the calling of an election to vote for the issue of bonds by the township in aid of a railroad, as authorized by the laws of Nebraska, were induced to sign the petition by representations on behalf of the railroad that it would locate a depot on a certain section. After the bonds were authorized the depot was located on another section and the aggrieved petitioners were granted an injunction restraining the issue of the bonds, on account of the false representations. In this case two agents of the company were engaged in the common purpose of soliciting the freeholders of a town to sign a petition for an election to vote bonds in aid of the railroad. One made promises and inducements to the freeholders, and shortly afterward the other secured their signatures to the petition. The court held that such promises and inducements were a part of the *res gestæ*. Wullenwaber v. Dunigan, 33 Neb. 477, s. c. 47 N. W. Rep. 420.

[5] State v. Lake City, 25 Minn. 404.

Corp. 76

seems to us that where there is no ground of estoppel and the vote in favor of the aid has been procured by the fraud of the beneficiary company it should be set aside upon opportune and appropriate application to the courts. But, of course, to warrant this conclusion, there must be fraud in all that the term implies on the part of the beneficiary.

§ 861. **Vote does not of itself constitute a contract.**—A vote in favor of granting aid, when a vote is required by the enabling act, is the foundation of the power to contract. It authorizes the municipality to enter into a contract but is not, of itself, a contract. In order that there may be an effective contract there must be appropriate action upon the vote by the municipality. Such a vote does not constitute a subscription, and the power to subscribe may be taken away by the legislature after the vote is taken and before a binding subscription is made,[1] or agreed to be made.[2] But after the agreement to subscribe has been fully entered into, it constitutes a contract which can not be impaired by the laws of the state.[3] Where the statute requires something to be done by the officers after the vote of the directors, wherein such officers are allowed any discretion, the preliminary vote confers no rights upon the company to which the aid is voted, until the officers have acted in making the subscription.[4]

[1] Aspinwall v. Commissioners, 22 How. (U. S.) 364; Town of Concord v. Portsmouth Savings Bank, 92 U. S. 625; Cumberland, etc., R. Co. v. Judge of Washington County Ct., 10 Bush (Ky.) 564; List v. Wheeling, 7 W. Va. 501; State v. Garroutte, 67 Mo. 445. Under the Indiana statute of 1869, the simple voting of aid by a township is not a subscription to the stock of a railroad company, but the subscription can be perfected only by the county board, and until the subscription is so made no liability attaches. Board of Com. of Hamilton County v. State, 115 Ind. 70, 17 N. E. Rep. 855.

[2] Town of Concord v. Portsmouth Sav. Bank, 92 U. S. 625. In Iowa it is held that if money be expended before the repeal of a statute, upon the faith of a tax provided for by it, the repeal does not invalidate the tax and it may be collected. Burges v. Mabin, 70 Iowa 633; Barthel v. Meader, 72 Iowa 125.

[3] Cases cited *supra*.

[4] Wadsworth v. St. Croix County, 4 Fed. Rep. 378; People v. Pueblo County, 2 Colo. 360; Cumberland, etc., R. Co. v. Barren County, 10 Bush (Ky.) 604. And so where the vote is for a subscription upon condition, the railroad company has a right to the voted aid

§ 862. **Aid authorized by popular vote—Duty of local officers.**—Where the statute requires that aid be granted by popular vote, and the voters are empowered to prescribe conditions and do prescribe conditions, the local officers must carry out the will of the voters. In such case the administrative officers appointed to carry the vote into effect can not make any change in the conditions upon which the subscription is voted.[1] It is the duty of such officers to obey the expressed will of the voters, and if they disobey it their proceedings will not be effective except where the doctrine of estoppel applies. Leaving out of consideration the principle of estoppel, it may be said that the conditions prescribed by the voters, where they are in accordance with the statute, constitute, in a great degree, the measure of power. Local officers can not, without statutory authority, organize taxing districts, and a vote by an arbitrarily organized district, and acts done in pursuance thereof, are not valid. It has been held that such a proceeding can not be validated by a subsequent enactment of the legislature, since such acts could not be said to be done by the representatives of the people affected by the tax.[2] It may, however, be doubted whether the broad doctrine of the case cited can be sustained since the general rule is that what the legislature can authorize it may validate,[3] but it is also to be kept in mind that acts which are absolutely void can not be validated by subsequent legislation.[4] Where commissioners are appointed, under authority

only upon a strict performance of the conditions. Brocaw v. Gibson County, 73 Ind. 543; Memphis, etc., R. Co. v. Thompson, 24 Kan. 170; Chicago, etc., R. Co. v. Aurora, 99 Ill. 205; People v. Hitchcock, 2 T. & C., (N. Y. Sup.) 134.

[1] People v. Supervisors of Waynesville, 88 Ill. 469.

[2] Williams v. Roberts, 88 Ill. 11.

[3] May v. Holdridge, 23 Wis. 93; Pelt v. Payne, 60 Ark. 637, s. c. 30 S. W. R. 426; State v. Guttenberg, 38 N. J. Law 419; Unity v. Burrage, 103 U. S. 447; Bennett v. Fisher, 26 Iowa 497; Allen v. Archer, 49 Me. 346; Commonwealth v. Marshall, 69 Pa. St. 328; Shaw v. Norfolk R. Co., 5 Gray 162; Brewster v. Syracuse, 19 N. Y. 116; Kunkle v. Franklin, 13 Minn. 127; Boyce v. Sinclair, 3 Bush 261.

[4] Kimball v. Rosendale, 42 Wis. 407; Maxwell v. Goetschius, 40 N. J. Law 383, s. c. 29 Am. R. 242; People v. Lynch, 51 Cal. 15; Thames, etc., Co. v. Lathrop, 7 Conn. 550; Abbott v. Lindenbower, 42 Mo. 162; Johnson v. Board, 107 Ind. 15; Andrews v. Beane, 15 R. I. 451. See Hasbrouck v. Milwaukee, 13 Wis. 37; Yeatman v. Day, 79 Ky. 186; Roche v. Waters, 72 Md.

of the enabling act, to make a subscription for a municipality they are the agents of the corporation to the extent of making the subscription, and it may adopt or reject their acts done outside the limits of their authority. If they annex to the subscription conditions beyond what are contained in the instrument of assent by which they received their appointment and authority, their act in so doing is not void, but such conditions are binding unless repudiated by the municipality.[1] Such commissioners can not bind the town by a waiver of any of the conditions imposed, or by an agreement that other terms and conditions shall be substituted.[2] And where a subscription, absolute in form, was made by commissioners appointed by a town to make the subscription upon certain conditions, and it appeared at the hearing of an application for a peremptory writ of mandamus to compel the delivery of bonds by the town, that the subscription was made under the belief, induced in part by the representations of the railroad company's officers, that the town could not be compelled to deliver the bonds until an agreement as to the performance of the conditions had been made, and that the conditions had not been performed by the relator, the writ was denied.[3]

§ 863. Contract granting aid—Subscription—Enforcement.—Where the statute conferring power to grant aid has been complied with, and the railroad company has fully complied with the terms and conditions of the statute and agreement, a contract exists which can not be annulled except, of course, for

264, s. c. 18 Atl. R. 866; State v. Doherty, 60 Me. 504; Pryor v. Downey, 50 Cal. 388, s. c. 19 Am. R. 656.

[1] Town of Danville v. Montpelier, etc., R. Co., 43 Vt. 144. Where a petition of tax-payers, relating to an issue of railroad aid bonds, provides that a certain quantity shall be issued when the road is located through the town, the commissioners appointed in pursuance of the petition are thereby authorized to postpone their issue to a later stage in the progress of the work, by contract with the company. Town of Cherry Creek v. Becker, 2 N. Y. Sup. 514.

[2] Falconer v. Buffalo, etc., R. Co., 69 N. Y. 491. Nor can they bind the town by any act not done in compliance with the authority conferred by the vote of the inhabitants. Horton v. Thompsen, 71 N. Y. 513.

[3] People v. Hitchcock, 2 Thompson & C., (N. Y.) 134.

§ 863   PUBLIC AID.   1199

sufficient legal or equitable cause. Thus it has been held that authority to make a subscription to be paid by the issue of municipal bonds only after the road is open for traffic will enable a town to make a binding subscription from which it can not be released without the consent of the railroad company, and that valid bonds may be issued after the completion of the road although the statute authorizing the subscription has, in the meantime, been repealed.[1] It may be laid down as a general rule that where the statute has been pursued in all its requirements, and the aid regularly voted, and the railroad company has complied with the conditions imposed, the corporation or its creditors may have a writ of mandamus to compel the issue of the bonds by officers whose only duties are ministerial, and who are given no discretion in the matter.[2]

[1] Town of Concord v. Portsmouth Sav. Bank, 92 U. S. 625; Livingston County v. First Nat. Bank, 128 U. S. 102, 126. The repeal of the law under which a tax was voted will not invalidate the tax where the proceedings have been regular, and the company has, on the faith of the vote, expended money in constructing its line in the town which voted the tax. Cantillon v. Dubuque & N. W. R. Co., 78 Iowa 48, 42 N. W. R. 613.

[2] Chicago, etc., R. Co. v. St. Anne, 101 Ill. 151; Brodie v. McCabe, 33 Ark. 690; Howland v. Eldeidge, 43 N. Y. 457; Louisville, etc., R. Co. v. County Court, 1 Sneed (Tenn.) 637; City of Mt. Vernon v. Hovey, 52 Ind. 563; Cumberland, etc., R. Co. v. Judge of Washington County, 10 Bush (Ky.) 564; Cincinnati, etc., R. Co. v. Clinton County, 1 Ohio St. 77; Raleigh, etc., R. Co. v. Jenkins, 68 N. C. 502; Napa Valley R. Co. v. Napa County, 30 Cal. 435; Selma, etc., R. Co., Ex parte, 45 Ala. 696; City of Muscatine v. Mississippi, etc., R. Co., 1 Dill. (U. S.) 536; United States v. Clarke County, 96 U. S. 211. Under the Kansas act of 1885, relating to municipal aid to railroads, providing that townships shall issue no more than $15,000 and five per cent. on its assessed value for such purpose, a subscription to the amount limited, duly made and accepted by the company, is a contract binding on the township, and the conditions being performed, the company is entitled to the township bonds to the exclusion of another road, to whose stock the town has afterwards subscribed, though the latter perform its conditions first. Chicago, K. & W. Ry. Co. v. Board, etc., 38 Kan. 597, 16 Pac. R. 828. In case of a subscription to the stock of a railroad company by the county board, the certificate of stock thus subscribed may be demanded as a condition of the payment of the money, and where the property of such company is sold on foreclosure, and bought in by a new company having no power to issue stock of the old company, such new company can not, by mandamus, compel the levy of a tax for the purpose of paying them the amount voted to be paid for stock in the original company. Board of Com-

If no conditions are imposed, the officers may be compelled to make the subscription as soon as it is fully authorized by a vote, and the rights of the beneficiary become vested.[1] But until there is an effective contract there is no right to a mandamus. The general rule is that the subscription will be held to have been made as of the date when it became the duty of the officers to make it. There is a sufficient subscription to entitle the railroad company to all the rights which a manual subscription on its books would confer, whenever the corporation, in the mode prescribed by the statute, directs its officers to subscribe for a certain amount of its stock, and there is either an actual or constructive acceptance on its part.[2] A manual subscription is not necessary on their part, however, but the agreement to take stock may be made binding by a resolution or vote of the municipal authorities or officers charged with discretion in the matter, if designed to have that effect, and passed for the purpose of completing the agreement.[3]

missioners v. State, 115 Ind. 70. If one whose land has been taken for use in the construction of a railroad without compensation so assents to the entry of the railroad as to waive his right to dispossess it, the omission to make such compensation can not be urged as a defense to an action by a railroad to recover money voted by a city to the railroad company to be paid on completion of the road. Manchester & K. Railroad v. City of Keene, 62 N. H. 81.

[1] People v. Cass County, 77 Ill. 438; People v. Logan County, 63 Ill. 374. The supreme court of Kansas has held that the vote of the people of a county to subscribe for the stock of a railroad company and to issue its bonds, does not create a contract between the county and the company, even though such vote was upon conditions which the company subsequently performed; and the court refused a mandamus to compel the subscription. Land Grant, etc., R. Co. v. Davis Co. Comrs., 6 Kan. 256.

[2] Nugent v. Supervisors, 19 Wall. (U. S.) 241; State v. Jennings, 48 Wis. 549. As to what constitutes an effective contract, see Nugent v. Supervisors, 19 Wall. (U. S.) 241; Justices of Clarke Co. Ct. v. Paris, etc., Turnpike Co., 11 B. Mon. (Ky.) 143; Shelby County Court v. Cumberland, etc., R. Co., 8 Bush (Ky.) 209; Welch v. Post, 99 Ill. 471; County of Clay v. Society for Savings, 104 U. S. 579. The mere vote by the inhabitants of a municipality to the effect that bonds shall be issued does not make the contract to issue them a binding one. State v. Lancaster County, 6 Neb. 214; Harshman v. Bates Co., 92 U. S. 569; Chesapeake, etc., R. Co. v. Barren Co., 10 Bush (Ky.) 604; Bound v. Railroad Co., 45 Wis. 543; Jeffries v. Lawrence, 42 Iowa 498; Land Grant R. Co. v. Davis Co., 6 Kan. 256.

[3] County of Cass v. Gillett, 100 U. S.

§ 864. Power of municipal officers where the statute requires submission to popular vote.—Municipal officers, as is well known, have only such powers as the statute confers upon them, and municipalities can only grant aid when expressly authorized by statute, so that it follows that where a vote is required there is no power to enter into a contract until the vote prescribed has been taken. It is correctly held that a contract with reference to the giving of aid made in advance of a popular vote will not be regarded as valid, even though it is made to procure such vote, and the vote is afterward obtained.[1] The vote is the foundation of the power and until it has been taken it can not be justly said that the municipality had any power to contract.

§ 865. Decision of local officers as to jurisdictional facts.—Some of the cases hold that a municipality is not bound by the decision of its officers as to jurisdictional facts, unless the rights of innocent third parties have so intervened as to estop it from disputing the correctness of such decision, and that a court of chancery may investigate the election and other preliminary acts conferring the alleged right to extend aid.[2] But

585; Illinois Midland R. Co. v. Barnett, 85 Ill. 313; Justices of Clarke County Ct. v. Paris, etc., Turnp. Co., 11 B. Mon. (Ky.) 143. Where the order is that a subscription be made with conditions and terms annexed, and it is not of itself final and complete, such order must be fully obeyed to render the subscription binding. County of Bates v. Winters, 97 U. S. 83. Where the law requires stock to be paid for at the time it is subscribed, the railroad company has no right to the voted aid until the stock is subscribed and the money paid. And it can not by mandate compel the levy of a tax voted by a municipality to pay for stock which the municipality proposes to take. Board, etc., v. State, 115 Ind. 64; Board, etc., v. Louisville, etc., R. Co., 39 Ind. 192. All the steps which precede the taking of stock, or the making of a donation by a county in such a case, are between the people of the county and its officers only, and only a voter can maintain a suit for mandate for this purpose. Board of Commissioners v. Louisville, etc., R. Co., 39 Ind. 192; Caffyn v. State, 91 Ind. 324.

[1] People v. County Board of Cass County, 77 Ill. 438. But see Chicago, etc., R. Co. v. Ozark Township, 46 Kan. 415.

[2] Winston v. Tennessee, etc., R. Co., 1 Baxter, Tenn., 60. See Horton v. Thompson, 71 N.Y. 513. An entry and order made by the board of county commissioners to the effect that a subscription in aid of railroads submitted to the sense of the "qualified voters" of the county had been carried by a ma-

there is conflict upon this general question, and we are of the opinion that where the attack is collateral the decision is conclusive, except, perhaps, where no action constituting a change of position has been taken by the railroad company, and no third persons have acquired rights.[1] As between the munici-

jority of such voters, while it can not be attacked collaterally does not so adjudicate the question of the legality of the election that it can not be contested by a direct proceeding for that purpose. Nor do the facts that the county commissioners have subscribed for shares of the capital stock of the railroads, and that the latter have made engagements and contracts based upon that subscription, prevent the election being contested and its validity determined by such a proceeding. Goforth *v.* Rutherford Ry. Const. Co., 96 N. C. 535, 2 S. E. 361; McDowell *v.* Rutherford Ry. Const. Co., 96 N. C. 514, 2 S. E. 351. The bonds in excess of the amount which a township was authorized to issue were obtained from the state treasurer on a false certificate by the township trustee that the conditions on which they were issued had been complied with. The railway company was cognizant of the fraud and receipted to the treasurer for the bonds, but never had actual possession of them, though it assented to their delivery to the contractor by the township trustee in payment for construction work. It was held that this did not constitute a negotiation of the bonds to an innocent purchaser; and, as the conditions on which they were issued had not been complied with, the consideration had failed, and the township was entitled to a decree for their surrender and cancellation. Wilson *v.* Union Sav. Assn., 42 Fed. Rep. 421. The acts of a Kentucky county court, in ascertaining the result of an election upon the question whether the county shall subscribe to the stock of the Kentucky Union Railway Company, under the Kentucky act of March 10, 1854, and in subscribing the stock, are ministerial, and not judicial, and the taxpayers are not confined to the remedy by appeal, but may maintain an action in the district court to declare the subscription void, and to enjoin the collection of the tax to pay it, on the ground of the illegality of the election. Holt, J., dissenting. Kentucky Union Ry. Co. *v.* Bourbon County, 85 Ky. 98, 2 S. W. 687. From this doctrine we dissent.

[1] Commissioners of Knox County *v.* Aspinwall, 21 How. (U. S.) 539; Town of Coloma *v.* Eaves, 92 U. S. 484; Commissioners, etc., *v.* Bolles, 94 U. S. 104; Town of Venice *v.* Murdock, 92 U. S. 494; Bissell *v.* Jeffersonville, 24 How. (U. S.) 287; Bank of U. S. *v.* Dandridge, 12 Wheat. 64, 70; Knox County *v.* Ninth, etc., Bank, 147 U. S. 91, s. c. 13 Sup. Ct. R. 267; Ryan *v.* Varga, 37 Iowa 78; Koehler *v.* Hill, 60 Iowa 543; Spaulding *v.* North San. Homestead Assn., 87 Cal. 40; Ela *v.* Smith, 5 Gray 121, s. c. 66 Am. Dec. 356; Tucker *v.* Sellers, 130 Ind. 514, 517; State *v.* Nelson, 21 Neb. 572, s. c. 32 N. W. R. 589; State *v.* Weatherby, 45 Mo. 17; City of Camden *v.* Mulford, 26 N. J. Law 49; Porter *v.* Purdy, 29 N. Y. 106, s. c. 86 Am. Dec. 283; Roderigas *v.* East River, etc., 76 N. Y. 316, s. c. 32 Am. R. 309; Landford *v.* Dunklin, 71 Ala. 594; Goodwin *v.* Sims, 86 Ala. 102, s. c. 11 Am. St. R. 21; Town of Cherry Creek *v.* Becker, 123 N. Y. 161; Henline *v.*

pality and innocent third persons, the decision of the board of officers who are appointed to determine whether the conditions precedent to the making of a subscription have been observed is final and conclusive on the municipality.[1] It has been held that where a petition is necessary, it must show that it is signed by the required number of the class authorized to present such a petition, or it will fail to confer jurisdiction.[2] We do not believe, however, that this can be the correct doctrine in cases where the local officers are empowered to determine jurisdictional facts.[3]

§ 866. Acceptance of aid.—The general rule is that where an act is beneficial to a party acceptance on his part may be presumed. This principle applies to cases where aid is granted

People, 81 Ill. 269; Chicago, etc., Co. v. Chamberlain, 84 Ill. 333; Brittain v. Kinnaird, 1 Brod. & Bing. 432; Betts v. Bagley, 12 Pick. 572; Martin v. Mott, 12 Wheat. 19; Vanderheyden v. Young, 11 Johns. 150. See authorities cited Elliott's Gen. Prac., § 260, notes. See Citizens', etc., Assn. v. Perry County, 156 U. S. 692, 15 Sup. Ct. R. 547.

[1] Comrs. Knox Co. v. Aspinwall, 21 How.(U. S.) 539, 544; Bissell v. Jeffersonville, 24 How. (U. S.) 287; Coloma v. Eaves, 92 U. S. 484. On a question as to the validity of certain bonds issued by a county to a railway company, it was claimed that the issue was not authorized by two-thirds of the qualified voters, as required by statute, and that such fact would appear from an inspection of the registration lists, although the board of supervisors, in the performance of their duties, had declared that two-thirds of the voters had voted for the measure. The court held that a *bona fide* purchaser was not required to go behind such returns, and one who purchased for value, without actual notice of any wrong, was entitled to recover. Madison County v. Brown, 67 Miss. 684.

[2] Wilson v. Caneadea, 15 Hun (N. Y.) 218; Angel v. Hume, 17 Hun (N. Y.) 374. See Williams v. Roberts, 88 Ill. 11. Where under the Kansas statutes an election is ordered in a county for the purpose of authorizing a subscription to the capital stock of a railroad company, and an issue of the bonds of the county in payment for such stock, the election is ordered upon a petition presented to the county board, which does not contain the requisite number of names, but which the county board declares to be sufficient, and the election is held, returns canvassed, and the result declared in favor of subscribing for the stock and issuing the bonds, and the clerk is ordered by the board to make the subscription, and does so, the election can not stand but must be deemed to be void because of a want of a sufficient petition. Chicago, K. & W. R. Co. v. Board of Com'rs, 43 Kan. 760, 23 Pac. R. 1064.

[3] Evansville, etc., R. Co. v. City of Evansville, 15 Ind. 395. See authorities cited in second preceding note.

to railroad companies. As a rule no formal acceptance of the subscription is necessary on the part of the company. If it complies with the terms upon which a subscription is voted by the municipality, an acceptance will be presumed.[1]

§ 867. Ratification of subscription.—Where there is an entire absence of power to subscribe to the stock of a railroad company, the municipal corporation assuming to make the subscription can not validate it by subsequent ratification. Possibly a statute might authorize a valid ratification, but even this is doubtful. It seems clear, at all events, that where there is no such statute and where the municipality had no authority to make the subscription, it can not ratify a subscription so as to give it any validity.[2]

§ 868. Stock subscribed by municipality—Legislative control of.—The legislative power over the property of a public or municipal corporation is, as we have seen, very broad and comprehensive. The rule that property held by a municipal corporation is under legislative control applies to stock subscribed by it in aid of a railroad company. The fact that such stock is already in the hands of the municipality will not prevent the legislature from transferring it to the tax-payers, at least in the case of imperfectly organized municipal corporations, such as counties and townships.[3] The legislative dis-

---

[1] State v. Town of Lime, 23 Minn. 521; State v. City of Hastings, 24 Minn. 78.

[2] Treadway v. Schnauber, 1 Dak. 236; Ryan v. Lynch, 68 Ill. 160. If a municipal corporation votes to subscribe for stock of a railroad before its own charter goes into effect, the vote is a nullity, and no ratification by its officers after the charter takes effect can give it validity. Clark v. Janesville, 13 Wis. 414, s. c. 10 Wis. 136; Berliner v. Waterloo, 14 Wis. 378; Winchester, etc., Co. v. Clarke County Ct., 3 Met. (Ky.) 140; Rubey v. Shain, 54 Mo. 207. But see County of Daviess v. Huidekoper, 98 U. S. 98, where bonds were held valid although authorized by a popular vote before the organization was completed.

[3] Lucas v. Board of Commissioners, 44 Ind. 524; Board of Commissioners v. Lucas, 93 U. S. 108. In New York the taxes collected from the railroad must be paid to the county treasurer to form a sinking fund for the payment of the bonds issued to aid it. Laws N. Y. 1869, c. 907, as amended by Laws 1871, c. 283, and c. 925. This act is constitutional. In re Clark v. Sheldon, 106 N. Y. 104; Vinton v. Board of Supervisors, 2 N. Y. Supp.

cretion, where discretion exists, is not subject to judicial surveillance, for the only question for the courts in such cases is power or no power. Under the general power which it possesses, the legislature may direct that the stock so taken by a municipality shall be divided amongst the tax-payers from whom the money with which it was purchased was collected, without laying the statute open to the objection that it compels persons to become stockholders in a private enterprise.[1]

367. It applies, not only in the case of railroads constructed under the act of 1869, but to all towns bonded in aid of railroads constructed in or through them. *In re* Clark *v.* Sheldon, 106 N.Y. 104, 12 N. E. 341. Taxes collected by a city from a railroad company, to aid which it had issued bonds, were paid over to the county treasurer and by him mingled with the county moneys, and never invested, but paid over by him to his successor. The court held that the successor was authorized, under the statute, to invest them for the benefit of the city. Spaulding *v.* Arnold, 6 N. Y. S. 336. The provisions of the North Carolina statute, by which the county taxes, levied on property and franchises of a railroad in a certain township, in aid of the construction of which railroad the township has voted its bonds, are to be applied to pay interest on such bonds, not interfering with the levy of taxes, are not unconstitutional and only direct the application of county revenue. Brown *v.* Commissioners, 100 N. C. 92, 5 S. E. 178.

[1] By an act passed March 15, 1851, the legislature of Kentucky incorporated the Shelby Railroad Company, and authorized the county of Shelby to subscribe for stock, and to levy taxes to pay therefor, each person paying such tax to become entitled to his *pro rata* share of the stock. By an amendment of February 3, 1869, a specified portion of Shelby county was authorized to subscribe for stock, issue bonds in payment thereof, and levy taxes, with the provision that stock for which certificates had been issued to tax-payers should be voted by the individuals holding the same. By act, March 11, 1870, the charter was again amended, so as to provide that any county, or part of a county, which had delivered bonds in payment of stock, should be entitled to representation, and to vote the amount of such stock through the county judge and justices of the peace. It was held that taxes paid and used merely to discharge the interest on the bonds did not entitle the tax-payer to stock, and the corporation itself was entitled to vote the stock represented by the amount of bonds still outstanding. Hancock *v.* Louisville & N. R. Co., 145 U. S. 409, s. c. 12 Sup. Ct. 960; Shelby R. Co. *v.* Louisville & N. R. Co., 145 U. S. 409. Tax-payers do not acquire an equitable lien upon the property of a railroad company, in the hands of a purchaser after a foreclosure sale subject to equitable liens, by reason of payments made by them upon a subscription of the county to the capital stock of such company, and the refusal of the company to issue stock to them therefor, whether such payments entitle them to stock or not. The fact that the payments were made to one of the contractors for building

§ 869. **Rights and liabilities of municipal corporations as stockholders.**—It is held that where a municipal corporation, under legislative authority, subscribes for stock without paying for it in full, it stands in the same relation to the company and its creditors that any other subscriber does who owes for an unpaid subscription.[1] But, of course, much depends upon the provisions of the statute which authorizes the municipality to subscribe, since the legislature has power to prescribe the rights and liabilities of the public corporation. In general, however, it takes its stock with all the incidents which attach to the position of a stockholder.[2] Thus it may be held liable for labor and material furnished to the company under a statute making stockholders liable therefor,[3] unless the statute authorizing the subscription expressly provides otherwise.[4]

§ 870. **Defenses to municipal subscriptions.**—Tax-payers may defend against subscriptions upon the ground that there has been a failure to comply with the requirements of the statute, and so, in some cases, may the municipality. It may be said that the general rule is that the same defenses to the payment of subscriptions, made upon condition, are open to municipalities that may be interposed by others making conditional subscriptions. It is true, as elsewhere indicated, that the municipality and the tax-payers may be estopped by their conduct to defend against the subscriptions.[5]

---

the road makes no difference. Spurlock v. Missouri Pac. Ry. Co., 90 Mo 199, 2 S. W. 219.

[1] County of Morgan v. Allen, 103 U. S. 498; Morgan County v. Thomas, 76 Ill. 120.

[2] Shipley v. City of Terre Haute, 74 Ind. 297. See Murray v. Charleston, 96 U. S. 432; National Bank v. Case, 99 U. S. 628.

[3] Shipley v. City of Terre Haute, 74 Ind. 297.

[4] Rev. Stat. Ind. 1894, § 5364, provides that no county or township which has become the owner of any stock, shall, in any case, be liable for work or materials furnished the railroad, though the assets of the company be exhausted.

[5] A township subscribed certain warrants in aid of a railroad, which were to be issued when the company should have built and put in operation, "with cars running thereon, by lease or otherwise, its said railroad, between two designated cities." The railroad company built its road from one to within 111 feet of the city limits of the other, at which point it intersected another road, and by running its cars over the

§ 871. **Estoppel of tax-payers.**—Tax-payers may by silence and acquiescence estop themselves from successfully objecting that the proceedings have not been conducted in conformity to the statute. If objections are seasonably and appropriately made they will often avail where they would be unavailing if made after rights have been acquired by the railroad companies or third persons. It may be safely said that the general rule is that if the tax-payers stand by without objection while considerable sums of money are expended in the construction of the road the courts will hold them estopped to aver that there were irregularities in the proceedings.[1] This doctrine can not apply, however, where there is an entire absence of power, but it does apply where power exists, although there may be many material errors and irregularities.

other road to its depot from this intersection, it continuously operated the road between the two cities. The court held that this was a substantial compliance with the conditions of the subscription, and that mandamus would lie to compel the issue of the warrants. Chicago, K. & W. R. Co. v. Makepeace, 44 Kan. 676. Where a county subscribes under an act authorizing counties to subscribe to the construction of a railroad, such county, and all the citizens thereof, must be taken to have acted with reference to the fact that the charter was liable to be amended as occasion should require. Powell v. Supervisors Brunswick County, 88 Va. 707, 14 S. E. R. 543. Amendments to the charter, which have not been acted upon by the company, do not release the county from its subscription. Taylor v. Board of Supervisors, 86 Va. 506, 10 S. E. R. 433. See, also, Kleise v. Galusha, 78 Iowa 310; Murfreesboro R. Co. v. Comrs. of Hertford Co., 108 N. Car. 56; Baltimore, etc., R. Co. v. Pumphrey, 74 Md. 86.

[1] Jones v. Cullen, 142 Ind. 335, s. c. 40 N. E. R. 124; Moulton v. Evansville, 25 Fed. R. 382; Ricketts v. Spraker, 77 Ind. 371; Kellogg v. Ely, 15 Ohio St. 64; Menard v. Hood, 68 Ill. 121; City of New Haven v. Fair Haven, etc., R. Co., 38 Conn. 422, s. c. 9 Am. R. 399; Rochdale Co. v. King, 16 Beav. 630; Dows v. City of Chicago, 11 Wall. 108; Muncey v. Joest, 74 Ind. 409; Johnson v. Kessler, 76 Iowa 411. After the collection and payment into the county treasury of taxes voted by a township in aid of a railway, the county can not set up the defense that the railway company had sold and disposed of its property and franchises before the taxes became due. Merrill v. Marshall County, 74 Iowa 24, 36 N. W. 778. Where a township voted bonds to aid in the construction of a railroad, made a subscription to the capital stock, and received and retains the certificates of stock issued to it, the proceedings having been regular and duly authorized, and the railroad was constructed through the township in strict compliance with the terms of the subscription, and is being regularly operated, the town-

§ 872. **Remedies of tax-payers.**—The validity of a municipal subscription or donation, or the issue of bonds thereunder, may in some jurisdictions be tested in many cases by *certiorari*,[1] bill of review, or writ of error.[2] But the remedy most often resorted to by tax-payers to prevent illegal municipal aid, or the unlawful levy of a tax to pay the same, is that by way of injunction. As a general rule, any one or more tax-payers of the municipality may institute a suit in behalf of all to enjoin the unauthorized levy of a tax or the illegal issue or payment of bonds.[3] So, the payment of bonds or a subscription may be enjoined by the tax-payers, in a proper case, where the company has not performed the conditions upon which the subscription was made or the bonds issued.[4] But it has been held that injunction will not lie until after a forfeiture has been declared.[5] Where the amount of taxes that may be voted and levied in aid of a railroad company is limited by law, no au-

ship is estopped in an action of mandamus to compel the issue and delivery of the bonds voted, from asserting that the petition presented to the board of county commissioners, requesting an election to be called at which to vote the bonds, was not signed by two-fifths of the resident tax-payers of the township, where the board of county commissioners had found and determined at the time of its presentation that it was so signed, and was legal in all other respects. Hutchinson & S. R. Co. *v.* Board of Comrs., 48 Kan. 70, s. c. 28 Pac. R. 1078; Chicago, etc., R. Co. *v.* Board of Comrs., 49 Kan. 399, 30 Pac. Rep. 456.

[1] Harris on Certiorari, §§ 28, 210, 215; 2 Beach Inj., §§ 1189, 1202.

[2] Anderson Co. *v.* Houston, etc., R. Co., 52 Tex. 228.

[3] Bittinger *v.* Bell, 65 Ind.45; Hill *v.* Probst, 120 Ind. 528; Alvis *v.* Whitney, 43 Ind. 83; Redd *v.* Supervisors of Henry County, 31 Gratt. (Va.) 695; New Orleans, etc., R. Co. *v.* Dunn, 51 Ala. 128; State *v.* Hager, 91 Mo. 452; Rutz *v.* Calhoun, 100 Ill. 392; Nefzger *v.* Davenport, etc., R. Co., 36 Iowa 642; Winston *v.* Tennessee, etc., R. Co., 1 Baxt. (Tenn.) 60; Campbell *v.* Paris, etc., R. Co., 71 Ill. 611. See, also, Morris *v.* Merrel, 44 Neb. 423, s. c. 62 N. W. R. 865; Gregg *v.* Sanford, 65 Fed. R. 151; Flack *v.* Hughes, 67 Ill. 384; Finney *v.* Lamb, 54 Ind. 1; Bronenberg *v.* Board, 41 Ind. 502; Cattell *v.* Lowry, 45 Iowa 478; Blunt *v.* Carpenter, 68 Iowa 265.

[4] Wagner *v.* Meety, 69 Mo. 150. See, also, Township of Midland *v.* County Board, 37 Neb. 582, s. c. 56 N. W. R. 317; Lamb *v.* Anderson, 54 Iowa 190; Peed *v.* Millikan, 79 Ind. 86; Chicago, etc., R. Co. *v.* Marseilles, 84 Ill. 145. But it is held that insolvency of the company does not necessarily render a tax previously levied invalid. Wilson *v.* Hamilton Co., 68 Ind. 508.

[5] Nixon *v.* Campbell, 106 Ind. 47, s. c. 4 N. E. R. 296, 7 N. E. R. 258; Pittsburg, etc., R. Co. *v.* Harden, 137 Ind. 486, s. c. 37 N. E. R. 324.

§ 872   PUBLIC AID.   1209

thority exists to submit to the electors the question of voting aid in excess of that amount, and taxes levied under such a vote may be enjoined.[1] But, as a general rule, injunction will not lie at the suit of tax-payers to prevent an election under legislative authority to enable the citizens of the municipality to vote to levy or not to levy a tax upon themselves in aid of a railroad.[2] And mere irregularities which do not prejudice any substantial rights will not be sufficient ground for an injunction.[3] So, it has been held that after a tax has been voted and levied, the sufficiency of the petition or the result of the vote as declared by the canvassing board can not be collaterally assailed or inquired into in a suit by the tax-payers to enjoin the collection of the taxes.[4] This is, indeed, the general rule.[5] As in other cases in which an injunction is sought, the plaintiff should act promptly and show the necessary grounds for the interposition of a court of equity.[6] If a tax-payer delays action until after the tax has been collected and the money paid over to the bondholders of the railroad company, when he might

[1] Burlington, etc., R. Co. v. Clay County, 13 Neb. 367. See, also, Hedges v. Dixon County, 150 U. S. 182, s. c. 14 Sup. Ct. R. 71.

[2] Roudanez v. New Orleans, 29 La. Ann. 271.

[3] Ricketts v. Spraker, 77 Ind. 371; Lafayette, etc., R. Co. v. Geiger, 34 Ind. 185; Louisville, etc., R. Co. v. County Ct. of Davidson Co., 1 Sneed (Tenn.) 637, s. c. 62 Am. Dec. 424; Milwaukee, etc., R. Co. v. Kossuth Co., 41 Iowa 57; Texas, etc., R. Co. v. Harrison Co., 54 Tex. 119. See, also, Chicago, etc., R. Co. v. Grant, Clerk, etc., 55 Kan. 386, s. c. 40 Pac. R. 654; Robinson v. City of Wilmington, 65 Fed. R. 856; 2 Beach Inj., §§ 1193, 1195, 1200.

[4] Ryan v. Varga, 37 Iowa 78; Dwyer v. Hackworth, 57 Tex. 245.

[5] Jones v. Cullen, 142 Ind. 335, s. c. 40 N. E. R. 124, and numerous authorities there cited; Board v. Hall, 70 Ind. 469; Pittsburg, etc., R. Co. v. Harden, 137 Ind. 486, s. c. 37 N. E. R. 324; Bell v. Maish, 137 Ind. 226; Citizens' Sav. & L. Assn. v. Perry County, 156 U. S. 692, s. c. 15 Sup. Ct. R. 547. But see Kentucky Union Ry. Co. v. Bourbon County, 85 Ky. 98; People v. Spencer, 55 N. Y. 1; McPike v. Pen, 51 Mo. 63; DeForth v. Wisconsin, etc., R. Co., 52 Wis. 320, s. c. 5 Am. & Eng. R. Cas. 28; Harding v. Rockford, etc., R. Co., 65 Ill. 90.

[6] Chamberlain v. Lyndeborough, 64 N. H. 563, s. c. 14 Atl. R. 865; Vickery v. Blair, 134 Ind. 554, s. c. 32 N. E. R. 880; Jones v. Cullen, 142 Ind. 335, s. c. 40 N. E. R. 124; Trustees, etc., School Dist. v. Garvey, 80 Ky. 159; Menard v. Hood, 68 Ill. 121; Moulton v. Evansville, 25 Fed. R. 382; 10 Am. & Eng. Ency. of Law, 802, 857, et seq.; ante, § 871.

have obtained an injunction restraining the collection of the tax by acting in time, he can not recover the amount of the tax paid by himself from the treasurer of the municipality,[1] but there are cases in which the payment of the tax to the company may be restrained even after it has been collected.[2] After bonds have been issued and a tax levied to pay them, a taxpayer can enjoin its collection in a suit against the municipality and its treasurer only upon grounds constituting a good defense on the part of the city to the payment of the bonds in the hands of the present holders.[3]

§ 873. **Remedies of municipalities.**—The rights and remedies of a municipal corporation which has subscribed for stock in aid of a railroad are, in the main, the same as those of an individual subscriber.[4] As a general rule any act of the railroad company that would release an individual subscriber will release the municipality as between it and the company, and, in a proper case, a bill will lie for the rescission of the subscription.[5] So, the municipality may, in a proper case, obtain an injunction restraining the company from violating conditions upon which the subscription was made,[6] or a rescission of a fraudulent contract into which it has entered.[7] The municipality may enforce the delivery of the stock in the same manner, and, as a rule, under the same circumstances as an individual subscriber.[8] A provision in the enabling act that the

---

[1] Butler v. Fayette County, 46 Iowa 326.

[2] Missouri, etc., R. Co. v. Miami Co., 12 Kan. 230.

[3] Wilkinson v. City of Peru, 61 Ind. 1.

[4] It occupies, in general, the same position as any other subscriber—no better and no worse. Pittsburg, etc., R. Co. v. Allegheny County, 79 Pa. St. 210; Shipley v. City of Terre Haute, 74 Ind. 297; Noesen v. Port Washington, 37 Wis. 168; County of Morgan v. Allen, 103 U. S. 498; Murray v. Charleston, 96 U. S. 432; Morgan County v. Thomas, 76 Ill. 120; State v. Holladay, 72 Mo. 499. Part of a county may be considered as a municipality for the purpose of owning and voting stock in a railroad company. Hancock v. Louisville, etc., R. Co., 145 U. S. 409, s. c. 12 Sup. Ct. R. 969.

[5] County of Crawford v. Pittsburgh, etc., R. Co., 32 Pa. St. 141.

[6] Town of Platteville v. Galena, etc., R. Co., 43 Wis. 493. See, also, Perkins v. Port Washington, 37 Wis. 177.

[7] People v. Logan County, 63 Ill. 374.

[8] County of Wapello v. Burlington, etc., R. Co., 44 Iowa 585.

§ 874   PUBLIC AID.   1211

citizens who pay the tax shall receive from the municipality, with its consent, the stock delivered to it by the railroad company has been held not to invalidate the tax or relieve the municipality of the obligation to pay its subscription.[1] Where bonds have been issued fraudulently or without authority of law, the municipality may maintain a suit to have them declared void and canceled by making the bondholders parties.[2] As we shall hereafter show a municipality which has authority to issue negotiable bonds may be estopped from questioning their validity in the hands of *bona fide* purchasers; but it has been held that it is not estopped from enjoining the officers of a railroad company from disposing of bonds irregularly issued by the mere fact that it has accepted the stock, and levied a tax to pay the interest upon the bonds.[3] It has also been held that an officer of a railroad company, who, with full knowledge that the bonds have become invalid because the company has ceased to exist, negotiates them to innocent purchasers, is liable to the municipality for what it is compelled to pay such purchasers,[4] and a county may have the assistance of a court of equity to restrain its treasurer from wrongfully applying funds in his hands to the payment of void bonds.[5]

§ 874. **Remedies of railroad companies.**—Where all the preliminary steps requisite to the valid issue of bonds or the col-

[1] Talbot v. Dent, 9 B. Mon. (Ky.) 526; Slack v. Maysville, etc., R. Co., 13 B. Mon. (Ky.) 1.

[2] City of Waverly v. Auditor, 100 Ill. 354; Paola, etc., R. Co. v. Comrs. of Anderson County, 16 Kan. 302; Comrs. of Anderson County v. Paola, etc., R. Co., 20 Kan. 534. See Brooklyn v. Insurance Co., 99 U. S. 362; Roberts v. Bolles, 101 U. S. 119; Town of Springport v. Teutonia, etc., Bank, 75 N. Y. 397; Chester, etc., R. Co. v. Commissioners of Caldwell County, 72 N. Car. 486. An action may also lie to correct errors in the bonds and make them conform to the vote authorizing their issue. Town of Essex v. Day, 52 Conn. 483.

[3] Madison County v. Paxton, 57 Miss. 701.

[4] Farnham v. Benedict, 107 N. Y. 159. So where the company unlawfully and fraudulently negotiates the bonds. Town of Plainview v. Winona, etc., R. Co., 36 Minn. 505, 517.

[5] Missouri River, etc., R. Co. v. Miami County, 12 Kan. 230. See, also, Township of Midland v. County Board, 37 Neb. 582, s. c. 56 N. W. R. 317.

CORP. 77

lection of the money voted in aid of a railroad company have been taken, and nothing remains but the ministerial duty to issue the bonds, levy the taxes, or make the collection, the company, having performed all necessary conditions on its part, may compel the performance of such duty by mandamus.[1] It has been held, however, that, unless the law makes it the duty of the municipality or its proper officers to make the subscription or issue bonds,[2] so that they have no discretion in the matter, the mere fact that an election has resulted in favor of making such subscription or issuing the bonds creates no contract with the company, and mandamus will not lie.[3] But when the subscription has once been legally made, mandamus will lie, upon tender of the stock, to compel the municipality to issue bonds[4] or take steps to raise the money to pay the subscription in accordance with the statute.[5] If, however, the aid is unauthorized,[6] or necessary conditions have not been com-

---

[1] Cherokee County v. Wilson, 109 U.S. 621; United States v. County of Clark, 96 U. S. 211; Chicago, etc., R. Co. v. Town of St. Anne, 101 Ill. 151; People v. Getzendaner, 137 Ill. 234, s. c. 34 N. E. R. 297; California, etc., R. Co. v. Butte Co., 18 Cal. 671; Napa Valley R. Co. v. Napa County, 30 Cal. 435; Louisville, etc., R. Co. v. County Ct. of Davidson County, 1 Sneed (Tenn.) 637, s. c. 62 Am. Dec. 424; Raleigh, etc., R. Co. v. Jenkins, 68 N. Car. 502; People v. Batchellor, 53 N. Y. 128; People v. Allen, 52 N. Y. 538; Jager v. Doherty, 61 Ind. 528; Duncan v. Mayor, 8 Bush (Ky.) 98; County Comrs. of Columbia Co. v. King, 13 Fla. 451; Commonwealth v. Pittsburgh, 34 Pa. St. 496; High Ex. Rem., §§ 282, 393. Mandamus will lie to compel the proper officers to promulgate the result of an election to determine whether a tax shall be levied in aid of a railroad. State v. Mayor of Monroe, 46 La. Ann. 1276, s. c. 15 So. R. 625.

[2] People v. Dutcher, 56 Ill. 144; People v. Holden, 91 Ill. 446; People v. Logan Co., 63 Ill. 374.

[3] Land Grant R., etc., Co. v. Davis Co., 6 Kan. 256; State v. Roscoe, 25 Minn. 445; People v. Fort Edward, 70 N. Y. 28. See, also, Chicago, etc., R. Co. v. Town of St. Anne, 101 Ill. 151; Board, etc., of Crawford County v. Louisville, etc., R. Co., 39 Ind. 192; Chicago, etc., R. Co. v. Olmstead, 46 Iowa 316; State v. Garoutte, 67 Mo. 445; Cumberland, etc., R. Co. v. Barren County, 10 Bush (Ky.) 604.

[4] State v. Jennings, 48 Wis. 549; Atchison, etc., R. Co. v. Jefferson Co., 12 Kan. 127; State v. Lake City, 25 Minn. 404; Ex Parte Selma, etc., R. Co., 45 Ala. 696, s. c. 6 Am. R. 722.

[5] Justices of Clarke Co. v. Paris, etc., Co., 11 B. Mon. (Ky.) 143; Osage Valley, etc., R. Co. v. County Ct. of Morgan Co., 53 Mo. 156; Cincinnati, etc., R. Co. v. Clinton Co., 1 Ohio St. 77.

[6] State v. Highland, 25 Minn. 355; State v. Minneapolis, 32 Minn. 501; State v. Tappan, 29 Wis. 664; Norton v. Town of Dyersburg, 127 U. S. 160, s.

plied with,[1] the writ will be refused. But mere delay on the part of the railroad company in enforcing its rights, where no one is injured thereby, has been held insufficient to prevent it from afterwards enforcing them by mandamus.[2] It has been held that where a perpetual injunction has been granted prohibiting the officers from making a subscription, mandamus will not afterwards lie at the suit of the railroad company to compel them to do so,[3] and so, on the other hand, it has been held that if a mandamus has first been awarded, injunction will not lie to prevent them from doing what they have been ordered to do by the mandate of the court.[4] The mere pendency of *quo warranto* proceedings against the company or the individuals composing it is not, however, a good defense to mandamus proceedings instituted by the company to compel the municipality to issue its bonds in a proper case.[5] Other remedies may doubtless be resorted to in some cases, but mandamus is usually the most desirable remedy, and is frequently the only remedy of the railroad company.[6]

c. 8 Sup. Ct. R. 1111. See, also, Clay Co. v. McAleer, 115 U. S. 616; United States v. County Ct. of Macon Co., 99 U. S. 582; Supervisors v. United States, 18 Wall. (U. S.) 71; State v. Rainey, 74 Mo. 229; People v. Logan Co., 63 Ill. 374; Commissioners of Brownsville v. Loague, 129 U. S. 493, s. c. 9 Sup. Ct. R. 327.

[1] People v. Waynesville, 88 Ill. 469; People v. Holden, 91 Ill. 446; People v. Glann, 70 Ill. 232; Essex Co. R. Co. v. Luneuburgh, 49 Vt. 143. See Casady v. Lawry, 49 Iowa 523.

[2] State v. Jennings, 48 Wis. 549. See, also, Merrill v. Marshall Co., 74 Iowa 24; Merrill v. Welsher, 50 Iowa 61.

[3] Ohio, etc., R. Co. v. Commissioners, 7 Ohio St. 278. See, also, *Ex Parte* Fleming, 4 Hill 581. But compare Knox County v. Aspinwall, 24 How. (U. S.) 376.

[4] Cumberland, etc., R. Co. v. Judge, 10 Bush 564. But see Commissioners of Brownsville Tax Dist. v. Loague, 129 U. S. 493.

[5] Oroville, etc., R. Co. v. Plumas County, 37 Cal. 354.

[6] See Smith v. Bourbon County, 127 U. S. 105, s. c. 22 Am. & Eng. Corp. Cas. 74, 78.

CHAPTER XXXV.

MUNICIPAL AID BONDS.

§ 875. Power to issue aid bonds.
876. Legislative authority requisite.
877. Constitutional questions — Completed road.
878. Governmental subdivision may be authorized to issue bonds.
879. Execution of the power to issue aid bonds—Generally.
880. Execution of the power to issue aid bonds—Implied powers.
881. Formal execution of bonds.
882. Nature of municipal aid bonds.
883. Proceedings of municipal officers must conform to the statute.
884. Want of power—Definition.
885. Conflict of authority.
886. Consolidation does not take away right to bonds.
887. Purchasers of aid bonds—Duty to ascertain that power to issue bonds exists.
888. Bonds issued in excess of the limits prescribed by the constitution.
889. Limitation of amount — Construction of statute.
890. Bonds in excess of the limit prescribed by statute.
891. Bonds running beyond time prescribed.
892. Bonds payable out of a specific fund.
893. Performance of conditions.
894. Ratification of bonds irregularly issued.
895. When bonds are void.
896. *Bona fide* holders of aid bonds.
897. Estoppel by recitals in bonds —General doctrine.

§ 898. Estoppel by recitals in bonds—Illustrative cases.
899. Recitals in bonds not always conclusive.
900. Official certificates — Conclusiveness of.
901. Recitals in bonds to constitute an estoppel must be of facts.
902. No estoppel where the officer ordering bonds to issue had no jurisdiction.
903. Estoppel otherwise than by recital—Illustrative instances.
904. Estoppel by retention of stock.
905. Recitals in bonds—Effect of against bondholders.
906. Refunding—Substitution.
907. Discretionary powers and peremptory duty.
908. Registration.
909. Rights of *bona fide* holders not affected by sale of bonds at less sum than that prescribed by statute.
910. Subrogation of holder of invalid bonds.
911. Liability of municipality to purchaser of invalid bonds.
912. Right of municipality to recover money paid because of wrongful acts of the railroad company.
913. Defenses to aid bonds.
914. Bondholders not bound by proceedings to which they are not parties.
915. Following state decisions.
916. Jurisdiction of federal courts.
917. Compelling the issue of bonds.
918. Remedies of bondholders.

§ 875. **Power to issue aid bonds.**—The power of a municipality to aid a railroad company, as we have elsewhere shown, is not an ordinary or implied corporate power, but exists only in cases where it is expressly granted by statute.[1] The whole subject of granting aid is a statutory one, and it is always necessary to look to the statute to ascertain the nature and extent of the power.[2] The rule which is, as we believe, supported by principle, and sanctioned by authority, is that there is no power to issue bonds to aid a railroad company unless the power is clearly conferred by statute.[3] A municipal corporation is in no sense a business or trading corporation, but is a governmental instrumentality, so that the true and just view

---

[1] *Ante,* §§ 825, 829.

[2] See Hutchinson *v.* Self, 153 Ill. 542, s. c. 39 N. E. R. 27; City of Columbus *v.* Dennison, 69 Fed. R. 58; United States *v.* County of Macon, 99 U. S. 582; United States *v.* County of Clark, 96 U. S. 211; State *v.* Shortridge, 56 Mo. 126; State *v.* Macon County Court, 41 Mo. 453. It has been held that general authority to subscribe to the stock of a railroad company or to make a donation of money to aid in the construction of its road, carries with it by necessary implication the power to borrow money for that purpose, and to issue bonds and sell them as a means to that end. Seybert *v.* City of Pittsburg, 1 Wall. (U. S.) 272; United States *v.* City of New Orleans, 98 U. S. 381; United States *v.* County of Macon, 99 U. S. 582; Thompson *v.* City of Peru, 29 Ind. 305; Hancock *v.* Chicot County, 32 Ark. 575; Nichol *v.* Mayor of Nashville, 9 Humph. (Tenn.) 252. Authority "to obtain money on loan on the faith and credit of the city for the purpose of contributing to works of internal improvement," was held to confer upon the city the power to guarantee payment of the bonds of a railroad company. City of Savannah *v.* Kelly, 108 U. S. 184. And it was held that an act which authorized a town to subscribe for shares in the capital stock of a railroad company, and to raise by loans or taxes the money required to pay the installments of the subscription, conferred on the town by implication the power to issue bonds. Commonwealth *v.* Inhabitants of Williamstown, 156 Mass. 70, 30 N. E. 472. But it has also been held that power to levy a tax, and make a donation to a railroad, or purchase its stock, confers no authority to issue bonds in anticipation of the tax. Town of Middleport *v.* Ætna Life Ins. Co., 82 Ill. 562; Lippincott *v.* Town of Pana, 92 Ill. 24; Winston *v.* Tennessee, etc., R. Co., 1 Baxter (Tenn.) 60; Daviess County Court *v.* Howard, 13 Bush (Ky.) 101; Leavenworth, etc., R. Co. *v.* Commissioners of Douglas County, 18 Kan. 169; Town of Wellsborough *v.* New York, etc., R. Co., 76 N. Y. 182; Concord *v.* Robinson, 121 U. S. 165; Wells *v.* Supervisors, 102 U. S. 625; Katzenberger *v.* Aberdeen, 121 U. S. 172; Kelley *v.* Milan, 127 U. S. 139.

[3] *Ante,* § 839.

is, that it has no power to issue bonds to aid in the construction of a railroad, unless the power is expressly conferred by statute.[1] The power to issue negotiable bonds is a high and important one, and there is strong reason for holding that unless expressly conferred it does not exist. Some of the cases take a different view of the general question, but, in our opinion, they are not well decided.

§ 876. Legislative authority requisite.—There is no power, as elsewhere demonstrated, to issue bonds to aid a railroad company except where it is conferred by express statute.[2] Thus, a mere voluntary vote of the people of a city under a city ordinance, and without any authority from the legislature, will not confer any rights upon the city to extend aid to a railroad.[3] Authority to issue bonds to pay debts or to borrow money for municipal purposes does not confer power to issue bonds as a donation to a railroad.[4] It may be said generally

---

[1] *Ante*, § 839. The rule that is best sustained by authority is thus stated by the supreme court of the United States. "It is well settled that a municipal corporation, in order to exercise the power of becoming a stockholder in a railroad corporation, must have such power expressly conferred upon it by a grant from the legislature; and that even the power to subscribe for such stock does not carry with it the power to issue negotiable bonds in payment for the subscription, unless the power to issue such bonds is expressly or by necessary implication conferred by statute." Kelley *v.* Milan, 127 U. S. 139, citing Pulaski *v.* Gilmore, 21 Fed. Rep. 870; Tax Payers *v.* Tennessee Central R. Co., 11 Lea (Tenn.) 329; Marsh *v.* Fulton County, 10 Wall. (U. S.) 676; Wells *v.* Supervisors, 102 U. S. 625; Ottawa *v.* Carey, 108 U. S. 110; Daviess County *v.* Dickinson, 117 U. S. 657. The grant of power to a municipality to subscribe for stock in a railroad does not imply the power to issue bonds therefor. Norton *v.* Town of Dyersburg, 127 U. S. 160; Hill *v.* Memphis, 134 U. S. 198.

[2] *Ante*, §§ 827, 839; Young *v.* Clarendon Tp.,132 U. S. 340; Kelley *v.* Milan 127 U. S. 139; Corcord *v.* Robinson, 121 U. S. 165; Norton *v.* Dryersburg, 127 U. S. 160; Daviess County *v.* Dickinson, 117 U. S. 657; Hill *v.* Memphis, 134 U. S. 198; Wells *v.* Supervisors, 102 U. S. 625. See City of Lafayette *v.* Cox, 5 Ind. 38; People *v.* Coon, 25 Cal. 635; Milan *v.* Tennessee, etc., R. Co., 11 Lea 329; Justices of Campbell County *v.* Knoxville, etc., R. Co., 6 Coldw. 598; City of Ottawa *v.* Carey, 108 U. S. 110; Fisk *v.* Kenosha, 26 Wis. 23; Pennsylvania R. Co. *v.* Philadelphia, 47 Pa. St. 189; Clay *v.* Nicholas County, 4 Bush 154; Jeffries *v.* Lawrence, 42 Iowa 498; City of Savannah *v.* Kelly, 108 U. S. 184.

[3] Quincy, etc., R. Co. *v.* Morris, 84 Ill. 410.

[4] Ryan *v.* Lynch, 68 Ill. 160. A city was duly authorized, by a popular

that if no power to issue the bonds existed at the time they were issued, they are void in whatever hands they may be.[1]

§ 877. **Constitutional questions — Completed road.** — The decisions which support the doctrine that a municipal corporation may be empowered to aid in the construction of a railroad proceed upon the theory that the road will be a benefit to the local community. It is doubtful whether the principle can apply where the road has been completed and all the benefit that can accrue has been secured.[2] It is, at all events, quite clear that bonds can not be issued to an insolvent company which has completed its road in order to enable it to pay claims of creditors, since that would be to authorize the levy of a tax for a private purpose and this the constitution will not permit.[3]

---

vote, to subscribe $100,000 to the stock of a railroad company, and to issue its bonds to an equal amount in payment therefor. Afterward the city council passed a resolution binding the city to sell to the company all this stock for $5,000, to be paid by a return of its bonds to that amount. The bonds were issued, and by direction of the council placed in escrow, to be delivered to the company upon the performance of certain conditions, the depositary being authorized and directed, upon receipt of the stock, to sell the same to the railroad company for $5,000 of the city bonds. There was nothing to show that the railroad company had agreed to purchase the stock, but, after the stock and bonds were duly exchanged, the stock was sold in the manner proposed. The court held that this transaction did not convert the "subscription," which was authorized by the statute, into an unauthorized donation of $95,000, and, if any wrong was done by the council in thus disposing of the stock, it did not vitiate the bonds in the hands of a *bona fide* purchaser. City of Cairo v. Zane, 149 U. S. 122, s. c. 13 Sup. Ct. R. 803. See, *ante*, § 841, note 2.

[1] Anthony v. County of Jasper, 101 U. S. 693; McClure v. Township of Oxford, 94 U. S. 429; Township of Elmwood v. Marcy, 92 U. S. 289; Thomas v. Richmond, 12 Wall. (U. S.) 349; Marsh v. Fulton County, 10 Wall. (U. S.) 676; Weismer v. Douglas, 64 N. Y. 91; State, *ex rel.* Beckel, v. Union Township, 15 Ohio St. 437; Hopple v. Hipple, 33 Ohio St. 116; Hancock v. Chicot County, 32 Ark. 575; Hamlin v. Meadville, 6 Neb. 227; Lippincott v. Pana, 92 Ill. 24; Williams v. Roberts, 88 Ill. 11; Williamson v. Keokuk, 44 Iowa 88; Woodruff v. Okolona, 57 Miss. 806; Steines v. Franklin County, 48 Mo. 167; Missouri River, etc., R. Co. v. Miami County, 12 Kan. 230; Burhop v. Milwaukee, 21 Wis. 257; Board, etc., of Delaware County v. McClintock, 51 Ind. 325.

[2] Baltimore, etc., R. Co. v. Spring, 80 Md. 510, s. c. 27 L. R. A. 72.

[3] Baltimore, etc., R. Co. v. Spring, 80 Md. 510, s. c. 27 L. R. A. 72. The decision in the case referred to asserts, as we believe, a just conclusion, but

§ 878. **Governmental subdivisions may be authorized to issue bonds.**—The power of the legislature over the subject of taxation is very broad and comprehensive and it may organize taxing districts. Upon the same principle it may, where there is no constitutional interdiction, provide for the formation of districts for the purpose of aiding railroad companies. Thus it has been held that "magisterial precincts" may be authorized to subscribe to the stock of railroad companies and to issue bonds to pay such subscriptions.[1]

§ 879. **Execution of the power to issue aid bonds—Generally.**—In our opinion the true rule is that the power to issue railroad aid bonds must be as strictly pursued as any part of the power to extend aid to a railroad enterprise,[2] and in cases where the statute has not been substantially followed in making the subscription or in issuing the bonds, such bonds will be invalid.[3] We do not mean to say that there may not be

we are inclined to think some of the statements of the opinion go too far. It seems to us that the court trenches somewhat upon the rule that where a question is a legislative one the decision of the legislature is conclusive. There is reason for affirming that the legislature has power to decide what railroad companies may receive aid, and if the power exists it is not subject to judicial surveillance or control.

[1] Breckinridge County v. McCracken, 61 Fed. R. 191, 194, citing City of Lexington v. McQuillan's Heirs, 9 Dana 513; County Judge v. Shelby R. Co., 5 Bush 225; Kreiger v. Shelby Railroad Co., 84 Ky. 66; County of Carter v. Sinton, 120 U. S. 517, s. c. 7 Sup. Ct. R. 650; Hancock v. Louisville, etc., Railroad Co., 145 U. S. 409, s. c. 12 Sup. Ct. R. 969. But, as a rule, it is only governmental corporations that can be authorized to grant aid to railroad companies. *Ante*, § 847.

[2] Mayor, etc., City of Kokomo v. State, 57 Ind. 152, 163; City of Madison v. Smith, 83 Ind. 502; Town of Wheatland v. Taylor, 29 Hun (N. Y.) 70; Cairo, etc., R. Co. v. Sparta, 77 Ill. 505. It is not necessary that the commissioners to sell the bonds should act personally in selling them and investing the proceeds, but they may do so through the medium of a broker. Brownell v. Town of Greenwich, 114 N. Y. 518, s. c. 22 N. E. R. 24. Where the act authorizing a city to issue bonds is silent as to the kind of currency in which such negotiable bonds shall be paid, the city has power to make them payable "in gold coin of the United States of the present standard weight and fineness." Judson v. City of Bessemer, 87 Ala. 240, s. c. 6 So. R. 267.

[3] People v. Smith, 45 N. Y. 772; People v. Hurlburt, 46 N. Y. 110; Horton v. Thompson, 71 N. Y. 513; Williams v. Roberts, 88 Ill. 11; People v. Santa Anna, 67 Ill. 57; Sinnett v. Moles, 38 Iowa 25.

§ 880   MUNICIPAL AID BONDS.   1219

cases where the statutory provisions are so clearly directory that a failure to comply with them may be justly regarded as unimportant, nor do we mean to say that there may not be instances where a deviation from a mandatory provision may be so plainly immaterial as to be justly held not to affect the validity of the bonds, but we do mean to say that such cases and instances form exceptions to the general rule, for, as we believe, the general rule is that the provisions of such statutes are mandatory unless the context clearly shows the contrary, and must be substantially pursued. We may add, to prevent misunderstanding, that we are here considering the question entirely independent of the doctrine of estoppel.

§ 880. **Execution of the power to issue aid bonds—Implied powers.**—It is very seldom that the enabling act goes into detail, for in almost all cases, power to issue bonds is granted in general terms. It is sometimes provided that bonds shall run for a designated length of time, or shall be of a particular tenure, and where this is so, and there is no effective estoppel, a material departure from the statute may be cause for refusing to enforce the bonds. But as a general rule, the power is a general one, and matters of detail are left to the municipality, and where this is so, there are, necessarily, implied powers conferred upon the municipality. Such a general power will, as a rule, authorize the bonds to be made payable at any place within or without the state.[1] So, too, such a general power

[1] Evansville, etc., R. Co. v. City of Evansville, 15 Ind. 395, 412; Maddox v. Graham, 2 Met. (Ky.) 56; Meyer v. Muscatine, 1 Wall. (U. S.) 384. It is held in Illinois, under the provisions of an act which authorizes the interest on such bonds to be made payable at any place which the county court may direct, that the principal be made payable only at the office of the treasurer. Prettyman v. Supervisors of Tazewell County, 19 Ill. 406; City of Pekin v. Reynolds, 31 Ill. 529. But it is held that a provision making them payable at another place will not invalidate the bonds, although the provision will be void. Sherlock v. Winnetka, 68 Ill. 530. Nor will it affect their negotiable character. Enfield v. Jordan, 119 U. S. 680. Municipal bonds, in the absence of any provisions as to the place of payment, are payable at the treasury of the municipality. Friend v. Pittsburgh, 131 Pa. 305, s. c. 6 L. R. A. 636. The fact that the act authorized the bonds to be issued, bearing interest at the legal rate where they were payable, which

will authorize the municipality to determine the form and tenure of the bonds, provided the municipality does not, in executing the bonds, go beyond the general power conferred upon it. And where this power exists and is exercised, and bonds payable at a particular place are issued and sold, neither the legislature nor the municipality can change the place of payment without the consent of the holders of the bonds.[1]

§ 881. **Formal execution of bonds.**—So far as concerns the mere formal parts of bonds, the courts are very liberal in upholding the rights of *bona fide* holders, and will not allow those rights to be defeated because of formal defects. Thus, in one case the municipality was enjoined from setting up the defense that the corporate seal was not affixed to the bonds.[2] Bonds should be executed by the proper officers of the municipality, and, if there is no estoppel, bonds executed by other representatives are not enforceable.[3] It is held that where the statute specifically provides what the denomination of the bonds shall be it must be obeyed.[4]

§ 882. **Nature of municipal aid bonds.**—It is competent for the legislature to provide that aid bonds shall not be negotiable. This it may do by directly declaring that they shall

is in another state, where the legal rate is larger than in Tennessee, did not render them void for usury. Nelson v. Haywood County, 3 Pickle (Tenn.) 781. Where the statute fixes the rate of interest that the bonds shall bear, the municipal officers can not contract to pay a greater rate. English v. Smock, 34 Ind. 115, s. c. 7 Am. R. 215.

[1] Dillingham v. Hook, 32 Kan. 185.
[2] Bernards Township v. Stebbins, 109 U. S. 341, s. c. 3 Sup. Ct. R. 252.
[3] Walnut v. Wade, 103 U. S. 683; People v. Smith, 45 N. Y. 772; Town of Danville v. Montpelier, etc., R. Co., 43 Vt. 144; Town of Douglas v. Niantic, etc., Bank, 97 Ill. 228. See

Mayor, etc., of Wetumpka v. Winter, 29 Ala. 651; Mercer County v. Pittsburg, etc., R. Co., 27 Pa. St. 389; First National Bank v. Arlington, 16 Blatchf. 57; Bank of Statesville v. Statesville, 84 N. Car. 169. As to what officers may execute. County of Kankakee v. Ætna Life Ins. Co., 106 U. S. 668, s. c. 2 Sup. Ct. R. 80. As to *bona fide* holders, it is sufficient if bonds are signed by officers *de facto*. County of Ralls v. Douglass, 105 U. S. 728. See Middleton v. Mullica Tp., 112 U. S. 433; Sauerhering v. Iron Ridge, etc., R. Co., 25 Wis. 447; Town of Wayauwega v. Ayling, 99 U. S. 112.

[4] County of Greene v. Daniel, 102 U. S. 187.

§ 882   MUNICIPAL AID BONDS.   1221

not be negotiable, or by clearly making them payable out of a specific fund and no other.[1] Ordinarily municipal bonds issued in aid of a railroad are commercial paper and *bona fide* holders for value take them freed from all equities of which they do not have notice.[2] Being commercial paper they are not within the rule of *lis pendens*.[3] But of course, where there is actual notice to the purchaser, he is not protected as a *bona fide* holder of commercial paper. It has been held that even where a subscription to the capital stock can not legally be made until after the railroad corporation is organized, bonds may be valid in the hands of *bona fide* holders,[4] and it is also held that the fact that the popular vote authorizing the subscription was taken before the organization was completed will not be a de-

---

[1] Blackman v. Lehman, 63 Ala. 547.

[2] Mercer County v. Hacket, 1 Wall. 83; County of Cass v. Gillett, 100 U. S. 585; Cromwell v. County of Sac, 94 U. S. 351, 96 U. S. 51; Board v. Texas, etc., R. Co., 46 Tex. 316; Tucker v. New Hampshire Sav. Bank, 58 N. H. 83; Arents v. Commonwealth, 18 Gratt. (Va.) 750; State v. Union Township, 8 Ohio St. 394. See, generally, Clapp v. County of Cedar, 5 Iowa 15; Hannibal,etc.,R.Co.v.Marion County, 36 Mo. 294; City of Aurora v. West, 22 Ind.88; Society, etc.,v.New London, 29 Conn. 174; Barrett v. County Ct. of Schuyler County, 44 Mo. 197; Consolidated Association,etc.,v.Avegno,28 La. Ann. 552; City of Elizabeth v.Force, 29 N. J. Eq. 587; Lindsey v. Rottaken, 32 Ark. 619. It will be presumed, in the absence of proof, that members of a railroad commission not present at a meeting at which bonds were ordered to be issued had notice that the meeting was to be held in accordance with the statute, authorizing a majority to act at any meeting of which all had notice. Hill v. Peekskill Sav. Bank, 46 Hun 180. Though all the bonds were dated on the same day, and payable twenty years from date, while the amendatory act provided that but ten per cent. of them should mature during any one year, they would not be invalid as to plaintiff, who was not shown to have knowledge of the irregularity, or that any other bonds were issued besides those he purchased. Brownell v. Town of Greenwich, 114 N. Y. 518, 22 N. E. R. 24. The fact that a vote of the people of a town for the issuing of railroad aid bonds, pursuant to lawful authority, was upon the condition that the road build its shops in the town, will not invalidate the bonds, the purpose for which they were issued not being changed by such condition. Casey v. People, 132 Ill. 546.

[3] Tucker v. New Hampshire Sav. Bank, 58 N. H. 83; Board v. Texas, etc., R. Co., 46 Tex. 316; County of Warren v. Marcy, 97 U. S. 96; County of Cass v. Gillett, 100 U. S. 585; Winston v. Westfeldt, 22 Ala. 760; Kieffer v. Ehler, 18 Pa.St. 388; Stone v. Elliott, 11 Ohio St. 252; Leitch v. Wells, 48 N. Y. 586.

[4] Ruhey v. Shain, 54 Mo. 207.

fense to an action by an innocent holder upon bonds issued after its completion.[1]

§ 883. **Proceedings of municipal officers must conform to the statute.**—Where there is no estoppel the rule is that the officers of the municipality must in all material respects obey the requirements of the enabling act.[2] Thus the provisions of the act in respect to elections, petitions, and the like must be complied with, but unimportant deviations from the act will not invalidate the bonds.[3] But it is to be kept in mind that where, as is generally true, third persons have purchased the bonds, the question as to whether there has been a compliance with the provisions of the statute is seldom of practical importance since the doctrine of estoppel cuts off inquiry.

§ 884. **Want of power—Definition.**—Confusion has arisen from a failure to discriminate between a want of power and an irregular or defective exercise of power. In considering the doctrine of *ultra vires* we pointed out the distinction between a want of power and a defective or irregular exercise of power conferred by statute. It is difficult to precisely define the meaning of the term "want of power" as used in relation to the rights of *bona fide* holders of municipal bonds. Judge Dillon, whose learning and ability always command respect, says that the term means "the want of legislative power, under any

---

[1] County of Daviess *v.* Huidekoper, 98 U. S. 98. Where there is an entire absence of power to issue bonds recitals therein will not estop the municipality. Hancock *v.* Chicot County, 32 Ark. 575; Anthony *v.* Jasper County, 4 Dill. 136.

[2] *Ante*, § 856.

[3] *Ante*, §§ 858, 859. As to elections see Claybrook *v.* Board, 114 N. C. 453, s. c. 19 S. E.R.593; Sampson *v.* People, 141 Ill. 17; Hill *v.* City of Memphis, 134 U. S. 198, s. c. 10 Sup. Ct. R. 562; Norton *v.* Taxing District, 129 U. S. 479, s. c. 9 Sup. Ct. R. 322. As to specifying place of hearing petition, Town of Andes *v.* Ely, 158 U. S. 312, s. c. 15 Sup. Ct. R. 954. Presumptions as to notice of elections, Knox County *v.* Ninth National Bank, 147 U. S. 91, s. c. 13 Sup. Ct. R. 267, citing Bank *v.* Dandridge, 12 Wheat. 64, 70. See, generally, Dallas County *v.* McKenzie, 110 U.S.686,s.c. 4 Sup.Ct.R. 184; Town of Oregon *v.* Jennings, 119 U.S. 74, s. c. 7 Sup. Ct. R. 124; Carroll Co. *v.* Smith, 111 U. S. 556, s. c. 4. Sup. Ct. R. 539; Gilson *v.* Town of Dayton, 123 U. S. 59, s. c. 8 Sup. Ct. R. 66; Grenada Co. Super. *v.* Brogden, 112 U. S. 261, s. c. 5 Sup. Ct. R. 125.

circumstances or conditions, to do the particular act in question."[1] This definition is, perhaps, as good as can be framed, but it is, we venture to say with great deference, somewhat broader than the decisions warrant. It is unquestionably true, however, that there are cases holding that there is a "want of power," although there is a general statute conferring authority. The definition we have quoted will not always apply, nor can any general definition be formulated upon which it will be safe to act in all cases.

§ 885. **Conflict of authority.**—Upon the question as to what shall be deemed "want of authority" there is much conflict of opinion. There is, it is evident, a failure on the part of some of the courts to discriminate between an entire absence of power and a defective exercise of a power conferred by statute. The decisions of many of the state courts are not in harmony with those of the United States courts above cited, for the reason that a failure to observe the precedent conditions imposed, which the latter hold to be a defective exercise of an existing power, is in many cases held by the former to prevent such power from vesting in the municipality or its officers.[2] Some of the decisions referred to in the note confuse the want of power with a defective exercise of power and the courts have fallen into error.

§ 886. **Consolidation does not take away right to bonds.**— The general rule that a consolidated company succeeds to the rights of the constituent companies requires the conclusion

---

[1] Dillon on Munic. Corp. (4th ed.), § 548.

[2] Mercer County v. Pittsburgh, etc., R. Co., 27 Pa. St. 389; City of Aurora v. West, 22 Ind. 88; Marshall County v. Cook, 38 Ill. 44; City of St. Louis v. Alexander, 23 Mo. 483; Hancock v. Chicot Co., 32 Ark. 575; Veeder v. Lima, 19 Wis. 280; State v. Goshen Tp., 14 Ohio St. 569. In Williams v. People, 132 Ill. 574, the court, in an opinion holding that bonds issued by authority of an election held without proper notice are void even in the hands of innocent purchasers, says: "Persons purchasing such bonds are bound to take notice of the provisions of acts of the legislature authorizing the election and the subscription, and of the proceedings on record in the county court in relation thereto, and of the requirements of the fundamental law upon the subject."

that aid bonds voted to one of the constituent companies belong to the consolidated company. It is necessary, of course, for the consolidated company to possess the substantial rights of the constituent company to which it is voted to the extent, at least, that it may build and operate the line of road for which the aid was granted. The authorities are in substantial agreement upon the general question,[1] but there are cases which hold that, under peculiar statutes, the consolidated company is not entitled to the bonds.[2] There are other cases which hold that a consolidation which works such a fundamental change as to release stockholders will deprive the consolidated company of a right to the bonds.[3]

[1] City of Columbus v. Dennison, 69 Fed. R. 58; Livingston County v. First National Bank, 128 U. S. 102, s. c. 9 Sup. Ct. R. 18; State v. Greene County, 54 Mo. 540; County of Scotland v. Thomas, 94 U. S. 682; Town of East Lincoln v. Davenport, 94 U. S. 801; County of Bates v. Winters, 97 U. S. 83; Wilson v. Salamanca, 99 U. S. 499; Menasha v. Hazard, 102 U. S. 81; Harter v. Kernochan, 103 U. S. 562; New Buffalo v. Iron, etc., Co., 105 U. S. 73; Empire v. Darlington, 101 U. S. 87; County of Tipton v. Locomotive Works, 103 U. S. 523; County of Henry v. Nicolay, 95 U. S. 619; Nugent v. Supervisors, 19 Wall. 241; Atchison, etc., R. Co. v. Phillips Co., 25 Kan. 261; City of Mt. Vernon v. Hovey, 52 Ind. 563; Scott v. Hansheer, 94 Ind. 1; Jussen v. Board, 95 Ind. 567. It has been held that a company which purchases the road of the company to which the aid is granted can not secure bonds. Board v. State, 115 Ind. 64. See Cantillon v. Dubuque, etc., R. Co., 78 Iowa 48, s. c. 35 N. W. R. 620; Nelson v. Haywood County, 87 Tenn. 781; Manning v. Mathews, 66 Iowa 675; Barthel v. Meader, 72 Iowa 125; Southern Kansas R. Co. v. Towner, 41 Kan. 72; Chicago, etc., Co. v. Shea, 67 Iowa 728; Sparrow v. Evansville, etc., R. Co., 7 Ind. 369; Bishop v. Brainerd, 28 Conn. 289; Schenectady, etc., Co. v. Thatcher, 11 N. Y. 102; Buffalo, etc., Co. v. Dudley, 14 N. Y. 336; South Bay, etc., Co. v. Gray, 30 Me. 547; Terre Haute, etc., R. Co. v. Earp, 21 Ill. 291; Illinois, etc., R. Co. v. Beers, 27 Ill. 185; Noyes v. Spaulding, 27 Vt. 420; Pacific, etc., R. Co. v. Renshaw, 18 Mo. 210; Fry v. Lexington, 2 Metcf. (Ky.) 314; Agricultural, etc., R. Co. v. Winchester, 13 Allen 29.

[2] Harshman v. Bates County, 92 U. S. 569; County of Bates v. Winters, 97 U. S. 83. See Marsh v. Fulton County, 10 Wall. 676.

[3] Lynch v. Eastern etc., R. Co., 57 Wis. 430. It is upon this principle that it is held that where a company sells all of its property the right to aid bonds is lost. Cantillon v. Dubuque, etc., R. Co., 78 Iowa 48, s. c. 35 N. W. R. 620. But where there is nothing more than a mere change of name the right to the bonds is not impaired. Society, etc., v. New London, 29 Conn. 174. See, also, Howard County v. Booneville, etc., Bank, 108 U. S. 314; Commonwealth v. Pittsburgh, 41 Pa. St. 278; Lewis v. Claren-

§ 887. **Purchasers of aid bonds—Duty to ascertain that power to issue bonds exists.**—As we shall hereafter show, the doctrine of estoppel exerts an important influence upon the rights of holders of municipal aid bonds, but this doctrine will not protect such holders where there is an entire want of power to issue the bonds. It is the duty of persons who are about to become purchasers of municipal aid bonds to ascertain whether the municipality had power to issue them.[1] It is obvious that, as the question of power or no power depends upon the decision of the question whether there was a valid statute authorizing the issue of the bonds, the purchaser must at his peril ascertain whether there is or is not such a statute.

§ 888. **Bonds issued in excess of the limits prescribed by the constitution.**—The authorities make a distinction between cases where bonds to an amount beyond that limited by the constitution are issued and cases where the limit prescribed by statute is exceeded. The rule in relation to bonds issued beyond the constitutional limit is that they are void even in the hands of a *bona fide* holder. The rule goes further, for it denies that there can be an estoppel in cases where the limit prescribed by the constitution is exceeded.[2] We believe the rule to rest on solid principle, but it is somewhat difficult to perceive why the same rule should not apply where the bonds exceed the limits prescribed by statute. Where aid bonds are issued in violation of the constitution, there can be no recov-

---

don, 5 Dill. 329; Chickaming *v.* Carpenter, 106 U. S. 663; Chicago, etc., R. Co. *v.* Putnam, 36 Kan. 121, s. c. 12 Pac. R. 593; Rochester, etc., R. Co. *v.* Cuyler, 7 Lans. 431; Taylor *v.* Board, 86 Va. 506; Muscatine, etc., R. Co. *v.* Horton, 38 Iowa 33.

[1] Dixon County *v.* Field, 111 U. S. 83, s. c. 4 Sup. Ct. R. 315; Town of Coloma *v.* Eaves, 92 U. S. 484, 490; Marst *v.* Fulton County, 10 Wall. 676; Northern Nat. Bank *v.* Porter Township, 110 U. S. 608, 615, s. c. 4 Sup. Ct. R. 524; Anthony *v.* County of Jasper, 101 U. S. 693, 697; McClure *v.* Township of Oxford, 94 U. S. 429.

[2] Hedges *v.* Dixon County, 150 U. S. 182, s. c. 14 Sup. Ct. R. 71, 9 Am. R. & Corp. R. (Lewis) 520; Hedges *v.* Dixon County, 37 Fed. R. 304; Buchanan *v.* Litchfield 102 U. S. 278 Quaker City Nat. Bank *v.* Nolan County, 59 Fed. R. 660; Millsaps *v.* City of Terrell, 60 Fed. R. 193; Risley *v.* Village of Howell, 57 Fed. R. 544. See State *v.* Town of Columbia, 111 Mo. 365, s. c. 20 S. W. R. 90.

ery against the municipality upon an implied contract.[1] The advantages derived from the construction of the railroad do not constitute such an equitable consideration as will entitle the bondholders to relief.

§ 889. **Limitation of amount—Construction of statute.—** Where the constitution limits the amount of aid which may be granted it is, of course, controlling, and bonds issued in excess of the amount fixed by the constitution can not be enforced. The legislative power is limited by such a constitutional provision, and, as everyone knows, if the legislature assumes to transgress the provisions of the constitution its enactments are void, but where a statute can be so construed as to prevent its being brought into conflict with the constitution, the courts will so construe it provided the construction be at all reasonable.[2] This general doctrine supports the ruling in the case wherein it was held that where the constitution limited the amount of aid to a designated per cent. of the taxable property a statute providing that aid "to any amount" might be granted was not invalid, insomuch as the courts must construe the statute to mean any amount within the constitutional limitation.[3]

---

[1] Hedges v. Dixon County, 150 U. S. 182, s. c. 14 Sup. Ct. R. 71, citing Magniac v. Thomson, 15 How. 281; Ætna Life Insurance Co. v. Middleport, 124 U. S. 534, s. c. 8 Sup. Ct. R. 625; City of Litchfield v. Ballou, 114 U. S. 190, s. c. 5 Sup. Ct. R. 820.

[2] Ferguson v. Borough of Stamford, 60 Conn. 432; Jamieson v. Indiana, etc., Co., 128 Ind. 555, 569; Dow v. Norris, 4 N. H. 16, 18; Cooley's Const. (6th ed.) 218.

[3] Atlantic, etc., Co. v. Town of Darlington, 63 Fed. R. 76, 82. In the course of the opinion it was said: "Is it in conflict with section 17, article 9, because no limit is fixed as to the amount of aid to be given to railroads? The constitution and the act must be read in *pari materia.* The legislature must be presumed to have enacted the act in view of the constitution. It can not be assumed that the legislature went in the teeth of the constitution. Such a construction must be put on this act as will reconcile it with the constitution. '*Ut res magis valeat quam pereat.*' We must hold it to mean, 'may issue bonds in any amount within the constitutional limitation.' As a conclusion of law, the act is not in conflict with section 17, article 9, in this respect." The judgment in the case from which we have quoted was affirmed in Town of Darlington v. Atlantic, etc., Co., 68 Fed. R. 849, where the cases of State v. Neely, 30 So. Car. 587, s. c. 9 S. E. R. 664; Floyd v. Perrin, 30 So.

§ 890. **Bonds in excess of the limit prescribed by statute.**— As we have said, a distinction is made between bonds issued in excess of the constitutional limit and bonds issued beyond the limit prescribed by statute, and it is held in the one case that there can be no estoppel, but that there may be in the other. Where bonds are issued in excess of the amount limited by statute and there is no estoppel, the bonds are void, although purchased before maturity and for a valuable consideration.[1] The prevailing rule is that all of the bonds are void where there is no estoppel and they are beyond the limit fixed by law.[2] It is held, however, that if the municipality authorizes an issue of the proper amount, but the officers wrongfully issue a greater amount than that authorized, the bonds are not all void.[3]

Car. 1, s. c. 8 S. E. R. 14, and State v. Whitesides, 30 So. Car. 579, s. c. 9 S. E. R. 661, are reviewed.

[1] Merchants' Bank v. Bergen County, 115 U. S. 384; Buchanan v. Litchfield, 102 U. S. 278; Dixon County v. Field, 111 U. S. 83; Lake County v. Graham, 130 U. S. 674; Gould v. Paris, 68 Tex. 511, s. c. 17 Am. & Eng. Corp. Cas. 340; Cumins v. Lawrence County, 1 So. Dak. 158, s. c. 46 N. W. R. 182.

[2] Hedges v. Dixon County, 37 Fed. R. 304; Reineman v. Covington, etc., R. Co., 7 Neb. 310. See McPherson v. Foster, 43 Iowa 48, s. c. 22 Am. R. 215; Hedges v. Dixon County, 150 U. S. 182, s. c. 14 Sup. Ct. R. 71, 9 Am. R. & Corp. R. (Lewis) 520; Reynolds, etc., Co. v. Police Jury, 44 La. Ann. 863, s. c. 11 So. R. 236; Borough of Millerstown v. Frederick, 114 Pa. St. 435. See City of Iola v. Merriman, 46 Kan. 49; Perrin v. New London, 67 Wis. 416.

[3] In Hedges v. Dixon County, 37 Fed. R. 304, it was said: "Counsel cites the case of Daviess County v. Dickinson, 117 U. S. 657, in which the county having authority to issue bonds to the amount of $250,000, the county officers issued $320,000, and the county was held liable for the $250,000, but the cases were not all parallel. In that the principal had proposed a valid contract. It had done that which it had a right to do, and the wrong or misconduct of its agents, the county officers, was held not to invalidate that which the county had lawfully authorized. In this there is no breach of duty charged upon the county officers. The agents have not departed from their instructions. The trouble lies in the action of the principal itself. Its act was unauthorized, and, being without warrant of law, or rather in defiance of law, created no valid obligation." In the case of Hedges v. Dixon County, 154 U. S. 182, affirming judgment below, the cases of Louisiana v. Wood, 102 U. S. 294; Read v. City of Plattsmouth, 107 U. S. 568; Daviess County v. Dickinson, 117 U. S. 657, were distinguished, and the court said: "Recitals in bonds issued under legislative authority may estop

§ 891. **Bonds running** beyond time prescribed.—The highest tribunal of the nation has held that where the enabling act provides that bonds shall be payable in a designated number of years, the municipality has no power to issue bonds payable after a longer period, and that the bonds are void.[1] The reasoning of the court is that the limitation is a restriction upon the power of the municipality, and so operates to invalidate the bonds. We believe this doctrine to be sound, but it is difficult to harmonize it with some of the rules declared in other cases.

§ 892. **Bonds payable out of a specific fund.**—Where a specific fund is provided by statute for the payment of the bonds, and the bonds on their face convey notice of the purpose for which they were issued and of the statute under which they are issued, purchasers are bound to take notice of the provisions of the statute and can not treat the bonds as the general obligations of the municipality. But it is not of itself sufficient to take from the bonds the character of general obligations of the municipal corporation that they show on their

---

the municipality from disputing their authority, as against a *bona fide* holder *for* value, but when the municipal bonds are issued in violation of a constitutional provision no such estoppel can arise by reason of any recitals contained in the bonds." Lake County v. Rollins, 130 U. S. 662, s. c. 9 Sup. Ct. R. 651; Lake County v. Graham, 130 U. S. 674, s. c. 9 Sup. Ct. R. 654; Sutliff v. Lake County Commissioners, 147 U. S. 230, s. c. 13 Sup. Ct. R. 318.

[1] Barnum v. Town of Okolona, 148 U. S. 393. In the case cited it was said: "That municipal corporations have no power to issue bonds in aid of a railroad except by legislative permission; that the legislature, in granting permission to a municipality to issue its bonds in aid of a railroad, may impose such conditions as it may choose; and that such legislative permission does not carry with it authority to execute negotiable bonds except subject to the restrictions and conditions of the enabling act—are propositions so well settled by frequent decisions of this court that we need not pause to consider them. Sheboygan Co. v. Parker, 3 Wall. 93, 96; Wells v. Supervisors, 102 U. S. 625; Claiborne Co. v. Brooks, 111 U. S. 400, 4 Sup. Ct. R. 489; Young v. Clarendon Township, 132 U. S. 340, 10 Sup. Ct. R. 107. Accordingly, if in the present instance, the legislature of Mississippi, in authorizing the town of Okolona to subscribe for stock in a railroad company and to pay for the same by an issue of bonds, prescribed that such bonds should not extend beyond ten years from the date of issuance, such limitation must be regarded as in the nature of a restriction on the power to issue bonds. Norton v. Dyersburg, 127 U.

face that they were issued for a special purpose.[1] If, however, the purpose for which the bonds are issued appears on their face, and the statute under which they are issued is referred to and that statute expressly provides that they shall be payable out of a special fund, and limits the power to tax to particular persons or property they can not be enforced as general obligations of the municipality.[2]

§ 893. Performance of conditions.—We have elsewhere shown that the conditions imposed by the enabling act must be substantially performed.[3] It is evident that, as the authority of the municipality depends upon the enabling act, the requirements of the act must be obeyed. The authority is not, as we have repeatedly said, general, but is an express statutory authority. It is generally held that if the preliminary conditions necessary to give jurisdiction to issue the bonds have not been fully performed, their issue may be enjoined at the suit of a tax-payer,[4] provided there are no facts creating an estoppel. So it is held that payment of such bonds may be enjoined after their issue at the suit of one or more of the tax-payers, if the suit is brought while the bonds remain in the hands of the railroad company to which they were originally issued.[5] But

S. 160, 8 Sup. Ct. R. 1111; City of Brenham v. German-American Bank, 144 U. S. 173, 12 Sup. Ct. R. 559."

[1] Olcott v. Supervisors, 16 Wall. 678; United States v. County of Clark, 95 U. S. 769, s. c. 96 U. S. 211; Supervisors v. United States, 18 Wall. 71; County of Macon v. Huidekoper, 99 U. S. 592, note; Knox County v. Harshman, 109 U. S. 229.

[2] United States v. County of Macon, 99 U. S. 582; United States v. Macon County Ct., 35 Fed. R. 483; State v. Macon County Ct., 68 Mo. 29; Braun v. Board, 66 Fed. R. 476, s. c. 70 Fed. R. 369; Strieb v. Cox, 111 Ind. 299, s.c. 12 N. E. R. 481. But see Kimball v. Board, 21 Fed. R. 145; Fowler v. City of Superior, 85 Wis. 411, s. c. 54 N. W. R. 800; State v. Commissioners of Fayette County, 37 Ohio St. 526.

[3] Ante, §§ 856, 858, 859.

[4] Redd v. Henry County, 31 Gratt. (Va.) 695; Wagner v. Meety, 69 Mo. 150; Lawson v. Schnellen, 33 Wis. 288; Wright v. Bishop, 88 Ill. 302; Daviess County Court v. Howard, 13 Bush (Ky.) 101; Town of Wellsborough v. New York, etc., R. Co., 76 N. Y. 182. See State v. City of Morristown, 93 Tenn. 239; Board v. Chesapeake, etc., Railroad, 94 Ky. 377. There may be acts creating an effective estoppel, and there may also be a conclusive adjudication upon jurisdictional facts which will repel a collateral attack. Ante, §§ 865, 871.

[5] Mercer County v. Pittsburgh, etc., R.

even as to the railroad company the doctrine of estoppel may often be available. So, too, the enforcement of the bonds may sometimes be enjoined while they are in the hands of a purchaser with notice.[1]

§ 894. Ratification of bonds irregularly issued.—The weight of authority is that the municipality may, where it has power to issue bonds, ratify them by subsequent action although the proceedings were irregular or defective. But where a vote of the inhabitants is required in order to authorize the execution of bonds the municipal officers can not, of their own motion, validate bonds issued in cases where the proceedings prior to the election were substantially defective. There may, however, be such acts on the part of the representatives of the munici-

Co., 27 Pa. St. 389; Nefzger v. Davenport, etc., R. Co., 36 Iowa 642; New Orleans, etc., R. Co. v. Dunn, 51 Ala. 128; Campbell v. Paris, etc., R. Co., 71 Ill. 611; Winston v. Tennessee, etc., R. Co., 1 Baxt. (Tenn.) 60; Redd v. Henry County, 31 Gratt. (Va.) 695. Where, under the law of its organization, a railroad company becomes extinct for failure to begin construction, municipal bonds issued in its aid become void in the hands of itself and its agent, at the date of its extinction. Farnham v. Benedict, 107 N. Y. 159, s. c. 13 N. E. 784. Where no part of the road was built in the township as required by the enabling act it was held that the railroad company was not entitled to the bonds. Township of Midland v. County Board, 37 Neb. 582, s. c. 56 N. W. R. 582. See State v. City of Morristown, 93 Tenn. 239, s. c. 24 S. W. R. 13; Echols v. City of Bristol, 90 Va. 165, s. c. 17 S. E. R. 943.

[1] A town for which railroad aid bonds have been issued may sue in equity to restrain the payment of interest, and to require them to be surrendered and canceled, and the town need not await a suit on the bonds in order to deny their validity. Town of Cherry Creek v. Becker, 2 N. Y. Supp. 514. The court will, in a proper case, decree the cancellation of bonds illegally issued. Town of Springport v. Teutonia Savings Bank, 75 N. Y. 397. But an injunction to restrain payment of bonds after they have been issued will not be granted unless the municipality has a valid defense to them. Wilkinson v. City of Peru, 61 Ind. 1. Where, by the statute, a tax-payer is authorized to sue to prevent the payment of certain railroad aid bonds, it is no defense to the suit that the objection set up as a ground for canceling the bonds might be shown as a defense in a suit on the bonds. Strang v. Cook, 47 Hun 46. Where the statute provides that the president of the company shall give bond to secure the application of the avails of bonds issued by a municipal corporation, the fact that the president does not execute such a bond does not invalidate the aid bonds where the road is completed before their delivery. Breckinridge County v. McCracken, 61 Fed. R. 191.

§ 895.   MUNICIPAL AID BONDS.   1231

pality as will constitute an estoppel.[1] Acts of the municipality or its officers when invested with authority,[2] or of the legislature, ratifying and making valid a municipal subscription, may validate the bonds issued in payment thereof.[3]

§ 895. When bonds are void.—We have heretofore shown that bonds issued in cases where there is an entire absence of power can not be enforced even by one who has bought them in good faith, and this is substantially equivalent to saying that they are void, but we do not mean to say that bonds issued without statutory authority are incapable of ratification by an effective curative statute. We employ the term "void" in this connection in the sense in which it is often used, although the term "voidable" would, perhaps, be the more

[1] Ante, §§ 843, 844, 845; Treadway v. Schnauber, 1 Dak. 236; Town of Andes v. Ely, 158 U. S. 312, s. c. 15 Sup. Ct. R. 954, citing Williams v. Town of Duanesburgh, 66 N. Y. 129; Horton v. Thompson, 71 N. Y. 513; Rogers v. Stephens, 86 N. Y. 623.

[2] Marcy v. Oswego, 92 U. S. 637; Converse v. City of Fort Scott, 92 U. S. 503; County of Randolph v. Post, 93 U. S. 502; Orleans v. Platt, 99 U. S. 676; Gause v. Clarksville, 1 Fed. R. 353.

[3] County of Bates v. Winters, 97 U. S. 83; Town of South Ottawa v. Perkins, 94 U.S. 260; St. Joseph Tp. v. Rogers, 16 Wall. (U. S.) 644; January v. Johnson County, 3 Dill. (U. S.) 392; City of Bridgeport v. Housatonic R. Co., 15 Conn. 475; Alexander v. McDowell County, 70 N. Car. 208; Sykes v. Columbus, 55 Miss. 115; Shelby County Ct. v. Cumberland, etc., R. Co.,8 Bush (Ky.) 209; Keithsburg v. Frick, 34 Ill. 405. Where railroad aid bonds were issued after the adoption of the Illinois constitution of 1870, which forbade the issuance of such bonds except where they had been authorized before such adoption by a vote of the people under "existing laws," but such bonds were authorized at an election irregularly held, which, however, was ratified by the legislature before the adoption of the constitution, such ratification does not validate the bonds issued after the constitution was adopted, since the "existing laws" referred to in the constitution are the laws in force when the election was held. Williams v. People, 132 Ill. 574, disapproving Jonesboro City v. Cairo, etc., Railroad Co., 110 U.S. 192. But an act which declares the aid proposed to be given to be a debt on the township, and provides for its payment, but does not validate the bonds illegally issued under a void vote to give such aid, and does not legalize the proceedings by which such bonds were issued, will not entitle the railroad company to a writ of mandamus to compel the township officers to sign a certificate of the completion of the road by means of which the company may obtain delivery of the bonds. State v. Whitesides, 30 S. Car. 579, s. c. 9 S. E. R. 661; State v. Harper, 30 S. Car. 586.

accurate one. We think that where there is legislative power to authorize a municipality to issue bonds, but the bonds are issued without a statutory grant of power, they are not absolutely void, that is to say, they are not "a mere nothing incapable of ratification" by legislative enactment. Bonds issued without statutory authority[1] or by authority of an unconstitutional statute[2] are often said to be void, even in the hands of *bona fide* purchasers,[3] and that no recitals which they contain can so estop the municipality as to give them validity. We say, to avoid possible misunderstanding, that bonds which can be ratified are not, in the strict sense, void, but bonds that can

---

[1] German Savings Bank v. Franklin County, 128 U. S. 526; Purdy v. Lansing, 128 U. S. 557; Ottawa v. Carey, 108 U. S. 110; Citizens etc., Loan Assoc. v. Topeka, 20 Wall. (U. S.) 655; St. Joseph Tp. v. Rogers, 16 Wall. (U. S.) 644; Aspinwall v. Commissioners, 22 How. (U. S.) 364; Borough of Millerstown v. Frederick, 114 Pa. St. 435; Duke v. Brown, 96 N. Car. 127; Eddy v. People, 127 Ill. 428; Williamson v. Keokuk, 44 Iowa 88; Sykes v. Columbus, 55 Miss. 115; Agawam Nat. Bank v. South Hadley, 128 Mass. 503.

[2] Harshman v. Bates County, 92 U. S. 569; Wells v. Supervisors, 102 U.S.625; Ogden v. County of Daviess, 102 U. S. 634; Allen v. Louisiana, 103 U. S. 80; Jarbolt v. Moberly, 103 U. S. 580; Howard County v. Paddock, 110 U. S. 384. Since the constitution of Missouri requires the consent of two-thirds of the qualified voters before a municipality can grant aid to a railroad, a statute is void which assumes to give authority to issue bonds without any vote. Hill v. Memphis, 134 U. S. 198. The United States courts have held the "Township Aid Act" of Missouri of March 23, 1868, to be constitutional and that bonds issued by authority of that act are valid. County of Cass v. Johnston, 95 U. S. 360. And this decision was adhered to after the supreme court of Missouri in State v. Brassfield, 67 Mo. 331, had held the act unconstitutional. Foote v. Johnson County, 5 Dillon (U. S.) 281. This being the case it is held that bonds issued under the act are proper subjects of compromise, and a tax levied to pay such compromise bonds issued under 2 Rev. St. Mo. 1879, p. 848, is valid. State v. Hannibal & St. J. R. Co., 101 Mo. 136.

[3] A distinction is taken between an entire absence of power to issue bonds and a defective execution of an existing power, acts done under the latter being held to bind the corporation in certain cases, while acts done in the absence of power to perform them never do. German, etc., Bank v. Franklin County, 128 U. S. 526; St. Joseph Township v. Rogers, 16 Wall. (U. S.) 644; and cases cited *supra*. In Northern Bank of Toledo v. Porter Township, 110 U. S. 608, the court says: "The question of legislative authority in a municipal corporation to issue bonds in aid of a railroad company, can not be concluded by mere recitals; but, the power existing, the municipality may be estopped by the recitals to prove irregularity in the exercise of that power."

not be ratified by legislative enactment are absolutely void. It is, therefore, strictly accurate to say that bonds issued in violation of the constitution are absolutely void. Upon the principle that an act which violates the constitution is entirely destitute of force, the federal courts hold that an issue of bonds in excess of the limit of indebtedness prescribed by the state constitution is void, and that no acts of the municipality, nor any recitals which may appear in the bonds, can give such bonds any validity.[1] The distinction which is made between such a case and the cases where an issue of bonds is allowed only upon certain conditions prescribed by statute has been thus stated: "In this case the standard of validity is created by the constitution. * * * These being the exactions of the constitution itself it is not within the power of the legislature to dispense with them, either directly or indirectly, by the creation of a ministerial commission whose finding shall be taken in lieu of the facts."[2]

[1] Buchanan v. Litchfield, 102 U. S. 278; Dixon County v.Field,111 U.S.83; Litchfield v. Ballou, 114 U. S. 190; Katzenberger v. Aberdeen, 121 U. S. 172; Lake County v. Rollins, 130 U. S. 662. Where an issue of county bonds for donation to a railroad has been adjudged void because in excess of the constitutional limit of indebtedness, equity has no power to reduce the issue to the limit, and enforce it against the county, the contract being indivisible, and void *in toto*, and there being no executed consideration to support an implied promise. Hedges v. Dixon County, 37 Fed. Rep. 304.

[2] Lake County v. Graham, 130 U. S. 674. The reasons here assigned would seem to cover a failure to observe any other precedent conditions prescribed by the constitution, such as a failure to hold a required election, etc. See Hill v. Memphis, 134 U. S. 198. An agreement entered into between a railway company and the authorities of a town, upon petition of a majority of the tax-payers in pursuance of the laws of Minnesota, for the issuance of the bonds of such town, but which was not submitted to a vote as required by a section of the law, is invalid, and imposes no legal obligation upon the town, by reason of the unconstitutionality of the statute; and the town in its corporate capacity, is not estopped to resist the enforcement of bonds so issued by the completion of a line of railroad under the agreement by such company. Town of Plainview v. Winona & St. P. R. Co., 36 Minn. 505, 32 N. W. 745; Town of Elgin v. Winona & St. P. R. Co., 36 Minn. 517, 32 N. W. 749; Harrington v. Plainview, 27 Minn. 224, 6 N. W. Rep. 777. Under the law of Mississippi, which declares that the legislature 'shall not authorize any county, city, or town to aid any corporation, unless two-thirds of the qualified voters of such municipality shall assent thereto at a special election, it was held railroad aid bonds were not invalidated in the hands of innocent purchasers by the fact that less than

§ 896. **Bona fide holders of aid bonds.**—The courts have gone very far in protecting *bona fide* holders of aid bonds. They have extended the doctrine of estoppel to great lengths for the protection of that class of persons. They have also liberally construed statutes in order to give validity to bonds in the hands of *bona fide* holders, and the federal courts have held that where a state court gives a construction to a statute which upholds the bonds, it will not be allowed to change its decision so as to invalidate the bonds in the hands of a *bona fide* holder who had acquired the bonds while the earlier decision was in force.[1] "To be a *bona fide* holder, one must be himself a purchaser for value without notice, or the successor of one who was. Every man is chargeable with notice of that which the law requires him to know, and of that which, after being put upon inquiry, he might have ascertained with reasonable diligence. Every dealer in municipal bonds, which upon their face refer to the statute under which they are issued, is bound to take notice of the statute and its requirements."[2] The general rule is that no one can claim to be a *bona fide* holder when the bonds themselves contain recitals showing that they were not issued in accordance with any existing law.[3] Thus, where the bonds recited that they were

such majority voted for them, where more than two-thirds of the votes cast were in favor of issuing the bonds. Madison County *v.* Priestly, 42 Fed. R. 817.

[1] Douglass *v.* County of Pike, 101 U. S. 677; Gelpcke *v.* Dubuque, 1 Wall. 175; Taylor *v.* Ypsilanti, 105 U. S. 60; Insurance Co. *v.* De Bolt, 16 How. 115; Anderson *v.* Santa Anna, 116 U. S. 356.

[2] McClure *v.* Township of Oxford, 94 U. S. 429. In the case cited the purchaser of bonds was held bound to take notice of the time the enabling act went into force. In the course of the opinion it was said, "The statute under which the bonds now in question were issued, and which is referred to in the bonds, though passed and approved March 1, 1872, was not by its terms to go into effect until after its publication in the 'Kansas Weekly Commonwealth.' Of this every purchaser of the bonds had notice, because it was part of the statute he was bound to take notice of. A purchaser would, therefore, be put upon inquiry as to the time of the publication, and by reasonable diligence could have ascertained that this did not take place until March 21. This being the case, the law charges him with knowledge that the statute did not go into effect until that date."

[3] Harshman *v.* Bates County, 92 U. S. 569; McClure *v.* Township of Ox-

issued under a statute which had been declared to be void, it was held that such a recital was notice to the purchaser of their invalidity.[1] But such a recital will not prevent the holder of the bonds from showing that they were really issued by authority of a different act than the one referred to, in which case they may be valid.[2]

§ 897. Estoppel by recitals in bonds—General doctrine.—The courts regard with favor *bona fide* holders of aid bonds, and liberally apply the doctrine of estoppel, in order to protect such holders. Recitals are given great force and effect. It is an established rule in the United States courts, where most of the litigation involving the validity of such bonds is carried on, that where power exists to issue bonds upon certain conditions, and the question of compliance with those conditions is left to the officers issuing the bonds for decision, or where the existence of the facts warranting an exercise of the power is peculiarly within the knowledge of such officers, the munici-

ford, 94 U. S. 429; County of Bates v. Winters, 97 U. S. 83; Anthony v. County of Jasper, 101 U. S. 693; Barnes v. Lacon, 84 Ill. 461; Johnson v. Butler, 31 La. Ann. 770; Woodruff v. Okolona, 57 Miss. 806; Dodge v. County of Platte, 82 N. Y. 218.

[1] Gilson v. Dayton, 123 U. S. 59; Crow v. Oxford, 119 U. S. 215. In this latter case it is held that the certificate of the state auditor, as to matters which he was not authorized by the statute under which the bonds were issued to certify, is of no avail against the municipality, although it procured such certificate to be indorsed upon the bonds. The New York act of 1869 was amended in 1871, so as to authorize the issuance of railroad aid bonds upon the petition of a majority of the tax-payers "who are taxed or assessed for property, not including those taxed for dogs or highway tax only, upon the last preceding assessment roll, * * and who * * * represent a majority of the taxable property." It was held, in a suit to enforce bonds issued after the amended act was passed, that a petition, after the enactment of the later statute which followed the language of the act of 1869, and did not show that petitioners were a majority of the tax-payers exclusive of those "taxed for dogs or highways only," conferred no power on the county judge, and an adjudication thereon which was similarly defective, and bonds issued on it, which recited that they were issued under the act of 1869, were void. Rich v. Town of Mentz, 134 U. S. 632, 10 Sup. Ct. R. 610.

[2] Anderson County Commrs. v. Beal, 113 U. S. 227; Ninth Nat. Bank v. Knox County, 37 Fed. R. 75; Knox County v. Ninth National Bank, 147 U. S. 91, s. c. 13 Sup. Ct. R. 267.

pality will be bound by the recital of the bonds as to such matters.[1] The rule has been thus stated· "Where legislative authority has been given to a municipality, or to its officers, to subscribe for the stock of a railroad company, and to issue municipal bonds in payment, but only on some precedent condition, such as a popular vote favoring the subscription, and where it may be gathered from the legislative enactment that the officers of the municipality were invested with powers to decide whether the condition has been complied with, their recital that it has been made in the bonds issued by them and held by a *bona fide* purchaser, is conclusive of the fact and binding upon the municipality, for the recital itself is a decision of the fact by the appointed tribunal."[2] The doctrine of the federal tribunals is very generally adopted and asserted by the state courts.[3]

[1] New Providence *v.* Halsey, 117 U. S. 336; Menasha *v.* Hazard, 102 U. S. 81; Pompton *v.* Cooper Union, 101 U. S. 196; Hackett *v.* Ottawa, 99 U. S. 86; County of Daviess *v.* Huidekoper, 98 U. S. 98; County of Warren *v.* Marcy, 97 U. S. 96; San Antonio *v.* Mehaffy, 96 U. S. 312; Comrs. of Douglas County *v.* Bolles, 94 U. S. 104; Town of Coloma *v.* Eaves, 92 U. S. 484; Mayor, etc., of Columbus *v.* Dennison, 69 Fed. R. 58; Block *v.* Commissioners, 99 U. S. 686; Commissioners *v.* January, 94 U. S. 202; Commissioners *v.* Clark, 94 U. S. 278; Brooklyn *v.* Insurance, 99 U. S. 362; Moran *v.* Commissioners, 2 Black 722.

[2] Town of Coloma *v.* Eaves, 92 U. S. 484; Buchanan *v.* Litchfield, 102 U. S. 278; Northern Bank *v.* Porter Township, 110 U. S. 608; Dixon County *v.* Field, 111 U. S. 83; Anderson County *v.* Beal, 113 U. S. 227; Phelps *v.* Lewiston, 15 Blatchf. 131; Irwin *v.* Town of Ontario, 3 Fed. Rep. 49. Where the county court has been designated by the statute as the proper authority to determine the existence of the conditions necessary to authorize the subscription by the township to the railroad company's stock, and the consequent issuance of bonds, the fact of the issue thereof by the county court under its seal, with the recital that all the necessary steps have been taken, together with the fact that the county has for several years paid interest on the bonds, estop it from setting up, as against a *bona fide* holder, any mere irregularity in making the subscription or issuing the bonds. Livingston County *v.* First Nat. Bank, 128 U. S. 102, s. c. 9 Sup. Ct. Rep. 18; Hopper *v.* Covington, 8 Fed. Rep. 777; Carrier *v.* Shawangunk, 10 Fed. Rep. 220; Anderson County *v.* Houston, etc., R. Co., 52 Tex. 228; Lane *v.* Embden, 72 Me. 354.

[3] Burlington, etc., R. Co. *v.* Stewart, 39 Iowa 267; Sauerhering *v.* Iron Ridge, etc., R. Co., 25 Wis. 447; New Haven, etc., R. Co. *v.* Chatham, 42 Conn. 465; Chicago, etc., R. Co. *v.* Shea, 67 Iowa 728; Kerr *v.* Corry, 105 Pa. St. 282; Johnson *v.* County of

§ 898.   MUNICIPAL AID BONDS.   1237

§ 898. Estoppel by recitals in bonds—Illustrative cases.—

In a recent case it was held that a recital in aid bonds estopped the municipality from questioning the qualifications of the county judge,[1] and from questioning the corporate existence of the railroad company.[2] In the case referred to the court carried the doctrine of estoppel very far, holding that the municipality was estopped, although the bonds were signed by commissioners appointed by the county judge and not by the regular municipal officers.[3] We can not escape the conclusion that the

Stark, 24 Ill. 75; Clarke v. Hancock County, 27 Ill. 305; Leavenworth, etc., R. Co. v. Comrs. of Douglass County, 18 Kan. 169; Lamb v. Burlington, etc., R. Co., 39 Iowa 333; Dodge v. County of Platte, 16 Hun 285; Jefferson County v. Lewis, 20 Fla. 980; Lane v. Emblen, 72 Me. 354; Gould v. Sterling, 23 N. Y. 456; Williams v. Roberts, 88 Ill. 11; Clark v. Janesville, 10 Wis. 136; Chicago, etc., R. Co. v. Commissioners, 49 Kan. 399, 30 Pac. R. 456; Kansas City, etc., R. Co. v. Rich. Township, 45 Kan. 275. But see Cagwin v. Hancock, 84 N. Y. 532. See, generally, State v. Commissioners, 37 Ohio St. 526; Shelby County v. Jarnagin, (Tenn.) 16 S. W. R. 1040; Gaddis v. Richland County, 92 Ill. 119; Lippincott v. Pana, 92 Ill. 24; State v. School Dist., 10 Neb. 544; Lindsey v. Rottaken, 32 Ark. 619.

[1] Town of Andes v. Ely, 158 U. S. 312, s. c. 15 Sup. Ct. R. 954. It was said in the opinion in the case cited: "But further, in view of the recitals on the bonds, are these questions open for inquiry? Ample authority was given by the statutes of the state referred to. Whether the various steps were taken, which, in this particular case, justified the issue of the bonds, was a question of fact; and when the bonds, on their face, recite that those steps have been taken, it is the settled rule of this court that in an action brought by a *bona fide* holder, the municipality is estopped from showing the contrary. See the multitude of cases commencing with Commissioners v. Aspinwall, 21 How. 539, and ending with Citizens', etc., Asso. v. Perry Co., 156 U. S. 692, s. c. 15 Sup. Ct. R. 547.

[2] In the case referred to in the preceding note the court cited, upon the point that a party contracting with a corporation is estopped to aver that it is not a corporation *de jure*, the cases of County of Leavenworth v. Barnes, 94 U. S. 70; Commissioners v. Bolles, 94 U. S. 104; Casey v. Galli, 94 U. S. 673; Chubb v. Upton, 95 U. S. 665. As to the effect of legislative recognition, the court cited Comanche County v. Lewis, 133 U. S. 198, s. c. 10 Sup. Ct. R. 286; State v. Commissioners, 12 Kan. 426; State v. Hamilton, 40 Kan. 323, s. c. 19 Pac. R. 723. See, also, County of Macon v. Shores, 97 U. S. 272, 276; Dallas County v. Huidekoper, 154 U. S. 655, s. c. 14 Sup. Ct. R. 1190; Smith v. County of Clark, 54 Mo. 58.

[3] Town of Andes v. Ely, 158 U. S. 312, s. c. 15 Sup. Ct. R. 954. It was said in the opinion that, "It may be said that those decisions are not wholly in point, inasmuch as these bonds were signed, not by regular officers, but by commissioners specially appointed, and that, before a recital made by them can be held to conclude the town,

case referred to is an extreme one, and that its doctrine should be limited rather than extended. It seems to us that where the statute provides that a municipality shall be represented by officers selected by its electors, a county judge has no authority to appoint agents to execute negotiable bonds in its behalf. It may, perhaps, be true that if the municipality secures the benefit of the bonds in tangible property or money, it should be held liable therefor, but we can not believe that the bonds can be considered as the obligations of the public corporation, unless executed by the officers constituted by law the representatives of the public corporation. If there is power to appoint corporate agents and to delegate to them authority to execute negotiable bonds in behalf of the municipality, then it may well be held that bonds executed by such agents are the obligations of the municipality. It is held that a municipality is estopped to dispute its liability upon bonds in the hands of *bona fide* holders, upon the ground that the election authorizing their issue was not properly conducted,[1] or that the per-

it must appear that they were duly appointed, and thus had authority to act. Doubtless this distinction is not without significance. Yet they were acting commissioners, and their authority was recognized, for each bond was registered in the office of the county clerk, and attested by the signature of the county clerk with the seal of the county; and if we go back of that to the records of the county judge—the appointing power—there appears a separate order in due form, appointing them commissioners, which order recites a prior adjudication of all the essential facts. Giving full force to the distinction which exists between the action of general and special officers, there must be even in respect to the latter, some point in the line of inquiry, back of which a party dealing in bonds of a municipality is not bound to go in his investigations as to their authority to represent the municipality, and that point, it would seem, was reached when there is found an appointment, in due form, made by the appointing tribunal named in the statute."

[1] Commissioners of Knox County v. Aspinwall, 21 How. (U. S.) 539; Mercer County v. Hacket, 1 Wall. (U. S.) 83; Supervisors v. Schenck, 5 Wall. (U. S.) 772; Lynde v. The County, 16 Wall. (U. S.) 6; Town of Coloma v. Eaves, 92 U. S. 484; County of Leavenworth v. Barnes, 94 U. S. 70; County of Cass v. Johnston, 95 U. S. 360; Hackett v. Ottawa, 99 U.S. 86; Anthony v. County of Jasper, 101 U. S. 693; Northern Bank v. Porter Township, 110 U. S. 608; Webb v. Commissioners of Herne Bay, L. R. 5 Q. B. 642. A recital in a bond issued in payment of a subscription to railway stock, that it is authorized by a certain statute, will not estop the municipal corporation from asserting that the issue was

§ 898   MUNICIPAL AID BONDS.   1239

sons giving their written assent did not constitute two-thirds of the resident tax-payers,[1] or that the required proportion of the voters had not signed the necessary petition,[2] or that the amount of bonds issued was a greater per cent. of the taxable valuation of the municipality than it was empowered to issue,[3] or that the proper recommendation of the grand jury as to the amount of bonds to be issued was not had,[4] where the bonds, as issued, contained a recital that such prerequisite conditions had been observed.[5] It has been held that where the bonds

not authorized by a proper vote, as required by law. Carroll County v. Smith, 111 U. S. 556. But see Commissioners v. Aspinwall, 21 How. (U. S.) 539.

[1] Town of Venice v. Murdock, 92 U. S. 494.

[2] Bissell v. Jeffersonville, 24 How. (U. S.) 287.

[3] Marcy v. Township of Oswego, 92 U. S. 637; Humboldt Township v. Long, 92 U. S. 642; New Providence v. Halsey, 117 U. S. 336; Coler v. Board of Commissioners, 27 Pac. R. 619. But where the amount to be issued was limited to a certain fixed sum, bonds containing no recitals, issued in excess of that sum, were held void for lack of power to issue them, even in the hands of *bona fide* holders. Daviess County v. Dickinson, 117 U. S. 657; Merchants' Bank v. Bergen County, 115 U. S. 384.

[4] Mercer County v. Hacket, 1 Wall. (U. S.) 83.

[5] Northern Bank v. Porter Township, 110 U. S. 608; Ottawa v. Nat. Bank, 105 U. S. 342; Menasha v. Hazard, 102 U. S. 81; Foote v. County of Pike, 101 U. S. 688, note; Douglass v. County of Pike, 101 U. S. 677; Pompton v. Cooper Union, 101 U. S. 196; Roberts v. Bolles, 101 U. S. 119; Anthony v. County of Jasper, 101 U. S. 693; Lyons v. Munson, 99 U. S. 684; Block v. Commissioners, 99 U. S. 686; Orleans v. Platt, 99 U. S. 676; Wilson v. Salamanca, 99 U. S. 499; Supervisors v. Galbraith, 99 U. S. 214; Hackett v. Ottawa, 99 U. S. 86; County of Daviess v. Huidekoper, 98 U. S. 98; County of Macon v. Shores, 97 U. S. 272, 279; County of Warren v. Marcy, 97 U. S. 96; San Antonio v. Mehaffy, 96 U. S. 312; Township of Rock Creek v. Strong, 96 U. S. 271; County of Cass v. Johnston, 95 U. S. 360; Com's. of Douglas County v. Bolles, 94 U. S. 104; County of Randolph v. Post, 93 U. S. 502; Town of Venice v. Murdock, 92 U. S. 494; Town of Coloma v. Eaves, 92 U. S. 484; Pendleton County v. Amy, 13 Wall. (U. S.) 297; St. Joseph Tp. v. Rogers, 16 Wall. (U. S.) 644; Kenicott v. Supervisors, 16 Wall. (U. S.) 452; Lynde v. The County, 16 Wall. (U. S.) 6; Grand Chute v. Winegar, 15 Wall. (U. S.) 355; City of Lexington v. Butler, 14 Wall. (U. S.) 282; Supervisors v. Schenck, 5 Wall. (U. S.) 772; City of Cincinnati v. Morgan, 3 Wall. (U. S.) 275; Meyer v. Muscatine, 1 Wall. (U. S.) 384, 393; Van Hostrup v. Madison, 1 Wall. (U. S.) 291; Mercer County v. Hacket, 1 Wall. (U. S.) 83; Bissell v. Jefferson, 24 How. (U. S.) 287; Commissioners v. Aspinwall, 21 How. (U. S.) 539; Third Nat. Bank v. Seneca Falls, 15 Fed. R. 783; Cary v. Ottawa, 8 Fed R. 199; Nicolay v. St. Clair County, 3 Dill. (U. S.) 163; Mygatt v. Green Bay, 1 Biss. (U. S.) 292; Moran v. Commissioners,

contained a recital that they had been issued in pursuance of a subscription to the capital stock of a railroad company, made under the authority of a certain statute, the corporation was estopped from setting up the fact that the subscription was made after the authority to make it had expired, as a defense to a suit by a *bona fide* holder of such bonds.[1] In the case referred to three of the members of the court dissented, and, as it seems to us, with good reason, for we believe that the question was one of power to be determined by an examination of public laws. Bonds were held valid in a case where the subscription was made upon conditions which the municipality had power to impose, and bonds were issued reciting that such conditions had been performed, when, in fact, they had not; and it was held that the application of the rule was not affected by the fact that the statute declared that such bonds should not be binding until after the performance of the prescribed conditions.[2] And the purchaser is held not to be charged with constructive notice of anything in the public records of the municipality, which would show that such recitals are really false.[3]

§ 899. **Recitals in bonds not always conclusive.**—As we have elsewhere seen, recitals in bonds or statements in certificates of officers are not conclusive where the municipality has no power to issue bonds, but there are also other cases in which they are held not to be effective as an estoppel. Where there is notice of defects and no change of position made in good faith, and no laches or acquiescence, there can be no estoppel, notwith-

---

2 Black (U. S.) 722; Woods *v.* Lawrence County, 1 Black (U. S.) 386; City of St. Louis *v.* Shields, 62 Mo. 247; Smith *v.* County of Clark, 54 Mo. 58, 81; Shorter *v.* Rome, 52 Ga. 621; Wilkinson *v.* Peru, 61 Ind. 1; Bargate *v.* Shortridge, 5 H. L. Cas. 297; *In re* Imperial Land Co., L. R. 11 Eq. 478; Webb *v.* Commissioners of Herne Bay, L. R. 5 Q. B. 642; Royal British Bank *v.* Turquand, 6 El. & Bl. 325.

[1] County of Moultrie *v.* Rockingham Ten-cent Sav. Bank, 92 U. S. 631. The court discriminates the case before it from that of Town of Concord *v.* Portsmouth Savings Bank, 92 U. S. 625, but it seems to us that the principle is the same in both cases.

[2] Insurance Co. *v.* Bruce, 105 U. S. 328.

[3] Marcy *v.* Township of Oswego, 92 U. S. 637; Humboldt Township *v.* Long, 92 U. S. 642.

standing the recitals in the bonds. Where the enabling act expressly requires that the bonds shall be registered and provides that if not registered they shall be void, the certificate of the officer is held not to estop the municipality from showing that the provisions of the enabling act were not complied with.[1] In other cases bonds have been held void and the doctrine of estoppel denied application.[2]

§ 900. **Official certificates—Conclusiveness of.**—Where the law imposes upon a municipal officer the duty of certifying that certain facts exist or that certain proceedings have been had, or invests him with authority to make such a certificate, the general rule is that as to *bona fide* purchasers of bonds, the certificate is conclusive.[3] In order that a certificate shall be conclusive in itself, it is essential that it should be made by

---

[1] In German Savings Bank v. Franklin County, 128 U. S. 526, s. c. 9 Sup. Ct. R. 159, the case was distinguished from Lewis v. Commissioners, 105 U. S. 739, and it was said: "The registration of the bonds by the state auditor has nothing to do with any of the terms or conditions on which the stock was voted and subscribed. Neither the registration nor the certificate of registry covers or certifies any fact as to compliance with the conditions prescribed in the vote, on which alone the bonds were to be issued. The recital in the bonds does not contain any reference to the act of April 16, 1869, or certify any compliance with the provisions of that act; and the certificate of registry merely certifies that the bond has been registered in the auditor's office pursuant to the provisions of the act of April 16, 1869. The statute does not require that the auditor shall determine or certify that the bonds have been regularly or legally issued."

[2] County of Randolph v. Post, 93 U. S. 502; Town of Concord v. Robinson, 121 U. S. 165, s. c. 7 Sup. Ct. R. 937. In German, etc., Bank v. Franklin County, 128 U. S. 526, s. c. 9 Sup. Ct. R. 739, the cases of Insurance Co. v. Bruce, 105 U. S. 328; Pana v. Bowler, 107 U. S. 529, s. c. 2 Sup. Ct. R. 704, and Oregon v. Jennings, 119 U. S. 74, s. c. 7 Sup. Ct. R. 124, are reviewed and their effect defined.

[3] Block v. Commissioners, 99 U. S. 686; State v. Comrs. of Hancock county, 12 Ohio St. 596; Town of Ontario v. Hill, 99 N. Y. 324; Hannibal v. Fauntleroy, 105 U. S. 408; Gelpcke v. Dubuque, 1 Wall. 175; Bank of Rome v. Rome, 19 N. Y. 20, s. c. 75 Am. Dec. 272; City of San Antonio v. Lane, 32 Tex. 405; Hannibal, etc., R. Co. v. Marion County, 36 Mo. 294; Humboldt Tp. v. Long, 92 U S. 642. See, generally, Wilson v. Salamanca, 99 U. S. 499; Davis v. Kendallville, 5 Biss. 280; Nicolay v. St. Clair County, 3 Dill. 163; Sherman County v. Simons, 109 U. S. 735; Pollard v. City of Pleasant Hill, 3 Dill. 195; Van Hostrup v. Madison, 1 Wall. 291.

an officer or agent invested with authority, since the certificate of a person having no authority whatever to make such a certificate is, of itself, of no force or effect.[1] It is important to bear in mind, in applying the rule stated, that it applies only in cases of persons who acquire rights without notice of defects in the proceedings. It is evident that it can not apply in any case where there is an entire absence of power to issue bonds.[2] Where there is power to issue bonds the rule is of general application, since a purchaser of bonds is not bound to examine the municipal records in cases where the recitals of the bonds show a compliance with the law, or the certificate of an authorized officer or agent recites that the steps required by law have been taken.

§ 901. Recitals in bonds to constitute an estoppel must be of facts.—To constitute an estoppel the recitals in bonds must be of matters of fact. Thus it has been held that a recital which amounts to no more than a statement, "that a subscription to the capital stock of the company was authorized by the statutes mentioned, and that the sum mentioned in the bond was part of it," will not constitute an estoppel.[3] It is quite difficult to reconcile the statements found in the opinions delivered in the many cases upon this subject. It may, however, be safely said that to be sufficient to work an estoppel the recitals must always be of matters of fact, but what shall be

[1] Dixon County v. Field, 111 U. S. 83, s. c. 4 Sup. Ct. R. 315; Anthony v. County of Jasper, 101 U. S. 693; Daviess County v. Dickenson, 117 U. S. 657; County of Jefferson v. Lewis, 20 Fla. 980; State v. Commissioners, 11 Ohio St. 183.

[2] Allen v. Louisiana, 103 U. S. 80; Lippincott v. Pana, 92 Ill. 24; Chicago, etc., R. Co. v. Aurora, 99 Ill. 205; Ogden v. County of Daviess, 102 U. S. 634; Sherrard v. Lafayette County, 3 Dill. 236; Clay v. Hawkins County, 5 Lea (Tenn.) 137; State v. School Dist., 10 Neb. 544; People v. Jackson County, 92 Ill. 441; Wells v. Supervisors, 102 U. S. 625; Phillips v. Albany, 28 Wis. 340. See Town of Farview v. Winona, etc., R. Co.,36 Minn. 505; Harrington v. Plainview, 27 Minn. 224; Cromwell v. County of Sac., 96 U. S. 51; State v. Montgomery, 74 Ala. 226; Cagwin v. Hancock, 84 N. Y. 532; Lincoln v. Iron Co., 103 U. S. 412; Williams v. Roberts, 88 Ill. 11; People v. Oldtown, 88 Ill. 202; Ryan v. Lynch, 68 Ill. 160; Treadway v. Schnauber, 1 Dak. 236.

[3] Carroll Co. v. Smith, 111 U. S. 556, s. c. 4 Sup. Ct. R. 539.

considered matters of fact it is not easy to determine with accuracy or precision. In one of the cases it was held that estoppels can result only from " matters of fact, which the corporate officers have authority to certify," but it was also held that it is "not necessary that the recital should enumerate each particular fact essential to the existence of the obligation." It was said in the case referred to that, "A general statement that the bonds have been issued in conformity with the law will suffice so as to embrace every fact which the officers making the statement are authorized to determine and certify."[1]

§ 902. No estoppel where the officer ordering bonds to issue had no jurisdiction.—It has been held that where it appears that the officer directing bonds to issue had no jurisdiction of the subject, the bonds are void even in the hands of a *bona fide* holder.[2] It is not easy to reconcile some of the broad statements made in the opinions given in the cases referred to, by the federal courts of original jurisdiction, with some of the

---

[1] Dixon County v. Field, 111 U. S. 83, s. c. 4 Sup. Ct. R. 315. The statement copied in the text asserts the rule as generally enforced, but there is some conflict in the cases as to the application of the rule. Van Hostrup v. Madison City, 1 Wall. 291; Hayes v. Holly Springs, 114 U. S. 120, s. c. 5 Sup. Ct. R. 785; Ogden v. County of Daviess, 102 U. S. 634; Commissioners of Knox County v. Aspinwall, 21 How. 539; County of Moultrie v. Rockingham Savings Bank, 92 U. S. 631; Marcy v. Township of Oswego, 92 U. S. 637; Town of Coloma v. Eaves, 92 U. S. 484; School District v. Stone, 106 U. S. 183, s. c. 1 Sup. Ct. R. 84; County of Clay v. Society, etc., 104 U. S. 579; County of Warren v. Marcy, 97 U. S. 96; Town of Pana v. Bowler, 107 U. S. 529; Quincy, etc., Railroad Co. v. Morris, 84 Ill. 410. *Ante*, § 900, authorities cited in notes.

[2] Rich v. Mentz Tp., 134 U. S. 632; Cowdrey v. Town of Caneadea, 16 Fed. R. 532; Rich v. Town of Mentz, 19 Fed. R. 725. See, also, People v. Smith, 45 N. Y. 772; Town of Mentz v. Cook, 108 N. Y. 504, s. c. 15 N. E. R. 541; People v. Smith, 55 N. Y. 135; Town of Wellsborough v. New York, etc., Railroad Co., 76 N. Y. 182; Metzger v. Attica, etc., Railroad Co., 79 N. Y. 171; Hills v. Peekskill, etc., Bank, 101 N. Y. 490, s. c. 5 N. E. R. 327. In the first case cited, the court declared that it was bound to follow the decisions of the state court, and referred to the cases of Meriwether v. Muhlenburg County Court, 120 U. S. 354, 357, s. c. 7 Sup. Ct. R. 563; Claiborne County v. Brooks, 111 U. S. 400, 410, s. c. 4 Sup. Ct. R. 489.

Corp. 79

statements in other cases, but the conclusion reached is, as we believe, unquestionably correct. We think that dealers in municipal bonds must always ascertain that the power to execute the bonds has been conferred upon the municipal officers who assume to issue them,[1] and that the rule protecting such dealers has been in some instances unjustly extended. It is known to every one that municipal officers exercise limited delegated powers,[2] and hence there is reason for requiring persons who purchase municipal bonds to ascertain that the authority assumed to be exercised has been conferred by a valid statute.

§ 903. **Estoppel—Otherwise than by recitals—Illustrative instances.**—Estoppel may be created by acts which make it against equity and good conscience to permit the municipality to deny the validity of the bonds. It is impossible to lay down accurate general rules, for cases are usually to be determined upon particular facts. We refer to some of the cases upon the general subject. It has been held that the levy by town officers of taxes to pay interest on railroad aid bonds does not of itself estop tax-payers from contesting their validity,[3] but on this point there is an apparent, if not actual, conflict of authority.[4] Payment of interest on bonds is not of itself sufficient to create an estoppel, but the fact that the county has paid interest on such bonds is a circumstance to be considered in deciding whether the acts of the municipality work an estoppel against it.[5] Where interest has been paid for a long period of

[1] In Cowdrey v. Town of Caneadea, 16 Fed. R. 532, the court said: "Purchasers of municipal bonds, executed by agents, must ascertain at their peril that the delegated authority assumed has been conferred."

[2] Union School Township v. First National Bank, 102 Ind. 464, 470; Lowell, etc., Bank v. Inhabitants of Winchester, 8 Allen 109; Dickinson v. Inhabitants of Conway, 12 Allen 487; Benoit v. Inhabitants of Conway, 10 Allen 528; Railroad Nat. Bank v. City of Lowell, 109 Mass. 214.

[3] Town of Cherry Creek v. Becker, 2 N. Y. Sup. 514; Citizens' Sav., etc., Assn. v. Topeka, 20 Wall. 655; Lippincott v. Pana, 92 Ill. 24.

[4] Town of Eminence v. Grasser, 81 Ky. 52; County of Cass v. Gillett, 100 U. S. 585; County of Moultrie v. Rockingham, etc., Bank, 92 U. S. 631.

[5] Livingston County v. First Nat. Bank, 128 U. S. 102, 9 Sup. Ct. 18; Moulton v. City of Evansville, 25 Fed. R. 382.

§ 903   MUNICIPAL AID BONDS.   1245

time it has been held that it will estop the municipality to take advantage of irregularities or defects.[1] Voting as a stockholder has been regarded as sufficient to create an estoppel,[2] but there is authority to the contrary.[3] It has been held that substituting bonds for those originally issued will estop the municipality from setting up as a defense that the original proceedings were defective or irregular.[4] It is to be noted, however, that where there was an entire absence of power to issue the original bonds, and no curative statute or statute authorizing substitution, there can be no effective exchange or substitution of bonds.[5] Where there is an exchange of bonds for stock, or of stock for bonds, and long acquiescence, an estoppel arises.[6] Where there has been no change of position, and no acquiescence the general rule is that there can be no estoppel.[7] The general rule is that tax-payers who stand by, and without objection, see expenditures of money made upon the faith that the subscription or bonds are valid and enforceable are estopped from denying their validity, and we can see no reason why

[1] A county which issued bonds containing a recital that they were issued under the act, delivered them to the railroad company and paid interest on them for fifteen years, can not set up an irregularity in the election, as against an innocent purchaser of the bonds. Nelson v. Haywood County, 3 Pickle (Tenn.) 781, s. c. 11 S. W. Rep. 885; State v. Anderson County, 8 Baxter 249; Portsmouth Savings Bank v. Springfield, 4 Fed. R. 276; County of Clay v. Society, etc., 104 U. S. 579.

[2] County of Cass v. Gillett, 100 U. S. 585.

[3] Supervisors v. Paxton, 57 Miss. 701.

[4] County of Jasper v. Ballou, 103 U S. 745. See Washington, etc., R. Co. v. Cazenove, 83 Va. 744; County of Randolph v. Post, 93 U. S. 502; Leavenworth, etc., R. Co. v. Commissioners, 18 Kan. 169. See County of Warren v. Marcy, 97 U. S. 96; Town of Solon v. Williamsburgh, etc., Bank, 114 N. Y. 122; Hills v. Peekskill, etc., Bank, 101 N. Y. 490; Deyo v. Otoe County, 37 Fed. R. 246; City of Plattsmouth v. Fitzgerald, 10 Neb. 401; Commissioners Douglass County v. Bolles, 94 U. S. 104; Marcy v. Township of Oswego, 92 U. S. 637; Gause v. Clarksville, 1 McCrary 78.

[5] Horton v. Thompson, 71 N. Y. 513; McKee v. Vernon Co., 3 Dill. 210. The decision in the first of the cases cited is, as elsewhere shown, of doubtful soundness upon some of the questions involved, but as to the immediate point to which it is here cited it is not justly subject to criticism.

[6] Pendleton Co. v. Amy, 13 Wall. 297.

[7] Portland, etc., R. Co. v. Hartford, 58 Me. 23; Union, etc., R. Co. v. Lincoln County, 3 Dill. 300; Union, etc., R. Co. v. Merrick County, 3 Dill. 359.

this general doctrine should not apply to the municipality.[1] The tendency of the decisions is to extend the principle of estoppel for the protection of *bona fide* holders of municipal aid bonds. Circumstances which in ordinary cases would hardly be regarded as sufficient to constitute an estoppel are often held to create an estoppel in favor of bondholders.[2]

§ 904. **Estoppel by retention of stock.**—The doctrine of some of the cases is that if the stock received for the bonds is retained by the municipality it is estopped to deny the validity of the bonds. We incline to think this doctrine of doubtful soundness. If there was no power to issue the bonds then it seems clear that there could be no estoppel, although the municipality might be liable for the value of the stock. We can not assent to the broad doctrine that so long as the municipality retains the stock which it received in exchange for bonds, it will be estopped from defending against them on the ground that they are invalid.[3] It seems to us that the doctrine of estoppel can not apply where there is an entire absence of power, but that it does apply where there is power although it is improperly or irregularly exercised. There may be cir-

---

[1] *Ante*, § 871; Planet, etc., Co. v. St. Louis, etc., R.Co., 115 Mo. 613, s. c. 22 S. W. R. 616; Simpson Co. v. Louisville, etc., R. Co., (Ky.) 19 S. W. R. 665; Jones v. Cullen, 142 Ind. 335, s. c. 40 N. E. R. 124; Vickery v. Blair, 134 Ind. 554, s. c. 32 N. E. R. 880. See, generally, New Orleans, etc., R. Co. v. City of New Orleans, 44 La. Ann. 748, s. c. 11 So. R. 77, and 44 La. Ann.728,11 So. Rep. 78; City of Seattle v. Columbia, etc., R. Co., 6 Wash. 379, s. c. 33 Pac. R. 1048, 56 Am. & Eng. R. Cas. 618; Spokane, etc., R. Co. v. Spokane Falls, 6 Wash. 521, s. c. 33 Pac. R. 1072; Fort Worth, etc., Co. v. Smith Bridge Co., 151 U. S. 294, s. c. 14 Sup. Ct. R. 339, 44 Am. & Eng. Corp. Cas. 604.

[2] Supervisors v.Schenck, 5 Wall. 772.

But see Supervisors v. Cook, 38 Ill. 44; Redd v. Henry County, 31 Gratt. 695. See, also, County of Ray v. Van Sycle, 96 U. S. 675; Luling v. Racine, 1 Biss. 314; Beloit v. Morgan, 7 Wall. 619; Butler v. Durham, 27 Ill. 473; McPherson v. Foster, 43 Iowa 48; New Haven, etc., R. Co. v. Chatham, 42 Conn. 465; Goshen Township v. Shoemaker, 12 Ohio St. 624; Lane v. Schomp, 20 N. J. Eq. 82; Alvord v. Syracuse, etc., Bank, 98 N. Y. 599; Belo v. Commissioners, 76 N. C. 489; Whiting v. Town of Potter, 18 Blatchf. 165.

[3] Pendleton County v. Amy, 13 Wall. (U. S.) 297; Whiting v. Potter, 2 Fed. R. 517; Munson v. Town of Lyons, 12 Blatchf. (U. S.) 539.

§ 905   MUNICIPAL AID BONDS.   1247

cumstances in addition to the retention of the stock which will create an estoppel, but we think that the mere retention of the stock will not, of itself, create an estoppel. It has been held that the corporation will be estopped to deny the validity of the bonds issued in exchange for stock, where it has held the stock for years and exercised the rights of a stockholder by virtue of holding such stock.[1]

§ 905. **Recitals in bonds—Effect of against bondholders.**—The principle upon which rests the doctrine that recitals in bonds estop the municipality does not apply, in full vigor at least, as against the bondholder. Thus a recital in a bond that it was issued under a particular statute may estop the municipality, but it does not, according to the adjudged cases, estop the holder of the bond.[2] Where there are two statutes the bondholder may show under which of the two the bonds were issued.[3] It has been held that where there is a valid statute and the bonds recite that they are issued "in pursuance of an act of the legislature" it will be presumed that the bonds were issued under a valid act and not under an invalid act.[4] It is somewhat difficult to reconcile the doctrine of the cases referred to in the notes with the elementary principle that an estoppel must be reciprocal, but there may possibly be some reason for denying the application of this general principle. The bondholder relies upon the recitals and may derive benefit from them, and it is not easy to perceive how he can assert an estoppel against the municipality and yet affirm that the recitals do not operate against him. If there is a clear, express and unmistakable identification of a particular statute, we can

---

[1] Munson v. Town of Lyons, 12 Blatchf. (U. S.) 539; Whiting v. Potter, 2 Fed. R. 517; Pendleton County v. Amy, 13 Wall. (U. S.) 297.

[2] Knox County v. Ninth National Bank, 147 U. S. 91, s. c. 13 Sup. Ct. R. 267; Commissioners v. January, 94 U. S. 202.

[3] Ninth National Bank v. Knox County, 37 Fed. R. 75, 79, citing Commissioners v. January, 94 U. S. 202; Anderson Co. Comrs. v. Beal, 113 U. S. 227, s. c. 5 Sup. Ct. R. 433, and distinguishing Crow v. Oxford, 119 U. S. 215, s. c. 7 Sup. Ct. R. 180; Gilson v. Dayton, 123 U. S. 59, s. c. 8 Sup. Ct. R. 66.

[4] Moulton v. City of Evansville, 25 Fed. R. 382, 387.

not conceive on what ground, except, perhaps, that of fraud or mistake, the purchaser of the bonds can be heard to aver that they were issued by authority of some other statute than that designated. Where there is no specific designation of a statute and a general or indefinite reference to legislative acts, there is reason for permitting the bondholder to show under which of two statutes the bonds were issued.

§ 906. **Refunding—Substitution.**—Where the statute specifically prescribes how the power to issue bonds shall be exercised, and upon what conditions, it must be substantially complied with, and if there be no element of estoppel, bonds issued in a mode not authorized by the statute are voidable. But where a choice of means and methods is left to the municipality it may adopt such means or methods, within the range of the power conferred, as it may deem best. It has been held that a municipal corporation which has issued legal bonds in aid of a railroad may lawfully take them up and issue others in their stead without any additional grant of authority, where the exchange can be made on terms favorable to the municipality.[1] We can see no reason why there may not be a refunding where the statute does not expressly or impliedly interdict it, but, of course, if the statute, either expressly or by implication, forbids a refunding, then there can be no valid refunding. It has also been held that bonds of the new series may be en-

---

[1] Rogan v. City of Watertown, 30 Wis. 259; Commonwealth v. Commissioners, 37 Pa. St. 237; Merchants' etc., Bank v. County of Pulaski, 1 McCrary (U. S.) 316; Gause v. Clarksville, 5 Dill. (U. S.) 165. When bonds, issued in aid of a railroad, are afterwards replaced by new bonds issued in place of those that had matured, under an act authorizing the issue of the new bonds and declaring them to be a continuation of the former liability, it is not necessary that the question of issuing the new bonds should be submitted to the voters of the county in pursuance of this section having reference to the contracting of debts, and not to antecedent obligations, or the use of the means necessary for their discharge. Blanton v. Board of Commissioners, 101 N. Car. 532, s. c. 8 S. E. Rep. 162; County of Jasper v. Ballou, 103 U. S. 745; Little Rock v. National Bank, 98 U. S. 308; Portland, etc., v. Evansville, 25 Fed. R. 389; Sullivan v. Walton, 20 Fla. 552; People v. Lippincott, 81 Ill. 193; City of Galena v. Corwith, 48 Ill. 423.

forced even though the manner of issuing them as prescribed by law was not followed,[1] but we suppose this doctrine can not obtain where there has been a substantial departure from the statute unless there is an effective estoppel. We regard statutes granting power to give aid to railroad companies as within the rule that grants of corporate power are to be strictly construed, and for that reason we think the doctrine of the case referred to should be limited rather than extended. The power is one of an extraordinary nature and is liable to great abuse, so that courts are bound to require a substantial compliance with the provisions of the enabling act. Courts move on dangerous ground when they assume to dispense with obedience to such statutes or to adjudge their provisions to be merely directory.

§ 907. **Discretionary powers and peremptory duty.**—There is, it is obvious, a clear distinction between the exercise of a discretionary power and the performance of a peremptory duty. Courts can not control the action of officers invested with discretionary powers, but they may compel the performance of a specific duty. The general rule is that if a discretionary power is conferred upon the officers of a municipality as to whether they will issue bonds in pursuance of the authority contained in a popular vote, they will not be compelled to do so.[2] Where the power of determining the course to be pursued is vested in the municipal authorities, they are the judges of what will best promote the interests of the municipality. It has been held that where bonds are issued they may be exchanged directly for stock of the railroad company without any special power in the act authorizing their issue,[3]

---

[1] See McKee v. Vernon County, 3 Dill. (U. S.) 210, where the bonds substituted were engraved instead of being signed as required by law, but the county retained the consideration for which the original bonds were given, and paid interest for two years on the engraved bonds.

[2] People v. County Board of Cass County, 77 Ill. 438.

[3] Evansville, etc., R. Co. v. City of Evansville, 15 Ind. 395; Slack v. Maysville, etc., R. Co., 13 B. Mon. 1; Commonwealth v. Councils of Pittsburgh, 41 Pa. St. 278; Meyer v. City of Muscatine, 1 Wall. (U. S.) 384. Even where there is a doubt as to the right to make the exchange under the strict terms of the statute, the municipality can not deny the validity of the bonds

but this doctrine can not prevail where the statute expressly or impliedly forbids such exchange. Where the duty to execute bonds is peremptory and all the preliminary conditions have been fulfilled, a writ of mandamus will be awarded to compel the municipal officers to act.[1]

§ 908. **Registration.**—The decisions of the courts place great stress upon provisions in enabling acts requiring bonds to be registered, and hold that such provisions must be strictly obeyed. It seems difficult to harmonize the statements found in the decisions referred to with those made in the many cases broadly asserting and enforcing the doctrine of estoppel by recitals.[2] It is held where all bonds issued to aid a railroad company were required by law to be registered with the state auditor before being negotiated, and bonds which were not so registered were declared by statute to be void, that bonds issued after the act went into force were void although they were dated as of a time prior to the passage of the act.[3]

merely upon that account after having received full consideration, and after making use of the stock to carry its purposes into effect. City of Bridgeport v. Housatonic R. Co., 15 Conn. 475. Where a town subscribes for shares in the capital stock of a railroad, and issues bonds for the payment thereof, it is not necessary that the bonds be sold in the market for cash, in order that the money be paid to the railroad company, when the latter is willing to take the bonds at their full value. Commonwealth v. Inhabitants of Williamstown, 156 Mass. 70.

[1] People v. Cline, 63 Ill. 394; People v. County Board of Cass County, 77 Ill. 438.

[2] This is especially true of the case of German Savings Bank v. Franklin County, 128 U. S. 526, s. c. 9 Sup. Ct. R. 159.

[3] Anthony v. County of Jasper, 101 U. S. 693, affirming Anthony v Jasper Co., 4 Dillon 136; Hoff v. Jasper County, 110 U. S. 53; German Savings Bank v. Franklin County, 128 U. S. 526, s. c. 9 Sup. Ct. R. 159.; Bissell v. Spring Valley Township, 124 U. S. 225; Crow v. Oxford, 119 U. S. 215; Dixon County v. Field, 111 U. S. 83; Town of Eagle v. Kohn, 84 Ill. 292; Richeson v. People, 115 Ill. 450, s. c. 5 N. E. R. 121; Parker v. Smith, 3 Bradw. (Ill.) 356. In the case of Concord v. Portsmouth Savings Bank, 92 U. S. 625, the opinion is expressed that a recital in the bonds that a subscription had been made before a constitutional provision forbidding such subscriptions took effect, and that the bonds were issued in pursuance of such subscription and in conformity with the provisions of the act under which that subscription purported to have been made, being a recital of matters of fact peculiarly within the knowledge of the municipal officers, would operate as an estoppel against

§ 909. **Rights of bona fide holders not affected by sale of bonds at a less sum than that** prescribed by statute.—A *bona fide* holder of aid bonds who acquires them in the usual course of business is entitled to enforce them against the municipality, although they were originally sold at a sum less than that prescribed by the enabling act. In one of the cases the statute provided that the railroad company should not sell the bonds "at less than their par value," but the court held that the fact that the company did sell the bonds for less than their par value did not constitute a defense on the part of the municipality.[1] In another case which arose under a statute similar to that acted upon in the case referred to, the court held that the bonds were enforceable in the hands of a *bona fide* holder, although the railroad company had sold them for sixty-four cents on the dollar.[2]

§ 910. **Subrogation of holder of invalid bonds.**—As we have seen, the power to grant aid does not necessarily carry with it the power to issue negotiable bonds, so that there may be power to subscribe to the stock of a railroad company and pay the subscription in money, but no power to issue negotiable bonds in payment of the subscription. The power to issue bonds depends entirely upon the statute, and if there be no power the bonds are void. But where bonds are acquired in good faith, and in the belief that they were valid, the holder may be entitled to be subrogated to the rights of the municipality to the extent of the interest represented by his bonds. The general principles of subrogation authorized this conclusion, for the person who purchases the bonds is not a mere volunteer. In accordance with this general doctrine, it has been

the municipality which would prevent it from denying its liability upon the bonds. A recovery of the sum actually paid for the bonds was allowed in a case where the public corporation had power to borrow money, and the avails of the bonds were used by the corporation for legitimate corporate purposes. Wood *v.* Louisiana, 5 Dill. 122; Louisiana *v.* Wood, 102 U. S. 294, citing Moses *v.* McFerlan, 2 Burr. 1005; Marsh *v.* Fulton County, 10 Wall. 676.

[1] Woods *v.* Laurence County, 1 Black 386, 410.

[2] Richardson *v.* Laurence County, 154 U. S. 536, s. c. 14 Sup. Ct. R. 1157.

justly held that where there was power to subscribe to the stock of a railroad company, but no power to issue bonds, the purchaser of such bonds was entitled to stock.[1]

§ 911. **Liability of muncipality to purchaser of invalid bonds.**—It is held that where a municipality having power to issue bonds disposes of bonds which, by reason of a defective execution of the power it possesses, are invalid, the holder of the bonds may recover back the sum actually paid for them in an action for money had and received.[2] But where the issue of the bonds is positively forbidden by law, as where the municipality is forbidden by the state constitution, to incur the debt for which they are issued, the purchaser is without remedy, since the corporation can not indirectly become liable on an indebtedness which it is forbidden to assume directly.[3]

§ 912. **Right of municipality to recover money paid because of wrongful acts of the railroad company.**—It seems just to hold that where the wrongful acts of the railroad company compel the municipality to pay illegal bonds, it may have an action for the recovery of the money it has been compelled to pay. In a case where a railroad company procured negotiable bonds to be illegally issued by the officers of a town, which were in form the obligations of the town and recited that they

---

[1] Illinois, etc., R. Co. v. Wade, 140 U. S. 65, 70, s. c. 11 Sup. Ct. R. 709. To the point that the bonds were void the court cited Wade v. Walnut, 105 U. S. 1.

[2] Wood v. Louisiana, 5 Dillon (U. S.) 122; Louisiana v. Wood, 102 U. S. 294; Paul v. Kenosha, 22 Wis. 266; Gause v. Clarksville, 5 Dillon (U. S.) 165. A municipality which issued bonds in payment of a stock subscription can not, in an action on such bonds, when they have been held void as *ultra vires*, be held to liability on the subscription. Norton v. Town of Dyersburg, 127 U. S. 160, s. c. 8 Sup. Ct. Rep. 1111.

[3] Litchfield v. Ballou, 114 U. S. 190. In this case bonds were sold in excess of the constitutional limit of city indebtedness and the proceeds were used in part payment for a system of water-works which the city erected on land previously acquired. The bonds having been declared void, a suit was brought to have the purchase-price declared a lien in equity against the water-works, but the court held that the city could not render itself or its property liable in any way for the debt which the bonds evidenced. See Agawam Nat. Bank v. South Hadley, 128 Mass. 503; Railroad Nat. Bank v. Lowell, 109 Mass. 214.

were legally issued and such bonds were negotiated and transferred by it for the full face value thereof, and were subsequently negotiated and sold to the citizens of another state, who, in an action in the circuit court of the United States, brought against the town to recover overdue interest, and tried upon the merits, recovered final judgment therefor, which fixed the liability of the town for the whole amount of such bonds to the holders thereof it was held that, by reason of such wrongful acts of the company, a cause of action arose in favor of the town, and against the company, for the recovery of the amount of such bonds, with interest.[1] We think that while there may possibly be cases where money can be recovered from a wrongdoing company they are very rare. We do not believe that there can be a recovery where the company acts in good faith and the loss is solely attributable to a mistake of law. In a case where an officer of the company, after the corporate existence of an alleged railroad corporation had ceased by failure to comply with the law regulating such corporations, knowing its condition, and having in its hands bonds given by plaintiff village to such corporation, and knowing that such bonds were void, and could not be enforced by such corporation, fraudulently sold them to innocent parties, representing them to be *bona fide* securities, and valid bonds of plaintiff village, it was held that such officer, by his fraud, became liable to the village for the value of the bonds negotiated by him, and the fact that he had accounted to his company for the proceeds did not release him.[2] We regard the doctrine of the case referred to as sound, for there was clearly actionable fraud causing damages.

§ 913. **Defenses to aid bonds.**—It may be said, generally, that the entire absence of power to issue bonds is always a suf-

[1] Town of Plainview v. Winona, etc., R. Co., 36 Minn. 505. As the bonds in this case were issued under a statute which was declared unconstitutional, and the town had received the benefits from the construction of the road, it is doubtful if this case can be sustained on principle. It seems to us that the case cited carries the doctrine too far, for, as we conceive, there was no actionable wrong, nor anything more than a mere mistake of law.

[2] Farnham v. Benedict, 107 N. Y. 159.

ficient defense to an action on the bonds, but that, as a rule, the irregular or improper exercise of a power duly conferred does not furnish sufficient grounds for a defense against bonds in the hands of a *bona fide* holder. Payment of the bonds can not be successfully resisted upon grounds which are insufficient to release the corporation from its subscription, such as the wrongful acts of the corporation or its officers,[1] or any acts done by it in pursuance of a power to lease, consolidate, increase the capital stock, or the like, which existed at the time the bonds were issued.[2] The failure of the officer issuing the bonds to annex to his signature words indicating his official position does not invalidate the bonds, but the fact that he is an officer of the municipality may be proven by extrinsic evidence.[3] And the fact that the officers by whom the bonds were executed were not legally elected will not avail as a defense against a suit to enforce payment, if they were serving as *de facto* officers with the acquiescence of the municipality.

[1] Ottawa, etc., R. Co. v. Black, 79 Ill. 262; Illinois Midland R. Co. v. Barnett, 85 Ill. 313,

[2] Menasha v. Hazard, 102 U. S. 81; Wilson v. Salamanca, 99 U. S. 499; County of Henry v. Nicolay, 95 U. S. 619; Town of East Lincoln v. Davenport, 94 U.S. 801; Nugent v. Supervisors, 19 Wall. (U. S.) 241, 3 Biss. 105; City of Mt. Vernon v. Hovey, 52 Ind. 563; Edwards v. People, 88 Ill. 340; Illinois Midland R. Co. v. Barnett, 85 Ill. 313; State v. Greene County, 54 Mo. 540. The fact that a railroad company to whom bonds were authorized to be issued was consolidated by statute with another, after notice of an election began to run, does not render the bonds void because issued to the consolidated company, where the consolidation act took effect before the election. Nelson v. Haywood County, 3 Pickle (Tenn.) 781. An agreement by a railroad company, executed after a county had subscribed to its stock, to sell and transfer its road after completion, in order to obtain money for its construction, does not release the county from the payment of its subscription which was payable when the road was completed "and in operation by lease or otherwise." Southern Kansas & P. R. Co. v. Turner, 41 Kan. 72, 21 Pac. R. 221. Under the Missouri act to authorize the consolidation of railroad companies in that state with companies in adjoining states, the consolidated company is entitled to the same privilege under the laws of Missouri that the Missouri corporation was entitled to at the time of the consolidation, including the privilege of collecting a subscription to stock by a township. Livingston County v. First Nat. Bank, 128 U. S. 102.

[3] County Commissioners v. King, 13 Fla. 451.

§ 914. **Bondholders not bound by proceedings to which they are not parties.**—The familiar elementary rule is that no person is bound by a judgment or decree rendered in an action or suit to which he is not a party or privy. It is necessary, therefore, in order to secure a judgment or decree binding a bondholder, that he should be brought into court. The rule is that the court will not pass upon any questions touching the bonds unless the bondholders are before the court. And it has refused to adjudge bonds fraudulent as between the railroad and the municipality, and to decree that the railroad should pay them, in the absence of those to whom the bonds had been assigned.[1]

§ 915. **Following state decisions.**—Questions as to the validity of municipal aid bonds very often depend upon the construction given state statutes by the courts of the state by which the statute is enacted. The federal courts, as a rule, follow state decisions, construing state constitutions or statutes, but do not, unless they regard them as sound, follow them upon general questions of law. The supreme court of the United States holds itself bound by the construction given to a state statute, in so far as it affects the validity of bonds issued after the statute has been so construed,[2] but it holds that it is not concluded by any decisions of the state courts made after the bonds have been negotiated, at least where such decisions are based upon general principles of law. And it will decide the case according to its own rules of construction, where the points raised have never been adjudicated in the state courts.[3]

§ 916. **Jurisdiction of federal courts.**—It is not our pur-

---

[1] County of Ralls v. Douglass, 105 U. S. 728.

[2] Board v. Texas, etc., R. Co., 46 Tex. 316.

[3] German Savings Bank v. Franklin County, 128 U. S. 526, 538; Anderson v. Santa Anna, 116 U. S. 356; Green County v. Conness, 109 U. S. 104; Burgess v. Seligman, 107 U. S. 20; Douglass v. County of Pike, 101 U. S. 677, where the court says: "After a statute has been settled by judicial construction, the construction becomes, so far as contract rights acquired under it are concerned, as much a part of the statute as the text itself."

pose to enter into any extended discussion of the question of the jurisdiction of the federal courts, nor indeed to do more than make a very few brief suggestions.[1] It is barely necessary to say that the jurisdiction in suits and actions upon municipal bonds depends upon the same principles as those which prevail in ordinary cases. There is nothing in the nature of a municipal bond that of itself gives federal jurisdiction. Bonds of this character are so generally in the hands of persons living in other states than those authorizing the issue, that for this reason, and also for the reason that the current of judicial decision of the United States courts is favorable to the bondholders, nearly all the litigation of this character is carried on in those courts. There must, however, in all cases where relief is sought upon municipal bonds, be diverse citizenship, or the federal courts will not have jurisdiction.[2] The fact that so much of the litigation is in the federal courts makes it desirable that the rules established by the supreme court of the United States should be accepted as the law by the state courts. The decisions of that court, except as to federal questions, are, it is true, not binding on the state tribunals, but if they were followed much confusion would be avoided.

[1] Olcott v. Supervisors, 16 Wall. (U.S.) 678; Township of Pine Grove v. Talcott, 19 Wall. (U. S.) 666; Claiborne County v. Brooks, 111 U. S. 400. But possibly the holding would be different if the decision of the state court was based upon the peculiar construction of a local statute and not upon general principles. Township of Elmwood v. Marcy, 92 U.S. 289. See Town of Venice v. Murdock, 92 U. S. 494. In Gelpcke v. Dubuque, 1 Wall. (U. S.) 175, and City v. Lamson, 9 Wall. (U. S.) 477, the decisions of the court are placed upon the ground that the supreme courts of Iowa and Wisconsin, respectively, had been so vacillating that there was authority for either view of the question that the United States court chose to take.

[2] Federal courts have jurisdiction over a suit brought by an assignee of a municipal bond which is in form a simple acknowledgment of indebtedness and an unconditional promise to pay a certain sum at a certain time. Porter v. Janesville, 3 Fed. Rep. 617. But no recovery can be had upon municipal bonds transferred by citizens of the state where the municipality is situated, to a citizen of another state, for the sole purpose of giving jurisdiction to the courts of the United States. New Providence v. Halsey, 117 U. S. 336. And the same rule applies to assignments of coupons. Farmington v. Pillsbury, 114 U. S. 138.

§ 917. **Compelling issue of bonds.**—The well known general rule that where municipal officers are under an imperative duty to perform an act mandamus will lie to coerce performance, but will not lie where the duty is purely discretionary, applies to cases where railroad companies or purchasers are entitled to municipal bonds. If there is a mandatory duty resting on the municipal officers to execute and deliver bonds the party entitled to the bonds may compel their delivery by a writ of mandamus.[1] The party who asks the writ must show that there is a duty to issue the bonds, otherwise the writ will be denied. Thus, where the notice of the election was insufficient the writ was refused although the aid had been voted.[2] But we suppose that the doctrine of the case just referred to can not apply where there are acts constituting an estoppel, since errors and irregularities in conducting the election can not be made available to defeat the rights of one who has acted in good faith without notice and who would suffer loss if the municipality were permitted to take advantage of errors and irregularities.

§ 918. **Remedies of bondholders.**—Where the bonds are issued by municipal corporations and are the general obligations of the corporations issuing them, the holder may maintain an ordinary action at law and secure judgment. He can not, according to some of the decisions, resort to mandamus in

[1] Smith v. Bourbon Co., 127 U. S. 105; Massachusetts, etc., Co. v. Township of Cherokee, 42 Fed. R. 750; State v. Jennings, 48 Wis. 549; People v. Ohio Grove Township, 51 Ill. 191; Santa Cruz, etc., R. Co. v. Board, etc., Santa Cruz County, 62 Cal. 239; People v. Walter, 2 Hun 385; Humphreys County v. McAdoo, 7 Heisk. 585; Chicago, etc., R. Co. v. Mallory, 101 Ill. 583; People v. Oldtown, 88 Ill. 202; State v. Lake City, 25 Minn. 404. In Massachusetts, etc., Co. v. Township of Cherokee, supra, it was held that specific performance of the duty to deliver would be decreed, but it seems to us that mandamus is the appropriate remedy where there is a peremptory official duty. Analogous cases support this conclusion. Selma, etc., R. Co., Ex parte, 45 Ala. 696; Pfister v. State, 82 Ind. 382; Commissioners v. Hunt, 33 Ohio St. 169; Carpenter v. County Commissioners, 21 Pick. 258; Cincinnati, etc., R. Co. v. Commissioners of Clinton County, 1 Ohio St. 77; Osage Valley, etc., R. Co. v. County Ct., 53 Mo. 156.

[2] McMahon v. Board, etc., 46 Cal. 214.

the first instance in cases where the bonds are general corporate obligations, since he has an adequate remedy at law.[1] Where a judgment is obtained on the bonds, and the municipal officers refuse to levy a tax to pay the judgment, mandamus will lie to compel the municipal officers to make the proper levy.[2] The right of the bondholders to have a tax levied can not be defeated by the resignation of the municipal officers.[3] It was held by a federal circuit court that where bonds are void, but a judgment by default has been rendered upon the coupons, that the municipality will not be allowed to set up as a defense to a mandamus on the judgment that there is no statute requiring the tax to be levied.[4] But the judgment in the case referred to was reversed.[5] Some of the courts will not

[1] Sharp v. Mayor, etc., 40 Barb. 256; People v. Hawkins, 46 N. Y. 9; Ex parte Lynch, 2 Hill 45.

[2] Board, etc., v. Aspinwall, 24 How. (U. S.) 376; City of East St. Louis v. Amy, 120 U. S. 600, s. c. 7 Sup. Ct. R. 739; State v. Police Judge, 111 U. S. 716, s. c. 4 Sup. Ct. R. 648; Kelley v. Milan, 127 U. S. 139; Norton v. Dyersburg, 127 U. S. 160; United States v. Jefferson County, 5 Dill. 310; Commonwealth v. Councils of Pittsburgh, 88 Pa. St. 66; State v. City of Davenport, 12 Iowa 335; Flagg v. Mayor, etc., Palmyra, 33 Mo. 440; Morgan v. Commonwealth, 55 Pa. St. 456; State v. Gates, 22 Wis. 210; Commonwealth v. Pittsburg, 34 Pa. St. 496; Robinson v. Butte County, 43 Cal. 353; Maddox v. Graham, 2 Metcf. (Ky.) 56; State v. New Orleans, 34 La. Ann. 477. A return to the alternative writ that the tax has been levied is sufficient. Bass v. Taft, 137 U. S. 458, s. c. 11 Sup. Ct. R. 154.

[3] Meriweather v. Muhlenburg County Ct., 120 U. S. 354, s. c. 7 Sup. Ct. R. 563. But it is difficult to reconcile the doctrine of the case cited with the cases which hold that courts can not levy taxes. Upon the general subject of compelling by mandamus county officers to levy a tax to pay municipal bonds or subscriptions, see United States v. Lincoln County, 5 Dill. 184; United States v. Jefferson County, 1 McCrary 356; Shelby County v. Cumberland, etc., R. Co., 8 Bush 209; Commonwealth v. Commissioners, 32 Pa. St. 218; State v. County Judge of Johnson County, 12 Iowa 237; Brodie v. McCabe, 33 Ark. 690; Moore v. New Orleans, 32 La. Ann. 726; McLendon v. Comrs. of Anson County, 71 N. C. 38.

[4] Loague v. Taxing Dist. of Brownsville, 36 Fed. Rep. 149.

[5] Comrs., etc., of Brownsville v. Loague, 129 U. S. 493, s. c. 9 Sup. Ct. R. 327. See Hill v. Scotland County, 32 Fed. R. 716; Harshman v. Knox County, 122 U. S. 306, s. c. 7 Sup. Ct. R. 1171; Moore v. Town of Edgefield, 32 Fed. R. 498; Hill v. Scotland County, 32 Fed. R. 714; Ralls County Ct. v. United States, 105 U. S. 733. See Scotland County v. Hill, 132 U. S. 107, s. c. 10 Sup. Ct. R. 26. As to the rule where the municipal officers have a discretionary power as to the mode of paying a judgment, see Grand County Commissioners v. King, 67 Fed. R. 202.

issue a writ where the liability on the bonds is doubtful and is controverted until a judgment has been obtained on the bonds,[1] nor will the writ issue, except perhaps to put the officers in motion, where the municipal officers have a discretionary power as to the mode of payment or the like.[2] Where there is a judgment rendered by a court possessing jurisdiction adjudging the bonds to be valid, the municipality can not set up the invalidity of the bonds as a defense to the action for mandamus.[3] The supreme court of the United States has modified if not denied the doctrine of some of the earlier cases, for it has held that where the bondholder goes behind the judgment upon some of the points adjudged, he can not successfuly aver that the judgment conclusively establishes the validity of the bonds.[4] The bondholder entitled to money collected to pay bonds and in the hands of a municipal officer can compel its payment to him by mandamus,[5] for in such a case there is a

See, generally, upon the subject of mandamus to compel levy of taxes, State v. Yellowstone County, 12 Mont. 503, s. c. 31 Pac. R. 78; Wells v. Commissioners, 77 Md. 125, s. c. 26 Atl. R. 357, 20 L. R. A. 89; Wayne County, etc., Bank v. Supervisors, 97 Mich. 630, s. c. 56 N. W. R. 944; State v. Tappan, 29 Wis. 664; Wilkinson v. Cheatham, 43 Ga. 258; Bassett v. Barbin, 11 La. Ann. 672; Meyer v. Porter, 65 Cal. 67; Pegram v. Comrs. Cleveland County, 64 N. C. 557; State v. Beloit, 20 Wis. 79; County Comrs. v. King, 13 Fla. 451.

[1] Commonwealth v. Pittsburgh, 34 Pa. St. 496; State v. Mayor, etc., 52 Wis. 423; State Board v. West Point, 50 Miss. 638. See, generally, Leach v. Comrs. of Fayetteville, 84 N. C. 829; State v. Clay County, 46 Mo. 231; Mansfield v. Fuller, 50 Mo. 338; School Dist. v. Bodenhamer, 43 Ark. 140; Coy v. City Council of Lyons City, 17 Iowa 1; People v. Clark County, 50 Ill. 213.

[2] Board of Commissioners v. King, 67 Fed. R. 202. See, generally, as to the right to exercise an option, Queen v. Southeastern R. Co., 4 H. L. Cas. 471; State v. Township of Union, 43 N. J. Law 518. As to the exercise of discretionary powers, United States v. Seaman, 17 How. 225; Heine v. Levee Commissioners, 19 Wall. 655; United States v. Lamont, 155 U. S. 303, s. c. 15 Sup. Ct. R. 97.

[3] United States v. New Orleans, 98 U. S. 381; Ralls County Ct. v. United States, 105 U. S. 733; Loague v. Taxing District of Brownsville, 36 Fed. R. 149; State v. Gates, 22 Wis. 210. See Boyd v. Alabama, 94 U. S. 645.

[4] Comrs., etc., of Brownsville v. Loague, 129 U. S. 493, s. c. 9 Sup. Ct. R. 327, citing Norton v. Board, etc., 129 U. S. 479, s. c. 9 Sup. Ct. R. 322, and distinguishing Harshman v. Knox County, 122 U. S. 306, s. c. 7 Sup. Ct. R. 1171.

[5] State v. Craig, 69 Mo. 565; State v. McCrillus, 4 Kan. 250.

peremptory duty to pay the money over to the party entitled to it. It is held by the supreme court of the United States that where the specific tax is insufficient to pay the bonds, the holder is entitled to payment out of the general funds of the municipality,[1] but it seems to us this can not be the rule where the statute under which the bonds are issued clearly and unequivocally confines the right to payment from a specific fund.[2] The right of a *bona fide* holder of bonds to compel the municipal officers to levy the necessary tax is not defeated by the repeal of the statute under which the bonds were issued.[3] Where the bonds have been held invalid in a proceeding for writ of mandamus, the judgment concludes the plaintiff from successfully prosecuting an action on the bonds themselves,[4] but the question of the validity of the bonds must be one which was litigated or which might have been litigated in the mandamus proceedings, and there must be jurisdiction of the subject-matter and of the person in order to make the judgment conclusive. The courts will not compel municipal officers to do that which they have no power to do under the law.[5] Where the power of a municipality is specifically limited to a given percentage on all taxable property and it is confessed by the demurrer to the answer that the entire sum realized from the tax is required for the proper maintenance of the municipal government, a mandamus will not be awarded.[6] It is held that the court will not itself appoint

---

[1] United States *v.* Clark, 96 U. S. 37; Olcott *v.* Supervisors, 16 Wall. 678.

[2] *Ante*, § 892. Quill *v.* City of Indianapolis, 124 Ind. 292, 299; Spidell *v.* Johnson, 128 Ind. 235, 238, 239; United States *v.* County of Macon, 99 U. S. 582.

[3] Deere *v.* Rio Grande County, 33 Fed. 823.

[4] Block *v.* Commissioners, 99 U. S. 686; Louis *v.* Brown Township, 109 U. S. 162, s. c. 3 Sup. Ct. R. 92; Corcoran *v.* Chesapeake, etc., Co., 94 U. S. 741.

[5] Supervisors *v.* United States, 18 Wall. 71, 77; United States *v.* County of Macon, 99 U. S. 582; County of Macon *v.* Huidekoper, 99 U. S. 592, note; Comrs., etc., of Brownsville *v.* Loague, 129 U. S. 493. See United States *v.* Clark, 96 U. S. 37; Butz *v.* City of Muscatine, 8 Wall. 575; State *v.* Whitesides, 30 So. Car. 579; Board of Commissioners *v.* King, 67 Fed. R. 202, 205.

[6] Clay County *v.* McAleer, 115 U. S. 616, s. c. 6 Sup. Ct. R. 199. See McAleer *v.* Clay County, 42 Fed. R. 665; Board of Commissioners *v.* King, 67 Fed. R. 202; United States *v.* Miller Co., 4 Dill. 233.

officers to levy the tax.[1] This doctrine proceeds upon the ground that the duty of levying taxes is not judicial and can not be exercised by the courts.[2] The decisions establish the rule as we have stated it, but it seems to us that courts have power to do complete justice and to make their writs effective, and that where there is a clear, unquestionable right to relief, they have power to grant it, even though they may be compelled to appoint ministerial agents to perform the duties of municipal officers who refuse to perform the duties enjoined on them by law. The power to "do justice and that not by halves," is, as we believe, ample foundation for the authority to provide for the assessment and collection of taxes where there is a clear right in the creditor and a peremptory duty resting on the municipality and its officers. The principle which empowers a court to appoint receivers and take control of property, is, as we conceive, broad enough to authorize courts to appoint officers or agents to levy and collect a tax.[3] Where there is no statute authorizing a tax, then, of course, the courts are powerless, but where there is a statute and a refusal to perform official duties required by law, courts ought to have power to award complete relief. Giving force to a state statute, it has been held that where the municipal officers refuse to act, in obedience to a peremptory writ of mandamus, a marshal or commissioner may be appointed to act.[4] This power should, as we have substantially said, reside in the courts, otherwise cases might arise in which payment might be delayed, or possibly avoided by a municipal corporation, and justice defeated. Officers who refuse to obey a writ of man-

---

[1] Heine v. Levee Commissioners, 19 Wall. 655; Rees v. Watertown, 19 Wall. 107; Board of Commissioners v. King, 67 Fed. R. 202, 205.

[2] Thompson v. Allen County, 115 U. S. 550, s. c. 6 Sup. Ct. R. 140; Rees v. Watertown, 19 Wall. 107, 124; Meriweather v. Garrett, 102 U. S. 472, 518. But see Meriweather v. Muhlenburg County Ct., 120 U. S. 354, s. c. 7 Sup. Ct. R. 563.

[3] Garrett v. City of Memphis, 5 Fed. R. 860, and cases cited. See Thompson v. Allen County, 13 Fed. R. 97, and authorities cited in the dissenting opinion in Thompson v. Allen County, 115 U. S. 550, s. c. 6 Sup. Ct. R. 140.

[4] Supervisors v. Rogers, 7 Wall. 175; Lansing v. County Treasurer, 1 Dill. 522.

1262   THE CORPORATION.   § 918

date may, it is true, be punished as for contempt, but punishment for contempt may not always be an adequate remedy for the enforcement of payment of the bonds. The duty to levy taxes to pay bonds is ordinarily a continuing one, and if one or more levies will not produce a sum sufficient to pay the bonds, the municipal officers may be compelled to make another levy.[1]

[1] State v. City of Madison, 15 Wis. 30; Benbow v. Iowa City, 7 Wall. 313; Robinson v. Butte County, 43 Cal. 353. As to the power of the federal courts, see Welch v. St. Genevieve, 1 Dill. 130; United States v. Muscatine County, 2 Abbott (U. S.) 53; Riggs v. Johnson County, 6 Wall. 166. As to the necessity of first reducing the claim on the bonds to judgment, see County of Greene v. Daniel, 102 U. S. 187, s. c. 3 Am. & Eng. R. Cas. 105. See, generally, East St. Louis v. Underwood, 105 Ill. 308. As to presentation of bonds for allowance, see County of Greene v. Daniels, 102 U. S. 187, s. c. 3 Am. & Eng. R. Cas. 105; Commissioners' Court v. Rather, 48 Ala. 433. Matters of pleading, People v. Colorado, etc., R. Co., 42 Fed. R. 638; United States v. City of Elizabeth, 42 Fed. R. 45. Actions on bonds, New Providence v. Halsey, 117 U. S. 336, s. c. 6 Sup. Ct. R. 764; Ninth National Bank v. Knox County, 37 Fed. R. 75. Evidence on part of plaintiff, Hannibal v. Fountleroy, 105 U. S. 408; Massachusetts, etc., Co. v. Township of Cherokee, 42 Fed. R. 750. See, generally, Houston v. People, 55 Ill. 398; People v. Jackson County, 92 Ill. 441; Lamoille Valley R. Co. v. Fairfield, 51 Vt. 257; County of Morgan v. Allen, 103 U. S. 498; Smith v. Railroad, 99 U. S. 398.

END OF VOLUME II.